the
AMERICANA
ANNUAL

1985

GROLIER

AN ENCYCLOPEDIA OF THE EVENTS OF 1984

YEARBOOK OF THE ENCYCLOPEDIA AMERICANA

This annual has been prepared as a yearbook for general encyclopedias. It is also published as *Encyclopedia Year Book.*

Grolier Enterprises, Inc. offers a varied selection of both adult and children's book racks. For details on ordering, please write:

Grolier Enterprises, Inc.
Sherman Turnpike
Danbury, CT 06816
Attn: Premium Department

EDITORIAL

Editorial Director	Bernard S. Cayne
Executive Editor	James E. Churchill, Jr.
Editor	Jeffrey H. Hacker

Managing Editor   Doris E. Lechner   **Art Director**   Richard Glassman

Associate Editors

Saundra France	Richard N. Morehouse
David T. Holland	Nathan H. Pletcher
Virginia Quinn McCarthy	Edwin F. Sparn

Copy Editor   Grace F. Buonocore   **Proofreader**   Stephen Romanoff

Chief Indexer   Jill Schuler   **Indexer**   Vitrude DeSpain

Production Editor   Cynthia L. Pearson   **Manuscript Typist**   Joan M. Calley

Head, Photo Research   Ann Eriksen   **Manager, Picture Library**   Jane H. Carruth

Photo Researcher   Jane DiMenna

Administrative and Financial Manager   S. Jean Gianazza

Staff Assistants

Carol Arnold   Mickey Austin   Jennifer Drake

MANUFACTURING

Director of Manufacturing	Joseph J. Corlett
Production Manager	Alan Phelps
Production Assistant	Marilyn Smith

Contents

Feature Articles of the Year

The Alphabetical Section

Separate entries on the continents, major nations of the world, U.S. states, Canadian provinces, and chief cities will be found under their own alphabetically arranged headings.

The
Year
in
Review

By Peter Jennings, ABC News
Anchor and Senior Editor, "World News Tonight"

There were events in the first six weeks of 1984 which, in retrospect, made it clear what sort of year it was going to be. The Rev. Jesse Jackson, the first black American to run seriously for the presidency, convinced Syria's President Hafez al-Assad to release a black U.S. Navy flier, Lt. Robert Goodman, Jr., who had been shot down over Lebanon. President Reagan decided, under pressure from Congress, to withdraw the remaining U.S. Marines from Lebanon. Cubans celebrated the 25th anniversary of their revolution, and a U.S. helicopter was forced down by Nicaraguan gunfire along the Nicaragua-Honduras border. Ronald Reagan made it official: he was running again for the presidency. And the Soviet president, Yuri Andropov, died in Moscow.

By the end of 1984, President Reagan had defeated his Democratic opponent, Walter Mondale, in a landslide, but he had still not had a summit with the new Soviet leader, Konstantin Chernenko. The United States had virtually abandoned *all* its efforts to support the peace effort in the Middle East. To add insult to injury—and causing more injury—the temporary U.S. Embassy in Beirut was attacked again by Islamic terrorists. In Central America, the United States and Cuba made no progress in reconciling their different views of the region, and by year's end there was considerable nervousness that conflict between Nicaragua and the United States might lead to the open involvement of U.S. troops.

The American election results came as something of an anticlimax, but 1984 was still a historic year in U.S. politics. Not only did the Reverend Jackson make a creditable showing in the contest for the Democratic nomination, but when Walter Mondale was finally chosen—somewhat bloodied and bowed even before confronting President Reagan—he chose a woman as his running mate. Geraldine Ferraro, a congresswoman from New York, became the first woman to run for the vice-presidency as the nominee of a major national party. The Democratic ticket ultimately did not do very well, but Ferraro made it clear to most Americans that never again would a candidate be automatically excluded from the highest offices in the land simply because of her sex. As for the 1984 presidential race, Americans appeared to prove again that they vote for personalities rather than issues.

Elsewhere around the globe, 1984 was a watershed year in political affairs.

Canada's Prime Minister Pierre Elliott Trudeau resigned from office after more than 15 years on the job. In the subsequent election, his Liberal Party suffered the worst defeat in its history. A Conservative businessman named Brian Mulroney was elected Canada's new leader.

In Central America, the people of El Salvador, visibly weary of civil war, elected José Napoleón Duarte as president. By year's end, Duarte had held two face-to-face meetings with the antigovernment guerrillas. While there was no obvious sign that civil war was ending, both sides had indicated willingness to negotiate. In Nicaragua, meanwhile, the Sandinista government also held elections, but most of the opposition boycotted them. The more dangerous contest remained that between the Sandinistas and the Reagan administration. U.S.-supported anti-Sandinista military forces scored no major victories against the government, and by year's end the Reagan administration was sounding more threatening.

In India political change was violent. In late October, Prime Minister Indira Gandhi was assassinated by her own

The Strait of Gibraltar and Mediterranean Sea are seen in an oblique, easterly view from the space shuttle "Discovery" during its November flight. The success of the shuttle program was one of the bright spots of 1984.

NASA

Sikh bodyguards. In retrospect, many Indians believe they saw it coming. In June, Indian government troops had stormed the holiest Sikh shrine, the Golden Temple at Amritsar in the Punjab, and killed perhaps hundreds of Sikh separatists. Gandhi's assassination was seen as revenge, to which Hindus responded by murdering Sikhs. Not to the surprise of those who believe India's democracy is firmly embedded, the violence died down within a month. Mrs. Gandhi's only surviving son, Rajiv, was named to succeed her.

Some of the most bitter political tussling of the year took place in Great Britain. The government of Prime Minister Margaret Thatcher continued to hold a commanding majority in Parliament, but coal miners and the Irish Republican Army (IRA) launched major efforts to bring the government down. In October the IRA claimed responsibility for a massive bomb explosion at a British resort hotel, which came very close to killing or wounding the prime minister and much of her cabinet. Meanwhile, British miners were on strike for most of the year. It was an increasingly violent test of wills, which by year's end the government appeared to be winning. The leader of the mineworkers, a lifelong Marxist, made it clear that he was intent on overthrowing the government. And indeed it was less a miners' strike than class warfare. Towns and even families were divided by it.

Once again, the most crucial political battle of the year was between the United States and the Soviet Union on the subject of arms control. However, 1984 saw no progress in arms control because no negotiations even took place. Only in the waning months of the year did Washington and Moscow show signs of being prepared to try again. At the same time, the leaders of both nations were determined that their defense budgets would continue to grow. And both superpowers were concerned about the other's capacity to wage war in space.

Meanwhile, the world was reminded again of just how many people could be fed for the price of one nuclear weapon. Millions of people in more than 20 African nations were facing death from starvation. When mothers and babies were seen dying on television, much of the world responded with short-term aid. The long-term problems of drought and mismanagement of land, however, had still not been addressed.

As always, there were bright spots, Bishop Desmond Tutu, the black South African opponent of apartheid, won the Nobel Prize for Peace, overdue recognition of a struggle for equality that was reaping little attention outside the African continent. The summer Olympic Games in Los Angeles, despite a retaliatory boycott by the Soviet Union and some of its allies, were a great success for all the nations that did attend. They were a particular rejuvenation for Americans, who used the Games as a launching platform for an outburst of patriotism which by year's end had not waned. Americans also had reasons to cheer the continuing success of the space shuttle, which had stopped being an experiment and became a full-fledged delivery system for space. In November, the second man in history to receive an artificial heart reminded many citizens how far science could go in the service of mankind.

January

1 Brunei, a small Islamic sultanate on Borneo's northern coast, is granted independence by Great Britain.

3 Responding to the "human appeal" of visiting U.S. presidential candidate the Rev. Jesse Jackson, the Syrian government releases Lt. Robert O. Goodman, Jr., a U.S. Navy flier captured by Syria in Lebanon on Dec. 4, 1983.

4 Paul Thayer resigns as U.S. deputy secretary of defense amid allegations that the Securities and Exchange Commission planned to charge him with illegally distributing privileged stock information during his tenure as chairman of the LTV Corporation and director of four other companies.

10 The United States and the Vatican establish complete diplomatic relations.

11 The National Bipartisan Commission on Central America, chaired by Henry A. Kissinger, presents its report, recommending a broad five-year, $8 billion (U.S.) economic-aid program for the region.

A U.S. helicopter is forced down near the Nicaraguan border in Honduras, killing the pilot, Chief Warrant Officer Jeffrey C. Schwab.

12 As Prime Minister Zhao Ziyang concludes a three-day visit to Washington, China and the United States sign a science and technology agreement and a new accord on industrial cooperation.

Matsumoto, Sygma

Oil-rich Brunei gained independence, and its sultan, pictured above, became prime minister. In Syria, Jesse Jackson negotiated the release of U.S. Navy pilot Robert Goodman (waving).

Hartwell, Gamma-Liaison

16 France announces that it has agreed to sell Saudi Arabia more than $4 billion in arms.

17 The U.S. Supreme Court rules that the noncommercial home use of video recorders does not violate federal copyright law.

18 Malcolm H. Kerr, president of the American University of Beirut, is killed by unidentified gunmen in Beirut, Lebanon.

In Stockholm, Sweden, for the 35-nation East-West conference on European security, U.S. Secretary of State George Shultz and Soviet Foreign Minister Andrei Gromyko confer for some five hours.

Gen. Mohammed Buhari, chairman of Nigeria's Supreme Military Council, appoints an 18-member cabinet. Shehu Shagari was ousted as president in a coup on Dec. 31, 1983.

19 In Casablanca, Morocco, the Organization of the Islamic Conference agrees to readmit Egypt as a member. Egypt had been suspended after signing a peace treaty with Israel.

22 The Los Angeles Raiders defeat the Washington Redskins, 38–9, to win the National Football League's Super Bowl XVIII.

23 Chile and Argentina sign a friendship pact, pledging to resolve peacefully their dispute over the Beagle Channel.

24 Israel's Prime Minister Yitzhak Shamir welcomes West German Chancellor Helmut Kohl to Jerusalem.

25 President Reagan delivers the annual State of the Union address to Congress.

27 Voters in the Philippines approve a referendum on constitutional amendments, including the restoration of the office of vice-president.

29 President Reagan officially announces his candidacy for reelection.

February

1 President Reagan presents to Congress his budget for fiscal year 1985. Revenues are estimated at $745.1 billion and expenses at $925.5 billion.

2 Jaime Lusinchi is inaugurated as president of Venezuela.

Venezuela's new President Jaime Lusinchi and his wife, Gladys, wave to the crowd in the inauguration parade. Lusinchi, 59, won election in December 1983.

Sygma

5   In Lebanon, the nine-member cabinet of Prime Minister Shafik al-Wazan, a Muslim, resigns as pressure from Muslim groups opposed to the policies of President Amin Gemayel grows.

6   In Lebanon, Shiite and Druze forces opposed to President Gemayel seize key bases. U.S. President Reagan orders the use of U.S. air and naval forces against antigovernment positions near Beirut.

7   President Reagan orders the 1,600 U.S. Marines in the Beirut, Lebanon, area to begin "shortly" a phased redeployment to Navy ships offshore.

8   Great Britain withdraws its 115 troops from Lebanon, and Italy orders a gradual pullback of its 1,600-man force.

10   The Soviet Union announces the death of President Yuri Andropov on February 9.

China and the USSR sign a $1.2 billion (U.S.) trade agreement.

11   The space shuttle *Challenger* lands at Cape Canaveral, completing an eight-day mission. The mission was highlighted by two free-flying excursions outside the spacecraft by astronauts Capt. Bruce McCandless 2d and Lt. Col. Robert Stewart, but was marred by the failure of two communication satellites.

13   Konstantin U. Chernenko is named to succeed Yuri V. Andropov as general secretary of the Soviet Communist Party.

Panama's President Ricardo de la Espriella resigns without explanation and is succeeded by Vice-President Jorge Illueca.

14   President Reagan meets jointly with Egypt's President Hosni Mubarak and Jordan's King Hussein at the White House.

15   Leamon R. Hunt, 56-year-old U.S. director general of the multinational force in Egypt's Sinai Peninsula, is fatally shot in Rome, Italy.

17   Following the resignation of Richard B. Stone as special envoy to Central America, the White House names Harry W. Shlaudeman to the post.

Robin Moyer, Black Star

The 18-month mission of U.S. Marines in Lebanon came to a close February 26. Critics asked what had been accomplished.

18 Italy and the Vatican sign a new 14-article concordat under which Roman Catholicism ceases to be Italy's state religion.

19 The XIV Olympic Winter Games conclude in Sarajevo, Yugoslavia.

22 David, a 12-year-old who because of an immune deficiency syndrome spent his entire life except for 15 days in a sterile plastic bubble, dies in Houston, TX.

26 The U.S. Marine contingent stationed in Beirut, Lebanon, completes its pullout.

29 Pierre Elliott Trudeau announces that he plans to step down as prime minister of Canada. The action will be effective as soon as the ruling Liberal Party elects a new leader.

The USSR vetoes a French-sponsored proposal before the UN Security Council that would have sent a UN peacekeeping force to Lebanon.

Lebanon's President Gemayel and Syria's President Hafez al-Assad confer in Damascus.

March

3 Peter V. Ueberroth is named to succeed Bowie Kuhn as commissioner of baseball, effective Oct. 1, 1984.

5 Lebanon formally cancels its troop withdrawal accord with Israel.

The U.S. Supreme Court rules that a city may include a Nativity scene as part of its Christmas decorations without violating the constitutional clause calling for the separation of church and state.

8 In Poland, protests against the removal of crucifixes from the schools become more widespread.

11 Syria's President Hafez al-Assad shuffles his cabinet, naming his brother, Rifaat al-Assad, and two others as vice-presidents.

12 João Clemente Baena Soares of Brazil is elected secretary-general of the Organization of American States.

14 Gerry Adams, 36-year-old president of Sinn Fein, the political wing of the Irish Republican Army, is shot and wounded in Belfast.

16 South Africa and Mozambique sign a nonaggression treaty—the first such pact between South Africa and a black-ruled African nation.

William F. Buckley, first secretary of the U.S. Embassy's political section in Beirut, is kidnapped at gunpoint in Beirut.

20 A session of the Lebanese national unity talks, which convened in Lausanne, Switzerland, on March 12, breaks up without results.

The U.S. Senate rejects a White House-supported constitutional amendment to permit vocal prayer in public schools.

21 Taiwan's National Assembly reelects President Chiang Ching-kuo to a second six-year term.

In Ottawa, Canada, representatives from nine European nations and Canada sign an acid-rain agreement.

22 French President François Mitterrand confers with President Reagan in Washington.

25 Presidential elections are held in El Salvador. Since no candidate received more than 50% of the vote, a runoff is to be held in late April or early May.

26 Japan's Prime Minister Yasuhiro Nakasone concludes a series of talks with Chinese leaders in Peking.

Britain's Queen Elizabeth begins a state visit to Jordan.

29 A giant storm sweeps across the East Coast of the United States; some 67 persons are killed in a series of tornadoes in North and South Carolina.

Léopold S. Senghor, former president of Senegal, becomes the first black to be admitted to the French Academy.

31 Gen. Gustavo Alvarez Martínez, commander of the Honduran armed forces, is forced to resign.

Boyd, Gamma-Liaison

Salvadoran voters went to the polls to elect a president, but the initial balloting produced no clear winner. The turnout was heavy, but a shortage of ballot forms caused confusion.

April

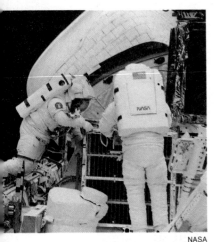

NASA
U.S. space shuttle astronauts James Van Hoften (right) and George Nelson perform midorbit repairs on the damaged "Solar Max" satellite recovered by Challenger *in its April mission.*

2 Washington lawyer Jacob A. Stein is named as an independent counsel to conduct a special investigation of charges against Edwin Meese 3d, who was nominated attorney general by President Reagan on Jan. 23, 1984.

3 The armed forces of Guinea announce that they have seized power in the West African nation. Ahmed Sékou Touré, the president of Guinea since 1958, died on March 26.

6 Residents of the Cocos Islands in the Indian Ocean vote to become part of Australia.

7 The United States and Japan reach an agreement regarding the amount of beef and citrus products to be exported to Japan.

10 The U.S. Senate approves a sense-of-the-Senate resolution opposing the use of federal funds to mine Nicaraguan waters. Americans working for the Central Intelligence Agency (CIA) reportedly were overseeing the mining of Nicaraguan waters.

11 Soviet party secretary Chernenko is named to the additional post of president (chairman of the Presidium of the Supreme Soviet).

13 The space shuttle *Challenger* lands safely at Edwards Air Force Base, completing a seven-day flight.

15 In west Beirut, members of Amal Shiite militia rescue two persons who had been kidnapped—Frank Regier, an American professor, and Christian Joubert, a French engineer.

Two U.S. diplomats are killed in a bomb explosion at a gas station in Namibia (South-West Africa).

Brian Dickson, 67, a native of Yorkton, Saskatchewan, became chief justice of the Supreme Court of Canada. Considered a moderate liberal, Dickson has served on the court since 1973.

Chris Schwarz

18 Two U.S. Army helicopters, one carrying two U.S. senators, are shot at near the El Salvador-Honduras border. No one is injured.

The Public Service Company of New Hampshire lays off 5,200 workers and halts work on both reactors at the Seabrook (NH) nuclear power plant.

19 Brian Dickson is sworn in as the 15th chief justice of Canada.

22 Great Britain announces that it is breaking diplomatic relations with Libya and is ordering the occupants of the Libyan Embassy in London to leave the country by April 29. On April 17, shots were fired from the embassy into a crowd of Libyans demonstrating against the government of Muammar el-Qaddafi, killing a police officer and injuring 10 other persons.

25 David A. Kennedy, the 28-year-old son of the late Sen. Robert F. Kennedy, is found dead in a Palm Beach (FL) hotel room.

26 In the Dominican Republic, at least 60 persons are dead and hundreds are injured following three days of rioting over government-ordered increases in the prices of food, medicine, and imported goods.

27 The Rhode Island Supreme Court overturns the 1982 attempted-murder convictions of Claus von Bülow and orders the socialite to face a new trial on charges of attempting to murder his wife.

29 Sudan's President Jaafar al-Nemery declares a state of emergency to "enable the government to achieve a maximum level of security and stability."

May

1   President Reagan concludes a five-day visit to China, highlighted by accords on nuclear cooperation and cultural exchange.

Colombia's President Belisario Betancur Cuartas declares a state of siege following the assassination of his justice minister.

6   Conservative Leon Febres Cordero Rivadeneira wins a narrow victory in a presidential election runoff in Ecuador.

7   Vietnam veterans agree to an out-of-court settlement of $180 million in their class action suit against seven chemical companies for injuries allegedly caused by Agent Orange.

The Soviet Union announces that it will not participate in the 1984 Summer Olympics in Los Angeles.

8   A gunman opens fire inside the Quebec National Assembly; three persons are killed and 13 wounded, none of them legislators.

Antigovernment guerrillas attack one of the residences of Libyan leader Muammar el-Qaddafi. Loyalist troops quell the attack.

On his 100th birthday, the late President Harry S. Truman is remembered in a joint session of Congress.

9   Martin Feldstein, chairman of the President's Council of Economic Advisers, announces his resignation.

10   The International Court of Justice rules that the United States should halt all mining and blockading of Nicaraguan ports.

11   José Napoleón Duarte of the Christian Democrats is declared the winner of El Salvador's May 6 presidential election runoff.

12   Pope John Paul II ends an 11-day pilgrimage to Alaska, where he met President Reagan on May 2, South Korea, Papua New Guinea, the Solomon Islands, and Thailand.

The Louisiana World Exposition opens in New Orleans.

AP/Wide World

Pope John Paul II receives a gift of arrows from a native tribesman after saying Mass at a remote highlands town in Papua New Guinea, May 7.

Bill Fitz-Patrick, The White House

During his "journey for peace" to China, President Reagan met with Premier Zhao Ziyang at the Great Hall of the People in Peking. Zhao was critical of U.S. foreign policy.

Escalation of the war between Iran and Iraq led to intensified air attacks against commercial oil shipping in the Persian Gulf. Raids continued throughout the spring.

14 In legislative elections in the Philippines, the New Society Movement of President Ferdinand Marcos retains a majority, but the opposition makes a surprisingly strong showing.

16 During a four-day visit to the United States, Mexico's President Miguel de la Madrid Hurtado addresses a joint session of Congress and warns against the use of force in Central America.

Nicolas Ardito Barletta Vallarina is declared the winner of Panama's first presidential election in 16 years.

19 The Edmonton Oilers win the National Hockey League's Stanley Cup, defeating the New York Islanders four games to one.

28 A solemn state funeral service is held at the Arlington (VA) National Cemetery for the last unidentified U.S. serviceman killed in the Vietnam war. President Reagan presides.

29 President Reagan authorizes the sale of 400 Stinger antiaircraft missiles to Saudi Arabia, citing "grave concern" over the escalating Iran-Iraq war and the danger to neutral vessels in the Persian Gulf. Attacks on Gulf shipping have been intensifying sharply since late April.

The United States and Japan announce a series of measures to raise the value of the yen and open Japan's financial markets.

The spring meeting of NATO foreign ministers convenes in Washington, DC, as the alliance marks its 35th anniversary.

June

1 U.S. Secretary of State George Shultz makes an unexpected trip to Nicaragua, where he meets with junta leader Daniel Ortega.

The Dutch cabinet votes to postpone until Nov. 1, 1985, a decision on whether to deploy U.S. cruise missiles.

6 Indian army troops storm the holiest Sikh shrine, the Golden Temple in Amritsar, the state of Punjab, in an attempt to put down escalating violence by Sikh separatists. More than 300 persons are reported killed.

President Reagan, France's President François Mitterrand, and six other Western leaders commemorate the 40th anniversary of D-Day on the beaches of Normandy, France. The U.S. president arrived in France after a four-day visit to Ireland.

9 The tenth annual summit conference of the seven major industrialized democracies ends in London after three days of talks.

Santosh Basak, Gamma-Liaison

In India, the increasingly militant campaign of Sikh separatist extremists in the state of Punjab finally moved the government to harsh countermeasures during early June.

12 Lebanon's parliament approves the new "national unity" cabinet of Prime Minister Rashid Karami. It also grants Karami special authority to reform the political system and armed forces.

The U.S. Supreme Court rules that courts may not order employers to protect the jobs of recently hired minorities at the expense of employees with greater seniority.

The Boston Celtics win their 15th National Basketball Association championship by defeating the Los Angeles Lakers, 111–102, in the seventh game of their final play-off series.

14 South Africa's Prime Minister P. W. Botha concludes a 17-day, eight-nation tour of Western Europe. The trip was intended to reduce isolation over his country's apartheid policy.

15 The United States withdraws a $300 million loan guarantee for Argentina. The move comes four days after Argentina rejected austerity measures proposed by the International Monetary Fund.

16 The second-ever direct elections for the 434-seat European Parliament are held in six member-nations; voting had been held in the other four member-nations on June 14.

17 Swale, winner of the 1984 Kentucky Derby and Belmont Stakes, dies suddenly after a light workout at Belmont Park, NY.

20 On his first official visit to Moscow, France's President Mitterrand rankles Soviet leaders by raising the issue of Andrei Sakharov, the rights activist reportedly on a hunger strike.

22 At Cartagena, Colombia, 11 Latin American nations agree to establish a task force and a consultation process to find solutions for the Third World foreign debt crisis.

Officials in the United States and El Salvador report that a right-wing plot to assassinate U.S. ambassador Thomas Pickering had been uncovered during the month of May.

26 The maiden flight of the U.S. space shuttle *Discovery* is aborted four seconds before liftoff because of an engine malfunction.

27 In talks in Havana with Cuba's President Fidel Castro, U.S. presidential candidate the Rev. Jesse Jackson arranges for the release of 22 U.S. citizens being held in Cuban prisons, as well as 26 Cuban political prisoners.

30 John Napier Turner is sworn in as the 17th prime minister of Canada. The 55-year-old corporate lawyer and former cabinet minister was elected leader of the Liberal Party on June 16.

Bolivia's President Hernan Siles Zuazo is kidnapped and then freed in an aborted coup attempt by army and police officers.

At Canada's Liberal Party convention in Ottawa, John Napier Turner won election as party leader and the nation's next prime minister. He succeeds Pierre Elliott Trudeau.

Brian Willer

July

3 Air Florida files for protection under Chapter 11 of the federal bankruptcy code, leaving many passengers stranded.

4 In the first phase of the peace plan adopted by Lebanon's new national unity government, army units begin taking over positions that had been held by warring factions in Beirut.

The 13 member-nations of the Caribbean Community and Common Market (CARICOM) convene in Nassau for a four-day summit.

5 Umaru Dikko, former Nigerian transport minister, is found unconscious inside a crate at a London airport. Wanted by the Nigerian government, Dikko had been kidnapped near his London home.

The U.S. Supreme Court rules in two cases that there is a good-faith exception to the 70-year-old "exclusionary rule," the principle that criminal evidence is inadmissible at trial if it is obtained unconstitutionally.

6 The U.S. Labor Department reports that the nation's unemployment rate fell in June to a seasonally adjusted 7.0%, its lowest level in more than four years.

7 The much-ballyhooed, four-week "Victory" concert tour of the Jackson Brothers kicks off in Kansas City, MO.

8 John McEnroe wins his second consecutive Wimbledon men's singles tennis championship. Martina Navratilova took her third straight women's crown the day before.

12 In their first substantive negotiations since the Reagan administration took office, the United States and Cuba open talks in New York on issues of immigration.

13 China and Vietnam report heavy fighting along their border.

14 In general elections in New Zealand, the Labor Party, led by 41-year-old David Lange, ousts the conservative National Party government of Prime Minister Robert Muldoon.

18 James Oliver Huberty, an unemployed 41-year-old husband and father, goes on a shooting rampage at a McDonald's restaurant in San Ysidro, CA, leaving 22 persons dead.

19 At the Democratic National Convention, former Vice-President Walter F. Mondale accepts the party nomination for president. Rep. Geraldine A. Ferraro (NY) is nominated for vice-president.

France's recently appointed Prime Minister Laurent Fabius names a new Socialist-led coalition cabinet. Fabius, 37, was appointed premier after the resignation of Pierre Mauroy on July 17.

21 Marking the 40th anniversary of Communist rule, the Polish Parliament grants amnesty to 652 political prisoners.

23 Vanessa Williams announces her resignation as Miss America. Pageant officials had asked her to step down upon learning that nude photographs of her would be published in a magazine.

Two Amtrak trains collide in Queens, NY, killing one person and injuring 125. It is the fourth major Amtrak crash in a month.

25 Soviet cosmonaut Svetlana Savitskaya, 36, becomes the first woman to walk in space.

AP/Wide World

Vanessa Williams answers reporters' questions after relinquishing her title of Miss America. She had been asked to resign—the first of 57 Miss Americas to be so requested—after it was learned that nude photographs of her would be published.

26 The U.S. government commits itself to a $4.5 billion rescue package for the ailing Continental Illinois National Bank of Chicago. It is the largest federal support package for any private enterprise in U.S. history.

28 The Games of the XXIII Olympiad in Los Angeles are declared open.

August

1 After talks in Peking with Chinese leaders, Britain's Foreign Secretary Sir Geoffrey Howe announces an accord between the two countries on the future of Hong Kong. Britain's lease on the colony expires in 1997; China will take control.

3 In response to Poland's declaration of amnesty for political prisoners July 21, the United States lifts some of its economic sanctions against the country.

After a week of record volume trading on the New York Stock Exchange, the Dow Jones industrial average closes at 1202.08, a record 87.46-point increase over the previous Friday.

4 On the first anniversary of the coup that brought him to power, President Thomas Sankara of Upper Volta declares that the name of the country will be changed to Burkina Faso.

6 The second UN International Conference on Population convenes in Mexico City, with delegates representing 149 nations.

10 Judge Harry E. Claiborne, a U.S. district court judge in Nevada, is found guilty of tax evasion. He is the first active federal judge ever to be convicted of a crime.

13 King Hassan II of Morocco and Col. Muammar el-Qaddafi of Libya sign an accord establishing in principle a "union of states."

15 British and French minesweepers join Egyptian and U.S. ships and helicopters in the Red Sea to search for the cause of a series of explosions that damaged more than a dozen ships in recent weeks.

During a nationwide tour, U.S. Olympic medal winners are honored with a ticker-tape parade in New York City, August 15. The event was marred by a collapsing construction scaffold, which injured about 100 spectators.

AP/Wide World

16 A federal jury in Los Angeles finds former automobile manufacturer John Z. De Lorean not guilty on eight charges related to an alleged sale of cocaine in 1982.

22 At the 33d Republican National Convention in Dallas, President Ronald Reagan and Vice-President George Bush are formally nominated for reelection.

24 The M-19, Colombia's best-known guerrilla group, signs a cease-fire agreement with the government. It is the country's third major leftist rebel organization to sign a truce in two days.

29 Six days before the first production model is to be unveiled, a prototype of the controversial B-1 bomber crashes during a test flight near Edwards Air Force Base in California. One crewman is killed and two injured.

September

1 Nicaraguan forces shoot down a U.S. helicopter during a rebel raid against a government military camp. Three persons, two of them U.S. citizens, are killed.

4 Brian Mulroney and the opposition Progressive Conservatives (PCs) win a landslide victory in Canada's parliamentary elections. The PCs win a record number of seats.

5 The U.S. space shuttle *Discovery* completes a highly successful, six-day maiden flight.

Soviet party leader Konstantin Chernenko makes his first public appearance in nearly two months, awarding medals to three cosmonauts in Moscow.

South Africa's Prime Minister Pieter W. Botha is elected executive president under the nation's new constitution. Mixed-race and Asian voters went to the polls August 22 and 28 to elect their representatives to the new tricameral parliament.

6 President Chun Doo Hwan becomes the first South Korean leader to make an official visit to Japan since 1945.

Soviet Chief of Staff Marshal Nikolai Ogarkov is dismissed from his post. Marshal Sergei Akhromeyev, his deputy, replaces him as the senior military officer.

Nearly 1,400 people are killed as Typhoon Ike ravages the southern Philippines.

Canapress

M. Brian Mulroney and wife Mila wave thanks to Progressive Conservative supporters after he won a landslide victory in Canada's general elections, September 4. Mulroney was sworn in as prime minister on September 17.

Pete Souza, The White House

9 Pope John Paul II begins a 12-day tour of Canada, becoming the first pontiff ever to visit that country.

John McEnroe defeats Ivan Lendl to win his fourth U.S. Open men's singles tennis championship. Martina Navratilova won her second straight women's title by beating Chris Evert Lloyd the day before.

14 Israel's parliament approves a national unity government of the Labor Party and the Likud bloc. In the unprecedented power-sharing arrangement, Shimon Peres of the Labor Party is sworn in as prime minister for 25 months.

18 The UN General Assembly convenes its 39th annual session.

20 The U.S. Embassy annex outside Beirut, Lebanon, is bombed in a suicide car attack, leaving at least 23 persons dead and dozens of others injured.

21 The United Auto Workers (UAW) union and General Motors Co. reach agreement on a new, three-year contract. After a week of selective strikes, union members go back to work.

25 Jordan announces that it will resume full diplomatic relations with Egypt; ties had been broken after Egypt signed a peace treaty with Israel in 1979.

Under an accord signed September 17, France and Libya begin withdrawing their troops from Chad.

28 President Reagan holds three and a half hours of "forceful and direct" talks with Soviet Foreign Minister Andrei Gromyko at the White House. It is Reagan's first meeting with any ranking Soviet official since becoming president. Gromyko held a 90-minute conference with Democratic candidate Walter Mondale the day before.

29 In one of the stiffest crackdowns ever on the Mafia, Italian law enforcement authorities begin arresting dozens of suspected organized crime figures. The roundup follows the confession of former high-level Mafia drug trafficker Tommaso Buscetta.

North Korea begins sending relief supplies to flood victims in South Korea. It is the first aid to pass across the border since before the Korean War.

Soviet Foreign Minister Andrei Gromyko and President Reagan conferred for three and a half hours at the White House on September 28. Secretary of State George Shultz described the meeting as "a very strong personal interchange between two individuals."

October

AP/Wide World

Raymond Donovan announces that he is taking a leave of absence as U.S. secretary of labor to fight a 137-count indictment which he says is not "worth the paper it's written on."

1 China celebrates 35 years of Communist rule with a massive military and civilian parade through Tien An Men Square in Peking.

2 Three Soviet cosmonauts return to earth after spending a record 237 days in space.

U.S. Secretary of Labor Raymond Donovan announces that he is taking a leave of absence after being indicted by a Bronx (NY) County grand jury. The charges relate to work done on a subway project by his former construction company.

3 The Marxist government of Mozambique and the rebel National Resistance movement reach agreement on a cease-fire, to be policed by South Africa.

FBI agent Richard W. Miller is arrested in San Diego on charges of providing classified U.S. documents to the Soviet Union. He is the bureau's first agent ever to be arrested for spying.

5 The West German government announces that more than 80 East Germans have entered its embassy in Prague, Czechoslovakia, seeking political asylum.

11 Kathryn D. Sullivan becomes the first U.S. woman to walk in space, as she leaves the space shuttle *Challenger* during its eight-day mission. Seven astronauts, the most ever, are on the flight.

12 Britain's Prime Minister Margaret Thatcher and her entire cabinet escape assassination as a bomb explodes at a hotel where they are staying in Brighton, England. The Irish Republican Army claims responsibility for planting the bomb.

The 98th U.S. Congress adjourns.

14 The Detroit Tigers win baseball's World Series with an 8-4 triumph over the San Diego Padres in Game 5.

15 El Salvador's President José Napoleon Duarte meets in La Palma with top rebel leaders for four and a half hours. The parties agree to form a joint commission to seek an end to civil war. It is the first meeting of government and guerrilla leaders.

Breaking with Eastern European allies and with Soviet policy, Rumania's President Nicolae Ceauşescu travels to Bonn, West Germany. It is the first top-level contact between a Warsaw Pact nation and a NATO member since the USSR broke off arms-control talks in 1983.

16 Bishop Desmond Tutu, a leader of the antiapartheid movement in South Africa, is named the winner of the 1984 Nobel Peace Prize.

18 Chile and Argentina initial a treaty settling their long-standing dispute over the Beagle Channel.

20 China announces major reforms in its urban industrial economy, limiting central planning and introducing free-market forces.

24 A commission investigating the August 1983 assassination of Philippine opposition leader Benigno Aquino, Jr., concludes that the military had been involved in a "criminal plot."

29 Members of the United Auto Workers (UAW) in Canada end a 13-day strike against General Motors, as they ratify a new contract.

Japan's Yasuhiro Nakasone is reelected leader of the Liberal Democratic Party, assuring him two more years as premier.

30 The body of Poland's missing pro-Solidarity priest, Father Jerzy Popieluszko, is found in a reservoir 11 days after he was kidnapped by three state security police officers.

31 India's Prime Minister Indira Gandhi is shot and killed by Sikh bodyguards. Rioting breaks out as Hindus seek revenge. The late prime minister's son, Rajiv Gandhi, is sworn in as her successor.

At the end of a two-day emergency meeting in Geneva, oil ministers of the Organization of the Petroleum Exporting Countries (OPEC) announce reductions in output quotas for most member nations.

November

1 Svetlana Alliluyeva, daughter of the late Soviet leader Stalin, has returned home to the USSR 17 years after defecting to the West, according to reports in the official Soviet press.

2 Margie Velma Barfield, a 52-year-old North Carolina grandmother convicted of murdering her fiancé in 1978, becomes the first woman to suffer the death penalty in the United States in 22 years.

4 Nicaraguan junta leader Daniel Ortega Saavedra is elected president and his Sandinista National Liberation Front (FSLN) wins 61 of 91 National Assembly seats in the nation's first election since 1974. The U.S. administration calls the voting a "farce."

6 President Ronald W. Reagan and Vice-President George Bush are returned to the White House with a landslide victory over the Democratic ticket of Walter F. Mondale and Geraldine A. Ferraro.

Chile's President Augusto Pinochet declares a state of siege and names a new cabinet following a major outbreak of violent public protests and a national strike.

With her son and successor, Rajiv (far left), *at her side, slain Indian Prime Minister Indira Gandhi lies in state.*

J. Langevin, Sygma

Tannenbaum, Sygma

In mid-November, amid mounting tensions with the United States, Nicaragua's armed forces were placed on full combat alert and prepared for possible war. U.S. officials had charged that Soviet MiG fighter planes were being shipped to Nicaragua, an accusation which Managua and Moscow labeled "provocative."

8 Israeli and Lebanese officials open talks on the terms of withdrawal for the remaining 10,000 Israeli troops in southern Lebanon.

14 Six unnamed employees of the U.S. Central Intelligence Agency are reported to have been disciplined for their role in producing and distributing a manual on guerrilla tactics to Nicaraguan rebels.

15 Baby Fae, a two-month-old girl whose defective heart had been replaced by the heart of a baboon on October 26, dies at Loma Linda (CA) University Medical Center, where the operation was performed.

19 A storage area for liquefied natural gas in a suburb of Mexico City explodes in flames just before dawn, destroying a heavily populated 20-block area and killing more than 500 people.

20 South Africa announces that it will negotiate with Angola on the withdrawal of its troops from that country. On November 11, Angola offered to remove most Cuban troops stationed there.

22 The United States and Soviet Union announce the scheduling of arms negotiations in early January 1985 between Secretary of State Shultz and Foreign Minister Gromyko in Geneva.

25 William J. Schroeder, a 52-year-old retired federal employee, becomes the second person to receive a permanent artificial heart.

In Uruguay's first election in 13 years, Julio Mariá Sanguinetti, a centrist, is elected president.

26 The United States and Iraq restore full diplomatic ties.

27 Great Britain and Spain announce an agreement to normalize relations between Spain and Gibraltar.

28 Senate Republicans elect Robert J. Dole as majority leader, to take over from Howard Baker, who is retiring from the Senate.

Lee M. Thomas is named to replace William D. Ruckelshaus as head of the U.S. Environmental Protection Agency. Ruckelshaus announced his resignation the day before.

December

1 Prime Minister Bob Hawke and his Australian Labor Party easily win parliamentary elections, though with a reduced majority.

3 In what is described as the worst industrial accident ever, a poisonous gas leak from a pesticide plant in Bhopal, India, leaves more than 2,000 people dead.

4 Centrist candidate Herbert Augustus Blaize is sworn in as prime minister of Grenada, one day after his election.

Leaders of the ten European Community nations conclude a two-day summit in Dublin, with little result.

9 Iranian security forces storm a hijacked Kuwaiti airliner at Tehran airport, freeing the last nine hostages on board and capturing the hijackers, believed to be Lebanese Shiite Muslims. Two American passengers were killed during the five-day drama.

12 In a bloodless coup in Mauritania, Col. Maouya Ould Sidi Ahmed Taya takes control from Lt. Col. Mohammed Khouna Ould Haidalla.

14 Manuel Esquivel of the United Democratic Party upsets Prime Minister George Price of the People's United Party in national elections in Belize.

The United States and Cuba announce an agreement on the repatriation to Havana of 2,746 Cuban criminals and mental patients who came to the United States in the 1980 Mariel boatlift.

16 Britain's Prime Minister Margaret Thatcher meets in London with visiting Soviet official Mikhail Gorbachev, believed to be the second-in-command at the Kremlin and the eventual successor to Konstantin Chernenko. Talks center on arms control.

18 After a five-year absence, Egypt takes its seat at the 15th annual summit meeting of foreign ministers of the Islamic Conference Organization, held in Sana, North Yemen.

19 The United States confirms that it will be withdrawing from UNESCO at the end of the year.

In Peking, Chinese Premier Zhao Ziyang and Britain's Prime Minister Thatcher sign an agreement giving China sovereignty over Hong Kong in 1997 but preserving the capitalist system there.

22 Marshal Sergei L. Sokolov, 73, is chosen to succeed Dmitri F. Ustinov as Soviet defense minister. Ustinov died December 20.

23 During a visit to Peking by Soviet First Deputy Prime Minister Ivan V. Arkhipov, China and the USSR announce four new cooperation agreements, indicating a slight thaw in relations.

At least 25 people are killed and 50 injured when two bomb explosions rock a packed train passing through a tunnel between Florence and Bologna, Italy. Political terrorism is suspected.

25 Vietnamese troops mount a major attack against Cambodian rebel camps along the Thai-Cambodian border.

29 Returns from nationwide parliamentary elections in India show Prime Minister Rajiv Gandhi and his Congress (I) party the winners in a landslide.

31 Bernhard Hugo Goetz, a 37-year-old Manhattan man, turns himself in to police in Concord, NH, confessing to be the "vigilante" gunman of four teenagers on a New York City subway ten days before.

AP/Wide World

Rosa Parks, who sparked the U.S. civil rights movement in Montgomery, AL, nearly 30 years before by refusing to give up her bus seat, joins an anti-apartheid march in front of the South African Embassy in Washington. The Reagan administration also came under new pressure late in the year for its policy toward South Africa.

THE 1984 U.S. ELECTIONS —AN OVERVIEW

By Robert Shogan

Aboard the same train used by Harry Truman in 1948, Ronald Reagan went on a 200-mile (320-km) "whistle stop" of Ohio in October. Like Mr. Truman's, the president's campaign was an overwhelming success.

The 1984 presidential campaign had the distinction of being the longest in U.S. history, its origins going back to early 1983. Long before a single vote had been cast in 1984's Democratic primaries and caucuses, eight contenders for the Democratic nomination had between them spent millions of dollars and traveled thousands of miles to promote their candidacies.

The unprecedented intensity of this early activity represented the culmination of two major developments in the nation's political system. One was the breakdown over the past two decades of the influence of regular party organizations and leadership that in the past had been able to dominate the outcome of the nominating process. In this power vacuum candidates have been obliged to build their own organizations to seek support on their own among rank and file voters. The other development was the post-Watergate campaign finance reforms that limited the size of individual contributions to campaigns and forced candidates to work longer and harder to collect smaller contributions from more donors.

Both these trends had been evident in recent previous presidential campaigns. And in 1984 the contenders for the Democratic nomination, mindful of past experience and determined not to be outdone by their competitors, launched their efforts earlier than ever before. The Republicans were spared such a prolonged and fractious struggle because it had long been assumed that President Reagan could have their nomination for the asking and generally expected that he would seek reelection. Any lingering doubts on that score were ended on January 29 when the president, in a paid political telecast from the Oval Office, told the nation's voters: "Vice-President Bush and I would like to have your continued support and cooperation in completing what we began three years ago."

By the time Reagan formally announced his candidacy, the Democratic contest was already in high gear. Former Vice-President Walter F. Mondale was regarded universally as the front-runner. He was the best known of the presidential prospects, had raised far more money than his rivals during 1983, and had received the endorsement of several powerful Democratic constituency groups, notably the AFL-CIO. Mondale's rivals were former Florida Gov. Reubin Askew, California Sen. Alan Cranston, Ohio Sen. John Glenn, Colorado Sen. Gary Hart, South Carolina Sen. Ernest Hollings, civil-rights leader Jesse Jackson, and 1972 nominee George McGovern.

About the Author: Robert Shogan has been national political correspondent in the Washington Bureau of the *Los Angeles Times* since 1973. Previously he was an assistant editor of *The Wall Street Journal* and a correspondent for *Newsweek* magazine. Mr. Shogan's most recent books include a biography of former President Jimmy Carter, *Promises to Keep,* and a study of the American presidency, *None of the Above: Why Presidents Fail & What Can Be Done about It.*

Jack Kightlinger, The White House

Displays of patriotism went with the GOP theme: "America is back, a giant on the scene, powerful in its renewed spirit, powerful in its growing economy, and secure in its peace."

With dramatic and unexpected victories in several early Democratic primaries and caucuses, Gary Hart was the big surprise of the 1984 political season. The senator from Colorado sought to project the message that he was the candidate with youth, vigor, and new ideas.

The Democratic Caucuses and Primaries. The focus of the campaign in its early stages was on televised debates between the Democratic candidates, the first two of which were held at Dartmouth College in New Hampshire, site of the first primary, and in Des Moines, IA, the first caucus state. In both these encounters Mondale's rivals joined in attacking him, while the former vice-president concentrated on outlining his differences with the Reagan administration. In the Des Moines debate on February 11, Hart raised a point that was to become a particular vulnerability for Mondale when Hart challenged the front-runner to name an important issue on which he disagreed with the AFL-CIO. Mondale did not respond directly, and the issue of his closeness to organized labor and other interest groups was to haunt him throughout the political season.

At first, though, the debates did not appear to have damaged Mondale. He won the Iowa caucuses on February 20 with 49% of the vote, while Glenn, who had been expected to give Mondale his strongest competition, finished fifth with only 3.5%. Hart finished second with 16.5%, thus strengthening his position in the forthcoming primary in New Hampshire where Hart had forged a strong personal organization. The

Colorado senator's efforts in that state were rewarded in the February 27 primary when he scored a stunning upset victory, getting 39% of the vote to 29% for Mondale. In the wake of his defeat, the former vice-president declared that he was no longer the front-runner, and momentum shifted dramatically to Hart. Askew, Cranston, and Hollings dropped out of the competition.

In swift succession Hart won the Maine caucus on March 4 and the nonbinding Vermont primary on March 6, and opinion polls showed him gaining support across the nation, leading many observers to believe that he would drive Mondale out of the race and clinch the nomination for himself. The critical test came on March 13, dubbed Super Tuesday, because it was the date of five primaries and four caucuses around the country. Though Hart won the primaries in Rhode Island, Massachusetts, and Florida and appeared to finish ahead of Mondale in most of the caucus states, the former vice-president rallied to win the Georgia and Alabama primaries. Glenn and McGovern both abandoned their candidacies, and the campaign became a three-way contest, involving Mondale, Hart, and Jesse Jackson.

Having survived Super Tuesday, Mondale lashed out at Hart during a continuing series of televised debates. He argued that Hart's Senate voting record showed that he had failed to support the nuclear freeze and measures to combat unemployment. He also challenged Hart's claim to be the spokesman for "new ideas" with a line borrowed from a fast-food commercial: "Where's the beef?"

Helped by the backing of the United Auto Workers, Mondale won a major victory in the Michigan caucuses on March 17 with 50% of the vote and finished first in two other caucuses in Arkansas and Mississippi. Jackson came in first in South Carolina. Meanwhile, Hart's campaign, which lacked Mondale's financial and organizational resources, was showing the

AP/Wide World

At the John F. Kennedy School of Government on January 31, contenders for the Democratic presidential nomination (left to right), Jesse Jackson, George McGovern, Gary Hart, John Glenn, Walter Mondale, and Ernest Hollings debated foreign policy. Alan Cranston also participated; Reuben Askew was absent. The Rev. Jackson (below) appealed to his "rainbow" constituency, including "the desperate, the disinherited, and the despised."

Mark Phillips, Picture Group

At the convention in San Francisco, Democratic leaders came together to congratulate their ticket.

strain of the intense competition. In the campaign leading up to the March 20 Illinois primary, Hart became involved in a distracting dispute over campaign commercials, and Mondale defeated him, getting 40.5% of the vote to 35.2% for Hart. Jackson finished a strong third, and his candidacy helped foster a heavy black turnout in Chicago.

Mondale followed up his Illinois success with impressive victories in New York on April 3 and in Pennsylvania on April 10, where he was aided by backing from labor leaders and local Democratic leaders. Mondale's victories were all the more impressive because Jackson was getting the support of most black voters, many of whom, it was generally presumed, would otherwise have backed Mondale.

But Jackson could not get a significant portion of white votes and thus was unable to achieve his goal of forging a "rainbow coalition." Jackson had gained favorable attention early in the year when he traveled to Syria and helped in gaining the release of Navy flier Robert Goodman who had been held prisoner by the Syrians after his plane was shot down while it was on a mission over Lebanon. Nevertheless, many whites apparently still regarded Jackson's rhetoric on the campaign stump as too strident. And his chances of broadening his support also were damaged by charges of anti-Semitism leveled against him. This criticism stemmed from Jackson's reference to New York City as "Hymietown" in a conversation with a reporter, and from various remarks made by one of his supporters, black Muslim leader Louis J. Farrakhan, who accused Jewish groups of trying to harm Jackson's campaign. Although Jackson disavowed any anti-Semitic intent, his reluctance to repudiate Farrakhan was a continuing problem for him.

For his part, Hart had at least as much difficulty winning black support as Jackson had in getting white votes. And the Colorado senator could not match Mondale's appeal to other traditional Democratic constituencies, such as Jews, union members, and the elderly. Nevertheless, Hart continued to get backing from independent-minded Democrats and from the so-called "yuppies"—young, upwardly mobile professionals. The yuppie vote helped him score narrow upset victories over Mondale in May 8 primaries in both Ohio and Indiana, while Mondale was winning in North Carolina and Maryland.

Though Mondale, who had also won the Texas caucuses, by now had a commanding lead in delegates, Hart's success in the two Midwest states, and subsequent victories in primaries in Nebraska and Oregon, helped keep his candidacy and the Democratic campaign alive until the final primaries on June 5. In these contests Hart defeated Mondale in California, the nation's largest state; New Mexico; and South Dakota. But Mondale won the West Virginia primary and gained an overwhelming victory in New Jersey, enough to give him more than the 1,967 delegate majority needed for nomination at the convention.

AP/Wide World

In a rousing keynote address at the Democratic Convention, Gov. Mario Cuomo of New York called on Americans "to look past the glitter, beyond the showmanship" of the Reagan presidency.

Benson, "The Arizona Republic"

The Democratic Ticket. Though Hart and Jackson continued to pursue their candidacies, Mondale's nomination was no longer in serious doubt, and he turned his attention to the selection of a running mate. After a much-publicized series of interviews with prospective candidates, he announced just before the Democratic convention that he had decided on Congresswoman Geraldine Ferraro of New York. She would become the first woman nominated by a major party for national office.

The selection of Ferraro, who was serving her third term in the House, came under criticism from those who contended that Mondale had yielded to the pressure of women's groups in picking her, and who argued that she lacked the experience to serve as understudy to the president. But these criticisms, at least at first, were overshadowed by the widespread enthusiasm for Mondale's decision to break new ground by choosing a woman.

Mondale distracted attention from these positive feelings on the eve of the convention's July 16 opening in San Francisco by attempting to replace Democratic National Chairman Charles Manatt with Bert Lance, Georgia Democratic chairman. Lance, who had been forced to leave his Carter administration post as director of the Office of Management and

At the GOP convention, a video screen was used for closed-circuit projection and an 18-minute film on the president.

J. L. Atlan, Sygma

Budget because of a scandal over his previous operations as a Georgia banker, subsequently had been acquitted of criminal charges and had been a major factor in Mondale's victory in the critical Georgia primary. But party leaders objected so vigorously to the plan to make Lance national chairman that Mondale was forced to scrap the idea. Instead Mondale appointed Lance to a post in his own campaign from which he subsequently resigned.

At the convention itself both Hart and Jackson pledged to campaign for Mondale and appealed for party unity. Mondale himself in his acceptance speech said that the Democrats had learned from their 1980 defeat that the electorate was reluctant to support more government programs and increased federal spending. He promised to bring "a new realism" to politics and government. Polls immediately after the convention showed that the Mondale-Ferraro ticket trailed the Republicans by only a few points, and Democrats' hopes for victory rose.

This mood soon changed, however, in part because of a controversy over the financial affairs of Ferraro and her husband, John Zaccaro, who at first refused to make public his income tax returns. Ultimately he did so, and Ferraro, during a nationally televised press conference, sought to dispel questions about her finances. Nevertheless, the furor had an unsettling effect on the Democrats at a crucial moment in the campaign and, some analysts believed, diminished Ferraro's appeal as a candidate.

The GOP Convention and the Campaign. The Republican convention in Dallas was marked by some preliminary squabbling over the platform, notably about how firm the party should be in pledging its opposition to a tax increase in view of the huge federal budget deficit. But a compromise was reached, and a strongly conservative platform reflecting President Reagan's own views was adopted readily by the convention after it opened August 20. Reagan and Bush were renominated by acclamation. In his acceptance speech the president vowed that he would ask the voters "to renew the mandate of 1980, to move us further forward on the road we presently travel."

Polls at the start of the general election campaign in September showed the president ahead by about 15 to 20 points, a margin that Mondale was never able to diminish significantly. Reagan's chief assets were his personal popularity, the strength of the economy, and the fact that the nation was at peace. In his stump speeches the president frequently compared current conditions with the difficulties the nation had endured under the Carter-Mondale administration. He avoided specific commitment on most issues, relying instead on a general promise to continue his policies. Mondale, on the other hand, sought to make the budget deficit the major issue of his campaign. He contended that a tax increase would be needed to avoid economic decline and promised that the Democrats would enact fairer tax legislation than the Republicans. But Reagan, by insisting that he would not propose any tax

AP/Wide World

Throughout his tenure as vice-president and the campaign, George Bush remained the loyal Reagan partisan. Between Labor Day and November 6, he traveled some 35,000 mi (56 325 km) extolling the accomplishments of the Reagan administration. Analysts generally declared him the winner of his debate with his Democratic opponent.

Two presidential debates high-lighted the campaign. Rep. Phil Gramm (R-TX), a former Democrat, was elected to the U.S. Senate. But all in all, the Reagan coattails were not long.

Photos, AP/Wide World

increase except as "a last resort," appeared to blunt Mondale's attack, and the challenger was unable to develop another effective message.

Most public interest in the campaign centered on the two televised debates between the presidential candidates. In the first encounter, October 7, Mondale seemed poised and crisp while Reagan was uncharacteristically awkward. Polls showed that Mondale was judged the winner by viewers, and media analysts suggested that by his faltering performance the 73-year-old Reagan had made voters wonder whether he was alert enough to serve a second term. But in the second debate, October 21, Reagan turned aside a question about his age with a joke, quipping that he would not exploit Mondale's "youth and inexperience." Polls showed that he had won the return match. Bush and Ferraro also debated on television on October 11, and polls indicated that the incumbent vice-president came out ahead.

The Results. The actual results at the ballot box closely matched the preelection findings of the pollsters. Reagan won a landslide victory, getting 52.6 million votes amounting to 59%, as against 36.4 million and 41% for Mondale. The president swept 49 states with Mondale carrying only his native Minnesota and the staunchly Democratic District of Columbia.

Republicans were not nearly so successful in the congressional contests, however. They had hoped to recapture all, or nearly all, of the 26 House seats they had lost to the Democrats in the 1982 elections. Instead they gained only 14 seats, leaving the Democrats firmly in control of the House with a majority of 252 seats to 182 (1 undecided). In the Senate the Republicans suffered a net loss of two seats, reducing their majority to 53 to 47. Of the 33 Senate races, 19 were for seats controlled by Republicans. Two Republican incumbents were defeated—Charles Percy of Illinois who lost to Democratic Rep. Paul Simon, and Roger Jepsen of Iowa who was defeated by Democratic Rep. Tom Harkin. In addition, in Tennessee, Democratic Rep. Albert Gore won the seat that had been held by retiring Republican Majority Leader Howard Baker. The only Democratic incumbent senator to lose was Walter D. Huddleston of Kentucky, who was defeated by Mitchell McConnell. Other new senators elected were Democrats John F. Kerry, who took over the Massachusetts seat held by retiring Democrat Paul Tsongas, and John D. (Jay) Rockefeller IV, who won the seat of retiring Democrat Jennings Randolph, and Republican Rep. Phil Gramm, who will replace retiring Republican John Tower of Texas.

In the gubernatorial races, the Republicans scored a net gain of one, giving them 16 governorships to 34 for the Democrats. Four Republicans won governorships in states where Democratic incumbents did not seek reelection. They were James G. Martin in North Carolina, Edward D. DiPriete in Rhode Island, Norman H. Bangerter in Utah, and former Gov. Arch Moore in West Virginia. Two Republicans also won governorships in states where GOP incumbents left office—Michael N. Castle in Delaware and John Ashcroft in Missouri. But in Vermont, Democrat Madeleine Kunin won the seat formerly held by a retiring Republican incumbent, and in North Dakota George Sinner defeated Republican incumbent Allen I. Olson, while in Washington, Democrat Booth Gardner defeated another Republican incumbent, John Spellman.

Following the elections, 28 state legislatures were under Democratic control. The GOP picked up more than 250 lower-house seats and about 20 on the upper-house level.

A number of surveys taken of voters as they left the polls suggested that the GOP, which has long been the country's minority party, had gained in the percentage of voters identifying themselves as Republicans, moving close to parity with the Democrats. And some Republican strategists said these figures might suggest at least the beginning of a broad realignment toward their party. Other analysts pointed out that the GOP had made similar advances linked to President Reagan's 1980 election victory, only to lose most of this ground during the 1982 recession. These observers pointed to the limited Republican gains in the Congress and argued that any judgment on realignment would have to await the conclusion of President Reagan's second term.

See also articles on individual states; United States Congress (pages 586–87).

From *Herblock Through the Looking Glass*
(W.W. Norton, 1984)

"WE WEREN'T WATCHING—ACTUALLY, WE'RE ALL PRIMARIED, CAUCUSED, POLLED, PREDICTED, DISCUSSED AND ANALYZED OUT"

©1984 HERBLOCK

WOMEN IN POLITICS

© Randy Taylor, Sygma

Walter Mondale's selection of Geraldine Ferraro as his running mate was greeted with a wave of euphoria at the Democratic National Convention in San Francisco in July 1984. Party activists hoped Mondale's bold decision to name the first woman to a major political ticket would fuel his uphill race for the presidency and transform a lackluster campaign into a history-making crusade. "If we can do this, we can do anything," the three-term congresswoman from Queens, NY, told the cheering delegates in her acceptance speech.

The 1984 Results. But when the votes were counted on November 6, the notion that a woman could catapult Mondale to victory was buried under President Ronald Reagan's 49-state avalanche. And there was even some evidence that Ferraro's candidacy was a net minus for the Democratic ticket. Not only did she fail to turn out record numbers of women, as originally anticipated, but her lack of foreign-policy experience in particular may have turned away some voters. Lamenting the lopsided results, feminist leader Gloria Steinem said, "I feel as if I have no country." CBS News correspondent Diane Sawyer, noting that women candidates on the whole fared poorly, called the election "the revenge of the white male."

Of ten women running for the Senate, only one was victorious. Kansas Sen. Nancy Landon Kassebaum was elected to a second term by a wide margin, making her an instant contender for the vice-presidential nomination in 1988. Kassebaum is one of two women senators; the other is Paula Hawkins of Florida, also a Republican, who faces reelection in 1986. Incumbency appeared to be a far more potent force than gender in determining winners. Twenty female incumbents in the House of Representatives were returned to office, but only 2 of 41 new women candidates for the House were successful. Although women account for more than 50% of the population, only 22 out of 435 House members are women. There were some gains at the state level. Women doubled their number of governorships —from one to two—with Madeleine Kunin of Vermont joining Martha Layne Collins of Kentucky in the elite sorority. Arlene Violet, a lawyer and a former nun, became attorney general of Rhode Island, the first woman to hold that post.

But the dramatic strides that many thought would accompany the appearance of the first woman on a major national ticket just did not happen. Instead, women stayed roughly even in the Congress and captured only a small number of additional seats in state legislatures. As a result of the 1984 elections, there would be 939 women serving in state legislatures across the country, compared with 911 in 1982 and 344 in 1972. Asked why the drive for electoral equality seemed to be taking so long, former New York Rep. Bella Abzug said, "A transition has to take place. . . . Americans are not ready for change overnight."

Although women voted for President Reagan with less enthusiasm than men, giving him 55% of their vote compared with 62% from their male counterparts, Reagan was still the clear winner. "It's not that we lost it, but that he won it—won it handily," said Ferraro. The "gender gap" that plagued Reagan in 1980, the measurable difference in his greater appeal to men than to women, narrowed from ten points to seven in the 1984 landslide. No longer regarding the gap as a bonus of women for Democrats, the Democratic Party began its own soul-searching to discover why men had defected in such large numbers from the presidential ticket.

Ferraro drew huge crowds and generated a great deal of enthusiasm, but she was unable to translate the emotional outpouring into votes. Party officials credited her with bringing in 10,000 new contributors and $4 million from eager supporters, but there was little evidence of women power on Election Day.

The Ferraro Selection and Campaign. Indeed, polls showed that Mondale's historic decision to appoint Ferraro was regarded by many Americans as just one more capitulation to a special-interest group. Mondale was under considerable public pressure from women's groups to choose a woman as his running mate. With women composing 54% of the electorate, a delegation of women leaders made a July 4 pilgrimage to Mondale's Minnesota headquarters to argue the case, as National Organization for Women (NOW) President Judy Goldsmith put it, "A woman appeared to mean the margin of victory."

Mondale took until July 12 to make up his mind, an agonizing process that prompted fellow Democrat Gary Hart to accuse him of "pandering" to special interests, notably women. But when Ferraro met Mondale in St. Paul, MN, all was forgiven, at least temporarily, in the exuberance of the moment. "In America, anything is possible if you work for it," Ferraro declared. "American history is about doors being opened, doors of opportunity for everyone, no matter who you are, as long as you're willing to earn it."

The daughter of Italian immigrants, Ferraro was the embodiment of the American dream. After a decade as a housewife, she had become a prosecutor in her home district of Queens, NY. Against odds that traditionally favored men, she had won election to the Congress as a liberal in the conservative, working-class neighborhoods that had given rise to the television series, *All In The Family*. Feisty and outspoken, she was perhaps the only woman who could have won the legendary Archie Bunker's confidence. After learning that she was in the running for the vice-presidency, Ferraro said, "I'm happy there is no longer a sign, 'white males only need apply.' It's our turn, folks."

OTHER HISTORIC FIRSTS

By becoming the first woman to be nominated by a major political party for the vice-presidency of the United States, U.S. Congresswoman Geraldine Ferraro (D-NY), shown page 36 addressing the National Organization for Women, notched a special place in history books, joining Sandra Day O'Connor, Frances Perkins, Ella Grasso, and other pioneers.

Culver

UPI/Bettmann

AP/Wide World

Jeannette Rankin (1880–1973) was the first woman to be elected to the U.S. House of Representatives. A Republican from Montana, she served two terms, 1917–19 and 1941–43.

Hattie Wyatt Caraway (1878–1950) was the first woman to be elected to the U.S. Senate. Appointed to her late husband's seat in 1931, she twice won election and served until 1945.

Ella Grasso (1919–81) was the first woman to be elected a state governor without having her husband precede her in office. She was governor of Connecticut, 1975–80.

Frances Perkins (1882–1965) was the first woman to be a member of a president's cabinet. A former chemistry teacher, she was FDR's secretary of labor, 1933–45.

Shirley Chisholm (1924–) was the first black woman member of the U.S. House of Representatives, 1969–83. Her name was put in nomination for the presidency in 1972.

Sandra Day O'Connor (1930–) is the first woman to be an associate justice of the U.S. Supreme Court. Appointed by President Reagan, she was sworn in Sept. 25, 1981.

UPI/Bettmann

UPI/Bettmann

© Lester Sloan, "Newsweek"

But after a first burst of euphoria, Ferraro's candidacy was sidetracked almost immediately by questions about her husband's real-estate business, an illegal loan to her first congressional campaign, and a number of omissions in her financial disclosure forms. Complicating matters further, her husband, John Zaccaro, initially refused to make his income-tax returns public.

As the furor over Ferraro's finances threatened to permanently obstruct Mondale's presidential bid, Zaccaro relented, releasing most of his financial data; and Ferraro answered questions in such detail during a 90-minute televised press conference that sympathetic reporters booed a fellow journalist when he appeared to press her too hard. Her performance under pressure defused the family's finances as a major issue, but the subject could still play a role in her political future. As the campaign ended, a Manhattan (NY) Grand Jury was investigating two of Zaccaro's real-estate transactions. In early December, the House Ethics Committee found that she had unintentionally violated the government's ethics act. Since the violation was unintentional, no reprimand was issued.

Candidate Ferraro won high marks for her general decorum during the campaign. A curiosity at first, she forged new paths for women in everything from etiquette to proper voice modulation. She and Mondale agreed never to embrace in public lest her image be confused with that of a first lady. In her debate against Vice-President George Bush, Ferraro deliberately slowed down her normally hurried speech in order to sound more authoritative. Conscious of her place in history, Ferraro said she felt she was "standing in for every woman in this nation."

On the campaign trail, Ferraro had her share of hecklers as well as organized protests by antiabortion groups. Although a Catholic, Ferraro said she personally opposed abortion but was pro-choice as a matter of public policy. Catholic bishops held news conferences to denounce her stand on the issue. Ferraro also drew flack for proclaiming that Reagan was "not a good Christian" because of some of the budget cuts he had made in social programs. The remark kicked off a debate about religion that cost the Mondale-Ferraro ticket precious time and did little to enunciate the real differences between Mondale and Reagan.

In fact, a Reagan-Bush campaign official had written, "It's all over, folks," in a July memo assessing the impact of Ferraro on the fall campaign. Accurately judging that the Bible Belt South would reflexively reject a liberal northeastern woman as a potential president, he concluded that Mondale had just ceded the South to Reagan, making his reelection all but certain. Republican pollster Linda DiVall ran a "feelings thermometer" check on Ferraro in the Deep South. She discovered the Queens congresswoman measured a frigid 43 degrees on a scale of one to a hundred.

Mondale, of course, ran even worse among Southerners. But the traditional idea of a vice-president is to balance the ticket and add pluses where there are minuses. Ferraro did little of that, except that she added excitement where Mondale was perceived as dull. There was also the realization that Ferraro was chosen because she was a woman. Conceding that she would never have been in the running if her name was Gerald instead of Geraldine, Ferraro said candidly, "Obviously, if I were not a woman I would not be discussed." In an interview shortly before the election, she acknowledged that Bush was more qualified to be vice-president than she was. "No doubt about it," she said. "He's been there four years." The admission did not help Ferraro in the "heartbeat away" issue. Voters had difficulty imagining her ready to step into the presidency at a moment's notice.

With the benefit of hindsight, victory was never within Mondale's reach and the addition of Ferraro to the Democratic ticket made it even less so. But another barrier had fallen for women, and both Ferraro and Mondale deserve credit for making that happen. For Mondale, knowing that he had lent his hand to the advancement of women's rights was one of the few bright spots in his otherwise dismal showing. "We didn't win, but we made history. And that fight has just begun," he declared in an emotional concession speech.

Ferraro's candidacy signaled the entrance of women into another previously all-male preserve. Already, political experts are speculating that the vice-presidency may have a female stamp on it, that both the Republicans and the Democrats may feel compelled to name a woman in 1988 to satisfy the expectations raised in 1984. It is also more likely that a woman will enter the primaries in 1988 and earn a crack at the number-two spot instead of waiting for the nod.

Women were courted as never before in the 1984 election, and that is likely to continue. In the 64 years since women gained the right to vote, they have been transformed from an auxiliary cadre to be tolerated but not encouraged to an important element of the electorate. Women held the balance of power in several key Senate races, giving liberal Democrats the margin of victory in Iowa (Tom Harkin), Illinois (Paul Simon), and Massachusetts (John Kerry). Although women, just like men, overwhelmingly supported Ronald Reagan, the election showed that their votes cannot be taken for granted. Women tended to split their tickets, preferring Democrats for the Congress along with more humanistic policies on the economy, the environment, and foreign policy.

ELEANOR CLIFT, *Newsweek*

BLACKS AND THE VOTE

TOTAL BLACK VOTER REGISTRATION

millions

1968 1972 1976 1980 1982

In his drive for the presidency, Jesse Jackson (left) worked hard to continue the trend toward increased black voter registration. The civil-rights activist told his black audiences that "there's a freedom train a-coming' but you've got to register to ride."

The black vote had virtually no impact on the outcome of the 1984 presidential election, but in the congressional elections there was dramatic evidence that it continues to be a major factor in the national political equation.

The 1984 Results. As they have since 1964, blacks in 1984 voted overwhelmingly for the Democratic nominee, Walter Mondale, giving him about 90% of their votes. President Reagan received 9%, about the same as in 1980. Had the white vote been more evenly divided between the Republican and Democratic candidates, the size and cohesiveness of the black vote might have made it critical to the outcome. But with the rest of the electorate lined up solidly behind President Reagan, 67–33%, blacks did not come close to exercising a pivotal role.

In 1984 blacks were 10.5% of the voting-age population and cast nearly 10 million votes in the election, mainly in the South and the large industrial states of the Northeast and Midwest. The sheer size of the black vote makes it a critical determinant of strategy for both parties. When the Republican Party is not directly or vigorously competing for that vote, it must compensate by winning other key segments of the electorate. Thus Richard Nixon developed his "southern strategy," and Ronald Reagan in two campaigns went even further in appealing to traditionally Democratic white ethnic voters

in all regions. The black vote, then, is a powerful force in the political dynamics of the country.

While neither the outcome of the presidential election nor the lopsided black vote was surprising, some observers were surprised that black voter turnout in 1984 was not much higher than in 1980, given blacks' emphasis on increasing voter registration and turnout and their antipathy toward the Reagan administration. Although by year-end there were no completely reliable data on black turnout, preliminary indications were that the black vote increased substantially in the South and in a few cities outside the South, including Chicago and Washington, DC. Nationally, however, it was only slightly higher than in 1980. In this respect, black turnout was similar to turnout for the total electorate, which was reportedly up by only 0.3% over 1980.

Despite its lack of effect on the presidential race, the black vote was very influential in other races. It helped to secure a two-seat gain for Democrats in the Senate, to limit Republican gains in the House of Representatives, and to prevent an erosion in the ranks of black members of Congress and state legislatures.

The impact of the black vote was most conspicuous in three crucial Senate races: the successful reelection bids of Democrats Howell Heflin of Alabama and Carl Levin of Michigan

Former Vice-President Walter Mondale appealed for support before the Black Caucus at the Democratic Convention. On Election Day, about 90% of black voters pulled the lever for the Democratic nominee.

and in Congressman Paul Simon's defeat of GOP incumbent Sen. Charles Percy in Illinois. In all three cases the defeated Republican candidates won the white vote handily, but overwhelming black support for their Democratic opponents cost them the election. In Illinois, Senator Percy won about a third of the black vote in 1978, but in 1984 he got only 6% compared with Simon's 86%.

In the House races, the black vote was critical to Democratic victories in five districts in North Carolina, Alabama, Mississippi, and South Carolina. Such support in these and other closely contested races helped to limit Republican inroads in the House. The black vote also was instrumental in helping reelect black members of Congress. Their numbers were reduced by one, from 21 to 20, as Indiana's first-term Congresswoman Katie Hall lost the primary to a white challenger, but all incumbents who stood for reelection won by wide margins. The only formidable black challenger for a congressional seat held by a white incumbent, State Sen. Robert Clark in Mississippi's second district, lost a close race because of unusually high white turnout in support of the incumbent. And in state legislative races, blacks increased their number of seats by six, bucking the tide of Republican strength at the polls.

Polarization, Questions, Concerns. The presidential election results pose several questions for blacks. One concerns an apparent increase in racial polarization. Many analysts point to the fact that while 90% of blacks voted for Mondale, about 67% of whites voted for President Reagan, and in the South the racial polarization was even greater. This kind of polarization is not new; it has been especially pronounced at least since 1968. It may have increased somewhat in 1984 over previous years, partly in response to such developments

as Jesse Jackson's bid for the Democratic presidential nomination. Some analysts believe that the increasing prominence of blacks in the Democratic Party also may have influenced the white vote. Of course it is not known exactly how much race affected the vote or how it is likely to affect partisan alignment in the future, but deepened or prolonged racial polarization will seriously retard black political influence.

Although racial polarization is a concern, too much probably has been made about the impact of race in the election. The cleavage that showed up at the polls seems to reflect much deeper causes than merely an antiblack mood of the electorate. It reflects the sharply different experiences of the black and white populations during 1981–84 and their differing expectations for the future. A survey conducted for the Joint Center for Political Studies by The Gallup Organization in August 1984 underscored these differences in a way that predicted the voting trends with remarkable precision. While 48% of whites felt satisfied with the way things were going in the United States and a plurality felt better off financially than they were four years ago, only 14% of blacks felt satisfied and a plurality felt worse off; 57% of whites approved of the way the president was handling his job and 32% disapproved, while 82% of blacks disapproved and 8% approved; and 31% of whites but 72% of blacks considered President Reagan prejudiced. In view of the sharp divergence of views between blacks and whites, their widely different votes are far from surprising.

A second question concerns turnout. Why did not more blacks vote? The dramatic success of black mayoral candidates in Chicago and Philadelphia in 1983, partly on the strength of sharp increases in black turnout, had stirred expectations of high turnout. Moreover, one of the explicit goals of Jesse Jackson's candidacy was to increase black registration and turnout. The Joint Center for Political Studies national survey in August indicated that the Jackson candidacy did indeed mobilize large numbers of new black voters, and according to Election Day exit polls, about 12% of black voters were voting for the first time. A higher overall turnout may have been discouraged by the absence of issues in the campaign that generate enthusiasm among blacks and by the failure of the Mondale organization to campaign vigorously in black neighborhoods or to stress traditional get-out-the-vote drives. Many blacks also may have been influenced by the widespread perception from the preelection polls that the outcome of the presidential race had been settled.

A third question is whether continued monolithic support by blacks for the Democratic Party, while the rest of the electorate is shifting away from its traditional loyalties, will isolate and further limit the political influence of blacks. Some argue that the Republican Party's ability to win presidential elections without significant black support may encourage Republicans to maintain a strategy of ignoring blacks and appealing to the white electorate. The Democratic Party, on the other hand, may find it unnecessary to be responsive to blacks since it will not need to compete for their support.

But black allegiance to the Democratic Party has existed for some time. While it does have adverse effects, it has been less damaging to blacks than most analysts suggest. For one thing, blacks continue to be a critical force in the nomination of the Democratic Party's candidate for president, since they cast close to 25% of the party's votes. Easily the most serious handicap Gary Hart experienced in his bid for the Democratic Party's nomination was his failure to win significant support from blacks. (He received only about 4% of the black primary vote nationwide). Had he won substantially greater support in a few Southern states or in Illinois during the primaries, he might well have won the nomination.

Furthermore, winning the presidency is not the only measure of partisan success. Had the president been more attractive to blacks, for example, he might very well have seen elected a more favorable Congress with which to implement his program. Unless the Republican Party competes effectively for the black vote, it is unlikely to be a truly governing party with control of both Congress and the White House.

The Future. Blacks, like the rest of the population, will be forced by the outcome of the presidential election to consider seriously how they might adjust their electoral strategies to increase their influence on the executive branch. One adjustment almost certainly will involve new steps to increase turnout by blacks. In spite of the massive efforts made to register eligible blacks in 1984, almost half the

TOTAL NUMBER OF ELECTED BLACK OFFICIALS

Includes U.S. and state legislators; state administrators and agency heads; city and county officers; judges, magistrates, constables, marshals, sheriffs, and justices of the peace; college and school board members.

Year	Number
1984	5,700
1983	5,606
1982	5,160
1981	5,014
1980	4,890
1979	4,584
1978	4,503
1977	4,311
1976	3,979
1975	3,503
1974	2,991
1973	2,621
1972	2,264
1971	1,860
1970	1,472

Source: Joint Center for Political Studies

black voting-age population still failed to vote. Blacks cannot afford this level of nonvoting if their political influence is to increase significantly. For the future, blacks are likely to seek to augment traditional registration and get-out-the-vote efforts by getting state and local governments to play a larger role in simplifying registration procedures.

Another adjustment might be to de-emphasize racial rhetoric and campaign strategies aimed solely at black voters and instead stress the development of new coalitions based on common interests. In this way they can take the initiative in efforts to reduce racial polarization of the electorate.

Finally, the blacks will almost certainly be exhibiting renewed interest in the Republican Party. As the Republican Party prepares for a future beyond Ronald Reagan, it might find the black vote an attractive vehicle for maintaining its success at the presidential level and increasing its strength in Congress. Blacks may well be more recruitable now than at any time during the past two decades.

EDDIE N. WILLIAMS and MILTON D. MORRIS

Editor's Note: Eddie N. Williams is president of the Joint Center for Political Studies, and Milton D. Morris is the center's director of research. The Joint Center is a national research and public policy institution that focuses on social, economic, and political issues of concern to Black Americans.

Church and State

by Fred Graham

Darryl Heikes, "U.S. News & World Report"

Proponents of school prayer hold an all-night vigil at the U.S. Capitol.

About the Author: Fred Graham has been law correspondent of CBS News, Washington, since 1972. Prior to that he was supreme court correspondent for *The New York Times* for seven years. Mr. Graham is the holder of an LL.B. degree from Vanderbilt University (1959) and a diploma in law from Oxford University (1960). He is the author of *The Self-Inflicted Wound* (1970), *Press Freedom Under Pressure* (1972), and *Alias Program* (1977). Mr. Graham has been honored with a Gavel Award from the American Bar Association, a George Foster Peabody Award, and several Emmy Awards.

After decades in which principles of separation of church and state seemed established and secure in the United States, the mid-1980s appeared to promise a pronounced—and to some, troubling—change. Suddenly, the familiar notion that the government should be neutral to religion—to preserve, as Thomas Jefferson had put it, "the wall of separation between church and state"—was being challenged by a popular president and an activist Supreme Court. The result was a surge of legal and political change, as the law shifted away from separation of church and state toward government accommodation of religious practices and groups.

The force behind these winds of change was obvious. Christian fundamentalism had, in recent years, turned fervently political. In the form of the Moral Majority and other political groups, evangelicals had insisted that the government and its laws should reflect the prevailing Christian views of the United States. The Conference of Catholic Bishops adopted the position that Catholic political leaders should advocate the Church's position on such issues as abortion and nuclear arms, disapproving the view of many Catholic politicians that they should not attempt to impose their personal moral or religious values on the general public.

Some observers saw this as a reflection of a deep religious revival among the American people. Others viewed it as a broad public reaction against the rapid cultural changes and moral and sexual permissiveness of the 1970s. But for whatever reason, the result was a ground swell of public pressure for greater governmental accommodation of Christian objectives—and signs began to appear of a substantial erosion of the doctrine of separation of church and state.

The Supreme Court. The winds of change swept most sharply through the Supreme Court. Traditionally, in interpreting the 1st Amendment, the court had placed its primary emphasis on the "establishment clause," which says that "Congress shall make no law respecting an establishment of religion." Construing this to encompass the state legislatures as well as Congress, the Supreme Court handed down a series of rulings over the years that sought to define the proper "wall" of separation between church and state.

The court used a stringent test to determine the constitutionality of government actions that were alleged to amount to an "establishment of religion." The test held that to be constitutional, any such action must have a secular purpose, must have a principal effect that does not advance religion, and must not create an excessive entanglement between government and religion. Under this type of rigid scrutiny, many government efforts to foster religion were struck down. The most celebrated, of course, were the decisions of the early 1960s, *Abington School District v. Schempp* (1963) and *Engel v. Vitale* (1962), that declared unconstitutional Bible reading and officially sponsored prayer in the public schools. Among the other measures struck down were public payments to underwrite teaching or construction in parochial schools, taxpayer subsidies to cover testing and record-keeping in church schools, and the posting of prayers in public schools.

In the rhetoric that ran through these Supreme Court opinions, the justices always maintained that they were groping for the proper line to separate church and state. But despite insisting that a constitutional barrier did exist, if it could only be identified, the court approved a number of laws that had clearly been passed to aid religion. In a caustic dissent, Robert Jackson, a member of the court (1941–54), compared the court to "Byron's Julia, who, saying 'I will ne'r consent,' consented."

In fact, the court did consent to a number of arrangements that had been challenged as violative of the separation of church and state. It permitted states to pay for transportation and books for parochial-school students, to finance construction at church-related colleges, to grant tax exemptions to churches and church-owned businesses, to extend tuition tax deductions to parents of parochial-school students, and to employ Protestant ministers as chaplains in the legislatures. The reason why the Supreme Court did not consider these measures to be invalid "establishments of religion" was that the

"I believe that faith and religion play a critical role in the political life of our nation and always has. . . . The truth is, politics and morality are inseparable. And as morality's foundation is religion, religion and politics are necessarily related."

Ronald Reagan
Aug. 23, 1984

"I believe in an America that honors what Thomas Jefferson first called the 'wall of separation between church and state.' That freedom has made our faith unadulterated and unintimidated. . . . Today, the religion clauses of the 1st Amendment do not need to be fixed; they need to be followed."

Walter F. Mondale
Sept. 6, 1984

Bryce Flynn/Picture Group

The constitutionality of using public funds to pay for the Paw-tucket, RI, Christmas decora-tions, including the above nativity scene, was decided by the U.S. Supreme Court in 1984. The court ruled that such Christ-mas displays are permissible within the "establishment clause" of the Constitution's 1st Amendment.

1st Amendment contains another provision, which forbids any governmental action "prohibiting the free exercise" of religion. The court felt that this "free exercise" clause allowed the government to do things that acknowledged the religious roots of American society. For instance, nobody seriously questioned the constitutionality of "In God We Trust" on the coins, or the morning prayer in Congress. By the same token, the court held that the government could foster the public's free exercise of religion by providing the benefits listed in the paragraph above. But the court still insisted, in its opinions, that these benefits must meet its test for the separation of church and state. However, during its 1983–84 term the Burger court announced an apparent willingness to lower the constitutional barrier that had separated church and state.

It developed out of a nativity scene that had been a fixture of the annual Christmas celebration in Pawtucket, RI, for 40 years. Each year the city government purchased, erected, and maintained Christmas decorations to adorn the city square. The display included Santa Claus, his reindeer, even Mickey Mouse—and also a nativity scene.

A suit was filed, sponsored by the American Civil Liberties Union and alleging that the publicly sponsored and financed nativity scene was an "establishment of religion" by the city government. The lower courts agreed. They applied the Supreme Court's long-standing test and held that the public sponsorship of a nativity scene violated it in every respect: it had no secular purpose, its basic result was to advance religion, and it threatened to promote religious strife by encouraging other sects to lobby for recognition of their religious

holidays, too. But the Supreme Court upheld the constitutionality of the nativity scene and used the occasion to announce
a new emphasis in the relationship between church and state.
First, the court pointed out that the nativity scene was more
in the nature of a symbol of a national holiday than an official
"establishment of religion." The government has every right
to acknowledge such religious aspects of the nation's heritage,
Chief Justice Warren Burger wrote for the majority. "Nor
does the Constitution require complete separation of church
and state," Burger continued. "It affirmatively mandates accommodation, not merely tolerance, of all religions, and forbids hostility toward any."

An important shift had taken place. By stressing that government should not impede the "free exercise" of religion,
the Supreme Court was saying that the state could accommodate religious groups, so long as it did not discriminate between them. Quickly, three related church-state issues came
before the court to be decided during the term scheduled to
end in July 1985. If all three were decided along the same
lines, it could mark a watershed in the relationship between
government and religion.

One case concerns the constitutionality of a moment of
silence for prayer and meditation in the public schools. At
issue is a law enacted in Alabama, which, like 22 other states,
has adopted the moment of silence as a substitute for the
outlawed school prayers. The states argue that the students
are free to pray, meditate, or doze as they wish, and thus any
religious exercise is truly voluntary. Critics say the moment
of silence has no secular purpose, and thus has the primary
effect of advancing religion. In a friend-of-court brief, the Reagan administration urged the court to approve the practice and
to use the occasion to elaborate on the justices' new emphasis
on government "accommodation and toleration for private religious beliefs and practices." Some legal observers speculated that if the court were to uphold the moment of silence, it
would then be asked to overturn its decisions against school
prayer and Bible reading.

Chick Harrity, "U.S. News & World Report"

Billy A. Melvin (left) and Art Gay,
the executive director and outgoing president, respectively, of
the National Association of
Evangelicals, flanked President
Reagan during a moment of
prayer at the association's 1984
convention in March. Addressing the meeting, the president
lobbied for passage of "an
amendment to the Constitution
to allow voluntary vocal prayer"
in U.S. schools.

The second case involves a Michigan school district's "shared time" program, which sends public-school teachers into parochial schools to teach remedial and enrichment classes. In past years the justices have struck down similar arrangements, and the lower courts invalidated this one, too. The Supreme Court's willingness to review this decision raised the possibility that it may be preparing to shift its position on this issue, also.

The third case up for review concerns a Connecticut law that gives employees of private companies the absolute right not to work on the day designated by the worker as his or her sabbath. This case appeared to bring into sharper focus the church-state problems that can arise from governmental accommodation of religion. For while the law was neutral as to different religions with their separate sabbaths, it did favor religious workers at the expense of those who profess no religion. Those employees would have to work on the days assigned by their companies, while their coworkers who professed religious beliefs had a right to their sabbath off. This led the Connecticut Supreme Court to strike the law down as a governmental "establishment of religion," a decision that the Supreme Court agreed to review.

The Reagan administration's position, expressed in its friend-of-court brief, revealed the problems lurking in the trend toward governmental encouragement of the "free exercise" of religion. The administration argued that this gives religion a "special status" and that "the government may seek to accommodate or protect religiously motivated claims of conscience, even where it does not accord the same treatment to other strongly held beliefs." This would mean that the traditional constitutional goal of governmental neutrality toward religion would give way to a doctrine under which the state could affirmatively place its weight on religion's side.

The Reagan Administration and Congress. In the political arena outside the Supreme Court, the Reagan administration unabashedly pursued its goal in favor of the religious side. President Reagan pressed for a constitutional amendment that would overturn the school prayer decision, lobbied for a fed-

AP/Wide World

Sen. Orrin Hatch (R-UT) is a leading spokesman for right-wing causes. A bishop of the Mormon church, he not only has sponsored an amendment that would give states the right to outlaw abortions but also has worked for passage of a silent-prayer in school amendment.

A cartoonist ties together the debate over the abortion issue and the increasing role of religious topics and personalities in the 1984 campaign. Debate regarding church and state was a hallmark of 1984 politics.

"THE COMMITTEE HAS DETERMINED THAT LIFE BEGINS AT THE MOMENT OF ELECTION"

James Margulies/Rothco Cartoons

AP/Wide World

Pope John Paul II greets the recently named U.S. ambassador to the Holy See, William A. Wilson. U.S.-Vatican diplomatic relations, which had been broken for more than a century, were restored in 1984.

eral law granting tuition tax breaks to parents of children in church schools, and advocated tight restrictions on women's abortion rights.

Congress shifted in the same direction. After 116 years in which the United States had not granted full diplomatic status to the Vatican, Congress in 1983 endorsed the appointment of a U.S. ambassador to the Holy See. In 1984, President Reagan appointed William Wilson the first ambassador to the Vatican since shortly after the Civil War, when the United States had cut off diplomatic relations. Congress in 1984 also passed a law giving students the right to hold religious services during free time in public schools—this, even though the new legislation opened the way for such groups as the Ku Klux Klan and the Communist Party to demand the same privilege.

The Rev. Moon Case. This entanglement of the goals of mainstream Christianity with the interests of other groups seeking advantageous relationships with the state came to the surface in an unexpected way in 1984. It arose in connection with the tax evasion conviction of the founder of the Unification Church, the Rev. Sun Myung Moon. He had been prosecuted amid charges by his followers that the "Moonie" church had been targeted by prosecutors because of the sect's unpopularity. The charges focused on Rev. Moon's failure to report as personal income interest payments that had accrued on church bank accounts held in his personal name. Rev. Moon's

O. Franken, Sygma

Followers of the Unification Church were persistent in their support of their leader, the Rev. Sun Myung Moon, who was convicted in 1982 of tax fraud and obstruction of justice. Moon claimed the income on which he had not paid taxes belonged to his church and not to him and that he was the victim of religious persecution. The U.S. Supreme Court refused to review the case, and Moon began an 18-month jail term in 1984.

lawyers claimed that this was the proper way for the Unification Church to handle funds, since he was the personification of the church. They also objected to the Justice Department's insistence that the case be heard by a jury, rather than by a judge, who they felt would be less affected by bias.

The jury found Rev. Moon guilty, and when he appealed to the Supreme Court, a surprising coalition of other religious groups rallied to his cause. Organizations as diverse as the National Council of Churches, the United Church of Christ, the Southern Baptist Convention, and the Mormon church joined in friend-of-court briefs, declaring that the conviction of Rev. Moon potentially threatened them all. They said that many religious groups handled funds in ways that the government might not approve, and that if the leader of an unpopular sect could be imprisoned for this, all of them were potentially at risk. The Supreme Court, rejecting the claim that the conviction amounted to religious persecution, refused to review Rev. Moon's case. He entered prison to serve an 18-month term, declaring that he would continue to run his church from behind bars.

Overview. By the middle of the 1980s, there could be little doubt that the concept of a neutral zone between government and religion was no longer the dominant guiding principle of church and state relations in the United States. What was unclear was how far the trend toward governmental accommodation of religion would go, and whether the new relationship would prove divisive, or just different from earlier practices. Those who encourage this trend argue that it is actually a return to the concept of church-state relations that was held by the founders of the nation, and that the growing association of government with religion is primarily symbolic and peripheral. They point out that Congress had chaplains from its earliest days, that official oaths have always used the pledge "so help me, God," and that the Supreme Court begins each day with the prayer that "God save the United States, and this honorable court." They insist that the recent changes are as symbolic or innocuous as the traditions of the past. For instance, they say that nativity scenes on public property are traditional in scattered U.S. communities; that the moment of silence has been noncontroversial in most communities; and that the National Park Service's policy of allowing religious gatherings on public land has provoked little public controversy.

On the other hand, oganizations such as the American Civil Liberties Union, the American Jewish Congress, and Americans United for Separation of Church and State have issued a series of warnings and protests. They assert that traditional principles of separation of church and state are being abandoned, and that the dangers are both individual and national. Individuals will suffer, they say, by being offended or embarrassed by governmental sponsorship of religious observances that offend their beliefs. The national fabric could be damaged, they argue, if religious groups begin to compete for, and squabble over, favors from the state.

Madalyn Murray O'Hair, the atheist who won the Supreme Court's decision that closed the schools to prayer and Bible reading, summed up these concerns in characteristically pungent terms. "We are headed," she said, "into a legally bound theocracy that you would not believe." Even for some of those who held no commitment to either side of the controversy, it appeared that the timing of the current trend was awkward, if not ominous. For during an era in which the government was developing a closer official identity with Christianity, the United States was becoming an increasingly less "Christian" nation. The flow of immigration—legal and illegal—was bringing in millions of people of other faiths and was, for the first time, substantially altering the Christian homogeneity that had always been assumed before. At the dawn of the 1980s, the U.S. population included 2 million Muslims, nearly 7 million Jews, and hundreds of thousands of Hindus, Buddhists, and Confucians—and their numbers were rapidly growing. That meant that as the law was being changed to permit government to favor religion, more religious groups were present to compete for the favors. It also helped to explain why there was some concern over changes in the relationship between church and state.

Now as much as ever, atheist Madalyn Murray O'Hair promotes the widest possible separation between church and state.

AP/Wide World

TORNADOES

by Robert Davies-Jones

About the Author: Robert Davies-Jones is a member of the staff of the National Severe Storms Laboratory of the U.S. National Oceanic and Atmospheric Administration (NOAA) in Norman, OK. Dr. Davies-Jones has written on meteorology for a variety of publications, including the *Encyclopedia of Science and Technology.*

Tornadoes are the most violent and mysterious of atmospheric storms. They swoop down from the sky and shatter people's lives in a minute. After years of relative quiet, a record number of tornadoes battered the United States during the spring of 1984. The worst single day was March 28, when 23 tornadoes cut a path of destruction through Georgia and the Carolinas, killing 63 persons. Then, during a two-week period in late April and early May, an onslaught of 303 tornadoes struck the Southern states. After a month's lull, on June 7, a strong jet stream across the northern United States brought a fresh barrage from Iowa to Wisconsin. On that day, the most intense twister of the year leveled the town of Barneveld, WI (*photo above*).

The average number of tornadoes in the entire United States is about 750 per year. During the last 30 years, the annual average number of tornado-related fatalities has been 104. In 1983 the national death toll was only 34. In 1984 the count had reached 120—far exceeding the yearly average—by mid-June.

Forms and Patterns. A tornado is defined as a tall, narrow, violently rotating column of air, averaging about 100 yds (91 m) in diameter, that extends downward from a thunderstorm cloud to the ground. The typical tornado lasts only a few minutes and causes relatively minor damage. It moves along the ground for about 1 mi (1.6 km) in a northeasterly direction at some 30 mph (48 km/h) and has maximum wind speeds of approximately 125 mph (201 km/h). Although people living in the path of a tornado can be at risk, tornadoes usually do not pose a major threat to large populations. Only about 3% of tornadoes are extremely violent and capable of devastating entire communities; those 3% account for the lion's share of the annual death toll. Violent tornadoes last for tens of minutes, cutting paths up to 1 mi wide and often tens of miles long as they move across the land at speeds of up to 70 mph (113 km/h). Scientists have measured winds up to 250 mph (402 km/h) in these violent whirlwinds. Tornadoes come in many forms—from slender ropes of cloud to elephant trunks, dust-filled columns to dark, boiling cloud masses on the ground, and multivortex structures (several small tornadoes rolled into one). The transformation of a broad, almost vertical form into a thin, severely tilted, sinuous rope typically signals the imminent decay of the tornado.

What made 1984 such a bad year for tornadoes? The answer is a complicated one, lying in some unusual large-scale weather patterns. The simple answer is to blame it on the jet stream (though this is somewhat unfair because the jet stream

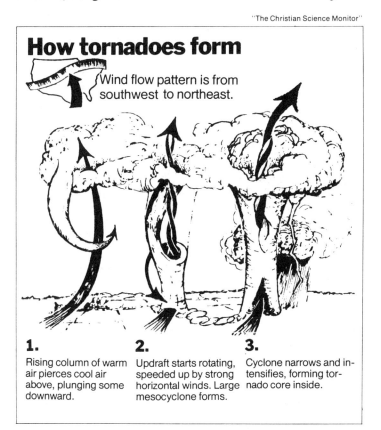

"The Christian Science Monitor"

How tornadoes form

Wind flow pattern is from southwest to northeast.

1.
Rising column of warm air pierces cool air above, plunging some downward.

2.
Updraft starts rotating, speeded up by strong horizontal winds. Large mesocyclone forms.

3.
Cyclone narrows and intensifies, forming tornado core inside.

On the day before Easter, ten counties in northern Mississippi were ravaged by tornadoes. Worst hit was the farming town of Water Valley, which suffered $20 million in damage.

and other atmospheric features, such as fronts and lows, are interdependent). During 1984 the jet stream was stronger and farther south than usual, and its position was steady compared with the marked fluctuations characteristic of most years. The result was a rapid succession of cyclones (lows on the weather map) steered by the jet stream from west to east across the southern half of the nation. The lack of deviation by the jet stream was significant because the warm, moist air necessary for fueling severe thunderstorms was never pushed far south and was drawn northward in advance of each cyclone.

Upper-air disturbances, which help trigger severe storms, tend to track along the jet stream. Another prime ingredient for tornadoes, vertical wind shear (variation in wind speed and/or direction with height), also is strong in the vicinity of the jet. The presence of dry air at intermediate levels (10,000–15,000 ft; 3 000–4 000 m) is yet another key forecast parameter for tornadoes. With the lee side of the Rockies a source region for dry air, cyclones moving eastward away from the mountains draw this air into their circulations. In 1984 all the above conditions—warm, muggy air at low levels; weather disturbances; strong wind shear; and cool, dry air aloft—combined regularly to pound the United States with severe tornado outbreaks.

Prediction. Weather forecasters have developed considerable skill in identifying the weather patterns that spawn widespread tornado outbreaks. This is fortunate, since such outbreaks contain a disproportionate number of violent and menacing twisters. Isolated and weak tornadoes occur more randomly and are correspondingly more difficult to predict. When conditions warrant, meteorologists at the National Severe Storms Forecast Center in Kansas City, MO, issue tornado watches one hour in advance. Typically a watch is valid for six hours and covers a rectangular area of about 25,000 sq mi (65 000 km²); several watches may be in effect simultaneously. The forecast unit in Kansas City is responsible for overall U.S. tornado prediction.

Tornado warnings for specific counties are issued by the nearest National Weather Service office and are made for tornadoes that are either imminent or already in progress. They are valid for about one hour and are based on actual sightings or radar observations. Even in this technological age, observations by trained spotters provide the basis for most warnings. The present radar network is scheduled to be replaced within the next decade by Doppler radar, which is better equipped to detect tornado rotation. Current radar measures only the spatial distribution of precipitation, with rotation inferred by examining the shape of the radar echo, an imprecise method. With Doppler radar, the velocity component of raindrops and hailstones along the radar beam also can be measured. This allows meteorologists to recognize the signatures of two types of vortex within the storm—the mesocyclone and the tornado itself.

The mesocyclone is the parent, large-scale circulation of the tornado. It has maximum tangential wind speeds of about

45 mph (72 km/h) at a radius of 1–3 mi (1.6–4.8 km) from its axis of rotation. Strong tornadoes invariably form within the confines of a mesocyclone, usually close to its axis. Because a radar beam is broad in comparison with a tornado, even Doppler radar does not "see" the tornado clearly and has a limited range for tornado detection (varying from zero for very small tornadoes to more than 100 mi—160 km—for very large ones). Since 50% of mesocyclone signatures are associated with tornadoes, and since mesocyclones can be detected at long range (150 mi—241 km—or more), tornado warnings can be issued on the basis of mesocyclone identification alone. Tests have shown that this procedure results in an average lead time of 20 minutes before tornado touchdown with a relatively low false-alarm rate, a significant improvement over current operational methods.

The mesocyclone is first detected at midlevels within the storm, descending to the surface over time. Strong tornadoes await the development of the larger-scale rotation at low levels. The tornadic-vortex signature (TVS), when it can be detected, is a highly reliable indicator that a tornado is forming. For a strong tornado, it is first observed aloft and builds both upward and downward, reaching the ground in about 20 minutes. The TVS is the only current source of information about the invisible part of the tornado above cloud base. For violent tornadoes, the TVS has been observed to heights of 40,000 ft (12 000 m). Doppler radar does miss some tornadoes, but these are generally small and fairly weak ones which form without mesocyclones and do not pose a great threat.

Tornado Formation. Exactly how tornadoes form is still largely a mystery, though a great deal has been learned from Doppler radar observations, computer models of severe thunderstorms, visual observations by scientific intercept teams, and laboratory tornado simulators. By using two or more Doppler radars in separate locations and invoking the principle of mass conservation, meteorologists are able to synthesize the three-dimensional airflow within a storm down to a scale of one or two miles. The computer models possess roughly the same resolution and are able to reproduce the gross features that appear in the radar data, while allowing researchers the

UPI/Bettmann

Tornado funnels extend downward from a thunderstorm cloud to the ground. The spinning column of air moves at an average speed of about 30 mph. Wind speeds reach 125 mph.

flexibility to examine different effects separately and to control different parameters (e.g., if the earth's rotation were stopped). To study the flow inside a tornado, investigators must either intercept (come within close range of) the tornado and obtain data firsthand, analyze films, examine the patterns of damage and debris, or simulate the tornado in miniature in the laboratory. This last approach has yielded vortices with many of the same characteristics as real tornadoes, but the artificial means by which they are formed may not model the genesis of tornadoes even remotely.

Observations have established that tornadoes generally form on the southwest side of their parent thunderstorm from a distinctly lowered cloud base known as a "wall cloud." Strong tornadoes form near the center of a mesocyclone, which at the surface resembles a low-pressure area on a weather map with a warm front extending eastward and a cold front southward. The contrasting temperatures are generated by warm, moist, light air flowing along the ground into the storm from the southeast, and rain-chilled air sinking to the ground in the northern sector of the storm. The tornado usually forms close to, but outside, the precipitation region. Over time a curtain of rain spirals cyclonically into the mesocyclone center and wraps around the tornado. Thus, many tornadoes end their lives in rain. The tornado is found on the southwest side of the storm's main updraft, with downdraft close by.

For years it was thought that tornadoes acquire their rotation through direct amplification of the earth's rotation (vertical component). But this explanation has been shown to be incorrect. Modern theory is based on the realization that, because of the large increase and turning of the winds on tornado days, small parcels (or blobs) of air spin more rapidly about one of their horizontal axes than about the vertical. The thunderstorm, with its columns of rising warm air and descending cool air, tilts the parcels' axes of rotation toward the vertical. When the winds turn clockwise, theory dictates that the updrafts rotate counterclockwise, the downdrafts clockwise. This explains the initial formation of the mesocyclone. How the mesocyclone descends to the ground is currently under investigation. Tornado formation is not completely understood, but it is known to involve the longitudinal stretching of a rotating column of air. As the column narrows, it spins faster and faster, eventually creating a tornado.

Research engineers, meanwhile, are concerned with the practical matter of data collection—such as wind speeds and pressure deficits. Although a number of quite reliable measurements of wind speeds—up to 250 mph (402 km/h)—exist from remote sensors and damage assessments, pressure and temperature inside a tornado can only be obtained through direct probing. That has yet to be achieved. Instruments have either not survived or have responded too sluggishly to the rapid changes. Tornadoes are difficult to study because they are short-lived, usually small, and—most of all—dangerous to approach. Meteorologists expect that advances in techniques and instrumentation will produce a greater understanding of the most violent and mysterious of atmospheric storms.

FAME

**The Making
and Meaning
of Household
Names**

By Jeffrey H. Hacker

Jane DiMenna

They perform under the glaring lights of a movie set, theater or concert stage, sports arena, or political press conference. Their faces cover magazines and gossip tabloids. They show up in TV commercials and presidential campaigns. They are mobbed by autograph seekers everywhere. Their romances, personal problems, and contract negotiations are chronicled in newspapers and TV talk shows.

They are the famous, and there is an intense fascination with everything they do and say. They are the Michael Jacksons, Tom Sellecks, Brooke Shieldses, Christie Brinkleys, O. J. Simpsons, Robert Redfords, and Princess Dianas whose faces *everybody* knows. They are larger than life.

The famous are scrutinized, idolized, and furiously pursued. Redford describes the problem: "You go into a little diner for breakfast, and suddenly the waitress' hand was shaking on the dish when she put your coffee down, and you knew the jig was up. The next thing you know . . . cars and pickups are pulling into the place, and you've got to get out fast."

Glamorous, rich, envied, or simply well known, the famous set styles and trends. Dorothy Hamill, Farah Fawcett, and Bo Derek each started a rage in women's hair styling. John Kennedy popularized touch football, Jimmy Carter made country music fashionable, and Ronald Reagan piqued the public's taste for jelly beans.

And finally, when a famous person dies—especially young, as John Kennedy, Elvis Presley, or John Lennon—the grief is homefelt. Tears are shed as if for a family member.

Why are celebrities the objects of such fascination and idolization? What makes a person famous? What are the possible consequences of becoming a celebrity?

A boom in "celebrity journalism" betrays the public fascination with fame and the famous. The "name game" is big business.

About the Author. Jeffrey H. Hacker is not only editor of this annual but also serves as a free-lance writer and editor for other publications. Mr. Hacker has written three books for young adults—*Government Subsidy to Industry* (1982), *Franklin D. Roosevelt* (1983), and *Carl Sandburg,* (1984).

The power of the media in creating household names is not lost to politicians. New York City Mayor Edward Koch (left), for example, appeared on the Johnny Carson Show *in March 1984. His autobiography,* Mayor, *meanwhile, was on the best-seller list.*

AP/Wide World

Making a Name. Fame today means something different from what it once did. In times past, a person became famous for some special talent, accomplishment, or act of courage. From Benjamin Franklin to Thomas Edison, Charles Lindbergh, and Jesse Owens, figures in many fields won worldwide acclaim for their outstanding achievements. Today, however, fame is as much *created* as it is earned. A celebrity is simply somebody in the public eye. The famous may possess some measure of talent, but public attention is largely the work of press agents, publicists, and advertisers.

The making and meaning of fame today can be attributed to the power and reach of the mass media. That first media exposure—the mere fact of being in a magazine or on television—may begin the avalanche of public attention.

Nearly a decade after his death, Elvis Presley is idolized by two generations of rock 'n' roll fans. Elvis memorabilia abound.

Ira Berger, Black Star

The public preoccupation with fame has been evidenced by a boom in "celebrity journalism." *People,* born in 1973, is now among the 20 widest-circulating magazines in the United States. The major news weeklies carry such regular columns as "People" or "Newsmakers." Newspaper gossip columns have made a strong comeback. Celebrity biographies and autobiographies dot the best-seller lists. And how many Americans can wait in a supermarket line without taking a look at the headlines of *The National Enquirer* or *The Star*? On television, *The Johnny Carson Show, Merv Griffin Show,* and like fare draw big audiences. Newscasts and morning talk shows are devoting more time to celebrity interviews. And epitomizing the entire trend is a one-hour weekly program, *Lifestyles of the Rich and Famous,* which puts viewers poolside and topdeck with the stars.

The "Name Game." Fame is also big business. Name recognition creates markets, both for the individual whose name it happens to be and for any company or commodity with which the name is associated. Baseball players file as corporations. Tennis players earn millions for sporting designer labels on their sleeves or a particular set of stripes on their sneakers. Rock stars and fashion models have high-priced licensing agreements with poster, T-shirt, button, and doll manufacturers. Such income combines with salaries, purse money, or record sales to make some celebrities veritable business conglomerates. "By the end of the year," according to *Newsweek* (Feb. 27, 1984), "Michael Jackson Inc. will probably earn its 25-year-old chairman more than $50 million —and that's on top of the more than $45 million that poured into his corporate treasury last year."

The value of a familiar face is not lost to companies with high-budget advertising campaigns. Pepsi-Cola paid $1.5 million to Jackson for a commercial which itself got headlines when the young singer's hair caught fire. Joan Collins vamps for Scoundrel perfume. Karl Malden won't go anywhere without his American Express card.

So closely intertwined are advertising and the "name game" that some celebrities are created *by* commercials. Frank Perdue and the "Where's the Beef?" lady, Clara Peller, are current advertising cult stars. The balding scalp, prominent nose, and droopy eyes of Frank Perdue first appeared on television in the early 1970s. The public came to love him as the "chicken man," and his family chicken farm grew into an empire with annual sales of hundreds of millions of dollars. Peller, the gravel-voiced octogenarian who also happens to have a conspicuous nose, became a celebrity almost overnight. For the lifelong resident of Chicago and grandmother of two, a simple three-word utterance won the affection of the TV-viewing public. Since the first commercial appeared in early January 1984, there have been Clara Peller posters, coffee mugs, T-shirts, dolls, and a fan club. For the product itself, Wendy's Old Fashioned Hamburgers, Peller and the slogan meant a 15% growth in sales during that first month.

The Price to Pay. Wealthy and successful, the famous are reminders of the American Dream. In the public mind they are images and symbols rather than real people. They are treated as part of the public domain. For the private individuals behind the public roles, being famous puts strains and pressures on daily life.

Celebrities live in a fishbowl. Everywhere they go they are on stage; their every move is watched. Fingers are pointed, and excited whispers are heard behind their backs. Anonymity is lost. Robert Redford walks into a diner, and the pickup trucks start pulling into the parking lot. Michael Jackson looks out the window of his Encino, CA, estate and sees teenage fans packed six deep at the front gate. Jacqueline Onassis walks down a street, and camera lenses are thrust in her face.

And the loss of privacy runs deeper than that. Personal matters become grist for the media mill. Divorce settlements and drinking problems make splashy headlines. Though the stories are often untrue or exaggerated, there is little recourse. In March 1981 the actress Carol Burnett won a libel suit against a well-known news tabloid for printing a damaging gossip item, but such rulings are relatively rare. In U.S. libel law, "public figures" cannot win a libel suit "as long as the comments are made without malice and without reckless disregard for the true facts."

The biggest pop phenomenon since Elvis and The Beatles, Michael Jackson has created a larger-than-life image. His huge following, however, often forces him into reclusion.

AP/Wide World

You Can't Fly Without It

Traveling Cards for Traveling Feds, p. 15

Celebrity sells. Actors do it, athletes do it, even American vice-presidents do it. Right: *On the cover of a government publication, George Bush holds up the credit card distributed to officials for use on government business.* Below: *Answering the question "Where have you gone, Joe DiMaggio?", the former baseball star rehearses for a TV endorsement of a coffee maker.*

Some celebrities naturally yearn for escape. At the same time, "life in the fast lane" may mean increased exposure to drugs and alcohol. Moreover, public idolization may breed an unreal sense of power and immunity. The combination can be literally lethal. Examples of drug overdose and suicide by the famous unfortunately abound. Beyond that, the threat of outside physical harm also exists. John Lennon, for example, was murdered by a psychopath who by some twist of thinking sought to be identified with him.

If nothing else, fame can have adverse effects on the celebrity's career itself. For actors and actresses, winning fame in a specific role may mean getting stuck in a stereotype and having trouble finding other parts. For famous writers, the advantage of anonymous observation, so essential to the literary craft, may be lost. For athletes, the pressure of being in the spotlight can be a distraction from field performance.

Famous Last Words. The reasons for which certain individuals become famous, the ways in which celebrities are treated, and the rewards and punishments of being in the limelight all say less about the individual than about the dreams, yearnings, and shifting temperaments of the whole society. Fame, therefore, is often short-lived. Many celebrities fizzle out like shooting stars. Yesterday's media darlings may be today's "Where Are They Now?" column. Fame is a special place in which some celebrities manage to thrive for decades. Others, however, are overwhelmed or dismissed in the blink of a flashbulb. "In the future," said Andy Warhol, "everybody will be famous for fifteen minutes."

The Small Business
−The Backbone of the U.S. Economy

by Sen. Lowell P. Weicker, Jr.
Chairman, U.S. Senate Committee on Small Business

The backbone of the U.S. economy has always been the small business enterprise. From the colonial period of blacksmith and apothecary shops to the present "postindustrial" economy, small and moderate-size businesses have provided the great majority of the land's goods and services and have employed more Americans than any comparable sector. Small businesses have cultivated the entrepreneurial spirit and creativity that have led the United States to greatness.

Dramatic Growth. The number of small businesses and their importance as a whole to the American economy have increased significantly in recent years. In 1983, 98% of all nonfarm businesses in the United States were classified as small (fewer than 500 employees) by the U.S. Small Business Administration (SBA), and such firms accounted for approximately 47.9% of the country's total employment. The recession of the 1970s and early 1980s witnessed a decline of basic industry and a substantial loss in employment. America's traditional industries and their assembly lines have experienced a challenge from high technology and automation that

About the Author: A U.S. senator (R-CT) since January 1971, Lowell P. Weicker, Jr., has been a member of the Senate Committee on Small Business since 1977 and its chairman since 1981. A graduate of Yale University (1953) and the University of Virginia School of Law (1958), Senator Weicker served in the Connecticut General Assembly (1963–69) and the U.S. House of Representatives (1969–71).

is unprecedented. International competition has taken a toll on the market for the goods of heavy industry. But while older, traditional industries are declining, new businesses are continually forming. Often the capital-intensive, heavy research conducted by big business inspires potential entrepreneurs and creates markets that are then captured by small business people. Thus, while the *Fortune* 1000 companies employ fewer workers now than they did in 1970, a new generation of small business innovators and operators has been created. Figures for 1981–82 demonstrate that an estimated 1 million new businesses were formed. The percentage of new businesses among total businesses grew from 6.3% in 1978 to 10% in 1981. Further, in fiscal years 1981 and 1982, small business firms created approximately 2.6 million new jobs, while larger industries lost more than 1.6 million employment opportunities—resulting in a net gain of 1 million jobs. It should be noted that this occurred during the worst recession in decades.

Greater automation in the workplace, vast technologies, and the advent of a "service economy" offer great opportunity to entrepreneurs, and, as has always been the case, individuals have responded to opportunity by establishing their own companies. As a result, newly formed small and moderate-size businesses dominate the changing U.S. economic landscape, and the most prosperous entities in the 1980s are finding profits in small and aggressive manufacturing ventures and, particularly, service-oriented opportunities. Concomitantly, job creation has been greatest among the new "high-tech" and service industries. Service enterprises—including such areas as financial operations, insurance, food production and processing, and transportation—now account for approximately two thirds of the U.S. gross national product (GNP) and employ 70% of the nation's work force.

Many American students find enterprising schemes to pay for the increasing cost of a higher education. By being reliable and less expensive than their larger competitors, such entrepreneurs successfully operate their own small businesses.

UPI/Bettmann

In part because the decision-making process is limited to fewer individuals, small business firms can develop their goods—from the research stage to the finished product—with great quickness. This accelerated course of development is especially important in the technology industry, where the United States is a world leader. Quickness and efficiency stimulate more exports and buffers against high rates of imports. Cutting into the market enables entrepreneurs to develop new innovative products. Their new products and innovations create new markets, while big business normally reacts to marketplace activities.

The People Involved. The men and women of small business today are a diverse and self-reliant group. A significant number of small businesses are traditionally family owned and operated. These people manage traditional businesses—shops, restaurants, etc.—and pass the leadership from generation to generation. Others are individuals who founded small companies during the 1950s and 1960s and continue to prosper today. Many of the recent entrepreneurs are part of the post-World War II "baby boom" generation. They are frequently young and, in most cases, college educated. A desire for independence and self-expression often leads these people to go out on their own, become their own boss, and develop a distinctive product or service. Others of these young entrepreneurs will join larger companies and corporations early in their careers but later will leave and use their experience to establish new business entities, or "spin-offs." These individuals, usually with formal training in business that orients them toward finance and accounting, are transformed into aggressive entrepreneurs geared toward production and the marketplace. Those willing to try it on their own will sacrifice the security of the corporate setting and frequently will employ bold and innovative actions in their pursuit of success.

The Problems. Small businesses face numerous and varied problems. The chances for failure are significant. In recent years, businesses with between 20 and 50 employees have had a 50% chance of succeeding, while those with 20 employees or less have a 37% chance of surviving.

A prerequisite facing any individual starting a new business, and a primary obstacle to the establishment of a successful small business, is start-up capital. Thousands and often hundreds of thousands of dollars are required to lease or purchase work space and equipment, acquire initial raw material or data, and pay salaries sufficient to establish production and delivery of goods and services. The sources of capital most frequently available to the aspiring entrepreneur are either personal or family wealth, commercial banks, the SBA direct or guaranteed lending programs. and venture capitalists. If the small business person is fortunate enough to have access to personal or family savings, he or she undoubtedly will use them to avoid the expense and constraints of borrowing. Although capital is available for start-up businesses through commercial institutions, there is usually an insufficient track

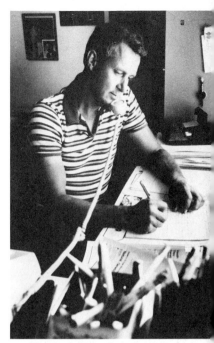

Robert Frerck, Odyssey Productions

The freedom of working for oneself and the convenience of working at home or in a small office lead many people to form their own business. As the 1980s began, there were 12.7 million sole proprietorships in the United States.

The growth of the computer industry has had a tremendous effect on the small business world. It not only has simplified the daily routine of the independent employer but also has been responsible for the birth of many small companies.

record to convince banks to grant a loan. In addition, in periods of high interest rates, even if the small business can qualify for a loan, the terms can be so burdensome as to be prohibitive and will discourage even the more established small business from borrowing. So-called venture capital is money invested in entrepreneurial activities of great potential growth and recognized risk, such as ventures in futuristic computer technology. In return for an instant infusion of capital, the business hands over a certain amount of control to the investor. The amount of venture capital available to small businesses is limited, however, because of the select nature of the types of businesses invested in, and the extremely high rate of return frequently sought by, the venture capitalist.

Another obstacle faced by small businesses is sometimes brought about by their own success. When small firms pioneer in a new market and provide goods and services previously not produced, other companies, usually larger, are attracted into the new market as well. Depending upon the degree of competition, small firms involved in the new market may be crowded out simply because they do not have either the capital or the existing business network to compete with the larger, more established companies. This process has been illustrated in the microcomputer industry. Whereas only a handful of firms fought for position in that market a short time ago, there now are several hundred competing companies.

The relative inexperience of some new small business people and their frequent lack of expertise in a new field also can create problems in establishing an enterprise. An unfamiliarity with a particular market or industry means that the start-up business entrepreneur starts out with an immediate disadvantage. Added to costs and overhead that are always higher for start-up businesses, this limits the new firm's ability to compete effectively from the outset. At the same time, many young business people are able to learn a market and its particular needs, earn a good track record with suppliers and consumers, and prosper completely on their own.

The Government's Role. The attitude and role of the federal government have not traditionally served the needs of small business. The primary concern of the government has generally been the large, visible corporations that employ thousands of individuals. In addition, the lobbying networks of these giants and their vast political and economic strength command the attention of the federal and state policymakers. In the meantime, small business grows and remains unappreciated for being the force that it is. Thus, the problems and needs of small business have often been overlooked. The result has been a lack of competition and creativity, a loss of market share to foreign firms, and a decline in overall U.S. productivity. Only recently, with the troubles experienced by some large corporate industries in difficult economic times and the emergence of small business as a recognized economic stabilizing force, has this attitude been forced to change.

Broad and constraining regulations that favor larger companies the often burdensome federal tax laws and a federal orientation toward macroeconomic policies all reflect the built-in governmental bias against small business. Many regulations, though intended to be reasonable and constructive, drain small businesses of their resources and limit their overall productivity. The cost of compliance with those regulations is frequently high, and many small businesses find it extremely difficult to spread out these and other costs. At the same time, big corporations, with their greater ability to absorb overhead costs, are not as threatened by compliance with rules and regulations. In addition, many large corporations are protected by the delayed implementation of such regulations adopted during the 1960s under so-called ''grandfather clauses.'' Thus, small businesses are burdened continually by the new regulations. The guidelines provided by the Occupational Safety and Health Administration (OSHA) are intended to prevent work-related accidents and protect employees, but to the small business the cost and time required to conform adequately to these standards can be extremely damaging. The small business simply does not have the same resources available with which to set up and maintain often complicated and complex compliance procedures. Further examples of burdensome regulations mandated by the government are those involving record keeping and the supplying of information. Often the flood of paperwork requires hours, even days, to complete—time that the small business cannot afford.

Federal-tax policy also sometimes serves to discourage small business entrepreneurship. One of the underlying problems is the tax code's encouragement of capital investments that usually assists larger companies but does not sufficiently aid small businesses, which frequently are labor-intensive. Large corporations that receive substantial infusions of investors' capital and ideally use those funds to expand their operation often are rewarded with tax benefits. The small business owner whose operation is often dependent on labor receives no such reduction. In addition, small businesses normally bear

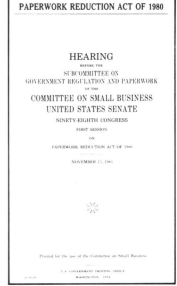

In 1980 legislation was enacted to reduce the amount of information collection and record keeping required by the government. In 1983 hearings were held to determine how the act was ''affecting America's small businesses.'' It was concluded that there ''had been some progress'' in reducing the burden but that more needed to be done.

Robert Frerck, Odyssey Productions

Worldwide, street selling is probably the oldest and most common small business. Historically, the flower has probably been the best-seller.

the brunt of the burden of other types of taxes such as estate taxes, which make it difficult for the small firms to stay within a family, and taxes on social security, which drive up labor costs. Unfortunately, small business is frequently only an afterthought when amendments to the tax code are adopted.

The macroeconomic policies of the federal government also are affecting the status of America's small businesses. Recent massive federal budget deficits have hurt all businesses, but smaller companies in particular. Most importantly, the government's indebtedness requires it to enter the capital markets and to borrow extensively to fund that debt. This results in increased demand and competition for credit and higher interest for all private-sector borrowers. This is substantially harder on smaller businesses, which are more susceptible to the problems and failures generated by high interest rates. For small businesses, which, unlike larger borrowers, must pay 2–5% above the prime rate, it becomes a struggle to survive. Further, the constant pressure for budgetary restraint and increased revenue results in frequent changes in regulatory and tax standards. The small business, less informed of the detailed alterations and less able to respond to them, stands to suffer more than the larger competitors.

Fortunately, appreciation for the importance and needs of small businesses on the part of the federal government has increased gradually in recent years. The Small Business Administration is the only federal government agency solely committed to the needs of small business. It was established in 1953 and is an independent agency that reports directly to the president. The agency maintains more than 100 offices throughout the United States and has approximately 4,300 employees. Although the SBA administers various programs, a major aspect of its responsibility is to offer a variety of guaranteed loans and financial assistance to small businesses. SBA's loan guarantee programs have helped many small businesses sustain and expand operations. In recent years the total amount of guaranteed loans made by the SBA has exceeded $2 billion (U.S.) annually.

The U.S. Congress also has become more involved in looking after the interests of the country's small businesses. Committees to review the needs of small business have been established in both the Senate and the House. Their job is to oversee the SBA to ensure its efficient and purposeful management, initiate pertinent legislation, and protect small business interests in the shaping of national and international fiscal and budgetary policy.

Whether American small business will continue to thrive in the future is contingent upon a combination of factors. As in the past, there must be the incentive for entrepreneurs to pursue their goals, to innovate, and to take risks. The economic horizon must reveal signs of continued growth, available credit, and free commerce and foreign trade. Finally, the federal government must consider the impact of its actions on small business and seek to ease the path to success for the small, independent businessman. Indeed the small business is one of the most important sectors of the economy.

"America's strength lies in the ingenuity and perseverance of its people. No other group of Americans better exemplifies these qualities than the nation's small business owners, who contribute daily to our economic well being."

**Ronald Reagan
Small Business Week
1984**

CHINA
—A Time of Change

About the Author: Donald S. Zagoria is professor of government at Hunter College and at the Graduate Center of the City University of New York. He was the author of *The Sino-Soviet Conflict* and editor of *Soviet Policy in East Asia.* Professor Zagoria last visited China in December 1983 and observed first-hand the current changes occurring there. His detailed analysis of "China's Quiet Revolution" appeared in the spring 1984 issue of *Foreign Affairs,* published by the Council on Foreign Relations. The editors of the Annual are most grateful to *Foreign Affairs* for granting them permission to adapt Professor Zagoria's commentary.

Liu Heung Shing, Contact

by Donald S. Zagoria

A young man wearing a suit and tie walks down a busy Peking street, enters a large store, and emerges 15 minutes later carrying a new television set. A farmer takes his produce to market in Shanghai, sets up a private stall, and sells the goods for profit. A souvenir shop at the Great Wall sells T-shirts and Coca-Cola to busloads of Western tourists.

The late Chairman Mao Zedong might not have believed it —he certainly would not have allowed it—but these are some of the scenes being witnessed in China today. A new revolution, quieter than the Communist takeover of 1949, is beginning to take hold. Since Mao's death in 1976, and particularly since the rise of Deng Xiaoping in 1978, the leaders of China have sought to develop a new strategy and new institutions for modernizing the nation. Maoist egalitarianism is being replaced by an emphasis on material incentives for hard work, and revolutionary zeal is giving way to a pragmatic quest for efficiency and productivity. Along with these ideological shifts, there have been important changes in Chinese politics, economy, lifestyle and culture, and foreign affairs.

In the economy, the post-Mao leadership has sought a more decentralized, quasi-market socialist system better suited to Chinese conditions than the highly centralized, Soviet-type system adopted in 1949. Perhaps the most significant step has been a de facto decollectivization of agriculture. There has been a legalization of some private commerce and trade, and some private ownership, particularly in the service industries. This has coincided with a greater use of indirect mechanisms, such as price scales rather than output quotas and commands, to influence the allocation of resources. And there has been an upgrading of light industry and the beginning of a sweeping "consumer revolution."

In the political sphere, the post-Mao leaders have sought greater stability and reliability so that China never again has to go through the chaos of a Cultural Revolution. Younger, better educated, and more professionally trained officials are slowly replacing the older generation in the party, government, and military, and top Mao loyalists have been removed.

Accompanying these internal reforms has been an opening up of the system to foreign economic and cultural influences on an unprecedented scale—what the Chinese call the "open-door" policy. This stands in sharp contrast to two and a half decades of Maoist insularity and "self-sufficiency."

The changes that have occurred are significant, and the direction of change, if it is sustained, is very encouraging both for the welfare of China and for its external relations.

Seeds of Change. The catalyst for the reforms in post-Mao China was an economic and social crisis accompanied by a loss of popular confidence in the ruling Communist Party and its ideology. The catalytic event was, of course, the Cultural Revolution, which ran from about 1966 until shortly after Mao's death. The Cultural Revolution was a far-reaching— and disastrous—campaign to keep China from slipping back into the corrupt, bourgeois ways of pre-Communist life.

The situation inherited by Mao's successors was nothing short of calamitous. The economy was in serious difficulty. Industrial production was of low quality. Agricultural production was barely keeping abreast of population growth, and per capita food consumption had not improved since the 1950s. One Chinese leader conceded that 100 million Chinese peasants did not have enough to eat. Continual harassment of intellectuals had set back science and technology perhaps several decades. The educational system was in shambles. The society was embittered, exhausted, and alienated.

During the Cultural Revolution, it has been estimated, close to one million people were killed or driven to suicide. Millions of others were sent to labor camps or to work in remote rural areas. By 1979 the very legitimacy of Communist Party rule was in question among large numbers of Chinese. Respect for the party and the socialist system was at an all-time low. The picture was desperate enough so that even some Old Guard leaders recognized that political survival required drastic action. The post-Mao leaders thus embarked on a series of radical reforms designed to raise the abysmally low standard of living, open safety valves for mass dissatisfaction, and gradually restore popular confidence in the ruling party.

Agriculture and Industry. At the heart of the post-Mao reforms, under the leadership of Deng Xiaoping, have been far-reaching changes in the agricultural and industrial sectors of the Chinese economy. By far the most far-reaching has been the de facto decollectivization of agriculture. Because some 80% of the Chinese population are peasants and China remains predominantly rural, this reform clearly affects the largest number of people. Land has not been returned to private ownership—it cannt be bought or sold—but since 1979 most of the countryside has adopted one or another version of the so-called "household responsibility" system. By this system, individual families or households are assigned parts of collective fields to farm on contract with local officials.

Reforms in China's agricultural system provide economic incentives for individual farmers. Left: Liu Wancong got rich (by Chinese standards) from his abundant cotton crops.

Already these incentives are creating a new, albeit small, class of rich peasants in the countryside. In the Chinese press one reads today of individual peasants who earn more than 10,000 yuan (about $5,000 U.S.) per year, an income at least 15 to 20 times the national average. The new rural incentives are also having a dramatic impact on Chinese agricultural efficiency generally. Agricultural output per capita, according to Wharton Economic Forecasting Association, rose from $166 in 1978 to $226 in 1983, a gain of about 36% in five years.

A second important change in China is that the traditional Stalinist priorities—heavy industry, defense, and production over consumption—have been replaced by new emphases on light industry, consumer goods, and raising the standard of living.

The economic transformation was fully extended to industry in October 1984. Central government control was eased just as it had been for agriculture a few years before, and basic reforms were instituted to introduce capitalist-style market forces: state-run enterprises would now compete for survival, plant managers would be free to plan production and marketing, extensive state subsidies would be phased out, and the price of many commodities would be determined by supply and demand.

And there have been other changes. Since 1979, enterprises in China have been permitted to retain a percentage of their profits for use in any way they see fit, provided they meet certain state guidelines; the excess profits may go into worker bonuses, new technology, new plant construction, marketing, or other areas. Another promising experiment has been to let factories sell some of their products directly to the

To spur production, raise personal income, and reduce urban unemployment (at about 9%), the post-Mao regime has allowed private enterprise on a modest scale. In "free markets," ordinary Chinese sell everything from food and clothes to buttons, kitchen utensils, and pet birds. Small shopkeepers are helping meet the high demand for such items as household furniture. The number of self-employed businessmen in China today is more than 8 million.

market instead of to the state. Perhaps even more significantly, the Chinese are now demonstrating a very un-Marxist willingness to close down inefficient enterprises. The whole system of hiring, firing, and promoting workers is being reformulated, with a new, distinctly un-Maoist emphasis on skills and competence rather than ideological "purity."

Another set of reforms has been instituted to decentralize much economic decision making to local authorities. The post-Mao leaders have increased significantly the rates of budget revenue retained by local authorities and given these local authorities greater freedom to adjust tax rates and even to determine how their retained revenue is to be spent.

Still another set of reforms designed to stimulate production has been the rapid expansion of out-and-out private enterprise. Farmers, for example, can now purchase their own trucks and engage in a variety of private enterprises. In the cities and towns, individuals and families can now open tailor shops, restaurants, and other private enterprises provided they do not hire more than a certain number of people. Cooks, maids, and nannies are now being hired in the households of some middle-income and wealthy professional families. Entrepreneurs are even opening up small private inns for travelers.

At the macroeconomic level, there is growing use of indirect economic levers rather than administrative orders to influence the economy. Thus, a newly created Central Bank now seeks to manipulate the Chinese money supply and fine-tune the economy. Loans, interest rates, and even prices are being used, though modestly, to guide economic decision making.

Open-Door Policy. In their quest for a more successful modernizing strategy, the post-Mao leaders have opened up the Chinese economy and society to the West in a host of new ways. One is the creation of special economic zones in which foreign investment is accepted (indeed encouraged), foreign technology is absorbed, and Western techniques are learned. In effect the zones are enclaves of capitalism within China, though the official press rejects this characterization. To lure foreign firms, the Peking government has offered special profit incentives, and about 100 equity joint ventures were formed in 1983 alone.

China has also begun a major effort to expand its trade with the United States, Japan, and Western Europe. Chinese trade with the United States, for example, increased from $1.1 billion (U.S.) in 1978 to $4.4 billion in 1983.

An important aspect of the new open-door policy has been an effort to increase tourism and bring in foreign currency. Top-notch Western-style hotels are being constructed, domestic air travel has been improved, and the Chinese people are encouraged to show friendliness and hospitality toward tourists. In 1983 more than 872,000 foreigners—about one fifth from the United States—visited China, spending about $930 million in hard currency.

Perhaps equally important, the Chinese are sending thousands of research scientists and students abroad for advanced professional training. In the United States alone, there were

Early-morning shoppers line up for fresh beans on a Shanghai street corner. Farm workers from a nearby collective sell the surplus from their production contract with the state.

Photos Jeff Hacker

Photos Jeff Hacker

The "opening up" of China to foreign trade and culture has brought changes to the drab and spartan lifestyle of the Maoist system. Under the new "pragmatic" leadership, imported and domestically produced consumer goods—such as TVs, stereos, and sewing machines—are available to the average Chinese. In fashion, once pervasive blue and green "Mao jackets" are giving way to Western-style suits—albeit of an earlier era.

more than 10,000 Chinese students in 1984. Not only will these students and scientists continue to bring new ideas and modern techniques back with them to China, but the long-term value of their training will preserve China's interest in keeping an open door to the outside world.

Even in the cultural realm, the number and variety of books, films, plays, and operas now available—including many from foreign countries—are greater than at any time since 1949. There has been a revival of traditional dance and opera and a greater willingness to import Western techniques in music and art—outright heresy during the Cultural Revolution. Much greater religious freedom is now allowed, with Buddhist temples and Christian churches being reopened in many parts of China. The expansion of foreign trade and domestic production of consumer goods have made such items as televisions, stereos, and sewing machines more available. And most conspicuously of all, the people have slowly begun to throw away their blue and green "Mao jackets" in favor of more colorful and stylish Western clothing.

Politics and Ideology. There has been a series of substantial changes in the political and ideological spheres as well. At the very top of the leadership, Hua Guofeng and other key opponents of economic reform have been removed from the top decision-making bodies; they have been replaced by strong reform advocates such as Premier Zhao Ziyang and Party Secretary Hu Yaobang.

In the party, government, and army, there has begun what one China specialist in the U.S. Embassy in Peking described as the beginning of a "sea change" in the Chinese leadership. The old, semieducated peasant revolutionaries who went through the Long March and were Mao's most trusted cadres for two and a half decades are giving way to a new generation of younger, better educated, more technically competent leaders. The attitudes and perspectives of the new generation are bound to be quite different from the generation of leaders they have succeeded. Their primary goal will be modernization and development. And they are bound to be more innovative.

The Big Picture. The impact of political and economic reforms should not be exaggerated. Many things still have not changed. There are no free elections at any level of the Chinese political system. Civil liberties in the Western sense are not recognized. Political indoctrination is still a major element of education at all levels. The media are controlled, though more loosely than before. Birth control measures are extraordinarily strict, including forced abortion. The major instruments of totalitarian rule, while weakened, have not been eliminated. Labor camps for political prisoners still exist, and many of the "democratic activists" who were encouraged to dissident action by the loosening of controls in 1978–79 have been jailed. Recently there have been showcase executions of substantial numbers of criminals. A conservative Old Guard still entrenched within the ruling party is fearful that the reform effort may weaken party control. Events in Eastern

Owen Franken, Sygma

With a population of more than 1 billion, China faces the future with a heavy economic burden. To lower the birth rate, the government in 1979 began promoting a "one child per family" policy. Economic incentives are provided for couples who agree to have only one child, while pressures are brought to bear on those who want more. Continuing a steady decline, China's population growth rate fell to 1.3% in 1984.

Europe and the Soviet Union caution that genuine and lasting reform of Leninist systems is extremely difficult because any real relaxation of decision-making authority challenges the vested interests of the ruling party.

Still, the changes now in progress in China are very great, have strong popular support, and go further than many Western observers realize. As *The New York Times'* Peking correspondent Christopher Wren has written: "In four years, Mr. Deng has brought China around to virtually a mixed market economy and opened its doors to Western investment. One official likened his country to a great ship in a storm. It was trying to change course, he said, but it could not do so all at once or the ship might capsize."

Obstacles. While the pace of reform has been impressive, substantial obstacles remain. First among these is the resistance of much of the bureaucracy. The impetus for the reforms comes largely from the very top leadership, yet it is the middle and lower levels of the bureaucracy that are responsible for carrying them out. Much of the resistance within the party undoubtedly comes from some 15 million of its 40 million members—those who were recruited during the Cultural Revolution in a totally different atmosphere from that prevailing today. They came into the party as "revolutionary purists," not as overseers of technocratic reform.

Another key problem is what happens after the 79-year-old Deng Xiaoping passes from the scene. If Deng were to die in the near future, it is conceivable that a power struggle might develop, thus introducing a new note of instability into the picture. On the other hand, if he remains in effective control for another few years, the reform process is likely to be more institutionalized than it is now and therefore more difficult to reverse.

There are other reasons to be cautious about the future. While the changes so far constitute a thoroughgoing de-Maoization of the system, it is still not clear how far the reform coalition intends to depart from the orthodox Soviet economic model. The true tests lie ahead. Will the Chinese move further in the direction of a market socialist economy of the Hungarian or Yugoslav variety, or will they tightly restrict the market forces now being unleashed? There is still no coherent strategy for combining planned and market economies, and the problems of running a mixed system are bound to be enormous.

The new reforms also are bringing with them a host of serious social problems. In the countryside, the agricultural decollectivization risks polarizing a new class of richer peasants against the great majority of poor peasants. Regional tensions likewise may grow. The provinces and regions most likely to benefit from decentralizing reforms will be pitted against those least likely to benefit. Also, tensions are growing between people in some of the most affluent rural areas adjacent to urban centers and the urban workers and intellectuals who feel they are not keeping up with recent increases in peasant income.

Jeff Hacker

The Future. Despite these uncertainties, there is reason for cautious optimism about the future of reform. The post-Mao leaders introduced such drastic measures not so much because they were ideologically committed to reform as such, but because the existing system was an economic failure and they wanted to restore popular faith in the Communist Party's ability to modernize China. The whole reform process must be regarded as a response to a perceived crisis of stagnation that, sooner or later, would have undermined the very basis of Communist power.

As for the opening up to trade, tourism, and the world community in general, the West should not delude itself about the likely consequences of China's new posture. No matter how far it goes down the path of reform, China under the Communist Party will remain independent in world affairs and not a Western ally. It will remain highly authoritarian, and its interests and values will conflict with those of the West in many areas. Still, the present trends are very hopeful. A reformist China—more decentralized, market oriented, and culturally tolerant—will also want to continue its "open-door" policy and to develop substantial new trade and cultural ties with the West. Such a China will want also to be drawn increasingly into the new Pacific community that is emerging in the Far East. All of these developments will increase China's incentives for a long-term relationship with the West. Properly nurtured on both sides, it could carry into the 21st century, when China is almost certain to become a major world power.

A rapidly expanding tourist trade has contributed vast sums of foreign currency to China's development. While Westerners have been able to observe first-hand the sweeping changes taking place, ancient ways and deeply etched Communist values still persist. The extent of future development, reform, and participation in world affairs remains uncertain.

People, Places, and Things

Anniversaries: Government leaders and military veterans from eight Western nations gathered on the beaches of Normandy, France (top), to commemorate the 40th anniversary of the D-Day invasion, June 6. Among the year's most celebrated birthdays was Donald Duck's 50th; five decades had passed since Donald's debut in a Walt Disney cartoon called "The Wise Little Hen." And in the nation's capital, the centennial of the Washington Monument was observed; the 555-ft (169-m) obelisk was completed on Dec. 6, 1884.

Kaleta, Gamma-Liaison

People and Pastimes: Michael Wittkowski (above), a 28-year-old printer from Chicago, holds up the lucky ticket after winning a record $40 million in the Illinois State Lottery. With a general lottery craze sweeping the nation, ticket sales increased by some 26% in 1984. Joe W. Kittinger (right, at left), a 56-year-old Floridian, completed the first solo balloon crossing of the Atlantic on September 18. His ten-story helium-filled balloon, "Rosie O'Grady's," crash landed in the mountains of the Italian Riviera after the 3,535-mi (5 689-km), 84-hour journey; Kittinger suffered a broken ankle. For less adventurous souls, the year's hottest pastime was "Trivial Pursuit" (below). The board game was expected to sell 22 million copies—at about $750 million—during 1984. It was developed by two Canadian journalists in 1979.

Arnaud Borrel, Gamma-Liaison

Jane DiMenna

Robert R. McElroy, "Newsweek"

Hazel Hankin

Amusement parks and a grand old library made news during 1984. June 16 marked the 100th anniversary of the first American roller coaster at Coney Island, NY. The original ride no longer stands, but its successor —the wooden-frame "Cyclone" (above)—remains a favorite of roller coaster aficionados. Meanwhile, a frightening series of accidents at carnivals and theme parks across the country prompted Congress to consider legislation on tougher safety regulations. In quieter surroundings, the New York Public Library—also nearly a century old —completed the first phase of a $45 million renovation project. The inaugural event was an exhibition called "Censorship: 500 Years of Conflict," shown at left.

Harrison Funk, Retna

Break-dancing—born literally on the streets of the inner city—moved its acrobatic, spinning, high-stepping act onto the stage and under the lights. There were music videos, feature-length motion pictures, and even how-to books. As seen above, local discos drew crowds with break-dancing contests. Also drawing huge crowds—several hundred thousand people, in fact—were the International Games for the Disabled, held June 16–30 in Nassau County, NY. Some 1,500 handicapped competitors from more than 50 countries took part. President Reagan attended the opening ceremony.

Bruce Bennett

The Alphabetical Section

Martine Franck, Olympic Arts Festival
Tony Whitmann, Olympic Arts Festival

The Los Angeles Olympic Organizing Committee presented the Olympic Arts Festival, June 1–Aug. 12, 1984. With the motto "the arts belong to everyone," the Times Mirror acted as official sponsor.

Festival director Robert Fitzpatrick traveled worldwide for three years seeking varied talent that "might catch people off guard." Some 1,500 performers in many art forms—including the theater, opera, acrobatics, and dance—participated. Mexico's Teatro Taller Epico, Japan's Sankaijuku, West Germany's Pina Bausch Wuppertaler Tanztheater, Australia's Circus Oz, China's Chengdu Acrobatic Troupe, and Britain's Royal Shakespeare Company and Royal Opera were among the groups and companies represented.

For the Olympic Arts Festival, the Twyla Tharp Dance Company offered "Performing Nine Sinatra Songs," left. France's Théâtre du Soleil presented "Richard II" as a Kabuki play; Georges Bigot, above, was Richard. A colorful sculpture, page 78, served as the festival's logo and was on display throughout Los Angeles and its environs.

79

ACCIDENTS AND DISASTERS

AVIATION

Feb. 28—In northeast Spain, a U.S. Air Force transport plane crashes, killing 18.

March 24—A U.S. military helicopter crashes into a South Korean mountainside, killing 29.

Aug. 24—Two planes collide in flight near San Luis Obispo, CA; 17 are killed.

Sept. 18—An Ecuadorian cargo jet crashes on takeoff from Quito, killing 60 persons.

Dec. 6—A Provincetown-Boston Airline plane crashes soon after takeoff from Jacksonville, FL, killing 13.

FIRES AND EXPLOSIONS

Jan. 14—In Pusan, South Korea, a hotel fire kills at least 38 persons.

Jan. 18—Fire in Japan's Miike coal mine, located off the island of Kyushu, under the ocean floor, kills 83.

Feb. 25—In the San José shantytown of Cubatao, Brazil, an oil-pipeline explosion kills at least 508 people.

March 24—Fire in Mandalay, Burma, is believed to have killed 10 persons; about 2,700 buildings are destroyed.

April 23 (reported)—At the Resavica coal mine southeast of Belgrade, Yugoslavia, a mine blast kills at least 33.

May 11—At Six Flags Great Adventure amusement park in Jackson Township, NJ, eight persons are killed when fire strikes a haunted-house attraction.

Mid-May—An explosion at a Soviet naval supply depot located in Severomorsk is believed to have killed more than 200 people.

May 23—A methane gas explosion in an underground water station in Abbeystead, England, killes at least 15.

May 28—In Taipei, Taiwan, a hotel fire kills 19.

June 20—Near Taipei, Taiwan, a coal mining explosion kills 74.

July 4—In Beverly, MA, a fire in a three-story rooming house kills 14 persons.

July 10—Near Taipei, Taiwan, a fire sweeps through a coal mine; at least 101 persons are dead.

July 21–22—In Pilgrim's Rest, South Africa, 13 girls are killed in a fire when lightning strikes their hut.

July 23—Explosions in the Union Oil Co. refinery in Illinois kill 17.

Oct. 18—In Paterson, NJ, a fire in a residential hotel kills 13 persons.

Oct. 23—In Baguio, Philippines, fire sweeps through a luxury hotel, killing 17 persons.

Nov. 19—Near Mexico City, Mexico, gas explosions at a storage area for liquefied gas kill 452 people.

Dec. 3—A toxic gas leak from a pesticide plant in Bhopal, India, kills more than 2,000 people and injures many others.

Dec. 5—Near Taipei, Taiwan, a coal mine explosion kills at least 33; 61 other miners are believed trapped.

LAND AND SEA TRANSPORTATION

Jan. 5—A minibus skids off a road 125 mi (201 km) south of Katmandu, Nepal, killing 15.

Jan. 21—Near West Glacier, MT, a fuel-tank truck and a school bus collide, killing 10.

Jan. 24—A Greek-owned freighter capsizes during a storm in the English Channel, killing at least 16.

Feb. 10—Two trains collide about 18 mi (29 km) west of New Delhi, killing at least 43 persons.

June 3—North of Bermuda a British square-rigged racing ship is abandoned and lost in tossing seas; one person is dead and 18 are missing.

June 6—A sailboat carrying refugees from Haiti capsizes north of Haiti after it is boarded by the U.S. Coast Guard; six are dead and several others are missing.

June 18—In Angola, a speeding passenger train derails and crashes, killing at least 50 people.

July 7—An Amtrak passenger train enroute to Montreal derails near Williston, VT, killing five.

July 7—A triple-deck excursion boat on the Tennessee River near Huntsville, AL, capsizes, killing 11.

July 14—A freight train and a passenger express train collide in Divaca, Yugoslavia, killing 36.

July 30—Three cars of an express train derail near Polmont, Scotland, killing 13 persons and injuring 44.

Aug. 13—A ferry capsizes off the coast of the eastern Malaysian state of Sabah; 200 people are missing.

Sept. 20 (reported)—A passenger boat capsizes in the Rapti River in Nepal; nearly 100 are feared dead.

Sept. 23—In the Indian state of Uttar Pradesh a bus plunges into a gorge in the Himalayan foothills, killing 34 Hindu pilgrims.

Sept. 24—An overloaded passenger launch sinks off the island of Nossi-Be (Madagascar), killing at least 31.

Oct. 28—In the Philippines off the island of Marinduque a ferry sinks; more than 100 persons are missing.

STORMS AND FLOODS

Jan. 2–4—A winter storm across Europe disrupts transportation and causes at least 10 deaths.

Jan. 29—A hurricane strikes in Mozambique, Swaziland, and South Africa, killing more than 100 persons.

Feb. 28—Heavy snow hits the U.S. Middle West and East, killing at least 29 people.

March 18–24—Wintry storms—from a Rocky Mountain snowstorm to Texas and Oklahoma thunderstorms—move into the Midwest and are blamed for 27 deaths.

March 28–29—Spring storms of snow, wind, and floods hit the eastern United States; tornadoes in the Carolinas kill at least 61 persons; another 1,000 are injured.

April 21—Tornadoes and thunderstorms sweep through ten counties in northern Mississippi, killing 15 persons.

April 26–29—From Oklahoma to Minnesota a spring storm system producing 130 tornadoes kills 17 persons.

May 6–8—Flooding of swollen rivers in northern Alabama, Tennessee, Kentucky, and West Virginia, and an Eastern Seaboard storm system producing tornadoes kill 17.

May 13–June 21—Monsoon floods in Bangladesh and northeast India kill 200 people and leave thousands homeless.

May 27—A landslide caused by heavy rains in Dongchuan, Yunnan Province, China, kills about 100 people.

May 27—In Tulsa, OK, 12 inches (30 cm) of overnight rain causes flooding, killing 13 persons.

June 8—Forty-nine tornadoes sweep the U.S. Plains states and upper Midwest, killing at least 16 persons.

June 9—Tornadoes hit the western Soviet Union, particularly near the town of Ivanovo, killing at least 400.

June 25 (reported)—In Indonesia in the island of Amboina, heavy rains kill 11 persons; 11 others are missing.

Aug. 31–Sept. 2—Torrential rains cause widespread flooding in South Korea; at least 200 are dead or missing.

Sept. 3—Typhoon *Ike* hits the southern Philippines, killing 1,363 people.

Sept. 24 (reported)—Floods and landslides in Nepal kill more than 150 people and block a major supply road.

Oct. 9—A tornado hits Maravilha, Brazil, killing 10.

Nov. 24 (reported)—Storms with hurricane-force winds sweep across Europe, killing 14 persons.

MISCELLANEOUS

Nov. 7 (reported)—In Munnar in the Indian state of Kerala, a rope bridge spanning a swollen stream collapses; about 125 school children who had been on the bridge are reported missing.

See also GEOLOGY.

Wendy's "Where's the Beef?" ad, with Clara Pellar (right), *was so successful that a follow-up aired in the fall.*

ADVERTISING

The U.S. economy smiled kindly on the advertising industry in 1984. With the inflation rate steadying around 6%, advertising spending forecasts were up by nearly 15%. In the healthy economic environment of 1984, advertising was a star growth industry.

Laws and Regulations. The country's deregulatory mood, which coincided with the dismantling of the National Association of Broadcasters (NAB) in 1982, was reflected in a more laissez-faire attitude in the courts toward marketing and advertising cases.

In January the U.S. Supreme Court overturned the Ninth Circuit Court of Appeals' 1983 decision, which had held it illegal to copy television programs off the air. In *Sony v. Universal Studios,* the Supreme Court in a 5–4 decision found that the practice was not unlawful when done for one's own convenience and not for resale. They also said that companies that make and sell videocassette recorders (VCRs) do not violate the copyright law. The decision was favorable to the booming consumer VCR market.

The trend towards a hands-off policy in the courts was further in evidence in other cases. Procter & Gamble and Chesebrough Ponds brought actions against one another over hand-and-body lotions. Each claimed the other's advertising was misleading under Section 43(a) of the Lanham Act, which prevents a company from saying anything deceptive about its own products in its advertising. The decision by the U.S. District Court for the Southern District of New York called the dispute a market controversy that would be better settled by consumers than judges.

When the rights of the individual were in jeopardy, however, the courts were less hesitant to intervene and set guidelines for advertising. Jacqueline Onassis' ongoing attempts to protect her privacy resulted in a legal action against the Christian Dior-New York company, which had used a model who looked like Mrs. Onassis in their product advertising. The New York Court ruled in favor of the former first lady; the case was appealed.

In May the advertising industry learned that the easing of government regulation sometimes opens the doors for increased litigation. The approval by the U.S. Food and Drug Administration (FDA) of ibuprofen as an over-the-counter analgesic resulted in at least two legal actions, as a number of companies tried to gain a competitive edge with the introduction of ibuprofen-based brands. With American Home Products and the Upjohn Company the only two American firms licensed to market such brands in 1984, Johnson & Johnson moved to delay their one-year advantage. Its McNeilabs brought an action against the FDA, challenging the FDA's approval of the over-the-counter sale of ibuprofen. The agency approved the product provided that manufacturers followed certain advertising rules, but McNeilabs contended that the FDA had no authority to regulate consumer advertising of nonprescription drugs. Both American Home Products and Upjohn began advertising their products in early summer.

Still not finally decided by late 1984 was Godfather's Pizza's action against advertising agency Chiat/Day/Hoefer Inc., challenging the traditional process of agency reviews and new business efforts. A lower California court enjoined ten Chiat employees from working on the agency's big new Pizza Hut account because they had access to Godfather's confidential files during a review for the company's advertising account. Chiat had withdrawn from the Godfather's review in order to compete for the much larger Pizza Hut account, which the agency later succeeded in winning. Chiat, concerned that the suit would prompt Pizza Hut to rescind the assignment, countersued Godfather's Pizza for $10 million in punitive and exemplary damages. In the meantime, the ten Chiat people were at least temporarily barred from helping or working on the new account as the case was appealed.

Media. The economic recovery, which was accompanied by delayed consumer hunger for goods and services, together with a year of Olympic Games and elections, created a strong surge in advertiser demand for media in 1984. Network television volume increased dramatically, especially for news, daytime, and late-night programming. Partially as a result of the pressure on network television, demand for spot TV and barter syndication was high. Although some spots for the Olympics went unsold, spot TV increased overall for the year as a result of heavy spending by local retailers competing for freer consumer dollars. Barter syndication continued to attract significant spending away from network outside prime time as a result of consumer popularity of syndicated programming and its lower cost to advertisers.

The magazine industry had its second strong year after a poor showing in 1982. Volume was up 15% in 1984. Newspapers also held their own, primarily due to increased local spending, as well as heavy national spending by regional telephone companies.

Cable TV's rate of wiring additional homes slowed slightly, stemming the growth rate of advertising revenue and subscriber growth. Advertisers, however, increased their cable purchases, reflecting their growing confidence in the major cable networks as avenues to sell products and services. Three of the majors—MTV, Nickelodeon, and CBN—turned profits for the first time in 1984.

Radio continued to be considered a viable alternative to more expensive media. Outdoor advertising managed a relatively modest, although respectable, 10% volume growth.

New media technology produced two major issues that affected media in 1984. (1) The controversy continued over the effectiveness of split-30-second commercials (two messages for unrelated products in a 30-second unit), although the activity in the purchase of split-30s indicated a gradual acceptance by some advertisers. (2) With the increased sales of home VCRs, there was a growing concern over elimination of commercials from television programming by consumers who tape shows to watch later.

Volume. Advertisers were expected to increase total outlays by 15% to $87.83 billion (U.S.) in 1984, a rate of growth similar to 1983. Once again newspaper buys represented the largest share of overall outlays with $23.67 billion, a 15% increase over 1983. Both radio and magazine advertising were up 15% in 1984, to $4.86 billion and $5.99 billion, respectively. Television buys showed the strongest gains, up 18% overall, reflecting increased spending in network (up 19% to $8.37 billion), local (up 19% to $5.15 billion), and spot (up 14% to $5.46 billion). Cable television expenditures, although representing only $510 million, have doubled since 1982. The weakest gains were posted by business publications (up 7% to $2.13 billion) and outdoor advertising (up 10% to $870 million). Growth in direct mail and miscellaneous (everything from bus-shelter ads to skywriting) was about the same as in 1983, with direct mail up 14% to $13.45 billion and miscellaneous up 15% to $17.37 billion.

Canada. Gross advertising revenues for 1984 rose 7.6% in 1984 to $5.6 billion, from $5.2 billion in 1983. These revenues lagged slightly behind the growth in GNP, a trend which has been in evidence since 1982. Percentage shares of net advertising revenues remained fairly constant: newspapers accounted for 32%, broadcast for 28%, direct mail/catalogs for 20%, periodicals for 15%, and outdoor for 6%.

There were major developments in Canadian pay television. Following the 1983 bankruptcies of two of the four original noncommercial channels launched earlier that year, the two remaining competitors, First Choice and Superchannel, merged in July 1984 and split the country into two regional monopolies. A further development occurred in September with the launching of two national commercial channels: Much Music, a 24-hour music channel, and TSN (The Sports Network), a 24-hour sports channel. Unlike the noncommercial channels that have no advertising and charge a premium subscription rate of approximately $15 per month, these new channels allow eight minutes of advertising per hour (compared with the 12 minutes on broadcast commercial television) for a much reduced subscription price of approximately $2.50 per month.

EDWARD H. MEYER, *Grey Advertising Inc.*

P. Manoukian, Sygma

Two Afghan guerrillas take time out from the war. The mujahidin *continued to hold their own against Soviet forces.*

AFGHANISTAN

During 1984 the Soviet Union escalated the violence in Afghanistan and tried to administer a knockout blow to the resistance. In the fifth year of hostilities, however, the overall stalemate continued.

Military Operations. In early spring the Soviets launched a campaign to destroy the resistance and pacify the country. An estimated 70,000 elite commando and heliborne troops, mostly from the Baltic and European Russian fronts, were deployed into Afghanistan. Their principal objectives were the strategic Panjshir, Logar, Shomali, and Andarab valleys. Lesser attacks took place in Paktia province and in the cities of Herat and Kandahar. Simultaneously aerial bombing and artillery shelling across the Pakistan border sought to interdict resistance reinforcements and intimidate Pakistan. Soviet troops were backed by high-level bombers from bases in the USSR as well as large numbers of helicopters, tanks, artillery pieces, and armored vehicles. The Soviets also carpet bombed and launched ground attacks on civilian villages, destroying crops and livestock and scorching the earth so as to deprive the *mujahidin* (guerrillas) of the aid and comfort of the local population.

However, more than 200 Soviet soldiers deserted to the resistance. Several, granted asylum in the West, revealed their revulsion against Soviet atrocities and mass killings. They also described the general disaffection among Soviet troops, high drug use, alcoholism, illness, and demoralization. In contrast, the Afghan resistance was better armed, better

organized, and better led. The Soviet high command hoped to reverse these trends by scoring a major victory against the resistance. But the big offensive did not succeed and actually backfired. In the Panjshir, for example, the resistance commander had advance notice of the attack and cleared the entire valley of civilians and *mujahidin*. The Soviets took control of the valley floor and left garrisons there, but the *mujahidin* were back to harass them. Similar inconclusive military results were reported in other areas. On the other hand, the Soviet attacks tended to unite the various resistance factions, a result that the Afghans themselves had been unable to achieve. And the Soviet escalation also brought a response from the United States. The Senate issued a report strongly urging increased aid for the *mujahidin,* and in August the House voted $50 million in additional covert aid.

Soviet efforts to revive the moribund Afghan army also failed. Desertions increased, and attempts to increase recruitment led to wholesale flight of Afghan youths to join the resistance or emigrate. In desperation, the government began to draft previously exempt Communist Party members and meted out four-year prison sentences to draft dodgers, three years of which could be commuted by army service. An attempt to extend the period of service of those already in the military resulted in several mutinies and desertions of entire units. Differences over these failures had provoked a quarrel between Deputy Defense Minister Gen. Khalilullah and Defense Minister Abdul Qadir, in which the latter was severely beaten or shot in 1983. The aftermath

83

was a wholesale shakeup of the Afghan military establishment in which the chief of staff, the chief of operations, and the deputy defense minister were all replaced.

The Resistance. Field operations by the *mujahidin* during 1984 were better organized and more successful. Frequent attacks on Soviet supply lines, including cutting the fuel pipeline to Kabul, resulted in severe shortages. Urban guerrilla activities also were stepped up. Kabul became less secure, with frequent assassinations of Afghan and Soviet officials and numerous attacks on government installations.

Though efforts failed to join all resistance factions under a United Front led by former Afghan King Zahir, there was more cooperation among feuding *mujahidin*. Also, two of the most adamant fundamentalist groups in Peshawar—Gulbuddin Hekmatyar's *Hezb-i-Islami* and Burhanuddin Rabbani's *Jamiat-i-Islami*—pledged cooperation and urged all other resistance groups to join.

The resistance continued to face major problems: shortages of weapons and ammunition, lack of defenses against the new Soviet high-altitude carpet bombing, and, most damaging, the wholesale Soviet attack on civilians.

U.S. support for the Afghan resistance increased during 1984. The Senate passed, 98–0, a nonbinding resolution urging all nations to provide food and medical aid to the resistance. Visits to the Khyber Pass by Secretary of State George Shultz and Vice-President George Bush evoked strong statements of support for the resistance. In October, Congress approved an "effective support" resolution to ensure adequate military aid for the *mujahidin*.

Political Developments. Soviet political objectives were clarified during 1984: to change the country from a loosely knit, tribal-based society into a socialist state governed by the Afghan Communist Party subservient to Moscow; to make Afghanistan into a secure, cooperative buffer on its southern border; and to prepare Afghanistan to serve as a forward base for future operations in southern Asia, the Middle East, and the Indian Ocean.

The first step is to "Sovietize" Afghan society. Copying its success in its Central Asian Muslim republics, the Soviets are trying to subdue the resistance by a combination of naked force, starvation and depopulation, division, and bribery. New cadres are being trained in the USSR; young women are being used as a surrogate proletariat with promises of liberation from Islamic and feudalist constraints; overlapping security services are being consolidated; and local militias and young revolutionary guards are being established. Cultural ties also are being expanded; more than 10,000 Afghans went to the USSR for training during 1984. The Afghan government, meanwhile, is trying, through heavy-handed propaganda, bribery, promises of local autonomy, and promotion of "Fatherland Front" organizations, to increase popular support for the Communist regime. But these measures were having little impact on Afghan society.

Diplomacy. After several visits to Kabul and Islamabad by UN mediator Diego Cordovez and a visit to Moscow by UN Secretary-General Javier Pérez de Cuellar, proximity talks between Pakistan and Afghanistan finally resumed in Geneva. By this time, however, it had become clear that the Soviet position had hardened. Soviet leader Konstantin Chernenko had snubbed Pakistani President Zia ul-Haq during the latter's visit to Moscow for Yuri Andropov's funeral. In an obvious attempt to intimidate Pakistan, aerial and artillery attacks were launched across the Pakistani-Afghan border. Finally, the escalation of Soviet troops in Afghanistan and the spring offensive clearly indicated a Soviet search for a military rather than a diplomatic solution. Indeed, in Geneva the Afghans would not budge on the issues of consultation with refugee and *mujahidin* groups and refused to provide a schedule for withdrawal of Soviet troops.

Economy. During 1984 the most devastating Soviet attack on the resistance was on the economic front. The self-sufficient Afghan economy is based on a network of villages that provide the resistance with food, shelter, medicines, staging areas, and hiding places. These villages now found themselves the targets of the Soviet scorched-earth attacks, and the economic destruction reached vast proportions. The Soviet strategy was to wait until the crops were ready for harvest and then deploy specially equipped helicopters, planes, and tanks to burn and trample them. Livestock was rounded up and killed or removed. The British Overseas Development Corporation, which sent clandestine observers into Afghanistan during the year, reported widespread famine; two of every three children examined were suffering from starvation. Some 3,000 tons of food per month is needed to feed the estimated 100,000 *mujahidin* combatants inside Afghanistan. With domestic agriculture being ravaged, food—as well as weapons—would now have to come from external sources.

LEON B. POULLADA
University of Nebraska, Omaha

AFGHANISTAN • Information Highlights

Official Name: Democratic Republic of Afghanistan.
Location: Central Asia.
Area: 251,773 sq mi (652 225 km²).
Population (mid-1984 est.): 14,400,000.
Chief Cities (March 1982): Kabul, the capital, 1,036,407; Kandahar, 191,345; Herat, 150,497.
Government: *Head of state,* Babrak Karmal, president (took power Dec. 1979). *Head of government,* Soltan Ali Keshtmand, prime minister (named June 1981). *Policy-making body*—57-member Revolution Council.
Monetary Unit: Afghani (50.6 afghanis equal U.S.$1, July 1984).

AFRICA

As 25 years of independence approaches for most African countries, assessment of their political and economic performance is inevitable. In many ways the year 1984 epitomized the problems and potential of the post-independence period. The year had its share of successful and unsuccessful coup attempts, and the continent continued to be an arena for big power politics. Authoritarian political systems still far outnumbered democratic states, white supremacy remained the guiding principle in South Africa, and opposition to South African apartheid was perhaps one of the few issues that all African states were able to agree on.

As in previous years, leaders were forced to compromise their ideological positions and to make pragmatic concessions in some cases to ensure the very survival of their regimes. The prime examples were the Accord of Nkomati, which established an uneasy détente between a reluctant Mozambique and South Africa, and the return to a more centrist position in Guinea after the military seized power following the death of President Sekou Touré.

The Organization of African Unity (OAU) entered its third decade with an uncertain future, not unlike the prognosis for Africa as a whole. The $45.5 million deficit in 1984 was the most serious financial crisis in its 21-year history, and at least one member state, Zaire, called for the dissolution of the organization in favor of a "League of the States of Black Africa" that would exclude the Arab north. If the OAU is to survive as an effective international organization, it must not only address the ideological differences between member states but must find an immediate solution to its unpaid membership fees and operating deficit.

Electoral and Constitutional Change. Significantly, the facade of democracy, if not its substance, was maintained in nearly all African states. Elections in Zaire in 1984 returned President Mobutu Sese Seko with 99.16% of all votes cast, and Jean-Baptiste Bagaza, the president of Burundi since a 1976 coup, was elected with a similarly large plurality. In the People's Republic of Congo, the Congolese Labor Party unanimously reelected President Denis Sassou-Nguesso, and in the People's Republic of Benin, President Mathieu Kerekou was reelected by an electoral college. Lesotho announced plans to hold its first election in 14 years. Finally, in a contested democratic election in Botswana, President Quett Masire was returned to power while Foreign Minister Archie Mogwe lost his parliamentary seat to a relative unknown.

Liberia took its first tentative steps toward a return to civilian rule in 1984. On July 3 a referendum was held on a new draft constitution that established the framework for civilian rule. Following its acceptance, Liberia's head of state Samuel K. Doe dissolved the ruling People's Redemption Council (PRC) and the constitutional advisory committee and personally selected the members for a new interim National Assembly and declared himself its president. Not surprisingly, all members of the dissolved PRC were among those appointed to the new assembly. On July 26 the ban on political activities was ostensibly lifted on the condition stipulated by Doe that "political activities had to be left to the politicians and anyone else caught engaging in politics would be arrested and detained without trial." Subsequently, in August and September, political and military leaders who represented a potential challenge to Doe in the general election scheduled for the fall of 1985 were alleged to have been plotting a coup and were arrested or detained.

On August 4, the first anniversary of the 1983 Upper Volta coup, Capt. Thomas San-

John Chiasson, Gamma-Liaison

In Upper Volta on August 4, the first anniversary of the coup establishing the current government, citizens celebrate as the country's name is changed to Burkina Faso, a new flag is adopted, and a new national anthem is introduced.

South Africa's Prime Minister Pieter W. Botha (center) is installed as the first executive state president under a new national constitution.

A. Nogues, Sygma

kara, head of state and chairman of the National Revolutionary Council (CNR), officially changed the name of the Republic of Upper Volta to Burkina Faso, "the land of men of integrity." The national flag, anthem, and motto also were changed in response to the new president's desire for a symbolic break with the past, "a declaration of second independence."

In September, Ethiopia celebrated the tenth anniversary of the overthrow of Emperor Haile Selassie and the reorientation of the country along Marxist lines. While Lt. Col. Mengistu Haile Mariam remained in control, Ethiopia continued to confront Eritrean and Tigre liberation movements and remained in the ambiguous situation of being closely allied with the Soviet Union while at the same time dependent on Western aid to alleviate widespread drought and starvation. Cuban troops, so important in maintaining the Mengistu regime in the past, were expected to be reduced to close to 3,000 by the end of 1984 from a maximum of 20,000. The reduction was caused by the belief that a renewed Somali attack in the Ogaden region was considered unlikely and because of the high cost to Ethiopia of maintaining the Cuban presence. The creation of a new Workers Party of Ethiopia (WPE) and the adoption of a new constitution reaffirmed the power of Mengistu Haile Mariam and the former Provisional Military Administrative Council.

In August the ruling Zimbabwean African National Union (ZANU) held its first Congress since the party was created 20 years ago. The 6,000 delegates reaffirmed the party's commitment to scientific socialism and to the establishment ultimately of a one-party state. Prime Minister Robert Mugabe was not willing to meet the demands of those who favored changing the existing parliamentary system immediately. On August 12 the prime minister announced the composition of the newly created 15-member Politburo and ZANU's 90-member Central Committee, the two most important decision-making bodies within the party. Their membership reflects Mugabe's efforts to achieve a political balance among differing ideological factions and competing clans within the majority Shona ethnic group.

In September a new constitution was introduced in South Africa creating a tricameral parliament that extended a modicum of power to so-called Coloureds and Indians while continuing to exclude blacks, who constitute more than 73% of the population. Effective power will remain in white hands, concentrated in the new office of executive state president. The prime minister, Pieter W. Botha, was inaugurated as South Africa's first president under the new constitution on September 14. Elections were held for the Coloured House of Representatives and the Indian House of Delegates, but the government considered an election for the all-white House of Assembly unnecessary, and thus the previous legislature continued in office. Significantly, 80% of the eligible voters in the Indian community and 70% in the so-called Coloured community boycotted the August elections for members of Parliament to the newly created tricameral legislature. By staying away from school on election day, Coloured children and subsequently young blacks joined the boycott. Several leaders of the boycott campaign were arrested by the government and remained in preventive detention. The extremely low voter turnout was a clear rejection of the new constitutional formula and an indication of the strength of the United Democratic Front (UDF), a coalition of antiapartheid groups and the single most important force behind the boycott.

Coups d'état. Where successful coups occurred in 1984, military rulers were quick to promise a return to civilian rule, although it was more likely that the new leaders would either fall victim to a countercoup or maintain power by transforming themselves into civilian regimes. The CNR of the then Republic of Upper Volta announced on June 7 that there had been an attempt to overthrow the regime of Capt. Thomas Sankara by Col. Didier Tiendrebeogo and other military officers and civil servants. The plot, which had been planned for May 28, failed and resulted in the execution of seven of the conspirators.

There was also an attempted coup in Cameroon, led by rebel elements within the presidential guard. After several days of fighting, troops loyal to President Paul Biya were able to restore order. It is alleged that the failed coup attempt was instigated by forces loyal to the previous president, Ahmadou Ahidjo, who was forced into exile in 1983, after which a Cameroonian court found him guilty in absentia of plotting against the government.

In Ghana in March, a group of soldiers tried to overthrow Flight Lt. Jerry Rawlings' three-year-old military government, but troops were able to contain the attempt. The dissidents, at least 11 of whom were killed, were mainly Ghanaian military exiles who crossed over from the Ivory Coast and Togo. There had been growing unrest in Ghana because of the austerity program introduced by Rawlings in 1983 when the government turned to the International Monetary Fund (IMF) for assistance. Ghana in turn received $600 million in exchange for implementing corrective economic measures, including a 90% devaluation of the cedi.

The 26-year rule of President Ahmed Sekou Touré of Guinea ended with his sudden death in a U.S. hospital on March 26. Within one week, a group of military officers under the leadership of Col. Lansana Conté seized power in a bloodless coup. The Military Committee for National Rectification (MCNR) took immediate steps to free political prisoners and promised a return to "genuine democracy" and an economy based on free enterprise.

A bloodless coup in Mauritania occurred in December, when President Mohammed Khouna Ould Haidalla was out of the country. Army chief of staff Maouya Ould Sidi Ahmed Taya, a former premier, took control of the Military Committee for National Salvation.

On Dec. 31, 1983, Nigeria experienced its fifth coup since it became independent in 1960. This coup, which appears to have been the direct result of the worsening economic situation and an unprecedented level of corruption, ended more than four years of civilian rule. A measure of Nigeria's economic malaise is reflected in the fact that the country's annual oil revenues, which provided more than 90% of its foreign-exchange earnings, had been reduced by an estimated $12 billion (U.S.) since the dramatic decline in oil prices in 1980. At that time oil earnings were more than $22 billion. Maj. Gen. Mohammed Buhari, the former federal commissioner for petroleum, became the head of the 19-member Supreme Military Council, Nigeria's new federal military government, on New Year's Eve, only four months after the August 1983 election in which President Shehu Shagari and his National Party of Nigeria (NPN) government had been reelected.

An elaborate funeral was held for Sekou Touré, president of Guinea since 1958, at Conakry's Grand Mosque, March 30.

Pierre Perrin, Gamma-Liaison

Political Violence. There were significant outbreaks of political, racial, religious, and ethnic violence throughout 1984.

The most serious violence since the Soweto riots of 1976 erupted in black townships around Johannesburg, South Africa, in September, resulting in more than 80 deaths and hundreds of injuries. Ostensibly a response to rent increases, the riots were symptomatic of the much deeper black frustration over exclusion from political power, discrimination in education, and increasing black unemployment. The government's response was to impose a ban on public gatherings in the Johannesburg area and to detain hundreds of blacks, many of whom were arrested while attending a funeral during the ban on public gatherings.

In Zimbabwe, a report from Catholic bishops accused the army of terrorizing Matabeleland, stronghold of opposition leader Joshua Nkomo. The government's response to these allegations was that it was simply trying to suppress South African–backed dissidents, formerly members of Nkomo's Zimbabwe African People's Union (ZAPU). Government troops were withdrawn from Matabeleland by August.

Even though the 17-year civil war between Sudan's predominantly Muslim north and Christian and animist south ended in 1972, tensions between these two regions have continued to surface sporadically. President Jaafar al-Nemery's plan, announced late in 1983, to create an Islamic state and redivide southern Sudan into three administrative units reinforced southern fears of discrimination by the northern Arab-dominated government and precipitated renewed tensions in 1984. Indications that Sudan was heading for a period of open, protracted hostilities include an army mutiny in January, the emergence of the Sudan People's Liberation Movement (SPLM) in the south in the spring, and the declaration of a state of emergency on April 29. In an about-face to ease tensions, President Nemery, in late September, ended the state of emergency and reversed his earlier decision to redivide the southern region.

The year 1984 was the fifth year since Milton Obote was returned to power as president of Uganda following the downfall of dictator Idi Amin. By 1984 neither the political stability nor the economic recovery that was anticipated with the return of Obote had materialized. Indeed, allegations were made that the level of violence continued to be extremely high, in part the result of the army's overzealous efforts to eliminate anti-Obote guerrillas in the Luwero Triangle north and west of Kampala, the capital city.

For the third time since 1980, Islamic fundamentalists turned to violence in northern Nigeria, posing the first major crisis for Nigeria's new military regime. It was estimated that more than 1,000 people lost their lives in religious riots in February and March before the military restored order.

Regional Political Accommodation. In a year of relative political turmoil and uncertainty in some parts of Africa, there was an apparent rapprochement between Kenya and Somalia and Kenya and Ethiopia. Kenya's President Daniel arap Moi met with Somali President Mohammed Siad Barre in July, the first such visit by a Kenyan head of state to Somalia. The meeting resulted in an official memorandum of understanding and cooperation and signaled a move toward more cordial relations. Diplomatic relations between Kenya and Ethiopia also continued to improve with the renewal of a commitment to respect the inviolability of the region's borders.

A possible break in the military and diplomatic stalemate in Chad between the forces of President Hissène Habré in the south and the northern opposition Transitional Government of National Unity (GUNT) occurred in 1984. There were indications that the French, who were supporting President Habré, and the Libyans, who were backing Goukouni Oueddi's coalition (GUNT), engineered an agreement in September for a simultaneous withdrawal of their respective troops by mid-November as a way of extricating themselves from the apparently worsening situation. Peace talks began on October 20 in Brazzaville, Congo. President Habré appeared to have benefited most from this reshuffling because of the splintering among opposition groups.

Mozambique, facing a third year of drought, economic crisis, and continuing attacks by South African-backed guerrillas of the Mozambique National Resistance (MNR), was maneuvered into signing a nonaggression pact with white-ruled South Africa on March 16. The Nkomati accord charged each of the signatories to deny sanctuary and support to one another's enemies. Through the agreement, the South African government sought to weaken the African National Congress (ANC), a black nationalist group fighting South Africa. While Mozambique was added to the countries denying the ANC bases for its guerrilla operations, the level of violence in South Africa did not seem to have abated. Five months after the pact had been signed it was alleged that the rebel MNR forces in nine of Mozambique's ten provinces were still being supplied by South Africa and the MNR actually seemed to have widened the war. In September when the Nkomati accord seemed threatened, Pretoria convened a cease-fire conference aimed at ending eight years of hostilities. Under this new agreement, "armed activity and conflict within Mozambique" would be ended and South African troops would monitor the process.

The Southern African Development Coordination Conference (SADCC) marked its fifth year with a donor's conference in Lusaka,

Zambia, in February and its fifth annual summit conference in Gaborone, Botswana, in July. Donor response to requests for emergency assistance for drought relief and regional food security programs as well as other development projects was positive. The SADCC secretariat estimated pledges in 1984 in excess of $500 million. The July summit was marred by differences of opinion on member states' relationships with South Africa.

Once again little progress was made on implementing UN Security Council Resolution 435, which calls for independence for Namibia. As in the past, the stalemate resulted from irreconcilable differences between South Africa's perception of its security needs and the South West African People's Organization's (SWAPO) demand for Namibian independence free of South African–imposed conditions. South Africa's demands included the withdrawal of Cuban troops from Angola, which the Luanda government continues to see as essential for its survival; the removal of SWAPO guerrilla bases from southern Angola; SWAPO disarmament; and an insistence that representatives of South African–backed internal Namibian parties be included in any ruling coalition.

In February, South Africa and Angola signed a disengagement agreement calling for South African troops to leave southern Angola and for the withdrawal of South African support from Jonas Savimbi's rebel National Union for the Total Independence of Angola (UNITA) in return for Angolan assistance in controlling SWAPO guerrillas in the border areas. By year-end, however, South African troops were still 20 mi (32 km) within Angola's

Cynthia Johnson, Gamma-Liaison

Severe drought causing widespread famine severely affected some 150 million people in 24 African nations. With the great need for aid, U.S. wheat from the Food for Peace Program was transported to Mauritania from Senegal (above) and some 2,000 starving Ethiopians were housed in metal shelters at a distribution center in the Gondar region.

Anthony Suau, Black Star

borders, the result, according to South Africa, of continued SWAPO activity inside the country.

Economic Decline and Conditionality. The economic and financial conditions in Africa continued to deteriorate in 1984 and reached near-crisis proportions. In addition to the worst drought in almost a century that has affected nearly half of the countries on the continent, Africa has suffered the effects of a world recession, a decline in commodity prices, worsening terms of trade with the industrialized nations of the world, the long-term effects of devastating oil price increases in the 1970s, as well as internal government mismanagement and corruption. The extent and severity of the economic crisis were hidden for several years by the massive injection of international bank loans. However, as the forecast for Africa's future economic growth worsened and African recipients were unable to meet interest payments on loans, international lending agencies, led by the International Monetary Fund (IMF), began to impose conditions on subsequent loans. This "conditionality," requiring drastic changes in domestic monetary and fiscal policies, created severe strains on internal political stability and on the viability of certain regimes. Some of the more untenable conditions included the removal of agricultural subsidies, increases in the price of staple foods, the reduction of nonfood imports, the freezing of wages, and the devaluation of currencies. African leaders were being forced to make austere monetary reforms, one of the most drastic of which was Ghana's 90% devaluation of the cedi. The new military regime in Nigeria, on the other hand, continued to resist devaluation, as had its civilian predecessor, despite IMF pressures.

It was clear that by 1984 the IMF had emerged as one of the most significant influences on the economic and political life of many African countries. This is particularly true since other international donor agencies and commercial banks now wait to see whether IMF terms have been met before proceeding with their own programs. The IMF thus has assumed an importance far in excess of its basic mandate to lend funds to correct balance-of-payments deficits. Critics of the IMF's insistence on a free-market approach and its opposition to government intervention into the economy allege that conditionality has become tantamount to a new form of colonialism.

South Africa's historically strong economic position has not insulated it from the effects of the current world economic crisis. Soaring interest rates, a rising rate of inflation, a negative balance of payments, a depressed world gold market, excessive government expenditure, and the worst drought in a century have combined to create the deepest economic recession since the 1930s. Critics point out that the apparatus to maintain white supremacy exacts an inordinately high price; the defense budget for 1984–85, for example, was twice as high as it was four years earlier, and the provision of services to the different racial groups required costly bureaucratic duplication and a government bureaucracy that employs more than one third of all white workers. If the economy continues its downward spiral, white unemployment and backlash would likely confront black unemployment and increasing unrest.

Zimbabwe's economic crisis worsened in 1984. Its gross domestic product and exports fell, inflation and government debt service rose, and the availability of critical foreign exchange declined. Exacerbating these economic problems were the continued emigration of whites with skills essential to the economy, almost no new major foreign investment since 1980, a third consecutive year of drought, which forced Zimbabwe to become an importer of food, and the influx of an estimated 100,000 refugees from Mozambique.

Drought. In 1984, UN officials estimated that 150 million Africans currently were living in the 24 countries most severely affected by endemic drought, the worst in Africa in a century. This natural disaster has been exacerbated by mismanagement and corruption, emphasis on cash crop production at the expense of food production, the absence of land conservation efforts, inadequate storage facilities, and poor transportation.

Countries particularly hard hit by the drought include Mauritania, Senegal, Mali, and Niger in the Sahel on the edge of the Sahara desert; Kenya and Ethiopia in the Horn of Africa; and Mozambique and Angola in southern Africa. The UN Food and Agricultural Organization (FAO) reported that while prospects for the 1984 harvest in the Sahel improved, the harvest in southern Africa had failed for the third year in a row. Zimbabwe's 1.8-million-metric-ton maize harvest in 1981 had been reduced to 500,000 tons in 1984, while an even worse situation in Mozambique resulted in nearly 100,000 refugees. In Lesotho one out of every two persons are said to be in need of emergency food aid, while in Ethiopia drought-related famine appears to have become a permanent feature of Ethiopian life as it has in a number of West African nations bordering the Sahara desert. Even Kenya, which normally has been able to provide for its domestic food needs, had to apply for food aid, the result of the recent failed harvest.

Finally, given Africa's population growth rate, which is the highest in the world, the population of many African countries will double within 20 years. This, viewed in the context of declining food production, seems to be leading to some future Malthusian catastrophe.

PATRICK O'MEARA
N. BRIAN WINCHESTER
Indiana University

Jeff Lowenthal, "Newsweek"

As a result of a high number of farm foreclosures and bankruptcies, many American farms were sold at auction.

AGRICULTURE

The growing proficiency of modern agriculture was demonstrated again in 1984, when the world's farmers harvested twice the amount of grain produced only 15 years earlier. However, the benefits of agricultural growth did not adequately reach millions of undernourished citizens.

Also failing to benefit from this increased productivity were some of the most efficient producers. For farmers in the highly developed democratic countries, now the world's major food exporters, 1984 was a year of uncertainty and, in many cases, financial hardship. Many efficient commercial farms experienced losses despite improved weather, increased yields, and some governmental income supports.

In the United States, farmers' losses were also felt by agribusinesses and farm town retailers. Producers of agricultural equipment, chemicals, and hybrid seed were obliged to make internal adjustments in order to survive another year of low sales volume. Farm credit institutions came under severe stress, and a few rural banks were declared insolvent. Rural community institutions were mobilized to alleviate psychological as well as economic distress, but there were relatively few of the farmer "protest" activities such as had previously resulted from hard times on the farm. In France, however, farmers blockaded roads in January to sabotage meat imports, which they blamed for falling meat prices.

Agricultural sectors in the developed democratic countries, despite increasing productivity and efficiency, did not wholly share in the recovery felt in other sectors during 1984. The agricultural problem was to be explained in part by the fact that productive capacity was growing faster than effective demand. Productivity had been stimulated by government income-support programs, both in the United States and in the European Community (EC). In addition, new knowledge from agricultural research was continually being applied to improve productive capacity, and yet another wave of proficient technology was forthcoming from biogenetic breakthroughs. With food consumption stable or even declining in the United States and Europe, democratic governments were under pressure from their farmers to be aggressive in the competition for export markets.

United States. A second explanation for 1984 farm troubles in the United States was a sharp change in federal monetary and fiscal policy, which shrank U.S. export markets even while increasing the cost of agricultural credit. Under the Nixon administration, a decade earlier, the U.S. dollar has been weakened with abandonment of the gold standard, substantially improving U.S. farmers' access to a growing world market. At that time land values were rising and "real" interest rates (after discounting for inflation) were low, encouraging commercial farmers to borrow heavily for modernization and expansion. During the Reagan administration, by contrast, fiscal and monetary policies strengthened the dollar, reducing exports. "Real" interest rates were raised to historic highs. Meanwhile, farmland values declined by as much as 20% in 1984. Up to one fourth of all commercial farmers had become heavily indebted, hardly able to pay interest costs. Lenders become reluctant to extend loans. It was difficult for these farmers or their creditors to recoup the loans by selling their land and other devalued assets.

In 1984 the major new U.S. farm policy proposal was a program under which lenders would forgive a portion of farm loans in return for the government's guarantee that the remainder of the loan would be repaid. Interest payments would be stretched out or temporarily suspended. Thus, attention was being given to preserving the existing structure of efficient, medium-size farms, whose numbers were suffering an alarming decline.

In 1984 also, there was renewed concern about reducing the many occupational hazards in the modern farm environment. In addition to injuries and deaths from farm machinery accidents, some farmers were suffering lung illness traceable to the polluted air within animal confinement operations. Farm chemicals, though safer than earlier ones, were suspected as a cause of the higher incidence of leukemia among farmers.

In 1984, U.S. farmers planted 11% more acres to crops with the end of the 1983 payment-in-kind (PIK) program, which had reduced acreage while clearing surpluses. Feed-grain acreage (largely corn) jumped 17 million acres (7 million ha) from the previous year, to total plantings of 120 million acres (49 million ha). However, Midwestern feed-grain crops were inundated by spring rains and damaged by midsummer drought, so that 1984 production was projected at less than 1982 (pre-PIK) production. Uncertainty about crop size slowed expansion of cattle and hogs, resulting in a strengthened livestock market. Broiler production increased about 5% over 1983.

Because of a continuing wheat surplus, the federal government authorized a continuation of production control programs for wheat in 1983–1984. Excellent yields, however, resulted in one of the largest U.S. wheat crops in history. This unexpected production was partly absorbed by unexpected increases in foreign demand for U.S. grains, especially large Soviet purchases.

U.S. imports were up in 1984, in part as substitutes for Texas and Florida citrus lost in a massive freeze-out during December 1983, but also because of increased demand for foreign food products, spurred by the general economic recovery and the strong U.S. dollar.

Western Europe. The European Community (EC), which includes most Western European countries, continued its strong thrust toward self-sufficiency in major agricultural products. Increased production was projected within virtually all European countries for beef, pork, mutton, broilers, and combined grains. The EC was expected to become a net exporter of feed grains in 1984, and continuing exports of wheat, sugar, and other agricultural products had established Europe as a producer region.

The end of the 1983 payment-in-kind program led to an 11% increase in the number of crop acres planted.

Kevin Horan, Picture Group

European productivity had been stimulated by the EC's Common Agricultural Policy (CAP), which supports prices on various commodities at levels well above world prices. The EC internal market was preserved through use of import restrictions. Market surpluses were devoted to secondary uses (such as using wheat for animal feed) or were sent abroad under export subsidies. However, the growing costs of CAP, which already consumed two thirds of the EC's budget, led to a 1984 decision to cancel all price increases. Even so, the EC was unable to fund its agricultural programs, and members disputed over the prospect of a special assessment. Still, the EC seemed resolved to continue subsidizing its agriculture, to the dismay of competitors in the United States, Australia, Canada, New Zealand, and other countries.

Other Exporters. Most other grain exporters were favored in world markets over the United States, which was hindered by the strong dollar. Australia, with sharply increased wheat production; Canada; and Argentina all increased wheat exports in 1984. Overall, the 1984 world wheat reserve, or carryover, was moderately high. However, total grain reserves fell below the standard generally considered necessary for world food security, mainly due to short supplies of corn and other feed grains.

Eastern Europe. Although Eastern European governments lately have striven for a more abundant agriculture, increases in that region's productivity have been modest. Among the more vigorous measures taken in 1984 was Poland's new agricultural law, which for the first time offered to independent farmers (who predominate in Poland) both the promise of continuity and the opportunity for growth. In the Soviet Union the administrative foundation was laid in 1984 for an "agro-industrial complex" that would be given responsibility for organizing and implementing agricultural development. Meanwhile, the Soviet Union and the United States had ended their trade hiatus, concluding a second long-term trade agreement in October 1983. Under the terms of the agreement, the Soviets would purchase at least 9 million metric tons of U.S. wheat and corn each year and would be permitted to buy up to 12 million metric tons without special permission. The United States waived this ceiling for 1984 and 1985. Actual Soviet purchases worldwide in 1984, in response both to need and favorable prices, were projected to be 46 million metric tons, some 20 million of these from the United States.

Asia. In the dynamic economies of Japan, Taiwan, and South Korea, domestic agriculture prospered even while food imports increased. In South Korea, continued rapid expansion of meat and milk production required growing imports of U.S. feed grains and soybeans. These countries were also major markets for U.S. "high-value" products, including meat and citrus fruit. In April, Japan signed an agreement with the United States that more than doubled the size of scheduled increases of these U.S. products under import quotas over the next four years.

Food supplies became more abundant in the world's two most populous countries, China and India. China continued to seek and achieve large, consistent gains in agricultural production. Its pragmatic government began to turn away from the commune structure of agriculture. Projected 1984–1985 Chinese production was 50% larger than that of 1974–1975. India's per capita production, too, continued to grow, at a less spectacular level.

World rice production continued its upward trend in 1983–1984. The international rice trade increased sharply, with Thailand the world's leading exporter.

Africa. Drought in Ethiopia, Morocco, South Africa, Kenya, and Zimbabwe exacerbated the food deficits that have characterized virtually all African countries. There were large increases in food imports—including a 50% increase for Ghana—despite existing heavy debt burdens remaining from previous food purchases. U.S. food donations increased, particularly to stem famine in Ethiopia. An increase was expected under the Food for Peace program for which immediate cash payment is not required. Higher world prices for cocoa and tea were favorable notes for some African countries.

South America. Central and South America, like Africa, are observed to possess undeveloped agricultural resources. Also as in Africa, however, productivity in these regions has hardly kept pace with population growth. Several countries, including Argentina, Mexico, and Brazil, did make strides in their goal of generating more exchange through agricultural exports. Chile, too, though faced with a $20 billion foreign debt, was able to look forward to a projected trade surplus in 1984.

Food Problems as Income Problems. Countries with many malnourished people were generally to be found among those regions with low productivity and increasing food imports. Typically, these same countries already had large trade deficits and monumental indebtedness. Thus they found it difficult to buy more food. While no solution to the problems of food-deficit nations appeared in 1984, it became clearer to decision makers in exporting nations such as the United States that food demands abroad are elastic, determined more by income than by per capita caloric need, and therefore, that industrializing countries such as China and South Korea may increase their demand enough to absorb the world's increasing food production.

See also FOOD.

DON F. HADWIGER, *Iowa State University*

ALABAMA

Politics dominated Alabama news during 1984.

Elections. President Reagan's smashing November win was the number-one political story in Alabama, as it was elsewhere in the nation. The incumbent captured approximately 61% of the popular vote, Walter Mondale only 38%. Reagan carried 54 of Alabama's 67 counties, Mondale just 13 (including nine Black Belt counties). Reagan campaigned twice in Alabama during the 1984 election year. Mondale visited the state frequently during his successful effort to win the state's presidential primary in March.

In the U.S. Senate race Democratic incumbent Howell Heflin easily overwhelmed former Republican Congressman Albert Lee Smith. Only three U.S. House seats were seriously contested. In these races, Birmingham Democratic Rep. Ben Erdreich defeated Republican Jabo Waggoner, a former Democratic state legislator; H. L. Callahan, another Democrat turned Republican, beat Frank McRight in Mobile in a contest to succeed retiring Republican Rep. Jack Edwards; and incumbent William Dickinson (R) defeated Larry Lee (D) in the Montgomery district.

Legislative Sessions. The Alabama legislature met in both regular and special session in 1984. Few pieces of major legislation emerged from the regular session, which began in February. However, the education budget was notable for providing sufficient appropriations for a fully funded state kindergarten program for the first time. The most controversial law passed over the governor's veto allowed larger cities within counties prohibiting the sale of alcoholic beverages to vote separately on the

question of liquor sales. Several cities quickly held referenda in the summer and most voted to go "wet." On November 6, Decatur, which had the distinction of being the largest legally "dry" community in the nation, also approved alcoholic beverage sales for the first time since Prohibition.

In a May special session the legislature defeated an industry-backed bill that would have made it more difficult for employees injured on the job to file lawsuits.

Horse Racing. In voting in Birmingham and Jefferson County on June 12, horse racing with pari-mutuel betting was approved by an overwhelming margin. Although three dog-racing tracks were in operation in the state, no horse racing had occurred in Alabama since the 19th century. The horse-racing track was expected to open in mid-1986.

Federal Intervention. Because of state enforcement inadequacies due to personnel shortages, the U.S. Environmental Protection Agency on July 30 took over administration of federally imposed hazardous waste disposal standards from the Alabama Department of Environmental Management. Problems associated with the disposal of toxic wastes were most notable in connection with a 2,400-acre (972-ha) landfill near Emelle, AL.

In several localities, federal suits were filed that sought to enhance prospects for the election of blacks to city and county councils and commissions. The anticipated result was considerable movement from at-large to district elections among Alabama local governments.

In November, an agreement was reached on a 13-year-old lawsuit involving conditions in Alabama prisons. A four-person committee created by a federal district court in 1983 to resolve the issue met with Gov. George Wallace to recommend dismissal of the lawsuit. The court's jurisdiction in the lawsuit was terminated, but the committee was authorized to continue monitoring the Alabama prison sys-

In July, Selma Mayor Joe Smitherman won a sixth term, defeating a black minister and former backer, F. D. Reese.

AP/Wide World

tem for three years, during which time the suit could be reactivated.

Unemployment. Alabama's jobless rate continued to be in double digits during 1984. In midyear the rate was 10.9%, one of the highest rates in the nation. A decline was noted from the same point in 1983, however, when the rate was 14.1%.

Accident. In July, 11 people were drowned when a triple-deck excursion boat capsized in the Tennessee River near Huntsville, AL. A freak wind of hurricane force caused the riverboat to tip over.

WILLIAM H. STEWART
The University of Alabama

ALASKA

Jan. 3, 1984, marked the 25th anniversary of Alaska statehood, an event that occasioned large ceremonies and celebrations.

Energy. The most expensive well every drilled, the Standard Oil of Ohio Mukluk well in the Beaufort Sea, came in dry. The cost of drilling was $1.6 billion, but the disappointment did not appear to have long-term negative effects on future exploratory efforts. However, decreases in the price of crude oil by Organization of Petroleum Exporting Countries (OPEC) nations forced downward the projections of revenues the state expected to derive from North Slope oil.

In a related matter, the U.S. Supreme Court handed down a decision that constrains the ability of the state to oppose offshore oil and gas exploration. This, following an earlier decision disallowing Native sovereignty over outer continental shelf areas, was viewed as a serious blow to efforts designed to protect fisheries, marine mammal habitats, and other ecological considerations. Some of these concerns were eased when Secretary of the Interior William P. Clark reduced the extent of the offshore

AP/Wide World

As congressional adjournment neared, Sen. Ted Stevens' office was nothing but paper. The Alaskan Republican won reelection but lost his bid to become majority leader.

lease areas originally offered by his predecessor James Watt.

Politics and Government. The state legislature, as a result of the November elections, featured a Democratic leadership structure in the House of Representatives and a Republican-led coalition in the Senate. The election also saw the restoration of Libertarian Party representation to the state legislature with the election of a representative from southeast Alaska. While the election resulted in an increase of Democrats in both houses, Alaska's congressional delegation remained firmly Republican. The lone representative survived a strong challenge from the widow of former Congressman Nick Begich, while Sen. Ted Stevens breezed by his opponent and looked beyond the election to his bid for the majority leader post in the Senate. The latter bid was unsuccessful, however.

A law raising the legal age for drinking alcoholic beverages from 19 to 21 went into effect in 1984, following patterns established in other states. The legislature also passed a law prohibiting smoking in all public buildings, except for specifically designated areas.

Legislation was passed enabling the state of Alaska to accept transfer of the Alaska Railroad from the federal government. The state eventually would assume control of the only rail line able to claim the distinction of being built, maintained, and operated by the federal government.

The federal government had a more direct impact on Alaska during 1984. On the one

---

ALASKA • Information Highlights

Area: 591,004 sq mi (1 530 700 km²).
Population (July 1, 1983 est.): 479,000.
Chief Cities (1980 census): Juneau, the capital, 19,528; Anchorage (July 1, 1982 est.), 194,675; Fairbanks, 22,645; Sitka, 7,803.
Government (1984); *Chief Officers*—governor, William Sheffield (D); lt. gov., Stephen McAlpine (D). *Legislature*—Senate, 20 members; House of Representatives, 40 members.
State Finances (fiscal year 1983): *Revenues,* $5,247,000,000; *expenditures,* $3,836,000,000.
Personal Income (1983): $8,238,000,000; per capita, $17,194.
Labor Force (May 1984): *Civilian labor force,* 242,900; *unemployed,* 25,600 (10.5% of total force).
Education: *Enrollment* (fall 1982)—public elementary schools, 63,211; public secondary, 26,202; colleges and universities (fall 1983), 26,045. *Public school expenditures* (1982–83), $625,817,760 ($7,325 per pupil).

hand, the Environmental Protection Agency, after much negotiating, established that federal air quality standards must be met in the larger cities in the state—specifically Anchorage and Fairbanks, where climatic and geographical characteristics combine to trap pollutants above the cities during the winter months. On the other hand, after a great deal of maneuvering at the national level, Alaska was chosen as one of the locations for a new Light Infantry Brigade.

Economy. The effects of deregulation of the airline industry began to be felt in 1984. Wien Air Alaska, Alaska's oldest airline, withdrew from the bush areas of the state, selling its airport facilities to MarkAir, a new airline in the field. Wien, in the meantime, dropped "Alaska" from its name and ventured south in search of more profitable markets. Subsequently, Wien filed for reorganization under federal bankruptcy laws.

The Supreme Court decision overturning residency requirements as a basis for determining eligibility for participation in the Permanent Fund distribution continued to affect state programs. The Pioneers Pensions, known as the Longevity Bonus, were the latest of such programs to be deemed unconstitutional by the attorney general's office. Attempts were under way to redraw the program to include those not formerly eligible.

While oil had been the basis for economic growth and stability in Alaska, coal began to acquire a new status as a potential market item.

Contract negotiations between a major coal producer in interior Alaska and Korean interests were under way for the better part of the year.

Social. Between 1983 and 1984 the state's population, according to the Department of Community and Regional Affairs Census, increased by approximately 15%—some 50,000 additional people having moved to the state, and the majority to the Anchorage area. Coincidentally, 1984 saw a construction boom in rental units as well as owner-builder starts. However, this positive evidence of economic health was more than offset by the governor's report that approximately one of every five persons living in Alaska was below the U.S. government's poverty line in terms of income.

An issue receiving much attention over the year was the status of Alaska Natives as a consequence of the passage of the Alaska Native Claims Settlement Act (ANCSA) in 1971. The impact study due before Congress in 1985 as a condition within ANCSA was completed during the summer, and public hearings were scheduled for December or January. In the meantime, the Alaska Federation of Natives, in response to the selection of an outside consultant firm to prepare this report, commissioned a well-known Canadian jurist, Thomas Berger, to conduct an inquiry into the same subject matter.

CARL E. SHEPRO
Department of Political Science
University of Alaska, Fairbanks

ALASKA—25 YEARS OF STATEHOOD

The Territory of Alaska was admitted to the Union on Jan. 3, 1959, as the 49th state. In the 25 years since then, the sturdy inhabitants of our largest state have continued with distinction the work of developing this vast storehouse of abundant resources, while preserving its special environment. As a result of their efforts, Alaska now produces one eighth of the nation's gold, one fifth of its petroleum, and two fifths of its harvested fish. Ten of the 16 strategic minerals vital to our nation's security are produced in Alaska. The millions of dollars worth of minerals, forest and food products, and energy resources produced each year have long since repaid many times over the $7 million paid by the United States to purchase Alaska in 1867.

The people of Alaska constitute a special resource. . . . Native Alaskans and immigrants from every state, as well as foreign countries, have worked together to build the cities, pipelines, rail, water, air, and ground transportation facilities which are the basis of Alaska's prosperity. . . .

In recognition of the importance of Alaska's people and its scenic and natural resources to the United States and in honor of the 25th anniversary of the admission of Alaska into the Union, the Congress . . . has authorized and requested the president to proclaim Jan. 3, 1984, as "Alaska Statehood Day. . . ."

A Presidential Proclamation, Jan. 3, 1984

1959	Alaska is admitted to the Union on January 3, becoming the 49th state.
1964	A Good Friday (March 27) earthquake severely damages the Gulf Coast region, killing 131.
1967	Alaska celebrates its centennial.
1968	The Prudhoe Bay oil field discovery is confirmed.
1971	The U.S. Congress approves the Alaska Native Land Claims Settlement Act, providing Alaska Natives title to 40 million acres (16 million ha) of land and payment of more than $900 million.
1977	The trans-Alaska oil pipeline from Prudhoe Bay to Valdez is completed.
1978	A 200-mile fishing limit goes into effect.
1980	The Alaska legislature votes to repeal the state personal income tax and provides for refunds of 1979 taxes. A Permanent Fund is established as a repository for one fourth of all royalty oil revenues for future generations.
	The Alaska Lands Act of 1980 puts 53.7 million acres (21.7 million ha) into the national wildlife refuge system, parts of 25 rivers into the national wild and scenic rivers system, 3.3 million acres (1.3 million ha) into national forest lands, and 43.6 million acres (17.6 million ha) into national park land.
1983	Alaska's four time zones are changed to two. The U.S. government ends its control over the Pribilof Islands.

Still one of the most insulated and mysterious countries in the world, Albania marked 40 years of Communist rule in 1984. Posters to the glory of the Albanian Workers' Party (PPSH) were prevalent in the capital city of Tiranë, left, and throughout the country.

Ferdinando Scianna, Magnum

ALBANIA

Little change was evident in Albania's domestic affairs or in its relationship with the rest of the world in 1984.

Domestic Affairs. The aging (76) Stalinist leader of Albania, First Secretary of the Albanian Workers' Party Enver Hoxha, seemed to be approaching the end of his 40-year-long rule. He did not appear in public from May to October, apparently because of poor health. Day-to-day governmental functions seemed to be in the hand of his heir-apparent, Ramiz Alia, head of state since 1982 and secretary of the Central Committee and member of the Politburo of the AWP. Governmental changes included the appointment in February of Qirjaki Mihali as a third deputy premier and his replacement as minister of finance by Niko Gjyzari.

Although Albania continued to have the lowest standard of living in Europe, official prognoses for 1984 were optimistic. The economic plan and budget for 1984 envisaged an 8.5% rise in industrial production and a 14% rise in agricultural production. In January, Minister of Foreign Trade Shane Korbeci announced that 70% of Albania's exports now consisted of finished and semifinished goods, and that the country imported more mechanical equipment than raw materials.

Rumors persisted of continuing trials and purges of the allies of former Premier Mehmet Shehu, who was alleged to have plotted the overthrow of the Hoxha regime and to have committed suicide in December 1981. Subsequently, some 30 high-ranking political figures were said to have been executed or imprisoned. Modest official relaxation of domestic tension was seen in the allowing of Italian and Turkish films to be shown in Albania and the signing, in July 1984, of a two-year agreement for the exchange of programs and for technical cooperation with the Austrian broadcasting corporation.

Foreign Relations. Albania also seemed willing to make cautious changes in its self-imposed isolation in 1984. In February, Greek Premier Andreas Papandreou protested alleged Albanian mistreatment of the Greek minority in southern Albania, asserting that Greece had no territorial claims against Albania and was eager to discuss formal termination of the state of war that technically existed between the two countries since 1940. Albanian Deputy Foreign Minister Muhamet Kapllani traveled to Greece in the spring. Subsequently, legal border crossing between the two countries was made easier, and Albania announced that it would train Greek-language teachers for the Greek minority. However, Albania refused to participate in a conference of Balkan states, sponsored by Greece, to discuss the creation of a nuclear-weapons-free zone in the Balkans.

In February, Albania and Turkey signed an agreement on trade and air links. In March, three months after the inauguration of ferry service between the Albanian port of Durrës and the Italian port of Trieste, a trade agreement was signed with Italy. In August, Bavarian Premier Franz Josef Strauss visited Tiranë and met with Deputy Premier Manush Myftiu, apparently to discuss possible diplomatic relations between Albania and West Germany.

JOSEPH F. ZACEK
State University of New York at Albany

ALBANIA • Information Highlights

Official Name: People's Socialist Republic of Albania.
Location: Southern Europe, Balkan peninsula.
Area: 11,100 sq mi (28 748 km²).
Population (mid-1984 est.): 2,900,000.
Chief City: (1981 est.): Tiranë, the capital, 220,000.
Government: *Head of State,* Ramiz Alia, president of the Presidium (took office November 1982). First secretary of the Albanian Workers' Party, Enver Hoxha (took office 1941). *Head of government,* Adil Çarçani (took office January 1982). *Legislature* (unicameral)—People's Assembly, 250 members.
Monetary Unit: Lek (7 Leks equal U.S.$1, June 1984).
Gross National Product (1981 est. U.S.$): $2,380,-000,000.

ALBERTA

Alberta showed some signs of pulling out of the current recession. However, in the first half of the year, net emigration, reversing recent trends, amounted to almost 20,000, about equal to the natural increase, for a zero population growth.

Politics and Government. In the federal election, Alberta returned a full slate of Conservative candidates to Parliament, their party being overwhelmingly successful and forming the government.

Grant Notley, leader of Alberta's New Democratic Party since 1968, was killed in a plane crash on October 20. Among the four survivors of the crash was the provincial housing minister, Larry Shaben. At a convention in November, Ray Martin, the NDP's only member in the provincial legislature, was elected NDP's permanent leader. He had been serving as interim leader since Notley's death.

Agriculture. In common with other prairie provinces, Southern Alberta experienced drought conditions compounded by grasshopper plagues. Central Alberta, however, produced satisfactory crops, as did the Peace

The Alberta legislature paid tribute to Grant Notley, the provincial NDP leader who died in a plane crash. Ray Martin (head bowed) succeeded him in the party post.

Canapress Photo Service

River area, which received adequate moisture for the first time in four years.

Employment. Alberta's unemployment levels were virtually the same as the national average of 11–12%, but in Calgary and Edmonton they ranged to more than 14%. With little new residential or commercial construction, workers in these fields were most seriously affected.

Collective agreements in both public and private sectors showed wage and salary increases below the inflation rate of about 5%. However, despite threats of work stoppages, there was little overt labor unrest.

Transportation. With both national railways double-tracking west from Alberta, prospects for improved freight movement to the west coast in the near future appeared bright.

Through rail passenger service from Winnipeg to Edmonton, discontinued in 1981, was restored, with prospects of renewal of Edmonton-Vancouver service shortly.

Oil and Gas. Lessened restrictions on extraction, price, and export of natural gas and increased production, planned or begun, from oil sands and heavy oil deposits indicated improvement in the oil and gas industry.

Rental Occupancy. In cities, residential apartment vacancies were in the 15% range, up from less than 1% in 1981. Office vacancies ranged from 20–40%.

Education. Tight provincial funding—below inflation levels—and increased enrollments at postsecondary institutions caused serious problems, but the use of general admission quotas was averted.

Sports. For the first time, Edmonton hosted the Canadian Football League's annual Grey Cup game in November; however, the five-year supremacy of the Edmonton Eskimos in the CFL had ended in 1983. The 1984 Grey Cup was taken by Winnipeg. The Blue Bombers defeated the Hamilton Tiger-Cats, 47–17. Edmonton's fall in football was balanced in 1984 by the Edmonton Oilers' win of the Stanley Cup, emblematic of the National Hockey League championship.

In Calgary, preparations for the 1988 Winter Olympics proceeded apace. Meanwhile, Alberta athletes did well in the Olympic Games in Los Angeles.

Papal Visit. In fine September weather, large and enthusiastic crowds welcomed Pope John Paul II on the occasion of his visit to the province.

JOHN W. CHALMERS
Concordia College, Edmonton

ALGERIA

While Morocco and Tunisia experienced serious riots, and while Libya and Morocco signed a controversial "treaty of union," Algeria preserved its enviable reputation for stability. Quiet diplomacy abroad and patient economic progress at home helped the government retain its popularity. Meanwhile, however, the population continued to expand at the rapid rate of 3.2%, and unemployment in nonagricultural industries remained at about 14%.

Foreign Relations. Algeria was surprised and chagrined by the treaty signed by Libya and Morocco in August. The treaty clearly was intended to weaken Algeria diplomatically and to steal its momentum of regional leadership. By signing the treaty with Morocco, Libya left Algeria isolated in its support for the Polisario guerrillas, who were seeking to seize control of the Western Sahara away from Morocco.

At first, Algeria angrily denounced the treaty, suggesting that it was part of a "Zionist plot" to undermine Maghreb (North African) unity. But by mid-September, Algeria's anger began to yield to the more realistic perception that the Libyan-Moroccan treaty probably would have a limited effect. Morocco opened its border with Algeria, keeping a promise made in 1983, and the roar of rhetoric died down as Algeria sought to stabilize its regional position.

Relations with the United States, which had been improving steadily since 1980, continued to grow warmer. In February, U.S. Secretary of Agriculture John R. Block led a delegation that discussed cooperation in agricultural technology. And in October, Gen. Kenneth Burns, U.S. assistant secretary of defense for North African and Middle Eastern Affairs, met with Algerian officials on his regional itinerary. General Burns was believed to have discussed the possibility of providing Algeria with U.S. weapons. Algeria was pleased that the 1985 Pentagon budget included a substantial appropriation for training Algerian military staff.

Politics. President Chadli Benjedid was elected to a second five-year term in January, winning more than 95% of the vote. He then made several important cabinet changes, naming the American-educated Abdelhamid Brahimi, a former minister of planning, to replace Mohamed Abdelghani as prime minister. The promotion of Brahimi, who was considered a political moderate, came soon after the purge of several hard-line leftists from the ruling party's central committee. Chadli's confidence in the security of his rule was displayed in May when he amnestied 92 political prisoners—many of them Islamic fundamentalists.

The Economy. Recognizing the severe structural imbalances in the economy, the Algerian government began to shift its emphasis away from hydrocarbons and grandiose expenditures on heavy industry. Agriculture, light industry, rural development, and urban social projects received greater emphasis in the 1985–1989 development plan, which was approved in late 1984. The new plan also called for private investment and small businesses to be encouraged for the first time.

Unlike co-members of OPEC that export only crude oil, Algeria has diversified its hydrocarbons industry, concentrating on the exportation of natural gas and petroleum by-products. In 1984, Algeria was able to refine more than half of its oil, selling the by-products for prices substantially higher than those of crude oil.

Natural-gas exports had doubled since 1980, but Algerian sales in 1984 were snarled in contractual disputes. The French state utility, Gaz de France, went to international arbitration to obtain a 10% cut in purchases specified in its long-term contract with Algeria. Enagas, the Spanish state gas company, also insisted on reducing its purchases from Algeria, which retaliated by canceling a construction contract it had awarded to a Spanish firm.

Algeria was also investing in a 630-megawatt thermal power plant and a massive expansion of the telecommunications system. Plans to build a subway in Algiers were being considered.

MICHAEL MAREN, *"Africa Report"*

ALGERIA • Information Highlights

Official Name: Democratic and Popular Republic of Algeria.
Location: North Africa.
Area: 950,000 sq mi (2 460 500 km²).
Population (mid-1984 est.): 21,400,000.
Chief Cities (1980 est.): Algiers, the capital, 2,200,000; Oran, 633,000; Constantine, 384,000.
Government: *Head of state,* Chadli Benjedid, president (took office Feb. 1979). *Head of government,* Abdelhamid Brahimi, prime minister (appointed Jan. 22, 1984).
Monetary Unit: Dinar (4.931 dinars equal U.S.$1, June 1984).
Gross Domestic Product (1982 U.S.$): $42,900,-000,000.
Foreign Trade (1982 U.S.$): *Imports,* $10,754,-000,000; *exports,* $13,182,000,000.

ANTHROPOLOGY

A spate of human and ape fossil finds and intensified debate and theorizing over fossil specimens made 1984 an important year in the field of anthropology.

Fossil Finds. In northern Kenya, anthropologists uncovered the remains of an apelike creature previously known to have existed only in Asia. Approximately 17 million years old, the fragments of jaws, teeth, and skulls seemed to point to an apelike form similar in many ways to the orangutan. The discovery was made by a team led by Alan Walker of Johns Hopkins University and Richard Leakey, director of the National Museums of Kenya. Walker believes the new specimen is a creature known as *Sivapithecus,* thought to be part of the evolutionary branch that led to the orangutans of Asia. As a result of the new discovery, however, it is considered possible that orangutans originated in Africa and that *Sivapithecus* was a more generalized form ancestral to all apes and humans. This would also mean that gorillas and chimpanzees, rather than similar to the last common ancestor of apes and humans, are only specialized apes, while the orangutan is a living fossil.

Walker and Leakey made another notable discovery in 1984. On the island of Rusinga in Lake Victoria, Kenya, they unearthed thousands of fossilized bones of 18-million-year-old creatures called *Proconsul africanus.* Sharing characteristics of both apes and monkeys, *Proconsul* apparently played a key role in the course of human evolution. The adult creature weighed 20–25 lbs (9–11 kg) and was about 18 inches (46 cm) high at the shoulders when walking on all fours. Because only a skull and a few other bones had previously been discovered, the 1984 find was expected to provide important new insights into *Proconsul's* appearance and behavior.

Also in Kenya, at a site called Tabarin in a remote region near Lake Baringo, a jaw fragment dated at five million years was discovered. That would make it about one million years older than any previously found fossil of possible human ancestry. The 2-inch (5-cm) piece of jawbone is similar to that of the species *Australopithecus afarensis,* also known as "Lucy."

In the Fayum region of the Sahara, about 50 mi (80 km) southwest of Cairo, Elwyn L. Simons of Duke University discovered four skulls of the early species *Aegyptopithecus.* This small primate, about the size of a house cat, lived in Africa more than 30 million years ago. Simons reported that the newly discovered skulls show different proportions and variations and that they exhibit progressive brain sizes characteristic of primates related to humans. He believes that the human ancestry of *Aegyptopithecus* is evidenced by its facial and tooth structures, which appear in later apes and monkeys.

Finally in October, again in Kenya, archaeologists unearthed the skull and bones of a "strapping" youth of about 1.6 million years ago. The fossil bones were described as the most complete skeleton of an early human ancestor ever found. They were said to be the remains of a 12-year-old boy who stood between 5'4" and 5'6" (1.63 and 1.68 m), surprisingly tall for a *Homo erectus.*

Debate. The discovery of certain fossils revived the debate as to the time of evolutionary divergence between the African apes and the hominid line (humans). Paleoanthropologists have considered this to be about 15 million years ago, but molecular analysis of blood proteins and DNA of apes and humans has led molecular biologists to claim a time of divergence of 4.5 million years ago. The extreme age of recent fossil finds, however, now suggests that the divergence may have taken place about 10 million years ago.

At the May meetings of the American Association for the Advancement of Science, the debate between the molecular biologists and the paleoanthropologists intensified. Jeffrey H. Schwartz of the University of Pittsburgh said that his research showed that the genus *Homo* (humans) has many more similarities in form and structure with the orangutan than with the chimpanzee or gorilla. However, a proponent of the molecular theory, Morris Goodman of Wayne State University, said that the morphological evidence may only mean that humans and orangutans are similar because of convergent evolution.

Wild Man of China. In remote parts of central and southern China, there were reported sightings of a creature called "Ye Ren," or Wild Man. The reports describe a hairy creature 7–8 ft (2.13–2.44 m) tall, with human features, no tail, and an ability to laugh. Li Jian, secretary general of the Society for the Survey and Research of the Chinese Wild Man, says that the creature is not human, though it walks like a man. According to one theory, Wild Men are survivors of a species of giant ape whose fossils have been found in China.

Other. The year 1984 saw the publication of two insightful books about the late anthropologist Margaret Mead: *With a Daughter's Eye—A Memoir of Margaret Mead and Gregory Bateson,* by Mary Catherine Bateson (William Morrow); and *Margaret Mead—A Life,* by Jane Howard (Simon & Schuster). When she died in 1978, Mead was world-famous for her far-ranging work in cultural anthropology and ethnology, but few people really knew her well. Both new biographies do much to explain Margaret Mead the person. Bateson's book is a tribute to her famous parents.

HERMAN J. JAFFE
Brooklyn College, CUNY

The "Ancestors" Exhibition

The cranium of an adult female "Cro-Magnon Man" (upper right), the cranium and lower jaw of an adult male "Mount Carmel Man" (lower left), and a selection of Late Paleolithic tools were among the many important specimens on display at a unique anthropological exhibition in New York City.

AMNH

From April 13 to Sept. 9, 1984, the American Museum of Natural History in New York City was the scene of an unprecedented exhibition: "Ancestors: Four Million Years of Humanity." In the exhibit, the museum brought together, for the first and probably the only time, more than 40 of the most complete and spectacular of the fossils that document the long course of human evolution. Although the total number of known human fossils is probably in the thousands, only a very few consist of more than a fragment of jaw with a few teeth, a small piece of skull, or part of a long bone. The specimens on display in "Ancestors" represented a substantial proportion of the more complete human fossils known. For the first time, the public and scientists alike were able to see and compare for themselves many of the most important among the original, tangible pieces of evidence on which the understanding of human evolution is based. Most of the fossils had never before traveled from their home institutions, and virtually all had been available for examination only to scientists.

Organizing "Ancestors" required the active cooperation of 20 institutions worldwide, and preparations took more than three years. Each fragile specimen was hand-carried to New York by its curator and returned home the same way. The simultaneous presence of the fossils and the scientists responsible for them made possible an unprecedented scientific event: four days of formal comparison sessions in which paleoanthropologists from around the world could examine the specimens side by side, rather than compare them secondhand by means of casts, photographs, and notes. The opportunity to discuss the myriad outstanding problems in human evolution in the presence of primary evidence proved revelatory, as many attested during the four-day symposium that followed the comparison sessions.

The main visual focus of the exhibition was on the fossils themselves, but much supplementary and explanatory material was provided. The spectrum of fossils on display covered all major phases of human evolution, from prehuman beginnings more than 30 million years ago to the present. The emphasis was on the last four million years, the documented span of the human family. Included were early hominoids (broadly, apes); both robust and gracile australopithecines; *Homo habilis; Homo erectus* from both Asia and Africa; "archaic *Homo sapiens*" from Europe and Africa; Neanderthals from sites ranging from France to Israel; "transitional" forms from Africa and the Levant; early modern humans from Europe and Africa; and representatives of the earliest human inhabitants of the Americas. Each group of fossils subsequent to the origin of stone tool-making was displayed with original artifacts. Among the most famous fossils on exhibit were the original Neanderthal skullcap; the skull of the "Taung child," the first australopithecine ever discovered; "Java Man" specimens; the jaw of "Heidelberg Man"; and a Cro-Magnon skull.

IAN TATTERSALL, *Co-curator*

ARCHAEOLOGY

Many important discoveries made in 1984 came from well-organized research projects, most of which, especially in the Eastern Hemisphere, received support from various national governments. The U.S. space program also provided assistance, as radar images from the shuttle *Challenger* in October were to be used in the search for Nordic ruins on an island in the Baltic Sea.

Eastern Hemisphere

Ice Age Hunters. Old Stone Age people with simple chopper and flake technology are now known to have lived much farther north than previously suspected, thanks to a Soviet find 160 km (99 mi) north of the Siberian city of Yakutsk on the Lena River. Fireplaces and other debris were found under deposits one million years old; the site, it was concluded, could not have come later than the Gunz glaciation. For humans, presumably the form called *Homo erectus,* to have survived under such conditions, archaeologists surmise that crude clothing must have been fashioned.

In Swaziland, Africa, English archaeologists examining stratified deposits at Siphio Rock Shelter found an industry dating from 16,000 years ago, a previous blank in the prehistory of southern Africa. This new Lubombo Culture is distinguished by microlithic blades and scrapers and ostrich shell beads, made at a time when the climate was very dry; most of the charcoal came from the drought-tolerant Ironwood tree.

Creative Farmers. The known remains of the Near Eastern Pre-Pottery Neolithic "B" culture had been immensely pragmatic dwellings, tools for farming, and defensive fortifications. The stone walls at Jericho were impressive but still did not prepare American archaeologists for the discovery, at Ain-Ghazal, Jordan, of a cache of plaster statues left behind in a large farming village. The first set includes ten statues nearly one meter (3.3 ft) tall, while another set includes 12 busts less than 0.5 m (1.6 ft) high. A particularly interesting large statue is of a nude female holding her right hand to a breast. Such a statue appears to foreshadow the Astarte fertility cult known in ancient civilizations 4,000 years later.

A detailed survey of the high mountains of southeastern Turkey located thousands of rock engravings or petroglyphs dating back 10,000 years or more. Most of them depict mammals, but some show symbolic and abstract designs or human beings. The most impressive, called Bison Rock, shows two bison and a hart deer etched on a bluish slab 2.2 m (7.2 ft) tall.

At Twann, Switzerland, archaeologists salvaged a carbonized, but still intact, loaf of bread accidentally burned by a Neolithic Cor-

taillod Culture (ca. 3,500 B.C.) baker. The bun-shaped loaf of finely sifted, leavened wheat flour measures 6.5 cm (2.6 inches) in diameter and must have been 2.4 cm (.9 inch) thick.

In Zhengzhou, China, an intact hen's egg was recovered at late neolithic levels, dating from just before 2,000 B.C. Chinese archaeologists interpreted the find as evidence of the practice of storing eggs for decades to improve their flavor.

Nile Valley Finds. A Cairo University project at Saqqara explored the best-preserved graves found in Egypt since the opening of Tutankhamun's grave. Five tombs made of massive stone blocks contained stone sculptures and finely executed murals. The tombs date to the time of Rameses II (ca. 1305–1227 B.C.). More paintings and inscriptions came to light when a sandstorm at Siwa Oasis uncovered a 2,000-year-old Greco-Roman temple.

Up the Nile in the Sudan, Swiss archaeologists digging at Kerma uncovered traces of an ancient kingdom, called Kush by the Egyptians, which flourished around 1800–1500 B.C. The settlement's round wattle and daub houses were protected by stone fortification walls and a dry ditch. The best-preserved tomb held the flexed burial of a 16-year-old bowman, desiccated by the sands, while another tomb contained a wooden bed, table, stools, and a funeral meal of lamb and other meats.

Asiatic Civilization. In southwest Asia, on the West Bank of the Jordan River, Israeli archaeologists discovered an altar on an 820-m (2,700-ft)-high mountain overlooking Wadi Pharaoh. The altar is a large stone with a central depression filled with ashes and sheep bones, debris left from sacrifices. Artifactual evidence in the compound holding the altar indicates a date in the 12th century B.C., about the time of the exodus of the ancient Israelites from Egypt.

The results of long-running Danish expeditions to Bahrain, ancient Dilmun, finally were synthesized. The Barbar temple there is seen to be dedicated to Enki, the ancient Sumerian god of groundwater. The temple, established ca. 2200 B.C., was built on the ziggurat principle near a sweet water spring. From that spring was retrieved a bronze male figurine, 12 cm (5 inches) tall. Copper ingots, adzes, alabaster vases, and a copper bull's head—an ornament for a lyre—were found in the temple.

Chinese archaeologists excavated the site of the royal palace of the first Chinese dynasty, that of the Qin (Chin). The palace is near the ancient city of Xi'an in central China's Shanxi Province. The 400-m (1,312-ft)-long site yielded tiles, hollow bricks, and pottery and mural fragments from ca 220 B.C., the time of Emperor Qin, whose tomb east of Xi'an produced the famous terra-cotta soldiers and horses.

Also in Shanxi Province, archaeologists found 91 km (57 mi) of one of the oldest parts

At Rio Azul in the jungles of northeast Guatemala, archaeologists opened a Mayan tomb from the Early Classic period (A.D. 250 to 600). Twenty-nine other tombs at the site, like the one right, had been looted.

of the Great Wall of China. This portion was built in the 7th century B.C. during the Chu dynasty, a forerunner of Qin.

Cave Temple. Greek investigations of Mt. Ida on the island of Crete—the legendary birthplace of Zeus—revealed layers of deposit about 10 m (33 ft) thick, made greasy black by centuries of food and oil offerings. Artifactual votives include cauldrons, ivory seals, ceramic cups, a stone altar, and rings and pins of gold. While the cave was used for rituals from the Bronze Age until the Christian era, most of the finds date from the Geometric Period (1,000–700 B.C.).

Viking Finery. A skeleton grave at Esbjerg on the west coast of Denmark contained one of the most richly equipped Viking burials yet found. Upon his death about A.D. 900, the man was furnished with fine weapons and horse gear, most of it inlaid with silver.

Western Hemisphere

Early Hunters. Continued delving by University of Kentucky scientists at boggy Monte Verde, Chile, brought forth additional wooden tools used by Paleo-Indians ca. 11,500 B.C. The relics include two handles for stone endscrapers, wooden planks for house foundations, and three crude wooden mortars. Other finds included mastadon bones, chopping tools, and plant remains.

The Gainey site of southern Michigan provided local archaeologists with new insight into Clovis hunter-foragers. Seven clusters, possibly tent sites, yielded 25 fluted points. Charcoal-rich features revealed some of the plants utilized by these hunters ca. 11,000 B.C., who acquired flint from as far away as central Ohio's "Flint Ridge."

Woodland Indians. At Santa Rosa Sound on the Florida Panhandle, condominium construction opened a major site of the Deptford Phase, an early Woodland culture of Florida. The first known house from this culture was revealed, along with numerous stone tools and ceramics, including a four-legged pot.

Mesoamerican Civilization. In a grave field riddled by looters in Río Azul in northeastern Guatemala, one tomb from the Early Classic period (420–470 A.D.) had been left unscathed. In 1984, University of Texas researchers opened that burial chamber to reveal pottery, jade beads, and red-painted murals and inscriptions. The skeleton, with tattered shroud remnants still adhering, lay atop the decayed wooden bier. Among the 15 pots were six tripods and a stirrup-handled jar with screw-top lid. Unique among pre-Columbian artifacts, the lid worked on the modern "child-proof" principle; anyone who could have opened this jar would have seemed a powerful magician indeed.

Reports by University of Missouri archaeologists concerning excavations at Tula, Mexico, made public an important bas-relief sculpture of Quetzalcoatl, one of the main gods of the Toltecs and related peoples. In this same house, dated ca. 1,000 A.D., a headless skeleton was found seated inside a household altar decorated with a shard and stone mosaic.

Spanish Explorers. At Long Bay, San Salvador island, U.S. archaeologists recovered European artifacts from an Indian site. The historic artifacts include three glass beads, brass rings, iron spikes and hook, and shards of Spanish pottery. The artifacts date from ca. 1500, making this the oldest known European contact site in the Bahamas. It is only 180 m (590 ft) from the popularly supposed first landing site of Columbus.

With the help of a nuclear reactor, scientists confirmed that bones and artifacts found in 1977 at a cathedral in Lima, Peru, were in fact those of the Spanish explorer Francisco Pizarro. The remains had been found in boxes, one of which had an inscription identifying the skull inside as that of Pizarro. The conqueror of the Incas was killed in a sword fight with former followers in 1541. Cut-marks on the skeleton matched perfectly the historic account of how the sword entered him.

RALPH M. ROWLETT
University of Missouri-Columbia

ARCHITECTURE

In the architecture of 1984 there was a maturing of trends that had appeared revolutionary and possibly transitory a few years before. Entering the mainstream were not only romantic, classic, and decorative designs—as epitomized by Post-Modernism, called by many a reaction to the square lines of the International Style—but greater respect for the country's cultural and natural heritage. The concern for the latter was demonstrated by a high level of activity in architectural restoration and the design of new buildings to fit in with their environments instead of dominating them, as so many mid-20th century projects had done.

The latter approach, known as contextual design, produced such brilliant examples as architect Emilio Ambasz's proposals for Schumberger Research Laboratories, structures with earth mounded up and over them to make them appear part of a natural, rolling terrain. When the approach was taken in cities, it was often called infill design, although the new construction could be many times the size of the existing—as was the case of the Mid-Continent Tower by architects HTB, Inc., built to top in similar style a 1918 Beaux-Arts office building in Tulsa. It was also the case with the 500 Park Avenue Tower in New York City by James Stewart Polshek and Partners, a building designed to sit comfortably beside a relatively new landmark, the petite office building by architects Skidmore, Owings & Merrill built for Olivetti in 1960. Similar noteworthy large projects started in 1984–all in classic early 20th-century, commercial palace garb—included an office and retail condominium in Alexandria, VA, designed by Zinser & Dunn Associates to blend in with ''Old Town''; a 500,000 sq ft (46 450 m²) residential and commercial building on the Boston Public Garden by the Architects Collaborative; and two office towers in San Francisco's older commercial district by Gensler & Associates and Kaplan/McLaughlin/Diaz, respectively.

Modest projects, even more within the original intention of infill to produce sympathetic scale, were a series of low office buildings in Washington, DC, woven by David M. Schwarz/Architectural Services between existing low buildings, many of historic character and residential size. A dramatic hybrid of natural and traditional design was the plan by architects Shepley Bulfinch Richardson for the Smithsonian Institution's 368,000 sq ft (34 187 m²) addition. To be built mostly under the broad front gardens of the original Victorian main structure, the new massive construction would protrude at street level only as two pavilions of classical design.

The maturing of Post-Modernism as a style was seen in debate over its nature—some contending, as did museum director Heinrich Klotz of the Gwerman Museum of Architecture in Frankfurt, that its ornamental forms were only a revision of modernism (International Style) while others, including Charles Jencks of Moore Ruble Yudell, believed Post-Modernism to be a fresh reaction to modernism.

Allowing that the controversial ''Chippendale'' skyscraper for AT&T in New York City by Johnson/Burgee Architects was substantially complete in 1983, possibly *the* Post-Modern building completed in 1984 was the General Foods Corporation headquarters in Rye, NY, by architects Kevin Roche John Dinkeloo and Associates; the million-square-foot building was likened to a Palladian country house on a giant scale. Another building completed in the style included the Justice Center in Portland, OR, designed by the Zimmer Gunsul Frasca Partnership and located across a central park from the pioneering Post-Modern Portland Building by Michael Graves; the new building lacked the latter's decorative exuberance. Two major projects begun in 1984 were located in Florida—the Poynter Institute for Media Studies in Saint Petersburg, a group of pavilions with traditional high-pitched tile roofs and deep eaves by Jung/Brannen Architects, and a 9-million-sq-ft (836 100-m²) medical exhibition and learning center of mixed historic and modern styles between Fort Lauderdale and Hollywood by architects RTKL Associates. It promised to be, when finished, the second-largest building in the United States after the Pentagon.

The popular acceptance of Post-Modernism was seen at the World's Fair in New Orleans, where gigantic figures on allegorical themes and eclectic buildings of many historic styles were gathered, and at the Olympics sites in Los Angeles where facades of columns and flat, cut-out pediments were applied to utilitarian structures.

Not every major new building conformed. The High Museum of Art in Atlanta by Richard Meier & Partners received much attention in the press. Its crisp white sculptural forms could be seen to have their historic precedent, if any, in the 1920's Modernist movement in Europe. Meier was the recipient of the 1984 Pritzker Prize for excellence in architecture. Similarly, the triangular skyscraper for IBM in New York City by Edward Larrabee Barnes was designed in a straightforward utilitarian vernacular. Both buildings were far from the commercial box forms that the International Style had produced.

The year also was one in which—after much debate and soul searching—the National Council of Architectural Registration Boards decided to limit candidates for licensing to graduates of accredited schools of architecture and not include those qualified by equivalent practical experience.

CHARLES HOYT, *''Architectural Record''*

American Institute of Architects
1984 Honor Awards

Project and Locale: *Shelly Ridge Girl Scout Center,* Miquon, PA
Architect: Bohlin Powell Larkin Cywinski
Jury Comment: ''.... The architect has taken a light-hearted approach, creating an atmosphere of fun through the use of color, columns, gables, and other elements, while simultaneously using the structures themselves as active learning tools. . . . ''

Project and Locale: *Gainesway Farm,* Lexington, KY
Architect: Theodore M. Ceraldi
Jury Comment: '' . . . a masterly example of the great beauty and elegance that can result from simple design done well. . . . ''

Project and Locale: *Vietnam Veterans Memorial,* Washington, DC
Architect: Cooper-Lecky Partnership, designed by Maya Ying Lin
Jury Comment: '' . . . . The power of the memorial is derived from its contemplative simplicity and the almost magical way this most economical of designs transmits enormous meaning.''

Project and Locale: *R.J. Reynolds Tobacco Company Building,* Winston-Salem, NC
Architect: Croxton Collaborative/Hammill-Walter Associated Architects
Jury Comment: ''The preservation, restoration and reconstruction of the Art Deco exterior facade and ground floor . . . exemplify a superb solution to the difficult problem of harmonizing an old style with a contemporary interpretation. . . . ''

Project and Locale: *Carver-Hawkeye Sports Arena,* University of Iowa, Iowa City, IA
Architect: CRS/Caudill Rowlett Scott
Jury Comment: '' . . . . By placing the bulk of the structure underground in the contours of a natural ravine, the architects have retained a human scale . . . and have reduced the intrusion of what would otherwise be a massive structure on the campus environment. . . . ''

Project and Locale: *Taft Residence,* Cincinnati, OH
Architect: Gwathmey Siegel and Associates
Jury Comment: '' . . . The architect has deftly composed the indoor and outdoor spaces . . . integrating the house into the landscape. . . . ''

Project and Locale: *Addition to North Shore Congregation Israel,* Glencoe, IL
Architect: Hammond Beeby and Babka Inc.
Jury Comment: '' . . . The designers . . . draw freely from a rich mixture of historical references, giving the design itself religious significance.''

Project and Locale: *333 Wacker Drive,* Chicago, IL
Architect: Kohn Pederson Fox/Perkins and Will
Jury Comment: '' . . . the architects have responded to a difficult and complex triangular site. . . . The different faces it presents . . . are each brilliant . . . , making this truly a building with no front or back, only multiple inviting fronts. . . . ''

Project and Locale: *High Museum of Art,* Atlanta, GA
Architect: Richard Meier and Partners
Jury Comment: '' . . . is an artistic, sculptural and architectural tour de force that asserts itself as a work of art, while not overwhelming its contents. . . . ''

Project and Locale: *Saint Matthew's Church,* Pacific Palisades, CA
Architect: Moore Ruble Yudell
Jury Comment: '' . . . is an excellent example of how modern religious architecture can remain within the context of a proud historical tradition and blend harmoniously with its site. . . . ''

Project and Locale: *Fragrant Hill Hotel,* Peking, China
Architect: I. M. Pei and Partners
Jury Comment: '' . . . harmonizes traditional Chinese architecture with contemporary elements to produce a structure totally at home with its site. . . . ''

Project and Locale: *Weekend House,* Southwest Michigan
Architect: Tigerman Fugman McCurry
Jury Comment: '' . . . While the form is simple . . . the house is delightfully and meticulously detailed inside and out. . . . ''

Otto Baitz, Croxton Collaborative
R. J. Reynolds Tobacco Company Building

Richard Payne, Gwathmey Siegel & Assoc.

Taft Residence

Project and Locale: *Gordon Wu Hall,* Princeton University, Princeton, NJ
Architect: Venturi, Rausch and Scott Brown
Jury Comment: ''Situated in a subtly complex and architecturally contradictory site on a campus with a variety of building styles, the architect's imaginative design very successfully mediates between the surrounding international style and traditional collegiate Gothic structures, fitting . . . into the overall campus fabric. . . . ''

In his first year in office, President Raúl Alfonsín asserted government control over the military and settled a long-standing territorial dispute with Chile. His biggest worry, meanwhile, was the economy.

Villalobos, Gamma-Liaison

ARGENTINA

Enjoying popular support, President Raúl Alfonsín attempted to honor his 1983 campaign promises. The military establishment reeled under the repeal of its "self-amnesty" law covering human-rights abuses. Economic policy remained a problem area. And a settlement on the Beagle Channel was reached with Chile.

Politics. By midyear President Alfonsín had negotiated a "nonaggression pact" with the nominal leader of the opposition Peronistas, Isabel Martínez de Perón, who had returned from self-imposed exile in Spain in order to sign the national unity agreement. In addition to the government and the principal opposition party, representatives of 15 other centrist political entities affixed their signatures to the pact, which outlined a limited austerity program at home and established a national position on important foreign policy matters. Perón, who had established a working relationship with the new president, then returned to Spain, leaving her party splintered and analyzing its 1983 election defeat.

Among the first actions of the incoming chief executive had been the issuance of decree on Dec. 13, 1983, to prosecute nine former military junta members—including former presidents Jorge Videla, Roberto Eduardo Viola, and Leopoldo Galtieri—for excesses committed during the civil strife (1976–82). Proceedings against the military officers began at the end of December 1983, following the repeal of an amnesty that had been decreed by the military junta serving under Gen. Reynaldo Bignone. Charges against the military leaders included murder, illegal deprivation of liberty, and the use of torture on persons under arrest.

Also in December 1983, President Alfonsín appointed new military commanders and forced more than half of Argentina's active generals, admirals, and brigadiers into retirement. Under a reformed command structure, the president would become the commander in chief of the armed forces, and military commanders would report to a civilian minister of defense. The military code. of justice was amended at the beginning of 1984 to allow cases involving violations of human rights by military men to go to civilian courts on appeal. And the military high command was shaken up again in July, when Alfonsín replaced the army chief of staff and three other top generals.

Persistent friction between the Alfonsín government and its armed forces heightened with another round of coup rumors and the mass resignation on November 14 of all 11 judges on the nation's highest military tribunal, which had been considering the cases of officers accused of committing human-rights violations. Failure of the court to bring forth any convictions during a year of deliberations provoked sharp attacks on its lack of progress by human-rights groups, political parties, and some public officials. Tribunal members claimed that the government had failed to comply with a promise to shield the body from public criticism. When the tribunal ruled in September that nine former military junta members were only "indirectly responsible" for human-rights abuses during their tenure, leftist periodicals published the names of 1,351 armed forces personnel, policemen, and civilians who had systematically kidnapped, tortured, and murdered thousands of suspected terrorists, leftists, and dissidents. The civil-rights violators had been identified by a 16-

member "blue-ribbon" commission appointed by President Alfonsín. Six participants were selected by Congress.

The presidential commission on human-rights violations presented a 50,000-page report on its findings to the chief executive on September 20. The report documented 8,780 cases of disappearances and located 280 secret prisons. Hundreds of military and police personnel were implicated in the human-rights abuses. Coinciding with the presentation of the report was a mass demonstration at the Plaza de Mayo in Buenos Aires by several thousand political-party and human-rights activists chanting "We Want Justice." The commission was headed by Ernesto Sábato, a noted novelist.

Economy. Probably the biggest problem facing the Alfonsín government was the economy, but this proved to be the area in which the new administration was least eager to move. The regime's economic program featured inflation control, wage lids, debt renegotiation, reduced unemployment, cuts in defense spending, improved tax collection, and banking reforms. In order to reach the ambitious growth rate of 5% (the rate in 1983 was 2.5%), the government pledged to reduce inflation by a cut in the public sector deficit from 14% of Gross Domestic Product (GDP) in 1983 to 8% in 1984. Wage adjustments were to allow some real improvement in income, consistent with official anti-inflationary and deficit-reduction policies. It was the intention of the government to lower the 20% unemployment rate through economic revitalization, job creation, and new foreign investment. Military expenditures were to be reduced from 5% to 2% of GDP. More rigorous tax collections were called for, and levies on luxury items, capital gains, and property were to be increased. The banking system was changed to reduce the number of participating institutions and to give industry greater access to credit.

On September 25, Argentina and the International Monetary Fund (IMF) came to an agreement on an economic plan to help the country manage its foreign debt and reduce inflation. The agreement was announced at the 39th annual joint meeting of the World Bank and the IMF in Washington, DC. At more than $45 billion (U.S.)—90% of it owed to private banks—Argentina's debt was the third largest in the world (behind Brazil and Mexico). Under the terms of the IMF agreement, Argentina became eligible for $1.42 billion in standby credit over 15 months, to be applied toward nearly $2 billion due in interest and principal on previous loans, including $750 million that had come due on September 15 from a $1.1 billion bridge loan obtained in 1982. Argentina was obligated to bring its annual inflation rate down from nearly 700% to 150% by the end of 1984.

As the year ended, the IMF approved $20 million in aid for Argentina. Under the plan, Argentina would receive $1.7 billion from the IMF (including the $1.42 billion in credit), $4.2 billion from commercial banks, and $14 billion from rescheduled loans.

Relatives of the thousands of people who disappeared during military rule demonstrate in the streets of Buenos Aires.
Gamma-Liaison

President Alfonsín (right) and former President Arturo Frondizi look on as Isabel Perón, who returned temporarily from self-imposed exile, signs a national unity accord. The leaders of 14 other opposition parties pledged cooperation.

Labor. Following up on another campaign commitment, President Alfonsín called on the legislature to pass a major labor reform bill. His plan called for democratization of the nation's unions by providing for proportional representation and direct, government-supervised elections of union officials. Seeing the plan as a blueprint for reducing the power of Peronistas, however, the Senate rejected the bill in March. Thereafter union heads became bolder in expressing their demands for higher wages, as workers had to face runaway inflation rates. A series of small-scale strikes led to a general work stoppage called by the General Confederation of Labor (CGT) on September 3. The Alfonsín administration saw the strike as only a partial success, however, and negotiators went ahead on talks with the IMF, counting on the president's personal popularity as a buffer against union demands. Under the agreement reached with the IMF, the government pledged itself to holding wage adjustments to 14% per month for the remainder of the year.

Foreign Affairs. On October 18 in Vatican City, Argentina and Chile initialed a treaty settling the century-old Beagle Channel dispute along lines recommended in 1980 by Pope John Paul II, who acted as mediator. Although Chile would not gain any territorial waters in the Atlantic, it was awarded sovereignty over the three main disputed islands—Pictón, Lennox, and Nueva—as well as other islands and the first six miles of water adjacent to the ceded lands. Exploration and exploitation rights over the next six miles would be shared between Chile and Argentina. And the latter was to have exclusive jurisdiction over the next 188 miles of waters. Chile would not be able to press further border claims against Argentina for five

years following approval of the treaty. The accord was subject to ratification by the Argentine Senate, dominated by Peronistas. On November 25, Argentine voters approved the treaty by an overwhelming majority, 81%.

At the pope's insistence, both Argentina and Chile resubscribed to a lapsed agreement turning over to the International Court of Justice any future dispute between the two countries that could not be resolved through bilateral negotiations. There remained more than 50 unresolved border conflicts between the Southern Cone neighbors.

The Malvinas (Falkland) Islands issue returned to the United Nations General Assembly at the end of October, as mediation efforts by Switzerland and UN Secretary-General Javier Pérez de Cuéllar failed to resolve the longstanding conflict. Great Britain offered to remove the 150-mile exclusion zone around the

---

ARGENTINA • Information Highlights

Official Name: Republic of Argentina.
Location: Southern South America.
Area: 1,070,000 sq mi (2 771 300 km²).
Population (mid-1984 est.): 29,100,000.
Chief Cities: (1980 census): Buenos Aires, the capital, 2,908,001; Córdoba, 990,007; Rosario, 935,-471.
Government: *Head of state and government,* Raúl Alfonsín, president (took office Dec. 10, 1983). *Legislature*—Senate and Chamber of Deputies.
Monetary Unit: Peso (148.60 pesos equal U.S.$1, Dec. 3, 1984).
Gross National Product (1981 U.S.$): $130,000,-000,000.
Economic Indexes (1983): *Consumer Prices* (1974 = 100), all items, 1,404,578; food, 1,513,108. Industrial Production (1975 = 100), 87.
Foreign Trade (1982 U.S.$): *Imports,* $5,337,000,000; *exports,* $7,798,000,000.

islands, repatriate Argentine war dead, and restore trade in exchange for a cessation-of-hostilities agreement from Argentina. The Alfonsín government, however, was unwilling to engage in discussions with Great Britain that were not linked to the sovereignty issue. The Argentine hard line was attributed to an attempt by the foreign ministry to placate rightists who were critical of concessions made by its negotiators in the Beagle Channel settlement with Chile. British intransigence was attributed to the extraordinary pressure that the Falkland Islands Company exerted over Britain's parliament.

Meanwhile, relations with the United States warmed as democracy was restored in Argentina. U.S. Vice-President George Bush attended President Alfonsín's inaugural in December 1983. In private talks, the two discussed improvements in relations between their governments and the resumption of U.S. arms sales to Argentina. Alfonsín requested Bush's assistance in getting international banks to extend the payback periods on its debt and also to lower interest rates. Bush reiterated U.S. concern over a lack of international safeguards on Argentina's growing nuclear program. After an address to the UN General Assembly in September—in which he called for closer contact between Latin American debtor nations and the industrialized countries—President Alfonsín met briefly with President Reagan.

LARRY L. PIPPIN
University of the Pacific

ARIZONA

Arizonans turned out and voted in numbers exceeding the national average for President Ronald Reagan's reelection. The president drew 67% of the popular vote and carried 14 of 15 counties. In other state races, Congressmen John McCain (R), Morris Udall (D), and Bob Stump (R) easily won reelection. Only incumbent Jim McNulty (D) was defeated in the closest of four congressional races by Jim Kolbe (R), who had lost to McNulty by a narrow margin two years earlier.

Republicans remained in control of both houses of the state legislature. Voters rejected 14 of 15 initiatives on the statewide ballot. The only measure approved was one to repeal the requirement that local governments pay the prevailing wage rates on construction projects.

Water. Construction continued on the Central Arizona Project, which will carry water from the Colorado River east to Phoenix and Tucson. About 60% of the state's rapidly growing population depends on water pumped from diminishing underground aquifers. Earlier in the year testing by the Department of Health Services revealed that 114 of 800 public wells were contaminated by ground pollutants, thus contributing to present concerns about the state's limited water supply.

In August, President Reagan signed legislation that provided residents of parts of Arizona, California, and Nevada with 30 more years of low-cost hydroelectric power from the Hoover Dam. For 50 years, under a Depression-era contract, consumers had paid rates that were much less than the national average. The legislation had been opposed by eastern and midwestern states, which supported the sale of the power at market rates.

Immigration. National debate over the proposed Simpson-Mazzoli immigration bill focused attention on the thousands of immigrants from Mexico and Central America who continue to enter the state illegally along its vast southern border. The bill, which would have made employers criminally liable for hiring illegal aliens, divided politicians and the Hispanic community. The predominant view of Hispanic leaders was that such a provision would invite job discrimination against all Hispanics.

The Economy. With one major exception, 1984 was a good year for the state economy. Retail sales increased by 11%; personal income was up 12%; and unemployment dropped below 6%. The exception was the ailing copper industry. Foreign competition and declining demand resulted in lower prices and, in turn, seemingly unresolvable labor problems in what had been the state's leading industry. The outlook was not good.

Other Matters. The U.S. Department of Interior formally gave up its site claims for dam construction in the Grand Canyon National Park. In an effort to reduce the carnage on the state's highways, the legislature raised the legal drinking age to 21. The legislature continued to grapple with serious funding and management problems within the state's health-care and prison systems.

JAMES W. CLARKE, *University of Arizona*

ARIZONA • Information Highlights

Area: 114,000 sq mi (295 260 km²).
Population (July 1, 1983 est.): 2,963,000.
Chief Cities (July 1, 1982 est.): Phoenix, the capital, 824,230; Tucson, 352,455; Mesa, 171,695; Tempe, 112,514; Glendale, 106,420.
Government (1984): *Chief Officers*—governor, Bruce E. Babbitt (D); Secretary of State, Rose Mofford (D). *Legislature*—Senate, 30 members; House of Representatives, 60 members.
State Finances (fiscal year 1983): *Revenues,* $3,969,000,000; *expenditures,* $3,589,000,000.
Personal Income (1983): $31,575,000,000; per capita, $10,656.
Labor Force (May 1984): *Civilian labor force,* 1,402,800; *unemployed,* 71,600 (5.1% of total force).
Education: *Enrollment* (fall 1982)—public elementary schools, 359,229; public secondary, 151,067; colleges and universities (fall 1983), 213,437. *Public school expenditures* (1982–83), $1,208,045,927 ($2,524 per pupil).

Gov. Bill Clinton, a liberal Democrat who once was Arkansas state Attorney General, was elected to a third term.

ARKANSAS

Politics and improvements in the quality of public education were the center of attention in Arkansas during 1984. Unemployment remained high despite signs of economic recovery.

Elections. Although the state cast its six electoral votes for President Ronald Reagan, his personal appearance in Little Rock on the preelection weekend did little to assist Republicans. Democrats decisively won all statewide elective offices, including two positions on the Arkansas Supreme Court. Republicans kept only the uncontested U.S. House seat held by John Paul Hammerschmidt. Sen. David Pryor (D) won 58% of the vote to defeat Congressman Ed Bethune (R) for the U.S. Senate. Sheriff Tommy Robinson of Pulaski County defeated two-term state Rep. Judy Petty, Republican from Little Rock, for the House seat vacated by Ed Bethune. Gov. Bill Clinton (D), obtaining 62% of the vote, defeated Woody Freeman (R) to become the third Arkansas governor elected to a third term. Republicans increased their number in the state Senate from three to four and in the House from seven to nine.

Voters ratified constitutional amendments increasing the terms of governor and the six other state executives from two to four years and permitting local governments to pay higher interest rates on their bonds. They rejected proposals to abolish the personal property tax, to levy a 1/8¢ sales tax for the Game and Fish Commission, and to legalize casino gambling in Garland County.

State Government. In the longest special session in state history (38 days), the General Assembly adopted most of Governor Clinton's legislative agenda. It revised the formula distributing state aid to public schools, required public-school teachers to pass a controversial basic skills competency test, mandated changes in public school programs such as a longer school year, and increased the sales tax from 3¢ to 4¢. The legislature turned down the governor's severance tax and corporation income tax bills.

Judiciary. The Arkansas Supreme Court cast doubt on the validity of local government tourism bonds by invalidating a Little Rock revenue bond issued to construct a motel. The court removed from the general election ballot the antiabortion Unborn Child Amendment because of its deceptive title.

Education. A Quality Higher Education Study committee proposed a basic general education program and development of a basic competency test for college students. Four of Arkansas' state-supported universities celebrated their 75th anniversaries: Arkansas State University in Jonesboro, Arkansas Tech University in Russeville, the University of Arkansas in Monticello, and Southern Arkansas University in Magnolia.

Federal District Judge Henry Woods, ignoring public outcries and overriding efforts to prolong court proceedings, ordered immediate consolidation of the three public school districts in Pulaski County to remedy purposefully committed acts that increased racial segregation in the Little Rock school district.

Utilities. State residents were upset when an administrative law judge of the Federal Energy Regulatory Commission (FERC) ruled that the Arkansas Power and Light Company, a subsidiary of Middle South Utilities, should bear 36% of the $3 billion cost for the Grand Gulf nuclear power plant in Mississippi, even though the state did not need or plan to use its power. The decision, if approved by the FERC, could increase AP&L electric rates by some 30%.

WILLIAM C. NOLAN
Southern Arkansas University

ARKANSAS • Information Highlights

Area: 53,187 sq mi (137 754 km²).
Population (July 1, 1983 est): 2,328,000.
Chief Cities (1980 census): Little Rock, the capital (July 1, 1982 est.), 167,974; Fort Smith, 71,626; North Little Rock, 64,288; Pine Bluff, 56,636.
Government (1984): *Chief Officers*—governor, Bill Clinton (D); lt. gov., Winston Bryant (D). *General Assembly*—Senate, 35 members; House of Representatives, 100 members.
State Finances (fiscal year 1983): *Revenues,* $2,739,000,000; *expenditures,* $2,488,000,000.
Personal Income (1983): $20,875,000,000; per capita, $8,967.
Labor Force (May 1984): *Civilian labor force,* 1,083,100; *unemployed,* 93,100 (8.6% of total force).
Education: *Enrollment* (fall 1982)—public elementary schools, 304,443; public secondary, 128,122; colleges and universities (fall 1983), 76,702. *Public school expenditures* (1982–83), $801,194,009 ($1,971 per pupil).

ARMS CONTROL

For arms control, 1984 was a bleak year. Neither the Strategic Arms Reduction Talks (START), designed to place limits on strategic nuclear weapons, nor the intermediate nuclear forces (INF) negotiations was reopened. Both had become stalled in 1983 when the Soviets left them in protest over the deployment of U.S. cruise missiles and Pershing II's in Western Europe. Further, efforts to open discussions on the control of weapons based in space were a failure. However, in June the Soviets proposed negotiations to ban the militarization of space. The American response was that the Soviets were merely attempting to thwart the beginning U.S. effort to research the development of space defense weapons—the Strategic Defense Initiative—and to block testing of an antisatellite (ASAT) weapons system. Washington tried to link the discussion of arms control in space to the Soviets' returning to the START and INF talks, which Moscow refused to do.

In September a flurry of arms-control excitement was caused by the announcement that Soviet Foreign Minister Andrei Gromyko would meet with President Reagan and Secretary of State George Shultz. Although prior to the meetings both sides proclaimed their interest in resuming arms-control negotiations, little was accomplished. Later it was announced that Shultz and Gromyko would meet for arms control talks in Geneva in January 1985.

Debate over U.S. Arms Policy. Within the United States considerable argument took place regarding the utility of the Reagan administration's arms policy, which was designed to move the Soviets to the bargaining tables. The controversy centered on Washington's belief that a buildup of U.S. military power would compel the Soviet Union to negotiate in good faith on arms-control measures. Those opposing the administration's policy contended that the American arms buildup would only increase Soviet intransigence and provoke a reciprocal arms increase. Although the Reagan administration was successful in obtaining from Congress much of the funding for the arms buildup, the Soviets did not negotiate. Moscow claimed that the American buildup was a disguised effort to achieve military superiority. This perspective was set forth by Chairman Chernenko in a *Pravda* statement of September 2: "Also unrealizable today are [U.S.] calculations of acquiring military superiority in the hope of prevailing in a nuclear war. I repeat: The Soviet Union itself is not seeking military superiority over others, but it will not allow anyone else to achieve superiority over it. It is possible that some people in the United States still find it difficult to accustom themselves to this, but they will have to acknowledge the fact that our two states can con-

duct matters only on equal grounds, on the basis of consideration for each other's legitimate interests. There is no reasonable alternative to this."

Another subject of debate within the United States was the impact on the 1972 Anti-Ballistic Missile (ABM) Treaty that would occur should the United States pursue the Strategic Defense Initiative (SDI). Opponents of the SDI contended that moving from research on space-based defense systems to the development of such technologies would violate the ABM Treaty; they maintained that the United States should seek to preserve the treaty—both on its merits and because, they claimed, it was the most important agreement between the two superpowers. In favor of the SDI, others argued that undue emphasis on preserving the ABM Treaty was unwise. Their point was that in the face of possible Soviet efforts to move ahead of the United States in ABM technology, Washington should not constrain its counterefforts by blind adherence to a treaty not being honored by Moscow.

Alleged Violations of Agreements. A problem for future arms control was made public by President Reagan on January 23, when he accused the Soviet government of both "violations" and "probable violations" of arms-control obligations. The accusations were contained in a classified report sent by the administration to Congress and later published in a declassified four-page fact sheet. According to the government's information the Soviets had repeatedly violated the Biological Warfare Convention and the Geneva Protocol banning the use of chemical weapons in war. Further, Washington charged that a new Soviet radar "almost certainly" violated the ABM Treaty; that the SS-X-25 ICBM was "probably" a violation of the SALT II agreement; and that Soviet nuclear testing constituted a "likely violation" of the Threshold Test Ban Treaty.

The president's charges were followed by another accusatory report, issued in October by the General Advisory Committee on Arms Control and Disarmament, an independent body advising the administration. The new allegations prompted responses by both the Soviet government and American arms-control experts outside the government. Moscow denied the U.S. charges of Soviet cheating and went on to distribute a statement claiming at least eight instances of American violation of arms-control agreements. Two Americans, former chief U.S. arms negotiators Gerard C. Smith and Paul C. Warnke, stated in the fall their opinion that "the record of both sides is very good so far as living up to the letter of the agreements." The former negotiators added, however, that there had been some "technical" violations by both sides.

ROBERT M. LAWRENCE
Colorado State University

New York City's Museum of Modern Art (MoMA) reopened in the spring after a four-year, $55 million renovation.

ART

The expansion of existing museums and the opening of new ones, the continuing trend toward cooperatively sponsored, traveling exhibitions, and the success at auction of 20th-century decorative pieces were among the highlights of the art world in 1984.

MoMA. New York City's Museum of Modern Art (MoMA), the most important institution of its kind in the world, was reopened in May after a $55 million renovation for which most of the building was closed for several years. The original 1939 structure on West 53rd Street and the east wing added in 1964 had become inadequate for showing the collection and maintaining the museum's other services. The new construction, designed by Cesare Pelli, has added a six-story west wing, a garden wing to the east on 53rd Street, and a north wing on 54th. The west wing also serves as a base for a 52-story residential condominium tower. The total exhibition area is now more than twice that of the original museum. There are two film theaters; separate galleries for prints, drawings, architecture and design, and photography; and a two-story structure for sculpture, providing four times the former space. The

lobby, sales, and restaurant areas have been enlarged, and glass-enclosed escalators solve the circulation problems of the old building. In spite of these changes, the intimate character and scale of the museum have been preserved by means of low ceilings and small rooms.

The galleries on the second and third floors display about 800 paintings and sculptures, including many never shown before. Among them are works left to MoMA by Nelson Rockefeller in 1979. This permanent exhibition includes masterpieces by Cézanne, Van Gogh, Brancusi, Mondrian, Matisse, Miró, and Pollock. In the temporary galleries on the first and basement floors, the first show at the new MoMA was "An International Survey of Recent Painting and Sculpture," consisting of more than 150 new works loaned by 16 nations.

Coinciding with the opening celebration came the announcement of a large gift from the McCrory Corporation: 249 paintings and sculptures—to be known as the Riklis/Lindner Collection of McCrory Corporation—and $1.75 million. MoMA selected the art from about 1,000 works assembled by the chairman and vice-chairman of the corporation. The collection is representative of Constructivism and related styles; it includes works by such artists as Kandinsky, Albers, and Malevich, as well as some lesser-known ones that the museum had lacked. A part of the McCrory Collection was exhibited at the Albright-Knox Gallery in Buffalo, the Indianapolis Museum of Art, and the Herbert F. Johnson Museum of Art in Ithaca, NY, in 1983. It will travel to Japan before coming to MoMA in the fall of 1985.

The Getty. With its plans for new buildings and activities nearing completion, the J. Paul Getty Museum in Malibu, CA, became increasingly influential in the international art scene. As in 1983 when it acquired the Ludwig Collection of medieval manuscripts and overnight became one of the world's major repositories of art in that field, so in 1984 it entered into another new field, photography. With the purchase of several complete collections—totaling about 18,000 pieces—the Getty now rivals the International Museum of Photography at Eastman House in Rochester, NY.

Allaying fears that rival collectors would no longer be able to compete for new acquisitions, the Getty Trust did demonstrate its stated intention of cooperating with rather than dominating other institutions. Although the Getty did acquire 7 of the 70 Old Master drawings from the collection of the Duke of Devonshire at Chatsworth, auctioned at Christie's in London in July, it dropped out of the bidding for the two most hotly contested drawings: a Raphael and a page from Vasari's notebook with drawings by Filippino Lippi, which went to private collectors for $4.8 million and $4.4 million, respectively. And at the auction of the collection of the famous art historian Lord Kenneth Clark, a seascape by J. M. W. Turner was sold for more than $10 million to a private collector after the Getty had dropped out of the bidding. The sum was the highest ever paid at auction for any painting.

In another case, a painting already purchased by the Getty from a private collector in Great Britain was the subject of a fund-raising campaign to match the purchase price and keep it in England. The painting, a Crucifixion attributed to the Sienese painter Duccio, had long been on loan to the Manchester City Art Gallery, and the museum waged a gallant battle to keep it there. Money was raised from public and private sources, but the decisive contribution came, curiously enough, from J. Paul Getty 2d, the son of the founder of the Getty Trust.

Other U.S. Museum News. The Los Angeles Museum of Contemporary Art acquired an important group of 80 works of Abstract Expressionism and Pop Art from the Count and Countess Panza di Biumo of Milan for $11 million. Many of the works—including pieces by Rothko, Kline, Rauschenberg, Oldenburg, and Segal—were originally bought in Los Angeles during the 1950s and 1960s, and it was considered fitting that they return as a unit to form the nucleus of the new museum. Although its building is not scheduled for completion until 1989, the museum already has mounted a major show in temporary quarters: "Automobile and Culture," featuring 30 vintage cars and 200 works of art from 1896 to the present.

At the Los Angeles County Museum, more than 100 Impressionist and Post-Impressionist paintings were assembled into a show called "A Day in the Country," presented as part of the Olympics Arts Festival. The show moved to the Chicago Art Institute in October, and then would be seen in Paris from February through April 1985.

In January 1984 the Center for the Fine Arts, the first in a complex of three buildings to include also a museum of local history and a

"Seascape: Folkestone" by J.M.W. Turner sold for a record $10,023,020 at an auction at Sotheby's in London on July 5. A private collector purchased the painting, formerly owned by the late Lord Clark.

public library, opened in Miami, FL. Designed by Philip Johnson, the $6 million structure was planned specifically to house traveling exhibitions. For the opening, 200 objects from 60 museums—ranging from an Egyptian bronze of 1600 B.C. to a Duane Hanson painting dated 1981—were assembled under the title "In Quest of Excellence."

Later in January, the new 9-acre (3.6-ha) Dallas Museum of Art, designed by Edward Larrabee Barnes, was opened. Built at a cost of more than $50 million, it houses a collection of 19th- and 20th-century paintings and sculptures.

In Washington, DC, the newly renovated galleries of the Phillips Collection presented "Pierre Bonnard: The Late Paintings." Originating in Paris at the Pompidou Center and later set to go to Dallas, it was the first exhibition of the later works of Bonnard (1867–1947).

Daniel Barsotti, Dallas Museum of Art

New museum openings across the United States demonstrated the vitality of the art world. The Dallas Museum of Art, above, designed by Edward Larrabee Barnes, was called by Time *the "latest and most successful example of integrating community activity with the display of objects." Miami's Center for the Fine Arts, with Philip Johnson as architect, is Dade County's "first publicly built and supported visual arts facility."*

Steven Brooke, Center for the Fine Arts

"Porte-fenêtre ouverte, Vernon" was featured at a major international exhibition of Pierre Bonnard paintings.

At the Metropolitan Museum in New York, the Jack and Belle Linsky galleries were opened in June. In rooms specially designed to simulate a private home collection, the permanent display includes 373 works—paintings by Rubens and Crivelli and a rich variety of furniture, bronze statuettes, procelains, and jewelry from the Middle Ages through the 19th century. And in 1984 the Met announced the gift of another collection to be separately maintained and exhibited. Put together by Geneva art dealer Heinz Berggruen, this collection emphasizes the work of Paul Klee (1879–1940). It is comprised of some 90 objects, including paintings, drawings, watercolors, and gouaches.

Museums in Europe. The New State Gallery, a somewhat unusual building designed by British architect James Stirling, was inaugurated in Stuttgart, West Germany. The museum already possesses the leading collection of Picassos in the country, and it is assured of steady future growth as the beneficiary of about $1 million annually from the state lottery.

In Brussels, where the large assemblage of 19th- and 20th-century French and Belgian paintings at the Museum of Fine Arts had outgrown its allotted space, a Modern Art Museum was opened in October.

Paris celebrated the reopening of the Orangerie after seven years of renovation. Formerly used to accommodate temporary exhibitions, it is now devoted to the collections of Paul Guillaume and Jean Walter, early discoverers and collectors of such artists as Soutine, Modigliani, Cézanne, Renoir, and Picasso. Meanwhile, the unveiling of the plans by U.S. architect I. M. Pei to reorganize the Louvre caused consternation and debate. Questions were raised in particular about the most visible part of the

project: a large glass pyramid to be built in the center of the courtyard as a museum entranceway. The pyramid, some maintained, would mar the view—one of the city's most famous —across the Tuileries Gardens to the Arc de Triomphe.

Exhibitions. Continuing a now well-established trend, most major exhibitions are cooperatively sponsored by two or more museums and shown in several cities internationally. This makes it possible for the world's top curators and scholars to work together in planning shows and writing the catalogs, facilitates the exchange of works among institutions, and results in more new and more comprehensive shows than otherwise might be organized.

Thus, in spring 1984, the Metropolitan Museum in New York featured a retrospective of the French painter Balthus, a show that had originated at the Pompidou Center in Paris. Although his paintings had been exhibited regularly at the Pierre Matisse Gallery in New York since 1958, Balthus had never before been the subject of a comprehensive show. It was a great hit on both sides of the Atlantic.

Another international show celebrated the 300th birthday of Jean Antoine Watteau (1684–1721) with a comprehensive assemblage of paintings and drawings from the Louvre, the Berlin Charlottenburg Museum, and the National Gallery (Washington, DC). The show opened in Washington in June and then was to move to Paris in October and Berlin in February 1985. Similarly, "Kandinsky: Russian and Bauhaus Years 1915–1933" was seen at the Guggenheim Museum in New York from December 1983 to February 1984, in Atlanta from March through April, in Zurich from May to July, and in Berlin from August through September.

Also celebrated in 1984 were the 150th anniversaries of James Whistler and Edgar Degas. Several commemorative shows were organized in the United States and elsewhere.

Chinese art and artifacts were featured in shows throughout the United States. A major loan exhibition from the Shanghai Museum highlighted items from the Neolithic period, including carved jade and pottery, excavated during the 1950s. Bronze vessels, vases, and paintings from later periods also were shown. The exhibit was organized in concert with the Asian Art Museum of San Francisco and was seen also at the Field Museum in Chicago, the Museum of Fine Arts in Houston, and the Smithsonian in Washington, DC. Another exhibition from the People's Republic of China, "Contemporary Chinese Painting," was seen in San Francisco, Ithaca (NY), Denver, Indianapolis, Kansas City, and Minneapolis. It gave American audiences their first chance to see the combination of traditional and Western influences characteristic of Chinese art today. New Yorkers were treated to three shows de-

Freer Gallery of Art

Chinese Culture Center of San Francisco

The 150th anniversary of the birth of James McNeill Whistler was marked in 1984. His "Rose and Silver: The Princess from the Land of Porcelain," top, was part of a show at Washington's Freer Gallery of Art. Contemporary Chinese painting, influenced by both traditional and Western cultures, was on view in several U.S. cities, including San Francisco, bottom, Denver, and Kansas City.

voted to the China trade: "Silk Roads—China Ships," organized by the Royal Ontario Museum of Toronto and presented at the Museum of Natural History, covering 2,000 years of commerce between East and West; "New Yorkers' Taste: Chinese Export 1750–1865" at the Museum of the City of New York, showing Chinese objects used in the homes of wealthy New Yorkers; and "New York and the China Trade" at the New York Historical Society, demonstrating the influence of U.S. buyers on Chinese objects made for export.

Auction News. The big news at the art auction block during the 1983–84 season was the high prices commanded by 20th-century decorative arts objects, which came to rival those paid for the finest 18th-century pieces. For example, a silver spoon made by Josef Hoffmann of the Wiener Werkstätte was sold by Phillips in London for $24,410, a record for a spoon. A silver vitrine, also by Hoffmann, was auctioned at Sotheby's for $275,000. At Christie's, a Frank Lloyd Wright stained glass door sold for $110,000, a record for a Wright design at auction and for a stained glass of any period.

Christie's, Sotheby's closest rival, expanded its base in New York City. Sales at the New York branch, led by the Impressionist and Modern Art department, rose by 48% in the 1983–84 season to top sales at the London branch.

Forgeries. New York's Metropolitan Museum and the entire art world were startled to hear that at least 45 objects of art and jewelry that had been considered Renaissance masterpieces, including the so-called Rospigliosi Cup attributed to Benvenuto Cellini (1500–71), are in fact forgeries. The discovery was made by a curator at the Victoria and Albert Museum in London, who identified a series of working drawings by a late 19th-century German goldsmith, Reinhold Vasters. The drawings were plans for pieces of jewelry that came to be displayed as genuine Renaissance works in the world's foremost museums.

Other Developments. The end of a long dispute over the estate of Mark Rothko came with the announcement by the new trustees of the Rothko Foundation that the more than 1,000 paintings and drawings under its jurisdiction would be given to 19 museums. The lion's share, 285 paintings and more than 500 sketches, went to the National Gallery of Art in Washington, DC.

The uncertain fate of Thomas Benton's panoramic murals of life in the United States, sold in 1983 by New York City's New School for Social Research (for which they had been painted), finally was resolved. The Equitable Life Assurance Society of the United States bought all ten panels, reportedly for more than $3 million, and planned to display them in their new building in New York.

ISA RAGUSA, *Princeton University*

ASIA

Peaceful postcolonial map changing continued in Asia during 1984, as Great Britain relinquished two remnants of its former empire. But violence also flared, as religious unrest in India led to the assassination of Prime Minister Indira Gandhi and as international conflict or domestic upheaval continued in Afghanistan, Sri Lanka, Indonesia, the Philippines, Burma, and Cambodia.

Changing of the Guard. A new nation joined the ranks of the free states of Asia in February —tiny, oil-rich Brunei on the northern coast of the island of Borneo. The Muslim sultanate had been protected militarily and represented in foreign relations by Great Britain.

More important, however, was the agreement in September between Great Britain and China on the status of Hong Kong after Britain's lease of the territory expires in 1997. The two parties agreed that, for the 50 years following the colony's return to China, the "current social and economic systems of Hong Kong will remain unchanged." The territory would become a "Special Administrative Region" in which private ownership—of property and of business enterprise—would continue.

China's subsequent announcement of sweeping internal economic reforms—reduced government control over industry and a shift to supply-and-demand pricing—suggested that Hong Kong's economic system might be less different from that of China by 1997 than might have been expected. Peking's almost immediate offer of similar terms to Taiwan indicated that the Chinese clearly intended to continue their pursuit of "lost territories."

Two deaths also reflected the changing of the guard in Asia: Souvanna Phouma, the last pre-Communist premier of Laos; and Adam Malik, the former foreign minister of Indonesia and one of the chief architects of unity among Southeast Asia's non-Communist states.

International Conflict. No new wars broke out in Asia in 1984, but the bloody Soviet-Afghan conflict, in its fifth year, intensified. The number of Soviet troops in Afghanistan rose to 150,000, and clashes between the invaders and the anti-Communist guerrillas increased in number and severity. Moreover, the Soviet strategy involved greater intimidation of the non-Communist civilian population. No end of the standoff seemed to be in sight.

Vietnam's on-again, off-again border clashes with Thailand and China flared anew but did not dramatically escalate. In one of their largest military moves ever on that front, the Vietnamese briefly sent battalion-sized forces into Thailand in March in an effort to wipe out a concentration of anti-Hanoi Cambodian insurgents. Thailand issued a strong warning, and China—a supporter of the Cambodian resistance movement—sent troops of its own across the northern Vietnamese border in retaliation. China also held naval exercises in the Gulf of Thailand.

The Cambodian resistance coalition of historically anti-Communist and previously ruling Communist (but anti-Hanoi) elements persisted in externally aided armed opposition to the Vietnamese-installed Heng Samrin government in Phnom Penh. The Association of Southeast Asian Nations (ASEAN)—Indonesia, Thailand, Malaysia, Singapore, the Philippines, and Brunei—called for "national reconciliation" and the "withdrawal of foreign forces"— meaning Vietnamese troops. Thailand, however, and, to lesser degrees, Malaysia and Singapore themselves encouraged the Cambodian irregular forces.

Reconciliations. The fighting in Afghanistan and Cambodia notwithstanding, the emphasis elsewhere in Asia was very much on peacemaking and reconciliation. The two major states of East Asia, China and Japan, were leaders in such efforts.

The Chinese, besides joining with Great Britain in a solution to the Hong Kong question, hosted Japanese Premier Yasuhiro Nakasone in March and President Ronald Reagan in April; Premier Zhao Ziyang had visited Washington in January. China also played host to a Soviet deputy foreign minister in the fifth round of talks to "normalize" relations between the two estranged Communist nations, while continuing negotiations with India over long-standing border differences. President Li Xiannian traveled to Pakistan in March, and Pakistani Foreign Minister Sahabzada Yaqub Khan returned the visit in July. China's Foreign Minister Wu Xueqian paid calls on the non-Communist Southeast Asian states of Burma, Thailand, and Malaysia.

Improved relations were the object of the Chinese diplomatic calling, but Peking had other interests in mind, too: the April visit by President Reagan was followed in June by a U.S. agreement to sell sophisticated arms to Peking; and President Li's pledge to defend Pakistan on his trip to that country sent a message to both India and Soviet forces in Afghanistan. Party Secretary Hu Yaobang traveled to pro-Soviet North Korea in May, and the North Korean foreign minister was among several Asian leaders and officials to call on Peking.

In other diplomatic contacts, Japan's Premier Nakasone traveled to India and Pakistan as well as China, and in early September he hosted South Korea's President Chun Doo Hwan, the first South Korean leader ever to make an official visit there. There were also Japanese-Soviet talks in Moscow, but these accomplished very little in light of territorial and other differences between the two states.

South Korea resumed nonpolitical relations with the USSR; ties had been suspended following the Soviet downing of a Korean airliner

The October 31 assassination of India's Prime Minister Indira Gandhi was followed by outbreaks of violence in New Delhi, left, and many other parts of the country. Most of the attacks were by Hindus against Sikhs as revenge for Gandhi's killing.

Baldev, Sygma

in September 1983. Of even greater importance, however, were new direct contacts between North and South Korea, stemming from North Korea's offer of aid to flood victims in the South. That action, which contrasted sharply with the attempted murder of South Korea's president and top cabinet leaders in Burma in late 1983, may have been encouraged by Japan's peacemaking efforts.

The latter activity also was reflected in Japan's hosting in October of Vietnamese Foreign Minister Nguyen Co Thach, paralleling a diplomatic trip by Hanoi's Communist party secretary Le Duan to India a month earlier. Japan and, to a lesser extent, India were earnestly seeking an end to the warring on the Indochinese peninsula and normalization of Vietnam's relations with non-Communist Asia. The Vietnamese foreign minister also visited Indonesia and Australia, two of the non-Communist western Pacific countries most sympathetic to the regularization of Vietnam's relations with neighboring states.

Other regional travelers in 1984 included U.S. Vice-President George Bush and Secretary of State George Shultz, who separately visited India, Pakistan, and key Southeast Asian states. Peacemaking Indonesian Foreign Minister Mochtar Kusumaatmadja met with Soviet Foreign Minister Andrei Gromyko in Moscow, but the USSR's relations with Bangladesh significantly worsened as nine diplomats and five other Soviet nationals were expelled from Dhaka.

Internal Problems. Two Indian leaders, Prime Minister Gandhi and Sikh extremist Jar-

nail Singh Bhindranwale, died political deaths. The latter's death occurred during the June 6 storming of the Golden Temple in Amritsar, the state of Punjab, by Indian army troops; the temple had become an arsenal for autonomy-seeking Sikh militants. Several hundred of Bhindranwale's coreligionists and government troops died in the fighting. It was the attack on the temple that led to Prime Minister Gandhi's own demise—murder at the hands of Sikh bodyguards—on October 31. Hindus subsequently slaughtered Sikhs by the thousands—in the days following Gandhi's slaying.

In October a Philippine judicial panel rejected President Ferdinand Marcos' claim that Communists had been responsible for the August 1983 murder of opposition leader Benigno Aquino, Jr. All the panelists agreed that Aquino had been killed as a result of a military conspiracy.

At least 20 persons died in Muslim instigated rioting against ethnic Chinese in Jakarta, Indonesia, the worst violence in that country in ten years. In Sri Lanka extremists among the Tamil Indian minority continued their terrorism, with the majority Sinhalese army responding no less violently.

The communal violence in Sri Lanka, Indonesia, and the Punjab, like that between Hindus and Muslims in Bombay and warring Assamese and Bengalese in northeastern India, represented the continuing legacy of imperfectly integrated nations that emerged from the colonial era.

RICHARD BUTWELL
California State University, Dominguez Hills

ASTRONOMY

Plans for building the world's two largest telescopes made great advances in 1984. One of them will be constructed by the University of California, thanks to a $36 million bequest. Its main mirror will have a diameter of 10 m (32'10")—twice that of the famous 200-inch (508-cm) reflector at Mount Palomar in California—and will be formed from 36 2-m (6'7") nested hexagons. The other instrument is to be a U.S. national telescope with an effective diameter of 15 m (49'3"). Its light-gathering surface will involve four mirrors, each 7.5 m (24'7") in diameter.

Terrestrial Extinctions. Over the past few years, evidence has rapidly accumulated that the earth's plants and animals have suffered at least 12 major extinctions over the past 250 million years. Similar eras of death can be traced 2½ times further back in the history of our planet. What made headlines in 1984 was the announcement that these mass extinctions may occur at intervals of about 26 million years. If this is true, we now are living about halfway through such a period.

Two explanations have been proposed for the periodic extinctions. One is that the Sun has a companion star, dubbed "Nemesis," whose gravitational influence disrupts perhaps billions of comets in the far reaches of the solar system and sends them on collision courses with the earth. The resulting cometary bombardment flings enormous quantities of debris into the earth's atmosphere, thus dimming the Sun's light and destroying food chains. The alternative hypothesis is that the Sun, as it circles the nucleus of our galaxy, periodically encounters huge clouds of interstellar matter. Again, the gravitational influence of such clouds would stir up the comet swarm and cause the same catastrophe.

Halley's Comet. This long-awaited visitor will not become widely visible until December 1985, though it may be five times brighter than anticipated. The latter prediction stems from a study of Halley's Comet over the past 2,000 years and observations made in September 1984, at Kitt Peak (AZ) National Observatory.

Also in September, comet-hunter Tsutomu Seki of Japan, using only a 24-inch (61-cm) telescope, became the first amateur astronomer to photograph Halley's Comet on its present return. That same month, Kitt Peak astronomers discovered that the icy nucleus of Halley's Comet had begun to evaporate, with the vapors extending outward some 17,000 mi (27 000 km). The comet at that point was 576 million mi (927 million km) from the Sun, more than six times farther away than the earth is. Few comets have been observed undergoing evaporation at such great distances from the Sun.

The Soviet Union, Japan, and a consortium of European nations, meanwhile, planned to send spaceprobes to Halley's Comet. But the United States will be the first to reach a comet. An old satellite now known as the International Cometary Explorer has been retargeted to pass through the tail of Comet Giacobinni-Zinner in September 1985, six months before the other spacecraft arrive at Halley.

Heliopause? The most plausible explanation for radio noise discovered in 1983 and 1984 by the Voyager 1 and 2 spacecraft is that it originates at the heliopause. This elongated "bubble" in our solar system marks where the wind of electrically charged particles from the Sun is contained by pressure from the interstellar environment. If these observations are confirmed, it will have been shown that at least part of the heliopause lies about 4.3 billion mi (6.9 billion km) from the Sun (about 46 times the earth's distance). This is where "deep" space can be said to truly begin.

IRAS Results. Whenever astronomers explore a new region of the electromagnetic spectrum, a host of unexpected discoveries is made. In 1984 many results became available from the Infrared Astronomical Satellite (IRAS), which observed at wavelengths between 0.01 and 0.1 millimeter. This portion of the spectrum samples relatively cold material in the universe, radiating at temperatures from 30° above absolute zero (-459.7°F) to the freezing point of water (32°F).

During its 10 months in operation, IRAS discovered five comets—an unprecedented harvest for one instrument in so short a time. This success was attributed to IRAS' extreme sensitivity to warmed dust and to the fact that many comets are much dustier than had been previously believed.

In 1983, IRAS detected a warm dust cloud around the star Vega. At first the cloud was believed to be a nascent planetary system, but later studies showed that the observations also could have been caused by a swarm of comets. In 1984 an examination of the star Beta Pictoris yielded better evidence for another planetary system. Observations with the Carnegie 100-inch (2.54 m) telescope in Chile revealed a circumstellar disk containing thousands of earth masses of material. Said Richard Terrile, one of the investigators, "It's hard not to form planets from material like this."

IRAS also found that our own galaxy contains vast clouds of very cold dust. Some of the dust forms stringy filaments. Another component of the clouds is rather sheetlike, and it is more pervasive throughout the galaxy. The discovery of this material at least doubles the amount of nonluminous matter known to exist in the Milky Way. It thus accounts for some of the "missing" matter astronomers have long anticipated but could not detect.

IRAS also revealed that some distant galaxies produce more than 1,000 times more infrared energy than a "normal" galaxy like our

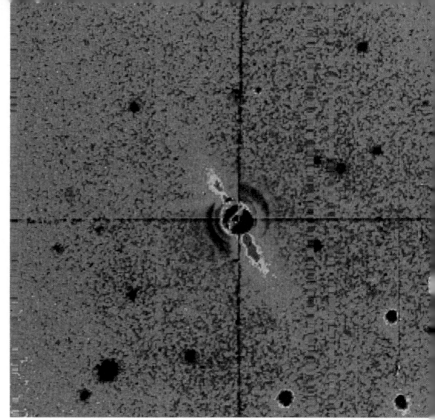

A computer-processed photograph of the star Beta Pictoris, located 293 trillion miles from earth, shows a cloud of solid particles orbiting the fireball. Astronomers think the cloud is another solar system, in the early stages of formation.

University of Arizona/JPL

Milky Way. One such object, called Arp 220, emits 99% of its energy at infrared wavelengths. Extensive observations by many ground-based astronomers have indicated that this galaxy is probably undergoing an enormous burst of star formation.

Heart of the Milky Way. The nucleus of our galaxy is hidden from human eyes by intervening dust and gas, which can be penetrated only by infrared light and radio waves. Observations at these wavelengths have uncovered a bizarre collection of features near the nucleus, including streams of high-velocity gas and a massive star cluster. A source called IRS 16 is presumed to lie at the very core of the Milky Way. In 1984 it was discovered that this object emits eight million times as much radiation as the Sun and may be responsible for most, if not all, of the radiation from the center of our galaxy.

Perhaps the most unusual feature yet discovered in the heart of our Milky Way is an arc of parallel filaments, each some 130 light-years long and three light-years wide. Their emission, restricted to the radio region of the spectrum, is highly polarized, a characteristic of radiation generated in a magnetic field. In this case the field is perpendicular to the plane of our galaxy. Thus, the rotation of the Milky Way carries gas across the magnetic-field lines and thereby converts mechanical energy into electricity. In other words, the hub of the Milky Way acts like a dynamo.

Quasars and Gravitational Lenses. For more than 20 years quasars have perplexed astronomers. The question has been whether these starlike objects are relatively nearby and moderately bright, or lie at vast distances and have enormous luminosities. Recent research has made it clear that at least some of the quasars lie at great distances.

One implication of Einstein's general theory of relativity is that a massive object, such as a galaxy (or a cluster of galaxies), can gravitationally bend light from a more distant object and thereby act as a lens. Six lensed quasars have now been found, three in 1984 alone. One of these, in the constellation of Pisces, is so closely aligned with a foreground galaxy that its light passes through that object's stellar halo. In this case, individual stars can gravitationally image the quasar's light. Such alignments are temporary and should cause short, sudden outbursts of brightness. Two such episodes have already been observed.

Possible Planet. Late in the year, astronomers at the University of Arizona at Tucson reported the discovery of what they believed to be the first planet to be detected outside the earth's solar system. The gaseous object, called Van Biesbroeck 8, was discovered orbiting a star in the constellation Ophiuchus an estimated 21 light years from earth. It is about nine tenths the size of Jupiter but 30-80 times more massive, with a surface temperature of some 2,000°F (1,100°C). Some astronomers contend that it may be too massive and hot to be considered a planet.

LEIF J. ROBINSON, *"Sky & Telescope"*

AUSTRALIA

Political events dominated the scene, and an election called by Prime Minister Robert J. Hawke resulted in the Australian Labor Party (ALP) retaining office in December. ALP's 16-seat majority in the considerably enlarged new 148-seat House of Representatives was halved, however. In the concurrent poll for approximately half of the Senate, the ALP and the opposition Liberal-National Party coalition secured equal numbers, but Democrats and independents retained a "balance of power," thus thwarting one of Hawke's prime aims in holding the premature election. The overall 2% drop in ALP support to below 48% belied the forecasts by media commentators of a landslide victory for the party in view of Hawke's consistently high personal ratings (70%).

A slowing economy and investigations into various aspects of crime and corruption allegedly involving some ALP figures worked against the government. Other disruptive developments included sharpened factional differences within the party over Hawke's pragmatic policies and in particular his determined support for continued mining of uranium and for close ties with the United States.

Lower interest rates were a positive development, but a hight cost structure hampering business and lowering international competitiveness plus a massive deficit with federal borrowings reaching close to 5% of gross domestic product (GDP) placed a drag on the economy.

Political Round. A pivotal factor in the political arena was the formal accord on prices and income endorsed by the government and the Australian Council of Trades Unions as representatives of the labor movement. The agreement brought a slow but steady escalation of wages.

The general election on December 1 came after months of speculation during which the public was encouraged to believe that Hawke would capitalize on a prevailing buoyancy and his popularity by holding an early election. Opinion polls supported Hawke's confidence. After a major redistricting, combined with an increase in the number of parliamentary seats, and what was seen as a "preelection budget," Hawke announced a House of Representatives election to coincide with half-Senate polls. The ALP had no specific issue to run on, forcing Hawke to rely on a "trust me" strategy.

The Liberal-National Party coalition, led by Liberal leader Andrew Peacock, had an extensive platform that formalized the long-running parliamentary attack on Labor's legislative program. The government was forced to become defensive on tax policy and ad hoc decisions on Aboriginal land rights. Other emergent issues proved damaging to the ALP. Swirling intrusions included immigration policy (with Hawke defending the tilt toward Asian sources), and proposals for a Bill of Rights designed to have overriding powers over legislation by state governments as well as over federal law. The opposition attacked the ALP on what it termed that party's "declared war" on the elderly and pensioners, its program of "socialist medicine," its burdens on the family, a failure to maintain a bipartisan approach to immigration, a concentration of support for government schools, the drift in the U.S. alliance, and the party's efforts "to turn Australia into a socialist republic."

Meanwhile newspapers gave prominence to what was headlined as "the 1984 debate on justice and crime." Federal Attorney General Sen. Gareth Evans criticized publication by the *Age* of details from tapes secured from police telephone taps which suggested a vast network of influence reaching into the New South Wales state judicial system. Evans said such publication "outraged privacy and threatened human rights." The allegations of corruption were extended in parliamentary debate to implicate a High Court judge, Justice Lionel Murphy, a former Labor appointee. He denied any wrongdoing and remained in office during a Senate inquiry into the allegations. The matter was left in abeyance when the Senate adjourned for the election. Allegations of union-linked crime involving drugs and money manipulation continued. One official report resulted in indictment of a New South Wales judge; another substantiated evidence of links between certain union leaders and organized crime.

The December poll left Peacock in firm control as Liberal leader.

Economic Course. Economic performance was marked by somewhat lowered inflation (6–7%); an overall recovery best described as patchy and uncertain, with manufacturing results falling back from midyear; a worsening balance of trade; and a deficit combined with continuing upward pressure on costs which

---

AUSTRALIA • Information Highlights

Official Name: Commonwealth of Australia.
Location: Southwestern Pacific Ocean.
Area: 2,970,000 sq mi (7 692 300 km²).
Population (mid-1984 est.): 15,500,000.
Chief Cities (June 30, 1982): Canberra, the capital, 251,000; Sydney, 3,310,500; Melbourne, 2,836,800; Brisbane, 1,124,200.
Government: *Head of state,* Elizabeth II, queen; represented by Sir Ninian Martin Stephen, governor-general (took office July 1982). *Head of government,* Robert Hawke, prime minister (took office March 11, 1983). *Legislature*—Parliament: Senate and House of Representatives.
Monetary Unit: Australian dollar (1.2121 A$ equals U.S. $1, Dec. 31, 1984).
Gross National Product (1982 A$): $153,000,000,000.
Economic Indexes (1983): *Consumer Prices* (1970 = 100), all items, 361.3; food, 351.3. *Industrial Production* (1975 = 100), 101.
Foreign Trade (1983 U.S.$): *Imports,* $19,393,-000,000; *exports,* $20,594,000,000.

lessened competitiveness. Unemployment remained at about 9%. A growing level of sporadic industrial stoppages reflected restlessness within unions that negated the restraints of the wages-prices accord that Hawke regarded as the centerpiece of his economic policy. The Arbitration Commission continued to struggle with recalcitrant unions seeking rewards beyond the accepted indexed levels of wages and workers' associated benefits.

From midyear a 1% fall in GDP marked the first reversal in more than a year. The decline reflected the spotty performance of the manufacturing sector plus a lowered level of investment outlays and a leveling out in farm production after 1983's bumper post-drought yields. Mining experienced its third successive adverse year due to intensified competition in international markets and an unfavorable cost structure. The industry's overall return barely reached 4% of sales revenue. Because of the dismal profit picture, investment in mining was 11% lower, with exploration outlays cut fully 40%. Influenced by slackness in commodity markets, the rural sector showed a decline of A$1.2 billion in overall farm product returns.

Two major initiatives were the freeing of the Australian dollar early in the year and subsequent moves toward deregulation of the banking system. The latter action cleared the way for foreign banks and other financial institutions to become more active in Australia.

In presenting the fiscal 1985 budget in August, Treasurer Paul Keating said it was aimed at setting the economy on a new path of noninflationary, sustainable economic growth. Keating forecast a deficit of $6.745 billion, $1.6 billion less than the previous year.

Meanwhile, gross foreign debt was estimated to have gone from $34 billion to $40 billion (up 18%). Most commentators believed the budget would have little impact in improving the economic picture.

One counterview to government optimism was that expressed by the chairman of a broad-based investment company. The government should have curbed the very high level of government spending, he said. "Budget spending in 1983–84 was more than 7% higher in real terms; for 1984–85 the budget plans a rise of another 6% in real terms. That is a very rich diet for any economy and the danger is that, rather than provide energy for growth, the rich spending may simply put on fat." He saw failure to cut the deficit sharply as basic to underlying problems.

A Brookings Institution study found that labor was overpriced and unemployment benefits too generous, while national distrust of market influences, together with a strong belief in equality, continued to inhibit any move toward a more effective system.

Foreign Affairs and Defense. The thrust of foreign and defense policy remained unchanged. Prime Minister Hawke's warm embrace of the ANZUS defenses pact with New Zealand and the United States continued after New Zealand's newly elected Labour Party government decided to ban visits by nuclear-powered or nuclear-armed ships. Policy differences between Australia and New Zealand on the operation of the U.S. alliance remained.

In the South Pacific, Hawke also won respect for his promotion of a nuclear-free zone in the region and his support for the eventual independence of New Caledonia.

It was announced in November that high-level teams from the Soviet Union and the United States would visit Australia early in 1985 to discuss arms control and disarmament —a move calculated to draw support to the ALP from the newly formed Nuclear Disarmament Party.

A report prepared for the government by businessman Sir Gordon Jackson suggested that the Pacific region should again become the main, almost exclusive, focus of Australian aid. The efficiency of aid administration should be improved. Aid should favor integrated, planned "project or program" support. Total aid commitment should rise from 0.5% of national income to the international goal for industrialized countries of 0.7%.

Election to the UN Security Council was taken as an indication that Foreign Minister Bill Hayden was planning to augment Australia's international role. It was the first time in ten years that Australia had sought council membership. .

Trends and Events. Using an electron microscope, a researcher at the Australian National University recorded on film the oldest fossilized organism yet discovered: the remains of a type of primitive bacteria believed to be 3.4 billion years old. The photographs, showing the bacteria to be closely associated with oil-shale deposits, appeared to confirm a theory that fossil fuels arose mainly from bacteria rather than the remains of marine plankton.

The new Parliament House under construction in Canberra, at a cost estimated at more than $500 million by its completion in 1988, attracted nearly 2 million sightseers. Other major tourist complexes were opened including one on an island off the Queensland coast adjacent to the Great Barrier Reef and another, described as "a spectacular gem set in the heart of the Outback," at Ayers Rock, central Australia.

Signs of inflationary times included introduction of a $100 note and abandonment of the $1 note in favor of a coin.

In April residents of Cocos Island in the Indian Ocean voted to join Australia following the government's move in 1983 to acquire all the land of the island from the former sole owner, John Clunies-Ross.

R. M. YOUNGER, *Australian Author*

AUSTRIA

The year in Austria was quiet and uneventful, with slow economic improvement.

Economy. In 1983, mounting federal deficits, 36% higher than budgeted, caused the federal debt to rise by 21.8% to 416.2 billion schillings (ca. $20 billion). The deficits led the Socialist-Freedom Party government headed by Chancellor Fred Sinowatz to enact a series of fee and tax increases to go into effect on Jan. 1, 1984. Postage, telephone rates, rail fares, and other charges were increased, while a new savings withholding tax of 7.5% was enacted, and the value-added tax was raised by 2%. The latter brought a rush of consumer buying at the end of 1983 to beat the tax, with a consequent rise in prices and a marked decline in consumer purchasing in the first quarters of 1984. The inflation rate, 3.3% in 1983, stood at 5.6% in January 1984. The new tax on interest brought a decline in savings deposits and an increase in bond purchases.

The 1984 budget of 436.5 billion schillings (ca. $22 billion) called for a decline in the deficit to 62.1 billion schillings (ca. $3.2 billion), which nevertheless was expected to raise the federal debt to 476.2 billion schillings (ca. $25 billion). The budget allotments were: social welfare, health, and housing, 26.1%; public transport and road construction, 22.6%; government debt, 15.6%; education, science, research, and culture, 12.2%; economic sector, 7.4%; national security and law enforcement, 6.5%; other expenditures, 9.6%.

Unemployment fell to a new low of 3% in June. Restrictive measures in regard to foreign workers led to their decline by about 11,000 in 1983, and about 7,000 were expected to leave in 1984. The social security system was under financial strain, especially in respect to pensions, where 26.6% of the total expenditure was financed out of the federal budget. A 2.5% growth in the gross domestic product (GDP) was predicted at midyear.

Government. On July 1, a new law requiring automobile drivers and front-seat passengers to wear seat belts went into effect. In September, Chancellor Sinowatz replaced four ministers in a Cabinet shuffle, but denied reports of political infighting.

Foreign Affairs. At the end of February, President Rudolf Kirchschläger began a nine-day state visit to the United States, meeting with President Ronald Reagan on February 28. It was the first state visit by an Austrian president to the United States. This visit of friendship was followed by a most successful U.S. tour by the Vienna Volksoper, April 10–May 20.

At a conference in Ottawa, March 20–21, Austria, along with eight other European countries and Canada, signed a five-point agreement to reduce sulfur dioxide emissions, linked to acid-rain problems, by at least 30% by 1993.

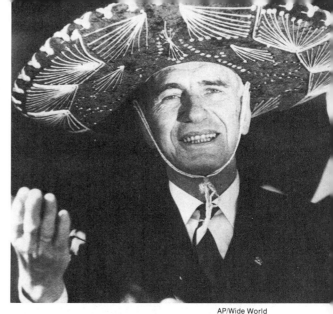

AP/Wide World

Austria's President Rudolf Kirchschläger was presented with a sombrero during a March visit to Los Angeles, CA.

Prime Minister P.W. Botha of South Africa made an unofficial visit to Vienna on June 7 and met with Chancellor Sinowatz, prompting some minor anti-South African demonstrations.

Austrian relations with Israel improved. Along with the United Nations, Austria acted as intermediary in the Israeli-Syrian exchange of prisoners and war dead that took place on June 28. Austria continued to be the mecca for East Bloc refugees. During the first half of 1984, 4,240 sought asylum, compared with 2,497 in 1983. In recognition of its great services over the years to more than 200,000 Jewish emigrants from the Soviet Union, the Austrian government on April 29 received the annual Humanitarian Award of the International Jewish Rescue Organization (Rav Tov).

Ernst C. Helmreich, *Professor of History Emeritus, Bowdoin College*

AUSTRIA • Information Highlights

Official Name: Republic of Austria.
Location: Central Europe.
Area: 32,370 sq mi (83 835 km²).
Population (mid-1984 est.): 7,600,000.
Chief Cities (1981 census): Vienna, the capital, 1,531,346; Graz, 243,166; Linz, 199,910; Salzburg, 139,426; Innsbruck, 117,287.
Government: *Head of State,* Rudolf Kirchschläger, president (took office July 1974). *Head of government,* Fred Sinowatz, chancellor (took office May 24, 1983). *Legislature*—Federal Assembly: Federal Council and National Council.
Monetary Unit: Schilling (21.82 schillings equal U.S. $1, Oct. 11, 1984).
Gross National Product (1982 U.S.$): $66,890,000,000.
Economic Indexes (1983): *Consumer Prices* (1970 = 100), all items, 214.0; food, 193.1. *Industrial Production* (1975 = 100), 123.
Foreign Trade (1983 U.S.$): *Imports,* $19,364,000,000; *exports,* $15,431,000,000.

AUTOMOBILES

The U.S. auto industry left the recession of the early 1980s a dim memory during 1984, chalking up its highest model-year sales in five years and racking up record profits.

For the 12-month model year ended Sept. 30, 1984, the nation's six domestic automakers reported 7,914,738 retail sales, a 22.4% gain from the 6,466,897 in the 1983 model year. Sales volume in 1983 marked the first upturn from the 1982 low of only 5,447,135 domestic cars—the depth of the industry's long downturn. The industry's sales had plunged sharply since the 1979 model year, when 8,620,400 new cars were sold. Adding to the lusty automotive performance were trucks, vans, and utility vehicles. U.S. truck production in the first nine months of 1984 rose by a sizable 36.8% from the comparable 1983 period to 2,333,552 units and seemed likely to finish the year at close to the 3.5 million mark.

The combined car and truck upsurges sent Big Three (Chrysler, Ford, and General Motors) earnings and profits soaring in the first half of 1984. The increases also cleared the way for GM and Ford to negotiate three-year contracts with the United Auto Workers (UAW) restoring many of the economic concessions granted by the union in early 1982 and introducing "job-security" provisions guaranteeing laid-off workers income for periods up to six years. Profit-sharing plans pioneered by GM and Ford in 1982 were broadened in the 1984–87 contracts.

First-half profits at giant GM rose to $3.2 billion on sales of $44.5 billion, surpassing the prior 1979 records. Ford netted $1.8 billion on sales of $27.1 billion. Chrysler Corp., which had flirted with bankruptcy in 1981 and 1982, turned in a net profit of $1.5 billion on sales of $10.2 billion and paid back in full the $1.2 billion in federally guaranteed loans that had been enacted to keep the Number 3 automaker solvent. Even American Motors wound up in the black to the tune of $9.8 million on sales of $2.1 billion, ending a string of 14 red-ink quarters.

GM finished the 1984 model year with 4,659,818 domestic new-car sales, up 20.2% from 1983's 3,876,006; Ford, 1,906,806, up 28.7% from 1,481,382; Chrysler Corp., 946,575, up 15.5% from 819,206; AMC, 201,275, up 10% from 183,005; Volkswagen, 83,084 Rabbit cars made in Pennsylvania, compared with 83,222; and American Honda, 117,180 Accord cars built in Ohio, up 386.8% from 24,073.

Although Chevrolet's Cavalier subcompact dethroned Ford's Escort from the Number 1 sales spot in the model year, with 371,836 sales, Ford outsold Chevrolet in trucks and vans by 1,150,474 to 1,108,340.

The 1985 Models. "Young upwardly mobile professionals," increasingly attracted to higher-priced imported cars, formed a common target for the Detroit-headquartered automakers as the time came to introduce mid-decade cars. But competition also came on stream for hottest new body style of all in 1984—Chrysler's seven-passenger minivans, which exceeded all expectations with first-year sales of nearly 150,000 units.

Aiming at the young affluent market, GM led the 1985-model attack with the introduction of three new sports coupes—the Buick Somerset Regal, Oldsmobile Calais, and Pontiac Grand Am. These European-looking front-wheel-drive cars were to be followed early in 1985 by the Chrysler LeBaron GTS and Dodge Lancer, front-drive hatchback sedans assembled in a new Chrysler plant at Sterling Heights, MI.

Volkswagen retooled its assembly plant at New Stanton, PA, for the 1985-model Golf compact, successor to the Rabbit, which the new car resembles. The Golf is an upscale front-drive compact and moves VW a second step further into the U.S. market. The Rabbit replaced the Beetle and had been marketed in the United States since 1975.

The 1985-model year was largely a carryover cycle for Ford, which had led the way in 1984 with an "aerodynamic" look on three distinct lines—the Lincoln Mark VII, Ford Tempo and Mercury Topaz, and Ford Thunderbird and Mercury Cougar. Ford planned to facelift its Ford Escort and Mercury Lynx subcompacts for 1985½, however, and to redesign its midsize Ford LTD and Mercury Marquis sedans into front-drive 1986 models to be called Ford Taurus and Mercury Sable.

In line with a resurgence in the convertible market, which domestic automakers abandoned in 1976, AMC added a Renault Alliance softtop body style for 1985. The burgeoning

American Motors introduced the 1985 Renault Alliance, a two-door, four-passenger, 1.7-liter-engine convertible.

American Motors

Leasing

Leasing a new car or truck, rather than buying one outright, has become an entrenched part of the American automotive scene. A record 20% of 1983-model domestic new cars sold in the United States were leased to fleets or individuals, amounting to 1,115,000 units. Lease sales have exceeded the one million mark in each of the past ten years, prompting auto observers to forecast continued growth because of the personal and tax advantages afforded by the leasing method.

The attractiveness of leasing was boosted in the postrecession recovery year of 1984 by higher prices for both domestic and imported cars. Higher product prices spell increased purchase down payments, and not the least of leasing's pluses is elimination of the down-payment requirement that accompanies financed individual purchases.

Types.   There are essentially two types of leases used in automotive marketing—the net-lease or closed-end lease and the finance or open-end lease.

Under the more prevalent net lease, usually for a period of 24 or 36 months, the selling dealer takes back possession of the vehicle at the end of the contract period. Usually the car or truck is replaced by another leased vehicle, eliminating the need for the user to trade in the vehicle or sell it individually when a new unit is purchased. Terms of the net lease call for the lessee to pay for any damages beyond normal wear and tear. This liability normally does not exceed three monthly payments or a predetermined figure set forth in the contract for liquidated damages.

The open-end or finance lease allows the customer to buy the vehicle at the end of the lease at a predetermined wholesale value. The lessee has the option in most open-end arrangements to refuse purchase, but then the dealer lessor can charge the lessee for any difference in the wholesale book value set forth in the lease and the actual value at the end of the agreement. Fluctuating market conditions make this type of lease especially risky for the individual lessee.

Popularity.   Leasing has risen in popularity despite the fact that monthly costs of leasing contracts exceed those of individual finance contracts as a rule. The American Automotive Leasing Association estimated that the average cost of closed-end leases in its fleet was $328.13 per month in 1983, compared with an average finance cost of $245 per month.

Higher costs for leasing new vehicles reflect administrative expenses by the dealer, a loss factor for closed-end-lease units that the dealer eventually reclaims, and liability insurance. On the other hand, lessees are attracted by the fact that no down-payment requirement exists; the total cost is generally accepted as a tax-expense write-off; the dealer takes care of most insurance and all service even after the factory warranty period; and the used lease automobiles remain the responsibility of the lessor.

Leasing to business fleets and companies engaged in daily rental of cars and trucks accounts for a substantial number of domestic new-vehicle sales, although not of imported makes. The trade magazine *Automotive Fleet* estimated that 3,650,000 cars and 1,660,000 light trucks and vans were in overall fleet use as of Jan. 1, 1984. Most of these vehicles were on lease from manufacturers through franchised dealers.

Fleet sales of imported cars in the United States, however, continued to hold below 2% in the 1983-model year, or fewer than 44,000 units. But as many as 25% of the imports were delivered to individuals on personal leases in the same period, with higher-priced sedans from Europe a major beneficiary of leasing's advantages.

Historically larger models have been most sought by lease-type buyers, and 1983 proved no exception to this rule. Statistics for the 1983-model year showed that intermediate-size cars constituted the largest lease segment at 446,846 units, exceeding compacts at 316,042. Intermediate and full-size cars accounted for 53% of all domestic fleet/lease sales in the 1983-model year, with subcompacts taking only 12.2%.

In 1979 the all-time volume record for leased domestic cars was set when 1,423,807 went into lease operation through fleets or individuals. This equaled only 13.8% of total sales, however, as 1979 registrations of 10,356,695 new cars preceded four straight years of auto-industry recession.

Outlook.   With domestic automakers offering substantial incentives to fleet and lease buyers of 1985 models, it was forecast that up to two million domestic cars could be leased in 1984 and again in 1985 for new volume records.

Such dramatic achievements would give automobile leasing 25% market shares and extend leasing's impact into small-car segments that hitherto have not shared in the growth of the "nonownership" way to possess vehicles.

Maynard M. Gordon

The Merkur, Ford's new German-made model with a 2.3-liter, 175-horsepower turbocharged engine, debuted in November.

Ford

minivan market pioneered by Chrysler with the Dodge Caravan and Plymouth Voyager attracted two 1985 entries from GM, the Chevrolet Astro and GMC Safari, as well as a 1985½ competitor from Ford, the Aerostar.

With sales of full-size and midsize cars surging in 1984, both GM and Ford failed to meet the federal Corporate Average Fuel Requirement (CAFE) levels of 27 miles per gallon. The CAFE rose to 27.5 m.p.g. for 1985 models. GM extended production of 1984-model small-car lines into December so as to reduce the penalty for noncompliance with the CAFE law.

The Imports. Sales of imported new cars in the United States finished virtually even with 1983 results for the first nine months of 1984. The reason for the import sales "plateau" was indisputably the fourth year of the voluntary restraints by the Japanese government on car shipments to the U.S.

The 1984–85 export quota to the United States was raised about 10% from 1983–84 to 1,900,000 cars, but as domestic car sales spurted during the year, the import share of the U.S. market declined from 27.3% in 1983 to 23% in 1984. Import sales in the first nine months totaled 1,829,484 in 1984, compared with 1,838,698 the previous year.

While most Japanese imports showed modest sales declines, due to the quotas, European makes continued to advance. Major sales gains were recorded by Volvo, the Volkswagen imports, Audi, BMW, and Saab.

A "Far East" import and domestic production strategy was initiated by GM, which began import of the Suzuki-built Sprint minicompact and Isuzu-made Spectrum subcompact from Japan. A GM-Toyota joint-venture compact car, called the Chevrolet Nova, entered production at Fremont, CA, in December 1984. GM also signed an agreement with South Korea's Daewoo auto operation for a 1986-model subcompact import.

Ford, not to be outdone, began import from its West German subsidiary in November 1984, of the "Merkur" sports sedan for U.S. Lincoln-Mercury dealers. Chrysler Corp. filed an antitrust suit in Federal District Court against the GM-Toyota joint venture but said it might be compelled to follow GM's lead with its own Japanese Mitsubishi partner if the litigation was unsuccessful.

Sporty and upscale models also were enroute from several importers. Toyota planned to send the United States a two-seater coupe called the MR-2 in midyear, competing with the successful year-old Pontiac Fiero and the Mazda RX-7. Honda and Britain's BL Ltd were codeveloping a midsize sedan for 1986, when AMC would bring in the Renault Espace seven-passenger minivan.

MAYNARD M. GORDON
Editor, "Motor News Analysis"

WORLD MOTOR VEHICLE DATA, 1983

Country	Passenger Car Production	Truck and Bus Production	Motor Vehicle Registrations
Argentina	128,260	30,915	4,750,000
Australia	310,542	26,533	7,955,200
Austria	6,148	6,059	229,861
Belgium	260,711	24,767	3,571,092
Brazil	576,356	319,926	10,646,620
Canada	968,867	555,546	13,838,579
Czechoslovakia	172,349	57,832	2,831,703
France	2,960,823	375,039	23,109,500
East Germany	182,930	41,223	3,221,976
West Germany	3,877,641*	292,910	25,683,717
Hungary	–	13,321	1,328,982
India	44,613	109,025	1,808,125
Italy	1,395,521	179,620	21,257,812
Japan	7,151,888	3,959,771	41,336,379
Korea	121,987	99,032	634,164
Mexico	207,137	78,348	6,585,439
The Netherlands	105,597	12,000	5,018,000
Poland	260,000	54,000	3,572,000
Rumania	99,000	55,000	380,000
Spain	1,141,581	147,140	9,859,486
Sweden	344,702	51,995	3,142,726
United Kingdom	1,044,597	244,514	17,930,777
United States	6,781,184	2,424,191	159,509,825†
USSR	1,317,700	860,500	17,934,400
Yugoslavia	210,059	37,919	3,153,455
Total	29,670,193	10,057,126	436,532,496‡

* Includes 315,904 micro-buses. † U.S. total includes 123,697,863 cars and 35,811,962 trucks and buses. ‡ World total includes 337,951,455 cars and 98,581,041 trucks and buses, of which 389,289,818 are from countries shown above. U.S. total does not include Puerto Rico, 1,116,921 cars and trucks. Other countries with more than 1 million vehicle registrations were Denmark, 1,602,290; Greece, 1,525,908; Indonesia, 1,516,654; Malaysia, 1,146,406; New Zealand, 1,653,409; Nigeria, 1,150,000; Norway, 1,518,492; Portugal, 1,371,000; Saudi Arabia, 1,585,500; South Africa, 3,712,000; Switzerland, 2,658,628; Turkey, 1,060,133; and Venezuela, 2,200,000. Source: Motor Vehicle Manufacturers Association of the United States, Inc.

BANGLADESH

Military ruler Lt.-Gen. H. M. Ershad, who assumed the additional title of president in December 1983, continued in 1984 to move haltingly toward an end to martial law in Bangladesh. Economic growth fell short of expectations, but export earnings brought foreign-exchange reserves to an all-time high.

Political Developments. Local elections were completed with relatively little violence, but upazilla (subdistrict) elections scheduled for March 24 were postponed because of political opposition. The 15-party alliance led by Hasina Wajed's Awami League and a seven-party coalition led by Begum Khaleda Zia's Bangladesh National Party (BNP) both demanded that parliamentary elections precede those for either upazillas or the presidency. Ershad eventually scheduled, but afterward canceled, parliamentary elections for Dec. 8, 1984.

Ershad continued in 1984 to maneuver for a place in the postmilitary order. He shuffled his cabinet several times, appointed veteran politician Ataur Rahman Khan as prime minister in March, and dropped Foreign Minister A.R.S. Doha from the cabinet in June. Ershad publicly endorsed the Janadal Party but stopped short of formal affiliation. A loose amalgam of diverse interests, including numerous defectors from both the leftist Awami League and the rightist BNP, the Janadal was supportive of the military regime but was plagued by serious factional conflicts.

Student violence and tribal unrest persisted. To counter tribal separatism in the Chittagong Hills, Ershad appointed prominent tribal leader Upendra Lal Chakma as a presidential adviser on tribal affairs.

Economic Concerns. The economy grew by approximately 4.5% in fiscal 1984, less than the original target of 6% but up from the 1983 and 1982 figures of 3.7% and 0.9%. Extensive flooding in May, which affected 403 of the country's 406 upazillas, cut food production and sent prices soaring. In June, major public protests took place in Dhaka over price rises as high as 20%.

Export earnings increased to $825 million, raising foreign-exchange reserves to a record $518 million. At the same time foreign-aid disbursement increased to $1.35 billion (U.S.), and the government projected that 80% of its 1985 development plan would be financed by such assistance.

Foreign Affairs. Bangladesh permitted the USSR to replace diplomats expelled in December 1983. Armed clashes occurred over India's attempts to fence its border with Bangladesh, to prevent illegal immigration, but a military stand-down agreement between the two countries in June seemed to relieve tensions. India also agreed to permit Bhutan to ship goods freely through India to Bangladesh.

BANGLADESH • Information Highlights

Official Name: People's Republic of Bangladesh.
Location: South Asia.
Area: 55,125 sq mi (142 775 km²).
Population (mid-1984 est.): 99,600,000.
Chief Cities (1981 census): Dhaka, the capital, 3,458,602; Chittagong, 1,388,476; Khulna, 623,184; Rajshahi, 171,600.
Government: *Head of state,* Hossein Mohammed Ershad, chief executive (assumed power March 24, 1982) and president (Dec. 1983). *Head of government,* Ataur Rahman Khan, prime minister (took office March 30, 1984).
Monetary Unit: Taka (25.2 taka equal U.S.$1, May 1984).
Gross National Product (fiscal 1982 U.S.$): $11,000,000,000.
Economic Indexes: *Consumer Prices* (1983, 1972 = 100), all items, 536.7; food, 511.0. *Industrial Production* (1982, 1975 = 100), 132.
Foreign Trade (fiscal 1983 U.S.$): *Imports,* $2,300,000,000; *exports,* $650,000,000.

In November, President Ershad represented Bangladesh at the funeral of India's Prime Minister Indira Gandhi. By sending Indian troops into East Pakistan in 1971, Mrs. Gandhi had helped Bangladesh win its independence.

WILLIAM L. RICHTER, *Kansas State University*

BANKING

The year 1984 was a dramatic one for American banking. It witnessed the collapse and governmental rescue of Continental Illinois (one of the nation's ten largest banks), the failure of many smaller institutions, and the need to reschedule a large number of foreign loans—mainly to Latin America, at great expense to bank earnings.

One basic problem: energy prices had fallen and banks had made loans, both domestically and internationally, without taking into consideration what lower oil prices would do to the companies and countries that had taken out huge bank credits for petroleum development projects. As a result of the government's rescue of Continental Illinois, however, the United States has its first quasi-governmentally owned bank in more than 150 years.

The impact of these failures on the rest of the banking industry has been a turn to conservatism, a building up of reserves at the expense of earnings, and a policy of caution in lending policies.

A likely event in the future, therefore, is a change in the way banks are insured. Developments in 1984 showed that while a small bank can be allowed to fail, a large bank is too important to public confidence in the financial structure for the regulators to let it go under. The public has been told by regulatory statements and actions, in effect, that "size is strength." The large bank will be rescued, but the small will not. This could hurt the growth

AP/Wide World

Customers wait to collect their funds from the Orange County (CA) Heritage Bank, which was liquidated in March.

of smaller banks, unless insurance and protection policies are altered.

This situation is paradoxical, for 1984 saw a continuation of the trend to chartering new banks to meet changing and varied public needs. When the United States had 13,500 banks, many observers predicted the death of most smaller so-called "community banks," but now the nation has 15,300 banks, a development caused by the chartering of new institutions. Despite problems with rising interest rates, the number of thrifts has been rising because of new chartering of savings and loans.

The regulatory structure of American banking in 1984 has witnessed as much turmoil as has the operation of American banks.

The attempts of banks to get into other areas—notably insurance, investment banking, and general discount brokerage sales—and the efforts of nonbank companies (such as brokerage firms, Sears Roebuck, and many others) to get into commercial banking have led to the need for new laws to define what a bank is and who can own a bank. What has brought this need for new regulation to a head has been the effort of many nonbanks to get around legal restraints against their owning banks. They have done this by setting up so-called "nonbank banks"—banks that have deleted one service, usually commercial loans, from their portfolio—so that they no longer are legally considered banks under congressional definitions. In this way these nonbank banks are able to offer almost every bank service.

Congress tried to deal with this effort to take advantage of legal loopholes, but the House and Senate failed to agree on what action to take and proposed legislation died.

Another major trend during the year was the continuing geographical expansion of banks. Some large banks, notably Citibank of New York, have been able to become more and more nationwide organizations through the purchase of failing institutions in other states. Some states, moreover, have passed laws allowing their banks to be bought by out-of-state banks if their own banks are allowed to make similar purchases in the other state. Regional pacts have developed by means of which various states allow their banks to move interstate. These pacts generally have excluded large and powerful New York and California banks, out of fear that they would swallow the industry. These regional pacts are being tested in the courts, however, by banks that feel they have been illegally excluded from a region. In time, truly national banking is likely to develop if these regional pacts are ruled illegal.

Electronic banking continued to expand in 1984, notably through the growth of networks connecting Automatic Teller Machines (ATMs). While current law does not allow an individual to deposit money in a bank through an ATM unless the machine is located in his or her state, customers of banks that have joined networks can make withdrawals of cash anywhere in the nation. Banking in the home, through TV and telephone, has not advanced far, however, so it was in ATM growth that most customers in 1984 saw their banking service affected by electronics.

One consumer service trend whose growth has disturbed the banks is called "lifeline banking." Legislatures of certain states have declared that people unable to afford banking, or the young and the elderly, regardless of wealth, should get free banking service. Banks argue that no other industry is forced to give away service just because some people cannot pay for it. Banks are concerned about this trend of government to tell banks whom to serve and how much to charge.

Canada. A similar trend in expansion of operations has been apparent in Canada, and the rigid boundaries that have separated that nation's financial institutions for decades are tending to disintegrate. Banks, brokers, insurance, and trust companies—known as the "four pillars"—were taking advantage of legal loopholes to do business in competitors' territories, thereby blurring traditional regulatory boundaries.

Events in 1984 have continued to make the structure and differences more and more vague, while the growth of foreign bank operations in Canada has further developed the same type of "scrambled finance" that has been apparent in the United States.

PAUL S. NADLER, *Professor of Finance Rutgers—The State University of New Jersey*

BELGIUM

Economic recovery continued in Belgium during 1984, while terrorism and environmental issues were interjected into daily life.

Economy. The partial resurgence of the Belgium economy was the paramount factor throughout the year in this highly industrialized state. In 1981–82 the government had established a comprehensive austerity program to restore not only productivity but also international competitiveness. In 1984 there were many indications that Belgium was emerging successfully from its recession. Industrial output rose 2.7% in 1983 and approached 4% by the end of 1984. A rapid improvement in the balance of payments indicated a strong showing in world markets, and the current accounts deficit was turned into a modest surplus. The national deficit, which was 122 billion Belgian francs (ca $2.2 billion) in 1982, dropped to 10 billion (ca $180 million) in 1983 and was forecast to reach a surplus of 10 to 20 billion by the end of 1984.

Recovery was spotty, however, especially in the area of unemployment. Even though the growth of joblessness leveled off at 14%, there was concern because that figure appeared to be based mostly on structural problems in the traditional sunset industries of Wallonia. Rather dismal prospects in the smokestack areas of the south, combined with a continued decline in real wages, reduced consumer spending by over 2% per year. The coalition government of Prime Minister Wilfried Martens found itself in a dilemma, unable to decide whether to cut back business taxes to aid recovery or to respond to unemployment demands through social payments. Although the former approach has been stressed, political pressures from the political left, the trade unions, and Walloons in general have caused the government to modify its original emphasis on aid to business.

The gradual recovery has been based to a large extent on the emergence of a small but vibrant scientific and technological sector of the Belgian economy. Although the nation imports a vast majority of its advanced equipment, some high-tech items such as computers, software, and office equipment are emerging in the expanded telecommunications area.

Bombings. Terrorism reappeared in Belgium in 1984. A series of five bombings in both public and private buildings in October and November resulted in a tightening of security, particularly at NATO headquarters and the various multinational firms located in the nation's capital. Responsibility for the explosions, which did not result in any deaths, was not clearly determined but generally believed to be the acts of the Communist Combatant cells.

Environment. Belgium experienced a potential environmental crisis during 1984. In August the French freighter *Mont Louis* collided with

Isopress/Pictorial Parade

In Belgium in June, China's Zhao Ziyang met with King Baudouin. The two nations signed an investment accord.

a car ferry off the coast of Ostend in the English Channel and sank. Although the cargo included 240 tons (220 metric tons) of crystallized uranium hexafluoride, a form of uranium used to make fuel for nuclear reactors, assurances were given that the dangerous materials had not been released into the environment. No traces of radioactivity were found by Belgian public health authorities, but the accident caused great worries at a time when many Belgians were vacationing at the popular seaside resorts.

PIERRE-HENRI LAURENT
Tufts University

BELGIUM • Information Highlights

Official Name: Kingdom of Belgium.
Location: Northwestern Europe.
Area: 11,792 sq mi (30 540 km²).
Population (mid-1984 est.): 9,900,000.
Chief Cities (Dec. 31, 1981): Brussels, the capital, 994,774; Ghent, 237,687; Charleroi, 219,579; Liège, 211,528; Antwerp, 183,025; Bruges, 118,048.
Government: *Head of state,* Baudouin I, king (acceded 1951). *Head of government,* Wilfried Martens, prime minister (formed new government Dec. 1981). *Legislature*—Parliament: Senate and Chamber of Representatives.
Monetary Unit: Franc (62.25 francs equal U.S. $1, Oct. 22, 1984).
Gross Domestic Product (1982 U.S. $): $85,420,-000,000.
Economic Indexes (1983): *Consumer Prices* (1970 = 100), all items, 256.4; food, 225.2. *Industrial Production* (1975 = 100), 114.
Foreign Trade (1982 with Luxembourg U.S. $): *Imports,* $58,239,000,000; *exports,* $52,364,00,000.

129

BIOCHEMISTRY

The year 1983–84 saw significant discoveries in the field of biochemistry. Progress was made in biochemical understandings of cancer, Huntington's disease, Alzheimer's disease, and the role of RNA as a biological catalyst.

Cancer. Biochemists in recent years have identified more than 20 different oncogenes in cancer-causing animal viruses. These genes have the ability to transform normal cells into a cancerous state; similar genes—called proto-oncogenes—perform important functions in normal cells. Oncogenes are acquired by the viruses during the course of infection of the host cell. It is generally agreed that cancer develops in several steps and involves at least two oncogenes—one causing the cells to grow indefinitely and the other making them malignant. In 1983–84 biochemists attempted to find out what causes the genes to become oncogenic and make the cells cancerous, and what functions proto-oncogenes perform in normal cells.

A study conducted at the National Cancer Institute in Bethesda, MD, provided evidence that a single chemical change (point mutation) in a proto-oncogene can make normal cells become cancerous. Investigators analyzed a proto-oncogene called *ras* in the tumor tissue of a lung-cancer patient and in the normal tissue of the same patient. The *ras* gene consists of about 45,000 nucleotides, the building blocks of its DNA. The study showed that the gene from the tumor tissue differed from that in the normal tissue in just one nucleotide, suggesting that a single mutation activated the *ras* gene in the patient. Further evidence of this came from another study by the same biochemists. The *ras* gene from tumor cells of a female rat with mammary cancer was compared with the *ras* gene from normal tissue, and again they differed in a single nucleotide.

Not all cancers, however, are caused by point mutations in oncogenes. In some cases, it is caused by amplification of oncogenes—that is, when too many copies of a specific oncogene are made in the cell. This was reported by three different groups of biochemists, who found that in neuroblastomas (tumors of nerve cells), the cells contain many copies of an oncogene called *myc*.

Progress also was made in determining the function of proto-oncogenes in normal cells and how it is related to the development of cancer. First it was discovered that a protein synthesized under the direction of the *sis* oncogene has chemical similarities with a growth substance called PDGF, which helps heal wounds. Then a team of scientists found another link between a cancer gene and a natural substance that promotes cell growth. This link is considered critical because cancer is a process in which cell growth goes awry and cannot be turned off. What the team found was that the viral oncogene erb-B may be derived from the cellular gene that controls the formation of the receptor for epidermal growth factor (EGF). Receptors are proteins located in cell surfaces to which growth factor and other substances bind and elicit a specific response in the cell. The new research shows that erb-B causes production of a substance resembling part of the EGF receptor. But the substance is defective and acts as a signal to turn on cell growth abnormally, apparently without the EGF.

Alzheimer's and Huntington's Diseases. Alzheimer's disease (AD) is the most common form of dementia among the aged and is often responsible for senility. Huntington's disease (HD), also involving the brain, is a fatal nervous system disorder characterized by involuntary movement, intellectual impairment, and severe depression. In important breakthroughs, scientists identified a biochemical abnormality in AD and located the gene for HD.

Scientists at Harvard University compared samples of brain frozen at autopsy from six AD patients and from four persons with no history of AD. The AD brain was found to have half the normal level of RNA, a key chemical needed for protein synthesis. The diseased brain cells also contained increased levels of the active form of an enzyme, alkaline ribonuclease, that breaks down RNA. In the normal brain cells, the activity of this enzyme is relatively low because of the presence of an inhibitory protein. But in the diseased cells, the inhibitor was found to be either absent or ineffective. As a result, the ribonuclease is free to destroy RNA, leading to decreased protein synthesis. That decrease presumably interferes with proper brain function.

Using a recombinant DNA technique, biochemists succeeded in finding a genetic marker lying close to the gene for HD on chromosome 4. The finding is expected to allow diagnosis of HD before any symptoms appear. What the scientists did was use a restriction enzyme that cuts DNA at characteristic places. Depending on the DNA, the specific restriction enzyme can give one of four different patterns of DNA fragments; one of these patterns is linked with the HD gene. An individual whose DNA shows the same cutting patterns with that restriction enzyme is likely to have the disease.

RNA as Catalyst. Biochemists have recently discovered that RNA can carry out a catalytic function. A cell contains a variety of RNA molecules, of which three types are known to participate in assembling amino acids into a proper sequence in proteins. The new discovery shows that a specific RNA, without the presence of any protein, can act as a catalyst to trim segments of another specific RNA—transfer RNA—into their final and active form. The finding may help answer questions regarding the origin of life some 3.5 billion years ago.

PREM P. BATRA, *Wright State University*

BIOGRAPHY

A selection of profiles of persons prominent in the news during 1984 appears on pages 131–45. The affiliation of the contributor is listed on pages 589–92; biographies that do not include a contributor's name were prepared by the staff. Included are sketches of:

Alfonsín Foulkes, Raul	Lauren, Ralph	Peres, Shimon
Bombeck, Erma Louise	Lewis, Carl	Reagan, Ronald Wilson
Bush, George Herbert Walker	Ludlum, Robert	Sauvé, Jeanne
Chernenko, Konstantin Ustinovich	MacLaine, Shirley	Sondheim, Stephen Joshua
Ferraro, Geraldine Anne	Martins, Peter	Trudeau, Garry B.
Gandhi, Rajiv	Mondale, Walter Frederick	Trump, Donald John
Gromyko, Andrei Andreyevich	Mulroney, Martin Brian	Turner, John Napier
Hamilton, Scott	Nichols, Mike	Tutu, Desmond Mpilo
Hart, Gary Warren	O'Connor, John Joseph	
Jackson, Michael Joe	Payton, Walter	

ALFONSÍN FOULKES, Raúl

Raúl Alfonsín Foulkes became the 45th president of Argentina on Dec. 10, 1983, ending a series of military juntas that had exercised power since 1976. Alfonsín quickly responded to the dilemmas of contemporary Argentina, which included a serious debt problem and human-rights abuses by the unrestrained armed forces and military, as well as labor unrest.

The tough line that President Alfonsín took in mid-1984 against a debt repayment plan proposed by the International Monetary Fund (IMF) pleased Argentines. But his stance made it impossible for the country to obtain development loans from international sources or reschedule the $20 billion (U.S.) of its $43.6 billion foreign debt due in 1984. After Argentina announced its inability to pay $750 million due September 15 on a $1.1 billion bridge loan, Alfonsín hosted a conference of 11 debtor nations and appealed for regional solidarity on the economic crisis. In September, Alfonsín reached an agreement with the IMF on an austerity program in exchange for a $1.4 billion loan.

The chief executive rescinded an amnesty law for men in uniform decreed by the last military junta and ordered courts-martial for military commanders accused of the illegal arrest, torture, and murder of thousands of Argentines. All nine members of the three juntas ruling Argentina between 1976 and 1983 were to be prosecuted. An ambitious human-rights committee appointed by Alfonsín was able to document 8,800 cases of abductions and disappearances under military rule. The resulting unrest in military circles caused President Alfonsín to dismiss four generals from the military high command on July 4, thus reasserting civilian supremacy over the armed forces.

A general strike by organized labor occurred on September 3, nine months after Alfonsín's inauguration. The 24-hour stoppage was about 50% effective. Its purpose was to demand greater wage and salary increases.

On the foreign policy front, little was accomplished by the Alfonsín government in reopening negotiations with Great Britain over the future of the Falkland (Malvinas) Islands. Another international dispute that Alfonsín was attempting to resolve involved three tiny islands in the Beagle Channel that were claimed by both Argentina and Chile. A settlement reached on October 19, awarding the disputed islands to Chile, was approved by congress and the people. Despite the various difficulties, President Alfonsín's personal popularity remained strong.

Background. Alfonsín was born in Chascomús, a small town in Buenos Aires province, on March 12, 1927. A military-school graduate and lawyer, he has been active in the Radical Civic Union (UCR) since the 1950s. By 1972 the future president had organized a reform movement within the UCR that challenged the dominance of veteran party leader Ricardo Balbín. After Balbín's death

in 1981 the party leadership gravitated toward Alfonsín, who was nominated as its presidential candidate in July 1983. In a hard-fought campaign to return democracy to Argentina, underdog Alfonsín upset his Peronist opponent, Italo Luder. The UCR victory ended the longtime dominance of Argentine politics by the Peronist party.

Alfonsín is married to María Lorenza Barreneche, and they have six children.

LARRY L. PIPPIN

BOMBECK, Erma Louise

Finding humor in the humdrum concerns of the suburban housewife and mother, Erma Bombeck has emerged as one of America's most popular comic writers. The latest of her seven books, *Motherhood: The Second Oldest Profession,* was published in 1983 and stayed on the best-seller lists well into 1984. Her thrice-weekly newspaper column is syndicated in more than 900 papers in the United States and Canada. She has written numerous articles for major magazines, as well as television scripts, lectures, and a record album. Bombeck also appears regularly on ABC-TV's *Good Morning America* show.

"My type of humor is almost pure identification," Bombeck has said. "A housewife reads my column and says 'But that's happened to *me*.' I know just what she's talking about." With a pathos born of personal experience and a style based on wild exaggeration, Bombeck cracks cathartic one-liners about everything from ironing ("my second favorite chore, my first being hitting my head on the top bunk bed until I faint") to the husband who watches too much football ("like a dead sponge surrounded by bottle caps").

The 5'2", 125-lb (1.57-m, 57-kg) resident of Phoenix lists her age as "somewhere between estrogen and death" and describes herself as quiet, simple, and ordinary. "Everyone thinks of ordinary as some kind of skin disease," she jokes.

Background. Born Feb. 21, 1927, in Dayton, OH, Erma Louise Fiste knew what she wanted to do from the eighth grade on. At Patterson Vocational High School she wrote a humor column for the school paper, and after graduating she went to work as a copy girl for the Dayton *Journal Herald.* A year later Erma enrolled at the University of Dayton, where she majored in journalism and continued writing humor. After getting her B.A. in 1949, Bombeck went back to work as a reporter for the *Journal Herald.* In that same year, she was married to William Lawrence (Bill) Bombeck, who later became a school administrator.

When her first child, Betsy, was born in 1953, Bombeck left work to become a housewife and mother. At age 37, following the births of sons Andrew and Matthew, Erma was bored and yearning for something else to do. "Too old for a paper route, too young for social

Rod Moyer, McGraw-Hill

Erma Bombeck

administration's "crisis manager." He chairs the Special Situation Group, which is convened to deal with foreign-policy crises such as the role of the U.S. Marines in Lebanon. Bush helped persuade Reagan to order the withdrawal of the Marines in February 1984 when it became apparent the Lebanese government was on the verge of collapse.

Background. George Herbert Walker Bush was born June 12, 1924, in Milton, MA. He attended Phillips Academy and Yale University, graduating Phi Beta Kappa in 1948. A Navy pilot in World War II, he was decorated with the Distinguished Flying Cross after being shot down over the Pacific in 1944. Bush made his fortune in the oil drilling business in Texas. He served two terms (1967–1971) as a Republican representative to the House from Houston. Bush, who lost races for the Senate in 1964 and 1970, was named UN ambassador and then chairman of the Republican National Committee by President Richard Nixon. President Gerald Ford appointed him U.S. envoy to China and head of the CIA. After losing his bid for the presidency in 1980 to Reagan, he gained enough strength among moderate Republicans to become Reagan's logical choice for vice-president.

The son of the late U.S. Sen. Prescott Bush (R-CT), George Bush married the former Barbara Pierce in 1945. They have four sons and a daughter.

ELEANOR CLIFT

security, and too tired for an affair," she persuaded a small local paper to print her humor articles on what she called the "utility-room beat." The next year the *Journal Herald* hired her for two columns a week, and shortly thereafter she was syndicated by Newsday Specials. In 1970 her thrice-weekly articles were taken over by Publishers-Hall Syndicate and then the Field Newspaper Syndicate.

Bombeck's first book, *At Wit's End* (1967), was a selection of her newspaper columns. That volume was followed by *Just Wait Till You Have Children of Your Own* (with cartoonist Bil Keane, 1971); *I Lost Everything in the Post-Natal Depression* (1974); *The Grass is Always Greener Over the Septic Tank* (1976); *If Life is a Bowl of Cherries, What Am I Doing in the Pits?* (1978); *Aunt Erma's Cope Book* (1979); and *Motherhood (1983)*.

BUSH, George

With the 1984 reelection of President Ronald Reagan, Vice-President George Bush became a leading candidate for the presidency in 1988. Although his views are more moderate than Reagan's on everything from abortion to taxes, his loyalty and unflagging enthusiasm on the campaign trail should guarantee him Reagan's endorsement. As the president's chief surrogate, Bush traveled full-time during the 1984 campaign, reminding voters that Democratic candidate Walter Mondale was Jimmy Carter's vice-president and that he should be held accountable for the failures of the Carter administration.

Because his rival for the job was a woman, Geraldine A. Ferraro, more attention than usual was paid to Bush's campaign style. His press secretary described his approach as "hard-nosed and high-road." Although Bush attacked the opposition, his natural reserve and Ivy-League demeanor softened the blows. In a nationally televised debate with Ferraro, Bush demonstrated his familiarity with foreign policy. Polls showed Bush triumphed in the "heartbeat away" issue, meaning that voters felt he was more qualified to step into the presidency at a moment's notice than Ferraro.

Bush has one of the most impressive résumés in government. Among the positions he has held are ambassador to the United Nations (1971–72), U.S. representative to the People's Republic of China (1974–75), and director of the Central Intelligence Agency (1976–77).

In the White House, Reagan has tapped Bush's knowledge, particularly in foreign affairs. Bush is the

CHERNENKO, Konstantin Ustinovich

When the ailing Yuri Andropov died on Feb. 9, 1984, after only 15 months as general secretary of the Communist Party of the Soviet Union, four days passed before Konstantin Chernenko, a colorless 72-year-old Brezhnev loyalist, was confirmed as the new Soviet leader. The Politburo apparently had been divided between those who favored a return to the conservative policies of Brezhnev and younger men who wanted to continue Andropov's reforms. Thus, Chernenko began his tenure as head of party and state significantly weaker politically than either of his immediate predecessors and was in no position to disavow the recent reforms. A transitional figure, Chernenko filled the gap between the stagnant stability of the Brezhnev years and the changes expected to come with a new generation of leaders. In his first months at the top, he took a hard line toward the United States, refusing to renew arms-control talks suspended in late 1983 after the U.S. deployment of Cruise and Pershing II missiles in Western Europe. Analysts in the West believed that Foreign Minister Andrei Gromyko (see BIOGRAPHY) and the Soviet defense establishment were playing the dominant role in the formulation of Soviet foreign policy and that Chernenko was merely acting as chairman of an aging collective leadership. Chernenko himself was the oldest man ever to take over the top seat in the Soviet hierarchy. The general secretary's first public appearances were marked by hesitancy, and in subsequent months he was absent from public view for long periods. There was growing speculation in the West that, as had been the case with his predecessor, Chernenko was in failing health.

Background. Konstantin Ustinovich Chernenko was born in the village of Bolshaya Tes in the Krasnoyarsk region of Siberia on Sept. 24, 1911. He came from a large peasant family, and he left school at age 12 to work as a farmer. Chernenko joined Komsomol, the Young Communist League, in 1926 and the Communist Party five years later. He held several party positions in Krasnoyarsk, becoming regional secretary in 1941. Chernenko was transferred in 1948 to the new Moldavian Republic, where two years later Leonid Brezhnev became the party leader. As Brezhnev's career flourished, so did that of his close collaborator.

In 1956, Chernenko followed Brezhnev to Moscow and was named propaganda chief of the Central Committee apparatus. When Brezhnev became chairman of the presidium (president) in 1960, Chernenko became a member of that body. In 1964, Brezhnev succeeded

Khrushchev as first secretary of the party, and Chernenko was made head of the important General Department of the Central Committee. In 1971, Chernenko became an actual member of the Central Committee, in 1976 he joined the party Secretariat, and in 1978 he was made a full member of the Politburo. Brezhnev was thought to favor Chernenko as his successor, but when he died in November 1982, the Politburo majority chose Chernenko's rival, Andropov. Most Western observers believed that Chernenko's career had ended with this defeat, and his 1984 appointments as general secretary of the party and president of the Soviet Union came as a surprise. Because of Chernenko's advanced age and uncertain health, maneuvering for his successor may have already been underway from the first days of his administration.

RONALD GRIGOR SUNY

FERRARO, Geraldine Anne

As the first woman on the national ticket of a major political party, Geraldine A. Ferraro brought a much-needed sense of excitement to Walter Mondale's uphill race for the presidency. Mondale's choice of Ferraro as his running mate was greeted with euphoria at the Democratic Convention in San Francisco. Polls taken soon after showed that the addition of the three-term congresswoman from Queens, NY, had narrowed the gap against President Ronald Reagan to within five points. But those heady gains soon gave way to Ferraro's finances became the subject of intense focus in the press. Her husband, New York real-estate developer John A. Zaccaro, reluctantly agreed to release some of his tax returns. In a 90-minute televised press conference, Ferraro defended the propriety of family loans to her first congressional campaign, an inadvertent underpayment of taxes, and her husband's business practices. Her candor quieted the controversy. However the House Ethics Committee conducted an investigation and found that she unintentionally violated the ethics in government act. No sanctions were imposed.

Ferraro was also embroiled in a controversy with the bishops of the Roman Catholic Church over her stand on abortion. While a Catholic herself and opposed to abortion, Ferraro nevertheless embraces freedom of choice in public policy. The bishops held press conferences to denounce her position, and antiabortion pickets dogged her at every campaign stop.

A lawyer and a former prosecutor, Ferraro conducted herself well in a 90-minute debate with Vice-President George Bush in October. Despite the overwhelming defeat in November of the Mondale-Ferraro ticket, she remains a strong poltical force for the future.

Background. Geraldine Anne Ferraro was born Aug. 26, 1935, in Newburgh, NY. Her father, an Italian immigrant, died when she was eight years old. The family moved to the Bronx, where Ferraro's mother eked out a living as a seamstress. After graduating from Marymount Manhattan College in 1956, Ferraro got a teacher's certificate from Hunter College and taught English in New York public schools. She attended Fordham Law School at night and passed the New York Bar exam in 1960. To honor her mother, who made her schooling possible, Ferraro continued to use her maiden name after marrying John Zaccaro in 1960. The couple has three children.

In 1974, Ferraro's cousin, Queens District Attorney Nicholas Ferraro, hired her as an assistant district attorney. She specialized in cases of child abuse, rape, and domestic violence. In 1978, Ferraro ran for Congress in Queens, the working-class community that was the home of Archie Bunker in the television series *All In The Family.* Her campaign slogan was "Finally, A Tough Democrat." Although Ferraro is liberal on most issues, she won reelection twice (in 1980 and 1982) from her conservative district. In accepting her party's nomination, Ferraro noted her humble beginnings and declared, "I stand before you to proclaim tonight: America is a land where dreams can come true for all of us."

ELEANOR CLIFT

GANDHI, Rajiv

On Oct. 31, 1984, Rajiv Gandhi, a relative newcomer to Indian politics, was sworn in as prime minister of India, following the assassination of his mother, Prime Minister Indira Gandhi. In 1980, Rajiv reluctantly gave up his position as a pilot with Indian Airlines to "help Mummy," after his younger brother, Sanjay, who was obviously being groomed as Mrs. Gandhi's successor, was killed in an airplane crash in June. A year later he was elected to Parliament from the Amethi constituency in Uttar Pradesh, a seat that his brother had previously held. Thereafter he became more active in political affairs, assisting his mother in running the government and in reorganizing her Congress (I) party. In February 1983 he became a general secretary of the party.

A quiet, soft-spoken man, unlike his more assertive and abrasive brother, Rajiv developed an image as "Mr. Clean." He was soon recognized as the central figure in the move to revitalize the Congress (I) party and to deal with problems of demoralization, corruption, and venality. Increasingly he became a spokesman for the government and his party on a wide range of national and international issues. Thus his political experience was intensive, if brief. He was the obvious choice to replace his mother, especially during the troubled period following her assassination. As *The New York Times* New Delhi correspondent observed shortly after Rajiv assumed office: "He now wears both the mantle of a martyr's son and that of the Nehru dynasty."

As 1984 ended, the new prime minister led his Congress (I) party to overwhelming victory in parliamentary elections and began preparing to "swiftly take India forward." (*See* INDIA.)

Background. The first of two children of Indira and Feroze Gandhi, Rajiv was born on Aug. 20, 1944. When his grandfather, Jawaharlal Nehru, became prime minister of newly independent India, his mother became her father's hostess and comrade, and Rajiv was brought up in the prime minister's official residence in New Delhi. He attended the prestigious Doon School in India and then spent two years each at the Imperial Scientific and Technical College in London and at Cambridge University, where he received a degree in mechanical engineering in 1965. Returning to India, he trained to be a commercial pilot, and he served as a pilot with Indian Airlines for about ten years. Throughout this period he and his wife, Sonia, daughter of an Italian businessman who became a naturalized Indian citizen, and their two children—a son, Rahul, and a daughter, Priyaka—lived with his mother, who was then prime minister. Prior to his brother's death, Rajiv had shown little interest in politics.

NORMAN D. PALMER

GROMYKO, Andrei Andreyevich

After the death of Soviet party chief Yuri Andropov in February 1984 and his replacement by Konstantin Chernenko, responsibility for key foreign policy decisions fell inevitably to longtime Foreign Minister Andrei Gromyko. The 74-year-old Politburo member had been a central figure in world politics for more than four decades, and he had met every U.S. president since Franklin Roosevelt. In recent months he had played a key role in Soviet-American relations, which went from bad to worse after the Soviet walkout from Geneva arms-limitation talks in November 1983.

With the change in Soviet leadership, the difficult times in East-West relations, and the jockeying for position by U.S. presidential candidates, Gromyko was much in the news in 1984. His stolid appearance and serious demeanor seemed to convey Soviet toughness. Early in the year, he warned of a "perilous slide into the abyss" unless the United States reversed its decision to deploy nuclear missiles in Europe. In September at the United Nations, he cited "Washington's deliberate intention to

Andrei Gromyko

wreck the negotiations on strategic arms." At the same time, however, Gromyko's words often stressed willingness to explore possibilities for compromise. On September 28, the Soviet foreign minister met with President Ronald Reagan at the White House in the first contact between top U.S. and Soviet leaders since Reagan took office. The previous day, Gromyko met in New York with Democratic candidate Walter Mondale.

Background. The future foreign minister was born on July 18, 1909, in Starye Gromyk in Byelorussia. He was educated at the Minsk Institute of Agriculture and entered the Communist Party in 1931. He worked as an economist until entering the foreign ministry in 1939. Like many of his generation, he benefited from the Stalin purges of 1937–1939 and rose rapidly through the party ranks. By 1943, at the age of 34, he became ambassador to the United States. He participated in the Dumbarton Oaks Conference, the Big Three meetings at Yalta and Potsdam, and the founding conference for the United Nations in San Francisco. In 1946, Gromyko became the permanent Soviet representative to the UN Security Council. He returned to Moscow two years later and was made first deputy foreign minister.

It was during the regime of Nikita Khrushchev that Gromyko's career really accelerated. He was raised to the Central Committee of the party in 1956 and named foreign minister in 1957. A loyal functionary for the post-Stalin leadership, Gromyko was involved in the implementation and coexistence and détente policies of the 1960s and 1970s. Under President Leonid Brezhnev he was elevated to membership in the Politburo (1973) and was involved in the negotiations for the SALT I and SALT II agreements. As U.S.-Soviet relations deteriorated after the invasion of Afghanistan in December 1979, Gromyko began taking a harder line with the West.

Cultured and well-read, Gromyko speaks English fluently and is said to have a good sense of humor. At home in the Soviet Union, he enjoys playing chess with his wife, Lidiya, and hunting boar. Even his adversaries admire his diplomatic skills. He is considered tough and shrewd, a master tactician.

RONALD GRIGOR SUNY

HAMILTON, Scott

A childhood disease stunted his growth, and physicians feared it might kill him. He survived the illness and became one of the most dynamic, most admired, and most successful figure skaters in the history of the sport. On Feb. 16, 1984, Scott Hamilton capped a brilliant amateur career by winning a gold medal in the Olympic Winter Games at Sarajevo, Yugoslavia. The following month he won the world championship in Ottawa, Canada. It was his 17th consecutive victory in major competition, going back to 1981. All in all, he captured four U.S. championships and four world titles—as well as the Olympic gold.

Hoping to change the unmasculine image of his sport, Hamilton abandoned the traditional figure-skating costume with beads and sequins in favor of a one-piece stretch suit similar to those worn by speed skaters. His performances combine dazzling athletic ability with personal charisma, charm, and a pixieish sense of humor. At only 5'3", 115 lbs (1.60 m, 52 kg), he brings a giant determination onto the ice. Preparing for the Olympics, Hamilton would sometimes work out for six hours a day.

Background. Scott Hamilton was born Aug. 28, 1958, in Toledo, OH. He was a few weeks old when he was adopted by Ernest and Dorothy Hamilton, professors at Bowling Green University in Ohio. When Scott was two, the Hamiltons realized that he had stopped growing. Doctors determined that his body was not properly absorbing the nutrients from his food. Six years went by, however, before the ailment was diagnosed precisely as Shwachman's syndrome, a rare illness similar to cystic fibrosis.

About that time, Scott went to a nearby rink to watch his sister Susan ice skate. Although he had a feeding tube leading to his stomach, Scott wanted to try skating. He did, and he loved it.

A few more casual outings were followed by lessons. Perhaps because of the exercise and cold air, his illness began to disappear and Scott began to grow. So did his fondness for skating.

Scott Hamilton

With dedicated training and expert coaching, Hamilton qualified for the 1980 U.S. Olympic team. The up-and-coming star finished a respectable fifth in the 1980 Games and carried the U.S. flag in the opening ceremonies. He had been elected for his struggle in overcoming his childhood disease.

Four years later at Sarajevo, Hamilton again carried an American flag. This time it was during his victory lap after being awarded the gold medal.

Later in 1984, Hamilton began his professional skating career with a touring ice show.

FRANK LITSKY

HART, Gary Warren

Sen. Gary Hart (D-CO) was the surprise of the 1984 presidential primary season. His upset victory in New Hampshire over former Vice-President Walter Mondale set the stage for a bitter struggle for the Democratic nomination. Hart's appeal was greatest among younger, white-collar Democrats and Independents—called "yuppies," political shorthand for "young, upwardly mobile professionals." Although his campaign was underfinanced and poorly organized compared with that of front-runner Mondale, Hart won almost as many states (24 to Mondale's 25), carrying all of New England and every Western primary and caucus with the exception of the one in Texas. Hart also did not carry the state of Kentucky.

Senator Hart said that he spoke for a new generation of Americans and that his presidency would be one of "new ideas." But he was unable to successfully articulate those ideas against a barrage of negative campaigning by Mondale, who borrowed the slogan "Where's the beef?" to challenge Hart to come up with specifics. Hart fought back, charging Mondale with being unduly influenced by Big Labor and "pandering" to minorities and women in his vice-presidential selection process. But lingering questions over Hart's age (he sometimes presented himself as a year younger) and why he had changed his name (from Hartpence) undermined his credibility.

Hart went to the Democratic Convention in San Francisco more than 800 delegates behind Mondale and $3.5 million in debt. He refused to withdraw, however, arguing that public opinion polls showed him stronger than Mondale against President Ronald Reagan. When the Democrats nominated Mondale on the first ballot, Hart bowed out quietly, promising he would not be "a spoiler."

Background. Gary Hart was born Nov. 28, 1937, in Ottawa, KS. He was raised in the fundamentalist Christian Nazarene religion and attended Bethany Nazarene College in Bethany, OK. He went to Yale Divinity School and then to Yale Law School, graduating in 1964. After a brief stint in Washington at the Justice and Interior Departments, Hart moved to Denver in 1967 to practice law. In 1972 he quit his practice to run the presidential campaign of George McGovern. Although McGovern was beaten badly by Richard Nixon in the general election, Hart gained national recognition for his role in securing him the Democratic nomination. His book *Right From The Start* describes the tactics he used to steer McGovern through a maze of newly created primaries and caucuses.

His immersion in politics complete, Hart won election to the U.S. Senate from Colorado in 1974 and was reelected in 1980. His record in the Senate has been consistently liberal on such issues as civil rights and abortion, but he considers himself a "New Generation" Democrat on defense and economic affairs, favoring tighter fiscal controls and a measured military buildup. His book *A New Democracy*, published in 1983, sketches his positions on various issues.

Hart married the former Lee Ludwig in 1958. They have two children, Andrea and John.

ELEANOR CLIFT

Gary Hart

AP/Wide World

JACKSON, Michael Joe

By 1984 pop singer Michael Jackson's phenomenal international success merited comparison with that of The Beatles and Elvis Presley. At 25, Jackson had surpassed many of their achievements. His unique fusion of R&B, rock, and pop musical styles defied categorization. His appeal cut across barriers of age and race.

Jackson's 1983 album *Thriller* was the largest-selling album in history at 35 million copies worldwide. It produced seven Top Ten singles, smashing his own previous record of four, set in 1979 with *Off the Wall*. In 1984 the singer also received an unprecedented eight Grammy awards and a Presidential Special Achievement Award. Jackson's videos of the songs "Billie Jean," "Beat It," and "Thriller" were fast-paced visual vignettes spotlighting his spectacular vocals and dancing. *Making Michael Jackson's Thriller* became the best selling home music video in history.

Jackson's summer 1984 Victory Tour with his brothers was both technically and commercially the largest concert tour ever mounted. Jackson's personal attention to his career brought him an estimated fortune of more than $75 million. His business acumen and flamboyant public image—sequined costumes, dark sunglasses, and the trademark single glove—were in marked contrast to his reclusive private life.

Background. Born in Gary, IN, on Aug. 29, 1958, Michael became lead singer and focal point of The Jackson 5 by age 11. Managed by their father, Joseph, the five brothers between 1969 and 1975 recorded 11 albums and numerous hit singles on Motown Records—among them "I Want You Back," "ABC," and "I'll Be There." Michael began a parallel solo career on Motown in 1971 with the hit single and album *Got To Be There*. During the early 1970s, Michael and The Jackson 5 appeared frequently on television—they even had their own series—and headlined in Las Vegas. By 1975, however, their popularity was on the wane.

In 1976 they moved to Epic Records and became The Jacksons. With Michael at the helm, the group returned to the Top Ten with "Enjoy Yourself." The LP *Destiny* in 1978 marked a turning point for Jackson; it tapped his abundant writing and production skills for the first time. In 1978, Michael appeared in the film *The Wiz* with mentor Diana Ross. There he met producer Quincy Jones, with whom he recorded his Epic solo debut, *Off the Wall*, in 1979. A runaway critical and commercial success, it produced a record-breaking four Top Ten singles. One of these, "Don't Stop 'Til You Get Enough," won Jackson a Grammy. Michael's ascendancy became ever more clear as *Off the Wall*'s sales topped $7 million.

The year 1983 marked both the release of the meticulously crafted *Thriller* and the emergence of Michael Jackson as a charismatic adult entertainer. Motown's 25th Anniversary TV special showcased Jackson's breathtaking dancing and vocals. Videos confirmed his extraordinary talent and kept him in the public eye despite few personal appearances.

PAULETTE WEISS

LAUREN, Ralph

Some fortunes may have been built on a shoestring; that of fashion designer Ralph Lauren began with a tie. In 1967 he designed a line of expensive handmade ties for the firm of Beau Brummel. He named the collection "Polo" because, to him, the sport epitomizes a lifestyle of elegance. To further this concept, in 1969 he established Polo as a separate menswear design company, and, based on its success, he introduced his ready-to-wear collection for women in 1971. By 1981 this image had propelled the Polo logo into one of the more popular men's and women's fashion-accessory categories as well as into children's wear, furs, cosmetics, and fragrances.

In 1983, feeling strongly that his clothes were an accurate reflection of the lifestyle of his clients, he expanded the Polo name into home furnishings by creating what he called "a total environment." This included the design of sheets, towels and related textiles, tableware, decorating accessories, and wall coverings. He also established a network of shops across the United States carrying only Polo merchandise as a showcase for his design point of view. And, in conjunction with Diana Vreeland and The Costume Institute of the Metropolitan Museum, he sponsored an exhibition of clothing, painting, and sculpture titled "Man and the Horse" in late 1984.

With no formal design training but a profound appreciation for the classics of fashion, Ralph Lauren has become a force. A purist who works only in natural fibers and traditional fabrics, his strength is in the way he reworks these classics—refining their lines, recoloring their fabrics, and updating their proportions. Whether it is an English hacking jacket, Ivy League campus clothes, or American Western wear, he elevates them to new fashion significance by his styling and his attention to detail in order to achieve a total look. His list of awards is impressive.

He also costumed the male stars in the film *The Great Gatsby* (1974) and designed the wardrobes of Woody Allen and Diane Keaton for *Annie Hall* (1977), a film that sparked the menswear look for women.

Background. Ralph Lauren was born in the Bronx, NY, Oct. 14, 1939. His fashion career began as a department store salesman where he worked during the day while taking business courses at night at the City College of New York. After a tour in the Army, he worked as an assistant buyer at Allied Stores before becoming the neckwear designer at Beau Brummel in 1967.

He is married to Ricky Law Beer (1964) and has two sons, Andrew and David, and a daughter, Dylan. Their residences include an apartment in Manhattan, a Montauk, NY, home, a Colorado ranch, and a cottage in Jamaica.

ANN ELKINS

LEWIS, Carl

Not since the legendary Jesse Owens in 1936 had any track-and-field athlete won four gold medals in a single Olympics. Yet when 23-year-old Carl Lewis accomplished the feat at the 1984 Games in Los Angeles, there was a vague sense of anticlimax. In the eyes of many, the result had been a foregone conclusion. For a year or more there had been talk of Lewis winning gold in the 100-m dash, 200-m dash, long jump, and 4 x 100-m relay. And when it came down to the actual competition in the LA Coliseum, there was little in the way of real challenge. Lewis was a cut above—and steps ahead of—the world's best.

Sporting a new flat-top haircut, the 6'3", 180-lb (1.9-m, 82-kg) Lewis flashed to his first victory in the 100 meters. His time of 9.9 seconds gave him the widest winning margin in the history of the Olympic event. Next came Carl's favorite event, the long jump. His very first leap of 28'1¼" (8.54 m) gave him the gold by nearly a foot. Then came an Olympic record of 19.80 seconds in the 200. And to close out his performance, Lewis ran the anchor leg for the winning U.S. 4 x 100-m relay team, which set a new world record of 37.83 seconds.

Cool, independent, and abundantly self-confident, Lewis stood at the top of the track world even before the 1984 Olympics. Taking full advantage of the relaxed rules of amateurism for track-and-field athletes, Carl amassed a modest fortune endorsing products, making personal appearances, and competing in major U.S. and international meets.

Shunning the media, he spends much time at his plush, Victorian-style house in suburban Houston, where his collection of fine china and crystal is prominently displayed.

Background. Carl Lewis was born and raised in the suburban, middle-class community of Willingboro, NJ. His parents, Evelyn and Bill, had both been accomplished runners, and his two older brothers and older sister also excelled in sports. (Carol, in fact, also competed in the 1984 Olympics but fell short of a medal.)

Carl was short, skinny, and shy as a boy, but at age 8 he was running for a club track team coached by his parents. It wasn't until he was 15 that Carl showed any exceptional talent. He grew 2½ inches (6 cm) in two months and proceeded to run a 100-yd dash in 9.3 seconds and long jump 25 ft (7.62 m). By his senior year in high school he leaped an astonishing 26'8" (8.13 m).

Carl continued his exploits at the University of Houston, where he majored in radio and TV but left during his junior year. Training under coach Tom Tellez, Lewis gave notice of his imminent Olympic heroics by winning three individual events at the 1983 World Track and Field Championships in Helsinki, Finland.

See also SPORTS (page 465).

LUDLUM, Robert

Since the publication of *The Scarlatti Inheritance* in 1971, Robert Ludlum's novels of intrigue and derring-do together have sold more than 60 million copies in 23 languages. When his latest novel, *The Aquitaine Progression,* climbed to the top of best-seller lists in 1984, it confirmed his position as one of the most popular authors in the world.

A former actor and theater producer, Ludlum did not turn to writing until the age of 42. He then chose a genre that has since snowballed in popularity—the spy thriller. *The Scarlatti Inheritance,* his first novel, is set in pre-World War II Germany and details an international plot to finance the Nazis. It set the pattern for the string of tales that followed. In *The Aquitaine Progression,* for example, a young American lawyer unearths a ruthless scheme to take over the world. Ludlum's novels have been criticized for being plodding in style and incredible in plot, but the rate at which they are being snapped up makes it clear that his readers are loyal and find them spellbinding.

Robert Ludlum

Background. Robert Ludlum was born on May 25, 1927, in New York City, the son of a successful businessman. He attended private high school and had his first taste of acting in a school play. The taste proved addictive; at 14 he ran away from school and, under an assumed name, took a part in the 1941 New York farce *Junior Miss.* Eventually he returned to school, served in the U.S. Marine Corps during World War II, and earned a B.A. degree at Wesleyan University. In 1951, while still in college, he married Mary Ryducha, an aspiring actress.

During the 1950s, Ludlum acted in productions at New England repertory theaters and in New York City. He also appeared in a number of live television dramas, on such shows as *Studio One* and *Kraft Television Theatre.* By 1960, however, he had determined that he was better suited to producing plays, and he went on to produce more than 370. He also was a founder of the Playhouse-on-the-Mall in Paramus, NJ.

Despite his success, Ludlum became increasingly unhappy with the financial pressures of theatrical life, and in 1969 he gave up the theater to write full time. Following the success of *The Scarlatti Inheritance,* he went on to write *The Osterman Weekend* (1972), *The Matlock Paper* (1973), *The Matarese Circle* (1979), *The Bourne Identity* (1980), *The Parsifal Mosaic* (1982), and other novels, some under the pen name Jonathan Ryder. Several of the novels have been made into films.

Without firsthand experience of espionage, Ludlum gleans most of the factual material for his tales through travel and library research. He lives in Connecticut with his wife; they have three grown children.

ELAINE PASCOE

MacLAINE, Shirley

Shirley MacLaine marked her 50th birthday in 1984 by scoring a triple success—as a stage entertainer, a best-selling author, and a film actress. Her stage revue, *Shirley MacLaine on Broadway*—an evening of songs, dancing, and recollections of past movie roles—brought critical raves. Her book, *Out on a Limb,* a mixture of autobiography and spiritualism, climbed to the top of *The New York Times* paperback best-seller list. And her role in the James Brooks film *Terms of Endearment* won her an Academy Award as best actress.

The Oscar confirmed MacLaine's status as an accomplished dramatic actress. Once dubbed the "queen of kooks," in *Terms* she portrayed Aurora Greenway, an overbearing but in the end likable character who ages ungracefully, fighting all the way. But the actress did not view her achievement as the culmination of her career. "I love the idea of being 50," she told interviewers, "because the best is yet to come."

Background. Shirley MacLean Beaty was born April 24, 1934, in Richmond, VA. She began studying ballet at age 3—at about the time her brother, actor Warren Beatty, was born. By the age of 12, Shirley was attending the Washington School of Ballet five afternoons a week. When she grew too tall for ballet, however, she opted for musical theater. During and after high school she landed several chorus-line parts in New York.

Her first break came in 1954, when, as understudy for Carol Haney in *The Pajama Game* on Broadway, she had a chance to perform as the lead dancer. Her success brought a movie contract and led to her first film role, in Alfred Hitchcock's *The Trouble with Harry* (1955).

Films that followed included *Some Came Running* (1958), *The Apartment* (1960), and *Irma La Douce* (1963), each of which earned her Academy Award nominations. By the mid-1960s, MacLaine had established a reputation as an impishly attractive and highly individual star with a flair for comedy. But she was dissatisfied, as she put it, with playing "hookers and doormats." She slowed down her film career and became increasingly involved in politics, campaigning for Democratic candidates. She traveled widely and became an outspoken critic of the Vietnam War and a strong supporter of civil rights. In 1973 she toured the People's Republic of China and produced an acclaimed documentary film, *The Other Half of the Sky,* about that country.

In the mid-1970s, MacLaine put together a nightclub act that toured in the United States and abroad. She also starred in several television specials and continued to act in films; she again was nominated for an Academy Award for *The Turning Point* (1977). Still active in poli-

Shirley MacLaine

Photos, AP/Wide World

tics, she also became interested in spiritualism—reincarnation, out-of-the-body experiences, and other occult phenomena.

MacLaine divides her time among homes in New York, California, and the state of Washington. She was divorced in 1982 and has one daughter. In addition to *Out on a Limb,* she has written two other autobiographical books, *Don't Fall Off the Mountain* (1970) and *You Can Get There from Here* (1975).

ELAINE PASCOE

MARTINS, Peter

When Peter Martins danced at a gala in Clearwater, FL, on Jan. 7, 1984, it was a performance, he said, that marked his last appearance onstage as a ballet dancer. Martins' retirement from dancing at the age of 37 was widely considered premature and came as a shock to those who had admired him as an internationally acclaimed star with the New York City Ballet for more than 15 years.

In March 1983 the Danish-born dancer had become, with Jerome Robbins, co-director of the company. Each was given the new title of balletmaster-in-chief. George Balanchine, the City Ballet's artistic director, had been ill by then for many months. When Balanchine died on April 30, 1983, Martins found himself entrusted with the day-to-day operations of the troupe while Robbins concentrated on creating new ballets and on overall policy. Faced with his new duties, Martins also made clear that his prime interest was choreography, a "passion" that had grown since he created his first ballet, *Calcium Light Night,* in 1977. Performing was no longer a priority, Martins said.

Three ballets by Martins had premieres in 1984: *A Schubertiad* and the Bach *Réjouissance* for the City Ballet, as well as *Mozart Violin Concerto* for the Pennsylvania Ballet, where Martins had been artistic adviser since 1982. With these, Martins had now choreographed 19

Peter Martins

Martha Swope

ballets; a solo on ice for the skater John Curry; the dancing in *Dido and Aeneas* for the New York City Opera; and numbers in two musicals, *Dream of the Twins* and *On Your Toes.*

Martins entered this watershed year in his career with public recognition as one of ballet's most eloquent classical male dancers. In the summer of 1983, Queen Margrethe II of Denmark made him a Knight of the Order of the Dannebrog. Martins ended his dancing career with the City Ballet in *The Nutcracker,* in which he had made his New York debut with the troupe in December 1967. After his final performance on Dec. 6, 1983, Robbins crowned him with a laurel wreath.

Background. Martins was born in Copenhagen on Oct. 27, 1946. He entered the Royal Danish Ballet school when he was eight, joined the company at 18, and became a principal dancer at 21. His son, Nilas, now a student at the school, was born during Martins' brief marriage to Lise La Cour, a dancer in the company.

Martins first danced with the City Ballet at the 1967 Edinburgh Festival, flying from Denmark to substitute for an injured dancer in Balanchine's *Apollo.* He spent three years as a guest with the New York Company before he resigned from the Royal Danish Ballet and joined the company as a principal in 1970. His bold, noble presence, the purity of his training, and his outstanding technique made him a star in a company that played down stars.

Balanchine created eight ballets for him and Robbins. Three among the 58 he danced in the City Ballet. Balanchine went out of his way to encourage Martins to choreograph, and Martins regarded Balanchine as a mentor who taught him the virtues of "directness, clarity, and simplicity" in ballet.

ANNA KISSELGOFF

MONDALE, Walter Frederick

After a surprise loss to Gary Hart in New Hampshire, Walter F. ("Fritz") Mondale made a stunning comeback in the Democratic Party primaries. With the catchy slogan "Where's the Beef?", the former vice-president demolished Hart's claims of policy innovation and, after a long and grueling campaign, won the party's nomination. As the fall campaign got underway, however, polls showed Mondale 20 points behind President Reagan, and political analysts questioned whether the "Fightin' Fritz" of the primaries could come from behind again. Mondale's strategists regarded two televised debates with Reagan—one on domestic policy and the other on foreign policy—as his best chance to break through the personal charm that surrounds Reagan and to pin down the president on issues.

Although noted for his political caution, Mondale made history by naming the first woman vice-presidential candidate to a major party ticket, Rep. Geraldine A. Ferraro from New York (*see* BIOGRAPHY). In another break with election-year political tradition, Mondale spelled out the tax increases he would seek to reduce the federal budget deficit. In his acceptance speech at the Democratic Convention in San Francisco, Mondale declared, "Mr. Reagan will raise taxes, and so will I. He won't tell you. I just did." Reagan characterized Mondale as a big spender and pledged to further reduce personal income tax rates. Following the November election in which he was defeated overwhelmingly by the Reagan ticket, the former vice-president left for a Caribbean vacation. He announced that he would not run for public office again.

Background. Walter Frederick Mondale was born on Jan. 5, 1928, in Ceylon, MN, and reared in the nearby town of Elmore. His father was an impoverished Methodist minister of Norwegian ancestry. Mondale attended Macalester College in St. Paul but was forced to drop out for lack of money when his father died in 1949. He received his B.A. cum laude from the University of Minnesota in 1951 and, after two years in the army, returned there under the G.I. Bill to study law.

AP/Wide World

Walter Mondale

Mondale began dabbling in politics early, organizing campus volunteers in 1947 for "The Diaper Brigade" in support of Hubert Humphrey and other mainstream Minnesota Democrats. In 1956, the same year he graduated from law school, Minnesota Gov. Orville Freeman named him state attorney general, the first of several appointive positions Mondale held. When Humphrey resigned his U.S. Senate seat in 1964 to become vice-president, Freeman chose Mondale to fill the vacancy. Mondale went on to spend 12 years in the Senate (1964–1976), gaining a reputation as an outspoken advocate of civil rights and other liberal concerns. His voting record with the AFL-CIO and the liberal Americans for Democratic Action never fell below 80%.

In 1974, Mondale made a run for the presidency but dropped out, declaring a disdain for the rigors of the campaign trail. "I'm not ready to spend the rest of my life in Holiday Inns," he said, confessing that he lacked an "overwhelming desire to be president." In 1976, Jimmy Carter chose him as his vice-presidential running mate, the perfect Washington insider to complement the man from Plains, GA. In the White House, Carter referred to him as "my partner," and Mondale claimed to be in on every decision of consequence. That claim would haunt him in his 1984 race against Reagan, who tagged him with every failure of the Carter administration.

Mondale is married to the former Joan Adams. They have three children, Theodore, Eleanor, and William.

ELEANOR CLIFT

MULRONEY, Martin Brian

On Sept. 4, 1984, Brian Mulroney led his Progressive Conservative (PC) party to one of the largest landslide victories in Canadian history. A fortnight later, on September 17, he became Canada's 18th prime minister and only the fourth Tory in the office in the 20th century. Though Mulroney had never even run in a municipal election before becoming party leader on June 11, 1983, the former Montreal lawyer's long association with Tory backrooms and his experience as a company negotiator in Quebec's tough labor scene qualified him as leader for a fractious party and a divided country. As a politician without perceptible ideological commitment, Mulroney easily captured the center of Canadian politics, professing an unalterable commitment to social programs while reassuring more right-wing followers by a devotion to free enterprise and a promise to restore good relations with Ronald Reagan's United States.

Background. The son of an electrician and the third of six children, M. Brian Mulroney was born on March 20, 1939, in the northern Quebec town of Baie Comeau. He grew up in a comfortable Catholic, Liberal, working-class home, spoke English with his parents, French at school and emerged with an easy, colloquial command of both languages that proved to be a valuable political asset. At 13 he went to St. Thomas College in New Brunswick, and in 1955 to St. Francis Xavier University in Antigonish, N.S. It was there that he became a Conservative. At 19, Mulroney went to Dalhousie University to study law. He switched to Laval University in Quebec, where he completed his training in French and gathered many of the friends who would help shape his later political career.

As a young lawyer in Montreal, Mulroney specialized in labor relations and circulated in a Quebec Conservative party driven to the edge of annihilation by the dominant Liberals. At 34, he married Mila Pivnicki, the 19-year-old daughter of a Serbian émigré.

Fresh from a high-profile role as management representative on Quebec's Cliche Commission investigation into union violence and corruption, Mulroney became a surprise candidate at the Tories' 1976 leadership convention. By his eloquence, freshness, and skillful organization, Mulroney won third place. Next he became president of the Iron Ore Company of Canada, a troubled subsidiary of Cleveland's Hanna Corporation. The company remained in the red, but Mulroney's skills as a manager and conciliator were most evident. Even his shutdown of a company town, Schefferville, was accepted by most of its workers. Meanwhile, as his personal finances recovered, Mulroney was building strong Tory backing. Party leader Joe Clark, unable to increase party support, put his leadership to a convention test in June 1983; a smooth campaign and a pledge to win Quebec seats gave Mulroney the victory.

In his first year as Conservative leader, Mulroney did a great deal to restore party unity. Meanwhile, Liberal Prime Minister Pierre Elliott Trudeau gave way to John N. Turner, who called for a general election shortly after taking office on June 30, 1984. During the two-month campaign, Mulroney reversed a large deficit in the polls and made good on his promise to deliver Quebec support. He took office with the biggest parliamentary majority—211 of 256 seats—in Canadian history. (*See* CANADA).

DESMOND MORTON

NICHOLS, Mike

The versatile Mike Nichols had an exceedingly prolific year in 1983-1984, his 21st as a Broadway stage and film director. His film *Silkwood*, which earned him a third Academy Award nomination, marked a return to film directing after an eight-year hiatus. Soon thereafter Tom Stoppard's powerful play *The Real Thing* brought Nichols his sixth Tony Award. Almost simultaneously the Nichols creative surge continued with the 1984 Off-Broadway and Broadway openings of *Hurlyburly*, a David Rabe play featuring a prestigious cast. The Nichols-Rabe collaboration previously had proved successful with the 1976 production of *Streamers*.

Background. Born Michael Igor Peschkowsky in Berlin on Nov. 6, 1931, he was four when a rare reaction to a whooping cough shot caused him to lose his hair. He and a younger brother were brought from Germany to the United States in 1939 by their Russian-born Jewish physician father. Upon his arrival, he was so shocked by a Hebrew sign in a New York delicatessen that he wondered, "Is that allowed here?" He was sent to boarding school at age ten, where he was "quietly unhappy." His classmates remember his sense of humor as well as his baldness. He attended the University of Chicago from 1950 to 1953, but his theatrical ambition intervened and he left to study at New York's Actors Studio.

He later returned to Chicago and began a three-year stint at a nightclub within a group of six that included

Elaine May. By 1957, Nichols and May had decided to team up. They headed for New York and performed in clubs there, acquiring a following. Soon they were acclaimed national television comics. The two successfully opened on Broadway in 1960 in *An Evening with Mike Nichols and Elaine May,* but they split professionally in 1962.

Despite his success as an improvisor, Nichols does not believe that he "grew up" professionally until he began directing. His Broadway directorial debut came with Neil Simon's *Barefoot in the Park* (1963), for which Nichols won his first Tony Award. He later directed other Simon plays, *The Odd Couple* (1965), *Plaza Suite* (1968), and *The Prisoner of Second Avenue* (1971), and picked up three more Tonys for them. He also was awarded a Tony for *Luv* (1964). In 1977 he directed *The Gin Game* and produced the musical *Annie.*

Who's Afraid of Virginia Woolf? (1966) marked his start as a film director and was followed by *The Graduate* (1967), which won him an Academy Award. His other important films include *Catch-22* (1970) and *Carnal Knowledge* (1971).

A wealthy man (he coproduces his plays and films), he has a New York apartment and two farms. His third wife is the novelist Annabel Davis-Goff. He is the father of three children.

O'CONNOR, John Joseph

After an unusually brief tenure as bishop of Scranton, PA, the Most Rev. John J. O'Connor—who spent most of his priestly career as a Navy chaplain—succeeded the late Terence Cardinal Cooke as archbishop of New York. He was formally named to this prestigious Roman Catholic post on Jan. 31, 1984, just two weeks after his 64th birthday.

During his first year in New York, the Philadelphia-born prelate was characterized mainly by his firm stand on the politics of abortion, even to the point of challenging such Catholic political leaders as New York's Gov.

Archbishop John O'Connor

AP/Wide World

Mario Cuomo and Democratic vice-presidential candidate Geraldine Ferraro on their pro-choice positions on abortion. At the same time, Archbishop O'Connor was visible on the controversial issue of war and peace, having been part of the U.S. bishops' committee that drafted the well-known pastoral letter, "The Challenge of Peace: God's Promise and Our Response," in 1983.

Combining what some in the Church see as the best of the pre-Vatican II Church—its firm, unwavering teaching voice—with a deep sense of compassion for individuals under his pastoral care, the archbishop is said to blend a sparkling personality with an oft-unfettered sense of humor, even when discussing thorny issues.

The former chief of Navy chaplains has made it clear, both in Scranton where he served as ordinary for eight months and in New York, that his top priority is the defense of the unborn. At the same time, he is an enthusiastic ecumenist who has been cited by B'nai B'rith as Man of the Year and is a published author on many topics, drawing upon his graduate degrees in ethics, clinical psychology, and political science.

In 1984, the archbishop was serving as head of the U.S. bishops' Committee on Social Development and World Peace. He also was a member of the administrative committee of the National Conference of Catholic Bishops and head of the New York Catholic Conference. Late in the year, reports indicated that he would soon become a cardinal.

Background. Born in Philadelphia on Jan. 15, 1920, John O'Connor studied for the priesthood at St. Charles Borromeo Seminary in the Overbrook section of Philadelphia. He was ordained a priest of the Philadelphia archdiocese on Dec. 15, 1945, and then taught on both the high school and college levels, while also serving as a parish curate. He also did graduate work at Villanova University, the Catholic University of America, and Georgetown University.

Father O'Connor joined the Navy in 1952 and served in various capacities with the Marine Corps and the Navy, including stints in both Korea and Vietnam. For four years, he was an auxiliary of the Military Vicariate, then headed by Cardinal Cooke. The vicariate serves as a diocese for all U.S. Catholics in the armed forces. He retired from the Navy on June 1, 1979, with the rank of rear admiral, after four years as head of the chaplains corps. The future leader of the New York archdiocese, who was ordained a bishop by Pope John Paul II on May 27, 1979, had received the Legion of Merit with Combat V and the Meritorious Service and Distinguished Service medals.

ROBERT L. JOHNSTON

PAYTON, Walter

The play was called "Toss-28 Weak," and films of it would go to the Professional Football Hall of Fame in Canton, OH. On Oct. 7, 1984, in the third quarter of a game against the New Orleans Saints, running back Walter Payton of the Chicago Bears took a quick toss from the quarterback and blasted into the left side of the line. He gained six yards on the play to increase his career total to 12,312—five more than the legendary Jim Brown. In the sixth game of his tenth season, Payton thereby became the all-time leading rusher in the history of the National Football League (NFL).

The 5'10", 202-lb running back went on to gain 154 yards in that contest, breaking another of Brown's records: it was the 59th time in his career that Payton had rushed for at least 100 yards in a game. Earlier in the season, the Bear star had surpassed Brown's career record of 15,459 all-purpose yards (rushing, receiving, and kick returning). Nicknamed "Sweetness," the 30-year-old Mississippian combines the speed and slick moves of a halfback with the brute force and durability of an old-fashioned fullback. Said an admiring teammate, "He runs with a fever."

Background. Walter Payton was born on July 25, 1954, in Columbia, MS. As a boy growing up in Missis-

Walter Payton

sippi, he developed a mean stiff-arm to keep the bigger kids from messing up his clothes in sandlot games. He was a high-school standout in Columbia, and his coach there, Charles Boston, has remained a close friend through the years and an ardent fan. Boston was on hand at Chicago's Soldier Field to see Payton's record-breaking performance in 1984.

Walter stayed in Mississippi to attend college, starring at Jackson State. During his career there, Payton did everything from rushing to catching touchdown passes, returning punts, and even punting and kicking. He also set an NCAA record for career points. After receiving his B.A. in communications, Payton was the first-round draft choice of the Bears in 1975. During his nine-plus seasons in Chicago, he has played in six Pro Bowls (1976, 1977, 1978, 1979, 1980, and 1983) and won several major awards, including league Most Valuable Player honors in 1978. In perhaps his greatest performance, Payton rushed for a single-game record of 275 yards against the Minnesota Vikings on Nov. 20, 1977. Before the 1983 campaign, the battered star underwent successful arthroscopic surgery on both knees. "I had my 11,000-mile tune-up," he said, "and I feel great." After setting the all-time rushing record, the soft-spoken, goal-oriented Payton set his sights on the 15,000-yard plateau. Others wondered whether 18,000 wasn't within reach.

Payton lives with his wife, Corinne, and son, Jarrett, at homes in Chicago and Jackson. He is one of the highest-paid athletes in professional sports, enjoying a contract that pays a reported $240,000 a year—for the rest of his life.

See SPORTS—Football.

PERES, Shimon

The election of a new Israeli government on Sept. 14, 1984, marked the end of a seven-week political stalemate, the institution of a novel concept in the nation's system of leadership, and the high point in the career of one of Israel's most enduring political figures. Inconclusive national elections on July 23 had been followed by long, unsuccessful interparty negotiations. The Knesset (parliament) on September 14 finally approved a na-

tional unity government in which the nation's two largest political blocs—the Likud and the Labor Party—both would take part. According to the power-sharing arrangement, the premiership would rotate between the two parties—25 months for the leader of one, followed by 25 months for the other.

Taking the oath for the first "term" was 61-year-old Shimon Peres of the Labor Party. Having lost two elections to Likud (1977 and 1981) and having gained only a narrow plurality in 1984 despite being far ahead in the polls, Peres assumed office as Israel's eighth prime minister with a special sense of urgency. He called for "immediate and vigorous action" to get the economy under control, and he called on Jordan's King Hussein to join the Middle East peace process as soon as possible. As for the prospects of the coalition cabinet, Peres said, "Our aim now must be to serve the nation instead of just our parties."

Background. Shimon Persky was born Aug. 16, 1923, in a province of Poland that today is part of the Soviet Union. His merchant father, Isaac, and his mother, Sarah, moved the family to Palestine in 1934, where Shimon hebraized his surname to Peres.

In 1941, Peres helped found a kibbutz in the Lower Galilee, where he worked as a herdsman. While still in high school, however, Peres had joined Haganah, the underground Jewish resistance organization. Prior to Israeli independence in 1948, Peres was in charge of arms purchasing and manpower mobilization for the entire Haganah movement. After independence he was appointed to the defense ministry, where he moved up to director general in 1953. A protégé of Israel's first prime minister, David Ben-Gurion, Peres was named deputy defense minister after his first election to the Knesset in 1959.

At the same time that he was becoming one of Israel's top defense experts and building the nation's arms industry, Peres was also gaining prominence in the party. During the 1960s he played an important role in unifying the Labor movement. In 1974, Peres was appointed defense minister in the government of Prime Minister Yitzhak Rabin, who had narrowly defeated him for the party leadership. Rabin again defeated Peres for the Labor nomination in 1977, but the prime minister was forced to resign in a financial scandal a few months later. The mild-mannered, hard-working Peres was voted to replace him and lost his first national election later that year.

Shimon Peres is married to the former Sonia Gelman. They have three children.

See ISRAEL.

Shimon Peres

REAGAN, Ronald

With the proclamation that "America is back and standing tall," Ronald Reagan officially began his quest for a second White House term. As the nation's 40th president, Reagan enjoyed higher popularity ratings on the eve of election battle than any incumbent since Dwight Eisenhower. His ability to escape personal blame for policy failures and the scandals surrounding some of his top officials earned him the title, "the Teflon president," meaning nothing negative sticks. In his campaign against former Vice-President Walter Mondale, Reagan stressed patriotism, family values, and hard work. He claimed credit for a recovering economy and pledged to raise taxes in a second term "only as a last resort."

A former Hollywood actor, Reagan's talent for television produced a campaign that was said to be long on "photo opportunities" and short on substance. Mondale accused Reagan of being isolated and "ducking" issues. But Reagan did agree to two 90-minute televised debates, one on domestic policy, the other on foreign affairs.

While Reagan appeared vulnerable on some issues, his personal charm exceeded any negatives. Polls showed that voters preferred Reagan as a leader even when they disagreed with his policies. Midway through the fall campaign, the U.S. embassy in Beirut was bombed for the third time during Reagan's presidency. Reagan compared the lack of fortifications at the embassy with a kitchen remodeling job that was behind schedule. That kind of remark led to renewed hope among Democrats that Reagan could yet torpedo his 20-point lead with a thoughtless observation or off-the-cuff comment.

On September 28, just five weeks before the election, Reagan met with Soviet Foreign Minister Andrei Gromyko at the White House, his first session with a top Russian leader. Although no agreements were reached, Reagan's softened tone made it more difficult for Mondale to argue that Reagan's bellicose rhetoric had derailed arms talks.

As president, Reagan called for the largest military buildup in peacetime. His slogan was "Peace through Strength." Unlike his immediate predecessors, Reagan did not shy away from committing American military resources abroad. He sent U.S. Marines to Lebanon, propped up a fragile democracy in El Salvador with military and economic aid, and sought covert assistance for a guerrilla movement in leftist Nicaragua. His most notable success as commander in chief was the 1983 invasion of the tiny island of Grenada, where U.S. troops rescued the students of an American medical school from what appeared to be an imminent takeover by Soviet surrogates. His most glaring foreign-policy failure occurred in Lebanon, where 241 Marines were massacred in a terrorist attack on Oct. 23, 1983. In February 1984, Reagan announced the withdrawal of U.S. forces.

In his four years, Reagan presided over both the worst recession in 40 years and the most robust recovery since World War II. Unemployment dropped from a high of 10.8% in late 1982 to 7% in June 1984. Inflation virtually vanished. But a series of tax cuts, which his critics claimed benefited the rich more than the middle class, helped contribute to record deficits of $174 billion.

Following the president's reelection, it was revealed that legislation establishing a "flat rate" tax and a nuclear-arms agreement with the Soviets would be the prime objectives of his second term.

Background. Ronald Wilson Reagan was born Feb. 6, 1911, in Tampico, IL, the younger son of an adoring mother and an itinerant father. In his biography, *Where's The Rest of Me?*, Reagan writes of his father's alcoholic bouts and the family's struggles during the Depression. After graduating from Eureka College in 1932, Reagan served as a sports announcer in Davenport and Des Moines, IA. His movie career began in 1937 when he took a screen test with Warner Brothers. Of the 55 feature-length films he made, his most famous part was that of Notre Dame football star, George Gipp, in the movie *Knute Rockne—All American.*

A liberal Democrat in his early years, Reagan officially switched his party affiliation to Republican in 1962. He served two terms as California governor (1967–1975), setting a pattern of pragmatism that continued through his years in the White House and that belied his often sharply conservative rhetoric. He made two losing efforts for the GOP presidential nomination (1968 and 1976) before his victorious race against Jimmy Carter in 1980. Reagan survived an assassination attempt on March 30, 1981.

President Reagan has four children, Maureen (by) and Michael (adopted) during his first marriage to actress Jane Wyman, and Patti and Ronald, Jr., by his present marriage to former actress Nancy Davis.

ELEANOR CLIFT

SAUVÉ, Jeanne

Canada's 23d governor-general and commander in chief is the sixth Canadian to hold the post, the third Westerner, and the first woman. Bilingual and cultivated, Madame Sauvé was a popular choice for the almost wholly ceremonial role of the queen's representative in Canada. Though a strong Liberal, she had achieved at least a measure of nonpartisanship as the presumably neutral speaker of the House of Commons since February 1980. Observers predicted that her sophistication would reverse the folksy and somewhat dull atmosphere of Rideau Hall, the governor-general's official residence, under her predecessor, Edward Schreyer.

Background. Jeanne Benoit was born in Prud'homme, Sask., on April 26, 1922. Her father was a prosperous contractor who built churches, convents, and private homes. She grew up in Ottawa and was active in the radical Jeunesse Étudiante Catholique (Young Catholic Students), moving to Montreal in 1942

Jeanne Sauvé

Canapress

to become the organization's national president. In 1948, she married Maurice Sauvé and went with him to Paris. While he completed his doctorate in economics at the University of Paris, she received a diploma in French civilization and worked for UNESCO. The couple returned to Montreal in 1952, where Sauvé worked briefly with her husband in trade-union organizing before beginning a brilliant career as journalist and commentator with Radio Canada and a succession of media outlets. The Sauvés have one son, Jean-François.

Jeanne Sauvé was first elected to Parliament in 1972, representing a Montreal riding. (Her husband had been politically active as a Liberal member of Parliament and cabinet minister from 1962 to 1968 before becoming a business executive.) Almost at once, Prime Minister Pierre Elliott Trudeau made her minister of state for science and technology. She was appointed minister of the environment in 1974 and minister of communications in 1975. In the latter important portfolio, she sponsored Canada's Telidon videotext system and the first stages of Pay-TV. In 1980, Jeanne Sauvé was Trudeau's choice for speaker. The first woman in the post faced an unhappy tenure in a rancorous House of Commons. Her main victory was the reform of Parliament's internal administration. The experience damaged Jeanne Sauvé's health, and she took up her role as governor-general only after a prolonged struggle with illness.

DESMOND MORTON

SONDHEIM, Stephen Joshua

Drawing on sources as diverse as the works of the Greek playwright Aristophanes and the Swedish filmmaker Ingmar Bergman, composer and lyricist Stephen Sondheim has had a profound impact on Broadway musical theater. The year 1984 saw a new Sondheim musical in New York—*Sunday in the Park with George,* based on the life of the French painter Georges Seurat and directed by James Lapine. At the same time, the New York City Opera was preparing to restage *Sweeney Todd,* a 1979 Sondheim work, and his *Pacific Overtures* was a fall-season Broadway revival.

Sondheim's earliest mentor was Oscar Hammerstein II. But by the time he turned 30, he was ready to break with the traditional, romantic type of musical that had made Hammerstein famous. Most of Sondheim's 13 shows have dealt bluntly with contemporary themes, including marital problems and the loss of idealism. As the composer once described his work, "I like to write in dark colors about gut feelings." His often avant-garde music and lyrics have won numerous awards. But while many of his shows have enjoyed long runs, few have had great financial success.

Background. Stephen Joshua Sondheim was born on March 22, 1930, in New York City. His father, a dress manufacturer, and his mother, a fashion designer and interior decorator, divorced when he was 10. Not long after that, Stephen moved with his mother to Doylestown, PA, where Hammerstein was a neighbor. It was Hammerstein who introduced Sondheim to musical theater and critiqued his first work—a school play written at age 15—with the words, "It's the worst musical I ever heard." But the master also showed him how to write songs for the stage, and Sondheim served as his apprentice and assistant for *South Pacific* and *The King and I.*

Sondheim earned a degree in music at Williams College in 1950 and then studied for two years in New York with composer Milton Babbit, who also had a strong influence. In 1953, Sondheim wrote the music and lyrics for a musical called *Saturday Night,* but plans for staging the show fell through when the producer died suddenly. Sondheim found work as a TV scriptwriter in Hollywood but two years later got a chance to write the lyrics for Leonard Bernstein's *West Side Story* (1957). The show was an immediate success, and Sondheim found himself in demand. He wrote the lyrics for *Gypsy* (1959) and then managed to convince director Harold

AP/Wide World

Stephen Sondheim

Prince to do a show based on the comedies of the Roman playwright Plautus. The result was *A Funny Thing Happened on the Way to the Forum* (1962).

Forum was followed by other Sondheim shows that won wide acclaim. At one point he won Tony awards for best lyricist and composer three years in a row (1971, 1972, and 1973)—for *Company,* a musical that viewed marriage through a jaundiced eye; *Follies,* which explored show girls' broken dreams; and *A Little Night Music,* a romantic comedy based on Ingmar Bergman's film *Smiles of a Summer Night.*

ELAINE PASCOE

TRUDEAU, Garry B.

Michael, Zonker, B.D., Joanie, Duke, and the rest of the gang were back. After a 21-month sabbatical for their creator, Garry Trudeau, the characters of the comic strip "Doonesbury" made their return in 735 newspapers across the United States on Sept. 30, 1984. Much had transpired during their absence from the funny pages. A Broadway musical about them—*Doonesbury,* lyrics and book by Trudeau—had opened in November 1983 and run until February 1984. And the characters themselves, college students since their creation 14 years earlier, had finally graduated and moved into "the larger world of grown-up concerns." They just needed time, Trudeau had said, to "make the journey from draft beer and mixers to cocaine and herpes."

The first comic strip artist ever to be awarded a Pulitzer Prize for cartooning (1974), Trudeau brings to the funny pages a brand of political and social satire that had always been reserved for the editorial pages. Over the years, many of his strips have been a source of journalistic controversy—with some editors in fact choosing to run them on the editorial page and others refusing to run them at all. But by the time "Doonesbury" returned

UPI/Bettmann

Garry Trudeau

from its 21-month absence in late 1984, 60 million readers—many of them under 35—could not wait to find out what was happening with Michael, Zonker, Joanie, and the rest.

Background. Garry B. Trudeau was born in 1948 in New York City and grew up in Saranac Lake, NY. Little is known about his youth or other details of his life, because Trudeau is intensely protective of his privacy, refusing all requests for interviews.

As an undergraduate at Yale University in 1968, Trudeau began doing a strip, called "Bull Tales," for the campus newspaper. Though "Bull Tales" was confined largely to life on the Yale campus, it came to the attention of one syndicator as a possible new property with national appeal. Trudeau entered the Yale School of Art in 1970 to pursue his M.F.A. degree, and that October "Doonesbury" made its debut in 30 newspapers under the Universal Press Syndicate. The strip was named after one of the holdover characters from "Bull Tales," Michael Doonesbury, and its subject matter was expanded to the Vietnam War, racism, and other issues of national concern.

In addition to his daily newspaper strips, Trudeau has published more than a dozen books in the "Doonesbury" series. He is married to Jane Pauley, co-host of NBC's *Today* show. In December 1983 the couple welcomed the birth of twins, Ross and Rachel.

TRUMP, Donald John

Fred Trump, who in the 1920s started the family real-estate business with modest apartment buildings in Brooklyn and Queens, NY, said of his son Donald: "He has great vision, and everything he touches seems to turn to gold." As president of the company, Donald J. Trump expanded the Trump Organization into a billion-dollar New York City real-estate empire. Following three rules for success—"location, location, location"—the think-big developer built or bought luxury hotels and condominiums, shopping centers, and tens of thousands of apartments in Manhattan. In spring 1984, Trump and Harrah's opened a 39-story, 614-room hotel and casino in Atlantic City; it is one of the largest facilities of its kind in the world. The previous September, Trump bought the New Jersey Generals franchise of the fledgling United States Football League.

The showpiece of Trump's holdings is the plush, 68-story Trump Tower at Fifth Avenue and 56th Street in New York. The $200 million concrete, bronze, and glass structure opens into a six-story marble atrium with an 80-ft (24-m) waterfall. The 263 condominium units sell for $600,000 to $10 million each. A similarly luxurious cooperative apartment building, the $125 million Trump Plaza at Third Avenue and 61st Street, was opened in 1984. On the drawing board is the 60-story, gold-leafed Trump Castle—with moat and drawbridge—to be built at Madison Avenue and 60th Street.

The handsome, 6-ft (1.8-m), 38-year-old Trump is married to a Vienna-born former skier and model, Ivana, who is now executive vice president of the Trump Organization, in charge of interior design. They have three children and live in a triplex atop Trump Tower.

Background. One of five children, Donald Trump was born in 1946 and raised in the exclusive Jamaica Estates section of Queens, NY. The family minister, the Rev. Norman Vincent Peale, was an important influence. "The mind can overcome any obstacle," says Trump today.

Somewhat of a discipline problem, young Donald was sent to New York Military Academy in Cornwall-on-Hudson, where he excelled at baseball. After attending Fordham University for two years, he transferred to the Wharton School of Finance at the University of Pennsylvania. He graduated first in his class in 1968 and then joined his father's business.

Refinancing the company's apartment holdings and making some lucrative land deals, Trump moved into the Manhattan market in the early 1970s. His first big move was to buy the dying Commodore Hotel in a 50-50 deal with the Hyatt Corporation. The building, on 42nd Street near Grand Central Station, was gutted, renovated, and reopened as the Grand Hyatt luxury hotel.

A financial supporter of New York Democratic politicians, Trump is the object of some controversy for his tax abatements and grandiose plans. "I like to create great things," he says. "Money is an offshoot. . . ."

Donald Trump

AP/Wide World

TURNER, John Napier

Not since Sir Charles Tupper in 1896 has a Canadian prime minister served a shorter term of office than John Napier Turner: from June 30, 1984, to Sept. 17, 1984. Nor in the annals of political polling has a Canadian party leader experienced such a rapid decline in public support.

Background. Born in Richmond, Surrey, England, on June 7, 1929, Turner was raised by his mother, a Canadian economist, who took him to Canada following his father's death in 1931. Turner was graduated from the University of British Columbia in 1949. He won a Rhodes Scholarship to Oxford University and also attended the University of Paris.

Turner was admitted to the Quebec bar in 1954 and practiced law in Montreal. He was first elected to Parliament in 1962 as part of a Liberal recovery and was appointed to Prime Minister Lester Pearson's cabinet in 1965. He also met and married Geills Kilgour, daughter of a well-known and wealthy Winnipeg family.

In the 1968 Liberal leadership convention, Turner placed third behind Pierre Elliott Trudeau. Under Prime Minister Trudeau, he served as solicitor general, minister of justice, and minister of finance. In 1975, after sharp differences with Trudeau, Turner resigned to become a partner in a prominent Toronto law firm.

Turner's political career was in eclipse. Trudeau's restoration to power in 1980 seemed to spell an end to Turner's hope of vindication; the disastrous fall in Liberal popularity after 1982 restored it. When Trudeau announced his resignation in February 1984, much of the Liberal establishment believed that Turner, with his good looks, business connections, and apparently right-wing views, might be the party's savior. On March 16, Turner announced his candidacy for the party's leadership.

Three months later, on June 16, after an unexpectedly awkward performance and much organizational turmoil, Turner won on the second ballot. On June 30, he became prime minister and within a week called a general election for September 4. With polls showing Liberal support at 46% to 49%, victory seemed certain. Instead, disaster followed. Turner's acceptance of a long list of Trudeau patronage appointments undermined his claims of independence from the old regime. His apparent conservatism worried traditional Liberal supporters. Above all, Turner proved to have little influence in the traditional Liberal stronghold of Quebec. On election night, he presided over his party's most memorable debacle, cheered only by the unexpected news that voters in his own affluent Vancouver constituency of Quadra had defied the trend and given him a seat in Parliament. From that frail base, Canada's 17th prime minister began planning his party's comeback.

DESMOND MORTON

TUTU, Desmond Mpilo

The 1984 Nobel Peace Prize was awarded to Bishop Desmond Mpilo Tutu, an outstanding black South African leader who has vigorously campaigned against his country's apartheid system. The bishop's middle name, Mpilo, meaning "life," is appropriate for a man who preaches nonviolence as he seeks an open, free, and just society for South Africa.

Bishop Tutu is the second black South African to receive the Peace Prize. In 1960 the award was given to Albert John Luthuli, former president of the African National Congress. The text of the 1984 Nobel announcement emphasized that the award "should be seen as a renewed recognition of the courage and heroism shown by black South Africans in their use of peaceful methods in the struggle against apartheid." Bishop Tutu will use the $190,000 award for educational scholarships for the poor.

The prize selection committee based its decision on the nonviolent campaign waged by Bishop Tutu to end apartheid in South Africa. His philosophy is based on the belief that South Africa is a violent society but that blacks have not been responsible for introducing violence there. He calls for international economic, political, and diplomatic pressures against South Africa. The committee considered his approach to be of vital importance to the whole continent of Africa and for the cause of peace in the world. In 1981 the bishop was awarded the Athinai Prize of the Alexander Onassis Foundation but was not able to accept the prize personally because his passport had been withheld.

Background. Tutu was born in Klerksdorp, in the Transvaal, on Oct. 7, 1931, into a Methodist family that later converted to the Anglican Church. His father was a teacher at a mission school that his son attended. Tutu wanted to become a doctor, but his family could not afford to send him to medical school. Instead, he attended the Bantu Normal College, in Pretoria, where he received a Higher Teacher's Diploma. At the same time he completed a B.A. correspondence degree from the University of South Africa.

At the age of 25, Tutu decided to study for the Anglican priesthood. In 1960 he was ordained and subsequently studied for an M.A. at King's College, London. In 1975 he became the first black Anglican dean of Johannesburg. He was bishop of Lesotho from 1976 to 1978, when he was appointed assistant bishop of Johannesburg. In 1978 he also became the first black general secretary of the South African Council of Churches, an organization with a membership exceeding 12 million, which has been investigated by the government and subjected to continual harassment because of its opposition to apartheid. In mid-November the 1984 Nobelist was elected as the first black Anglican bishop of Johannesburg.

PATRICK O'MEARA

Bishop Desmond Tutu

UPI/Bettmann

BOLIVIA

The government of President Hernán Siles, Bolivia's first democratically elected regime in two decades, remained in power throughout 1984. It did so despite one of the severest economic crises the country had ever faced and amid an exceedingly turbulent political situation as well.

The Economic Crisis. On April 6, President Siles announced a package of economic measures demanded by the International Monetary Fund as a condition of help in dealing with the country's foreign debt of at least $4.4 billion (U.S.). The proposed measures included currency devaluation, ending of price subsidies for essentials such as food and energy, and a reduction of the government's deficit. Siles called this "an effort for national salvation." A week later the government decreed a 75% devaluation of the peso and a fivefold increase in prices of basic foods and fuel.

Meanwhile, the Bolivian Labor Confederation (COB) mounted a major protest against these measures. A three-day general strike began on April 14. When it ended, the COB gave Siles until April 23 to reverse his policies or face a general strike of indefinite duration. On April 30, it called another three-day walkout. However, on May 30 the government and the COB reached a tentative agreement temporarily to postpone payment of $1 billion owed to private foreign banks until new terms were negotiated for the debt. The agreement was conditional on the COB accepting a general wage increase of "only" 130%. This accord drew strong criticism from opposition parties, which called on Siles to resign.

In July, the Bank of America warned President Siles that if debt payments were not renewed within 90 days, the country would be declared in default, which would cut off all possibility of obtaining further credit. In August, the peso was further devaluated from 2,000 to 50,000 per U.S. dollar—a move intended to circumvent trading on the black market, where the rate was between 9,000 and 10,000 to the dollar. Both the opposition parties and the COB opposed this new devaluation.

Some easing of the situation was evident at the September joint meeting of the IMF and the World Bank in Washington, where the atmosphere was described as "more conciliatory." At that meeting, also, it was reported that the Siles government was seeking loans in Europe and from other Latin American countries.

Politics. The year had begun with a political crisis, caused by congressional censure of the cabinet. President Siles reappointed 13 of the 18 outgoing ministers. The government's political base was somewhat strengthened in April, when Siles again reorganized his cabinet to make room for members of the Movement of the Revolutionary Left (MIR) headed by Vice-

AP/Wide World

Strife between President Siles (right) and labor leader Juan Oquendo continued to paralyze Bolivia economically.

President Jaime Paz Zamora. The new cabinet, besides representing the president's MNRI party and the MIR, included members of the Christian Democratic party and the pro-Soviet Communist party.

Another political crisis occurred on June 30, when President Siles was kidnapped and held for most of the day by a group of military men and police. Particularly involved were the U.S.-trained special narcotics police. U.S. ambassador Edwin Corr played a key role in negotiating release of the president. After this incident more than 100 conspirators were arrested.

See also LATIN AMERICA.

ROBERT J. ALEXANDER, *Rutgers University*

BOLIVIA · Information Highlights

Official Name: Republic of Bolivia.
Location: West-central South America.
Area: 424,000 sq mi (1 098 160 km²).
Population (mid-1984 est.): 6,000,000.
Chief Cities (1982 est.): Sucre, the legal capital, 79,941; LaPaz, the actual capital, 881,404; Santa Cruz de la Sierra, 376,912; Cochabamba, 281,962.
Government: *Head of state and government,* Hernán Siles Zuazo, president (took office Oct. 10, 1982). *Legislature*—Congress: Senate and Chamber of Deputies.
Monetary Unit: Peso (50,000 pesos equal U.S.$1, August 1984).
Gross National Product (1983 U.S.$): $5,600,-000,000.
Economic Index (1983): *Consumer Prices* (1970 = 100), all items, 6,225.1; food, 7,453.7.
Foreign Trade (1983 U.S.$): *Imports,* $514,000,-000,000; *exports,* $789,000,000,000.

BRAZIL

The transition from military to civilian rule continued as the candidate of Brazil's major opposition party emerged as the odds-on favorite to capture the presidency.

Government and Politics. Brazil had lived under military rule since 1964, when the armed forces ousted a mercurial civilian chief executive. But soon after becoming president in 1979, Gen. João Baptista Figueiredo committed himself to an *abertura,* or democratization of the political system.

However, the military government ruled out the possibility of direct popular elections for 1984, favored by 90% of respondents in public-opinion surveys. Instead, the chief executive was to be selected in January 1985 by a 686-person electoral college. Despite three months of public demonstrations in favor of direct elections, an opposition-backed constitutional amendment calling for direct elections in November 1984 was rejected by Congress on April 26. The president had proposed an alternative amendment scheduling free elections for 1988, but this was withdrawn in June.

At its August 1984 convention, the ruling, military-backed Social Democratic Party (PDS) chose as its standard-bearer Paulo Salim Maluf, a 52-year-old conservative loyal to Figueiredo and supported by elements of the army, including the National Intelligence Service. Maluf, a former governor of São Paulo, received 493 votes to 350 for his rival, Interior Minister Mario Andreazza.

Meanwhile, the leading opposition group, the Brazilian Democratic Movement Party (PMDB), nominated Tancredo Neves, 74, the governor of Minas Gerais state and a lawyer, citing four decades of political experience. Joining the PMDB in this nomination was the Democratic Alliance (AD), a dissident faction of the PDS led by Vice-President Antonio Aureliano Chaves de Mendonça. Formerly a presidential aspirant himself, Chaves resigned from his party because of disputes over both the succession procedure and the PDS's antipathy toward direct popular elections. The AD named José Sarney, who stepped down as the PDS's president, as its vice-presidential nominee.

A confluence of factors augured well for Neves: the PDS's hostility to direct popular voting, the breakup of the governing party, the joining of the PMDB and AD in a Liberal Front, and—above all—the unpopularity of the allegedly corrupt Maluf, who represented continuity of the military regime in a nation starved for change.

Not only did Neves enjoy the support of the PMDB governors, concentrated in populous southern states, he also benefited from endorsements by many PDS state executives, including those in Maranhão, Bahia, and Rio Grande do Norte. Indeed, of the nine governors elected by the PDS in the northeast, only one—Wilson Braga of Paraiba—threw his support to Maluf. While unable to dictate the makeup of state delegations to the electoral college, the governors could exert sufficient strength to ensure Maluf's defeat.

Protests disrupted early campaign appearances by the PDS's nominee. In Aracajo, capital of northern Sergipe state, a crowd of several thousand engulfed Maluf for 90 minutes before security men could whisk him away in a car bombarded by eggs and chunks of wood.

Alarmed at his dismal performance, Figueiredo reportedly gave Maluf 30 days in which to prove his electability or release the government from further support of his candidacy. The weakness of the documentation that Maluf presented in his behalf increased the chances of his being forced from the race by disgruntled officers—with the elections postponed until the armed forces could field a stronger candidate, possibly a military man.

Economics. Political uncertainties aside, Brazil's badly depressed economy showed signs of recovery thanks to a 25% growth of sales abroad, consisting mostly of manufactured goods. The upswing in exports meant that by August 31 the country boasted a $9 billion (U.S.) trade surplus—a goal not expected to be reached until year's end under a 1983 belt-tightening stabilization plan negotiated with the International Monetary Fund.

The nation's arms industry helped generate $3 billion, up from $1 billion in 1983. Saudi Arabia alone purchased $50 million worth of arms in August and, less than two months later, signed a contract whose value to Brazil is expected to reach $200 million. The second deal may permit the Saudis, employing Brazilian technology, to develop and manufacture various types of armaments in Brazil. Reportedly, a similar arrangement existed with Iraq, which invested heavily in the production of a multiple rocket launcher, the Astros II, deployed successfully against Iran in the Gulf war.

The continuing decline in energy prices as a result of the persistent petroleum glut spurred Brazil's economic rebound even as the country moved to achieve energy self-sufficiency within a decade. An ambitious program of exploration and drilling raised domestic production, which totaled 200,000 barrels a day during 1980 when oil imports devoured $10 billion in foreign exchange, to 500,000 barrels a day, driving the nation's oil-import bill below the $5 billion mark in 1984.

The use of alcohol in 1.2 million vehicles saved some 160,000 barrels of oil daily. In October the Brazilian Air Force unveiled an aircraft propelled by "prozene," a substance derived entirely from oils extracted from sunflower, peanuts, palms, soya, and other plants. Commercially unfeasible at current prices, the fuel will serve as a strategic reserve.

The president of the Central Bank of Brazil (third from left) and New York bankers discuss Brazil's financial needs.

The enormous Itaipú hydroelectric facility on the Paraná River between Brazil and Paraguay began operations despite charges by the opposition that this was the kind of "pharaonic" project that nearly bankrupted the country. The $18 billion plant will become the world's largest generating station in 1990 when all of its 18 generators are in place.

Although high unemployment and triple digit inflation rate blemished the economic picture, Brazil's impressive trade performance encouraged creditors to reschedule an important part of the country's $98 billion foreign debt, the largest in the Third World. The model for a "multi-annual" renegotiation is Mexico: international bankers, delighted by that nation's good-faith adherence to a tough austerity plan, stretched out the repayment period, trimmed interest rates, and waived the commission normally charged for restructurings.

Foreign Affairs. U.S. Secretary of State George Shultz visited Brazil in February as part of a nine-day trip to Latin America. While in Brasilia, Shultz signed bilateral scientific and technical agreements. The pacts strengthened cooperation in several areas, including military technology. Seven years before, Brazil had terminated a military assistance treaty with Washington because of U.S. legislation linking aid to respect for human rights. Indeed, in its 1984 report on that subject the U.S. State Department praised Brazil's progress in the field of human rights.

In mid-September, Brazilian Foreign Minister Ramiro Saraiva Guerreiro welcomed President Reagan's rejection of strict quotas or higher tariffs on U.S. steel imports from Brazil and other suppliers. The diplomat voiced support for the voluntary export restraints preferred by the White House.

Brazilians took pride in the unanimous election, on March 12, of one of their country's diplomats, João Clemente Baena Soares, as secretary general of the Organization of American States.

Secretary of State Shultz joined the foreign ministers of the various Latin nations at the annual convention of the OAS in Brasilia in mid-November.

See also LATIN AMERICA.

GEORGE W. GRAYSON
College of William and Mary

BRAZIL • Information Highlights

Official Name: Federative Republic of Brazil.
Location: Eastern South America.
Area: 3,286,486 sq mi (8 512 000 km²).
Population (mid-1984 est.): 134,400,000.
Chief Cities (1980 census): Brasilia, the capital, 1,176,908; São Paulo, 7,032,547; Rio de Janeiro, 5,090,700; Salvador, 1,491,642.
Government: *Head of state and government,* João Baptista Figueiredo, president (took office March 1979). *Legislature*—National Congress: Senate and Chamber of Deputies.
Monetary Unit: Cruzeiro (2,724.0 cruzeiros equal U.S.$1, Nov. 19, 1984).
Gross National Product (1982 U.S.$): $295,000,-000,000.
Economic Indexes (1983): *Consumer Prices* (1972 = 100), all items, 11,541.6; food, 14,344.1. *Industrial Production* (1975 = 100), 108.
Foreign Trade (1983 U.S.$): *Imports,* $16,311,-000,000; *exports,* $21,253,000,000.

In Vancouver, B.C., construction was underway at the site of Expo 86, a world exposition scheduled to open during 1986. The construction continued despite escalating costs and disruptive labor disputes over the use of nonunion contractors.

Canapress

BRITISH COLUMBIA

The settlement of labor disputes reduced some of the political tensions during 1984.

Budget. The February 1984 budget continued the same "restraint" themes as those of 1983. Operating expenditures for the next fiscal year were placed at C$7.9 billion and for the first time in 31 years were at a level below that of a previous year. Despite the 6.2% reduction in spending and an 8.6% projected increase in revenues, a deficit of $671 million was forecast for 1984–85. While $470 million was transferred to retire the debt of the British Columbia Railway, health was the only service to receive an increased budget. A new 4% "health care maintenance" surtax on personal income tax was imposed effective July 1984 rising to 8% in 1985. This was said to be required to make up for the federal government's underfunding of health care costs.

Government forest management functions, child-care facilities, and institutional laundry facilities were transferred to the private sector. Travel agency, real estate, insurance, and securities licensing also were to be deregulated. Student financial assistance in the form of grants was discontinued and replaced by a loan scheme. Controls over the number of medical practitioners also were imposed.

Legislature. Legislation passed during the spring session included the reintroduced Human Rights and Residential Tenancy Acts, amendments to the Labor Code, and a Constitution Act amendment establishing an electoral commission to review regularly the need for additional representation in the Legislative Assembly. In April the government legislated an end to a nine-week lockout in the pulp and paper industry. It recalled the legislature for a special sitting in September for similar action to end a 13-week Metro-Transit strike-lockout, which had shut down public bus services in Victoria and the Lower Mainland.

Politics. At the New Democratic Party leadership convention held in May, Bob Skelly, 41, with 12 years experience in the legislature, was chosen to succeed the retiring leader, Dave Barrett. One of the five defeated leadership candidates, Graham Lea, said he would leave the party to sit as an independent. In two November by-elections the NDP retained one seat and captured another from Social Credit.

Economy. Recovery from the 1982 recession continued to elude the British Columbia economy in 1984. Forest industry output was projected to fall by 9%, and, while pulp and paper showed some strength, lumber producers faced weak markets and low prices. The shutdown of a major open-pit copper-molybdenum mine brought the number of mine closures during 1983–84 to 13. The first shipments of coal to Japan were made on schedule from the North-East coal development, but falling world prices forced reductions in the contract price.

The recession also resulted in a major surplus of electric power, and proposals for a new Peace River dam were shelved by B. C. Hydro. A new provincial energy policy would permit for the first time long-term exports of surplus power to the United States.

Construction work continued for the world exposition Expo 86 in Vancouver. In August the Expo site was designated as a special economic development project.

BRITISH COLUMBIA • Information Highlights

Area: 366,255 sq mi (948 600 km²).
Population (April 1984 est.): 2,863,200.
Chief Cities (1981 census): Victoria, the capital, 64,379; Vancouver, 414,281; Prince George, 67,559; Kamloops, 64,048; Kelowna, 59,196; Nanaimo, 47,069.
Government (1984): *Chief Officers*—lt. gov., Henry Bell-Irving; premier, William R. Bennett (Social Credit Party); atty. gen., L. Allan Williams. *Legislature*—Legislative Assembly, 57 members.
Provincial Finances (1985 fiscal year budget): *Revenues,* $6,500,000,000; *expenditures.* $8,300,-000,000.
Personal Income (average weekly earnings, May 1984): $432.29.
Labor Force (July 1984, seasonally adjusted): *Employed workers,* 15 years of age and over, 1,203,000; *Unemployed* 207,000 (14.7%).
Education (1984–85): *Enrollment*—elementary and secondary schools, 531,370 pupils; postsecondary (1984–85)—universities, 52,590; community colleges (full-time), 21,300.
(All monetary figures are in Canadian dollars.)

In May, the Supreme Court of Canada confirmed the province's jurisdiction over the seabed resources between Vancouver Island and the mainland.

NORMAN J. RUFF, *University of Victoria*

BRUNEI

The oil-rich Sultanate of Brunei cut its remaining ties with Britain on Jan. 1, 1984. A proclamation declared Feb. 23, 1984, as Brunei's national day, and independence celebrations were held in the capital, Bandar Seri Begawan. The sultan, Sir Muda Hassanal Bolkiah, assumed the office of prime minister of the 2,226-sq-mi (5 788-km²) enclave bordered by Malaysia and facing the South China Sea.

Southeast Asia's newest nation ranked as its richest on a per-capita income basis ($22,000 annually) and its smallest in population (200,000). Brunei has a thriving economy and a treasury swollen by revenues from bountiful resources of oil and gas. A flurry of hotel and office-building construction transformed the capital.

British protection began in 1888, but at no time was Brunei's status that of a colony. From 1959 the sultanate enjoyed full self-government in local matters, and in 1979 agreement was reached on the transition under which the sultan would assume responsibility for the final elements of sovereignty—foreign affairs and defense—at the end of 1983. British-educated Sir Hassanal, the 29th sultan, made it clear that independence would not be followed by elective government. Key government posts were assigned to members of the sultan's family.

Brunei became a member of the Commonwealth of Nations, the Association of Southeast Asian Nations (ASEAN), and the United Nations.

R. M. YOUNGER

BULGARIA

With a low foreign debt, abundant food supplies, and a high rate of economic growth, Bulgaria enjoys an enviable position among Soviet-bloc countries.

Domestic Affairs. In 1984, Bulgaria's current five-year plan appeared to be proceeding beyond expectations, with an annual economic-growth rate of 4.6%. In March, Todor Zhivkov, general secretary of the Bulgarian Communist Party (BCP) and chairman of the State Council, affirmed that the reforms begun in 1982 would continue. He criticized "unadventurous officials" and advocated the brigade system for industry. At the end of March, Yakov Ryabov, chairman of the Soviet Union's State Committee for Foreign Economic Relations, met with Zhivkov in Sofia. The two discussed various kinds of cooperation, especially in regard to the construction of nuclear power projects.

Much of the reshuffling of high party and government officials in January stemmed from economic considerations. Yordan Yotov and Chudomir Aleksandrov were appointed full members of the BCP's Politburo. The latter was also appointed first deputy chairman of the Council of Ministers, with primary responsibility for the economy. Four ministries dealing with economic matters were merged into two.

Five bombing incidents from July through October in various cities apparently were connected with the 40th anniversary of Communist rule in Bulgaria. To stimulate a sluggish population growth, especially among "intellectuals," the government offered married students incentives to have more children, including higher family allowances and priority in the allocation of apartments. On January 10 a Balkan Air flight from East Berlin crashed on approach to Sofia, killing 45 persons.

Foreign Relations. Bulgaria continued to encounter widespread disapproval abroad. On June 19, Italy charged that Bulgaria, possibly with Soviet support, masterminded the plot to assassinate Pope John Paul II in 1981, apparently to eliminate the pope's support for the independent Polish labor union, Solidarity. Three Bulgarians and four Turks were indicted for the crime on October 26.

In March, Bulgaria was censured by the United States for its involvement in international terrorism, smuggling arms and drugs, espionage in the United States, and attempts to subvert U.S. export laws. A scheduled American trade fair was held in Sofia in May, but in July the U.S. State Department banned all nonessential governmental travel to Bulgaria.

In January, Bulgaria attended a conference of Balkan states in Athens to discuss the creation of a nuclear-weapons-free zone in the area. Closely following the Soviet lead, it boycotted the Summer Olympic Games in Los Angeles. It also canceled a scheduled visit by Zhivkov to West Germany in September.

JOSEPH F. ZACEK
State University of New York at Albany

BULGARIA • Information Highlights

Official Name: People's Republic of Bulgaria.
Location: Southeastern Europe.
Area: 42,823 sq mi (110 912 km²).
Population (mid-1984 est.): 9,000,000.
Chief Cities (Dec. 31, 1981): Sofia, the capital, 1,070,358; Plovdiv, 358,176; Varna, 293,950.
Government: *Head of state,* Todor Zhivkov, chairman of the State Council and general secretary of the Communist Party (took office July 1971). *Head of government,* Georgi (Grisha) Filipov, chairman of the Council of Ministers (took office June 1981).
Monetary Unit: Lev (0.985 lev equals U.S.$1, July 1984).
Foreign Trade (1982 U.S.$): *Imports,* $11,527,-000,000; *exports,* $11,428,000,000.

As the Rangoon government tries to run a centralized economy, the black market thrives on smuggled goods. About 80% of the country's imported consumer goods enter illegally.

AP/Wide World

BURMA

Burma continued to feel political repercussions of an October 1983 incident in which North Korean agents exploded a bomb in Rangoon, killing 17 senior South Korean officials and four Burmese.

Domestic Affairs. As a result of the bombing, Col. Aung Koe was deposed as Burma's military intelligence chief. Neither he nor his replacement, Col. Maung Hlu, had the qualifications or political contacts of their predecessor, Gen. Tin Oo, who, however, had been given five life sentences on corruption charges in September 1983. Tin Oo appealed to the Supreme Court but failed to win a reversal. He was confined in comfortable quarters, however, and was allowed to receive reading materials not publicly available in Burma. His largely political punishment, reflecting fear of a younger rival on the part of aging strongman Gen. Ne Win, seriously weakened Burmese intelligence and security and was regretted by many other soldiers.

Burma's reduced intelligence capability was mirrored in greater insurgency as well as in the 1983 bombing. The government reported that 2,731 clashes, including 16 major ones, cost the lives of 2,464 rebels between April 1983 and March 1984. Army deaths were believed higher than the officially acknowledged 528. In eastern Burma, heavy fighting against 5,000 Karen rebels continued into the rainy season. The army also had to contend with Peking-aided Communists, opium-trading Shans, and former Nationalist Chinese.

About 80% of Burma's consumer-goods imports entered illegally. The government tolerated such smuggling because discontent was bound to accompany the severe shortages that would otherwise exist. As it was, the illegal imports were insufficient to meet demand. Textiles, automobile parts, medicines, shoes, radios, and plastic products were the chief items smuggled in. Paying for these were rice (the main legal export as well), timber, precious stones, and seafood. Bangladesh imported six times as much Burmese rice illegally as through government channels.

Foreign Relations. Burma continued its policy of steering clear of U.S.-Soviet and Sino-Soviet differences, but the USSR made that difficult. Moscow falsely charged that North Korean responsibility for the bombing incident was an American-Japanese fabrication. Chinese Foreign Minister Wu Xueqian paid an official visit to Rangoon, strengthening Burma's ties with China while those with the Soviet Union were weakening. U.S.-Burmese relations also improved.

The death sentences of the two surviving (of three) North Korean assassins were upheld by the Supreme Court, but Burma would not join with South Korea in bringing the incident before the United Nations. However, Burma no longer maintained embassies in both Seoul and Pyongyang, having broken diplomatic relations with North Korea over the bombing incident.

RICHARD BUTWELL
California State University, Dominguez Hills

BURMA · Information Highlights

Official Name: Socialist Republic of the Union of Burma.
Location: Southeast Asia
Area: 261,300 sq mi (678 576 km²).
Population (mid-1984 est.): 38,900,000.
Chief City: Rangoon, the capital.
Government: *Head of state,* U San Yu, president (took office Nov. 1981). *Head of government,* U. Maung Maung Kha, prime minister (took office March 1977). *Legislature* (unicameral)—People's Assembly.
Monetary Unit: Kyat (8.353 kyats equal U.S.$1, June 1984).
Gross National Product (1981–82 est. U.S.$): $5,601,000,000.
Economic Index (1982): *Consumer Prices* (1970 = 100), all items, 288.8; food, 294.3.
Foreign Trade (1983 U.S.$): Imports, $268,000,000; exports, $378,000,000.

BUSINESS AND CORPORATE AFFAIRS

The U.S. business climate during 1984 continued the upward trend from the serious recession of 1981–82. The overall economy was definitely "upbeat," but there continued to be serious problems in several sectors. The most serious problem continued to be the decline in the U.S. steel industry. In the past ten years U.S. steel production has declined from 151 million tons (137 million metric tons) to 85 million tons (77 million metric tons). Only those living in the steel-producing areas of the country could be fully aware of how serious the situation had become.

While the national unemployment rate dropped from 9.5% in 1983 to 7.3% in September 1984, the unemployment rate in some of the steel producing regions was almost double that rate. The housing industry also was not experiencing the kind of economic expansion that much of the rest of the economy was having. An indication of the strength of the economy was reflected though in the increase in employment. The number of persons gainfully employed increased by 3.3 million persons during the year. Inflation was running at an annual rate of 4.2%, only a slight deterioration from 1983's 3.8%, and personal income was increasing more rapidly than inflation. Automobile sales were particularly strong throughout the year.

Continuing high interest rates not only had an adverse effect on the housing industry, but also a negative effect on the stock market. The Dow Jones Industrial Average dropped from about 1,200 at the beginning of the year to a low of 1,087 in late July, but then recovered to just about where it had been.

Economists, as usual, had varied predictions about the economy for 1985. A majority of those polled were predicting that the U.S. economy would grow at a 3% to 4% annual rate through most of 1985 and slump into a recession by the summer of 1986. A minority were predicting an earlier date for a recession. The slight slowing up of economic activity that took place during the second half of 1984 was considered a favorable trend that was needed to prevent the economy from overheating and stimulating more inflation.

Profits and Losses. The turnaround in the economy that took place in 1983, which was reflected in a sharp increase in corporate profits after taxes, continued in 1984. Corporate profits after taxes were running at a rate of about 18% higher than 1983. Corporate after-tax profits, which totaled $127.4 billion in 1983, were estimated to be $150.2 billion in the second quarter of 1984. The automobile industry reported record profits during the first part of the year, and the way sales were holding up, the industry was hoping for its best year ever.

Losses were cropping up for the less fortunate companies. Even though 1984 was a turnaround year for a number of airlines, it was not that for Pan American, Braniff, or Air Florida. Air Florida filed for bankruptcy during the year, and was taken over by Midway. More than 65 banks failed during the year, which is more than for any full year since the Depression. Business failures were down, however, by about 14% from 1983.

Many firms in the computer software industry were in financial trouble due to the influx of 20,000 programs for the 5 million or so personal computers in use. The shakeout process already had hit the personal computer market; now a shakeout was in process in the personal computer software industry.

Mergers and Divestitures. During 1984 the entire merger-divestiture situation was taking on a different look from that in previous years. Mergers and takeovers continued, but there were serious questions being raised about such acquisitions and there was considerable movement toward divestitures. A number of companies were finding out that what they hoped would happen through mergers and takeovers was not happening, so they were divesting themselves of some of the companies they had previously taken over. Serious questions were being raised both by the public as well as the U.S. Congress as to whether there was really much benefit to the U.S. economy as a whole through the rash of mergers and acquisitions that had taken place.

The largest mergers and acquisitions included the $13 billion takeover of Gulf by Chevron; the $10 billion takeover of Getty by Texaco; the $2.5 billion takeover of Electronic Data Systems by General Motors; and the $2.4 billion takeover of Utah International by Broken Hill Proprietary. Champion International's proposal to buy St. Regis for $1.84 billion would create the nation's largest forest-products company and, analysts were saying, set the stage for an expected flurry of mergers and acquisitions in the industry. International Business Machines, for the first time in 20 years, acquired another company, Rolm Corporation, a telephone-equipment manufacturer, for $1.5 billion.

Mergers also took place in the food industry. The Swiss food giant Nestlé agreed to acquire Carnation Company for $3 billion in a bid to strengthen its presence in the U.S. market. Beatrice acquired Esmark at a price of $2.7 billion. Esmark had bought out Norton Simon in 1983 for about $1 billion. Ralston Purina had agreed to buy ITT's Continental Baking Company for about $475 million.

While many mergers were taking place, divestitures also were occurring. A number of major companies' acquisitions were turning out to be liabilities, so parts of companies were being spun off. Warner Communications sold nearly all of its Atari unit to a new company headed by the former chief executive of Commodore International. Raytheon sold its Raytheon Data Systems division to Telex for about $200 million, taking a $95 million write-off in its second quarter. In one of the biggest divestitures, R. J. Reynolds Industries, the second-largest U.S. cigarette manufacturer, took a back-to-basics step by selling its energy businesses to Phillips Petroleum for $1.7 billion. Earlier in the year, Reynolds had divested itself of its containerized shipping subsidiary Sea-Land to its shareholders.

A different kind of divestiture was the court-ordered breakup of the American Telephone and Telegraph Company. Seven independent regional Bell operating companies were created by the breakup: Ameritech, Bell Atlantic, BellSouth, Nynex, Pacific Telesis, Southwestern Bell, and US West. AT&T will continue to be a competitor in long-distance telephone business, will continue its Bell Laboratories and Western Electric Company operations, and, most important to AT&T, will have the right to compete in the mammoth computer industry. The architects of the AT&T divestiture wanted more competition, but there is a serious question as to whether the breakup will make more problems for the public than the benefits that may accrue from a more competitive telecommunications industry.

Greenmail and Golden Parachutes. Investors have been disturbed as they see what they perceive to be two very questionable practices in the business community—greenmail and golden parachutes. Greenmail is the term applied when an investor buys a large block of shares in a company and indicates the possibility of taking over control of the company. Top management becomes worried because they may lose their jobs. So the top men frequently capitulate and offer to buy back the greenmailer's stock at a premium price in exchange for a promise that the raider will not go after it again, at least not in the near future. A classic case of greenmail was the attempt of investor Saul Steinberg to take control of Walt Disney Productions. He bought a large block of Disney stock, and Disney management "persuaded" him to sell it back to the company at a price that netted him $31.7 million plus $28 million in expenses. All of this occurred in one month's time.

Because of greenmailing, golden parachutes were developed. Golden parachutes are rich severance contracts granted to a company's officers and directors in case the company is taken over and the officers are left without a job. Many of these golden parachutes have been in the multimillion dollar range. Congress approved and President Reagan signed legislation that would severely curtail greenmail and restrict golden parachutes for corporate execu-

AP/Wide World

During a tumultuous year for Walt Disney Productions, Michael D. Eisner, 43, took over as president and CEO.

tives. It was believed that the measure would help ensure the fairness of the takeover process.

Management Personnel. Significant changes were taking place among top corporate officials. United Technologies' board of directors named Robert F. Dantell as president and chief operating officer. Citicorp, the nation's largest bank holding company, named John S. Reed as its new chairman. A divided Walt Disney Productions board named Michael D. Eisner as chairman and chief executive officer.

Following the government's multibillion-dollar rescue of the Continental Illinois National Bank and Trust Company, John E. Swearingen, former chairman of Standard Oil of Indiana, was named chairman and chief executive officer of the new holding company for the Chicago banking concern. American Motors gave the additional post of chief executive officer to its president, Jose J. Dedeurwaerder; International Business Machines named John F. Akers as its new chief executive.

For corporate women there are still problems in getting promoted to top corporate positions. Women managers have become a significant part of the corporate pyramid in the past decade, but they are still concentrated in its lower half. A Market Opinion Research vice-president said a survey showed that women make up about 50% of entry management and 25% of middle management but account for only a tiny percentage of upper management.

STEWART M. LEE, *Geneva College*

Health inspector Bruce Tsutsui oversees enforcement of San Francisco's new law, establishing smoke-free zones.

CALIFORNIA

The state elections focused almost entirely on ballot propositions in 1984. The financial condition of the state was sound. Few dramatic events occurred other than the ultimately unsuccessful effort to save the life of "Baby Fae" at Loma Linda University Hospital through the first transplantation of the heart of a baboon to replace the baby's own. (*See also* MEDICINE AND HEALTH.)

Elections. In the June primary election, Sen. Gary Hart carried the state in the Democratic presidential contest. The voters adopted an initiative that permanently cut 30% from the legislature's lavish budget and guaranteed the minority party proportional representation on all committees. Legislative leaders decided not to challenge the new rules.

In the general election the Republicans gained only one seat in each house of the legislature and one in Congress. The congressional delegation was so effectively gerrymandered by the late Rep. Philip Burton (D-San Francisco) that only four of the 45 house members won by less than 60%. The delegation was Democratic by 27 to 18. On issues, the public approved a state lottery, which had been rejected in the past. Voters rejected a proposal by Howard Jarvis designed to further restrict local taxing powers and another to restrict state welfare payments severely.

A balanced-budget initiative had been removed from the ballot by the state Supreme Court in August. If the measure had passed, California would have been the 33d state of the 34 required to petition Congress to call a constitutional convention for the purpose of passing a balanced-budget amendment.

San Diego Mayor Roger Hedgecock was easily reelected, even though he faced felony charges of accepting illegal campaign contributions. He had been indicted in September on one count of conspiracy and 12 counts of perjury and went on trial in December while continuing in office. If convicted of any charge, he would automatically be removed from office.

Voters in West Hollywood created a new city, with a majority of the new council proclaiming themselves homosexuals. The new city also had a large number of elderly persons who wanted municipal rent control.

The antitax and antidebt mood of a few years before seemed to have passed. Voters approved four large state bond issues in June and six more in November.

State Budget. The legislature passed a $31.3 billion budget, a 15% increase over 1983, but Gov. George Deukmejian vetoed $743 million of it, and the vetoes were sustained. The budget increases were concentrated on education from kindergarten through graduate work and on law enforcement, especially for prison guards. The governor's actions left the state with a reserve of about $950 million.

Disasters. One quite severe earthquake, 6.2 on the Richter scale, occurred April 24. Its epicenter was 12 mi (19 km) east of San Jose. Some 25 people were injured and nine homes were moved off their foundations.

On April 11, California's coastal Highway 1 through the scenic Big Sur country was reopened after 13 months of intense effort following four gigantic winter storms. Workers had struggled seven days a week to clear the route, which had been blocked by landslides. The tourist area had suffered economic losses.

Reagan Presidential Library. On February 14, after foot-dragging by some faculty and alumni, the trustees of Stanford University agreed to have the Ronald Reagan presidential library and museum located on campus. A White House decision to postpone plans for a Reagan public-affairs center hastened the agreement.

CALIFORNIA • Information Highlights

Area: 158,706 sq mi (411 049 km²).
Population (July 1, 1983 est.): 25,174,000.
Chief Cities (July 1, 1982 est.): Sacramento, the capital, 288,597; Los Angeles, 3,022,247; San Diego, 915,956; San Francisco, 691,637; San Jose, 659,181; Long Beach, 371,426; Oakland, 344,652.
Government (1984): *Chief Officers*—governor, George Deukmejian (R); lt. gov., Leo McCarthy (D). *Legislature*—Senate, 40 members; Assembly, 80 members.
State Finances (fiscal year 1983): *Revenues,* $43,768,000,000; *expenditures,* $42,493,000,000.
Personal Income (1983): $333,741,000,000; per capita, $13,257.
Labor Force (May 1984): *Civilian labor force,* 12,433,700; *unemployed,* 898,200 (7.2% of total force).
Education: *Enrollment* (fall 1982)—public elementary schools, 2,801,818; public secondary, 1,263,668; colleges and universities (fall 1983), 1,730,847. *Public school expenditures* (1982–83), $11,050,353,922 ($2,733 per pupil).

Criminal Justice. Results of the state's 1982 revision and stiffening of its drunk-driving laws were evaluated in 1984. Drunk-driving convictions in the state increased by 14% and deaths caused by drunk drivers decreased by 15.8%, but the number of persons in jails increased. This figure increased by 55% between 1978 and 1983 and was higher than the national rate of 41%; of these, 11% were women, compared with a national figure of 7%. In June, voters approved bond issues for both new county jails and new state prisons.

The homicide rate in the state dropped a full 27% during 1981-1984. The trend was statewide, but opinions varied as to the exact reasons.

Disney Productions. Walt Disney Productions fought off a takeover attempt by New York financier Saul P. Steinberg, March 9-June 11, at great cost to the firm. Afterward, the board of directors hired two film executives to take the top offices. It was the first time since the firm was founded in 1923 that it had sought outside executive talent. (*See also* BUSINESS AND CORPORATE AFFAIRS.)

CHARLES R. ADRIAN
University of California, Riverside

CAMBODIA

The political and military struggle in Cambodia followed very much the same pattern in 1984 as it has since the Vietnamese invasion in 1979. A Vietnamese army occupied the country and attempted to defeat a Cambodian resistance force that was backed by China and the Association of Southeast Asian Nations (ASEAN). The fighting was more intense than usual in 1984, but there was no breakthrough in the long diplomatic stalemate.

Politics. Heng Samrin remained at the head of the Vietnamese-backed People's Republic of Kampuchea (PRK) government and its small Communist Party. Not a forceful personality, he was apparently acceptable to both Hanoi and Moscow, Cambodia's two main supporters. Defense Minister Bou Thang was the most prominent of a group of Hanoi-trained Cambodians who held most of the other key positions in the PRK.

Military Developments. Vietnam began a major offensive against Cambodia during mid-April, attacking rebel camps near the Thai-Cambodian border. An estimated 100,000 Cambodian refugees fled into Thailand as a result of the attacks.

In a speech broadcast by the PRK radio in August 1984, Bou Thang acknowledged that PRK and Vietnamese forces were fighting a difficult war against the Cambodian resistance. Bou Thang claimed that the resistance suffered 10,000 casualties in the first half of 1984. A quarter of these, he said, were inflicted by the PRK army and the rest by Vietnamese forces in Cambodia.

The Vietnamese occupation army numbers about 150,000 men. The PRK adds another 30,000. The resistance is composed of about 30,000 Communist troops who are followers of Pol Pot and 15,000 non-Communist soldiers.

In late December, the dry season in Southeast Asia, Vietnam launched its largest attack yet against Cambodian guerrilla camps along the Thai-Cambodian border. The Vietnamese forces bombarded the camps and then took control of the area, sending at least 60,000 Cambodian civilians fleeing to relief shelters in Thailand.

Economy. According to limited published data, the PRK expected a serious shortfall in rice production in 1984, mainly because of the flooding. Before 1970, Cambodia exported a substantial surplus of rice, natural rubber, corn, pepper, and other food stuffs.

The resistance made the recovery more difficult by attacking convoys on the highways and interrupting traffic on the two railway lines. Nevertheless, the PRK government claimed that some of Cambodia's factories had resumed limited production, despite a continuing shortage of raw materials, spare parts, and trained personnel.

Another sign of recovery was the PRK's claim that 1.5 million children were attending school by 1984. Many older students were being sent to Soviet-bloc countries for training.

Foreign Affairs. Vietnam continued to supervise the foreign affairs of its PRK client state while attempting to shift some of the burden for fighting the resistance to the PRK army. Several hundred Soviet and East European advisers remained in Cambodia, but they did not openly seek to supplant Vietnamese influence.

The ASEAN and China continued to support the Cambodian resistance militarily and diplomatically. Vietnam and ASEAN each claimed a willingness to negotiate an end to the struggle, but they made no progress toward a settlement in 1984. The UN General Assembly once again voted overwhelmingly to support the position of the ASEAN states on Cambodia.

PETER A. POOLE
Author, "Eight Presidents and Indochina"

CAMBODIA • Information Highlights

Official Name: The People's Republic of Kampuchea or Democratic Kampuchea.
Location: Southeast Asia.
Area: 70,000 sq mi (181 300 km²).
Population (mid-1984 est.): 6,100,000.
Chief City (1983 est.): Phnom Penh, the capital, 600,000.
Government: *Head of state and government,* Heng Samrin (took office 1981).
Monetary Unit: Riel (4 riels equal U.S.$1, Dec. 1983).

In the presence of Governor-General Jeanne Sauvé and other dignitaries, M. Brian Mulroney was sworn in as Canada's 18th prime minister by Privy Council Clerk Gordon Osbaldeston (left) in Ottawa on September 17.

CANADA

The year 1984 in Canada was one for the history books. Memories of papal and royal visits, Olympic medals, prairie drought, and persistent high unemployment all might fade, but the political transformation would remain as a chronicler's watershed.

Spectacles. Several events during the year distracted Canadians from their domestic discontents and political differences. A national lottery fever ended when an elderly Brantford couple won C$13,890,588, tax-free under Canada's laws. In the Winter Olympics at Sarajevo, Yugoslavia, Gaeten Boucher became a national hero by winning two gold medals in speed skating. At the Summer Games in Los Angeles, the Canadians did even better: swimmers, boxers, divers, canoeists, kayakers, and a woman sharpshooter collected a total of 10 gold, 18 silver, and 16 bronze medals. For another two weeks, in September, Canadians were transfixed by the visit of Pope John Paul II, a mixed reminder of the new dominance of Catholics within Canada's mosaic and of the divisions of conservatism and reform among Catholics themselves. Following the pope, as a reminder of an older national tradition, was a two-week visit by Queen Elizabeth II. Meanwhile, Comdr. Marc Garneau of the Canadian Navy was performing experiments as a payload specialist on the October mission of the U.S. space shuttle *Challenger*.

A number of the year's spectacles served as counterpoints to a growing conservative pressure for law and order. In New Brunswick, the province's Conservative premier, Richard Hatfield, was charged with possession of marijuana. In Saskatchewan, a former Conservative minister of energy, Colin Thatcher, was convicted of murdering his American-born former wife and was sentenced to 25 years in prison. Canada's abortion crusader, Dr. Henry Morgenthaler, was acquitted by a Toronto jury on a charge of procuring a miscarriage.

Political Maneuvering. Such spectacles provided respite from the year's ongoing main event, the battle between the Liberal Party and the Progressive Conservatives (PCs) for control of the federal government. The sparring began early in the year in Parliament with a shrewd assault by the opposition PCs on the tactics of federal tax-collectors, and a budget from the Liberal government that sought to reassure business while offering meager benefits to the elderly and the self-employed. In particular, the Liberal government set out to destroy the untried new Tory leader, Brian Mulroney (*see* BIOGRAPHY). Polls showed that most Canadians opposed the extra-billing and deterrent fees that Conservative and right-wing provincial governments had introduced to curb the rising cost of Medicare. A Canada Health Bill, designed to penalize such provinces, was a test for the national Tory leader, as was the strident Conservative campaign against the concessions offered by Manitoba's New Democratic Party (NDP) government to a French-speaking minority. Would Mulroney oppose western Tories or alienate potential support in Quebec? The Tory leader had no problem deciding: he would uphold Medicare and bilingualism. With the polls promising a Tory election victory, even his traditionally fractious backbenchers held their tongues. As for the Conservative premiers, they directed their fire at the Liberals, confident that in time they could deal more amicably with a Mulroney administration.

Who to Lead? For months Canadians had wondered whether Prime Minister Pierre Elliott Trudeau would lead the Liberal Party into a sixth election. Why else would he launch a highly publicized "peace offensive," circling the globe in search of world leaders who shared his concern? Trudeau continued to dominate government and Parliament, appointing a new governor-general, Jeanne Sauvé (*see* BIOGRAPHY), without even a pretense of consultation. Then, on February 29, after "a walk in the snow" during an Ottawa blizzard, he announced that he had asked Liberal Party President Iona Campagnolo to call a leadership convention. The news brought unseemly rejoicing in such circles as Calgary's Petroleum Club, where Trudeau's Canadianization policies were detested, and discreet anxiety in Tory circles, where the prime minister was judged to be the opposition's greatest asset.

Liberals agreed with that judgment. While six cabinet ministers, led by Trudeau's trusted workhorse Jean Chrètien, emerged as candidates, most of the party establishment and some of the most powerful ministers backed a man who had left Parliament eight years earlier and who appeared to be the antithesis of Trudeau. John Napier Turner and his fabled organization were promised a virtual coronation and perhaps a repetition of Trudeau's own national victory in 1968. If Canadians really were turning conservative, who better to win their votes than a handsome, silver-haired corporation lawyer with a business image and a preoccupation with deficits and waste.

The faith of Turner backers was soon strained. Their man was rusty after eight years, and his fabled organization was a myth. By June 16, when Liberal Party delegates met in Ottawa to choose a leader, the coronation had become a real contest with Jean Chrètien, who claimed that he represented "Main Street" against Turner's Bay Street, the locale for Toronto's corporate elite. But hard work by Turner's powerful backers, plus opinion poll evidence that Liberal fortunes had shot ahead of the Tories, gave Turner a second-ballot victory after everyone but Chrètien and Treasury Board President Don Johnston had withdrawn.

Candidate	Ballot	
	1st	2d
John Turner	1,593	1,862
Jean Chrètien	1,067	1,368
Donald Johnston	278	192
John Roberts	185	to Chrètien
Mark MacGuigan	135	to Turner
John Munro	93	to Chrètien
Eugene Whalen	84	to Chrètien

Election. The resignation of Prime Minister Trudeau took effect on June 30, and John Turner was sworn in with a slightly reshuffled cabinet that day. Prime Minister Turner could have spent the summer meeting the pope and the queen, looking prime ministerial and distancing himself from the Trudeau style as preparation for a fall election. Instead, buoyed by polls showing the Liberals with 46%–49% of the vote (enough for a landslide in a three-party system), Turner chose a summer election campaign. Economic difficulties might be worse in the autumn, he felt, and his predecessor had robbed the Liberals of their parliamentary majority by insisting on a long list of Senate and judicial appointments for loyal members of Parliament (MPs). With the Tories ten points be-

Canapress

John Paul II, the first Roman Catholic pontiff to visit Canada, went on a coast-to-coast tour September 9–20. Right: the papal entourage travels down the Rideau Canal in Ottawa.

THE CANADIAN MINISTRY

M. Brian Mulroney, prime minister
George H. Hees, minister of veterans affairs
Duff Roblin, leader of the government in the senate
Joe Clark, secretary of state for external affairs
Flora MacDonald, minister of employment and immigration
Erik H. Nielsen, deputy prime minister and president of the queen's privy council for Canada
John C. Crosbie, minister of justice and attorney general
Roch LaSalle, minister of public works
Donald F. Mazankowski, minister of transport
Elmer MacKay, solicitor general
Jake Epp, minister of national health and welfare
John A. Fraser, minister of fisheries and oceans
Sinclair Stevens, minister of regional industrial expansion
John Wise, minister of agriculture
Ramon J. Hnatyshyn, minister of state (government house leader)
David E. Crombie, minister of Indian affairs and northern development
Robert R. de Cotret, president of the Treasury Board
Perrin Beatty, minister of national revenue
Michael Wilson, minister of finance
Robert C. Coates, minister of national defence
Jack B. Murta, minister of state (multiculturalism)
Harvie Andre, minister of supply and services
Otto J. Jelinek, minister of state (fitness and amateur sport)
Thomas Siddon, minister of state for science and technology
Charles J. Mayer, minister of state (Canadian Wheat Board)
William H. McKnight, minister of labour
Walter F. McLean, secretary of state
Thomas M. McMillan, minister of state (tourism)
Patricia Carney, minister of energy, mines and resources
André Bissonnette, minister of state (small businesses)
Suzanne Blais-Grenier, minister of environment
Benoit Bouchard, minister of state (transport)
Andrée Champagne, minister of state (youth)
Michel Côté, minister of consumer and corporate affairs
James F. Kelleher, minister for international trade
Robert E. Layton, minister of state (mines)
Marcel Masse, minister of communications
Barbara J. McDougall, minister of state (finance)
Gerry S. Merrithew, minister of state (forestry)
Monique Vézina, minister for external relations

hind in the polls and the New Democrats at an abysmal 11%, Turner could be confident.

Turner and his party were deceived. Whatever election organization the Liberals possessed retired with Trudeau. To the Liberals' own surprise, the long list of patronage appointments by Trudeau had given the Tories their first big campaign issue. National resentment at the former prime minister fastened on the new Liberal leader. While the Turner supporters tried to cleanse their party machinery instead of putting it to work, a superbly planned Mulroney organization went to work across the country, including Quebec, which hitherto had yielded a single Tory seat in 1980. Most surprisingly of all, the NDP did not die. Faced, as he claimed, with two indistinguishable conservative parties, NDP leader Ed Broadbent claimed to be speaking for "ordinary Canadians." His chosen issues—relieving unemployment, full equality for women in the work force, and a fairer tax system—became dominant themes for all three major parties in the election. Two major television debates, one in French and the other in English, gave a boost to Mulroney and Broadbent and a blow to Turner, who limply confessed that he could not refuse Trudeau's patronage demands.

By midsummer there was little doubt as to the outcome of the elections. Canadians clearly wanted a change, and they had lost their brief faith in John Turner. Polls consistently showed the Tories with 50% of the vote, the New Democrats climbing back to their old plateau of 18%, and the Liberals in a free fall. Most astonishing was Quebec, where the Tories had pulled past the Liberals; few experts could believe so massive a shift in allegiance. Former Trudeau strategists such as Sen. Keith Davey, summoned to the rescue, struggled to reshape Turner as a populist and to launch brutal portrayals of the Tory leader as the one-time business executive who closed an entire town.

Brian Mulroney was untouched by their attacks. Canadians saw him as a politician in the center, more devoted than Turner to such popular programs as Medicare. The budget deficit, he insisted, was a problem to be tackled once the economy had improved. In Quebec, his easy colloquial French marked him as a native son while Turner's stiff diction reminded listeners that he was an outsider. Tories with right-wing or eccentric views were discreetly silenced. The media, after some early Mulroney gaffes, were kept at a polite distance, brilliantly managed and tuned to deliver whatever message the Conservatives wished. The New Democrats, too, managed their campaign with unusual and unexpected efficiency, conscious that their fortunes were on the rise.

Turner's advisers counted on a quiet, even boring summer campaign. Certainly there was little evidence of public participation, except in Mulroney meetings in Quebec. An NDP rally of 6,000 was the biggest of the campaign. Yet, on election day, the turnout was an impressive 76%. The final outcome confirmed the opinion polls.

In Brantford, Ont., Indian children present Queen Elizabeth with flowers. The queen and Prince Philip spent 14 days in Canada in 1984, marking some historic anniversaries.

Canapress

Party	Seats	Percent Vote Share
Progressive Conservative	211 (103)	50 (33)
Liberal	40 (146)	28 (44)
New Democrat	30 (32)	19 (20)
Other and Independents	1 (–)	3 (3)

—(1980 results in brackets; election for one seat was delayed.)

The Progressive Conservatives won a majority of votes in every province. Their landslide began in the Maritimes, continued through Quebec (where they rose from a single seat to 58), and carried through Ontario. Only in the West did their already overwhelming support rise only a little, allowing the threatened NDP to retain most of its seats. Liberal support remained strong only in parts of Montreal, in the ethnic communities of Ontario, and, to surprise, in John Turner's prosperous Vancouver constituency of Quadra.

New Government. By prior arrangement, the 17th Canadian prime minister, John Turner, handed over to the 18th prime minister, Brian Mulroney, on September 17. Mulroney knew that both John Diefenbaker in 1957 and Joe Clark in 1979 had sown the seeds of later defeat by their manner of taking power, and his own transition planning was detailed and thoughtful. His new cabinet, with 40 ministers, was the largest in history, and there were no surprises among the recipients of the major portfolios. Joe Clark, whom Mulroney had deposed in 1983, was awarded External Affairs for his subsequent loyalty. He and Flora MacDonald in Manpower and Immigration were among the moderates in the new government; Sinclair Stevens at Regional Industrial Expansion and John Crosbie in Justice were too restlessly radical in their conservatism to reassure the business community. That was the role of Michael Wilson, the new minister of finance.

How far did Canadians want change and of what kind? The polls—vital to the generation of party managers who had brought Mulroney to power—were ambiguous. Alan Gregg, chief Tory pollster, warned that Canadians were hostile to many of their institutions but that they were not very keen on the alternatives, either. They did want better relations with the United States—nationalism was too expensive if it cost jobs—but they also wanted an independent line in world affairs. An early visit to a warmly welcoming President Reagan, followed by promises of Canadian military buildup, allowed the Mulroney government to proclaim a new era of harmony with Canada's powerful neighbor. Speeches by Joe Clark and the appointment of former Ontario NDP leader Stephen Lewis as Canada's voice at the United Nations promised that Canada would still seek to play its role as intermediary.

Canapress

Comdr. Marc Garneau, 35-year-old bilingual native of Quebec City, served as a payload specialist aboard the October flight of the U.S. space shuttle "Challenger."

Canadians also appeared to welcome an end to the federal-provincial wrangling of the Trudeau years. With Tory or sympathetic governments running eight out of ten provinces and René Lévesque's independentist Quebec government openly welcoming a Mulroney government, the new regime in Ottawa could at least deliver temporary harmony. As a first gesture, the new prime minister invited the provincial premiers to set their own agenda for a federal-provincial conference on the economy. How far a financially constrained central government could go to meet provincial demands was a question largely deferred to 1985.

Strategy led the new government to emphasize the scale of the economic troubles it had created. Though Mulroney had claimed from the hustings that the federal deficit had reached $34 billion, he professed indignation that it was so high. Certainly a government compelled to borrow for a third of its annual spending would have to forgo its costly election promises.

While the prime minister and his colleagues strove, on the whole, to present a moderate and conciliatory image in their first months in office, Canada's business community had no hesitation in presenting its demands to a government that professed itself pro-business. If Mulroney had insisted that "jobs" were his priority, business and financial leaders insisted that the deficit was the only issue that mattered and that public spending cuts, not tax increases, were the only acceptable remedy for its reduction. Business lobbyists echoed most of the shibboleths of Reagan conservatism, from deregulation to "down-sizing." A brief from the Canadian Manufacturers' Association

Canapress

With the unemployment rate in double digits in 1984, "jobs, jobs, jobs" became a theme of the Mulroney campaign.

even demanded an end to Canada's unemployment insurance system and repeal of child labor laws.

When Parliament opened on November 5, it was obvious that the new Conservative government had been listening. While the opening speech from the throne, read by Governor-General Sauvé, emphasized the Mulroney themes of reconciliation and consultation, a lengthy statement by Finance Minister Wilson on November 8 gave a much more forceful indication of government intentions. As business had demanded, the deficit had indeed become the priority. Spending cuts of $4.2 billion affected almost every government activity, from defense to the Canadian Broadcasting Corporation. Oil and gas prices moved at once to world levels. Access to unemployment insurance was tightened. Wilson promised even more drastic cuts and debate on a series of fundamental questions, from universality in Canada's social programs to the possibility of a free-trade arrangement with the United States.

In the new Mulroney style, hard decisions would, however, follow consultation with labor, business, and, above all, the provinces, recipients of the largest chunk of Ottawa's $103 billion annual expenditure. The prime minister's November meeting with his provincial colleagues would be limited to setting an agenda. Hard bargaining would come in 1985.

What Canadians Wanted. Assessing what Canadians wanted in 1984 was as difficult as determining the direction of their new government—and the two were intimately related. Faced with persistent high unemployment, especially among the young, a debt burden that had crushed East Coast commercial fishing and menaced much of Canadian agriculture, Canadians had looked to governments for answers. The year saw completion of complex restructuring of Newfoundland and Nova Scotia fishing companies with heavy public participation.

Conservatives, as much as Liberals, were expected to solve the farm debt problem and to cope imaginatively with the aftermath of a severe prairie drought. A year after British Columbia's Social Credit government had slashed public and social services, Progressive Conservative spokesmen had gone out of their way to disassociate themselves from such ideological extremism. Still, on many social and moral issues, Canada was in a right-wing mood. Scattered episodes in which police or prison guards were slain revived demands for a return to the death penalty. Amendments to the Criminal Code promised to curb pornography, street soliciting, and sexual assaults on children.

At the same time, higher courts began confirming the sweeping provisions of Canada's Charter of Rights and Freedoms, adopted in 1982, to overthrow traditional police and criminal court practices. When Canada's Chief Justice Bora Laskin died on March 26 after ten years on the bench, Trudeau's choice of successor, Brian Dickson, was another liberal, described as having "an empathy for the little man, an impatience with technicalities that impede justice." Thanks to Trudeau's constitutional changes, Canada's Supreme Court and its chief justice now occupied a central political role that could not be reversed.

A Year of Change. All in all, Canadians in 1984 had plenty of opportunity for distraction from the dreary, persistent problems of their environment and economy. If the papal visit was a celebration of Canada's acceptance of cultural and linguistic diversity, the 1984 election was a symbol of national unity. Every region of Canada voted strongly for a party and a leader who promised an end to the weary federal-provincial battles of the Trudeau years. For a time at least, Canadians united in giving a mandate to a single leader though the content of that mandate was as good-natured and as unspecific as Brian Mulroney himself.

DESMOND MORTON
Erindale College, University of Toronto

CANADA · Information Highlights

Official Name: Canada.
Location: Northern North America.
Area: 3,851,809 sq mi (9 976 185 km²).
Population (mid-1984 est.): 25,100,000.
Chief Cities (1981 census): Ottawa, the capital, 295,163; Montreal, 980,354; Toronto, 599,217.
Government: *Head of state,* Elizabeth II, queen; represented by Jeanne Sauvé, governor-general (took office May 14, 1984). *Head of government,* M. Brian Mulroney, prime minister (took office Sept. 17, 1984). *Legislature*—Parliament: Senate and House of Commons.
Monetary Unit: Canadian dollar (1.3221 dollars equal U.S. $1, Oct. 22, 1984).
Gross National Product (second quarter 1984 C$): $418,900,000,000.
Economic Indexes: *Consumer Prices* (July 1984, 1981 = 100), all items, 122.9; food, 119.4.
Foreign Trade (1983 C$): *Imports,* $75,586,600,000; *exports,* $90,963,000,000.

The Economy

During 1984 the Canadian economy grew at a lackluster pace. High real interest rates deterred the economy from achieving fast recovery. While inflation was being licked, unemployment remained in double digits.

Real Gross National Product (GNP) rose at an annual rate of 3.0% in the second quarter compared with 2.8% in the first quarter. A slight increase in employment accompanied by faster labor-income growth, falling nominal interest rates, and a declining personal saving ratio caused final domestic demand to rise at an annual rate of 3.5% during the second quarter. This upturn in demand was offset partly by a weaker growth in business investment and government expenditure on current goods and services.

Among the remaining expenditure components of GNP such as inventory investment and export trade, the latter made a far more significant contribution toward improving the level of economic activity than the former. While the monthly change in the level of inventories by the end of August touched a low of .1%, the Canadian trade sector continued to perform well. It showed a goods surplus of C$1.9 billion (seasonally adjusted) in September as the total surplus for the first nine months rose to an annual rate of $20.4 billion well above 1983's $17.7 billion. Exports of auto and auto parts, machinery and equipment, chemicals, and forest products rose significantly.

Despite a modest economic upturn, Canadians continued to experience double-digit unemployment. With October's seasonally adjusted unemployment rate of 11.3%, more than 1.3 million people were looking for jobs. Employment in the primary industries of fishing, forestry, and mining was down 8%; manufacturing was off 7%; and agriculture down 4%. Unemployment indeed is one of the most serious challenges facing Canada in the mid-1980s.

High unemployment, however, created an almost-perfect economic environment for moderating wage expectations and reducing inflationary pressure. The Consumer Price Index was up by only 0.2% between September and October, leaving it 3.4% ahead of a year earlier. That was the lowest year-to-year increase since September 1971. The low inflation rate paved the way for relaxing monetary strings and lowering interest rates. By late 1984, however, real interest was topping the 9% mark, which was a shade lower than 10% in mid-1981, when the prime reached 22.75%.

The high cost of credit was affecting consumer confidence, dampening business investment, and government's ability to reduce debt. Business confidence reflected through business spending intentions already had shown sagging signs. Canada's industrial output slipped in August after showing a strong surge in July.

Canadians could expect tough times ahead. Minister of Finance Michael Wilson's economic statement offered the taste of unpleasant things to come. Consumers faced inevitable price increases for gasoline and heating fuels. The government also set the stage for reducing the bulging Canadian deficit and public debt by reviewing all programs including the "social safety net" program accounting for 40% of federal outlays.

R. P. SETH
Mount Saint Vincent University, Halifax

THE CANADIAN ECONOMY

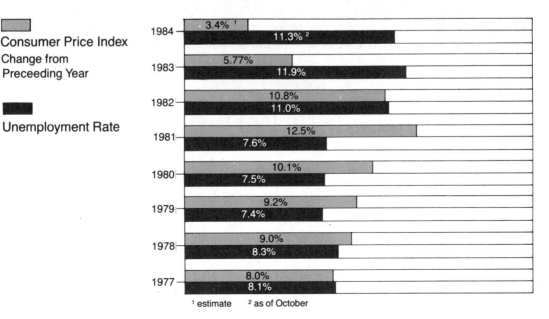

Consumer Price Index
Change from Preceeding Year

Unemployment Rate

Year	CPI	Unemployment
1984	3.4% [1]	11.3% [2]
1983	5.77%	11.9%
1982	10.8%	11.0%
1981	12.5%	7.6%
1980	10.1%	7.5%
1979	9.2%	7.4%
1978	9.0%	8.3%
1977	8.0%	8.1%

[1] estimate   [2] as of October

Canapress Photo Service

THE TRUDEAU YEARS

Sixteen years of colorful but at times unpredictable leadership by Pierre Elliott Trudeau ended in 1984. After a "great walk" in heavy snow in late February, the former Montreal constitutional lawyer concluded that "this is the appropriate time for someone else to assume" the leadership of Canada's ruling Liberal Party.

Except for the period June 4, 1979, to March 3, 1980, Trudeau had served in the premiership since April 20, 1968. His tenure was marked by a struggle between the federal government and French separatists in the province of Quebec; the birth of a new constitution, including a Charter of Rights; and a desire by Canadians to become less economically dependent on the United States. At the same time, the flamboyant Trudeau freely expressed his views on the international scene, seeking a greater role for his nation and for himself. He also advocated greater dialogue between the world's rich and poor nations.

Canapress Photo Service

Brian Willer, "Maclean's"

P. Breese, Gamma-Liaison

According to his biographer, Pierre Elliott Trudeau became "central to the Canadian imagination as no other prime minister before him." A highlight of his leadership occurred April 17, 1982, when Queen Elizabeth II signed the Constitution Act, granting Canada complete independence from Great Britain (top right). An internationalist, the prime minister traveled to India in 1971 (page 162) and to Asia, including Thailand, in 1983 (above left), and was host to the 1981 summit of the leaders of the six major industrial democracies (right). An ardent campaigner, Trudeau enjoyed particular political success in Quebec (below left). A stylish but informal dresser, the divorced parent is said to be highly devoted to his three sons.

J. P. Lafont, Sygma

Canapress Photo Service

The Arts

The rapid turnover in prime ministers, from Pierre Trudeau to John Turner to Brian Mulroney, had Canadian artists wondering not only what the government would do for them but also what government would be doing it. The Canadian Conference of the Arts, representing 600 organizations, met in Ottawa and heard speakers ask that government give a higher priority to the arts. Two main anxieties were a tightening of federal funds and the increasing number of artists from the United States who were taking Canadian jobs. To be sure, politicians promised help to the arts, but the promises often were short on specifics.

Visual Arts. The Art Gallery of Ontario celebrated the province's bicentennial with its exhibition *From the Four Quarters: Native and European Art in Ontario 5000 B.C. to 1867 A.D.,* arranged by Joan Vastorak and Dennis Reid. It also mounted *Toronto Painting '84,* showing the work of 32 Toronto artists. At the same gallery, *The Mystic North,* an exhibition of symbolist landscape painting, demonstrated the likenesses between Northern European and North American canvases. Still another exhibition, entitled *Norval Morriseau and the Emergence of the Image Makers,* paid tribute to Morriseau, a northern Ontario Indian, whose paintings drew on Indian mythology.

In other news the Royal Ontario Museum's exhibition *Georgian Canada: Conflict and Culture 1745–1820* brought that era to life with paintings, fine furnishings, swords, and statues. Painter and skating star Toller Cranston had an exhibition of his works in his native Hamilton, Ont. After four years of fund-raising, the Northern Arts and Cultural Centre in Yellowknife, N.W.T., opened with a gala show. At the Montreal Museum of Fine Arts, Louise d'Argencourt arranged a highly popular exhibition of works of Adolf William Bouguereau, a classical painter of late 19th century Paris. *Canadian Art,* a quarterly, made its debut as Canada's only national arts magazine.

Less than a year after the splendid new Vancouver, B.C., Art Gallery opened, its director, Luke Rombout, resigned and was appointed by *Expo '86,* Vancouver's 1986 world's fair, to handle all of its visual arts. Paintings worth $500,000 and given over a five-year period to the gallery by timber executive and former gallery president Ron Longstaffe were to be exhibited in early 1985. The mostly Canadian paintings were given after the gallery committed itself to gaining new quarters. Among numerous exhibitions in the gallery's first year was *Alex Colville: a Retrospective.*

An exhibition scheduled at the gallery was Paul Wong's *Confused/Sexual Views,* consisting of videotapes showing head and shoulders views of 27 people giving their thoughts on human sexuality. Entry was to have been restricted to viewers 18 years old or over. Two days before the show's opening, the gallery canceled it as unsuitable. Wong took his case to the British Columbia Supreme Court, which refused to grant an injunction ordering the gallery to show his exhibition.

Another show canceled—but for engineering reasons—was Blair Atwell's sculptural exhibition, consisting mostly of big rocks from a river, at the Coburg Gallery, Vancouver. Called *Primary Interface,* the show was canceled only hours before its scheduled opening when an engineering study indicated that the exhibit's great weight could cause it to crash through the floor, to the peril of viewers.

Popular painter Toni Onley was again in the news. In 1983 he had managed to ease Canadian tax regulations regarding artists by threatening to burn publicly $1 million worth of his prints to protest tax regulations that classed him as a manufacturer whose unsold works had to be assessed for taxation. His current adventure was far more hazardous. Fond of painting glaciers, he and photographer John Reeves had piloted a plane to a landing on Cheakamus Glacier in Garibaldi Park, B.C. Taking off for the return trip, Onley's plane was swept down by a wind current and crash landed, with the body of the plane perched over the only narrow part of a deep crevasse, supported precariously by a wing on either side of the cleft. The pair were rescued the next day.

Performing Arts. The 32nd Stratford Festival at Stratford, Ont., opened with Shakespeare's *A Midsummer Night's Dream,* directed by John Hirsch, with sets by Desmond Heeley. Gilbert and Sullivan's *Iolanthe,* directed by Brian Macdonald, featured the insertion of Canadian political references. Gilbert and Sullivan's *The Gondoliers* and *The Mi-*

Katharina Megli and Paul Massel duet in Gilbert and Sullivan's The Gondoliers, *performed at the Stratford Festival.*

Clifford Jones, Toronto International Festival

Salt Lake Mormon Tabernacle Choir

The Toronto International Festival featured 185 performances of music and dance from around the world. Among the presentations was the Kathakali dance drama, left, traditionally performed only by men since its creation in India around 1650. The 340-member Salt Lake Mormon Tabernacle Choir, above, was another participant.

kado, both of which had been enormously popular, were repeated. Other Shakespearean offerings included *Love's Labour's Lost,* directed by Michael Langham, and *Romeo and Juliet,* directed by Peter Dews.

In another successful season at Niagara-on-the-Lake, Ont., the Shaw Festival included George Bernard Shaw's *The Devil's Disciple,* directed by Larry Lillo; Thornton Wilder's *The Skin of Our Teeth,* directed by Christopher Newton, with sets by Michael Levine; and Noel Coward's *Private Lives,* directed by Denise Coffey.

Montreal writer Mordecai Richler adapted his popular novel *The Apprenticeship of Duddy Kravitz* to the musical stage as *Duddy* with music by Mike Stoller and lyrics by Jerry Leiber. Canada's most expensive musical at $1 million, it was scheduled to tour Canada but closed after a run at the Citadel Theatre in Edmonton, Alta. On a more hopeful note, in Toronto the Adelaide Court Theatre and producer Marlene Smith formed a company to encourage new musicals. Another company in the same theater, the Group of Several, under artistic director Jim Betts, encouraged workshops in musical theater.

For ten years Saskatchewan farmer Charles Keeling loved singer Anne Murray and imagined that she loved him and that her songs contained secret messages for him. The law took a hand when Keeling was jailed for three months and fined $500 for disobeying a court order not to communicate with her. Later Paul Ledoux and David Young made Keeling's story into a well-received stage play at Thunder Bay, Ont.

Honoring Ontario's bicentennial and Toronto's sesquicentennial, the Toronto International Festival presented 3,000 performers from many countries, with the Metropolitan Opera Company of New York giving seven operas. The Canadian Opera Company presented the North American premiere of the early Italian opera *Representation of Soul and Body* in St. Michael's Cathedral, with the cathedral choir and the Mainly Mozart Orchestra participating. The National Ballet performed John Cranko's *Onegin.* The festival, under director Muriel Sherrin, cost more than $9 million to mount, and attendance for the events varied.

The Canadian Opera Company gave the Canadian premiere of *Death in Venice,* with music by Benjamin Britten and libretto by Myfanwy Piper.

The Montreal Symphony Orchestra, under Charles Dutoit, celebrated 50 years with a highly successful European tour. The Winnipeg Symphony Orchestra, under its new musical director Kazuhiro Koizumi, opened its season debt free for the first time in its history. Rudolph Barshai was to succeed Kazuyoshi Akiyama in September 1985 as music director of the Vancouver Symphony Orchestra.

Les Grands Ballets Canadiens made a lengthy and successful tour of Asia. The National Film Board made a documentary film of the tour, which marked the farewell appearance of prima ballerina Annette av Paul.

Film. Hollywood moviemakers, lured by the low value of the Canadian dollar in relation to the American one, were busy in Canada, especially in British Columbia. The province had a record influx of U.S. producers and their crews, who spent approximately $60 million and provided several hundred jobs for local actors and technicians.

DAVID SAVAGE
Simon Fraser University

Matthew Naythons, "Time"

In October, one year after the overthrow of a Marxist government on Grenada, the Point Saline International Airport (below), begun by Cuba and completed with U.S. aid, opened officially. By then, luxury cruise liners also had begun returning to the island. Generally, the Caribbean tourist industry enjoyed a profitable year.

Susanna McBee, "U.S. News & World Report"

CARIBBEAN

The economies of the Caribbean countries were mired in a continuing recession during 1984. Prices of such principal commodities as bauxite, alumina, and bananas improved slightly during the year, but not enough to boost export earnings to prerecession highs. The sugar industry remained depressed, with prices well below the cost of production for most exporters. There were, however, a few hopeful signs in a generally gloomy panorama.

CBI. Preliminary data suggested that the United States' Caribbean Basin Initiative (CBI), which went into force on Jan. 1, 1984, has the potential for opening new markets for Caribbean products. The CBI offers duty-free entry into the United States for a wide variety of goods produced in the region. In the first three months of 1984, total exports from the Caribbean basin countries (including Central America) increased by 31% over the same period in 1983, from $1.7 billion to $2.2 billion. Individual countries fared even better than the regional average. Exports from Barbados were up by 176%; from St. Lucia by 160%; from Grenada by 149%; and from Jamaica by 147%. The trend continued through the first half of the year, with Jamaica alone reporting a six-month jump of 130%.

Economists emphasized that the export improvement merely represented a recovery from the depressed levels of the previous three recession-bound years. Caribbean exports to the United States dropped from $10.3 billion in 1980 to $7.1 billion in 1983. The projected 1984 level of $9.3 billion would still be considerably below the pre-1981 totals. In addition, the economists pointed out that the strength of the U.S. dollar may have as much to do with the higher U.S. import level as does the CBI. Department of Commerce officials nonetheless reported that investment in the Caribbean has risen since the approval of CBI.

Tourism. The strong U.S. dollar also lay behind a resurgence of tourism, a key Caribbean money-maker. The region was host to 7.3 million tourists in 1983, a 2.6% rise over 1982. Tourism earnings were up by $208 million, to a total of $4.5 billion. Tourism officials reported that the growth continued through the first half of 1984. The biggest increases were registered by Jamaica and the Bahamas, while Puerto Rico and Barbados were relatively unchanged. The Bahamas and Puerto Rico are the tourism volume leaders in the Caribbean, each with annual gross earnings of about $700 million.

Sugar Cane. World free market prices for sugar plummeted as low as five cents per pound in 1984, plunging cane growers and sugar producers into economic doldrums. In July the sugar-exporting member countries of the Organization of American States (OAS) held a three-day meeting in the Dominican Republic to identify alternative uses for sugar cane. The emphasis was on the production of ethanol, a fuel-grade alcohol made from sugar cane by biomass conversion. Ethanol can be used by itself as a fuel for automobiles or mixed with gasoline to produce gasohol. OAS technicians said that the Latin American and Caribbean countries can produce up to 160 million gallons (606 million 1) of ethanol per year using existing resources and facilities, and the output could be raised to 300 million gallons annually through more efficient operations.

In another energy-related development, Mexico and Venezuela extended until mid-1985 the four-year old "San José Agreement," under which the two countries supply petroleum on concessional terms to nine smaller countries in the Caribbean and Central America. Beneficiaries pay only 80% of the cost of oil supplied under the agreement. The remainder is treated as a low-interest, five-year loan.

Commission. In July, 15 heads of Caribbean countries met with U.S. President Ronald Reagan on the campus of the University of South Carolina in Columbia, SC. The Caribbean leaders asked the president to appoint a high-level commission, similar to the Kissinger Commission on Central America, to formulate proposals for substantial long-term assistance to the Caribbean islands. The government chiefs praised President Reagan's CBI but said trade concessions need to be accompanied by concrete development projects. They reminded the president that the invasion of Grenada had demonstrated the "strategic" value of the Caribbean to U.S. security interests.

Trade Problems. Despite the trade concessions of the CBI, several trade disputes between the United States and Caribbean countries smoldered during the year. The U.S. Environmental Protection Agency banned imports of tropical fruits containing residues of ethylene dibromide (EDB), a plant fumigant that is a suspected carcinogen. About $30 million worth of Caribbean fruit exports annually were affected. The U.S. Federal Aviation Administration said it would begin to enforce strict new aircraft noise control rules on Jan. 1, 1985. Caribbean governments protested that their older planes could not meet the standards and they could not afford new equipment. Officials at Miami airport said the rules would effectively ban 37 Caribbean and Latin American airlines from landing there. In October, Congress legislated a one-year delay in enforcement of the rules.

New meat inspection rules that took effect on Jan. 1, 1984, temporarily interrupted shipments of fresh meat from the Dominican Republic to the United States. It was several months before the Dominican Republic obtained the new inspection equipment mandated by the rules. Several Caribbean countries also balked at a provision written into the CBI requiring them to exchange tax information with the United States. The Bahamas and the Cayman Islands declined to participate in the CBI as a result. An agreement was reached with Barbados only after difficult negotiations. A Barbadian official said the dispute had been a "major source of acrimony."

Hispaniola. The two-country island of Hispaniola was beset by violence and depressed conditions in 1984. In April at least 30 people in the Dominican Republic were killed in riots brought on by price increases for all imported goods and many basic foodstuffs. In June rioting also erupted in Haiti for the first time in the more than quarter of a century of rule by the Duvalier family. Tourism, once a mainstay of the Haitian economy, plummeted as visitors were repelled by Haiti's image of state terrorism and reports that the country was a focus of AIDS, a deadly immunological disease.

Church. Pope John Paul II visited the Dominican Republic and Puerto Rico in October. In the Dominican Republic the pontiff attended a meeting of CELAM, the Conference of Latin American Bishops.

St. Kitts. The twin-island state of St. Christopher (St. Kitts) and Nevis became the 32d member country of the OAS in March. St. Kitts became independent in September 1983.

RICHARD C. SCHROEDER, *"Visión" Magazine*

CENTRAL AMERICA

In the spring of 1983 several U.S. congressmen proposed the creation of a bipartisan commission to investigate America's role in Central America. President Ronald Reagan established the National Bipartisan Commission on Central America later in the year and placed it under the chairmanship of former Secretary of State Henry Kissinger. Eleven men, plus Kissinger as chairman and career diplomat Harry Shlaudeman as executive director, and a number of advisers spent many months of study, including visits to Central America. Their report was presented to President Reagan in January 1984. Some members filed minority comments on specific items, but in general, great agreement was reached about the major issues as well as possible solutions to specific problems. Broadly, the report recommended massive socioeconomic assistance, increased military aid, a huge cultural and academic exchange, assistance in political maturation, a strict human-rights policy, and the establishment of a new umbrella agency, the Central American Development Organization.

Generally, both liberal and conservative members of the commission agreed that the roots of the Central American problem were complex, that a Marxist threat existed in the area, but that Central America's socioeconomic problems were basic and historic. The report's most significant proposal sought external financing of $24 billion (U.S.) to be awarded before 1990 to the seven countries of Central America. One third of the funds would come from the United States, the rest from other nations and international financing agencies. Greatly expanded military aid to El Salvador, continued assistance to the anti-Sandinista governmant rebels, the "Contras," of Nicaragua, but no invasion of Cuba were other measures agreed on. Although President Reagan asked Congress for about $750 million in mixed economic and military aid as a start, the U.S. elections slowed action on the report's recommendations.

Personality conflicts were reported as the reason for the resignation of Richard Stone as special envoy to Central America and his replacement by Shlaudeman, who had served in three Latin American nations as ambassador.

Several events provoked disagreements between the administration and Congress, including some members of the Republican Party. The Central Intelligence Agency (CIA) was accused of directing the mining of Nicaragua's harbors without keeping Congress informed and in probable violation of international law. The U.S. Senate condemned the action as did the International Court of Justice. The mining was halted in April. In September two U.S. civilians were killed by Nicaraguan government troops. Denying charges that the CIA was trying to overthrow the Sandinista government, the administration contended that the men were acting on their own.

President Duarte called his meeting with rebel leaders "among the most transcendental hours in Salvadoran history."

Frank Fournier, Contact Press Images

With voting mandatory in Guatemala, some 1.7 million of the nation's 2.5 million registered voters cast ballots in July 1 elections for a Constituent Assembly. The new legislature was to write a constitution in preparation for presidential elections.

Claude Urraca, Sygma

The Kissinger Commission had favored the acceptance of the Contadora process for bringing peace in Nicaragua. This was an effort of an outside group—five Central American republics (Costa Rica, El Salvador, Guatemala, Honduras, and Nicaragua) plus Mexico, Panama, Venezuela, and Colombia—to get all the participants, including the United States, to agree to some principles and procedures. In September the Sandinistas surprised the United States by suddenly announcing their willingness to accept a Contadora treaty and called for the United States to do the same. Now the Reagan administration refused, raising objections to certain terms, but Sandinista propaganda made it appear as though the United States opposed the very notion of peace.

Considering the turbulence in the region, the existence of a fairly general economic recession was not surprising. The Central American Common Market in particular suffered as relations among several pairings of nations remained strained. Most trade became bilateral as a result. But Central America did benefit from closer ties with Western Europe.

Belize. The Kissinger Commission did not address the relationship between Belize and its neighbors, in particular, Guatemala. In spite of Belize's backward economy, large numbers of Central Americans increasingly were migrating into this former British colony in 1984. The government of Prime Minister George Price in midyear gave all undocumented foreigners 90 days in which to register and indicate whether they preferred provisional, permanent, or refugee status. An estimated 26,000 foreigners were residing in Belize; more than 3,000 registered during the first two weeks of the program. It should be remembered that the entire population of the young nation is only about 155,000, so many citizens were alarmed at the numbers.

Economic as well as racial tensions were aggravated. Most of the migrants were Latin from Guatemala, Honduras, or El Salvador and even poorer and less skilled than the blacks of Belize. The migrants ostensibly came seeking work as cane cutters, but they often drifted off into the jungle and found more lucrative work raising and selling marijuana to the international market. This business became so large that the United States threatened to cut off its aid to Belize under the Caribbean Basin Initiative (CBI), which demands such action when a nation does not do its share in fighting the drug trade. Meanwhile, many black natives left Belize for Canada, the United States, or Great Britain in search of better jobs.

To get help from the International Monetary Fund (IMF), Belize tried to meet the austerity demanded by that agency and raised taxes on many imports, as well as gasoline, beer, soft drinks, and utilities. For these measures Price was criticized from the left and the right, and he sought to strengthen his administration by adding more leftists to his government. The strict measures seemed to help the economy, but exports were still down about 20% from 1983. On the positive side it could be noted that the important peanut crop had grown dramatically in 1982–84, several U.S. loans had been approved, and an increase in banana prices late in the year was making the trade balance look better.

In spite of the improvements, Price and his People's United Party suffered a major defeat in the nation's first parliamentary elections since independence in 1981. In mid-December, the opposition United Democratic Party, led by Sen. Manuel Esquivel, a 44-year-old physics teacher, captured 21 parliamentary seats to 7 for Price's party. The outgoing prime minister even lost his own seat from Belize City. Increased foreign investment and a freer economy were Esquivel's campaign themes.

Belize also needed assurance that it would be safe from possible incursions by Guatemala, which still claims the land as a descendant of the old Spanish empire. This protection has come from Great Britain, with modest amounts of military supplies from the United States. During the political campaign, Esquivel expressed his eagerness that the 1,800 British force should remain in Belize.

Costa Rica. Maintaining its neutrality in a region at war with itself continued to pose many problems for Costa Rica in 1984. The nation was pressured by the United States to give greater support to the Contras against the Nicaraguan government. The presence of thousands of Nicaraguans in Costa Rica plus a dozen or more border clashes along the San Juan River separating the two nations prompted the delivery of American jeeps, patrol boats, light weapons, and two helicopters to the Costa Rican government. Since Costa Rica has no army—only a sort of national guard of about 8,000—the value of these items was questionable. The guard's equipment was considered "antiquated."

Seeking alternatives to closer ties with the United States, President Luis Alberto Monge visited Western Europe in June. He was well received in Spain and West Germany but treated cooly by many Dutch and French diplomats. He received little in loans and grants, the major purpose of his visit. In August he asked for, and received, the offers of resignation of his entire cabinet and many agency heads. His exact purpose was unclear, for many leaders were reappointed, but four cabinet members and some department heads were not. Although there were rumors that the changes were to prevent a coup, Vice-President Armando Arauz Aguilar declared that the matter concerned the continuing economic malaise.

At the time a strike of banana workers was about one month old. The workers were asking for a 57% increase in wages. But the strike dragged on and the unions lowered their demands as many workers drifted back to the plantations. An affiliate of United Brands faced the longest strike in the nation's history—three months—and complained that the company and the government were losing millions in revenues. Two workers were killed in strike-related activity. By the end of September the government insisted that the strike had ended, but many workers still picketed. At the peak about 3,000 workers had walked out.

Costa Rica faced an enormous external debt, originating in easy loans and the sudden increase in energy costs in the late 1970s. After many months of negotiations the government was able to reach an accord with the IMF and various banks to reschedule the debt and receive additional financing. In return, austerity measures had to be enacted at home, and they turned out to be politically unpopular. In addition, the government was able to arrange bilateral trade agreements with a number of American and European nations to restore some of the trade lost in sickness of the Central American Common Market. Industry showed some signs of recovery from the oil crisis, and inflation had modified. Coffee production rose slightly, and prices appeared to have leveled off. All of these elements should be assisted by the new Caribbean Basin Initiative (CBI). President Monge continued to push for his "Back to the Land" movement, to save the value of the colón by making the nation more self-sufficient in foods.

El Salvador. Late in 1983 the Constituent Assembly presented the nation a new constitution, the 36th since 1824. Larger issues concerned a better balance of power among the three branches of government and the means of completing the dragging land reform program. The most important matter concerned the election of a president. The large number of candidates prevented anyone from achieving a majority at the first election in March. Of the two leaders, José Napoleón Duarte received the plurality and a vote of about 43%; second was Roberto d'Aubuisson who had about 30%. A third candidate, Francisco José Guerrero, gained nearly 20%. In the May runoff Duarte defeated D'Aubuisson 53% to 46% out of a popular vote of 1,403,000. The latter accused the CIA of stealing the election from him because of its contribution of more than $2 million to some of the candidates. Rumors of coups and terrorist action proved false, and Duarte was inaugurated without incident on June 1.

				CENTRAL AMERICA • Information Highlights	
Nation	**Population (in millions)**	**Area**		**Capital**	**Head of State and Government**
		(sq mi)	**(km²)**		
Belize	0.2	8,870	22 963	Belmopan	Elmira Minita Gordon, governor-general
					Manuel Esquivel, prime minister
Costa Rica	2.5	19,700	51 022	San José	Luis Alberto Monge, president
El Salvador	4.8	8,292	21 476	San Salvador	José Napoleón Duarte, president
Guatemala	8.0	42,000	108 780	Guatemala City	Oscar Humberto Mejía Victores, chief of state
Honduras	4.2	42,301	109 560	Tegucigalpa	Roberto Suazo Córdova, president
Nicaragua	2.9	57,143	148 000	Managua	José Daniel Ortega Saavedra, president
Panama	2.1	29,208	75 650	Panama City	Nicolas Ardito Barletta, president

The United States continued to hold military exercises in Honduras in 1984, causing some Hondurans to hold protests against the increasing U.S. presence on their soil.

His problems remained enormous. In addition to strong right-wing opposition, there was vast unemployment, a civil war now five years old, and civil-rights questions that determine the rate of financial assistance from the United States and probably other nations as well. In May and July he visited Washington and discussed military aid with the president and congressional leaders.

At home, President Duarte moved to bolster the weak civil-rights program. He established commissions to investigate the "death squads," took personal command of many military programs, and fired or transferred officers suspected of violations. The number of abuses seemed to drop, although one Catholic Church agency found no change. Five soldiers were convicted of murdering three American nuns and a lay worker in December 1980. Unresolved was the degree of responsibility of superior officers in the deaths.

In October, President Duarte issued a surprise invitation to leaders of the Salvadoran left to meet with him and discuss measures that might lead to peace. The invitation was accepted, and an all-day session was held in a church at the little town of La Palma. San Salvador's Archbishop Arturo Rivera y Damas acted as a witness. Thousands of people waited outside the church. The rebels were represented by Guillermo Ungo and Rubén Zamora. There were no incidents. The men discussed major issues but agreed on nothing substantive. Other meetings were planned to work on the basic issues dividing the factions. Although the violent war continued, the fact of the meeting encouraged many to believe that a cease-fire was possible. Ungo has been quoted as favoring a unilateral cease-fire and rebel participation in a future election, but only if the left-wing groups are given a share in the government. He also went to the United States and appealed for his cause.

The civil war has taken an economic toll on the land in addition to the terror it has brought to the people. The gross domestic product dropped every year from 1978 until a near-leveling took place in 1983. In spite of many controls over most salaries and basic foods, inflation remained a double-digit problem, and there were many scarcities. To encourage manufacturing, the Inter-American Development Bank lent the nation $60 million on long, easy terms.

President Duarte continued to receive support from both the U.S. Congress and the Reagan administration but was frustrated by lack of control of his own congress. This could come to a head in March 1985 when the next legislative election is scheduled. At that time 80 seats would be contested.

Guatemala. On July 1, Guatemalans went to the polls to choose delegates for a Constituent Assembly. So close was the vote that the first count had the wrong parties leading, and two weeks passed before the final count was accepted. Approximately 1.7 million voters gave the extreme-right-wing National Liberation Movement 23 delegates, the National Union of the Center 21, and the Christian Democrats (originally thought to be the winners) 20. Not only did no party have a majority, the vote showed that more ballots were blank or improperly marked than the number received by any single party, a standard Latin American demonstration of dissatisfaction with the options. Chief of State Gen. Oscar Humberto Mejía Victores announced his hope that presidential elections would be held in March 1985 at which time he would retire.

Meanwhile the Constituent Assembly would write the fifth Guatemalan constitution in 40 years. These events gave hope, but no promise, of a restoration of a bit of civilian authority in Guatemalan affairs. No leftist candidates ran in the 1984 election, incidentally. For

Claude Urraca, Sygma

Daniel Ortega of the Sandinista National Liberation Front (FSLN) ran successfully for Nicaragua's presidency.

about 30 years the military has ruled in Guatemala, and Congress has not met since 1982. Much of the time the rule has been most repressive, especially under the regime of President Gen. Romeo Lucas García, beginning in 1978. Because of U.S. charges of violations of human rights, Guatemala has received no U.S. military assistance since 1977. Nevertheless, the Guatemalan government has been surprisingly successful against some reported 5,000 guerrillas. By late 1984, however, the regime had begun asking about military assistance again, and it might be forced to adopt less repressive measures against its populace in order to receive such help. One bishop stated that kidnappings and massacres still continued, and the new archbishop, Próspero Penados del Barrio, did not believe that the civil war was over. Contrary to his predecessor, who urged Catholics to support the government, the archbishop announced his intention to keep his distance from the military. One step intended to make the government look better was the dismissal in September of about 400 officers of the national police force for various crimes.

The repression, a per capita income that had not risen in eight years, and an official underemployment figure of 40% led to the continuation of a massive refugee issue. The Mexican government stated that about 46,000 Guatema-

lans, mostly Indian, have moved into Mexico, presumably for increased security. (The U.S. estimate was about 150,000.) Raiding from either side and an increasing number of border incidents prompted the Mexican government to initiate a program of forced migration farther into Mexico. The Indians have been living in several dozen United Nations–sponsored camps in Chiapas province; in July, Mexico commenced transporting a few hundred at a time to Campeche, about 435 mi (700 km) to the northeast. Some accepted the option to go home, but Mexico planned to have all of them away from the border by early 1985.

Honduras. In April, just one day before Honduran-U.S. military exercises were to begin, a group of young officers arrested Gen. Gustavo Alvarez Martinez, the commanding general of all Honduran forces, and sent him into exile in Costa Rica. The general, a close friend of the United States, was accused by some of sharing control of Honduras with U.S. Ambassador John Negroponte. The episode came as a surprise to the Reagan administration. What role, if any, Honduras' President Roberto Suazo Córdova played in the overthrow was unclear. By a vote of 78 to 0, the Congress agreed on a successor to finish the five-year term. The new commander, Gen. Walter López Reyes, 46-year-old commander of the air force, was certainly no enemy of the United States but was expected to be much more independent of the Pentagon and the American embassy than his predecessor.

The people of Honduras became increasingly concerned over the continued and growing presence of U.S. and Salvadoran troops on their soil. The Salvadorans were receiving training from the North Americans, an operation not popular with Hondurans whose many disputes with El Salvador have not been settled since the 1969 Soccer War.

Now López Reyes was asking for new arrangements with the United States, including the removal of the Salvadorans, better military facilities for Honduras at Puerto Castilla, a reexamination of the program to train Nicaraguan Contras, and a revision of the 1954 military agreement between his nation and the United States.

The U.S. presence was substantial. Military assistance to Honduras in 1983 amounted to $37 million; for fiscal 1984, President Reagan asked for $78.5 million. Economic aid for 1984 was about $72.5 million. There were 1,700 American troops in Honduras, the number expanding greatly during the many maneuvers held in Honduras each year. In 1983 the United States trained 700 Hondurans and 1,500 Salvadorans, and in 1984, 3,400 Hondurans and 4,350 Salvadorans; an estimated 12,000 Nicaraguans are based in Honduras for U.S. help. U.S. task forces patrol both coasts, and Americans are improving two air bases at La Ceiba and Palmerola. Honduras returned to civilian government in 1982 after nine military governments; many Hondurans fear that continued U.S. presence might bring the return of army rule to Honduras.

While the infrastructure has been improved in places, the U.S. use of Honduras as a "permanent" base has done little for the economy. Inflation ranged at about 21% for 1983 and 1984, the foreign debt was more than $2 billion, unemployment was about 20%, and underemployment much worse. In June, President Suazo Córdova, whose term ends in 1985, proposed to Congress a new tax package, originally demanded by the IMF. The president also wanted a requirement that all public workers would have to buy government bonds. When tens of thousands of workers threatened a strike, he called off the measure and sought more U.S. aid. In August he completely shook up his cabinet, amid complaints that his advisers wanted his term extended and that his party was deliberately mishandling registration of voters in order to delay the election.

The economy still suffered from the decline in the Central American Common Market as well as the general slowness of demand for the tropical agriculture on which Honduras relies. Honduras also suffered from a rapidly increasing population growth, helping to produce the lowest per capita gross domestic product in the region.

Nicaragua. There was no improvement in relations between the United States and Nicaragua in 1984, as each side seemed to take its turn in calling the other's bluff. In April the U.S. government admitted that the CIA had directed the mining of Nicaraguan harbors by Contras. The mines did little damage, but the episode stirred a great deal of bitterness. Some European nations delighted in offering to remove the mines. Some congressmen, including Republicans, condemned the CIA for not following congressional guidelines.

In August the Sandinistas admitted that they were building a 12,000-ft (3 600-m) runway, large enough to handle any Soviet airplane. Then they shot down a helicopter attacking Nicaraguan bases and discovered that two of the persons killed were Americans. The fact that they were civilians made their presence in a combat zone a matter of questionable legality. The Reagan administration denied that the CIA played any role in the episode. More investigations began. And in the course of the year each side changed its attitude toward the Contadora Group's peace effort. The United States had at first favored the proposals of the group, and the Sandinistas opposed them; then, later in the year, when the Nicaraguan government agreed to the terms, the United States found objections. Gradually, the United States became more isolated in its Nicaraguan policy, especially when 21 European and Latin American nations agreed to support the Contadora peace plan as well as to give aid to Nicaragua, a step that President Reagan would not take.

Another episode brought humiliation to the Reagan government when it was learned that the CIA had produced a manual for the Nicaraguan rebels teaching methods of terror and "neutralization," a term that meant whatever the reader wanted. The United States insisted that assassination is prohibited as foreign policy and always has denied intentions of overthrowing the Sandinistas. All concerned tried to dodge responsibility for this event, and more investigations began.

Tempers rose again in November when the Reagan government claimed that Soviet freighters were bringing unnecessarily large amounts of offensive weapons to Nicaragua, including MiG-21s in crates. A war of nerves began as American planes made many flights over the ships and the land to check on the cargo or frighten the Nicaraguans, depending on the version. Both sides rattled their sabers,

Neveu, Gamma-Liaison

A billboard indicates that the May 6 presidential race in Panama is extremely tight. It took until mid-May for an electoral tribunal to declare Nicolas Ardito Barletta, a vice-president of the World Bank, the winner.

Judy Sloan, Gamma-Liaison

A controversial CIA manual "Psychological Operations in Guerrilla War" was circulated among Nicaraguan rebels.

and the Nicaraguan government ordered 20,000 civilians from the coffee harvest—where they were doing emergency duty—to arm for the U.S. invasion. The rumor of the MiGs proved false, and the invasion never came.

Nicaragua staged elections on November 4; the strongest opposition boycotted the election, but about 80% of those eligible voted. They chose José Daniel Ortega Saavedra, the junta leader, to be president and endorsed the government party's candidates for the 90-seat National Assembly by a wide margin.

The government's struggle with the Contras continued throughout the year. One group captured San Juan del Norte and held it for a week, the first time that the opposition had taken a town from government control. The leader of this faction, Edén Pastora, was wounded and five others were killed when a bomb exploded at a press conference he was holding near the Costa Rica border. His army, which shunned the use of former Somoza followers, received no help from the United States, which instead had (until blocked by Congress in November) given significant support to the Nicaraguan Democratic Force operating out of Honduras.

In spite of the turmoil, 1984 was the most productive year so far for the Sandinista regime, except in livestock. Food supplies rose 9%, and the overall gross domestic product increased 5%. But food was still scarce, and

there was much rationing and black marketeering. Inflation remained about 25%. The government controlled the economy tightly, but perhaps 50% of the production was in private hands, including U.S. firms. The rest of the nation's business was in co-ops and state-run companies. The government bought most goods, established priorities on raw materials, and controlled wages. Strikes were prohibited. Production had yet to reach prerevolutionary days.

Panama. Panamanian politics behaved "normally" in 1984. In February, President Ricardo de la Espriella, who had assumed office after a nonviolent coup in 1982, resigned without explanation in favor of his vice-president, Jorge Illueca. This took place just four months before the presidential election in which 100,000 voters were challenged and 11 days were required to count the ballots, as the two leading candidates claimed victory. The election, the first in 16 years, resulted in the victory of Nicolás Ardito Barletta, the representative of the National Democratic Union, who took office in October. Second by about 1,700 votes was Arnulfo Arias Madrid of the Democratic Opposition Alliance. Arias, 83, had been elected three times in the past but had never been able to finish his term of office because of action by the Panama military.

The new president is well known in diplomatic circles; for the previous seven years he had been a vice-president of the World Bank. After his election he traveled in the United States and Asia seeking trade for his nation.

In April, after more than six years of construction, the Fortuna dam and hydroelectric power project was finished. This dam, built by Italian and Japanese firms, checks the Chiriqui River and should result in more and cheaper power.

The pride and nationalism associated with the transfer of the Panama Canal to the republic of Panama, now in a transitional stage, emerged in other ways in 1984. Although a part of Central America, Panama chose to join with Mexico, Colombia, and Venezuela as partners in the Contadora process. The fact that Panama is an intermediary in a dispute involving the United States adds to Panamanian feelings of importance. Additionally, in late July, President Illueca announced that the U.S. Army School of the Americas would have to close under terms of the 1978 treaty. The United States was eager to keep the school operating as it has since the 1940s. More than 44,000 Latin American military personnel have attended the school and nearly 2,000 were still enrolled. In August, Gen. Manuel Antonio Noriega, chief of the defense forces, announced that the school would continue to operate, but under Panama's auspices.

THOMAS L. KARNES
Arizona State University

A French paratrooper guards the desert fort of Biltine in eastern Chad. Withdrawal of the 3,000-man French force, which was supporting President Habré, began in the fall.

Gysembergh, Photo Trends

CHAD

French President François Mitterrand's decision in August 1983 committing troops to support Chadian President Hissène Habré's government stopped the Libyan-backed dissident forces loyal to ousted President Goukouni Oueddei. By the spring of 1984 more than 3,000 French ground troops and air units were in Chad. The hostile forces faced each other at the 16th parallel—the "red line"—each being content with patrol action. The stalemate continued, since the major decisions were no longer made by Habré or Oueddei, but by President Muammar el-Qaddafi of Libya and Mitterrand. Neither wished escalation.

Economy. The economy improved slightly during the lull in fighting because of the influx of foreign capital. In 1983, Habré's government received 249 million francs (ca. $27 million) and was promised over 70 million (ca. $8 million) more from France in April. The United States contributed $22 million for national reconstruction. These funds and the money spent for foreign troops helped in rebuilding parts of Ndjamena, the capital, and encouraged resettlement of abandoned areas. Production of cotton, one of the important exports, reached 150,000 tons, equivalent to the amounts grown before the civil war's disruption. Serious economic dislocations still existed, however. Large portions of Ndjamena and other southern towns needed to be rebuilt, and agricultural production of major food crops was far below normal. Famine conditions resulted in hundreds of deaths in normally prosperous southern Chad.

Political Affairs. The second anniversary of Habré's assumption of power on June 7 was a day of official rejoicing. Habré's control was increased because his opposition was divided into hostile factions, although attempts were made in August to bring these critics into a united front by forming the Committee for Action and Condemnation. Even the fighting units supporting Oueddei were divided into groups whose primary allegiance was to leaders other than Oueddei. The lack of unity of the government in exile was shown by its complete reorganization by Oueddei in September.

The accidental loss of nine French soldiers in April fueled public and official criticism of President Mitterrand's policies. This, combined with the mounting cost of the operation, estimated at $300,000 per day, and Libya's détente with Morocco, convinced Mitterrand to seek an agreement with Libya. It had become obvious that a conference in Brazzaville proposed by the Organization of African Unity would not convene, so in early September Mitterrand flew to Morocco for talks with King Hassan II. These resulted in an agreement with Libya, and the French defense minister on September 17 announced that France would begin withdrawing troops from Chad. By the end of September the French evacuated their forward posts. This retrograde movement was halted since there were no signs of a concomitant Libyan withdrawal. Mitterrand's actions, nevertheless, appeared to ease international tensions and focused the responsibility for ending the long, costly war upon the Chadian leaders.

HARRY A. GAILEY, *San José State University*

CHAD • Information Highlights

Official Name: Republic of Chad.
Location: North-central Africa.
Area: 496,000 sq mi (1 284 640 km²).
Population (mid-1984 est.): 5,000,000.
Chief City: Ndjamena, the capital.
Government: *Head of state and government,* Hissène Habré, president (seized control June 7, 1982).
Monetary Unit: CFA franc (427.23 CFA francs equal U.S.$1, June 1984).
Gross National Product Per Capita (1982): $80.

CHEMISTRY

Advances in chemistry in 1984 included measurement of an elusive equilibrium, synthesis of a long-sought compound, and elaboration of new techniques for preparing chiral compounds and polymers.

Measurement. Acetone, a common solvent, is a compound composed of three carbon, one oxygen, and six hydrogen atoms. In water solution it exists almost entirely in its "keto" form, with the oxygen atom doubly bonded to a carbon atom. However, a very tiny fraction of the acetone molecules in water are present in another form, the "enol" form, with a hydrogen atom shifted and attached to the oxygen. The keto and enol forms are in dynamic equilibrium, rapidly interconverting. In the past, a number of attempts have been made to measure the small fraction of enol molecules present, but all efforts relied on an assumed value for some unknown quantity. In 1984 a group of chemists from the University of Toronto and the University of Basel, Switzerland, reported that they had measured the fraction of enol acetone molecules by a method in which all necessary values were determined. The enol was produced by flashing an alkaline methyl butyl ketone solution with laser light. Measurement of its decay rate and other factors showed that only about six of every billion acetone molecules were in the enol form.

Synthesis. Methylenecyclopropene (MCP), the simplest cross-conjugated cyclic hydrocarbon, has long been used by theoretical chemists to illustrate basic ideas of pi-electron theory. The real compound, however, had resisted all efforts at preparation. In 1984 two groups, one at Rice University in Houston and the other at the University of Nebraska, Lincoln, announced that they had succeeded in preparing small amounts of the compound. The synthetic routes used by the two groups were similar, involving preparation of a halogenated precursor and subsequent removal of halogen and hydrogen atoms. MCP collected as a white solid at low temperatures. Thus far, MCP's measured properties agree closely with values predicted by theoretical calculations.

Chiral Compounds. Many chemical compounds can exist in two forms, one the mirror image of the other. These are termed chiral compounds. Nature in its biochemical processes often employs just one member of the pair, selectivity being controlled by highly specific enzymes. Laboratory syntheses, in contrast, tend to produce equal amounts of the two forms, which are then difficult to separate.

In 1984 chemists at Purdue University announced that they had discovered a general method for producing chiral, or "optically pure" compounds. The method starts with alpha-pinene, a pine tree product which itself comes in mirror-image versions. Treatment with borane yields a product that crystallizes out of solution in 100% optically pure form. Additional steps yield chiral alkyl boranes, which in turn can be used to produce a wide variety of optically pure compounds by standard methods. The technique should be especially valuable for the manufacture of drugs and other biologically active compounds.

Polymers. Polymers are giant molecules from which plastics, textiles, and other modern materials are produced. Polysilane, a polymer with a backbone of silicon atoms, may find a role in the production of other polymers as a result of work by Robert West of the University of Wisconsin, Madison. When struck with ultraviolet light, polysilane breaks up into reactive fragments called radicals, which can initiate polymer-producing reactions. According to West, polysilanes have two advantages over other compounds for this important role: they are highly efficient and thus only small amounts are needed, and, unlike many other photoinitiators, they work even in the presence of oxygen.

A team of University of Pennsylvania chemists reported new developments with polymers that conduct electricity. Polyaniline, when treated with an acidic electrolyte solution, becomes oxidized and conducting. When treated with an alkaline solution, the polymer converts to a reduced, insulating form. The process can be reversed and the cycle repeated. Eventually this may permit the creation of lightweight, rechargeable, plastic batteries. The Pennsylvania chemists have already simulated a dry cell, a storage battery, and a fuel cell with their plastic conductors.

Other Developments. A group of Cornell University scientists turned a laboratory mistake into a discovery. Working on a mixture of graphite and potassium bromide compressed between two diamond anvils, a graduate student accidentally set a laser used for heating the sample to a higher power than planned. Analysis showed that a small part of the diamond anvil had been melted, producing an apparently new material. According to the researchers, this was the first evidence that diamond melts under high pressure. It may help answer the question of whether liquid carbon can exist in the earth's interior.

Catalysts are substances that speed up chemical reactions. By one estimate, catalysts are responsible for the production of materials representing one fifth of the U.S. gross national product. Not surprisingly, therefore, catalysis continues to be a "hot" area of research. Among the year's developments in this area was the synthesis by Kansas State University chemists of a new bimetallic manganese-cobalt catalyst with unusual properties. The manganese, though relatively inactive itself, increased the catalytic hydrogenation activity of the cobalt by 100-fold.

PAUL G. SEYBOLD, *Wright State University*

CHICAGO

Political bickering, court corruption, and the near collapse of the city's biggest bank made news in Chicago in 1984.

Mayor vs. City Council. The ongoing war between Mayor Harold Washington and the majority bloc in the City Council centered around the award of lucrative city contracts. Chicago mayors traditionally have held a firm grip on these contracts, often passing them out to political cronies. In July the council resisted this practice by attaching control amendments to three ordinances for $820 million in public works projects, including the expansion of O'Hare International Airport. Mayor Washington vetoed the measures, but the two sides went on to work out a compromise.

Bank Crisis. Chicago's business community was jolted by the near collapse in May of Continental Illinois Bank and Trust Co. A series of bad loans, including $1.07 billion in energy-related loans through Penn Square Bank of Oklahoma City, which was closed by federal regulators, led to a run on deposits. Continental's stock tumbled, and Moody's Investment Service lowered the bank's debt rating. Continental lost its standing as Chicago's largest bank, falling to second place. An infusion of $7.5 billion in cash and credit from 28 banks and the Federal Deposit Insurance Corporation helped keep the bank's doors open.

Court Corruption. A Federal Bureau of Investigation (FBI) "sting" operation in the Circuit Court of Cook County led to the indictments of four judges and 13 others, including lawyers, policemen, court personnel, and just plain fixers. The charges included bribery, extortion, tax fraud, and racketeering. It was the most far-reaching investigation of judicial corruption in the city's history. As the accused went to trial, the U.S. Attorney's office had mixed success in the prosecutions.

Other Developments. The Chicago Board of Education voted not to renew the $120,000-a-year contract of Schools Superintendent Ruth Love. Love blamed her firing on Mayor Washington and his followers. She was replaced by Dr. Manford Byrd, a deputy superintendent who had been passed over for the top spot twice before.

A strike by the Chicago Teachers' Union left the city's schools teacherless from December 3–16. The walkout in the nation's third largest school system affected more than 430,000 students.

Labor Day 1984 will be remembered for the worst car accident in the city's history—in which seven people were killed—and for the awarding of the biggest lottery prize in history—$40 million to 28-year-old Chicago printer Michael Wittkowski. (*See also* PEOPLE, PLACES, and THINGS, page 75.)

ROBERT ENSTAD, *Chicago Tribune*

CHILDREN

The "generation gap" may be a thing of the past, according to a 1984 survey. A study of U.S. junior and senior high school students showed that young people today are adopting the traditional values of their parents and looking forward to career success and marriage as adults. Such views may reflect the stable environments in which most children are raised. But the fact remains that less fortunate children continue to be plagued by serious problems— abuse, poverty, and others.

The year 1984 saw new efforts to solve some of these problems. Congress passed a new law aimed at enforcing child-support payments, and a federal child-protection bill sparked intense debate. Meanwhile, the problem of child abuse came under the spotlight, as social agencies and the news media gave increasing attention to beatings and sexual assaults on children.

Child Abuse. Approximately 1 million cases of child abuse are reported each year in the United States. The difficulties faced by government and social agencies in dealing with this widespread problem were highlighted in 1984 by a case in Island Pond, VT, where members of a small Christian sect regularly caned their children for, they said, the children's own salvation. State officials took 112 children into custody to examine them for signs of abuse, but a district court held that the detention violated the children's rights. The children were ordered released, leaving open the question of whether the canings represented discipline or abuse.

The possibility that government agencies might overstep their bounds in dealing with cases of suspected abuse was countered by the fear that they might do too little. Negligence on the part of social agencies was cited as a factor in some other cases of abuse. In New York City, for example, a government report charged that social workers had failed to investigate properly in cases that led to the deaths of nine children.

Child psychologists also expressed concern over a less obvious form of abuse, emotional deprivation. But the most publicized aspect of the problem was sexual abuse. Experts at a national conference on sexual abuse of children, sponsored by the Children's Hospital National Medical Center in April, cited grim statistics: A child is sexually abused somewhere in the United States every two minutes; one in every five victims is under age seven. Perhaps the most shocking cases of 1984 involved day-care centers in New York, California, Illinois, Alabama, and Nevada. Tougher penalties for child molesters and better education for children were among the solutions proposed.

Rising concern over child abuse was a force behind House and Senate versions of a new

Incidents of child abuse were exposed at day-care centers in several states during 1984. In one highly publicized case, the operators of a preschool in suburban Los Angeles were charged with 208 counts of child molesting over a ten-year period.

AP/Wide World

child-protection bill. The main purpose of the bill was to renew funding for child-abuse prevention and adoption services. But the legislation was held up through much of the year by debate on provisions to protect handicapped infants, an issue sparked by the 1982 "Baby Doe" case. In that case, an infant born with Down's syndrome and a malformed esophagus was allowed to die after his parents, backed by Indiana courts, chose not to feed him. A compromise bill, agreed to in late September, included provisions that addressed the needs of the handicapped. Congress also voted to stiffen laws against child pornography.

Day Care. The incidents of child abuse at day-care centers prompted questions about the overall quality and regulation of such care. With 52% of the mothers of children under age six now working, demand for day care continues to increase. Some experts contend that cuts in federal funding have reduced day-care opportunities for low-income families and that other budget cuts have affected the states' abilities to enforce day-care regulations.

At a House hearing on the problem in September, child abuse expert Kee MacFarlane of the Children's Institute International in Los Angeles voiced fears that some centers had served as covers for child pornography rings. Other witnesses proposed solutions to the day-care problem, including stricter licensing, better monitoring of centers, and better training, pay, and pre-hiring checks for employees.

Child Support. Census figures show that nearly $4 billion (U.S.) in court-ordered child support goes unpaid each year. Less than half of the 4.5 million women entitled to such payments receive the full amount, and nearly one fourth receive nothing. Families on welfare have for some years received federal help in collecting past-due payments, but in 1984 a new law extended such help to all families.

The new law, signed by President Reagan in August, requires employers to withhold past-due child support from employees' wages. It also empowers states to place liens on property and withhold state income-tax refunds when money is owed, and it permits child-support obligations to take priority over other debts. The legislation was the product of two years of congressional work and passed both houses unanimously.

Missing Children. Some 1.8 million children are reported missing each year in the United States. The vast majority are runaways, while about 150,000 are abducted by parents in custody disputes. The exact number taken by strangers is not known; estimates range from 5,000 to 50,000. What is known is that most of the children in this last group are never found.

Concern over the situation has led to the formation of nearly 100 action groups that help investigators and act as clearinghouses for information on missing children. They range from small volunteer agencies to such large registries as Child Find in New Paltz, NY, which charges fees for its services. But the efforts of state agencies and such private groups are often poorly coordinated, and many parents pay exorbitant fees to private investigators—with little result. To help alleviate the problem, a national clearinghouse—the National Center for Missing and Exploited Children—was founded in 1984 with a grant from the Justice Department.

Adoption and Foster Care. The federal government reported success in its drive to find permanent homes for foster children. The number of children in foster care dropped from 500,000 in 1977 to 243,000 in 1982. But social welfare agencies said that they found it increasingly difficult to place older and handicapped children and those with behavioral problems.

ELAINE PASCOE, *Free-lance Writer*

CHILE

The end of 1984 saw Gen. Augusto Pinochet more secure in power than at any time in recent years despite continued monthly protest meetings, violence, and a scandal involving government land purchases near his costly home at Lo Corro. Pinochet benefited from a divided opposition and an improved economy under the direction of two new ministers.

Political Liberalization Blocked. In several August-September speeches, General Pinochet warned opponents that his 1973 coup could be repeated and ruled out congressional or presidential elections before 1989. His remarks effectively dampened talks between Interior Minister Sergio Onofre Jarpa and the Democratic Alliance of centrist parties headed by Gabriel Valdés. Pinochet extended the "internal disturbance" decree in September, prolonging for another six months the government's power to exile persons without trial and to restrict assembly and the press. In addition, the government charged ten opposition leaders with attempting to overthrow it by means of September 4–5 protests in which 19 people died. The interior ministry also told foreign airlines not to sell tickets to 4,942 exiles abroad without its approval.

Fourteen Chilean bishops sent a letter on August 24 supporting Santiago Archbishop Juan Francisco Fresno against accusations by Pinochet. The Chilean leader had charged that the Vicariate of Solidarity, a church human rights defense organization, was "more Communist than the Communists themselves, beginning with its leader."

Chile suffered a new wave of terrorist attacks despite passage of tough antiterrorist decrees on May 15. More than 250 bombings and terrorist acts took place in Santiago alone through July. Left-wing guerrilla groups claimed responsibility for most of the attacks. But 12 churches and a seminary were the targets of shootings, arson, and graffiti threats by anti-Communist groups unhappy with priests in Santiago slums who opposed Pinochet.

Air Force Commander Gen. Fernando Matthei repeated 1983 statements on September 23 that the government should "establish a clear timetable" for a political transition, including creation of a "supervisory Congress" and "true participation" by the population in political decisions. Otherwise, he warned, "we will destroy the armed forces much more efficiently than any Marxist infiltration would be able to."

After a week of renewed violence and protest in late October, the cabinet resigned on November 5 and Pinochet declared a state of siege the next day. A new cabinet was formed with only minor changes. On November 15 troops conducted a lightning raid on the Santiago slum neighborhood of La Victoria, a center of antigovernment activities. Houses were searched, and some 5,000 men and boys were rounded up for questioning. Although all but 237 were released, the sweep signaled Pinochet's determination to curb dissidence.

New Economic Team. New Finance Minister Luis Escobar Cerda and Economy Minister Modesto Collados were sworn in April 2. Escobar was successful in arranging $780 million of standby credits from the International Monetary Fund to meet interest payments of $2.3 billion (U.S.) on the overall foreign debt of $22 billion. Chilean officials hoped copper prices would increase from the 60–62 cents a pound current in September—the lowest in several years—after President Reagan had refused demands by a group of American companies to restrict copper imports to the United States. Reduction of Chilean exports to the United States from 290,000 tons in 1983 to 121,000 tons annually would have impaired Chile's ability to pay its foreign debt.

Increased production in the agricultural, construction, and industrial sectors during the first four months of 1984 led to projections that the year's gross domestic product would show a gain of 4.5%, compared with declines of 14.5% in 1982 and 15.5% in 1983. Exports increased to $1.35 billion the first four months of 1984, a 10.2% increase over the same 1983 period. Unemployment declined from 14.6% in the last three months of 1983 to 12.3% in the first four months of 1984; but 750,000 persons —13% of the labor force—were still employed on emergency work projects. Real wages started to grow again, after a two-year decline, as inflation was projected to rise at an annual rate of 16.5% compared with 23.1% in 1983.

Foreign Relations. Relations with Argentina improved considerably with the signing of a friendship agreement on January 23 and of a treaty settling the Beagle Channel islands dispute on November 29. Relations with France continued to be sour as two French priests were beaten by police in March and May and another was shot in September.

NEALE J. PEARSON, *Texas Tech University*

CHILE · Information Highlights

Official Name: Republic of Chile.
Location: Southwestern coast of South America.
Area: 293,386 sq mi (759 871 km²).
Population (mid-1984 est.): 11,900,000.
Chief Cities (June 30, 1983 est.): Santiago, the capital, 4,132,293; Viña del Mar, 298,663.
Government: *Head of state and government,* Gen. Augusto Pinochet Ugarte, president (took power Sept. 1973). *Legislature*—Congress (dissolved Sept. 1973).
Monetary Unit: Peso (126 pesos equal U.S. $1, official rate, Dec. 31, 1984).
Economic Index (1983): *Consumer Prices* (1970 = 100), all items, 702,623; food, 745,673.
Foreign Trade (1983 U.S.$): *Imports,* $2,754,000,000; *exports,* $3,836,000,000.

J. P. Laffont, Sygma

The 35th anniversary of the People's Republic was celebrated October 1 with a parade in Peking's Tien An Men Square.

CHINA, PEOPLE'S REPUBLIC OF

The year in China was marked by efforts on the part of Chairman Deng Xiaoping and his colleagues to consolidate and extend the political and economic reforms introduced in recent years, and to pursue the "open door" policy of increased interaction with Western nations.

Domestic Affairs

Political Reform. A campaign to oppose "spiritual pollution" came to an abrupt end in April. Although initiated by Deng himself in October 1983, the campaign had come to be used by opponents of his effort to extend China's interaction with the West to criticize what they saw as the injurious effects of that interaction. Meanwhile, party rectification—a three-year program also begun in October 1983—moved from the higher to the middle and lower levels of the party apparatus. In the party, the military, and state institutions in every sector, elderly leaders were removed from their positions—often to be given "advisory" positions in which they maintained their privileges and perquisites—and replaced with younger, more qualified individuals.

Economic Reform. In October the Third Plenum of the 12th Central Committee adopted a program for restructuring the urban econ-

omy. Seen as parallel to the revamping of agriculture under the program adopted by the Third Plenum of the 11th Central Committee in 1978, the new proposals substitute market forces, taxation, and interest rates for the economic controls previously exerted by state planning. More than one million enterprises would be affected by the new regulations. The number of industrial products subject to planned targets and prices would be reduced from 120 to 60, and the number of agricultural products would drop from 29 to 10. Only basic commodities such as steel and energy would continue to be state-regulated. In order to increase productivity and eliminate inefficient units, enterprise managers are to be given significantly expanded freedom and responsibility. One effect of the program will be gradually to reduce the very substantial subsidies for housing, food, transportation, and energy enjoyed by China's urban dwellers. These subsidies had represented up to 40% of state expenditures.

Rural Reorganization. Changes in the political and economic administration of China's rural areas also continued in 1984. With the institution of the "responsibility system" of agricultural production, the communes, brigades, and teams under which rural production had been organized since 1958 were replaced with township and village governments. In order to solve the problem of rural underemployment,

Chinese economists suggested that 30 to 40% of the rural work force might have to be moved from agricultural pursuits to work in village- and township-based, collectively owned industrial and commercial enterprises by the year 2000. According to statistics released in September 1984, there were some 1.33 million of such enterprises; their revenue in the first half of 1984 was 84.4 billion yuan ($316 billion, U.S.), up 20% over the previous year.

Crime. In January 1984 the Ministry of Public Security released statistics to show the effectiveness of a campaign against crime launched the preceding fall. The crime rate during the period September through November 1983 was said to be down 43% from the comparable period one year earlier. It was reported that some 50,000 persons had been arrested during the campaign, of whom 5,000 were executed. Others estimated that arrests during the period may have totaled as many as 100,000. Amnesty International, in its first report on China since 1978, deplored the fact that, in conjunction with this campaign, the number of crimes punishable by death had risen to 44 and, despite efforts at enhancing the rule of law in China, procedures ensuring the rights of the accused at the time of arrest were frequently ignored.

Other. On October 1 the 35th anniversary of the founding of the People's Republic of China was celebrated with a parade involving some 500,000 participants. Deng Xiaoping presided over a military review that included some 10,000 troops and China's most advanced military equipment. It was the first time that a celebration of this sort had been held in Peking since the Cultural Revolution.

In July the People's Republic sent its first full-fledged team to the summer Olympics. Chinese athletes returned home from Los Angeles with a total of 32 medals.

Foreign Affairs

Pursuing an "open door" policy of increased interaction with Europe, Japan, and the United States, China moved very slowly toward improving relations with the Soviet Union in 1984. An agreement was reached in China's negotiations with Great Britain over the future of Hong Kong, but the hope in Peking that this would serve to move Taiwan toward reunification proved ill-founded.

United States. Chinese Premier Zhao Ziyang visited the United States in early January, becoming the highest-ranking Chinese official to make such a visit since the establishment of the People's Republic in 1949. Two agreements were signed during his tour, one covering cooperation in industry and technology, the other renewing scientific and technological exchanges between the two governments. At a news conference at the conclusion of his visit,

Zhao expressed his surprise at the "mass following" he had observed in the United States for the development of Sino-U.S. ties. Noting differences between the two governments on the question of Taiwan, the *People's Daily* nonetheless described the talks held during Zhao's visit as "candid, serious and friendly."

In late April, U.S. President Ronald Reagan made a six-day visit to China. While in Peking, he formalized three agreements: a treaty on corporate income taxes; the renewal of a cultural exchange pact; and a long-awaited nuclear cooperation accord. The Chinese press assessed the visit favorably, saying that it "broke ground for an enduring and steady growth in Sino-U.S. relations." Shortly after the president's return to Washington, however, the question of whether or not China was assisting Pakistan in developing a nuclear capability in violation of its verbal assurances to the contrary delayed the administration's submission of the nuclear pact to Congress. This, in turn, delayed negotiations by U.S. firms seeking to sell nuclear-related equipment to China and, some said, gave the edge in these sales to French and German firms.

The National Council for U.S.-China Trade projected in January that two-way trade between the two countries would reach $5.5-$6 billion in 1984. In 1983, U.S. firms were granted a total of 3,300 export licenses for goods valued at $1.2 billion, up from 1,500 licenses for $469 million in goods in 1982. It was estimated that 3,600 licenses would be granted in 1984, worth $2 billion. The Chinese Enterprise Management Association announced in late January that it would seek to sign a total of 3,000 new contracts with foreign firms during 1983–85, including some 1,000 contracts in 1984, totaling $1 billion. Subsequently, the Ministry of Foreign Economic Relations and Trade announced greater centralization of foreign trade arrangements. Affected by the change would be Chinese imports of steel, chemical fertilizer, grain, and sugar, and export of crude oil, coke, grain, and cotton.

Soviet Union. Although China did express an interest in improving relations with the USSR, the "obstacles" that Peking insisted must be removed before relations could improve served to block any significant progress. These obstacles included the occupation of Afghanistan, assistance to Vietnam in its conflict with Cambodia, and the stationing of troops and missiles on China's northern border. Press reports estimated that Soviet troops on the Chinese border numbered in excess of 720,000 (plus 50,000 troops in Mongolia), while Chinese troops in the area numbered about 810,000.

Hanoi and Peking accused one another of launching attacks over the Sino-Vietnamese border in April and again in July. Outside observers estimated Chinese troop strength on the southern border at 330,000, and Vietnamese strength at 600,000. Perhaps caused in part by the deterioration of Sino-Vietnamese relations, Soviet First Deputy Premier Ivan Arkhipov, scheduled to visit China in mid-May, postponed his visit with one day's notice. Deputy Foreign Minister Qian Qichen paid a four-day visit to Moscow in early July, but again no apparent progress was made in improving relations.

In September, Soviet Foreign Minister Andrei Gromyko and Chinese counterpart Wu Xueqian met in New York in conjunction with the opening of the UN General Assembly. The following month, the fifth in the series of normalization talks was conducted in Peking—again without result.

Finally, in late December, during a nine-day visit to Peking by Soviet Deputy Premier Arkhipov, there was a breakthrough. A series of accords was signed on scientific and technological exchange, increased trade, and Soviet assistance in the modernization of Chinese factories.

Hong Kong. Negotiations between China and Great Britain concerning the future of Hong Kong continued as the year began. (Britain's lease on the territory expires in 1997, when it returns to Chinese sovereignty.) In March, Roger Lobo, an unofficial member of Hong Kong's Legislative Council, introduced a resolution calling for that body to review and comment on any agreement reached between Peking and London. However, objections to the resolution were raised in both London and Peking.

In late July, British Foreign Minister Geoffrey Howe visited Peking and, following his visit, announced in Hong Kong the outlines of the Sino-British agreement. Details of the agreement were not published until after a draft was initialed on September 26. The agreement provides for the transfer of sovereignty from Great Britain to China on July 1, 1997, after which Hong Kong would become a "special administrative region"—with its own political and economic system—for 50 years. An elected legislature will have authority over all areas except foreign affairs and defense; a chief executive will be appointed by Peking; and Hong Kong citizens will continue to enjoy civil rights, including the right to leave the zone at will. Although such problematic issues as civil aviation regulations and nationality also were resolved in the agreement, details remained to be worked out to establish a basic law for Hong Kong. The agreement did provide for a Sino-British joint liaison group that would oversee the implementation of the agreement.

Europe. Through the exchange of several visits, China's interest in further developing its relations with European nations was effectively demonstrated in 1984. In June, Premier Zhao Ziyang visited France, Belgium, Sweden, Norway, Denmark, and Italy. President Li Xiannian visited Yugoslavia in September, and the following month West German Chancellor Helmut Kohl visited China.

Early in the year, China submitted bids to three German companies for the storage of up to 4,000 tons of radioactive waste from European nuclear plants. If the bids are accepted, the Chinese stand to realize up to $5.45 billion from the deals. During Zhao's visit to France and Kohl's visit to Peking, French and German participation in the development of major new nuclear power plants in China was discussed, though contracts were yet to be signed. In October, Volkswagen signed a 25-year joint-venture contract with Shanghai Tractor and Automobile Company, with an initial production target of 20,000 passenger cars per year; the plant was ultimately expected to produce 100,000 cars for the Chinese domestic market. This was the first contract signed for the production of passenger cars by a foreign manufacturer in China.

Korea. Chinese leaders confirmed to foreign visitors during the year that they were interested in developing informal ties with South Korea. Trade between China and South Korea increased markedly during 1984, though most of it was conducted through Hong Kong. The developing relationship suffered a setback in August, however, when Seoul released a group of Chinese citizens arrested the preceding summer for highjacking a Chinese aircraft. The highjackers were transported to Taiwan, where they were given a hero's welcome and paid cash rewards for their defection. The Republic of Korea is one of the few countries that still formally recognize Taipei and not Peking.

Peking, for its part, was proceeding cautiously in developing ties with Seoul so as to avoid adversely affecting its relationship with North Korea. Party General Secretary Hu Yaobang traveled to Pyongyang immediately after Reagan's departure in May to help shore up this relationship.

See also feature article, page 65; Hong Kong; Taiwan (Republic of China).

John Bryan Starr, *Yale-China Association*

CHINA · Information Highlights

Official Name: People's Republic of China.
Location: Central-eastern Asia.
Area: 3,706,560 sq mi (9 600 000 km²).
Population (mid-1984 est.): 1,034,500,000.
Chief Cities (1982 census): Peking, the capital, 9,230,687; Shanghai, 11,859,748; Tianjin, 7,764,-141.
Government: *Head of state,* Li Xiannian, president (took office June 1983). *Heads of government,* Zhao Ziyang, premier (took office Sept. 1980); Deng Xiaoping, chairman, Central Military Commission. *Legislature* (unicameral)—National People's Congress.
Monetary Unit: Yuan (2.332 yuan equal U.S.$1, July 1984).
Foreign Trade (1983 U.S.$): *Imports,* $21,324,-000,000; *exports,* $22,150,000,000.

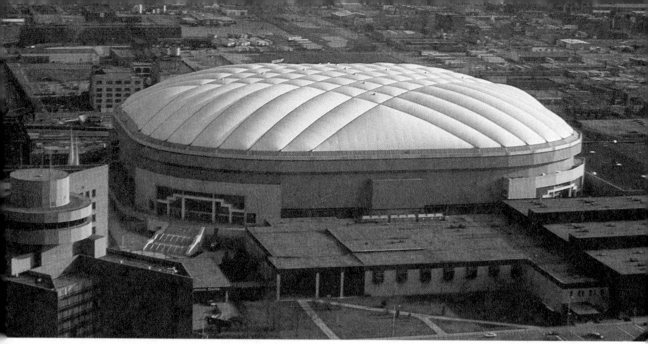

Indiana Convention Center & Hoosier Dome

U.S. cities are looking to the private sector. In Indianapolis the $80 million Hoosier Dome, above, was built to bring in business. In Hartford, CT, construction of the Metro One Center office complex, below, signaled economic growth. And in Baltimore, local businesses support the Blue Chip-In jobs program, left, for low-income youths.

City of Baltimore

Scott Thode, "U.S. News & World Report"

CITIES AND URBAN AFFAIRS

In an election year dominated by foreign affairs and budgetary matters, urban issues tended to get lost on the national agenda. Nevertheless, 1984 was a significant year for U.S. cities as they continued to adjust to post-industrial dislocation and federal cutbacks. The adjustment was uneven, with some cities faring better than others; within cities, downtown development overshadowed neighborhood investment and industrial realignment.

The major theme of 1984 was urban self-help. Mayors begrudgingly adapted their agendas to the realities of President Reagan's New Federalism and the continued transfer of power to the states. Cities concentrated on the maintenance of existing federal urban programs—such as Urban Development Action Grants (UDAGs), general revenue sharing, and Community Development Block Grants (CDBGs)—and on the crafting of innovative, effective, locally based economic development strategies. Based on an improved national economy, the overall mood was clearly more bullish in 1984 than in the preceding two years, but the outlook for 1985 and beyond in the face of a $200 billion national budget deficit remained quite uncertain.

Intergovernmental Relations. Although cities have more or less accepted the cutbacks imposed by Reaganomics, they continued to lobby aggressively to prevent state and federal policies from making their problems worse.

For example, in late November the National League of Cities took serious exception to a Treasury Department study that contended that state and local economies were stronger than that of the national government. The Treasury report suggested that the definition of federal aid be expanded to include "hidden subsidies"—such as the deductions taken on individual income returns for taxes paid to state and local government, estimated to be $31 billion annually and to cost the Treasury $6 billion in revenue. Fearful that the groundwork was being laid for further cuts in federal appropriations and programs, the mayors in a show of bipartisan unity protested that cities had done "more than their share" to reduce the growing national deficit. Arguing that decisions should be made on the basis of real urban needs rather than the fluctuating fiscal conditions of the cities, the League called for reduced military spending and a bipartisan commission of federal, state, and local officials to examine the budget deficit problem and to recommend equitable solutions.

A report to the Joint Economic Committee of Congress titled "A New Urban Agenda" called for a reordering of federal priorities away from defense and toward new social programs to alleviate the oppressive conditions of the urban poor and to provide cities with more funds through tax reform.

In June the U.S. Conference of Mayors proposed reducing the federal deficit through tax reform, defense cuts, and, for the first time, lower automatic increases in entitlement programs, such as Medicare and Social Security. At the same time, increases in specific programs for the poor and unemployed were demanded.

By December the Reagan administration was floating other proposals to reduce the budget deficit, including elimination of all loans and other financial assistance provided by the Small Business Administration; dropping most subsidies for railroads, ports, and waterways; elimination of the UDAG programs; and major cutbacks in the Economic Development Administration of the Commerce Department. All of these cuts would be protested vigorously.

The ability of local governments to cope with severely reduced federal aid was further eroded by antitrust litigation engendered by a 1982 Supreme Court decision making the regulatory actions of city governments subject to triple damages. When in May the Federal Trade Commission brought the first-ever antitrust charge against local governments—New Orleans and Minneapolis for violating antitrust provisions in setting taxi fares—local officials complained to Congress that this was disruptive "federal meddling." Congress responded by removing financial damages in private suits and barring the FTC from using its 1985 appropriations for municipal antitrust cases.

The cities continued to be caught between conflicting assessments of the effects of federal regulatory relief under the Reagan administration. An Urban Institute report concluded that "state and local governments have been the big winners in regulatory relief," while a study by the Advisory Commission on Intergovernmental Relations found that federal laws and regulations continue to place administrative and federal burdens on local governments.

In fact, the easing of regulatory burdens has often been accompanied by significant reductions in federal aid. Some argue that reducing federal oversight, with or without aid reduction, may mean sacrifices for underprivileged groups, the environment, and safety in the workplace. On the other hand, it is asserted that federal controls have actually increased and that the burden of "cross-cutting" rules, which impose social and economic requirements on grants, and "crossover" sanctions, which deny funds to one program because of violations in an unrelated program, are severe.

Changing intergovernmental relations have caused local governments to seek new remedies for urban problems. While the states have picked up some of the financial slack caused by federal cutbacks, state controls over urban policies also have increased. Thus, the cities have become extraordinarily creative and more aggressive in pursuing strategies for survival. They have become more entrepreneurial in the development of local economies, enlisting the cooperation of the private sector, often in joint-venture partnerships. Incentive financing for both local business and industry and outside and even overseas investors has become common. An attractive business climate has become a priority for bringing in new investment, and city governments must seek a competitive advantage through strategic planning and creative uses of capital for economic development.

Louis H. Masotti
Northwestern University

obverse

U.S. Olympic Commemorative

reverse

American Numismatic
Association

British Royal Mint

New British Coinage

COINS AND COIN COLLECTING

Early 1984 saw the U.S. Bureau of the Mint, established by the Department of the Treasury under the Coinage Act of 1873, revise its name to United States Mint. Mint director Donna Pope cited a need to identify more clearly the Mint and its products worldwide as the reason for the change.

Following a two-year hiatus, the Mint reinstituted its sale of uncirculated sets containing specimens of all current U.S. coinage from the cent through half dollar. Housed in new, innovative packaging inspired by suggestions from the collecting public, the sets officially were released for sale on Labor Day.

Months of heated controversy preceded the Mint's official acknowledgment that the 1983 "doubled-die reverse" Lincoln cent is indeed a genuine doubled die produced as a result of the coin being struck with an improperly made reverse die. It is estimated that only about 500 to 1,500 pieces exist, the error having been discovered by Mint personnel early in the production process and subsequently corrected. Manufactured at the Philadelphia Mint during the first quarter of 1983, the coins commanded premium prices throughout 1984.

Midyear marked the discovery of a second doubled-die piece—the 1984 "doubled-die ob-verse" Lincoln cent. Little information is known about the coin, though it is believed to have originated at either the Philadelphia Mint or the U.S. Bullion Depository at West Point, NY. Net yet acknowledged by Mint officials, the coin is recognized by the American Numismatic Association Certification Service (ANACS) as a genuine doubled die.

The Olympics. Legal tender issues commemorating the 1984 Olympic Games were produced by many countries, most notably Yugoslavia, which hosted the XIV Olympics Winter Games at Sarajevo, and the United States, host of the 1984 Summer Games in Los Angeles, CA.

The National Bank of Yugoslavia issued a collector set containing 15 sterling silver and 3 gold coins, released in 3-coin sets during a two-year period beginning in January 1983. Bearing common-obverse designs picturing the Yugoslavian coat of arms beside the Olympic logo, the coins feature reverses depicting various winter sports, Yugoslavian landmarks, and political figures. Mintage of each silver coin was limited to 110,000, while gold coins were produced in limited quantities of 55,000 each.

Olympic commemoratives produced by the U.S. Mint included 1983 and 1984 silver dollars and a 1984 $10 gold piece, the first legal tender gold coin struck in the United States in 50 years and the first to carry the W mintmark of the U.S. Bullion Depository at West Point. Struck in both proof and uncirculated conditions, the coins carry distinctive obverse and reverse designs and were sold in record numbers throughout 1984.

Great Britain. A new portrait of Her Majesty Queen Elizabeth II, designed in 1984 by Raphael Maklouf, will grace all United Kingdom coinage issued after Jan. 1, 1985, and will replace the Arnold Machin rendering that has appeared on British coins since 1968. The new portrait marks a return to the "couped bust" (cut off above the shoulders) that was featured on British coinage during the first half of this century.

LISA A. SUNDERLIN, *The Numismatist*

COLOMBIA

The year 1984 marked a major turning point in the Colombian government's attempts to quell guerrilla insurgencies. Truces were signed with all but one of the major guerrilla groups, and by year-end the truces seemed to be holding. Another turning point may have been reached in the government's attempts to deal with the country's narcotics problem. The murder of Justice Minister Rodrigo Lara Bonilla in late April led to a government crackdown on the "drugs Mafia." However, the dismal performance of the Colombian economy offset the political gains of the year. In foreign affairs, President Belisario Betancur's leadership of the Contadora initiative for a peace settlement in Central America enhanced his image at home but adversely affected relations with the United States.

Politics. Most of the political news in Colombia was good, as Betancur continued his activist presidency. An April agreement, which took effect on May 28, resulted in a year-long truce with the Revolutionary Armed Forces (*Fuerzas Armadas Revolucionarias Colombianas,* or FARC). The FARC was the largest guerrilla organization in the country, with 15,000 members, and the April compact paved the way for similar accords with other insurgents. In late August three guerrilla groups— the M-19, the Popular Liberation Army, and the Workers' Self-Defense Force—all accepted truces under the same conditions as the FARC. The government in turn agreed to conduct a "national dialogue" with the rebels and also to establish programs for the poor, to end civil rights abuses by such groups as Death to the Kidnappers (*Muerte a Secuestradores,* or MAS), and to grant pardons to those guerrillas who would voluntarily lay down their arms. The truce was opposed by elements within the army, and in September talk of a military coup abounded. However, Betancur's personal popularity appeared to make a coup unlikely.

Colombia's President Belisario Betancur (right) meets a member of the Nicaraguan junta to discuss the peace plan for Central America proposed by the Contadora group.

AP/Wide World

COLOMBIA • Information Highlights

Official Name: Republic of Colombia.
Location: Northwest South America.
Area: 440,000 sq mi (1 139 600 km²).
Population (mid-1984 est.): 28,200,000.
Chief City: Bogotá, the capital.
Government: *Head of state and government,* Belisario Betancur Cuartas, president (took office Aug. 1982). *Legislature*—Congress: Senate and House of Representatives.
Monetary Unit: Peso (96.15 pesos equal U.S.$1, Nov. 26, 1984).
Gross National Product (1983 U.S.$): $40,000,-000,000.
Economic Index (Bogotá, 1983): *Consumer Prices* (1970 = 100), all items, 1,305.2; food, 1,597.1.
Foreign Trade (1983 U.S.$): *Imports,* $5,030,200,000; *exports,* $3,176,000,000.

Progress also was made in 1984 in dealing with the growing power of the "drugs Mafia." In March and April the government uncovered two enormous drug-processing complexes in the southern jungles. The murder of Minister Lara Bonilla (the man responsible for the drug raids) brought a declaration of "war to the death" by President Betancur against drug traffickers. Colombia quickly agreed to extradite several suspected drug dealers to the United States.

Local-council elections in March were inconclusive. Betancur's Conservatives received 42% of the vote, while the divided Liberals garnered 52%. Abstention in the election hovered at 70%.

The Economy. Worsening economic problems plagued Colombia in 1984. Foreign-exchange reserves dropped by midyear to a low of $1.8 billion (U.S.). Foreign debt rose to $10.7 billion, two thirds of which was owed by the government. Colombia's negative balance of trade was expected to top $1.54 billion for the year. Massive new government deficits, amounting to 92.1 billion pesos ($960 million) through May, resulted from the failure of tax reform to generate new revenues. Unemployment remained in the neighborhood of 13%, while inflation continued at 19% for the year. About the only bright economic news was a major oil find in the department of Arauca near the Venezuelan border.

Foreign Affairs. In June the president hosted the first debt meeting of Latin American nations, at Cartagena. Betancur continued to be openly critical of U.S. policy in Central America and the Caribbean, arguing that a more conciliatory approach by the United States would produce greater stability in the area. The refusal of the Reagan administration to accept the draft peace treaty for Central America, proposed in October 1983 by the Contadora Group (Colombia, Mexico, Panama, and Venezuela), further worsened relations between Colombia and the United States.

ERNEST A. DUFF
Randolph-Macon Woman's College

COLORADO

The political season in Colorado opened with a surge of enthusiasm among Democrats when the state's senior senator, Gary Hart, won the New Hampshire presidential primary. But Hart, the first major contender for the presidential nomination in either party from Colorado, ultimately lost the Democratic nomination to Walter Mondale. Republicans further dampened the spirits of Colorado Democrats by sweeping the November election.

Besides capturing Colorado's eight electoral votes for Ronald Reagan, the GOP reelected U.S. Sen. William Armstrong and gained a congressional seat. Republicans confirmed their victory by expanding their previous majorities in both chambers of the Colorado General Assembly.

Unofficial returns handed Reagan 63% of the vote, with a 769,241 to 434,698 margin over Mondale. Armstrong won his second Senate term with a slightly wider margin over his Democratic challenger, Lt. Gov. Nancy Dick.

Republicans also gained a 4–2 edge in Colorado's delegation to the U.S. House of Representatives by picking up the third congressional district seat vacated by retiring Democratic Rep. Ray Kogovsek. The giant district sprawls over mountainous western Colorado as well as the city of Pueblo. Registered Democrats outnumber Republicans in the district. But Democrats were unable to unite after a divisive primary fight in which environmentalist W Mitchell narrowly defeated State Sen. Richard Soash, who had been backed by labor and business groups. Carbondale rancher Mike Strang had an easier Republican primary win over Grand Junction city councilman Phil Klingsmith, and Strang's well-financed campaign went on to defeat Mitchell with 58% of the vote. All five incumbent U.S. representatives who sought reelection won new terms: Republicans Dan Schaefer, Hank Brown, and Ken Kramer and Democrats Patricia Schroeder and Tim Wirth.

In the state legislature, Republicans picked up three seats in the Senate for a 24–11 margin and an even more lopsided edge in the House, where they gained six seats for a 47–18 majority. Despite talk of a "veto-proof" legislature, however, veteran GOP legislative leaders cautioned it would not be a simple task to meld the party's moderate and conservative wings into a solid ideological phalanx.

The election also brought victory to the Right-to-Life movement in Colorado. Voters narrowly approved, 627,067 to 616,815, an amendment to the state constitution prohibiting the use of state tax dollars to pay for abortions, except to save the life of a pregnant mother or an unborn child. But voters rejected a proposal by a two-to-one margin to legalize casino gambling on a tract near Pueblo.

COLORADO • Information Highlights

Area: 104,091 sq mi (269 595 km²).
Population (July 1, 1983 est.): 3,139,000.
Chief Cities (July 1, 1982 est.): Denver, the capital, 505,563; Colorado Springs, 231,699; Aurora, 184,372; Lakewood, 118,498.
Government (1984): *Chief Officers*—governor, Richard D. Lamm (D); lt. gov., Nancy Dick (D). *General Assembly*—Senate, 35 members; House of Representatives, 65 members.
State Finances (fiscal year 1983): *Revenues,* $4,203,000,000; *expenditures,* $4,062,000,000.
Personal Income (1983): $40,085,000,000; per capita, $12,770.
Labor Force (May 1984): *Civilian labor force,* 1,705,300; *unemployed,* 85,800 (5.0% of total force).
Education: *Enrollment* (fall 1982)—public elementary schools, 379,599; public secondary, 165,610; colleges and universities (fall 1983), 172,650. *Public school expenditures* (1982–83), $1,605,885,020 ($3,171 per pupil).

Economy. The state's economy generally recovered from the recent recession. AMAX Corp. reopened two large molybdenum mines in Climax and Henderson. But Colorado's hopes of sharing in the high technology boom were undercut when a "shakeout" in the computer industry prompted three Boulder County firms—Miniscribe, Otrona, and Storage Technology—to lay off a combined total of 3,500 workers in the fall. By contrast, downtown Denver's economy received a boost with the opening of the Tabor Center retail complex.

Efforts to produce petroleum from Colorado's huge oil shale reserves inched forward in 1984 as Union Oil Co. completed construction on a large mine and retort facility in Parachute Valley. The project has been backed by a guarantee from the federal government to buy its output at above-market prices. But "teething troubles" delayed the start of commercial production.

Urban and Other News. Suburban Aurora lifted a "blue line" that had blocked annexations to it for ten years and agreed to consider annexation requests in a 117-sq mi (303-km²) area mostly to the east and south.

Denver and suburban officials continued to try to work out differences over how to expand the congested Stapleton International Airport, now ranked as the nation's sixth-busiest airport. Denver-based Frontier Airlines joined the list of carriers struggling to cope with deregulation. Frontier competes directly with Continental Airlines on 70% of its routes and was expected to ask its employees to accept sharp pay cuts similar to those imposed by Continental in 1973 after that company had filed for bankruptcy.

Gov. Richard D. Lamm received national publicity for a speech in which he declared that the incurably ill have a "duty to die" rather than allow their sufferings to be prolonged by extraordinary and costly medical procedures.

Bob Ewegen, *"The Denver Post"*

COMMUNICATION TECHNOLOGY

The U.S. telecommunications industry underwent a major transformation on Jan. 1, 1984, when the Bell System and its parent organization, American Telephone and Telegraph Co. (AT&T), were officially restructured. AT&T was divested of its 22 previously-owned local Bell Telephone companies, which were formed into seven independent, regional holding companies. AT&T retained its long-distance communication network; its research and development organization, Bell Laboratories; and its equipment-manufacturing subsidiary, Western Electric. The divestiture, however, opened a new era of deregulation and competition in local and long-distance service.

In technology, 1984 was a year of advances in lightwave systems—both local and long-distance, improved satellite and microwave radio systems, and growth of computer-controlled electronic switching. Dramatic changes were being brought about by the use of digital techniques in both transmission and switching, using the high-speed on-off (1 and 0) pulses that constitute the language of computers. And basic to the new communication technology are year-by-year advances in microelectronics and optoelectronic devices, such as improved lasers, lower-loss optical fibers, and more efficient photo-detectors and signal processors.

Transmission and Switching. In 1984 a new modulator developed by AT&T increased the capacity of lightwave loop carrier systems from 96 simultaneous conversations per pair of optical fibers to seven times that number, and the equivalent in data or television signals.

A new digital data transmission technique called Time Compression Multiplexing also was introduced. It allows computer users to transmit and receive high-speed digital data over the public switched network using the same two-wire loops normally supplied for conventional telephones. At a rate of 56 kilobits per second, it is six times faster than the previous maximum speed.

A digital microwave radio system with a capaity of 14,000 simultaneous telephone calls was developed by AT&T Bell Laboratories. The new system adds 50% to the capacity of existing digital radio routes, both for telephony and long-distance data communications.

Plans for the first undersea lightwave cable system to span the Atlantic Ocean moved ahead in 1984 when telecommunication officials of the United States, Great Britain, and France signed contracts for construction of TAT-8. Scheduled to begin service in 1988, it will have a capacity of 37,800 simultaneous conversations or an equivalent amount of high-speed data and television signals. This is four times the capacity of the most recent cable, TAT-7.

A new technique for satellite transmission, Companded Single Sideband (CSSB), was demonstrated in a transoceanic field trial conducted between international switching centers in Pittsburgh and Frankfurt, West Germany. AT&T, COMSAT, and Deutsche Bundpost (DBP)—the German communication agency—participated. The new system will increase the capacity of international satellites tenfold.

Significant advances also were made during the year in the field of electronic switching and network operation through the increasing use of programmed, computer-controlled facilities. One example is the Local Area Network (LAN), used by large corporations for communication between offices within a building and between buildings at distant locations. Microprocessors control the Private Branch Exchanges (PBXs) and other terminals, and coaxial cables and optical fibers provide the necessary broad-band transmission capabilities. Another step forward in switching tech-

Roy Stanek, Illinois Bell Telephone Co.

A new high-capacity mobile communication system—called "cellular" radio—employs low-power microwave transmitters. The system, put into operation in 20 cities, greatly expands the use of car radio telephones.

nology was a field trial of Local Area Switching Services (LASS) conducted by Bell of Pennsylvania in Harrisburg. LASS makes use of the existing high-speed digital signaling network that carries call-handling instructions for routing telephone calls. It automatically transmits the number of the caller as well as the number being called. Users can program their local switching system to have certain selected calls announced by a distinctive ring or by a call-waiting tone, and to have certain preselected calls transferred to another telephone. They can trace anonymous harassing telephone calls, and, with a small attachment, they can see the phone number of an incoming call.

Communication Services. The new high-capacity mobile radio communication system went into service in about 20 major cities in 1984. Known as "cellular" radio, it uses low-power microwave transmitters to cover small geographic "cells." With automatic electronic switching as the car moves from cell to cell, available radio frequencies can be used and reused many times in the same area. With the new system, more than 100,000 car radio telephones can be served in a given city instead of the less than 1,000 in the older VHF bands.

Telephone communication entered a new realm in October, when service was introduced on 20 commercial airliners. The new pay service employs cordless radio phones in wall-mounted consoles; small antennas are installed on the underside of the plane. Passengers can call anywhere in the United States while flying over the continent. The system is also designed to receive calls from the ground, a service expected to be introduced shortly.

Television with stereophonic audio was on the way as a result of an FCC authorization for the use of subcarriers in the audio channel of the TV signal. Previously, "simulcast" with another local FM station was the only way in which a TV viewer could get a stereo sound channel. The split channel can also be used for a second-language track or for simultaneous translation from one language to another. Already in use in Japan, the system was expected shortly in the United States, Great Britain, France, Italy, and the Netherlands.

Microelectronics and Microprocessors. As the dimensions of microelectronic structures shrink, their costs come down and the number of functions they can perform, their speed, and their reliability all increase. In 1984, 32-bit microprocessors were put into production by several manufacturers in the United States and Japan, replacing the earlier 16-bit chip in minicomputers and telecommunication equipment. Capable of processing 32 bits of information simultaneously, the device is smaller than a dime, yet it contains the circuit equivalent of 180,000 transistors.

AT&T continued to increase production of its 256K dynamic access memory chip. This device can store and retrieve as many as 256,000 bits of computer information on a single small piece of silicon containing more than 600,000 microscopic components. Meanwhile, IBM fabricated an experimental silicon chip that can store more than one million bits.

M. D. FAGEN, *Formerly, Bell Laboratories*

COMPUTERS

The rapid pace of innovation and evolution of the computer industry continued into 1984. Some firms, unable to compete in the quickly changing marketplace, floundered and fell by the wayside. No one—not manufacturers, not retailers, not computer magazine publishers—was immune to bankruptcy court. But the industry continued to lure newcomers, and for most firms the year was an upbeat one. Sales continued to increase as people became ever more comfortable with and dependent on computers.

Hardware. The year's major new computer was Apple's Macintosh, a 32-bit personal computer with a high-resolution display of exceptional clarity and crispness. The well-received "Mac" came with 128K of random-access memory (RAM) and 64K of machine-language read-only memory (ROM). It had a 3½-inch disk drive and a detached keyboard with 58 keys, all programmable. Designed for easy use with a desktop "mouse" (pointing device to control the screen cursor), the Macintosh is appealing to inexperienced computer users. In September, an enhanced version with 512K RAM became available.

IBM began shipping its PCjr, a scaled-down version of the popular PC, with 64K RAM and two ROM cartridge slots. The machine's "chicklet" keyboard, its preclusion of a second disk drive, and its limited memory expansion capabilities were severely criticized, and later in 1984 the firm announced a new version of the PCjr that incorporated a number of improvements. IBM also unveiled the PC AT (Advanced Technology), a high-speed desktop computer that can be used by up to three persons simultaneously, with two of them at remote terminals. The machine has a disk drive capable of storing 1.2 megabytes of information. An advanced model also includes a 20-megabyte hard disk.

Several firms introduced lap-size "notebook" computers that have as much power as desktop models. Most of the machines are 16-bit and compatible with the IBM PC. They have liquid-crystal display screens, built-in disk drives, and as much as 512K RAM.

Software. Large publishing companies entered the home-computer software market in force, introducing entertainment, educational, and home productivity products. These firms were major participants in the rush to license

Apple Computer

Apple's new Macintosh is a 32-bit personal computer with 128K of RAM and 64K of ROM. It has a "mouse" for easy use and a detachable keyboard with 58 programmable keys.

well-known fictional characters. Random House introduced a line of software featuring the Peanuts cartoon characters. Simon & Schuster came out with educational software featuring The Muppets.

A lucrative market developed for one of the newest genres of home software: self-help programs and "life-enrichment software." Aerobic exercise programs afford a variety of basic routines or a customized routine that provides extra toning in specific body areas. Biofeedback programs are designed to teach people how to handle stress, how to relax, even how to control blood pressure and heart rate. Parenting products present strategies for guiding child development. "Mind Prober," released by Human Edge Software, lets a user analyze personality traits of other people and prints out the results, including such things as attitudes toward work and sex, how well they cope with stress, and what makes them tick.

Among business users of computers, the hottest products in 1984 were integrated software packages—programs that combine a number of major business applications, such as word processing, file management, graphics, and spreadsheet analysis. With such software a person can write a report, generate a graph from the spreadsheet, insert the graph and the spreadsheet into the report, and then print the entire thing. If the software has telecommunications capabilities, the report can be transmitted by telephone to a distant office without having to change programs and reenter the information.

Data base management packages also were popular. These make it easier for people to maintain and access collections of information. For example, "Pulse 1000," an information management system introduced by Computers

in Medicine, enables doctors in a group practice to call up color graph displays of patient blood pressure, weight, and medication over time and, a moment later, check an appointments calendar or examine a graph of the group's finances—all by pressing only a few keys on the computer.

To overcome some of the problems inherent in conventional selling of software, several firms began to distribute software electronically. Instead of buying the packaged product off a retailer's shelf, a buyer calls up a mainframe computer and indicates what program is desired. The mainframe then sends the program over the telephone line to the buyer's microcomputer or other type of receiving device. One such system, introduced by Network Applications, is designed for large corporations that want a specific software title for many employees. Such a firm may need 100 copies of a program but has no desire to pay for 100 packages and 100 instruction books. Electronic distribution thus promises to reduce a business's software costs. The system also should simplify distribution of updated software.

Robotics. As their capabilities increase, programmable robots are assuming new and more significant roles in industry, businesses, and even homes. A supermarket that opened in Nokendai, Japan, in 1984 uses robots to greet customers, slice meats, unload trucks, and stack shelves. While customers push shopping carts through the store, their children can listen to a piano-playing robot or enjoy educational games on a laser videodisc system.

"Personal robots"—small creatures designed for home use—can walk, talk, play games, detect smoke, act as watchdogs, serve food, and fetch the morning newspaper. They are equipped with sensors to determine distances and to detect and avoid objects in their path. Though the 1984 models were still comparatively primitive, analysts predicted that it would not be long before robots are considered essential household helpers.

As the use of robots and other computer technologies becomes increasingly common, many people are concerned about their impact on society and the economy. A report prepared by the U.S. Congressional Office of Technology Assessment indicated that the increased use of computer-based automation over the next decade will aggravate regional unemployment but will not generate massive nationwide unemployment. Furthermore, the use of automation will gradually alter the mix of occupations and skills needed by manufacturers and may consequently limit the mobility of manufacturing employees. The report states that while the use of automation is likely to improve physical working conditions, its effects on psychological aspects of work will depend on how the technologies are implemented.

JENNY TESAR, *Free-lance Science Writer*

CONNECTICUT

President Ronald Reagan's margin of victory in Connecticut of more than 320,000 votes over the Democratic candidate Walter F. Mondale was the state's largest plurality for a presidential candidate in 20 years and helped put Republicans in control of both houses of the state legislature for the first time since the 1972 landslide of Richard M. Nixon.

The Republicans won 86 seats, the Democrats 65, in the House of Representatives; they won 24 seats to the Democrats' 12 in the Senate. Despite those majorities, the GOP does not have enough votes of its own to override a veto by Democratic Gov. William A. O'Neill.

In addition to winning the legislature, the Republicans picked up one congressional seat with the defeat of three-term Danbury Democrat William R. Ratchford by John G. Rowland of Waterbury, a former state representative. The state's congressional delegation is now divided equally, with three Democrats and three Republicans, for the first time since the 1972 election.

The Judiciary. Ellen Ash Peters, the first and only woman named to the Connecticut Supreme Court, was appointed the state's chief justice on November 13 by Governor O'Neill. Peters, 54, succeeded John A. Speziale, 62, who resigned to return to private law practice. Before she was appointed to the court in 1978, Peters was a Yale Law School professor.

Labor. On September 26, 1,500 clerical and technical workers at Yale University went on strike. Most of the strikers were women, and a major issue was comparable pay for women doing the same work as men. In early December the strikers returned to work without a settlement.

Crime. Barry Dov Schuss, 17, charged with four counts of arson in connection with fires in the summer of 1983 at two synagogues, the home of a rabbi, and the home of a Jewish state

Office of Court Administrator

Gov. William O'Neill named Ellen Ash Peters chief justice, adding a "new dimension" to the state court's history.

legislator, received a suspended sentence in February of a total of 21 years in prison. He avoided imprisonment by agreeing to remain in a mental institution until he is no longer considered a threat to himself or the community. All the arsons were in West Hartford where Schuss lived. He was a member of one of the synagogues he burned.

Victor M. Gerena, whom police suspect in the theft of $7 million in cash from Wells Fargo Armored Services Corp. in West Hartford, was still at large more than a year after the Sept. 12, 1983, incident. He has been placed on the FBI's list of the ten most wanted fugitives, and a $500,000 reward has been offered for information leading to his arrest.

Business. After 12 years as chairman of Aetna Life & Casualty, Hartford, John H. Filer, 60, retired on November 30. James T. Lynn, 57, a Washington lawyer and Aetna director, was chosen to succeed Filer. Lynn had been a cabinet officer and presidential assistant in the Nixon and Ford administrations.

Robert Carlson resigned as president of United Technologies Corp., Hartford, on September 17. He was replaced by Robert Daniell, who had been a senior vice-president. Harry J. Gray continues as chairman and chief executive officer.

Other. The state legislature approved a $5.5 billion, ten-year program to repair the state's roads and bridges. To help pay for the program, the gas tax will rise to 23 cents a gallon over the next decade, and motor vehicle fees will be doubled.

ROBERT F. MURPHY
"The Hartford Courant"

CONNECTICUT • Information Highlights

Area: 5,018 sq mi (12 997 km²).
Population (July 1, 1983 est.): 3,138,000.
Chief Cities (July 1, 1982 est.): Hartford, the capital, 136,334; Bridgeport, 143,745; New Haven, 125,348; Stamford, 103,614.
Government (1984): *Chief Officers*—governor, William A. O'Neill (D); lt. gov., Joseph J. Fauliso (D). *General Assembly*—Senate, 36 members; House of Representatives, 151 members.
State Finances (fiscal year 1983): *Revenues,* $4,707,000,000; *expenditures,* $4,427,000,000.
Personal Income (1983): $46,733,000,000; per capita, $14,895.
Labor Force (May 1984): *Civilian labor force,* 1,646,800; *unemployed,* 68,200 (4.1% of total force).
Education: *Enrollment* (fall 1982)—public elementary schools, 335,997; public secondary, 150,473; colleges and universities (fall 1983), 164,344. *Public school expenditures* (1982–83), $1,711,012,766 ($3,636 per pupil).

CONSUMER AFFAIRS

A turnaround in the U.S. economy continued through 1984. This turnaround was reflected in a continuing upsurge in consumer spending, particularly for new automobiles. Personal consumption expenditures were running at an annual rate of more than $2.29 trillion during 1984. The moderating rate of inflation gave consumers a feeling of optimism, as did a slight reduction in the unemployment rate.

Family Purchasing Power and Poverty. The typical American family had $539 more to spend in real purchasing power in 1984 than when President Reagan took office in 1981. This was due in part to federal tax cuts and the slowing of inflation. However, the most recent figures on poverty released in 1984 revealed that the number of poor people, those below the poverty threshold of $10,178 for a family of four, grew by 868,000, from 34.4 million in 1982 to 35.3 million in 1983. The rate increased from 15% in 1982 to 15.2% in 1983. This was the highest rate since the start of President Johnson's antipoverty program in 1965.

The Presidential Election. During the 1984 presidential campaign neither candidate paid much attention to consumer issues. President Reagan emphasized that during his first term his administration had taken numerous steps to get the government "off the back" of business and consumers and let the marketplace and consumer education play a more significant role. The Democrats criticized the Reagan administration for relaxing government rules and regulations too much, particularly in the area of product safety.

Auto Safety. Secretary of Transportation Elizabeth Dole ruled that air bags or automatic seat belts would have to be provided in all automobile models by 1990, with the program to be phased in over four years. This rule would be rescinded if states representing two thirds of the U.S. population enact mandatory seat-belt laws before April 1, 1989.

The Department of Transportation also ruled that after Sept. 1, 1985, all new passenger cars will be required to have a third brake light mounted at the rear of the car at the driver's eye level. Three studies of cars so equipped have shown reductions of 50 to 58% in rear-end collisions. It is estimated that the device could lower rear-end crashes by 90,000 a year, reduce damage to cars in such collisions by $434 million a year, and reduce personal injuries by 40,000 annually.

Protection Regulations. By late 1984, 33 states had passed "lemon" laws. There are variations in the various laws, but basically they all provide for the replacement or refund for a new car that has been out of service for a total of 30 days or has been brought back four times for the same repair job.

A Federal Trade Commission (FTC) funeral rule went into effect during 1984, requiring funeral homes to issue itemized price lists and give price information over the telephone and in written disclosures. The rule also includes a provision that prohibits funeral homes from saying that a casket, other than an unfinished wooden box, is required for direct cremation, and another that directs funeral directors to inform customers that embalming is not always required.

Eight states have passed item-pricing legislation, requiring that items sold in supermarkets where electronic scanning checkout counters are used must have prices stamped on the packages. New York State became the first state to rule that banks and savings and loan associations must clear checks that have been deposited to an account more quickly. Checks must be cleared within two days by commercial banks and within three days by thrift institutions.

Credit. Congress passed a bill extending until May 31, 1985, the ban against merchants adding a surcharge on credit card purchases.

Telephone Deregulation. Probably few court decisions have created quite the stir among consumers as the decision to break up the American Telephone and Telegraph Corporation. Only time would tell the long-range benefits of the action. Meanwhile consumers were having to make many decisions concerning phone service, and there continued to be much confusion.

Bank Deregulation. Consumers also were very directly affected by government deregulation of the banking industry. As a result of deregulation, commercial and savings banks were looking more and more alike. Consumers now benefit from the interest being paid on checking accounts and the higher interest rates being paid on various savings accounts. However, they are paying for this, as banks are charging fees for a variety of services that had been free, the fees on many other services are going up, and interest rates on loans are continuing at a high rate. The more than 65 bank failures during 1984 were cause for concern, but in general the public has faith in the banking system. This was due in considerable measure to the confidence consumers have in the Federal Deposit Insurance Corporation and the Federal Savings and Loan Insurance Corporation.

Consumer Complaints. The Council of Better Business Bureaus reported in 1984 that 7.8 million consumers contacted the Better Business Bureau offices for assistance with inquiries and complaints in 1983. Inquiries accounted for nearly 6.1 million of the contacts, and complaints totaled 1.7 million. Mail-order companies led as the subject of inquiries and complaints.

STEWART M. LEE
Geneva College

In a major crackdown against the Mafia, law enforcement officers arrested dozens of alleged organized crime figures in Italy and the United States during September and October. Left: Italian police arrest a leading member of the Camorra, a Neapolitan version of the Mafia.

UPI/Bettmann

CRIME

According to figures released by the Federal Bureau of Investigation (FBI), the number of crimes committed in the United States decreased 7% from 1982 to 1983, with decreases in all major categories except rape. Offenses showing a decline were murder, robbery, aggravated assault, burglary, larceny, car theft, and arson. The total number of major crimes dropped from approximately 12.9 million in 1982 to about 12 million in 1983. In 1982 the decrease had been 3% from the previous year. The 1983 decline was the largest since the present FBI record-keeping system was begun in 1924, and it marked the first time in 24 years that the crime rate declined for two consecutive years. The FBI statistics are compiled from reports submitted by nearly 16,000 law-enforcement agencies, which police 97% of the nation's population.

The decline in major crime took place in all geographic regions of the country and held for cities, suburbs, and rural areas. The largest percentage drop, 8%, was recorded in the Northeast.

A total of 19,308 homicides were committed in the United States during 1983, 8% fewer than the year before. Handguns, involved in 44% of the slayings, continued to be the most frequently employed weapons in homicides. Of every 100 homicide victims, 76 were male, 55 white, 20 Latin, and 33 between the ages of 20 and 29. Detroit replaced Gary, IN, as the city with the highest per-capita homicide rate. Miami dropped from second to third, and New Orleans moved from sixth to fourth place.

The total of 78,918 reported rape and attempted rape cases was about the same number as in the previous year. The reason for the lack of decline, according to some, was that women were becoming less reluctant to report sexual assaults to law-enforcement authorities. According to others, however, the rape rate remained high because of growing hostility between men and women rooted in emerging redefinitions of sex roles.

Further statistical tabulations for the year showed that 46% of violent crimes were solved, compared with only 18% of property crimes. The number of law-enforcement officers slain in the line of duty, 80, was the lowest in a decade.

Crime Report Criticized. The Police Foundation, a research organization based in Washington, D.C., issued a report during the year maintaining that the FBI crime statistics are highly inaccurate. The major source of error was said to lie in the complex and vague instructions given by the FBI to the nation's police departments in regard to what constitutes an arrest. Some departments were said to report an arrest when a suspect is stopped by a police officer, others only when a person is booked, and still others only when there is a court arraignment. The report also cited a high number of clerical errors. The Police Foundation emphasized that general crime rates from different jurisdictions ought not be compared because of variations in reporting methods and statistical accuracy.

Nonetheless, differences in the national crime totals from year to year are believed to represent accurately the overall trends, since the same kind of reporting procedures are regularly repeated. This point was underlined in 1984 by the National Crime Survey, which also reported a 7% decline in crime in 1983. The survey is conducted twice a year by means of interviews with 128,000 persons in 60,000 households nationwide. Respondents are asked about personal experiences as crime victims. The survey calculated that there were a total of 36.9 million rapes, robberies, assaults, personal larcenies, household burglaries, and motor vehicle thefts. This figure is much higher than the FBI's because it includes cases not reported to the authorities. According to the survey, 27% of U.S. households experienced a major crime during the year. About 5.3 million households—6.1% of the total—were burglarized.

Explaining the Decrease in Crime. Two major explanations were offered for the reported drop in crime in the United States. The first was that the "baby boom" generation has aged out of its crime-prone years. Violent and property offenses are notoriously committed by persons between the ages of 14 and 24; when there is a lower percentage of such persons in the population, the overall crime rate can be expected to drop. Nonetheless, as pointed out by Steven R. Schlesinger and Jeffrey L. Sedgwick of the Bureau of Justice Statistics in the U.S. Department of Justice, the decrease in crime rates cannot be totally credited to demographic changes. They note that from 1978 to 1983, crimes against persons and households, as measured by the National Crime Survey, declined 18.2% and 14.1%, respectively, while the number of persons aged 14 to 24 went down only 8.7%.

Schlesinger and Sedgwick suggest that the rate of imprisonment also has played a significant role in the crime decrease. They note that in 1960, 18% of the arrests for major crimes resulted in imprisonment. By 1970, as the crime rate skyrocketed, that number had fallen to 6.2%. In 1980 it rose to 7.3%, and in 1984 it surpassed 8%. High rates of imprisonment are said to reduce the incidence of crime because potential offenders may already be behind bars and because others may be deterred by fear of imprisonment.

Anticrime Law. In October, President Reagan signed into law what Attorney General William French Smith called "the most far-reaching and substantial reform of the [federal] criminal justice system in our history." At the center of the legislation were measures to make it easier for federal judges to keep convicted criminals and defendants deemed to be "dangerous" behind bars. Parole was abolished, the bail and sentencing systems were overhauled, and pretrial detention of "dangerous" suspects was allowed. In addition, the measure curbs the insanity defense by shifting the burden of proof to the defendant; gives prosecutors wider authority to seize and sell the property of convicted drug dealers; increases penalties for drug dealers; makes credit-card fraud a federal crime; outlaws the use of computers to obtain illegal profits or unauthorized access to national security data; authorizes up to $170 million for state and local anticrime programs; creates a $100 million fund for aid to victims of federal offenses; and enacts dozens of other changes. Law enforcement officers generally praised the legislation, while critics regarded some provisions as threats to civil liberties.

Crime and the 1984 Election. Unlike earlier elections, the 1984 presidential campaign afforded a relatively minor role to the issue of crime. Polls indicated that for the first time in several decades the public was not intensely concerned about the matter. The *Wall Street Journal*, analyzing the election, offered the following explanation:

Neither party has a monopoly on solutions, and many of the proposed antidotes to crime are too complex to translate into election slogans. But the main reason, experts say, may be that an increasingly savvy electorate doesn't believe that crime, as it affects them personally, is really a federal issue.

Mass Murder. On July 18, a heavily armed gunman killed 22 persons and wounded 15 at a crowded McDonald's restaurant in the California town of San Ysidro, near the Mexican border. It was the worst mass slaying in U.S. history. The killer, James Oliver Huberty, 41, was finally shot dead by a police sniper perched on the roof of a nearby post office. Huberty used a shotgun, pistol, and semiautomatic hunting rifle in the massacre.

In the wake of the slaughter, experts looked for explanations for such mass killings. James Alan Fox and Jack Levin of Northeastern University examined 156 episodes between 1976 and 1980 in which four or more persons were slain. They found that only four of the 156 mass murderers were women and that a majority were white. Blacks committed 50% of single-victim murders, they noted, but only 22% of multiple murders. Multiple murderers tend to be in their thirties, about ten years older than other murderers. Like most killers, those slaying four or more persons were usually found to kill people they knew, most often out of rage or frustration or in a misguided fit of jealousy.

Dr. Helen Morrison, a Chicago psychiatrist, believes that mass murderers are marked by grandiose ideas about their power and that they display strong obsessive traits. She points out that John Gacy, a building contractor who was convicted in 1980 of murdering 33 young men, kept notebooks recording what he did minute by minute and even wrote down the precise moment he mailed a letter. "This tremendous organization is about the only structure they have," Dr. Morrison believes.

One contributing factor, according to some sociologists, is that America is becoming a nation of strangers. Others blame television depictions of violence for making persons insensitive to the feelings of their fellow human beings. It is generally agreed, however, that it is impossible to predict whether any particular person will become a mass murderer.

Violence in the Schools. President Reagan during the year called crime in schools a major impediment to excellence in education. A report to the president, "Chaos in the Classroom: Enemy of American Education," observed: "Discipline is the public's foremost concern about schools. Three million secondary schoolchildren are victims of crime each month." The cost of school vandalism was said to exceed the expense of textbooks. The president noted in a radio broadcast that "the problem is so bad that almost 8% of urban junior and senior high school students missed at least one day in the classroom per month because they are afraid to go to school." He pointed out that each month 6,000 teachers are robbed, 125,000 are threatened with physical harm, and 1,000 require medical attention. The president contended that campaigns against school crime were handicapped by recent court decisions, such as one in New Jersey which ruled that the search of a student's locker was a violation of that student's rights.

In a report for the National Institute of Justice, Jackson Toby of Rutgers University noted that "the traditional expectation that schools arc safe places for children is changing." According to the report, 12% of U.S. secondary school teachers said that they had hesitated to confront misbehaving students during the previous month out of fear for their own safety. In the largest cities, that figure rose to 28%. Violent acts in schools, however, are most likely to be committed by persons Toby labels "intruders": predators, who perhaps are not even neighborhood residents; angry parents; and suspended students who return to the building. Toby found that junior high schools are more dangerous for students than high schools, largely, he believes, because they contain a higher proportion of involuntary students, persons forced to be at school because of compulsory attendance laws.

Critics of the focus on school violence charge that the schools are being unfairly portrayed as "blackboard jungles," and that, instead of merely deploring the violence, the government should provide resources for better counseling, higher teacher salaries, and other measures that would upgrade the educational environment. While parents rate discipline as the major problem of schools, teachers have singled out lack of parent interest as the biggest stumbling block to improved education.

Family Violence. "A person beaten in the home is no less a victim than a person beaten on the sidewalk in front of the home," noted the 1984 report of the U.S. Attorney General's Task Force on Family Violence. The report called for more arrests, trials, and imprisonments for perpetrators of family violence. It recommended the creation of special units to process family violence cases and asked for the elimination of the requirement that a victim must sign a formal complaint before charges can be filed in a family violence case. The federal panel also advocated that a child's testimony at a trial should be presented on videotape rather than in person.

The Bureau of Justice Statistics indicated that there are upward of 450,000 cases of family violence annually, and that a majority involve lower-income women and their spouses or former spouses. Violence was found to be four times more likely in households with yearly incomes of less than $7,500 than in households with incomes of more than $25,000. Weapons were used in 30% of episodes.

Death Penalty. The use of the death penalty increased dramatically in 1984, reaching the highest point in 20 years. More than 1,300 U.S. prisoners continued to await execution, with their number increasing by about 250 each year. Some two thirds of the death row inmates were being held in the southern states, with Florida, Texas, and Georgia having the most. About 40% of the death-row population is black, compared with a 12% nationwide black population. Only about 1% of the death row population is made up of women. Among the inmates put to death in 1984 was 51-year-old Margie Velma Barfield, convicted in 1978 of killing her fiancé with arsenic. Her November execution in North Carolina marked the first time in 22 years that a woman was put to death in the United States.

Mafia Crackdown. In one of the most sweeping anti-Mafia campaigns ever, Italian police rounded up dozens of alleged organized crime figures in late September and early October. Arrest warrants were issued following the confession of Tommaso Buscetta, a Mafia leader extradited to Italy from Brazil in July. A total of 366 warrants were issued, but about 200 of the cited individuals were already in jail. Assisting in the operation, the U.S. Justice Department ordered the arrest of 28 Americans and Italians on U.S. soil. Extradition would be possible under a treaty approved by the Senate in early July. That treaty was part of a series of cooperative efforts to crack down on organized crime in both countries.

GILBERT GEIS
University of California, Irvine

Convicted murderer Margie Velma Barfield, 51, became the first U.S. woman in 22 years to suffer the death penalty.

Robbin D. Hyde, Picture Group

En route home from the funeral of Soviet President Yuri Andropov, Cuba's President Fidel Castro stopped in Spain and was received warmly by Premier Felipe González (left). East-West relations and Central America were reported to be topics of their discussions.

Agencia EFE/Photo Trends

CUBA

U.S. policy on Cuba was the main concern of President Fidel Castro's Marxist government in 1984. Domestically, the country suffered an economic setback due chiefly to declining sugar prices.

Foreign Relations. While at the beginning of 1984 Castro appeared defiant and declared that "if the United States wants to invade it would have to kill all of the Cuban people," in his traditional July 26 address to the nation he sounded conciliatory and held out an offer of peace to the Reagan administration. Although Cuba, following the Soviet lead, boycotted the Los Angeles Olympic Games, at the same time formal U.S.-Cuban diplomatic discussions began in New York. The talks dealt principally with the American demand that Cuba take back several thousand unwanted refugees who had arrived in Florida during the 1980 boatlift. On its part, Cuba wanted the United States to discuss the issue of more than 1,000 former political prisoners and tens of thousands of relatives of Cuban Americans stranded in Cuba after the United States Interests Section in Havana stopped issuing them visas. The bilateral conversations started partly as a result of a June visit to Cuba by the Rev. Jesse Jackson, who persuaded Castro to free 48 American and Cuban prisoners.

In October, as it appeared that the New York meetings would produce no immediate results, Cuba announced that it was conducting large-scale maneuvers and civilian-evacuation drills, which included digging trenches and shelters in anticipation of a U.S. attack.

In mid-December an agreement was reached on the repatriation to Cuba of 2,746 criminals and mental patients who had arrived in the United States in the 1980 Mariel boatlift. The accord also opened the way for resumption of normal immigration from Cuba.

According to a new Pentagon study, the Soviet Union had been stepping up its military assistance to Cuba. Among the most important Soviet weapons delivered to the Havana government in 1984 were 12 new jet interceptors (7 MiG-21s and 5 MiG-23s), 22 military helicopters, 100 tanks, 11 multiple-rocket launchers, and 83 antitank guns. Cuba's military force, the report said, consisted of 25 divisions and 950 tanks, 270 combat aircraft, 208 surface-to-air missiles, and other weapons. Cuban seapower, U.S. Naval sources said, had expanded to three submarines, two frigates, and a fleet of 80 missile, torpedo, and attack boats. The armed forces were larger, if not better equipped, than those of Mexico, Brazil, or Canada.

Cuba and China agreed to improve trade, cultural, and scientific exchanges despite differences on international matters. Havana also made efforts to improve relations with Argentina, Ecuador, and Panama, among other countries. Relations with Mexico continued cordial.

Losses in Angola. Cuban government news media began referring more frequently to military and civilian losses in Angola, where the Castro government had some 20,000 soldiers and civilian workers. In March, when President José Eduardo dos Santos visited Cuba, Havana said that more than 150,000 Cubans had worked in Angola "in military and civilian fields" since Cuba's 1975 military intervention in support of the Luanda Marxist regime. According to Western experts, some 3,000 Cubans had been killed or wounded in Angola. In 1984, these experts said, Cubans became increasingly involved in that country's civil war, in which pro-Western guerrillas supported by South Africa were fighting government forces propped by Cuban military units.

Economic Developments. A large harvest of 8.2 million metric tons of sugar, Cuba's main export, was offset by a decline in world market prices for sugar from about 8 cents a pound in

1983 to less than 5 cents in 1984. "The economy is going to be affected by a setback in [our] sugar plans," commented Castro in reference to Cuba's resultant losses in foreign currency earnings.

Higher interest rates forced Havana to ask Western banks to reschedule the $250-million service charges on its debt due in 1984. Some 100 creditors, mostly in Europe, agreed to the postponement. The total of Cuba's debt to Western private institutions and governments was estimated in 1984 at $2.5 billion (U.S.).

Havana tried to expand one sure source of foreign currency: tourism. Cuba was said to be attracting numerous visitors from Spain, Canada, Mexico, and West Germany, in addition to those from the Communist bloc.

Under an agreement with East Germany, between 1986 and 1990 experts from that country would help Cubans refurbish Havana and rebuild the city's infrastructure. Plans were also announced for a start before the year 2000 on construction of a subway in the capital, whose population had grown to about 2 million.

Political Prisoners. Among the Cuban political prisoners released in 1984 and allowed to leave the island was Jorge Valls, a poet who had won numerous awards for works written in prison since 1964 after he testified against the Castro government in a political trial in Havana. Later in 1984, however, Castro indicated to a delegation of Hispanic Americans visiting Cuba that some of his political prisoners may never be released. Among them were Eloy Gutiérrez Menoyo, a former major in Castro's guerrilla forces who later turned against him.

Pollution. In 1984, for the first time, Cuba showed deep concern over environmental pollution. According to the Communist party newspaper, *Granma,* Nipe Bay had been polluted by industrial waste to a point where marine life was rapidly dying in its waters. The bay, Cuba's largest and most beautiful, is located in the northeastern part of the island. The worst thing about the situation, said a Cuban Academy of Science expert, was that at the current rate of pollution it would take only about a year and a half for the damage to become irreparable.

GEORGE VOLSKY, *University of Miami*

CYPRUS

With intercommunal talks having failed to produce a compromise since the de facto division of the island republic in 1974, the minority Turkish Cypriots of the north and the majority Greek Cypriots of the south undertook a new form of negotiation, "proximity talks," under the aegis of UN Secretary General Javier Pérez de Cuéllar during 1984.

The newly formed Turkish Republic of Northern Cyprus, proclaimed in November 1983, exchanged ambassadors with Turkey in April 1984. The move was strongly denounced by Greek Cypriot President Spyros Kyprianou and by the government of Greece.

Negotiations. In May the United Nations, which continues to maintain a peacekeeping force on the island, was called on by the Greek Cypriots to condemn the Turkish Cypriot move. On May 11 the UN Security Council passed a resolution, 13 to 1 with the United States abstaining, decrying the Turkish Cypriot efforts at secession and requesting that UN Secretary-General Javier Pérez de Cuéllar re-initiate negotiations between the two sides.

Pérez de Cuéllar, who had been involved in some of the earlier intercommunal negotiations, undertook a new effort. In August he met separately with members of the two groups in Vienna. To each he presented "working points" for further discussions. After disagreements broke out among the Greek Cypriot political parties over the future of the negotiations, President Kyprianou went to Athens for discussions with Greek President Constantine Caramanlis. Indeed, Kyprianou maintained contact with Athens throughout the year, making several trips. When the Greek Cypriots and Turkish Cypriots decided to continue their negotiations through the mediation of the secretary-general, Pérez de Cuéllar met in New York with Kyprianou and the Turkish Cypriot leader, Rauf Denktas. Since Greek Cypriot representatives refuse to meet officially with Turkish Cypriot representatives lest that imply some form of recognition, Pérez de

Cuéllar met separately with the principals in these "proximity talks."

The negotiations lasted several weeks and to all appearances seemed to be without results. A second round of "proximity talks," begun in October, proved to be equally fruitless. Finally in the third round, started in November, the Turkish Cypriots presented very concrete proposals which President Kyprianou, his government, and the Greek government all took under serious consideration. As a result, Pérez de Cuéllar could announce in December that Kyprianou and Denktas would meet directly, under his auspices, in New York City in mid-January 1985.

Royal Visits. Britain's Queen Elizabeth II and Prince Philip stopped at Cyprus briefly in March. In October, Prince Philip visited the British contingent stationed on Cyprus. Britain has maintained its own bases on Cyprus apart from the Cypriot administration since the island gained its independence in 1960.

GEORGE J. MARCOPOULOS, *Tufts University*

CZECHOSLOVAKIA

As indicated by the government report on the results achieved in the first half of 1984, Czechoslovakia's economy performed somewhat better than in the previous few years. Compared with the first half of 1983, gross national income rose by 3.2%, industrial production by 4.1%, construction by 2.1%, labor productivity in industry by 2.6% and in construction by 0.4%, and retail trade by 3.7%. Deliveries for export to socialist countries increased by 8.3% and to nonsocialist countries by 8.1%. Highest rates of growth were attained in the electrotechnical industry (11.3%) and general machinery (7.1%). Monetary income of the population grew by 2.7%, wages by 2.8%, and personal consumption by 2.4%. On the other hand, output of black coal was down by 0.7% and freight transportation by 0.8%. The annual plan for the construction of apartments was fulfilled only by 35.8% in the first six months of 1984, and decreases were registered in the quantity of cows, pigs, and poultry.

Foreign Relations. The year was marked by a lively exchange of official meetings with representatives of a number of other countries. In the course of the year Prague served as a host to UN Secretary General Javier Pérez de Cuéllar, Vatican representative Archbishop Luigi Poggi, the presidents of Malta and North Korea, the premier of Greece, the Swedish foreign minister, and two members of the Soviet Politburo.

During his customary summer pilgrimage to the Soviet Union, Czechoslovakia's President Gustáv Husák was awarded Lenin's Order, the Golden Star Medal, and the title of Hero of the Soviet Union on the occasion of his 70th birth-

day. Czechoslovak Premier Lubomír Štrougal journeyed to India, Burma, Yugoslavia, Libya, Syria, and Bulgaria, while his foreign minister paid visits to Zimbabwe, Angola, Brazil, Argentina, Colombia, France, West Germany, and Poland. Agreements on economic cooperation were concluded with Syria, Libya, and Greece. In July a high-level Czechoslovak government delegation led by the premier and three deputy premiers traveled to Moscow for talks with the Soviet leaders about the next Czechoslovak five-year plan, to begin in 1986.

Church Affairs. A worrisome problem landed in the government's lap when František Cardinal Tomášek of Prague invited the pope to visit Czechoslovakia in 1985 for the commemoration of the 1,100th anniversary of the death of Archbishop St. Methodius, the Greek missionary who first brought Christianity to Bohemia-Moravia. A campaign launched to collect signatures for a letter inviting the pope triggered a wave of harassment and detention of those involved. A suggestion was made by the regime's spokesmen that the orthodox Patriarch Pimen of Moscow be invited instead.

Continued Dissidence. In spite of recurrent arrests of its members, Charter 77, the Czech human rights movement, continued its criticism of the regime for its violations of human rights. In February 1984 it angered the government by issuing, together with the Polish dissidents and Solidarity supporters, a joint declaration appealing to "the people of the world" to join them in the struggle for the liberation of political prisoners in Poland and Czechoslovakia. Protests also continued against the stationing of Soviet missiles on Czechoslovak soil.

The Nobel Prize. The poet Jaroslav Seifert became the first Czechoslovak writer ever to be awarded the Nobel Prize for literature. (*See also page 320.*)

EDWARD TABORSKY
The University of Texas at Austin

CZECHOSLOVAKIA • Information Highlights

Official Name: Czechoslovak Socialist Republic.
Location: East-central Europe.
Area: 49,370 sq mi (127 870 km²).
Population (mid-1984 est.): 15,500,000.
Chief Cities (Dec. 31, 1982 est.): Prague, the capital, 1,185,693; Bratislava, 394,644; Brno, 378,722.
Government: *Head of state,* Gustáv Husák, president (took office 1975). *Head of government,* Lubomír Štrougal, premier (took office 1970). *Communist party, secretary-general,* Gustáv Husák (took office 1969). *Legislature*—Federal Assembly.
Monetary Unit: Koruna (13.04 koruny equal U.S.$1, July 1984).
Gross National Product (1982 U.S.$): $147,-100,000,000.
Economic Index (1983): *Industrial Production* (1975 = 100), 134.
Foreign Trade (1983 U.S.$): *Imports,* $15,-800,000,000; *exports,* $16,507,000,000.

Martha Graham's illustrious modern dance troupe gave its premiere performance of Stravinsky's "The Rite of Spring."

DANCE

The dance world appeared to be in transition in 1984. The deaths of major dance figures and conflicts between artistic directors and boards of trustees suggested that dance was entering a new era. Artistically, there was a diminishing dominance by pure-dance works and a new interest in pieces that explored narrative or emotional relationships. The foremost trend in this direction was exemplified by the new "dance-theater" aesthetics of foreign companies such as those of Pina Bausch from West Germany and Sankai Juku from Japan.

Modern Dance. The Pina Bausch Wuppertaler Tanztheater opened the Olympic Arts Festival in Los Angeles. The highly acclaimed festival made California a temporary dance capital with the appearances of (in addition to North American companies) the London Contemporary Dance Theater, the Korean National Dance Company, the Groupe Emile Dubois from France, Les Ballets Africains from Guinea, and other troupes.

Miss Bausch's works caused the most controversy during her company's East Coast debut at the Brooklyn Academy of Music. The violence of her images was disturbing to those who felt that in her "dance-theater" she condoned the maltreatment men and women inflicted on one another. For others, Bausch was a powerful innovator whose roots lay in German Expressionism but whose formal structures bore a distinctly contemporary stamp. Her version of Stravinsky's *The Rite of Spring* still used conventional dance movement, but more recent works used dialogue or nondance movement.

Sankai Juku, headed by Ushio Amagatsu, also eschewed conventional dance idioms. As part of an experimental "dance-theater" trend in Japan known as "butoh," the company focused typically on themes of creation and destruction, metamorphosis and transcendence. Four of the five-member male troupe caused a sensation when they hung, upside down, from the roof outside New York's City Center theater. The same symbolic birth image was repeated inside in the work *Jomon Sho* (Homage to Pre-History). Another work—(*Kinkan Shonen* (The Cumquat Seed)—treated its images of evolution with more humor.

For sheer drama, it was difficult to match the theatricality of America's modern-dance pioneer Martha Graham. In a triumphant New York season, Miss Graham, just short of her 90th birthday, presented her first treatment of *The Rite of Spring*. Rejecting the references to Russian folklore in the Stravinsky ballet score, the Graham *Rite* seemed set in a desolate clime in the American Southwest.

Inspired by American Indian rites, Miss Graham's fertility ritual was nonetheless more abstract than specific. The National Endowment for the Arts, whose refusal to give Miss Graham's company a Challenge Grant in 1983 sparked a wide protest, awarded her a $500,000 Challenge Grant in 1984 and a special grant of $250,000 to film her works.

Modern dance had other highlights. Merce Cunningham's premieres were *Pictures* and *Inlets 2*. Erick Hawkins recalled Americana themes in the new *The Joshua Tree, or Three Outlaws* and revivals of *Trickster Coyote* and *God's Angry Man, The Passion of John Brown.* Other premieres included Paul Taylor's *Equinox* and . . . *Byzantium,* Alwin Nikolais' *Liturgies* and *Persons and Structures,* and Murray Louis' *Frail Demons* and *Four Brubeck Pieces.*

The Alvin Ailey American Dance Theater presented new works such as Judith Jamison's *Divining,* Donald McKayle's *Collage,* Ulysses Dove's *Nightshade,* Loris Anthony Beckles' *Anjour,* and (on tour) Ailey's *For Bird-With Love.* Patrick Dupond, a guest from the Paris Opera Ballet, was flamboyant and outstanding as the rock star in *Precipice,* an Ailey ballet created in Paris that received its American premiere at the Metropolitan Opera House.

Twyla Tharp's company had two New York seasons where she presented the premieres of *Telemann, Fait Accompli, Bad Smells,* and a big hit to Frank Sinatra's recordings that explored ballroom dancing, *Nine Sinatra Songs.* She was also more active than usual in ballet companies. American Ballet Theatre gave most viewers a first glimpse of her reworked *The Little Ballet* and *Bach Partita,* created in late 1983. Less substantive but very much a popular novelty was *Brahms/Handel,* which Jerome Robbins choreographed with her for the New York City Ballet to Brahms' *Variations and Fugue on a Theme of Handel.*

Ballet. The New York City Ballet's regular choreographers remained faithful to the plotless neoclassic style of George Balanchine, who was the troupe's artistic director until his death in 1983. Peter Martins (*see* BIOGRAPHY) was more successful with his Bach *Rejouissance* than his *A Schubertiad.* Helgi Tomasson's *Menuetto,* premiered in Saratoga, NY, was impressively fluent as was Martins' *Mozart Violin Concerto* for the Pennsylvania Ballet. Bart Cook's *Seven by Five* was also seen during the City Ballet summer season in Saratoga. Jerome Robbins, codirector of the company with Martins, created *Antique Epigraphs* to Debussy and revived his *Moves.*

American Ballet Theatre's *Cinderella* by Mikhail Baryshnikov and Peter Anastos received lukewarm reviews but proved a commercial success. Martine van Hamel, a dancer in the company, choreographed *Amnon V'Tamar.* Based on a biblical story, it was her first ballet for the troupe. Gelsey Kirkland, one of America's leading ballerinas, unexpectedly left the company in the spring.

A newsworthy production was the Dance Theater of Harlem's version of *Giselle.* Although the choreography, restaged by Frederic Franklin, was traditional, the scenery and costumes by Carl Michel transferred the action from Germany to 19th-century Louisiana among the free black population. The company also performed Glen Tetley's *Voluntaries* for the first time. The Feld Ballet's premieres by

Eliot Feld were *The Jig Is Up* and *Adieu.* A new group, Finis Jhung's Chamber Ballet U.S.A., presented the premiere of Helgi Tomasson's *Contredances.*

Rudolf Nureyev returned to New York with *Nureyev and Friends,* a small ensemble that presented nothing new and that showed him in poor form. His earlier appearance at the Pennsylvania Ballet's 20th anniversary gala in Philadelphia showed him in a solo—*Bach Suite*— that better suited his present capabilities.

Other News. In a gesture of reconciliation at the sama gala, Robert Weiss, the Pennsylvania Ballet's artistic director, paid public tribute to Barbara Weisberger, the company's founder who had resigned in 1982 in a conflict with the board of directors. During 1984, Violette Verdy, criticizing her own board, resigned as artistic director of the Boston Ballet. In the New York area, Edward Villella left the Eglevsky Ballet's artistic directorship after a sharp dispute that led him to file suit against some members of the board. An attempt by the board of the San Francisco Ballet to oust Michael Smuin as codirector failed as a result of pressure from the company's membership association. Smuin was taken back for one year.

Shortly afterward, Lew Christensen, director of the San Francisco Ballet since 1951 and who had invited Smuin as his codirector in the 1970s, was hospitalized and died. In Boston, E. Virginia Williams, the founder of the Boston Ballet, died soon after relinquishing control to Miss Verdy.

Other deaths that saddened the dance world were those of David McLain, artistic director of the Cincinnati Ballet; Vera Nemtchinova, a former star of Serge Diaghilev's Ballets Russes who became a well-known teacher in New York; and Balasaraswati, the great classical dancer from India who had taught and performed in the United States.

On the brighter side, the American Dance Festival in Durham, NC, celebrated its 50th anniversary with commissioned premieres and guest companies from Asia. Its beginnings at Vermont's Bennington College were recalled when Hanya Holm, one of the modern-dance pioneers associated with the Bennington period, was presented with the Samuel H. Scripps-American Dance Festival Award.

New projects included the first New York International Ballet Competition, which was held at the City Center, and the "National Choreography Project" to encourage companies to work with choreographers new to them. Twenty-eight experimental groups or choreographers were honored with the first "Bessies," established by Dance Theater Workshop in New York as the dance equivalent of the "Obies" in theater. The prizes were named after Bessie Schönberg, a dance teacher who has trained many innovative choreographers.

ANNA KISSELGOFF, *"The New York Times"*

Democrat S.B. Woo, 47-year-old physics professor, staged a successful bid for Delaware's lieutenant governorship.

DELAWARE

History was made in Delaware in 1984 as its voters elected the first Chinese-American lieutenant governor in the United States. S. B. Woo defeated by a narrow margin D. Battle Robinson, the first woman to run for the state's second-highest-ranking office.

Elections. Gov. Pierre duPont IV (R) could not succeed himself for reelection. Lt. Gov. Michael N. Castle (R) was elected to the office, defeating Supreme Court Justice William Quillen. The Republican Party wrested control of the state's House of Representatives from the Democrats by electing five new members. The Republicans will lead the House by a 22–19 margin, but control of the state Senate remained with the Democrats (13–8).

Wilmington's Mayor William McLaughlin declined to run for reelection. City Council member Daniel Frawley was elected easily to the post after a razor-thin victory in the primary. In populous New Castle County, County Executive Richard Collins, a Republican, chose not to seek reelection. He will be succeeded by Rita Justice (R), who defeated veteran County Councilman Joseph F. Toner.

President Ronald Reagan carried the state easily. His coattails, however, seemed to have little impact in Delaware as two Republican challengers with close identification with the president's policies, John M. Burris and Elise duPont, were unable to defeat incumbents Sen. Joseph R. Biden and Rep. Thomas R. Carper, respectively.

Legislative Session. The second session of the 132d Delaware General Assembly ran from January through June 1984. It operated in a fiscal atmosphere dramatically different from that which prevailed in 1983. In 1983, revenues were so limited that state employees were forced to forego a pay increase and spending for state programs had to be cut. However, in 1984 sharply rising revenues allowed the legislature to provide a tax cut, provide money for projects that had to be foregone in previous years, and still end the fiscal year with the highest surplus in the state's history. Tax cuts include a 10% across-the-board cut in personal income taxes, an increase in the personal exemption from $600 to $800, and decreases in tax rates for top-bracket earners with incomes exceeding $50,000. A package of tax incentives to certain types of business employing blue collar workers also was adopted.

The legislature also authorized new money for equalizing teacher pay and for increases in a variety of programs to upgrade the quality of the state's education system. The legislature also adopted a system of formulas to allocate money to senior centers based on a newly designed formula.

Economy. The Chrysler Corporation, with one of its largest automobile assembly plants located in Delaware, was able to pay back a $5 million loan to the state. The state also was able to pay back a debt of $34.5 million due the Unemployment Trust Fund. As of October 1984, Delaware's seasonally adjusted unemployment rate stood at 5.5% of the work force, compared with the October 1983 figure of 6.8%.

The Environment. Delaware and Pennsylvania received a historic acquisition of land in 1984. The duPont Company donated 1,700 acres (687 ha) of wilderness land in the beautiful White Clay Creek Valley to the two states. The land has been designed as an "intrastate park preserve."

JEROME R. LEWIS, *University of Delaware*

DELAWARE • Information Highlights

Area: 2,044 sq mi (5 295 km²).
Population (July 1, 1983 est.): 606,000.
Chief Cities (1980 census): Dover, the capital, 23,507; Wilmington, 70,195; Newark, 25,247; Elsmere, 6,493.
Government (1984): *Chief Officers*—governor, Pierre S. du Pont IV (R); lt. gov., Michael N. Castle (R). *General Assembly*—Senate, 21 members; House of Representatives, 41 members.
State Finances (fiscal year 1983): *Revenues,* $1,315,000,000; *expenditures,* $1,072,000,000.
Personal Income (1983): $7,673,000,000; per capita, $12,665.
Labor Force (May 1984): *Civilian labor force,* 308,300; *unemployed,* 15,000 (4.9% of total force).
Education: *Enrollment* (fall 1982)—public elementary schools, 59,527; public secondary, 33,119; colleges and universities (fall 1983), 31,945. *Public school expenditures* (1982–83), $294,222,012 ($3,456 per pupil).

Denmark's Poul Schlüter (right) and a glum Anger Jørgensen confer during a debate following January elections.

DENMARK

Since taking office in September 1982, the four-party minority government headed by Conservative Poul Schlüter has struggled with such perennial problems as inflation (which has been somewhat reduced), budget deficits, an unfavorable balance of payments, and continued high unemployment. Moreover, the government's defense and foreign policies have not been fully supported at all times by the opposition.

Elections. As a result of a parliamentary vote rejecting the proposed state budget late in 1983, Prime Minister Schlüter was compelled to call a parliamentary election, which was set for Jan. 10, 1984. The results showed that the four government parties managed to hold their own but failed to gain enough seats to form a majority coalition in the Folketing (parliament). The Conservatives were the main winners, their seats in parliament increasing from 26 to 42. The other three government parties fared as follows: the Liberals gained two for a total of 22 seats; the Center Democrats lost 7 seats to end up with only 8; and the Christian People's Party went up from 4 to 5 representatives.

The opposition parties all suffered losses: the Social Democrats lost 3 members for a total of 56; the Progress Party lost 10, ending up with 6; and the Radicals lost 1 for a total of 10. The Socialist People's Party retained 21 seats, and the Left Socialists retained 5 seats. The founder of the Progress Party, Mogens Glistrup, was elected while still serving a prison term. However, when he attempted to take his seat in parliament, he was rejected by a vote of 139 to 18.

The election of Danish representatives in the European Parliament in Strasbourg was held on June 14, with a very low turnout of voters. More than 60% of Denmark's new representatives in the body favored Denmark's continued membership in the European Community (EC), which at times has been a point of contention.

Greenland. Greenlanders went to the polls on June 6 to elect a new Landsting (parliament). The elections, in which 65% of the electorate took part (compared with 75.1% in 1983), did not bring any changes in the composition of the legislature. The socialist Siumut Party won 11 seats; the more conservative Atassut Party also ended up with 11 seats; and the radical Inuit Ataqatigiit Party increased its representation from 2 to 3. The party representation in the smaller governing Council was to remain as before.

After years of dissatisfaction with EC fisheries policies, Greenland finally left the EC when the Danish Parliament on May 7 ratified this unprecedented step. However, Greenland will be an associate member of the EC after it gives up full membership on Jan. 1, 1985.

Other. Queen Margrethe and Prince Henrik visited the Faroe Islands May 11–15, for the first time in several years. French President François Mitterrand made an official visit to Denmark on February 17 and discussed the finances of the European Community with Prime Minister Schlüter. Spain's Prime Minister Felipe Gonzalez visited Copenhagen May 7–8 and conferred with Danish officials.

K. B. Andersen, one of Denmark's most popular and admired politicians, died on March 23. Born in 1914, Andersen served at various times as president of parliament, minister of education, and foreign minister and took part in many cultural activities as well as the work of the Social-Democratic Party.

ERIK J. FRIIS
"The Scandinavian-American Bulletin"

DENMARK • Information Highlights

Official Name: Kingdom of Denmark.
Location: Northwest Europe.
Area: 16,632 sq mi (43 076 km²).
Population (mid-1984 est.): 5,100,000.
Chief Cities (1982 est.): Copenhagen, the capital, 1,377,064; Århus, 181,518; Odense, 137,427.
Government: *Head of State,* Margrethe II, queen (acceded Jan. 1972). *Head of government,* Poul Schlüter, prime minister (took office Sept. 1982). *Legislature* (unicameral)—Folketing.
Monetary Unit: Krone (11.13 kroner equal U.S. $1, Oct. 22, 1984).
Gross National Product (1982 U.S.$): $56,400,-000,000.
Economic Indexes (1983): *Consumer Prices* (1975 = 100), all items, 336.2; food, 211.9. *Industrial Production* (1975 = 100), 124.
Foreign trade (1983 U.S.$): *Imports,* $16,256,-000,000; exports, $16,029,000,000.

DRUG AND ALCOHOL ABUSE

A significant shift in attitudes toward drunk driving has occurred in the United States during the past few years. Legal penalties for those convicted of driving while intoxicated (DWI) have become more severe. Perhaps as a result of the publicity given to the DWI problem, a trend toward a gradual decrease in frequency and amount of alcoholic beverage use was noted. Since an estimated 14.7% of Americans are either problem drinkers or alcoholics, and since alcohol has been linked with incidents of family violence and a decline in workers' productivity, the trend toward moderation was welcomed. At the same time, authorities continued to be concerned with the problem of drug abuse, giving special attention to drug trafficking. In July, Brazil and Colombia signed an agreement to combat drug traffic between the two nations, and Colombia began spraying thousands of acres of marijuana fields with herbicide. About 60% of the marijuana used in the United States was said to come from Colombia. The Reagan administration congratulated Colombia on its action.

Alcohol. The seriousness of the DWI problem was highlighted after it was revealed that 53% of all traffic deaths in 1983 were attributed to drunk drivers. This means that 22,500 people lost their lives and hundreds of thousands were injured in connection with DWI. Since about 5,000 of the 1983 DWI deaths were in the 16-21 age group, the issue of the legal age for the purchase, possession, and consumption of alcoholic beverages received special attention.

It has been demonstrated that after a state raises the legal drinking age to 21, a 28% decrease occurs in nighttime fatal crashes by drivers over 21. Accordingly, a federal law to encourage states to fix the minimum age at 21 was signed by President Reagan on July 17, 1984. According to the act, a portion of federal highway construction funds will be withheld from states that do not enact a minimum drinking age of 21 by 1987, and there will be financial incentives for states to establish mandatory minimum sentences for drunk driving. By late 1984, approximately half of the states had enacted such legislation, and similar bills were pending in most other states.

A few states also enacted "dram shop" laws. They provide that anyone who sells or serves alcoholic beverages to an individual who is visibly intoxicated is liable for the subsequent drunken acts of the consumer. Similarly, most states have enacted a *"per se"* law. This means that a blood alcohol concentration (BAC) of .1% is, in itself, proof of intoxication. Translated into number of drinks, .1% represents four or five average-size drinks (a 12-oz. can of beer, four ounces of wine, or one ounce of whiskey) taken within an hour without food. Beginning mental and motor impairment will take place at half the .1% level, or .05%. It is definite in drivers at a BAC of .1%.

Meanwhile the military has taken a leading role in the problem of alcohol in the workplace. A BAC of .05% (two drinks) is *per se* evidence of unfitness for duty at that time. The .1% level is retained for other purposes. Commanders are mandated to prepare separation papers for those individuals found to be intoxicated from alcohol or other drugs on more than one occasion. Education-rehabilitation opportunities are offered first.

Cocaine. By 1984, most illicit drug use had leveled off. The one exception was cocaine. One out of every ten Americans has tried it at least once. It is estimated that each day, 5,000 people try it for the first time. A hot line, 800-Cocaine, receives about 1,000 telephone calls per day. In a few metropolitan areas, deaths from cocaine now exceed heroin deaths.

The unusual aspect of cocaine use is the compulsion to continue use as long as access to supplies is available. Some 20% of all users find it impossible to stop despite the presence of serious family, job, health, or legal difficulties. Although physical dependence (tolerance and withdrawal) occur at high doses, it is the psychological craving to continue sniffing, injecting, or smoking cocaine that locks the person into cocaine-seeking behavior. The reason for the intense urge to continue usage is multiple. The immediate euphoria is very attractive but brief, especially when the intravenous or the cocaine free-base smoking routes are employed. Coming down after a series of cocaine "hits" becomes an unpleasant, sometimes an anguished, experience. Following a "coke run" of many hours or days, a considerable depression (the coke blues) can emerge. Finally, after the cocaine user has stopped, he or she is unable to enjoy the ordinary pleasures of existence, a condition called anhedonia. All of these mood changes—the euphoria, the dysphoria, the depression, and the anhedonia—drive the consistent user back to cocaine. The mood changes are based on stimulation, and later exhaustion, of the reward centers of the brain and similar fluctuations of the neurotransmitter to that area, dopamine.

The cost of cocaine ($50–$150 a gram) has been the major deterrent to inordinate use. In such Latin American countries as Bolivia, Peru, and Colombia, the smoking of coca paste is inexpensive, and an unchecked epidemic of destructive use has broken out. A majority of the beds in the psychiatric hospitals in these nations are occupied by psychotic coca-paste smokers. Although coca-bush destruction and many laboratory seizures have occurred, the overbundance of supplies in the local and world markets remains.

SIDNEY COHEN
Neuropsychiatric Institute
UCLA School of Medicine

León Febres Cordero of the Christian Social Party reads of Ecuador's presidential elections. He won the runoff.

ECUADOR

National elections and the foreign debt were the centers of attention in Ecuador during 1984. There were also some significant developments in the country's foreign relations.

Elections. The first round of the presidential election and contests for the one-house national legislature were held on Jan. 29, 1984. Nine candidates ran for president, although only two were major nominees. One was conservative León Febres Cordero of the Christian Social Party, backed by a coalition that included most of the country's traditional parties. The other was Rodrigo Borja, nominee of the Democratic Left. Borja won the initial balloting with 28.7% of the vote, to 27.8% for Febres Cordero. Borja's party also did well in the congressional poll. The Democratic Left won 25 seats in the legislature, while the parties backing Febres Cordero placed only 16 members in Congress. The remaining 32 seats were scattered among a number of small groups, including pro-Soviet and Maoist Communist parties.

Because neither presidential candidate won an outright majority, a runoff election was held May 6. This time Febres Cordero was the victor, getting 52.2% of the valid vote to 47.8% for Borja. Another 10% of the ballots were blank, apparently in response to left-wing urgings for a boycott. Febres Cordero's victory was generally attributed to his ability to associate Borja's position with the widely unpopular economic policies of outgoing President Osvaldo Hurtado, whose party did support Borja. Febres Cordero, a wealthy 53-year-old former businessman, was inaugurated without incident on August 10.

Debt. One of the most important issues facing the country was the renegotiation of debt payments due in 1984. In March an agreement was reached with foreign commercial banks on more than $600 million due during the year. The accord called for the money to be repaid over a nine-year period, with four. years of grace and at an interest charge of 1.5% above the U.S. prime rate. Another agreement was announced in May, whereby $353 million in government debt payments would be spread over eight years, also with four years' grace and 1.5% above the U.S. prime. An additional $270 million owed by the Ecuadorean private sector was not negotiated.

Ecuador also participated in meetings of the major Latin American debtor countries. The first of these was held in January in Quito, Ecuador. The second was held in June in Cartagena, Colombia, and was attended by representatives of seven nations.

Oil. The Ecuadorean government continued negotiations with foreign oil companies for joint enterprises to explore and exploit the nation's oil reserves. Texaco reached an agreement with the government oil firm, CEPE, to sell it 37.5% of the oil it produced for $4.50 per barrel, to supply the domestic market.

Oil workers in two provinces went on strike in late February and early March, demanding that the government make substantial investments in roads and public services. The strike was called off March 17, three days after President Hurtado declared a nationwide emergency and sent army troops to guard the oil fields against sabotage.

Foreign Affairs. In January, Ecuadorean and Peruvian troops clashed along a contested frontier area, and at least one Ecuadorean soldier was reported killed. Also that month, President Hurtado reestablished full diplomatic relations with Cuba, suspended in 1981.

ROBERT J. ALEXANDER, *Rutgers University*

ECUADOR • Information Highlights

Official Name: Republic of Ecuador.
Location: Northwest South America.
Area: 109,483 sq mi (283 561 km²).
Population (mid-1984 est.): 9,100,000.
Chief Cities (1982 census): Quito, the capital, 1,110,248; Guayaquil, 1,300,868; Cuenca, 272,-397.
Government: *Head of state and government,* León Febres Cordero Rivadeneira, president (took office August 1984). *Legislature* (unicameral)—Congress.
Monetary Unit: Sucre (63.23 sucres equal U.S.$1, official rate, Oct. 22, 1984).
Gross National Product (1982 U.S.$): $13,300,-000,000.
Economic Index (1983): *Consumer Prices* (1981 = 100), all items, 116.3; food, 117.1.
Foreign Trade (1983 U.S.$): *Imports,* $1,465,000,000; *exports,* $2,203,000,000.

EDUCATION

Major efforts at school reform dominated 1984 education news in the United States, USSR, France, Japan, and elsewhere. Serious church-state issues affected U.S. public schools. (*See* feature article, pages 42–49.)

United States

School Reform. By late 1984, one year after the release of several studies criticizing education in the United States, at least 40 states had upgraded high school diploma requirements, 32 had changed curriculum standards or textbook adoption procedures, 24 had increased their school day or year, 42 had raised teacher certification requirements, and 17 were raising teachers' salaries (often tied to merit). "We have so many reforms on the platter that we may have indigestion," said U.S. Education Secretary Terrel H. Bell. Many governors, particularly in the South, have acted on state-level education reports. More state education laws and new financing were shifting power from local to state levels. Some people noted a backlash against overregulation and new standards imposed from the top, threatening local control. Post-Sputnik (1957) school reform upgraded science and math for the gifted. Current reform is aimed at the total curriculum and at all students. Past reform was more teacher-initiated. Current reform is led by governors, legislatures, and other noneducators. Some experts say that reform momentum and success will depend on funding, finding and training talented teachers, and restoring a sense of command to the teaching force.

Upgrading Teachers. To attract and keep talented teachers, a Rand Corporation report recommended in August a $20,000–$50,000 teacher salary range and such recruitment incentives as scholarships and forgivable loans. A sharp drop has occurred in the number of college students majoring in education; older teachers are retiring; and abler younger teachers are leaving for better-paying jobs. In face of these losses, an upsurge in elementary school enrollment is anticipated. The report said that the teaching profession must have "rigorous entry requirements, supervised induction, autonomous performance, peer-defined standards of practice, and increased responsibility with increased competence."

A study by the National Center for Education recommended replacing disparate state teacher certification procedures with a national certification standard, including a national proficiency exam. Of 800 teacher education programs surveyed, half were not up to standard, only 60% required a program admission test, and less than 50% required a program exit test.

A Howard University report saw blacks threatened by the teacher-testing movement. In Florida in 1980, 85% of whites passed the test for new teachers, but only 40% of blacks passed. Blacks score lower on the National Teachers Examination, required by 24 states. The result is that some blacks in education switch to nonteaching jobs; others, unless they are better prepared, will avoid majoring in education. The report urged that education colleges improve preparation of black students and that state and national exams not be the sole basis for selecting teachers.

Poll on Public Schools. In a May Gallup Poll of 1,515 American adults, 42% gave their local public schools an A or B grade approval (compared with 31% in 1983), 25% rated the nation's public schools A or B grade (19%, 1983), and 52% of those with children in public schools judged their local schools to be A or B. It was the largest confidence vote for the schools since 1976.

Of those polled, 41% would pay higher taxes for their local schools (39%, 1983; 30%, 1981); 50% gave public school teachers A and B grades (39%, 1981); 47% gave principals and

AP/Wide World

Anthony Copas (left) and Harold Ingels attend a new Harvard University program aimed at training professionals, retirees, and housewives as math and science teachers. Those fields remained areas of prime concern; in fact, federal legislation was enacted to upgrade the specialties.

AP/Wide World

Like many U.S. educators, California School Superintendent Bill Honig calls for better textbooks.

administrators A and B (36%, 1981); and 41% gave A and B to local school boards. The poll found growing support for recent education reform proposals; 44% favored adding a month to the school year (37%, 1982); 42% would add an hour to the school day (37%, 1982); 65% favored a nationwide high school diploma exam (69%, 1981); and 37% thought teachers' salaries are too low (29%, 1981).

Desegregation. On the 30th anniversary of the May 17, 1954, Supreme Court school-desegregation decision, liberals hailed the ruling as having evoked the most pervasive civil-rights movement in U.S. history and as having given self-confidence and hope to black students. Critics saw it as an illegal use of power by high court justices and lesser federal judges in amending rather than interpreting the U.S. Constitution, something only Congress and the people can legally do. Declaring the Constitution color blind in 1954 was right, some say, but federal judges went beyond the Constitution in making social policy by mandating integration schemes, such as busing and school redistricting. The results were violence, school disorder, and lowered academic standards. Since 1954, it is said, school segregation has increased rather than decreased, as whites fled to suburbs, leaving blacks in inner cities. The long-term effect, some believe, was to move the American majority into the present conservative coalition.

College Aid and Draft. On July 5 the U.S. Supreme Court upheld by a 6-2 vote a 1982 law denying federal student aid to males 18 years and over who fail to register for the military draft. Two groups of Minnesota college students had brought suit against the law as discriminatory toward those opposed to the draft. A St. Paul federal judge agreed. But a government appeal resulted in the Supreme Court's upholding the law. Those favoring the ruling applauded connecting a college student's right to federal aid with his responsibility to obey federal law.

College Costs. After three years of 10%–11% annual increases, the increase in college costs dropped to 6% in 1984–85. A College Board report gave as the average cost for four years of college (including dormitory costs) $4,881 at public colleges (which enroll 80% of all college students) and $9,022 at private colleges. At public four-year colleges, tuition alone averaged $1,126. The most expensive U.S. college was Massachusetts Institute of Technology at $16,130 annually.

Sex Discrimination. On February 28 the Supreme Court affirmed by a 6–3 vote the right of Pennsylvania's private Grove City College not to sign antisex discrimination forms required under Title IX of a 1972 Education Act. Some students received federal grants and loans, but the college received no direct federal aid and claimed not to discriminate. The court sided with the Reagan administration's view that Title IX should not be applicable to an entire school, but should be "program specific." This first Reagan Justice Department victory in a major civil-rights case was criticized by liberals, who saw the program-specific interpretation as threatening other civil-rights laws and gains made by women, blacks, and the poor. A bill to overturn the court's Grove City College decision and so restore Title IX's broad scope passed in the House in May but was shelved by the Senate just prior to adjournment.

Teacher Strikes. September teacher strikes affected at least 145,000 students and 8,000 teachers in nine states, including Illinois (hardest hit), Michigan, Pennsylvania, New Jersey, New York, Rhode Island, Louisiana, Indiana, and Washington.

International

USSR. The Soviet Union enacted major school reform in April. The program would try to heighten students' work ethic and patriotic enthusiasm for building a new society. Vocational skills would be strengthened among the 45 million Soviet schoolchildren in 143,000 elementary and secondary schools; millions of children would be steered away from white-collar careers into semiskilled blue-collar jobs, where a critical labor shortage exists. High school graduates entering higher education, down from 56% in 1960 to under 20% in 1984, would be reduced further. The age for starting school would be changed from age 7 to age 6 in 1986, extending general education to 11 years. On entering school, all children will combine regular studies with some work experience; 10th graders will do factory work one day a week and part of summer vacation, returning part of their pay to their school. The plan calls for more Marxist, atheistic ideology in the already highly politicized national curriculum and more military training in the last two years of high school. Russian language is to be stressed because many speak only a native language at home and are taught in that language at school, with Russian a second language.

The reforms appeal to those Russian adults who see the younger generation as lazy, undisciplined, and obsessed with consumer goods but not willing to work for them. U.S. school reformers see their students as not getting enough academic content. USSR reformers see their students as getting too much academic education, which creates undesirable socioeconomic and political divisions.

France. The socialist government sought to gain greater control over the nation's private schools (93% of them Roman Catholic; serving 1 child in 6). Under the plan, private school budgets would have been under regional control and their teachers would have been civil servants. The reform plan was defeated in July, after massive demonstrations forced its withdrawal and the resignation of the minister of national education.

Japan. Japan's schools, praised abroad but criticized at home for overstressing memorization and testing, were under pressure in 1984 to soften their severe demands. The 27.8 million students in 58,150 schools at all levels are locked into a competitive system of study, cramming, "examination hell," expensive tutors, and special preparatory schools. The pattern is to enter the right kindergarten, which leads to the right elementary school linked to high schools with good records at getting their graduates into a prestigious university and thence into lifetime jobs with the best companies and government ministries. At the urging of Prime Minister Yasuhiro Nakasone, parliament in August established a three-year commission to study ways to improve Japan's schools. The fault with the system, some say, is that it was strongly influenced by Americans after World War II. The prime minister and others would like the schools somehow to recapture Japan's Confucian, Buddhist, and Shinto roots. Japanese who like the present system say it has produced an educated, disciplined work force who have made the country economically strong.

Comparison. According to the findings of a University of Michigan study released in June, Japanese and Taiwanese schoolchildren in the first and fifth grades do better in reading and math than do U.S. schoolchildren. Researchers found no evidence at the elementary school level for U.S. educators' claim that they promote creativity and social skills as well as academic subjects. By the fifth grade, U.S. children spend less time in school and on academic subjects, more time on extracurricular activities and in general "wandering." Outside school, U.S. children play more, do more home chores, read less, and do less homework. While U.S. children achieve less than do Japanese and Taiwanese children. U.S. mothers have a higher opinion of their children's school work than do Japanese and Taiwanese mothers. U.S. parents, more of them college-educated than in Japan and Taiwan, place less value on homework and are less eager to push their children to achieve. The study concluded that U.S. parents are not sufficiently dissatisfied with public schools and that school reform must start in the early grades.

FRANKLIN PARKER, *West Virginia University*

U.S. Public and Private Schools

	1984–85	1983–84
Enrollment		
Kindergarten through Grade 8	30,250,000	30,600,000
High school	13,700,000	13,600,000
Higher education	12,330,000	12,400,000
Total	56,280,000	56,600,000
Number of Teachers		
Elementary and secondary	2,400,000	2,400,000
Higher	700,000	700,000
Total	3,100,000	3,100,000
Graduates		
Public and private high school	2,650,000	2,740,000
Bachelor's degrees	960,000	980,000
First professional degrees	74,000	75,000
Master's degrees	295,000	300,000
Doctor's degrees	33,000	33,000
Expenditures		
Public elementary-secondary school	$134,500,000,000	$124,700,000,000
Private elementary-secondary	10,000,000,000	16,300,000,000
Public higher	63,000,000,000	59,000,000,000
Private higher	32,500,000,000	30,000,000,000
Total	$240,000,000,000	$230,000,000,000

Source: National Center for Education Statistics

SOURCES OF EDUCATION EXPENDITURE 1984–1985

- 28% tuition, fees, endowments, private gifts and grants
- 8% federal government
- 24% local governments
- 40% state governments

EGYPT

In 1984 there was some, though not much, change on the Egyptian domestic scene, while in foreign relations there was real improvement.

Domestic Affairs. Egypt's underlying problems, though alleviated by U.S. aid (running at about $1 billion, U.S., annually), continued unsolved and basically untouched by government policies. These intractable problems included a high rate of population growth; heavy subsidies, which keep low the prices of food and energy but use up 11% of the gross national product and discourage domestic food production; disorganization and decay in the cities; and an overblown and underworked bureaucracy.

The government's dilemmas were neatly illustrated by an incident in early October. The regime announced higher food prices and heavier payroll deductions for state pensions, and riots immediately swept a town near Alexandria, leaving at least one person dead and 13 injured. The next day, the food price increases were rescinded.

Events just after the October 1981 assassination of President Anwar el-Sadat were the subject of a 21-month criminal trial that concluded on Sept. 30, 1984. The trial, the longest in Egypt's history, was of 281 Islamic fundamentalists charged with fomenting riots and attempting to overthrow the government. The prosecution had sought the death penalty for all defendants, but the court acquitted 174 and sentenced 107 to prison terms ranging from two years to hard labor for life. In another trial, 176 men were accused of being members of Jihad, an Islamic underground radical group. In October the state of emergency was renewed for another year.

Politics and Elections. President Mubarak demonstrated a desire to move toward a multiparty system, though his government did try to obstruct one party. The Wafd ("delegation") Party, founded in 1918 and for decades a nationalistic thorn in the side of British control of Egypt, had suspended its activities in 1978 but announced its intention in August 1983 to resume an active role. A legal struggle for survival met with success on Jan. 2, 1984, when the State Council's Administrative Court ruled —against the government—that Wafd had the status of a legal political party. Then on April 11, the New Wafd forged an alliance with the fundamentalist Muslim Brotherhood, which did not have legal party status.

A general election, the freest in Egypt in some 30 years, was held on May 27. Mubarak's ruling National Democratic Party scored a landslide with 73% of the vote and 391 of the 448 elective seats in the new parliament. The New Wafd-Muslim Brotherhood alliance gained 15% of the vote and took 57 seats. Though there were a number of incidents of violence and opposition charges of government pressure, the election was a notable event in the context of the Arab world. As permitted by the constitution, President Mubarak on July 19 nominated ten additional members to parliament. The ten appointees—one from his own party, four from the Socialist Labor Party, and five from the Coptic Christian Community— demonstrated his interest in a multiparty system.

Prime Minister Ahmed Fuad Mohieddin, 58, died on June 5. Foreign Minister Kamel Hassan Ali became acting premier and was confirmed as prime minister on July 17.

Foreign Relations. The effort to regain Egypt's status as a leader of the Arab world made clear progress in 1984. The isolation that had followed the peace treaty with Israel in 1979 was largely at an end, as formal links began to be reestablished with Arab neighbors. In early January, Prince Talal ibn Abd al-Aziz, the first member of the Saudi royal family to visit Egypt since 1977, was given a warm welcome; he reciprocated by proclaiming Egypt "the heart of the Arab world." On January 30, Egypt accepted an invitation to rejoin the Islamic Conference, from which it had been expelled in 1979; it formally rejoined that body on April 2.

The most striking breakthrough was the September 25 decision by King Hussein of Jordan to restore full diplomatic ties; two weeks later the king visited Mubarak in Egypt. Syria and Libya, however, remained hostile. The latter's threats to Sudan caused concern, as did the internal instability of Egypt's southern neighbor. In August and September, Egypt cooperated with the major Western powers in minesweeping operations in the Red Sea to locate mines that Libya was suspected of having laid. Egypt's relations with Israel remained formally correct but very cool. After a three-year break, Egypt and the Soviet Union agreed on April 19 to exchange ambassadors.

ARTHUR CAMPBELL TURNER
University of California, Riverside

EGYPT • Information Highlights

Official Name: Arab Republic of Egypt.
Location: Northeastern Africa.
Area: 386,660 sq mi (1 001 449 km²).
Population (mid-1984 est.): 47,000,000.
Government: *Head of state,* Hosni Mubarak, president (took office Oct. 1981). *Head of government,* Kamel Hassan Ali, prime minister (took office July 1984). *Legislature* (unicameral)—People's Assembly.
Monetary Unit: Pound (0.8316 pound equals U.S.$1, Oct. 31, 1984).
Gross National Product (1982 U.S.$): $30,800,000,000.
Economic Index (1982): Consumper Prices (1970 = 100), all items, 310.1; food, 387.8.
Foreign Trade (1982 U.S.$): *Imports,* $9,078,000,000; *exports,* $3,120,000,000.

Oil is in abundant supply, prices are dropping, and gas stations are trying clever ads to attract customers.

ENERGY

Optimism and stability characterized the U.S. energy situation during 1984. All forms of energy were in abundant supply, and during the latter half of the year regular gasoline prices dropped below one dollar a gallon in some regions. This favorable energy situation contributed to a vigorous economic recovery with the lowest rate of inflation in years. Further, most analysts expected low-cost, abundant energy to be the pattern for the immediate future. The major qualifier to this positive outlook was the possibility of a cutoff of oil exports from the Persian Gulf.

Consumption and Production

For both the world and the United States, the key contributor to the favorable energy situation was reduced consumption. Triggered by the oil shocks of the 1970s, consumers learned both to use energy more efficiently and to substitute other forms for petroleum. In addition, the worldwide economic recession of the early 1980s had reduced consumption. U.S. energy consumption in 1984 was nearly 10% less than the 1979 peak. With improved efficiency the quantity of energy needed to generate a dollar's worth of economic activity had decreased by roughly 25% between 1973 and 1984.

Projected Consumption Increase. Data available in 1984, however, indicated that the 1979–83 pattern of absolute decline in consumption of all forms of energy was at an end, with coal, the nation's most abundant source, growing at twice the rate of other forms. Growth in U.S. consumption outpaced the rest of the world. It was generally expected, however, that the U.S. boom would stimulate world economic growth and therefore energy consumption.

Any increase in petroleum consumption would be supplied primarily by exports from the Organization of Petroleum Exporting Countries (OPEC), since they control most of the world's unused production capacity. Even with substantially increased demands for OPEC oil, prices were expected to remain stable. Faced with a need for increased oil revenues, the OPEC producers, according to most analysts, would do nothing to disrupt the growing market for their oil.

For the world's oil importers two dark clouds hung on the horizon. First, economic recovery meant ever greater dependence on OPEC. In the United States each additional barrel of consumption must be imported, since the nation has no reserve production capacity. Further, domestic production was likely to experience a slow but steady decline. During the first five months of 1984, net U.S. petroleum imports increased by 38%.

Mideast Instability. The second and much more unpredictable dark cloud was continuing instability in the Middle East. Traditional tensions in that area increased significantly with new developments in the war between Iran and Iraq. Early in the year the Iraqi military position was seen as eroding. With financial support from a number of Arab Persian Gulf neighbors, the Iraqis acquired new military equipment. Among this equipment were new French-built Mirage jets equipped with Exocet missiles.

Armed with these new weapons, the Iraqis expanded the conflict into the Persian Gulf, attacking tankers carrying Iranian oil. The Iraqi goal was to undercut the financial ability of the Iranians to carry on the war.

The Iranian government responded by announcing that if their exports were cut they would block all exports from the Gulf. Since Iraq was not exporting through the Gulf, this Iranian threat was aimed at Saudi Arabia and the other Arab Gulf exporters. Following a number of attacks on tankers headed to or from Arab states, tensions in the area increased. Although Gulf exports were maintained, the prospect of a widened war created worldwide concern about a third oil disruption.

Possible U.S. Response. With roughly 25% of the non-Communist world's oil coming from the Persian Gulf, any shutdown of exports would clearly be disruptive. Just how disruptive, however, was a source of debate. U.S. officials took the position that a Persian Gulf oil disruption would not have serious consequences. They noted that only 10% of U.S. oil consumption was supplied from the Gulf. Further, they noted that many oil consumers in the United States now had the capability to switch to other fuels. Finally, they argued that the government's Strategic Petroleum Reserve of roughly 450 million barrels could easily fill the gap created by a denial of Persian Gulf oil. The administration of President Ronald Reagan stated that in the event of a disruption it would immediately make oil from the Strategic Petroleum Reserve available to the highest bidder. The administration's view was that with this oil the marketplace could readily manage the disruption.

A number of analysts expressed skepticism about what they called the sanguine view of the administration. First, they noted that under the terms of international agreements the United States would be required to fill some of the demand of its more import-dependent European and Japanese allies. Second, the skeptics noted that, although the government's Strategic Petroleum Reserve had been growing steadily, privately held stocks were declining at about the same rate. The overall supply of oil in storage, then, was about the same as it had been before the vigorous government effort to fill the Strategic Petroleum Reserve. Third, a number of critics questioned whether delivery facilities existed to move oil from the Strategic Petroleum Reserve into the nation's supply system. Finally, the skeptics argued that the real problem flowing from a disruption would be a sudden price increase. These critics maintained that, even though U.S. dependence on Persian Gulf oil was small, the U.S. price of oil would inevitably reflect the world price, which they believed would be bid up by more import-dependent nations. In sum, observers using the same information came to quite different conclusions about the nation's security in the face of an oil disruption. Oil continued as it had for the last decade to be the uncertain factor in the nation's energy situation.

U.S. Energy Policy

Three issues dominated the political debate over energy during the year. They were natural gas price deregulation, the Synthetic Fuels Corporation, and acid rain.

Natural Gas. Natural gas price deregulation historically has been one of the most contentious energy issues, and events in 1984 suggested that nothing had changed. In 1978 the U.S. Congress initiated a process of partial price deregulation with the Natural Gas Policy Act. It was the view of the Reagan administration that the Congress should complete the process of deregulation. Those supporting deregulation made two arguments. First, the free market would provide much better management of natural gas; and second, with a surplus of gas available, deregulation could occur without any significant increase in price. Throughout the year a variety of proposals were made in the Congress aimed at deregulation, but, consistent with the history of gas price regulation, each of those proposals mobilized strong opposing interests, and it was not possible to find a majority in Congress to support any of the proposed pieces of legislation.

Synthetic Fuels Corporation. Following the second oil crisis triggered by the Iranian Revolution, in an effort to reduce the heavy dependence of the United States on imported oil, Congress created a federal Synthetic Fuels Corporation (SFC). The legislation creating the SFC set a production goal of 500,000 barrels per day of synthetic oil equivalent by 1987 and two million barrels per day by 1992. To accomplish those goals the SFC was provided with an initial appropriation of $22 billion (U.S.). Most of the initial appropriation remained uncommitted at the end of 1984.

Faced with a world surplus of oil at a price of roughly $29 per barrel, the prospect of spending federal funds to produce synthetic fuels that might cost more than $60 a barrel had generated substantial opposition to the SFC. Additional opposition grew during 1984 as a result of growing allegations of mismanagement.

The SFC had been established with a seven-member governing board. By midyear, resignations had reduced the board membership to three, one less than the quorum required to make decisions. President Reagan stated that he would appoint no new members until the Congress withdrew $9 billion from the initial appropriation. Some Congressional opponents sought even deeper cuts, proposing a $10.5 billion reduction. The SFC, then, spent the year in a condition of legal and political stalemate.

Some members of Congress, while agreeing with the charges of mismanagement, nonetheless argued that significantly reducing the corporation's funding was shortsighted. They argued that the present oil surplus would be of short duration, while the nation's need for oil was continuing, and the SFC was a way to protect against a future oil shortage.

Acid Rain. Evidence continued to accumulate that acid rain was damaging both forests and lakes in the northeastern United States. Although controversy continued over the source of acid rain, studies released by both the National Academy of Sciences and the Environmental Protection Agency found strong associations between emissions from coal-fired facilities in the Midwest and acid rain. Pressures increased for controlling these industrial emissions. The Reagan administration responded by increasing funding for research on acid rain, arguing that no scientific cause-and-effect relationship had been proven. Critics argued that the reason for the administration's inaction was not scientific uncertainty but rather the economic costs that emissions regulations would impose on the depressed economies of many of the Midwestern states.

Party Platforms. The platforms of both major parties included planks on energy. The Democrats proposed a federal role in the management of any oil disruption and in the development of alternative resources for the long term. The Republicans proposed leaving these choices to the marketplace and, in addition, proposed total natural gas price deregulation, the elimination of the oil windfall-profits tax, and the elimination of the Department of Energy. At neither convention, however, did energy receive major attention.

The Private Sector

In the private sector two developments received primary attention. They were the mergers of a number of the nation's largest oil companies and the deteriorating financial condition of several electric utilities.

Oil Company Mergers. In the case of the oil industry, giants swallowed giants. For example, Standard Oil of California bought Gulf Oil, and Texaco bought Getty Oil. Such takeovers would have been inconceivable not many years before. That they were occurring appeared to

L. Gubb, Gamma-Liaison

Financial problems were common at some nuclear power plants. The uncompleted Shoreham plant, above, on Long Island was ten years behind schedule and over budget.

be the result of two developments. First, a combination of reduced oil prices and a recession had caused the stock value of the companies taken over to drop to less than the value of their oil and gas reserves.

Second, in the past the monies used to pay for these takeovers would have been invested in the search for new oil and gas reserves. In recent years, however, many of the large oil companies have found that, even with vigorous exploration programs, they have been unable to add sufficient new reserves of oil and gas to replace the oil and gas they produce. With exploration costing more and finding less, the takeover companies found that they could buy already proven oil and gas reserves through these takeovers more cheaply than they could find new reserves.

Critics of the takeovers argued that, while it might be in the interest of the takeover companies to buy existing reserves, it was not in the national interest. Such takeovers, they pointed out, do nothing to increase the nation's reserves; rather, they divert funds that might pay for new finds.

Utility Woes. A number of the nation's utilities involved in building nuclear power plants were experiencing financial problems. One frequently cited case was Long Island Lighting, which announced during the year that it faced the prospect of bankruptcy. That company's Shoreham Nuclear Plant, presently estimated to cost $4.1 billion, was the source of the financial problem. Although the Shoreham plant was nearly complete, local and state opposition made the plant's eventual opening uncertain. If it were opened and the full cost of the plant were built into the customers' rates, estimates were that the price of electricity could jump as much as 60% in one year. Although Long Island Lighting represented an extreme case, it was only one of several instances of utilities facing similar problems.

DON E. KASH, *The University of Oklahoma*

ENGINEERING, CIVIL

New cost-cutting designs and construction techniques enabled the United States and other nations to continue building major bridges, canals, dams, and tunnels during 1984.

Bridges

United States. At Bonners Ferry, ID, close to the Canadian border, work was completed on a new highway bridge to carry U.S. 95 over the Kootenai River. The four-lane, lightweight cable-stressed steel structure, including four steel girders, is 1,378 ft (420 m) long with spans varying in length from 100 to 155 ft (30 to 47 m). At a cost of about $9 million, the new structure replaces a span built in 1933.

Work was also completed on a concrete, asymmetrical stayed-girder bridge over the Ohio River, connecting East Huntington, WV, and Proctorsville, OH. The two-lane vehicular structure, 2,841 ft (866 m) long, has a 900-ft (274-m) main span supported by cables fanning out from a single A-shaped tower built on one pier and anchored in the 608-ft (185-m) stayed back span. The 41-ft (12.5-m)-wide concrete deck is supported by concrete box girders. The approach spans were built by the conventional balanced cantilever erection method. The final cost of the project was about $40 million.

Canada. In British Columbia, construction continued on a four-lane, high-level bridge over the Fraser River, linking Annacis Island with Vancouver on the mainland. The $80 million, stayed-girder structure will have a 1,526-ft (465-m) main span rising 184 ft (56 m) above the river. With approaches, it will be more than 9,000 ft (2 743 m) long. Work is scheduled for completion in 1986.

India. A cable-stayed vehicular bridge with a 1,499-ft (457-m) main span and 600-ft (183-m) side spans is being built over the Hooghly River between Calcutta and Howrah. The $158 million structure will be completed in 1986. The two main piers support two-leg steel towers rising to a height of 443 ft (135 m). Cables support the deck 113 ft (34 m) above the river.

Canals

United States. The Bureau of Reclamation is involved in considerable canal work in Nebraska. Nearing completion is a 19-mi (31-km) diversion section of Mirdan Canal to conduct water from Colamus Dam, near Burwell in the central part of the state, to the North Loup area. More than 2 million yd³ (1.5 million m³) of excavation was removed for the 13-ft (4-m)-deep waterway, which is 65 ft (20 m) wide at the top and 13 ft (4 m) wide at the bottom.

Also underway in Nebraska is a $15.5 million project for 28 mi (45 km) of unlined canal —involving 4.4 million yd³ (3.4 million m³) of excavation—at Sections 2 and 3 of the Mirdan Canal in Valley County. The irrigation water-

Construction progresses on a stayed-girder bridge over the Ohio River. Completed in late 1984, the $40 million structure connects West Huntington, WV, and Proctorsville, OH.

way provides water to lands between Colamus Dam and Davis Creek Dam.

In Montezuma County in southwest Colorado, Burec is building a 12-mi (19-km) stretch of Dove Creek Canal, part of the Dolores Project, to carry water from the Dolores River for irrigation, municipal, and industrial use. The $10 million job involves 1.5 million yd³ (1.1 million m³) of excavation.

Rumania. A ship canal begun nearly 40 years earlier was completed in 1984 to connect Cernavoda, a new port on the Danube River, and the Black Sea. The 40-mi (64-km) channel, 24 ft (7 m) deep, flows southeast to the recently expanded port city of Constanta.

Dams

United States. In Texas the U.S. Army Corps of Engineers is constructing Ray Roberts Dam on the Elm Fork of the Trinity River to supply water to the cities of Denton and Dallas. The earthfill structure is 15,250 ft (4 648 m) long, with a maximum height of 139 ft (42 m). The embankment totals 18 million yd³ (16 million m³) and will create a 29,350-acre (11 878-ha) lake. Started in 1982, the $49 million dam is scheduled for completion in 1986.

The Alaska Power Authority is building the $190 million, 193-ft (59-m)-high Terror Lake Dam on Kodiak Island. Located in a national wildlife refuge, the compacted rockfill dam faced with concrete will provide electricity to the cities of Kodiak and Port Lion and to a U.S. Coast Guard station. A 5-mi (8-km) power tunnel will conduct water to a 3,100-ft (945-m) inclined penstock and a 20-Mw powerhouse.

In Utah the Bureau of Reclamation is constructing Upper Stillwater Dam in the Uinta Mountains east of Salt Lake City. The cold climate permits only a six-month construction schedule. When completed in 1987, the structure may be the world's largest roller-compacted concrete gravity dam—2,670 ft (814 m) long, 275 ft (84 m) high, and 180 ft (55 m) wide at the base. It will require a total of 1.5 million yd³ (1.1 million m³) of rollcrete, spread with tractor-dozers and compacted with vibratory rollers in 12-inch (30-cm) lifts. The storage dam will impound a reservoir of the Central Utah Project. Its estimated cost is $61 million.

France. Electricité de France, builder of the Grand Maison Dam in the French Alps east of Lyon, has had to contend with avalanches and a harsh climate at an elevation of 5,500 ft (1 676 m); the construction season lasts only from June through October. The rockfill gravity dam is 1,800 ft (549 m) long and 525 ft (160 m) high, involving 17 million yd³ (13 million m³) of material, and will impound a 112,600 acre-ft reservoir. When earthwork for the $600 million hydroelectric project is completed in 1985, tunnels and sloping penstocks will carry the water to a 1,680-Mw powerhouse.

Sri Lanka. The need for hydropower and irrigation development on the island nation of Sri Lanka has spurred dam construction on the Mahaweli River and its tributaries. A four-dam project will store water to irrigate 350,000 acres (141 640 ha) and develop 400 Mw of power at an estimated cost of $2 billion (U.S.). Most notable among the four barriers is Victoria, a double-curvature, thin-concrete arch dam 393 ft (120 m) high and with a crest length of 1,700 ft (518 m). It will impound a 600,000 acre-ft reservoir to produce 210 Mw of power from an underground powerhouse. The project is scheduled for completion in 1986.

Tunnels

United States. As a flood-control measure to protect the new Papago Freeway I-10 in Phoenix, 5.5 mi (8.9 km) of drainage tunnels are being bored 50 ft (15 m) underground. The tunnel is in three sections—2.6, 2.2, and 0.7 mi (4.2, 3.5, and 1.1 km) long—with a 21-ft (6.4-m) diameter. Boring is being handled with tunneling machines at a cost of about $50 million. The tunnels will be lined with cast-in-place reinforced concrete. With drainage to the Salt River already underway, construction will proceed to completion of the 20-mi (32-km) freeway section, the last remaining segment of Interstate 10 running from Florida to California.

In Virginia a second two-lane vehicular tunnel is being constructed under the Elizabeth River between Norfolk and Portsmouth on I-264. The $310 million project parallels an existing 32-year-old tube. The new 3,813-ft (1 162-m) tunnel includes eight concrete-lined sunken steel tubes flanked by cut-and-cover sections. The tubes range in length from 280 to 332 ft (85 to 101 m) and are 40 ft (12 m) wide by 34.5 ft (10.5 m) high. Fabricated in Texas, the tubes were barged to the job site and there lined with concrete. Each tube, weighing about 2,000 tons (1 814 metric tons), was sunk into a trench dredged to depths of 40 to 105 ft (12 to 32 m). The entrenched, connected tubes were then backfilled.

West Germany. Deutsche Bundesbahn, the German Federal Railway, is reconstructing a 265-mi (426-km) rail line from Hanover, at the north end, to Würzburg, at the south. The double-track, high-speed line will relieve congestion on the nation's main north-south axis. It will have 63 tunnels totaling 73 mi (117 km). The line will carry both passenger and freight trains in tunnels 42 ft (13 m) wide and 25.5 ft (8 m) high. The tunnels are being blasted through rock at depths to 30 ft (9 m) and are being lined with concrete 12 inches (30 cm) thick. The longest bore is the 6.7-mi (11-km) Landrücken Tunnel, requiring 1.8 million yd³ (1.4 million m³) of excavation.

WILLIAM H. QUIRK, *Construction Consultant*

ENVIRONMENT

The year 1984 was marked by continuing efforts on the part of world conservation groups to promote joint, coordinated programs of environmental conservation. Among the major meetings held during the year were one on wetlands preservation and another of the General Assembly of the International Union for the Conservation of Nature and Natural Resources (IUCN).

In the United States, there was not as much conflict or controversy between environmental groups and the Reagan administration as during the year before. Observers attributed the relative calm to the 1983 departure of two administration figures anathema to environmentalists—former Interior Secretary James Watt and Environmental Protection Agency (EPA) head Anne Gorsuch Burford. In their places during 1984 were appointees more palatable—or at least less objectionable—to environmental groups. Interior Secretary William P. Clark and EPA Administrator William D. Ruckelshaus shunned confrontation with environmentalists and took a more conciliatory approach.

World Developments

The IUCN General Assembly session, held in Madrid, Spain, during November, was centered around the theme "Partnership in Conservation: Toward a World Conservation Plan." The IUCN, with membership from governmental agencies and environmental groups in most countries, has for several years backed coordinated conservation planning among the world's nations, treating national problems individually but in the context of a worldwide conservation strategy.

At the November meeting, participants reviewed progress and problems in global conservation planning. Among the areas discussed were protection of endangered species and important ecological areas, conservation law, monitoring of ecosystems, and helping individual countries with their conservation strategies. The IUCN has encouraged nations, especially in the developing world, to establish long-term strategies for conserving natural resources in a manner consistent with economic development.

More than 50 nations were represented at the May meeting of the Second Conference of Contracting Parties to the Convention on Wetlands of International Importance Especially as Waterfowl Habitat—usually referred to as the Ramsar Convention. Held in Groningen, the Netherlands, the meeting was devoted to developing ways to implement the convention, designed to help nations preserve key wetlands.

The meeting adopted a resolution toward convention implementation. Major points included the need for a system of wetlands classification and common criteria for gauging the importance of wetlands locally, nationally, and internationally.

Saving Plants. The IUCN and World Wildlife Fund (WWF) used the first day of spring to launch an ambitious campaign to save rare and endangered plants around the world. The effort will be carried on by the IUCN with financial support raised by the WWF. Both public education to spread awareness of the need to conserve plants and field research and conservation projects will be included in the program. More than 25,000 species of plants are threatened with extinction, and, conservationists warn, the list is growing rapidly—especially in tropical rain forests, which continue to be destroyed throughout many parts of the developing world.

The focus of the campaign is plants that can be used for food, those with potential as energy sources or industrial raw materials, and those of medicinal value. Typical of the individual projects undertaken under the program is one in which the threatened plants of Nepal will be inventoried.

Plants are imperiled by a wide spectrum of pressures, including habitat destruction, overgrazing by domestic stock, and collecting for private and commercial purposes. Some cacti, for instance, have been pushed to the brink of extinction because so many of them have been taken from the wild for sale as garden and house plants.

Saving Rhinos. Action was taken in several parts of the world in behalf of rhinoceroses, all five species of which are considered to be in danger of extinction. During March, four great one-horned Asian rhinos were captured in Assam, India, and translocated to Dudhwa National Park near the Nepal border. The rhino once ranged the Dudhwa area but vanished there about a century ago. Another translocation of great one-horned rhinos took place between Nepal and Pakistan. Two rhinos from the Chitwan National Park in Nepal were taken to Lal Suhanra, a reserve in Pakistan, and freed. And five black rhinoceroses from Natal, South Africa, were shipped to ranches in Texas where conservationists will attempt to breed them. The translocation was arranged by Game Conservation International, a Texas-based organization of hunters, fishermen, and others interested in fish and wildlife.

World Bank Sets Rules. The World Bank, which supports development projects such as dam construction and irrigation systems in various countries around the world, announced that it would not finance activities that are potentially harmful to people or the environment without precautionary safeguards. The bank established a set of standards for estimating the environmental impact of projects and for keeping the damage to a minimum.

Acid Rain Pact. At a meeting in Ottawa, Canada, in March, ministers from nine European countries and Canada signed a pact agreeing to reduce sulfur emissions into the air by 30% in the next ten years. The two-day meeting was intended, in part, to put pressure on the United States and Great Britain to pledge cuts in atmospheric emissions that cause acid rain.

U.S. Developments

New Leadership. Starting his second year as the head of the EPA, William Ruckelshaus received mild accolades from environmental groups for restoring morale and efficiency in the agency, but he was also criticized for not rolling up his sleeves and tackling such tough environmental problems as acid rain.

Praise for Ruckelshaus came from one of the sharpest critics of the Reagan administration's environmental policies, Jay D. Hair, executive vice-president of the National Wildlife Federation. Hair said the EPA chief "is doing a heck of a job," particularly in his attempts to remove lead from gasoline and in his support of clean water. Russell W. Peterson, president of the National Audubon Society, was more cautious. He credited Ruckelshaus with shoring up the EPA but chided him for being an apologist for the administration's environmental policies. Congressional critics faulted the EPA chief for failing to pressure the administration to deal more forcefully with acid rain.

Battling between environmentalists and the Interior Department also cooled off. To many environmentalists, Secretary Clark seemed a marked contrast to his predecessor. Clark personally maintained a low profile while demonstrating a willingness to work with conservationists on environmental problems. Reversing Watt policies, the Interior Department began to acquire new land for national parks, curbed offshore oil leasing, and promised not to allow oil leasing in wildlife refuges and wilderness areas. Two activist environmental groups, however, the Sierra Club and the Friends of the Earth, both expressed dismay with Clark's performance on the occasion of the first anniversary of his succession.

Declaring to the president that "the ship called EPA is righted and is now steering a steady course," Ruckelshaus announced in late November that he was resigning from EPA. Lee M. Thomas, the agency's assistant administrator, was named his successor. And as plans for the president's second term proceeded, Secretary Clark also said that he would resign. The president then announced that he would nominate Secretary of Energy Donald P. Hodel to be interior secretary. Hodel had been undersecretary of interior in the early days of the Reagan administration.

New Priorities Urged. According to a report on the state of the environment issued in June by the Conservation Foundation, pollution problems such as acid rain and toxic wastes require new environmental policies and approaches. "Environmental policy at mid-decade is suspended between old problems and new, between progress and retrogression, between cooperation and polarization," said foundation President William K. Reilly.

Policies developed during the 1970s to cope with environmental threats are outmoded, the report said, because of new information and insights into the types of pollution affecting air and water. Present regulations were designed to cope with pollutants affecting either air or water but not both, according to the foundation. Progress has been made, the report went on, but policies must be more sophisticated to deal with the complexities of, for instance, acid rain.

By way of example, the report suggested that incentives might be established for industries that conduct their activities according to methods that do not harm the environment. Environmental laws and agencies need to be reshaped, the report said, if they are to challenge major pollution problems.

Wilderness Protection. In 1984 the Congress passed, and President Reagan signed, more legislation creating new wilderness land than in any year since 1964. Separate bills were passed for 20 different states, designating 8.3 million acres (3.3 million ha) of new wilderness. That brought the total U.S. wilderness area to 88.6 million acres (35.4 million ha). The legislation was made possible by a compromise between environmentalists and developers in longstanding negotiations. Developers were granted permission to timber and drill on 13.5 million acres (5.4 million ha) that had been off limits.

The California Wilderness Act designated 23 new wildernesses and other special land areas, including the Mono Basin National Forest Scenic Area (below). Federal legislation gave wilderness protection to land in 19 other states.

Bob Tribble, USDA Forest Service

Toxic Wastes. A major report issued by the Environmental Protection Agency seemed to lend credence to the Conservation Foundation's view of the complexity of environmental problems facing the United States today. The report, based on a study during 1981, led to a revision of the EPA's definition of toxic wastes to include not only hazardous chemicals but also vast amounts of wastewater. Under the new definition, the amount of hazardous wastes produced in the country annually is estimated at 71 billion gallons, or 290 million tons, six times the former assessment.

Prior to adjourning in early October, the U.S. Senate refused to reauthorize the Superfund toxic waste cleanup program. However, the 98th Congress did pass, and President Reagan did sign, a bill that renewed and tightened federal laws regulating the disposal of hazardous wastes. The measure reauthorized the Resource Conservation and Recovery Act of 1976, one of the nation's major antipollution laws, and lowered the regulatory threshold to cover at least 130,000 small companies that previously had been allowed to dispose of small amounts of hazardous wastes without federal regulation.

Acid Rain. Acid rain, according to a report published by the National Wildlife Federation, is no longer only a major environmental problem in the northeastern United States but across much of North America. Abnormally high levels of acid precipitation were recorded in "every state east of the Mississippi River, many western states, and every province of Canada," the federation said. Fog in some parts of California, the report noted, is acidic enough to burn the eyes and throat. Virginia's rain in 1983 was twice as acidic as during the year before. And in Houston, rain with 400 times the natural acidity level was reported.

Black Duck Problem. A decline in the number of black ducks, among the nation's best-known waterfowl, continued to puzzle biologists. Black ducks traditionally have been one of the most common species east of the Mississippi, especially in the northeast. About 30 years ago, however, their numbers began to decline, and at last count there were only about 300,000 of them—down 60% in three decades.

Among the reasons for the decline, biologists speculate, are acid rain, which kills the insects eaten by the young black ducks; the use of pesticides; hunting; and, most likely, several of these forces in combination. Recently, biologists also suggested that an even more insidious threat to black ducks is that they can interbreed with mallards. Mallards have become increasingly numerous, partly because thousands have been propagated and released by state fish and game agencies. According to the United States Fish and Wildlife Service, 13% of black ducks today may really be mallard-black hybrids.

Federal and state wildlife officials have attempted to cope with the problem by reducing the number of black ducks in hunters' bag limits. Biologists working on the problem say, however, that until all the causes of the black duck's decline are clearly identified—and broader problems of pollution solved—the outlook for the species seems clouded.

Wood Stork Endangered. After a long campaign by the National Audubon Society, the wood stork, which nests in Florida, Alabama, Georgia, and South Carolina, has been added to the federal list of endangered species. Wood storks, the Audubon Society reported in May, have declined from 20,000 nesting pairs to about 4,000. The society attributes the drop in stork numbers to the logging of cypress swamps in which the bird breeds and to the manipulation of water in wetlands where the bird feeds. A federal and state effort was begun in Florida to manage properly the remaining stork habitats in the hope that its numbers would increase.

EDWARD R. RICCIUTI
Environment, Science, and Outdoor Writer

Leonard Lee Rue III, Bruce Coleman

Efforts were under way to save two dwindling species—the black duck, above, and the wood stork, below.

Wendell Metzen, Bruce Coleman

ESPIONAGE

A dispute arose in the United States over the mining of Nicaraguan waters. Anti-Sandinista rebels had carried out the operation, but the mines were traced back to the Central Intelligence Agency (CIA). After President Reagan stopped CIA participation, the World Court in May condemned the United States and Congress refused to vote any more money for covert activities in Nicaragua.

The CIA Primer. Another dispute concerned CIA guidelines for the Nicaraguan rebels. The primer gave advice on "neutralizing" Sandinista officials and creating anti-Sandinista martyrs. Critics in Congress charged that it violated CIA rules forbidding plots to assassinate foreign leaders. Reagan called the dispute "much ado about nothing," and did not dismiss anyone. A CIA comic book urging sabotage in Nicaragua added heat to the controversy

The Czech Spy. In November a former employee of the CIA, Karl F. Koecher, was arrested in New York and charged with passing secret information to Czech intelligence. His wife was described as a courier in the case.

Spy Planes. When a U.S. spy plane crashed in El Salvador, Reagan described the flights as a defense of freedom. Opponents retorted that they added to the danger of the United States becoming involved in a war in Central America.

The FBI. In October, Richard W. Miller became the first agent of the Federal Bureau of Investigation (FBI) to be accused of spying for

In a major 1984 spy case, five persons were charged with conspiring to smuggle classified U.S. info to China.

AP/Wide World

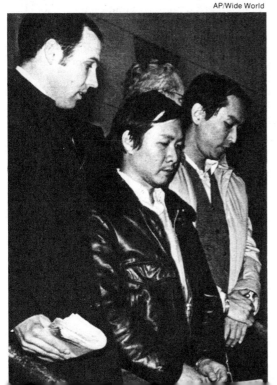

the Soviets. Arrested with Soviet émigré Svetlana Ogorodnikova and her husband, Miller was said to have given her classified information, which she passed on to a Soviet diplomat.

Assassins at the Vatican. The attempt to kill Pope John Paul II in 1981 reentered the news when evidence presented in Rome implicated four Turks and three Bulgarians. Two of the Turks, Mehmet Ali Agca and Oral Celik, were said to have fired the three bullets that struck the pontiff. Agca was seized by members of the crowd in front of St. Peter's, while Celik escaped. The Italian prosecutor speculated that the State Security Committee (KGB) was behind the Bulgarians in the plot. The USSR and Bulgaria denied any role in the crime. The Italian authorities went ahead with their investigation of the two men they held, Agca and a Bulgarian named Sergei Antonov.

Communist Espionage. East bloc diplomats accused of spying were expelled from the United States, Britain, Belgium, Denmark, Ethiopia, and Norway. Iran executed ten "self-confessed spies" for the Russians. Accused agents for the Soviet Union included Roger Craig Smith and James Durward Harper, Jr., in the United States, Arne Treholt in Norway, and Dieter Gerhardt in South Africa.

The Swedish underwater alarm system indicated that, as in 1981, a Soviet submarine spied on the Karlskrona naval base. However, attempts to locate the sub failed.

Nigeria. A bizarre espionage incident occurred in July in London when officials at the airport prevented two crates from being loaded aboard a Nigerian Airways plane. In one crate they found a drugged Nigerian defector, Umaru Dikko, and an Israeli with a syringe. In the other they found two Nigerians. One Nigerian and three Israelis were charged with kidnapping. Nigeria and Israel denied that the accused belonged to their espionage agencies.

Technological Espionage. The biggest spy case involving technology was broken in the United States when five persons were arraigned for conspiring to smuggle to China classified information on radar, missiles, and bugging gadgets. A U.S. spy satellite intercepted a message from Libya, ordering the staff of the Libyan embassy in London to use force against anti-Qaddafi demonstrators. In April somebody in the embassy fired on the crowd, killing a British policewoman, but under diplomatic immunity, no one could be held.

The United States and the Soviet Union launched additional spy satellites during the year. The Soviet embassy in Washington erected sensitive antennas to intercept American messages. As a result, the National Security Agency (NSA) called for more stringent measures to protect those systems.

VINCENT BURANELLI,
Coauthor, Spy/Counterspy

AP/Wide World

Lt. Col. Mengistu's portrait dominated as Ethiopia marked the tenth anniversary of its Marxist government.

ETHIOPIA

Famine continued to engulf Ethiopia during 1984. In spite of the disaster, elaborate celebrations were held in the capital, Addis Ababa, in September to mark the tenth anniversary of Ethiopia's Marxist government. Also during 1984, the third Congress of the Commission to Organize the Party of the Working People of Ethiopia (COPWE) announced the formation of a vanguard political (Communist) party, and Ethiopia and the USSR signed a new economic agreement.

Famine. Because of the worst drought in a decade more than 7 million people faced starvation in Ethiopia. The UN Children's Fund (UNICEF) reported that eight of Ethiopia's regions had been declared disaster areas. Tens of thousands died during the year. In 1984, the United States contributed $65 million worth of food; UNICEF and voluntary organizations contributed more than $100 million in emergency relief; and the USSR, Ethiopia's ally, contributed $3 million in aid.

International Relations. Sudanese President Jaafar al-Nemery accused Ethiopia of waging a secret war against his country by helping Sudanese rebels who wish to overthrow his government. Discussions between the two countries, brokered by Egypt, were canceled by Ethiopia in March because, according to the Ethiopian foreign minister, the United States and the Sudan were in "collusion and conspiracy" against Ethiopia. In March, at the time of the canceled meeting, the United States announced that it would increase its military aid to the Sudan to protect it against "increased security threats" from Ethiopia. In January and May, Ethiopia's air force pounded the northwest region of Somalia in its continued but intermittent assault on Somalia, which it maintains is aiding rebels in the Ogaden who oppose the Ethiopian government.

Tesfaye Demeke, chargé d'affaires at Ethiopia's embassy in Washington, sought and received political asylum in the United States. He stated that he had become "isolated within a government established with Soviet power and perpetuated by Soviet arms." Demeke was the highest-ranking diplomat from Ethiopia in the United States. Two months earlier, Ethiopia expelled four U.S. diplomats accusing them of fomenting domestic discontent. The United States responded by expelling two Ethiopian diplomats, but one, the Commercial Counselor Gelagay Zawde, requested and received political asylum.

Despite the fact that Ethiopia has received more than $4 billion (U.S.) in military aid from the USSR since 1978, *The New York Times* reported that Cuba was withdrawing 11,000 of its 13,000 troops from Ethiopia because they were no longer necessary to oppose the Somalis and Ethiopia could no longer afford to pay for them. Most were reported to have left by June.

Domestic Politics. On September 10, the Workers' Party was established, replacing COPWE. Mengistu Haile Mariam became the secretary general. An 11-member Politburo and 136-member Central Committee were appointed. Seven Politburo members and 20% of the Central Committee were from the military.

Amnesty International reported that Tsehai Tolessa, a leader of the Ethiopian Evangelical Mekane Yesus Church, had been held without charge for four years. The church itself has been labeled counterrevolutionary. The U.S. House of Representatives Foreign Affairs Committee passed a resolution calling attention to the plight of Ethiopian Jews, now reduced to 25,000. The war against secessionist rebels in Eritrea and Tigre continued.

PETER SCHWAB
State University of New York at Purchase

ETHIOPIA • Information Highlights

Official Name: Socialist Ethiopia.
Location: Eastern Africa.
Area: 455,000 sq mi (1 178 450 km²).
Population (mid-1984 est.): 32,000,000.
Chief Cities (July 1980): Addis Ababa, the capital, 1,277,159; Asmara, 424,532; Dire Dawa, 82,024.
Government: *Head of state and government,* Mengistu Haile Mariam, chairman of the Provisional Military Administrative Council (took office Feb. 1977).
Monetary Unit: Birr (2.07 birr equal U.S. $1, May 1984).
Gross Domestic Product (1982–83 U.S. $): $4,500,000,000.
Economic Index (Addis Ababa, 1983): *Consumer Prices* (1970 = 100), all items, 275.9; food, 302.7.
Foreign Trade (1982 U.S. $): *Imports,* $787,000,000; *exports,* $404,000,000.

ETHNIC GROUPS

Politics, in different ways, dominated the year for America's diverse ethnic groups. While Italian-Americans took pride in the nomination of Geraldine Ferraro as the Democratic vice-presidential candidate, black Americans rallied around the landmark campaign of Rev. Jesse Jackson. Hispanic-Americans looked to the 1984 elections to consolidate their growing political influence in the midst of what has been called "the decade of the Hispanic" and also fought a bitter political battle over a controversial immigration bill. Asian-Americans found themselves at a crossroads of political identification. And even the relatively small population of Native Americans began organizing to overcome the effects of recent governmental policies.

Hispanics. Many political observers agreed that the biggest untapped source of voting strength lay in the Hispanic population that increased 61% between 1970 and 1980. Only 2.2 million of the 6.6 million eligible Hispanic voters cast ballots in 1980. Yet their potential for influence is great, especially in the big, key states.

But there was a more immediate political issue facing Hispanic-Americans in 1984, the Simpson-Mazzoli Bill. Sen. Alan K. Simpson (R-WY) and Rep. Romano L. Mazzoli (D-KY) had cosponsored the bill, the first major attempt by Congress to reform immigration law in more than 30 years. The bill had passed in the Senate previously and was finally passed by the House of Representatives in the summer of 1984 but not before creating odd alliances of backers and opponents. The two key elements of the bill were a fine on employers ($1,000 per alien) who knowingly hired illegal immigrants, and amnesty for illegal immigrants who had entered the country before 1982. Hispanic groups and Congressional liberals were joined by manufacturers and farmers in opposing the employer sanctions, intended to minimize the job opportunities that lure most illegal immigrants to the United States. Those opponents charged that the sanctions were unfair to employers and would encourage discrimination against all Hispanics. On the other hand, black groups, environmentalists, and political conservatives attacked the amnesty provision of the bill, because it would legitimize immigrants who compete with poor blacks for jobs and social services, lead to a drain on natural resources, and reward lawbreakers. Some Hispanics also opposed the amnesty as a sham, pointing out that few would qualify.

Simpson-Mazzoli also generated controversy beyond the United States. Mexican officials expressed resentment at the unilateral attempt to solve an international problem. Some U.S. border communities, for example, are dependent on Mexican consumers as well as Mexican labor, and the Mexican economy is dependent on the American currency sent home by illegal-immigrant workers. The furor inspired by the bill led to its being deadlocked in Congressional conference committee.

Asians. Asian-Americans, whose numbers have swelled to nearly 4 million, also were courted by both political parties in 1984. But the group, which ranges from generations-old Japanese-American families to recent immigrants from Vietnam and Laos, was difficult to categorize. Many Asian-Americans identified with the Democrats because of that party's social policies concerning ethnic minority groups; others preferred the Republican emphasis on economic opportunity. But regardless of their politics, Asian-Americans were clearly blazing trails of achievement, particularly in education. In 1984, Asian-Americans were the fastest-growing population in U.S. higher education. Nine of 40 Westinghouse Science Talent Search semifinalists were Asian-American, and that group topped all others in math scores on the Scholastic Aptitude Test.

But those accomplishments were seen by many as a mixed blessing. The "smart Asian" was a stereotype in itself that placed a burden on many young people. And as many Asian-American students noted, there were several reasons for their academic successes. Asian culture traditionally emphasizes scholarship, and families tend to have high expectations for their children. Asian immigrants, like other newcomers to the United States, tend to have a strong motivation to get ahead; science and mathematics, in particular, are accessible fields for people overcoming a language barrier.

Native Americans. With 1.4 million people (one fourth living below the poverty line), Native Americans have never been much of a political force; only nine states have a Native American population that exceeds 1%. But in 1984, Native American rights were under increasing attack in state courts and legislatures, and the federal government had cut the budget for social services on the reservations. As a result, tribal leaders were concerned about signing up new voters and coping with the unique challenges facing their people. Because the Reagan administration's policies stressed self-reliance, the 288 reservations in 26 U.S. states were scrambling to develop such commercial ventures as industrial parks, trailer courts, tourist stops, and bingo halls. The biggest potential economic resource was coal. Native Americans owned 200 billion metric tons, half the U.S. reserves. But the difficulties in exploiting that resource were exemplified by the Crows of Montana; the tribe owned 17 billion metric tons of coal and was $1 million in debt, with 70% unemployment and 50% of its people on welfare.

See also pages 26–41.

DENNIS A. WILLIAMS, *"Newsweek"*

Liechtenstein's Prince Hans Adam (left) *took over as regent in August after his father, Prince Franz Josef II (second left),* the longest reigning monarch in Europe, *relinquished his responsibilities but not his title to the throne. The 39-year-old, Swisseducated Prince is married to Princess Marie, and they have four children.*

EUROPE

In 1984, after a decade of gloom and self-doubt dominated by an economic depression that was deepened and perhaps directly caused by the escalating oil prices posted by the Organization of the Petroleum Exporting Countries (OPEC), Europeans glimpsed the possibility of renewed economic progress. But despite evidence of falling inflation and, in many countries, of real economic growth, anxiety remained general. Terrorism, for political ends or material gain, seemed ubiquitous. Social conflict turned violent, often between labor unions protecting employment in outmoded industries and governments determined to force economic modernization.

For the first part of the year, the European Community seemed on the edge of not merely political but financial bankruptcy. Most dangerous of all, in the view of most Europeans, détente between the superpowers had been replaced by a bitter confrontation, in which West and East Europeans were compelled, often unwillingly, to make concrete gestures of allegiance to either the American-led or the Soviet-led alliance.

A Faltering Recovery. The West European economic recovery was real, if small in scale. Most welcome was a drop in inflation. Strict monetary policy in West Germany and Britain held their inflation rates to 3% and 5%, respectively, while Italy was able to hold its price rises to 10%. Western Europe as a whole was expected to achieve a 3% growth rate, stimulated by a strong revival of exports, especially to the United States as a result of the continually strengthening U.S. dollar. The economic growth did not, however, reduce the unemployment rate, largely because labor unions preferred to translate the gains into higher wages or, in the case of West Germany, into shorter working hours for employed workers. However, most countries were able to stabilize the unemployment rate, although often at high levels.

Although the strong dollar stimulated exports, European governments blamed American economic policy for many of their difficulties. In June at the economic summit meeting in London of the government heads of the seven major non-Communist industrial powers (Britain, Canada, France, Italy, Japan, United States, West Germany), the American budget deficit was blamed for the high interest rates that were attracting European capital away from job-creating investment at home. Moreover, the strong dollar was held responsible for exacerbating the repayment problems of Third World debtor countries, whose real interest rates in dollars were rising while commodity prices were falling, and thus for endangering the European banks that had earlier collaborated with American banks in making the $700 billion (U.S.) loans still outstanding.

Attempts by European governments to handle longstanding economic problems exacerbated social tension. Both the Conservative government of Prime Minister Margaret Thatcher in Britain and the Socialist government of President François Mitterrand in France attempted to close down money-losing coal mines, even at the risk of increasing unemployment. An unusually violent strike by the British miners' union not only reduced coal and steel production but provoked sympathy strikes by dockworkers that virtually closed British docks and brought the pound to its lowest value ever. In France, Mitterrand's efforts to cut 25,000 jobs in the steel industry by closing out-of-date plants provoked strikes that closed down the Lorraine mining district and cut border contacts with France's neighbors. Determined, like Thatcher, to face down the unions, Mitterrand remodeled his government in July, without Communist participation, and authorized the new premier, Laurent Fabius, to press on with the unpopular measures of austerity and industrial modernization. In West Germany, a seven-week strike by the metalworkers unions hampered recovery.

The European Community in Crisis. For much of the year, the European Community (EC), which had been founded to stimulate economic development, seemed to be yet another obstacle to recovery. The EC budget expanded to $25 billion, which provoked not only disputes between the members as to their share of that burden but even profounder quarrels on the purpose of the EC expenditures. British Prime Minister Thatcher had argued, since taking power in 1979, that Britain was paying an unfair share of the budget, since 66–68% of the EC expenditures were support and rebate payments made to continental farmers to maintain artificially high farm prices. At the summit meeting of EC heads of government in Athens in December 1983, Thatcher demanded a massive reduction in the British contribution and a gearing of each member country's payments to its output of goods and services; she made clear that unless satisfied she would bring the EC into bankruptcy as a result of failure to reach budget agreement. Meeting in Brussels in March 1984, the EC leaders again reached deadlock on the budget, even though a small start was made in reducing the high costs of the agricultural subsidies on dairy products. The elections for the European Parliament held in June gave the electorate the chance to show their disillusionment with the performance of the EC leaders both at home and in the Community. In France, Mitterrand's Socialist-Communist coalition received only 32% of the vote. In Italy, the Communists received a larger share of the vote than the Christian Democrats for the first time. Thatcher's Conservatives in Britain lost 14 seats. But the most significant message was voter apathy. Less than 60% voted overall. In Britain, with the lowest turnout, only 32% went to the polls.

Perhaps chastened by these results, at their meeting in Fontainebleau, France, in July, the EC leaders gave in to most of Thatcher's demands. Britain was to receive a rebate of $800 million in 1984, with further rebates of two thirds of its contributions in future years. Agricultural spending was to be slowed, and Community income was to be increased by raising the EC's share of value-added taxes. With financial difficulties finally faced, the EC leaders attempted to revive the Community's momentum by calling for new policies to complete their economic integration, most notably in the monetary sphere, and to negotiate the membership of Spain and Portugal by 1986.

European Reaction to U.S.-Soviet Confrontation. Perhaps more forcefully than at any period since the first Cold War confrontations of the late 1940s, both West and East Europeans felt themselves to be largely passive participants in an increasingly dangerous trial of strength between the superpowers. The rigidity of Soviet policy seemed partly explicable by a leadership hiatus after the death of President Leonid Brezhnev in November 1982. Brezhnev's successor, Yuri Andropov, disappeared from public view in August 1983 and died in February 1984. The new president and party secretary, 72-year-old Konstantin Chernenko, appeared unable or unwilling to change the tough line of strategy followed by the Soviet Union since its invasion of Afghanistan in December 1979; and in fact, the most devastating attack of Russia's war against Afghan rebels was launched in May.

Supposed American security laxness was given as an excuse for the Soviet boycott of the Olympic Games in Los Angeles in July, and most East European Communist countries unwillingly showed their allegiance by joining the boycott. The Soviet leaders refused to return to the Strategic Arms Reduction Talks (START) or the talks on intermediate-range nuclear forces (INF), which they had left in December 1983 after the deployment of the first American Pershing and cruise missiles to NATO forces in Britain and West Germany. They began deployment of new intermediate-range missiles in East Germany and Czechoslovakia. West Germany in particular became the target of Soviet criticism; East German party Secretary Erich Honecker in September canceled his long-awaited visit to West Germany.

Some West Europeans agreed with the Soviet leaders that American intransigence was responsible for the international tension. In West Germany the Green Party joined with some Social Democrats in criticism of the government's willingness to accept American missiles on German soil, and small numbers of activists attempted to harass U.S. troops. But, like their governments, most West Europeans seemed resigned to taking concrete steps to counter the imbalance in military strength between NATO and Warsaw Pact forces in Europe. At the same time, like the leaders at the London economic summit, they called for a "search for extended political dialogue and long-term cooperation" with the Soviet bloc.

Terrorism Unabated. Britain seemed to have replaced France as the prime target for terrorist activity. In December 1983 the Irish Republican Army (IRA) set off a car bomb outside a London department store during the Christmas shopping season. In April 1984, an unidentified gunman shot a London policewoman from the windows of the Libyan embassy. And in October the IRA attempted to kill the entire British cabinet during the Conservative party conference in Brighton by setting off a bomb in their hotel. But few parts of Western Europe were totally spared from terrorist attack, and Mrs. Thatcher persuaded the economic summit participants to issue a declaration condemning terrorism and promising increased cooperation in preventing it.

F. ROY WILLIS
University of California, Davis

Today's Grandparents

With the elderly population set to double in 60 years, attention is focusing on the changing role of grandparents in the American family.

Traditionally, grandparents have been a major resource for both parents and children —dispensing advice and family history, providing child care and other support, and serving as a focal point for family reunions. Now high mobility, increased divorce rates, and a tight economy have altered the part played by older relatives in rearing children. In some cases, the generations have been driven apart; in others, they have been brought closer together.

Moving Apart. Long distance moves have become common for younger and older Americans alike. It is almost the norm for families with young children to move thousands of miles to new jobs, and in recent years older people have headed in droves to retirement communities and new homes in the Sun Belt. As a result, many grandparents have found their roles in the day-to-day lives of their families reduced to occasional letters and telephone calls.

Divorce also has helped split the generations in many families. Some 50% of marriages now end in divorce, with custody of children awarded to one partner or the other. Because of emotional pain and conflict between the parties or because of remarriage and gradual drifting apart, ties with former in-laws often dissolve as well. For many grandparents, the result has been loss of contact with grandchildren.

Grandparents' Rights. More and more, however, grandparents are suing for visiting rights and even custody of their grandchildren. In one widely publicized case, Harvey and Marcia Kudler of Queens, NY, spent five years in court attempting to gain the right to visit their two grandchildren. They then turned to the media and to Congress, where they testified before the House Subcommittee on Human Services. The subcommittee hearings led to a resolution calling for a federal law to protect grandparents' rights, which was passed by the House in 1983. However the Senate refused to act on the proposal.

Forty-seven states already have such laws. In general these statutes do not guarantee grandparents the right to visit their grandchildren; rather, they require family courts to consider the grandparents' rights. Courts in California, Massachusetts, Michigan, New York, and other states have used social workers and psychologists to iron out generational disputes and set up workable visitation schedules.

Don Folland, FPG International

Moving Closer. Increased separation from younger family members is not always unwelcome to grandparents. Many older people prefer to concentrate on travel and leisure or to continue working rather than to help raise their grandchildren. Nor is the separation universal. In many families, ties between the generations have grown stronger.

The recession and high interest rates of the early 1980s made it increasingly difficult for young families to set up homes of their own. Many young couples—with and without children—solved the problem by moving in with their parents. Similarly, family finances now often require both parents to hold jobs. With daycare expensive and difficult to find, grandparents in many families have stepped in to play an increased role in child care. The rising numbers of divorced and single parents are apt to rely even more heavily on grandparents for emotional and financial support.

Coupled with these various economic factors is a growing awareness of the importance of intergenerational relationships for young children, sparked in part by press coverage of the problem.

The federal Foster Grandparent Program has enrolled more than 18,000 older people to give advice and companionship to disabled children. State and local programs have brought older people into schools to serve as tutors and paired them with young people for public-service work. Similar projects have been started by such groups as the Future Homemakers of America, the Girl Scouts, and the Foundation for Grandparenting—a Mount Kisco, NY, group.

ELAINE PASCOE

Pleated skirts in the muted colors and fine fabrics of classic menswear were popular fashion items for fall 1984. Mid-calf lengths predominated, and a soft woolen sweater or flannel shirt jacket completed the look.

FASHION

The fashion world, ever fond of buzzwords to define and classify a trend, latched onto "androgynous" to sum up the direction of fashion in 1984. Defined as possessing both male and female characteristics, the word seemed apt in a year that not only featured menswear looks for women but in which designer Jean-Paul Gaultier appeared at a New York presentation of his fashions in his pin-striped, double-breasted business suit that had an ankle-length wrap skirt in place of the usual trousers.

In 1984, women strode the fashion runways dressed aggressively in oversized coats worn over jackets and trousers that were as well tailored as the men's and fabricated of the same coverts, serges, twills, gabardines, and flannels. Sleek, polished, and elegant, the new fashions had none of the waifish, ragtag, costumed look of the "Annie Hall" menswear trend of the late 1970s.

Apparel. Pants were omnipresent, the pivotal piece in every collection. Cuffed and softly pleated, they fell into straight and easy lines and featured wide or shaped waistbands. Jackets were square-shouldered, hip-length versions of single- or double-breasted blazers, high- or V-necked cardigans, or Norfolk jackets. Coats were boxy, often ankle-length versions of traditional balmacaans in checks, tweeds, or plaids, as well as classic trenches, dusters, and polo coats of camel's hair or cashmere. Their common denominator was dash and a built-in sense of ease and assurance.

The menswear influence was carried through into evening as the wrap, styled on the lines of the classic men's dressing gown, became the dress of the year. Elegantly casual, it was shown everywhere in sensuous silks and satins, but nowhere more spectacularly than at Ralph Lauren, where it was done in luxurious silk velvet with a shawl collar of mink. Another superb velvet version by Gloria Sachs featured lapels and cuffs of gold lamé.

Other evening looks projected a more distinctly feminine sexiness than did the wrap. Black lace or jersey conveyed a seductive message. Lace in strapless or décolleté gowns was a formal evening essential, while clinging jerseys in deceptively demure "little" dresses outlined the body in a sensual way.

Skirts, though overshadowed by pants, did provide news for fashion watchers. Lengths ranged from mid-thigh minis to just above the ankle, with the predominant length hovering mid-calf. Lean in look, they were nevertheless made easy to wear via pleats, slits, or sarong styling. The culotte or split skirt was also a popular item shown in most sportswear groups.

Important sweater looks included long, lean tunic vests in cashmere shown by Anne Klein

G. H. Bass

The black leather penny loafer was back, thanks to the trend-setting style of pop star Michael Jackson.

and evening versions of the cardigan worn backbuttoned over full lace or satin skirts at Bill Blass. Beaded Fair Isle sweaters were shown over crepe pajama pants at Bill Haire.

Softening Touches. Blunting the hard-edged tailoring and mannish styling of the androgynous look were a number of alluring and softening touches. In fabrics, texture was one of the mellowers. Napped flannels, nubby tweeds, and mixtures of wool with angora or mohair tempered the tailoring, and pliant jerseys added body awareness. White—number one on the fashion palette—and pastels were feminine, and patterns in sophisticated combinations or more conservative matchings gave the trouser suits and greatcoats a womanly touch. Shirts of supple silk and soft cashmere sweaters further counterpointed the mannish suit styles.

The masculine styling could be softened additionally with accessories. Jewelry included pearl and chain necklaces, bold bracelets, and big, bright pins in heraldic modes adorning lapels or hats. Colorful silk or challis shawls blurred the sharp lines of the haberdashery look. And, as though acknowledging that the fedora and the tie were too much the male symbols, designers ignored both in favor of the banded beret and the muffler or scarf of silk or wool. The latter wrapped the throat or tucked into a shirt or sweater neckline.

Color Trends. Beyond haberdashery looks and the chiaroscuro of black and white, secondary trends appeared on the fashion landscape. Bright color relieved the omnipresent black and white and the classic menswear palette. In the collections of Emanuel Ungaro and Bill Blass, coats and jackets were vibrantly colored in cobalt blue, cherry red, emerald green, and canary yellow; Yves Saint Laurent's satin evening coats and gowns blazed with the same

brightness. At Bill Haire, blazers and sweater dresses were brilliant in turquoise, fuchsia, and acid green. Bold color was the electrifier in the abstract patterned sweaters of Perry Ellis and the plaid knit ensembles by Adrienne Vittadini; Stephen Sprouse in his retrospective mini-dresses revived the Day-Glo neon colors of the 1960s. Color came through, too, in heavily stone-studded jewelry and in scarves, gloves, and hats.

Shoes and Handbags. Important accessories in every wardrobe, shoes and handbags were elegantly in keeping with the menswear look. Flat or low-heeled oxfords and gillies in suede or highly polished leathers suited the trousers, as did tailored shoulder bags and totes in glazed calfskin or snake. The news here was less in the style than in the materials used. The more novel and interesting types included real or imitation buffalo, elephant skin, ostrich, or crocodile. Textured, embossed, or printed suedes and kidskin were featured, as were stenciled calfskin, woven or perforated leathers, mesh, cork, and even rubber—ribbed or bubbled like tub mats. For evening, satin shoes and bags were ornamented with lavish beading and rhinestones in pavé settings. Lace and lamé were other gala materials used.

Yet the most popular, most talked-about shoe owed less to a designer or fashion trend than it did to a pop star. Michael Jackson made the black leather penny loafer the number-one shoe just by wearing it and created a market for moccasins that ranged from the classic version to the soft, flexible Italian driving shoe.

Menswear. Androgyny aside, menswear became staid and proper in 1984. Business suits were dark—navy, charcoal gray, or brown—and more frequently single-breasted than double-breasted, with a lightly relaxed fit and cuffed trousers. White or pastel shirts with French cuffs, understated ties, polished wingtips or loafers, and the classic trenchcoat or cashmere chesterfield completed the look.

British influences were seen in the lapeled or double-breasted vests that seemed to be a part of every business suit and in the braces, silk pocket squares, and Windsor-knotted ties worn with spread-collared shirts.

Tweeds, patterns, sweaters, or mismatched suits, no matter how discreet, were strictly for weekends, as was rugged outerwear or any other casual garb. Jewelry did not exist except for cuff links and a tasteful watch, the only function of which was to tell time.

It appeared that the appropriation of menswear looks by women had caused men to become more rigid and conservative in their own dress. But early indications were that women's clothes might return to a more feminine mien, freeing men to take a more relaxed and adventuresome attitude toward fashion.

ANN M. ELKINS
Fashion Director, "Good Housekeeping"

Top right: *The menswear look for women was given a luxurious treatment by Bill Blass, whose gray satin balmacaan coat featured a mink lining.* Bottom right: *A trend toward vibrant color was manifested in boldly tinted coat and skirt ensembles.* Below left: *Evening wear included elongated cashmere sweater sets and backbuttoned cardigans worn over flounced satin or taffeta skirts.*

Photos, Gideon Lewin/Bill Blass Ltd.

FINLAND

Politically, the year 1984 proved to be one of the more quiet periods in recent Finnish history. However, in November 1983, President Mauno Koivisto had managed to ruffle the feelings of Finnish editors and journalists with his confidential letter to the heads of more than 30 newspapers, reprimanding them for their irresponsibility and poor judgment when reporting on Finland's foreign policy. Indignation was the immediate public response; Koivisto's letter was regarded widely as an attempt to introduce a measure of veiled censorship. Others cited presidential weariness at having to explain, interpret, and correct what he considered distorted presentations of his statements. A subsequent meeting on January 18 between the president and 51 editors served to placate journalistic feelings.

Two party conventions held during the summer may have important consequences for the future activities of the parties involved. The Social Democratic Party reelected Kalevi Sorsa, the current prime minister, as its chairman for the next three years. This indicated Sorsa's firm hold on power within his party. The Finnish Communist Party, which is split into majority and minority factions, elected as its chairman Arvo Aalto, a former party secretary. This was held to forebode more intraparty dissension in the future.

Elections for municipal and rural councils were held on October 21 and 22, with a voter turnout of 73.6%, the lowest since 1956. No great changes were registered by any of the parties, with the exception of the Rural Party which lost 4.4% of their former representation to end up with 5.3% of the vote.

Åland, the Swedish-speaking archipelago in the Baltic Sea, which the League of Nations awarded to Finland in 1921, has ever since been protective of its autonomy. Åland now has its own flag and is represented officially in the Nordic Council; the islands also are being considered as the headquarters of another Nordic House. The latest symbol of Åland autonomy was the issuance on March 1 of the first Åland postage stamps. The first issue comprised seven stamps with five different motifs.

Economic Affairs. Dissatisfaction with wages and other working conditions led several Finnish unions, in spite of protracted negotiations with the Employers' Confederation, to threaten a one-day strike for March 6. Such a strike, involving 800,000 union members, would not only have affected factory workers, the post office, and transportation personnel but also teachers and university professors. The strike, however, finally was warded off on March 5, through the persistent efforts of State Mediator Matti Pekkanen.

In May another strike did occur, this time by physicians at municipal hospitals and health centers. The seriousness of the situation led to a threat of national legislation to force the doctors to go back to work; as a result the strike was over by the end of the month.

Other. Paavo Haavikko, one of Finland's leading writers, was selected as the 1984 winner of the $25,000 American Neustadt Prize. This prestigious prize is awarded by the University of Oklahoma and the periodical *World Literature Today*.

Eight Finns made exploration history in May when they traveled on skis across the ice from Resolute Bay in northern Canada to both the Magnetic North Pole and the North Pole itself. The round trip took two and a half months and was an unprecedented achievement.

ERIK J. FRIIS
"The Scandinavian-American Bulletin"

FINLAND • Information Highlights

Official Name: Republic of Finland.
Location: Northern Europe.
Area: 130,160 sq mi (337 113 km²).
Population (mid-1984 est.): 4,900,000.
Chief City (Dec. 31, 1982): Helsinki, the capital, 484,399.
Government: *Head of state,* Mauno Koivisto, president (took office Jan, 27, 1982). *Head of government,* Kalevi Sorsa, prime minister (took office May 6, 1983). *Legislature* (unicameral)—Eduskunta.
Monetary Unit: Markka (6.46 markka equal U.S. $1, Oct. 18, 1984).
Gross National Product: (1982 U.S.$): $49,100,000,000.
Economic Indexes (1983): *Consumer Prices* (1970 = 100), all items, 388.7; food, 407.8. *Industrial Production* (1975 = 100), 137.
Foreign Trade (1983 U.S.$): *Imports,* $12,847,000,000; *exports'*. $12,550,000,000.

FLORIDA

Judicial action ending a tax revolt, issues involving national politics, citrus-growing problems, and growth management dominated Florida headlines in 1984.

Tax Revolt. Proposition One, calling for a state constitutional amendment that would roll back all taxes to the 1980 level, was scheduled for the November 1984 ballot. However, in March the Florida Supreme Court ordered it stricken from the ballot. The court ruled that the proposed amendment was too wide ranging, whereas Florida's constitution limits citizen initiatives to single issues. Proponents vowed to try again.

Politics. In the March Democratic presidential primary, Gary Hart scored a surprising victory over Walter Mondale. Former Florida Gov. Reubin Askew and Sen. John Glenn, both of whom had hoped for a strong showing, failed to win a single convention delegate, and they soon dropped out of the Democratic presidential race. Based on Mondale's weak showing, few observers gave him much chance of carrying the state in the general election, which President Reagan won with 65.3% of the votes.

While President Reagan demonstrated his popularity in Florida, his coattails did not carry along many other Republicans. They won no additional seats in Congress (Florida delegation: 12 Democrats, 7 Republicans—all incumbents) and managed to win only six new seats in the Florida legislature, all in the House. Most of the gains were in south Florida, possibly reflecting Reagan's popularity among the Hispanic voters there. Democrats remained in control of the legislature, however.

Citrus Problems. As the citrus industry worked to recover from the devastating December 1983 freeze, the dreaded Mediterranean fruit fly was sighted in Dade County, a threat that was eliminated by November through the rapid response of agricultural officials. There was no celebrating, however, because an equally dangerous threat had been identified in September in a central Florida nursery—citrus canker. The preceding citrus canker infestation, in 1913, required 20 years to eradicate.

Citrus canker, which is harmless to humans but defoliates and kills citrus trees, was probably introduced from groves in Asia or Mexico. Since the disease is caused by bacteria, it spreads easily, and there is no "cure." Consequently, infected and "suspect" trees must be burned. Trees from the original infected nursery have been traced to several other nurseries, and almost seven million trees have been burned. To prevent spreading the disease, only fruit from canker-free groves can be harvested and shipped.

Temik, a pesticide widely used in citrus groves, was banned in 1983 because of fear of toxic pollution of drinking water. The ban was lifted by state officials after testing demonstrated that the danger posed by Temik was exaggerated. However, as a precaution, minimum-distance requirements have been established for its use near drinking-water wells.

Environment. The 1984 legislature was expected to enact a comprehensive growth-management policy that would enable Florida to continue its rapid growth yet protect sensitive environmental areas and water supplies. No such policy emerged, but a Groundwater Protection Task Force was created and a wetlands bill was approved. The wetlands law grants the Department of Environmental Regulation (DER) power to consider the cumulative impact of development and to reduce the scope of proposed development in order to protect the environment. DER also has more control over dredge and fill operations, especially in the Everglades.

Child Abuse. There was growing concern in Florida about child abuse. This concern resulted in laws that impose more severe penalties for sex crimes against children and new

AP/Wide World

The cruise ship "Scandinavian Sun" embarks from Miami, a growing port of call for the seafaring cruise liners.

regulations governing child-care centers. In addition, a Missing Children Information Clearinghouse was created to help locate missing minors.

Education. As a result of legislative efforts, high school students began the 1984-1985 school year with a longer school day, consisting of seven class periods rather than the former six. More academic credits will be required for graduation, and a "merit" pay plan was being formulated that would financially reward teachers and schools who excel. Teacher unions oppose the merit plan, but the legislature felt it necessary in order to encourage excellence in education.

J. LARRY DURRENCE
Florida Southern College

FLORIDA • Information Highlights

Area: 58,664 sq mi (151 939 km²).
Population (July 1, 1983 est.): 10,680,000.
Chief Cities (July 1, 1982 est.): Tallahassee, the capital, 102,579; Jacksonville, 556,370; Miami, 382,726; Tampa, 276,413; St. Petersburg, 241,214.
Government (1984): *Chief Officers*—governor, Robert Graham (D); lt. gov., Wayne Mixson (D). *Legislature*—Senate, 40 members; House of Representatives, 120 members.
State Finances (fiscal year 1983): *Revenues,* $10,569,000,000; *expenditures,* $9,874,000,000.
Personal Income (1983): $123,815,000,000; per capita, $11,593.
Labor Force (May 1984): *Civilian labor force,* 5,032,100; *unemployed,* 304,500 (6.1% of total force).
Education: *Enrollment* (fall 1982)—public elementary schools, 1,038,998; public secondary, 445,736; colleges and universities (fall 1983), 443,436. *Public school expenditures* (1982–83), $3,667,785,894 ($2,680 per pupil).

FOOD

In 1984, as in past years, the whims of nature and political turmoil joined forces to create changes in the world's food-growing areas and in the total supply of food. In late 1983 and early 1984, the United States was staggered by cold, snow, and floods. In 1983, weather damage amounted to $14 billion (U.S.) in losses to agriculture. Although totals are not yet available, 1984 could prove to be equal or worse. In the Sunbelt alone, the December 1983 freeze caused an estimated loss of $500 million to citrus and other tender crops and raised retail prices. In northern areas, livestock losses were high, leading to the expectation that meat prices might be affected. In the West, snow, cold, floods, and fire all contributed to the problems of producing food as well as lowering yields.

In the rest of the world, currency values, high interest rates, lowered crop yields, and conflicts in the Middle East and Afghanistan created much uncertainty in the availability of food, and its role in combating hunger. Throughout the world, 1984 weather and crop conditions appeared to be more promising than in the previous two years.

Food Supply. The supply of food for the world appeared to be better than in 1983. The 'Food and Agricultural Organization (FAO) forecast world cereal production at 1,765,000,000 metric tons,[1] up about 8% from 1983. Coarse grains were expected to increase 16% to 800 million tons, and both wheat and rice up 2% or 505 and 460 million tons, respectively. As with any forecast, weather conditions between the time of forecast and harvest can drastically change crop yields. Of crucial importance in the food-supply arena is the level of world cereal trade, where it was expected that volume would be equal to, or slightly higher than, the previous two years. If so, the carryover stocks would be down below the minimum level necessary for world food security.

In the United States, the September estimate by the Department of Agriculture (USDA) showed the corn crop at 7.55 billion bushels, or 81% more than 1983. As such, the corn harvest would be the fourth largest in U.S. history, exceeded only by the 1979, 1981, and 1982 crops. Wheat was forecast at 2.57 billion bushels, or 6% above 1983, and down slightly from the 1982 record crop of 2.81 billion bushels. The 1984 soybean crop was estimated at 2.03 billion bushels, or 29% higher than 1983.

In related food areas, the USDA reported a 4% decline in cattle on feedlots in 13 major cattle-producing states and a 2% increase in cattle being sent to slaughter.

[1] 1 metric ton equals 1.102 short tons. All tonnages given in this article are metric.

Food Production and Population. Since 1950 the world population has grown from 2.5 billion to 4.7 billion in 1984. Of the 80 million people born each year, the majority are born in less developed countries where domestic food production cannot, or barely, support them. Per capita cropland availability has dropped during the past 30 years in Central America, China, Iran, Mexico, North Africa, and South Asia. In such areas as Argentina, Brazil, Uruguay and certain parts of North America, Oceania, Southern Africa, and Southeast Asia cultivated cropland could expand. However, it is expected that future increases in output will be the result of new technology and increases in productivity. As a particular example of change, per capita food production in Africa has declined 16% in the past 30 years, while in Sub-Saharan Africa a population growth rate of 3.1% has been recorded. Due to droughts, unstable economic conditions, and political changes, cereal imports there doubled between 1975 and 1983 and now account for one fifth of the cereal consumption.

U.S. Food Supply. The U.S. food supply, other than being affected by weather, remained relatively stable in terms of wholesale prices until costs rose 0.3% in July. However, for the first seven months of the year, the annual rate of 2.9% was under that predicted. As the year progressed, more acute problems arose. In Florida, the citrus industry, after being hit with a harsh freeze at Christmastime 1983 and a Medfly outbreak in the spring, was affected by citrus canker, a bacterial disease that defoliates and kills trees. The disease threatened the $1.2 billion Florida citrus industry, which supplies more than half the orange juice, 90% of the limes, and 75% of the grapefruit used in the United States. To eradicate the disease, federal and state authorities ordered the burning of diseased nursery stock; the defoliation, spraying, and burning of trees adjacent to diseased seedlings; and a ban on harvesting and shipping of fruit until each grove or grower is cleared. Since the wholesale price of juice was much higher than in 1983, it was feared that the disease would raise prices even higher and affect the industry for years to come.

In Florida, California, Massachusetts, and other states early in 1984, numerous name-brand cake mixes, flour, grits, and similar products were removed from store shelves. The cause was the chemical ethylene dibromide (EDB) used by farmers to control insects in grain and citrus fruit. An effective pesticide, EDB is also a carcinogen, a fact known for ten years. In early February the Environmental Protection Agency (EPA) banned EDB as a pesticide for grain and set limits for tainted grain products. EPA pointed out that tainted grain could be made safe by airing or extending storage time. The question of what level of risk is acceptable remained unanswered, however.

After a bacteria called citrus canker was found in several Florida nurseries in late August, the federal government halted the shipment of all citrus from the state and ordered the burning of diseased trees and stock.

Pierre Ducharme, Gamma-Liaison

In a more complex situation, Chesapeake Bay, an area well known as a food producer, was described as dying or in decline. A prolific food producer in the 19th century, the bay today is producing much less in fish, game birds, shellfish, and crab. Currently the EPA, the contiguous states, and the producer associations are attempting to formulate a plan to save the bay. While the bay problems stem partially from natural causes, most are man-made or man-related. Sewage, increased population, and pollution of all types have contributed to the bay's lowered harvest.

U.S. Food Industry. Worldwide, the U.S. food industry influences packaging, processing, and production, but in late 1983 a new venture was initiated. The joint production of foods by Beatrice Foods and China's Guangzhou Company is in the form of a 15-year contract, jointly operated and designed to provide products needed both in the United States and China. This is the first joint U.S.-Chinese venture in the food area since diplomatic relations were established between the two nations.

In other developments, business mergers were creating new and huge companies from large, single corporations. Nestlé and the Carnation Company combined in a $3 billion deal. This consolidation is the largest of a number of mergers occurring within the food industry and may indicate a trend. In the past year, Beatrice acquired Esmark (Swift, Hunt's); CPC became the owner of C.F. Mueller, making CPC the largest U.S. pasta maker. Conagra absorbed four large companies, while General Foods bought up six companies in the same period.

Food Irradiation. In February 1984, Margaret Heckler, secretary of Health and Human Services, announced the clearance of the safe use of irradiation for processing of food. The proposal acknowledged the time and money that had been expended in investigating irradia-tion and also noted that the levels of treatment are conservative. The regulations would permit food to be irradiated to kill insects in fruits or vegetables or slow the growth, ripening, and spoilage of fresh produce. The food industry viewed the proposal as a step that would add new technology but also reduce spoilage.

Packaging. Food packaging is a growing and changing field. Aseptic packaging has been accepted by the consumer to the extent that some 800–900 million units were produced in 1983 and used for various liquids. Currently such foods as yogurt, soup, tomato products, sour cream, and other foods are being tested in aseptic flexible packages. The latest products to appear in this package that requires no refrigeration are fruit juice or drink concentrates. These products are similar to the frozen concentrate with the container being lower in cost and ready to use.

Nutrition. The elderly in America, or specifically those over 65, are increasing in numbers yearly and are now being regarded as a marketing force by the food industry. While many new foods are directed toward the elderly, nutritional surveys have shown that caloric intake is low and vitamin and mineral intake is inadequate in this group. At a 1984 conference, suggestions were made to develop foods to meet elderly taste and nutritional requirements, to set up test markets using the elderly, and to have food processors contribute to programs that would help the elderly.

The role of salt in the diet has come under examination. Salt was implicated in high blood pressure until a recent study disputed the theory and states that deficiencies of calcium, potassium, and vitamins A and C cause hypertension. The scientific community did not fully accept the study.

KIRBY M. HAYES
University of Massachusetts

J. Langevin, Sygma

France's President Mitterrand (right) *played a key role in reaching a budget accord at the EC summit in Fontainebleau.*

FRANCE

The political scene in France during 1984 was marked by a steady shift to more restrictive, conservative economic policies by the Socialist government. This shift triggered intense opposition from both rightist and left-wing groups, amid growing unpopularity of government leaders. Following a cabinet reorganization in July, the Communists withdrew from the ruling coalition. In foreign affairs, the single most outstanding achievement in 1984 was France's successful leadership at the Fontainebleau summit meeting of Common Market leaders in June.

Domestic Affairs. Layoffs in the automobile industry and other ailing sectors of the economy, such as steel and shipbuilding, were to become a major political issue throughout 1984. In his New Year's message, President François Mitterrand reiterated the government's commitment to recovery and industrial modernization, but both the Communists and right-wing opposition groups repeatedly attacked the government's policy of economic austerity.

Throughout January 1984, French farmers violently protested falling prices of pork and other meats. In Normandy and Brittany, they hijacked trucks carrying British lamb and severely disrupted rail traffic. On January 24, about 3,000 shipbuilders marched throughout Paris in protest against a plan to eliminate about 6,000 jobs. A day earlier, Premier Pierre

Mauroy announced that the government would offer a two-year retraining program to offset the heavy layoffs in the automobile, steel, shipbuilding, and coal sectors. Farmers were promised relief from imports, which they blamed for sliding prices.

As part of steady skirmishing with right-wing opposition parties, Mauroy announced at a January news conference that former President Valery Giscard d'Estaing and his prime minister, Raymond Barre, had covered up and obstructed investigations into an unsuccessful oil-prospecting project. Both Giscard d'Estaing and Barre denied the charges.

Amid growing unemployment and spreading labor unrest, the Communist Party and most of the labor unions began to pressure the Socialist government to reverse its policy of austerity in favor of an expansionary, job-creating approach. Public-opinion polls began showing that austerity remained highly unpopular and that the government increasingly was being perceived as unable to govern effectively. While the polls reflected virtually no personal animosity, they showed that Mitterrand had become the least popular French president since the Fifth Republic was established in 1958.

Throughout the spring, the government's plan to increase government control over France's predominantly Roman Catholic private schools touched off more mass demonstrations in major cities. A controversial proposal in the bill would have submitted the budgets of private schools to the control of regional bodies. Despite the opposition, the cabinet on April 18 approved the bill with some modifications.

Opposition to the government's economic austerity program again erupted in violence in early April, when riot police fired tear gas to disperse steel workers protesting layoffs in the Lorraine region of eastern France. Mitterrand insisted that "either France is capable of facing up to international competition and ensuring its independence and well-being, or it will be pulled down toward decline."

Seeking to test Communist loyalty to the government, Prime Minister Mauroy called for, and won, a vote of confidence in the National Assembly on April 20. Forty-four Communist deputies approved, effectively assuring that four Communists holding ministerial portfolios would remain in the government. But party leaders emphasized that they would continue to oppose the government's economic policy.

Mauroy triggered a heated political debate on May 20 when he renewed a Socialist proposal to establish a 35-hour workweek in business and industry for the purpose of reducing unemployment. Officials of the Communist-led General Confederation of Labor (CGT) supported the initiative, but it was immediately criticized by business leaders.

In the first major defeat for the government, the Socialists polled only 20.8% of the vote in June 18 elections for the European Parliament, losing three seats. The Communists received 11.3%, retaining 10 of their former 19 seats; it was the party's lowest showing in a national

Laurent Fabius was named prime minister on July 17. At age 37, he became modern France's youngest premier.

A. Nogues, Sygma

election in more than 50 years. The National Front, a right-wing party led by Jean-Marie Le Pen, won seats in the parliament for the first time, gaining 11% and 10 seats.

Several weeks of intense speculation ended on July 17 with the resignation of Prime Minister Mauroy and his government. President Mitterrand immediately named Industry Minister Laurent Fabius as the new head of government. A Mitterrand protégé and son of a wealthy antique dealer, Fabius at age 37 became modern France's youngest prime minister.

Two days later the Communist Party announced that it was leaving the government, having turned down four ministerial posts. Party leaders said they would offer selective support to the government in the parliament. Meanwhile, Fabius named a cabinet made up of Socialists and two smaller leftist groups. Key ministers remained from the previous government, notably Minister of External Relations Claude Cheysson and Defense Minister Charles Hernu. Jacques Delors resigned as finance minister to become president of the EC Commission in Brussels, a post he was scheduled to assume in January 1985. Delors was replaced by Pierre Beregovoy, who promised to further reduce the budget deficit.

On July 19 the cabinet approved a package of tax cuts for business and individuals. Political observers said that the cuts were intended to dramatize the government's commitment to conservative economic policies. They also reflected President Mitterrand's determination to capture the middle ground in French politics prior to parliamentary elections in 1986.

Throughout September and October, Prime Minister Fabius moved to defuse centrist opposition by withdrawing the government's support for a controversial press reform bill and by postponing action on the school-reform measures.

Economy. The French economy began 1984 with a virtually stagnant gross domestic product (GDP) growth rate of 0.7%, steadily rising unemployment, an inflation rate of just over 9%, and deficits in trade and the current account of the balance of payments. Having reversed its expansionary policy only in the second half of 1983, the government clearly was out of phase with most of its trading partners, whose economies were beginning to show signs of recovery with lower inflation rates. The Organization for Economic Cooperation and Development (OECD) and the International Monetary Fund (IMF) agreed, however, that France was on the right track in pursuing conservative policies.

Many Frenchmen disagreed. Jean-Pierre Chevenement, the former industry minister and outspoken leader of the Socialist Party's leftist-leaning faction, in February renewed his call for an expansionary policy of "mobilization.'' (Chevenement rejoined the cabinet in July as education minister and dropped his criticism of the government's economic policy.) Former Prime Minister Barre expressed his fears over the government's failure to improve industrial productivity and competitiveness in export markets; he said the French economy was gripped by ''paralyzing recession and fierce corporatism.'' Yvon Gattaz, president of France's employers' association, the Patronat, urged the government to reduce or eliminate a wide range of business taxes to spur capital spending.

The much-awaited July economic-outlook report of the OECD had encouraging words for the government, particularly for the declining inflation rate (7¾% in the first half of the year), an improving trade picture, and cutbacks in government spending. But the OECD, among others, warned that unemployment would continue to increase and possibly surpass 11% by the end of 1985. That compared with 9¼% during the first half of 1984 and 8.4% in 1983.

Meanwhile, the finance ministry released figures showing that the pace of France's external borrowing had slowed during the first half of 1984. Total gross foreign debt had climbed to about 600 billion francs ($70 billion), a record. First-half net borrowing had totaled the equivalent of $1.9 billion, compared with $6.4 billion in the second half of 1983. Government officials said that they expected the downward trend to continue.

In what became a heated controversy, Creusot-Loire, France's largest privately owned engineering group, was placed in receivership on June 28. It was the largest industrial bankruptcy case in recent French history. The ailing company, an affiliate of the Empain-Schneider group, employs about 30,270 people, with an additional 10,000 working as subcontractors. By December, Creusot-Loire was still operating under the supervision of the

Paris Commercial Court, as the government sought to find support among private and state-owned companies and labor unions for a financial rescue package.

The 1985 budget, approved by the National Assembly in mid-November, was aimed at moderately stimulating the economy through cuts in taxes and government spending, while keeping inflation relatively low. Spending was projected to rise by 6% to 995.2 billion francs. The deficit was expected to rise to just under 140 billion francs from the estimated 1984 level of 135 billion francs. Finance Minister Beregovoy said his goal was to keep the 1985 deficit to 3% of GDP, compared to the 1984 rate of just over 3.3%. Growth would be modest, with GDP rising to 2% from an estimated 1.3% in 1984. Inflation would fall from 7.6% in 1984 to 5.2% in 1985. Conservatives and Communists challenged the figures and forecasts.

Foreign Affairs. In contrast to public opinion regarding his handling of economic and social policy, President Mitterrand received wide support for his handling of foreign policy, notably the intervention in Lebanon and Chad, deeper involvement in the Atlantic alliance, and leadership as president of the European Community Council of Ministers, a rotating, six-month position that he assumed on Jan. 1, 1984. The October 26 release of a French television journalist, Jacques Abouchar, who had been imprisoned in Kabul while filming near the Afghanistan-Pakistan border, also was viewed as a victory for the government.

In a joint announcement on January 2, the ministries of defense and external relations said that France would cut by one fourth its troop strength in the multinational peacekeeping force in Beirut. The government emphasized that the mission of the French contingent was not changing, even though its troops had become a prime target for terrorist groups. Finally on March 24, with 86 of its soldiers killed,

A. Nogues, Sygma

In May about 2,000 automobile workers peacefully occupied a Citroën plant at Aulnay-sous-Bois, near Paris, to protest job cuts. Layoffs in the automobile industry and other ailing sectors of the French economy were a major political issue of 1984.

France announced that it was withdrawing its remaining 1,250 troops from Beirut.

Joint participation in the Lebanon peace force helped create a friendly atmosphere for President Mitterrand's eight-day visit to the United States in late March. In his welcoming address to the French leader at the White House, President Ronald Reagan praised Mitterrand for his "courage and decisiveness" in handling "international challenges that tested the character of Western leadership." In subsequent talks, top French and U.S. officials reaffirmed their commitment to seeking solutions to the world arms buildup, yet without making new concessions to the Soviet Union. While Mitterrand generally avoided areas of conflict with the United States, he did raise controversial issues in his March 22 speech to a joint session of Congress. He cited the disputes between Washington and the European Community (EC) over farm policy; he voiced the EC's concern about rising U.S. budget deficits and the strong dollar; and he warned that Central America should be allowed to develop itself "without interference or manipulation."

Probably the most important diplomatic achievement of the year for France was the successful outcome of the June 25–26 EC summit meeting held in Fontainebleau, near Paris. Ending four years of bitter dispute, the leaders of the ten member nations agreed to reduce Britain's contribution to the EC budget over the following three years. The British also were to receive a rebate on their 1983 and 1984 payments; the 1983 rebate at first was blocked by the European Parliament but finally approved in October. President Mitterrand, who presided over the May meeting, said that the agreements also established ad hoc committees whose goal would be "relaunching Europe" through such measures as trade liberalization, simplified border procedures, establishment of an EC radio and television network, issuance of a community passport, and construction of a space station.

A series of preliminary meetings in the early spring between Mitterrand, Thatcher, and Chancellor Helmut Kohl of West Germany produced a key result a week before the Brussels summit in March. EC farm ministers agreed to a package of measures aimed at reducing subsidized, surplus agricultural production, notably milk. France, acting through its farm minister, Michel Rocard, again played a crucial role in winning support for the cutbacks, both among other EC ministers and with French farmers.

In another key diplomatic event just prior to the Fontainebleau summit, President Mitterrand visited the Soviet Union on June 20–23. It was his first visit to the Soviet Union since he took office in 1981 and the first by a NATO leader since President Konstantin Chernenko came to power in February. The French leader had considered canceling his trip to protest the plight of dissident physicist Andrei Sakharov, who had staged a hunger strike to obtain permission for his wife to travel abroad for medical treatment. In his discussions with Chernenko at the Kremlin, Mitterrand pressed the Sakharov issue, but during a dinner on June 21 the Soviet leader cautioned against "those who are trying to give us advice in respect of human rights." The French leader responded by saying that "we must not disappoint our peoples. That is why we raise the cases of people who are sometimes symbolic." The bombshell effect of bringing up the Sakharov case at the Kremlin immediately created a sensation in the media, bolstering Mitterrand's image. In subsequent conversations, the French leader also cited the Soviet military presence in Afghanistan and the occupation of Cambodia by Soviet-allied Vietnam but emphasized that he hoped for an improvement in strained French-Soviet relations. He reiterated his rejection of a Soviet demand that France's nuclear arsenal be included in arms-reduction talks affecting NATO forces.

The French-Libyan agreement to withdraw forces from Chad, announced on September 17, was regarded for a time as France's second most important diplomatic achievement of the year after the EC accords. The withdrawal promised to end a confrontation that pitted as many as 5,000 Libyan troops against 3,200 French soldiers. The goal had been to prevent a Libyan-backed rebel group, led by former President Goukouni Oueddei, from overthowing the government of President Hissène Habré. However, in a political embarrassment to Mitterrand, both Habré and the U.S. State Department reported in November that Libyan troops were still in Chad. The French leader met with Qaddafi on Crete and upon his return to Paris admitted that two Libyan battalions, totaling about 2,000 men, remained.

AXEL KRAUSE
"International Herald Tribune," Paris

FRANCE · Information Highlights

Official Name: French Republic.
Location: Western Europe.
Area: 213,000 sq mi (551 695 km²).
Population (mid-1984 est.): 54,800,000.
Chief City: Paris, the capital.
Government: *Head of state,* François Mitterrand, president (took office May 1981). *Chief minister,* Laurent Fabius, prime minister (took office July 1984). *Legislature*—Parliament: Senate and National Assembly.
Monetary Unit: Franc (9.1225 francs equal U.S.$1, Nov. 16, 1984).
Gross Domestic Product (1982 U.S.$): $542,000,-000,000.
Economic Indexes (1983): *Consumer Prices* (1970 = 100), all items, 349.3; food, 356.4. *Industrial Production* (1975 = 100), 113.
Foreign Trade (1983 U.S.$): *Imports,* $105,422,-000,000; *exports,* $91,278,000,000.

Beginning in June 1984, the public could enjoy the beautiful new National Country Garden at the National Arboretum in Washington, DC.

John Neubauer

GARDENING AND HORTICULTURE

According to a 1984 survey, impatiens became the most popular bedding plant in the United States, with petunias moving to the second position and marigolds a strong third. Among the year's other highlights were continuing space research, a new national garden, new plant varieties, a major festival, and important new additions to the field's literature.

Seeds in Space. Nine million tomato seeds were sent into space aboard NASA's Long Duration Exposure Facility (LDEF) in April 1984, to return to earth in April 1985. The seeds were sent by George W. Park Seed Co. of Greenwood, SC, as part of a continuing test of the effects of exposure to outer space on plant life. Park scientists selected an open pollinated variety because it would breed true in successive generations and facilitate the identification and isolation of mutations that result from radiation exposure. The seeds will be distributed by NASA's Educational Services Branch to more than 130,000 science classes, fifth grade through college, throughout the world. Seed kits will include space seeds and control seeds, as well as experiment instructions. The Educational Services Branch will collect, analyze, and publish the results.

New Garden. The National Country Garden was officially opened in June 1984 at the National Arboretum in Washington, DC. Designed by landscape architect Guy L. Rando and Associates, Inc., the garden includes displays and demonstrations for home vegetable and flower gardening. Of particular interest are demonstrations of gardening in limited space—townhouse or patio gardening, vertical gardening, and balcony and clothesline gardening.

New Plant Varieties. Two new introductions were made to the impatiens family: Super Elfin "Blush," an apple-blossom pink with a splash of red in the center of each blossom, and "Lipstick," a rich raspberry color. The Super Elfin impatiens are the most popular of all and come in nine other colors—pure white, pink, orchid, rose, red, salmon, scarlet, fuchsia, and orange.

The only flower to receive the All-America award for 1984 was the Border Beauty Rose Hybrid zinnia, introduced by W. Atlee Burpee Co. of Warminster, PA.

Exposition. The International Garden Festival, "Liverpool '84," was held on the banks of the River Mersey in Liverpool, England, from May 2 to Oct. 14, 1984. The largest flower and garden festival ever held in England, "Liverpool '84" saw the transformation of a 250-acre (101-ha) tract of derelict waterfront property into a magnificent display of international theme gardens and horticultural/floral excellence. More than 3 million visitors from some 140 countries visited the exposition.

New Publications. *The Ortho Problem Solver,* a horticultural reference published in 1983 by Ortho Information Services of Chevron Chemical Co., sold out its first edition. October 1984, therefore, saw the publication of a new edition, with more than 1,040 pages, 300 new color photographs (a total of more than 2,500), solutions to 170 more plant and insect problems (total more than 2,000), and a simplified index.

The world's most extensive gardening book series, *Plants and Gardens,* written and published by the Brooklyn (NY) Botanic Garden, expanded its list of titles with "Oriental Herbs and Vegetables" and an updated edition of "Propagation." The series includes more than 60 titles, each devoted to a specific type or aspect of gardening—specialty plants and gardens, Bonsai, Japanese gardens, trees and shrubs, herbs, vegetables, arts and crafts, indoor gardening, and others. Each publication is a well-illustrated manual of 64 to 104 pages.

R.L. SNODSMITH, *Ornamental Horticulturist*

GENETICS

The year 1984 saw advances in the understanding of genetic processes and continuing controversy in the field of genetic engineering. The discovery that RNA can act as a catalyst, the development of a procedure for early detection of the gene for Huntington's disease, the cloning of gene fragments from an extinct animal, and new studies on the genetic bases of alcoholism and criminal behavior were some of the notable advances in research. Among other developments was a court ruling on the use of gene-spliced organisms in a field experiment.

RNA as a Catalyst. Catalysts are substances that alter the rate of a chemical reaction but remain unchanged at the end of the process. Chemical reactions in living organisms are catalyzed by *enzymes,* which consist of proteins and, in some cases, other compounds.

Scientists working with the enzyme *ribonuclease P,* consisting of protein and RNA (ribonucleic acid), discovered that the RNA component alone can perform the catalytic activity of the enzyme, whereas the protein alone cannot.

The discovery suggests that RNA may have been the original "information molecule." The earliest such molecule, it is generally agreed, must have been both simple and capable of catalytic activity. RNA, the simplest known molecule with the capacity to store and transmit information, was now shown to meet the last requirement of the original information molecule.

Huntington's Disease. A dominant genetic disorder that manifests itself in adult life (usually after parenthood), Huntington's disease is a progressively debilitating disease of the nervous system. It usually leads to death. Although there is no known cure, scientists have developed a procedure that permits early identification of individuals who have the gene.

The technique uses a group of enzymes, called *restriction enzymes,* that cut DNA (deoxyribonucleic acid) only at specific "recognition sites." The recognition sites may vary among family lines, yielding DNA fragments of a size that characterize the particular lineage. Thus if a gene causing a disease in one parent's family line happens to be associated with a particular DNA fragment, the presence of such a fragment in a child identifies that child as having the gene for the disorder. In order for this procedure to yield accurate information, the families under study must be large and must include members from several generations.

Extinct Species. Scientists have been able to take salt-preserved muscle tissue of the quagga, an extinct species, and extract fragments of its DNA. These were cloned in bacteria and then retrieved, analyzed, and compared with the DNA of closely related living species. The quagga DNA was found to be most similar to that of the zebra. Cloning techniques in the future should permit the study of genetic material obtained from extinct species.

Alcoholism. The results of a recent study suggest that alcoholism might be a genetic metabolic disease that might be treatable with enzyme replacement therapy. A group of severe alcoholics was found to have elevated blood levels of the chemical compound 2,3 butanediol after consuming a fixed amount of alcohol, while a control group of social drinkers showed no such excess under the same conditions. Animal studies have demonstrated that 2,3 butanediol is produced when the normal chemical pathway for alcohol breakdown is blocked. The implication of the study is that such blocking in humans somehow predisposes an individual to alcoholism. Assuming that the blockage results from the absence of an enzyme, as occurs typically in genetic metabolic diseases, one might conclude that at least some, if not all, alcoholics are genetically incapable of producing an enzyme normally used in alcohol breakdown.

Criminal Behavior. Evidence of a genetic rather than an environmental predisposition to crime was found in a study of criminal conviction rates among 14,427 adoptees in Denmark and both their biological and adoptive parents. Compared with a control group, the adoptees whose adoptive parents had been convicted of a crime showed no statistically significant increase in criminal convictions. However, there was a significant association between criminal convictions in adoptees and biological parents.

In the same study, it was found that siblings who had been placed in different adoptive homes tended to have the same conviction rate. However, in a comparison of half-sib brothers (same mother, different fathers) and full-sib brothers (same parents), it was found that the closer the genetic relationship between adoptees, the greater was the similarity in conviction rates. The association was found to exist in convictions for property crimes (such as theft) but not violent crimes (assault, etc.).

Gene-Splicing Decision. The controversy over genetic engineering continued with a lawsuit over the proposed release of a genetically modified strain of the bacterium *Pseudomonas syringae* on rows of potato plants; scientists wanted to test whether the bacteria could protect the plants from frost in the field as they had in greenhouse experiments. The project had been approved by the Recombinant-DNA Advisory Committee of the National Institutes of Health (NIH).

A U.S. federal court ruled against release of the bacteria because NIH had not conducted an environmental-impact study. The decision has only a limited effect, however, since it applies only to genetic material altered by gene-splicing and not to identical mutants produced by other methods or found in nature.

Louis Levine, *City College of New York*

GEOLOGY

Major explorations of the earth's ocean, crust, and mantle, and widely distributed volcanic and seismic events kept geologists busy during 1984.

Ocean Projects. With the U.S. Senate proclaiming 1984 the "Year of Water" and the year beginning July 1 the "Year of the Ocean," several ambitious ocean research projects were continued or planned.

Joint Oceanographic Institutions, Inc. was awarded a five-year, $141 million contract by the National Science Foundation (NSF) to manage and operate the Ocean Drilling Program (ODP). This major international program, involving ten major oceanographic institutions and expected to last a decade, succeeds the 15-year-long Deep Sea Drilling Project (DSDP), which ended in 1983.

Well under way was Operation Deep Sweep, a project to explore the Pacific Ocean from pole to pole. As part of the program, 50 scientists of the marine geology branch of the U.S. Geological Survey (USGS) planned a 41,000-mi (64 000-km) cruise from above the Arctic Circle off Alaska to McMurdo Sound, Antarctica. An additional 150 scientists from West Germany, France, Australia, and New Zealand eventually will take part. Meanwhile the project made an important discovery southwest of Hawaii. Geologists found nodules with concentrations of cobalt as high as 2.5%. Smaller but still significant concentrations of nickel and platinum also were recorded. It was proposed that a similar ten-year exploration and survey be made to inventory the resources of the 3.9 billion acres (1.6 billion ha) between the U.S. shoreline and the 200-mi offshore limit. (*See also* OCEANOGRAPHY.)

Probing the Continental Crust and Mantle. Though the oil and gas industry in the United States drills more than 10,000 wells each year, little drilling has been done for purely scientific purposes. Now, with improved technology and a pressing need to solve problems revealed by exploratory geophysics, the drilling of deep holes is becoming a reality. Three government agencies took concrete action by signing an agreement by which duplication of, and gaps in, federal studies of the earth's crust would be avoided. The NSF, USGS, and Department of Energy (DOE) signed the pact to create The Interagency Coordinating Group for Continental Scientific Drilling.

Soviet researchers drilling on the Kola Peninsula in the northwest USSR have produced the deepest hole in the world—more than 12 km (7.5 mi). The project, already under way for more than 14 years, has a goal of 15 km (9.3 mi). A turbodrill drives only the bit at the bottom of the hole, not the entire string of pipe. And the project has yielded some interesting discoveries. For example, the researchers did not find the three classic crustal layers—a sedimentary-volcanogenic layer down to 4.7 km (2.9 mi), a granitic layer down to about 7 km (4.3 mi), and a basaltic layer below that. What the researchers found was the granitic layer at 6.8 km (4.2 mi), while the basaltic layer was not yet encountered at all. Unanticipated also was the rapid rise in heat, which could exceed 300°C (572°F) at 15 km (9 mi). Most surprising of all was the discovery of circulating fluids where none were thought possible. Gases, including methane, and strongly mineralized

The September eruption of Mayon volcano, Albay Province, the Philippines, was its worst since 1814.

AP/Wide World

Significant Earthquakes of 1984		
Date	Location	Magnitude (Richter Scale)
Jan. 1	Japan, off south coast of Honshu	6.6
Jan. 8	Indonesia (Sulawesi)	6.7
Feb. 1	Afghanistan	5.9
Feb. 8	Solomon Islands	7.7
Feb. 16	Hindu Kush Mountain region (Asia)	6.0
March 5	Mindanao, Philippines	6.6
March 6	Japan, south of Honshu	6.6
March 20	Central Asia (Uzbek SSR)	7.1
March 25	Kuril Islands (USSR)	7.0
March 28	Papua New Guinea	6.8
April 24	Central California, USA	6.2
April 29	Central Italy	5.3
May 7	Southern Italy	6.0
May 11	Southern Italy	5.4
May 13	Adriatic Sea	5.1
May 26	Prince Edward Island region (south Indian Ocean)	6.5
June 24	Dominican Republic region	6.7
June 24	Dominican Republic region	5.1
July 5	Solomon Islands	6.8
Aug. 7	Kyushu, Japan	6.9
Sept. 9	Northern California, off coast	6.7
Sept. 14	Honshu, Japan	6.2
Sept. 17	South of Kermadec Islands (southwest Pacific)	6.5
Sept. 18	Turkey	5.6
Sept. 19	Japan, off Honshu	6.9
Sept. 28	South of Fiji Islands	6.8
Oct. 15	Tonga Islands	6.5
Oct. 18	Turkey	5.4
Nov. 1	Central Mid-Atlantic Ridge	7.2
Nov. 15	Loyalty Islands region (southwest Pacific)	6.5
Nov. 17	Northern Sumatra	7.4
Nov. 20	Mindanao, Philippines	7.1
Nov. 23	Vanuatu Islands region	6.7
Dec. 28	Near East Coast of Kamchatka (USSR)	6.7

Source: National Earthquake Information Center

waters were found even at depths of 11.5 km (7.1 mi).

In the United States, meanwhile, geologists were laying plans for a 10-km (6.2-mi) hole to be drilled in the southern Appalachians. There, according to intensive seismic investigations, crustal layers were piled up by massive tectonic movements, forcing a slice of sedimentary rocks and the upper part of the underlying basement onto sediments still in their place of origin. The proposed hole would test the thrust theory and provide other major information.

Relying chiefly on seismic data, geophysicists from the California Institute of Technology and Harvard University worked on three-dimensional models of the earth's mantle. Already there was evidence that lateral inhomogeneities prevail and that these are related to slow convective processes. Surface hot spots such as Iceland and Hawaii underlie immense ascending currents that reach deep into the mantle.

Volcanic and Seismic Events. Although geologic events took relatively few human lives in 1984, the year was notable for an unusually wide geographic distribution of earthquakes (*see* accompanying list) and eruptions. Hawaii's Kilauea, probably the world's most ac-

tive volcano, erupted in January and continued spewing lava with Old Faithful–like regularity through most of the year. Nearby Mauna Loa began erupting on March 25 for the first time in nearly nine years. A lava flow 17 mi (27 km) long for a time threatened Hilo, the largest city on the island. The eruption of Mauna Loa marked the first time since 1868 that the two Hawaiian volcanoes were active simultaneously. On the U.S. mainland, Mount St. Helens in the state of Washington also was active. Elsewhere, the Mayon volcano in Albay Province, the Philippines, began a series of violent eruptions on September 12. Lava, ash, and steam were expelled, and thousands of persons were forced to leave their homes.

WILLIAM LEE STOKES
University of Utah

GEORGIA

In 1984, Georgians witnessed the continued growth of Atlanta's economy, the establishment of regional banking, the indictment of state officials and consequent reform legislation, and a pronounced shift toward Republican candidates in the general election.

Economy. Population and employment figures for metropolitan Atlanta revealed a booming economy. Ranked third in population growth among the nation's cities, Atlanta also provided more new jobs than had been expected. The annual income in Atlanta outpaced the national average by approximately $1,000 per person, and residential construction permits soared.

Regional Banking. Gov. Joe Frank Harris signed into law a bill making Georgia the first southeastern state to allow regional interstate banking. As a result, Georgia's banks can buy or merge with banks in any of the nine regional states with similar laws, and banks in those states have similar privileges in Georgia. One of the three largest bank holding companies, Trust Company of Georgia, has announced plans to merge with Sun Banks of Florida.

Indictments. Labor Commissioner Sam Caldwell was indicted on various fraud and racketeering charges. The legislative fiscal officer Cary Bond was indicted for conspiring to defraud the state in connection with a renovation of the state capitol.

Reform Legislation. The capitol renovation scandal, abuses in the pension system, and corruption in the Labor Department led to the passage of several reform bills. One such bill mandated competitive bidding on legislative construction and purchase contracts. Pension reform legislation was prompted by the controversy in 1983 over former Gov. George Busbee's invoking the state's involuntary separation rule so that he would qualify for a pension. It also resulted from the fact that in-

Walter Mondale hoped to gain support in the South by having Georgia's Bert Lance (right) serve as general chairman of his presidential campaign. However, the appointment was criticized by other Democrats and was short-lived.

dicted officials like Bond and Caldwell were, under existing laws, eligible to receive pension benefits. Two proposed constitutional amendments that redefined pension eligibility to meet these concerns were ratified by voters in the general election.

Other Legislation. The first statewide curfew bill for children under 17 was approved as was a bill to reinstate Georgia's compulsory school attendance law. The General Assembly passed legislation giving legal standing to "living wills." A decade-long effort by supporters of Dr. Martin Luther King, Jr., to have a state holiday set aside for him was rewarded in 1984 as the legislature approved a Harris administration measure commemorating King's birthday.

Elections. President Ronald Reagan, who captured 60% of the vote in Georgia, won strong support from white voters in suburban and rural sections. Walter Mondale drew most of his backing from urban areas and the Black Belt of central Georgia. Blacks turned out in record numbers. More than 60% of the regis-

tered black voters went to the polls, the majority of them supporting the Democratic ticket.

Republicans swept most posts in the Atlanta suburbs, but the GOP gain statewide was modest despite Reagan's appeal. A net Republican gain of only five seats in the General Assembly and the failure to oust two Democratic incumbents on the Public Service Commission disappointed Republican leaders. The GOP did provide the major upset in the election when Republican challenger Pat Swindall defeated six-term Congressman Elliott Levitas in the fourth district. Most analysts noted that the defeat came as a result of the reapportionment of the district two years earlier when black areas were joined to the fifth district, leaving the fourth a district of predominantly white, wealthy, college-educated voters.

In the sixth congressional district Republican Newt Gingrich won an easy victory, and the popular U.S. Sen. Sam Nunn was reelected by a wide margin.

Education Review Commission. After 16 months of deliberation, a blue-ribbon group of citizens presented a plan to Governor Harris containing a sweeping set of educational reforms, including full-day, mandatory kindergarten, stiffer standards and more pay for teachers, and a radical new system of school finance. The governor hailed the plan as a "campaign of excellence in Georgia education," but lawmakers and teacher groups immediately announced opposition to some of the proposals.

Death of Rev. Martin Luther King, Sr. Georgians mourned the death of "Daddy King," father of civil rights leader Martin Luther King, Jr. Testimonials poured in from around the nation for the 84-year-old Atlanta pastor, who suffered a heart attack on November 11.

KAY BECK
Georgia State University

GEORGIA · Information Highlights

Area: 58,910 sq mi (152 576 km²).
Population (July 1, 1983 est.): 5,732,000.
Chief Cities (July 1, 1982 est.): Atlanta, the capital, 428,153; Columbus, 174,348; Savannah, 145,699.
Government (1984): *Chief Officers*—governor, Joe Frank Harris (D); lt. gov., Zell Miller (D). *General Assembly*—Senate, 56 members; House of Representatives, 180 members.
State Finances (fiscal year 1983): *Revenues,* $6,992,000,000; *expenditures,* $6,563,000,000.
Personal Income (1983): $59,494,000,000; per capita, $10,379.
Labor Force (May 1984): *Civilian labor force,* 2,771,900; *unemployed,* 162,300 (5.9% of total force).
Education: *Enrollment* (fall 1982)—public elementary schools, 739,178; public secondary, 314,511; colleges and universities, (fall 1983), 201,453. *Public school expenditures* (1982–83), $2,123,-585,842 ($2,169 per pupil).

In a year of extensive travel, Chancellor Helmut Kohl (center, right) *made a six-day visit to Israel in January.*

GERMANY

In 1984, bilateral relations between the two German states, the Federal Republic of Germany (West Germany) and the German Democratic Republic (East Germany), continued to improve. Following West Germany's guarantee of a one billion mark ($400 million) loan to East Germany, East Germany eased travel restrictions for visiting West Germans and lowered the minimum age limit for its own citizens wishing to travel to West Germany. In the first five months of 1984, a record 30,000 East Germans were allowed to emigrate to West Germany, the highest number since the Berlin Wall was built in 1961. Economic and trade activity between the two states also expanded. An agreement between the Volkswagen company and East Germany called for the construction of a large plant manufacturing automobile engines in East Germany. About half of the engines produced were to be used in East German cars, with the remainder exported to West Germany. In July, Bonn announced a second loan guarantee to East Germany for an additional one billion marks. Finally, Erich Honecker was scheduled to visit Bonn in September; it would have been the first visit by an East German head of state to West Germany.

But the rapid pace of this German détente was unsettling to Moscow. Following a strong anti–West German press campaign in *Pravda,* which was in fact also directed at East Germany, East Germany announced in September that the Honecker trip had been postponed. Apparently the reluctance of East Germany to follow Moscow's hard line toward the West in the wake of the deployment of new North Atlantic Treaty Organization (NATO) missiles aroused Soviet suspicions about the loyalty of its East German ally to the socialist camp. Both German states, however, appear determined to continue on this course of closer economic and cultural ties, albeit with less fanfare.

The improvement in intra-German relations as pursued by the West German government of Chancellor Helmut Kohl could, however, also rekindle old fears of a revived nationalism among Germany's neighbors. In September, the Italian foreign minister, Giulio Andreotti, like Chancellor Kohl a Christian Democrat, caused a sensation in West Germany when he commented in Rome that while ''West Germany's quest for better relations with East Germany was welcomed, it should not be overdone.'' He added that ''Pan-Germanism must be put behind us. There are two German states and that is the way it should remain.'' The government officially reacted with shock and dismay to the statement, which sounded similar to the approach Moscow had taken to the German détente. Andreotti later explained that he had been quoted out of context and that he did not intend to link ''Pan-Germanism'' to the policies of West Germany, or to suggest that West Germany was not committed to the existing political division of Europe as set down in postwar treaties. Some West Germans felt that Andreotti was simply stating openly

President Karl Carstens accepts the resignation of Economics Minister Otto Lambsdorff (right) on June 27. Lambsdorff had been indicted for corruption in the political payoff scandal known as the "Flick affair."

Gaby Sommer, Gamma-Liaison

what most Western leaders have long thought privately about German reunification, namely that it would create more problems than it would resolve.

Although the Social Democratic Party (SPD) had been as dismayed as the government by Andreotti's comments, the party did criticize the Kohl administration for its lack of long-range perspective in its policies toward East Germany and for failing to consider the effect a sudden improvement in intra-German relations would have in both Eastern and Western Europe. The Social Democrats have stressed that policies toward East Germany must be in tune with West Germany's general approach to Eastern Europe and the Soviet Union. Failing this, the Moscow leadership hoped to be able to use the specter of a reunited, "revanchist" Germany to keep its East European allies in line.

WEST GERMANY • Information Highlights

Official Name: Federal Republic of Germany.
Location: North-central Europe.
Area: 96,346 sq mi (249 535 km²).
Population (mid-1984 est.): 61,400,000.
Chief Cities (June 30, 1982): Bonn, the capital 292,200; West Berlin, 1,879,100; Hamburg, 1,630,400; Munich, 1,228,200.
Government: *Head of state,* Richard von Weizsäcker, president (took office July 1, 1984). *Head of government,* Helmut Kohl, federal chancellor (took office Oct. 1982). *Legislature*—Parliament: Bundesrat and Bundestag.
Monetary Unit: Deutsche mark (3.095 D. marks equal U.S.$1, Dec. 5, 1984).
Gross National Product (1982 U.S.$): $658,400,-000,000.
Economic Indexes (1983): *Consumer Prices* (1970 = 100), all items, 189.7; food, 175.1. *Industrial Production* (1975 = 100), 115.
Foreign Trade (1983 U.S.$): *Imports,* $151,276,-000,000; *exports,* $169,422,000,000.

Federal Republic of Germany (West Germany)

For the ruling Christian Democratic–Free Democratic (CDU-FDP) coalition of Chancellor Kohl, 1984 was a difficult year. The government's troubles began in January when the defense minister, Manfred Wörner, dismissed a high-ranking army general for alleged homosexual activity. The general vehemently denied the charges, and a subsequent investigation found them to be groundless. Chancellor Kohl ordered the general reinstated (he later retired), but Kohl refused to accept the resignation of Defense Minister Wörner.

In May the government announced it would introduce a bill granting an amnesty to party officials and contributors involved in past violations of the party finance laws. The ensuing public uproar over the proposal prompted the government to withdraw the bill. The Free Democrats were especially vocal in their opposition, and many in the party demanded the resignation of Hans-Dietrich Genscher, foreign minister and vice-chancellor, as the leader of the FDP. To avoid a major intra-party conflict, Genscher agreed to step down as party chairman in early 1986. In June, the economics minister, Otto Lambsdorff, who was also a Free Democrat, resigned after being indicted for malfeasance in office. Lambsdorff was charged with accepting illegal contributions to his party from the Friedrich Flick Industrial Holdings Co., in exchange for a favorable tax ruling by his ministry.

The government's difficulties continued into October, when the CDU leader and president of the Bundestag, Rainer Barzel, resigned because of allegations that he too had received extensive financial support from the ubiquitous

Flick company. The Barzel affair provoked widespread demands that West German politicians, like their counterparts in the United States, be subject to financial disclosure laws.

The Greens, who entered the Bundestag for the first time in 1983, were the major political beneficiaries of the government's problems. In several local and state elections throughout the year and in the June election for the European Parliament, the Greens received more than 8% of the vote, well above their 5.6% in the 1983 national election. In spite of various organizational and leadership problems, the Greens' emphasis on environmental protection and disarmament struck a responsive chord among increasing numbers of German voters.

The largest opposition party, the Social Democrats, made little progress in 1984 toward returning to power. Intraparty conflicts over how to deal with the Greens, the party's economic policies, and its own involvement in the Flick affair all undercut its efforts to attract support. For many voters desiring to send a message to the government in Bonn, the Greens, and not the Social Democrats, had become the more effective opposition party.

The Economy. In 1984 the West German economy continued the modest recovery that began in early 1983. Expectations of a healthy 4% growth rate, however, were dimmed by a six-week strike of 300,000 metal workers in the spring. The strike practically shut down the German automobile industry and other impor-

The first five months of 1984 saw the largest wave of legal migration from East to West Germany since 1961.

Regis Bossu, Sygma

tant manufacturing sectors. Ironically, the high unemployment rate was a major reason for the work stoppage. It was not the usual concerns about wages and fringe benefits that were at issue, but rather the length of the workweek. In order to create more jobs, the trade unions called for a reduction of the normal workweek from 40 to 35 hours, with no loss of pay. Employer associations flatly rejected this demand as unrealistic, given the fragile condition of the economy. They also argued that a reduced workweek would not produce a significant number of new jobs but instead would increase costs and decrease productivity.

In a departure from its position in past labor disputes, the Bonn government clearly favored the employers. Chancellor Kohl called the strike incomprehensible in light of the general economic situation. A settlement was finally reached according to which the metal workers received a reduction in the workweek to 38.5 hours, with a modest wage increase. Vacation, sick leave, and "free" day provisions were increased to further reduce the actual time spent on the job.

Continued high interest rates in the United States also siphoned off much domestic capital that could have been used to expand the domestic economy. Little significant progress was made in 1984 in reducing unemployment, which remained at about 8.5%. Two bright spots in the economy were the inflation rate, which dropped to about 2% by the fourth quarter, and a booming export market, which produced a balance-of-trade surplus for 1984 of more than $15 billion.

Social Conditions. Continued high unemployment among young people and growing resentment against the large number of legal and illegal foreign residents in West Germany were two of the major social issues in 1984. Traditionally, German business and industrial enterprises together with the government and the schools have prided themselves on providing a sufficient number of apprenticeship and trainee positions for those young people who wish to embark on vocational careers. Indeed, the German system of vocational training has been regarded as a model by other countries. In recent years, however, there has not been an adequate number of these positions. The prospect of an alienated youth subculture is very disturbing to German policymakers. In an attempt to meet this problem, a shorter workweek and early retirement plans were under serious consideration in 1984 by the trade unions and the government, respectively.

The Kohl government's program of bonuses and severance payments to foreign workers who decided to return, with their families, to their homeland produced a major drop in 1984 in the number of foreign residents. In all, about 250,000 foreign workers and their families were repatriated to their countries of origin.

The German Democratic Republic marked its 35th anniversary with a vast military parade in East Berlin in October.

The Environment. Throughout 1984 public concern about the environment continued to grow. The most pressing issue was acid rain and its effect on Germany's fabled forests. Government-sponsored studies found that about one third of all trees were affected by it. To help meet this problem, the Kohl government introduced legislation requiring lead-free gasoline in all automobiles produced after Jan. 1, 1986. From 1989 on, all cars, new and used, that are registered in the country must be fitted with catalytic converters. To encourage the voluntary use of converters, the tax on unleaded gas will be reduced beginning in mid-1985 and the tax on leaded fuel will be increased. Also, buyers of new cars with converters will be exempt from car taxes for up to ten years; the tax on ordinary cars, however, will increase.

Foreign Policy. West Germany in 1984 continued its efforts to reduce tensions between the United States and the Soviet Union. In May, Foreign Minister Genscher met with Soviet leaders in Moscow, but his proposals for a resumption of arms-control talks were rejected. Indeed, shortly after Genscher's visit the Soviet Union launched a press and media campaign against West German "revanchism," in an attempt to revive the image of a militarist, expansionist German state. In addition to its impact on East Germany, the "revanchism" campaign was a signal to West Germany that Moscow was not willing to forgive and forget the 1983 deployment of new NATO missiles on West German soil. Yet in spite of all the rhetoric, economic ties between the two countries continued to grow. In October a consortium of West German banks agreed to lend about $250 million to the Soviet Union, a loan that was guaranteed by the West German government.

Within the European Community (EC), West Germany attempted in 1984 to mediate the dispute between Britain and the other European Community members over agricultural price supports. The government of Prime Minister Margaret Thatcher threatened to withdraw from the EC unless changes were made in the amounts Britain had to pay to support West Europe's farmers. The West Germans who, like the British, pay more into the agricultural fund than they receive in benefits, supported the compromise agreement reached at Fontainebleau in June.

In 1984 the West German government also sought to play an active role in Latin America. In July, Chancellor Kohl visited Argentina and Mexico. He was the first major Western leader to visit Argentina since the election of President Raúl Alfonsín. The chief purpose of the trip was to urge the Argentine government to impose austerity measures as a condition for the rescheduling of its large Western debt. West Germany is the largest single government lender to Argentina. In Central America, West Germany emerged in 1984 as the strongest European supporter of the new Duarte government in El Salvador. Following Duarte's election in March, the Kohl government released $28 million in development assistance. West Germany's aid to Nicaragua, however, was suspended.

German Democratic Republic
(East Germany)

In 1984, East Germany celebrated its 35th anniversary. In October a huge parade of goose-stepping troops accompanying Soviet-built tanks and missiles was held in East Berlin to commemorate the event. Soviet Foreign Minister Andrei Gromyko offered congratulations from the Soviet Union, and a new 15-year trade and economic pact was signed by both countries. These surface events, however, could not obscure the dramatic developments in East Germany's relationship to the West and the Soviet bloc that had taken place earlier in the year. East German leader Erich Honecker, in spite of opposition from Moscow, attempted to salvage détente at least with regard to West Germany.

Honecker's policy of "damage limitation" following the 1983 collapse of U.S.–Soviet arms talks in Geneva produced East Germany's first serious rift with the Soviet Union in its history. While Moscow talked of a "palisade of missiles" between the two German states, Honecker intensified his efforts to normalize and improve intra-German relations. In the fall of 1984, Moscow attempted to put a halt to this independent policy. A series of articles in *Pravda,* echoed by the Soviets' surrogate press in Prague, attacked West Germany for its attempt to subvert the East German regime through economic aid. *Pravda*'s real target, of course, was East Germany. A few weeks later, Honecker announced the postponement of his planned trip to Bonn. Yet East Germany also stressed that its policy of improving relations with West Germany would continue. After the 1983 missile deployment, the East Germans clearly had taken advantage of the leadership vacuum in Moscow—created by the lingering and ultimately fatal illness of Yuri Andropov—to pursue a more independent foreign policy. By the end of 1984, however, with Konstantin Chernenko installed as head of both the party and the state, the Moscow leadership question had apparently been clarified to the point where a strong signal could be sent to Honecker.

Political Conditions. The détente with West Germany has been very popular with East Germans. The ruling elite in East Germany probably enjoys more popular support than at any time in its history. Honecker's policy toward West Germany further undercut East Germany's own dissident peace movement, which had been weakened by arrests and forced deportations. Public resentment against East Germany's decision to join the Soviet Olympic boycott was also somewhat offset by this policy.

Economy. From its inception, détente has been closely connected with East Germany's economic situation, specifically its large debt to the West and its domestic supply problems. In 1984, East Germany did make some progress in reducing its Western debt, but it did so at the expense of a domestic austerity program that has resulted in stagnating levels of domestic consumption and growing shortages of quality consumer goods.

Foreign Policy. East Germany in 1984 also attempted a cautious opening to other Western nations. For the first time, a U.S. secretary of state formally met with the East German counterpart. Similar meetings at this level took place in London and Paris. East Germany remained, however, an important assistant to the Soviet Union in the Third World. The most technically proficient of the Eastern bloc countries, East Germany has widespread economic and technical assistance missions throughout Asia and Africa.

West Berlin

The improvement in intra-German relations and the continued modest economic recovery in West Germany also benefited West Berlin in 1984. Unemployment declined, while industrial production increased. For the first time since 1978 there was no net loss of jobs in the city, as 1,500 new employment positions were created.

The city, however, lost its popular lord mayor, Richard von Weizsäcker, who became president of West Germany. His successor, Eberhard Diepgen, became the youngest man ever to hold the office. Diepgen could expect strong opposition in the 1985 city elections from Hans Apel, the former West German defense minister, who will seek to regain the city for the Social Democrats. Both major parties must also contend with the strong opposition of the Greens. Drawing upon the large number of students and a radical "alternative" youth subculture, the Greens will probably become the third-strongest party in the city and will hold the balance of power in the Berlin parliament.

DAVID P. CONRADT, *University of Florida*

EAST GERMANY • Information Highlights

Official Name; German Democratic Republic.
Location: North-central Europe.
Area: 41,612 sq mi (107 774 km²).
Population (mid-1984 est.): 16,700,000.
Chief Cities (June 30, 1981): East Berlin, the capital, 1,157,600; Leipzig, 561,900; Dresden, 516,600.
Government: *Head of state,* Erich Honecker, chairman of the Council of State. *Head of government,* Willi Stoph, chairman of the Council of Ministers. General secretary of the Socialist Unity (Communist) Party, Erich Honecker (took office 1971). *Legislature* (unicameral)—Volkskammer (People's Chamber).
Monetary Unit: DDR mark (2.9 DDR marks equal U.S.$1, Aug. 1984).
Gross National Product (1982 U.S.$): $165,600,-000,000.
Economic Index (1983): *Industrial Production* (1975 = 100), 143.
Foreign Trade (1983 U.S.$): *Imports,* $21,524,-000,000; *exports,* $23,793,000,000.

Stuart Franklin, Sygma

A bitter strike by coal miners, the longest major strike in British history, had far-reaching political effects.

GREAT BRITAIN

As 1984 began, there was no reason to believe that it would be other than a typical dull and uneventful postelection year in Great Britain. The government had a huge majority, and the opposition was divided. Yet by November, Britons were looking back on one of the most tumultuous years in their history, a year which almost saw the whole cabinet wiped out in an audacious assassination attempt by the Irish Republican Army (IRA).

The Tories began the year with an overall parliamentary majority of 144, a superiority rarely seen in Britain and one that made Her Majesty's ''loyal opposition'' almost an irrelevance. To the disappointment of some of its supporters and most of its critics, the government began and ended the year with the same rigid monetary policy that had characterized its first term in office, and at year's end the huge unemployment figure of more than 3 million persisted.

It was perhaps because the Labour Party had been reduced to impotence by the large Conservative majority in Parliament that the next major challenge to Prime Minister Mar-

garet Thatcher's government came from two left-wing leaders who were outside of Parliament: Arthur Scargill, the leader of the miners' union, and Ken Livingstone of the Greater London Council, the municipal authority that directs much of the day-to-day life of the capital. Scargill's challenge came in the form of a strike, and Livingstone's in a highly effective propaganda campaign against the government's attempt to destroy his power base by abolishing his council.

The Miners' Strike. The miners' strike developed into the longest major strike in British history, and the most bitter since the general strike of 1926. The strike began when the National Coal Board, the controlling body of the state-owned coal mines, decided to close down 20 of the most unproductive of Britain's coal mines. Scargill and the executive board of the National Union of Mineworkers called a strike in all the coalfields. The call was controversial inasmuch as the general membership had not been asked to vote on it. Although the executive board argued that as an elected body it had the authority to call a strike, Scargill's critics replied that a vote had not been taken because two previous strike proposals had been voted down.

The strike began in March, the worst time for the miners because coal stocks then were very high, and summer, which is a period of low demand, was approaching. The union membership split over the decision, and many miners, especially in the Nottingham coalfields in the Midlands, continued to work, producing about one quarter of the normal national output. Small groups and even individual miners in other areas also decided to work on. The scene was set for some of the most violent confrontations between police and strikers ever seen in Britain.

Mrs. Thatcher, a confrontational politician, said that every miner had the right to work and would be entitled to state protection if he so chose. The country's police forces were sent from their home bases to mining areas to open avenues through picket lines for those miners who wished to cross them.

The battles between thousands of miners and the police force were frequently so violent that by year's end 13 men had died and more than 3,000 had been injured.

Both the coal board and the union met periodically throughout the strike, but neither seemed ready to compromise. Scargill insisted that no mines—except those that were unsafe or those whose ores were exhausted—should be closed. He argued that the surrender of one mine would lead to the wholesale closure of others, and if the mines were closed hundreds of small villages that existed wholly on the earnings from them would be destroyed. The National Coal Board, led by the dour and taciturn Scottish-American Ian MacGregor, refused in turn to alter its plans to close the 20 mines. He contended that all mines had a limited life and that to insist that each one, no matter how inefficient, be permanently maintained would only devastate the industry because its coal would become so expensive that customers would turn either to other forms of energy or other coal suppliers.

In Scargill the miners had a leader who not only wanted to save coal mines but had political ambitions as well. His hardline tactics suggested that he was aiming at a rerun of the miners' strike of 1974. At that time the ruling Conservative government of Thatcher's predecessor, Edward Heath, was forced to limit industry to a three-day workweek because the lack of coal for power stations had drastically reduced the supply of electricity. Heath had been forced by the strike to call a general election on the issue of "who runs the country," and he was resoundingly defeated.

Thatcher is made of sterner stuff, and with her huge parliamentary majority she has no need to call an election. But she was badly served by MacGregor, the coal board chairman, who had made his reputation as a ruthless cost cutter in the U.S. coal industry. MacGregor, not accustomed to dealing with powerful unions and underestimating the strength of Scargill's own support among miners, made little attempt to explain his case to the public. But toward the end of the year he was pressured into appointing Michael Eaton, an experienced negotiator, to handle the coal board's presentation of its case to the public.

Scargill did not play his own cards particularly well. He persistently refused to call a vote by the union members, despite constant demands that he do so, and in October his union was fined £200,000 and he himself £1,000 for contempt of court. The fines were levied after Scargill insisted his strike was legal, despite an earlier court ruling declaring that it was illegal. When the union refused to pay, the court ordered its total assets of about £9 million to be sequestered. Scargill made his cause even more unpopular by sending emissaries to Libya to request aid from "Libyan trade unionists." As there are no free trade unions in Libya, the assumption was that the union was asking Libya's leader, Col. Muammar el-Qaddafi, a man thoroughly disliked in Britain, for funds to support the strike.

Scargill's position was further eroded in November when the mine foremen's union refused to join the walkout. By the middle of the month a back-to-work movement was under way, although the National Union of Mineworkers denied the claim of the coal board that 69,000 union members were returning to work.

Effect on Labour and the Tories. The miners' strike colored all political life in Britain. Its fallout was most noticeable in the Labour Party where a new and inexperienced leader, Neil Kinnock, a 42-year-old Welshman, was trying to assert his authority in the wake of Labour's overwhelming defeat in the 1983 election. The party was split in its reaction to the strike. The left wing of the party, led by the veteran Tony Benn, demanded full party support for the strikers. However, the right wing held back, arguing that Scargill was behaving undemocratically. The strike also split the trades union movement. Because of the divided opinion in these two major British socialist institutions, Kinnock, a vigorous leader and compelling speaker, was seen to be having trouble controlling his own party. Thatcher and the Conservatives, on the other hand, were well ahead in the polls, by nine points near the end of November.

The Economy. Tory government popularity had little to do with Thatcher's legislative program, which had done nothing to solve the country's major problem, namely its huge unemployment rate. The number of unemployed never dropped below 3 million, Britain's largest total since World War II. Tens of thousands of workers had been jobless for more than three years, and many in the over-50 group never expected to work again. The government had contended that once it brought inflation under control, business would prosper as prices stabilized. The government had in fact reduced inflation to 5.0%, one of the lowest rates in Europe. But industry, handicapped by rigid unions and unsophisticated management and debilitated by interest rates of about 10%, failed to respond as had been expected. Unemployment remained high and showed no sign of decreasing. Meanwhile the government resisted all calls to pump up the economy by injecting money into state-financed projects. Unemployment will clearly be the major problem facing the government as it moves toward the next election. This problem was even acknowledged by the Conservatives at the grassroots level. At the party's annual conference in October, delegate after delegate warned that the party was increasingly being viewed as cold, indifferent, and uncaring about joblessness.

Terrorism. The conference, held in the seaside resort of Brighton, would have been a relatively uncomfortable one for Mrs. Thatcher, who on the whole had a lackluster year to look back on. But the dull speeches and party unease over unemployment were forgotten when the IRA exploded a huge bomb in the ornate Grand Hotel where Mrs. Thatcher and most of her cabinet were staying. The bomb, which was triggered by a delayed timing device, was in a fifth floor bathroom and could have been planted days before the conference, exploded just before 3 A.M. on Friday, October 12. A central section of the hotel facade and a huge chimney cascaded into the basement, killing five, including one member of Parliament, and injuring 32.

Photos, UPI/Bettmann

The Irish Republican Army claimed responsibility for the bombing of the Grand Hotel in Brighton, left, where Prime Minister Thatcher and much of her cabinet were staying during the Conservative Party conference. Unscathed, Thatcher later addressed the conference, saying "all attempts to destroy democracy by terrorism will fail."

Mrs. Thatcher's own bathroom was badly damaged by the falling rubble, and a prominent cabinet minister, Norman Tebbit, regarded by many as Mrs. Thatcher's natural successor as Tory leader, was buried under tons of rubble and only taken to safety after firemen had scrabbled in the wreckage for four hours to extract him. Mrs. Thatcher, who was still working when the bomb went off, appeared live on television within an hour, looking as immaculate in a dark suit and pearls as if she had just come from a beauty salon. Her attendance at the conference within hours of the blast and her final speech to the delegates—in which she offered no new economic initiatives but said that democracy would never give in to bombers—was greeted with almost hysterical applause and adulation by her supporters. In a sense the bombing was a miniature rerun of the Falklands War, when Mrs. Thatcher was overnight turned into the "Iron Lady" heroine of the country. Her defiance of the Brighton bombers produced much the same effect, and her standing in the polls jumped to its highest for the year.

The bombing was a propaganda triumph for the IRA. Although the bomb did not kill a major political figure, the assassination attempt showed that the organization had the capability of striking at the heart of the British govern-

ment with the most sophisticated weapons. Until the Brighton bombing, the IRA had not had an especially good year by its own standards: the number of soldiers and police killed by the IRA in Northern Ireland in 1984 was one of the lowest recorded since the British army had gone into Ulster in 1969. The bombing was seen, however, as a great morale booster for the IRA and came, perhaps predictably, after the IRA had suffered a major military setback. This setback had been the seizure at sea by the Irish navy of a trawler loaded with seven tons of modern weapons that the IRA had bought in the United States.

The IRA bombing was the most serious of the terrorist acts launched in Britain in 1984, but by no means the only fatal one. Because Britain traditionally has been a haven for political refugees from all over the world, foreigners have tended to fight their battles there. Scotland Yard's antiterrorist branch finds that about three fourths of the cases it investigates involve groups other than the IRA. In February, for example, the assistant commissioner for India in the Midlands city of Birmingham was kidnapped and later found murdered. His killers claimed to be members of a previously unknown group, Kashmir Liberation Army, which said it was fighting for the independence of the Indian state of Kashmir.

In March, a series of nonfatal bombings was launched against Libyan opponents of Muammar el-Qaddafi. In July, at the small Stansted airport to the east of London, police seized a crate about to be loaded onto a cargo plane bound for Nigeria. Inside the crate was the current Nigerian military regime's "most wanted man," Umaru Dikko, who was bound and drugged. A former transport minister, he is alleged to have embezzled millions of dollars worth of government money. In the crate with Dikko was a well-known Israeli anesthetist, and in another crate were two more Israeli nationals. The three Israelis and a Nigerian were indicted for Dikko's kidnapping.

Before the Brighton bombing, however, the terrorist affair that had most outraged the country was the shooting on April 17 of an unarmed policewoman, Constable Yvonne Fletcher, in the heart of London. Fletcher was one of a group of police monitoring a demonstration against the Qaddafi regime outside the embassy in St. James's Square. As the demonstrators shouted anti-Qaddafi slogans, a burst of submachine gun fire was sprayed into the square from the first floor of the embassy. Yvonne Fletcher was the only person killed. Her death in the arms of other police officers was shown on television screens across the country.

Because the embassy was diplomatic property, the police were unable to storm it. Instead the police laid siege to it, waiting for the gunmen to come out. The problem for the British government, however, was that more than 8,000 British nationals were living in Libya, mainly working in the oilfields and on construction projects. They were all "potential hostages." After 11 days the government reluctantly had to face diplomatic reality, and 30 Libyans, the killer of Yvonne Fletcher among them, were allowed to march out of the embassy and return to Libya, undoubtedly taking the murder weapon in their diplomatic baggage. Diplomatic relations between the two countries were broken shortly after the killing.

The Value of the Pound Sterling. While stories of bombings and murders made spectacular headlines, the longest running story, apart from the miners' strike, was the continuing decline of the pound sterling. The currency began the year at what was then regarded as a low level of $1.43 to the pound sterling, then fell in value throughout most of the year, at one point in December reaching an all time low of just over $1.16. The fall was so inexorable that City of London dealers planned "parity parties" to mark the day when the currency would reach a rate of one pound for one U.S. dollar.

Politicians and economists gave two reasons for the decline of the pound, which was joined in its fall by most major European currencies. The major cause was seen as high U.S. interest rates, which attracted speculators and dealers to move away from other currencies to invest in U.S. dollars. Even the most conservative British politicians were critical of huge U.S. budget deficits, which contributed to the high interest rates in the United States. Nigel Lawson, the most rigid of monetarist British chancellors of the exchequer, said testily of U.S. fiscal policy in early June, "It's rather an old fallacy that the only way you can have a recovery is by having a budget deficit." The second major cause of the decline in the pound sterling, which is supported by Britain's earnings from its North Sea oil, was the fall in world oil prices. In October, Britain was forced to drop the price of its oil by $1.50 a barrel to match a similar decrease by Norway.

The decline in the value of the currency had some beneficial effects, the main one being that Britain's exports, especially to the United States, became much cheaper. On the other hand, imported raw materials increased in price. An unwelcome side effect of the currency's slide was the spiraling cost of the Trident submarine-launched nuclear missile system, which Britain is buying from the United States to replace its aging Polaris strategic missile system. As the pound lost value against the U.S.

W. Achtner, Sygma

The siege of the Libyan Embassy in London, where pro-Qaddafi "student revolutionaries" and accredited diplomats were holed up for 11 days after the shooting of an unarmed policewoman in the street below, ended on April 28. With the British government concerned for the safety of British nationals living in Libya, the 30 men inside the embassy were set free and allowed to return to Tripoli.

dollar, the cost of the Trident system increased, raising the question of whether the system should be scrapped before its increased price caused too much distortion of the budget.

Diplomacy. In May the New Ireland Forum, a group of politicians, clerics, and other interested parties from both Northern Ireland and the Republic of Ireland, who had been meeting under the republic's auspices, produced their final report on the future of the divided island. The report suggested alternative ways of governing Northern Ireland: by joint rule by London and Dublin or with Northern Ireland as a federal state under the republic. The British reaction was lukewarm, and in late November Prime Minister Thatcher said that neither unification, nor confederation, nor joint authority over Northern Ireland would be acceptable.

In March, Britain had its annual disagreement with its fellow Common Market members on the size of Britain's payments into the European Community (EC). Britain again asserted that its payments were far too high. At a meeting in Fontainebleau, France, in June the community agreed to rebate to Britain $800 million on its 1984 payments and $600 on its 1983 payments. But when Britain vetoed a proposal agreed on by the other nine members of the community for covering the community's budget deficit for 1984, the European Parliament in July blocked payment of the $600 million rebate. However, by the time of the Dublin summit in December, Britain and the EC seemed to have solved the repayment problem.

The major diplomatic achievement of the year was undoubtedly the conclusion of an agreement with the People's Republic of China over the future of Hong Kong, much of which has to revert to China in accordance with a treaty leasing the land to Britain until 1997. All experts agreed that the British got the best deal that they could have expected for the 5.3 million people of their last major colony. The Chinese government agreed that Hong Kong would become a special administrative region after 1997, with a high degree of autonomy. This autonomy would preserve the basic freedoms that now exist in Hong Kong, including freedom to travel and to strike, a freely convertible currency, independent finances, and the laissez-faire business rules that now make it one of the world's major trading centers.

Observers agreed that Britain had no choice but to take Chinese guarantees at face value. Pessimists pointed out that China had made similar promises to the people of Shanghai when they took power in 1948, promises that they broke within a year of making them. Optimists argued that China would not interfere with Hong Kong because the colony was the major source of foreign currency and because China's long-term target was the repossession of Taiwan. If China went back on its promises to Hong Kong, it was unlikely that the Tai-

wanese would ever agree to a peaceful unification with the mainland.

Sports. The year, dominated by the Olympics, was one of great triumphs and failures. The English national rugby team was roundly defeated by almost every other major rugby nation, including Australia, South Africa, and France. These setbacks, however, were balanced by the performance of the Scottish national team, which beat all the other major European teams in the winter championship to win an international "grand slam." The ice dancers Jayne Torvill and Christopher Dean became possibly the most televised skating team in history when their ravishing rendition of Ravel's *Bolero* won them a gold medal at the Sarajevo Winter Olympics. But Britain's cricket team suffered the ultimate humiliation of losing all five test matches to the West Indies.

National honor was restored by the Los Angeles Olympic team, which included among its four gold medalists Daley Thompson in the decathlon and Sebastian Coe in the 1,500-m run, repeating their performances in Moscow in 1980. However, the most publicized athlete of all was a failure, Zola Budd. Banned as a South African from international competition, she was flown to Britain by a Fleet Street newspaper and was hurriedly given a British passport, for which she was eligible because her father was English. At Los Angeles she was booed around the track after being either the victim or the villain in the fall of Mary Decker in the 3,000-m race. The Welshman Steve Jones recorded a new world's best time when he won the Chicago marathon in October.

The Royal Family. On September 15, Diana, Princess of Wales, gave birth to a second son, Henry Charles Albert David, known almost immediately to the royal family and the media as Harry. He will be third in line to the throne after his father, Prince Charles, and his elder brother, Prince William.

TONY CLIFTON
London Bureau Chief, "Newsweek"

GREAT BRITAIN · Information Highlights

Official Name: United Kingdom of Great Britain and Northern Ireland.
Location: Island, western Europe.
Area: 94,200 sq mi (243 977 km²).
Population (mid-1984 est.): 56,500,000.
Chief Cities (mid-1982 est.): London, the capital, 6,765,100; Birmingham, 1,017,300; Glasgow, 765,000; Leeds, 716,100; Sheffield, 545,800.
Government: *Head of state,* Elizabeth II, queen (acceded Feb. 1952). *Head of government,* Margaret Thatcher, prime minister (took office May 1979). *Legislature*—Parliament: House of Lords and House of Commons.
Monetary Unit: Pound (0.8554 pound equals U.S.$1, Dec. 20, 1984).
Economic Indexes (1982): *Consumer Prices* (1970 = 100), all items, 458.4; food, 477.6. *Industrial Production* (1980 = 100), 101.
Foreign Trade (1983 U.S.$): *Imports,* $100,083,-000,000; *exports,* $91,653,000,000.

The Arts

On the initiative of two new leaders, Sir William Rees-Mogg who became chairman in 1982 and Luke Rittner who was appointed secretary general in 1983, the Arts Council, the fountain of arts patronage in Britain, announced a new strategy for the next decade under the title "The Glory of the Garden" (from a Kipling verse on the virtues of weeding). Basic to the strategy was to reduce from 156 to 94 the number of institutions looking to the council for vital financial support and to switch an increasing percentage of the total budget over the years from London to the regions.

In the end some of the cuts to artistic centers in London were not as drastic as feared. The Royal Court Theatre, seedbed of a generation of new playwrights, was reprieved with warnings; one of London's four major orchestras had to become a touring orchestra; and small music societies, like the English Sinfonia and Opera 80, were cut. The literature budget was halved, while contemporary art and dance gained in budgets. Among reactions to the policy statement, the *Financial Times* pointed out "of vital importance, it will help convince the government that there are strong men with fresh ideas running the Arts Council" and ensure government respect for Arts Council funds. Early in the year the Priestley report—a hardheaded government financial scrutiny into two of the Arts Council's most omnivorous cultural centers, the Royal Shakespeare Company and the Royal Opera House, Covent Garden—not only pronounced them not guilty to charges of extravagance but expressed some amazement that they achieve the standards they do on the money provided. The government immediately voted them a £5 million (ca. $8 million) bonus.

While the financial backdrop was being rearranged, the arts continued to perform with strenuous vitality.

Theater. A year that produced new plays by Alan Ayckbourn, Michael Frayn, Tom Stoppard, Pam Gems, and Michael Hastings, to name only the most well known, cannot be considered anything but lively. In commercial terms also, London's theater boasted a 12% increase in the total theater-going audience over the previous year. The power and range of the great state-subsidized companies, the Royal Shakespeare Company and the National Theatre, continued to grow, but without casting a blight elsewhere. Instead, other groups have been stimulated to follow the principle of providing a staple fare at a set address. For example, Ray Cooney's new Theatre of Comedy bought the Shaftesbury Theatre and provided a hit in *See How They Run;* Ed Mirvish reopened the Old Vic with a loyal subscription audience; and Andrew Lloyd Webber purchased the Palace Theater as a center for musicals, although his hit *Starlight Express* opened elsewhere.

The year produced an outstanding list of high-caliber performances. Included were dazzling Maggie Smith in *The Way of the World* at the Chichester Festival, transferring to London's West End; a challenging Glenda Jackson in Eugene O'Neill's five-hour epic *Strange Interlude;* Anthony Sher as *Richard III* at the Royal Shakespeare Company in Stratford, finally wresting the part away from memories of Laurence Olivier; and the National Theatre actors Ian McKellan and Michael Pennington settling into a two-hand team of romantic acting in *Venice Preserv'd.* Later at the National, McKellan moved on to a quick-silver performance as Platonov in Chekhov's first play, newly translated by Michael Frayn under the title *Wild Honey.* McKellan ended the year as a heroic *Coriolanus* under Peter Hall's direction.

Donald Cooper, "Time" Magazine

Jeffrey Daniel stars in Andrew Lloyd Webber's "Starlight Express." The new roller skating musical was one of the hottest selling tickets of the London season.

The Glyndebourne Festival celebrated its 50th birthday in 1984, and its touring opera company presented a new children's work, "Where the Wild Things Are," based on a Maurice Sendak book. Oliver Knussen wrote the music.

Guy Gravett, Camera Five

Dance. Amid the new financial strategies, dance was selected for special favors, including extra Arts Council funds for promising regional groups, such as the black five-man "Phoenix" in Leeds. A study "The Turn of Dance" examined the proposal for a theater for dance in London. The main ballet companies, especially the Royal Ballet and its new wave of choreographers, staged a number of new works. With *Consort Lessons* and *Choros* the Royal's David Bintley cemented a rapidly rising reputation. Sir Kenneth MacMillan took up a post with American Ballet Theatre in New York but remained the Royal Ballet's principal choreographer. He created a ballet on the *Woyzeck* theme, *A Different Drummer,* to mixed reviews.

Music. The Royal Opera House, Covent Garden, had its best year in some time. Not only did the Priestley report confirm that the house was seriously underfunded, allowing the arts minister to write off its debts, but a number of its productions reached the high level that justifies the effort. The year began with a fine *Andrea Chénier,* a joint production with Cologne Opera, with José Carreras and Rosalind Plowright in fine voice. A disappointing *Aida* with Luciano Pavarotti was followed in the fall by a splendid *Turandot* with Placido Domingo and Gwyneth Jones that had been seen in Los Angeles at the Olympic Arts Festival. In addition to a successful tour of a number of U.S. cities, the English National Opera at the Coliseum staged some excellent home productions, notably *The Mastersingers of Nuremberg* directed by Elija Moshinsky with Gwynne Howell as Hans Sachs, Verdi's *Sicilian Vespers* directed by John Dexter with Rosalind Plowright, and Janacek's *Osud.* Among the many music festivals, Bath completed its tenth under the direction of Sir William Glock, former head of music at the BBC, with a rare program, opening with Handel's *Solomon* in Bath Abbey. Glyndebourne Festival Opera celebrated its fiftieth birthday, with Peter Hall's production of *Le Nozze di Figaro,* an opera central to the Glyndebourne tradition, and a new production of *L'incoronazione di Poppea,* also produced by Hall. The Adleburgh, Buxton, and Edinburgh festivals all presented many interesting opera and concert works. The London concert scene meanwhile enjoyed an acknowledged highlight in the series of concerts in which Simon Rattle conducted the Philharmonia Orchestra under the title *Mahler, Strauss and their Influence.*

Visual Arts. Trouble at the Tate Gallery led to the resignation of Peter Palumbo as chairman-elect of the trustees, after he accused director Alan Bowness of "buying too much fashionable work at very high prices." The Tate had to extend the run of its very popular Pre-Raphaelite exhibition and succeeded with a show of English traditional realism, "The Hard-Won Image." The year ended at the Tate with the largest George Stubbs exhibition ever mounted. The Victoria and Albert Museum showed English Rococo, "Art and Design in Hogarth's England," and the Royal Academy exhibited "The Age of Vermeer and de Hooch." A sculpture show of Anthony Caro started in London at the Serpentine Gallery and moved to Manchester and Leeds before touring Europe. Bridget Riley's touring exhibition "Working with Colour" focused on this painter's newest development.

Film and Television. The reawakening film industry felt more under attack than supported by the government's proposal to end the National Film Finance Corporation and replace it with a private consortium financed by Thorn, EMI, and Rank along with Channel Four television. Television itself produced a number of notable events, including blockbuster series such as *The Jewel in the Crown,* based on Paul Scott's novels of the last days of the British in India. But all of the series were eclipsed by the brilliance of one play written for BBC television by Alan Bennett, *An Englishman Abroad.* It was directed by John Schlesinger and starred Alan Bates as the defector Guy Burgess.

MAUREEN GREEN, *Free-lance Writer, London*

AP/Wide World

Andreas Papandreou (left) was welcomed to Warsaw by General Jaruzelski. The premier praised the Polish regime.

GREECE

During 1984, Prime Minister Andreas Papandreou and his socialist party, the Panhellenic Socialist Movement (PASOK), continued to follow their moderate leftist course.

Politics. Throughout the year, Prime Minister Papandreou was criticized by opponents who represented a wide range of political beliefs. Within PASOK itself he had to be mindful of the extreme left, which generally pushed for a more rapid expansion of socialism and a greater detachment from the Western powers. In the conservative opposition New Democracy Party, Evangelos Averoff resigned as party leader in August and was replaced by Constantine Mitsotakis, toward whom Prime Minister Papandreou held a longstanding personal antipathy.

Elections were held in Greece on July 17 to fill the country's 24 seats in the European Parliament. Papandreou's PASOK received 41.6% of the total vote and won ten seats. New Democracy's 38.1% of the vote gave it nine seats. Four seats went to Communists and one to a far-right candidate. Since PASOK received a 6% smaller portion of the vote than in the Greek parliamentary elections of 1981, Papandreou's opponents could claim that he had been dealt a setback.

Foreign Affairs. Prime Minister Papandreou steadfastly maintained that Turkey was potentially a greater threat to Greece than any other outside power. Though he lived in the United States for many years and is married to an American, Papandreou also continued his barrage of anti-U.S. statements. He called the United States "imperialist" and maintained that the Korean airliner shot down by the USSR in 1983 was on a CIA spying mission.

In July some 1,600 Greek workers staged a 27-day strike at the four U.S. military bases located in Greece. Though this was not the first such work stoppage, it was notably rancorous, particularly at the Hellenikon air base near Athens. After the strike was settled, the Greek government accused U.S. military authorities of not complying with the agreement.

Despite a 1981 election pledge to take Greece out of NATO, Prime Minister Papandreou kept his nation in the organization during 1984. But he refused to participate in NATO maneuvers in the Aegean Sea because of the exclusion of the Greek island of Limnos, which Turkey believed should have a demilitarized status. With the ambivalence that many have come to expect of him, Papandreou first announced that he would allow NATO aircraft to use Greek bases for surveillance of Eastern Europe and then, following a visit to Poland in October, praised the Warsaw regime.

Papandreou stressed the need for friendship with Arab states. In September he visited Col. Muammar el-Qaddafi in Libya and signed a $1 billion (U.S.) economic accord.

In October, President Constantine Caramanlis was warmly received in Spain by King Juan Carlos I and Queen Sofia, sister of the deposed Greek King Constantine II.

Economy. Greece suffered double-digit inflation during 1984, though the rate had dropped since Papandreou took office in 1981. His government was accused of policies that were impeding investments, particularly by foreign investors. The Greek drachma, which sold at about 50 per U.S. dollar in late 1981, stood at 121 in mid-November 1984.

GEORGE J. MARCOPOULOS, *Tufts University*

GREECE • Information Highlights

Official Name: Hellenic Republic.
Location: Southwestern Europe.
Area: 51,199 sq mi (132 608 km²).
Population (mid-1984 est.): 10,000,000.
Chief Cities (1981 census): Athens, the capital, 885,136; Salonika, 402,443; Piraeus, 187,458 (1971).
Government: *Head of state,* Constantine Caramanlis, president (took office May 1980). *Head of government,* Andreas Papandreou, prime minister (took office Oct. 1981). *Legislature*—Parliament.
Monetary Unit: Drachma (121.0 drachmas equal U.S.$1, Nov. 13, 1984).
Gross National Product (1982 U.S.$): $38,600,000,000.
Economic Index (1983): *Consumer Prices* (1970 = 100), all items, 688.7; food, 791.2. *Industrial Production* (1975 = 100), 123.
Foreign Trade (1983 U.S.$): *Imports,* $9,519,000,000; *exports,* $4,412,000,000.

GRENADA

Peace and order returned in 1984 to Grenada, the tiny Caribbean spice island that was invaded by U.S. troops in October 1983.

Cruise ships, the backbone of Grenada's tourism industry, once again began to dock at St. George's, the island's capital. Grenadian authorities estimated that at least 100 liners would stop at Grenada in 1984. No ships called at St. George's for more than four months after the American invasion.

The U.S.-backed interim government began to repair the island's disintegrating road network. The Reagan administration asked Congress for $57 million to improve Grenada's electric and water systems. Order was maintained by a 280-man U.S. military police force, backed by 300 constabulary officers from neighboring islands. The 300-man Grenadian police force underwent retraining by Britain.

The jet airport that was started by Cuban construction workers began operations on October 25, the anniversary of the U.S. intervention. But terminal facilities, being completed by an American firm under contract to the U.S. government, would not be ready until 1985.

The Future. Despite the encouraging signs, it was clear as the year ended that Grenada was not yet ready to fend for itself. The political scars of the previous five turbulent years were still visible, and the economic distortions brought about by Grenada's flirtation with Cuba and the Soviet Union virtually guaranteed that Grenada would remain dependent on outside help for some time to come. The estimated cost of running the new airport, for example, was $10 million a year, a formidable sum on an island with a gross domestic product of only $100 million a year. Although the island's economy is substantially oriented toward tourism, there are only about 450 hotel rooms in all of Grenada.

The island's interim government carried out its promise to hold elections by the end of 1984. On December 3, Herbert A. Blaize, head of the centrist, coalition New National Party, swept to victory. He defeated the supporters of former Prime Minister Eric Gairy and the followers of assassinated Prime Minister Maurice Bishop. Blaize was strongly supported by the Reagan administration.

RICHARD C. SCHROEDER

GUINEA

The unexpected death of President Ahmed Sekou Touré in Cleveland, OH, on March 26, 1984, brought far-reaching changes to Guinea. Touré, the country's only president, and the Partí Démocratique de Guinée (PDG), the only legal party, had controlled the affairs of state since 1958 when he engineered independence from France. Touré instituted a type of autocratic socialism. At the same time, however, his government remained uncommitted in the Cold War. Guinea's early foreign policy was a mixture of bombast and pragmatism. Touré broke relations with France, Senegal, and the Ivory Coast and withdrew from the franc zone in the 1960s. Later he adopted a more conciliatory attitude and became active in African affairs. His regime had survived a number of assassination and coup attempts.

New Regime. After Touré's death Premier Louis Lansana Beauvogui became the interim head of state. Before a new president could be chosen, middle-rank officers of the army led by 39-year-old Col. Lansana Conté on April 3 seized the government in a bloodless coup. In the midst of reported calm and popular rejoicing, Conté denounced Touré's long regime as one that led the people astray and had no concern for human rights. The PDG was dissolved as was parliament and all mass organizations. A new 33-man legislature was created, but the ruling body of the state was the army-dominated, 18-member Committee for National Rectification, which contained representatives of the three major national groups—the Fulani, Malinke, and Susu. Touré had always favored the Malinke. Beauvogui and others close to Touré were placed under arrest. Conté stated that the object of his government was to "banish all the harm" done by Touré's regime. Political prisoners were released and freedom of speech and press promised.

Most importantly the economic system, which was on the verge of collapse, was to be changed, giving priority to producers in a limited, free-enterprise system. Guinea immediately sought outside assistance to improve its economic infrastructure. Response was immediate, with Morocco, Saudi Arabia, and the Soviet Union moving to supply direct aid.

HARRY A. GAILEY

Honolulu Mayor Eileen Anderson speaks at the dedication ceremony for a stamp marking 25 years of Hawaiian statehood.

HAWAII

Hawaii's silver anniversary of statehood, which was observed in 1984, had fireworks unmatched anywhere in the nation: Mauna Loa spewed fiery magma into the air and surged almost to the doorsteps of Hilo, county seat of the Island of Hawaii. Nature's fireworks far exceeded in noise and brilliance those that were fired to mark the 25th anniversary of the signing of the Statehood Proclamation by President Dwight D. Eisenhower on Aug. 21, 1959.

Economy. Hawaii had many other milestones to mark on the anniversary. Its population (estimated by the State Department of Planning and Economic Development at 1,040,400 residents and visitors) was up nearly 50% from 1959. Tourism was booming along at its fastest rate in more than a decade. In 1960, Hawaii had 296,517 visitors; some 4.5 million were expected in 1984.

Diversified agriculture, such as flowers, foliage, and nuts, has replaced the old standbys of sugar and pineapple. Movie production, which seldom averaged more than one picture a year before statehood, now contributes $35 million annually to the economy. The expenditures for federal civilian employees (other than those working at military installations) have increased 40%.

Astronomy and astrophysics now occupy a prominent spot atop Haleakala Volcano on the Island of Maui and on Mauna Kea on the Island of Hawaii. Some $200 million worth of telescopes and other celestial-mapping equipment were to be installed at Mauna Kea on completion of the University of California's 10-meter reflector (the world's largest).

Other milestones on this anniversary were not so welcome. For example, food prices, never low in the islands, have become the highest in the United States. Housing costs also top those elsewhere in the United States, with the average price of a single-family home selling for about $160,000, compared with a national average of $90,000. The average price in 1959 was $23,560.

Other changes throughout the 25 years have given Hawaii a new look. High-rise hotels, condominiums, and apartments now dot the Waikiki skyline. Rapid construction techniques pioneered by Henry J. Kaiser and other builders have brought Waikiki out of the Polynesian-style era into the modern age of concrete and steel, not without criticism.

Hawaiian Activists. Hawaiians comprise only 20% of the population (much less if pure Hawaiians are counted). Hawaiians dominate the welfare lists, school dropouts, and crime statistics. Young activists, often with the support of their elders, have agitated for reparations from Congress in the same way the American Indians have done. The indemnities are believed to be due because of the "illegal takeover and seizure" of Queen Liliuokalani's throne by plantation executives and their supporters in 1893. The crown was restored, but the action paved the way for the annexation of Hawaii in 1898 by the United States. The activists also have targeted the military in Hawaii for their demonstrations.

Politics. An upset of major proportions occurred in the general election, when more than 83% of the state's voters turned out to give the Republican presidential team of Ronald Reagan and George Bush a stunning 55% victory over the Democratic team of Walter Mondale and Geraldine Ferraro. It was only the second time that predominantly Democratic Hawaii had opted for a GOP presidential ticket. The first was in 1972, when the Nixon-Agnew slate beat the McGovern-Shriver team. The Republican landslide in 1984 carried over to the Honolulu mayor's race, where incumbent Democrat Eileen Anderson, serving her first term, was defeated by Frank F. Fasi (R).

The Republicans also gained three seats in the state House of Representatives but still were outnumbered by the Democrats, 40 to 11. The Republicans lost one seat in the state Senate, and the Democrats held a 21–4 edge in that body.

Incumbent representatives Daniel K. Akaka (D) and Cecil Heftel (D) won reelection and increased their chances of running for the governorship in 1986. Mrs. Anderson also was considered to be a prime candidate for the governorship, but her loss to Fasi left that in doubt.

Court Ruling. In a May ruling, the U.S. Supreme Court upheld the Hawaii Land Act of 1967. The land reform program allows a state to break up large estates, using its power of eminent domain, and transfer land ownership to the estates' tenants. It had been challenged by the Bishop Estates, a charitable trust that owns 9% of Hawaii's land.

Taxes. The Hawaii Tax Review Commission, created by the 1978 State Constitutional Convention, recommended in 1984 that taxpayers get a one-time, $83 million adjustment in their taxes to offset the effects of inflation. It would not be a rebate, since one already is provided when the state's general revenues exceed specified limits. Rather, it would result from changes in the income tax brackets and in standard deductions. The commission suggested that the lost revenue be recovered through a state lottery and a hotel-room tax.

CHARLES H. TURNER
"The Honolulu Advertiser"

HONG KONG

After two years of difficult negotiations, Britain and China finally signed a treaty on the future of Hong Kong.

Impact of Negotiations. In October 1982 the two powers began the first phase of talks on Hong Kong. Britain's lease on the New Territories—90% of the colony—would expire in 1997, leaving the remainder of Hong Kong crippled. After the fourth round of the second phase of talks ended in August 1983, London and Peking remained silent. Apparently little progress had been made in the negotiations. A general lack of confidence in Hong Kong's future was reflected by an outflow of capital, reduction of new investments, delay of big government projects, and increasing efforts of Hong Kong Chinese to emigrate to the United States, Canada, or Australia.

The people of Hong Kong had never been consulted by the Chinese and British governments during their talks. Accordingly, the Legislative Council passed a motion in March 1984 that any proposals for the future of Hong Kong should be debated in the council before a final Sino-British agreement was reached. The unofficial (noncivil-servant) members of the Executive and Legislative councils sent delegations to London and Peking to express the anxieties of Hong Kong's people. But neither Britain nor China recognized the delegates as speaking for Hong Kong since they were not the people's official representatives. Moreover, the Chinese government would not permit "external interference" in the negotiations and therefore rejected the concept that the Hong Kong government itself should have a place at the bargaining table.

During the first half of the year, fears were deepened by several events. Jardine, Matheson & Co., one of Hong Kong's oldest trading firms, stated that in March it would reorganize as a holding company registered in Bermuda. The next month, Britain officially announced that it would relinquish all of Hong Kong when the New Territories lease expired. The Hang Seng Index, the colony's economic barometer, immediately plunged by nearly 46 points. After Deng Xiaoping, China's de facto leader, announced in May that China would station troops in Hong Kong after 1997, the index fell another 30 points. In June the China-financed Ever Bright Industrial Corp. called off a deal to purchase land for the development of its $128 million City Garden Residential Project. The index then dropped 21 points.

On June 21 the British working team headed by David Wilson and the Chinese team led by Ke Zaishuo met to begin drafting the Sino-British declaration. One of their major disagreements was that the British team insisted on a detailed declaration, whereas the Chinese wanted only a statement of broad principles.

Jeff Hacker

Hong Kong's thriving capitalist economy seemed threatened by Chinese takeover in 1997, when Britain's lease expires. But on Dec. 19, 1984, Margaret Thatcher and Zhao Ziyang (r) signed an accord guaranteeing a free market for 50 years.

AP/Wide World

Another major obstacle was the Chinese proposal to set up a Sino-British commission purportedly to study the administration of Hong Kong during the period to 1997. The British feared that such a commission might develop into a transitional government. Other major issues were land leases, nationality, and aviation.

To break an apparent deadlock, China stated that if agreement was not reached by September it would announce its own plans for Hong Kong's future. Throughout the summer the atmosphere in the colony was tense as the deadline set by China approached.

The Declaration. The joint declaration, with three annexes, was initialed on September 26 and signed by Prime Ministers Margaret Thatcher and Zhao Ziyang in Peking on December 19. It contained a comprehensive range of assurances promised to post-1997 Hong Kong. The joint declaration would come into force upon its ratification by the National People's Congress of China, some time before July 1, 1985. The British Parliament has ratified it.

The first annex presented details of the 12 basic points proposed by China. For example, the Hong Kong Special Administrative Region (SAR) of China would be autonomous and vested with executive, legislative, and independent judicial powers. Its government would be composed entirely of people from Hong Kong, with a chief executive appointed by Peking on the basis of elections or local consultations. The current socioeconomic system and lifestyle would continue. Rights and freedoms would be ensured by law. The Hong Kong SAR would run its own finances independently and remain a free port and a separate customs ter-

ritory. Peking would not levy taxes on it. The SAR would retain the existing system of aviation management and continue to keep its own registry of aircraft. It would have specific authority to renew or amend air-service agreements previously in force. All policies outlined in the first annex would last for 50 years after 1997.

The second annex spelled out the operation of the Sino-British Joint Liaison Group to be set up to help implement the policies of the joint declaration, which would come into force before July 1, 1985. The liaison group would continue its work until Jan. 1, 2000. It would not be an organ of power and would play no part in the administration of Hong Kong.

The third annex dealt with leases on land. Leases granted by the British Hong Kong government and expiring before July 1, 1997, would be extendable for up to 50 years.

China refused to grant dual nationality to Chinese nationals in Hong Kong, whether they held British Dependent Territories Citizen's (BDTC) passports or not. In a memorandum attached to the joint declaration, China agreed that from July 1, 1997, Chinese nationals could use travel documents issued by Britain but would not be entitled to British consular protection in the SAR or other parts of China. In a separate memorandum, Britain stated that all BDTCs would lose that status on July 1, 1997, but the British government would seek parliamentary approval to give them a new status. However, only those born in Hong Kong before July 1, 1997, could apply for such status, and they could not pass it on to their children. The future of Hong Kong was now clear. But many residents feared that radical Communist leaders might control China again after Deng's death and not fulfill the declaration.

The Economy. The deficit for fiscal year 1984 was $385 million, and that for 1985 was expected to be nearly $80 million higher. About $1 billion (U.S.) was invested in Hong Kong by more than 500 foreign concerns. This amount did not include $4 billion invested by China. In the first six months of 1984, exports increased by 45%, imports by 39%, and re-exports by 55%, compared with the same period in 1983.

Major projects were under construction in 1984: expansion of the Kwai Chung Container Terminal, which would become the world's second-busiest such facility; the Hong Kong-Macau Ferry Terminal, with two 41-story skyscrapers; and the second Man Kam to Bridge, providing another road link with China.

CHUEN-YAN DAVID LAI
University of Victoria, British Columbia

HOUSING

Housing, especially the purchase of a home, is often viewed as an American birthright—the fulfillment of the American dream. In the last decade, the achievement of this dream has become more difficult, while its realization, in terms of the type of unit produced and occupied, has changed.

Production of housing in the United States often proceeds on a "boom" and "bust" cycle. In the early 1970s, the number of housing starts peaked at approximately 2.3 million; by 1975 starts plummeted to 1.2 million. By 1978, however, production returned to a robust annual level of 2 million units. The 1980s have witnessed similar reversals. Housing starts dropped to 1.1 million in 1981–82; by 1984, declining interest rates and an improving economy stimulated housing production to an estimated 1.7 million starts.

While housing production has fluctuated, its cost has moved inexorably upward. In 1970, the median price for a new single-family home was $25,700. The inflation of the 1970s drastically increased delivery costs. By 1975, the median price for a new single-family home was $39,500; by 1980, it was $63,100. As of 1983, it had climbed to $75,900. While median family income also increased dramatically during the 1970s and early 1980s, it did not match the inflation in housing costs. Many families were finding it increasingly more difficult to realize the dream of purchasing their own home.

One response to this cost pressure has been modification of the dream to encompass dwellings other than a single-family detached house. In the late 1970s, about 30% of total housing starts consisted of multifamily units; as of 1984, the latter share had increased to approximately 43%. Numerous configurations of multifamily housing are becoming more commonplace and include townhouses, garden apartments, garden condominiums, and patio homes.

The growing popularity of multifamily housing is partially a result of economics—it costs less to produce an attached as opposed to a detached dwelling unit. Changing demographics are a second underlying influence. American families are having fewer children resulting in a steady decrease in household size from 3.52 in 1950, to 3.38 in 1960, 3.11 in 1970, and 2.75 in 1980. This decline has diminished shelter space needs so that the smaller detached unit is often more appropriate to today's demographics as opposed to the larger single-family home.

Another change in the American housing dream is that it is increasingly realized in the form of manufactured housing, commonly called mobile homes. The latter comprise approximately one third of new single-family home sales. Whereas stick-built single-family units have a median price of more than $70,000, the mobile home is sold for slightly more than $20,000. In addition, mobile homes have become more attractive because of improved construction, durability, and financing terms.

Inclusionary Zoning Ordinances and Subsidies. The public sector also has joined the search for affordable housing delivery. Numerous communities have enacted inclusionary zoning ordinances. The latter mandate that a builder make available a portion of the total number of units in a development at below-market prices. For instance, Orange County, California, required that 25% of all units in developments of five or more homes be affordable by low- and moderate-income families.

Inclusionary zoning received a strong affirmation in the 1983 New Jersey State Supreme Court decision *Southern Burlington County NAACP vs. the Township of Mount Laurel.* The Mount Laurel ruling declared that "every municipality's land use regulations . . . must provide a realistic opportunity for decent housing for its indigenous poor . . . and for a fair share of the region's present and prospective low- and moderate-income housing need." This declaration has spurred numerous municipalities in the state to adopt inclusionary requirements as a means to realize the Mount Laurel mandate.

With the help of urban-renewal funding, the Ralston Purina Company has developed a 140-acre (56.6 ha) housing project in the LaSalle Park area of St. Louis, MO. The project includes new public-housing apartments as well as restored century-old brick houses. Restoration now plays an important part in the U.S. housing picture.

Inclusionary zoning requires residential builders to provide lower-cost housing. Some municipalities have decided that nonresidential developers have a housing responsibility as well and are exacting requirements to fulfil this obligation. San Francisco has taken the lead in this respect. In 1981 the city created an Office/Housing Production Program (OHPP) under which developers of at least 50,000 sq ft (4 645 m²) of office space must build, or cause to be built, housing units (640 sq ft, or 60 m²) for every 1,000 sq ft (93 m²) of office space. Other cities are considering similar provisions.

Another public response to housing costs and affordability is the provision of subsidies. From the late 1960s to the early 1980s, numerous federal housing programs were available that offered low-cost mortgages, operating cost write-downs, and other assistance. Examples included the Section 236 and Section 8 subsidies. Most of these offerings, however, either have been eliminated or reduced in scope. Some state and local housing subsidies remain available, but these are not significant.

Increased new housing costs and diminished public subsidy have encouraged greater investment to preserve the extant housing stock. In 1980, approximately $46 billion was spent on the upkeep and improvement of residential properties; by 1983 more than $49 billion was expended. Of the $49 billion, $18 billion was spent on maintenance and repairs, $20 billion on alterations and additions, and $11 billion on major replacements.

Financing. A significant influence on both the production of new housing and the preservation in the extant stock is the change in housing financing. Until the 1970s, mortgage monies typically were made available by thrift institutions—local savings and loans associations or mutual savings banks. By law as well as tradition, the thrifts focused on housing lending for their own investment portfolio. The mortgage interest rate they charged was often limited to a below-market ceiling by state usury statutes.

Housing buyers could thus draw on local financial institutions making available mortgages at favorable terms.

These relationships have been shaken by inflation and near-revolutionary changes in the financing industry. The steep inflation of the 1970s led depositors at thrift institutions to withdraw savings from relatively low interest rate savings accounts. To constrain such outflow, the thrifts were forced to offer higher interest rate investments such as certificates of deposit (CDs). Many lenders were thus caught in a financial squeeze whereby the deposits they attracted in the form of CDs cost them more (in terms of the interest rate paid) than the maximum interest rate they could charge for mortgages. This untenable situation ultimately forced the rescinding of severe usury restrictions. Instead of artificially being fixed at a low-interest ceiling, the mortgage interest rate now would be set at the market cost of money.

This change had profound effects. Homebuyers obtaining mortgages had to pay a market interest rate—higher than the traditional charge. Since mortgages now yielded a market rate, such additional financial institutions as commercial banks were willing to extend home financing. The mortgage market expanded in another dimension as well. Thrift institutions originating home loans traditionally kept most of these for their own investment portfolio. More recently, individual mortgages often are assembled into blocks and then sold on the secondary mortgage market to permanent investors, such as life insurance companies. Much of this secondary mortgage market trading activity is done by government or quasipublic agencies, such as the Federal National Mortgage Association (FNMA), Government National Mortgage Association (GNMA), and the Federal Home Loan Mortgage Corporation (FHLMC).

DAVID LISTOKIN
Rutgers University

HUNGARY

In 1984, Hungary took major steps to update its New Economic Mechanism, the very successful economic reform program followed since 1968.

Economic Affairs. In April the Central Committee of the Hungarian Socialist Workers' Party (HSWP) called for higher quality in production and further movement toward a free-market economy. It recommended a series of measures to improve industrial management and promote profitability, including increasing the role of workers in management, linking wages more closely to performance, and decreasing state subsidies. The Council of Ministers approved the proposal on May 10 and commissioned Lajos Faluvégi, deputy premier and president of the National Planning Office, to implement it over a two-year period beginning in 1985. In a related political change, László Kapolyi replaced Lajos Mékes as minister of industry. The economic plan for 1984 foresaw rises of 1.5 to 2% in national income and industrial production above 1983 levels, 0 to 1% in agricultural production, and 0 to 0.5% in personal consumption.

In February, the government praised the success of some 20,000 small business ventures, which employed about 3% of the total work force (about 150,000 people) and produced slightly more than 1% of the national income. It also announced plans to approve up to ten new joint ventures between Hungarian and Western firms. That same month, Hungary and the Soviet Union signed a contract for the delivery of 7,800,000 tons of Soviet oil and oil products in 1984.

Hungary continued to be very successful in securing foreign funding for its economic plans. In January, the International Monetary Fund (IMF) extended a standby credit worth $437 million for one year. In March, Hungary signed an agreement with 12 commercial banks for a credit of $50 million, repayable over five years. In April, the World Bank approved a $200 million credit to develop Hungary's export industries and petrochemical processing, and a consortium of commercial banks agreed to a medium-term credit of $210 million.

But economic progress had its drawbacks. A sharp rise in crimes against property was reported, reflecting popular resentment of the growing number of successful entrepreneurs in the country. In February, a two-day conference in Pecs discussed the rapid decline of "dwarf villages," settlements of less than 500 inhabitants, because of the exodus of young and trained people. In July, Hungary witnessed the largest environmental protest ever to take place in the Soviet sphere. About 6,000–7,000 Hungarians, including about 50 prominent intellectuals, fearing serious environmental damage and social dislocation, presented a petition against a governmental plan to dam or divert a 138-mi (222-km) stretch of the Danube for a hydroelectric and navigational project. A joint Hungarian-Czechoslovak venture begun in 1977, it would cost about $1.12 billion (U.S.).

Political Affairs. In December 1983, the National Assembly adopted a bill mandating a choice of candidates in all parliamentary and local elections. In April 1984, another bill established a Constitutional Law Council to scrutinize proposed legislation and verify its constitutionality. In July, the Lutheran World Federation held a two-week meeting in Budapest, the first such meeting in a Communist country. (Hungary has about 430,000 Lutherans.) Popular dissent continued, however. In March, 19 dissidents called for the release of all political prisoners in Eastern Europe and for improved conditions for the Hungarian minorities in Czechoslovakia and Rumania.

Foreign Relations. Hungary showed modest signs of independence in its foreign policy in 1984. In July and August, official Hungarian newspapers cautiously expressed support for a possible rapprochement between East and West Germany, risking Soviet displeasure. János Kádár, first secretary of the HSWP, visited France in October, the first such visit by a Soviet bloc leader since President François Mitterrand took office in 1981. In a low-key statement, the two leaders expressed agreement on the importance of reducing "overarmament" and limiting space, bacteriological, and chemical warfare. But Hungary followed the Soviet lead in refusing to send a team to the Summer Olympic Games in Los Angeles.

Visitors to Hungary in 1984 included UN Secretary-General Javier Pérez de Cuéllar, British Prime Minister Margaret Thatcher, Italian Premier Bettino Craxi, and Richard Burt, U.S. assistant secretary for European affairs.

JOSEPH F. ZACEK
State University of New York at Albany

HUNGARY • Information Highlights

Official Name; Hungarian People's Republic.
Location: East-central Europe.
Area: 35,900 sq mi (92 980 km²).
Population (mid-1984 est.): 10,700,000.
Chief Cities: (Jan. 1, 1983): Budapest, the capital, 2,064,307; Miskolc, 211,200; Debrecen, 204,891.
Government: *Head of state*, Pál Losonczi, chairman of the presidential council (took office April 1967). *Head of government*, György Lázár, premier (took office 1975). First secretary of the Hungarian Socialist Workers' Party, János Kádár (took office 1956). *Legislature* (unicameral)— National Assembly.
Monetary Unit: Forint (49.611 forints equal U.S.$1, July 1984).
Gross National Product (1982 U.S.$): $65,200,000,000.
Economic Indexes (1983): *Consumer Prices* (1970 = 100), all items, 186.4; food, 188.0. *Industrial Production* (1975 = 100), 125.
Foreign Trade (1983 U.S.$): *Imports*, $8,503,000,000; *exports*, $8,696,000,000.

ICELAND

Despite its success in reducing inflation dramatically, or because of it, the government, a Progressive-Independence Party (centrist-right) coalition headed by Steingrímur Hermannsson, faced gloomy prospects in late 1984. In office since the spring of 1983, the government had rolled back the annual inflation rate by some 100 percentage points in just 16 months. It hoped to reduce the inflation rate to 13% by year's end and to less than 10% by the end of 1985. By the beginning of November, however, it was clear these goals could not be achieved due to the new wage contracts won by state and municipal workers that promised them gains of an estimated 20% in 1985.

The workers' victory capped a massive, month-long strike that closed many schools, stopped bus services in Reykjavík, kept freighters from docking, disrupted telecommunications, and forced the state-run radio and TV off the air. The walkouts reflected dissatisfaction, which had apparently been building for a long time, with the prolonged belt-tightening the country had endured in an effort to bring the high inflation rate under control.

Fisheries. The fisheries, the mainstay of the national economy, faced an intractable combination of woes, including a shortfall in the cod catch and adverse trends in fishery export markets. Though the overall catch through August was up, thanks to the comeback of capelin fishing, export prices for capelin products—fish meal and oil—were sharply down. The day was saved for herring operators by a big advance sale to the Soviet Union.

Economy. Iceland's foreign trade benefited in 1984 by the rising world prices for aluminum, which is smelted in Iceland. But the level of imports remained high, and the trade deficit increased. Iceland's foreign debt at the end of 1984 was projected as 61.5% of the gross national product (GNP), up by a small margin from 1983. Payments on the debt rose to 23% of export earnings, as opposed to 21% in 1982 and 1983.

Farm subsidies continued to be a major drain on the economy. As usual, exported surpluses of lamb were sold at a fraction of the domestic wholesale price. The average unemployment rate stood at just over 1%, about twice the general level from 1972 to 1981. The GNP was expected to fall by about 1% in 1984, the third consecutive year of decline.

Energy. Work on a major new hydroelectric project continued. A settlement in a long dispute with Alusuisse, owner of an aluminum smelter that buys a large proportion of all electricity generated in Iceland, was in sight. Geothermal utilities served nearly 80% of the population.

HAUKUR BÖDVARSSON
Free-lance Journalist, Reykjavík

ICELAND · Information Highlights

Official Name: Republic of Iceland.
Location: North Atlantic Ocean.
Area: 39,749 sq mi (102 845 km²).
Population: (mid-1984 est.): 200,000.
Chief Cities (Dec. 1, 1982): Reykjavík, the capital, 86,092; Kópavogur, 14,279; Akureyri, 13,758.
Government: *Head of state,* Vigdis Finnbogadóttir, president (took office Aug. 1980). *Head of government,* Steingrímur Hermannsson, prime minister (took office May 1983). *Legislature*—Althing: Upper House and Lower House.
Monetary Unit: Krona (32.125 kronur equal U.S. $1, Aug. 1984).
Gross National Product (1983 U.S.$): $2,200,-000,000.
Foreign Trade (1983 U.S.$): *Imports,* $815,000,000; *exports,* $751,000,000.

IDAHO

The economic recovery that took place elsewhere in the United States in 1984 was slow to reach Idaho. Ink was hardly dry on the fiscal 1985 budget of $507.8 million when Democratic Gov. John Evans was forced to order a 3% holdback for most state agencies.

On April 7, Idaho lost a distinguished public servant, when former U.S. Sen. Frank Church died of cancer in Washington, DC. Church, who was 59, had served in the Senate from 1957 to 1981. His body was returned to Boise for burial.

On April 2, U.S. Congressman George Hansen (R) was convicted under the 1978 Ethics in Government Act for failing to report income and loans of nearly $334,000. Hansen, who immediately appealed the conviction, was later reprimanded by his House colleagues. Ignoring numerous appeals to resign, Hansen was renominated on May 22. On June 15 he was sentenced to up to 15 months and fined $40,000.

Legislature. Political skirmishing between Evans and the Republican-controlled legislature continued as in past years. The main battle was over a permanent increase in the sales tax from 3 to 4%. (A temporary 4.5% sales tax had been slated to revert to 3% on July 1.) The new sales tax won approval only after a bill supported by the Republican leadership appropriating $215 million to public schools was defeated in the House of Representatives. The final appropriation for public schools was $226 million; colleges and universities received $78.9 million.

The legislature failed to redistrict itself, with both of two attempts invalidated by the courts. A court-mandated redistricting plan expanded the Senate from 35 to 42 members and the House from 70 to 84. The court was firm in adhering to a constitutional prohibition against splitting counties between legislative districts.

Election. The big election news was the 130-vote defeat of embattled second district Representative Hansen at the hands of Democrat

IDAHO · Information Highlights

Area: 83,564 sq mi (216 432 km²).
Population (July 1, 1983 est.): 989,000.
Chief Cities (1980 census): Boise, the capital (July 1, 1982 est.), 104,586; Pocatello, 46,340; Idaho Falls, 39,590.
Government (1984): *Chief Officers—*governor, John V. Evans (D); lt. gov., David H. Leroy (R). *Legislature—*Senate, 35 members; House of Representatives, 70 members.
State Finances (fiscal year 1983): *Revenues,* $1,349,000,000; *expenditures,* $1,245,000,000.
Personal Income (1983): $9,450,000,000; per capita, $9,555.
Labor Force (May 1984): *Civilian labor force,* 461,700; *unemployed,* 31,500 (6.8% of total force).
Education: *Enrollment* (fall 1982)—public elementary schools, 145,416; public secondary, 57,557; colleges and universities (fall 1983), 42,911. *Public school expenditures* (1982–83), $395,430,436 ($2,052 per pupil).

Richard Stallings. In other races, Republican U.S. Sen. James McClure handily defeated challenger Peter Busch. Senator McClure won 72% of the vote, the identical percentage won in the state by President Reagan. In the first district, Rep. Larry Craig won reelection over Democratic challenger Bill Hellar with 69% of the vote.

Republicans increased their control of the legislature, by 50 seats in the House and 14 in the Senate. These margins provide them with a two-thirds majority in each chamber, allowing them to override vetoes by Governor Evans, who has used the veto effectively.

Voters turned down an initiative to remove the sales tax from food and defeated a proposed constitutional amendment to allow counties to be split for the purpose of redistricting. They approved a constitutional amendment shifting control over state water rights from the Water Resources Board to the legislature.

M. C. HENBERG
University of Idaho

ILLINOIS

Illinois voters gave President Ronald Reagan a strong victory in the November elections but ousted incumbent Republican Sen. Charles H. Percy. Reagan won his native state by more than 600,000 votes with about 57% of the vote.

Elections. The president and Walter Mondale both visited the state several times during the campaign. Mondale had hoped that Illinois, with its sagging economy, would help him put together a winning coalition of northern industrial states.

In the Senate race Percy, the chairman of the Senate Foreign Relations Committee, lost his quest for a fourth term to U.S. Rep. Paul Simon, a liberal Democrat from downstate Illinois. Simon won by 61,000 votes. It was a bitter campaign that cost the candidates more than $5 million. Simon capitalized on Percy's

move toward the political right. He accused Percy of "flip-flopping" on the issues as he moved from his earlier stances as a moderate and liberal Republican. Percy attacked Simon for advocating federal tax hikes that he said would cost $200 billion over four years.

Percy had put together a broad constituency during his terms in the U.S. Senate. But in 1984 many of those voters abandoned him. Simon picked up the votes of many liberals, Jews, and blue-collar workers who had helped Percy in the past. Thousands of conservative Republicans who never liked Percy very well voted for the Libertarian Party candidate for the Senate. The Libertarian got 1.3% of the vote as Simon squeaked through with just 50% of the vote for the U.S. Senate. Percy, who once aspired to the presidency, said he would never again seek election to public office. It was possible, however, that he would receive a presidential appointment, such as to a diplomatic post.

Economy. Illinois never fully recovered from the recession, and the long-range economic outlook for the state was not good. Unemployment remained high. It began an upward trend in June and rose from 8.7% in September to 9.4% in October. That was 2 percentage points above the national average, which held steady during the month of October.

A study released that month by The Commercial Club of Chicago painted a grim picture. The report said the growth in jobs in the Chicago area lagged behind the national norm in almost every category. Manufacturing jobs were dwindling faster than in such northern

Chicago Mayor Harold Washington (r) congratulates Senator-elect Paul Simon. A heavy pro-Simon vote by women and blacks helped the congressman defeat Charles Percy.

AP/Wide World

trouble spots as Detroit and St. Louis. From 1960 to 1982, the study said, those jobs declined 21% in the Chicago area. And the state was not experiencing a concurrent rise in jobs in high technology.

The situation also looked bad for Illinois farmers, the world's leading corn and soybean producers. Sagging commodity prices put an estimated 98,000 Illinois farmers, or 20% of the total, into financial trouble. Another 30% faced possible distress if commodity prices did not rise or if interest rates did not begin to fall significantly.

Bad times on the farm hurt the state's farm-implement manufacturers, such as International Harvester and Caterpillar Tractor Co. Farm-implement makers were running at only 50 to 60% of their levels of the late 1970s. The United Auto Workers union said its agricultural-implement membership fell from 122,000 in 1981 to 74,600 in August of 1984.

Income of Illinois farmers fell from $1.2 billion in 1977 to $732 million in 1982. The University of Illinois said average net income of the farmers fell from $35,000 in 1979 to $15,000 in 1983. And farm debts more than doubled from 1977 to 1983, going from $5.1 billion to $11.3 billion.

Crime. One of the nation's most massive manhunts ended in July with the capture of Alton Coleman, 28, and Debra Brown, 21, as they relaxed in a park in Evanston, IL. During a crime spree lasting almost two months, the pair were said to have terrorized six Midwest states. They were principal suspects in the deaths of at least seven people and in numerous kidnappings, beatings, assaults, and robberies.

A chance sighting of the pair by a high school acquaintance of Coleman, of Waukegan, IL, led to the end of the intensive manhunt. They offered no resistance.

See also CHICAGO

ROBERT ENSTAD,
Chicago Tribune

INDIA

The year 1984 in India saw much tragedy and upheaval. Growing unrest among Sikh extremists in the Punjab was dealt with harshly by the government at midyear, leading to the assassination of Prime Minister Indira Gandhi on October 31 (*see* OBITUARIES). In widespread violence that followed, primarily by Hindus seeking revenge against Sikhs, thousands of people were killed or injured. Then in early December, in the worst industrial accident in history, untold thousands were killed or injured by poisonous gas that leaked from an American-owned insecticide plant in the city of Bhopal (*see* special report, page 263).

Nevertheless, as the year came to an end, a note of optimism could be heard. Though the passing of Mrs. Gandhi had left a great void and created great uncertainties in Indian politics, parliamentary elections in late December gave her son and chosen successor, 40-year-old Rajiv Gandhi, also of the Congress (I) party, a clear mandate (*see* BIOGRAPHY). "There are many problems before India," said the new prime minister, "but with the power you have given us, we will be able to fight these problems."

Crisis in the Punjab. The rioting, killings, and other acts of violence that occurred in many parts of India during 1984 reached their most extreme and highly publicized form in the Punjab, India's wealthiest state and the homeland of the Sikhs. Although they constitute less than 2% of the total population of India, the Sikhs make up about 52% of the population of the Punjab. Led by the Akali Dal party, the Sikhs had long been demanding greater autonomy and recognition within the Indian union; some even advocated a separate Sikh nation. By early 1984, however, more extremist groups, led by Sant Jarnail Singh Bhindranwale, had replaced the Akali Dal as the directing force in the Sikh movement.

The extremists set up headquarters in the Golden Temple at Amritsar, the holiest Sikh shrine, and turned it into a veritable fortress. This came as a serious challenge to the national government of Prime Minister Indira Gandhi. In mid-February, the prime minister met with leaders of the Akali Dal and other opposition parties in an attempt to reach an agreement that would end the violence in the Punjab. But the Akali leader, Sant Harchand Singh Longowal, and his associates walked out of the meetings and refused to return. On March 19, President's Rule (direct rule by the central government), which had been imposed in the Punjab in October 1983, was extended for another six months. And the following day, Longowal was arrested on charges of sedition. These actions, along with curfews in major cities, widespread arrests of Sikh agitators, and other security measures, seemed only to inflame an already dangerous situation. From January 1 to June 3, according to official sources (invariably conservative), there were 775 violent incidents in the Punjab in which 298 persons were killed and more than 525 were injured.

On June 2, units of the Indian army were sent to the Punjab, and the entire state was declared off-limits to foreigners. Four days later, in an action that sent shock waves throughout India—and beyond—the army stormed the 72-acre (29-ha) Golden Temple complex to drive out the Sikhs. Hundreds of people, including Bhindranwale himself, were killed in the raid, and parts of the temple complex were destroyed. The government reported that 493 civilians and terrorists and 83 army personnel had been killed. Other estimates were much higher.

The government's action provoked violent protests by Sikhs throughout India and many other parts of the world. Hundreds of Sikhs in the Indian army mutinied or deserted. After the first shocks were over, however, the most violent resistance died down and most Indians seemed to approve of the government's stern actions. Prime Minister Gandhi contended that the action had been taken only as a last resort, after all efforts to settle the dispute through negotiations had failed. She charged that the events in the Punjab were greatly aggravated by "certain foreign forces inimical to India" and by "certain misguided and antinational elements within the country." On August 23 the Indian Parliament approved a constitutional amendment extending President's Rule in the Punjab for another year.

Other Unrest. Violence and rioting on a large scale also took place in several other Indian states, notably Andhra Pradesh, Assam, Kashmir, Maharashtra, and Uttar Pradesh. In May a major outbreak of Hindu-Muslim fighting occurred in Maharashtra. The violence began in Bhiwandi, a textile town northeast of Bombay, and soon spread to other nearby industrial towns and Bombay itself. After a week of fighting, a reported 216 persons had been killed, 756 injured, 13,000 left homeless, and 4,100 arrested. Bombay was described as a city under siege, with 6,000 army troops patrolling the streets.

In Kashmir, protests were staged in both Indian- and Pakistani-held sections following the February 11 execution in New Delhi of terrorist leader Mohammed Maqbool Butt, founder of the Kashmir Liberation Front, an organization fighting for Kashmir's independence. More serious violence erupted in Kashmir in July following the dismissal of Chief Minister Farooq Abdullah. Prime Minister Gandhi's Congress (I) party had long sought to depose him and to divide his party, the National Conference.

In Andhra Pradesh, Gandhi's efforts to bring down another chief minister boomer-

anged. The state had been a Congress party stronghold since India's independence in 1947, but in elections in 1983 a new state party, the Telugu Desam, headed by N. T. Rama Rao, a popular film star, won an overwhelming victory. Then on Aug. 16, 1984, the governor of the state, a Gandhi appointee, dismissed the Rama Rao ministry on the grounds that party defections had deprived the Telugu Desam party of a majority in the state assembly. Rama Rao's dismissal led to widespread rioting, strikes, and demonstrations not only in Andhra Pradesh but also in New Delhi and other parts of India; hundreds of people were killed and thousands arrested. Opposition leaders accused Mrs. Gandhi of attempting to "murder democracy." Thousands of Indian army troops were rushed to Hyderabad, the capital of Andhra Pradesh, and a "shoot-on-sight" curfew was imposed. Rama Rao led 162 members of the state assembly to New Delhi to protest his ouster. When his successor as chief minister, Bhaskara Rao, was unable to obtain a majority in the assembly, Mrs. Gandhi had to concede defeat. Rama Rao was reinstated as chief minister on September 16, and four days later he won an overwhelming vote of confidence.

Assassination and Aftermath. On the morning of October 31, as she came out of her residence in New Delhi, Prime Minister Gandhi, 66, was shot and killed by members of her own special security force. The gunmen were identified as Sikhs, and the assassination was apparently a retaliation for the June raid of the Golden Temple in Amritsar. At an emergency cabinet meeting the same day, Mrs. Gandhi's lone surviving son, Rajiv, was sworn in as the new prime minister, thus continuing the Nehru "dynasty." Because of his relative inexperience and untested abilities, however, Rajiv's political future and that of the Congress (I) party seemed quite uncertain.

During the first three days after the assassination, at least 1,000 people, mostly Sikhs, were killed in New Delhi and other places across India. The new prime minister appealed to the people for "maximum restraint," and the violence gradually subsided.

Rajiv Gandhi retained his mother's entire cabinet except for the planning minister and, like his predecessor, took over the foreign affairs portfolio himself. Among the many immediate tasks facing him were the restoration of law and order, the continuing disaffection in the Punjab, and a decision regarding the eighth national elections, scheduled to be held prior to Jan. 20, 1985.

Elections and Politics. The ruling Congress (I) party fared well at the ballot box in 1984. In March biennial elections to the Rajya Sabha, the upper house of Parliament, the Congress (I) got 47 of the 73 contested seats, plus 7 uncontested seats. The remaining 26 contested seats went to opposition parties, which now num-

The Disaster in Bhopal

Medical personnel and family members try to assist victims of a poisonous gas leak at a pesticide plant (rear) *in Bhopal.*

The worst industrial accident on record occurred in the early morning of Dec. 3, 1984, when toxic gas leaked from a storage tank at a pesticide plant in the central Indian city of Bhopal. The noxious fumes killed more than 2,000 people and injured an estimated 150,000 others.

The chemical, methyl isocyanate, is widely used in preparing pesticides. Even in small amounts, it is extremely irritating to human tissues, especially moist tissues such as those in the eyes and respiratory passages. It is easily absorbed through the skin and quickly enters the bloodstream. Initially, physicians feared widespread blindness and other severe medical problems among the survivors of the accident. By year's end, however, cases of vision loss and brain and nerve damage appeared to be limited. No significant damage to other internal organs was apparent. Because little is known about the long-term effects of exposure to methyl isocyanate, medical experts agreed that follow-up studies of Bhopal residents would be essential.

The Bhopal plant was jointly owned by Union Carbide, a major U.S. corporation, and Indian investors. In accordance with Indian law, the plant was built and operated by Indians. The methyl isocyanate was stored in refrigerated tanks, to keep it in liquid form. For unknown reasons, the temperature in one of the tanks rose above 100° F (38° C), at which point methyl isocyanate turns into a gas. The temperature continued to rise and the gas expanded, exerting more and more pressure against the inside of the tank. The plant had two automatic safety devices designed to neutralize the gas in such a situation. Whether through mechanical failure or human error, neither of the devices worked and the gas escaped into the air.

Following the accident, Indian officials sealed off the plant and placed some key personnel under arrest. They seized company documents that might play a role in legal prosecutions connected with the accident. They also announced that the plant would be closed permanently. First, however, the facility was reopened for several days so that some 15 tons of methyl isocyanate remaining in one of the storage tanks could be rendered harmless. This was accomplished by turning it into carbaryl, the chemical name for the pesticide known commercially as Sevin.

The effects of the Bhopal tragedy promised to be felt far beyond the stricken city. In the United States and India, thousands of lawsuits were filed on behalf of the victims and their surviving kin. Governments and firms that use or create dangerous chemicals began to reevaluate the often conflicting implications of technology transfer. One widely expected consequence was the imposition and enforcement of more rigid industrial safety regulations.

AP/Wide World

The Nehru dynasty goes on in India: Rajiv Gandhi, grandson of Jawaharlal Nehru and son of assassinated Indira Gandhi (portrait rear), began 1985 with an electoral mandate.

bered fewer than 10. All in all, the Congress (I) gained 20 seats, giving it 152 of the 244 total.

The Congress (I) did less well in May by-elections for 24 assembly seats in 16 states, winning only 9 seats. But it had no difficulty in securing the election of its candidate for vice-president of India, Ramaswami Venkataraman, a former finance and defense minister. On August 31, Venkataraman was sworn in as India's eighth vice-president, replacing Mohammed Hidayatullah, whom Mrs. Gandhi chose not to support for another term.

In February, August, and October, leaders of the main opposition parties (except the two main Communist parties) held talks to explore the possibility of forming a united front in the forthcoming national elections. But even though most of them agreed to merge their parties into a new political grouping, announced on October 21, the prospects for real unity were not bright because of ideological differences and personal rivalries.

Indira Gandhi had approached the upcoming national elections with confidence in spite of considerable disorganization and even demoralization in her party. On November 13,

two weeks after succeeding his slain mother, Rajiv Gandhi announced that the voting would be held December 24 and 27. It was hoped that the Congress (I) would benefit from national unity sentiment and sympathy for Rajiv Gandhi. When the last ballots were counted, it was clear that the government had won a major victory. Of 542 seats in the Lok Sabha (lower house of parliament), Congress (I) had won 396, increasing its majority by 30. (A total of 508 seats were at stake in the December balloting. There were no elections in the states of Punjab and Assam, which have 27 seats, and another 7 seats were to be decided in 1985).

Inheriting an improved but still tenuous economy and an important role in international —especially Third World—affairs, the new prime minister said that there would be some change in domestic policy but that foreign policy would remain essentially the same.

Economy. With some exceptions, the general economic situation was brighter in 1984 than it had been for several years. The overall growth rate was reported to be 5–6%, or even higher. Food-grain production reached a record high of approximately 150 million tons. In January, Mrs. Gandhi announced that because of an increase in foreign-exchange reserves, India would waive the final $1.1 billion (U.S.) installment of the $5.8 billion loan pledged by the International Monetary Fund in 1981. Inflation was generally still under control, though it did reach 9.3% in March. In April the government announced a new export-import policy, featuring a relaxation of trade restrictions on some key exports. In spite of a dock strike that closed India's ten largest ports for nearly two months, both exports and imports increased substantially.

In the budget for 1984–85, presented to the Lok Sabha by Finance Minister Pranab Mukherjee on February 29, total expenditures were estimated at 420 billion rupees (U.S. $42 billion). The budget called for a 7% in-

---

INDIA • Information Highlights

Official Name: Republic of India.
Location: South Asia.
Area: 1,269,340 sq mi (3 287 590 km²).
Population (mid-1984 est.): 746,400,000.
Chief Cities (1981 census): New Delhi, the capital, 4,865,077; Bombay, 8,227,332; Calcutta, 3,291,-655.
Government: *Head of state,* Zail Singh, president (took office July 1982). *Head of government,* Rajiv Gandhi, prime minister (took office Oct. 31, 1984). *Legislature*—Parliament: Rajya Sabha (Council of States) and Lok Sabha (House of the People).
Monetary Unit: Rupee (7.82 rupees equal U.S. $1, Dec. 31, 1984).
Gross National Product (1982 U.S. $): $146,000,-000,000.
Economic Indexes (1983): *Consumer Prices* (1970 = 100), all items, 289.1; food, 282.0. *Industrial Production* (1975 = 100), 144.
Foreign Trade (1983 U.S. $): *Imports,* $13,162,-000,000; *exports,* $7,922,000,000.

crease in military spending, emphasized energy projects and rural development, and provided new benefits for the poor and middle class. It also gave added impetus to the Twenty-Point Program of national development through substantial increases for the last year of the Sixth Five-Year Plan.

A Draft Approach Paper on the Seventh Five-Year Plan, approved by the National Development Council (NDC) in July, envisaged a total investment of 3.2 trillion rupees during the Plan period (1985–90). In an address to the NDC, Mrs. Gandhi said that the basic priorities of the Seventh Plan would be food, work, and productivity.

India's economic policies were praised by the World Bank, the Asia Development Bank, and various foreign private banks. In June the World Bank and the International Development Association promised to provide loans of $784.7 million, and in October a consortium of nine foreign banks agreed to lend India $300 million.

Foreign Policy. Although preoccupied with internal problems, Mrs. Gandhi continued to be active in world affairs, especially in her role as chairman of the nonaligned movement. In February she traveled to Moscow for the funeral of late Soviet President Yuri Andropov. In April she made official visits to Libya and Tunisia. In May she joined the prime ministers of Greece and Sweden and the presidents of Argentina, Mexico, and Tanzania in an appeal to the world's nuclear powers to halt all testing, production, and deployment of nuclear weapons and to reduce their nuclear stockpiles. India's President Zail Singh made official visits to Mexico and Argentina in late April.

India's relations with its neighbors were particularly troubled in 1984. Relations with Pakistan had seemed to improve as a result of the renewal of high-level talks on India's draft of a friendship treaty and Pakistan's proposal for a nonaggression pact. But relations were soon soured by several developments, including reports in the Pakistani press that India had deployed 29 army divisions along the border, Indian allegations of Pakistani involvement in the crisis in the Punjab, and clashes along the cease-fire line in Kashmir.

India and Bangladesh held several productive meetings in 1984, but relations were strained because of tensions along the frontier. In 1984, India began to construct a barbed wire fence along its entire border with Bangladesh, an action that the Dhaka government protested bitterly.

Heightened tensions in Sri Lanka between Sinhalese and Tamils led to unprecedented strains in India's relations with that country. The Indian government denied Sri Lankan charges of interference in Sri Lanka's internal crisis, but there was no doubt that the Indian government was disturbed by the communal tensions in Sri Lanka and that many Indians were sympathetic to the Tamil cause. Thousands of Tamils from Sri Lanka—perhaps as many as 40,000—took refuge in India, mainly among their fellow Tamils in the south. Mrs. Gandhi denied persistent reports that several thousand Tamils were being trained in guerrilla warfare training camps in the Indian state of Tamil Nadu. Official relations between the two countries did improve somewhat as a result of several high-level contacts, including a visit by President Junius Jayewardene to New Delhi in late June and early July.

Highlights in Indo-Soviet relations in 1984 were the six-day official visit to India in March by the late Soviet Defense Minister Dmitri Ustinov, and the signing of a contract in August under which India would receive about 40 new supersonic MiG-29 "Fulcrum" jet fighter planes, with the first to arrive before the end of the year.

Indians continued to be critical of the United States because of its military aid to Pakistan and what Mrs. Gandhi described in February as "indifference" to India. The visit of U.S. Vice-President George Bush in May seemed to have little effect in improving relations. Indians were particularly incensed by U.S. news reports that India was contemplating an attack on Pakistan's nuclear installations at Kahuta; government spokesmen characterized the reports as "utterly baseless and ridiculous."

Limited contacts between India and the People's Republic of China continued throughout the year. In January a 12-member Chinese delegation, led by the president of the Chinese Academy of Social Sciences, visited India on a "study tour." The following month, a high-level Chinese delegation participated in a conference of Asian parliamentarians in New Delhi. And in September the fifth round of bilateral talks since 1981 was held in Beijing.

An official visit by Japan's Prime Minister Yasuhiro Nakasone in May also was of special interest. He was the first Japanese prime minister to visit India in 23 years.

In early November nearly 100 foreign leaders, including the prime ministers of Great Britain, Japan, and the Soviet Union; the presidents of Bangladesh, Pakistan, Poland, and Sri Lanka; the U.S. secretary of state; and the secretary-general of the United Nations, attended the funeral ceremonies in New Delhi for Indira Gandhi.

Other. The third and largest Indian expedition to Antarctica, in February–March, left behind a 12-member party that established India's first permanent station on that continent. In April, air force pilot Rakesh Sharma became India's first man in space when he joined two Soviet cosmonauts on a one-week mission.

NORMAN D. PALMER, *Professor Emeritus*
University of Pennsylvania

INDIANA

Republicans dominated the national, state, and local elections in Indiana in 1984. The dominant issue in the state's 30-day, alternate-year "short session" of the General Assembly was a local government financing bill. An improving economy, a banner agricultural year, the transfer of professional football's Baltimore Colts to Indianapolis, and a controversial pornography ordinance also headlined events during the year.

Election. President Ronald Reagan carried 91 of the state's 92 counties to defeat Democrat Walter Mondale by more than 500,000 votes, an even larger win than that over Jimmy Carter in 1980. Gov. Robert D. Orr's victory over Democratic challenger state Sen. Wayne Townsend put Republicans in the statehouse for an unprecedented fifth consecutive term, but Orr's less-than-expected 6% margin of victory indicated considerable cross-party voting in the state. The Democrats also made political history by nominating a woman, Ann Delaney, for lieutenant governor. Democrats retained four of Indiana's ten congressional seats, with the eighth district race still undecided late in the year. Republican challenger Rick McIntyre contested the 73-vote victory of incumbent Frank McCloskey. Republicans maintained clear majorities in both houses of the General Assembly—60–40 in the House of Representatives and 31–19 in the Senate.

Voters allowed Chief Justice of the state Supreme Court Richard Given to retain his judgeship for ten more years despite his controversial decision in favor of the parents of Baby Doe, a Down's syndrome infant with other medical complications who was not fed or given medical care.

Indiana's senior senator, Richard M. Lugar, was selected as chairman of the Senate Foreign Relations Committee in November.

Legislature. A local government funding measure, hailed as the most substantive change in local financing in more than a decade, occupied much of the lawmakers' time during the legislative session. In addition to allowing cities, towns, and counties to increase their property-tax levies by at least 5% annually, the new law gave counties the option of imposing a local income tax that could eventually reach 1% of a resident's income. Although the net result of the measure will be higher property taxes for homeowners and businesses, the law also continues a 2% property-tax homestead credit through 1985 and raises it to 4% in 1986. Support for the measure, considered a "significant victory for local home rule" by some and a "turkey" by others, cut across party lines.

Also passed were bills relating to reforms in education and drunk driving. Failing to pass was a hotly contested bill setting up an experimental merit-pay program for teachers. A highly controversial utility-regulation measure removing a legislative ban on charging customers for local telephone calls on the basis of number and length died in committee.

Budget. The 1984 supplementary budget bill added more than $161 million to the $14.1 billion two-year state budget adopted in 1983. The increase was the largest for a nonbudget year since legislators started annual sessions in 1971. Included were $12 million for Project SAFE, the assistance program for residential heating bills; $25 million for highway paving; and $8.9 million to improve the state's mental health facilities. Although legislators approved $27 million for new educational programs proposed by Governor Orr, many Democrats charged that the budget measure shortchanged education at all levels. Members of both parties criticized the $8 million appropriation for a White River State Park in Indianapolis. Passed without debate were significant pay raises for the governor, judges, legislators, and other elected state officials.

Other. Despite harvesting problems resulting from unseasonal autumn rains, most Indiana counties experienced a banner year in corn and soybean production. Lower unemployment and inflation rates contributed to an improved economy in the state.

Amid much controversy with Baltimore and the National Football League, Robert Irsay moved his professional football team franchise from Baltimore to Indianapolis. Although the Colts played the 1984 season in the newly opened Hoosierdome, an impending court battle would determine the team's right to remain in Indiana.

Also in the capital, an ordinance outlawing pornography on the grounds that it violated women's civil rights was signed into law and immediately challenged in federal court. It was declared unconstitutional in November.

LORNA LUTES SYLVESTER
Indiana University

INDIANA • Information Highlights

Area: 36,185 sq mi (93 720 km²).
Population (July 1, 1983 est.): 5,479,000.
Chief Cities (July 1, 1982 est.): Indianapolis, the capital, 707,655; Fort Wayne, 167,633; Gary, 147,537.
Government (1984): *Chief Officers*—governor, Robert D. Orr (R); lt. gov., John Mutz (R.) *General Assembly*—Senate, 50 members; House of Representatives, 100 members.
State Finances (fiscal year 1983): *Revenues,* $6,166,000,000; *expenditures,* $5,843,000,000.
Personal Income (1983): $57,401,000,000; per capita, $10,476.
Labor Force (May 1984): *Civilian labor force,* 2,663,300; *unemployed,* 234,900 (8.9% of total force).
Education: *Enrollment* (fall 1982)—public elementary schools, 663,547; public secondary, 335,995; colleges and universities (fall 1983), 256,470. *Public school expenditures* (1982–83), $2,239,068,800 ($2,414 per pupil).

266

INDONESIA

The political calm of recent years was abruptly broken on September 12, when at least 1,500 devout Muslims attacked a police post in the Jakarta harbor area. The immediate cause of the attack was the arrest a day earlier of four men charged with assaulting an official who was removing antigovernment posters from a mosque. According to the government, nine persons were killed and 53 injured by security forces defending the post.

Some analysts argued that the larger cause of the incident was a continuing government effort to push Muslims out of the political arena. For more than a year, President Suharto and his lieutenants had been attempting to persuade all political parties and mass membership associations to accept the state ideology of *Pancasila* as their basic doctrine. The government's declared purpose was to quash forever the idea of an Islamic state in Indonesia.

Muslims could take little comfort from the first Congress of the Development Unity Party, held in Jakarta in September. Development Unity is an assemblage, created at government insistence in 1973, of four Islamic parties. As a result of trends, confirmed and extended at the 1984 Congress, among the four constituent parties and the government, the Muslim community will be less well represented in parliament and other institutions than at any time in the history of independent Indonesia.

Longtime foreign minister (1966–1977) and vice-president (1978–1983) Adam Malik died of liver cancer on September 5 (*see* OBITUARIES).

Economy. As in 1983, economic policy decisions reflected concern with slowed national growth and shrinking budget revenues. State banks were permitted to remove credit ceilings and raise interest rates, generating a substantial flow of new capital and adding about $2 billion (U.S.) to the country's net foreign exchange reserves. Income and sales tax reforms, designed to make up for losses in oil revenue caused by the world recession, were passed early in the year, though implementation of the sales tax was later postponed for administrative reasons. A new contract was signed with Indonesia's largest oil producer, Caltex, by which the government would get 88% of production after costs and Caltex would get 12%. Both the new Five-Year Plan and the 1984–85 budget emphasized austerity and called for further reductions in oil subsidies.

The World Bank and the Inter-Governmental Group on Indonesia (IGGI), a consortium of creditor nations, again approved the government's basic economic policy direction. The IGGI granted a new loan package of $2.45 billion, an 11% increase over 1983.

Foreign Policy. Independence movements in Irian Jaya and East Timor continued to plague Indonesia's relations with Papua New Guinea

AP/Wide World

Indonesian Marines remove an unexploded bomb from an ammunition warehouse in Jakarta. An October explosion at the site killed some 25 persons and injured 100 others.

and Australia. In Irian Jaya the issue was Jakarta's plan, already being implemented, to resettle a million Javanese and Balinese within five years, many of them along the northern and southern border with Papua New Guinea. Ongoing clashes between the Free Papua Movement and the Indonesian armed forces around the provincial capital of Jayapura led to flights of several thousand refugees across the border.

In 1984, Indonesia first negotiated with and then launched a major campaign against *Fretilin,* the leftist nationalist movement in East Timor. The Australian Labor Party government, whose left wing includes many *Fretilin* supporters, attempted with little success to persuade the Indonesian government to change its policies. In the United Nations, debate on the Timor issue was postponed for another year at the request of Portugal and Indonesia.

R. WILLIAM LIDDLE
The Ohio State University

INDONESIA • Information Highlights

Official Name: Republic of Indonesia.
Location: Southeast Asia.
Area: 736,000 sq mi (1 906 240 km²).
Population (mid-1984 est.): 161,600,000.
Chief Cities (1980 census): Jakarta, the capital, 6,480,000; Surabaya, 2,017,000; Bandung, 1,461,-000; Medan, 1,373,000.
Government: *Head of state and government,* Suharto, president (took office for fourth five-year term March 1983). *Legislature* (unicameral)— People's Consultative Assembly.
Monetary Unit: Rupiah (1,033.00 rupiahs equal U.S.$1, Oct. 22, 1984).
Gross National Product (1983 U.S.$): $70,000,-000,000.
Economic Index (1983): *Consumer Prices* (1980 = 100), all items, 137.4; food, 132.6.
Foreign Trade (1983 U.S.$): *Imports,* $16,352,-000,000; *exports,* $21,146,000,000.

Business equipment, especially the latest in office machinery, was being produced and sold at an increasingly rapid pace.

Xerox Corporation

INDUSTRIAL PRODUCTION

U.S. industrial production in 1984 recovered sharply throughout most of the year but slackened in the closing months. Still, the 11% gain raised the capacity-utilization level in manufacturing to nearly 82% from the 75.2% recorded for 1983. That helped fuel a capital investment boom that was sparked by the tax cuts of 1981.

Industrial production in the six major Western European countries rose about 2% in 1984 after drifting down 0.1% in 1983. Growth was strong in Japan, equaling the U.S. rate of gain. Industrial production spurred the economies of such rapidly industrializing countries as Taiwan, South Korea, and Singapore and the colony of Hong Kong, fostering growth rates in the 8–10% range.

U.S. industrial production continued to rise strongly throughout most of 1984 but faltered in September and October, primarily due to strikes against General Motors both in the United States and Canada. After rising 6.5% in 1983 to 147.6 (1967 = 100), the Federal Reserve Board's index of industrial production increased 11% in 1984.

Among products, the fastest pace was set by business equipment, with production up some 18% compared with a 3% drop in 1983. Defense-equipment output rose 12% after posting a 9.7% increase in 1983. Consumer-goods output was up 6.5%, just about matching the preceding year's growth.

While manufacturing production overall rose almost 11.5%, compared with a 7.8% gain in 1983, the best record was by durable goods with a 15% increase, almost double the 1983 rise. Nondurables manufacturing posted an almost 7.5% gain, almost matching the 1983 increase.

Utilities increased output more than 5%, after a 2.2% gain in 1983. Mining output grew 9%, reversing the 7.7% drop of 1983. Oil and gas extraction, after plummeting 11.1% in 1983, posted a 4.4% gain. Other mining, after rising a mere 1.1% in 1983, increased 19%, thanks to a nearly 40% step-up in iron-ore mining. Nonferrous-ore production grew 4%.

Among durable-goods producers, the non-electrical machinery group led with a nearly 21% increase in 1984, following a 1.1% uptick in 1983. The best performance was by office machinery, up 20% following an 8.9% increase. General industrial machinery rose nearly 19% after a 2.8% increase. Engines and turbines recovered from their 12.7% drop in 1983 by posting an almost 25% increase. Output of farm equipment showed a 13.3% drop for 1983 and registered a 1984 increase of equal percentage. Still, farm equipment unit sales amounted to just 45% of the 1979 level. Construction equipment came up with a 26% increase, offsetting the 16.7% loss in 1983. Metalworking machinery was up 21%, after a 4% decline.

Electrical-machinery producers posted a production gain of almost 18%, after a 9.6% increase in 1983. Output of electronic components shot up 25% following a 14.2% step-up. Radio and TV set producers showed a 21% growth after increasing 15.4%. Communication equipment was up nearly 16% after increasing 6.3%. Household appliances recorded a 12% increase following a 15% rise.

Transportation equipment racked up a 16% gain after a 12.4% growth. Motor vehicles and parts producers recorded a 21% gain after a 25.2% jump in 1983, as domestic passenger car assemblies rose from 6.8 million to 7.8 million in 1984. The hottest sellers were Chrysler's minivans and sporty models such as General Motors' Fiero and Ford's Thunderbird. U.S. truck production also rebounded from 2.4 million in 1983 to slightly more than 3 million. Aircraft and parts production was up 8% after a 1.7% drop. Railroad-equipment production zoomed by 115% following a 50.5% collapse in 1983. Ships and boats were up almost 20% after a 1.5% increase. Mobile-home production edged up only 1.7% following a 25.1% jump in 1983.

Instrument production rose nearly 10% after a 2% drop. Consumer-instrument products reversed the 8.3% drop of 1983 and increased 7% in 1984. Equipment-instruments output rose nearly 12% after rising 2.6%.

Fabricated-metal-products production rose 14% after a 4.7% increase. Output of metal cans was up about 1.5%, just about the same rate of gain as in the preceding year. Production of hardware, plumbing, and structural materials was up 12% after a meager 0.6% increase in 1983. Other fabricated-metal-products production rose almost 20%, double the increase in the preceding year.

Lumber and wood products were up almost 8% after a 21.8% rise. The increase in household furniture output was 6% compared with a 17.9% step-up in 1983. Fixtures and office-furniture output raced ahead at a 23% increase, more than fivefold the growth shown for the preceding year. Production of ordinance increased 8% after rising 9.7%.

Stone, clay, and glass products production rose 11% after posting an 11.6% increase for 1983. Glass products were up more than 9% following a 2.6% gain, but cement and structural-clay products slowed their rate of increase from 15.7% to 12%.

Primary metals as a group rang up a 10% increase after snapping back by 13.9% in 1983. Basic steel and mill products output rose 7% after a 17.8% growth. Shipments of steel products rose 9.8% in 1983 to 67.6 million tons, and a 15% increase was posted for 1984. Iron and steel foundries pushed their production up by 20% after an 11.6% increase. Nonferrous-metal producers raised production 10.2% in 1983 and increased by a roughly like percentage in 1984.

Among producers of nondurable goods, rubber and plastic products as a group repeated their 1983 growth performance of 14.7%. Tire output jumped by 24% after a 10.8% gain in 1983. Rubber products excluding tires registered a 12% increase after rising 5.4%. Plastics products were up 13% following a 17.2% increase.

Output of chemicals was up 7% after rising 9.6%. In the group, the fastest rise was in paints, up nearly 17% after a 2.6% increase in 1983. Synthetic materials and basic chemicals recorded increases of 7%, after respective gains of 19.1% and 11.4%. Agricultural chemicals output rose nearly 10% after dropping 5.4%. Drugs and medicines were up 6% after a 5% gain. Soaps and toiletries posted a 2% increase after rising 4.3%.

Food-products production grew about 4.5% following a 3.6% growth in 1983. Tobacco products crept ahead 2% following a decline of 4.6%. Textile-mill products were practically unchanged after a 13.1% increase in 1983.

Petroleum-products production was up nearly 4% after declining 1.3%. Paper and paper products production climbed 6% after rising 9%. Leather and leather products output declined 0.7% after eking out a 1.8% gain in 1983.

Employment. While total private nonagricultural employment had topped the prerecession, July 1981, job count by 5.5% by September 1984, manufacturing jobs at 19.9 million were still 2% below the previous business cycle peak.

Employment in durable-goods manufacturing rose 7% between September 1983 and September 1984 to 11.8 million, but that was still 3.3% lower than when the recession began in July 1981. Electrical and electronic-equipment industry employment grew 9.7% over the year to 2.2 million, or 8% above the prerecession level. Lumber and wood-products job count was 730,000, or 3% above the year-before level, and topped the prerecession level by 7.7%. Employment in furniture and fixtures was 486,000 in September 1984, 4.8% above the year earlier count, and 2.7% higher than before the last recession began. Jobs in transportation equipment reached 1.95 million in September, 8% higher than the year-before job count and also 1.7% higher than in July 1981.

Industry groups with job counts still below the prerecession level were primary metals, where jobs totaled 877,000 in September, 2.7% higher than in September 1983 but 23% below the prerecession level. The nonelectrical-machinery group reported September jobs at 2.2 million, up nearly 9% from the year before but 10.6% lower than in July 1981. The job count in the fabricated-metals group was 1.5 million,

A new locomotive is prepared for transport. Generally, transportation equipment production increased in 1984.

an over-the-year gain of 6.7% but still 6.6% below when the recession began. Jobs in the instruments group grew 3.8% over the year to 727,000 in September, but remained 1% below the prerecession level. Stone, clay, and glass products manufacturers increased their over-the-year employment by 4% to 623,000, but that fell short of the prerecession count by 2.8%.

Nondurable-goods manufacturing industries added 1.9% more jobs over the year, but the total of 8.1 million was 0.5% short of the prerecession level. Employment in leather and leather goods dropped 5% over the year to 203,000 in September 1984, almost 18% below the July 1981 level. Textile mills saw payrolls decline by 1% over the year, putting the job count of 752,000 some 10% below the prerecession level. Despite an over-the-year gain of 1% to 1.2 million, apparel-industry jobs remained 4.6% short of the July 1981 total. Jobs in the petroleum- and coal-products industry dropped 4% from the year before and were 13% below the prerecession level. Chemicals producers increased employment 1.5% over the year, but the 1.1 million total was still 4% below the count as of July 1981. The paper and allied products group gained 2.3%, and the job count of 685,000 fell only 1% short of the prerecession level.

Employment in the printing and publishing industry grew 5% over the year, putting the total of 1.37 million 8% over the July 1981 level. Jobs in the rubber and plastics-products group increased 8.7% from September 1983 to September 1984 to 810,000, some 8% higher than before the recession began. Tobacco manufacturers added 1% to their job count over the year, and their employment of 73,000 was nearly 3% above the prerecession level.

Mining employment bounced back with a 7.5% increase between September 1983 and September 1984, but it was still 12% below the prerecession peak. Employment in public utilities crept up 1.9%, to 903,000.

New Equipment and Investment. Reflecting the growth of industrial production as well as giving it a strong boost was the 14% increase in the 1984 business investment in new plant and equipment. The increase came after a decline of 4.8% in 1983. Measured in current dollars, the investment total for 1984 was $308 billion.

Manufacturing industries spent $130 billion for capital investment, up 17.5% from 1983. A large increase was by producers of durable goods, 22% for the whole group as compared with an 8% drop. Transportation-equipment producers showed the largest gains: motor vehicles producers invested $11 billion for a 53% increase as compared to a 14% drop in 1983. Aircraft manufacturers boosted investment by 12% after an 18% drop. Electrical-machinery industry's investment increased 23% following a 2.6% gain. Nonelectrical-machinery manu-

facturers raised spending by 16% after a 4% drop. Fabricated-metals producers showed a 16% increase after a 14% fall-off. Producers of primary metals registered a 12% increase following a 14% decline. Stone, clay, and glass manufacturers showed a 6% increase after a 6% drop. Other durables producers, such as lumber, furniture, and instrument, increased capital spending by 22% after a 13% cutback in 1983.

While nondurable producers as a group hiked capital spending by 14% after a 5.5% decline, the largest increase was posted by textiles, up 22% after a gain of 4% in 1983. The paper industry continued its expansion, up 20% following a 3.5% increase. Chemicals were up nearly 13% after practically no change. The rubber-industry investment was up 23% after a 12% gain. The petroleum industry raised capital spending by 11% following a 12% retrenchment. Food and beverage producers boosted spending by 13% after cutting back by 14.7%. Other nondurables, such as apparel, tobacco, leather, and printing and publishing, increased capital spending by almost 15% after a 5.9% gain in 1983.

After cutting capital investment by 23.4%, the mining industry increased outlays by 9% in 1984. Electrical utilities reduced capital expenditures by 1%, after a 4.8% increase in 1983. Gas and other utilities rebounded with a 35% increase from an 18% drop.

Among transportation industries, railroads pumped up spending by 36% after a 10.6% decline. Air transportation cut back by 20% after a 4% decline. Other transportation industries, such as pipelines, increased spending by 30% after a 3.6% slide.

International Developments. Among major industrial countries, Japan raised industrial production by nearly 11% after a 3.5% gain in 1983. Following a 5.9% increase, Canada's production rose 7.5% in 1984. West German and British production performances were dampened by strikes in 1984. A metalworkers' strike in the second quarter held West Germany's gain to 3.3% in 1984, following an anemic increase of 0.6% in 1983. Production in the United Kingdom rose only 0.9% in 1984, after posting a 3.3% increase in 1983.

Industrial production continued to slide in France, down 0.2% after a 0.3% drop in 1983. Italy recorded a 4% gain after a drop of 5.3% in 1983. Belgium posted a 6.5% gain after a 7.1% increase in 1983. The Netherlands showed a 3.5% increase in 1984 following a 2.8% growth in 1983.

Among centrally planned economies, the industrial production plans called for the following increases in 1984: Soviet Union, 3.8%; East Germany, 3.6%; Czechoslovakia, 2.9%; Poland, 5%; Rumania, 6.7%; Hungary, 2%; and Bulgaria, 5%.

AGO AMBRE, *U.S. Department of Commerce*

The Venturi Collection
Knoll International

Wendell Castle's Coffee Table
Si Chi Ko, Workbench

INTERIOR DESIGN

The important trends in contemporary furniture design all appear to evince the Post Modern notions of diversity and ambiguity. But while the most noteworthy new designs have certain characteristics in common—such as odd or exaggerated forms and brilliant applied color—there are fundamental differences in approach and emphasis. One style is distinctly historical in inspiration, another gives emphasis to more purely artistic forms, and a third gives vent to a variety of impulses.

The controversial Philadelphia architect Robert Venturi designed a series of chairs for Knoll International with exaggerated historic references. The collection follows a series of historical styles—including Chippendale, Queen Anne, Directoire, and Art Nouveau—adapted for industrial manufacture. The chairs are made of molded, laminated plywood, with surfaces that are ornamentally perforated and contoured, in an uninhibited range of color.

Noted Post Modern neo-classicist Michael Graves chose the soft, plump, sensuous profiles of the 1940s for his latest furniture designs. The large-scale patterned upholstery almost gives the appearance of camouflage.

No less controversial are the recent one-of-a-kind furniture designs by artists and artist-craftsmen concerned with basic form, line, texture, and proportion. When Formica invited artists to create furniture utilizing the company's latest surfacing material, the original intention was to retail the pieces through Workbench stores. The results—including Wendell Castle's well-publicized coffee table, Mitch Ryerson's Victorian hall stand, and Gary Knox Burnett's partner's desk—proved so intriguing that they were sent on the road for exhibition in museums and galleries. But the marriage of art and furniture design does not stop there. Interior design publications have been showing an astonishing array of furniture work by geographically isolated artists.

Perhaps even more astonishing is the Memphis series—chairs, tables, storage, and lighting from followers of the Italian designer Ettore Sottsass, Jr. Also called Il Nuovo Design, the style refers to such diverse schools of art as Cubism, Pointillism, and the Surrealism of Giorgio de Chirico. The Italian designers emphasize that their work is *not* Post-Modernist. A major design objective has to do with the production process: there is no tooling. All surfaces are colored sheets of Melamine cut and bent into odd shapes and ornamented with printed silk-screen designs sometimes embedded with faceted colored glass chips.

JEANNE WEEKS

INTERNATIONAL TRADE AND FINANCE

In 1982 the severe debt problems of several major developing countries threatened an unraveling of the international financial system. By the end of 1984, however, those rifts were largely patched up, and the world's leaders heaved a cautious sigh of relief.

"The worst aspects of the debt crisis may be behind us," World Bank President A. W. Clausen told the finance ministers of the 148 nations that are members of his institution at their late September annual meeting in Washington, DC. "But," he added, "many nations, as well as the global banking system, remain exposed to risks of high indebtedness which must be made more manageable."

Recovery. Helping the developing nations deal with their problem was a solid world economic recovery. Indeed, the staff of the International Monetary Fund (IMF) noted in September: ". . . activity in the world economy is strengthening more rapidly than projected by the staff six months ago."

This, the staff noted, was especially true of the United States. Expansion there was so strong that many observers were afraid it would lead to a renewal of inflation unless it was slowed down. That slowdown occurred. Growth in real gross national product (GNP, the output of goods and services after subtracting the inflation rate) dropped from a 10.1% annual rate in the first quarter to 2.7% in the third quarter, according to the first GNP estimate. Most economists anticipated some increase in that level of activity as the year continued. Growth for the year was estimated at about 7% in real terms.

The IMF staff also boosted its growth projections for most other industrial nations. It was figuring on a real 5% increase in output in the industrial nations as a group. In turn, this growth was boosting the exports and business activity in the developing countries.

Adding to the cheer as the year wore on was a substantial drop in interest rates in the United States. The rate on federal funds, the interest rate banks charge on their overnight loans to each other, fell below 10% in mid-October. The U.S. dollar, which had been embarrassingly strong, also dropped somewhat. Inflation remained modest. Even oil prices were weakening. All this was good news for President Reagan, seeking reelection. He boasted to the joint annual meeting of the World Bank and the IMF: "The United States has enjoyed 21 straight months of economic growth—the strongest growth since 1950."

Trade. President Reagan also noted that rapid growth in the United States, the world's largest single market, had meant increased

AP/Wide World

Jacques de Larosière addresses annual IMF meeting.

trading opportunities for other nations. Total U.S. imports, he noted, were going to be up about 25% in 1984 over the level of 1983. Indeed, 1984's trade deficit of more than $100 billion was considered troublesome, and one reason for the slowdown.

As the year ended, Western Europe was expecting an average growth in 1984 of around 3% in real terms, Japan about 5%, and Canada something over 4%. As a whole, the industrial world was enjoying its strongest economic growth in eight years. Economists estimated that the developing countries as a group would grow in constant dollars by some 3.5%, the best performance since the 1970s.

As measured by volume, world trade was up 9% in the first half of 1984 from a year earlier, according to a report by the General Agreement on Tariffs and Trade (GATT) in Geneva. The international agency expected the value of world trade in 1984 to be up 5–7%, held back in statistical terms by the high value of the U.S. dollar. The percentage gain in actual physical volume of trade was somewhat higher. The dollar value of trade in 1983 (statistics for 1984 would not be available until late 1985) amounted to $1.8 trillion dollars, down 2% because of the stronger dollar.

The Debt. As for the world debt problem, there were several favorable developments. One was the happier financial outlook for the Eastern European bloc. Its total net debt in hard currencies stood at $61.1 billion (U.S.) at the end of 1983, down from $65.6 billion at the end of 1982. Western European bankers figured that the Soviet-bloc debt crisis was largely over, and West European countries began lending money voluntarily to the Soviet Union and its allies once more during 1984. These nations had cut back imports sufficiently to repair their international financial situation.

Another significant development was the rescheduling agreement between representatives of some 550 commercial banks and Mexican officials of almost $50 billion in public-sector debts. (Mexico's total foreign debts were running at about $96 billion.) The deal signified a new long-term approach to the debt problem. It signaled an end of short-term crisis management for at least one nation. The package spread out over 14 years the principal due on past loans, thereby permitting Mexico to plan much better payments on its debts and provide financial room for further expansion of the nation's economy. Indeed, Mexico did resume a modest rate of real growth in output, with more growth expected in 1985. That was a dramatic reversal from its 4.7% decline in gross domestic product in 1983. The new terms of the loans were expected to save Mexico about $400 million per year in interest charges.

In late September, after nine months of negotiation, Argentina reached agreement with the IMF on an economic adjustment program. Since Argentina had not been making all payments on time on its more than $45 billion in debts, many commercial banks were forced to declare some relatively modest losses. With the political risks involved in Argentina's change from a military regime to a democracy, the new government was slow to accept any degree of austerity, considered necessary by the IMF, to improve its balance of payments.

The Philippines was the last of the major debtors to reach agreement with the IMF on a package of economic reforms. That was pretty well worked out by mid-October, after more than two weeks of negotiations in New York between Prime Minister César Virata and representatives of nearly 400 commercial banks. The Philippines had started on its austerity program well in advance of the deal in June with a devaluation of the peso and a tightening of the budget. As often is the case in reschedulings, the Philippines got new money—nearly $1 billion—from the commercial banks, as well as a stretching out of the portion of the nation's $25.6 billion in debts coming due before the end of 1985. The IMF agreed to loan the Philippines about $600 million as soon as the package with the commercial banks was fully tied up.

Developing countries as a group were burdened by external debts exceeding $800 billion, with the Latin American nations accounting for more than $350 billion. Obviously, the decline in interest rates later in the year was a great relief to them, just as a rise in rates earlier in the year had caused them much anguish. The prime rate of commercial banks, a basis for many loans, started the year at 11% before climbing to 13% by summer.

Meetings and Summits. Some 11 Latin American debtor nations met in Cartagena, Colombia, June 21–22, and called for the adoption of measures leading to drastic and immediate reduction of real and nominal interest rates in international markets. They proposed a "compensatory window" at the IMF to provide funds offsetting high interest rates. They suggested that interest charges sometimes should be added to the capital of the loan.

In September the Latin debtors met again, as did the finance ministers of the Common-

wealth countries. Further, the "Group of 24" developing countries gathered just prior to the IMF–World Bank meeting. Each of these groups suggested a renewal of the "North-South dialogue" between the rich and poorer nations to deal with the debt crisis and other economic problems. The industrial countries agreed on a renewal of the dialogue, but only on their own terms. The talks, they insisted, must take place within the Interim Committee of the IMF, and the Development Committee of both the IMF and the World Bank, during their regular meetings in April 1985. (The industrial powers retain control of these bodies because of a system of weighted voting.) One boost to the mood at the IMF–World Bank joint meeting was a drop in the prime rate to 12.75% by Morgan Guaranty Trust Company on September 21, when many finance ministers and central bankers were already assembled in Washington. Other banks followed soon after. A few weeks later the prime rate in the United States notched down again to 12.5% and later headed lower.

At the IMF meeting, the United States and some other major industrial countries blocked the request of France and developing countries for a $15 billion increase in special drawing rights, a kind of international money issued by the IMF. The U.S. powers also managed to reduce slightly borrowing access to the IMF by nations in international payments trouble. Since it was considered unlikely that any IMF member will need the maximum access, the change was regarded as mostly symbolic.

At its meeting, the World Bank urged a program to help out Black African nations, most of which have been backward economically for years. Many also now face famine because of a drought. Though donor nations embraced the program, it was not immediately clear whether they would dig up the $2 billion in extra money that the Bank saw as needed. Shortly after the meeting, the United States announced that it was preparing to deal with the short-term famine emergency with extra supplies of grain.

The heads of government of the United States, Great Britain, West Germany, France, Canada, Italy, and Japan held their tenth annual economic summit in London, June 7–9. The idea of a spring 1985 renewal of the North-South dialogue was one of the proposals discussed. The London summit made more significant political declarations than economic ones. The seven democratic leaders sent a gentle invitation to the Soviet Union to come back to the arms negotiation table. They issued separate declarations on international terrorism, the Persian Gulf war, and democratic values. On the economic side, they released a 12-page communiqué which included, as British Prime Minister Margaret Thatcher put it, a ten-point program to "sustain the economic recovery, to create new jobs, and to spread our prosperity much more widely across the world." The communiqué included an agreement to go ahead with a new round of trade negotiations, although no date was set. The seven leaders also talked of increasing the flow of resources to Third World countries, though no new aid money was visible; urged developing countries to open their doors further to private investment; acknowledged the need to keep their markets open for the exports of developing countries; and devised a five-part program for dealing with developing country debts, including multiyear rescheduling (as followed later in the case of Mexico).

Protectionism, Deficits, Etc. The industrial countries, despite their noble-sounding statements, actually raised more barriers to imports. The Group of 24 developing countries complained that "protectionist measures continued to intensify, reducing access for developing countries' exports and rendering adjustment in their external accounts all the more difficult." In the United States, as other industrialized countries, the picture was mixed. President Reagan turned down requests for protection on tuna, stainless steel, flatware, shoes, and copper. He also rejected a recommendation by the International Trade Commission for quotas or tariff relief for the steel industry. However, he did promise to negotiate so-called "voluntary" quotas with such nations as Brazil, Spain, and South Korea that are not covered by previous agreements limiting steel imports. By October such talks had begun. (See also special report, page 275.)

IMF Managing Director Jacques de Larosière pointed to another problem area—an "explosion" of public debt throughout the world. He strongly urged policymakers to adopt measures to reduce their "structural deficits"—those that will not disappear with complete economic recovery. Such deficits, as they build up, can have "damaging consequences," he said. In the United States, Congress passed a "down-payment" package of spending cuts and tax increases, with more deficit reduction expected after the November election. The deficit, $175 billion in fiscal 1984, was a hot item of debate between Democratic candidate Walter Mondale and President Reagan, especially after Mondale made the unusual move of announcing that he would, if elected, trim the deficit by raising taxes as well as by cutting expenditures.

Oil prices were weak for most of the year on spot markets. The Organization of the Petroleum Exporting Countries (OPEC) was forced to call an emergency meeting October 22 in Geneva after Nigeria (a member of the 13-nation cartel), Norway, and Great Britain cut crude prices by up to $2 per barrel. Previously, OPEC had managed rather well in maintaining its benchmark price of $29 per barrel.

Around the world there was some tendency to adopt freer market practices, even in some Communist countries. China made a major move in that direction in the autumn, adopting capitalist-style policies for the industrial sector. As a result of similar free-market incentives in agriculture, China had seen its food output rise 10% annually for three years. In the United States, meanwhile, the advocates of "industrial policy" (calling for greater government management of the economy) were losing the battle for public opinion in 1984. And the weakness of the Soviet economy was becoming more evident as a poor crop once again required large grain imports from the West.

DAVID R. FRANCIS
"The Christian Science Monitor"

The Rising Value of the Dollar

In relation to the currencies of its major trading partners, the U.S. dollar continued its steady rise during most of 1984. According to economists, high interest rates attracted a heavy flow of foreign capital into the United States. The strong dollar raised the price of U.S. exports and reduced the price of imports, causing trade imbalance and the loss of perhaps a million or more jobs. The value of the dollar as against other major currencies is charted below for the years 1980–1984.[1]

					1984			
	1980	1981	1982	1983	Jan.	Apr.	July	Oct.
Argentina peso	0.199	0.725	4.854	23.261	26.304	37.526	61.261	110.600
Belgium franc	31.523	38.460	49.920	55.640	57.490	55.400	58.800	60.900
Canada dollar	1.195	1.186	1.229	1.244	1.249	1.284	1.312	1.315
France franc	4.516	5.748	6.725	8.347	8.609	8.338	8.934	9.240
Great Britain pound	0.419	0.524	0.619	0.689	0.713	0.716	0.766	0.815
Ireland pound	0.527	0.633	0.716	0.881	0.910	0.880	0.942	0.994
Italy lira	903.500	1,200.000	1,370.000	1,659.500	1,714.200	1,618.700	1,786.000	1,873.500
Japan yen	203.000	219.900	235.000	232.200	234.750	225.950	246.100	245.100
Netherlands guilder	2.129	2.468	2.624	3.064	3.169	3.041	3.292	3.400
West Germany mark	1.959	2.255	2.376	2.724	2.814	2.717	2.912	3.013

[1] end of period

Tariffs

The year 1984 should have seen a weakening of U.S. trade protectionism. A world recovery was well under way, and the U.S. economy was expanding nicely. Yet Washington witnessed a slam-bang fight between protectionists and those seeking to retain a more open trading system. "The pressures for protectionism now are greater than at any time since the 1930s," said C. Fred Bergsten, director of the Institute for International Economics (IIE).

Despite their pressure, the protectionists basically lost their battle in Congress. Under threat of a presidential veto, House-Senate conferees stripped an omnibus trade bill of most of its protectionist trappings before passing it in early October. Indeed, administration officials called the bill "pro-trade." It included authority for the president to negotiate a free trade agreement with Israel. (Such negotiations were already well along.) It renewed the so-called Generalized System of Preferences (GSP), extending for eight and a half years a program of duty-free treatment for selected products—such as raw materials and simple manufactures—entering the United States from some 140 developing nations. It strengthened the president's power to retaliate against unfair trade practices by other nations, such as abuses by firms in other countries of patents, copyrights, and trademarks held by U.S. firms. It further allowed the administration to eliminate tariffs on semiconductor imports from any nation granting reciprocal treatment to the United States.

More generally, the president was granted the power under the new law to negotiate a free-trade arrangement and investment-liberalizing accord with any country or group of countries if the House Ways and Means Committee and the Senate Finance Committee give advance approval to negotiations. Then, when a deal is complete, both houses of Congress would have to approve that agreement. A re-elected Reagan administration was expected to use this provision to go back to Congress in 1985 to seek permission to negotiate free trade in certain sectors with Canada, somewhat along the lines of the existing free trade in automobiles and car parts. Broadly, administration officials saw these liberal provisions as enabling them to counter protectionism and move toward freer trade, perhaps eventually to another series of global trade negotiations like the Tokyo Round of the 1970s.

In 1984 a new antiprotectionist force sprang up in Washington. The nation's leading retailers formed a new group, the Retail Industry Trade Action Committee (RITAC), to do

AP/Wide World

A veteran steelworker signs a piece of pipe that would go to Washington with a message supporting American steel.

battle with the protectionist movement. Representing some 2 million stores and 17 million employees, the retail organization was able to claim a partial victory in August—a decision by the administration to delay briefly enforcement of new customs regulations that would have hurt perhaps as much as $500 million of textile and garment imports from the developing countries.

J. Robert Brouse, managing director of RITAC, promised that his group would fight on behalf of the consumer in other trade disputes as well. RITAC has a million-dollar budget and hired lawyers with a public-relations firm to help it persuade the public, Congress, and the administration of its position.

Despite the formation of such a group, trade experts like the IIE's Bergsten worried that the protectionist wave could do more damage in 1985, especially if the U.S. dollar remains strong. Bergsten regarded the overvaluation of the dollar—"by 25 to 30 percent" —as the leading cause of the surge in protectionism by making imports cheap and exports expensive. A 1984 trade deficit estimated at $125–130 billion (U.S.) could reach $150 billion in 1985, Bergsten predicted. History indicates, he added, that an overvalued dollar "drives protectionism."

Altogether, there were more than 100 protectionist bills before Congress in 1984. Doreen L. Brown, president of Consumers for World Trade, feels that industries sometimes win special protection because "consumers in America don't know what it is about. They don't realize the effect of protectionism on their pocketbooks." If protectionist measures were to prevail, say those who favor open trade, the cost to consumers in higher prices could be huge. Already in 1984, according to Consumers for World Trade, the hidden tax of protectionism was costing each U.S. family of four at least $1,500 a year.

Surveys of the American public have shown that a majority of citizens support specific protectionist measures. For instance, the United Steelworkers union released a survey in summer 1984 showing that an overwhelming majority of voters (76%) in the nation's major industrial states believed that the United States should be "tougher" on restricting foreign steel imports.

The Reagan administration's record on trade in 1984 was mixed. In September the president rejected an International Trade Commission recommendation that he give the steel industry five years of trade relief that would place worldwide quotas and higher tariffs on 70% of the foreign steel entering the United States. However, the president did decide to seek so-called "voluntary quotas" from those countries exporting steel to the United States but not covered by earlier restraints. By October, U.S. trade officials had already begun talks with Argentina, Brazil, Spain, Japan, and South Korea.

U.S. steel imports were running at about 25% of the market during 1984. The House had passed a bill requiring the president to cut them back to 17% of the market, and the Senate bill did not include a steel provision. The conferees, dealing with the omnibus trade bill, made the House provision a nonbinding "sense of the Congress" that imports should be cut back to between 17 and 20.2% of the market. Special Trade Representative William E. Brock, meanwhile, set a goal of limiting imports to 18.5% of the U.S. market.

The copper industry also sought to ward off imports. But the president declined to give it any special protection, as recommended by the International Trade Commission. President Reagan also refused to restrict imports of tuna, stainless steel, flatware, and shoes.

Another measure that won the support of Democratic presidential candidate Walter Mondale but got nowhere in Congress was a domestic content bill for the automobile industry, requiring cars sold in the United States to have as much as 90% domestic-made parts by 1986. The Reagan administration did continue a system of quotas that limits imports of Japanese cars.

A bill to control exports of sensitive technology, aimed primarily at the Soviet bloc, foundered in a House-Senate conference in early October. One problem was a provision that would have banned loans by U.S. banks to the South African government and the compa-nies it owns. The U.S. Department of Commerce, however, acting under presidential emergency powers, tightened its vigilance on exports of sensitive technology.

Over time, the growing economic interdependence of the United States and its trading partners should reduce protectionism, said Bergsten, a former high-ranking economist in the Treasury Department. More industries and employees are deeply involved in exporting or servicing imports. The agricultural community, for instance, though benefiting from protection against imports of tobacco, soybeans, and other commodities, has been joining the fight against protectionism by industry out of fear of retaliation by other nations against farm exports. The proportion of U.S. manufacturing employment facing import competition rose from 8.4% in 1970 to 14.7% in 1980. The proportion of manufacturing employment related directly and indirectly to exports rose from 8.1% to 14.5% during the same time span.

As in the United States, protectionist pressures were strong in other major industrial democracies. Japan, enjoying large balance-of-payments surpluses, particularly with the United States, took various steps to open up its markets to foreign goods. But a U.S.-Japan Advisory Commission concluded that the difficulties that U.S. companies still find in marketing goods in Japan "call into question Japan's commitment to free or fair trade. Japan needs to develop stronger mechanisms to ensure that once commitments are given, they are implemented fully and on schedule."

In Western Europe, with unemployment running at approximately 11%, governments were under strong pressure to protect domestic industries. So-called voluntary quotas protected European film, tires, plates, forks, automobiles, and many other products. In 1955, for example, alarmed at the prospect of competition from Fiat, Japan asked Italy to agree to limit the automobile trade to 2,200 vehicles in each direction. With the shoe on the other foot now and Japan's auto industry being stronger than Italy's, the Italian government insisted on sticking to the voluntary commitment.

The ambition of the United States was to start another major round of trade negotiations under the auspices of the General Agreement on Tariffs and Trade (GATT), based in Geneva. Special goals would be liberalization of trade in services—such as engineering, insurance, banking, and consultancy—and agriculture. The United States got approval of such a round at the economic summit of the seven major industrial powers in London in June, but no date was set; some of the more important developing countries also gave approval to the idea.

DAVID R. FRANCIS

IOWA

The 70th Iowa General Assembly meeting in its second session in 1984 worked for a total of 103 calendar days. The session may go down in Iowa legislative history as the Veto Session, in that Gov. Terry Branstad (R) vetoed more bills either in toto or by item veto than any Iowa governor. Faced with a Democratic-controlled House (60–40) and Senate (28–22), the governor vetoed two bills and used his item veto on eight in 1983, and in 1984 he used the veto authority 19 times. Thus in two years Branstad was presented with 545 bills approved by the Iowa legislature and he vetoed 5.32% of them—an unprecedented number in Iowa. Only one of Governor Branstad's vetoes was considered for an override vote, and that failed to gain the required two-thirds majority. However, it should be noted that few vetoes have ever been overridden in Iowa. Among the more unpopular vetoes cast by the first term governor was the state lottery bill, which he also rejected in 1983.

The Republican governor sent a priority list of nearly 100 items to the Democratic legislature. More than 300 of the nearly 1,000 bills introduced were passed. Among the priorities enacted were statutes that continue funding math, science, and other priority educational programs in the elementary and secondary public schools, provide more controls and regulations on bingo operations within the state, require use of seat belts or child restraint devices for children age six and under, require law enforcement agencies to begin immediately to investigate reports of missing children, and make unauthorized access or damage to private computers a crime. The 1984 Iowa legislature passed budget and revenue measures to finance a 1985 fiscal year budget of $2.2 billion and assured that a deficit would be avoided. The package, very similar to that recommended by the governor, included $329 million for higher education, $795 million for elementary and secondary education, $278 million for social services, and $38 million for environmental programs. All were record highs for the state of Iowa.

Agriculture and Economy. In spite of having the driest month of August in the history of the Weather Bureau and a very wet May and early June, the corn harvest in Iowa was 84% larger than that of 1983. Much of the increase was due to the much larger number of acres in production.

Unemployment in the state continued to be below the national average. However, unemployment in the farm implement industry—John Deere and International Harvester—remained unusually high. State revenue recovered more slowly than in most of the other states, with revenue below projected estimates.

AP/Wide World

With his wife and daughter, Senator-elect Tom Harkin (D) attends a victory rally. The 44-year-old, five-term Congressman defeated Sen. Roger Jepsen by 154,100 votes.

Elections. Iowa gave its eight electoral college votes to the Reagan-Bush ticket. However, split-ticket voting continued in the state as Tom Harkin (D) defeated incumbent Roger W. Jepsen (R) in the U.S. Senate race. The state also saw the reelection of five U.S. congressmen—James Leach (R) in the first district, Tom Tauke (R) in the second, Cooper Evans (R) in the third, Neal Smith (D) in the fourth, and Berkley Bedel (D) in the sixth. Jim Ross Lightfoot (R) won in the fifth. Democrats retained control of the legislature.

RUSSELL M. ROSS, *University of Iowa*

IOWA • Information Highlights

Area: 56,275 sq mi (145 753 km²).
Population (July 1, 1983 est.): 2,905,000.
Chief Cities (July 1, 1982 est.): Des Moines, the capital, 191,506; Cedar Rapids, 109,086; Davenport, 103,799; Sioux City (1980 census), 82,003.
Government (1984): *Chief Officers*—governor, Terry E. Branstad (R); lt. gov., Robert T. Anderson (D). *General Assembly*—Senate, 50 members; House of Representatives, 100 members.
State Finances (fiscal year 1983): *Revenues,* $4,106,000,000; *expenditures,* $4,157,000,000.
Personal Income (1983): $31,092,000,000; per capita, $10,705.
Labor Force (May 1984): *Civilian labor force,* 1,440,300; *unemployed,* 97,400 (6.8% of total force).
Education: *Enrollment* (fall 1982)—public elementary schools, 337,728; public secondary, 167,255; colleges and universities (fall 1983), 152,968. *Public school expenditures* (1982–83), $1,474,443,207 ($3,095 per pupil).

AP/Wide World

Seven hostages, above, were released from a hijacked Kuwaiti airliner December 9 at Tehran airport. Hours later, Iranian forces stormed the plane and freed the last hostages. Questions remained about Iran's role in the whole affair.

IRAN

The year 1984 may well have turned out to be a watershed for the Islamic revolution in Iran. The major focuses of the Islamic Republic and its ruling party, the Islamic Republican Party (IRP), were in two main areas: how to keep the momentum of the regime and how to conduct the war with Iraq. The two concerns were closely tied.

Domestic Affairs. By midsummer it was clear that the strains of the war were taking their toll on the party leadership. Greater divisions began to appear between those who wished to prosecute the war full-scale and those who wished to wind it down even if they were not yet willing to reach an armistice.

The divisions among the leadership of the IRP became more evident in August when the *majlis* (parliament)—itself elected in April—failed to confirm 5 of 20 cabinet ministers. The five included the ministers of defense, education, interior, work, and commerce—all key posts in determining the direction of the Islamic revolution. While Defense Minister Mohammad Salimi may have lost his post for failure to achieve significant gains in the war, the others apparently lost their positions over differences in the direction the economy should go—toward more nationalization or toward a more capital-intensive orientation—and over a split in the IRP between the ultraconservative *hojjatieh* and less conservative groups. The replacement of the commerce and work ministers may have represented a shift away from the

nationalization policies implemented during the first three years of the revolution and necessitated by the war economy. Also, legislation regarding employer-employee relations had left workers with virtually no rights or grievance procedures, which caused worker dissent and some strikes. In the midst of the war with Iraq, unrest among workers was exactly what the leaders of the IRP—Prime Minister Hosein Musavi, President Ali Khamenei, and *majlis* leader Hashemi Rafsanjani, all of whom were members of the *hojjatieh*—did not want. Coupled with the high war casualties, it could have given rise to more widespread opposition.

The commerce and labor policies also had angered the traditional *bazaari*, the national bourgeois element that supported Ayatollah

---

IRAN • Information Highlights

Official Name: Islamic Republic of Iran.
Location: Southwest Asia.
Area: 63,600 sq mi (1 647 240 km²).
Population (mid-1984 est.): 43,800,000.
Chief Cities: (1980 est.): Tehran, the capital, 6,000,000.
Government: *Supreme faqih,* Ayatollah Ruhollah Khomeini. *Head of state,* Mohammad Ali Khamenei, president (took office Oct. 1981). *Head of government,* Mir Hosein Musavi-Khamenei, premier (took office Oct. 1981). *Legislature* (unicameral)—Parliament.
Monetary Unit: Rial (90.723 rials equal U.S.$1, August 1984).
Gross National Product (1982 U.S.$): $66,500,-000,000.
Economic Index (1983): *Consumer Prices* (1970 = 100), all items, 584.7; food, 683.1.

The War

The year 1984 was the most decisive in the Iran-Iraq war since its outbreak in September 1980. It became clear in 1984 that Iran would not be able to conquer Iraq, in particular the port city of Basra, Iraq's only outlet on the Persian Gulf. The conquest of Basra would have effectively split the Arab-dominated portions of Iraq—its two major cities, Baghdad and Basra, and its two major factions, Sunni and Shiite Muslims.

Iran calculated that the capture of Basra, first attempted in 1982, would have led to the fall of Iraq's President Saddam Hussein. It would also have placed Iran in a position to dominate the politics of the six other Gulf countries—Bahrain, Kuwait, Oman, Qatar, Saudi Arabia, and the United Arab Emirates. Because the eight countries of the Persian Gulf possess 60–65% of the world's oil reserves, and 20–25% of the West's oil passes through the Gulf, the consequences of such domination would have extended far beyond the region.

The Islamic Revolution. Conquering Basra was the goal of Iran's spring 1983 offensive against Al-Amarna, situated halfway between Baghdad and Basra, and of its limited offensive in the southern sector in October 1984. A victory in either battle would have allowed the revolutionary and populist form of Islam, called "The Islam of the People" *(Al-Islam Al-Shabi* in Arabic and *Islam-i-Khalk* in Persian), to penetrate all other Arab countries, as well as such Muslim countries as Pakistan and Sudan.

Since the commencement of its revolution in 1979, Iran has hoped to export—perhaps without war—its revolution and its popular form of Islam to the other Gulf countries. Although it was Iraq that launched the war in September 1980 with a surprise attack, Iran might well have picked that country as the best place to begin. Nearly 60% of Iraq's population is Shiite, and the major Shiite shrines are in the cities of Karbala and Najaf—in which there are also about 100,000 people of Iranian descent.

In addition to the eight million Shiites in Iraq, there are nearly one million in the six traditional Gulf nations, ranging from about 11,000 in Qatar to 450,000 in Saudi Arabia. But the Shiites are underrepresented in these countries, which are ruled by Sunni families of Bedouin origin who came to power with British support in the late 19th and early 20th centuries. The aim of the Islamic Revolution is to create a change in the political order of the Gulf region, then in the Arab West (especially Egypt, Jordan, and Lebanon), and then in Sudan, Pakistan, and other nearby states.

Overt attempts to topple foreign governments began soon after the revolution began in Iran. The Saudi government was challenged in November 1979, as was the Egyptian government in October 1981 with the assassination of President Anwar el-Sadat. An attempt to change the government in Bahrain was made in December 1981. And supporters of the populist Islam were behind the fierce resistance to Israeli and U.S. presence in Lebanon in 1983 and 1984. All in all, the Islamic revolution and the repoliticization of Islam is the greatest challenge to confront Arab Nationalism in the 20th century.

Critical Point. What happened in 1984 was not the collapse of the Iranian Islamic revolution or of populist Islam. They will continue for the next several decades. It did become clear, however, that Iran was unable to prosecute the war as fully as it wanted because of mounting casualties and other military and economic problems. In 1984, Iran was perhaps reaching the critical point in terms of human resource expenditures without military victory, i.e., the conquest of Basra. In battles during February and March, Iran may have lost 30,000 men, with at least that many more wounded. Since the beginning of the war, the total number of casualties suffered by Iran was estimated at 200,000–250,000 killed and 500,000–600,000 seriously wounded. Iraqi casualties were estimated at 70,000–80,000 dead and 245,000–280,000 wounded.

In addition to the loss of human life, Iran claimed that it had sustained nearly $100 billion (U.S.) in war damages by May 1983; other sources put the figure as high as $125 billion. And in 1984, Iran was still spending some $2 million per day to fund the war. Finally, damage to oil refineries and other facilities has been estimated at $50–$60 billion.

The high costs and casualties, combined with an inflation rate of about 40%, high unemployment, slow industrial development, and an economic policy hindered by a lack of skilled workers and management contributed to a scaled-down war effort by Iran in 1984. The offensive in late October seemed to be an effort to gain a stronger strategic position in case of an armistice or negotiations in 1985–86. In any case, the "final offensive" that Iran had proclaimed for 1984 did not materialize.

Iraqi Strategy. The winding down of the war was furthered by the strengthening of Iraq's position on the foreign front. Total aid from Arab countries was nearly $30 billion by 1984, and Egypt and Jordan had some 20,000 nationals actually fighting for Iraq. Under the direction of Foreign Minister Tarik Aziz, Iraq was able to improve strained relations with Moscow. And in late November, Iraq and the United States announced that they would resume full diplomatic relations. During the summer, the U.S. Export-Import Bank agreed to guarantee up to 85% of $500 million in commercial loans, half of the estimated construction cost of a new Iraqi oil pipeline to be laid through Jordan to the port of Aqaba. All of this was intended to encourage Iraq's trend toward pragmatism and modernization, and to solidify the alliance between Iraq, Saudi Arabia, Jordan, and Egypt—the Arab regimes most vulnerable to Islamic populism and most closely tied to the West.

As a result of its increased support from the West, Iraq was forced to stop employing Tabun, a nerve gas of World War II vintage, and mustard gas. Iraq's use of lethal chemical agents in the war had met with strong international disapproval when it was discovered in spring 1984.

Relying on five French-supplied Super Etendard warplanes equipped with Exocet missiles, Iraq in 1984 attempted to internationalize the war by attacking Gulf shipping to and from Iran. Baghdad hoped to increase the concern of the major oil-consuming countries, which obtain a large percentage of their oil from the Gulf, bringing international pressure on Iran to end the conflict or at least enter into earnest negotiations. In June two Saudi interceptors, backed by U.S. AWACS reconnaissance aircraft, shot down two Iranian warplanes. Iran's threat to close down the Gulf if Iraq persisted in its shipping attacks did not materialize. Saudi Arabia had called its bluff.

By April-May, Iraq's strategy had reduced Iranian oil exports to 500,000–600,000 barrels per day from a normal wartime production of 2.5 million barrels per day. Although its production returned to that level by fall, Iran had learned the lesson of vulnerability that Iraq had wanted to drive home. Iran could not close the Gulf because it was itself totally dependent on the Gulf's shipping lanes for all of its oil exports and for nearly all its imports of food and other supplies. To counter Iraq's strategy, Iran would have had to strike other Gulf countries, which would have invited intervention by the United States and other Western powers.

Iran's position was further weakened by the quota reduction announced by the Organization of the Petroleum Exporting Countries (OPEC)—of which Iran is a member—in late October. Since the beginning of the war, Iran had overproduced its quota and sold at a price lower than the official OPEC level. A drop in the spot market price of oil in 1985 would facilitate de-escalation of the war. The war would become one of attrition, with a reduced threat to disruption of world oil supplies.

ROBERT OLSON

Khomeini. But to placate the *hojjatieh,* whose support was essential, the Khomeini forces dismantled the Tudeh (Communist) Party. The *hojjatieh* had long been critical of alleged infiltration by the Tudeh Party into the government bureaucracy. The latter in turn did not conceal its disdain for the *hojjatieh* and their fundamentalist beliefs.

Foreign Affairs. The dismantling of the Tudeh turned Iranian-Soviet relations from frosty to icy and resulted in a strengthening of Soviet-Iraqi ties. By that action, the IRP and Khomeini tried to point up several policy objectives: 1) to assure the West that there was no Communist infiltration; 2) to signal Moscow of its displeasure with continued Soviet arms supplies to Iraq; and 3) to placate and keep the support of the *hojjatieh,* the consultative body of leading clergy, and the popular militia. These efforts were coupled with stronger defense agreements with Turkey and Pakistan to create a regional command defense.

Iran's foreign policies brought response from the West. In July, West German Foreign Minister Hans-Dietrich Genscher was in Tehran seeking increased trade. The European policy in general, however, was to keep trading and oil lines open to both Iran and Iraq.

On December 9, Iranian security forces ended a highly charged, six-day hijacking drama by storming the Kuwaiti airliner being held at Tehran airport and freeing the nine remaining hostages on board. The hijackers, said to be members of a Shiite Muslim terrorist group, had released 153 passengers during the six days but had killed two U.S. diplomats. Kuwait expressed its gratitude for the Iranian action. U.S. officials, however, criticized Tehran for not acting sooner, charged that Iran had taken actions that encouraged the hijackers, and even suggested that Iran might have been in league with the terrorists.

Economy. In light of the domestic and foreign trade situations, Iran moved to further privatize its economy. In 1983, 19.5% of Iran's total imports—worth $25 billion (U.S.)—were brought in by the private sector, largely *bazaari;* about $200 million in goods was imported from the United States. As a result of legislation approved in November 1984, a greater amount of trade will be handled by the private sector. And barring a major shift in government, Iran's economy will be more closely tied to the West. In 1985, trade with the United States could well jump to $500–$600 million.

ROBERT OLSON, *University of Kentucky*

Iraqi children leave their school in Baghdad wearing the standard white-shirt uniform. The murals depict the Iran-Iraq war as a new conflict between Persia and Arabia.

AP/Wide World

IRAQ

In 1984, Iraq greatly improved its position internationally—strengthening ties with and increasing arms supplies from the West, the Soviet Union, and its Arab neighbors—and continued to hold off Iranian forces in their four-year-old conflict. If the Iraqi government of President Saddam Hussein were to fall, it was clear by year's end that it would not be by military defeat but rather from internal upheaval or change.

Foreign Relations. Developments on the diplomatic front enabled Iraq to improve its military position against Iran. Baghdad increased its arms purchases from the West, especially France and Brazil. It also established warmer relations and increased arms supplies from the Soviet Union. And it strengthened its ties with its Arab neighbors of Saudi Arabia, Egypt, and Jordan. These measures enabled Iraq to internationalize the war by striking at Persian Gulf shipping to and from Iranian ports. Finally, culminating steadily improving ties, Iraq and the United States announced on November 26 that they had agreed to restore formal diplomatic relations.

Domestic Affairs. To prevent internal upheaval, the regime continued several policies that it had initiated in 1983. The government was unable to reconcile differences with Kurdish rebels, groups of whom were supported by Iran, and the Kurds continued to gather their own nationalist momentum and step up guerrilla activities. In March, Iraqi forces fired on Kurdish demonstrators in Sulaimaniyya, the administrative center of Kurdish areas, killing three persons. In March and October, there were reports that Iraq had allowed Turkish troops to penetrate up to 20 mi (32 km) into its northern border region to pursue Kurdish guerrillas. In late July it was reported that talks between the Iraqi government and a top Kurdish rebel leader had broken off.

The second major problem facing the Iraqi government in 1984 was the continued opposition of Shiite Muslims, who compose 60% of the population but are underrepresented in the government. In order to contain that opposition, the government in 1984 continued to encourage Iraqi patriotism and reduce the Shiite sectarian appeal coming from Iran. At the same time, the government kept up its attacks against Shiite underground movements.

There were other problems as well. In the face of the high casualties and increased opposition to the war, the regime was forced to stiffen the penalties for avoiding conscription. The great loss of life, meanwhile, resulted in a continuing labor shortage. This was exacerbated by the attrition of foreign workers, whom Iraq could no longer afford to pay.

Economy. One of the major developments in Iraq in recent years has been the increased privatization of the economy, especially in light and medium industry, the service industries, and, most significantly, agriculture. It seems clear that the new private and capitalist sectors of the economy have been encouraged, indeed necessitated, by the war effort. This in turn has gained more support for the Baathist government from private and professional sectors of the economy. It also has allowed for more economic and political cooperation with other Arab countries and the West.

ROBERT OLSON, *University of Kentucky*

IRAQ • Information Highlights

Official Name: Republic of Iraq.
Location: Southwest Asia.
Area: 167,924 sq mi (434 924 km²).
Population (mid-1984 est.): 15,000,000.
Government: *Head of state and government,* Saddam Hussein Takriti, president (took office July 1979).
Monetary Unit: Dinar (0.311 dinar equals U.S.$1, August 1984).
Gross National Product (1983 U.S.$): $30,000,000,000.

IRELAND

Hopes for an end to the Northern Irish crisis rose in May when the New Ireland Forum, made up of leaders of the four main Irish nationalist parties, unveiled a plan to unite the country. Although Protestant Unionists in the north refused to take part and all paramilitary parties, including Sinn Fein (the political wing of the Irish Republican Army), were excluded, the Forum served as a useful clearinghouse for ideas about reuniting the 32 counties by consent rather than force. And despite some dissension among members, the Forum did call for the creation of a "unitary state" based on a "nondenominational" constitution. Led by Prime Minister Garret FitzGerald, head of the coalition Fine Gael-Labour government, Charles Haughey, leader of the Fianna Fail party, and John Hume, leader of the Social Democratic and Labour party of Northern Ireland, the Forum also stressed the need to protect the rights of the Protestant minority and to preserve the identity of both the nationalist and unionist communities.

Predictably, the report provoked sharp criticism from socialists and republicans, as well as from Protestant militants in the north. The British government remained cool to the idea of unification without the support of northern Protestants.

Foreign Relations. On March 9, Prime Minister FitzGerald arrived in Washington, DC, for a series of meetings with U.S. politicians and businessmen. Deeply concerned about the flow of money and weapons from the United States to the IRA, he told a joint session of Congress on March 16 that he opposed all forms of aid to people engaged in acts of "horrific violence." He also reminded Irish-Americans of their "moral obligation" to reject violence.

In early June, U.S. President Ronald Reagan made an official visit to Ireland. Amid tight security he traveled to University College, Galway, where he received an honorary degree. A highlight of Reagan's tour was a stop at his ancestral home in Ballyporeen, county Tipperary. On June 3 at a state banquet in Dublin Castle, Prime Minister FitzGerald made it clear that the Irish people opposed U.S. intervention in Central America. The next day, President Reagan addressed the Irish Parliament, defending U.S. foreign policy, both in Central America and with regard to the Soviet Union.

Elections to the European Parliament on June 14 resulted in a voter turnout of 48%. Fine Gael won six seats; Labour lost all four seats won in 1979; Fianna Fail captured eight seats; and the Liberals retained their one seat. On July 1, Prime Minister FitzGerald became president of the European Community (EC) for a six-month term.

Trade and Economy. During March, Ireland became embroiled in a dispute within the Eu-

AP/Wide World

Parliamentary speaker Tom FitzPatrick applauds as President Reagan addresses a joint session of the Irish parliament June 4. Foreign policy was the president's theme.

ropean Community (EC) over agricultural subsidies. At a summit meeting of EC leaders, both Britain and Ireland criticized the system of subsidies to farmers on the continent. On March 20, FitzGerald walked out of a meeting to protest the EC's refusal to exempt Ireland from cuts ordered in milk production, arguing that the Irish economy depended too heavily on dairy produce to afford such reductions. After a week-long deadlock, EC members worked out an agreement that spared Ireland from a 7% production cut.

Rising prices, a heavy tax burden, and a weakened pound added to the country's economic problems. Middle- and lower-income families found it ever harder to make ends meet, and the job market was shrinking.

L. Perry Curtis, Jr., *Brown University*

IRELAND • Information Highlights

Official Name: Ireland.
Location: Island in the eastern North Atlantic Ocean.
Area: 27,136 sq mi (70 282 km²).
Population (mid-1984 est.): 3,600,000.
Chief Cities (1981 census): Dublin, the capital, 525,360; Cork, 136,269; Limerick, 60,721.
Government: *Head of state,* Patrick J. Hillery, president (took office Dec. 1976). *Head of government,* Garret FitzGerald, prime minister (took office Dec. 1982). *Legislature*—Parliament: House of Representatives (Dail Eireann) and Senate (Seanad Eireann).
Monetary Unit: Pound (0.9910 pound equals U.S.$1, Oct. 22, 1984).
Gross National Product (1982 U.S.$): $17,067,-000,000.
Economic Indexes (1983): *Consumer Prices* (1970 = 100), all items, 560.9; food, 518.6. *Industrial Production* (1975 = 100), 147.
Foreign Trade (1983 U.S.$): *Imports,* $9,182,000,000; *exports,* $8,611,000,000.

ISRAEL

The year 1984 was a historic one for Israel. Parliamentary elections in July seemed to fragment Israeli society but ultimately resulted in a national unity government which before year's end showed signs of tackling the country's two major problems—the economic crisis and the stalemate in Lebanon.

Politics and Domestic Affairs. Hopes for a stable government were frustrated by the July election results, which left Prime Minister Yitzhak Shamir's Likud Bloc with 41 seats in the Knesset (parliament) and Shimon Peres' Labor Alignment with 44 seats, each short of the 61 needed for a majority. After negotiating for seven weeks, Likud and Labor finally agreed to form a government of national unity with the premiership rotating between the two leaders. On September 14, Peres (*see* BIOGRAPHY) was sworn in as prime minister and Shamir as acting prime minister and foreign minister for the next 25 months; then their roles would be reversed. A 25-member cabinet was formed, consisting of 12 members of Likud, 12 members of Labor, and one member of the National Religious Party. The most important government decisions, however, would fall to a ten-member "inner cabinet," equally divided between Likud and Labor. In the Knesset, the coalition would hold 97 of 120 seats.

The July election had another interesting result—the emergence of the Sephardim as a growing political power. The surprise gain of four Knesset seats by the Sephardic Torah Guardians reflected a growing political awareness on the part of this religious group. Since the beginning of their migration from Middle Eastern countries in 1948, when they constituted 17%, the Sephardim have grown to 55% of the Israeli population.

Terrorism and domestic violence also took on new dimensions during the year. Members of the so-called "Islamic Jihad," in addition to the bombing of buses, random shooting on crowded streets, and stoning of passing vehicles, kidnapped and murdered Jewish soldiers, teenagers, and students hitchhiking on country roads. Meanwhile, the arrest in April and subsequent trials of 27 Israelis exposed the existence of a Jewish underground dedicated to stemming Arab terrorism. Considering themselves counterterrorists, the members of the Jewish underground, some of them reserve paratroopers and tank commanders in the armed forces, were charged with an attempt to plant bombs under Arab buses, a plot to blow up the Dome of the Rock mosque on the Temple Mount in Jerusalem, and the 1980 bombing attack on the Arab mayors of four cities in Judea and Samaria. The trials precipitated agonizing debates and polarized Israeli society. Even as the first long-term prison sentences were handed out, new incidents of Arab terrorism were occurring, with acts of retaliation by Jews unaffiliated with the underground.

Economy. Without question, however, the most serious matter facing Israel in 1984 was the economic crisis. Although devaluation of the shekel and government budget cuts had re-

Israeli Arabs cast their ballots in the July parliamentary elections. Neither Likud nor Labor won a majority.

Nackstrand, Gamma-Liaison

Resolving a seven-week political deadlock, Labor Party leader Shimon Peres (left) and Likud leader Yitzhak Shamir (right) agreed on a national unity government. By the arrangement, Peres assumed the premiership for 25 months, after which Shamir would take over.

AP/Wide World

duced the country's staggering trade deficit to 25% during the first five months of 1984, the annual inflation rate spiraled from 307% in July to 525% in August, 925% in September, and an estimated 1,300% in October. Immediately upon taking office in September, the cabinet announced a cut of $1 billion (U.S.) from the $23 billion budget, a 9% devaluation of the shekel, a six-month ban on the import of such luxury items as cars and major appliances, and a three-month freeze on all prices, wages, profits, and taxes. Israeli labor and management shared the economic squeeze, the former taking a one-third cut in the cost of living allowance and the latter making the necessary adjustment on the remaining two thirds of the allowance.

The United States took on a broader role in helping Israel manage its economic problems. In October, Washington agreed to speed up disbursement of $1.2 billion in economic aid, thereby increasing Israel's low foreign currency reserves. The United States and Israel also announced the establishment of a free-trade zone and the formation of a special committee comprising U.S. and Israeli business leaders to work out a plan for a long-range Israeli economic recovery.

Foreign Affairs. The 22,000 Israeli troops in southern Lebanon were another major national issue. Even before the July elections, both Shamir and Peres had come out in favor of withdrawal, but neither was willing to undertake this step without proper guarantees for the security of northern Israel. The unity government compromised on the Israeli position with regard to a simultaneous Syrian withdrawal, insisting instead that the Syrian forces refrain from moving into the territory vacated by Israel and prevent the Palestine Liberation Organization (PLO) from infiltrating the border region. Israel called for control of the area by the South Lebanese Army and the UN peace-keeping force. In November, Israeli and Lebanese military delegations opened negotiations on the terms of the withdrawal. In the meantime, border authorities reported a sharp increase in the number of Lebanese entering Israel. These were mostly workers seeking employment and patients seeking medical treatment.

Positive developments on the diplomatic front included a visit to Israel by two Nigerian tribal leaders, the king of the Uruba tribe in southern Nigeria and the emir of the Kanu Muslims in northern Nigeria. Their visit underscored Israel's expanding role in helping improve economic and health conditions in several Afro-Asian countries. Israel maintained diplomatic relations with Zaire, Lesotho, Liberia, Swaziland, and Malawi and economic contact with 12 other nations in Black Africa. Exports to those countries totaled more than $200 million in 1984. In Botswana, Israel embarked on a project to develop the country's arid zones and introduce poultry farming in order to improve the health standards of a population with beef as its principal diet.

The year also saw El Salvador and Costa Rica return their embassies to Jerusalem. The two nations had been among the 13 who moved their embassies to Tel Aviv in 1980 to protest the "Jerusalem Law," in which Israel declared sovereignty over undivided Jerusalem and affirmed the city as the nation's capital.

Following the move by the two Central American countries, Egypt announced that it would sever diplomatic relations with both of them; Israel lodged a strong protest with Cairo. All in all, Israeli-Egyptian relations were not good. The normalization process stipulated in the 1979 Camp David accords has been suspended, and in October Egyptian President Hosni Mubarak rejected Prime Minister Peres' call for a summit meeting.

Jerusalem

Perched high in the Judean hills, Jerusalem's ancient fortresses, medieval shrines, and modern housing developments are built in stylistic harmony of pink Jerusalem stone. Yet harmony has been largely absent during the 3,000-year history of this city sacred to three religions and with a name believed to mean "City of Peace." Ever since King David made it the capital of ancient Israel, Jerusalem has been the focus of veneration and rivalry. Here Solomon built the Temple, great Hebrew prophets preached universal peace, Jesus was crucified, and Mohammed symbolically rose to heaven. Babylonians, Persians, Greeks, Romans, Muslims, Crusaders, and Ottomans invaded Jerusalem in a centuries-long cycle of devotion and devastation. Today, Christians and Muslims flock to its shrines. Jews bewail its destruction and come to be buried in its soil. And governments continue to dispute its political status. All in all, the city of 468,000 is a unique blend of the past and the present, of problems and progress.

History. In the year 70 A.D., the Roman general Titus sacked Jerusalem and massacred and exiled its Jewish defenders. Fifty-five years later, the Emperor Hadrian razed it to the ground and built in its place a Roman city, which he called Aelia Capitolina. Helena, the mother of Emperor Constantine, restored the name Jerusalem, destroyed its pagan temples, and replaced them with churches.

To outdo Jerusalem's churches, Muslim Caliph Abd el-Malik in the 7th century built the Dome of the Rock Mosque, which still dominates the skyline. Four centuries later the Crusaders placed a gold cross atop its dome. But the Armenian Saladin, and later the Ottoman Suleiman, restored to Jerusalem a Muslim imprint which was to last into the 19th century.

Growing European influence in the 19th century brought Christian ascendancy to the city. The Latin churches under the protection of France, England, and Germany, and the Greek Orthodox Church under Russian patronage, vied for superiority. European powers set up consulates and erected several religious landmarks. In the Jewish quarter, meanwhile, magnificent synagogues were built. The 19th century also marked the beginning of Jerusalem's modern Jewish sector. On land purchased from the sultan, the first houses outside the city walls were built to ease crowding in the Old City. The growth of New Jerusalem was spurred by an influx of "Lovers of Zion." By 1856, Jews comprised a majority of the population, and New Jerusalem had outgrown the Old City.

With the defeat of Turkey in World War I, Palestine came under British mandate, and Jerusalem had a spurt of growth; the Hebrew University, Hadassah Hospital-Medical School, Rockefeller Museum, and other institutions were built. Growing tension between the Jewish and Arab communities erupted in violent conflict after World War II. A UN resolution in November 1947 to partition Palestine into Arab and Jewish states and to internationalize Jerusalem prompted an all-out attack on the Jewish sector by six Arab nations. At the end of the hostilities in 1949, Jerusalem was a divided city. East Jerusalem and the Old City belonged to Transjordan, and West Jerusalem became the capital of Israel. Then, in the Six-Day War of June 1967, Israel repelled a Jordanian offensive and reclaimed the entire city.

Jerusalem Today. An international team of experts has redesigned Jerusalem into a cohesive entity by blending new housing with restored archeological finds, renovating old neighborhoods, and skirting it all with a national park. One architectural feat was the adaptation of Cardo, an excavated Byzantine promenade, into a shopping mall. While construction on the West Bank remains a source of international and domestic dispute, the city itself has undergone extensive development.

Today Jerusalem is a center of industrial, social, and cultural growth for a mixed population. About one out of every four city residents is Arab. Although Jerusalem Arabs retain Jordanian citizenship, they receive welfare, pension, and child-care payments from the Israeli government. An Arab affairs adviser serves as a link between the two groups. New clinics, classrooms, dental laboratories, libraries, and community centers have been built in the Arab sector. An Arab theater group, dance troupe, art center, youth orchestra, and teacher-training course all have been set up.

But controversies continue. The Temple Mount, under the de facto control of the Supreme Muslim Council, has been a source of dispute. Some Jews have tried to hold prayer services there in the face of a Muslim ban.

A broader, diplomatic dispute has to do with a 1980 Israeli declaration affirming "undivided" Jerusalem as the nation's capital. In the aftermath, 13 countries moved their embassies to Tel Aviv (though two of them have since returned to Jerusalem). Evangelical Christians gave support to the Israeli action by establishing a "Christian Embassy" in Jerusalem. The U.S. Embassy has remained in Tel Aviv, but the matter continued to be debated in 1984.

LIVIA BITTON-JACKSON

A deterioration in Soviet attitudes toward Israel was reflected in an escalation of reprisals against Jews who had requested emigration permits to Israel and those who fostered Hebrew culture and Jewish religious observance. That deterioration was underlined in July by the detention of former Israeli President Ephraim Katzir, also a noted biochemist, and his wife, Nina, in Leningrad. On a visit to the Soviet Union as guests of the Russian Academy of Sciences, former President Katzir and his wife were intercepted by KGB agents before entering the home of a Jewish family in Leningrad and detained for prolonged interrogation. That incident was followed by the arrest and imprisonment of five Hebrew culture activists and attacks on several others on charges of drug abuse; according to the KGB, it is a "known fact that Jews use drugs in religious rituals." Israeli and U.S. rabbinic authorities issued a condemnation of the "outrageous accusation" as a Soviet attempt to distort understandings of the Jewish religion. They designated November 13 as a public fast in solidarity with Soviet Jewish prisoners and appealed to Soviet authorities to "release these men and allow them to emigrate to Israel with their families."

An official visit by West Germany's Chancellor Helmut Kohl in January evoked memories of the Holocaust. On the day of his arrival, Kohl paid his respects at the Yad Vashem Holocaust Memorial in Jerusalem, where he was confronted by some 200 demonstrators. During his six-day diplomatic visit, Kohl also faced official and popular protests over a proposed West German arms sale to Saudi Arabia.

Other. In a rare archaeological find, scientists from Tel Aviv University and Cornell University in New York discovered an urban settlement in central Israel dating from the Bronze Age. Tel Afek, one of the largest archaeological sites in Israel, yielded several important finds, among them the stage of Odeon, a small performing forum built by the Roman Emperor Julian the Apostate and destroyed by his Christian successors. The municipality of Petah Tikva undertook the restoration of the ancient stage for use in public performances. Some 100 votive plates with Summerian, Akkadian, Hittite, Egyptian, Canaanite, and Greek inscriptions were also unearthed.

Among the several prominent Israelis who died during the year were Yigal Yadin, 67, a former deputy prime minister, Israel's second chief of staff, and one of its foremost archaeologists; and David Hacohen, 85, a founder of the Israeli Labor movement.

LIVIA E. BITTON-JACKSON
Herbert H. Lehman College, CUNY

ISRAEL • Information Highlights
Official Name: State of Israel.
Location: Southwest Asia.
Area: 8,000 sq mi (20 720 km²).
Population (mid-1984 est.): 4,200,000.
Chief Cities (Dec. 31, 1982 est.): Jerusalem, the capital, 424,400; Tel Aviv-Jaffa, 325,700; Haifa, 226,100.
Government: *Head of state,* Chaim Herzog, president (took office May 1983). *Head of government,* Shimon Peres, premier (took office Sept. 14, 1984). *Legislature* (unicameral)—Knesset.
Monetary Unit: Shekel (552.6 shekels equal U.S.$1, Nov. 19, 1984).
Gross National Product (1982 U.S.$): $22,200,000,000.
Economic Indexes (1983): *Consumer Prices* (1970 = 100), all items, 37,971.3; food, 43,205.6. *Industrial Production* (1975 = 100), 133.
Foreign Trade (1983 U.S.$): *Imports,* $8,386,000,000; *exports,* $4,931,000,000.

AP/Wide World

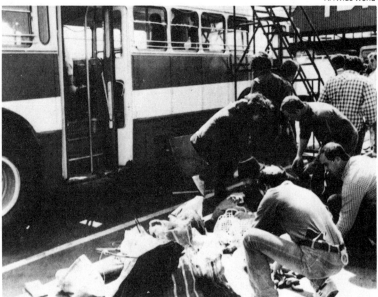

Three persons were killed in a bus bombing March 7 in the port city of Ashdod, south of Tel Aviv. Terrorist attacks against civilians escalated in 1984, but so did retaliations by Jewish underground counterterrorists.

ITALY

Italy negotiated a revision of its concordat with the Vatican governing church-state relations and launched a new campaign against organized crime, inflation, and unemployment.

Politics and Economics

Craxi Government. The five-party Left-Center coalition government headed by Socialist Premier Bettino Craxi since August 1983 tackled the stubborn problem of inflation, which was 14.7% at the end of 1983. Craxi sought legislation to partly freeze the system that links wage increases to the cost-of-living index. This led to the most serious split in 12 years among organized labor. The Catholic CISL and Socialist UIL labor unions supported Craxi, whereas the Communist CGIL opposed him. The Communists filibustered in Parliament for days until the government accepted a 6-month anti-inflationary measure instead of a 12-month one. Parliament approved this law on June 8.

In October the Craxi government submitted to Parliament its austere budget for 1985. It called for lowering inflation from the current 10.4% to 7% and for narrowing the deficit by cutting outlays for health, social security, and education. The government's 3 million employees would be limited to a 7% pay hike. Estimates indicated the 1984 deficit would total $50.42 billion (U.S.), wider than 1983's $47.27 billion. The 1984 deficit represents about 15% of Italy's GNP.

Death of Enrico Berlinguer. In the heat of the debate over economic measures, Enrico Berlinguer, leader of the Italian Communist Party (PCI) since 1972, suffered a cerebral hemorrhage while speaking in Padua on June 7. He died on June 11, after four days in a coma. Berlinguer had started the Eurocommunist movement for more autonomy from Moscow, and he advocated a "historic compromise" with Italy's ruling Christian Democrats. He almost brought the PCI to power in the 1976 parliamentary elections when his party got an unprecedented 34.4% of the vote.

Berlinguer's funeral in Rome on June 13 drew one million mourners. Among them were Italy's Socialist President Sandro Pertini, Premier Craxi, Christian Democratic Party leader Ciriaco De Mita, and leaders of many foreign Communist parties. The pope also expressed his sorrow. The United States was represented by a political secretary from its embassy.

Europarliament Elections. In the wake of Berlinguer's death, the Communist Party received a wave of sympathy votes in the European parliament elections of June 18. For the first time the PCI narrowly edged the hitherto dominant Christian Democratic (DC) party, receiving 33.3% of the votes to 33% for the DC.

AP/Wide World

Premier Craxi and the Vatican's Agostino Cardinal Casaroli cap the signing of a new concordat with a handshake.

Craxi's Socialist Party was third with 11.2%. Altogether, the five parties in the government coalition dropped about 2% from their 56.4% majority in the 1983 parliamentary elections.

Natta Named Communist Leader. On June 25 the PCI Central Committee elected Alessandro Natta to be Berlinguer's successor as secretary general. The 66-year-old Natta, an intellectual fond of quoting Latin classics, was the party's expert on education and headed its Central Control Commission, which keeps files on the party's 1.7 million members. Natta was expected to continue Berlinguer's Eurocommunist policy.

Continuing Scandals. On July 12, Italy's Budget Minister Pietro Longo, a Social Democrat, was linked by a parliamentary report to the P-2 Masonic Lodge scandal that had erupted in 1981 and brought an end to the Christian Democrats' long monopoly on the premiership. President Pertini accepted Longo's resignation and appointed Premier Craxi to take over Longo's duties temporarily.

Meanwhile, Licio Gelli, the fugitive grand master of the illegal P-2 Lodge, escaped from a Swiss jail in March.

One of Gelli's close associates was Michele Sindona, an Italian banker and financial adviser to the Vatican. In 1974 he fled to the United States after two of his banks went into liquidation. In New York he was found guilty of involvement in the failure of the Franklin National Bank in 1974 and was sentenced to a 25-year term. Italian judicial authorities finally succeeded in getting Sindona extradited to Italy in September 1984 for questioning (thanks to a new U.S.-Italian extradition treaty). It was thought that Sindona might shed light on both the P-2 scandal and the collapse of the Vatican-linked Banco Ambrosiano in Milan.

In October the Chamber of Deputies rejected a Communist motion to force the resignation of Foreign Minister Giulio Andreotti for his alleged connections with Sindona.

Terrorism. Though the incidence of political guerrilla warfare subsided, numerous crimes continued. The Red Brigades claimed responsibility for the February murder in Rome of Leamon Hunt, the United States head of the multinational peacekeeping force in the Sinai. In March they also claimed responsibility for a $25-million robbery of an American-owned security company in Rome, and in April for the murder of the education commissioner in Nardo.

In mid-August an investigating judge in Rome ordered 180 suspected Red Brigadesmen to stand trial, thus ending a two-year probe in connection with terrorism in Rome and the abduction of U.S. Gen. James Lee Dozier in Verona in 1981. In December, Italian police were investigating a reported plot to bomb the U.S. Embassy in Rome.

The Mafia. Even more troublesome than the Red Brigades was the expansion of organized crime syndicates from Sicily to the mainland, with drug trafficking now their most lucrative activity. The protection racket continued to be huge, with Italian businessmen paying more than the equivalent of $1 billion annually.

The Mafia's penetration of Sicily's regional government was graphically revealed in January when Deputy Premier Salvatore Stornello was charged with corruption. The regional government had to resign a few days later after revelations that the premier was also under investigation.

In northern Calabria, police arrested 51 Mafia suspects on June 29, while in August eight people were killed in a gun battle between rival Camorra gangs in Torre Annunziata near Naples.

A crackdown on organized crime in both Italy and the United States occurred in October with the arrests of dozens of *mafiosi* in both countries. This came as a result of the July extradition to Italy from Brazil of Tommaso Buscetta, a top Sicilian Mafia leader who had also been active in the United States. Buscetta broke the code of silence (*omertà*) after his two sons and a brother were killed in gang warfare. Buscetta provided Italian authorities with 3,000 pages of testimony, whereupon arrest warrants were issued for 366 suspects, 28 of whom were sought in the United States and are subject to extradition. In October, Interior Minister Oscar Luigi Scalfaro met in Washington with U.S. Attorney General William French Smith, who declared that the Italian crackdown was "the single most devastating assault on the Mafia in its entire history."

Pope John Paul II traveled to Calabria in October, where he called on Italians to break the "tragic chain of vendettas" and "to have the courage to wipe out *omertà*."

Church and State

Revision of Lateran Concordat. After 15 years of negotiations, draft revisions of Italy's 1929 Lateran concordat with the Vatican were presented to parliament in January. On February 17, Premier Craxi and Vatican State Secretary Agostino Cardinal Casaroli signed the new concordat. Under the new arrangements, Italy will continue to recognize Vatican City as an independent sovereign state, but Roman Catholicism will cease to be the state religion of Italy. Priests will no longer receive part of their pay from the state. Catholic religious education will be available in state schools only to those children whose parents specifically request it. Rome will no longer have the status of a "sacred city," and the Vatican will turn over Jewish catacombs to the Italian state. The new concordat reflects the significant secularization that has taken place in Italy in recent years, including the legalization of divorce and of abortion under certain circumstances.

Italy's Socialist President Pertini paid his first official visit to Pope John Paul II at the Vatican in May. On August 13 the Senate approved the revised concordat.

Soon thereafter, Italy's Protestant minority, the Waldensian church, signed a new understanding with the Italian government.

Foreign Relations

Peacekeeping Operations. Italy contributed 1,385 military personnel to the multinational peacekeeping force in Lebanon over a period of 17 months. The nation withdrew these forces in February when the French, British, and Americans also withdrew theirs in the face of the deteriorating situation.

Red Sea Mines. In August, at Egypt's request, Italy assisted other countries in efforts to sweep mines that had been laid in the Red Sea, presumably by Libyans.

East-West Relations. In April, Italy announced that the 16 cruise missiles deployed by

---

ITALY • Information Highlights

Official Name: Italian Republic.
Location: Southern Europe.
Area: 116,300 sq mi (301 223 km²).
Population (mid-1984 est.): 57,000,000.
Chief Cities (Dec. 31, 1982): Rome, the capital, 2,834,094; Milan, 1,580,810; Naples, 1,209,086; Turin, 1,093,384; Genoa, 754,432.
Government: *Head of state,* Alessandro (Sandro) Pertini, president (took office July 1978). *Head of government,* Bettino Craxi, prime minister (sworn in Aug. 4, 1983). *Legislature*—Parliament: Senate and Chamber of Deputies.
Monetary Unit: Lira (1873.5 lire equal U.S.$1, Oct. 31, 1984).
Gross Domestic Product (1982 U.S.$): $347,000,-000,000.
Economic Indexes (1983): *Consumer Prices* (1970 = 100), all items, 588.9; food, 548.9. *Industrial Production* (1975 = 100), 128.
Foreign Trade (1983 U.S.$): *Imports,* $80,367,-000,000; *exports,* $72,681,000,000.

NATO at Comisco, Sicily, the previous December were now operational.

That same month Foreign Minister Andreotti flew to Moscow for talks with Soviet President Konstantin Chernenko on East-West relations, and in May, Italy signed an agreement with the USSR to buy 155 billion cu ft (4.65 billion m³) of Siberian natural gas. Italy, which agreed to pay current market prices, got a better bargain than did other European states.

In May, Premier Craxi raised a storm in Italy and irritation in Washington when he abruptly announced an Italian initiative to revive East-West talks on deployment of intermediate-range missiles in Europe. Moscow's response, a week later, was to characterize the proposal as "timid and incomplete."

In the autumn Italy, along with various Western states, lifted the "diplomatic quarantine" on Poland that had been in effect since the suppression of "Solidarity." Foreign Minister Andreotti announced that he would visit Warsaw in December.

The "Bulgarian Connection." Italy continued its investigation of the attempted assassination of Pope John Paul II in 1981 by the Turk Mehmet Ali Agca. In June the report of the state prosecutor, Antonio Albano, was leaked to the press. Albano wanted the indictment and trial of four of Agca's alleged Turkish coconspirators, plus three Bulgarians, one of whom, Sergei Antonov, has been in custody in Rome since 1982. In October, Ilario Martella, the investigating judge, concluded that all seven must stand trial and that Agca should be tried on new charges.

Despite the investigation, Italy and Bulgaria decided to exchange ambassadors again.

German Reunification. Sharp words were exchanged between Bonn and Rome in September after Foreign Minister Andreotti, in a panel discussion sponsored by the Communist Party in Rome, decried "pan-Germanism" and declared that "there are two German states, and two there shall remain." West German Chancellor Helmut Kohl found Andreotti's remarks "absolutely incomprehensible," and German Foreign Minister Hans-Dietrich Genscher told the Italian ambassador that Andreotti's comments were a "serious insult."

In a letter to Kohl on September 17, Premier Craxi reaffirmed Italy's position of "friendship, cooperation and mutual trust," and Andreotti expressed regret that his remarks had led to "misunderstanding." Andreotti explained that he had not intended to speak against long-range goals of the German people.

The Common Market. British Prime Minister Margaret Thatcher went to Rome in January to discuss the amount that Britain should contribute to the Common Market. Premier Craxi was critical of Thatcher's position regarding this

P. Aventurier, Gamma-Liaison

The June 14 funeral of Enrico Berlinguer, leader of the Italian Communist Party, attracted Rome's largest crowd—about one million people—since the end of World War II.

issue. In February, President Pertini made a formal visit to England.

Antonio Giolitti, Italy's commissioner in the European Community (EC) in Brussels since 1979, announced he would resign in December and reenter Socialist Party politics.

Industrial "Big Seven." In June, Premier Craxi represented Italy at the annual summit meeting of the "Big Seven" industrial powers, held in London.

Austria. Great inconvenience was caused to truckers in February when Italian customs officers at the Brenner Pass staged a two-week slowdown on operations. An 80-mi (130-km) traffic jam built up on the Austrian side. The slowdown ended on March 9 when Italy agreed to augment the staff and pay of the customs collectors.

South Africa. When South Africa's Prime Minister P. W. Botha visited Rome in June, Premier Craxi strongly condemned apartheid.

CHARLES F. DELZELL, *Vanderbilt University*

JAPAN

Japan, which had already assumed status as a major economic power but had held the outside world at arm's length, began in 1984 to experiment with a new, vigorous political role in the world. The nation's unprecedented international stance was largely a product of Prime Minister Yasuhiro Nakasone's stated determination to convert Japan into a "respected and consulted nation."

The prime minister's activities both abroad and at home tended to boost his popularity with the Japanese public. According to a Kyodo News Service poll taken on October 3, on the eve of his bid for a second two-year term as president of the ruling Liberal-Democratic Party (LDP), Nakasone received the approval of 58% of respondents in the survey. More significant was the 83.1% popularity rating among those who supported the LDP. The favorable rating set a record for his 22-month-old administration and led to his reelection as party president, thus assuring that he would continue as prime minister. Nakasone became the first leader to survive more than a single term since Eisaku Sato left office in 1972.

Domestic Affairs

Prime Minister Nakasone's success seemed all the more remarkable in light of the LDP's earlier difficulties. In the general election in December 1983, the party had placed only 250 official candidates in the (lower) House of Representatives, six short of a majority. After the poll, the LDP picked up nine unendorsed conservatives and then, in effect, formed a coalition cabinet with the New Liberal Club (NLC), which provided eight additional seats in return for one post in the Nakasone administration.

Party Politics. When the 101st session of the Diet convened on Feb. 6, 1984, the LDP-NLC coalition controlled 267 seats in the lower house and 136 seats in the (upper) House of Councillors. Opposition forces were led by the Japan Socialist Party (JSP), with 113 seats in the lower house and 43 seats in the upper. Others included the Clean Government Party (Komeito), the Democratic Socialist Party (DSP), and the Japan Communist Party (JCP). Both the Komeito and the DSP announced that they were studying the possibility of joining the LDP-NLC coalition.

Early in the year, however, Nakasone's LDP encountered roadblocks in the Diet. Other factions within the party continued to criticize the prime minister for relying on the support of the powerful Kakuei Tanaka faction, the largest in the party. (Technically this faction was no longer led by former Prime Minister Tanaka, who in October 1983 had been found guilty of accepting bribes in the Lockheed aircraft procurement case. Tanaka, how-

ever, had remained in the Diet and had placed several of his faction members in the Nakasone cabinet.) In addition, opposition parties engineered a four-week legislative stalemate in protesting Nakasone's "negative growth" budgets.

Nonetheless, by compromise the LDP coaxed the opposition back to business on June 15, and thereafter Prime Minister Nakasone was credited with getting much of his legislative program through the Diet. Among the bills that passed were ones revising the national health-insurance system, establishing a special panel to undertake wholesale educational reform, and divesting the Japan Tobacco and Salt Public Corporation. Little headway was made in the effort to privatize the Nippon Telephone & Telegraph Corporation (NTT). The prime minister also succeeded in reorganizing most bureaus of his own executive office into the new Management and Coordination Agency. On July 2, State Minister Masaharu Gotoda (of the Tanaka faction) became the first director general of the new agency and pledged to carry out further administrative reform.

Buoyed by these domestic successes and with a growing reputation abroad, Prime Minister Nakasone on September 25 announced his plan to run for a second term as LDP president. His potential opposition within the party included former Foreign Minister Kiichi Miyazawa (Suzuki faction), who unveiled a plan to double Japan's assets by 1995; the incumbent Foreign Minister Shintaro Abe (Fukuda faction); the incumbent Finance Minister Noboru Takeshita (Tanaka faction); and the incumbent director general of the Economic Planning Agency (EPA) Toshio Komoto (who headed a small non-mainstream faction). Zenko Suzuki and Takeo Fukuda, former prime ministers, had both pressed Nakasone to "rid the government of Tanaka influence."

The threat of a bitter intra-LDP struggle was averted when senior party officials reached a behind-the-scenes compromise and renamed Nakasone as party president on October 29, without going through the primary process. Ironically, Abe and Takeshita, who had withdrawn their candidacies in the hope of assuming influential posts in the party, were reappointed foreign minister and finance minister, respectively. Party elders reportedly had agreed to Nakasone's reappointment only on condition that he fulfill his promise to reduce the influence of Tanaka in the government.

Economy. Estimates by the Japanese Economic Planning Agency (EPA) in June 1984 set the annual gross national product (GNP) at 221,009 billion yen ($903 billion U.S.). Japan's annual rate of growth, after adjustment for inflation, was projected by the EPA at 4.1%. Private research institutes like the Nikko Research Center predicted a 5.4% real rate of growth through the fiscal year ending March

Despite an austere budget for fiscal 1984, the government increased defense spending by a healthy 6.55%. Japan continued to be under pressure from the United States to expand its armed forces and overall defense capabilities.

1985. On the other hand, according to the Management and Coordination Agency, the unemployment rate in June reached a record high of a seasonally adjusted 2.81%.

For the first time, because of blockage in the Diet, the government received an approved budget only on April 15 (retroactive to April 1). Finance ministry officials described the budget as the most austere in 29 years, with an increase in expenditures of only 0.5% over the previous year. The general account total of 50,627.2 billion yen (about $207 billion) was to be financed by tax revenues (68%), nontax revenues (7%), and deficit bonds (25%).

Social Issues. Japan's population showed the slowest annual growth on record for the year ended March 31. The increase was 0.6%, to a total of 119,316,468, according to the Home Ministry. The average household consisted of only 3.15 members, down from 3.17 a year earlier. Meanwhile, the proportion of senior citizens (aged 65 and over) climbed to 9.9% of the population, creating new public-policy issues.

One of the major items on the Nakasone administration's agenda has been reform of the nation's educational system. Issues have included the rise in violence, particularly in the middle schools; the American-style, four-level pattern of formal education; and the notorious entrance examination system for the universities. After the Diet had passed enabling legislation, the first meeting of the *ad hoc* Council on Education began gathering data and holding hearings in September.

Early in August, Japan's antinuclear campaign reached a peak with services at Hiroshima Peace Memorial Park and silent prayers at Peace Park in Nagasaki. Prime Minister Nakasone was present at the Nagasaki ceremony.

On August 14 a strong earthquake rocked a wide area of Japan from northern Honshu down to the Kansai (surrounding Kyoto), leaving at least 28 persons dead or missing. Seismologists registered the magnitude at 6.9 on the Richter scale.

Foreign Affairs

Japan's newfound vigor in world affairs was revealed in many ways: at the United Nations and in its agencies; at the June summit meeting of seven industrialized nations in London; in mediation efforts in South Asia and the Middle East; and in its attempts to promote stability on the Korean peninsula. Common concern over Korea led to closer ties between Tokyo and Peking, but contacts between Tokyo and Moscow were strained. Meanwhile, U.S.-Japan relations, increasingly referred to in Tokyo as an "alliance," continued to be dominated by several issues of finance and commerce.

United Nations. In September in New York, Foreign Minister Abe represented Japan at the UN General Assembly and in talks with his counterparts from the United States, the Soviet Union, and China. In his UN speech, Abe urged protection for commercial ships in the Persian Gulf and a "just and honorable solution" to the Iran-Iraq conflict. The foreign minister supported the plan by which South Korea and North Korea would be admitted to the UN simultaneously, in order to encourage their unification. Abe, however, denied reports that Japan's self-defense forces might be used for overseas peacekeeping missions.

The foreign minister also represented Japan at a regional ministerial meeting held in Jakarta, Indonesia, in July. Abe proposed to delegates of the Association of Southeast Asian Nations (ASEAN) a three-stage plan for bringing peace to Cambodia. With stability in border zones, Japan would provide assistance for reconstruction of all Indochina.

On April 17 in Tokyo, Prime Minister Nakasone opened the 40th ministerial session of the UN Economic and Social Commission for Asia and the Pacific (ESCAP). Foreign Minister Abe was elected chairman of the conference. Both Nakasone and Abe pledged that Japan would continue to help developing nations in the region, which were receiving more than 70% of the nation's $2.4 billion in official development assistance (ODA).

United States. While Japanese watched party (LDP) elections at home, they also kept a wary eye on the national elections in the United States. Although President Ronald Reagan took a generally antiprotectionist stance, in July he did implement the International Trade Commission's five-year relief plan, which imposed quotas and possibly higher tariffs on steel products. Japanese bureaucrats and businessmen joined in deploring this step. They

were alarmed also by the earlier adoption of a strong protectionist position by Democratic presidential candidate Walter Mondale, who had endorsed local content legislation as applied to automobile imports. Mondale later softened his rhetoric. In any case, Japanese business quietly celebrated the reelection of President Reagan.

Nonetheless, the U.S. trade deficit for the first six months of 1984 had reached a record $58.9 billion, of which $16.4 billion—by far the largest component—was the trade deficit with Japan. On the positive side, the Japan External Trade Organization (JETRO) noted in a report released in September that Japan's import promotion policy was beginning to take effect. Imports of manufactured goods from the United States increased by 15.6% in the first half of the year. That growth, JETRO noted, came at the cost of high interest rates and a fiscal deficit, which could prompt changes in U.S. policy after the elections.

Meanwhile, detailed trade negotiations between Tokyo and Washington continued. Preliminary talks had been held when President Reagan visited Japan in November 1983. Follow-up negotiations involved Vice-President George Bush, Director General Komoto of the EPA, and Foreign Minister Abe. In Washington in early April, hard bargaining resulted in an agreement initialed by Japan's Minister of Agriculture Shinjiro Yamamura and U.S. Trade Representative William Brock. The net result was a considerable expansion of Japan's quota on high-grade American beef and an increase in imports of citrus fruit products. Japanese farmers organizations bitterly opposed the agreement and demanded price supports for domestic citrus fruit.

Vice-President Bush was in Tokyo again May 8–10, pressing for Japanese tariff reductions. He urged prompt action to liberalize Jap-

Sygma

Japan's Prime Minister Yasuhiro Nakasone (left) visited China in March. A shared interest in reducing tensions in Korea brought Tokyo and Peking closer together in 1984. In an unusual gesture of friendship, China's Party Secretary Hu Yaobang (right) held a luncheon for Nakasone at his own home.

anese financial markets, but Prime Minister Nakasone responded merely that Japan would "do its best." Conversations between Japanese and U.S. officials continued at an economic conference in Rome on May 21–22. Meanwhile, in a report announced simultaneously in Tokyo and Washington on April 29, Japan pledged to gradually deregulate interest rates, to ease restrictions on Euroyen contracts, and to allow foreign financial institutions to engage in trust banking activities in Japan. The chief issue yet to be resolved had to do with the growing importance of information systems (the so-called value-added networks, or VANs), and the degree of competition to be allowed in the two countries.

China, Korea, and South Asia. During Prime Minister Nakasone's visit to Peking on March 23–25, China joined Japan in expressing a common desire to reduce tensions on the Korean peninsula. The two sides voiced concern over the continuing Soviet military buildup in Northeast Asia. Nakasone met with Premier Zhao Ziyang and with Deng Xiaoping.

Early in July in Tokyo, China's Defense Minister Zhang Aiping consulted with his counterpart, Yuko Kurihara, director general of the Japan Defense Agency (JDA). It was the first visit to Japan by a Chinese defense minister. Zhang publicly supported the U.S.-Japan Security Treaty as important in strengthening Japan's defense.

On July 17 also in Tokyo, Chinese Foreign Minister Wu Xueqian expressed Peking's hope that the forthcoming visit to Japan by South Korea's President Chun Doo Hwan would contribute to easing tensions on the Korean peninsula. Wu told Foreign Minister Abe that North Korea was indeed seeking a peaceful solution to the division of Korea. Abe called on Peking to secure the peace and prosperity of Hong Kong, both before and after the Chinese takeover in 1997.

Foreign Minister Abe had returned from a visit to Seoul, on July 6–9. With Foreign Minister Lee Won Kyong he had officially confirmed the forthcoming "historic visit" to Tokyo by President Chun. In January 1983, Prime Minister Nakasone had been the first Japanese head of state to travel to Korea since World War II. President Chun, in turn, would be the first Korean leader to visit Japan since the 36-year occupation of Korea by Japan came to a close in 1945.

President Chun arrived in Tokyo for his two-day visit on September 6. At a reception banquet that night, Emperor Hirohito expressed regret at the "unfortunate past" between the two countries; President Chun said that he saw the "beginning of a new era of friendship." In talks with Prime Minister Nakasone, Chun maintained that the issue of Korean unification should be handled only by direct talks between the North and South.

Later in September, North Korea's President Kim Il Sung appeared to be conciliatory in three meetings with Japan Socialist Party leader Masashi Ishibashi in Panmunjom. Kim appealed for improved relations among the two Koreas, Japan, and the United States.

Japan's expanded role in global affairs was further evidenced by Nakasone's trip to Pakistan and India, on April 30–May 6. He became the first Japanese leader to visit Southwest Asia in 23 years. In talks with Pakistan's President Zia ul-Haq and India's Prime Minister Indira Gandhi, Japan's role as a "bridge" between the Nonaligned Movement and the industrialized democracies—between North and South—was emphasized.

USSR. Although Japan had normalized relations with the Soviet Union, the disposition of what Japanese call the "northern territories" —the lower Kurile islands, occupied by the USSR since World War II—remained a point of contention between Tokyo and Moscow. On August 31 in Moscow, Soviet Foreign Minister Andrei Gromyko denounced the Nakasone foreign policy, specifically a military buildup supposedly "in line" with U.S. purposes. He also reiterated Moscow's refusal to consider Japan's claims to the "northern territories." Gromyko's statements were made to former Foreign Minister Yoshio Sakurauchi.

Japan, however, did maintain contact with the USSR. Just before his selection as LDP president for another term, Prime Minister Nakasone on October 26 welcomed to Tokyo a Soviet delegation headed by Dinmukhammed A. Kunayev, a member of the Politburo. Kunayev, like Gromyko, brushed off territorial claims by Japan, urging instead the adoption of a good-neighbor treaty of cooperation. Prime Minister Nakasone responded that the territorial issue was something the Japanese simply could not ignore in any consideration of a friendship treaty.

ARDATH W. BURKS, *Rutgers University*

JAPAN • Information Highlights

Official Name: Japan.
Location: East Asia.
Area: 14,747 sq mi (381 945 km²).
Population (March 31, 1984): 119,316,468.
Chief Cities (Oct. 1, 1982 est.): Tokyo, the capital, 8,336,103; Yokohama, 2,848,155; Osaka, 2,623,124; Nagoya, 2,093,416.
Government: *Head of state,* Hirohito, emperor (acceded Dec. 1926). *Head of government,* Yasuhiro Nakasone, prime minister (took office Nov. 1982). *Legislature*—Diet: House of Councillors and House of Representatives.
Monetary Unit: Yen (246 yen equal U.S.$1, Nov. 26, 1984).
Gross National Product (1984 U.S.$): $903,000,-000,000.
Economic Indexes (1983): *Consumer Prices* (1970 = 100), all items, 259.3; food, 256.2. *Industrial Production* (1975 = 100), 144.
Foreign Trade (1983 U.S.$): *Imports,* $146,992,-000,000; *exports,* $146,676,000,000.

JORDAN

The breakdown of talks between Jordan's King Hussein and Palestine Liberation Organization (PLO) leader Yasir Arafat left Jordan on the sidelines of Middle East diplomacy at the end of 1983. Hussein began 1984 by pursuing a new approach to reestablish for himself a central role in peace negotiations.

Reconvening Parliament. In January, Hussein reconvened parliament (effectively suspended since 1974) to amend the constitution so that Palestinians from the Israeli-occupied West Bank could be appointed as members. Hussein also shuffled his 20-member cabinet to increase the number of Jordanians of Palestinian origin.

Hussein sought to strengthen his position as a spokesman for the Palestinians in any peace negotiations while encouraging the PLO to resume talks on a negotiated peace with Israel.

In early March, Hussein and Arafat met for the first time since April 1983 and agreed on a broad Jordanian-Palestinian formula for Middle East peace talks.

U.S. Relations. The king appealed to the United States for military aid and weapons to bolster his own regime and to assist Arab states in the Persian Gulf. In March the United States set plans to sell Stinger antiaircraft missiles to Jordan. As a result of restrictions placed on the use of these weapons and American support for Israel, Hussein attacked Reagan administration policies, stating that the United States had lost its credibility as a mediator in the Arab-Israeli conflict. The United States canceled the arms sale to Jordan, and Hussein suggested he might turn to the Soviet Union for military equipment.

Elections. Also in March, Jordanians voted in national elections for the first time in 17 years. Muslim fundamentalist candidates won three of eight vacant seats in the Lower House. The remarkably strong showing served as a reminder to Hussein of domestic constraints to entering peace negotiations before achieving a broader Arab and Palestinian consensus.

Following the Israeli elections on July 23, Hussein dismissed calls for peace talks by new Israeli Prime Minister Shimon Peres as "subterfuge and deception."

Renewed Ties with Egypt. On September 25, in a surprising move, Hussein restored full diplomatic relations with Egypt after a five-year hiatus. Jordan thus became the first Arab state that had broken ties with Cairo after the Egyptian-Israeli peace treaty of 1979 to restore full relations. Egypt's President Hosni Mubarak visited Amman in early October, and King Hussein was welcomed in Cairo in early December.

It was unclear whether Hussein's move would mark a new chapter in attempts at Arab solidarity or deepen splits in the Arab ranks.

JORDAN · Information Highlights

Official Name: Hashemite Kingdom of Jordan.
Location: Southwest Asia.
Area: 35,000 sq mi (90 650 km²).
Population (mid-1984 est.): 3,500,000.
Chief Cities (Dec. 1982): Amman, the capital, 712,000; Zarqa, 244,500.
Government: *Head of state,* Hussein ibn Talal, king (acceded Aug. 1952). *Head of government,* Ahmad Obeidat, prime minister (appointed Jan. 10, 1984). *Legislature*—Parliament: House of Representatives and Senate.
Monetary Unit: Dinar (.3995 dinar equals U.S.$1, Nov. 19, 1984).
Gross National Product (1982 U.S.$): $4,900,000,000.
Economic Index (1983): *Consumer Prices* (1980 = 100), all items, 121.5; food, 116.1.
Foreign Trade (1983 U.S.$): *Imports,* $3,030,000,000; *exports,* $579,000,000.

Relations between Jordan and Syria, already at a low ebb because of mutual accusations of subversion and Hussein's qualified approval of President Reagan's 1982 Middle East peace plan, were further exacerbated by Jordan's resumption of relations with Egypt.

Economy. The Jordanian economy has suffered as a result of the Iran-Iraq war and falling oil prices. Exports to Iraq, Jordan's chief trading partner, and other Arab states fell sharply in 1983 and continued to decline in 1984.

Foreign aid, an important component of Jordan's economy, failed to reach expected levels. The 1978 Baghdad summit promised Jordan $1.25 billion (U.S.) in annual aid. However, Jordan expected to receive only $600 million in 1984, including $117 million from the United States.

At the end of 1984 it remained to be seen whether the renewed ties with Egypt would create a new market for Jordanian goods to boost its slowed economy as well as provide new political opportunities for an overall settlement of the Arab-Israeli conflict.

STEVEN M. RISKIN
Middle East Specialist, Washington, DC

KANSAS

The Kansas economy was relatively stable in 1984, although depressed prices in the agriculture industry continued to be a concern. The destructive forces of nature gained their share of newspaper headlines.

Agriculture. The 1984 wheat crop was the third largest on record, totaling 429 million bushels (15.1 billion liters). The crop was down 4% from 1983, but it was the fifth year that production had exceeded 400 million bushels (14 billion liters). Dry conditions at planting time resulted in sparse stands of wheat in some parts of the state, but spring growing and moisture conditions were generally favorable. Farmers harvested a total of 11 million acres

(4.4 million ha) of wheat. This was only 81% of the acreage planted in the fall of 1983, with acreage reduction and payment-in-kind programs accounting for the sizable amount of unharvested acreage. Wheat yields averaged 39 bushels (1 374 liters) per acre, and Sumner County led the state with a total of 13.5 million bushels (475.7 million liters) harvested.

Weather. A late winter snow and ice storm hit Kansas on March 18, 1984, causing damage to trees, television towers, and electrical lines. The worst ice damage was along a wide line from Dodge City to Atchison. An estimated 100,000 residents in the Kansas City area were without electricity because of the storm, and 110,000 homes were without power across the state. The ABC television affiliate in Topeka was knocked off the air when its transmitting tower collapsed from a coating of ice. Efforts to restore service were hampered by winds and falling chunks of ice that snapped power lines that had survived the storm itself. It took almost two weeks to restore power throughout the state, and the clean-up of tree limbs continued for a number of weeks.

Several destructive tornadoes struck towns in Kansas, causing extensive damage in Effingham in the spring and the loss of several lives in Carbondale in late October.

Legislation. In a relatively harmonious session, the Kansas legislature approved a record $1.66 billion budget and addressed several major issues. Educational concerns resulted in a $36 million increase in aid to public schools, and another bill raised the percentages by which school districts can increase their budgets. This will allow salaries for public school teachers to be raised by approximately 9%.

Attempts to prohibit the burial of all hazardous wastes were defeated, but a superfund for clean-up of hazardous waste sites was created. The Kansas Corporation Commission was given broad authority to determine what costs of utility plant construction can be passed on to ratepayers, in view of the approaching completion of the Wolf Creek nuclear power plant near Burlington. Attorney General Robert Stephan announced in December that his office would intervene in the Wolf Creek rate case if prohibitive rate hikes were to be imposed on consumers.

Prison overcrowding was addressed through the creation of prerelease centers; a law reducing minimum sentences to one year for less serious, nonviolent crimes; and a variety of measures for remodeling and expanding facilities and for hiring additional staff.

Elections. More than 1 million Kansans voted in the November election. The record turnout contributed to another record when U.S. Sen. Nancy Landon Kassebaum was reelected for her second term with approximately 77% of the vote. Incumbent Congressmen Pat Roberts (R), Jim Slattery (D), Dan Glickman

UPI/Bettmann

Sen. Nancy Kassebaum (R-KS) discusses air-traffic problems with Federal Aviation Administrator Donald Engen. The daughter of Alf Landon won a second term in 1984.

(D), and Bob Whittaker (R) were reelected. In the third district, Jan Meyers (R), a former state senator from Overland Park, defeated Kansas City Mayor Jack E. Reardon.

In late November, the state's senior senator, Robert Dole, was elected Senate Majority leader.

PATRICIA A. MICHAELIS
Kansas State Historical Society

KANSAS • Information Highlights

Area: 82,277 sq mi (213 098 km²).
Population (July 1, 1983 est.): 2,425,000.
Chief Cities (July 1, 1982 est.): Topeka, the capital, 120,269; Wichita, 288,723; Kansas City, 162,211.
Government (1984): *Chief Officers*—governor, John Carlin (D); lt. gov., Thomas R. Docking (D). *Legislature*—Senate, 40 members; House of Representatives, 125 members.
State Finances (fiscal year 1983): *Revenues,* $2,990,000,000; *expenditures,* $2,864,000,000.
Personal Income (1983): $29,703,000,000; per capita, $12,247.
Labor Force (May 1984): *Civilian labor force,* 1,200,500; *unemployed,* 59,600 (5.0% of total force).
Education: *Enrollment* (fall 1982)—public elementary schools, 282,879; public secondary, 124,195; colleges and universities (fall 1983), 141,709. *Public school expenditures* (1982–83), $1,131,758,425 ($3,058 per pupil).

KENTUCKY

The 1984 Kentucky political scene was dominated by the question of improving the quality of primary and secondary education and paying for the improvements. National educational studies had shown Kentucky lagging behind most other states, including those in the South, and a number of Kentucky organizations had recommended reforms.

Tax Proposals. At the start of the 1984 legislative session, Gov. Martha Layne Collins opposed tax increases and proposed that the state find ways of improving the schools that did not require large sums of money. Late in January, however, revenue estimates for the 1984–86 biennium were revised downward. Governor Collins became convinced that new taxes were necessary and that the increase should be large enough to make progress in education possible. She recommended tax increases that would produce $324 million in new revenue during the biennium, with 70% of the new funds going for education. She also proposed wide-ranging reforms to improve the quality of education.

The proposal for tax increases met strong resistance in the state legislature. Governor Collins made several changes in the tax package in an effort to win legislative support, and the final package included increases in the income tax and corporate license fees. In mid-March, when it became clear that there were not enough votes in the Democratic caucus to pass the tax measure in the House, the gover-

nor withdrew it. The legislature then adopted its own version of the budget, which did not include any tax increase.

Educational Reform. The legislature provided some additional funding for education, in part by minimizing pay increases for state employees. More funds were allocated to mandatory kindergartens, remedial education, and assistance to poorer school districts.

The legislature also adopted educational reforms with minimum costs to the state. These measures included competency tests and one-year internships for new teachers, standardized educational requirements for school board members, and a requirement that school districts support education with at least a minimum property tax.

The most controversial—and potentially expensive—part of the governor's educational plan was her proposal for a career "ladder" for state teachers. It was designed to identify the best teachers and provide them with substantially higher salaries. Critics questioned whether an equitable and nonpolitical method could be developed to select the best teachers. The legislature set up a committee to study methods of implementing the proposal.

Elections. President Ronald Reagan carried the state by more than 280,000 votes, the sixth Republican victory in Kentucky in the last eight presidential elections. Perhaps the major upset of the 1984 Senate elections was the defeat of Democratic Sen. Walter D. Huddleston by Republican Mitch McConnell, Jr., the county judge-executive of Jefferson County (Louisville), by a margin of less than 6,000 votes. It was the first statewide victory of a Republican candidate (other than a presidential candidate) since 1968. The Democrats, however, retained their solid control of the state legislature. They lost only three House seats, giving them a 74–26 margin.

MALCOLM E. JEWELL
University of Kentucky

In a close U.S. Senate race, Republican Mitch McConnell, Jr., 42, tied himself closely to Reagan policy and won a major upset over Democrat incumbent Walter Huddleston.

AP/Wide World

KENTUCKY • Information Highlights

Area: 40,409 sq mi (104 660 km²).
Population (July 1, 1983 est.): 3,714,000.
Chief Cities (July 1, 1982 est.): Frankfort, the capital (1980 census), 25,973; Louisville, 293,531; Lexington-Fayette, 207,668.
Government (1984): *Chief Officers*—governor, Martha Layne Collins (D); lt.gov., Steven L. Beshear (D). *General Assembly*—Senate, 38 members; House of Representatives, 100 members.
State Finances (fiscal year 1983): *Revenues,* $5,364,000,000; *expenditures,* $5,165,000,000.
Personal Income (1983): $34,903,000,000; per capita, $9,397.
Labor Force (May 1984): *Civilian labor force,* 1,746,100; *unemployed,* 156,100 (8.9% of total force).
Education: *Enrollment* (fall 1982)—public elementary schools, 457,505; public secondary, 193,579; colleges and universities (fall 1983), 146,503. *Public school expenditures* (1982–83), $1,233,797,475 ($2,100 per pupil).

Don Hunt (right) of the International Animal Exchange supervised an operation in Kenya to corral 25 reticulated giraffes and save the subspecies from eventual and complete extinction.

AP/Wide World

KENYA

President Daniel arap Moi continued to consolidate his power, seeing to the removal from office of Attorney General Charles Njonjo, and neutralizing Njonjo's powerful Kikuyu tribe. The Kikuyu had dominated Kenya during the rule of the late Jomo Kenyatta (1963–78) and were increasingly resentful that other ethnic groups were winning some of the political and economic advantages they had long enjoyed.

To prove his popularity, President Moi called a sudden election in September 1983, which he won without opposition. Moi then began a campaign against a "traitor," who turned out to be Njonjo, the leading Kikuyu in the government. By the end of 1984, Njonjo had been dismissed from office in disgrace and Kikuyu resentment of the action artfully negated. Although Moi seemed secure, the unsavory revelations about corruption at Njonjo's trial could eventually reach the president.

Ethnic Rivalries. Besides the political rivalry of different tribes, Kenya in 1984 was shaken by ethnic violence, some of it perpetrated by the Kenyan army. In the Wajir district of northern Kenya, two ethnic Somali clans, whom the Nairobi government suspected of separatist desires, were attacked by police and army troops in February. Reports put the number of dead at between 300 and 1,000. In addition, thousands were made homeless and many were subject to brutal interrogation. The government denied the figures and denounced the local political leaders who reported them, but the situation remained tense.

Kenyan troops also cooperated with Ugandan forces in harshly suppressing banditry and general disorder in the border area of the two countries. The main victims were the pastoral Pokot, Karamojong, and Turkana tribes, whose traditional grazing lands have been infiltrated by Kikuyu and Luhya farmers and who have responded by large-scale raids. The number killed was not known, but nearly 40,000 were made refugees.

East African Community. The moribund East African Community (EAC) finally was dissolved in 1984, after a last-minute attempt at revival. The EAC—the union of Kenya, Uganda, and Tanzania—had not really functioned since 1977, but early in 1984 the leaders of the three nations met to look into the possibility of renewed cooperation. The only result was the reopening of the Kenya-Tanzania border. It was finally seen that the community was beyond recall, and the three states proceeded to divide the assets and debts of the EAC, the lion's share of both going to Kenya. The economic ideological differences between Kenya and Tanzania and the former's overwhelming economic superiority in the region contributed to the community's end.

Economy. Kenya recorded a small economic upturn in 1984. It saw its balance-of-payments deficit reduced to under $400 million and was buoyed by an 85% rise in the world price of tea, one of its major exports. Assistance from the United States, Britain, and the International Monetary Fund provided enough foreign exchange to permit a new four-year plan to begin in 1984. At the same time, however, Kenya was hit by the devastating drought that was affecting other African nations.

ROBERT GARFIELD, *DePaul University*

KENYA • Information Highlights

Official Name: Republic of Kenya.
Location: East Coast of Africa.
Area: 225,000 sq mi (582 750 km²).
Population (mid-1984 est.): 19,400,000.
Chief Cities (1979 census): Nairobi, the capital, 827,775; Mombasa, 341,148.
Government: *Head of state and government,* Daniel arap Moi, president (took office Oct. 1978). *Legislature* (unicameral)—National Assembly, 170 members.
Monetary Unit: Kenya shilling (13.227 shillings equal U.S.$1, May 1984).
Gross Domestic Product (1982 U.S.$): $6,300,-000,000.
Economic Index (1983): *Consumer Prices,* (1975 = 100), all items, 216.3; food, 211.0.
Foreign Trade (1982 U.S.$): *Imports,* $1,683,000,000; *exports,* $979,000,000.

During an official September visit to Japan by South Korea's President Chun Doo Hwan (center), Japan's Emperor Hirohito (right) expressed regret for the "unfortunate past" between the two nations. Responding, Chun said that he saw the "beginning of a new era of partnership."

UPI/Bettmann

KOREA

Both North and South Korea enjoyed a peaceful, relatively prosperous, and politically stable year in 1984 without drastic sociopolitical or economic change. In the North, the transition of power from 72-year-old President Kim Il Sung to his son, Kim Jon Il, made apparently smooth progress. For the most part free from the violence that marred 1983 and shadowed 1984's first half, both Koreas were able in the second half of the year to approach and speak to each other on several issues virtually for the first time since 1973.

South Korea

The year's greatest accomplishment in the Republic of Korea (ROK) may have been intimations of progress in relations with North Korea. As the year ended, South Korea began mounting an attempt to become a full United Nations member.

International Relations. South Korea's enhanced international position was amply reflected in the year's events and visitations. Most significant of these was the September 5–8 state visit of President Chun Doo Hwan to Tokyo, a historic first for a Korean chief of state. During the visit Japanese Emperor Hirohito, who ruled Korea for 18 years, expressed regrets "that there was an unfortunate past between us for a period in this century" and added that this "should not be repeated." This equivocation was accepted reluctantly as the required apology for 40 years of harsh colonial rule, especially when reinforced by far more forthright references by Japanese Prime Minister Yasuhiro Nakasone to the "great sufferings" of the Korean people. Though efforts were discussed for improved treatment of Japan's 1,600,000 Korean minority, practical results mattered less than psychological clearing of the atmosphere, allowing closer relations for two nations bereft of any other compatible neighbors. In August, meetings of the Korean-Japanese Cooperative Council and the Korea-Japan Parliamentarians took place in Tokyo. These were followed by a visit to Seoul by Japanese businessmen seeking redress of mounting Japanese trading profits with Korea, which ran to $1.74 billion (U.S.) in the first half of 1984 alone.

Another historic first visit was made by Pope John Paul II in May. The pope commemorated the 200th anniversary of Catholicism in

SOUTH KOREA · Information Highlights

Official Name: Republic of Korea.
Location: Northeastern Asia.
Area: 38,190 sq mi (98 913 km²).
Population (mid-1984 est.): 42,000,000.
Chief City (1983 est.): Seoul, the capital, 9,454,825.
Government: *Head of state,* Chun Doo Hwan, president (formally inaugurated March 1981). *Head of government,* Chin Iee Jong, prime minister (appointed Oct. 14, 1983). *Legislature*—National Assembly.
Monetary Unit: Won (811.4 won equal U.S.$1, July 1984).
Gross National Product (1982): $70,800,000,000.
Economic Indexes (1983): *Consumer Prices* (1975 = 100), all items, 606.2; food, 682.3. *Industrial Production* (1975 = 100), 284.
Foreign Trade (1983 U.S.$): *Imports,* $26,192,-000,000; *exports,* $24,445,000,000.

Korea with a mass canonization ceremony for 93 Korean and 10 French Catholics martyred in the peninsula during the first century of Christianity. Protestantism celebrated, less spectacularly, its 100th Korean jubilee. With some 10 million Protestants and 1,700,000 Catholics, South Korea moved toward the Christianization of a third of its population.

Even greater public acclaim accompanied the dispatch of a 203-member team to the Olympic Games in Los Angeles, where it finished with 6 gold, 6 silver, and 7 bronze medals and provided great advertising for the 1988 Olympics in Seoul. (*See also* SPORTS—The Olympic Games, page 464.)

Publicized visits during the year of the Australian and Belgian prime ministers, the Sri Lankan president, the British foreign secretary, the German economics minister, U.S. Secretaries George Shultz and Caspar Weinberger, and the emir of Qatar expanded President Chun's image of legitimacy, questionable because of his 1979–80 seizure of power. The completion of 30 mi (48 km) of Seoul subway, the Olympic stadium, major highways, and irrigation facilities symbolized further welcome advances.

Economy. Economically, the year began with a continuation of the high level of growth of more than 9% that had characterized 1983. Electronic gear, chemicals, glassware, fish, cars, and machinery showed the export strength that put Korea in 12th place in world trade. GNP per person reached $2,000 by year's end, more than twice North Korea's. Economic activity continued to be concentrated in large, integrated corporations, ten of which had joint ventures with American conglomerates and placed within the world's top 500.

In the year's second half, rising protectionism in the United States and elsewhere against such items as televisions, steel, machinery, and textiles and the deepening Japan trade deficit began to threaten export earnings. Orders in shipbuilding, Middle East construction, and

synthetic textiles fell sharply, forcing the government to save larger numbers of heavily indebted companies from bankruptcy and plunging third-quarter GNP growth to 4.7% (compared with 11% in 1983) and export growth to 1.6% (15.3% in the third quarter of 1983). Foreign debt increased to $43 billion, fourth in the developing world, though Korea continued its high credit ratings. With inflation holding near the 2% level and a record rice crop, internal prosperity was maintained.

Government. Political progress was measured. Party, parliamentary, and press institutions for peaceful grievance remained sharply controlled and grossly inadequate, though press curbs relaxed a bit. In June, party prestige was weakened by a scandal over the accumulation by the former government party head of a fortune of nearly $20 million in real estate. Government majorities—partly appointed—voted down all important opposition demands for more democratic press, election, and judicial procedures, though some revisions to the nation's basic press law were promised in late November.

Students accordingly demonstrated throughout the year in most of Korea's 99 colleges and universities, protesting general curbs on freedom and student organization and the punishment of more than 1,000 students by drafting them into the military, where six students died.

In February and November the government lifted its political ban on a further 286 of the 567 politicians banned in 1980; 15 remained banned. From March on, the government gave up arresting student activists, releasing most and declaring a policy of campus independence and noninterference of the police except when summoned by university authorities. Many hundreds of student activists and most of the 87 dissident professors forced from teaching by the government were allowed to return for the fall semester. Yet demonstrations, by a mounting minority of students, escalated and forced Seoul National and Hannam universities to recall the police briefly, threatening basic stability and the durability of lenient policies. Mild anti-Americanism continued. Labor discontent, shackled by strict laws, still lacked unions and freedom sufficient to allow it major expression.

Military. Military affairs continued to be quiet. From February 1, the annual "Team Spirit" ROK-U.S. combined military exercises were held well below the demilitarized zone. The number of troops involved was increased to 147,300 Koreans and 60,000 Americans—36,400 from outside Korea. The 16th annual U.S.-ROK Security Consultation, May 9–10 in Seoul, noted progress in the military capabilities of South Korea and promised continuance of U.S. support with its 40,000 troops in South Korea.

In September, North Korean trucks and freighters transported relief supplies to victims of severe flooding in South Korea. After first refusing the assistance, Seoul accepted the offer, citing the need to "improve inter-Korean relations."

Kaku Kurita, Gamma-Liaison

North Korea

The lockstep impression of policy in the Democratic People's Republic of Korea (DPRK) during the first half of 1984 reflected the need to preserve the status quo during the gradual succession process of Kim Jong Il from his father, Kim Il Sung, who, through 40 years, had become one of the world's most durable leaders. Succession adjustments needed to be gradual, bureaucratic, and undramatic if they were to proceed. They were so in 1984, thus bringing the state an important step further toward the smooth transition hoped for in Pyongyang. Meanwhile, economic, international, and military events waited, making 1984 a year lacking in external drama until the month of October.

Economy. Social and economic news seemed sparse. Some progress was made generally and in the servicing and repayment to Scandinavian nations of small portions of the DPRK's $2 billion foreign debt. Otherwise, the economy appeared to remain sluggish with GNP at about $15–16 billion, about 1/5th that of South Korea. Foreign trade was little more than 1/20th of the South Korean total.

The DPRK's chief customer for cement appeared to be Iran, which also purchased a quarter of its arms from Pyongyang.

International Relations. Improvements in foreign relations were stalled primarily by the aftermath of the dramatic attempted assassination of President Chun Doo Hwan by DPRK agents during an official visit to Rangoon, Burma, on Oct. 9, 1983. The president escaped, but 17 high ROK officials—including four ministers—were killed in the bomb explosion. Hoped-for dialogue and increased contact froze thereafter, and Burma itself broke relations with Pyongyang.

The first signs of adjustment came with the appointments of Kim Yong Nam as foreign minister in December 1983 and Kang Song-san as premier in January, marking the emergence of younger and more flexible associates of Kim Jong Il, who appeared set to forward pragmatic solutions and broaden internationalities.

Quickly reflecting this, on Jan. 10, 1984, Chinese Premier Zhao Ziyang delivered personally to President Reagan a DPRK proposal for three-way talks between Pyongyang, Seoul, and Washington on a peace treaty and improved relations between the two Koreas. Seoul attacked this proposal as not offering full equality to the South in a peace treaty, for evading direct North-South talks, and for covering up the crimes of Rangoon. Washington declined to accept such talks.

Meanwhile, January saw the start of policies calling for cooperation with capitalist countries and espousing capitalist investment in North Korea in joint ventures; this reflected DPRK concerns over the widening economic gap with South Korea. These policies were made into law on September 7. Deng Xiaoping counseled Japan on October 23 to invest in North Korea for the sake of peace.

From February 1 on, forward movement took its annual dip with the start of the "Team Spirit" joint ROK-U.S. military exercises in the South, which evoke strong DPRK fears of invasion and nuclear attack.

In an interview with the Soviet news agency Tass on March 31, Kim Il Sung implied that China was colluding with Pyongyang's enemies, Japan and the United States, while Moscow had shown better support for the DPRK's real strategic interests against such a trilateral alliance. The statement was regarded as a bid for Soviet support for Pyongyang's arms modernization needs and as preparation for President Kim's forthcoming journey to Moscow.

In April, during President Reagan's trip to Peking, U.S. Secretary of State Shultz delivered a message "intended for North Korea" proposing "confidence-building measures" between North and South Korea and the United States, such as prior notification of military maneuvers and exchanges of observers for military exercises. But prospects continued to be clouded when, in April and May, talks between South and North Korea on forming a joint team for the Los Angeles Olympics broke down over Seoul's insistence on Pyongyang's apology for the Rangoon bombing. In early June, Pyongyang joined Moscow—belatedly—in boycotting the Los Angeles Olympics. Meanwhile, Seoul and Peking were enjoying their first sports exchanges.

On May 4, Chinese Communist Party Secretary Hu Yaobang arrived in Pyongyang to explain China's athletic exchanges with Seoul and receive assurances that Kim Il Sung's forthcoming Moscow trip was not anti-Chinese. Chinese compromise was symbolized in photographs showing Hu "warmly shaking hands" with heir apparent Kim Jong Il toward whose succession Peking previously had evinced little warm.

The climax of the Kim Il Sung year came with Kim's unprecedented May 16–July 1 train trip to Moscow, Warsaw, Berlin, Prague, Budapest, Bucharest, and Sofia, where he made 12 major speeches and signed friendship treaties with East Germany and Bulgaria. While inveighing against tripartite threat, Kim did not call for U.S. troop withdrawal nor for the ousting of Chun, thus apparently keeping avenues for progress open. Though the trip was thought to be aimed at garnering support for the Kim Jong Il succession, the son did not accompany his father nor did his name appear in the communiqués. Fellow socialist enthusiasm for the heretical succession seemed undemonstrative. In Bulgaria, President Kim said he would retire in a year and turn things over to his son. It was apparent that Kim received Soviet assurances of more advanced MiG-23s and 25s, SA-6 missiles, and sophisticated electronic weaponry to counteract such advanced weaponry as F-16s being received by the ROK.

North-South Thaw. From August on, communication between the two Koreas began to unfreeze, making the greatest progress since 1972-73. On August 20, President Chun proposed economic and technical assistance for the North. Shortly after serious September flooding in South Korea, the North offered to deliver rice, medicine, clothes, and cement to the flood victims. After some false starts in Panmunjom meetings, appropriate delivery means were found, and the ROK Red Cross accepted. From September 30 to October 4, $12 million of such supplies moved by ship to Inchon and Pukpyong and by trucks to Panmunjom, ROK receptionists giving gift packages in return, all accompanied by worldwide publicity. In October the ROK Red Cross president proposed to his DPRK counterpart that the Red Cross talks on uniting families, which had been suspended on Aug. 28, 1973, be reopened. On October 6, both sides agreed to reopen a telephone hotline. On October 29 the DPRK Red Cross accepted the proposal for a preliminary meeting at Panmunjom on November 20 to discuss date, format, and agenda for eight official meetings between the two Red Cross societies. The meeting was amicable.

In the same weeks, the ROK prime minister proposed talks to form a permanent organization to promote trade and economic cooperation between South and North. Pyongyang similarly accepted, setting the date for the economic talks for November 15. On that date, basic goals were amicably outlined, many proposals were submitted, and further discussions were postponed for three weeks. Unfortunately, a severe fire fight broke out in Panmunjom on November 23 during the successful defection of a Soviet student, killing three North Korean and one South Korean personnel. In its wake, further economic talks were postponed though both sides refrained from their complete rupture. Meanwhile, representatives of sports delegations of each Korea talked briefly at an international sports meeting October 23 in China. While results were not disclosed, Geneva Olympic sources informally spoke of the possibility of compromises which could lead to the formation of a joint South-North Korean team for the 1988 Seoul Olympics. These remain to be explored.

On October 8, during his trip to the United Nations in New York, Foreign Minister Kim Yong Nam said that North Korea was willing to consider the "confidence-building" measures referred to by Secretary Shultz in the context of the three-way talks proposed in 1983-84.

GREGORY HENDERSON, *Harvard University*

NORTH KOREA · Information Highlights

Official Name: Democratic People's Republic of Korea.
Location: Northeastern Asia.
Area: 47,000 sq mi (121 730 km²).
Population (mid-1984 est.): 19,600,000.
Chief Cities (July 1980 est.): Pyongyang, the capital, 1,445,000; Hamhung, 780,000.
Government: *Head of state*, Kim Il Sung, president (nominally since Dec. 1972; actually in power since May 1948). *Head of government*, Kang Song-san, premier (took office Jan. 24, 1984). *Legislature* (unicameral)—Supreme People's Assembly. The Korea Workers' (Communist) Party: General Secretary, Kim Il Sung.

Charles Steiner, Picture Group

Walter Mondale and Geraldine Ferraro marched in New York City's Labor Day Parade with prominent state Democrats. The ticket counted on heavy support from labor, but in November it garnered only about 53% of the overall union vote.

LABOR

For American labor, 1984 was a year of frustration. Rewards were meager, if any, at the ballot box, the employment office, and the bargaining table.

National Election. The AFL-CIO's endorsed candidate for president, Walter F. Mondale, ran into early trouble in the Democratic primaries and was defeated decisively by Ronald Reagan in the November election. An unprecedented unity marked labor's campaign efforts. Among the AFL-CIO's 96 affiliated unions, only the Longshoremen and the National Maritime Union endorsed President Ronald Reagan. The president's principal union support came from the unaffiliated Teamsters, once expelled from the AFL-CIO.

AFL-CIO President Lane Kirkland took what comfort he could from exit polls that showed AFL-CIO households voted for Mondale over Reagan by 61% to 39%, almost the reverse of the popular vote. Of the labor-endorsed candidates for the U.S. Senate and House of Representatives, 62% were elected.

Employment. In November, a record 105.9 million Americans were employed, an increase of more than six million over the last two years. However, much of the increase came in the service and retail industries where wages are lower and unions less active.

The U.S. Bureau of Labor Statistics reported 8.2 million workers still jobless. That was 7.2% of the labor force compared with 8.4% a year earlier. By race, the unemployed rate was 6.1% among whites, 15% among blacks, and 10% among Hispanics.

In November the average workweek was 35.2 hours, with 5.5 million working only part-time. An additional 1.2 million "discouraged" workers had despaired of finding employment and were no longer counted among the nation's unemployed.

Earnings. For the third quarter, the Bureau of Labor Statistics (BLS) reported a 5.2% median increase in wages and salaries over a year earlier. The Consumer Price Index for the same period rose 4.2%, giving workers a meager increase in purchasing power. Union leaders blamed the workers' inability to advance in this second year of economic recovery on cheap imports, deregulation, sharper competition, and the Reagan administration's hostility.

Collective Bargaining. Resistance to management's push for concessions in work rules and cuts in wages and benefits stiffened during the year as business improved. Earlier, when union bargaining power was sapped by higher unemployment, some unions were forced to accept a "two-tier" wage scale under which new hires could be paid less than older hands for the same work.

The Bureau of National Affairs reported that while only 4.4% of contracts signed in 1983 included the two-tier wage system, that figure doubled in the first half of 1984. These agreements are not just in depressed industries but also in profitable high-tech operations.

More than 97% of all union-management agreements are reached without strikes or lockouts. The year 1984 was no exception.

Three-year contracts between the United Auto Workers (UAW) and General Motors (GM) and Ford Motors were renegotiated. They provide modest wage increases and additional job security. Part of the wage increase will be paid as bonuses tied to corporate profits. Management got a freer hand to automate production and adapt work rules to new technology.

For the first time in 20 years, the contract between the United Mine Workers and the coal operators was renegotiated without a nationwide strike. It calls for a raise of $10.25 a day spread over three years. By 1987, coal miners would earn $125 a day.

Negotiations for the nation's largest labor-management contract between the postal unions and the U.S. Postal Service were referred to final and binding arbitration, ensuring uninterrupted mail service. The result was a 2.7% annual wage increase for three years for 500,000 postal workers. (*See also* Postal Service.)

Strikes. The Auto Workers and the Machinists struck plants of McDonnell Douglas Aircraft. In February, UAW members ended their 17-week strike at Long Beach after holding out unsuccessfully against the two-tier wage system. The Machinists strike at the Fort Worth plant in November ended after 17 days with wage increases and no union concessions.

A 47-day strike by 52,000 workers in New York area hospitals and nursing homes ended when union members accepted a 5% pay increase in each of two years. In turn, the union agreed to a second-year freeze on starting pay for new hires.

A strike by 2,600 mostly female clerks and technicians employed by Yale University closed campus dining halls, libraries, and other buildings. The issues that attracted most attention were pay equity and comparable worth. Workers returned to work in early December without a settlement.

Organizations. The California State Employees Association with 50,000 members affiliated with the 750,000-member Service Employees International Union.

The Ohio Association of Public School Employees with 25,000 members joined the 1.3-million-member American Federation of State, County and Municipal Employees.

The National Union of Hospital and Health Care Employees, formerly a division of the Retail, Wholesale and Department Store Employees, was chartered as a national union by the AFL-CIO. The Association of Flight Attendants, with 21,000 members, became the AFL-CIO's 96th affiliate. The Cement, Lime, and Gypsum Workers merged with the International Brotherhood of Boilermakers and Blacksmiths to form a union of 144,000.

Leaders. Lynn Williams, a Canadian, was elected president of the United Steelworkers of America, succeeding Lloyd McBride who died in November 1983. Joseph M. Misbrenner was elected president of the Oil, Chemical and Atomic Workers. Former President Robert M. Goss and seven staff members took early retirement to cut staff costs.

Labor Law. Reversing earlier decisions, the National Labor Relations Board, now dominated by Reagan appointees, held that:

• An employer is not precluded from interrogating workers about union organizing activities and their union sympathies.

• An employer who commits an unfair labor practice in violation of the law cannot be ordered to negotiate with a union unless he or she has the support of a majority in the unit.

• An employer is not generally required to bargain with unions on the transfer of operations to another location.

Legislation. Unions won protection against abuse of the Bankruptcy Code when Congress limited its use to break union contracts. The legislation requires that a corporation in bankruptcy can abrogate its union contract only after it has tried to reach agreement with the union on contract changes. If none is reached, the judge may approve the company's request only if the union lacked "good cause" and if equity clearly favors management's request.

Before adjourning, Congress enacted three other laws sought by labor: to continue the tax-exempt status of important union benefits; to require as a condition of import relief that steel producers use their assets for plant modernization and set aside 1% of income to retrain workers; and to strengthen existing laws against labor racketeering.

International

International Labor Organization (ILO). In November, Poland gave notice that it would quit the International Labor Organization, a branch of the United Nations. Under ILO law a two-year notice is required before a member can resign. The ILO Governing Body had found that the Jaruzelski government's suppression of Solidarity, the Polish Labor federation, was a violation of the ILO conventions of freedom of association and the right of workers to form trade unions. The Governing Body acted on a recommendation of a Commission of Inquiry appointed by ILO Director General Francis Blanchard on complaint of a French labor federation, Fource Ouvrier. Other Soviet

Charlie Cole, Black Star

Rejecting a new contract that called for a two-year wage freeze, some 1,800 employees of Disneyland in Anaheim, CA, went on strike in late September. Management refused to give in, and three weeks later the unions ratified.

bloc nations had threatened to leave the ILO if Poland was censored.

Canada. Unemployment in Canada stood at 11.3% of the labor force in October. Inflation moderated to 3.8% in September.

At its convention in May, the Canadian Labor Congress (CLC) reaffirmed its opposition to any rollback in wages or benefits, to the two-tier wage system, and to any weakening of collective bargaining for public employees. The CLC called for economic and social measures to stimulate recovery, a shorter workweek without loss of pay, community action to assist the unemployed, and extension of social programs.

Union membership increased to 3,651,000 in January from 3,563,000 a year earlier. Of those, 56.1% belong to unions affiliated with the CLC. Canadian unions continued to move toward greater autonomy from U.S.-based unions. In ten years the proportion of workers represented by Canadian national unions rose from 40% to 60%. However, the rival Canadian Federation of Labor (CFL) maintains its ties with U.S.-based unions.

Canadian members of the United Auto Workers rejected a contract offered by General Motors on terms approved by GM workers in the United States. The resulting strike was settled after two weeks. The agreement follows the U.S. pattern except that there would be cash payments in the second and third years rather than one lump sum payment. Canadian workers traditionally have shown less interest in job security than their U.S. colleagues.

John Turner succeeded Pierre Elliott Trudeau as leader of the Liberal Party government, which soon was replaced. In a national election the Conservative Party, headed by Brian Mulroney, won a landslide victory. The Conservatives took 211 out of 282 seats. The Liberal Party dropped from 146 seats to 40. The New Democratic Party, with which the CLC is affiliated, won 30 seats, a loss of two. The new government promised an early summit meeting on economic matters, a step applauded by CLC President Dennis McDermott.

Great Britain. Unemployment rose above 3 million, or 12.9% of the labor force. The number of employees cut back to part-time increased. The government opposed job-creating programs, hoping to bring down unemployment by slowing the growth of labor costs, deregulating business, increasing competition and labor mobility, as well as enacting tax reform. The annual inflation rate was less than 5%. Worker productivity showed a remarkable 15.2% increase during the period 1981–84.

The year's most important labor event was the long strike against the nationalized coal mines. The Mine Workers Union was protesting the government's plan to close 20 mines considered unproductive. At stake were 20,000 miners' jobs. For its own reasons, the union did not seek membership ratification for the strike. As a result, 20% of the miners continued to work, producing 530,000 metric tons of coal a week. This led to violence on the picket line. A court declared the strike illegal and sequestered the union's assets.

A strike of 1,200 mine safety inspectors, whose presence in the mines is mandatory under British law, was called off much to the union's disappointment. The union also suffered from the disclosure in October that its leaders had secretly sought financial support from Libya, a country with which Britain severed diplomatic relations after a policewoman was killed by rifle fire from inside the Libyan embassy in London. Although both the Labour Party and the Trade Union Congress officially supported the miners' strike, they condemned the union's action of seeking Libyan assistance —as did the British public.

Union membership declined from a peak of 55% of the labor force (13.4 million) in 1979 to 50% (11 million). British unions were opposing the Conservative government's efforts to denationalize major industries. The Labour Party promised to renationalize them if it is returned to power. Labour's economic program called for government-financed investments, price controls, and revenue sharing to hold down inflation. On defense matters, the Labour Party supported unilateral nuclear disarmament, a nuclear freeze for Europe, and the removal of all U.S. bases. Labour supports a stronger conventional defense force.

The Trade Union Democracy Act became law. Its major provisions include a requirement for secret ballot elections of principal members of union executive committees and a limit on immunity for strikes not approved by secret ballots. Union political funds must be approved by membership vote at regular intervals.

France. Again in 1984, the emphasis in France was on austerity, further cuts in social programs, and encouragement of private initiative. Working hours were cut from 40 to 39 per week, but the government backed off from its promise of a 35-hour workweek. Price controls were continued through 1984. Unemployment was 10.6% in September, and inflation exceeded 7%.

In July the Communist Party withdrew from the coalition government in protest against its program to reduce direct taxes and to cut social programs again. The Communists have suffered a steady decline in voting strength since the party joined the government in 1981, falling from the traditional 20% to 11% of the votes cast.

West Germany. Reducing unemployment by shortening the workweek was the dominant issue in labor-management relations in West Germany in 1984. Joblessness reached 2.1 million, more than 9% of the labor force.

Some unions affiliated with the German Federation of Trade Unions pushed to lower the retirement age. Most affiliates, led by metalworkers and printers, demanded a cut in working hours from 40 to 35 per week with no cut in pay. Scattered wildcat strikes failed to budge management. In May, with more than 75% of its members approving, the metalworkers struck. The stoppage lasted for seven weeks, nearly paralyzing the German economy. The strike ended when both sides agreed to accept final and binding arbitration. In turn, the union gave management more latitude in scheduling work.

Sweden. Austerity measures introduced in 1982 and 1983, including devaluation of Sweden's currency, brought robust recovery to the national economy. Inflation and unemployment dropped, and the government pressed unions for moderation in wage demands. Unions and management moved away from the traditional system of centralized bargaining.

A 20% tax on profits and payrolls voted by parliament in December 1983 now is financing five wage-earner funds. These funds were expected to have available $247 million a year to buy shares in private companies. By 1990 wage earners may control from 8% to 10% of all publicly held stock in Swedish industry.

Japan. By world standards, Japan's economy did well. Unemployment was less than 3% of the labor force, and the Consumer Price Index rose less than 2%.

The annual spring offensive in collective bargaining resulted in a 4.4% wage increase, the same as in 1983. The traditional summer bonus amounted to more than 4%.

The Japanese labor force grew by an increased influx of women, often cited as the major cause of Japan's "high rate" of unemployment.

See also UNITED STATES—Productivity.

GORDON H. COLE AND JOSEPH MIRE

A 13-day strike against General Motors of Canada ended October 29 with ratification of a three-year contract.

Canapress

LAOS

Clashes between Communists and anticommunists dominated the foreign relations of Laos and continued to be an internal political annoyance.

Politics. Prince Souvanna Phouma died in January. The last of the pre-Communist premiers of Laos, he was the half brother of the communist president of Laos, Prince Souphanouvong. The major nationalist political figure in Laos before 1975, he had lived in retirement since the Communist takeover.

A few of his countrymen continued to oppose Communist rule of the land, however. Anticommunist guerrilla raids persisted, albeit intermittently, especially in the southern part of the country. A May rebel attack on a combined Laotian-Vietnamese military truck convoy resulted in the deaths of 40 government troops.

Refugees flowed across the border into Thailand in growing numbers: 10,000 in the first eight months of 1984 (double the number of such persons in the preceding two years). The refugees were almost wholly Hmong (or Meo) hill people who fought with the Americans against the Communists before 1975.

Economy. The chief obstacles to continuing Communist collectivization of the economy were not political but the inadequate infrastructure of the country, widespread corruption, and general administrative inefficiency. Top priority was accorded agricultural production: the government aspired to complete collectivization of rice growing by 1985. Low foreign-exchange reserves continued to be a problem, with the sale of locally generated electrical power the country's chief foreign exchange earner. Widespread smuggling persisted.

Foreign Relations. Laos and Thailand clashed repeatedly during the middle months of the year over three relatively isolated border villages. The villages—Ban Mai, Ban Klang, and Ban Sawang—were located 120 mi (193 km) west of Vientiane and 330 mi (530 km) north of Bangkok.

Laos brought the controversy before the United Nations Security Council in October, claiming the existence of a "serious threat to the peace, stability, and security of Southeast Asia." Thailand, in response, pledged that it would draw back its troops in the interest of "improved relations."

Tensions between the two countries partly reflected the location of Laos between bitter Communist rivals, Vietnam and China (the latter drawing increasingly closer to Thailand). Vietnam maintained 45,000 troops in Laos, a legacy of the Indochina war that ended in 1975, while China kept three divisions along its side of the northern border of Laos.

U.S.-Laotian relations improved—a consequence of the Laotian government's action in late December 1983 in turning over the remains of several American soldiers lost in the Vietnam War. This followed the first U.S. visit to a crash site in Laos since the 1975 Communist takeover.

RICHARD BUTWELL
California State University, Dominguez Hills

LATIN AMERICA

Latin America's economic and political climate improved moderately in 1984, but the region remained troubled by debt problems and terrorism and guerrilla warfare. U.S. involvement in the hemisphere continued at a high level and figured prominently in the 1984 presidential campaign.

Debt. The magnitude of the Latin American debt, variously estimated at from $350 billion to $400 billion (U.S.), and the economic consequences of the region's enormous debt-service load, caused ongoing concern in international financial circles throughout 1984. The Inter-American Development Bank, in its annual report on economic and social progress in Latin America, warned that a number of Latin American countries have avoided possible default only through "severe domestic adjustments" that have had high social costs in unemployment, inflation, and an overall deterioration in living conditions.

The World Bank reported that, "During the past year, the decline in the level of economic activity in Latin American countries became ever more acute. For the entire region, per capita gross domestic product (GDP) fell by about 6 percent. For a number of countries (Argentina, Bolivia, Brazil, Uruguay, most of Central America, and the Caribbean), and the region as a whole, 1983 was the third consecutive year of either stagnation or decline in the per capita GDP."

While there was a growing consensus that the worst of the Latin America debt crisis had passed, there was also general agreement that major obstacles to sustained economic growth persist. Little new capital flowed into the region during the year, and Latin America was a net exporter of capital to the industrialized countries. But at the same time, cooperation between the key Latin debtor nations and the

---

LAOS • Information Highlights

Official Name: Lao People's Democratic Republic.
Location: Southeast Asia.
Area: 91,430 sq mi (236 804 km²).
Population (mid-1984 est.): 3,700,000.
Government: *Head of state,* Prince Souphanouvong, president. *Head of government,* Kaysone Phomvihane, prime minister. *Legislature* (unicameral) —National Congress of People's Representatives.
Gross National Product (1982 U.S.$): $320,000,000.

In June ministers from 11 Latin nations gathered in Cartagena, Colombia, to discuss the region's foreign debt.

big international banks improved markedly. The four biggest debtor countries—Argentina, Brazil, Mexico, and Venezuela—engaged in negotiations with their creditor banks on rescheduling significant portions of their debt. All but Venezuela reached agreement with the International Monetary Fund (IMF) on economic austerity programs. Despite the lack of agreement with the IMF, Venezuela imposed its own severe adjustment plan, which won the approval of the creditor banks.

There were also signs of increasing cooperation on debt problems among the Latin American and Caribbean countries themselves. In March, when Argentina faced imminent default, Brazil, Colombia, Mexico, and Venezuela extended a $300 million rescue package to enable Argentina to meet its payment deadline. In June, in Cartagena, Colombia, and again in September, in Mar del Plata, Argentina, the debtor countries met to map common strategies to deal with the Latin American debt crisis. The Mar del Plata meeting produced a call for a conference of debtor and creditor countries to negotiate an easing of loan terms and a reduction of interest rates. A short time later, during the annual meetings of the World Bank and the IMF, U.S. Treasury Secretary Donald Regan proposed a special global conference in Washington, DC, in April 1985 to discuss world economic issues, especially Third World debt, development, and trade.

Trade. Despite a growing trend toward protectionism in the developed countries, Latin America significantly improved its balance of trade with the rest of the world. According to data compiled by the United Nations Economic Commission for Latin America and the Caribbean (ECLAC), the region registered a record trade surplus of $31.2 billion in 1983. But the surplus was achieved, ECLAC said, by drastically cutting imports rather than by sharply increasing exports. Despite the favorable trade balance, the balance of payments closed the year with a deficit of almost $4 billion. The net transfer of resources from Latin America to the exterior, including interest, debt amortization, and profit remittances, reached $29.5 billion in 1983, ECLAC said.

Because of the shortage of foreign exchange, according to the Organization of American States (OAS), Latin American countries have turned increasingly to countertrade, or barter, to buy and sell goods. In 1984, Colombia became the first Western Hemisphere country formally to require the use of countertrade, listing some 30 items, including tractors, whiskey, typewriters, and computers, that can be imported only if Colombia can sell an equivalent amount of its own products.

Political. Following the lead of Argentina, which ended military rule in 1983, several Latin American countries took steps to restore democracy in 1984, although in some cases the steps were considered insufficient by critics. Elections were held during the year in Ecuador, El Salvador, Guatemala, Nicaragua, Panama, and Uruguay. Brazil's electoral college, made up of the national congress and other public officials, was to choose a president from two civilian candidates on Jan. 15, 1985. In Colombia, the government of President Belisario Betancur signed a truce with the main elements of leftist guerrillas and began talks on reincorporating the guerrillas into the political life of the country.

Brazilian diplomat João Clemente Baena Soares was elected secretary general of the Organization of American States by unanimous vote. He is to serve a total of six years.

Organization of American States

Progress was also noted in resolving several international disputes. Argentina and Chile, negotiating under the auspices of the Vatican, reached a tentative agreement on sovereignty over a disputed group of islands in the south Atlantic Ocean. Bolivia and Chile met in Bogotá, Colombia, to discuss Bolivia's 100-year quest for access to the Pacific Ocean, which it lost in a tripartite war during the 19th century. The Contadora Group, consisting of Colombia, Mexico, Panama, and Venezuela, produced a draft agreement for easing tensions in Central America, although it was unclear late in the year whether the pact would win the wholehearted cooperation of the five Central American countries—Costa Rica, El Salvador, Guatemala, Honduras, and Nicaragua—and that of the United States.

The United States, in fact, remained heavily engaged in Central America in 1984. It strongly backed the government of El Salvador in its ongoing struggle against leftist guerrillas. Evidence also surfaced that the Reagan administration was continuing to aid antigovernment "contra" forces in Nicaragua, despite a congressional ban on such assistance. In October the Congress reiterated its opposition to the CIA-managed contra aid program, forbidding the use of U.S. funds until a congressional reexamination of the situation in February 1985. On the other hand, the Congress took no action in 1984 on the report of the National Bipartisan Commission on Central America, headed by former Secretary of State Henry Kissinger, which recommended in January that the United States mount an $8 billion economic development effort in Central America between 1984 and 1990.

Inter-American System. In June the Organization of American States (OAS), the political association of most of the countries of the Western Hemisphere, installed a new secretary general, João Baena Soares, the former deputy foreign minister of Brazil. Baena Soares, 53, is a veteran of 30 years in the Brazilian foreign service. He replaced Alejandro Orfila, an Ar-

gentine diplomat, who resigned unexpectedly during the annual OAS General Assembly in November 1983. Orfila's departure from the OAS became tainted with scandal when it was revealed that, during the last three months in office, he had been on the payroll of a Washington public relations and lobbying firm, drawing salaries from both the OAS and the private company. The OAS Council censured Orfila and sent a recommendation to the OAS General Assembly that his $36,000 annual pension be terminated.

Drug Traffic. In August seven Latin American countries—Bolivia, Colombia, Ecuador, Panama, Peru, Nicaragua, and Venezuela—delivered a joint declaration to UN Secretary General Javier Pérez de Cuellar, calling for the creation of an international organization to combat international drug trafficking. The document, called the Declaration of Quito, said that "the drug trade is connected to plans and actions aimed at subverting the juridical order and the social peace in our countries." Colombia, Peru, and Bolivia, the chief sources of cocaine and marijuana reaching the United States, initiated antidrug campaigns with financial and technical assistance from the United States.

At the OAS, Secretary General Baena Soares indicated that the organization would assume a "transcendental mission" in the fight against drug trafficking in the hemisphere. The Inter-American Institute for Agricultural Cooperation (IICA), a specialized agency of the OAS, announced that it would develop a program to introduce alternative crops in the cocaine-growing regions of the Andes.

Church. Early in September, the Vatican's Sacred Congregation for the Doctrine of the Faith released a sharply worded criticism of the Catholic social action movement known as the Theology of Liberation. It said that clerical adherents of liberation theology, some of whom actively support rebel guerrillas in Latin America, err by employing "Marxist analysis."

RICHARD C. SCHROEDER, *"Visión" Magazine*

LAW

In the United States, 1984 marked the first time in 16 years that the judiciary was a major issue in the national elections. With five of the nine Supreme Court justices over age 75, and with an incumbent president seeking judges at all levels who shared his opposition to busing, racial hiring quotas, elaborate protections for criminal defendants, and Supreme Court decisions on such issues as abortion and school prayer, the future course of the judiciary stood to be greatly affected by the outcome of the election. The year 1984 also marked the 30th anniversary of the *Brown v. Topeka Board of Education* decision, which began the process of school desegregation. In lower courts, the year saw some highly publicized criminal, 1st Amendment, and civil-rights cases. And in international law, the World Court and other bodies heard arguments on U.S. military involvement in Nicaragua, the 1983 downing of a Korean Air Lines plane by the Soviet Union, and a variety of other disputes.

United States

Supreme Court. In its review of the Supreme Court's 1983–84 term, the national newspaper of the American Civil Liberties Union (ACLU) characterized the trend of the court's decisions as "statist"; in conflicts between the individual and the government, the majority tended to rule in favor of the state. Unlike the preceding two years, in which the efforts of the Reagan Justice Department were often rebuffed by the high court, the solicitor general's office in 1983–84 won 85% of the cases it advocated for the government. Justice John Paul Stevens, in a speech to the American Bar Association, attacked his colleagues for casting aside judicial restraint in an effort to move the law to the right. Stevens decried the majority's "voracious appetite for judicial activism . . . at least when it comes to restricting the constitutional rights of the citizen." Other observers noted that the court had not squarely reversed any key decision of the Warren Court.

In the area of criminal justice, the Supreme Court ruled, 6–3, that there can be a good-faith exception to the 70-year-old "exclusionary rule"—by which evidence is inadmissible at trial if it is obtained unconstitutionally *(U.S. v. Leon; Massachusetts v. Sheppard)*. In one case the wrong warrant form had been used, while in the other case evidence had been based on outdated information provided by an informant of uncertain reliability. Because neither case involved police acting without a warrant, the finding of a good-faith exception was not expected to affect many other cases.

For the first time, too, the court created an exception to the "Miranda rule"—by which police are required to advise an apprehended suspect of his rights against self-incrimination before questioning begins. In a 5 to 4 decision, the court held that New York prosecutors could introduce as evidence a gun seized by police before they warned the suspect of his rights. According to the ruling, "overriding considerations of public safety" justified immediate questioning before the suspect was warned against self-incrimination *(New York v. Quarles)*.

In another "Miranda" case, the court extended the warning requirement to any case, no matter how minor, in which a suspect is held in custody. However, it did not extend the rule to a driver pulled over for a possible traffic-law violation *(Berkemer v. McCarty)*.

With a dozen executions carried out during the Supreme Court's 1983–84 term (out of more than 1,300 inmates on death row), capital punishment moved off the front pages. In view of the high court's ideological orientation, it came as little surprise when the justices ruled that state appeals courts have no constitutional obligation to review a death sentence to determine whether the punishment is proportionate to that imposed on others for similar crimes *(Pulley v. Harris)*. Only where the statute has no other safeguards against arbitrariness would the court have a "proportionality review."

The most crowded death row in the country was in Florida, which adds about 25 inmates per year. The governor and attorney general, responding to public sentiment, were strong advocates of execution. They blamed the U.S. Court of Appeals for becoming a bottleneck by its willingness to consider challenges to Florida justice. The U.S. Supreme Court, on the other hand, decided that a Florida judge could impose a death sentence even after a jury had already recommended only life imprisonment *(Spaziano v. Florida)*.

The highest court remained true to its course in 1984 cases involving the rights of inmates. It took a hard line regarding the rights of prisoners, concluding that the 4th Amendment does not protect prisoners' personal possessions from unreasonable destruction *(Hudson v. Palmer)* and that inmates awaiting trial have no constitutional right to "contact visits" with friends and family *(Block v. Rutherford)*. The court also permitted juveniles charged with delinquency to be held before trial to prevent them from committing additional crimes *(Schall v. Martin)*.

In the area of minority rights, the nation's disadvantaged received mixed messages from the Supreme Court. In one notable case, the court ruled that federal laws prohibiting sex discrimination by schools and colleges receiving federal funds apply only to specific departments receiving the aid and not to the institution as a whole *(Grove City College v. Bell)*. Justice White could find no evidence of

The videocassette industry was given a boost by a Supreme Court ruling in January 1984. The justices held, 5-4, that taping TV shows off the air is not a violation of federal copyright law (Sony v. Universal City Studios).

congressional intent in Title IX "to follow federally aided students from classroom to classroom," while Justice Brennan maintained that this was precisely what Congress had intended. In an effort to offset the *Grove City* decision, the House of Representatives swiftly passed the Civil Rights Act of 1984, but foes in the Senate and the Reagan administration kept the proposed legislation bottled up in committee.

Women's rights fared better. The Supreme Court agreed that state antidiscrimination laws could be used to force the U.S. Jaycees to admit women as full members. The judges found that Minnesota's "compelling interest in eradicating discrimination against its female citizens" justified requiring a large civic organization such as the Jaycees to admit women *(Roberts v. U.S. Jaycees)*.

The Supreme Court ruled unanimously that female attorneys could sue if they were denied a chance to become partners in law firms because of their gender *(Hishon v. King & Spalding)*. The plaintiff's position was supported by the U.S. Justice Department.

In an important ruling on the legal rights of the handicapped *(Irving School District v. Tatro)*, the court unanimously decided that public school systems must provide certain support services that enable disabled children to attend classes.

In a case balancing worker seniority rights against affirmative action politics *(Memphis Firefighters v. Stotts),* the Supreme Court backed the "last hired, first fired" system. However, the case did not mark an end to affirmative action plans in other contexts. Quotas and goals would still be legal so long as they do not result in the displacement or demotion of white workers. The justices earlier had refused to hear a case involving a Detroit Police Department plan that reserved for blacks half the promotions to the rank of lieutenant. The court had also left intact a ruling by a district court judge requiring the Buffalo, NY, School Board to hire one minority teacher for every white teacher until school faculties reflected the city's 21% minority population.

Aliens did not fare so well before the Burger Court. The justices decided that the exclusionary rule does not apply to civil deportation hearings *(INS v. Lopez-Mendoza)* and that surprise search-and-detain operations by federal agents were permissible in factories and other workplaces suspected of employing illegal aliens *(INS v. Delgado)*.

Several noteworthy rulings on freedom of expression also were handed down. The court upheld a Los Angeles ordinance forbidding the posting of signs, in this case political, on public property because posters create "visual clutter" *(City Council v. Taxpayers for Vincent)*. It also refused to permit homeless people to conduct a symbolic "sleep-in" in Washington, DC, parks because sleeping in the park might damage the grass *(Clark v. Community for Creative Non-Violence)*.

Rejecting a federal broadcast regulation for the first time, the high court struck down a law barring public television stations from airing editorials *(FCC v. League of Women Voters)*. And on the same day that the Senate began debating school prayer, the Supreme Court ruled that a city, in this case Pawtucket, RI, may include a Nativity scene as part of an official Christmas display *(Lynch et al v. Donnelly et al)*.

In the area of property rights, the justices upheld a controversial land-reform program in Hawaii. With 47% of the land belonging to 72 private landowners and trusts, the state legislature in 1967 passed a law that, on the basis of eminent domain, condemned these tracts of land and offered them for sale to sitting tenants. The plan was challenged by one estate as a violation of the 5th Amendment, but in 1984 the U.S. Supreme Court unanimously ruled that, so long as it had a good reason, the state legislature could apply its power of eminent domain *(Hawaii Housing Authority v. Midkiff)*.

In other cases, the court upheld the so-called "bubble policy" for meeting air quality standards *(Chevron USA Inc. v. Natural Resources Defense Council);* according to that standard, a factory can add boilers or smokestacks if they do not increase pollution within the bubble. And in a case of interest to football fans, the court found that the National Collegiate Athletic Association (NCAA) had violated antitrust laws by not allowing individual colleges to negotiate their own football telecasts *(NCAA v. Board of Regents)*.

Finally, in the area of federal powers, the justices sustained a law making college men who do not register for the military draft ineligible for government financial assistance *(Selective Service System v. Minnesota Public Interest Group)* and reinstated the Reagan administration's curb on tourist and business travel to Cuba *(Reagan v. Wald)*.

Local Justice. In 1984 there were a number of lower-court trials that lent themselves to sensationalist publicity.

The most controversial of all was a $120 million libel suit—the biggest ever—by Gen. William C. Westmoreland (ret.) against CBS. Westmoreland claimed that he had been defamed by a CBS Television documentary that accused him of misrepresenting to Washington the size of enemy forces before the Tet offensive in 1968. A decision in the case, held in Federal District Court in New York City, was still pending at year's end.

In New Bedford, MA, 4 of 6 defendants were found guilty of joining in the 1983 rape of

John and Christine De Lorean celebrated his acquittal on federal drug charges. Jurors felt he had been entrapped.

AP/Wide World

a woman in a local tavern. All of the defendants were Portuguese immigrants, and local Portuguese groups claimed that they had not been treated fairly. Women's groups protested the defense's efforts to discredit the rape victim and maintained that future victims would be discouraged from seeking justice. The trial itself was covered live on cable television.

In April the Rhode Island Supreme Court overturned the 1982 conviction of socialite Claus von Bülow for the attempted murder of his heiress wife. A key piece of evidence, von Bülow's shaving kit containing a used hypodermic needle with traces of insulin on it, had been turned over to authorities by von Bülow's estranged stepson. The court said that there should have been a warrant before the syringe was tested. In addition the trial judge had improperly suppressed some evidence that might have helped von Bülow's case.

In a Los Angeles federal court, the highly publicized 22-week trial of former automobile manufacturer John De Lorean ended in August with an acquittal on all eight charges stemming from an alleged sale of cocaine. De Lorean's lawyers contended that he had been framed by FBI agents who wanted to enhance their careers.

As in a similar case in 1980, a Miami police officer in March 1984 was acquitted by an all-white jury of killing a black man. The officer claimed self-defense. As in the previous instance, the verdict was followed by street violence, looting, and arrests.

Another controversial civil-rights case, this one in North Carolina, also was decided by an all-white jury, even though 25% of the district's voters were black. Six members of the Ku Klux Klan and three members of the American Nazi Party faced federal charges of violating the civil rights of pro-Communist demonstrators at an anti-Klan rally in Greensboro, NC, in November 1979. Though five demonstrators were killed and news videotapes seemed to show several of the defendants firing at them, the verdict was not guilty.

Other highly publicized criminal trials were of self-styled revolutionaries Kathy Boudin and Samuel Brown for a fatal 1981 Brink's armored-car holdup in New York (both guilty) and of a Texas nurse for murdering a baby in the clinic where she worked (also guilty).

In cases involving freedom of the press, an unusual coalition of radical feminists and conservative women politicians in Minneapolis and Indianapolis sought to enact local ordinances making purveyors of pornography subject to legal action for violating the civil rights of women. They were opposed by civil libertarians and publishing trade associations. The Minneapolis legislation was vetoed by Mayor Donald Fraser, while the Indianapolis statute was challenged in federal court on 1st Amendment grounds.

The highest court in New York ruled that freedom of speech allowed a news reporter to remain silent even if a grand jury wanted him to disclose a confidential source. The decision was the court's first ruling on New York's "shield law." In a related decision, the New York Court of Appeals ruled that a newspaper did not have to identify the author of an anonymous letter. The letter had led to a libel suit against the paper.

Antiabortion activists, including the Reagan administration, went to court to compel doctors to ignore the wishes of the parents of New York's "Baby Jane Doe" and perform surgery to correct some of her birth defects. The courts rejected the intervention but also rejected efforts by the parents to get the losers to pay their court costs. An uneasy alliance of advocates of the rights of the disabled and the rights of the "unborn" worked to get the federal Executive Branch and Congress to institute rules to guide hospitals in Baby Doe cases.

A U.S. District Court judge ruled that the Chicago Transit Authority (CTA) must accept advertising by Planned Parenthood that mentions abortion. He said the CTA's policy of rejecting controversial public messages was applied in an "invidiously discriminatory manner."

In New York City an executive order requiring private groups doing business with the city to affirm that they would not discriminate in employment or hiring because of "race, creed, color, national origin, sex, age, handicap, marital status, sexual orientation or affectional preference" was challenged in court by the New York Catholic Archdiocese. It charged that the executive order violated the principle of separation of church and state by forcing the church to employ active homosexuals.

International Law

On May 10, the International Court of Justice in The Hague, responding to a complaint brought by Nicaragua, ordered the United States to stop supporting military actions against the Nicaraguan government. The court was unanimous in ordering an immediate stop to CIA-directed mining of Nicaraguan harbors. The United States announced that it would not accept World Court jurisdiction over U.S. activities in Central America for the next two years. It was the first time the United States had tested the jurisdiction of the World Court. The United States also claimed that its actions against Nicaragua were based on the "collective self-defense against an armed attack" provision of Article 51 of the UN Charter. Inasmuch as the U.S. mining had actually ended several months earlier, the World Court's opinion afforded Nicaragua only what it termed "a moral victory."

Another instance of international lawlessness was the September 1983 downing of Korean Air Lines Flight 007 from Soviet airspace. A team of experts from the International Civil Aviation Organization (ICAO) determined in 1984 that the Korean airliner probably had gone off course because of an incorrect navigational setting. A special assembly of the ICAO endorsed an addition to the convention on international aviation that would bar the use of weapons against civil aircraft.

The East German government in 1984 defended its border guards' shooting at people trying to flee the country. It told the UN Human Rights Commission that shooting at escaping citizens was not a violation of international agreements and was necessary to counteract Western subversion.

Unlike the Helsinki Accord and the 1948 Universal Declaration of Human Rights, the UN Covenant of Civil and Political Rights (ratified by about 80 countries, not including the United States), is binding international law. The UN Human Rights Commission is the vehicle for seeing that the agreement is implemented in domestic legislation and practice.

An Italian magistrate investigating the May 1981 assassination attempt against Pope John Paul II alleged that international law had been violated when Bulgaria had used a diplomatically protected van to smuggle accomplices out of Italy. In 1984, West Germany contended that the USSR also was misusing such diplomatically protected vehicles. And in July, British authorities thwarted an effort by the Nigerian military government to fly home a kidnapped opposition leader inside a crate.

Another case before the International Court of Justice was a dispute between the United States and Canada over where the boundary between the two countries should be drawn through the Gulf of Maine. The disputed region, the Georges Bank, is a rich fishing ground with potentially enormous resources of minerals and petroleum. The United States had wanted jurisdiction over the entire area, while Canada claimed half. The World Court drew a boundary line that gave the United States about two thirds and Canada one third.

Another maritime controversy also was resolved in 1984. The European Council of Ministers reached agreement on national quotas for fish caught in the North Sea.

Another agreement, by the International Maritime Organization's London Dumping Convention, extended a ban on the disposal of low-level radioactive material through September 1985, when a report on the safety of such dumping was scheduled to be completed. However, efforts by ecologists to block a proposal to begin research into dumping highly radioactive waste on the ocean floor failed.

MARTIN GRUBERG
University of Wisconsin, Oshkosh

The Jury System

Since the early days of U.S. independence, the right to trial by jury has been guaranteed by Article III, Section 2, and the 6th and 7th Amendments of the Constitution. Today, though legal experts and sociologists generally agree on the fairness and efficiency of jury decision making, the system continues to undergo review, debate, and adaptation. In 1984 reform proposals concerning the selection and functioning of juries were being considered by court systems, legislative bodies, and independent research and advocate groups across the United States. These proposals were of interest not only to legal experts but also to the many citizens who have been called for jury service.

Selection. The traditional number of jurors in a criminal or civil case is 12, though some jurisdictions use fewer for certain kinds of proceedings. No aspect of the U.S. jury system has undergone more change or been the subject of more debate than the methods used to select that panel of 12.

The process begins with a list of potential jurors. While in times past only community leaders were called for jury duty, today names are drawn from voting rosters, tax rolls, and even telephone books. In many places the lists are computerized. Despite progress in this area, the right to a jury of one's peers has been widely understood as requiring a more diversified pool of potential jurors, one that is more representative of the community as a whole. Specific suggestions include the supplementary use of census and social service lists.

The same criticism has been made, and perhaps with greater poignancy, of the procedure by which lawyers question the competency of potential jurors and then accept or reject those individuals for the panel—the process of "voir dire." Defense attorneys and prosecutors alike tend to exlude persons whose social, religious, ethnic, or educational background might not suit their case strategy. In fact, there are firms that specialize in "jury research," using scientific criteria to help lawyers select jurors with the most desirable backgrounds.

The criticisms of this trend are manifold. The privacy of potential jurors is said to be compromised, costly jury research is said to favor the rich over the poor, and the whole approach is said to manipulate the judicial system unconstitutionally. To remedy these problems, several special commissions have recommended that judges—not trial lawyers— conduct the jury-selection process. In 1983 the American Bar Association approved a set of recommended guidelines to make juries more representative of the community. As for the problem of juror privacy, however, the U.S. Supreme Court ruled in January 1984 that trial judges must allow the public and the press to attend jury selection proceedings in most cases *(Press-Enterprise Co. v. Superior Court)*.

Service and Decision Making. Jury duty comes as bad news to many citizens. In addition to time away from work and possible financial sacrifice, the juror may face tedious waiting in unpleasant facilities, a trial that drags on for weeks or months, and the task of trying to decipher complex and highly technical legal principles.

One method for alleviating the waiting problem, in use for about 12 years, is called the "one-day/one-trial" system. Candidates not selected to sit on a jury are excused after one day; those who are selected are required to serve for only one trial. Modified versions may require potential jurors to be available for one or two weeks, regardless of whether they are actually chosen. As for the problem of coping with complex issues, experiments have been made in simplifying the judge's instructions to the jury and making them uniform on specific points. Some groups have even proposed that complex decisions—as in antitrust cases—be left entirely to judges.

More fundamentally, juries have been attacked for their lack of understanding of the basic rules of law and evidence, their inability to follow expert testimony, and their lack of motivation and effectiveness in maintaining their independence. On the whole, however, empirical evidence gained from some 30 years of study does not support such allegations. One study showed judges agreeing with jury verdicts in 80% of criminal cases and 79% of civil actions. Other studies concluded that juries give real weight to judges' instructions, that judges and juries have similar understandings of such key legal concepts as "beyond a reasonable doubt," and that juries are not easily swayed by the strong opinion of any one member.

Conclusion. Debates over the proper role and function of juries are as old as the institution itself. Though problems persist, U.S. juries still resolve many more legal disputes than in any other country in the world. Moreover, the system of direct public adjudication—despite its inherent need for adaptation—has been shown to produce decisions that are generally just and proper.

RITA J. SIMON

Lebanon's warring factions came together in March for reconciliation talks in Lausanne, Switzerland—without effect.

LEBANON

Persistent foreign occupation, lack of sovereignty by the central government—bordering on chaos—and a complicated maze of internal political and sectarian strife contributed to the ongoing violence which characterized life in Lebanon in 1984. The year began with Israel still occupying the south, Syria occupying the north, and the Multinational Force (MNF)—consisting of the United States, France, Great Britain, and Italy—patrolling in the Beirut area in an effort to prop up the Gemayel government. Significant changes occurred which fundamentally altered the politics of the country, though by year's end it was unclear whether these changes had brought Lebanon any closer to resolving its profound problems.

Renewed Crisis. Muslim, particularly Shiite, discontent with President Amin Gemayel (a Maronite Christian), growing since the early months of his rule in 1982, reached its height in early February. At that time the commander of the French MNF units decided to withdraw from along one section of the Green Line which divided Christian East and Muslim West Beirut. Clashes erupted between the Lebanese Armed Forces (LAF) and the Shiite Muslim militia (Amal). Lebanon's volatile political and religious schisms and imbalances were clearly reflected in the 37,000-man LAF. Although it was 60% Muslim, a significant percentage of which were Shiite Muslims (the Shiite population numbers about 1 million out of 3 million Lebanese), 60% of the senior officers and com-

manders were Christian. Amal leader Nabih Berri called on Muslim LAF officers not to fight fellow Muslims. On February 6, Shiite and Druze militia forces took control of much of West Beirut, and by February 7 it was clear that the LAF had divided along sectarian, i.e., Christian-Muslim, lines. In response, U.S. President Ronald Reagan that day announced plans for a "phased redeployment" of the 1,400 U.S. Marines from the Beirut airport to ships offshore, while the U.S. battleship *New Jersey* and other Navy ships bombarded Druze and Syrian batteries that were shelling Christian-held East Beirut. The British, French, and Italian MNF contingents also began withdrawing from Beirut.

During this crisis, failed attempts by the United States and Saudi Arabia to resolve sectarian differences led to the resignation of Sunni Muslim Prime Minister Chafiq al-Wazan on February 5, effectively dissolving the cabinet. Immediately following the resignation of Wazan and the cabinet, Gemayel issued an eight-point proposal for the creation of a new government and the resumption of the Geneva reconciliation talks. The Lebanese opposition, armed and supported by Syria, and Syria itself called for a new government and demanded the abrogation of the Israeli-Lebanese agreement of May 17, 1983. Under that agreement, Israel would withdraw its troops from Lebanon but would continue to police the southern region. With Gemayel's position weakened by the MNF withdrawal and the disintegration of his army, the president in late February turned to

Syria to prevent the total collapse of his government. Syria's price for helping Gemayel was the abrogation of the May 17 agreement.

National Reconciliation Conference. On March 2, following meetings in Damascus, Syrian allies Nabih Berri and Druze leader Walid Jumblat dropped their demand for Gemayel's resignation, and on March 5 Wazan's caretaker government formally abrogated the May 17 agreement. This cleared the way for a "national reconciliation" conference, which opened March 12 in Lausanne, Switzerland, under Saudi and Syrian auspices. The conference was attended by President Gemayel and Syrian-backed opposition leaders Jumblat, Berri, former Prime Minister Rashid Karami (a Sunni), and former President Suleiman Franjieh (a Christian). Also present were Muslim independents Adel Osseiran (a Shiite), former speaker of parliament, and former Prime Minister Saeb Salam (a Sunni), as well as Christian Party leaders Pierre Gemayel (Amin's father) and former President Camille Chamoun.

The conference ended after nine days with the Muslim, Druze, and Christian leaders able to agree only that the cease-fire in Beirut should be consolidated. The final statement made no mention of any political reforms demanded by the opposition. The main cleavage was clearly between those supporting a strong Maronite presidency and a Lebanon based on the 1943 confessional system favoring the Christians, and those favoring a political structure giving recognition to the present Muslim majority by increasing the powers of a new Muslim-dominated parliament and premier.

The cease-fire, however, had been broken even before the conference ended. By late March not only were there clashes between Christian-backed forces and Shiite Muslim and Druze forces but between Druze and Sunni Muslim forces as well. Nonetheless, by early July the Lebanese army was able to complete its takeover of the capital from militia forces, though intermittent fighting continued.

New Cabinet. President Gemayel, left to rely only on Syria and its Lebanese allies for his administration's survival, on April 26 named the pro-Syrian former Prime Minister Rashid Karami to form a national unity government. On April 30, Karami named a ten-member cabinet that included Berri, Jumblat, Pierre Gemayel, Chamoun, and Osseiran. The cabinet was balanced politically, geographically, and religiously—2 Sunnis, 2 Maronites, 2 Shiites, 2 Greek Orthodox, 1 Druze, and 1 Greek Catholic. (The death of Maronite Christian patriarch Pierre Gemayel on August 29 added to the burden of President Amin Gemayel.)

The cabinet, confirmed by the Lebanese parliament, approved a sweeping reorganization of the still-divided LAF. The plan, worked out with the help of Syria, now the chief political broker in Lebanon, specified that military decisions, formerly handled solely by the Maronite Christian commander, now would be managed collectively by a military council representing the different religious groups. In October, in another indication of Lebanon's reorientation toward Syria, the parliament ousted its speaker of 12 years, Kamal Assad, who had presided over the parliament that had approved the May 17, 1983, agreement with Israel. Assad's elected replacement, Hussein Husseini, from the Syrian-controlled city of Baalbak, immediately pledged to make the "liberation of south Lebanon from Israeli occupation" the goal of his one-year tenure.

Israeli Occupation. With the fundamental reorientation of Lebanese policy toward Syria and away from the West, Israel's hopes for a stable and friendly new order in Lebanon were

The U.S. Embassy annex outside Beirut was struck by a suicide car bombing September 20, killing two dozen. It was the third major bombing of a U.S. facility in 17 months.

F. Reglain, Gamma-Liaison

LEBANON · Information Highlights

Official Name: Republic of Lebanon.
Location: Southwest Asia.
Area: 4,000 sq mi (10 360 km²).
Population (mid-1984 est.): 2,600,000.
Government: *Head of state,* Amin Gemayel, president (took office Sept. 1982). *Head of government,* Rashid Karami, prime minister (took office May 1984). *Legislature* (unicameral)—National Assembly.
Monetary Unit: Lebanese pound (6.70 pounds equal U.S. $1, August 1984.)
Gross National Product (1981 U.S.$): $4,190,-000,000.

shattered. With the abrogation by Lebanon of the May 17 agreement and the closing of Israel's liaison office near Beirut in July, Israel's goals were reduced to ensuring the security of its northern border. Israel's occupation of southern Lebanon, at first welcomed by the southern Shiites to rid the area of Palestinians, faced growing opposition because the Lebanese under Israeli occupation felt increasingly isolated from the rest of Lebanon. This contributed to stepped-up attacks on Israeli soldiers, which by midyear were occurring almost daily. To combat these attacks, Israel poured in money, material, and training to build a Lebanese force that would fill the vacuum left by the gradual thinning out of Israel's forces in the south. The South Lebanon Army (SLA) emerged out of the remnants of the Israeli-supported militia commanded by Lebanese Army Major Saad Haddad. Gen. Antoine Lahad, who took over following Haddad's death in January, estimated that it would take up to two years to recruit and train a force strong enough to police southern Lebanon. The clear implication was that Israeli troops could spend another two years in Lebanon.

Israeli-Lebanese Negotiations. After the Marine withdrawal in February, the United States did not play a noticeable role in Lebanon until September. With the help of U.S. Assistant Secretary of State Richard Murphy and UN sponsorship, negotiations between Lebanon and Israel on security arrangements for the withdrawal of Israeli forces from southern Lebanon opened in the Lebanese border town of Naqura on November 8. Lebanon's initial position included demands for a total withdrawal of Israeli troops, Lebanese Army occupation of the south, disbanding of the SLA, and $8–$10 billion in war reparations. Israel dropped its demand for a simultaneous Syrian troop withdrawal from Lebanon but asked for continuing limited access to southern Lebanon and for the SLA to assume the primary security role along the frontier. The differences between the two sides notwithstanding, the inauguration of the talks and their continuation showed clearly that both sides saw it in their mutual interests to reach some agreement.

As the negotiations continued into December, differences focused primarily on two issues: the first concerned who would assume responsibility for security in the south—the SLA, the Lebanese Army, or the UN Interim Forces in Lebanon (UNIFIL); and the second, whether the Israelis would continue to cross the border and enjoy a cooperative relationship with whichever force existed there.

The Lebanese government insisted that the UN forces be deployed within a 15-mi (24-km)-wide strip between the Litani River and the Israeli border. The Israelis wanted the UN forces deployed farther north, in the area between the Zahrani and Awali rivers, with a pro-Israeli Lebanese force (the SLA) patrolling the southern strip. Despite the desire on all sides for a settlement, the only agreement reached by year's end was one to suspend negotiations for the holiday season.

For the Israelis, security on their northern border was the *sine qua non* for agreement on a withdrawal from their occupation of southern Lebanon. For the Lebanese, any agreement at Naqura would have to be acceptable to the Syrians or it would suffer the same fate as the May 17 agreement. In addition, any formula emerging from the Naqura process was likely to have a direct effect on the future shape of Lebanon as a whole, not merely its southern region. Even if an agreement on the withdrawal of Israeli troops were reached, Lebanon would be left to face the deep-rooted religious and political problems that challenged the concept of "nation" in this war-weary country.

Economy. The physical destruction caused by Israel's invasion, the continued Syrian occupation of northern and eastern Lebanon, and the failure of the government to fully implement its security plan for Beirut lost Lebanon much of its economic credibility. The business community, long a symbol of the resilience of Lebanon's war-torn economy, lost confidence in the central government's ability to solve the country's problems. Throughout 1984 the Lebanese pound declined significantly against the U.S. dollar. During 1983–84 there was a net capital outflow of between $2.5 billion and $3 billion, and the balance of payments continued to deteriorate. Unemployment increased to more than 30%. Lebanon received only a fraction of the aid promised by the Arabs at the 1979 Tunis summit, and remittances from Lebanese abroad fell markedly because of declining revenues in oil-rich Arab states. The United States budgeted $140 million in aid to Lebanon, but because of the unstable situation only $27 million was sent. And because of the central government's lack of control, an estimated $300 million in unpaid taxes and charges was owed to the state. All of this compounded Lebanon's grave difficulties.

STEVEN M. RISKIN
Middle East Specialist, Washington, DC

LIBRARIES

There was continuing controversy involving policy, proposed by the Office of Management and Budget (OMB), governing federal information management. As a fundamental principle, the OMB declared that "information is not a free good, but a resource of substantial economic value and should be treated as such." This assertion drew praise from the Information Industry Association and condemnation from the American Library Association (ALA).

Librarians welcomed deferment of a Reagan administration plan to impose prepublication review of the public statements of present and former federal employees having, or having had, access to classified information. The directive, which would have affected more than 100,000 persons and apply to lectures as well as books and articles, was thought by some to be unconstitutional.

An April 13, 1984, decision by the Texas Board of Education constituted victory for intellectual freedom. The board repealed a decade-old rule restricting references to evolution in public-school textbooks in Texas. Because of Texas' massive purchase of textbooks, that state's antievolution rule had diluted the coverage of evolution in high school biology texts.

Qualifications. On Dec. 29, 1983, U.S. Magistrate Charles M. Powers reversed the decision of a lower court by holding that a master's degree from a program accredited by the ALA "is a standard widely recognized by academic and professional employers, including the U.S. Supreme Court." The lower court had determined, in *Merwine v. Mississippi State University,* that Glenda Merwine, who holds a master's degree in education, had been a victim of discrimination by virtue of her sex when a man, with a master's degree in librarianship from a program accredited by the ALA, won out over her in the contest for the position of head librarian at the university school of veterinary medicine. Powers, in reversing a $10,000 award for damages against George Lewis, the director of the university library, affirmed that discrimination on the basis of sex had not been involved in the employment decision. Despite Merwine's specialty in library science within the master's degree in education, excellent academic record, biomedical training and experience, and good performance in the MSU library, she did not meet the established minimum educational requirements for the position. The plaintiff in *Merwine* appealed the decision.

After urging during much of 1983 that only librarians who have completed two-year master's degree programs be permitted to enter the federal service at the GS-9 level, the Office of Personnel Management decided in the spring that persons with experience in librarianship and master's degrees encompassing at least 38 semester credits could be admitted to GS-9 library positions. This decision could influence the practice of other employers.

American Library Association (ALA). How should the ALA be reorganized? That was the familiar question heard at the association's midwinter meeting in Washington and at its 103rd annual conference in Dallas in June. Complaints about the organization of the association by the American Association of School Librarians (AASL), the Association of College and Research Libraries (ACRL), the American Library Trustee Association (ALTA), the Public Library Association (PLA), and the ALA round tables could prompt a restructuring. The Future Structure Report of the AASL recommended in April 1984 that the school librarians consider secession from the ALA and perhaps the creation of an entirely new, independent organization. At about the same time, the Executive Committee of the ACRL proposed that the ALA become a federation of relatively autonomous associations and divisions rather than remain a set of organizations with limited independence. In the meantime, the ALA's constituent units continued to hold and plan for separate national conferences. E. J. Josey, chief of the Bureau of Specialist Library Services at the New York State Library, is to preside over the ALA in 1984–85.

International Activities. Librarians regretted the pending U.S. withdrawal from the United Nations Educational, Scientific, and Cultural Organization (UNESCO). Kenneth R. Cooper, director general of the National Federation of Building Trades Employers, England, replaced the retired Sir Harry Hookway as chief executive officer of the British Library in the late summer. The 50th council meeting of the International Federation of Library Associations and Institutions convened in Nairobi, Kenya, Aug. 19–25, 1984, while Toronto was the site of the annual conference of the Canadian Library Association.

DAN BERGEN, *University of Rhode Island*

LIBRARY AWARDS OF 1984

Beta Phi Mu Award for distinguished service to education for librarianship: Jane Anne Hannigan, School of Library Service, Columbia University

Randolph J. Caldecott Medal for the most distinguished picture book for children: Alice and Martin Provensen, *The Glorious Flight: Across the Channel With Louis Bleriot*

Melvil Dewey Award for creative professional achievement of a high order: Warren J. Haas, president, Council on Library Resources

Grolier Foundation Award for unusual contribution to the stimulation and guidance of reading by children and young people: Carolyn Sue Peterson, head, Children's Department, Orlando (FL) Public Library

Joseph W. Lippincott Award for distinguished service to the profession of librarianship: Nettie Barcrott Taylor, assistant state librarian, state of Maryland

John Newbery Medal for the most distinguished contribution to literature for children: Beverly Cleary, *Dear Mr. Henshaw*

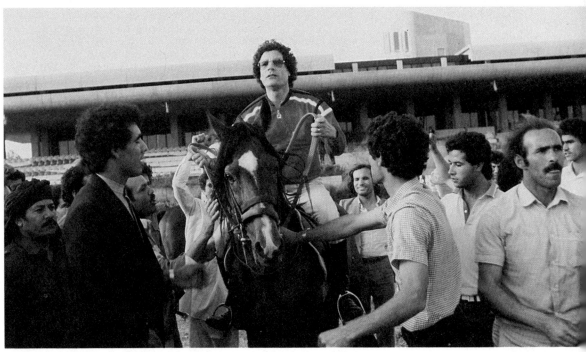

Following rebel attacks against the Tripoli headquarters of Muammar el-Qaddafi, the Libyan strongman appeared on television riding horseback and waving a fist. He accused Muslim Brotherhood extremists of carrying out the plot.

LIBYA

Domestic opposition to the government of Col. Muammar el-Qaddafi increased during 1984, triggering harsh responses both within Libya and abroad. Several European states blamed the Libyan regime for attacks on anti-Qaddafi groups and individuals on their soil, and one such attack involved Libya in a serious diplomatic rift with Great Britain. Some of Libya's African and Arab neighbors continued to accuse Colonel Qaddafi of meddling in their internal affairs, but late in the year Libya began to withdraw its military forces from Chad, where they had been engaged since 1982. In an effort to break out of the isolation in which his policies had placed his country, Qaddafi agreed to a "union of states" linking Libya with Morocco.

Domestic Affairs. Political alienation inside Libya involved primarily the middle class, which had been hurt by a decline in oil revenues that was not matched by curbs on high government expenditures, especially for military equipment. Other disgruntled groups included students, the army, and professional diplomats. Qaddafi had accused the army of corruption and had said he would phase it out in favor of a popular militia. Libyan embassies had been replaced by "People's Bureaus," and the functions of Libya's professional diplomats had been taken over by enthusiasts of the revolution who often lacked familiarity with the intricacies of diplomacy and international politics.

A wave of sabotage and arson spread through Libyan urban centers during 1984. Several organizations—including the National Front for the Salvation of Libya, a secular body composed largely of former government officials, and the Libyan Constitutional Union, which sought the restoration of the monarchy—were operating more overtly than other dissident groups. A coup attempt in May precipitated a five-hour gun battle in Tripoli between the police and insurgents. The attack came soon after the execution of a number of dissidents, and the National Front for the Salvation of Libya acknowledged responsibility for the assault. Three men accused of complicity in the abortive coup were hanged in June.

Foreign Relations. Even prior to the coup attempt, Colonel Qaddafi had pursued an energetic campaign against Libyan dissidents living abroad. In March several bombs exploded in England in places frequented by anti-Qaddafi exiles. In April, exiles demonstrating outside the Libyan embassy in London were fired on from the building. Several demonstrators were wounded and a policewoman killed. Relations between Great Britain and Libya were strained further when the Libyan diplomats refused to vacate the embassy or undergo questioning by British authorities, claiming diplomatic immunity. Britain broke relations with Libya and ordered the occupants of the embassy out of the country. But it agreed to honor international conventions that prevented its authorities from searching Libyan diplomatic pouches, which, they suspected, contained clues relevant to the shootings. Libya simultaneously expelled British diplomats. No reprisals were taken against the more than 8,000 Britons resident in Libya, although a few British subjects were arrested and detained for several months without having formal charges preferred against them.

Another dramatic incident occurred in November, when Egyptian authorities foiled a plot to assassinate a prominent Libyan exile in Cairo and tricked the Qaddafi government into announcing his "execution."

These were only two of the year's international confrontations involving Libya. Jordan severed relations in February when a mob attacked and burned its embassy in Tripoli after King Hussein had met in Washington with President Ronald Reagan and Egyptian President Hosni Mubarak.

Among Libya's closer neighbors, Sudan accused Colonel Qaddafi of responsibility for an air raid in March on Omdurman (across the Nile from Khartoum, the Sudanese capital) as part of a campaign to unseat the pro-Western government of President Jaafar al-Nemery. Agreeing that the aircraft had come from Libya, the United States temporarily assigned AWACS surveillance planes to Egypt, Sudan's ally, to thwart any new forays.

In late summer, after mines had damaged several merchant vessels in the Red Sea, Egypt suggested that a Libyan freighter had planted the mines, but the allegation was never proven. Nevertheless, this incident—along with accusations of Libyan interference in the domestic affairs of Mauritius, Mauritania, and other countries—indicated the tendency of the international community to regard the Libyan regime with suspicion and increasingly to isolate it.

Libyan officials sought a policy that would enable them to end this isolation. The desirability of such a policy increased as Egypt, long a political rival of Libya, proceeded with its reintegration into the Arab world after a period of ostracism caused by its peace treaty with Israel in 1979. Another concern was the continued adherence of Tunisia, Algeria, and Mauritania to their treaty of North African friendship and cooperation signed in 1983. As a counterweight, Libya entered into a "union of states" linking it with Morocco. Called the Arab-African Federation, the arrangement was the culmination of a rapprochement between Qaddafi and King Hassan, who until their meeting in Rabat in 1983 had disagreed bitterly over the future of Moroccan-occupied Western Sahara. The Treaty of Oudjda, which formally created the union, was signed in August 1984. It did not

envision a complete merger of the two nations but called instead for joint deliberative councils on political, economic, and cultural matters and a commitment to mutual defense.

While some observers speculated that this attempt at unity would end as unsuccessfully as similar ventures undertaken earlier by Colonel Qaddafi, the pact seemed carefully thought out and more realistic than previous ones and was, in fact, initiated by King Hassan, not by the Libyan leader. The move came as a surprise, particularly in that Morocco's constitutional monarchy held strong pro-Western and pro-American views, which seemed wholly antithetical to Libya's revolutionary attitudes. Nevertheless, both Colonel Qaddafi and King Hussein profited from the accord. Through Hassan, Qaddafi gained entrée into Arab circles in which he had recently been shunned, but at the same time Hassan was guaranteed Libya's abstention from interference in Western Sahara.

Conjectures that Hassan's more moderate policies might serve as a brake on Qaddafi seemed to be borne out in the fall when the Moroccan monarch acted as an intermediary helping Libya and France move toward agreement to remove their military forces from Chad. The two countries, which had backed opposing factions in the civil war in Chad, began a reciprocal withdrawal in September. When completed, this would free Libya of the continued costly maintenance of its 3,000 regular troops and an irregular "Islamic Legion" in northern Chad. Since French troops were also leaving, there was no loss of face, and Libya could claim that its objectives in Chad had been achieved. Qaddafi spokesmen stressed, however, that Libyan soldiers would remain in the mineral-rich Aouzou frontier strip, over which Libya had long claimed sovereignty.

See also CHAD; EGYPT; GREAT BRITAIN; MIDDLE EAST; MOROCCO.

KENNETH J. PERKINS
Department of History
University of South Carolina

LIBYA · Information Highlights

Official Name: Socialist People's Libyan Arab Jamahiriya ("state of the masses").
Location: North Africa.
Area: 679,000 sq mi (1 758 610 km²).
Population (mid-1984 est.): 3,700,000.
Chief Cities (1980 est.): Tripoli, the capital, 1,223,000; Benghazi, 530,000.
Government: *Head of state,* Muammar el-Qaddafi, secretary-general of the General People's Congress (took office 1969). *Legislature*—General People's Congress (met initially Nov. 1976).
Monetary Unit: Dinar (0.296 dinar equals U.S. $1, Aug. 1984).
Gross Domestic Product Per Capita (1983 est., U.S.$): $7,600.
Foreign Trade (1983 U.S.$): *Imports,* $9,000,000,000; *exports,* $12,000,000,000.

LITERATURE

Among the hottest-selling books of the year —and certainly *the* most discussed—was one that had first appeared 35 years before. George Orwell's novel about a totalitarian society of the future, *1984,* had come of age. During the first weeks of the year, copies of the books were selling at the rate of about 50,000 per day and the title hit the top of paperback best-seller lists. Meanwhile, in a deluge of articles, social and literary commentators discussed the extent to which Orwell's vision had become reality in today's world. A popular conclusion was that the author of *1984* had intended no prophecy, only a warning. Coincidentally, Orwell's reputation was further enhanced by the discovery in June of a cache of his writings from World War II. The find included some 250 letters, 62 radio commentaries on the war, and radio adaptations of stories by H. G. Wells, Anatole France, and others. Orwell, whose real name was Eric Blair, died of tuberculosis in 1950 at the age of 47.

Another major 20th-century English-language novel, James Joyce's *Ulysses,* was in the news in 1984. On June 16 ("Bloomsday"), after seven years of work, a team of scholars produced a new edition of the book that corrects several thousand errors—omissions, transpositions, and others—in previous editions. The reason for the mistakes was that Joyce had written the original manuscript in longhand.

Three giants of American letters—Emily Dickinson, Walt Whitman, and Washington

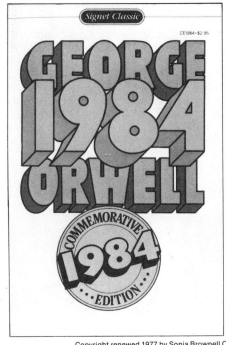

Copyright renewed 1977 by Sonia Brownell Orwell
Commemorative Edition *1984* published by The New American Library, Inc.

Irving—were the first writers to be memorialized in the new American Poets' Corner at New York City's Cathedral of St. John the Divine. The corner, which will enshrine two writers (not only poets) each year, is modeled after the English Poets' Corner in Westminster Abbey.

Among contemporary figures, 83-year-old Czech poet Jaroslav Seifert was awarded the 1984 Nobel Prize for Literature. The first Czech to be so honored, Seifert was cited for work that, according to the Swedish Academy announcement, "endowed with freshness, sensuality and rich inventiveness, provides a liberating image of the indomitable spirit and versatility of man." Born in Prague into a working-class family in 1901, Seifert supported himself as a journalist until 1950, though he had come into prominence as a poet in the 1920s. He has published nearly 30 volumes of poetry, but little of his work has been translated. Thus, while he is considered Czechoslovakia's national poet, he has not had great international recognition. In what has been described as a lyrical and at times colloquial voice, Seifert has written frequently on the subjects of love and the city of Prague. The poet was in the hospital when he learned of the award, suffering from a heart ailment and what his wife, Marie, described as overtiredness.

In England, 54-year-old Ted Hughes was named the new poet laureate, succeeding Sir John Betjeman, who died on May 19. Much of Hughes' poetry is about animals and birds. Perhaps his best-known collection is *The Hawk in the Rain* (1957).

Jaroslav Seifert, Czech poet
1984 Nobel Laureate in Literature

AP/Wide World

American Literature

The role of the university in the creation of American literature has become progressively more important. University writing programs are the biggest employers of novelists, short story writers, and poets, providing them with a relatively stable income. Although whether writing can be "taught" remains controversial, the programs have been an important source of young talent. Associated Writing Programs, a national organization that has grown to include about 100 universities, publishes a magazine, *Intro,* and a useful newsletter and awards its own series of literary prizes. The writing produced from these programs has been vital, accomplished, and diverse.

This current interest in the craft of writing was suggested in 1984 by the success of Eudora Welty's charming memoir, *One Writer's Beginnings,* and John Gardner's posthumous work, *The Art of Fiction: Notes on Craft for Young Writers,* both of which have useful advice for those who aspire to write fiction themselves.

Novels. From Trudy Gertler's sharply observed first novel about New York's publishing industry, *Elbowing the Seducer,* to octogenarian Helen Hooven Santmyer's compendious chronicle of generations of Midwestern lives, *. . . And Ladies of the Club* (originally published in 1982), it is clear that women novelists increasingly are important to American literature.

One of the most intriguing novels of the year was Joan Didion's *Democracy.* Didion puts herself in the novel as a character observing the manners of a curiously rootless set whose business always involves countries in crisis but whose only loyalty is to images and surfaces. Doris Grumbach's *The Ladies* comments obliquely on contemporary life through her depiction of two actual 18th-century women who defied the sexual and social codes of their own day. Alison Lurie demonstrates her wit in her masterful international novel, *Foreign Affairs.*

Jayne Anne Phillips' *Machine Dreams,* told from several points of view about a family torn by the strains of divorce and the Vietnam War, and Bette Pesetsky's *Digs* are remarkable first novels by writers formerly known only for their short stories. Jill McCorkle also made an impressive debut with the simultaneous publication of both her first and second novels: *The Cheer Leader* and *July 7th,* which successfully dramatized the complex network of relationships in a small southern town.

Other striking first novels were also by Southerners. Padgett Powell's *Edisto* is not only the story of a 12-year-old boy learning about life, but also a rich celebration of a language and a culture. Frederick Barthelme's *Second Marriage* brilliantly captures the flatness and sterility of the new South.

Among major figures who produced important work was Joseph Heller, whose audacious *God Knows* is a racy, poignant account of life in biblical times told from the point of view of King David. In *The Witches of Eastwick,* John Updike imagines a contemporary New England community in which several women really have supernatural powers, which they wickedly use for amusement and revenge. Norman Mailer tried his hand at a murder mystery with *Tough Guys Don't Dance.* Neither the Updike nor Mailer book represented the authors' best work, but both have a developed sense of place and make provocative social observations.

Short Stories. The rebirth of interest in the short story was striking. For the first time in its history *Esquire* magazine devoted an entire issue to fiction. Annual collections such as *Best American Short Stories* and *The O'Henry Awards,* usually thought of as only having a library market, sold well in paperback.

Saul Bellow's *Him With His Foot in His Mouth and Other Stories* has characters as cantankerous as they are articulate. The title story suggests Bellow's tragicomic view of life.

E. L. Doctorow's challenging *Lives of the Poets* contains six stories of varying style; the most touching is about a young boy forced by his family to write letters in the name of his recently dead father. Doctorow's collection is not fully understood without reading the title novella, a writer's monologue about his life, career, and the possibilities and limitations of fiction itself.

Thomas Pynchon's *Slow Learner* collects his first works. The stories make clear how Pynchon, early on, was haunted by the themes that pervade his novels and are prefaced by the author's critique of the stories' inadequacies.

John Hawkes' *Humors of Blood & Skin* contains both short stories and sections from the novels of one of America's most poetic writers of fiction. Hawkes' rich, highly metaphorical language creates a world of its own, but one that simultaneously comments on the tawdriness and barbarism of life.

Although much of her energy goes into her novels, Joyce Carol Oates' *Last Days* demonstrates her seriousness about the short story. Ranging in subject from private madness to political repression, the stories are intense, intelligent, and memorable. While Joyce Carol Oates is so prolific that her work is sometimes not given appropriate attention, Paule Marshall works so slowly that she tends to be forgotten between books. *Reena* makes available five stories by this careful, resonant writer.

Among posthumously published works were Elizabeth Bishop's *The Collected Prose* and Weldon Kees' *The Ceremony.* Miss Bishop, best known for her poetry, proved to be an accomplished essayist and short story writer. Mr. Kees committed suicide in 1955.

© 1984 Thomas Victor

William Kennedy won a Pulitzer Prize for Ironweed *(1983) and had his first novel,* The Ink Truck, *republished.*

Attesting to the vigor in short story writing was the diversity of form. Frederick Busch's *Too Late American Boyhood Blues* and Lynne Sharon Schwartz's *Acquainted With the Night and Other Stories* use traditional narrative to probe contemporary society. Max Apple's *Free Agents* mingles fiction and autobiography. James McCourt's *Kaye Wayfaring in "Avenged"* invents its own theatrical world. Michael Martone's *Alive and Dead in Indiana* has stories about the famous, including Alfred Kinsey and Whistler's father. Veronica Geng's *Partners*, Steve Katz's *Stolen Stories*, and Guy Davenport's *Apples and Pears* question the very definition of a short story.

Perhaps the year's most impressive work was in some ways the quietest. Mary Hood's *How Far She Went*, the winner of the Flannery O'Connor Award for Short Fiction, is effortlessly moving and true.

Poetry. Two of the most interesting books of poetry in 1984 were posthumous publications. William Faulkner's *Vision in Spring*, youthful poems that had never been published before, did not establish Faulkner as a major poet. It did give important insights into the development of his prose style, a topic dealt with in Judith Sensibar's critical study of his poetry, *The Origins of Faulkner's Art*. Sara Teasdale (1884–1933) was well known in the first decades of the 20th century for her love poetry and her association with Harriet Monroe and Vachel Lindsay. *Mirror of the Heart*, a new edition of her work containing many poems that she withheld from publication because she thought them too intimate, casts new light on her life.

Despite these historical highlights, poetry continued to be America's most forgotten literary art form. Major poets, who for decades have spoken eloquently and deeply of the human experience, are known only to a few. Karl Shapiro's *Love & War, Art & God* made clear that the work he has done since his famous World War II poems also deserves recognition. Nor could one accuse Richard Hugo of dry academicism in *Making Certain It Goes On*, a major collection filled with the pains and pitfalls of a hard life. Philip Levine added to his stature with his *Selected Poems*, drawn from the ten books he published between 1963 and 1981. The verbal brilliance of John Ashbery's *The Wave*, penetrating evocativeness of William Matthews' *A Happy Childhood*, or hypnotic reverie of Charles Wright's *The Other Side of the River* all tended to be experienced in limited circles, as well.

The subjects of contemporary poetry were not limited to introspective meditations. Mary Fell's *The Persistence of Memory* captures the voices of working women, present and past. Kate Daniels, with *The White Wave*, demonstrates (as many young poets do) a serious concern for the political as well as the personal. New voices showing a healthy range of interests included Paul Zarzyski's *The Make-Up of Ice*, Patricia Hooper's *Other Lives*, and Richard Kenney's *The Evolution of the Flightless Bird*.

Some critics in attempting to explain the limited appeal of current poetry argued that poetry was ignored because there was no establishment to rebel against and no avant-garde to create excitement. Instead, all was acceptable—from formal to free verse, obscurity to clarity, narration to pure image, and baroque and esoteric language to street talk and dialect.

Criticism. Alfred Kazin's *On Native Grounds* (1942) helped establish the importance of 20th-century American modernist fiction. His current work, *An American Procession*, ranges from Emerson to Faulkner in order to show that the modernist characteristics of irony, isolation, and a degree of cosmic alienation are central to American literature.

John Barth's first collection of essays, *The Friday Book*, starts out by spoofing itself by its subtitle, "Book-Titles Should be Straightforward and Subtitles Avoided," and follows that with a few pieces that might be called "meta-non-fiction." Most of the book, however, is devoted to more serious reflections on the nature of postmodernism.

Important works on feminism appeared. Susan Brownmiller's *Femininity* studied the complexity of the concept itself. Mary Daly's provocative *Pure Lust*, a densely brilliant and imaginative inquiry, is likely to draw comments for years to come. Annette Kolodny's *The Land Before Her* added significantly to the understanding of American culture, showing how women perceived and were affected by the frontier experience.

Two works of oral history, both dealing with war, received high praise. Studs Terkel's *"The Good War"* presents the voices of people from all walks of life who had been in World War II. In stark contrast with Wallace Terry's *BLOODS,* which records the often bitter and moving memories of black Vietnam War veterans.

History and Biography. A number of controversial biographies appeared. Patricia Bosworth's *Diane Arbus* presented the dark, manipulative side of the photographer whose haunting images have become part of American culture. Laurence Bergreen's *James Agee* brought charges of inaccuracy from his family. Dorothy J. Farnan's memoir, *Auden in Love,* was attacked. Susan Cheever's account of her father, John Cheever, in *Home Before Dark* made intimate revelations about his life.

Janet Malcolm's *In the Freud Archives* was itself a revealing account of a stormy controversy, a battle over the real nature of Freud's experiences and insights precipitated by a former projects director of the Freud Archives.

JEROME STERN, *Florida State University*

AMERICAN LITERATURE: MAJOR WORKS | 1984

NOVELS

Adams, Alice, *Superior Women*
Auchincloss, Louis, *The Book Class*
Banks, Russell, *The Relation of My Imprisonment*
Barthelme, Frederick, *Second Marriage*
Boyle, T. Coraghessan, *Budding Prospects: A Pastoral*
Brown, Rosellen, *Civil Wars*
Busch, Frederick, *Invisible Mending*
Carlisle, Henry, *The Jonah Man*
Dew, Robb Forman, *The Time of Her Life*
Didion, Joan, *Democracy*
Doerr, Harriet, *Stones for Ibarra*
Dubus, Andre, *Voices From the Moon*
Gertler, Trudy, *Elbowing the Seducer*
Gilchrist, Ellen, *Victory Over Japan*
Grumbach, Doris, *The Ladies*
Harrison, Jim, *Sundog*
Heller, Joseph, *God Knows*
Herbert, Frank, *Heretics of Dune*
Humphreys, Josephine, *Dreams of Sleep*
Just, Ward, *The American Blues*
Kenney, Susan, *In Another Country*
Lurie, Alison, *Foreign Affairs*
Mailer, Norman, *Tough Guys Don't Dance*
McCorkle, Jill, *The Cheer Leader*
McCorkle, Jill, *July 7th*
Nunn, Kem, *Tapping the Source*
Pesetsky, Bette, *Digs*
Phillips, Jayne Anne, *Machine Dreams*
Plante, David, *The Foreigner*
Powell, Padgett, *Edisto*
Robbins, Tom, *Jitterbug Perfume*
Santmyer, Helen Hooven, *. . . And Ladies of the Club*
Sennett, Richard, *An Evening of Brahms*
Slavitt, David R., *Alice at 80*
Updike, John, *The Witches of Eastwick*
Uris, Leon, *The Haj*
Vidal, Gore, *Lincoln*
Wharton, William, *Scumbler*

SHORT STORIES

Apple, Max, *Free Agents*
Bellow, Saul, *Him With His Foot in His Mouth and Other Stories*

Bishop, Elizabeth, *The Collected Prose*
Busch, Frederick, *Too Late American Boyhood Blues*
Davenport, Guy, *Apples and Pears and Other Stories*
Geng, Veronica, *Partners*
Hawkes, John, *Humors of Blood & Skin*
Katz, Steve, *Stolen Stories*
Lish, Gordon, *What I Know So Far*
Marshall, Paule, *Reena and Other Stories*
Martone, Michael, *Alive and Dead in Indiana*
McCourt, James, *Kaye Wayfaring in "Avenged"*
Oates, Joyce Carol, *Last Days*
Pynchon, Thomas, *Slow Learner*
Schwartz, Lynne Sharon, *Acquainted With the Night*
Thurm, Marian, *Floating*

POETRY

Ashbery, John, *A Wave*
Bell, Marvin. *Drawn By Stones, By Earth, By Things That Have Been In the Fire*
Blumenthal, Michael, *Days We Would Rather Know*
Daniels, Kate, *The White Wave*
Davison, Peter, *New and Selected Poems 1957–1984*
Dobyns, Stephen, *Black Dog, Red Dog*
Faulkner, William, *Vision in Spring*
Fell, Mary, *The Persistence of Memory*
Ferry, David, *Strangers*
Gallagher, Tess, *Willingly*
Hooper, Patricia, *Other Lives*
Howard, Richard, *Lining Up*
Hugo, Richard, *Making Certain It Goes On*
Kenney, Richard, *The Evolution of the Flightless Bird*
Kuzma, Greg, *Of China and Of Greece*
Levine, Philip, *Selected Poems*
Matthews, William, *A Happy Childhood*
McPherson, Sandra, *Patron Happiness*
Olds, Sharon, *The Dead and the Living*
Shapiro, Karl, *Love & War, Art & God*
Teasdale, Sara, *Mirror of the Heart*
Tillinghast, Richard, *Our Flag Was Still There*
Wright, Charles, *The Other Side of the River*
Zarzyski, Paul, *The Make-Up of Ice*

CRITICISM AND CULTURE

Barth, John, *The Friday Book*
Brownmiller, Susan, *Femininity*
Cox, Harvey, *Religion in the Secular City: Toward a Postmodern Theology*
Daly, Mary, *Pure Lust*
Evans, Mari, ed., *Black Women Writers (1950–1980) A Critical Evaluation*
Gardner, John, *The Art of Fiction: Notes on Craft for Young Writers*
Jackson, John Brinckerhoff, *Discovering the Vernacular Landscape*

Random House, Inc.

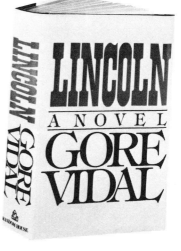

Harvard University Press

Children's Literature

Noteworthy trends in the estimated 2,600 children's books published in the United States during 1984 included the proliferation of toy and activity books aimed at bookstore (nonlibrary) consumers; a surge of computer-related books for children of all ages; and a burgeoning number of religious books. The year also saw a slight downswing in the popularity of the teenage paperback romance.

Foreign Books. Certain books originally published outside the United States made a strong showing in their American editions. One of the finest of these is Uri Orlev's *The Island on Bird Street*, from Israel, a gripping novel about a young boy's lonely vigil in a Polish ghetto hideout during the Holocaust. British imports included Warwick Hutton's *Jonah and the Great Fish*, a virtuoso picture-book retelling of an Old Testament story; Erik Christian Haugaard's surging, expansive novel of 16th century Japan, *The Samurai's Tale;* Philippa Pearce's exquisitely crafted story about enigmas of everyday life, *The Way to Sattin Shore;* and Margaret Mahy's absorbing novel of the supernatural, *The Changeover.*

Awards. The John Newbery Medal of the American Library Association (ALA) was presented to Beverly Cleary for *Dear Mr. Henshaw*, a book about a young boy who pours out his problems in letters to a favorite author. The ALA's Randolph Caldecott Medal went to Alice and Martin Provensen for *The Glorious Flight*, an evocative picture-book recounting of Louis Blériot's courageous flight across the English Channel in 1909.

Recommended Books. Outstanding books published for the picture-book set, aged 3 to 6, included two stunning books of photographs tailored for object identification and guessing games: *What's Inside?* by Duanne Daughtry and *Is It Rough? Is It Smooth? Is It Shiny?* by Tana Hoban. *Picnic*, Emily Arnold McCully's winsome, wordless picture book, is about a small mouse who falls unnoticed by the wayside when his large family embarks on an out-

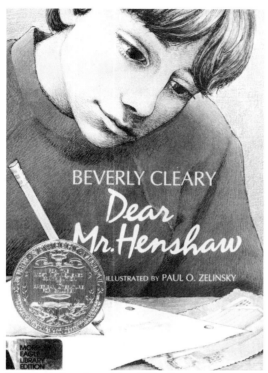

© 1983 Beverly Cleary. By permission of William Morrow and Company

set during the 1930s about a boy who carries a heavy load of guilt; Lloyd Alexander's masterful climax for his Westmark trilogy, *The Beggar Queen*, in which Theo and Mickle fight for the future of their kingdom; *Legend Days*, the first volume in a projected series by Jamake Highwater, detailing tragic hardships in the life of a 19th century Plains Indian girl; and Gary Bargar's *Life. Is. Not. Fair.*, a strikingly honest novel about racial prejudice in the 1950s.

KAREN STANG HANLEY, *"Booklist"*

SELECTED BOOKS FOR CHILDREN*

Ages 3–6
Chorao, Kay, *The Baby's Bedtime Book*
Kellogg, Steven, *Paul Bunyan*
Lobel, Arnold, *The Rose in My Garden*
Locker, Thomas, *Where the River Begins*
McPhail, David, *Fix-It*
Mikolaycak, Charles, *Babushka*
Ormerod, Jan, *101 Things To Do With a Baby*
Pomerantz, Charlotte, *One Duck, Another Duck*

Ages 7–10
Bunting, Eve, *The Man Who Could Call Down Owls*
Cole, Brock, *The Winter Wren*
Goble, Paul, *Buffalo Woman*
Hodges, Margaret, *St. George and the Dragon: a Golden Legend,* illustrated by Trina Schart Hyman
Isadora, Rachel, *Opening Night*
Miller, Jonathan and Pelham, David, *The Facts of Life*
Provensen, Alice and Martin, *Leonardo da Vinci*
Simon, Seymour, *The Earth* and *The Moon* (2 volumes)

Ages 9–12
Brenner, Martha, *Fireworks Tonight!*
Dowden, Anne Ophelia, *From Flower to Fruit*
Gaeddert, LouAnn, *Your Former Friend, Matthew,* illustrated by Mary Beth Schwark
Langton, Jane, *The Fragile Flag*
Lowry, Lois, *Anastasia, Ask Your Analyst*
Prelutsky, Jack, *The New Kid on the Block*

Young Teens
Bond, Nancy, *A Place to Come Back To*
Collier, James Lincoln and Christopher, *Who is Carrie?*
Hamilton, Virginia, *A Little Love*
Lasky, Kathryn, *Prank*
McKillip, Patricia, *Moon-Flash*
McKinley, Robin, *The Hero and The Crown*
Marrin, Albert, *War Clouds in the West*
Settle, Mary Lee, *Water World*
Thrasher, Crystal, *A Taste of Daylight*
Yolen, Jane, *Children of the Wolf*
*Works not cited in article.

© 1983 Alice and Martin Provensen. By permission of Viking Penguin Inc.

ing. Tomie de Paola's vividly colorful illustrations distinguish a new edition of a favorite nursery rhyme, *Mary Had a Little Lamb* by Sara Josepha Hale. *The Butter Battle Book* by Dr. Seuss is a pointed allegory about a ludicrous arms race. Audrey Wood's *The Napping House*, with pictures by Don Wood, is a witty tale extended by innovative artwork.

Books for older youngsters, aged 7 to 10, included *Animal Alphabet* by Bert Kitchen, a stylishly designed alphabet book juxtaposing ordinary and extraordinary creatures, and *The Mysteries of Harris Burdick*, which matches Chris Van Allsburg's highly atmospheric pencil drawings with his evocative captions that prompt children to invent corollary stories of their own. Lush oil paintings by Paul O. Zelinsky are featured in a new edition of the Grimm brothers' *Hansel and Gretel,* and Myra Cohn Livingston's poetry in *Sky Songs* is enhanced by Leonard Everett Fisher's paintings.

For readers aged 9 to 12, among noteworthy new titles were Beverly Cleary's *Ramona Forever!*, in which irrepressible Ramona Quimby is now a third grader, and *Julia's Magic*, a sensitively written installment in Eleanor Cameron's retrogressive series about Julia Redfern. *Downwind* by Louise Moeri is a potent novel about a family's flight from a threatened nuclear-reactor meltdown. Maxine Rosenberg compiled a profile of interracial child adoption in *Being Adopted*, with warm photographs by George Ancona.

Distinguished books for young teens were Paula Fox's *One-Eyed Cat*, a compelling story

THE GLORIOUS FLIGHT
ACROSS THE CHANNEL WITH LOUIS BLÉRIOT
BY ALICE AND MARTIN PROVENSEN

Canadian Literature: English

Many English-language Canadian writers published collections of short stories in 1984. In nonfiction, the federal general election inspired books on politics and political leaders.

Nonfiction. Pierre Elliott Trudeau, who in 1984 resigned after 15 years as prime minister, is the subject of Larry Zolf's *Just Watch Me: Remembering Pierre Trudeau.* It was Zolf's second book about Trudeau. Zolf also produced *Survival of the Fattest,* a saucy look at the Canadian Senate. Another book about Trudeau was *How Pierre and I Saved the Civilized World,* by humorist Gary Lautens. *John Turner,* by Jack Cahill, is a biography of the man who was elected Liberal leader and succeeded Trudeau as prime minister for two and a half months. *Mulroney,* by Ian MacDonald, profiles Progressive Conservative Brian Mulroney, who defeated Turner to become the next prime minister. *So You Want to Be Prime Minister,* by Ben Wicks, is a humorous antidote to the election seriousness. Another light-hearted volume is *The (Top Secret) Tory Strategy,* by Louise Dennys. Veteran newsman Charles Lynch contributed *Race for the Rose: The Liberal Leadership Campaign.*

The year's most talked-of Canadian book was George Jonas' *Vengeance,* subtitled *The True Story of an Israeli Counter-Terrorist Team.* Jonas claimed that his informant, who used the pseudonym "Avner," was the leader of an Israeli intelligence team that killed the terrorists who had caused the deaths of Israeli athletes at the 1972 Olympic Games.

Best-selling writer Pierre Berton's *The Promised Land—Settling the West 1896–1914* is the last of his four books about how the Canadian west was opened to settlers. Mordecai Richler's *Home Sweet Home* describes his feelings about Canadians and the Canadian character. *Canadian Writers in 1984,* edited by W. H. New, collects essays by Canadian writers to celebrate the 25th anniversary of the scholarly journal *Canadian Literature.* Robert A. Stebbins' *The Magician* treats an unusual topic: how magicians fare in Canada and how to become one. *The Film Companion,* by Peter Morris, discusses more than 650 Canadian films and those who made them. *Take Two, a Tribute to Canadian Film,* edited by Seth Feldman, is the second volume of an anthology about the industry.

Pirates and Outlaws of Canada, 1610–1932 demonstrates that the country has had its share of interesting villains. Lorraine Monk's *Ontario, a Loving Look* celebrates that province's bicentennial with selections from the writings of pioneers, together with an impressive collection of modern photographs. *Wet and Fat,* about whale watching, was written by the whale research team at Newfoundland's Memorial University and illustrated by Don

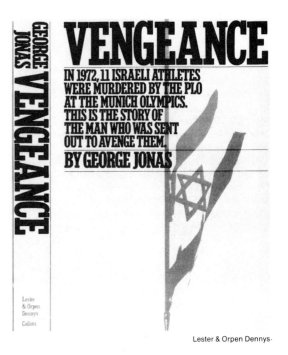

Lester & Orpen Dennys

Wright. Farley Mowat's *Sea of Slaughter* details man's decimation of whales, walruses, harp seals, and other ocean creatures. Creating a stir in universities was *The Great Brain Robbery—Universities on the Road to Self-Destruction,* by Professors David J. Bercuson, Robert Bothwell, and J. L. Granatstein, who believe education in Canadian universities has deteriorated because of relaxed entrance standards and inflated grades.

Jack Bush, by Karen Wilkin, is a handsomely illustrated tribute to the late Jack Bush and his paintings. G. Blair Lang's equally well illustrated *Morrice* is about painter James W. Morrice, who flourished in the early 1900s. Joan Murray's *The Best of the Group of Seven* is a lavishly illustrated treatise on Canada's pioneer painters of the modern era. *Sunlight in The Shadows: The Landscape of Emily Carr,* by Kerry Mason Dodd, has photographs by Michael Breuer of much of the scenery painted by Emily Carr. *The Last Buffalo,* edited by Joan Murray, is about western painter Frederick Verner.

My Son Wayne, by Walter Gretzky and Jim Taylor, is the biography of perhaps the greatest player in hockey, by his father and the sports columnist Jim Taylor. *Foul Balls,* by Alison Gordon, is about the Toronto Blue Jays in American League baseball, and incidentally about the author's eventual acceptance into the once all-male world of baseball reporting. The game of tennis receives humorous treatment by Eric Nicol and Dave More in *Tennis—It Serves You Right!*

Poetry. Margaret Atwood's *Interlunar* deals with human transitions, including some of her own. Lionel Kearns' ninth volume, *Convergences*, a long prose poem, illuminates two journeys: Captain Cook's voyage on the Pacific Ocean and humanity's voyage on the sea of life. Leonard Cohen's *Book of Mercy* comprises 50 poems he calls "psalms" because of their religious nature. Ralph Gustafson, who has written more than 20 volumes, contributed *Directions of Autumn*, a collection of new poems. Prolific Al Purdy's 27th volume was *Piling Blood*. Other new works included David McFadden's *The Art of Darkness* and Roo Bronson's *The Whole Night Coming Home*. Leona Gom published *Northbound* and Mary de Michele *Necessary Sugar*, her fourth book.

Fiction. W. O. Mitchell's *Since Daisy Creek* is about a professor who is mauled by a grizzly bear and becomes obsessed with hunting it down. Hugh Hood's *The Scenic Art* is the fifth novel of a projected 12 in a series entitled The New Age. *The Spanish Doctor*, by Matt Cohen, is a well-researched historical novel set in the 14th century. Sylvia Fraser's *Berlin Solstice* deals with the rise and fall of Hitler from 1923 to 1945. William Deverell's *The Dance of Shiva* tells of deaths in a cult group.

Among collections of short stories were W. P. Kinsella's *The Thrill of the Grass*, Norman Levine's *Champagne Barn*, Spider Robinson's *Melancholy Elephants*, Timothy Findley's *Dinner Along the Amazon*, and Robin Skelton's *The Man Who Sang in His Sleep*.

DAVID SAVAGE, *Simon Fraser University*

Canadian Literature: French

The year 1984 marked the 450th anniversary of Jacques Cartier's arrival in Quebec, and, fittingly, one of the most striking volumes was *Le Monde de Jacques Cartier*, in which some 20 French and Canadian scholars of different academic disciplines reinterpret Cartier's 16th century world. Beautiful illustrations accompany the text. Another major literary event was the posthumous publication of Gabrielle Roy's memoirs, *La Détresse et l'enchantement*.

French-Canadian music, traditional and contemporary, attracted much attention. Félix Leclerc published a third series of reminiscences, *Rêves à vendre*. In *Diane Dufresne*, Geneviève Beauvarlet, a French journalist, describes Dufresne's stunning success as a singer on the Paris stage. Donald Smith's essay, *Gilles Vigneault, conteur et poète*, offers new biographical and literary insights.

In the classical music field, a special issue of the journal *Dérives* (Nos. 44/45) explores 30 years of musical activity in Quebec. In a history of the Montreal Symphony Orchestra photos supplement Gilles Potvin's thorough text.

In the field of social commentary, Jacques Godbout bitterly castigates the materialism of North American marketing in *Le Murmure marchand*. In a lighter vein, Claude Jasmin's pamphlet *L'État-maquereau, l'état-Mafia* expresses indignation at paying taxes.

The major reference work was Maurice Lemire's fourth volume of *Le Dictionnaire des oeuvres littéraires du Québec*, which discusses the extraordinary literary explosion in Quebec from 1960 to 1969. In *Écrivains contemporains, entretiens 2: 1977–1980*, Jean Royer provides interesting interviews with present-day writers. Varied feminist literary perspectives appear in *Féminité, subversion, écriture*, edited by Suzanne Lamy and Irène Pages.

Two volumes examine literary relations between Quebec and France. Paulette Colette studies the attitudes of French novelists toward Canada in *Le Romancier français et le Canada, 1842–1981*, while Jacqueline Barrois-Gerol's *Le Roman québécois en France* analyzes the reception of Quebec writers abroad.

Among titles on individual figures, two deal with established writers: Hélène La France's *Yves Thériault et l'institution québécoise* and Lucille Roy's essay on Anne Hébert, *Entre la lumière et l'ombre*. An analysis of the poetry of Émile Nelligan, including poems written during his confinement in a mental hospital, is found in Jacques Michon's *Les Racines du rêve*.

Fiction. In *Crache à pic, la bootleggeuse!*, Antonine Maillet sketches a colorful Acadian female bootlegger of the Prohibition era. Violence and personal revolt characterize Marie-Claire Blais' *Pierre: La Guerre du printemps 81*. Michel Tremblay's chronicle of Mount Royal continues in *Des Nouvelles d'Édouard*, and Roch Carrier's imaginary world unfolds further in *De l'amour dans la ferraille*. Other interesting works included Jacques Poulin's *Volkswagen Blues*, Jacques Fillion's *Pourquoi cracher sur la lune?*, and Madeleine Ouellette-Michalska's *La Maison Trestler*.

Poetry. Among avant-garde works were *Intérieurs* by France Théoret, *Double Impression* by Nicole Brossard, and *Mahler et autres matières* by Pierre Nepveu. More traditional are Jacques Brault's *Moments fragiles* and Paul Chamberland's *Compagnons chercheurs*.

Children's Literature. Many volumes appeared in this burgeoning field, by both new and established writers. Among them were Toufik Ehm's *Jacques Cartier raconte. . . .*, Roch Carrier's *Ne faites pas mal à l'avenir*, and Gilles Vigneault's *Comptine pour endormir l'enfant qui ne veut rien savoir*.

Theater. Michel Tremblay's *Albertine en cinq temps* was the theatrical event of 1984. In his most lyrical and mature play thus far, Tremblay skillfully weaves together five decades in the life of an angry aged woman. Other plays of note were Jean Barbeau's *Les Gars*, Jean-Pierre Ronfard's *Don Quichotte*, and Marie-Laberge's *L'Homme gris*.

RAMON HATHORN, *University of Guelph*

English Literature

It is not every year that sees a "new" novel published by a long-dead master writer. But a work by D.H. Lawrence, *Mr. Noon*, was unveiled in September 1984 on what would have been Lawrence's 99th birthday. Written in 1921, to some extent as a sequel to *Sons and Lovers* and *The Rainbow,* the work was then split in half by Lawrence. The first part was rejected for publication in England as too short and in the United States as immoral. It was published as a fragment in the 1930s. The second half was given to Lawrence's American publisher, Thomas Selzer, for safekeeping and subsequently forgotten. It came to light when acquired among other Lawrence papers by the University of Texas in 1972 and was published by Cambridge University Press.

Fiction. A number of major writers published new novels in 1984, including Beryl Bainbridge, whose *Watson's Apology* was an essay in Victorian black farce, and Angela Carter, whose surrealist *Nights at the Circus* was considered a tour de force. William Boyd joined the band of writers describing desperate Englishmen adrift in the United States in the comic *Stars and Bars.*

Six authors were short-listed for the Booker Prize for fiction, Britain's most lucrative and most important annual literary prize. Penelope Lively was a candidate for *According to Mark,* a novel of tragic relationships, and David Lodge for *Small World,* an exercise in droll observations of the academic world. Julian Barnes pulled off a literary musing that only barely fulfilled itself as fiction in *Flaubert's Parrot.* Anita Brookner's novel *Hotel du Lac,* which also made the shortlist, was an evocation of a lonely woman writer on holiday in Switzerland observing women who are rich, idle, and infantile and the attenion paid to them by men. Anita Desai's contender was the moving novel *In Custody;* set in India, it portrays the friendship of a young scholar, Deven, and his literary hero, Nur, greatest poet of the dying Urdu culture. But perhaps the favorite and strangest of all the Booker challengers was J.G. Ballard's *Empire of the Sun.* A prolific science-fiction novelist, Ballard this time turned his attention to a nearer subject, the experience of a young English boy in and around Shanghai during the Japanese offensive in World War II. Separated from his parents, the 11-year-old learns how to survive as a prisoner of war and by 1945 has seen humanity in all its greed and brutality. As a picture of the blind helplessness of war, reviewers found Ballard's novel powerful and haunting. In a surprise choice, however, the judges opted for Anita Brookner's *Hotel du Lac,* praising her observation, humor, and elegant simplicity of style.

Among popular fiction, a clever and funny evocation of childhood in the sexually chaotic 1980s, *The Secret Diary of Adrian Mole Aged 13 3/4,* by playwright Sue Townsend, has topped the best-seller lists for some two years and was produced for the stage. The sequel, *The Growing Pains of Adrian Mole,* which takes our beleaguered hero to the age of 16, appeared in 1984.

Nonfiction. A distinguished curiosity, *Getting to Know the General,* was published by Graham Greene as he reached his 80th birthday. It is a celebration of his experiences in Panama with the late Panamanian leader Gen. Omar Torrijos. Among excellent biographies was the second volume of Hilary Spurling's life of novelist Ivy Compton-Burnett, *Secrets of a Woman's Heart,* which examines in detail the claustrophobic world of the writer and her woman companion. Peter Ackroyd published a life of T.S. Eliot, though without total access to family documents. The Bloomsbury saga never fails to produce some new biographies and memoirs, and 1984 was no exception. In *Deceived with Kindness: A Bloomsbury Childhood,* Angelica Garnett, Vanessa Bell's daughter, describes her idyllic childhood and later disillusionment among her mother's lovers. Light was cast on more minor Bloomsbury characters by Penelope Fitzgerald's description of *Charlotte Mew and Her Friends.*

Almost on the Bloomsbury scale was the attention paid during the year to H.G. Wells, with the republication by Faber of Wells' own two-volume *Experiment in Autobiography,* and at the same time from the same publisher, *H.G. Wells in Love* by G.P. Wells, the writer's son. Since Anthony West, Wells' son by Rebecca West, also revealed in *H.G. Wells: Aspects of a Life* his version of his father in love, detail has accumulated with some intensity. Critics felt that G.P. Wells' version might be the most important, and perhaps most truthful of all. Among more popular biographies, Janet Morgan's *Agatha Christie: A Biography* caused great interest. Among letters published in 1984, *A Very Private Eye: An Autobiography in Diaries and Letters* by Barbara Pym fueled the rising interest in this writer, as did a collection of letters by Jean Rhys for its author. In criticism and ideas probably the most telling book of the year was George Steiner's *Antigones.*

Poetry. A number of distinguished poets published new books in 1984. Among the most noteworthy were Charles Causley's *Secret Destinations,* personal reflections deriving from journeys in Australia and Canada, and James Fenton's *The Memory of War and Children in Exile,* technically assured poems on war and the victims of war, which were thought to be capable of finding large audiences. *Selected Poems* from Tony Harrison presents a rugged, distinctive voice reflecting compassionately on the relationship of the poet and society. Seamus Heaney's *Station Island,* an eagerly awaited new volume from a major poet, muses on the landscape and the problems of Ireland. Craig Raine's *Rich* contains poems of great brilliance, with jewel-like metaphors in his familiar style, referred to as "the Martian school of poetry" from Raine's earlier *A Martian Sends a Postcard Home,* an original look at everyday objects.

Other noteworthy collections published in 1984 were Philip Gross' *The Ice Factory,* Selima Hill's *Saying Hello at the Station,* and Michael Hofmann's *Nights in the Iron Hotel.*

MAUREEN GREEN, *Free-lance Writer, London*

World Literature*

The year 1984 was unusual in that many of its major literary events occurred among the so-called minor or marginal languages and geographical areas of the world: Bulgaria, Somalia, Finland, Egypt, Iran, and Vietnam. There were the usual and expected important new works by leading authors from the principal Western and Eastern literatures, but the year may well be remembered for the equally noteworthy successes among their smaller kin.

African. A wealth of excellent writing emerged from the African continent. Foremost were three works representing three languages and three widely separated regions. *Close Sesame,* by Nuruddin Farah of Somalia, completed a trilogy of novels collectively titled *Variations on the Theme of an African Dictatorship.* It tells the story of "the General," a former Soviet-leaning sloganeer turned pro-Western strongman, as viewed and criticized by a devout Muslim veteran of the anticolonial struggles, all wrapped in a superb, gripping plot. The work and its predecessors in the trilogy firmly establish Farah's reputation as Africa's best young anglophone writer of today.

Léopold Sédar Senghor, long an esteemed political figure as president of Senegal and, with Aimé Césaire, one of the instigators and leading exponents of the Negritude movement in African and Afro-Caribbean letters, was honored with a beautifully produced edition of his collected verse. The contents span nearly 40 years of creative work but also include several recent, personal poems, such as an elegy for his late son Philippe. The collection is a fitting tribute to an exemplary career and Senghor's 1984 induction into the French Academy.

The Afrikaans poet and prose writer Breyten Breytenbach, whose past work sometimes fell to amateurish and lamentably obscene levels, has steadily improved since his release from South African prison in 1982. The collection *yk* (a merging of the words for "you" and "I") is the fourth in his projected seven-part Undanced Dance series and offers a stunningly virtuosic array of poems whose verbal contortions are comparable perhaps only to the later

* Titles translated.

AGIP/Pictorial Parade

Léopold S. Senghor, the poet and former president of Senegal, became the first black member of the French Academy.

Joyce among major English-language writers. In both form and content, the volume is an exuberant affirmation of life and writing following the author's seven-year confinement, much of it solitary.

Asian. The Vietnam War has inspired fiction writers not only among U.S. veterans of that conflict, but also among Vietnamese vets. Tran Van Dinh's *Blue Dragon, White Tiger,* which appeared in a U.S. edition in 1984, recounts the story of a South Vietnamese soldier's return to his country following several years abroad after the South's defeat, his confrontation with the new world he finds there, his immersion in that world, and his rise to prominence in it. The result is an unmatched portrait of traditional and contemporary urban Vietnamese life amid war and its aftermath.

From elsewhere in Asia and the Pacific a spate of new works became available to the Western reader. Chief among them were Morio Kita's *House of Nire,* a prizewinning Japanese family saga à la *Buddenbrooks,* spanning three generations of upper-middle-class life in the first half of the 20th century; Yang Jiang's *Six Chapters from My Life "Down Under,"* possibly the best single work relating to the "re-education" movement of China's Cultural Revolution, under which intellectuals were sent to rural cadre schools and work farms to be purged of their elitism; and Albert Wendt's verse collection *Shaman of Visions,* which showed that New Zealand poetry is indeed alive and well.

Middle Eastern. Three books stood out among those emerging from the Middle Eastern countries in 1984. The most stunning was *Fear and Trembling* by the Iranian émigré author Gholam-Hossein Sa'edi; its six interlocking prose vignettes depict a small cast of poor Persian Gulf villagers in ill-fated encounters with

329

outside forces (a traveling mullah, a charlatan, a strange child), all told with an effect that is at once brutal, spare, and riveting. *Al-Mazini's Egypt,* meanwhile, represented a total contrast to Sa'edi's tragedy and squalor, bringing to the West's attention two short comic novels of Egyptian manners and several short stories by the most popular Arab satirist of the 20th century, Ibrahim al-Mazini (1899–1949). The best of the year's fiction from Israel was A. B. Yehoshua's novel *A Late Divorce,* in which a longtime Israeli expatriate who had been among the original settlers in 1948 returns to present-day Israel to obtain a legal divorce from a wife who had been institutionalized decades earlier; the country is one he no longer recognizes, a land of incongruence and contradiction yet still possessing a mythical unity— the grandson whose birth he awaits (and who is the cause of his need for a legal divorce) will be named Moses.

Caribbean. Trinidadian authors V. S. Naipaul and Derek Walcott have practically become part of Anglo-American literature by now, and both produced important new books in 1984: Naipaul's *Finding the Center,* containing strongly autobiographical narratives on the writer's beginnings and on a recent visit to the Ivory Coast; and Walcott's *Midsummer,* a sequence of 54 poems covering a single year, from one summer to the next. From the French-speaking area of the Caribbean came Guadeloupean author Maryse Condé's novel *Ségou,* a skillfully fictionalized historical account of Islam's conquest of animist peoples in Niger and the effects of that conquest on individual families and groups in the vicinity of the village of Ségou.

Eastern European. The marginal regions of Europe also produced several of the year's literary highlights. One of the most disturbing was *The Truth That Killed,* a condensed and somewhat sensationalized translation of Georgi Markov's posthumously published, two-volume *Reports in Absentia on Bulgaria,* which showed with extraordinary vitality how countless Bulgarian intellectuals struggled to preserve both personality and spirit in what had become by 1969 (when Markov departed for the West) a stereotypical totalitarian state. It was for just such accounts, broadcast to Bulgaria via Radio Free Europe, that Markov was assassinated in 1979 in a bizarre plot allegedly involving the highest Bulgarian authorities.

The fiction of noted Rumanian theologian and philosopher Mircea Eliade continued to emerge in a patchwork of foreign-language editions with the French publication of *The Three Graces,* a collection of playfully poetic tales exploring the frontiers of death, time, orphic mystery, and Kafkaesque encounters with bureaucratic quagmires. French publishers in 1984 also continued to promote the work of the Albanian writer Ismaïl Kadare, with the publi-

Thomas Victor, Knopf

Trinidadian author V. S. Naipaul writes about his visit to the Ivory Coast in his latest book, Finding the Center.

cation of *The Niche and the Shame,* a historical novel whose account of Albania's early 19th-century revolt against Ottoman rule strikes implicit parallels to contemporary geopolitics.

Scandinavian. The Finnish poet and prose writer Paavo Haavikko followed his receipt of the 1984 Neustadt International Prize (dubbed "the American Nobel" by many European critics) with a somberly poetic and intensely reflective volume of aphoristic prose titled *Darkness.* New novels by Sven Delblanc (*Canaan Land*) and Tove Jansson (*Stone Fields*), a collection of "imaginary and dream travels" by the Swedish Academy member Artur Lundkvist, and a new verse collection by Lundkvist's fellow Academician Östen Sjöstrand (*Directly Above the Water Line*) headed the year's production in Sweden. Iceland's flourishing literary marketplace, meanwhile, was set buzzing by two excellent but totally different novels: Jónas Kristjánsson's *Ordeal by Fire,* an action-filled saga of the 9th-century Nordic world, cast in what one reviewer termed "a seamless welding of imagination, style and erudition that far outstrips most recent prose"; and Oláfur Sigurdsson's *Dragons and Sparrows,* the final installment of a lengthy Dickensian trilogy about the youth and maturation of a young provincial in modern-day "occupied" Iceland.

German. In the major European literatures, 1984 was not a strong year, for the most part. None of the ranking international figures of the German-speaking world, for example, was represented in the year's principal publications, leaving the field to such excellent but less well-known authors as Günter Kunert and Thomas Bernhard. The latter's *Chopping Wood* is an embittered monologue that uses the setting of an "artistic dinner" among friends to comment on the Viennese cultural scene; the former's *Back to Paradise* is a collection of wry, often ironic stories and prose pieces straddling a fluid boundary between the normal and the extraordinary. Christine Brückner's *If You Had Spoken, Desdemona,* with its imaginatively recreated interior monologues of 11 famous women from the past (such as Clytemnestra, Sappho, and the Virgin Mary), from literature (Effi Briest), and from the present (the terrorist Ulrike Meinhof), brought critical acclaim to the author as the outstanding new talent of the year in German letters.

Russian. The year in Russian literature was weaker than usual as well. Characteristically, perhaps, the collected works of two of the finest and most renowned Soviet authors, Vladimir Soloukhin and Yevgeny Vinokurov, revealed mainly the unevenness in the oeuvre of both. Fazil Iskander, on the other hand, a native of the Caucasus region who writes in Russian rather than in his first language, Abkhazian, presented in *Chik's Defense* a delightfully imaginative, humorous, and sensitive collection of stories, novellas, and retold legends, all centered on the colorful invented village of Chegem on the eastern shore of the Black Sea. Abroad, the appearance of Sergei Dovlatov's ribald, autobiographical short-story collection *The Compromise* (plus publication of some of the individual pieces in the *New Yorker*) brought a major new émigré talent to the attention of Western readers.

French. Literature from France proved reasonably strong during the year, led by works from such big-name authors as Marguerite Yourcenar and Julien Green. In *Time, the Great Sculptor,* Yourcenar offered essays on a variety of subjects including art, history, language, politics, and psychology. Green's *Stories of Vertigo* contains previously unpublished materials from the author's earlier years, most of them Lovecraftian tales involving the irruption of the bizarre into ordinary life. On a rather different level, one of 1984's most sensational books was certainly *To the Best of My Recollection,* Françoise Sagan's thinly disguised *récits* about people she has known, experiences she has lived, the scandal of her early success with *Bonjour Tristesse,* and her life among the cultural jet set.

Spanish. Of greater substance and diversity, finally, was the year's harvest in Spanish-language works. In Spain itself, Juan Benet's *Broken Lances* proved to be by far the most imaginative of the many civil-war novels that have inundated the market since Franco's death. Set in Benet's fictive "Región," an isolated and forgotten Republican enclave largely bypassed by the war, the novel brings both that conflict and the era to life with a uniqueness and detail that have been compared to Faulkner

and his Yoknapatawpha County. Camilo José Cela's *Mazurka for Two Dead Men* is a more complex and difficult work on the same theme, with greater emphasis on the barbarity, cruelty, and irrationality that the civil war unleashed and on the human condition it both reflected and augured. A greater popular success than either of those works was Francisco Umbral's *Madrid Trilogy,* an inspired novelistic "memoir of one century in the life of Madrid's people, culture, and history."

Latin America could not match the volume and overall quality of works from Spain, but *Geographies* by Mario Benedetti did successfully combine prose and verse into an intriguingly unconventional mixed-genre work that explores the elusive topics of justice and love. His countryman Julio Cortázar, one of the principal figures of the so-called "Boom" in Latin American literature of the last two decades, passed away in February, leaving as his final legacy a collected edition of his poetry, *Except for the Twilight.* Cortázar's contemporary, the Mexican poet and essayist Octavio Paz, added luster to his reputation as the New World's outstanding man of letters with *Shadows of Things,* a collection of essays on art, literature, and much more. Ranging from the T'ang poets to Apollinaire, Simon Magus, Quevedo, Heraclitus, and others, and also touching on such subjects as glossolalia and panspermia theory, the volume represents Paz at his acute, challenging, and provocative best.

WILLIAM RIGGAN, *World Literature Today*

The celebrated Soviet poet Yevgeny Yevtushenko produced his first novel, Wild Berries, *about a geological expedition in the wilds of Siberia, where the author was born.*

Valentin Mastyukov, Tass/Morrow

UPI/Bettmann

Queen Elizabeth II presided at ceremonies opening the Thames River flood barrier at Woolwich, London.

LONDON

London's governing body, the Greater London Council (GLC), continued its fight for survival in 1984, combating the Thatcher government's program to abolish six metropolitan councils in Britain and the GLC by 1986. Most of the city councils are run by Labour Party majorities and have contested the Conservative government's financial policies.

The government's "paving" bill was introduced and passed by the built-in conservative majority in the House of Commons. It abolished the May 1985 elections to the GLC and paved the way for disbanding the GLC altogether by allowing for borough council appointees to take over from GLC councillors for the remainder of the GLC's life. The GLC mounted a spirited publicity defense, with the GLC's leader left-wing Ken Livingstone becoming a national figure. And in June, after a savage debate in the House of Lords, the "paving" bill was thrown out and the government forced to think again.

The government had to compromise but was determined to avoid elections and an opportunity for general debate; instead it conceded that present councillors should continue in office without a new election until 1986. Ken Livingstone and three other councillors resigned from the Council and successfully stood again at four by-elections in September.

In November the main bill to abolish the GLC and the six metropolitan councils came before Parliament and a bitter debate was foreseen. Public opinion polls showed that 66% of Londoners believe the GLC should not be abolished.

The Thames. In May, Queen Elizabeth joined Ken Livingstone at Woolwich in southeast London to open the Thames flood barrier. London is subsiding and increasingly threatened by flood water. The £464 million (ca. $675 million) barrier, designed by GLC architects and erected on a chalk section of the Thames River, boasts ten gates and nine silver domed piers to withstand the North Sea. Within half an hour of a storm warning, all ten steel gates can be raised to a defensive position, reaching a height of 52 ft (15.8 m).

MAUREEN GREEN, *Free-lance Writer, London*

LOS ANGELES

The people of Los Angeles took pride in hosting the 1984 Summer Olympic Games and in the smoothness with which the city's multifold activities, including traffic flow, functioned during the two-week period. Credit for this success belonged to many, but especially to executives of the California Department of Transportation, the Los Angeles Police Department, and the Olympic Organizing Committee. (*See also* pages 464–69.)

People. On April 8 the Bureau of the Census announced that the city was now the second largest in the United States, with a July 1, 1982, population of 3,022,247. Three weeks later the Department of Housing and Urban Development issued a report saying the city had up to 33,800 homeless persons, the most of any U.S. city. Of these, about 50% were alcoholics and 13% were single women.

Politics. The city budget was passed with less trouble than in many years, partly because the rising prosperity of the area resulted in higher receipts. A proposal to build the start of a subway system was stalled in controversies over cost and ridership potential. Mayor Tom Bradley hinted he would run for a third term in 1985.

Crime. Seven persons were indicted in March eventually on 208 counts of child molestation involving 42 children at a preschool in suburban Manhattan Beach.

Weather. After a nearly rainless winter and a warm spring, the city and its environs experienced an extremely hot and unusually humid summer, with many records set, especially in the first two weeks of September.

Prizes and Sports. The *Los Angeles Times* won two 1984 Pulitzer Prizes. In football, the Raiders, their court battles to stay in Los Angeles apparently won, captured the 1984 Super Bowl. In basketball, the Lakers reached the play-off finals for a third straight year but lost to the Boston Celtics.

CHARLES R. ADRIAN
University of California, Riverside

LOUISIANA

The Louisiana World Exposition ended its six-month run, from May 12 to November 11, bankrupt and $100 million in debt. In spite of its financial problems, the exposition, whose theme was "The World of Rivers—Fresh Water as a Source of Life," was regarded by many as an artistic, if not a fiscal, success.

Exposition. Fair officials had hoped that 12 million people would visit the exposition, which was located in New Orleans in a renovated warehouse district along the Mississippi River. But only 7.3 million attended, although 165,000 season tickets were sold—a world's fair record—to area residents. The fair's problems began even before it opened. Advance ticket sales lagged, and the state legislature had to lend the fair $10 million in April so that work could be completed in time for the opening.

Crowds lagged all summer, and money problems never ceased. The legislature provided an additional $15 million in June so contractors could be paid. The city of New Orleans temporarily froze the fair's bank accounts because the fair owed the city $1.6 million in back taxes.

Many blamed the poor attendance on the fair's $15 admission. Others said that world's fairs are becoming too common. Some commented that people today are too sophisticated or are jaded by television and other entertainments, including year-round theme parks, to be drawn to a fair that is a combination amusement park, theme park, and museum. However, in spite of its troubles, the fair ended with a bang, when almost 250,000 people attended during the last weekend. (*See also* page 525.)

New Orleans Projects. New Orleans will benefit from some fair residuals. The Rouse Company of Maryland, which has been responsible for urban-development projects in cities such as Baltimore and Boston, will spend $55 million to convert what was the upper level of the international pavilion into a Riverwalk mall of more than 200 shops, restaurants, and vending carts. An aerial cable-car system over the Mississippi will continue to operate, transporting commuters to and from downtown. The New Orleans Convention Center, while not built specifically for the fair, was one of its centerpieces and is expected to attract major exhibitions and trade shows.

Political Developments. In the November elections, all eight of Louisiana's members of congress were returned to office. All were unopposed, although several had faced opposition in the September primaries. Sen. J. Bennett Johnston (D) also was reelected without opposition.

Louisianians were faced with the biggest state tax increase in their history when the legislature passed $754 million in new revenues during a special session. Sales taxes were

AP/Wide World

Built for the New Orleans World's Fair, a $12 million aerial transit system across the Mississippi River will serve as a long-range commuter transportation facility.

raised one cent, the gasoline tax went up eight cents a gallon, tobacco and alcohol taxes were raised, corporate tax deductions were cut, and levies were raised on items ranging from sand and gravel to insurance premiums. Most of the money, still less than the $1.14 billion requested by Gov. Edwin W. Edwards, was designated to forestall a huge state deficit caused by a decline in petroleum revenues and lagging tax receipts caused by the national recession. In its regular session the legislature passed higher corporate franchise taxes by $135 million to pay for raises and pension hikes for teachers and other education workers.

JOSEPH W. DARBY III
"The Times-Picayune/States-Item"

LOUISIANA • Information Highlights

Area: 47,752 sq mi (123 677 km²).
Population (July 1, 1983 est.): 4,438,000.
Chief Cities (July 1, 1982 est.): Baton Rouge, the capital, 361,572; New Orleans, 564,561; Shreveport, 210,881; Houma, 100,346.
Government (1984): *Chief Officers*—governor, Edwin Edwards (D); lt. gov., Robert L. Freeman (D). *Legislature*—Senate, 39 members; House of Representatives, 105 members.
State Finances (fiscal year 1983): *Revenues,* $6,947,000,000; *expenditures,* $7,431,000,000.
Personal Income (1983): $45,576,000,000; per capita, $10,270.
Labor Force (May 1984): *Civilian labor force,* 1,930,700; *unemployed,* 171,500 (8.9% of total force).
Education: *Enrollment* (fall 1982)—public elementary schools, 555,978; public secondary, 219,688; colleges and universities (fall 1983), 179,647. *Public school expenditures* (1982–83), $1,954,086,520 ($2,739 per pupil).

Seeking reelection, Republican Sen. William S. Cohen (left) discusses agricultural problems with a Fort Fairfield potato farmer. The 44-year-old former mayor of Bangor and Congressman had no difficulty winning a second Senate term.

MAINE

Incumbent Republican Sen. William S. Cohen, up for his first reelection bid, proved to be a most popular politician. Outpolling President Reagan, who easily carried the state by 336,113 votes to Walter Mondale's 212,190, Senator Cohen won slightly more than 400,000 of the 543,000 votes cast in the race with Elizabeth H. Mitchell (D).

Both of the state's incumbents in the U.S. House of Representatives were reelected. In the first district, Republican John R. McKernan received 180,702 votes to Democrat Barry J. Hobbins' 102,588; in the second district, Republican Olympia J. Snowe trounced Democrat Chipman Bull by 192,231 to 57,220. As expected, the Democrats retained control of both houses of the state legislature. If there was a surprise at the polls, it was the 60–40 margin of defeat for the state's Equal Rights Amendment.

At the end of his constitutionally limited two terms, Democratic Gov. Joseph Brennan will step down in 1986. Speculation about his possible successor is already a lively topic of political conversation. Reports indicate that Congressman McKernan is favored to enter the race for the Republicans, while the Democrats have a number of prospective candidates, including current Attorney General James E. Tierney and State Planning Office Director Richard E. Barringer.

Population Increase. During 1983 and the first half of 1984, Maine continued the gentle population increase that has seen the state's 1.1-million base (1980 census) gain a bit less than 1% each year for the past three years. While the south-coastal sections, especially Cumberland County, which includes Portland, were growing at rates above the state average, even the sparsely populated easternmost counties, Washington and Aroostook, reported net gains.

Economy. The economy improved during 1983–1984 throughout the state. The overall unemployment rate, according to State Planning Office economist Lloyd Irland, was 4.9%, more than two points less than the national average. In Cumberland County the rate was less than 3%, a figure that, according to Irland, indicates a labor shortage.

With most of Maine at work, workers' incomes grew at a rate that was eighth best in the nation. Helped by a robust summer tourist season in 1984 and a spirited increase in service and high-technology jobs that filled the gap left by the loss of some manufacturing, Maine has enjoyed, as Irland put it, "Slow, steady, and manageable growth."

In one pivotal industry, however, the news was not so cheerful. According to a 1983 U.S. Forest Service report on the 17 million acres (7

MAINE • Information Highlights

Area: 33,265 sq mi (86 156 km²).
Population (July 1, 1983 est.): 1,146,000.
Chief Cities (1980 census): Augusta, the capital, 21,819; Portland, 61,572; Lewiston, 40,481; Bangor, 31,643.
Government (1984): *Chief Officer*—governor, Joseph E. Brennan (D). *Legislature*—Senate, 33 members; House of Representatives, 151 members.
State Finances (fiscal year 1983): *Revenues,* $1,685,000,000; *expenditures,* $1,671,000,000.
Personal Income (1983): $11,282,000,000; per capita, $9,847.
Labor Force (May 1984): *Civilian labor force,* 554,500; *unemployed,* 36,200 (6.5% of total force).
Education: *Enrollment* (fall 1982)—public elementary schools, 146,848; public secondary, 65,138; colleges and universities (fall 1983) 53,347. *Public school expenditures* (1982–83), $484,743,995 ($2,458 per pupil).

million ha) of Maine timber, the state's spruce and fir trees are headed for trouble. Poor management, combined with several years of spruce budworm epidemics, has left Maine with a population of overage trees. Unless "miracle" remedies are found, says the Forest Service, the industry will face cutbacks in several years. Because the industry accounts for some 30% of the state's jobs, a pulp and paper slump will have far-reaching effects.

Baseball. Some 182,200 Maine baseball fans turned out to watch the new Maine Guides, the state's first professional baseball team (Triple-A), perform in their brand new ballpark at Old Orchard Beach. Even though 19 home games were rained out in April and May, the attendance exceeded expectations and may have helped the Guides reach the league championship play-offs.

JOHN N. COLE, *"Maine Times"*

MALAYSIA

On Dec. 15, 1983, the federal cabinet and the nine royal rulers of Malaysian states settled their constitutional dispute. They agreed on limiting the power of the paramount ruler (king) to deny approval of federal legislation, provided that no such restriction be applied to the veto power of individual rulers over bills passed by their own state assemblies. Afterward, Prime Minister Mahathir Mohamad and his supporters swept party elections of their United Malays National Organization (UMNO). Other parties in the ruling National Front coalition faced internal struggles.

Politics. In May, Prime Minister Mahathir was reelected UMNO president without a contest, while Deputy President Musa Hitam extended his 1981 victory margin over Finance Minister Tengku Razaleigh Hamzah. Past party-power broker Harun Idris received only 34 of the 1,279 votes cast. Mahathir supporters won in vice-presidency and supreme-council contests, and loyalist Anwar Ibrahim retained his position as head of UMNO Youth.

The Malaysian Chinese Association (MCA), the largest Chinese party in the National Front, split over charges by challenger Tan Koon Swan that supporters of party president Neo Yee Pan were registering phantom members for upcoming MCA elections. Neo's expulsion of Tan and his associates from the party rallied more than half of the delegates to support Tan's reinstatement. Leaders of the Gerakan, the other major Chinese party in the coalition, narrowly survived election challenges. In the East Malaysian states, the United Sabah National Organization (USNO) was expelled from the National Front, and the newly formed Parti Bansa Dayak Sarawak won sufficient seats in a state election to gain admittance to the front.

MALAYSIA • Information Highlights

Official Name: Malaysia.
Location: Southeast Asia.
Area: 128,400 sq mi (332 556 km²).
Population (mid-1984 est.): 15,300,000.
Chief City (1980 census): Kuala Lumpur, the capital, 937,875.
Government: *Head of state,* Sultan Mahmood Iskandar (elected Feb. 9, 1984). *Head of government,* Mahathir Mohamad, prime minister (took office July 1981). *Legislature*—Parliament: Dewan Negara (Senate) and Dewan Ra'ayat (House of Representatives).
Monetary Unit: Ringgit (Malaysian dollar) (2.344 ringgits equal U.S. $1, July 1984).
Gross Domestic Product (1982 U.S. $): $25,936,-000,000.
Economic Indexes (1983): *Consumer Prices* (1980 = 100), all items, 120.4; food, 121.7. *Industrial Production* (1975 = 100), 171.
Foreign Trade (1982 U.S. $): *Imports,* $13,987,-000,000; *exports,* $13,917,000,000.

Verbal religious attacks on the government and UMNO leaders, made by the opposition Parti Islam (PAS), led to the detention of four PAS members and the banning of PAS meetings in the northern states. A public debate between Parti Islam and the prime minister, scheduled to be televised nationally on November 11, was canceled by the king.

Government. The sultans of Johor and Perak, major protagonists for the royalty in the constitutional struggle, were expected to vie for election as paramount ruler for the next five-year term. But the death of Sultan Idris

In Kuala Lumpur April 26, Sultan Mahmood Iskandar knelt as he became Malaysia's new paramount ruler.

Sipa/Special Features

Shah of Perak, shortly before the election, eased the choice of Sultan Mahmood Iskandar of Johor for the kingship.

A July cabinet reorganization elevated younger Mahathir loyalists. Political newcomer and wealthy businessman Daim Zainuddin became finance minister, replacing Tengku Razaleigh who was moved down to trade and industry. Abdullah Badawi was named education minister, traditionally a potent power base, and Anwar Ibrahim moved from culture, youth, and sports to become agricultural minister.

The Economy. Malaysia's economy continued to rebound from the international recession, with real growth in 1984 predicted at more than 6.5%. The government introduced the Fifth Malaysia Plan, outlining development policies for 1985–89, and announced a new agricultural policy.

Faced with almost $1 billion (U.S.) in bad debts owed to a subsidiary of Bank Bumiputra Malaysia, the National Equity Corporation sold its 86.7% interest in the bank to the national petroleum company, Petronas. Under a government-devised plan, Petronas was to pay about $1 billion to compensate National Equity and recapitalize the bank.

K. MULLINER, *Ohio University*

MANITOBA

Legislation introduced in mid-1983 by the New Democratic Party (NDP) government to make Manitoba a bilingual province created a political storm that went unabated during 1984. In February, 3,000 members of a mostly rural group called Grassroots Manitoba met in Winnipeg to protest the extension of French-language services. Supporters of the Grassroots viewpoint included two former Liberal Party leaders, a former Progressive Conservative (PC) premier, and the Manitoba-Progressive (MP) leader. Andy Anstett, who had chaired the language-legislation hearing in late 1983, took charge of the language question in the Legislative Assembly. He made some changes in the proposed legislation but did not satisfy the opposition PCs, who used procedural delays to prevent a vote.

In the House of Commons on February 24, the federal PC leader Brian Mulroney and Liberal Prime Minister Pierre Elliott Trudeau strongly urged Manitobans to endorse French language rights. However, the Manitoba PCs continued their filibuster, and after 263 hours and 10 minutes of continuous division bell-ringing in the Legislature, the NDP provincial government was forced to prorogue the session, thus shelving their proposals for the time being. In his first press conference after entering the contest to succeed Trudeau as Liberal Party leader, John Turner seemed to endorse the position of the Manitoba PCs, who were at odds with their own federal leader.

Two weeks later, Mulroney spoke to the Manitoba PCs in Winnipeg. His own party members gave him a hostile reception. In the federal election campaign, Jack Murta and Charles Mayer, members of Parliament (MPs) who supported Mulroney's stand on the language issue, faced strong opposition from their constituency parties but were reelected. Candidates from the new, anti-French party, the "Confederation of Regions," finished second against them. In the federal election, the PC vote was the second lowest in the country, mainly because of the strong showing of COR candidates, who got 8% of the total. However, the PCs gained four seats. Manitoba's new parliamentary representation consists of 9 PCs, 1 Liberal, and 4 from the NDP, compared with 5 PCs, 2 Liberals, 7 NDP following the 1980 polling.

Prime Minister Mulroney chose four Manitobans for his new cabinet, including Murta and Mayer as ministers of state for multiculturalism and for the Canadian Wheat Board, respectively. In addition, Duff Roblin, who had encouraged French-language services and schools when he had been provincial premier (1958–67), became leader of the government in the Senate and Jake Epp was named minister of national health and welfare. Many observers felt that Mulroney was attempting to strengthen the pro-French wing of his party by these appointments.

In early October 1984 the federal Supreme Court was about to issue its decision on the validity of Manitoba's unilingual legislation, and on the need for statutes and services to be in both French and English.

Manitoba had three prominent visitors in 1984—Pope John Paul II, Queen Elizabeth II, and Prince Albert of Monaco.

MICHAEL KINNEAR
The University of Manitoba

MANITOBA • Information Highlights

Area: 251,000 sq mi (650 000 km²).
Population (April 1984 est.): 1,054,400.
Chief Cities (1981 census): Winnipeg, the capital, 564,473; Brandon, 36,242; Thompson, 14,288.
Government (1984): *Chief Officers*—lt. gov., Pearl McGonigal; premier, Howard Pawley (New Democratic Party); atty. gen., Roland Penner. *Legislature*—Legislative Assembly, 57 members.
Provincial Finances (1984–85 fiscal year budget): *Revenues,* $2,968,950,900; *expenditures,* $3,457,-626,900.
Personal Income (average weekly earnings, May 1984): $374.66.
Labor Force (July 1984, seasonally adjusted): *Employed workers,* 15 years of age and over, 473,000; *Unemployed* 40,000 (7.8%).
Education (1984–85): *Enrollment*—elementary and secondary schools, 216,420 pupils; postsecondary (1984–85)—universities, 35,580; community colleges (full-time), 3,700.
(All monetary figures are in Canadian dollars.)

MARYLAND

The year 1984 marked the 350th anniversary of the founding of the Free State of Maryland. In 1634 two ships, carrying some 200 persons, landed at St. Clement's Island in the Potomac River. Celebrations marking the anniversary were held in St. Marys City, the state's first capital, in 1984. The Duke and Duchess of Kent represented Great Britain.

Election. President Reagan captured Maryland's ten electoral votes by winning 52% of the state's popular vote. Walter Mondale carried only Baltimore and Prince Georges County, a Washington suburb. Heavy preelection registration shifted the state's traditional Democratic voter advantage of 3½ to 1 down to 3 to 1, but in Baltimore the Democratic edge widened from 8 to 1 to 10 to 1. Maryland voters returned seven incumbents, six of them Democrats, to the U.S. House of Representatives. Clarence Long (D), a 22-year veteran of the House, lost his seat in a close race to Helen Delich Bentley (R), a former newspaper reporter and federal maritime commissioner.

Legislative Activities. Acting on the findings of a commission headed by former Attorney General Benjamin Civiletti, the Maryland General Assembly authorized $616 million in state aid to local school systems over five years. The aid was intended to help poorer jurisdictions offer public education equal in quality to that provided by wealthier counties. In another development, a joint legislative committee recommended to Gov. Harry Hughes that Maryland's 17 community colleges receive $77.8 million in state funds in 1985, representing a 13.5% ($9.3 million) increase over 1984 levels. Also studied by the legislature were methods to control the cost of health care.

Chesapeake Bay. Designation of the Chesapeake Bay shoreline as a "critical area" subject to special state protection was the centerpiece of ten bay cleanup measures Governor Hughes pushed through the legislature in 1984. President Reagan toured the bay in July, and U.S. House Speaker Thomas P. O'Neill visited the area in September. Both acknowledged the importance of the bay for food production and as a waterway. Congress had approved some $10 million to start cleanup.

Endangered Striped Bass. In October, President Reagan signed a Maryland-backed bill banning fishing for striped bass (rockfish) in Atlantic Coast states that fail to reduce catches of the endangered fish by 55%. The bill was passed after Governor Hughes imposed a ban on striped bass fishing in Maryland waters, effective Jan. 1, 1985, because bass stocks in the Chesapeake Bay were dangerously low. According to state natural resources officials, the commercial harvest of rockfish dropped from 5 million pounds (2.3 million kg) to 360,000 pounds (163 296 kg) in ten years.

MARYLAND · Information Highlights

Area: 10,460 sq mi (27 092 km²).
Population (July 1, 1983 est.): 4,304,000.
Chief Cities (1980 census): Annapolis, the capital, 31,740; Baltimore (July 1, 1982 est.), 774,113; Rockville, 43,811.
Government (1984): *Chief Officers—governor*, Harry R. Hughes (D); lt. gov., J. Joseph Curran, Jr. (D). *General Assembly*—Senate, 47 members; House of Delegates, 141 members.
State Finances (fiscal year 1983): *Revenues*, $6,598,000,000; *expenditures*, $6,921,000,000.
Personal Income (1983): $55,932,000,000; per capita, $12,994.
Labor Force (May 1984): *Civilian labor force*, 2,223,000; *unemployed*, 108,800 (4.9% of total force).
Education: *Enrollment* (fall 1982)—public elementary schools, 461,794; public secondary, 237,407; colleges and universities (fall 1983), 239,232. *Public school expenditures* (1982–83), $2,118,972,417 ($3,445 per pupil).

Naval Academy Scholar. Eight years after women were admitted to U.S. service academies, Midshipman Kristine Holderied of Woodbine, MD, an oceanography major with a 3.88 grade-point average, was first among 1,004 graduates at the U.S. Naval Academy in Annapolis.

The Colts Bolt. The Baltimore Colts of the National Football League secretly left the city in the middle of a March night and moved to Indianapolis, to which owner Robert Irsay transferred his franchise. City, state, and private organizations went to court to try to reverse the change.

PEGGY CUNNINGHAM
"Baltimore News American"

MASSACHUSETTS

Massachusetts joined in President Reagan's spectacular victory over Walter Mondale in the 1984 election. Some political analysts concluded that the president's personal popularity, coupled with the state's economic health (in September the unemployment rate was 4.2%, a 14-year low), led many voters to support him while remaining loyal to the dominant Democratic Party in state and local contests.

Senate Race. The race that drew the most attention was that for the U.S. Senate seat held by retiring Democrat Paul E. Tsongas. The Democratic contenders included Lt. Gov. John Kerry, Secretary of State Michael Connolly, former state House Speaker David Bartley, and Congressmen James Shannon and Edward Markey. Eliot Richardson, a former U.S. attorney general, and Raymond Shamie, a political newcomer and owner of a high-technology firm, were the Republican candidates in the September primary. Shamie easily defeated Richardson, the candidate of the Republican "Old Guard," while Kerry was the narrow winner among the Democrats. Republican leaders had high hopes for Shamie's candidacy,

Massachusetts' Lt. Gov. John F. Kerry (D), 40-year-old former county prosecutor and leader of the Vietnam Veterans Against the War, was elected to the U.S. Senate by a 10% margin.

but even a last-minute appearance in Boston by President Reagan on November 1 failed to marshal enough votes, and Kerry easily defeated Shamie after an occasionally bitter campaign.

Congressional Races. Another race attracted wide attention when Democrat Gerry Studds ran for reelection to the U.S. House of Representatives for a seventh term. Studds had been censured by the House in 1983 for having had sexual relations with a male congressional page. However, his popularity in his district overcame the issue, and he won reelection.

The 11-member Massachusetts congressional membership was returned nearly unchanged, with ten Democrats and one Republican. All the members but one, Chester G. Atkins (D), were incumbent candidates.

Speakership Fight. Republicans picked up six seats in the state House of Representatives, —their largest gain since 1964—but the House remained overwhelmingly Democratic: 126 to 34. Political observers closely watched the battle for the post of speaker of the House—a battle that had been going on all year long. The conflict pitted Speaker Thomas W. McGee against George Keverian, whom McGee removed as majority leader when Keverian announced his candidacy for the speaker's position. McGee, who had served as speaker for ten years, longer than anyone, has been a controversial figure in recent years. The speaker wields enormous authority in the House, and some members complained that McGee was insensitive to their needs.

Keverian accused McGee of reneging on an agreement whereby McGee would step down, allowing Keverian to succeed him. The fight over the speakership extended to the fall elections, in which both sides attempted to have supporters elected. At year's end, Keverian appeared to have an edge when the House votes on the issue in January 1985.

Other Events. In August, disturbances occurred in Lawrence, a city of 63,000 north of Boston, near the New Hampshire border. Fifteen persons were injured and 20 arrested in the disorders, which went on for several nights until a curfew was imposed over a ten-block area. The conflict involved newly arrived Hispanics, who clashed with long-time residents, many of whom were of French-Canadian extraction.

A new archbishop was appointed to head the archdiocese of Boston, one of the largest in the country. Bernard F. Law assumed the post in March, succeeding Humberto Cardinal Medeiros, who died in 1983.

In November, in an unusual lawsuit, British actress Vanessa Redgrave won damages of $100,000 from the Boston Symphony Orchestra in a breach of contract case. Her appearance as narrator with the orchestra was canceled after a storm of protest arose from her outspoken political views, especially her support of the Palestine Liberation Organization. The jury, however, did not find that her civil rights had been violated, as Redgrave's suit claimed.

Also in November, Gov. Michael Dukakis signed a bill controlling activities in Massachusetts' taverns and bars to reduce the toll from drunken driving. Among the provisions are a prohibition against "happy hours" and beer-drinking contests.

HARVEY BOULAY, *Rogerson House*

MASSACHUSETTS • Information Highlights

Area: 8,284 sq mi (21 456 km²).
Population (July 1, 1983 est.): 5,767,000.
Chief Cities (July 1, 1982 est.): Boston, the capital, 560,847; Worcester, 161,049; Springfield, 151,-586.
Government (1984): *Chief Officers*—governor, Michael S. Dukakis (D); lt. gov., John F. Kerry (D). *General Court*—Senate, 40 members; House of Representatives, 160 members.
State Finances (fiscal year 1983): *Revenues,* $9,383,000,000; *expenditures,* $9,332,000,000.
Personal Income (1983): $76,489,000,000; per capita, $13,264.
Labor Force (May 1984): *Civilian labor force,* 3,018,800; *unemployed,* 119,600 (4.0% of total force).
Education: *Enrollment* (fall 1982)—public elementary schools, 596,990; public secondary, 311,994; colleges and universities (fall 1983), 423,348. *Public school expenditures* (1982–83), $2,792,652,742 ($3,378 per pupil).

MEDICINE AND HEALTH

The pace of medical advances continues to quicken. But these advances are not without cost. According to a report by the Congressional Office of Technology Assessment, the use of medical technologies—drugs, devices, and medical and surgical procedures—has significantly affected Medicare costs. Payments for each Medicare enrollee rose 107% between 1977 and 1982. Although inflation was primarily responsible, one quarter of the increase was due to expanded use of medical technology.

One of the costliest—as well as one of the most dramatic—modern medical procedures is the still highly experimental implantation of a permanent artificial heart. On Nov. 25, 1984, doctors at the Humana Heart Institute in Louisville, KY, removed the diseased heart of 52-year-old William Schroeder and replaced it with a plastic-and-metal pump. The 6½-hour operation was performed by a 17-member surgical team headed by Dr. William DeVries. It was only the second such operation. The first, also performed by DeVries, took place in December 1982. That patient, Barney Clark, survived for 112 days with the implant.

The heart implanted in Schroeder was a modified version of the heart used in Clark. Designed by Dr. Robert Jarvik, a bioengineer at the University of Utah, it consists of two hollow chambers, each with a flexible plastic diaphragm. These chambers replace the natural heart ventricles (the lower, pumping chambers of the heart). Two plastic air hoses, one from each ventricle, connect the heart to an external power system. These hoses carry compressed air to the ventricles, alternately swelling and collapsing the diaphragms, which causes them to pump blood through the pulmonary arteries to the lungs and through the aorta to the rest of the body.

Prior to the operation, Schroeder suffered from congestive heart failure so severe that he was expected to die within days. He made an excellent recovery from the surgery, with the only serious setback on December 13, when he suffered three small strokes. But tests showed no problem with the artificial heart, and Schroeder's "slow, steady" recovery from the strokes led doctors to predict that he could be released from the hospital some time in early 1985.

Though offering many individuals hope for improved lives, artificial heart implants and other new medical technologies also raise profound social, ethical, and moral issues. There is a growing awareness in the medical community and the general public to confront and come to grips with such issues.

In Vitro Fertilization. In March 1984 the first baby produced from a frozen embryo—a 5½-lb (2.5-kg) girl—was born in Melbourne, Australia. The birth occurred following in vitro fertilization, a procedure by which an egg is removed from the woman's womb and fertilized in a laboratory dish. The embryo was then frozen, reportedly for two months, before being implanted in the woman's uterus.

The issue of hereditary rights of frozen embryos arose after a wealthy Los Angeles couple died in a plane crash, leaving two frozen embryos at a Melbourne clinic. Are doctors ethically obliged to try to bring such embryos to birth by implanting them in surrogate mothers? Do the embryos have rights of inheritance from the people who produced them?

Another dilemma is raised by the low success rate of in vitro fertilization when only one egg at a time is taken, fertilized, and implanted. With drugs, however, a woman can produce a number of eggs at one time. When mixed with semen, several embryos suitable for implantation may result. Should all viable embryos be implanted, even if the woman only wants one child? What should be done with "spare" embryos? Should they be used for research?

Pediatrics. Many premature infants must be given oxygen because they have trouble breathing. Unfortunately, the use of oxygen can leave these babies with eye damage and lung disorders. Studies indicated that the babies would benefit from vitamin E. However, the smallest and sickest of the babies could be treated only intravenously. Thus, when O'-Neal, Jones & Feldman Pharmaceuticals introduced E-Ferol Aqueous Solution in late 1983, doctors had high hopes of success. By April 1984, however, the company had recalled the solution, and government groups were scheduling hearings into charges that it was the cause of 38 infant deaths. The company had not sought approval from the Food & Drug Administration (FDA) for E-Ferol since, it claimed, the intravenous form was not a new drug but a variation of vitamin E preparations long on the market. Because the company did not seek FDA approval, it did not have to subject the drug to clinical trials to demonstrate that it was safe and effective.

In 1982 the FDA gave approval to Accutane, a drug that very effectively combats a severe skin disorder known as cystic acne. Because the drug was known to cause birth defects, the manufacturer, Roche Laboratories, warned that "patients who are pregnant or intend to become pregnant should not receive Accutane." Nonetheless, by mid-1984 there were at least 28 known cases of young women who delivered babies with severe birth defects that were almost certainly caused by the medication. Accutane is now labeled with red warning stickers, and dermatologists have been cautioned against prescribing the drug to sexually active women.

AIDS. French and U.S. scientists announced in April that they had isolated viruses thought

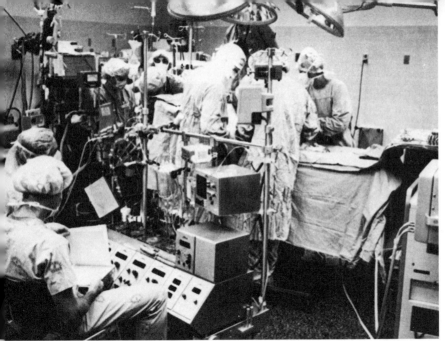

One of the most publicized and controversial stories of 1984 was the implantation of a baboon heart into a 12-day-old girl at Loma Linda (CA) University Medical Center. Baby Fae, as she was known, died 20 days later from transplant rejection.

AP/Wide World

to cause Acquired Immune Deficiency Syndrome (AIDS), a usually fatal disease that destroys the body's ability to fight infection. Scientists at the Pasteur Institute in Paris announced the discovery of a virus called LAV (lymphadenopathy-associated virus). Scientists at the U.S. National Cancer Institute called the virus they found HTLV-3 (human T-lymphotropic retrovirus 3). It was widely believed that the two viruses would eventually prove to be one and the same.

One of the groups primarily at risk of AIDS includes hemophiliacs, who risk getting the disease through blood transfusions from infected donors. Isolating the virus led to development of a test that can detect the virus in victims before symptoms arise and indicate if donated blood supplies are contaminated with the virus. The discovery also spurred work on a preventive vaccine.

Transplants. Similar to AIDS is an inherited disease called severe combined immunodeficiency (SCID). Children born with this rare illness can be killed by even the mildest cold virus. One such child, known to the public only as David, was born in 1971 and immediately placed in sterile isolation. He lived for 12 years in plastic enclosures, far longer than any other victim of the disease. His only hope of a normal life was a transplant of bone marrow cells. These cells produce the immune-system cells that SCID victims lack. In October 1983, David received specially treated bone marrow from his healthy sister. Whether the transplant was a success was never proven, for in February 1984 David became ill and needed fluids given intravenously, which could not be done in his plastic bubble chamber. So for the first time in his life, the "Bubble Boy" moved out of a sterile environment and was able to hug and kiss

his parents. But by February 22, David was dead, apparently of heart failure caused by unexplained fluid accumulation.

At least six other children with SCID have received marrow transplants. For at least one, T.J. Davis, the transplant appeared to be "working perfectly" in October, eight months after the operation.

On October 26, physicians at Loma Linda University Medical Center in California implanted a baboon heart in a 12-day-old girl named Baby Fae. (Her real name was not made public.) Only four ape-to-human heart transplants had been performed previously, all in adults. The longest–living of those recipients died 3½ days after the operation. Baby Fae was born with an underdeveloped heart and, according to her doctors, faced certain death without a transplant. She became the youngest person ever to get a heart transplant. She passed the critical post-operation period of 7 to 10 days without showing signs of rejecting the transplant. After two weeks, however, the infant began experiencing organ rejection, which finally led to her death on the 20th day. Dr. Leonard L. Bailey, who performed the surgery, said he would attempt another baboon heart transplant.

Medical Genetics. Genetic Systems, a biotechnology research firm based in Seattle, reported that it had produced the first commercial levels of highly specific antibodies called human monoclonal antibodies. These antibodies, made by cloned cells, attack disease organisms that cannot be overcome by the body's own antibodies or on which vaccines cannot be used. Their potential value, in both screening and treating disease, is considerable.

Genentec, a California firm, announced that it had artificially produced Factor VIII, a pro-

Trauma and Trauma Centers

One of the most serious and long-neglected public-health problems today is trauma: wounds caused by physical injury sustained in such events as vehicular and industrial accidents, firearm discharge, and suicide and homicide attempts. Many trauma incidents are relatively minor and do not require hospitalization. And, of those that are serious, only a small percentage are life threatening. Still, the number of such cases is substantial.

A study conducted by Eric Muñoz, assistant professor of surgery at State University of New York at Stony Brook, showed that in fiscal 1982 some 8 million Americans sustained trauma injuries and, of these, approximately 120,000 died. Trauma is the leading cause of death for Americans between the ages of one and 38. And according to Donald D. Trunkey, professor of surgery at the University of California at San Francisco School of Medicine, "trauma patients currently take up a total of about 19 million hospital days per year in the United States, more than the number needed by all heart-disease patients and four times the number needed by all cancer patients."

The economic costs are staggering. Muñoz calculated that trauma cost the United States approximately $61 billion in fiscal 1982. This included some $19 billion for medical expenses and more than $41 billion in lost wages. (The latter figure is as high as it is because many of those injured are just beginning their most productive work years.)

In an effort to reduce death rates, illness, disability, and costs, U.S. emergency medical systems are implementing major changes in their approach to trauma patients. The focal point of these changes is the trauma center—a regional, easily accessible hospital designed to provide around-the-clock care for critically injured patients. An in-house team of physicians and supporting staff enable the center to provide prompt, comprehensive treatment, including surgery if needed, to patients with life-threatening traumatic injuries.

Trauma Deaths. Numerous studies show that a significant number of trauma fatalities can be prevented if proper treatment occurs in "the golden hour," the time immediately following injury. Trauma deaths fall into three main categories. In the first, characterized as "immediate deaths," death occurs very soon after injury and results from severe damage to the nervous or circulatory system. Few of these victims could be saved, even under ideal medical conditions.

In the second category, "early deaths," death occurs within a few hours after injury.

The patients generally die from injuries that are treatable if procedures are instituted promptly. Various U.S. studies indicate that 30 to 40% of the deaths in this category can be prevented. After five trauma centers were established in Orange county, California, preventable deaths dropped from more than 70% to only 12%. Furthermore, whereas in 1974 only 20% of the trauma patients with surgically correctable problems received appropriate treatment, in 1980–81, after the trauma centers were established, 82% received treatment.

In the third category, "late deaths," death occurs days or even weeks after injury, usually from infection or multiple organ failure. In these mortalities, promptness of treatment generally is not a significant factor.

Trauma-Care System. A well-organized trauma-care system consists of much more than a trauma center. It begins with highly skilled in-field treatment of the victim by paramedics. Rapid transport of the patient to the trauma center is essential. Following surgery and other treatment, it is important to monitor the patient closely and to provide needed rehabilitation programs.

West Germany has established a particularly successful regional trauma-care system. Trauma centers are located along the nation's main highways. In fact, it is estimated that 90% of the West German population is within 15 minutes of such a center.

Trauma specialists also stress the importance of trauma prevention. Trunkey states that "perhaps as many as 40% of all deaths from trauma could be averted by the introduction of various prevention programs." Among the steps recommended are handgun control, efforts to reduce drunk driving, and legislation that mandates the use of automobile seat belts and motorcycle helmets. Data show that such steps effectively reduce trauma deaths and injuries. For example, a study in Nottinghamshire, England, showed that the introduction of legislation requiring the use of seat belts by drivers and front-seat passengers resulted in a 52% decrease in injuries and an 80% decrease in deaths. In contrast, after 27 U.S. states repealed or weakened their motorcycle-helmet laws, a 40% increase in motorcycle-accident mortalities in those states followed.

Trauma surgeons and others have developed a campaign to establish a trauma institute within the National Institutes of Health (NIH). Supporters believe that such a facility would offer "visibility, direction, and coordination" to the trauma field.

JENNY TESAR

tein that is missing or deficient in hemophiliacs. Currently, these people depend on donated blood as their source of Factor VIII.

Hepatitis. An experimental vaccine produced through gene-splicing methods has given healthy adults immunity to the virus that causes hepatitis B (formerly called serum hepatitis), a major cause of liver disease. The vaccine produced protective antibodies against the virus in 37 volunteers. The antibody levels were comparable to those obtained with the conventional vaccine, which is made from donated blood.

A team of U.S. and Venezuelan researchers discovered a lethal form of hepatitis caused by two viruses that act in concert in a manner never previously observed. The disease, called delta hepatitis, is due to a virus that cannot cause infection by itself. But when this virus interacts, or piggybacks, with the hepatitis B virus, the resulting illness can be more malevolent than that caused by hepatitis B virus alone. The discovery raises "an ominous specter for much of the world," said the researchers. They estimated that hundreds of thousands of people have delta hepatitis and that 200 million others may be at high risk because they have hepatitis B or are latent carriers of it.

Scientists from the FDA and the National Institutes of Health reported that they had identified the virus that causes non-A, non-B hepatitis. This is the type of hepatitis most commonly transmitted through blood transfusions. It accounts for more than 100,000 cases per year in the United States alone. The discovery is expected to lead to the development of a screening test to identify contaminated blood supplies.

Cancer. Studies continue to link diet and cancer. A study of 632 women conducted by scientists at the National Cancer Institute indicated that frequent consumption of fruits and vegetables helped protect against developing cancers of the mouth and throat.

The American Cancer Society issued new dietary guidelines, for the first time making explicit recommendations as to foods Americans should eat to prevent cancer. The society urged people to eat foods high in fiber and vitamins A and C, such as whole grains, fruits, and vegetables of the cabbage family. It also suggested that people avoid obesity, eat less fat, eat cured and smoked foods only in moderation, and limit alcohol intake.

The Centers for Disease Control (CDC) also reported that lung cancer will soon replace breast cancer as the leading cause of cancer deaths among women in the United States. The vast majority of lung cancer cases are caused by cigarette smoking, making the lung cancer epidemic "especially tragic because it is preventable," said the CDC.

A growing number of studies confirm that "passive" smoking also causes lung cancer.

The U.S. Environmental Protection Agency estimated that 500 to 5,000 nonsmoking Americans die each year of lung cancer caused by other people's cigarettes. This makes "passive" smoke the nation's most dangerous airborne carcinogen.

Researchers at the University of Southern California reported that the risk of developing cancer of the colon decreased as job activity increased. The researchers grouped 2,950 colon cancer patients into three job categories: sedentary jobs, moderate-activity jobs, and high-activity jobs. Men with sedentary jobs were found to have a 60% greater risk of developing colon cancer than men with active jobs.

A new screening test for liver cancer offers hope that tumors can be discovered soon enough to be removed surgically, thereby allowing long-term survival. The cancer, which is caused by the hepatitis B virus, is widespread in Asia and Africa. Usually, it cannot be detected until late in development.

A 1983 study came under criticism after researchers at the CDC and Boston University were unable to substantiate the results. The study reported that women who use birth control pills containing high levels of progestin ran an increased risk of developing breast cancer. "We don't feel the link . . . has been established," said a member of the FDA. Nonetheless, the FDA recommended that women who take oral contraceptives should ask their physicians to prescribe pills with the lowest possible dose of progestin that is effective in preventing pregnancy.

Heart Disease. Based on the recommendations of a committee of experts convened by the National Heart, Lung, and Blood Institute, the federal government recommended that greater emphasis be placed on nondrug treatments for high blood pressure (hypertension). The experts urged that therapies such as diet, exercise, and behavior modificaton be "pursued aggressively" in treating mild cases of the disease. They also suggested that such therapies be used as an adjunct in treating people with more severe hypertension. "We're responding to a lot of underlying concern about the toxicity of anti-hypertensive drugs and their side effects," explained Harriet Dunstan, chairperson of the committee. "There is also a growing appreciation of the fact that obesity and hypertension are closely related."

A ten-year federal study, the Lipid Research Clinics Coronary Primary Prevention Trial, followed 3,806 men with extremely high levels of cholesterol in their bloodstream. All the men went on a low-cholesterol diet. In addition, half of them were given an anticholesterol drug, called cholestyramine resin. Men in both groups significantly reduced their risk of heart disease, but those who received the drug had 24% fewer fatal heart attacks than those on the diet alone. They also had 19% fewer nonfatal heart attacks, 20% less pain from angina, and 21% fewer operations related to heart disease.

Contrary to earlier reports, findings from the Framingham Heart Study indicate that postmenopausal women who use estrogens have a 50% greater risk than nonusers of developing heart disease or suffering a stroke. Estrogens are frequently prescribed to postmenopausal women to relieve menopausal symptoms and to protect against bone loss.

Because they often confuse heart attack symptoms with indigestion, many victims of heart attacks do not get to the hospital as quickly as they should. As a result, treatment is delayed and may be ineffective. A study commissioned by the National Heart, Lung, and Blood Institute found that beta blockers, drugs commonly used to reduce heart muscle damage resulting from a heart attack, are ineffective if not given within the first four hours after an attack. Equally perturbing is the finding by the Framingham Heart Study that some 30% of all heart attacks go undetected by their victims. The attacks eventually show up on routine cardioelectrograms. Such quiet seizures, however, are just as likely as painful ones to foreshadow serious cardiac problems in later years.

Physical Fitness. The possible hazards of strenuous exercise became front-page news when James Fixx, author of *The Complete Book of Running* and a proponent of physical fitness, died of a heart attack while jogging. Fixx, who had a family history of heart disease, had apparently ignored chest tightness and other indications that he was suffering from severely clogged coronary arteries.

Researchers at Harvard and Stanford universities who have followed nearly 17,000 men since 1960 reported that inactivity—even among former varsity athletes—led to heart and lung diseases that shorten lives. "We can now prove that large numbers of Americans are dying from sitting on their behinds," said Dr. Bruce Dan.

According to scientists at the universities of Washington and North Carolina, men who engage in strenuous exercise reduce their risk of heart attack. The risk of cardiac arrest among men who exercise at least 20 minutes per week was only 40% that of more sedentary men. Among all groups, cardiac arrest was more common during exercise than at other times. But the more the men exercised, the less likely they were to suffer a heart attack during workouts. Those who exercised more than 2 hours and 20 minutes per week were five times as likely to suffer cardiac arrest during exercise than at other times. The likelihood was 56 times higher for men who exercised less than 20 minutes per week.

JENNY TESAR
Free-lance Science Writer

Dentistry

Dr. Donald E. Bentley, 1984 president of the American Dental Association (ADA), told a Senate subcommittee that dental prepayment coverage has encouraged cost-sharing by patients and proved cost-effective through required copayments and deductibles. He said that workplace dental plans might be a model for hospital and medical plans that have concentrated on first-dollar coverage, since the cost of dental care has increased at less than the cost of all health care services measured by the Consumer Price Index.

DNA Technology. Using recombinant DNA technology, a research team from the University of Southern California School of Dentistry, Los Angeles, has identified one of four genes responsible for the production of tooth enamel in humans. This research could eventually lead to the "cloning" of natural fillings for decayed teeth. Tooth enamel is produced by a careful blend of four different proteins—three amelogenins and one enamelin—each manufactured by its own gene. Drs. Malcolm Snead and Harold Slavkin isolated the tissues that produce these proteins and extracted the messenger RNA (mRNA). In studies with mice, they used the newly isolated mRNA to prepare a gene identical to the largest amelogenin. They spliced this mouse gene onto a strain of a common yeast, so that these living cell factories will begin to manufacture the enamel protein as programmed by the artificial genetic machinery. The investigators hope that this method will produce carbon copies of the mouse amelogenin protein.

Periodontal Disease. A powerful form of an over-the-counter pain killer may be a new weapon against periodontal, or gum, disease. This condition erodes the bone that supports the teeth and is a major cause of tooth loss. Researchers at the Harvard University School of Dental Medicine have found that the new drug, flurbiprofen, has reduced tooth loss in dogs by 66%. Flurbiprofen is a more potent version of ibuprofen, which was approved in 1984 for over-the-counter sales and has been used by prescription for ten years to treat arthritis and other problems.

Video Games and Dental Fear. What do video games and Buster Keaton have in common? When it comes to taking the anxiety out of dental treatment, both work equally well. Dental patients who played electronic Ping-Pong or viewed a montage of comedy film clips while having their teeth filled experienced less stress than did patients who merely listened to an audio tape of comedy routines, says Dr. Sait K. Seyrek of the School of Dentistry at the State University of New York at Buffalo. "We expected the two video conditions to be more distracting than the comedy tape. But we also expected the video game to be more distracting than the comedy film, which wasn't the case. Contrary to previous theory, distraction involving the performance of a motor task isn't necessary to lower dental anxiety." Dr. Seyrek and his colleague Dr. Norman L. Corah, an authority on behavioral science, concluded that the key ingredient in distraction is physiological arousal. By attaching electrodes to patient's fingers during treatment, they discovered that the video game and video comedy patients showed higher levels of physiological arousal than both the audio control groups. In fact, the highest levels were found in those watching the comedy films.

Soft Drinks and Tooth Decay. Can frequent consumption of soft drinks be detrimental to dental health? Yes, say Drs. A. I. Ismail, B. A. Burt, and S. A. Eklund of the School of Public Health, University of Michigan, Ann Arbor. Their research has shown that children and young adults reporting frequent consumption of soft drinks were at an increased risk of having high dental decay scores, even after accounting for differences in consumption of other sugary foods between those with low- and high-caries-causing capabilities. The scientists stressed that these findings challenge the belief that only highly retentive foods can be cariogenic and reinforce the concept that children should curb their consumption of soft drinks.

Lou Joseph, *Hill and Knowlton*

Mental Health

A skin test that may detect a genetic vulnerability to manic-depressive illness and related mood disorders that afflict an estimated 15 million Americans was announced by federal scientists in July. The test measures the density, in skin cells, of chemical receptors for the neurotransmitter acetylcholine, a substance known to be implicated in depressive illnesses. Skin cells, or fibroblasts, are used because of their accessibility for tests, as opposed to brain cells. Fibroblasts contain many of the same chemicals and receptors as brain cells because they share a common evolutionary origin. The test was developed on the basis of studies that showed that patients and their relatives with a history of affective illness had more receptors for acetylcholine in their skin cells than never-depressed relatives and normal persons participating in the study.

Drs. N. Suzan Nadi, John Nurnberger, and Elliot Gershon, who conducted the study at the National Institute of Mental Health (NIMH), said the findings offer the strongest evidence available to date of a specific genetic mechanism for affective illness. Of particular interest to the researchers is the test's potential for detecting risk for depression among children and adolescents, age groups in which symptoms of the illness may be masked by normal turmoils of growing up or by alcohol or drug abuse. For those with the inherited predisposition, doctors will be able to intervene earlier and more effectively. Early intervention assumes added significance in light of the alarming rise in suicide rates among American adolescents and young adults. Suicide is now the second leading cause of death in the 15- to 24-year-old age group.

Epidemiology. The results of the most comprehensive survey of mental disorders ever conducted in the United States reveal that about a fifth of all Americans suffer from at least one psychiatric disorder in a given six-month period. The study corrects the long-held but incorrect notion that women have higher rates of mental illness than men. Data indicate that rates between the sexes are comparable, but that men and women usually develop different types of illnesses.

The survey also found that fewer than 20% of Americans with a diagnosis of mental illness over the previous six months had received any treatment. Of those who were treated, most sought help from a general physician rather than a psychiatrist or other mental-health specialist.

The results indicate that anxiety disorders, which include phobias, panic disorder, and obsessive-compulsive behavior, are the most common forms of illness, affecting between 7 and 15% of randomly sampled respondents. Six to 7% of the population abuse alcohol or drugs, and 4 to 5% suffer affective disorders, such as depression and manic-depressive illness. The schizophrenic disorders, which can be among the most disabling forms of mental illness, affect 1% of the population.

The NIMH study, which is being conducted in collaboration with researchers in five areas around the country, is the first such survey to apply research-based criteria for mental illness to symptoms reported by study participants. A second phase of the project will attempt to define factors that place people at risk for developing disorders.

Psychic Stress in Children. A four- to five-year follow-up study of 25 children who had been kidnapped from their Chowchilla, CA, school bus in 1976 and held in a buried moving van for 16 hours before they escaped refuted the notion that children respond more flexibly than adults to a psychic trauma. Dr. Lenore Terr of the University of California found that, with few exceptions, the victimized children developed a "philosophical pessimism." Contrary to the bravado they expressed, the children were not toughened by the experience but "simply had narrowed their spheres of concern to their own rooms at night, to the local disasters in their home towns, and to other kidnap victims around the world," Dr. Terr reported.

Larry B. Silver, *Acting Director*
National Institute of Mental Health

METEOROLOGY

In addition to studying such phenomena as acid rain and wind shear, meteorologists in 1984 continued to utilize new instruments and make important advances in basic atmospheric measurement and weather forecasting.

Acid Rain. Joining fundamental chemical process equations with proven mathematical models of atmospheric circulations, meteorologists in 1984 launched a project to investigate computer simulation of the acid rain problem in the United States. Based on measurements of acidity in streams, other scientists reported that acid precipitation has steadied or slightly declined in the northeastern United States while increasing in most other regions of the country. Researchers also were investigating whether chemicals rising from the Gulf of Mexico and the Caribbean Sea help create acid rain in the United States.

Wind Shear. Sharp variations of wind with height, called wind shear, is a factor in the safety of aircraft landings and takeoffs. In 1984, three panels of the National Research Council were assessing current understandings of low-altitude wind shear, evaluating the use of wind shear-detection systems, and studying aircraft performance at low altitudes. The close of 1983 found about 60 major U.S. airports equipped with operational Low Level Wind Shear Alert Systems, with about 50 more scheduled for fitting by 1985. These systems have been a positive influence in averting potentially disastrous landing and takeoff situations related to adverse weather.

Atmospheric Measurement. A variety of new instruments are helping meteorologists make more accurate and reliable measurements of atmospheric phenomena. A laser-beam sensing device capable of distinguishing between rain and snow has been developed for use at unmanned weather stations. Dual-polarization radar may provide better estimates of rainfall amounts. Pulsed Doppler radar and coherent pulsed Doppler lidar both have been deployed in research aircraft to measure atmospheric winds from a roving platform. The U.S. National Oceanic and Atmospheric Administration (NOAA) announced that a laser-beam instrument for measuring winds globally may be placed aboard a weather satellite before 1990. And NOAA also announced plans to replace its aging network of operational radar with 145 new and more sophisticated radar using the Doppler technique. Meanwhile, a group of meteorological researchers planned to investigate the use of Doppler radar for observing the complete three-dimensional wind, temperature, pressure, and turbulence characteristics of the atmosphere's lowest mile.

An experimental automatic, self-contained weather station, housed in a standard 3m x 3m x 6m ship container, in 1984 completed very successful tests aboard commercial ships traversing the Pacific and North Atlantic oceans.

And a new network of lightning detectors, covering the region from Maine to North Carolina and as far west as Ohio, now provides useful information to air traffic controllers for routing commercial airliners away from lightning hazards.

Forecasting. Because of rapid population increases along the Atlantic and Gulf coasts, the evacuation time now required for high-population areas coming under risk of hurricane damage may exceed the maximum feasible warning time for hurricane forecasting techniques. Consequently, the Federal Emergency Management Agency and NOAA began working closely with state and local officials to develop operational procedures to relocate efficiently the millions of citizens at risk when a hurricane threatens.

In the area of tornado forecasting, NOAA's National Severe Storms Forecast Center reported a 20% increase in forecast accuracy with the use of new weather-satellite and computer-analysis tools. (*See* pages 50–54.)

According to a 1984 survey, only slightly more than half of U.S. daily newspapers print the official winter forecasts of the National Weather Service.

Climate and Weather. Four teams of meteorologists embarked on a study of ice-sheet behavior in West Antarctica and its effect on, and interactions with, global climate. The West Antarctic ice sheet is about four times the size of Texas and averages 1 830 m (6,000 ft) thick.

Research on seasonal atmospheric variability has shown that, because of differences in land/ocean distribution, surface temperature lags behind the seasonal solar cycle by about 28 days over the U.S. land mass, about 33 days over middle latitudes in the whole Northern Hemisphere, and about 44 days over middle latitudes in the whole Southern Hemisphere.

Arctic "winter hurricanes" also were under study by NOAA scientists. Like their tropical counterparts, typical major polar storms have a spiral cloud pattern, record winds in excess of 75 mph (121km/h), and may develop an eye.

Other Developments. The world's largest and most powerful wind-energy gathering turbines were dedicated in 1984 at Medicine Bow, WY. Plans call for a regional network of such turbines, capable of providing the average power requirements of 35,000 homes.

Finally, using computer models of the earth's atmosphere, U.S. and Soviet climatologists worked together in simulating the climatic effects of nuclear war. They concluded that the smoke and particulates from burning cities would so shield the earth from sunlight that the planet would be plunged into a long-term "nuclear winter" similar to the Ice Ages.

OWEN E. THOMPSON, *University of Maryland*

The Weather Year

December 1983–February 1984. Winter season temperatures were 2–4°F (1–2°C) below average throughout most of the United States. The Northeast and Southwest were slightly warmer than average, while the northern and central Rockies were colder. Precipitation was copious throughout the Rocky Mountains and the Southeast.

Arctic air covered much of the United States east of the Rockies during December. Record-breaking cold during the Christmas holidays froze citrus and vegetable crops in southern Texas and parts of Florida, as well as in northeastern Mexico, and triggered a significant fish kill along the inland waterways of the Gulf of Mexico. On Christmas Eve, Miles City, MT, recorded the highest surface atmosphere pressure ever measured in the continental United States.

January temperatures averaged 6–10°F (3–5°C) above normal in the northern Plains and along the West Coast. Precipitation was scarce except in the Rocky Mountains and coastal Southeast.

Unseasonably mild weather continued over the northern Plains in February and spread to the central Plains and Atlantic seaboard. Temperatures averaged 6–10°F (3–5°C) above normal in these regions. Abnormally heavy precipitation fell in the Appalachians, the western Great Lakes, and along an axis from western Oregon to central Missouri. At month's end, a major winter storm dumped considerable snow from the Plains through the Great Lakes to New England.

In Europe, Christmas seemed more like a spring holiday, with temperatures as high as 71°F (22°C) in Frankfurt, West Germany. Several major European cities broke high temperature records. Precipitation was heavy throughout Italy, Turkey, and Greece. In January, precipitation continued above average in England and western Europe. Heavy snows fell in Yugoslavia, Rumania, and Bulgaria. Record-breaking rainfall of more than 300% of normal caused flooding in parts of Argentina in February. Drought continued to plague parts of southern Africa.

March–May. Spring was cool and wet across the Corn Belt and throughout much of the Eastern coast. Precipitation was above average in the Pacific Northwest and central Rockies, while dry conditions prevailed in the upper Great Lakes, the Southwest, most of California, and southeastern Texas. A record number of tornadoes was reported. Deaths due to the storms reached the three-digit mark—the highest fatality total in more than a decade.

In early March a storm system triggered torrential rains in the Southeast, causing extensive local flooding. A series of storms continued to batter the Pacific Northwest, reintensify in the central Plains, and sweep across the midsection of the continent through much of the month, triggering heavy snows, high winds, and severe thunderstorms. At mid-month a strong winter storm dumped up to 36 inches (91 cm) of snow in New England. Late in the month a line of devastating tornadoes swept through the Carolinas.

In April monthly temperatures averaged 4–8°F (2–3°C) cooler than normal from the central Plains to the Appalachians and above average along the northern tier of states and in southern Texas. During mid-month abnormally warm temperatures accelerated the snowmelt along the front range of the Wasatch Mountains in Utah, triggering landslides and flooding around the Great Salt Lake. A late April storm spread heavy, wet snow through the central and northern Rockies and initiated intense thunderstorms in the central Plains. This was the worst spring snowstorm (24–36 inches; 61–91 cm) on record in Wyoming.

Wild weather continued in May. During the first week torrential rains touched off widespread flooding in Kentucky and Tennessee. Melting of the abnormally heavy snowpack in the Rockies continued to pose flooding problems for many Western towns. On May 26–27, rains totaling more than 8.5 inches (22 cm) fell in the Tulsa, OK, metropolitan area.

Torrential rains and landslides claimed more than 30 lives in northeastern India during May. Europe was cold and wet during the spring season, with temperatures 4–5°F (2–3°C) below normal.

June–August. The central United States had a generally dry summer, stressing crops and forcing water conservation. Parts of the Plains, south Texas, north central Montana, the Corn Belt, and central California received only half the average rainfall. Most of the southeastern Piedmont and the Great Basin were unseasonably wet.

In June a stationary high pressure ridge became established over the Southeast, funneling a flow of tropical air northward to the Great Plains and eastern United States. The clash of this air with a cold-air mass moving through the Rockies resulted in a severe weather outbreak with heavy rains that produced flooding along the lower Missouri River valley.

Drought conditions were prevalent from south Texas through Oklahoma into Kansas and Nebraska in July. During the first week of

In Florida on Thanksgiving weekend, a violent storm caused a Venezuelan cargo ship to crash into expensive beachfront property in Palm Beach. Earlier, residents of the Rocky Mountain states, including Denver (below), were fooled by an unusually early and powerful snowstorm.

Photos, AP/Wide World

the month, violent thunderstorms dumped up to 9 inches (23 cm) of rain along the lower Missouri valley from southeastern Nebraska to central Missouri. A heat wave in interior California sent afternoon highs above 100°F (38°C) during the first three weeks of July. In contrast, temperatures throughout the eastern half of the country were cooler.

Abnormally warm and dry weather in the central and northern Plains continued in August. Along the Appalachians, the central Gulf Coast, and the Intermountain states, precipitation was in excess of normal. Flooding occurred along the eastern slopes of the Appalachians, and flash floods developed in the desert Southwest.

Parts of Australia received rainfall totals of more than 400% average values during July. In August, Typhoon June caused extensive damage in the northern Philippines. Flooding also occurred in southeastern China. The prairie provinces of Canada suffered a dry, warm summer. Drought continued in Africa.

September–November. Autumn temperatures were warmer than average in the East and colder than normal in the West. Precipitation was light at first, but October and November were wet over much of the nation.

September was cooler than average, except in California. Precipitation was heavy in the lower Ohio Valley, coastal North Carolina, and central Arizona and Nevada. The rest of the country was drier than average. Hurricane Diana moved ashore at Wilmington, NC. Heavy beach erosion occurred due to high winds and tides. At the month's end, tropical storm Isidore caused heavy rains and localized flooding in Florida.

During the third week in October, a powerful autumn storm dumped heavy snow on the Rocky Mountain states, with record low temperatures for the month set in many cities. In contrast, southeastern cities basked in record warmth. Drought was declared in Hawaii.

During early November, severe thunderstorms struck the Mississippi Valley. Tornadoes roared through Arkansas and Louisiana. An intense Atlantic storm system brought high winds and heavy rain to northern Florida at Thanksgiving. Storminess near Juneau, AK, and the Hawaiian island of Oahu produced downpours with some flooding.

In Europe, precipitation was heavy in parts of France, Italy, and northern West Germany. A late November storm in Germany and Austria produced heavy rains and high wind gusts. Typhoon Ike and Typhoon Agnes struck the Philippines in early September and November, respectively, bringing death and destruction. Above-average rains in southeastern Australia were cited as a major reason for the dramatic increase in the rodent and mosquito populations there.

See also ACCIDENTS AND DISASTERS.

IDA HAKKARINEN

MEXICO

Mexico continued to show signs of recovery from its 1982 economic crisis, but progress was slow and painful for the bulk of the population. An agreement with its international creditors enabled the country to negotiate more favorable terms for repayment of debt principal and interest.

Politics. Corruption in government continued to be the major political issue in 1984. The May 30 murder of political columnist Manuel Buendia, who had been exposing scandal and corruption in the government oil company (PEMEX) and the oil workers union, spurred more exposés. The government continued its prosecution of Jorge Díaz Serrano, a former senator and head of PEMEX, and brought charges of tax evasion against former Mexico City police chief Arturo Durazo. President Miguel de la Madrid Hurtado, who has made moral renovation a major theme of his administration, barred subcontracting of public works, one of the most common areas of corruption, particularly in the oil industry. In addition, the president admitted that Mexicans were losing faith in law enforcement, ordered reforms in Mexico City, and asked state governments to institute similar reforms.

The government's Institutional Revolutionary Party remained strong and seemed sure of victory in the 1985 elections despite facing its own charges of corruption. The party's secretary general was forced to resign in March because of corruption. De la Madrid called for democratization of the party and opening of the political process.

Opposition parties of the left and the right tried to capitalize on the problems of the government party. The leftist Mexican Workers Party received official recognition and immediately criticized the government's conservatism. The rightist Authentic Party of the Mexican Revolution regained its official standing, which it had lost because of low voter support. And the major opposition party, the National Action Party, shifted further to the right under the leadership of Pablo Emilio Madero, nephew of the famous revolutionary hero Francisco Madero, by adopting a blatantly pro business, antistatist posture.

Potentially the most serious move of the year was President de la Madrid's efforts to decentralize the national educational system. Educational decentralization, if carried out as proposed, would put the daily administration of the nation's schools into the hands of state governors and would break the national teachers union into 31 separate units. The union has long been an active supporter of political bossism, and its leaders have been resisting educational reform.

President de la Madrid's September announcement that Mexico would relocate the 46,000 Guatemalan refugees who had settled in the border state of Chiapas after suffering public and private terrorism in their homeland brought complaints. Even though the process would take two years, many Mexicans complained that their government should not be aiding foreigners while its own citizens were suffering. Mexico sees the refugee problem as a serious one because Guatemala still lays claim to Chiapas, which is in the nation's new oil belt.

Economic Policy. To meet the requirements of its loan from the International Monetary Fund (IMF), Mexico adopted a strict austerity program. In real terms, government spending was cut and the budget deficit reduced to 6% of the gross domestic product, down from 18% in 1982. Prices for basic commodities and fuel were boosted, as were crop subsidies. Wage increases were held to 20%, producing a 40% decline in real wages. Devaluation of the peso at the rate of 13 centavos per day curbed imports and, by May, produced a $6 billion (U.S.) trade surplus. Petroleum, representing more than 70% of all exports, provided the bulk of funds necessary for debt service and imports,

In Mexico's worst industrial disaster ever, a storage and distribution center for liquefied natural gas outside Mexico City exploded in flames just before dawn on November 19. A 20-block area in the working-class suburb of Tlalnepantla was left in rubble. More than 500 people were killed and thousands of others injured. "It felt as if there was an earthquake," said one survivor.

but a drop in international oil prices during the fall created problems.

To encourage private capitalism and stimulate the growth of jobs, the government sold the nonbanking subsidiaries of banks it had nationalized in 1982. Foreign investment was encouraged by exempting 34 categories of industry from the 1973 law limiting foreigners to only a minority equity share in a business. Mexico made a concerted and often successful effort to increase investment from Japan and Western Europe and to increase trade with the Middle East, Africa, Cuba, and Europe.

In early September, Mexico announced that it had negotiated a very favorable repayment schedule for its $48.5 billion public sector debt. The new interest rate would be 1.11 percentage points above the London interbank rate. The repayment period was stretched out to 14 years instead of the original 1985–1990 schedule. Under the plan, Mexico would make no principal payments in 1985 and a high of $15 billion in 1988. In 1989, when President de la Madrid has left office, the nation will have to pay $3.7 billion. De la Madrid answered charges that he was setting a financial time bomb for his successor by claiming that he was buying the breathing space necessary to revive the economy. That the new loan agreement would free Mexico from the strictures of the IMF by the end of 1985 pleased nationalists.

Encouraging economic news included a drop in the inflation rate from 100% to 60%, reductions of food imports, growth in industrial production, and a substantial increase in tourist income.

Social Policy. The government planned to spend 425.4 billion pesos ($2 billion) to improve health care and began to decentralize health services to improve the efficiency of the national health care systen. The health services of the Health and Welfare Secretariat would be provided in every state, with state governors coordinating all public health systems. The long-term goal is to give state governments the responsibility for health care systems. The Health and Welfare Secretariat transferred its social welfare programs to the System for Integral Development of the Family in exchange for the latter's medical services program.

In February the National Housing Development Program was launched to aid the creation of owner-built housing. The program is nonsubsidized, with much of the necessary construction funds coming from banks.

In August the government announced a joint job training program with private enterprise to train 11 million workers over the next four years. Private companies will provide 150,000 job training sites.

In an effort to upgrade the national educational system, teacher training was raised to the university level, and academic standards of technical schools and universities were tight-

ened. The government announced plans to increase the use of instructional radio and televison at the primary and secondary levels.

Foreign Policy. Relations between Mexico and the United States deteriorated even further during 1984 in spite of talks between President de la Madrid and President Reagan in Washington in May. Mexico rejected the Reagan administration view that Nicaragua is a hemispheric threat, that the Soviets and Cubans are trying to subvert Central America, and that Mexico might become the principal security problem for the United States. Mexican officials were angered by reports of a Reagan directive asking the Central Intelligence Agency to get Central American leaders to pressure Mexico to support U.S. policy in Central America. Mexico argued that political unrest in Latin America stems from economic problems, social injustice, and political underdevelopment and that it is not an East-West issue. It also maintained that rising real interest rates in the United States were putting undue burdens on Latin economies.

On a different front, Mexico issued strong objections to the Simpson-Mazzoli immigration bill under consideration in the U.S. Congress. It feared that enactment would send hundreds of thousands of Mexicans back to Mexico, which was already plagued by massive employment problems. The proposed legislation died in conference committee.

Mexico and Venezuela agreed to modify their 1980 San Jose oil pact, through which they provide easy credit terms to other Central American and Caribbean countries. Under the new terms, oil shipments would be suspended for any country that "initiates warlike actions" or that does not strictly comply with payment agreements. Costa Rica and Nicaragua both had had payment problems, and, faced with its own economic crisis, Mexico could no longer afford to be as generous as it once was.

DONALD J. MABRY
Mississippi State University

MEXICO · Information Highlights

Official Name: The United Mexican States.
Location: Southern North America.
Area: 764,015 sq mi (1 978 800 km²).
Population (mid-1984 est.): 77,700,000.
Chief Cities (1980 census): Mexico City, the capital, 9,377,300; (1979 est.): Guadalajara, 1,906,145; Monterrey, 1,090,009.
Government: *Head of state and government,* Miguel de la Madrid Hurtado, president (took office Dec. 1982). *Legislature*—Congress: Senate and Federal Chamber of Deputies.
Monetary Unit: Peso (209.5 pesos equal U.S.$1, floating rate, Nov. 13, 1984).
Gross Domestic Product (1982 U.S.$): $168,000,-000,000.
Economic Indexes (1983): *Consumer Prices* (1972 = 100), all items, 1,716.8; food, 1,565.4. *Industrial Production* (1975 = 100), 142.
Foreign Trade (1983 U.S.$): *Imports,* $8,136,000,000; *exports,* $21,399,000,000.

MICHIGAN

Michigan's streamlined auto industry continued its spectacular comeback during 1984. Republicans made major gains in the November elections. Detroit's first municipal corruption trial in four decades ended with six convictions.

Economy. Despite costly strikes, General Motors Corporation had third-quarter profits of $416.8 million, a decline from the 1983 period but enough to give the firm a record profit of $3.64 billion for the first three quarters. Both Ford Motor Company and Chrysler Corporation also had record third quarters and record profits for the first nine months. In mid-December, Chrysler announced plans to build a $500 million technological center next to Oakland University near Rochester.

Consumers Power Company abandoned work on its $5.7 billion nuclear plant in Midland in mid-July. When construction began in 1969, the twin-reactor plant was estimated to cost $339 million and expected to be completed in 1975. Claiming it was near bankruptcy, the company asked the state Public Service Commission to approve rate increases that would enable it to charge its 1.34 million electric customers the entire investment in the plant. However, regulators indicated they expected Consumer stockholders to bear a major part of the cost.

Elections. Republicans made major gains in the fall elections. Incumbent U.S. Sen. Carl Levin retained his seat by soundly defeating former astronaut Jack Lousma, his Republican opponent. But Republican William D. Schuette of Midland upset incumbent U.S. Rep. Donald J. Albosta and trimmed Democratic control of the state congressional delegation to 11–7.

On the state level, four incumbent Democratic House members fell to Republican challengers as the GOP, aided by the Ronald Reagan landslide, made its best House showing in 12 years. Democrats would have a 58–52 margin over Republicans when the legislature convened in January, but this was still the best Republican showing since the 1971–72 session.

Corruption Trials. Six persons were found guilty in a retrial of Detroit's first municipal corruption case in four decades. The trials grew out of a multimillion dollar hauling contract awarded by the Detroit Water and Sewerage Department to Vista Disposal Inc., a firm owned by Darralyn C. Bowers, a confidante of Detroit Mayor Coleman A. Young. Mrs. Bowers was charged with two racketeering-bribery counts and sentenced to four years in prison. She also was ordered to forfeit $3.9 million in Vista profits. Among those convicted were Charles M. Beckham, director of the water department when the contract was awarded, three associates of Mrs. Bowers, and a lawyer who worked for the firm.

NAACP Decision. On July 25, Federal Judge Horace W. Gilmore ordered the City of Detroit to rehire more than 800 black police officers who had been laid off in 1979 and 1980. The judge acted to implement his earlier finding, in February, that the city breached its affirmative action obligations to the black officers.

In a 58-page decision, Gilmore called Detroit police unions "bitter opponents" of the city's affirmative action efforts and ruled that the Detroit Police Officers Association violated its obligation to provide fair representation to black officers. He ordered the association to bring a fair balance of blacks into its leadership structure within 12 months.

Gilmore's rulings came in a lawsuit filed against the city and the police union by the NAACP, ten individual police officers, and the Guardians, an organization of black officers.

Responding to the suit on November 7, the city offered a plan to rehire 724 officers, both black and white, on a staggered basis with all back on the job by mid-1985. The state legislature approved a city request to restore the city's 4% utility tax to 5% to finance the police rehiring.

World Series. A wild celebration, accompanied by sporadic violence, erupted in downtown Detroit in mid-October when the Detroit Tigers won the 1984 World Series.

Other Events. Construction of a 2.9 mi (4.7 km) automated rail line called the "People Mover" was started in downtown Detroit. But cost of the project, originally estimated at $135 million, threatened to hit $200 million.

The city of Flint celebrated in July the opening of Autoworld, a $70-million theme park dedicated to the history of the automobile. The park, partly financed by the Charles Stewart Mott Foundation, is considered to be symbolic of economic hope and renewal for the city.

CHARLES THEISEN, *"The Detroit News"*

MICHIGAN · Information Highlights

Area: 58,527 sq mi (151 586 km²).

Population (July 1, 1983 est.): 9,069,000.

Chief Cities (July 1, 1982 est.): Lansing, the capital, 128,338; Detroit, 1,138,717; Grand Rapids, 182,774; Warren, 156,131; Flint, 154,019; Sterling Heights, 108,482.

Government (1984): *Chief Officers*—governor, James J. Blanchard (D); lt. gov. Martha W. Griffiths (D). *Legislature*—Senate, 38 members; House of Representatives, 110 members.

State Finances (fiscal year 1983): *Revenues,* $16,097,000,000; *expenditures,* $14,789,000,000.

Personal Income (1983): $103,980,000,000; per capita, $11,466.

Labor Force (May 1984): *Civilian labor force,* 4,395,100; *unemployed,* 496,500 (11.3% of total force).

Education: *Enrollment* (fall 1982)—public elementary schools, 1,156,597; public secondary, 604,924; colleges and universities (fall 1983), 515,760. *Public school expenditures* (1982–83), $5,351,619,530 ($3,307 per pupil).

MICROBIOLOGY

The year 1984 was one of important discoveries in the field of microbiology. Scientists isolated the causative agent of AIDS (Acquired Immune Deficiency Syndrome), discovered a medicine that helps sufferers of genital herpes, and continued to develop synthetic vaccines to fight infectious diseases. Bacteria that can dispose of certain agricultural and industrial waste products also were found. And finally, the discovery of bacteria that live at 350°C (662°F) altered concepts about the environmental conditions needed for the origin and maintenance of living material.

AIDS Virus. By mid-1984, more than 4,000 cases of AIDS had been reported in the United States since the first documented case in 1978. In spring 1984, however, scientists announced the first major step toward a vaccine. Doctors at the Pasteur Institute in Paris and at the National Cancer Institute in Bethesda, MD, independently isolated a *human T-cell leukemia virus* (HTLV-3) from AIDS sufferers. They found that 90% of victims had antibodies in their blood serum that reacted with that virus.

In addition, the team of scientists at Bethesda also was able to develop a method for mass-producing the virus. Stocks of the AIDS virus would enable scientists to develop a way to test blood donors for the presence of antibodies against the virus. Anyone whose blood serum is found to contain the antibodies would be presumed to be infected with the AIDS virus. Such a test was expected to be available within six months. And although no cure for the disease appeared on the horizon, the new stocks of HTLV-3 may permit the development of a vaccine in an estimated three to five years.

Genital Herpes. Genital herpes is a disease caused by a DNA virus named *herpes simplex* Type II. When active, the virus produces sores on or near the genital organs. When inactive, the virus lies dormant in nerve cells. An estimated 10 to 20 million Americans are afflicted with genital herpes, with at least 300,000 new cases each year.

Although finding a cure for genital herpes remains a challenge for scientists, a medicine called *acyclovir* has been found to provide some relief. Acyclovir is completely ineffective against the virus in its dormant state, but the medicine apparently does help reduce the severity of disease flare-ups.

Synthetic Vaccines. The prevention of infectious diseases, especially those caused by viruses, is best accomplished through some form of vaccination. The vaccine, which consists of killed or altered viruses, stimulates the body to produce antibodies against the viruses and thus immunizes the individual against a particular disease. Research has shown that the production of antibodies is stimulated by the surface of the virus' protein coat.

Dr. Richard Lerner of the Scripps Clinic in La Jolla, CA, recently analyzed the coat protein *hemagglutinin* of the flu virus for those chains of amino acids that lie on its outer surface. Using on-the-shelf amino acids, he synthesized 20 different short chains which together accounted for most of the outer surface of the hemagglutinin. He then attached each of the short chains to a large protein molecule, which acted as a carrier, and injected each combination into a different rabbit. Seventeen of the 20 rabbits produced antibodies that reacted against the whole virus, indicating that even a small portion of the protein coat could function as an effective vaccine.

Waste Cleanup. Almost one billion tons of cellulose waste (corn stalks, sawdust, and other agricultural by-products) are produced in the United States each year. Bacteria of the genus *Thermomonospora,* it has been discovered, produce the enzyme cellulase, which converts cellulose into sugar. Unfortunately, these bacteria require a high temperature for optimum growth, making them inefficient for degrading cellulose waste. However, the gene for cellulase has been transferred to the laboratory bacterium *Escherichia coli,* and efforts will be made to modify the bacterium to achieve increased production of the valuable enzyme.

The synthetic compound polyethylene glycol (PEG) is another common pollutant. Used in antifreeze, detergents, plastics, and cosmetics, PEG often ends up as an industrial by-product that gets discharged into the nearest stream or lake. Scientists have discovered, however, that a number of bacteria, including *Desulfovibrio desulfuricans,* produce enzymes that can convert PEG into ethanol. The bacteria are anaerobic (live without oxygen) and can be used directly in many industries that have waste-management programs.

Life at 350°C. There are fissures in the earth's crust at the bottom of the ocean through which seawater circulates and becomes heated to temperatures as high as 350°C. The water is kept in its liquid state by the high pressure produced by the weight of the ocean water above it. This pressure prevents the superheated water molecules from separating from each other and forming water vapor (as would occur at 100°C, or 212°F, at sea level).

It was long believed that no living organism could survive at 350°C. In an astounding discovery, however, a team of scientists found that there are indeed bacteria living in these suboceanic "hydrothermal vents." The discovery indicates that the first organisms could have been formed and could have survived at temperatures and pressures that no organism presently living on the earth's surface could survive.

LOUIS LEVINE
City College of New York

MIDDLE EAST

The processes of history in the Middle East simmered rather than boiled over during 1984. Basic tensions and problems remained much the same as in previous years, with no striking denouements or solutions. But it was at least true that there were no great crises and no truly catastrophic changes.

The two major vortices of conflict and tension within the region remained the Iran-Iraq war and the situation in Lebanon. It no longer could be said, however, that either of these matters commanded the degree of attention from the outside world that they had formerly. The outside world had become less concerned because of the assumption that neither situation was likely to lead in the near future to Great Power intervention, with its threat of wider conflict.

Iran-Iraq War. The war between Iraq and Iran entered its fifth year in September. Always a somewhat curious conflict in several respects, in 1984 its oddity grew greater. The war had become increasingly pointless, in that hopes of decisive victory for either side could no longer be realistically entertained. The objectives for which Iraq had invaded Iran in September 1980—control of the Shatt al-Arab waterway and destruction of the radical Islamic regime in Tehran—were now clearly beyond reach. Iran's objectives, insofar as they were merely defensive and amounted to regaining the territory initially lost to Iraq's assault, had been attained as far back as 1982. The further Iranian war aim, destroying the detested secularist regime in Baghdad, seemed totally unlikely to be achieved. More than once, in 1982 and after, Iraq had offered to make peace on the basis of the *status quo ante bellum,* and even the payment of some kind of compensation was clearly negotiable, but these terms elicited no interest from the regime of the Ayatollah Khomeini. Innumerable attempts at mediation and peacemaking by other Middle Eastern states, and even by Japan (heavily dependent on Gulf oil), had come to nothing.

In fact, there was comparatively little serious land combat during the year. Fighting flared up on one or two occasions and then died away for months at a time. The most serious fighting of the year occurred in February and early March and centered on the island of Majnoon, site of a major oil field in southeast Iraq. On February 29 the Iraqi government admitted the loss of Majnoon, and, despite intense fighting in an Iraqi counterattack early in March, it was not recaptured. Iran did not, however, move any closer to capturing the important nearby city of Basra.

Throughout the next six months, Iran continued to talk of preparations for a "final offensive," but the threatened final blow was again and again postponed. On October 18, indeed,

Iran launched a major offensive in another area, on the central front about 70 mi (113 km) northeast of Baghdad, but Iraq claimed to have repelled the advance.

If the land fighting was indecisive and low-key for most of the year, other aspects of the war did claim attention. Deliberate attacks on civilian centers occurred during the first half of the year, breaking a tacit mutual avoidance of such steps. The attacks began on February 11, when Iraqi missiles hit the Iranian city of Dizful, about 90 mi (145 km) east of the south-central front. Iran retaliated, and there were several attacks by both countries over the next few days. A mutual agreement to desist from such action was worked out on February 18. A second wave of civilian attacks did take place in June, but they were broken off after an urgent appeal from UN Secretary-General Javier Pérez de Cuéllar.

During the first months of the year, Iraq was accused of employing lethal chemical agents, especially mustard gas. The speaker of the Iranian parliament claimed on March 4 that 400 Iranians had been killed by Iraqi chemical attacks in the fighting around Basra. These charges were upheld in general terms by the U.S. State Department on March 5, but the carefully balanced statement also took Iran to task for its "intransigent refusal" to end the war until the government of Iraq's President Saddam Hussein was overthrown. Tests on wounded Iranians conducted by various authorities in Tehran, Vienna, and Stockholm tended to confirm the allegations against Iraq, but not in any truly conclusive manner.

More serious, at least for a time, was the "tanker war" in the Persian Gulf. In February 1984, Iraq began a series of attacks on maritime traffic going to and from Iran, using French-built Exocet missiles and Super Etendard aircraft. Between February and the end of August, more than 20 merchant ships were hit in the Gulf. Iranian attacks on ships bound for Kuwait or Saudi Arabia also occurred, but usually as immediate retaliation for Iraqi attacks. Iraqi attacks were more than twice as numerous as those by Iran and were generally more damaging. Iranian attacks on shipping in the upper Gulf were abruptly abandoned after Saudi F-15 fighters downed two Iranian planes on June 5 off the Saudi coast. Thereafter Iranian attacks shifted to the lower Gulf. During the late summer and fall the incidents petered out.

All in all, the "tanker war" did not have serious consequences. It raised insurance rates, but it did not halt the flow of oil from Iranian or other sources in the Gulf and it did not bring any of the major powers into the conflict. Because its oil traffic was not seriously interrupted, Iran was not called on to carry out its retaliatory threat—closing the Strait of Hormuz to all traffic.

Egypt's President Hosni Mubarak (right) met with Jordan's King Hussein after the resumption of diplomatic relations in the fall. Jordan became the first Arab state to restore ties with Cairo since the 1979 Egyptian-Israeli accord.

All these short-lived initiatives by Iraq—the bombing of cities, the alleged use of chemical warfare, and the "tanker war"—had common objectives: to put pressure on Iran to come to the negotiating table, and to gain the attention of the major powers, with the same ultimate purpose. They did not, however, succeed in these aims.

Lebanon. With its complex problems, Lebanon still did not emerge from its troubles in 1984, though perhaps some progress was made. A security pact that would have disengaged the various factions had seemed near achievement shortly after the new year, but it foundered on the objections of the Druze militia leader Walid Jumblat. Fighting between the Lebanese army and the Muslim militias erupted again in the hills southeast of Beirut and continued through February. Meanwhile, on February 7, U.S. President Ronald Reagan announced plans to begin withdrawing U.S. Marines in Beirut to ships offshore and authorized naval artillery action against antigovernment forces. This move was completed by February 26, and the Sixth Fleet left Lebanese waters on March 30. Thus ended the major attempt, begun in August and September, 1982, to use a U.S. military presence to assist Lebanon toward stability. The U.S. withdrawal was paralleled by that of the other contingents in the multinational force —France, Great Britain, and Italy.

Lebanese President Amin Gemayel visited Damascus for talks with Syrian President Hafez al-Assad, February 29–March 1 and again April 19–20. In the meetings, Gemayel obtained Syrian agreement to put pressure on the warring Lebanese factions to support him and to join in a new government of national unity, the price being the cancellation of Lebanon's May 1983 pact with Israel. The outcome was Gemayel's appointment on April 26 of former Premier Rashid Karami, a pro-Syrian Sunni Muslim, to head a new government of national unity. The leaders of the factions had

In what President Mubarak called Egypt's most "free, honest, and sincere" elections, opposition parties were allowed to campaign openly for the first time in 30 years. The only opposition group to win assembly representation, however, was the New Wafd Party, left.

353

Reunification of Beirut was made possible in early July by the acceptance of a government peace plan by the major warring factions. The reopening of the city, however, was tied up by protesting Muslim women who demanded the return of the thousands of persons kidnapped during the fighting.

Greg Smith, Gamma-Liaison

agreed on April 9 to a new plan for the disengagement of their forces, à plan put into effect by the end of the month.

The new cabinet met for the first time on May 10 after long political haggling and compromises. The ten-member body, including Jumblat and the Shiite Muslim leader Nabih Berri, comprised five Christians and five Muslims and was carefully balanced to reflect all the major factions and divisions of Lebanon. In September the cabinet began talks on fundamental revisions of Lebanon's political structure, but progress was slow. Meanwhile, sporadic violence in various parts of the country continued.

All in all, the year did see a new stasis in Lebanese affairs. There was a government of national unity in which all major factions were represented. This marked the end of virtual control of Lebanese society and politics by the wealthier, Christian element. In foreign relations, the Israeli hope that its June 1982 invasion would lead to peace with a neutral Lebanon had disappeared. U.S. and European influence in Lebanon was virtually gone, replaced by Syrian predominance. The new order in Lebanon was a Syrian achievement.

Terrorism. The specter of terrorism continued to stalk the entire Middle East. Among many deaths, one of the saddest was the murder on January 18 of Malcolm Kerr, president of the American University of Beirut.

The U.S. embassy in Beirut, which had been occupying a building in a supposedly safer area in East Beirut since July 31, was bombed on September 20 by a truck loaded with explosives, leaving some 23 persons dead and more than 40 wounded. This was the fourth major terrorist attack on U.S. facilities in the Middle East in less than a year and a half. The first was the bombing at the Beirut embassy on April 18, 1983, killing 17 Americans and 33 Lebanese employees. Then on Oct. 23, 1983, a truck bombing at the U.S. Marine barracks at Beirut Airport left 241 servicemen dead. And on Dec. 12, 1983, the U.S. embassy in Kuwait was bombed, killing six persons.

Terrorist actions of another sort were seen in the mining of some 15 ships in the Red Sea during July and August. The attacks occurred in the Gulf of Suez at the north end of the Red Sea, and in the Strait of Bab el-Mandeb at the southern end. At the request of Egypt, the United States organized a major international effort to locate and eliminate mines using minesweepers and divers. In the end, however, only fragments of two mines were discovered, and their origin was not entirely clear. The episode of the mines was one of several happenings in the Middle East in 1984 that had a flavor of the unusual and the bizarre. An Egyptian government spokesman blamed "two countries" for laying the mines "to create confusion." The two countries were presumably Libya and Iran, and their aim was conjectured to be the embarrassment of Egypt, the only Arab state to make a formal peace with Israel. Tehran radio, meanwhile, said the mines were the work of the "Islamic Jihad" ("Islamic Holy War") terrorist group. Islamic Jihad had also claimed credit for the major attacks on U.S. facilities in 1983 and 1984, as well as for the murder of Dr. Kerr.

Islamic Fundamentalism. Islamic Jihad symbolizes something real and increasingly dangerous in the Middle East—the growing force of an Islamic fundamentalism suffused with hatred of the West and opposed to secularism and economic development. It is seen in its most fervent form in the regime in Iran, but it is also manifested elsewhere—in Col. Muammar el-Qaddafi's Libya; in the growing Turkish opposition to the secular state that was the legacy of Kemal Ataturk; and most recently in the Sudan, where President Jaafar al-Nemery has embarked on a policy of bringing the penal code into line with Islamic law *(sharia)*—a dangerous move in an unstable country where 40% of the population is non-Muslim. The confrontation between Islamic fundamentalism and secularism is embodied, of course, in the Iran-Iraq war, but it could become an issue that would split the whole Middle East into two camps and reduce to secondary importance the Arab-Israeli opposition.

Unpredictable Qaddafi. The eccentric and unpredictable ruler of Libya, Col. Muammar el-Qaddafi, continued to be the supreme maverick of the Middle East. In 1984 his minions continued to murder his Libyan political opponents on foreign soil. In April they machine-gunned protesters from the windows of the Libyan embassy in London, also killing a British policewoman. This led to the siege and then the closure of the embassy. Qaddafi also proclaimed that he had disposed of a former Libyan premier living in Egypt, but the Egyptian government demonstrated that the man was alive and well. Qaddafi made President François Mitterrand of France look foolish when the latter agreed to a mutual troop withdrawal from Chad but the Libyan troops were left in place. Probably never in history has the ruler of such a minor country created such a stir. Perhaps his supreme achievement in the realm of the bizarre, however, was the union proclaimed on August 13 between Qaddafi's Libya and King Hassan's Morocco—a "union" between two entirely antithetical regimes, one radical and the other conservative.

Role of Jordan. Another Mideast state of the second rank, Jordan, was much in the news in the latter part of the year because of the mediating role played by King Hussein, now 32 years on the throne. In September the king restored normal diplomatic links with Egypt, making Jordan the first Arab state to restore relations broken after the Egyptian-Israeli peace treaty of 1979. Egypt's President Hosni Mubarak and Jordan's King Hussein held a three-way meeting with President Reagan in Washington in mid-February. In early October, after the resumption of ties, President Mubarak visited Amman. And in early December, King Hussein reciprocated with a visit to Cairo.

King Hussein was also acting increasingly in concert with Yasir Arafat of the Palestine Liberation Organization (PLO). At the meeting of the PLO General Council in Amman, Jordan, at the end of November, Arafat was able to reassert his authority as chairman, discomfit his rival, Syrian-backed Ahmad Gibril, and re-

gain effective control of the organization. In subsequent statements King Hussein insisted on the Palestinians' right to self-determination and said that the PLO should be a "full partner" in any future peace talks. In fact, however, the precarious tenure of power by the new national unity government of Israel and its concentration on domestic economic issues made any major changes in the West Bank situation quite unlikely in the near future.

U.S.-Iraq Rapprochement. The United States and Iraq, which had not had normal diplomatic relations since the aftermath of the Six-Day War of 1967, announced the resumption of full ties on November 26. Iraqi policy, no doubt under the pressure of war, has become much more pragmatic and moderate in recent years, a trend that is in the interests of the West. The United States said that the move should not be understood as an expression of partiality in the Iran-Iraq war.

ARTHUR CAMPBELL TURNER
University of California, Riverside

An international minesweeping operation was begun in the Red Sea after 15 ships were damaged by explosions.

Milner, Sygma

MILITARY AFFAIRS

The tough rhetoric between Washington and Moscow cooled somewhat in the last several months of 1984. Observers attributed this to President Reagan's resolve to avoid military confrontation with the Soviets and to blunt the Democratic charge that he is reckless in military matters, and to the Soviets' realization that Reagan would be reelected and had to be dealt with for four more years. However, while the harshness in the war of words decreased, the preparations by both superpowers to increase their military strength continued.

Late in the fall of 1984, President Reagan signed a defense authorization bill for $211.5 billion (U.S.). This figure was down slightly from the $220 billion price tag that the administration originally requested.

Strategic Defense Initiative. A proposal by President Reagan in the spring of 1983 that the United States commence research that might lead to a defense against ballistic missile attack became, in 1984, one of the most hotly debated military questions in years. Termed the Strategic Defense Initiative (SDI) and called, somewhat derisively, the "Star Wars" defense by opponents, SDI officially was made a major component of American military policy when the president named a former associate administrator of the manned space flight program as director of the program's organization. Indicative of the importance the president attached to the SDI effort is the fact that the director, Lt. Gen. James A. Abrahamson, and his staff are part of the office of the Secretary of Defense. Persons outside of government opposing the SDI proposal include Dr. Hans Bethe, Nobel laureate in physics and a member of the atomic bomb program in World War II; Dr. Richard Garwin, prominent defense analyst; retired Adm. Noel Gayler, former deputy chief of Naval Operations for Research and Development; and physicist Henry Kendall.

The broad concept embodied in the SDI proposal is that the United States should ascertain whether it would be technically possible to build several types of defensive systems that could destroy large numbers of incoming nuclear warheads launched by intercontinental ballistic missiles (ICBMs) and submarine-launched ballistic missiles (SLBMs). Proponents of SDI claim that a successful SDI effort would enable the United States to prevent a nuclear attack by making nuclear weapons "impotent and obsolete." This, it is contended by SDI supporters, is preferable to the current policy of preventing an attack on the United States by threatening a massive nuclear retaliatory blow on the Soviet Union, which would kill and maim millions of Soviet civilians. Opponents contend that the technologies necessary for a ballistic missile defense will be very difficult to perfect, relatively easy to penetrate

if developed, and that an SDI effort would be seen by Moscow as an attempt to gain military superiority that would only provoke Soviet countermeasures and a heightened arms race in space.

Other Strategic Weapons Developments. The Reagan administration continued its policy of substantially upgrading U.S. strategic-weapons capability. The Navy commissioned the nation's fifth Trident nuclear-powered submarine, the *Henry M. Jackson,* named after the late U.S. senator, a longtime advocate of a strong national defense.

Despite the crash of a B-1A jet bomber prototype, the administration went ahead with production plans for the B-1B, an improved version of the supersonic, swing-wing bomber designed to carry the fastest cruise missiles. The controversial MX ICBM continued as a source of disagreement. In a series of compromises, Congress, eager to adjourn so that members could return home to campaign for the fall elections, agreed to postpone final votes on further MX funding until the spring of 1985.

In an effort to achieve a method of deployment for new ICBMs that would survive a massive Soviet nuclear attack, the Air Force showed interest in what is called the Strategic Reserve Force option. This concept involves the construction of missile bases more than .5 mi (.8 km) underground in areas of the western United States. The idea is to place missiles so deeply underground that even direct hits by Soviet warheads could not destroy the U.S. force. Initial plans for the underground survivable base call for the construction of possibly 400 mi (644 km) of tunnels in which the ICBMs would be housed, along with firing crews who could stay in their self-contained environment for as long as a year. After an attack the missile personnel would use machines to tunnel up to the surface and launch the ICBMs in a retaliatory attack.

As for the Soviets, they announced the deployment of long-range cruise missiles on strategic bombers and on submarines that operate off the east and west coasts of the United States. In a statement released by the Soviet Ministry of Defense, the justification for the new deployments was the need to offset the "massive deployment" by the United States of air-, sea-, and land-based missiles. This statement was perceived in Washington as being a reference to the deployment by the United States of cruise missiles and Pershing IIs in Western Europe to counter the earlier deployment by the Soviets of SS-20 missiles.

The ASAT. Military observers believed that the United States was preparing to test, unless arms control agreements preclude it, the world's most advanced ASAT (antisatellite) weapon. It would consist of an F-15 jet fighter, capable of flying at 1,500 mi (2 414 km) per hour, 10 mi (16 km) high, which would carry a

Chemical Warfare

A number of circumstances combined in 1984 to project the subject of chemical warfare back into the public consciousness. In the United States, some Vietnam veterans continued to contend that they had been physically harmed by a chemical herbicide, Agent Orange, used to defoliate jungle vegetation during the Vietnam conflict. A class-action lawsuit by veterans claiming negative health effects resulted in a $180 million out-of-court settlement with seven chemical companies involved in the production of Agent Orange.

In May the U.S. Defense Department reported that 14 to 16 countries—about 10 more than previously estimated—had chemical weapons. The Reagan administration, meanwhile, had been arguing for greater U.S. chemical warfare preparation. The most debated aspect of the administration's position was a proposal to start production of binary nerve gas—in which two inert gases are combined in the attacking shell to form a lethal gas. Exposure to nerve gas causes the central nervous system to cease functioning, which results in rapid death. According to Defense Department officials, safety and environmental considerations support the replacement of standard nerve gas stocks with the new binary agents. The latter do not pose a safety hazard until after they are combined, it is contended, making them more easily and safely disposed of than standard nerve gas. But the administration was not successful in making its case before Congress, and binary nerve gas was dropped from the defense budget for the year.

U.S. Policy. As a signatory to the Geneva protocol of 1925, the United States is committed to a "no first use" policy regarding specific lethal and incapacitating chemicals listed in the document. The United States is also a signatory to the Biological Weapons Convention of 1972, which commits it to work for the elimination of chemical weapons by means of negotiations with other nations. However, since no verifiable treaty banning chemical weapons has yet been signed, Washington's policy is to maintain a stockpile that will deter the use of chemicals by others and be used in retaliation if deterrence fails. The government also conducts research in medical therapy and casualty care, remote detection, protection, and decontamination procedures.

Reported Use. The Reagan administration firmly believes that the Soviet Union maintains a high level of chemical warfare capability. Since the late 1970s, the U.S. government has alleged that the Soviets have either used or directly furnished lethal and incapacitating

AP/Wide World

UN scientists concluded that lethal chemical weapons in the form of aerial bombs were used in the Iran-Iraq war.

chemical agents in Southeast Asia and Afghanistan. One of the most specific charges is that the USSR provided several chemicals, collectively called "yellow rain," which were sprayed on hill tribes in Laos; some scientists say that "yellow rain" may actually be bee excrement. Finally, there was new evidence that Iraq was using lethal chemical agents in its bitter war against Iran.

Negotiations. In spring 1984, U.S. Vice-President George Bush flew to Geneva to offer a new approach to the Soviets regarding a treaty to ban chemical weapons. The plan called for on-site inspection to verify treaty compliance. The Soviets rejected the proposal as discriminatory, since it required only the inspection of government facilities and not private companies. At year's end the two superpowers were still at an impasse in reaching a mutually acceptable treaty on limiting chemical weapons. Some Americans argued that in order to convince the Soviets to negotiate a treaty in good faith, the United States would have to produce new chemical weapons and increase its stockpile.

ROBERT M. LAWRENCE

two stage missile. The missile would release a small nonnuclear, nonexplosive warhead which would be guided on a collision course with Soviet satellites. White House spokesmen defended the ASAT test on the grounds that the Soviets previously have tested, and possibly deployed, their own ASAT system, thus necessitating the U.S. move to catch up with a potentially dangerous Soviet weapons advance. Secretary of State George Shultz rejected the suggestion by Soviet Foreign Minister Andrei Gromyko that the two superpowers initiate a freeze on ASAT research and development. According to Shultz, it would freeze the United States in an inferior position.

The Soviet ASAT system is thought by American defense experts to consist of an ICBM launcher that boosts a killer satellite into low-earth orbit up to 1,000 mi (1 600 km) above the earth's surface. The killer satellite makes several rotations about the earth as it is maneuvered near the satellite it is intended to destroy. When it is close enough, the killer satellite is exploded by electronic command, and the resulting debris destroy the target satellite.

The American scientific community was divided on whether the United States should develop the F-15-missile ASAT. Spokesmen from the Federation of American Scientists claimed that the Soviet system was relatively primitive and did not pose a threat to many American satellites, which orbit at distances of 25,000 to 60,000 mi (40 230 to 96 560 km) above the earth, while the U.S. ASAT would create a destabilizing situation by directly threatening many Soviet satellites, which operate in low orbits. Whether or not a ban on ASAT deployment could be monitored for compliance was another point that divided government spokesmen and members of the civilian scientific community.

Nuclear Winter. A number of scientists, including Cornell University astronomer Dr. Carl Sagan, continued their efforts to educate the public and government officials on the concept of nuclear winter. The core of the concept is that the smoke and soot that would rise into the atmosphere as a result of cities catching fire following a nuclear attack could form a dark cloud around the world, shutting out sunlight. It was believed by some that the effects of nuclear winter could be so severe that temperatures would be lowered appreciably and that plant life would die. Scientists were not in agreement regarding how many cities would have to burn simultaneously in order to bring on nuclear winter. In 1984 the U.S. government launched its own study of the nuclear-winter phenomenon, and nongovernment scientists awaited the publication of the study to ascertain if government research confirmed or negated the grim parameters set forth by Sagan and similar researchers.

Vietnam. Memories of the Vietnam War were recalled as a result of a libel suit brought by the former American commander in Vietnam, Gen. William Westmoreland. In a suit against CBS News, Westmoreland sought to prove that accusations about him in a CBS television documentary, *The Uncounted Enemy: A Vietnam Deception,* were false. Specifically, Westmoreland claimed that allegations in the documentary that there had been a conspiracy to suppress and alter intelligence information regarding enemy troop strength before the Tet offensive were unfounded. According to CBS, the alleged tampering with data was done to make it appear that the United States was winning the war of attrition. Beyond the immediate matter of whether Westmoreland had been libeled by CBS was the larger question concerning the degree of freedom the American media would have in reporting on future conflicts.

Other reminders of the Vietnam War occurred on Memorial Day and Veterans Day. On the former, President Reagan officiated at a state funeral in Arlington National Cemetery for an American serviceman, killed in Vietnam, whose identity is unknown. The serviceman was awarded the Medal of Honor as burial took place in the Tomb of the Unknowns. On Veterans Day, a bronze statue, "Three Servicemen," was dedicated at the Vietnam Memorial in Washington.

Middle East and Central America. The Iran-Iraq war and the strife in Lebanon dragged on with inconclusive results. Although U.S. Marines were withdrawn from Lebanon, sporadic terrorist attacks continued against U.S. installations, such as the embassy in Beirut.

The United States continued support for the El Salvadoran government in its war against the guerrillas, allegedly led by Communists. In neighboring Nicaragua, Washington sought to assist a rebel group, known as the Contras, in a campaign to overthrow the leftist Sandinista government. American military assistance to the government of El Salvador, although not always supported enthusiastically in the Congress, was continued in 1984. However, Congress voted to cut off further funding that would enable the Central Intelligence Agency (CIA) to assist the Contras in Nicaragua.

In the fall the status of U.S. support for the Nicaraguan Contras was confused further with the release of information that the CIA had produced a handbook in Spanish for the Contras in which it was urged that Sandinista officials be "neutralized." Sen. Daniel Moynihan (D-NY) stated that the word "neutralize" meant "assassinate" and that the CIA was thus instructing the Contras to violate a presidential directive that bans assassination as a tool of U.S. policy. The CIA denied that the word "neutralize" implies assassination but acknowledged publication of the handbook as a mistake.

ROBERT M. LAWRENCE
Colorado State University

Minnesota belonged to native son Walter Mondale in 1984. At left, the current owner of the Elmore boyhood home of the former vice-president prepares for a Mondale visit.

MINNESOTA

A native son's losing campaign for the presidency, mixed signals on economic recovery, and startling allegations of sexual abuse of children dominated events in Minnesota.

Elections. By a margin of less than 1%, Minnesota was the only state to give its presidential vote to Walter F. Mondale. He was Minnesota attorney general (1960–65) and U.S. senator (1965–77).

Although Independent-Republicans (IRs) failed to win the presidential vote, they took control of the Minnesota House of Representatives for the first time in 14 years, winning 68 seats to 66 for the Democrat-Farmer-Laborites (DFL). Gov. Rudy Perpich (DFL), midway through his four-year term, would face a divided legislature in the 1985 session, the DFL having captured the Senate, 42 to 25, in 1982.

The state's five DFL and three IR incumbent representatives were reelected, as was Sen. Rudy Boschwitz (R).

Economy. With officials forecasting a $1 billion state surplus by June 10, 1985, the stage was set for a political struggle over how large a cut the 1985 legislature would vote in the state income tax. IR leaders called for rebating the entire surplus, while Governor Perpich favored refunding $200 million and building a reserve of $500 million.

Profit, sales, and employment were generally up, compared with 1983. In August, retail sales were up 11%. In September the help-wanted index in Minneapolis was 78% higher than a year before. On the Iron Range, in Northern Minnesota, the year began on a bright note with iron ore, pulp, and paper production strong, but it ended with a layoff of 1,500 workers at the Mountain Iron mine.

Minnesota farmers harvested a record soybean crop and their third-largest corn crop, but many were nevertheless facing acute distress because of high interest rates, heavy indebtedness, and low crop prices. The state commissioner of agriculture predicted that 12,000 of the state's 100,000 farms would go under in the next two years.

Child Abuse. In Jordan, 30 mi (48 km) from the Twin Cities, 25 persons were charged with sexually abusing 40 children. After a jury found one couple not guilty, remaining charges were dropped by Scott County Attorney Kathleen Morris. In November investigators announced that they had found no evidence to support allegations that as many as six children may have been murdered, and that they intended to concentrate instead on allegations of a child pornography ring.

In an unrelated case, John Clark Donahue, founder and artistic director of the internationally acclaimed Children's Theater of Minneapolis, pleaded guilty to sexually abusing three minors, members of the company. He was

---

MINNESOTA • Information Highlights

Area: 84,402 sq mi (218 601 km²).

Population (July 1, 1983 est.): 4,144,000.

Chief Cities (July 1, 1982 est.): St. Paul, the capital, 270,443; Minneapolis, 369,161; Duluth (1980 census), 92,811.

Government (1984): *Chief Officers*—governor, Rudy Perpich (DFL); lt. gov., Marlene Johnson (DFL). *Legislature*—Senate, 67 members; House of Representatives, 134 members.

State Finances (fiscal year 1983): *Revenues,* $8,074,000,000; *expenditures,* $6,496,000,000.

Personal Income (1983): $49,371,000,000; per capita, $11,913.

Labor Force (May 1984): *Civilian labor force,* 2,256,600; *unemployed,* 131,600 (5.8% of total force).

Education: *Enrollment* (fall 1982)—public elementary schools, 471,670; public secondary, 243,520; colleges and universities (fall 1983), 214,219. *Public school expenditures* (1982–83), $2,075,572,146 ($3,085 per pupil).

given a 15-year sentence on probation and ordered to undergo psychiatric treatment. The judge strongly rebuked the community for failing to intervene when rumors of the trouble first circulated.

Major Projects. In Minneapolis, workers broke ground for what would be the nation's 11th tallest structure, the 70-story Norwest Center, home of the Norwest Bank System and its subsidiaries. In St. Paul, construction began on the Minnesota International Trade Center, intended to help the state become a center for serving foreign markets. A constitutional amendment having legalized pari-mutuel betting, a horse-racing track, Canterbury Downs, was being built in Shakopee.

Other. Hundreds of protesters, including the wife of Minneapolis' chief of police, were arrested for trespassing when they demonstrated against the Minneapolis Honeywell plant's manufacture of fragmentation bombs.

C. Peter Magrath, 11th president of the University of Minnesota, resigned to become president of the University of Missouri.

ARTHUR NAFTALIN, *University of Minnesota*

MISSISSIPPI

Federal elections marked by overwhelming Republican victories in both the presidential and senatorial contests, multiple legislative sessions dominated by pressing fiscal concerns, and an economy that consistently lagged behind that of the nation accounted for much of Mississippi's news in 1984.

Elections. Voting in record numbers, but still representing only 51% of the over-18 population, Mississippians gave incumbent Republican President Ronald Reagan 62% of the state's vote, the widest margin since the Richard Nixon landslide (78%) in 1972. Aided by white Democrats, Reagan carried more than 80% of the 82 counties. U.S. Sen. Thad Cochran, who had won his seat in 1978 with a plurality, became the first Mississippi Republican to capture a majority vote (61%) in a statewide race. His Democratic challenger, former Gov. William Winter, won only 13 counties.

In the second congressional district, where court-ordered redistricting earlier in the year had increased the black share of the voting-age population from 48% to 53%, first-term incumbent Webb Franklin (a white Republican) claimed 51% of the vote to defeat Robert Clark (a black Democrat) in a closely watched rematch of the 1982 contest. In the only other serious congressional challenge, Wayne Dowdy (D) won 55% of the vote to solidify his hold on the fourth district seat. A scattering of special legislative and county contests also were decided in the November balloting.

The Legislature. Despite an extension of its session from 125 to 129 days, the newly elected legislature ended its regular session May 10 with the state House of Representatives and the Senate unable to reach a compromise tax package to head off a budget crisis projected for the fiscal year beginning July 1. In late June, however, first-year Gov. William ("Bill") Allain, who had maintained a conspicuously low profile during most of the regular session, called legislators into special session to resolve the deadlock. Three days later, lawmakers had eliminated pending cuts in existing sales and income tax rates and had approved additional appropriations to relieve critical needs in the areas of higher education and mental health.

While the regular session ended in frustration, it was not without a number of significant accomplishments. Among these were a major governmental reorganization act and elimination of dual city-county voter registration. A constitutional amendment redefining ethical conduct for public officials was proposed by the legislature but was turned down by the electorate in November.

Economic Conditions. Unemployment levels, personal income, and consumer spending reflected a slow and painful recovery from the recession. By October, however, tax collections began to meet projections, giving some cause for optimism. The value of a near-record cotton crop was diminished by prolonged fall rains.

Other Highlights. Although the Tennessee-Tombigbee Waterway will not be completed until 1985, the Mississippi "divide section" joining the two river systems was dedicated in May. On November 13 the U.S. Supreme Court ended a three-year legal battle by upholding the Mississippi congressional redistricting plan adopted earlier in the year by a three-judge federal panel. The possible storage of high-level nuclear waste in Perry County salt domes continued to spark controversy.

DANA B. BRAMMER
The University of Mississippi

MISSISSIPPI • Information Highlights

Area: 47,689 sq mi (123 515 km²).

Population (July 1, 1983 est.): 2,587,000.

Chief Cities (1980 census): Jackson, the capital (July 1, 1982, est.), 204,195; Biloxi, 49,311; Meridian, 46,577.

Government (1984): *Chief Officers*—governor, William A. Allain (D); lt. gov., Brad Dye (D). *Legislature*—Senate, 52 members; House of Representatives, 122 members.

State Finances (fiscal year 1983): *Revenues,* $3,346,000,000; *expenditures,* $3,132,000,000.

Personal Income (1983): $20,951,000,000; per capita, $8,098.

Labor Force (May 1984); *Civilian labor force,* 1,051,500; *unemployed,* 99,500 (9.5% of total force).

Education: *Enrollment* (fall 1982)—public elementary schools, 326,998; public secondary, 141,296; colleges and universities (fall 1983), 109,728. *Public school expenditures* (1982–83), $812,671,198 ($1,849 per pupil).

Margaret Truman Daniel recalled her father, Harry S. Truman, in a joint meeting of the U.S. House and Senate on May 8, his 100th birthday. "The Man from Missouri" was remembered as an "uncommon common man."

MISSOURI

That Missouri voters pledged the state's eleven electoral votes to Ronald Reagan surprised no one, but Missouri Democrats were stunned by the magnitude of the Republican victory, which left only one state office in Democratic control. State Sen. Harriet Woods (D) was chosen lieutenant governor, becoming the first woman ever elected to a statewide office in Missouri.

Attorney General John Ashcroft (R) won the governorship in the most expensive and perhaps the most scurrilous campaign in recent Missouri history. After a primary victory over St. Louis County Executive Gene McNary in which each candidate attempted to prove the other unfit for high office, Ashcroft continued the same tactics against Lt. Gov. Kenneth Rothman, the Democratic nominee. At a declared cost of $3.12 million Ashcroft saturated radio and television time with what his opponents considered to be misrepresentations and distortions. Rothman retaliated in kind but he had roughly $1 million less to spend.

An admirer of Jerry Falwell, Ashcroft opposed the Equal Rights Amendment, fought desegregation of St. Louis schools, and favors a constitutional amendment to outlaw abortion. He supports the so-called Hancock amendment adopted in Missouri in 1980 to limit state revenues. Ironically its author, Mel Hancock, was the only Republican candidate for state office to be defeated, losing the lieutenant governorship to Harriet Woods, a liberal Democrat. Thus it is hard to characterize the election in Missouri as an unqualified endorsement for conservatism.

Furthermore, the return of all Missouri's congressional delegation with its six-to-three Democratic edge constituted some indication of Democratic viability in view of the fact that the national GOP had targeted two seats, those held by Harold Volkmer and Robert A. Young. Unprecedented expenditures—particularly in Volkmer's ninth district—to buy radio and TV time for ads failed to win those seats for Republican challengers.

A spate of initiative petitions on the November 6 ballot kept voters several minutes in the booths. Three measures generated considerable contention. In two cases opponents carried through the state courts efforts to keep the proposals off the ballot. One, offered by the Electric Ratepayers Protection Project, op-

---

MISSOURI • Information Highlights

Area: 69,697 sq mi (180 516 km²).
Population (July 1, 1983 est.): 4,970,000.
Chief Cities (July 1, 1982 est.): Jefferson City, the capital (1980 census), 33,619; Kansas City, 445,222; St. Louis, 437,354; Springfield, 134,453; Independence, 111,617.
Government (1984): *Chief Officers*—governor, Christopher S. Bond (R); lt. gov., Kenneth J. Rothman (D). *General Assembly*—Senate, 34 members; House of Representatives, 163 members.
State Finances (fiscal year 1983): *Revenues,* $5,319,000,000; *expenditures,* $4,780,000,000.
Personal Income (1983): $54,520,000,000; per capita, $10,969.
Labor Force (May 1984): *Civilian labor force,* 2,405,700; *unemployed,* 170,600 (7.1% of total force).
Education: *Enrollment* (fall 1982)—public elementary schools, 546,751; public secondary, 255,784; colleges and universities (fall 1983), 248,329. *Public school expenditures* (1982–83), $1,772,111,337 ($2,468 per pupil).

posed requests by Union Electric and Kansas City Power and Light for $639 million and $194.7 million, respectively, in rate increases for 1985. The utility companies' expenditure of more than $3 million to fight the proposition paid off, as voters rejected it by a margin of two to one. Church groups fighting proposals to legalize betting on horse racing and to permit a state lottery were unable to counter proponents' claims that the revenues from gambling would fill the state's depleted coffers. Both propositions won by a large margin.

Meanwhile, an issue on which politicians vied with each other to pledge undying opposition—the voluntary plan to desegregate St. Louis area schools—appeared to be working well. Even critics could complain about little except the cost of busing pupils from predominantly black inner city schools to suburban white schools. Supporters pointed to studies showing significant improvement in academic achievement on the part of the 2,300 students transferred in 1983–1984.

RUTH W. TOWNE
Northeast Missouri State University

MONTANA

Utility concerns, political races, and natural calamities marked the year in Montana.

The Public Service Commission rejected Montana Power Company's requested $96.4 million increase in electricity rates to cover its share of the cost of Colstrip 3 power plant. The commission ruled that there was no local need for the plant and granted only a $4 million increase. The ruling then went before the state Supreme Court. At year's end the power company was seeking an end to a running battle with the commission by phasing in substantially lower rate increases over a period of several years. Similarly, after several years of disagreement over unit trains and branch line abandonments, the Burlington Northern Railroad expected that new agreements on branch lines would produce better relations with the state commerce department, farmers, and grain shippers.

Elections. President Ronald Reagan swept his Democratic opponent by a 60–40% margin, comparable to his national proportion of the vote, but his landslide victory had no coattail effect as congressional and state incumbents won reelection. Sen. Max Baucus (D) easily defeated his Republican opponent. Democratic Rep. Pat Williams won reelection in the western district by a near-record margin, and Republican Ron Marlenee secured reelection in the eastern district more handily than anticipated. Democratic Gov. Ted Schwinden won a second term by taking some 70% of the vote in the most lopsided gubernatorial election since the turn of the century. The incumbent Democratic attorney general kept his seat, while Republicans won for secretary of state, state auditor, and superintendent of public instruction.

In the state legislature, Democrats picked up enough Senate seats to give them control of that body, but Republican gains in the House gave both parties 50 seats. In nonpartisan races, voters chose a new Supreme Court chief justice and a new associate justice. Voters approved constitutional amendments to speed up congressional district reapportionment following each decennial census and to expand the Supreme Court's power to enforce canons of judicial ethics on district court judges and justices of the peace.

Environment. Special water courts continued to adjudicate pre-1973 individual water rights to streams and rivers in Montana's 85 drainage basins, while the state's Reserve Water Rights Compact Commission continued attempts to negotiate water-rights agreements with Indian tribes, the U.S. Forest Service, and the National Park Service.

Natural phenomena added to the woes of farmers and rangers caught in a squeeze of rising costs and declining prices. A drought, in its third year in parts of the state, resulted in numerous forest and range fires. Fires in August darkened the sky, burned 30 rural homes, required importation of 5,000 out-of-state firefighters, and reduced some counties to disaster status. The drought reduced grain production and put adequate forage for cattle at a premium. The wheat crop was 22% less than a year before and barley 25% less.

Strip farming, long used to reduce soil blowing, began to give way to block farming, in which farmers plant from fence line to fence line and use massive farm machinery, which requires larger areas. Block plowing and tillage of marginal land contributed to soil erosion problems reminiscent of the 1930s. Blowing nearly doubled the rate of erosion in the previous five years.

RICHARD B. ROEDER
Montana State University

MONTANA · Information Highlights

Area: 147,046 sq mi (380 848 km²).
Population (July 1, 1983 est.): 817,000.
Chief Cities (1980 census): Helena, the capital, 23,938; Billings, 66,842; Great Falls, 56,725.
Government (1984): *Chief Officers*—governor, Ted Schwinden (D); lt. gov., George Turman (D). *Legislature*—Senate, 50 members; House of Representatives, 100 members.
State Finances (fiscal year 1983): *Revenues,* $1,376,000,000; *expenditures,* $1,263,000,000.
Personal Income (1983): $8,124,000,000; per capita, $9,949.
Labor Force (May 1984): *Civilian labor force,* 404,500; *unemployed,* 29,400 (7.3% of total force).
Education: *Enrollment* (fall 1982)—public elementary schools, 106,869; public secondary, 45,466; colleges and universities (fall 1983), 37,877. *Public school expenditures* (1982–83), $456,518,613 ($3,289 per pupil).

Moroccan soldiers view the heavily fortified wall stretching across the nation's desert frontier with Western Sahara. Morocco continued to claim the former Spanish possession.

AP/Wide World

MOROCCO

The new year began in Morocco with rioting in several cities. Students protesting tuition hikes took to the streets, and the violence quickly spread to the general population, which was disgruntled over rises in the prices of basic commodities. The increases had been gradually implemented since August 1983 in accordance with a wide-ranging austerity plan instituted at the behest of the International Monetary Fund. After three days of rioting and at least 29 deaths, King Hassan II came on television and rescinded the price hikes. Despite calls from unions and dissidents for continued unrest, the population fell back into a state of calm.

Foreign Relations. The war with the Polisario Front over the territory of the Western Sahara continued to be the primary issue on Morocco's agenda. The referendum to decide the future of the territory that was supposed to have been held at the end of 1983 never materialized, as Morocco continued to reject direct talks with Polisario to set the procedure for conducting the referendum. With diplomatic efforts stagnated, Morocco continued to expand the perimeter of its heavily fortified wall stretching across the desert frontier with Western Sahara. The expansion of the wall proved to be costly, as many Moroccan lives were lost before the new sections of the wall were completed in July. The expansion would also require Morocco to commit more troops and financial resources to controlling the territory. By the end of 1984, it was estimated that more than 100,000 Moroccan troops were committed to the Western Sahara and that the cost of holding on to the territory was between $1 million and $2 million per day. Moroccan officials said that they would continue to enlarge the perimeter of the wall unless an agreement could be reached with Algeria to prevent Polisario from attacking from across the Algerian border.

After the Organization of African Unity decided to seat a delegation claiming to represent an independent state in the Western Sahara, Morocco withdrew from the OAU in the fall.

Although Morocco's relations with Algeria had improved somewhat in 1983, Algiers' continued support for the Polisario Front led to renewed tensions in 1984. A brief skirmish broke out in July when Moroccan troops working on the defensive wall crossed into Algerian territory. When Hassan warned Mauritania of reprisals if Polisario forces were found operating from Mauritanian soil, Algeria said that it would come to Mauritania's defense.

On August 13, Morocco's King Hassan II and Libya's Muammar el-Qaddafi stunned both their allies and their foes by announcing that they had signed a treaty establishing a "union of states." The terms of the union called for a mutual defense pact and a rotating presidency between the two countries. Hassan quickly reassured the United States that his alliance with Qaddafi did not mean a change in Morocco's pro-U.S. stance. The union, he hoped, might serve to moderate Qaddafi's policies in Libya. Morocco hoped to receive subsidized oil or credits from Libya and, possibly, the financial aid it needs to continue the war in the Sahara.

Politics. In the first Moroccan election since 1977, supporters of King Hassan won a clear majority, though leftists increased their representation from 16 to 37 seats. The results were unlikely to affect Moroccan politics; Hassan remained very popular.

MICHAEL MAREN, *"Africa Report"*

MOROCCO • Information Highlights

Official Name: Kingdom of Morocco.
Location: Northwest Africa.
Area: 157,992 sq mi (409 200 km²).
Population (mid-1984 est.): 23,600,000.
Government: *Head of state,* Hassan II, king (acceded 1961). *Head of government,* Mohammed Karim Lamrani, prime minister (took office Nov. 1983). *Legislature* (unicameral)—National Assembly.
Monetary Unit: Dirham (8.821 dirhams equal U.S.$1, June 1984).
Gross National Product (1982 U.S.$): $14,-900,000,000.
Economic Indexes (1982): *Consumer Prices* (1974 = 100), all items, 228,0; food, 228.7.
Foreign Trade (1982 U.S.$) *Imports,* $4,315,000,000; *exports,* $2,062,000,000.

Robert Benton's critically acclaimed "Places in the Heart," starring Sally Field (second from right), was one of several movies set in rural America and affirming old-fashioned values.

Tri-Star Pictures

MOTION PICTURES

Once the months of summer escapism had ended, something exciting began to take place in American cinema. In what promised to be a fascinating trend, filmmakers were reaching into the heartland of the country to create stories recalling the struggles of brave and courageous men and women, past and present. They saw strength in old-fashioned values, sometimes undermined by injustice, but stubbornly reasserted by people with the kind of grit and spirit that fueled America's growth.

Astonishingly, three films dealt with farm life. The release of *Places in the Heart, Country,* and *The River* in one season contrasted dramatically with the chain of movies glorifying fantasy in space, tales of adventure, and other types of light entertainment. *Places in the Heart* starred Sally Field in a stirring performance as a plucky widow who fights to save her farm when threatened with foreclosure. Writer-director Robert Benton, who set the film in his hometown of Waxahachie, TX, during the Great Depression of the 1930s, was inspired by hand-me-down stories he had heard about generations of Bentons. More than just a drama about a woman's heroism, the movie dealt with race relations, compassion, and the simple ability of people to give each other strength in the face of hardship. It was another coup for the director, who in the 1960s had gained attention as the coauthor of *Bonnie and Clyde* and later was acclaimed as the writer-director of the popular *Kramer vs. Kramer.*

Country, chosen to open the New York Film Festival, materialized as a result of the dedication and determination of actress Jessica Lange, who coproduced it. Lange also excelled in the leading role of a contemporary Midwestern farm woman faced with foreclosure by the FHA (Farmers Home Administration). Sam Shepard, the playwright and occasional actor, made a powerful impression as her husband,

wracked with a sense of failure at not being able to meet the payments on a kind of loan that farmers had been encouraged to seek. Filmed with sincerity and simplicity, *Country* spoke eloquently against the plight of farmers unfairly squeezed by government bureaucracy.

The third film rooted in farm country was *The River,* teaming Sissy Spacek and Mel Gibson as yet another beleaguered couple, this time in Tennessee.

The most persuasive explanation for the upsurge of films dealing with struggling Americans was that times were not as rosy as some would believe. When acute economic and social problems persist, filmmakers tend to catch up with reality and dare to make movies of substance.

Regional Locales. Not only the subject matter of these films made them intriguing. They also illustrated the potential for making more films in diverse regions of the United States. Texas was emerging as a favorite locale. Eagle Pennell attracted attention with his low-budget, independently made *Last Night at the Alamo,* which examined assorted characters against the background of their favorite saloon, about to be torn down. Two young brothers in their twenties, Joel and Ethan Cohen, chose Texas for filming *Blood Simple,* a macabre Hitchcockian suspense yarn involving marital infidelity and revenge, which was also presented at the New York Film Festival.

The festival likewise spotlighted *A Flash of Green,* set in western Florida and dealing with a tenacious battle between real estate sharpies allied with politicians and people who want to preserve their bay environment. *Teachers,* using Columbus, OH, as an unspecified location, was a comic drama about the nation's overwhelming educational problems.

Taking a cue, numerous states, including Texas, Illinois, and South Carolina, were striving to lure filmmakers to their areas. Hollywood and New York could expect heightened competition.

Rating Change. A major development expected to have a lasting impact was the change in the rating system of the Motion Picture Association of America (MPAA). Its Classification and Ratings Administration instituted a new designation of PG-13, signifying that parents should pay heed to whether certain films are appropriate for children under 13. (Children under 13 were still allowed to view them without the accompaniment of a parent or guardian.) The change was precipitated by an outcry over *Indiana Jones and the Temple of Doom* and *Gremlins* as excessively violent. Both films were rated PG (parental guidance suggested) instead of the more stringent R (no one under 17 allowed without a parent or guardian). The introduction of an intermediate rating represented recognition that 17 is no longer an automatic demarcation line between child and adult in an age when teenagers tend to be more sophisticated. Special concern for younger children was gaining in importance.

The MPAA also strengthened its ratings grip by an agreement with the major manufacturers and distributors of video cassettes. When a movie is put on cassette the rating it had for theatrical distribution is to be cited on the package. Thus cassettes being brought into the home are treated differently from books, which are not rated.

The movie companies lost one key battle, however. They failed to convince the Supreme Court that videotaping movies from television, so long as the procedure is for personal use, violates copyright laws. The MPAA had sought royalties from the manufacturers of video equipment but later turned to Congress for action.

Boom. The movie industry had an extremely lucrative summer in 1984. Once again only a few of the films released accounted for the bulk of the box-office grosses. Leading the pack were *Ghostbusters, Indiana Jones and the Temple of Doom, Gremlins, The Karate Kid, Purple Rain, Bachelor Party,* and *Revenge of the Nerds.*

Another part of the entertainment business that promised a new, growing source of revenue was the field of music videos. There was a clear interaction with the movie medium. Videos on television, featuring pop singers, were coordinated with movies in release for purposes of promotion. Directors making names for themselves as music video specialists had opportunities to direct movies as well. The stylistic influence of videos on the movies (fast editing, a staccato beat) showed in pictures like *Electric Dreams, Flashdance* (1983), *Footloose,* and *Purple Rain.*

The Movie Business. Much of what the public sees on the screen is determined by the business aspects of the industry, increasingly dominated by conglomerates. The major executive shift of the year occurred when Barry Diller, extremely successful as the chairman of Paramount, resigned to become chairman and chief executive officer of 20th Century-Fox. He was replaced by Frank Mancuso. Michael Eisner also left his post as president of Paramount, choosing to join the Walt Disney company, which, in addition to fending off a takeover attempt, struggled to create a new image as a producer of more adult films.

An unsolved mystery of the year was the ultimate fate of *The Cotton Club,* a film that typified many of the insanities of the movie business. The project, initiated by producer Robert Evans, went through a series of crises, including legal battles for control, arguments between Evans and his director, Francis Ford Coppola, and problems with financing and budget. The cost of the movie soared to upwards of $48 million. The potential for success was there, however. *The Cotton Club* looked back on the era of the popular nightclub in Harlem that flourished during the 1920s and 1930s amidst bootlegging and the numbers racket. Mobsters as well as high society frequented the club, which specialized in entertainment by black performers, although no blacks were allowed as patrons. Robert Evans remained credited as producer and presenter, but his in-

Lucasfilm Ltd.

Parental outcry over violence in "Indiana Jones and the Temple of Doom," rated PG, was partly responsible for the creation of a new rating category, PG-13.

© Jurgen Vollmer/Tri-Star Pictures

After a four-year hiatus, Robert Redford returned to film acting in "The Natural," based on Bernard Malamud's novel.

MOTION PICTURES | 1984

THE ADVENTURES OF BUCKAROO BANZAI. Director, W. D. Richter; screenplay by Earl MacRauch. With Peter Weller, John Lithgow, Jeff Goldblum.

AFTER THE REHEARSAL. Director, Ingmar Bergman; screenplay by Mr. Bergman. With Erland Josephson, Ingrid Thulin, Lena Olin.

ALL OF ME. Director, Carl Reiner; screenplay by Phil Alden Robinson, based on the novel *Me Two* by Ed David. With Steve Martin, Lily Tomlin.

AMADEUS. Director, Milos Forman; screenplay by Peter Shaffer. With F. Murray Abraham, Tom Hulce.

AMERICAN DREAMER. Director, Rick Rosenthal; screenplay by Jim Kouf, David Greenwalt. With JoBeth Williams, Tom Conti.

AND THE SHIP SAILS ON. Director, Federico Fellini; original idea and screenplay by Tonino Guerra, Mr. Fellini. With Freddie Jones, Barbara Jefford, Janet Suzman.

ANOTHER COUNTRY. Director, Marek Kanievska; screenplay by Julian Mitchell. With Colin Firth, Rupert Everett.

BEVERLY HILLS COP. Director, Martin Brest; screenplay by Dan Petrie, Jr. With Eddie Murphy.

BIZET'S CARMEN. Director, Francesco Rosi, from the opera by Georges Bizet; libretto by Henri Meilhac, Ludovic Halévy; screen adaptation by Mr. Rosi, Tonino Guerra. With Julia Migenes-Johnson, Plácido Domingo.

BODY DOUBLE. Director, Brian De Palma; screenplay by Robert J. Avrech, Mr. De Palma. With Craig Wasson, Melanie Griffith.

THE BOSTONIANS. Director, James Ivory; screenplay by Ruth Prawer Jhabvala. With Christopher Reeve, Vanessa Redgrave, Madeleine Potter.

THE BOUNTY. Director, Bernard Williams; screenplay by Robert Bolt. With Mel Gibson, Anthony Hopkins, Laurence Olivier, Edward Fox.

BROADWAY DANNY ROSE. Written and directed by Woody Allen. With Woody Allen, Mia Farrow, Nick Apollo Forte.

THE BROTHER FROM ANOTHER PLANET. Written and directed by John Sayles. With Joe Morton.

CAL. Director, Pat O'Connor; screenplay by Bernard Maclaverty. With Helen Mirren, John Lynch.

CAREFUL HE MIGHT HEAR YOU. Director, Carl Schultz; screenplay by Michael Jenkins. With Nicholas Gledhill, Wendy Hughes, Robyn Nevin, John Hargreaves.

CHOOSE ME. Written and directed by Alan Rudolph. With Genevieve Bujold, Keith Carradine, Lesley Ann Warren.

CITY HEAT. Director, Richard Benjamin; screenplay by Sam O. Brown, Joseph C. Stinson. With Clint Eastwood, Burt Reynolds.

COTTON CLUB. Director, Francis Ford Coppola; screenplay by William Kennedy, Mr. Coppola. With Richard Gere, Gregory Hines.

COUNTRY. Director, Richard Pearce; screenplay by William D. Wittliff. With Jessica Lange, Sam Shepard.

CRIMES OF PASSION. Director, Ken Russell; screenplay by Barry Sandler. With Bruce Davison, John Laughlin, Anthony Perkins, Annie Potts, Kathleen Turner.

DUNE. Director, David Lynch; screenplay by Frank Herbert, Mr. Lynch. With Sting, Kyle MacLachlan, Francesca Annis.

EL NORTE. Director, Gregory Nava; screenplay by Anna Thomas, Mr. Nava. With Zide Silvia Gutiérrez, David Villalpando.

ENTRE NOUS. Director, Diane Kurys; screenplay by Miss Kurys. With Miou Miou, Isabelle Huppert, Guy Marchand.

ERENDIRA. Director, Ruy Guerra; screenplay by Gabriel Garcia Marquez. With Irene Papas, Claudia Ohana.

FALLING IN LOVE. Director, Ulu Grosbard; screenplay by Michael Cristofer. With Robert De Niro, Meryl Streep, Harvey Keitel.

FINDERS KEEPERS. Director, Richard Lester; screenplay by Ronny Graham, Terence Marsh, Charles Dennis. With Michael O'Keefe, Louis Gossett, Jr.

FIRSTBORN. Director, Michael Apted; screenplay by Ron Koslow. With Teri Garr, Peter Weller, Christopher Collet.

FIRST NAME: CARMEN. Director, Jean-Luc Godard; screenplay by Anne-Marie Mieville. With Maruschka Detmers, Jacques Bonnaffé, Jean-Luc Godard.

FOOTLOOSE. Director, Herbert Ross; screenplay and lyrics by Dean Pitchford. With Kevin Bacon.

THE 4TH MAN. Director, Paul Verhoeven; screenplay by Gerard Soeteman. With Jeroen Krabbe, Renee Soutendijk.

GARBO TALKS. Director, Sidney Lumet; screenplay by Larry Grusin. With Anne Bancroft, Ron Silver, Carrie Fisher.

GHOSTBUSTERS. Director, Ivan Reitman; screenplay by Dan Aykroyd, Harold Ramis. With Bill Murray, Dan Aykroyd.

GIVE MY REGARDS TO BROAD STREET. Director, Peter Webb; screenplay and music by Paul McCartney. With Paul McCartney, Ringo Starr.

THE GODS MUST BE CRAZY. Written and directed by Jamie Uys. With Marius Weyers, Sandra Prinsloo.

GREMLINS. Director, Joe Dante; screenplay by Chris Columbus. With Zach Galligan, Phoebe Cates.

GREYSTOKE: THE LEGEND OF TARZAN, LORD OF THE APES. Director, Hugh Hudson; screenplay by P. H. Vazak, Michael Austin. With Christopher Lambert.

THE HOTEL NEW HAMPSHIRE. Director, Tony Richardson; screenplay by Mr. Richardson, from a novel by John Irving. With Jodie Foster, Beau Bridges.

ICEMAN. Director, Fred Schepisi; screenplay by Chris Proser, John Drimmer. With Timothy Hutton.

INDIANA JONES AND THE TEMPLE OF DOOM. Director, Steven Spielberg; screenplay by Willard Huyck, Gloria Katz. With Harrison Ford, Kate Capshaw, Dan Aykroyd.

IRRECONCILABLE DIFFERENCES. Director, Charles Shyer; screenplay by Nancy Meyers, Mr. Shyer. With Ryan O'Neal, Shelley Long.

JOHNNY DANGEROUSLY. Director, Amy Heckerling; screenplay by Norman Steinberg, Harry Colomby, Bernie Kukoff, Jeff Harris. With Michael Keaton, Joe Piscopo, Marilu Henner.

THE KARATE KID. Director, John G. Avildsen; screenplay by Robert Mark Kamen. With Ralph Macchio, Noriyuki (Pat) Morita.

THE KILLING FIELDS. Director, Roland Joffe; screenplay by Bruce Robinson. With Sam Waterston, Dr. Haing S. Ngor, John Malkovich.

THE LITTLE DRUMMER GIRL. Director, George Roy Hill; screenplay by Loring Mandel, based on the novel by John le Carre. With Diane Keaton, Klaus Kinski.

A LOVE IN GERMANY. Director, Andrzej Wajda; screenplay by Boleslaw Michalek, Mr. Wajda, Agnieszka Holland. With Hanna Schygulla, Marie-Christine Barrault, Piotr Lysak.

LOVE STREAMS. Director, John Cassavetes; screenplay by Ted Allan, Mr. Cassavetes. With Gena Rowlands.

MASS APPEAL. Director, Glenn Jordan; adapted by Bill C. Davis from his play. With Jack Lemmon, Zeljko Ivanek, Charles Durning.

MICKI & MAUDE. Director, Blake Edwards; screenplay by Jonathan Reynolds. With Dudley Moore, Amy Irving, Ann Reinking.

MOSCOW ON THE HUDSON. Director, Paul Mazursky; screenplay by Leon Capetanos, Mr. Mazursky. With Robin Williams.

THE MUPPETS TAKE MANHATTAN. Director, Frank Oz; screenplay by Tom Patchett, Jay Tarses, Mr. Oz. With the Muppets (voices by Jim Henson, Frank Oz, and others).

THE NATURAL. Director, Barry Levinson; screenplay by Roger Towne, Phil Dusenberry. With Robert Redford.

1984. Written and directed by Michael Radford, from the novel by George Orwell. With John Hurt, Richard Burton, Suzanna Hamilton.

NOT FOR PUBLICATION. Director, Paul Bartel; screenplay by John Meyer, Mr. Bartel. With Nancy Allen, David Naughton, Laurence Luckinbill, Alice Ghostley.

OH GOD! YOU DEVIL. Director, Paul Bogart; screenplay by Andrew Bergman. With George Burns, Ted Wass.

ONCE UPON A TIME IN AMERICA. Director, Sergio Leone; screenplay by Leonardo Benvenuti, Piero de Bernardi, Enrico Medioli, Franco Arcalli, Franco Ferrini, Mr. Leone, based on the novel *The Hoods* by Harry Grey. With Robert De Niro, James Woods, Elizabeth McGovern.

PARIS, TEXAS. Director, Wim Wenders; screenplay by Sam Shepard. With Harry Dean Stanton, Hunter Carson.

A PASSAGE TO INDIA. Written and directed by David Lean, from the novel by E. M. Forster. With Dame Peggy Ashcroft, Judy Davis, James Fox, Sir Alec Guinness.

PLACES IN THE HEART. Written and directed by Robert Benton. With Sally Field, John Malkovich, Danny Glover.

THE PLOUGHMAN'S LUNCH. Director, Richard Eyre; screenplay by Ian McEwan. With Jonathan Pryce, Tim Curry, Rosemary Harris.

THE POPE OF GREENWICH VILLAGE. Director, Stuart Rosenberg; screenplay by Vincent Patrick. With Eric Roberts, Mickey Rourke, Daryl Hannah, Geraldine Page, Burt Young.

PROTOCOL. Director, Herbert Ross; screenplay by Buck Henry. With Goldie Hawn, Chris Sarandon, Richard Romanus.

RACING WITH THE MOON. Director, Richard Benjamin; screenplay by Steven Kloves. With Sean Penn, Elizabeth McGovern.

THE RAZOR'S EDGE. Director, John Byrum; screenplay by Bill Murray, Mr. Byrum. With Bill Murray.

THE RIVER. Director, Mark Rydell; screenplay by Robert Dillon. With Sissy Spacek, Mel Gibson, Scott Glenn.

ROMANCING THE STONE. Director, Robert Zemeckis; screenplay by Diane Thomas. With Michael Douglas, Kathleen Turner, Danny DeVito.

RUNAWAY. Written and directed by Michael Crichton. With Tom Selleck.

SIXTEEN CANDLES. Written and directed by John Hughes. With Molly Ringwald, Justin Henry, Paul Dooley.

A SOLDIER'S STORY. Director, Norman Jewison; screenplay by Charles Fuller. With Howard E. Rollins, Jr.

SPLASH. Director, Ron Howard; screenplay by Lowell Ganz, Babaloo Mandell, Bruce Jay Friedman. With Tom Hanks, Daryl Hannah.

STARMAN. Director, John Carpenter; screenplay by Ray Gideon, Bruce Evans, Dean Riesner. With Jeff Bridges, Karen Allen.

STRANGER THAN PARADISE. Written and directed by Jim Jarmusch. With John Lurie, Eszter Balint, Richard Edson.

A SUNDAY IN THE COUNTRY. Director, Bertrand Tavernier; screenplay by Colo Tavernier, Mr. Tavernier, based on the novel by Pierre Bost. With Louis Ducreux, Sabine Azéma.

SUPERGIRL. Director, Jeannot Szwarc; screenplay by David Odell. With Helen Slater, Faye Dunaway, Peter O'Toole, Peter Cook.

SWANN IN LOVE. Director, Volker Schlondorff; screenplay by Peter Brook, Jean-Claude Carrière, Marie-Hélène Estienne. With Jeremy Irons, Ornella Muti.

SWING SHIFT. Director, Jonathan Demme; screenplay by Rob Morton. With Goldie Hawn, Kurt Russell.

TEACHERS. Director, Arthur Hiller; screenplay by W. R. McKinney. With Nick Nolte, Jobeth Williams, Judd Hirsch.

THE TERMINATOR. Director, James Cameron; screenplay by Gale Anne Hurd, Mr. Cameron. With Arnold Schwarzenegger.

THIEF OF HEARTS. Written and directed by Douglas Day Stewart. With Steven Bauer, Barbara Williams.

TIGHTROPE. Written and directed by Richard Tuggle. With Clint Eastwood, Genevieve Bujold.

2010. Written and directed by Peter Hyams, from Arthur C. Clarke's novel. With Roy Scheider, Bob Balaban, John Lithgow, Helen Mirren, Keir Dullea.

UNDER THE VOLCANO. Director, John Huston; screenplay by Guy Gallo, based on the novel by Malcolm Lowry. With Albert Finney, Jacqueline Bisset, Anthony Andrews.

Gamma-Liaison

Director John Huston brought Malcolm Lowry's haunting 1947 novel "Under the Volcano" to the screen in 1984. Albert Finney (left) as The Consul gives a finely honed performance, ably supported by Jacqueline Bisset and Anthony Andrews.

terest was bought out by the film's principal financiers. *The Cotton Club* was to be released in December, but it would be sometime in 1985 before the verdict was in on whether it could make back its money or turn a profit.

Filming Literature. Several noteworthy films drew on classic works of literature. The team of producer Ismail Merchant and director James Ivory based their film *The Bostonians* on the novel by Henry James. The writings of Marcel Proust, considered nearly impossible for screen adaptation, yielded *Swann in Love,* directed by Volker Schlöndorff of Germany. Malcolm Lowry's difficult novel *Under the Volcano* was taken in hand by director John Huston, who made his movie with Albert Finney starring as "The Consul." Veteran director David Lean undertook E. M. Forster's challenging *A Passage to India.*

Prosper Mérimée's *Carmen* was rediscovered both by conventional and unconventional directors. Francesco Rosi of Italy took the traditional road with *Bizet's Carmen,* turning out a magnificent film opera. Jean-Luc Godard, famed French New Wave director who is still experimenting, used Mérimée's *Carmen* as a jumping off point for his own offbeat version, *First Name: Carmen.* Godard gave it a contemporary Parisian setting, making his Carmen a terrorist. These followed the dance-oriented *Carmen,* choreographed by and starring Antonio Gades.

The theater also was a source for two major films—Peter Shaffer's adaptation of his own *Amadeus,* directed by Milos Forman, and *A Soldier's Story,* based on the Pulitzer Prize-winning play by Charles Fuller and directed by Norman Jewison.

Awards. There seemed little doubt at Oscar time that *Terms of Endearment* would be a major winner. The movie, a blend of comedy, tragedy, and sentiment, proved enormously popular and did indeed win several awards. In addition to being voted best picture, it earned an award for James L. Brooks as best director. The best actress award went to Shirley MacLaine, and Jack Nicholson, to nobody's surprise, walked off with the best supporting actor Oscar. Ingmar Bergman, whose current film was *After the Rehearsal* (1984), about a director who reflects on his life and art, won the foreign film Oscar for *Fanny and Alexander.* (*See also* PRIZES and AWARDS.)

The New York Film Society bestowed its annual honor, celebrated at a gala, upon veteran actress Claudette Colbert.

Deaths. Motion picture personalities who died during 1984 included directors Joseph Losey and François Truffaut; actors Richard Burton, James Mason, former child star Jackie Coogan, Walter Pidgeon, William Powell, and Johnny Weissmuller; and actress Janet Gaynor. (*See also* OBITUARIES.)

WILLIAM WOLF, *Gannett News Service*

MOZAMBIQUE

Amid a worsening economy, dramatic developments took place in Mozambican foreign affairs during 1984. Mozambique entered into far-reaching agreements with its arch foe, the Republic of South Africa.

Domestic Affairs. After winning independence from Portugal in 1975, the Front for Liberation of Mozambique (FRELIMO) had instituted Marxist policies ending private ownership. The economy sharply declined. The year 1984 saw a strengthening of the trend away from collectivized agriculture to peasant farming. But the economic crisis remained severe. The government asked for rescheduling of debt payments on $862 million.

A three-year-old regional drought continued to cause famine in Mozambique. Thousands of starving Mozambicans entered neighboring Zimbabwe in search of food.

Rumors circulated of a split in the FRELIMO leadership in June when President Samora Machel dismissed the ministers of security and the interior amid a crackdown on the abuse of authority by the police and military.

Foreign Affairs. The Mozambique National Resistance (MNR), a guerrilla movement formed in the mid-1970s, spread sabotage in most of the country to oppose FRELIMO. It received support from South Africa. This war forced FRELIMO in March to sign the Nkomati accord, a ten-year "nonaggression and good neighborliness" pact with South Africa. In return for the withdrawal of South African support from the MNR, FRELIMO agreed to prevent the African National Congress, a black nationalist group, from using Mozambican bases to launch raids into South Africa. However, fighting continued in both countries.

In May, Mozambique signed a 32-year economic agreement to sell electricity from its Cabora Bassa hydroelectric plant to South Africa. The two countries agreed to jointly protect the dam, a frequent target of sabotage by the MNR.

The United States lifted a seven-year ban on direct economic assistance to Mozambique in June. Mozambique joined the World Bank and the International Monetary Fund in 1984.

See also AFRICA.

THOMAS H. HENRIKSEN, *Hoover Institution*

MOZAMBIQUE • Information Highlights

Official Name: People's Republic of Mozambique.
Location: Southeastern coast of Africa.
Area: 304,942 sq mi (789 800 km²).
Population (mid-1984 est.): 13,400,000.
Chief City (1984 est.): Maputo, the capital, 755,000.
Government: Head of state, Samora Moises Machel, president (took office June 1975). *Legislature* (unicameral)—People's Assembly.
Gross National Product (1981 U.S.$): $1,500,-000,000.

The Metropolitan Opera in New York opened its season with "Lohengrin," featuring Placido Domingo in the lead role.

MUSIC

Even as music videos, compact discs, and other innovations were fueling a boom in the recording industry, live performance remained vital to the major music forms in 1984. Classical and jazz festivals seemed to broaden their appeal, and extended concert tours were an overwhelming success for the top stars of rock.

Classical

Classical music festivals assumed a more significant role in U.S. cultural life, becoming "supra-institutions" embracing the genres of symphony, opera, and recital. As the number, variety, and scope of festivals increased, traditional lines between the forms became blurred. A move away from traditional institutions and styles of presentation also was evident.

New Music Festivals. Contemporary music was a major beneficiary of the emphasis on festivals. While new works, mostly premieres, continued to be offered in regular subscription series, a greater concentration and variety were performed in new music festivals.

The New York Philharmonic's contemporary music festival, titled "Horizons '84: The New Romanticism, A Broader View," encompassed the works of 40 composers in 10 concerts at Avery Fisher Hall, May 31–June 8.

The director, Jacob Druckman, placed works for traditional instrumental groups alongside computer and synthesizer music and "performance art." The N.Y. Philharmonic introduced George Crumb's *Landscapes,* a timbre exploration, and Oliver Knussen's opera, *Where the Wild Things Are,* based on Maurice Sendak's children's book.

The Juilliard School of Music produced a festival of five concerts, January 20–24, of modern music covering 50 years beginning in 1930—from Howard Hanson's *Second Romantic Symphony* to Milton Babbitt's *Canonical Forms* for piano. The sixth annual New Music America Festival in Hartford, CT, July 1–7, offered new music by 50 composers in jazz, rock, classical, folk, ethnic, gospel, and experimental formats.

The CalArts Contemporary Music Festival in California produced 12 programs over six days, March 8–13. Among the more than 20 composers represented, Italy's Giacinto Scelsi was singled out as exceptional. Among the other composers participating were Bernard Rands, Henry Brant, Kenneth Gaburo, R. Murray Schafer, Karl-Heinz Stockhausen, and Terry Riley.

Summer contemporary music festivals included one in late July at the Berkshire Music Center, and one at the Aspen (CO) Music Festival. The 1984 World Music Days, the annual festival of the International Society for Contemporary Music, was held in Toronto, September 23–27, and in Montreal, September 28–October 3.

Premieres. Donald Erb's Prismatic Variations for orchestra—and 80 young musicians around the hall playing unconventional and homemade instruments—was premiered by the St. Louis Symphony, Leonard Slatkin conducting, on January 28. Sir Michael Tippett's oratorio *The Mask of Time* was introduced by the Boston Symphony with the Tanglewood Festival Chorus on April 5, Sir Colin Davis conducting; the two-hour work was one of 12 commissioned by the Boston Symphony in celebration of its centenary year, 1981.

In a noteworthy joint enterprise, the Northeast Orchestral Consortium of the Albany (NY), Springfield (MA), New Haven (CT), and Hartford (CT) symphonies and the Hudson Valley (NY) Philharmonic commissioned six large orchestral works: John Harbison's *Ulysses' Raft,* Earl Kim's *Cornet,* Tobias Picker's *The Encantadas,* Charles Wuorinen's *Third Piano Concerto,* Ned Rorem's *Violin Concerto,* and Robert Starer's *Hudson Valley Suite.* The five orchestras were to play each work at least twice over a three-season period.

Major Festivals. Two general arts festivals in which music played a major role were the Olympic Arts Festival in Los Angeles, June 1–August 12, and the Toronto International Festival in June. The Olympic Arts Festival, sponsored by the Times Mirror Company and held in conjunction with the 1984 Summer Olympics, presented a broad program of music in addition to 22 dance groups, 30 theater companies, art exhibitions, films, and other events. The major musical offering was the exclusive U.S. appearance of the Royal Opera of Covent Garden, Sir Colin Davis conducting, in 11 performances of three works: Benjamin Britten's *Peter Grimes,* featuring Jon Vickers; Andrei Serban's controversial new production of Puccini's *Turandot,* combining kabuki, commedia

del l'arte, and other influences; and Mozart's *Die Zauberfloete.* The success of the Royal Opera's visit may have stimulated efforts to establish international opera in Los Angeles. It led directly to the appointment of Peter Hemmings, former director of the Welsh Opera and Australian Opera, as the first director of the L.A. Music Center Opera Association.

The Olympic Arts Festival produced two subfestivals. Of five concerts devoted to contemporary music, one was an outdoor performance of Stockhausen's *Sternklang;* two were devoted to music from the music world's high-tech center, the Institut de Recherche et Coordination Acoustique/Musique of Paris; and two to American and Canadian composers. The chamber music series focused on five string quartets—the Guarneri, Lydian, Colorado, Hagen, and Sequoia.

The Toronto International Festival, in celebration of the city's sesquicentennial and the province's bicentennial, produced 175 performances in all the arts. Visiting companies included the Metropolitan Opera, Hamburg Ballet, and Tanztheater Wuppertal. A high point was the Canadian Opera's production of Benjamin Britten's *Death in Venice.*

The San Antonio (TX) Festival, held May 18–June 9, offered a production of *Carmen* by the Berlin Opera; a San Antonio Opera production of Rossini's *William Tell;* Benjamin Britten's *Noyes Fludde;* the Dallas, Houston, and Austin symphonies; the Royal Swedish Ballet and Berlin Ballet; and two works by the English National Opera.

The new International Festival of the Americas, held October 14–30 at the University of Miami, was under the direction of Jose Serebrier and included 23 events. Featuring the American Symphony Orchestra and several local and visiting groups, it emphasized music from the United States (including three premieres) and Latin America (five premieres).

Martha Swope

"Akhnaten," a new minimalist opera by the acclaimed American composer Philip Glass, made its world premiere in Stuttgart, West Germany. It later appeared at the Houston Opera and the New York City Opera, left.

Opera. A major development in opera during 1984 was the wide adoption of the production device of supertitles, or surtitles, introduced by the Canadian Opera in 1983. During the performance, phrases of the text in English are projected on a small screen suspended below the proscenium.

Philip Glass, writing in his minimalist style, scored a success with the third in his series of protrait operas, *Akhnaten*. (The first two were *Einstein on the Beach* and *Satyagraha*.) *Akhnaten* premiered March 24 in Stuttgart, West Germany, with Dennis Russell Davies conducting. It made its U.S. debut at the Houston Opera on October 12, John DeMain conducting. Set in ancient Egypt, *Akhnaten* was described as a series of "living tableaux," the voices subordinated to the orchestral music and stage picture.

Hans Werner Henze's *We Come to the River* (1976), performed for the first time in the United States by the Santa Fe Opera on July 28, was a violent and polemical treatment of a sociopolitical morality theme. The production was highly unconventional, spilling over into the orchestra pit. The large cast (111 separate roles) and triple orchestra were conducted by Dennis Russell Davies.

Erich Korngold's *Violanta* and Alexander Zemlinsky's *A Florentine Tragedy* opened the Santa Fe Opera season as a double bill on June 30; they were perceived as heavily influenced by Wagner and Richard Strauss.

Handel's *Rinaldo* in January became the first baroque opera to be performed by the Metropolitan Opera. The first act of Rachmaninoff's unfinished *Monna Vanna* was given its world premiere August 11 at the Saratoga Performing Arts Center, with the Philadelphia Orchestra (Igor Buketoff conducting), Tatiana Troyanos, and Sherrill Milnes.

The first U.S. performance of Mussorgsky's *Khovanshchina* in the Shostakovich version, on November 11, was a major success of the San Francisco Opera's fall season.

The English National Opera made its first tour of the United States, giving 26 performances of five works in Houston, Austin, and San Antonio, New Orleans, and New York. Two of those works were grand, historical pageants—Britten's *Gloriana* (a U.S. premiere), and Prokofiev's *War and Peace*. The other three—Jonathan Miller's controversial production of *Rigoletto,* set in New York in the 1950s; *Patience;* and Britten's *The Turn of the Screw* —also were well received.

Names and Places. The new $18 million, 6,800-seat Filene Center at Wolf Trap Farm Park, VA, the U.S. national park for the arts, opened on July 30, replacing the auditorium that burned in 1982. On July 4 the Cincinnati Symphony inaugurated its new summer home, the Riverbend Music Center, seating 5,014 in the pavilion and 5,000 on surrounding lawns.

Laine Wilser

The Chamber Music Society of New York's Lincoln Center performs in a special Bach festival to commemorate the 300th anniversary of the composer's birth, in 1985.

Dennis Russell Davies, music director of the opera and orchestra of Bad Wuerttemburg, Stuttgart, and also of the Cabrillo Music Festival in Aptos, CA, was named principal conductor and program director of the Saratoga (NY) Performing Arts Center. The American conductor Lorin Maazel resigned as general manager, artistic director, and first conductor of the Vienna State Opera, charging "intolerable interference" by the Austrian minister of education and arts, Helmut Zilk. Soon after, Maazel was named music consultant of the Pittsburgh Symphony. Bruce Crawford, president of the Metropolitan Opera Association, was selected to succeed Anthony A. Bliss as the company's general manager beginning Jan. 1, 1986. Also in 1986, Ricardo Muti will become music director of La Scala opera house in Milan; this would not affect his position as music director of the Philadelphia Orchestra. Zubin Mehta's contract with the New York Philharmonic was extended four years until 1990, giving him the longest tenure of any music director in that orchestra's history. Gunther Herbig was named music director of the Detroit Symphony. André Previn, music director of the Pittsburgh Symphony since 1976, was appointed to the music directorship of the Los Angeles Philharmonic beginning with the 1986–87 season. Herbert Blomstedt, Swedish conductor of the Dresden Staatskapelle, was named music director of the San Francisco Symphony as of June 1985, succeeding Edo de Waart. Semyon Bychkov, 32, the Soviet émigré director of the Grand Rapids (MI) Symphony, was appointed music director of the Buffalo Philharmonic. Rudolf Barshai was appointed music director of the Vancouver Symphony. And Joseph Polisi became president of the Juilliard School of Music.

ROBERT COMMANDAY
Music Critic
"San Francisco Chronicle"

Jazz

In 1984 the jazz scene was enhanced by the reissuing of the great jazz recordings of the past. Especially interesting were the reissues of *The Complete Blue Note Recordings of Thelonious Monk,* the Dinah Washington sides on *Slick Chick,* the Gerry Mulligan-Chet Baker collaborations, and the classic music of Miles Davis, Count Basie, Duke Ellington, and Earl Hines.

Recording News. From France's Swing record label and various other early labels came the first six of a contemplated 320 albums reissued by the American Company, DRG Records. The most interesting album in the Swing series of reissues was *Ridin' in Rhythm,* produced originally by John Hammond in the early 1930s.

Led by pianist George Winston and the group "Shadow Fox," Windham Hill Records in 1984 achieved musical and financial success. Emphasizing the Oregon and Paul Winter tradition, the record company produced a new acoustic, relaxed, low-energy fusion small-group sound.

In the face of an overabundance of record labels, still more new labels surfaced, including Bruce Lundvall's Manhattan Records. Despite the advent of new labels, studio and recording work declined in 1984, resulting in potentially great jazz artists leaving the security of the recording studio and returning in a more active and creative way to performing. As such, studio trumpet player Jon Faddis formed his own jazz quintet, and trumpeter Randy Brecker started a new group with his wife, pianist Elaine Elias.

Noted Jazz Events. The most important, productive, and successful "jazztimes" convention was held in New York in March. The theme of the convention was the future of jazz. The subjects discussed were jazz in home video, building jazz societies, new horizons for jazz symphonic collaborations, overseas employment opportunities, record reissues, record-company practices, networking jazz support groups, and new technology.

The summer Kool Jazz Festival featured mostly swing music wedded to the early 1950s "Jazz at the Philharmonic" style. The festival's salutes were to Brazil, Django Reinhart, Harold Arlen, Benny Carter, and Illinois Jacquet. There was a tribute to Count Basie, who died in April, near the end of the festival.

With Pete Fountain as the host performer, the New Orleans World's Fair featured big bands from Lionel Hampton to Buddy Rich, small groups from Art Blakey to Wynton Marsalis, singers Mel Torme and Sarah Vaughan, and traditional jazz bands including the Preservation Hall Jazz Band and the Olympia Jazz Band. The groups were featured in the famous Reunion Hall and in the International Amphitheatre that had housed the International Jazz Festival in May.

Awards. The winners in the 32d Annual International *Down Beat* Critics Poll were: Charlie Haden, *The Ballad of the Fallen*—record of the year; Thelonious Monk, *The Complete Blue Note Recordings of Thelonious Monk*—reissue of the year; Count Basie—big band; Art Blakey—acoustic group; Weather Report—electric group; Carla Bley—composer; Gil Evans—arranger; Wynton Marsalis—trumpet; Jimmy Knepper—trombone; Steve Lacey—soprano sax; Phil Woods—alto sax; Sonny Rollins—tenor sax; Pepper Adams—baritone sax; Milt Jackson—vibes; Stephane Grappelli—violin; Cecil Taylor—acoustic piano; Josef Zawinul—electric piano; Joe Pass—guitar; Charlie Haden—acoustic bass; Steve Swallow—electric bass; Max Roach—drums; Joe Williams—male singer; Sarah Vaughn—female singer; Manhattan Transfer—vocal group.

DOMINIC SPERA, *Indiana University*

David Gahr

Miles Davis, long an influence on the jazz world, took top record honors in 1984 with his "Decoy." The highly inventive Davis continues to make inroads into jazz's future while codifying its past.

The Jackson brothers reunited for a four-month concert tour coinciding with the release of their "Victory" album.

Popular

Pop music was marked by overwhelming success for a relatively few artists and a Top 40 mentality in 1984, the second year of solid economic recovery for the music business. Although the restabilized industry concentrated on producing commercially viable "hit" material, renewed profits and exciting developments in audio and video technology encouraged exploration of new artists and new ways to present them.

Chief among the year's blockbuster concert tours was the Jacksons' controversial "Victory" tour. Both commercially and technically, it was the largest concert tour ever mounted. Drawing on the popularity of Michael Jackson, (*See* BIOGRAPHY), the tour raked in about $70 million from nearly 50 dates.

Bruce Springsteen's U.S. concert tour was a smash sellout. The double success of the *Born in the U.S.A.* album and tour, substantially supported by "Dancing in the Dark," the first video starring the Jersey-born rocker, firmly established Springsteen as a mainstream commercial act.

The Jacksons and Springsteen tours were the exceptions to a soft summer rock concert season, an indication that general attendance at

stadium-size rock concerts was declining in the face of high ticket prices and the proliferation of home music video sources. Arena rockers like Van Halen still drew, as did pop superstars of the stature of Kenny Rogers, Diana Ross, Barry Manilow, and Julio Iglesias. Although rock concert attendance picked up in fall and winter with major tours by Prince, Hall and Oates, Culture Club, Elton John, Billy Squier, U2, and Rick Springfield, the trend seemed to be more toward such mid-level acts as Scandal, John Waite, Stevie Ray Vaughan, and Lou Reed.

The influence of video grew even stronger, with the most popular acts having strong visual as well as musical appeal. Prince's visual charisma and extraordinary musicianship shot him and his band, the Revolution, to the top of the charts and made his autobiographical film, *Purple Rain,* the most commercially successful rock movie in history; his coterie of musical associates—The Time, Sheila E., Vanity, and Apollonia 6—achieved fame in his wake. The flamboyant Cyndi Lauper broke all records for a female rock singer with a series of alternately upbeat and tender hit singles and videos from her smash debut album, *She's So Unusual.* Although the Police maintained their popularity, their energies turned from group to individual

Rock superstar Bruce Springsteen, left, produced his seventh LP—"Born in the U.S.A."—and sold out his summer tour. Spanish crooner Julio Iglesias, probably the most popular singer in the world, won new fans with a 33-city U.S. tour.

projects; lead singer Sting seemed firmly headed for a film acting career. The smooth ballad style and expert videos of Lionel Richie kept him at the top of the pop charts for more than a year. A good-time rock sound and personable videos did almost the same for Huey Lewis and the News. While continuing to play acoustic jazz, Herbie Hancock crossed multiple musical boundaries with his hugely popular single and video "Rockit." "Rockit" swept the First Annual MTV Video Music Awards.

Video accelerated the popularity of such established and widely divergent pop artists as David Bowie, the Cars, Van Halen, Billy Joel, ZZ Top, and Chicago. Relative newcomers like Billy Idol, Madonna, Duran Duran, Culture Club, Eurythmics, Quiet Riot, and Ratt were firmly indebted to the video medium. MTV continued to be the chief disseminator of music video, with 24.1 million subscribers, but three other major channels arose to challenge its supremacy. Turner Broadcasting's Music Video Network was aimed at an older audience; MTV countered with its own network aimed at the 25–49-year-old market, Video Hits 1.

Spain's Julio Iglesias, one of the most popular vocalists in the world with international record sales of more than 100 million, finally conquered U.S. audiences, earning two platinum recordings in one year and launching a sellout U.S. tour. His Grammy-winning duet with country hero Willie Nelson and another with Diana Ross helped break the American barrier against foreign-language performers.

Internationally, most countries were still strongly influenced by U.S. and British pop artists. The United States continued to accept a British "invasion," encompassing artists as established as Paul McCartney and new, controversial ones like Frankie Goes to Hollywood.

Black artists smashed through industry-created categories and dominated the pop charts with a variety of sounds, from Prince's hard-rocking "Let's Go Crazy" to Stevie Wonder's lilting ballad "I Just Called to Say I Love You." Other black artists who were enormously popular in 1984 included Ray Parker, Jr., Lionel Richie, Chaka Khan, Deniece Williams, Billy Ocean, the Pointer Sisters, and Tina Turner, who made a strong comeback.

Original music from films became far more popular than in the previous peak movie-music year, 1978. Aided by exposure from video clips culled from the feature-length original, the soundtracks to *Purple Rain, Ghostbusters, Footloose, Breakin', Hard to Hold, The Big Chill,* and other films were popular.

Country music displayed a colorful palette of musical styles, from traditional to pop to folk-influenced modes. This was reflected in the 18th Annual Country Music Association Awards, which had the most varied slate of winners in years. Pop singer Anne Murray won in the best-single and best-album categories, Willie Nelson and Julio Iglesias won for best duet, while performers with a more traditional bent took most of the remaining categories.

PAULETTE WEISS, *Music Writer and Consultant*

Nebraska Gov. Bob Kerrey (left) and Minnesota Gov. Rudy Perpich listen as Sen. James Exon addresses the National Governor's Conference in February. In November, the senator won a second term.

AP/Wide World

NEBRASKA

The economy, legislative matters, and politics dominated state news in 1984.

Agriculture and the Economy. Uncooperative weather limited grain production, but corn, grain sorghum, and soybeans still surpassed the reduced yields of 1983. Prices remained low as costs increased and many farmers faced serious economic problems.

Late in 1983, Nebraska's largest industrial loan and investment firm, Commonwealth Savings Company of Lincoln, closed. It became apparent that the state-authorized, but privately funded, insurance corporation had less than $2 million to pay off insured deposits of about $59 million. Investigation suggested irregularities in management, and some managers became involved in litigation. Moreover, Nebraska Attorney General Paul Douglas appeared to be involved in questionable private business activities with Commonwealth. The legislature impeached him, but the state Supreme Court refused to remove him. He was later convicted of perjury and resigned from office. The failure of Commonwealth led to the closing or merger of other financial firms in the state.

Legislature and State Government. The regular legislative session dealt with numerous tough issues including the insolvency of Commonwealth. A budget 10% higher than that of 1983 was adopted, but the sales and income tax rates were lowered to 3½% and 19%, respectively. It provided pay raises for state employees and a homestead tax exemption for homeowners. Video-slot machines were banned; the drinking age was raised to 21; the burden of proof in the insanity defense was shifted from prosecution to defense; and the water law was amended to give the governor more authority over water management. However, property tax relief, a priority concern, was not achieved.

In August, Gov. Bob Kerrey called a special legislative session. It approved an amendment for reference to voters that would allow classification of farm property differently from urban property for tax purposes. The electorate approved the amendment by a 2–1 margin. A banking bill, allowing out-of-state banks to buy out troubled Nebraska banks, was not passed.

Election. In the November general election, President Reagan received 71% of the state's vote to Mondale's 29%. Incumbent Republican candidates for the House (Douglas Bereuter, Hal Daub, and Virginia Smith) easily defeated

---

NEBRASKA • Information Highlights

Area: 77,355 sq mi (200 350 km²).

Population (July 1, 1983 est.): 1,597,000.

Chief Cities (July 1, 1982 est.): Lincoln, the capital, 177,340; Omaha, 328,557; Grand Island (1980 census), 33,180.

Government (1984): *Chief Officers*—governor, J. Robert Kerrey (D); lt. gov., Donald McGinley (D). *Legislature* (unicameral)—49 members (nonpartisan).

State Finances (fiscal year 1983): *Revenues,* $1,881,000,000; *expenditures,* $1,807,000,000.

Personal Income (1983): $17,909,000,000; per capita, $11,212.

Labor Force (May 1984): *Civilian labor force,* 797,600; *unemployed,* 28,500 (3.6% of total force).

Education: *Enrollment* (fall 1982)—public elementary schools, 186,265; public secondary, 82,744; colleges and universities (fall 1983), 95,162. *Public school expenditures* (1982–83), $759,197,398 ($2,984 per pupil).

their Democratic rivals. Incumbent Sen. J. J. Exon (D) narrowly defeated his Republican challenger, Nancy Hoch. At the local level, only 2 of 12 cities voting on adopting a sales tax approved such a measure.

Miscellaneous. The conflict between Faith Christian School of Louisville and the state over certification of teachers continued, although the legislature passed a compromise bill to deal with the matter.

The University of Nebraska's undefeated football team lost to Miami in the last seconds of the 1984 Orange Bowl game. During the fall season, Nebraska was again ranked among the nation's top teams and was headed for the Sugar Bowl against Louisiana State.

ORVILLE H. ZABEL
Midland Lutheran College

NETHERLANDS

During the year 1984 economic life in the Netherlands showed signs of a limited and slow recovery, but political events were mixed in character, with uncertainties and indecisiveness continuing about the country's international role.

Domestic Affairs. The government led by Prime Minister Rudolph (Ruud) F. M. Lubbers, a Christian Democrat, remained firmly in control, hewing to its policy of gradually reducing the share of the public sector in the national economy, primarily through cuts in welfare programs. The cabinet drew its parliamentary support from an alliance of the Christian Democrats (CDA) and Liberals (VVD), backed by several small conservative religious parties. The opposition was led by the Labor Party (PvdA), which held fast to its position as the largest party but fell well short of a majority in the parliament.

The key measures in the government's restrictive policy were to uncouple the wages of government workers and the payments to recipients of various welfare programs (in particular old-age pensions and unemployment relief) from the earnings of workers in private industry and to reduce the welfare level about 3%. In addition to increased university tuition fees, charges scaled according to family income were introduced in public and private schools (which in the Netherlands receive identical payments from the state). The number of unemployed held steady at about 830,000, but the government gave special attention to the problem of widespread youth unemployment, encouraging both training and job-creation programs.

There was a modest improvement in the economic situation, largely as a result of increased exports. Despite deep anxiety in the ranks of labor, only a few widely scattered strikes occurred; most important was a strike of harbor workers in Rotterdam over a reduction of the work force in container terminals. Foreign workers from such countries as Turkey, Morocco, and Surinam were encouraged to return to their homelands by the grant of resettlement bonuses. But efforts were continued to integrate those who remained into the national life of the Netherlands, including a right to vote in local elections and support for maintenance of their traditional cultures. Resentment against the presence of these "guest workers" fed the appeal of a racist Center Party, which won seats in several local elections.

International Relations. The central problem facing the Dutch nation in world affairs during the year was the country's relations with the North Atlantic Treaty Organization (NATO), especially regarding the NATO proposal for placement of cruise missiles at the military base in Woensdrecht. There were clashes between antinuclear demonstrators and police at Woensdrecht. The Labor Party and the small left-wing parties were joined in their opposition to any extension of nuclear weapons by an antinuclear movement within the churches, endangering the government alliance. The cabinet preserved the unity of its parliamentary support by a resolution to delay a decision on deploying the missiles until November 1985. At that time the Netherlands would accept the installation of cruise missiles in 1988 if the Soviet Union continued to deploy SS-20 missiles. The number of missiles accepted would depend on whether a U.S.-Soviet arms limitation agreement had been reached. The hope was expressed that this policy would spur both Moscow and Washington to take desired measures of détente.

Full diplomatic relations with the People's Republic of China were restored in February when the government declined to permit building of additional submarines for Taiwan.

HERBERT H. ROWEN, *Rutgers University*

NETHERLANDS • Information Highlights

Official Name: Kingdom of the Netherlands.
Location: Northwestern Europe.
Area: 13,100 sq mi (33 929 km²).
Population (mid-1984 est.): 14,400,000.
Chief Cities (Jan. 1983 est.): Amsterdam, the capital, 687,397; Rotterdam, 558,832; The Hague, the seat of government, 449,338.
Government: *Head of state,* Beatrix, queen (acceded April 30, 1980). *Head of government,* Ruud Lubbers, prime minister (took office Nov. 1982). *Legislature*—States General: First Chamber and Second Chamber.
Monetary Unit: Guilder (3.4730 guilders equal U.S.$1, Oct. 22, 1984).
Gross National Product (1982 U.S.$): $137,300,-000,000.
Economic Indexes (1983): *Consumer Prices,* all items (1975 = 100), 235.9; food (1980 = 100), 116.2. *Industrial Production* (1975 = 100), 106.
Foreign Trade (1983 U.S.$): *Imports,* $61,573,-000,000; *exports,* $65,662,000,000.

Despite a strike by hotel and casino employees in spring and summer, left, Nevada gaming revenues increased 12% in fiscal 1984, fueling a strong recovery by the state's economy.

NEVADA

In 1984, the Republican Party continued to move toward its goal of dominating Nevada politics, and the state's economy rebounded from the recession of 1982–83.

The Elections. The overwhelming popularity of President Ronald Reagan in Nevada and the fact that the state's senior U.S. senator, Paul Laxalt, again served as his national campaign chairman meant that both parties ignored the state and its four electoral votes during the presidential campaign. President Reagan carried the state with 67% of the vote. In the only other statewide race, an incumbent state Supreme Court justice was defeated for the first time since 1950; Justice Noel Manoukian lost a close race with former Congressman and State Sen. Clifton Young of Reno. Nevada's two incumbent congressmen, Democrat Harry Reid of Las Vegas and Republican Barbara Vucanovich of Reno, were easily reelected.

The political issue that received the most attention during the 1984 campaign in Nevada was Question 12, a proposed constitutional amendment placed on the ballot by initiative petition. If it had been approved by the voters in 1984 and again in 1986, the amendment would have mandated that any tax or fee increase by state or local government entities would have had to be approved by a two-thirds vote of the legislative bodies and a vote of the people. Public employee groups and almost all elected officials in the state opposed the proposed amendment, and Democratic Gov. Richard Bryan and Republican Lt. Gov. Robert Cashell put aside their political feud to make an effective joint television ad urging the people to vote it down. Question 12 was rejected by 52% of the voters.

The Republican Party used President Reagan's coattails and a healthy campaign chest to help capture control of the Assembly for the first time since 1970 and only the third time since 1931. The GOP's 25–17 control of the lower house capped a remarkable comeback from a low of only five seats in 1977. Republi-

cans also picked up four seats in the Senate, reducing the Democratic margin to 13–8.

The Economy. Nevada's tourist-based economy rebounded sharply from the 1982–83 recession in fiscal 1984, led by an 11.5% increase in gross gambling profits. The total winnings of $2.99 billion by casinos resulted in a 12% increase in gaming revenues for the state's general fund. Retail sales also increased by a similar margin; however, both the gaming and sales tax revenues would have been even higher if it had not been for a strike of Las Vegas hotel-casino employees during the late spring and early summer. Nevada's unemployment during 1984 started at 8.2% in January, fell to 6.6% in May, and then rose to 8% in the fall at the end of the heavy tourist season.

Governor Bryan continued to push for diversification of the Nevada economy during 1984 and called the second special session of the legislature in 16 years to authorize Citicorp to set up a credit card center in Las Vegas. Several other major companies committed to build facilities in the state, including Porsche, which decided to establish its American headquarters in Reno.

DON W. DRIGGS
University of Nevada, Reno

NEVADA • Information Highlights

Area: 110,561 sq mi (286 352 km²).
Population (July 1, 1983 est.): 891,000.
Chief Cities (July 1, 1982 est.): Carson City, the capital (1980 census), 32,022; Las Vegas, 179,587; Reno, 106,748.
Government (1984): *Chief Officers*—governor, Richard Bryan (D); lt. gov., Robert A. Cashell (R). *Legislature*—Senate, 21 members; Assembly, 42 members.
State Finances (fiscal year 1983): *Revenues,* $1,696,000,000; *expenditures,* $1,570,000,000.
Personal Income (1983): $11,096,000,000; per capita, $12,451.
Labor Force (May 1984): *Civilian labor force,* 497,600; *unemployed,* 32,900 (6.6% of total force).
Education: *Enrollment* (fall 1982)—public elementary schools, 96,812; public secondary, 54,292; colleges and universities (fall 1983), 43,768. *Public school expenditures* (1982–83), $364,765,710 ($2,613 per pupil).

NEW BRUNSWICK

New Brunswick celebrated its 200th birthday in style in 1984. A year-long, $5 million party featured an endless succession of parades, cake-cutting ceremonies, and entertainment. The high point of the celebration was on June 18, the bicentennial of the day in 1784 when King George III created New Brunswick from territory that had been part of Nova Scotia. Throngs of people, many in 18th-century garb, gathered that day for ceremonies outside the legislature in Fredericton.

Pope John Paul visited the province for a day in September, followed by Queen Elizabeth for a few days later the same month.

Politics. The Conservative tide that swept Canada in the September 4 federal election included New Brunswick. Of the province's ten House of Commons seats, the Tories took nine, the Liberals one. Gerald Merrithew, a former provincial cabinet minister who won Saint John riding in his first try at federal politics, was named forestry minister in the new Tory cabinet.

Voting Scandal. Alleged voting irregularities resurfaced at the end of the legislative session. Liberal justice critic Frank McKenna drew attention to a police report on election wrongdoings—municipal, provincial, and federal—since 1978. One sworn affidavit in a Royal Canadian Mounted Police file cited by McKenna told of a person who voted about 50 times in a Saint John municipal election and was paid $500. The Conservative government rejected opposition demands for a public inquiry.

Journalism. A new French-language daily newspaper, *L'Acadie Nouvelle,* began publication in Caraquet on June 5, the only French-language daily east of Quebec. The tabloid's initial circulation was 7,000, which the owners hoped to expand to 15,000.

JOHN BEST
"Canada World News"

NEWFOUNDLAND

In March the Supreme Court of Canada unanimously ruled that the vast Hibernia oil field off Newfoundland belonged to the federal government. In June the court ruled that the Water Reversion Act was invalid; this decision ended the province's last attempt to force Hydro-Quebec to negotiate a better contract for power from Churchill Falls in the Labrador section of Newfoundland.

Gloom deepened when Bowater's Canada announced in June that it would close its huge newsprint mill in Corner Brook by the end of the year unless a buyer could be found. In January, Eastern Provincial Airlines had said that it was moving its corporate headquarters and maintenance staff out of Gander to Halifax.

Fishery catches were down, and the restructured Fishery Products International, the largest fish company in Atlantic Canada, was projected to lose $25 million in 1984. The company was hit by a protracted trawlermen's strike in July, and the 5,000 people directly affected added to a high unemployment rate.

When the legislature opened in March, the budget—some C$2.2 billion—imposed a wage freeze on 50,000 public servants and cuts in budgets for both hospitals and municipal governments. The hospital cuts came in response to recommendations of a royal commission, which called for the saving of $70 million and the elimination of 350 beds.

In the September election, the Tories won four of Newfoundland's seven seats in Parliament. In February a Tory cabinet minister, Leo Barry, had quit the provincial government, crossed the floor of the House of Assembly, and joined the Liberals. In October he became leader of the party in Newfoundland.

On September 12, Pope John Paul II visited Newfoundland.

SUSAN MCCORQUODALE
Memorial University of Newfoundland

NEW BRUNSWICK · Information Highlights

Area: 28,354 sq mi (73 437 km²).
Population (April 1984 est.): 712,300.
Chief Cities (1981 census): Fredericton, the capital, 43,723; Saint John, 80,521; Moncton, 54,743.
Government (1984): *Chief Officers*—lt. gov., George Stanley; premier, Richard B. Hatfield (Progressive Conservative). *Legislature*—Legislative Assembly, 58 members.
Provincial Finances (1984–85 fiscal year budget): *Revenues,* $2,454,000,000; *expenditures,* $2,759,700,000.
Personal Income (average weekly earnings, May 1984): $367.03.
Labor Force (July 1984, seasonally adjusted): *Employed workers,* 15 years of age and over, 249,000; *Unemployed* 42,000 (14.4%).
Education (1984–85): *Enrollment*—elementary and secondary schools, 144,750 pupils; postsecondary (1984–85)—universities, 19,050; community colleges (full-time), 2,070.
(All monetary figures are in Canadian dollars.)

NEWFOUNDLAND · Information Highlights

Area: 156,185 sq mi (404 517 km²).
Population (April 1984 est.): 578,900.
Chief Cities (1981 census): St. John's, the capital, 83,770; Corner Brook, 24,339.
Government (1984): *Chief Officers*—lt. gov., W. Anthony Paddon; premier, A. Brian Peckford (Progressive Conservative). *Legislature*—Legislative Assembly, 52 members.
Provincial Finances (1984–85 fiscal year budget): *Revenues,* $2,009,242,000; *expenditures,* $2,215,570,000.
Personal Income (average weekly earnings, May 1984): $387.01.
Labor Force (July 1984, seasonally adjusted): *Employed workers,* 15 years of age and over, 178,000; *Unemployed* 43,000 (19.5%).
Education (1984–85): *Enrollment*—elementary and secondary schools, 143,260 pupils; postsecondary (1984–85)—universities, 12,910; community colleges (full-time), 2,550.
(All monetary figures are in Canadian dollars.)

NEW HAMPSHIRE

In 1984 the two subjects debated more extensively than any others were politics and the fate of Public Service Company of New Hampshire (PSNH) and whether it could complete its Seabrook nuclear power plant.

Elections. The quadrennial apprearance of presidential candidates in the snows of New Hampshire was under way by January. As February 28 neared, the pundits were giving victory to Democrat Walter Mondale, but the voters had other ideas. Gary Hart emerged as the clear winner with 37% of the vote, 9% more than Mondale. His victory started the long battle between the two for the nomination.

The general election in November offered several major state races besides that for president. Gov. John Sununu (R) was challenged by Chris Spirou (D), longtime minority leader in the state House of Representatives. For the U.S. Senate, Rep. Norman D'Amours (D) sought the seat held by Gordon Humphrey (R). The moderate views of D'Amours contrasted sharply with those of the conservative Humphrey. D'Amours' House seat was sought by Dudley Dudley (D) and Robert Smith (R). The other House seat, held by Judd Gregg (R), was sought by Larry Converse (D). When the count was completed, Democrats had been routed at all levels. President Ronald Reagan won by a greater margin than did most major state candidates, capturing 69% of the vote. Sununu received 67% of the vote; Humphrey 59%; Smith won a surprisingly easy victory over Dudley with 60% of the votes; and Gregg was reelected overwhelmingly. In the General Court the GOP had its largest majority in the House since 1901 (292–108), while in the Senate Republicans had an 18–6 majority. The results indicated that the state was in the forefront of the trend to more conservative politics.

Utility Crisis. The financial status of PSNH was never absent for long from the news. During January, open discussion surfaced of the possibility of PSNH bankruptcy and whether it

could afford to complete its two Seabrook reactors. Projected construction costs continually escalated. From an estimated $5.2 billion at the start of the year, the total soared to $9 billion in March. Not only did this mean a financial dilemma for the company, but it would translate into much higher electric rates ("rate shock," as opponents styled it) when the plant was finished. Then in late March came the long-suspected cancellation of Unit 2 (only 22% complete). Other New England utility investors in the project had forced PSNH to take this action. Despite cancellation and the new estimate of completion costs for one unit at $6.1 billion, fund-raising problems continued, forcing PSNH to suspend all work at Seabrook in mid-April. The company appeared to be on the verge of bankruptcy. In May a new corporation (dubbed "Newbrook") was formed to complete Unit 1. A sale of bonds and rescheduling of payments in June temporarily alleviated the imminent danger of bankruptcy. Construction of Unit 1 resumed during the summer. By late fall the fate of PSNH seemed somewhat better, but the fiscal crisis remained. Much depended on the success of the sale of bonds set for late 1984.

Economy. A strong tourist year, the national economic recovery, and booming growth in the southern third of the state all contributed to a buoyant economic situation. From a statewide unemployment rate of 5.3% in January, the rate fell to 2.8% in September, the lowest in the nation. Some areas in the state, like Nashua, had rates as low as 2%, forcing the recruitment of workers from out of state.

WILLIAM L. TAYLOR
Plymouth State College

NEW JERSEY

Revitalization of decaying inner cities, public finance, and election politics dominated events in New Jersey in 1984.

Urban Aid. In January the legislature passed a bill providing $4.7 million for aid to the state's six major cities: Newark, Jersey City, Camden, Elizabeth, Paterson, and Trenton, as well as 22 smaller towns. The main purpose was to enable these communities to maintain adequate police and firefighting personnel, threatened because of financial problems.

Federal aid to Newport City, a residential and business development planned for the area around the entrance to the Holland Tunnel in Jersey City, aroused opposition from New York City's Mayor Edward Koch and other officials. They claimed that a $40-million Urban Development Action Grant was deliberately designed to favor Jersey City's job market at the expense of New York. New Jersey Gov. Thomas Kean and Jersey City Mayor Gerald McCann denied the charges, citing the social

---

NEW HAMPSHIRE • Information Highlights

Area: 9,279 sq mi (24 032 km²).

Population (July 1, 1983 est.): 959,000.

Chief Cities (1980 census): Concord, the capital, 30,400; Manchester, 90,936; Nashua, 67,865.

Government (1984): *Chief Officer*—governor, John H. Sununu (R). *General Court*—Senate, 24 members; House of Representatives, 400 members.

State Finances (fiscal year 1983): *Revenues,* $1,167,000,000; *expenditures,* $1,109,000,000.

Personal Income (1983): $11,525,000,000; per capita, $12,021.

Labor Force (May 1984): *Civilian labor force,* 510,900; *unemployed,* 24,100 (4.7% of total force).

Education: *Enrollment* (fall 1982)—public elementary schools, 107,349; public secondary, 52,848; colleges and universities (fall 1983), 53,143. *Public school expenditures* (1982–83), $402,306,643 ($2,750 per pupil).

U.S. Sen. Bill Bradley made education and children's issues central to his reelection campaign. The 41-year-old Democrat easily captured a second term.

Office of the Senator

and economic advantages for corporations wishing to locate on the west bank of the Hudson River.

Public Finance. Governor Kean introduced a $7.6 billion budget for fiscal 1985 that proposed higher spending in the areas of education, transportation, and mental health without tax increases. The greater spending would be paid for from a projected $96 million surplus and revenue increases due to economic growth, as well as from a bond issue to finance a $3.3 billion transportation program. Republicans greeted the budget message as a shrewd attempt to avoid conflict with the Democratic-controlled legislature, while Democrats criticized it because it did not provide enough aid for financially strapped localities. In June, budget statistics showed a far higher surplus than had been anticipated because of greater sales-tax revenues, prompting the governor to announce a program of tax rebates.

Election Politics. Redistricting of New Jersey's congressional districts, mandated in 1982, was still an issue in 1984. Democrats contended that a plan drawn up by the Republicans was overly weighted in favor of suburban areas and went to court to prevent compliance. However, the ruling of a three-judge Federal District Court upholding the plan was allowed to stand in a 6 to 3 decision by the U.S. Supreme Court.

The major statewide election was for the U.S. Senate seat held by Bill Bradley. The combination of his professional basketball career and a record as a hard worker in his first Senate term made him extremely popular, and there was only token opposition to his renomination in the June primary.

On the Republican side there was a spirited contest between Mary Mochary, former mayor of Montclair, and Robert Morris, a conservative lawyer from Mantoloking, with Mochary the winner. In the election campaign she em-

phasized she could do more for New Jersey than Bradley because of her close association with President Reagan and because Bradley would use his Senate seat as a springboard for a presidential campaign in 1988.

In the national campaign both parties made New Jersey one of the main battlegrounds, with President Reagan and Walter Mondale each paying several visits. The election's importance was emphasized by a successful drive to register new voters, and by the end of the campaign the New Jersey total of registered voters was approximately 4 million. Ticket splitting marked the election, with President Reagan and Senator Bradley each winning landslide victories. In the 14 congressional contests all the incumbents were reelected except Democrat Joseph Minish, who was defeated in the eleventh district by Republican Dean Gallo. This reduced the New Jersey Democratic Congressional delegation to eight.

HERMANN K. PLATT
St. Peter's College

NEW JERSEY • Information Highlights

Area: 7,787 sq mi (20 169 km²).
Population (July 1, 1983 est.): 7,468,000.
Chief Cities (July 1, 1982 est.): Trenton, the capital (1980 census), 92,124; Newark, 320,512; Jersey City, 222,881; Paterson, 138,986; Elizabeth, 106,803.
Government (1984): *Chief Officer*—governor, Thomas H. Kean (R). *Legislature*—Senate, 40 members; General Assembly, 80 members.
State Finances (fiscal year 1983): *Revenues,* $12,604,000,000; *expenditures,* $11,764,000,000.
Personal Income (1983): $105,455,000,000; per capita, $14,122.
Labor Force (May 1984): *Civilian labor force,* 3,885,600; *unemployed,* 243,100 (6.3% of total force).
Education: *Enrollment* (fall 1982)—public elementary schools, 776,608; public secondary, 395,912; colleges and universities (fall 1983), 314,468. *Public school expenditures* (1982–83), $4,340,959,702 ($4,007 per pupil).

NEW MEXICO

In 1984, New Mexicans were preoccupied with politics and voted in record numbers on November 6. They also took pride in Mai Shanley of Alamogordo, who won the Miss USA beauty contest title on May 17.

Politics. In the November general election all incumbents were returned to national office. They included representatives Joe Skeen (R), Manuel Lujan (R), and Bill Richardson (D); and Sen. Pete V. Domenici (R), who defeated Democrat Judy Pratt, the first woman to run for a Senate seat in the history of the state.

A three-judge panel in August found that the legislature's recent reapportionment plan for 16 state House of Representatives districts violated the Voting Rights Act because it diluted the effects of minority voters. The ruling came in response to a lawsuit.

Legislation. Increased education appropriations, three laws relative to drunk driving, and a new insurance code were enacted by the state legislature.

Indian Affairs. In June a federal law was passed returning a 25,000-acre (10 125-ha) tract in the Santa Fe National Forest to the Indians of Cochiti Pueblo north of Albuquerque. The longstanding claim was confirmed when a new document proving the Indians' ownership was discovered in the Mexican archives.

A special master in a 16-year-old water-rights suit, known as the Aamodt case, declared in August that Tewa Pueblos in the Pojoaque Valley near Santa Fe were entitled to first claim to all the irrigation water they needed. Neighboring non-Indian defendants in the suit expressed fears that the ruling would deprive them of all their rights and render their land worthless. Mindful of those concerns the special master held that after the Indians' basic needs were satisfied, decisions about control of scarce water resources should be made "with as little injury as possible to any party."

Jemez Pueblo and others filed a federal lawsuit claiming that the U.S. Forest Service is failing to protect hundreds of ancient ruins in the Southwest. The Indians asked for restoration of injured property, the fencing and monitoring of sites, and nomination of all eligible sites to the National Register.

Weather. Unseasonal rains in mid-August produced severe floods in parts of southeastern New Mexico. Hardest hit were the communities of Hobbs and Ruidoso. The Mescalero Apache Reservation in the Sacramento Mountains was under a state of emergency for several days. Earlier, spring flooding in the north, caused by a heavy snow melt, led Gov. Toney Anaya to declare Taos County a disaster area, allowing local officials to tap a $500,000 emergency fund. An October snowstorm trapped 200 hunters for several days in the wilderness along the Colorado border.

NEW MEXICO · Information Highlights

Area: 121, 593 sq mi (314 925 km²).
Population (July 1, 1983 est.): 1,399,000.
Chief Cities (1980 census): Santa Fe, the capital, 48,953; Albuquerque (July 1, 1982 est.), 341,978; Las Cruces, 45,086.
Government (1984): *Chief Officers*—governor, Toney Anaya (D); lt. gov., Mike Runnels (D). *Legislature*—Senate, 42 members; House of Representatives, 70 members.
State Finances (fiscal year 1983): *Revenues,* $3,343,000,000; *expenditures,* $2,692,000,000.
Personal Income (1983): $13,489,000,000; per capita, $9,640.
Labor Force (May 1984): *Civilian labor force,* 618,500; *unemployed,* 42,400 (6.9% of total force).
Education: *Enrollment* (fall 1982)—public elementary schools, 189,968; public secondary, 78,664; colleges and universities (fall 1983), 66,094. *Public school expenditures* (1982–83), $713,500,218 ($2,901 per pupil).

In October the Brantley Dam site on the Pecos River 15 mi (24 km) north of Carlsbad was dedicated. The $250 million project is intended to retain floodwaters.

Health. New Mexico experienced 15 cases of plague, among them two fatalities. Since the disease is endemic in wild rodents, state health officials warned hunters and other outdoor recreationists to avoid contact with any animals that appeared ill.

MARC SIMMONS
Author, "Albuquerque, A Narrative History"

NEW YORK

Nineteen eighty-four was the year that New York's Gov. Mario M. Cuomo brought his image of government as family to the American people and catapulted himself onto the national political scene.

In words that had become familiar to New Yorkers, Cuomo spoke in the keynote address at the Democratic National Convention of compassion and of the unseen cities of poor people across the nation. Cuomo's speech in July received rave reviews, as did his dissertation on issues of church and state a few months later at Notre Dame University.

Cuomo, who only two years before had been an underdog gubernatorial candidate often dismissed as a poor politician, was touted as a potential vice-presidential candidate for Democrat Walter Mondale. But the governor, who came out for Mondale early during the primary season, urged him to select Geraldine Ferraro instead. Cuomo did, however, keep his options open for 1988, and after Mondale's loss, the New York governor was mentioned frequently as a leading contender in the next presidential race.

The entire 211-member legislature was up for reelection. Democrats continued to dominate the 150-member Assembly overwhelmingly, and Republicans kept their 35-26 edge in

For the second year in a row, the legislature and the governor agreed on a budget before the April 1 deadline. It contained a record increase in state aid to local school districts. Legislators said it was the first year of a five-year plan to improve education by providing money for programs such as computers in classrooms and teacher training. For the first time, the state also voted to provide tuition aid to part-time students and tuition waivers for Vietnam veterans. Legislators also increased, for the first time in five years, the amounts of state scholarships and raised the income levels that determine eligibility.

Energy. The rate of the nearly completed Shoreham Nuclear Plant on Long Island remained a hot debate, as the Long Island Lighting Co., which built the plant, battled with government officials opposed to its opening. With billions of dollars at stake, the utility got some encouragement from the federal regulators who must license the plant and was able to avert a threatened bankruptcy in September. Suffolk County officials, who had adamantly opposed the plant on Eastern Long Island as unsafe, appeared to be softening their opposition toward the end of the year. But Cuomo and the state attorney general's office were reiterating their position that the plant should not open without a safe evacuation plan.

Politicians and businessmen continued to argue about whether cheap hydropower from state-owned plants should be redistributed when contracts expire at the end of the decade. Cuomo tried unsuccessfully to get the legislature to approve a plan taking some power away from upstate businesses. But a court decision during the summer lessened pressure for the state to act quickly. Officials were waiting to hear from the courts whether "paper utilities," such as one set up by New York City, would be eligible for the cheap power.

MIRIAM PAWEL, *"Newsday"*

AP/Wide World

New York is the first state to enact a law mandating the wearing of seat belts by adults riding in the front seat of a car. Assemblyman Vincent J. Graber, Sr. (above), a West Seneca Democrat, sponsored the bill.

the Senate. One state senator, Joseph Pisani, a Westchester Republican, resigned shortly before the election after being convicted of tax fraud. For the most part, incumbents were reelected to the U.S. House.

In early December, Alfred B. Del Bello announced his resignation, effective Feb. 1, 1985, as the state's lieutenant governor. Del Bello, a former Yonkers mayor and Westchester County executive, planned to accept a job in industry. With the resignation, Warren Anderson, Republican majority leader of the state Senate, would become the first in line of succession to the governorship.

Legislation. New York became the first state in the country to adopt a mandatory seatbelt law for adults riding in the front seat of a car. A bill to raise the minimum drinking age to 21 was narrowly defeated, and sponsors, including Governor Cuomo, vowed to bring the issue up again. In an effort to bolster New York's foundering wine industry, the legislature agreed to let grocery stores sell "wine coolers," if they are made with New York State wines. The governor also signed a bill to curb acid rain.

During his seventh year as mayor of New York City, Edward I. Koch remained as flamboyant as ever. On March 17 the appropriately dressed mayor and the city's new police commissioner Benjamin Ward (right) marched in the St. Patrick's Day parade.

NEW YORK CITY

Politics, a long hospital strike, and transportation and telephone services shared the front page with crimes, scandals, and some notable resignations and appointments in New York City during 1984.

Rep. Geraldine A. Ferraro (D) of Queens became the first woman vice-presidential candidate of a major party but was embroiled for much of the campaign in disputes over her family finances and her free-choice stand on abortion. In the November election, New Yorkers voted against the national tide that saw the Democratic ticket headed by Walter F. Mondale beaten by President Reagan and his running mate, George Bush.

The longest and costliest hospital strike in city history unfolded during the summer. The 47-day walkout affected 52,000 workers and 18,000 patients at 30 private, nonprofit hospitals and 15 nursing homes. It ended on August 28 with agreement on 5% raises in each year of a two-year contract and a workers' guarantee of every other weekend off.

Subway and bus fares rose from 75 to 90 cents, and commuter fares and bridge and tunnel tolls went up in January, but there were no notable improvements for the money. In fact, transit officials in February took all 851 of the city's Grumman Flxible buses out of service as unsafe. The cost of a pay-phone call jumped from 10 to 25 cents on July 1, the first increase in 33 years, but a bigger outcry was raised over another telephone company innovation: the division of the overloaded city into two area codes. Manhattan and the Bronx kept 212, but Queens, Brooklyn, and Staten Island were relegated to 718. The outer-borough subscribers complained of inconvenience.

The city's largest-ever mass murder occurred on April 15, Palm Sunday, when ten people were shot dead in a house in Brooklyn.

The alleged murderer was a man who wrongly suspected his wife, one of the victims, of infidelity. Meanwhile, the police cracked down on drug pushers on the Lower East Side and around public schools all over town, arresting hundreds. The police also reported that major crimes were down 9%.

The city also witnessed two big scandals in 1984. The director of Creedmoor Psychiatric Center in Queens was removed amid allegations of patient abuse. And some workers at a city-funded Bronx day-care center were charged with sexually abusing children, a case that figured in the resignation of James A. Krauskopf as head of the Human Resources Administration.

The year's most notable resignation, however, was that of Schools Chancellor Anthony J. Alvarado, who stepped down May 11 amid charges of professional misconduct. Also leaving office was Deputy Mayor Nathan Leventhal, who quit City Hall to become president of Lincoln Center.

The year's most prominent appointment was that of John J. O'Connor as archbishop of New York, succeeding the late Terence Cardinal Cooke. The archbishop denounced abortion in highly publicized colloquies with Representative Ferraro and Gov. Mario M. Cuomo. In other appointments, David L. Gunn became president of the Transit Authority, Robert Esnard and Stanley Brezenoff were named deputy mayors, and Benjamin Ward was sworn in as the city's first black police commissioner.

In other developments, an estimated two million people turned out for an August 15 ticker-tape parade for the U.S. Olympic team; the Museum of Modern Art reopened after a four-year, $55 million renovation; and Mayor Edward I. Koch's book *Mayor* remained a best-seller.

ROBERT D. McFADDEN
"The New York Times"

NEW ZEALAND

All the major events on the New Zealand political scene occurred in the second half of 1984.

The General Election. Polls in May and June had given the Labour Party a 3% lead over the ruling National Party. They had shown Prime Minister Robert Muldoon's margin slipping and had indicated that by a majority of two to one the electors believed that Labour could deal better with New Zealand's leading problem of unemployment. The election was due for November, but Muldoon advanced it to July on the grounds that the government's one-vote majority in Parliament could no longer be guaranteed. It was only the second snap election in 105 years.

A record field of 463 candidates from 20 parties was nominated, with four parties fielding full tickets. The state of the economy was the prime issue in the rather lackluster campaign. In the biggest turnout (91.9%) in more than 30 years, there was a 4.2% swing to Labour, which, however, won only 42.5% of the votes. Less than 50% of the winning candidates received majority support. With 56 seats, compared with 37 for National and the two retained by Social Credit, Labour had an overall majority of 17. The Labour leader, David Lange, 41, became the nation's youngest prime minister in the 20th century. Later, Jim McLay succeeded Muldoon as National Party leader.

The New Administration. In Labour's 20-member cabinet, average age 45 years, only four had previous experience holding portfolios. There were two Maoris, two women, and eight Aucklanders. Subsequently, two famous New Zealanders were appointed to diplomatic posts. Sir Wallace Rowling, Labour prime minister in 1974–75 and then leader of the opposition until 1980, became ambassador to the

NEW ZEALAND · Information Highlights
Official Name: New Zealand.
Location: Southwest Pacific Ocean.
Area: 103,885 sq mi (269 063 km²).
Population (mid-1984 est.): 3,200,000.
Chief Cities (March 31, 1983 est.): Wellington, the capital, 342,500; Auckland, 864,000; Christchurch, 322,200; Hamilton, 164,600.
Government: *Head of state*, Elizabeth II, queen, represented by Sir David Beattie, governor-general (took office Nov. 1980). *Head of government*, David Lange, prime minister (took office July 26, 1984). *Legislature* (unicameral)—House of Representatives.
Monetary Unit: New Zealand dollar (2.0576 N.Z. dollars equal U.S.$1, Dec. 3, 1984).
Economic Index (1983): *Consumer Prices* (1970 = 100), all items, 467.1; food, 464.9.
Foreign Trade (1983 U.S.$): *Imports*, $5,279,000,000; *exports*, $5,272,000,000.

United States, while Sir Edmund Hillary, in 1953 the first man to climb Mt. Everest, was appointed high commissioner to India. After assuming office, Lange attended the Commonwealth Heads of Government meeting, addressed the UN General Assembly, and met with U.S. Secretary of State George Shultz.

The Economy. Although inflation in the year ending June 1984 was held to 4.7%, other indicators were less assuring. In July nearly 5% of the work force was unemployed, the overseas deficit was reported as equaling 16.8% of the country's earnings, and New Zealand had climbed to 11th position on the table of external debt per capita.

During the election campaign there was a massive run on the dollar, and immediately afterward an economic crisis occurred. In July the new government announced three economic policy measures: the dollar was devalued by 20%, a temporary price freeze was imposed, and all interest rates were freed. The price of gasoline rose by 23%. An economic summit conference was held in September.

The Budget. In the first Labour budget, taxes or charges for liquor, gasoline, electricity, cigarettes, and road haulage were raised, some substantially. Low-income families were assisted, but employers offering fringe benefits, and the wealthiest 25% of superannuitants, were singled out for tax measures. While government gross spending was up by 13%, the budget foreshadowed the introduction in 1986 of a revolutionary all-embracing tax on goods and services, designed to partly replace income tax, and reduce the deficit by two thirds before the next election.

Nuclear Ban. Much debate centered on the Labour Party's pledge to ban visits to New Zealand waters by nuclear ships and how it would be translated into practice. Some feared that the policy would imperil the ANZUS (Australia, New Zealand, United States) defense alliance.

GRAHAM BUSH, *University of Auckland*

Labour's David Lange, 41, a lawyer who spent six years representing Auckland's poor, became prime minister in July.

AP/Wide World

NIGERIA

The military government led by Maj. Gen. Mohammed Buhari, which had overthrown the civilian regime of Alhaji Shehu Shagari on Dec. 31, 1983, struggled to cope with the manifold economic and social problems inherited from the previous government.

The Economy. The crisis in the economy, which first became acute in 1981, continued despite stringent remedial measures. The world's oversupply of petroleum had caused Nigeria's production, which accounted for more than 90% of foreign earnings, to fall to 900,000 barrels per day in the last quarter of 1983. Once the second-largest supplier to the United States, Nigeria had become only the seventh most important. The internal public debt had risen to 22.2 billion naira (₦), up from ₦4.6 billion in 1977, and the external debt was ₦7.7 billion, a sixfold increase during the same period. Foreign reserves had fallen in one year by ₦500 million to only ₦790 million. The new government needed to refinance ₦4.5 billion owed to foreign banks, which insisted the government comply with the demands of the International Monetary Fund (IMF) for a devaluation of the naira and liberalization of trade. Smuggling and the outflow of capital to foreign banks continued to be problems.

In March the government began to issue a series of harsh decrees. It sought to control foreign trade by placing all exports under specific license and by restricting imports to needed raw materials and spare parts. Excise duties were placed on 400 items, almost all goods manufactured in Nigeria. Foreign visitors were required to pay in foreign exchange, business travel allowances were suspended, and basic travel allowances were restricted to ₦100. University budgets were trimmed, four technical colleges were merged into existing universities, and school fees were reintroduced. Most drastic was the decision on April 23 to close Nigeria's borders and call in the old currency. The decree was aimed at smugglers and those Nigerians with large naira holdings outside the country. Between April 25 and May 6 old currency was exchanged for new notes to a limit of ₦5,000; all excess amounts had to be deposited in banks. Despite some problems, the exchange proceeded relatively efficiently. However, the Central Bank's decision to issue only ₦3.5 billion instead of ₦5.3 billion previously in circulation later restricted economic recovery.

The new budget for 1984–85 proposed a federal government expenditure of ₦10 billion. Top priority was given to agriculture, which received 21%; defense was budgeted at 15%. Despite cutbacks a deficit of ₦3.3 billion remained. In April an agreement was arranged with 350 creditors to give Nigeria a 2½-year grace period to pay on its foreign debts, thus

enabling the government to resist IMF demands for devaluation. In October, Nigeria broke the OPEC price arrangements by $2 per barrel and increased production to 1.2 million barrels per day. The following month Nigeria's oil minister refused to accept new quotas on production suggested by the majority of OPEC ministers at their meeting in Geneva. Improvement in petroleum production together with increased cocoa and oil palm exports and the new monetary controls improved the economy although major problems persisted. Currency was in short supply; restrictions on imports caused shortages of consumer goods; basic prices increased; and there was student unrest at the universities. Most disturbing was the reluctance of foreign investors to risk large amounts of capital in a state whose controlled economy was very restrictive.

Political Developments. In 1984, Nigeria's government was military and did not pretend to be democratic; it controlled all facets of life. The government isolated the major problems, the most serious being economic, and then issued decrees aimed at their solution. It also stringently controlled the media, the universities, and labor, and sought to punish those officials and businessmen who had enriched themselves during the Shagari period. Decree #3 of March 28 set up five special military tribunals to try those accused of graft. The tribunals were empowered to recover misappropriated funds and pass harsh sentences, ranging to life imprisonment, for those found guilty.

The government's zeal to punish malefactors led in July to difficulties with Britain when one of those accused, Umaru Dikko, then resident in London, was kidnapped. Discovered drugged in a crate, Dikko was rescued by British authorities, and London protested the involvement of Nigerian officials in the affair. Relations with neighboring states continued strained because of the decision to keep Nigeria's borders closed.

HARRY A. GAILEY
San José State University

NIGERIA • Information Highlights

Official Name: Federal Republic of Nigeria.
Location: West Africa.
Area: 356,667 sq mi (923 768 km²).
Population (mid-1984 est.): 88,100,000.
Chief City: Lagos, the capital.
Government: *Head of state and government,* Maj. Gen. Mohammed Buhari, leader, federal military government (took office Jan. 1, 1984). *Legislature* —Senate and House of Representatives.
Monetary Unit: Naira (0.768 naira equals U.S.$1, July 1984).
Gross Domestic Product (1983 U.S.$): $74,000,000,000.
Economic Index (May 1983): *Consumer Prices* (1975 = 100), all items, 328.4; food, 335.6.
Foreign Trade (1982 U.S.$): *Imports,* $20,846,000,000; *exports,* $19,739,000,000.

NORTH CAROLINA

Politics and nature provided the leading stories in North Carolina in 1984.

Politics. National attention was drawn to the heated senatorial race, and the candidates—Republican Sen. Jesse A. Helms and Democrat Gov. James B. Hunt, Jr.—lived up to their billing by conducting a memorable but disagreeable campaign costing a record $25 million, or about $11 for each vote cast. Incumbent Helms accused Hunt of being a "Mondale liberal" who favored higher taxes and flip-flopped on issues as the political winds changed; Hunt pictured Helms as out of step with North Carolinians, an ally of dictators and the "Religious Right," and callous toward individual liberties.

Helms' margin of victory was less than that of James G. Martin, who became the second Republican to be elected governor in the 20th century. Martin defeated Attorney General Rufus L. Edmisten, victor of a Democratic run-off so bitter that the loser, Charlotte Mayor Eddie Knox, joined the campaign of President Reagan, who swept the state with 62% of the votes. The GOP also captured five of eleven congressional seats, its largest number in the 20th century. Democrats, however, held onto the lieutenant governorship, electing Robert B. Jordan, and council of state and top judicial

NORTH CAROLINA • Information Highlights

Area: 52,669 sq mi (136 413 km²).
Population (July 1, 1983 est.): 6,082,000.
Chief Cities (July 1, 1982 est.): Raleigh, the capital, 154,211; Charlotte, 323,972; Greensboro, 157,337; Winston-Salem, 140,846; Durham, 101,242.
Government (1984): *Chief Officers*—governor, James B. Hunt, Jr. (D); lt. gov., James C. Green (D). *General Assembly*—Senate, 50 members; House of Representatives, 120 members.
State Finances (fiscal year 1983): *Revenues,* $7,662,000,000; *expenditures,* $7,232,000,000.
Personal Income (1983): $59,523,000,000; per capita, $9,787.
Labor Force (May 1984): *Civilian labor force,* 3,016,300; *unemployed,* 175,400 (5.8% of total force).
Education: *Enrollment* (fall 1982)—public elementary schools, 768,755; public secondary, 328,060; colleges and universities (fall 1983), 301,675. *Public school expenditures* (1982–83), $2,231,620,811 ($2,162 per pupil).

offices. Henry E. Frye became the first black ever elected to the state Supreme Court. The legislature remained Democratic 120 to 50. Thad Eure won his 13th four-year term as secretary of state.

Nature. Tornadoes in April roared into Robeson County from South Carolina and left an arc of destruction across eastern counties before exiting through Gates County on the Virginia border. Scores were killed, hundreds injured, and thousands left homeless in the Carolinas. In September southeastern coast communities were evacuated, but Hurricane Diana, which hovered over the area for three days, inflicted less damage than had been feared before finally veering back to sea.

Capital Punishment. After a lapse of 22 years, the death penalty was again administered in North Carolina. James W. Hutchins, convicted of killing three law enforcement officers, was executed in March. A concerted campaign by feminists and opponents of the death penalty failed to prevent the execution in November of Margie Velma Barfield, 51, a former private nurse, who admitted murdering her fiancé, her mother, and two patients. She thus became the first woman in 22 years to be executed in the United States. Both Hutchins and Barfield chose death by lethal injection rather than by gas.

Economy. The state's economy rebounded lustily, and the general fund was fattened by a 16.33% increase in collections over those of fiscal 1983. Income taxes accounted for $2.15 billion, and sales and use taxes brought in nearly $1 billion. The increased revenue permitted the General Assembly to provide larger appropriations for education, including substantial pay raises for teachers.

The number of farms in the state fell from more than 300,000 in 1948 to 92,000 in 1979, and to 79,000 in 1984; the 1979–1984 decrease was the largest of any state. Mechanization, corporate agricultural projects, and opportunities for other employment have contributed to the steady decline in the number of farms and an increase in their acreage.

Anniversaries. The four-year observance of the 400th anniversary of the Roanoke voyages, which led to the first English colony in the New World, began in April in Plymouth, England. Then in July, Princess Anne inaugurated activities in North Carolina, speaking at ceremonies on Roanoke Island and christening the *Elizabeth II,* a representation of a 16th-century sailing vessel. A 20-cent postage stamp commemorated the event. Wake Forest University observed its sesquicentennial.

Names in the News. Jane E. Milley became chancellor of the North Carolina School of the Arts, the first woman to head an institution of the state university system. William Friday, the only person to serve as president of the state's 16-campus system, announced plans to retire in 1985.

H. G. JONES
University of North Carolina at Chapel Hill

NORTH DAKOTA

North Dakota voters were firmly on the Reagan bandwagon in 1984, but they demonstrated a flair for independence by turning over to Democrats control of the governorship and a majority of executive-branch offices.

Elections. State voters gave President Ronald Reagan a 66%–34% victory over Walter Mondale. Gov. Allen Olson lost to the Democratic-endorsed state Rep. George Sinner, 45% to 55%. And U.S. Rep. B. L. Dorgan (D) was reelected easily.

Fargo attorney Nicholas Spaeth, a political newcomer, trounced Republican Attorney General Robert Wefald, 65% to 35%. Former Lt. Gov. Wayne Sanstead captured the superintendent of public instruction post for the Democrats, while state Rep. Earl Pomeroy (D-Valley City) was elected insurance commissioner and former state Treasurer Robert Hanson retook that office from Republican incumbent John Lesmeister. Tax Commissioner Kent Conrad, another Democrat, rolled to a crushing victory. Four Republican incumbents —Secretary of State Ben Meier, Agriculture Commissioner Kent Jones, Public Service Commissioner Dale Sandstrom, and Auditor Robert Peterson—held their posts. Voters affirmed a legislative action that brought three community colleges into the state higher education system.

Garrison. With congressional support waning for the Garrison Diversion plan, an ambitious program to divert Missouri River water to eastern and central parts of the arid state, Sen. Mark Andrews (R) sponsored an appropriations compromise that called on a federal com-

mission to recommend a plan for the project's future. Interior Secretary William Clark named the 12-member panel in mid-August, and it began work almost immediately. Commission chairman David Treen said he thought the federal government owed North Dakota a water project. But a commission staff report, released in November, indicated the project, as currently designed, would pay just 52 cents in benefits for each dollar invested. Commissioners were to formulate a new plan.

Law. A group of nine North Dakota farm families won their year-long battle to reform the Farmers Home Administration (FmHA) loan foreclosure procedures. The farmers had asked a federal judge to require FmHA to follow a 1978 law directing the federal lending agency to grant hearings before foreclosing on its loan customers, and to give them a chance to win deferrals by proving their financial difficulties were due to conditions beyond their control. U.S. District Judge Bruce Van Sickle of Bismarck had granted a temporary injunction against FmHA and expanded the suit to cover a nationwide class in 1983, and in February 1984 he made his order permanent.

Senator Andrews became the subject of daily statewide media attention when his family's $10.2 million medical malpractice lawsuit opened in a Fargo courtroom in April. Andrews and his wife, Mary, sued five Fargo doctors and four medical centers, contending they were malicious and negligent in the care of Mary Andrews after she contracted meningitis and a brain abscess that left her permanently impaired. A 12-member jury found two doctors and one medical center guilty of malpractice. But in an unusual move, jurors also ruled the negligence did not cause or exacerbate Mary Andrews' injuries and refused to award damages. The Andrewses filed an appeal.

Agriculture. North Dakota farmers produced a projected 281 million bushels of wheat, up 40% from 1983.

JIM NEUMANN, *"The Forum," Fargo*

NORTH DAKOTA • Information Highlights

Area: 70,702 sq mi (183 119 km²).
Population (July 1, 1983 est.): 680,000.
Chief Cities (1980 census): Bismarck, the capital, 44,485; Fargo, 61,383; Grand Forks, 43,765; Minot, 32,843.
Government (1984): *Chief Officers*—governor, Allen I. Olson (R); lt. gov., Ernest Sands (R). *Legislative Assembly*—Senate, 53 members; House of Representatives, 106 members.
State Finances (fiscal year 1983): *Revenues,* $1,330,000,000; *expenditures,* $1,302,000,000.
Personal Income (1983): $7,939,000,000; per capita, $11,666.
Labor Force (May 1984): *Civilian labor force,* 339,100; *unemployed,* 14,300 (4.2% of total force).
Education: *Enrollment* (fall 1982)—public elementary schools, 81,171; public secondary, 35,907; colleges and universities (fall 1983), 37,591. *Public school expenditures* (1982–83), $318,884,343 ($2,853 per pupil).

NORTHWEST TERRITORIES

A final land-claim agreement with the Inuvialuit (Eskimos) of the Western Arctic region of the Northwest Territories (NWT) was concluded in 1984.

Aboriginal Rights. An agreement between the Inuvialuit and the federal government was signed on June 5. Parliament acted speedily to pass the agreement into law, and on July 25 the Western Arctic (Inuvialuit) Claims Settlement Act created a new system of land ownership, wildlife management, and economic organization in the region—the first comprehensive Canadian land-claims settlement north of 60° latitude. The process of protecting aboriginal rights continued with the first ministers' conference in Ottawa in March, attended by the prime minister, provincial premiers, government leaders of the two territories, and representatives of aboriginal organizations.

Legislative Assembly. The 24-member Legislative Assembly of the Northwest Territories, elected in November 1983, met for the first time in January 1984. The assembly chose Richard Nerysoo as government leader, the first Déné (Indian) to be elected leader of a territorial government in Canada.

A major concern of the assembly was housing conditions, and a special committee was established that held public hearings throughout the NWT. The committee's recommendation that there be a substantial increase in funding for construction of public housing was accepted. Greater aboriginal language services was another issue of concern. The assembly passed an ordinance that, while establishing English and French as official languages in the NWT, recognized Chipewyan, Cree, Dogrib, North and South Slavey, and Inuktitut as official native languages.

Economy. Economic conditions improved in 1984, with all mines back in production following shutdowns in 1983 because of depressed mineral prices. Oil exploration with promising finds remained active in the Beaufort Sea, and there was extensive oil development in the Norman Wells area.

Ross M. Harvey
Government of the Northwest Territories

NORTHWEST TERRITORIES •
Information Highlights

Area: 1,304,903 sq mi (3 379 700 km²).
Population (April 1984 est.): 49,300.
Chief Cities (1981 census): Yellowknife, the capital, 9,483; Inuvik, 3,147; Hay River, 2,863.
Government (1984): *Chief Officer*—commissioner, John H. Parker. *Legislature*—Legislative Assembly, 24 elected members.
Public Finance (1985 fiscal year budget): *Revenues,* C$554,411,000; *expenditures,* C$550,703,000.
Education (1984–85): *Enrollment*—public and secondary schools, 13,050 pupils.

NORWAY

An important development in Norway's economy in 1984 was a far bigger than expected rise in revenues from offshore oil and gas, partly due to the strong U.S. dollar. The high value of the dollar also helped Norwegian exports to the United States and boosted kroner earnings from many of Norway's more traditional exports, such as aluminum and ferroalloys, forest products, fish, and shipping services. Exports to other markets benefited from the moderate world economic upswing, and the trade surplus for the first eight months of the year reached $3.15 billion (U.S.).

The Norwegian krone was twice devalued in 1984, each time by about 2%. The annual union-employer bargaining in the spring resulted in relatively moderate settlements, with most workers getting pay increases of 5.9%. The rate of inflation slowed from 8.5% in 1983 to just over 6% and was expected to fall below 6% in 1985. Industrial production, investment, and employment were all rising. Nevertheless, despite the fact that more people were working, the unemployment rate remained at slightly above 4%. This was high, by Norwegian standards.

Budget. With parliamentary elections due in September, 1985, and petroleum revenues pouring into the treasury at a record rate, the government did loosen the purse strings considerably in its draft budget for 1985.

Tabled on October 4, the budget proposed both higher spending and lower taxes, with social services, regional development, education, defense, and Third-World aid getting most of the extra money. Business and financial circles criticized the proposals as inflationary and said they could undermine the competitiveness of Norwegian industry, while the opposition said they did not go far enough. The budget envisaged expenditures of $20.8 billion—up 7.8% from a year earlier—while revenues were set to rise by only 2.5% to $21.6 billion. If offshore oil and gas income was discounted, the budget showed a deficit of $3.1 billion—the so-called "non-oil deficit"—up from an expected $2.7 billion in 1984.

Statoil Reform. On several issues the two small centrist parties leaned toward the views of the main opposition Labor Party. Their voice in the cabinet undoubtedly helped persuade the Conservative ministers to accept agreement with Labor on one of 1984's main political issues—the "reform" of Norway's state oil company, Statoil. The agreement separated Statoil's function as a revenue collector for the state from its role as Norway's largest oil company. Statoil's economic power was to be reduced by transferring to the state a share of the company's 50% stake in all Norwegian-shelf licenses granted since it was formed, in 1972.

In mid-October, Statoil cut its official crude oil price by $1.50 per barrel to $28.50, prompting world oil industry fears of a price collapse. Britain and Nigeria quickly followed suit, and the Organization of Petroleum Exporting Countries called an emergency meeting in Geneva to discuss countermeasures. Norwegian ministers ̈said that the cut had been forced on Statoil by weak price trends on the unofficial market.

Spy Scandal. Arne Treholt, a former Labor deputy minister subsequently employed in a senior foreign ministry job, was arrested on spying charges in January. He admitted to having contacts with KGB officials and to selling information to the Iraqi government.

An immediate consequence of the episode was the expulsion from Norway of five Soviet diplomats, and a much chillier climate between Oslo and Moscow.

THOR GJESTER, *Editor, "Økonomisk Revy"*

NOVA SCOTIA

During 1984, Nova Scotians reelected a Progressive Conservative government for the third consecutive term, were encouraged by the positive economic impact of oil and gas exploration activities on the Scotian Shelf, and greeted the visit of the "tall ships" in June and Pope John Paul II in September.

Provincial Election. Premier John Buchanan's Conservatives steamrolled their way to victory. For the first time in Nova Scotia history, three women—two Progressive Conservatives and the NDP leader—were elected to serve in the Legislative Assembly. Having captured 51% of the total vote, the Conservatives won 42 seats, while the Liberals took six seats, the NDP three, and the Cape Breton Labour Party one. This gave the Conservatives their largest majority since coming to power in 1978. Even Liberal leader Sandy Cameron was ousted from the electoral district he had retained since a 1973 by-election.

NORWAY · Information Highlights

Official Name: Kingdom of Norway.
Location: Northern Europe.
Area: 124,999 sq mi (323 750 km²).
Population (mid-1984 est.): 4,100,000.
Chief Cities (Jan. 1983 est.): Oslo, the capital, 448,775; Bergen, 207,292; Trondheim, 134,655.
Government: *Head of state,* Olav V, king (acceded Sept. 1957). *Head of government,* Kåre Willoch, prime minister (took office October 1981). *Legislature*—Storting: Lagting and Odelsting.
Monetary Unit: Krone (9.0 kroner equal U.S.$1, Oct. 18, 1984).
Gross National Product (1982 U.S.$): $56,200,-000,000.
Economic Indexes (1983): *Consumer Prices* (1970 = 100), all items, 306.7; food, 312.2. *Industrial Production* (1975 = 100), 140.
Foreign Trade (1983 U.S.$): *Imports,* $13,500,-000,000; *exports,* $17,979,000,000.

NOVA SCOTIA · Information Highlights

Area: 21,425 sq mi (55 490 km²).
Population (April 1984 est.): 868,100.
Chief Cities (1981 census): Halifax, the capital, 114,594; Dartmouth, 62,277; Sydney, 29,444.
Government (1984): *Chief Officers*—lt. gov., Alan R. Abraham; premier, John Buchanan (Progressive Conservative); att. gen., Ronald C. Giffen. *Legislature*—Legislative Assembly, 52 members.
Provincial Finances (1985 fiscal year budget): *Revenues,* $3,160,000,000; *expenditures,* $3,200,000,-000.
Personal Income (average weekly earnings, May 1984): $355.13.
Labor Force (July 1984, seasonally adjusted): *Employed workers,* 15 years of age and over, 343,000; *Unemployed* 47,000 (12.1%).
Education (1984–85): *Enrollment*—elementary and secondary schools, 173,810 pupils; postsecondary (1984–85)—universities, 29,660; community colleges (full-time), 2,760.
(All monetary figures are in Canadian dollars.)

Legislation. In 1984 the government secured legislative approval for 109 bills, of which 93 became law. Among the legislation were: amendments to the Health Services Act, under which Nova Scotia became the first province to ban extra billing by doctors; amendments to the Residential Tenancies Act, which entitle tenants to security of tenure after five years in a rental unit; and the amended Motor Vehicle Act, which requires Nova Scotians from January 1, 1985, to wear seat belts.

Economy. Various indicators showed that the provincial economy outperformed other parts of Canada. Despite high interest rates, consumer spending remained brisk. Prompted by a more than 10% increase in wages and salaries, retail trade during the first seven months of 1984 increased by 15.7%, as compared with the same period of 1983. New motor vehicles sales were up by 31%, while manufacturing increased its output by 17%. A decline in the value of residential building permits was balanced by a surge in nonresidential construction. Some 19,000 new jobs were created.

Energy. Nova Scotia's energy exploration —with seven drilling rigs currently searching for offshore oil and gas reserves—showed no sign of waning. Up until May 1984, the provincial government had signed 11 gas and oil exploration agreements with various oil companies—including PetroCan and Texaco— for spending an additional $632 million on exploration over the next three years. At the end of August, however, one group of companies canceled a $500 million drilling program because the wells drilled by the group were dry. Yet this setback did not mark an end of the Venture project, scheduled for execution by the end of 1988. In fact, fresh news of a gas discovery by Shell Canada reinforced the possibility of finding significant gas reserves south of Sable Island.

R. P. SETH
Mount Saint Vincent University, Halifax

OBITUARIES[1]

WEISSMULLER, Johnny

American swimmer and actor: b. Freidorf, Rumania, June 2, 1904; d. Acapulco, Mexico, Jan. 20, 1984.

The first swimmer to win five gold medals in Olympic competition, Johnny Weissmuller earned even greater fame as the bellowing, vine-swinging, chest-thumping star of nearly 20 Tarzan of the Jungle movies. During the 1920s, the tall, broad-shouldered freestyler won 51 U.S. national swimming championships and set 67 world records; the Associated Press later named him the outstanding swimmer of the half-century. Trading his swimsuit for a loin-cloth in 1932, Weissmuller built his image as the fearless protector of the animal kingdom, a mate named Jane (Maureen O'Sullivan), and a son named Boy (Johnny Sheffield) in the jun-

ANDROPOV, Yuri V.

Soviet leader: b. Stavropol province, Russia, June 15, 1914; d. Moscow, Feb. 9, 1984.

In November 1982 at the age of 68, Yuri Vladimirovich Andropov became the oldest man in Soviet history to become head of the Communist Party. After 15 years (1967–82) as head of the feared police organization, the KGB, he had managed to gain support from the military and prominent party officials to beat out his principal rival, Konstantin Chernenko, and succeed to the mantle of Leonid Brezhnev.

While the Brezhnev era (1964–82) had been marked by stability in foreign policy and polit-ical stagnation at home, Andropov's brief rule was characterized by new initiatives, the re-moval of many corrupt and inefficient officials, and economic reform. A campaign for labor

MERMAN, Ethel

American musical-comedy star: b. Astoria, NY, Jan. 16, 1909 (?); d. New York, NY, Feb. 15, 1984.

Perhaps more than any other Broadway star, Ethel Merman helped shape American musical theater. From 1930 through the 1950s, the singer with the booming, bell-clear voice— who never took a singing lesson in her life— brought down the house in 13 memorable shows, including Cole Porter's *Anything Goes* and Irving Berlin's *Annie Get Your Gun.*

Merman made her first Broadway appear-ance at the age of 21, in George Gershwin's *Girl Crazy.* When she belted out "I Got Rhythm," holding a high C for 16 bars, she became a star on the spot. Her talent for hold-

[1] Arranged chronologically by death date

gles of Africa. The image never faded. Though other actors played the role, Weissmuller was Tarzan, and Tarzan was Weissmuller.

His career as an actor was entirely unplanned, but the easy-going Weissmuller took to the part of Tarzan like a crocodile to water. "It was like stealing," he once said. "There was swimming in it, and I didn't have much to say. How can a guy climb trees, say 'Me Tarzan, you Jane' and make a million?"

Background. Born in 1904, Johnny Weissmuller was the son of Austrian immigrants making their way to Chicago. He learned to swim at age 8 at Fullerton Beach on Lake Michigan. His father, a saloonkeeper, died when Johnny was in eighth grade, forcing the boy to go to work at odd jobs.

At 16, Weissmuller came to the attention of swimming coach "Big Bill" Bacharach. Under Bacharach's iron hand, the 6'3", 190-lb (1.90-m, 86-kg) youth developed into a top freestyler.

At the 1924 Olympics in Paris, the 20-year-old won gold medals in the 100 meters, 400 meters, and 800-m relay. At the 1928 Games in Amsterdam, Weissmuller carried the U.S. flag in the opening parade and took two more gold medals —in the 100 meters and 800-m relay.

With a living to make, Weissmuller retired from amateur competition and became a pro. A $500-a-week job promoting swimsuits brought him to the attention of MGM, which offered a screen test for the Tarzan role. The first three jungle adventures—*Tarzan the Ape Man* (1932), *Tarzan and his Mate* (1934), and *Tarzan Escapes* (1936)—launched the series that lasted until 1949. Weissmuller then moved on to other films and a television series, *Jungle Jim*.

Following his death, it was revealed that Weissmuller was born in the Rumanian town of Freidorf, not Windber, PA, as he claimed. He came to the United States as an infant.

JEFF HACKER

---

discipline and productivity was begun, as Andropov promised workers more control over work and farmers greater incentives. In foreign affairs he tried to revive détente, even proposing a nuclear freeze, but the war in Afghanistan, tensions in Poland, the shooting down of a Korean airliner, and U.S. deployment of new missiles in Western Europe ended chances of improved East-West relations.

Just as his proposed reforms were being implemented, Andropov disappeared from public view. Only when he died was it revealed that he had been suffering from a devastating kidney ailment. He was succeeded by his aged rival, Chernenko, a loyal supporter of Brezhnev's policies. Observers began watching for indication of future Kremlin policy, especially in light of Chernenko's advanced age.

Background. Born the son of a railroad worker in southern Russia, Andropov began

his political career in the Komsomol, the Communist youth organization, in the 1930s. As senior officials were cut down in Stalin's Great Purges, he was rapidly promoted; by 1940 he was first secretary of the Komsomol in the Karelo-Finnish Republic. After Stalin's death in 1953, Andropov served as ambassador to Hungary, where he was involved in the crushing of the Hungarian Revolution of 1956. He was raised to the Central Committee in 1961 and became head of the KGB in 1967. Even as chief of the secret police, Andropov gained a reputation as a liberal and a reformer, as he attacked official corruption and arbitrary police practices. Just as former KGB men were appointed to clean up the Caucasian republics of Azerbaidzhan and Georgia, so—some say— Andropov was given a mandate to bring discipline to the Soviet Union.

RONALD G. SUNY

---

ing a note became a trademark; as she explained it, "I just stand up and holler and hope my voice holds out." Her voice had true pitch and a clarity that delivered every syllable.

Known as a hard worker at rehearsals, Merman also had a reputation for giving 100% at every performance and rarely missing a show. She was supremely self-confident and assertive, and, as her star status increased, she received as much as 10% of the gross as her fee. Her flashy style and flamboyant manner epitomized the Broadway of her time.

Background. Born Ethel Agnes Zimmerman, the singer shortened her name early in life because, as she put it, "If you put Zimmerman up in lights, you'd die from the heat." She trained as a stenographer and began singing in nightclubs while working as a secretary. She was headlined at the Brooklyn Paramount when she was hired for *Girl Crazy* in 1930.

As her Broadway career progressed, she compiled an impressive record of hits, including "I Get a Kick Out of You" and "You're the Top" from *Anything Goes* (1934); "There's No Business Like Show Business," "You Can't Get a Man with a Gun," and others from *Annie Get Your Gun* (1946); and "Everything's Coming Up Roses" from the 1959 Jule Styne-Stephen Sondheim musical *Gypsy*. Her favorite role was that of Mama Rose in *Gypsy*, and she was crushed when Rosalind Russell was given the part in the film version.

Merman herself made 14 films, including film versions of several of her Broadway shows, but was never the success on the screen that she was on stage. In 1966, she was the last of six stars to play the title role in Jerry Herman's *Hello Dolly*. Her last major appearance was in a 1982 benefit concert at Carnegie Hall.

ELAINE PASCOE

BASIE, Count

American bandleader: b. Red Bank, NJ, Aug. 21, 1904; d. Hollywood, FL, April 26, 1984.

One of the most famous of the big-band leaders, the legendary Count Basie was most responsible for the proliferation of the Kansas City jazz style, with its smooth articulations, improvised solos, and even 4/4 beat. With Basie guiding the rhythm section, the band produced an unequaled level of intense swing.

Background. Born William Basie, an only child, he started his musical training on the drums, but because of the presence in Red Bank of the talented future Duke Ellington drummer Sonny Greer, he switched to piano.

Fats Waller, an organist at the Lincoln Theater in Harlem, was an early influence.

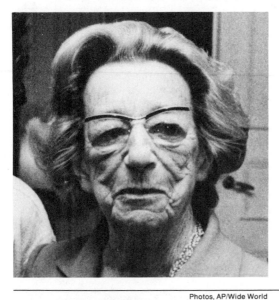

HELLMAN, Lillian Florence

American writer: b. New Orleans, LA, June 20, 1905; d. Martha's Vineyard, MA, June 30, 1984.

The most distinguished woman playwright in American theater, Lillian Hellman was also a noted memoirist and motion-picture scenarist. Influenced by Ibsen, Hellman believed that theater should do more than entertain. Her dramas force a consideration of the moral issues at the heart of evil and an awareness of the decency and integrity that are central to goodness and a better life.

The immediate Broadway success of *The Children's Hour* in 1934 opened Hellman's career. Of the eight original dramas and four adaptations that she wrote between 1934 and 1963, *The Little Foxes* (1939), *The Autumn*

Photos, AP/Wide World

GALLUP, George Horace

American public opinion pollster: b. Jefferson, IA, Nov. 18, 1901; d. Tschingel, Switzerland, July 26, 1984.

For more than 40 years, George Gallup was easily the world's most visible developer and advocate of public opinion polling. While the founder and chairman of the Gallup Organization liked to describe himself as just a "public opinion statistician" and colleagues described him as a kind of nontheoretical "tinkerer," Gallup was perhaps more responsible than anyone for setting in motion certain profound changes in politics as well as in both popular and scientific conceptions of public opinion. Gallup's early successes in predicting elections legitimized "modern" opinion polling. He argued that polling allowed the public to be heard.

Through Waller, Basie became a singer accompanist. Later he joined the touring Gonzel White show, which got stranded in Kansas City, where Basie played piano accompaniment to silent movies before joining Walter Page's Blue Devil Band in Tulsa, OK, in 1928. The band, with bassist Page and blues singer Jimmy Rushing, would provide two important members to future Basie bands. In 1935, for the Reno Club in Kansas City, Basie organized his first band. During a radio broadcast from the club, a program announcer decided that Bill was not a colorful enough name for a jazz musician and changed it to "Count." The broadcasts also brought Basie to the attention of jazz critic and enthusiast John Hammond who helped get the band into the Grand Terrace in Chicago, where it was expanded to 13 pieces.

From there, the band played a mediocre engagement at New York's Roseland Ballroom,

followed by an unsuccessful year on the road. In 1937 the group performed at New York's Famous Door, where with access to both local and national radio time they first stirred major interest and excitement. That same year, the band made its first recordings, including the classic hits *Jumpin' at the Woodside* and *One O'Clock Jump*.

The Basie Band "book" of the 1940s was based on the 12-bar blues structure, with driving riffs and brass "hits," and the band was built around a swinging core group of soloists. In 1950, Basie returned to a small-band format but in 1952 formed a new big band.

Highlights of his career included playing at President John Kennedy's inaugural ball, collaborating with Frank Sinatra (1965), and receiving a Kennedy Center honor for achievement in the performing arts (1981).

DOMINIC SPERA

Garden (1951), and *Toys in the Attic* (1960) perhaps best represent the remarkable talent and vision that Hellman brought to the theater. Her powerful characters, psychological insights, crisp dialogue, and sense of realism and irony moved audiences to a profound recognition of what being human means. *Watch on the Rhine* (1941), *The Searching Wind* (1944), and *Days to Come* (1936) examine the struggle against Fascism and reactionaryism, between love and appeasement, and between strikers and strikebreakers. They all testify to Hellman's social conscience and undying concern for integrity and decency.

In the early 1960s, Hellman turned to writing her memoirs. *Unfinished Woman* (1969), *Pentimento* (1973), *Scoundrel Time* (1976), and *Maybe* (1980) portray the dignity and pride, independence and spirit, courage, intellect, and compassion that enabled her to endure.

Background. The only child of Max and Julia Newhouse Hellman, Lillian was raised among relatives in New Orleans and Manhattan. After attending New York University and Columbia, she reviewed books and worked as a scenario reader for Metro-Goldwyn-Mayer. In 1930 she met Dashiell Hammett, who was her closest friend until his death in 1961.

Hellman was a controversial figure because of her anti-Fascist activities in the 1930s and 1940s, her pro-Soviet allegiance after other liberals denounced the evils of Stalinism, her 1952 appearance before the House Committee on Un-American Activities, and her outspokenness against the Vietnam War, the Watergate scandal, and political repression in general.

Hellman edited Chekhov's letters and Hammett's stories and adapted for the stage such works as *Montserrat, The Lark,* and *Candide.*

MARY MARGUERITE RIORDAN

At first, journalists resisted Gallup's polls as a threat to their own self-proclaimed insights about public opinion. Today, the media treat the polls done by their own organizations as major news events.

In the social sciences, the success of polls led public opinion scholars to believe that public opinion could be measured by simple frequency counts. Thus, a simple majority of individual citizens' opinions *is* public opinion.

Background. Born in a small railroad town in central Iowa, George Horace Gallup received his B.A. (1923), M.A. (1925), and Ph.D. (1928) degrees from the University of Iowa. During his doctoral study, which was of newspaper readership, he began to develop some of his ideas about survey sampling methods. After brief stints as a journalism professor in the Midwest, he became market research director for a New York advertising agency (1932–47).

With a partner who later sold out to him, Gallup began moonlighting in his own survey business in 1935. Undoubtedly the biggest boost to the firm was the free publicity generated when its poll successfully predicted that President Franklin D. Roosevelt would beat Alf Landon in 1936. Meanwhile, the *Literary Digest* magazine, with a much larger sample drawn from lists of more affluent Americans, had predicted that Landon would win. The error provided the object lesson about how wrong the old "unscientific" methods could be. Gallup's firm quickly used its success to "sell" its private market research to clients. Later the firm established branch offices overseas.

In contrast with his market research business, Gallup refused to do private polls for politicians, preferring to maintain his firm's reputation for impartiality.

JAMES B. LEMERT

BURTON, Richard

British actor: b. Pontrhydfen, South Wales, Nov. 10, 1925; d. Geneva, Switzerland, Aug. 5, 1984.

A lost promise of greatness shrouded actor Richard Burton at his comparatively early death. Laurels that perhaps should have been his were too late coming. He was nominated seven times for an Academy Award but never won; he was the most famous unknighted British actor. Despite this seeming unfulfillment, he had in fact appeared in many plays and by the age of 27 was considered one of Britain's greatest Shakespearean actors. Many critics thought him the greatest Hamlet of the era. He himself considered his best role that of Coriolanus. A romantic, Burton pursued living with as much vigor as he practiced his art. He was called a born actor, and yet his humble beginnings as the son of a Welsh coal miner appeared an uncanny start for such strivings. Philip Burton, a Welsh schoolteacher, became his legal guardian, giving him his name. Richard Jenkins became Richard Burton.

Background. Born the 12th of 13 children, Richard lost his mother when he was two. He spoke no English until age 10, but under the elder Burton's guidance he learned to speak, hold a knife and fork, and study the classics. His "coarse, rough" voice developed into a graceful baritone of incomparable quality.

After his London stage debut at age 18, Burton attended Oxford University and served as a wartime navigator before attracting serious attention in 1949 in Christopher Fry's *The Lady's Not for Burning.* Hollywood offers followed, and he appeared in the films *My Cousin Rachel* and *The Robe,* but he soon returned to England. He joined the Old Vic Company where he performed in a variety of roles, and he appeared in the British film *Look Back in Anger.* His success in the Broadway musical *Camelot* in 1960 brought an offer of the role of Antony in the expensive and ultimately ill-fated *Cleopatra.* During the filming he fell in love with his costar, Elizabeth Taylor. They became a favorite of the paparazzi, creating headlines with their two marriages to each other and extravagant lifestyle. During their years together, Burton made the film *Beckett* and had a triumphant 1964 Broadway run in *Hamlet.* The two were memorable in *Who's Afraid of Virginia Woolf?* and *The Taming of the Shrew,* but there were several forgettable pictures as well. With *Equus* (1977) and a 1980 stage revival of *Camelot,* Burton again succeeded. He teamed briefly with Taylor in 1983 in a Broadway production of *Private Lives.* Prior to his death he completed filming *Wagner* and *1984.*

He married five times; and was the father of three daughters, including an adopted one.

SAUNDRA FRANCE

CAPOTE, Truman

American writer: b. New Orleans, LA, Sept. 30, 1924; d. Los Angeles, CA, Aug. 25, 1984.

The celebrated career and public life of author Truman Capote spoke of a troubled genius. "I always knew that I wanted to be a writer and that I wanted to be rich and famous," he once said. Capote had his first story published at age 17, and at age 23 he scored a major critical and financial success with his first novel, *Other Voices, Other Rooms* (1948). His best-known and most admired work was the "non-fiction novel" *In Cold Blood* (1966), about the murderers of a Kansas farm family. And though his other novels, short stories, and reportage were acclaimed for their imagination and style, Capote's life work amounted to only 13 volumes—most of them small collections. An admitted alcoholic, drug addict, and homosexual, he was distracted from his literary vision by the perquisites of high society and media stardom. Capote died at age 59 without having finished what was to be his masterpiece, a lengthy novel about the rich and famous. The book was to be called *Answered Prayers.* Selected portions of the intended book had been published in various magazines.

Background. The future writer was born Truman Streckfus Persons. When he was still very young, his mother sent him away to live with relatives in Alabama. Truman would later say that in those years he felt like "a spiritual orphan." Much of his writing would be based on recollections of Monroeville, AL, where he spent several years of his lonely childhood.

Truman's parents divorced, and his mother married again to a Cuban businessman from New York, Joe Capote. At age 11, the boy was brought to New York to live with them. He was sent to several private schools, but he was bored and did not do well. It was a teacher at Greenwich High School in Connecticut who encouraged his fierce interest in writing. At age 17, Capote got a job as an errand boy at the *New Yorker* magazine and continued writing. Over the next two years he had several stories published in minor magazines.

Capote's breakthrough came in 1945, when *Mademoiselle* published his story "Miriam," which won him the first of his four O. Henry Memorial Awards. The appearance of *Other Voices, Other Rooms* in 1948 marked his arrival as a literary celebrity. Among his other notable works are the novels *The Grass Harp* (1951) and *Breakfast at Tiffany's* (1958); the short-story collection *A Tree of Night* (1949); *The Muses Are Heard* (1956), an account of his tour of the Soviet Union with a theatrical group; and *Music for Chameleons* (1980), a collection of nonfiction pieces.

JEFFREY H. HACKER

GANDHI, Indira

Indian political leader: b. Allahabad, India, Nov. 19, 1917; d. New Delhi, India, Oct. 31, 1984.

Indira Gandhi was prime minister of India (except for a 33-month interval) from 1966 until her assassination at the hands of two Sikh members of her own security guard. A child of the Indian revolution, she knew most of the leaders of the Indian independence struggle, including Mohandas K. Gandhi. From the time that her father, Jawaharlal Nehru, became prime minister of India (in 1946, even before independence) until his death nearly 18 years later, she was his hostess and confidante. A private, complex, enigmatic personality, she dominated Indian politics in her last two decades. She was internationally prominent.

Background. Indira Priyadarshini ("Dearly Beloved") Nehru was the only child of Jawaharlal and Kamala Nehru. Her childhood, as she later remarked, "was an abnormal one, full of loneliness and insecurity." She spent three unhappy years at a boarding school in Poona and a few memorable months at Santiniketan, an unusual university founded by Rabindranath Tagore. After some schooling in Switzerland, Indira entered Somerville College, Oxford, in 1937, but returned to India in 1941 without taking a degree.

While in London, she became reacquainted with a journalist from Allahabad, Feroze Gandhi, a Parsi, whom she had known in her childhood. In March 1942, despite almost universal opposition, the Hindu and the Parsi were married. Six months later they were arrested and jailed for their support of the Indian nationalist movement. In 1943 they returned to Allahabad, where they lived until 1946. During this period two sons, Rajiv and Sanjay, were born. She and her husband were estranged at the time of his death in 1960.

In 1955, Indira was made a member of the Congress Working Committee. Four years later she was elected president of the Congress party. After her father's death in May 1964, she became minister of information and broadcasting in the cabinet of Lal Bahadur Shastri. In January 1966, after the sudden death of Shastri, the Congress party bosses selected her as the new prime minister, apparently thinking that she could be controlled. For a time she seemed uncertain and ineffective, but later she moved decisively to challenge the old guard of the Congress. She was expelled from the party in November 1969 and organized her own wing, which had more supporters than the Congress old guard could muster. She consolidated her position by decisive victories in the general election in 1971 and state assembly elections in 1972, and by her strong stand during the crisis with Pakistan in 1971.

AP/Wide World

Having reached the peak of her power, she soon experienced a whole series of adversities, mainly because of growing economic and law and order problems. In June 1975—after a high court judge ruled that she must give up her seat in Parliament and stay out of politics for six years because of 1971 election abuses—she took the extraordinary step of imposing a state of emergency and taking coercive and repressive measures that were alleged to be violations of the Constitution. In January 1977 previously postponed elections were announced. In March the Indian voters repudiated her.

In October 1977 she was held briefly on charges of official corruption. Fourteen months later she was expelled from Parliament and confined in prison for the few remaining days of the parliamentary session. Thereafter her wing of the Congress—streamlined and renamed the Congress (I)—began to gather strength. She won a landslide victory in the January 1980 election.

Her last tenure of office was a troubled one. Her reluctance to denounce the Soviet invasion of Afghanistan was criticized widely, and she was unable to deal effectively with growing violence in several parts of India. In June 1980 she suffered a great personal tragedy when her younger son, Sanjay, who was rapidly emerging as her heir apparent, was killed in an airplane crash. Thereafter she turned to her older son, Rajiv, for assistance and for grooming as her eventual successor.

NORMAN D. PALMER

The following is a selected list of prominent persons who died during 1984.
Articles on major figures appear in the preceding pages.

AP/Wide World   UPI/Bettmann   Pictorial Parade   AP/Wide World

Walter Alston   *Brooks Atkinson*   *Enrico Berlinguer*   *Ellsworth Bunker*

Adams, Ansel (82), U.S. photographer: d. near Carmel, CA, April 22. (*See* page 414.)

Adams, Sir John (63), British-born particle physicist and executive director general of the European Organization for Nuclear Research (CERN) (1976–81): d. Geneva, Switzerland, March 3.

Aiken, George (92), U.S. senator (R-Vt, 1941–75); served in the Vermont House of Representatives and as governor of Vermont for two terms. As a senator he championed liberal legislation and was a strong supporter of the farmer, fighting for most of the farm legislation enacted. He was the chief architect of the food stamp program enacted in 1965: d. Montpelier, VT, Nov. 19.

Aleixandre, Vicente (86), Spanish poet; of the "Generation of 1927," he won the 1977 Nobel Prize for literature. His work surveyed the mysteries of death, love, and the unconscious and included *La destrucción del amor:* d. Madrid, Spain, Dec. 13.

Alston, Walter (72), baseball manager for the Brooklyn and later Los Angeles Dodgers from 1954 to 1976; guided the team to seven National League pennants and four World Series championships (1955, 1959, 1963, 1965). He was elected to the baseball Hall of Fame in 1983: d. Oxford, OH, Oct. 1.

Aries, Philippe (69), French historian and demographer; his best-known book is *Centuries of Childhood* (1960): d. Paris, Feb. 8.

Ashton-Warner, Sylvia (75), New Zealand writer; wrote books about teaching school children. Her first book *Spinster* (1959) was an international best-seller. Other books include *Teacher* (1963), *Greenstone* (1966), *Spearpoint: Teacher in America* (1972), and her autobiography *Myself* (1967): d. Tauranga, New Zealand, April 28.

Atkinson, Brooks (89), drama critic for *The New York Times* from 1925 to 1960 except for a four-year break in the 1940s during which he was a foreign correspondent. He won a Pulitzer Prize in 1947 for foreign correspondence. In 1960 Mr. Atkinson began a column "Critic at Large" that appeared in the *Times* for the following five years before his retirement, Mr. Atkinson wrote nearly a dozen books on theater, travel, and nature: d. Huntsville, AL, Jan. 13.

Balasaraswati (64), dancer; one of the greatest classical dancers of India. She performed and taught in the United States for a period of 20 years: d. Madras, India, Feb. 9.

Barry, Jack (66), television personality; was the producer and star of the television game shows *The Joker's Wild* and *21*. His company also produced *Concentration,* the longest-running daytime quiz show: d. New York City, May 2.

Barzini, Luigi (75), Italian author and journalist; he was also a member of the Italian parliament (1958–72). His best-known book was *The Italians* (1964). The son of a prominent Italian journalist, the American-educated Barzini worked as a journalist for newspapers and magazines in Italy and the United States. He founded the newspaper *Il Globo*, serving as editor and publisher from 1944 to 1947. In 1978 he became a regular columnist for *Corriere della Sera*. An early Mussolini supporter, he soon became disillusioned with Fascism and acquired a hatred of Mussolini: d. Rome, March 30.

Basehart, Richard (70), stage and film actor; made his Broadway stage debut in 1938 and in 1945 appeared in *The Hasty Heart*, for which he won the New York Drama Critics Circle Award. This triumph led to a Hollywood picture contract. He also appeared on television for four seasons beginning in 1964 in *Voyage to the Bottom of the Sea:* d. Los Angeles, CA, Sept. 17.

Bellonte, Maurice (87), early flier; was the navigator and radio operator on the first nonstop transatlantic airplane flight from Paris to New York in 1930: d. Paris, Jan. 14.

Ben Haim, Paul (86), German-born composer who fled to Palestine and became Israel's leading composer: d. Jerusalem, Jan. 15.

Beny, Roloff (Wilfred Roy) (60), Canadian photographer and artist; his acclaimed books include *To Everything There Is a Season* and *India:* d. Rome, March 16.

Berlinguer, Enrico (62), Italian Communist leader; started a movement among West European Communists for greater autonomy from Moscow. Since 1972 he was the leader of the largest Communist Party in Western Europe, which in 1979 elections took more than 30% of the vote: d. Padua, Italy, June 11.

Betjeman, Sir John (77), poet laureate of Great Britain: d. Trebetherick, Cornwall, England, May 19.

Brassai (born Gyula Halász) (84), Hungarian-born photographer; settled in Paris in 1924 and originally engaged in painting, sculpting, and writing. In 1930 he took up photography and later produced *Paris de Nuit,* with pictures of sailors, barflies, homosexuals, and prostitutes and their customers. The book created a sensation. Brassai photographed for *Le Minotaure* (1933–36) and *Harper's Bazaar* (1936–65). Between 1945–50 he designed for the stage, made films, and again took up sculpture. In 1982 the much-honored photographer came out with *The Artists of My Life:* d. near Nice, France, July 8.

Bratteli Trygve (74), prime minister of Norway (1971–72; 1973–76): d. Oslo, Norway, Nov. 20.

Brautigan, Richard (49), American writer; was a significant literary figure of the 1960s. His works include *Trout Fishing in America, In Watermelon Sugar, So the Wind Won't Blow It All Away,* and *The Pill Versus the Springhill Mine Disaster:* d. Bolinas, CA, Oct. 25 (found dead).

Bricktop (born Ada Beatrice Queen Victoria Louise Virginia Smith) (89), singer and entertainer; in her café society nightclubs in Paris in the 1920s and in Mexico City and Rome in the post–World War II years, she entertained royalty and writers: d. New York City, Jan. 31.

Brisson, Frederick (71), Danish-born theater and film producer. His Broadway successes included *The Pajama Game, Damn Yankees, The Pleasure of His Company,* and *Coco.* He was married to Rosalind Russell for 35 years, until her death in 1976: d. New York City, Oct. 8.

Brunot, James (82), first producer of the game Scrabble, which had been invented in 1933 by his friend Alfred M. Butts: d. Bridgeport, CT, Oct. 22.

Buckler, Ernest (75), Canadian novelist, essayist, and short-story writer; his best-known novel is *The Mountain and the Valley:* d. Bridgetown, Nova Scotia, March 4.

Bull, Peter (72), character actor and writer; he first appeared on the London stage in 1933 and made his Broadway debut in 1935. On Broadway he performed in *Luther* (1963), *Pickwick* (1965), and *Black Comedy* (1967). His film appearances included *Sabotage, Oliver Twist, The African Queen, Tom Jones, Dr. Strangelove,* and *Joseph Andrews.* His first book of reminiscences was published in 1956; it was followed by six others including the best-selling *I Say, Look Here!:* d. London, May 20.

Bunker, Ellsworth (90), U.S. diplomat; served as ambassador to South Vietnam between 1967 and 1973. Bunker, who had been a businessman for 30 years before becoming a diplomat, was trusted by all the presidents with whom he worked. The first was Harry Truman, who appointed him ambassador to Argentina (1951). Between 1952 and 1953, Bunker was ambassador to Italy. Under Eisenhower he served in India and Nepal (1956–61). In the administration of President Kennedy, Bunker helped settle a dispute between the Netherlands and

Indonesia over West New Guinea. He served in the Middle East and as a representative on the council of the Organization of American States before his assignment to Vietnam. His final effort as a diplomat was as the chief negotiator on the talks with Panama concerning a new and revised canal treaty, which resulted in two agreements: d. Brattleboro, VT, Sept. 27.

Burden, William (78), president of New York's Museum of Modern Art (1953–59; 1962–65); became a trustee of the Museum of Modern Art in 1943, remaining into the 1980s: d. New York City, Oct. 10.

Byers, Lord (Charles Frank) (68), the Liberal Party leader in the British Parliament's House of Lords since 1967: d. Lingfield, Sussex, England, Feb. 6.

Caldwell, Millard F. (87), governor of Florida (1945–49). A conservative Democrat, he had also been a state legislator, a U.S. representative (1933–41), the country's first federal civil defense administrator, and chief justice of the Florida Supreme Court (1967–69): d. Tallahassee, FL, Oct. 23.

Campbell, Clarence (78), president of the National Hockey League (1946–77): d. Montreal, Canada, June 24.

Case, Anna (95), Metropolitan Opera soprano, she made her debut there in 1909. In 1913 she sang the role of Sophie in the first American production of Der Rosenkavalier: d. New York City, Jan. 7.

Chivers, Howard P. (67), member of U.S. Ski Hall of Fame; was a U.S. and Canadian cross-country champion: d. Hanover, NH, March 8.

Christensen, Lew (75), former ballet dancer and director of the San Francisco Ballet. He danced in the 1930s with the American Ballet, the earliest company founded by George Balanchine and Lincoln Kirstein. His best-known ballet was Filling Station. He joined the faculty of the School of American Ballet in 1946 and was a ballet master of Ballet Society and the City Ballet. He became director of the San Francisco Ballet in 1952 and was its major choreographer for many years: d. Burlingame, CA, Oct. 9.

Church, Frank Forrester (59), U.S. senator (D-Idaho, 1957–81); was chairman of the Senate Foreign Relations Committee (1979–81). A liberal, he supported civil rights, equal rights for women, expanded benefits for the elderly, and the 1963 nuclear test ban treaty with the USSR. In 1966 he broke with the Johnson administration regarding the bombing in Vietnam and in the early 1970s continued his struggle against the war. In 1975, Senator Church became chairman of the Senate Select Committee on Intelligence, which examined activities of the Central Intelligence Agency and the Federal Bureau of Investigation: d. Bethesda, MD, April 7.

Clark, Mark Wayne (87), U.S. Army commander; served in both World Wars I and II and in the Korean conflict and was the last of the top five Army commanders of World War II. He was involved in the North African invasion of 1942 and in the capture of Rome in 1944. General Clark in 1952 became U.N. commander in Korea and commander in chief of the U.S. Far East Command. He signed the July 1953 Korean Armistice and initiated the prisoner exchange that followed. He retired in October 1953 and in 1954 became president of The Citadel, a military college in Charleston, SC, where he remained until 1965: d. Charleston, SC, April 17.

Cole, Kenneth S. (83), biophysicist; was a pioneer in the study of electrical properties of nerves and other living cells and a 1967 winner of the National Medal of Science: d. La Jolla, CA, April 18.

Commager, Steele (51), classics professor at Columbia University and the son of the historian Henry Steele Commager: d. New York City, April 2.

Coogan, Jackie (69), actor; famous as a child actor, he was responsible for a U.S. law that said that the money earned by child actors had to be deposited in court-administered trust funds. The law passed after his mother and stepfather announced that they would not turn over to Coogan the money he had earned as a child. He appeared with Charlie Chaplin in The Kid: d. Santa Monica, CA, March 1.

Cooper, Charles H. (Chuck) (57), basketball player for the National Basketball Association's Boston Celtics; became the first black player in the NBA when he joined the Celtics in 1950: d. Pittsburgh, Feb. 5.

Cooper, Douglas (72), internationally known British art historian, critic, and collector. He wrote several books, including Graham Sutherland (1961) and Picasso: Theatre (1968): d. London, April 1.

Corridan, John M. (73), Jesuit priest; crusaded against corruption on the New York City docks in the 1940s and 1950s, becoming known as the Waterfront Priest. His efforts led to labor reforms and the creation of a Waterfront Commission in 1953: d. New York City, July 1.

Cortázar, Julio (69), Argentine writer; famous for the novel Rayuela (Hopscotch) (1963). Other novels include Los Premios and Libro de Manuel. He wrote several collections of short stories as well, including Blow Up, later made into a movie. His works often dealt with reincarnation: d. Paris, Feb. 12.

Coveleski, Stanley (94), American League baseball pitcher; played 14 seasons, retiring in 1928. He pitched for the Philadelphia Athletics, the Cleveland Indians, the Washington Senators, and the New York Yankees. He was elected to the Baseball Hall of Fame in 1969: d. South Bend, IN, March 20.

Coxe, George Harmon, Jr. (82), writer of more than 60 mystery novels: d. Hilton Head, SC, Jan. 30.

Cronin, Joe (77), baseball player, manager, and American League president. Over a 20-year period he played for the Pittsburgh Pirates, Washington Senators, and Boston Red Sox and was a great clutch-hitter. With the Red Sox he was a manager and player; he retired as field manager in 1947. He served 11 years as a Red Sox executive before becoming president of the American League (1959–73). He was elected to the baseball Hall of Fame in 1956: d. Osterville, MA, Sept. 7.

Culver, Roland (83), British actor; appeared in more than 40 plays in Britain and more than 50 British and American movies: d. London, Feb. 29.

De Filippo, Eduardo (84), Italian playwright; wrote more than 50 plays; famous for his comedies of Italian family life. His works include Naples Millionaire, Filumena Marturano, and Inner Voices. Also an actor, along with his two brothers he formed the Company of Humorous Theater. He appeared in many Italian movies and wrote the screenplay of Yesterday, Today, and Tomorrow and Marriage Italian Style: d. Rome, Nov. 1.

Dirac, Paul (82), British-born Nobel laureate in physics in 1933; worked with Albert Einstein and Robert Oppenheimer and developed Dirac's equation, explaining the mechanics of the atom: d. Tallahassee, FL, Oct. 20.

Dors, Diana (born Diana Fluck) (52), British actress, popular in the 1950s, she was once described as Britain's answer to Marilyn Monroe: d. Windsor, England, May 4.

Dragon, Carmen (69), composer-conductor; made music for film, radio, television, and records; won an Academy Award for scoring the 1944 musical Cover Girl. He recorded more than 75 albums and conducted the Glendale Symphony Orchestra for 20 years: d. Santa Monica, CA, March 28.

Dunham, Theodore (86), astronomer; discovered in 1932 at the Mount Wilson Observatory in California, along with colleague W. S. Adams, that the atmosphere of Venus contained a large amount of carbon dioxide: d. Chocorua, NH, April 3.

Eckstein, Otto (56), economics professor at Harvard University who in 1968 was a founder of Data Resources Inc., an economic advisory service: d. Boston, MA, March 22.

Egan, William A. (69), Alaska's first elected governor after leading its drive for statehood. Egan was elected governor in 1959 and reelected in 1962. He ran again in 1966 but was defeated.

Frank Church

Mark Clark

Jackie Coogan

Diana Dors
Photos, AP/Wide World

Photos, AP/Wide World

Janet Gaynor   Martin Luther King, Sr.

Egan won a third term in 1970 but was defeated for a fourth: d. Anchorage, AK, May 6.

Ehricke, Krafft A. (67), German-born engineer and physicist; became involved in the American space program after surrendering to the U.S. Army in the closing days of World War II. At that time Ehricke was a member of the German V-2 rocket team. After coming to the United States in 1947 he worked for the Army's missile program but left to join private industry in 1952: d. La Jolla, CA, Dec. 11.

Elliot, Don (57), jazz vibraphonist, singer, and composer: d. Weston, CT, July 5.

Engelhardt, Vladimir A. (89), Soviet biochemist and director of the Soviet Institute of Molecular Biology. In 1979 he was given the title of Hero of Socialist Labor: d. Soviet Union, July 10.

Ernst, Jimmy (63), German-born American painter; was the son of the Dada and Surrealist painter Max Ernst: d. New York City, Feb. 6.

Evins, Joe (73), U.S. representative (D-TN, 1947–77): d. Nashville, TN, March 31.

Fagerholm, Karl-August (82), political leader of Finland; he was a member of Parliament for 36 years, speaker of the chamber five times, and was prime minister three times: d. Helsinki, May 22.

Ferencsik, Janos (77), Hungarian musical conductor; he helped establish and was director of the Hungarian State Symphony Orchestra: d. Budapest, June 12.

Fixx, James F. (52), writer of books on running, including *The Complete Book of Running*: d. Hardwick, VT, July 20.

Flame, Ditra (78), claimed to be the original "Lady in Black," who made an annual pilgrimage to the grave of Rudolph Valentino to leave a single rose: d. Ontario, CA; buried Feb. 28.

Flowers, Walter (51), member of the U.S. House of Representatives (D-AL, 1969-77); he was a member of the House Judiciary Committee during the Watergate hearings in 1974: d. Falls Church, VA, April 12.

Forbush, Scott (79), geophysicist; discoverer of a global effect on cosmic rays; he observed that a sharp decrease in the intensity of radiation that strikes the earth occurs one or two days after an eruption on the Sun. This effect became known as the Forbush effect: d. Charlottesville, VA, April 4.

Foreman, Carl (69), producer and screenwriter; wrote the scripts for *High Noon* and *The Bridge on the River Kwai*. He was blacklisted during the McCarthy era and lived in London for a number of years. Foreman wrote and produced *The Key* (1958), *The Guns of Navarone* (1961), *Young Winston* (1972), and wrote, produced, and directed *The Victors* (1963): d. Beverly Hills, CA, June 26.

Forsythe, Edwin B. (68), U.S. representative (R-NJ, 1970–84): d. Moorestown, NJ, March 29.

Foucault, Michel (57), French philosopher and historian. His books include *Madness and Civilization, Discipline and Punish: The Birth of the Prison, The Order of Things, The Birth of the Clinic, The Archaeology of Knowledge,* and *The History of Sexuality*: d. Paris, June 25.

Frampton, Hollis (48), avant-garde filmmaker and photographer; he produced more than 60 films in his career. He was a professor at the State University of Buffalo Center for Media Study although he had neither a high school nor college diploma. His essays were collected in the book *Circles of Confusion*: d. March 30.

Fraser, Hugh (66), British member of Parliament, was a prominent Conservative legislator and a friend of the family of John F. Kennedy. He was married to Lady Antonia Fraser until 1977 when the marriage was dissolved: d. London, March 6.

Friedrich, Carl J. (83), German-born professor of government at Harvard University (1926–71); was regarded as one of America's foremost thinkers on political ideology, particularly in his analyses of totalitarianism and Communism. His books include *Constitutional Government and Politics* (1937), *The New Belief in the Common Man* (1942), *Inevitable Peace* (1948), *Totalitarian Dictatorship and Autocracy* (coauthored with Zbigniew Brzezinski) (1956), *The Philosophy of Law in Historical Perspective* (1958), *Introduction to Political Theory* (1967), *The Pathology of Politics* (1972), and *Tradition and Authority* (1972): d. Lexington, MA, Sept. 19.

Garland, Red (William) (60), jazz pianist; worked in New York and Philadelphia with the major jazz musicians of the be-bop era before joining the Miles Davis group in 1955: d. Dallas, TX, April 23.

Garner, Peggy Ann (53), actress; won a special Academy Award for her performance in *A Tree Grows in Brooklyn*: d. Woodland Hills, CA, Oct. 16.

Gaye, Marvin (44), pop singer of soul music, with a beat of the old-time gospel singer; he had gained fame under the Motown label. Among his early hits was *I Heard It Through the Grapevine*. Other songs included *Let's Get It On* and *Sexual Healing*, for which he won two Grammy Awards in 1983. Gaye early in his career had been a member of the group the Marquees and also had made several successful duet recordings, especially with Tammi Terrell: d. Los Angeles, April 1.

Gaynor, Janet (77), film actress; won the first Academy Award for best actress (1927) for her roles in the silent films *Sunrise, Seventh Heaven,* and *Street Angel*. She was one of the most popular of Hollywood's leading ladies of the 1920s and 1930s, succeeding in the transition to talking pictures. She retired from acting in 1939, although she continued to perform on occasion: d. Palm Springs, CA, Sept. 14.

Gemayel, Pierre (78), Lebanese Maronite Christian political leader and the father of the current president of Lebanon. He was a founding member of the right-wing Phalange Party and a member of Lebanon's Parliament since 1960: d. Bikfeiya, Lebanon, Aug. 29.

Gobbi, Tito (68), Italian operatic baritone and operatic director; identified with the role of Scarpia in *Tosca*. He made his Metropolitan Opera debut in the role in 1956, and his last performance at the Met was also in that role in 1976. In addition to performing, he maintained a parallel career as a director: d. Rome, March 5.

Goldstein, Ruby (76), boxer and boxing referee; he fought professionally as a lightweight and a welterweight from 1925 to 1937, and beginning in 1943 was a boxing referee who worked in 39 championship fights: d. Miami Beach, April 22.

Goodman, Steve (36), folk singer and composer; wrote the song *City of New Orleans*: d. Seattle, WA, Sept. 20.

Goodrich, Frances (93), writer, who along with her husband Albert Hackett wrote the play *The Diary of Anne Frank*: d. New York City, Jan. 29.

Guillen, Jorge (91), Spanish poet, critic, teacher. His books of poetry include *Canticle, Clamour,* and *Homage*. He received the Cervantes Prize in 1976: d. Malaga, Spain, Feb. 6.

Guney, Yilmaz (47), film director; maker of *Yol*, which won top honors at the 1982 Cannes Film Festival and which Guney directed from his cell in a Turkish prison: d. Paris, Sept. 9.

Haddad, Saad (47), former Lebanese Army officer who for years ran his own militia force in southern Lebanon with the support of Israel. He was reinstated in the Lebanese Army in January 1984: d. Merj 'Uyun, Lebanon, Jan. 14.

Harden, Cecil (90), U.S. representative (R-IN, 1949–59): d. Lafayette, IN, Dec. 5.

Hathaway, Starke R. (80), codeveloper of the Minnesota Multiphasic Personality Inventory test, the world's most widely used psychological test: d. Minneapolis, MN, July 4.

Hauser, Gayelord (89), author of more than a dozen books on maintaining good health through natural foods: d. North Hollywood, CA, Dec. 26.

Hill, Lister (89), U.S. senator (D-AL, 1938–69); sponsored some of the most important post-World War II health and education legislation: d. Montgomery, AL, Dec. 20.

Himes, Chester (75), black American writer. Well known for *Cotton Comes to Harlem*, he wrote often on racial themes. His first novel was *If He Hollers Let Him Go*. Other works include *Lonely Crusade* and his autobiography *The Quality of Hurt*. He was also known for his Harlem detective stories: d. Moraira, Spain, Nov. 12.

Hoagland, John (36), American photographer, killed when caught in crossfire between government and rebel troops in El Salvador: d. near San Salvador, March 16.

Holland, Bill (76), automobile racer; was the 1949 winner of the Indianapolis 500 auto race; d. May 19.

Hoyt, Waite (84), baseball pitcher; played with the New York Yankees (1920–30) and with several other clubs in a 21-year major league career where he recorded 237 victories and 182 losses. He was elected to baseball's Hall of Fame in 1969: d. Cincinnati, OH, Aug. 25.

Hughes, Richard (77), Australian-born journalist and Far East expert; he was a foreign and war correspondent for Australian and British publications for more than 40 years: d. Hong Kong, Jan. 4.

Hunter, Alberta (89), blues singer and cabaret star; she had been internationally famous in the 1920s and 1930s and then had retired. She began a second singing career when she was in her 80s. Her repertoire included blues, pop songs, show tunes, gospel, and folk songs: d. New York City (Roosevelt Island), Oct. 17.

Hurd, Peter (80), American artist; painted subjects of the American southwest. He became well known as a result of a portrait he did of then President Lyndon Johnson, who turned down the work, calling it "the ugliest thing I ever saw." The painting was later acquired by the Smithsonian Institution: d. Roswell, NM, July 9.

Hutton, Ina Ray (67), band leader of the 1940s and 1950s; one of the first women to succeed in that capacity. She had a television weekly musical variety show on NBC in 1956: d. Ventura, CA, Feb. 19.

Huu, Trans Van (87), prime minister of Vietnam (1950–52): d. Paris, Jan. 17.

Jacoby, Oswald (81), contract bridge player; was a bridge author and newspaper columnist as well: d. Dallas, June 27.

Jaffe, Sam (93), character actor; best known for his role as Dr. Zorba in the television series *Ben Casey* (1961–65): d. Beverly Hills, CA, March 24.

Janco, Marcel (89), Rumanian-born abstract painter; was a founder of the Dada movement in Zurich in 1916, which dissolved in 1919: d. Tel Hashomer, Israel, April 21.

Jenkins, Gordon (73), composer, pianist, conductor, and arranger; wrote the popular hit *This Is All I Ask* and *Manhattan Tower.* He conducted for Nat (King) Cole and Frank Sinatra, among others: d. Malibu, CA, May 1.

Johnson, Budd (Albert) (73), jazz saxophonist and arranger: d. Kansas City, MO, Oct. 20.

Johnson, Uwe (49), East German-born novelist, he immigrated to West Germany in 1959. His books include *Two Views, Speculations about Jacob, The Third Book About Achim,* and *Anniversaries:* d. England, March 13 (reported).

Kapitsa, Pyotr L. (89), Soviet Nobelist in Physics; he was an outspoken advocate of free scientific thought. He studied at Cambridge University and then stayed in Britain to work in the physics of superpowerful magnetic fields and in low temperature physics. On a visit to Moscow in 1934 he was detained and thereafter worked in his own country. He was made director of the Vasilov Institute of Physical Problems in 1935, where he stayed until he fell from favor in 1946. After Stalin's death he was restored to his position (in 1955), where he remained until his death: d. Moscow, April 8.

Kaplan, Henry (65), radiologist who did pioneering research on Hodgkin's disease and was the coinventor of the linear accelerator, which enabled cancer patients to receive high-dosage radiation treatment. He was the first radiologist elected to the National Academy of Science: d. Palo Alto, CA, Feb. 4.

Kastler, Alfred (81), Nobel-prize-winning physicist; born in the then German-occupied Alsatian village of Guebwiller. His research helped set the stage for invention of the laser. He was awarded the Nobel Prize in 1966: d. Bandol, France, Jan. 7.

Kaufman, Andy (35), comedian; was seen in the television series *Taxi* and *Saturday Night Live:* d. Los Angeles, CA, May 16.

Keighley, William (94), theater and movie director; directed and coproduced the Broadway hit *Penny Arcade* (1930). Soon thereafter he began directing films. His movies include *The Prince and the Pauper, Green Pastures, The Man Who Came to Dinner, Street With No Name,* and *The Master of Ballantrae:* d. June 24.

Kennedy, David Anthony (28), third son of the late Sen. Robert Kennedy; found dead in a Florida hotel room: d. Palm Beach, FL, April 25.

Kerr, Malcolm (52), president of the American University in Beirut; was an expert on the Arab world. His books include *Islamic Reform* (1965) and *The Arab Cold War* (1968), and he was one of the authors of *The Economics and Politics of the Middle East* (1975). He was killed by gunmen in Beirut: d. Beirut, Jan. 18.

Khrushchev, Nina (84), widow of former Soviet leader Nikita Khrushchev: d. Moscow, Aug. 8.

King, Martin Luther, Sr., (84), influential black clergyman, the father of the late civil-rights leader Martin Luther King, Jr.: d. Atlanta, GA, Nov. 11.

Kirkpatrick, Ralph (72), harpsichordist and musicologist; he was an important figure in the modern revival of the harpsichord: d. Guilford, CT, April 13.

Knopf, Alfred (91), American publisher; his books were considered of high quality and his list of authors included more Nobel laureates in literature than that of any other publishing house. Knopf founded his firm in 1915. The company later became a subsidiary of Random House: d. Purchase, NY, August 11.

Krasna, Norman (74), playwright and screenwriter; he won the Academy Award in 1943 for *Princess O'Rourke*: d. Los Angeles, CA, Nov. 1.

Kroc, Ray A. (81), builder of the McDonald's hamburger empire and owner of the San Diego Padres baseball team. He started

UPI/Bettmann AP/Wide World

Ray Kroc *Mabel Mercer*

his first McDonald's in Chicago in 1955. In 1974, Kroc bought the San Diego Padres for $10 million, but he gave up operating control of the team in August 1979: d. San Diego, Jan. 14.

Kubik, Gail Thompson (69), composer of both serious and popular music; won several awards including the Pulitzer Prize for composition in 1952 for *Symphony Concertante*. Kubik wrote three symphonies, two violin concertos, a folk opera entitled *Mirror for the Sky,* and chamber music: d. Claremont, CA, July 20.

Kutakhov, Pavel (70), commander of the Soviet Air Force (1969–84): d. Moscow, Dec. 3.

Laskin, Bora (71), chief justice of the Supreme Court of Canada. The first Jew named to the Canadian Supreme Court, he joined the court in 1970, becoming chief justice in 1973: d. Ottawa, Canada, March 26.

Lawford, Peter (61), British-born actor; appeared in more than 30 films, including *Good News, Easter Parade, Exodus, Ocean's Eleven,* and *Advise and Consent,* and in two television series. He was the former brother-in-law of President Kennedy: d. Los Angeles, CA, Dec. 24.

Lewin, Ronald (69), British military historian; most famous for *Ultra Goes to War,* an account of the Allied decoding of German messages during World War II: d. Surrey, England, Jan. 6.

Lilienfeld, Abraham (63), epidemiologist. A leader in his field, he was a professor at the Johns Hopkins School of Hygiene and Public Health and was instrumental in moving epidemiology from a focus on infectious diseases to one involved with chronic diseases, including cancer, cerebral palsy, epilepsy, heart disease, and stroke: d. Baltimore, MD, Aug. 6.

Li Weihan (88), Chinese Communist Party figure; political leader of the army under Mao Zedong during the Chinese Civil War. He was branded a revisionist and purged from power in 1967, but reappeared on the political scene again in 1978: d. Peking, Aug. 11.

Lombardi, Riccardo (83), president of the Italian Socialist Party (1980); he served ten terms in Italy's lower house of Parliament and was a leader of the Italian Resistance during World War II: d. Rome, Sept. 18.

Lonergan, B. J. F. (79), Canadian-born Jesuit philosopher and theologian; taught at Gregorian University in Rome (1953–65). His first major work was *Insight: A Study of Human Understanding:* d. Pickering, Ont., Nov. 26.

Long, Avon (73), actor and singer; he had appeared for more than 50 years on the stage, in clubs, films, and on television. He danced at Harlem's Cotton Club, appeared on Broadway in the 1942 production of *Porgy and Bess:* d. New York City, Feb. 15.

Losey, Joseph (75), film director; was blacklisted during the McCarthy era and lived the last three decades of his life in Europe. His important films include *The Boy with Green Hair, The Big Night, The Servant, Modesty Blaise, Accident, The Damned, The Go-Between,* and *The Romantic Englishwoman:* d. London, June 22.

Low, George M. (58), headed U. S. Apollo space project and was president of Rensselaer Polytechnic Institute (1976–84). He served 27 years with the National Aeronautics and Space Administration and its predecessor the National Advisory Committee for Aeronautics and was an engineer and manager in the Mercury and Gemini programs: d. Troy, NY, July 17.

McDavid, Raven I., Jr. (73), editor and linguist; was a University of Chicago professor of English for 20 years and editor of the *Linguistic Atlas of the Middle and South Atlantic States* and of the *Linguistic Atlas of the North Central States,* both unfinished projects: d. Chicago, IL, Oct. 21.

MacEntee, Sean (94), Irish political leader; a founder of the Irish Republic. He was elected to the Irish Free State Parliament in

Photos, AP/Wide World

Snowdon/Camera Press

Liam O'Flaherty   *Walter Pidgeon*   *William Powell*   *J. B. Priestley*

1927 and held 27 different posts within the Fianna Fail Party governments until his retirement in 1969: d. Dublin, Ireland, Jan. 9.

McFarland, Ernest (89), U.S. senator (D-AZ, 1941–53); was Senate majority leader from 1951–53. He also served as governor of Arizona 1955–59, state Supreme Court judge 1964–67, and as the court's chief justice until his retirement in 1971: d. Phoenix, June 8.

McLain, David (51), artistic director of the Cincinnati/New Orleans City Ballet and head of the dance division of the University of Cincinnati College Conservatory of Music: d. Cincinnati, OH, Dec. 15.

Machito (born Frank Grillo) (76), bandleader of the Afro-Cubans dance band. He helped revolutionize Latin dance music, in the 1940s bringing together Latin rhythms with jazz harmony and improvisation: d. London, April 15.

Malik, Adam (67), Indonesian statesman and president of the United Nations General Assembly (1971); was Indonesia's foreign minister from 1966 to 1977 and vice-president from 1978 to 1983: d. Bandung, Indonesia, Sept. 5.

Maloney, Arthur (64), Canadian defense attorney. A former Conservative member of Parliament, he was one of the chief drafters of the Canadian Bill of Rights, passed in 1960: d. Rockwood, Ontario, Sept. 20.

Martin, Thomas (74), opera conductor; best known, however, for the many English-language opera translations he wrote with his wife: d. New York City, May 14.

Mason, James (75), British-born actor; appeared in more than 100 films including *The Seventh Veil, Odd Man Out, The Desert Fox, Julius Caesar, A Star Is Born, Lolita, Georgy Girl,* and *The Verdict*. He also acted on the stage, beginning in Britain at the Old Vic and with West End plays; he appeared on Broadway in 1978 in *The Faith Healer:* d. Lausanne, Switzerland, July 27.

Mayfield, Julian (56), black American novelist, playwright, and actor who became prominent in the 1950s. In the 1960s he expounded black power ideology and exiled himself twice —first in Ghana and then in Guyana: d. Takoma Park, MD, Oct. 20.

Mays, Benjamin (89), educator and civil-rights champion: d. Atlanta, GA, March 28.

Mercer, Mabel (84), singer of popular music; influenced many singers because of her phrasing and her ability to convey the emotional sense of a lyric. She received the U. S. Presidential Medal of Freedom in 1983: d. Pittsfield, MA, April 20.

Merrill, John (67), Boston physician and emeritus professor of medicine at Harvard who in 1954 led the medical team that did the first successful transplant of a vital organ. He was a pioneer in developing the artificial kidney: d. Bahamas, April 4.

Michaux, Henri (85), Belgium-born poet and painter; wrote more than 20 volumes of poetry and perhaps achieved his greatest success with *A Barbarian in Asia* (1933). He became best known as a painter in the 1950s when he showed works created while he was under the influence of mescaline and other drugs: d. Paris, Oct. 18.

Middleton, Ray (77), actor in musical theater; he made his Broadway debut in 1933 in the Jerome Kern musical *Roberta:* d. Panorama City, CA, April 10.

Mili, Gjon (79), Albanian-born photographer; was a longtime contributor to *Life* magazine: d. Stamford, CT, Feb. 14.

Milgram, Stanley (51), psychologist; known for his experiments on obedience to authority. His book *Obedience to Authority* (1974) was widely translated. He taught at Yale, Harvard, and the City University of New York: d. New York City, Dec. 20.

Mitchell, Clarence M. (73), leader of the civil-rights movement; was a lobbyist for the National Association for the Advance-

ment of Colored People between the years 1950 and 1978: d. Baltimore, MD, March 18.

Mohieddin, Ahmed Fuad (58), prime minister of Egypt (1982–84); also served as secretary general of President Hosni Mubarak's National Democratic Party: d. Cairo, June 5.

Morecambe, Eric (58), British comedian and television star; was part of the Morecambe and [Ernie] Wise comedy team. The two first teamed up in 1941 and first appeared on television in 1955. In 1961 they had their first television series: d. Tewkesbury, England, May 28.

Mujica Lainez, Manuel (73), Argentine novelist; known internationally for *Bomarzo*. His novel *Invitados en el Paraiso* won Argentina's national prize: d. Cordoba province, Argentina, April 21.

Naguib, Mohammed (83), Egyptian military figure who helped topple King Farouk in 1952 and who became Egypt's first president following the coup. He had served as president less than two years when Gamal Abdel Nasser ousted him from power. For 16 years following, until Nasser's death in 1970, he was under house arrest: d. Cairo, Egypt, Aug. 28.

Neel, Alice (84), painter, best known as a portraitist although she painted landscapes, seascapes, interiors, still lifes, and abstractions: d. New York City, Oct. 13.

Nemtchinova, Vera (84), ballerina and ballet teacher; she was a star of Sergei Diaghilev's Ballets Russes. Her most famous role was in *Les Biches* (1924). Since 1947 she had taught ballet in New York: d. New York City, July 22.

Niemöller, Martin (92), German Protestant theologian; he led church opposition to Hitler and in 1937 began eight years of Nazi internment because of his criticism of the Nazi Party and the Third Reich, especially for its persecution of the Jews. He was president of the Evangelical Church in Hesse and Nassau from 1947 until 1964. He saw military service during World War I but during the 1950s and 1960s became West Germany's most prominent pacifist. From 1961 to 1968 he was president of the World Council of Churches: d. Wiesbaden, West Germany, March 6.

O'Flaherty, Liam (88), prominent Irish writer; wrote of the Irish struggle for freedom and was a founder of the Irish Communist Party. His works include *The Informer* (1926; film 1935) and *Famine* (1937). Between 1924 and 1950 he wrote 36 novels, short story collections, and autobiographical volumes; thereafter he wrote very little: d. Dublin, Sept. 7.

Oppen, George (76), Pulitzer Prize-winning poet; won in 1969 for *Of Being Numerous:* d. Sunnyvale, CA, July 7.

Osmena, Sergio, Jr. (67), Filipino politician and businessman; was a governor of Cebu (1951–53) and mayor of Cebu City. In 1969 he ran for the presidency against President Ferdinand Marcos: d. Los Angeles, CA, March 25.

Owings, Nathaniel (81), founder of the architectural firm of Skidmore, Owings, and Merrill; was an early skyscraper advocate. Owings was awarded the American Institute of Architects Gold Medal in 1983. He also wrote two books—*The American Aesthetic* (1969) and *The Spaces in Between* (1973): d. Santa Fe, NM, June 13.

Parsons, Johnnie (66), auto racer; winner of the Indianapolis 500 auto race in 1950: d. Van Nuys, CA, Sept. 8.

Patriarca, Raymond (76), reputed boss of organized crime in New England: d. Providence, RI, July 11.

Peckinpah, Sam (59), movie director; known for his Westerns and graphic use of violence on film. His movies include *The Wild Bunch, The Ballad of Cable Hogue, Straw Dogs, The Killer Elite, Convoy,* and *The Osterman Weekend:* d. Inglewood, CA, Dec. 28.

Peerce, Jan (born Jacob Pincus Perelmuth) (80), American tenor; sang at the Metropolitan opera from 1941 until 1968, and after his retirement from the Met made his Broadway debut in 1971 in *Fiddler on the Roof*. He also made films, appeared on television, and in the early days of his career sang at the Radio City Music Hall: d. New York City, Dec. 15.

Peers, William R. (69), U.S. Army lieutenant general; headed the inquiry into the Army's handling of the My Lai massacre in Vietnam: d. San Francisco, April 6.

Penrose, Roland (83), art patron and biographer; he was the biographer and close friend of Pablo Picasso, Joan Miró, and Man Ray and the organizer of expositions for New York's Museum of Modern Art and London's Tate Gallery, among others: d. near Lewes, England, April 22.

Perkins, Carl (71), U.S. representative (D-KY, 1949–84); was a liberal who as chairman of the House Education and Labor Committee since 1967 helped push through major education legislation and labor measures: d. Lexington, KY, Aug. 3.

Pidgeon, Walter (87), Canadian-born actor; achieved great popularity in the 1940s in a series of eight movies he made with Greer Garson, including *Mrs. Miniver, Madame Curie,* and *That Forsythe Woman.* The urbane and courtly actor also appeared in *How Green Was My Valley, The Bad and the Beautiful, Executive Suite, Advise and Consent,* and *Funny Girl:* d. Santa Monica, CA, Sept. 25.

Pillsbury, Philip (81), former president and chairman of the Pillsbury Company; became president in 1940 and chairman in 1951, serving until 1965. He retired in 1968 and became chairman emeritus in 1974: d. Minneapolis, MN, June 14.

Pollock, Lee Krasner (75), abstract expressionist painter; was the wife and artistic partner of Jackson Pollock: d. New York City, June 19.

Porter, Hal (73), leading Australian writer: d. Sept. 29.

Powell, William (91), actor; famed as the suave sophisticate, he appeared as Nick Charles in six *Thin Man* movies, in which his costar was Myrna Loy. In all he made 13 films with Miss Loy. Other major films were *My Man Godfrey* (1936), *Life with Father* (1947), and *Mr. Roberts* (1955): d. Palm Springs, CA, March 5.

Priestley, J[ohn] B[oynton] (89), British novelist and playwright; wrote more than 100 books and plays. Some of his well-known novels are *The Good Companions, Angel Pavement, English Journey, Festivals at Farbridge, Lost Empires,* and *The Image Men.* His important plays include *Dangerous Corner, Time and the Conways,* and *I Have Been Here Before*—all of which speculate on the mystery of time, a favorite Priestley theme. His long-running plays included *Laburnum Grove* and *When We Are Married:* d. Stratford-on-Avon, August 14.

Prince Loewenstein (78), German historian and political figure; was an early opponent of Hitler. He wrote more than 40 books: d. Bonn, West Germany, Nov. 28.

Rahner, Karl (80), Jesuit Roman Catholic theologian; played a key role at the Second Vatican Council. A teacher at Austrian and German universities, he had 4,000 published works, including 30 books. His arguments were sometimes opposed by popes and cardinals, and he was for some time under a publication ban: d. Innsbruck, Austria, March 30.

Raskin, Judith (56), lyric soprano; was with the New York City Opera (1959–62) and the Metropolitan Opera (1962–72). She sang about 20 operatic roles, ranging from Mozart, through Stravinsky and Poulenc, and also appeared in concert: d. New York City, Dec. 21.

Rauff, Walter Herman Julius (77), former Nazi and accused war criminal of World War II; was thought to have been instrumental in the deaths of as many as 250,000 East Europeans, most of them Jews: d. Santiago, Chile, May 14.

Renault, Gilbert (79), French World War II hero: d. Guingamp, France, July 29.

Robbins, Lord (Lionel Charles) (85), British economist; he held a chair at the London School of Economics (1929–61). A liberal theorist who tended to blend various schools of thought, he considered scarcity to be the organizing principle in all aspects of economic activity; d. London, May 15.

Robin, Leo (89), song lyricist; received nine Oscar nominations for best song between 1934 and 1953, winning in 1938 for *Thanks for the Memory.* He also wrote the lyrics for the songs *Louise* and *Diamonds Are a Girl's Best Friend:* d. Los Angeles, CA, Dec. 29.

Robson, Flora (82), British actress; well known for her film performance in *Fire Over England* and her stage performance in *The Damask Cheek.* Her career spanned 50 years and included appearances in 60 films and more than 100 plays: d. Brighton, England, July 7.

Rock, John (94), human fertility pioneer; helped develop the birth control pill. Dr. Rock was the first scientist to fertilize a human egg in a test tube (in 1944): d. Peterborough, NH, Dec. 4.

Ronning, Chester (90), Canadian diplomat; in 1966 during the Vietnam war he made a confidential and unsuccessful attempt to get peace talks started. Born in China and fluent in Chinese, he saw diplomatic service in China (1946–51), Norway and Iceland (1954–57), and India (1957–64): d. Camrose, Alberta, Canada, Dec. 31.

Salan, Raoul (85), French general and once one of the country's most decorated soldiers. He led an attempt in 1961 to over-

Photos, AP/Wide World

Irwin Shaw *Mikhail Sholokhov*

throw President Charles de Gaulle and had organized a terrorist group opposed to independence for Algeria: d. Paris, July 3.

Samuels, Howard (64), industrialist and politician; along with his brother Richard founded the Kordite Company, which was later sold to the Mobil Corporation. He made three unsuccessful attempts for the Democratic nomination for governor of New York. At the time of his death, he was president of the North American Soccer League: d. New York City, Oct. 26.

Sánchez Albornoz, Claudio (91), Spanish historian and politician; was a foreign minister in 1933 and a leader of anti-Franco Republicans in exile: d. Avila, Spain, July 8.

Schneider, Alan (born Abram Leopoldovich) (66), Russian-born American theater director; was the primary American director of Samuel Beckett plays. He had directed the plays of Edward Albee and Harold Pinter, and also was associated with new plays and new playwrights: d. London, May 3.

Schonland, Herbert E. (84), rear admiral in the U.S. Navy; was awarded the Congressional Medal of Honor: d. New London, CT, Nov. 13.

Schwartz, Arthur (83), stage and film musical composer; probably most famous for his collaborations with lyricist Howard Dietz that began in the 1920s and ended with the Broadway show *Jennie* in 1963. He also composed with Ira Gershwin, Lorentz Hart, Frank Loesser, Dorothy Fields, Johnny Mercer, Sammy Cahn, E.Y. Harburg, and Oscar Hammerstein 2d. Among his Broadway musicals were *Three's a Crowd, The Band Wagon,* and *At Home Abroad:* d. Kintnersville, PA, Sept. 3.

Sharon, Arieh (84), Polish-born architect and town planner who established his office in Tel Aviv more than 50 years ago and influenced Israel's physical appearance: d. Paris, July 24.

Shaw, Irwin (71), writer of short stories, plays, screenplays, and novels; probably most famous for his first novel *The Young Lions* (1948). Acclaimed for such short stories as *The Girls in Their Summer Dresses,* he wrote the novel *Rich Man, Poor Man* as well: d. Davos, Switzerland, May 16.

Sheppard, Eugenia (80s), fashion writer of the 1960s and the 1970s: d. New York City, Nov. 11.

Shklovsky, Viktor (91), Russian writer; an early proponent of the value of form and structure over content; later a member of the Soviet literary establishment: d. USSR, Dec. 20 (reported).

Sholokhov, Mikhail A. (78), Soviet writer of the four-volume epic *And Quiet Flows the Don* and 1965 Nobelist in literature: d. Veshenskaya, Russia, Feb. 21.

Slipyj, Josyf Cardinal (92), the Major Archbishop of the Ukrainians; spent 18 years in Soviet prisons, until the Vatican obtained his release in 1963. He was elevated to cardinal in 1965: d. Rome, Sept. 7.

Sonoda, Sunao (70), leading member of Japan's Liberal Democratic Party; negotiated the Japan-China Peace and Friendship Treaty of 1978: d. Tokyo, April 2.

Souvanna Phouma (82), former prime minister of Laos, he served off and on in that post from 1951 until he was ousted in 1975 when the Communist Pathet Lao took power: d. Vientiane, Laos, Jan. 10.

Sperber, Manès (78), Austrian-born novelist and essayist; he settled in France in 1934 and became a French citizen: d. Paris, Feb. 5.

Steele, Freddie (71), former middleweight boxing champion; he had captured the title recognized by both the National Boxing Association and the New York State athletic authorities in 1936 by defeating the reigning champion Babe Risko. (European authorities continued to recognize France's Marcel Thil as champion.): d. Aberdeen, WA, Aug. 23.

Stern, Philip Van Doren (83), novelist, editor, and historian; wrote *The Greatest Gift* on which was based the movie *It's a*

Photos, AP/Wide World

François Truffaut   *Fred Waring*

Wonderful Life. He also wrote books on the American Civil War: d. Sarasota, FL, July 31.

Storrow, James, Jr. (66), publisher of *The Nation* magazine (1965–77): d. Stormville, NY, Jan. 13.

Stroh, John W. (91), president of the Stroh Brewery Company from 1950 to 1967, when he became chairman of the board and turned over much of the day-to-day operations to his nephew, Peter W. Stroh: d. Grosse Pointe, MI, Sept. 28.

Stuart, Jesse (76), poet laureate of Kentucky; he was considered one of the most significant U.S. regional writers: d. Ironton, OH, Feb. 17.

Taylor, Glen H. (80), U.S. senator (D-Idaho, 1945–51). He left the Democratic Party in 1948 to run as the vice-presidential candidate with Henry A. Wallace on the Progressive Party ticket: d. Burlingame, CA, April 28.

Tevis, Walter (56), novelist; best known for *The Hustler* and *The Man Who Fell to Earth*: d. Culver City, CA, Aug. 10.

Thill, George (86), French tenor. He spent two years at the Paris Conservatory and then two years in Naples under Fernando de Lucia, a great Italian bel canto tenor: d. Draghignan, France, Oct. 17.

Thornton, Willie Mae (57), blues singer; known as Big Mama, she did renditions of *Hound Dog* and *Ball and Chain* that inspired Elvis Presley and Janis Joplin: d. Los Angeles, CA, July 25.

Tidyman, Ernest A. (56), author and screenwriter; his screenplay of *The French Connection* won him an Academy Award: d. London, July 14.

Tizol, Juan (84), Puerto Rican–born trombonist who played with Duke Ellington's orchestra for nearly 20 years; was the composer of one of the Ellington band's most popular tunes—*Caravan.* He also played with the Harry James orchestra: d. Inglewood, CA, April 23.

Touré, Sékou (62), president of Guinea (1958–84); had been a union leader before entering politics and was black Africa's longest-serving head of state. He entered the Guinean Legislative Assembly in the 1950s and in 1958 led his nation to independence from France, serving as its only president until his death. A radical, he pursued Marxist policies, rejecting at the time of independence continuing ties with France, although he took aid from both the Soviet Union and the West, and late in his tenure encouraged American investment in Guinea. His Democratic Party of Guinea was the only legal party, but despite accusations of oppressive rule by Amnesty International and other organizations he was able to withstand various attempted coups and assassinations: d. Cleveland, OH, March 26.

Truffaut, François (52), French film director; was a leader of the New Wave group of French movie makers that emphasized the director's role in filming. Truffaut drew on his own life for his first full-length feature *The 400 Blows* (1959), which introduced the character of a self-reliant little boy. In five related movies the character is continued. Truffaut's *Day for Night* (1973) won an Academy Award for best foreign film. Other important films include *Shoot the Piano Player* (1960), *Jules and Jim* (1961), *Stolen Kisses* (1968), *The Wild Child* (1970), *The Story of Adele H.* (1975), *Small Change* (1976), and *The Woman Next Door* (1981). As a youth he was a film addict and spent hundreds of hours in movie theaters. He left school at age 14 and was briefly in a reformatory for stealing metal door knobs. The son of an architect, Truffaut was later taken in by the French film critic André Bazin and his wife and went into journalism. He wrote film criticism before starting his motion picture career: d. Neuilly-sur-Seine, France, Oct. 21.

Tsarapkin, Semyon K. (78), Soviet diplomat; served in the United States, West Germany, and the United Nations. He had been a member of the Soviet foreign service since 1937: d. Moscow, Sept. 19 (reported).

Tubb, Ernest (70), country western singer; a pioneer of the "honky tonk" sound. His song *I'm Walking the Floor Over You* sold a million records. He appeared at the Grand Ole Opry in Nashville, TN, and in 1965 was elected to the Country Music Hall of Fame: d. Nashville, TN, Sept. 6.

Tully, Grace (83), secretary to U.S. President Franklin D. Roosevelt during his years as governor of New York and as president of the United States. Her book of memoirs, *F.D.R.—My Boss,* was published in 1949: d. Washington, DC, June 15.

Ulam, Stanislaw Marcin (75), Polish-born mathematician; a key figure in the development of the hydrogen bomb: d. Santa Fe, NM, May 13.

Ustinov, Dmitri F. (76), Soviet defense minister (1976–84). Marshal Ustinov became head of production of conventional weapons throughout the USSR in 1941 and continued that role for 17 years. He later was a deputy prime minister and in 1965 began service in the Secretariat, heading the military-industrial complex. He was a powerful member of the Politburo: d. USSR, Dec. 20.

VanDerBeek, Stan (57), filmmaker; highly acclaimed for his experimental films, including *Science Friction* and *Newsreels of Dreams,* part of a 1984 show on independent movies at the Whitney Museum: d. Columbia, MD, Sept. 19.

Voorhis, Horace Jeremiah (Jerry) (83), U.S. representative (D-CA, 1937–47); lost his bid for reelection to Richard Nixon: d. Claremont, CA, Sept. 11.

Wallace, Lila Acheson (94), philanthropist and cofounder and cochairman for many years of *Reader's Digest;* her philanthropic endeavors totaled in excess of $60 million. Some of her special philanthropic interests included the Juilliard School of Music; the New York Zoological Society; Boscobel, an 18th-century mansion on the Hudson River; temples at Abu Simbel in Egypt; the painter Monet's house and grounds in Giverny, France; and New York's Metropolitan Museum. She and her husband DeWitt (who died in 1981) published the first *Reader's Digest* in February 1922; she retired as cochairman of the Reader's Digest Association, Inc. in 1973 but continued as a director: d. Mount Kisco, NY, May 8.

Waring, Fred (84), musical conductor and inventor of the Waring blender; Waring's group—the Pennsylvanians—performed for nearly seven decades. The group scored several firsts in the entertainment world, including the first electronic recording of a song, the first all-musical film *Syncopation,* the first vocal orchestra to have its own national radio show, and the first orchestra to have its own television show. In 1981, Waring was presented with the Congressional Gold Medal: d. Danville, PA, July 29.

Webster, Paul F. (77), lyricist; wrote more than 500 songs, including *Secret Love* and *Love Is a Many Splendored Thing*: d. Beverly Hills, CA, March 22.

Weisberger, Siegfried (88), Baltimore bookseller; ran a bookstore—the Peabody Bookshop and Beer Stube—that had a restaurant in the back. He sold the store in 1954, gaining national attention when he remarked, "the age of the boob is upon us": d. Cambridge, MA, March 23.

Werner, Oskar (61), Austrian stage and motion picture actor; best known for his film roles in *Jules and Jim* and *Ship of Fools.* He also appeared in *The Spy Who Came in from the Cold, The Shoes of the Fisherman,* and *Voyage of the Damned.* His stage work included a classic *Hamlet,* as well as other Shakespearian and classical works, and *Danton's Death*: d. Marburg, West Germany, Oct. 23.

West, Jessamyn (81), writer of short stories and novels, particularly known for her stories of Quaker life set in her native Indiana. She wrote *The Friendly Persuasion* (1945), later made into a motion picture: d. Napa, CA, Feb. 23.

Willson, Meredith (82), composer; probably best known as the composer, librettist, and lyricist of the Broadway musical *The Music Man.* He also wrote the score to *The Unsinkable Molly Brown* and later adapted the film *Miracle on 34th Street* into the musical *Here's Love.* In his early years he had toured with John Philip Sousa's band and in 1924 became the first flutist with the New York Philharmonic under Arturo Toscanini: d. Santa Monica, CA, June 15.

Wilson, Charles H. (67), U.S. representative (D-CA, 1963–81); was censured in 1980: d. Clinton, MD, July 21.

Wilson, Jackie (49), rock singer who became prominent in the 1950s with such songs as *Lonely Teardrops*: d. Mount Holly, NJ, Jan. 21.

Wilson, Peter C. (71), English auctioneer; head of Sotheby's, the London art-auction house (1958–80): d. Paris, June 3.

Winwood, Estelle (101), English-born actress of stage, screen, and television; appeared in the 1955 movie *The Glass Slipper* and in the 1949 Broadway production of *The Madwoman of Chaillot*: d. Los Angeles, CA, June 20.

Yadin, Yigael (67), Israeli military hero of the war of independence and a foremost archaeologist; served as deputy prime minister from 1977 to 1981: d. Hadera, Israel, June 28.

Zivic, Ferdinand (Fritzie) (71), world welterweight boxing champion; held the title nine months after winning it from Henry Armstrong in 1940. He was elected to the Boxing Hall of Fame in 1973: d. Aspinwall, PA, May 16.

OCEANOGRAPHY

Understanding the interrelationship between ocean circulation and atmospheric wind patterns has been a major goal of oceanographers and meteorologists. New efforts were stimulated by the dramatic effects of the "Pacific Warm Event," or El Niño, in the eastern Pacific Ocean in 1982–83. The Tropical Ocean Global Atmosphere (TOGA) Experiment, a ten-year project, is seeking to define the interaction by studying the two fluid media as a single system. The first need has been to increase the data base by establishing satellite observational networks for sea surface temperature, surface wind stress, and sea surface height. On a computer, oceanic and atmospheric general circulation models (GCMs) can then use the data to simulate the response of the tropical atmosphere to ocean warming. Programs closely reflecting observed patterns of the last 15 years show that ocean temperature variations account for up to 70% of the variance in tropical weather patterns. It is hoped that better knowledge of the conditions of the air-sea boundary will extend the range of forecasting beyond the present 12 to 15 days.

The Long-Term Upper Ocean Study (LOTUS) was in its second year at a site in the middle of the Sargasso Sea, about halfway between Cape Hatteras (NC) and Bermuda. From an array of moored buoys, a profile of eddy and internal wave energy from surface to bottom shows correlation with surface wind stress. The projected World Ocean Circulation Experiment (WOCE) will employ a network of satellite, ship, moored buoy, and acoustic observations to obtain an overall picture.

In polar latitudes, seven ships and seven aircraft were deployed in 1984 in the international Marginal Ice Zone Experiment (MIZEX), following a preliminary project in 1983. The United States, West Germany, Norway, Canada, France, Great Britain, and Denmark all contributed to the scientific effort, which examined the ice margin in Fram Strait, between Greenland and Svalbard. Here sea ice from the Arctic Ocean is carried far south into the Atlantic Ocean by the cold, low-salinity East Greenland current on the west side of the strait. On the east side, the warm, highly saline West Spitzbergen current keeps the coast nearly ice-free throughout the year. Unique features of the marginal ice zone include eddies and upwelling along the ice edge, with intrusions of polar or Atlantic water. The MIZEX program included a drifting phase with an array of monitoring instruments deployed on the ice, and landing sites where a sensor probe could be lowered by helicopter through ice openings to 500 m (1,640 ft). These surveys were then closely compared with shipboard results in open water to show the structure of the entire zone, both open and covered. In 1983 an eddy

about 500 km (311 mi) across and drifting southward beneath the ice at a rate of 7 km (4.3 mi) per day was tracked over a five-day period. Such eddies can provide exchange of temperature and salt across the ice margin and thus affect its location. Computer studies to model the ice edge involve the interrelationships among ice, air, and water. By obtaining a better understanding of the physical processes along the ice edge, such data can be introduced into a GCM for improved climatic forecasting.

The Circumpolar or Southern Ocean surrounding Antarctica has special significance in world geography. The physical and chemical character of most of the water in the world ocean is determined by exposure to the atmosphere over the Southern Ocean. In 1981 a joint U.S.-Soviet expedition for the first time surveyed the winter sea ice cover along the Greenwich meridian. In 1984, plans were being made for a U.S.-German expedition in the austral winter of 1986. The expedition would utilize the latest technology in icebreaker design. Direct observations of oceanic conditions well within the winter sea ice are needed to confirm trends that are otherwise determinable only from satellite data.

The ocean floor is another major area of research. The Ocean Drilling Program (ODP) will be undertaken as a joint project by the United States, France, West Germany, and the European Science Foundation (Italy, the Netherlands, Norway, Sweden, and Switzerland)—and possibly Canada, Great Britain, and Japan. ODP follows the Deep Sea Drilling Project (DSDP), which concluded in late 1983. A new vessel with facilities greatly expanded over those of the *Glomar Challenger* (used for DSDP) will be able to drill to depths of 9 000 m (29,500 ft). It will operate in the summer in the Weddell Sea near Antarctica. The first scientific cruise was scheduled for January 1985.

Much excitement in recent years has come from the study of the exotic marine life clustered around deep sea vents. A new community —the first found outside the eastern Pacific— was discovered in 1984 in the Gulf of Mexico southwest of Florida at a depth of some 3 500 m (11,500 ft). As in the Pacific vents, the Gulf community contains white surface mats, presumably of bacterial origin, large red-fleshed clams, dense beds of mussels, crabs, eel-like fish, and an abundance of tube worms. In the Pacific, the vent communities exist where new crust is being formed; the organisms survive by obtaining food chemically from the geothermal activity. The site off Florida is not in a geologically active area, but dissolved sulfur may be supplied from aquifers. The discovery raises questions about how widespread such communities might be and how they might be related to the origin of life forms on earth.

DAVID A. MCGILL,
U.S. Coast Guard Academy

OHIO

President Reagan's personal popularity in this "pivotal" unionized industrial state helped return Ohio Senate control to the Republicans in the 1985–1986 legislative session. Their narrow margin in the Ohio General Assembly upper house will be 18 to 15, compared with 17 Democrats to 16 Republicans in 1983–84.

Leadership in the Ohio House of Representatives, however, will remain in Democrat hands, 59 to 40, compared with 62 to 37.

An immediate reaction to the Senate leadership change was a promise by state Sen. Paul E. Gillmor of Port Clinton, a Republican spokesman, to reduce Ohio's income tax rates. These had been increased by as much as 90% in 1983 at the insistence of Gov. Richard F. Celeste (D). With the return of more prosperous times, the hike had resulted in embarrassingly large treasury surpluses, so that small refunds were mailed to taxpayers in 1984. Gillmor proposed slicing the rates with three 10% cuts, to be made at the beginning of 1985, 1986, and 1987.

Members of the two major presidential tickets made Ohio a major battleground, crisscrossing it often and drawing large audiences, particularly in the campaign's last two weeks. The Reagan-Bush ticket won on November 6 with 59.2% of the ballot, to 40.3% for the Mondale-Ferraro slate—or, in number of votes, by more than 2.67 million to about 1.82 million. Six counties out of 88 favored Mondale. These were Belmont, Jefferson, Mahoning, Monroe, and Trumbull counties, in eastern Ohio, and Cuyahoga (Cleveland). The six had been hard hit by the steel slump.

Ohio's Sen. John H. Glenn, Jr. (D), whose presidential campaign ran out of momentum early, and Sen. Howard M. Metzenbaum (D) were not on the ballot. Glenn's term continues through 1986, Metzenbaum's through 1988.

Other Election Results. James P. Celebrezze, an Ohio Supreme Court incumbent and Greater Cleveland Democrat, brother of the court's chief justice, was defeated by Franklin County (Columbus) Common Pleas Judge Craig Wright. The other high court race was won by Appeals Court Judge Andy Douglas of Lucas County (Toledo), who upset Cuyahoga County Common Pleas Judge John F. Corrigan.

Voters elected 11 Republicans and 10 Democrats to the 1985–1986 Congress. A newly elected congressman, Mahoning County (Youngstown) sheriff James A. Traficant, a maverick Democrat, had become something of a folk hero for refusing to enforce court-ordered mortgage foreclosures of homes, and because he acted as his own lawyer in a federal trial in Cleveland in which he won acquittal. He had been charged with taking $183,000 in bribes from gangsters and not paying taxes on the money.

Redistricting. Ohio lawmakers were ordered to redraw congressional districts' boundaries by April 15, 1985, in compliance with U.S. Supreme Court population equality standards. The deadline was delayed to avoid interference with the November 6 election.

Taxes. Cleveland voters gave double evidence that they opposed higher local taxation. They rebuffed Mayor George V. Voinovich's pleas for a 2.5% municipal income tax, up 0.5%, at a special election February 7 and emphasized their verdict May 8. The first rejection was by a 54% to 46% ratio, the second by nearly 2 to 1. A measure for construction of a $150-million multipurpose domed stadium in downtown Cleveland also lost on May 8 by nearly 2 to 1, in a Cuyahoga County vote.

Other Events. The Cincinnati Education Board unanimously approved a voluntary program for racial balance in its public schools as a first step in resolving a 1974 desegregation suit. Mandatory busing was not included in the initial requirements.

Honda Motor Co. and Japan-based suppliers announced several projects for Ohio in mid-1984, including part-making facilities and a doubling of Honda's assembly plant in Marysville to produce 300,000 cars a year.

Cleveland's renovation of its downtown Playhouse Square building treasures continued with the reopening of the State Theater. In June the annual Metropolitan Opera's Cleveland season opened at the State, rather than in the barn-like Public Hall. Improvements in waterfront areas were made in Cincinnati and Toledo.

Mayors of three small suburbs of Cleveland were indicted for gambling-related felonies as a result of three years of investigation by the FBI. One pleaded guilty, another was convicted, and the third was acquitted.

JOHN F. HUTH, JR. *Former Reporter,*
"The Plain Dealer," Cleveland

OHIO • Information Highlights

Area: 41,330 sq mi (107 044 km²).

Population (July 1, 1983 est.): 10,746,000.

Chief Cities (July 1, 1982 est.): Columbus, the capital, 570,588; Cleveland, 558,869; Cincinnati, 380,118; Toledo, 350,565; Akron, 231,659; Dayton, 188,499.

Government (1984): *Chief Officers*—governor, Richard F. Celeste (D); lt. gov., Myrl H. Shoemaker (D). *General Assembly*—Senate, 33 members; House of Representatives, 99 members.

State Finances (fiscal year 1983): *Revenues,* $17,682,000,000; *expenditures,* $15,901,000,000.

Personal Income (1983): $120,525,000,000; per capita, $11,216.

Labor Force (May 1984): *Civilian labor force,* 5,086,000; *unemployed,* 493,300 (9.7% of total force).

Education: *Enrollment* (fall 1982)—public elementary schools, 1,258,642; public secondary, 601,603; colleges and universities (fall 1983), 535,592. *Public school expenditures* (1982–83), $4,600,474,824 ($2,676 per pupil).

OKLAHOMA

President Ronald Reagan won 68.6% of Oklahoma's vote in the November election, but his victory did not help his party's congressional candidates. U.S. Sen. David Boren (D) was reelected to a second term by securing 75.6% of the vote. Incumbent congressional Democrats James R. Jones, Mike Synar, Wes Watkins, Dave McCurdy, and Glenn English were reelected. Republican incumbent Mickey Edwards won in the fourth district. All congressional races were won by landslide margins except for Jones's hotly contested race in the first district against Frank Keating, former U.S. district attorney. Voter independence was thought to be the reason Jones garnered 52% of the vote in this heavily Republican district.

Democrats retained control of both state legislative chambers, though Republicans gained seven House seats.

Legislature. The legislature, which met for 88 days, imposed a temporary one-cent increase in the state sales tax, to expire on Dec. 31, 1985. It also appropriated $1.65 billion from the general fund for a total budget of more than $2.1 billion. This represented a $3 million decrease for fiscal year 1985.

Many state agencies received second-year funding cuts (averaging 7.4%) or were left with "standstill" budgets. Partial restoration of cuts was made in "critical" areas: public schools, higher education, correctional affairs, human services, and the tax commission. For a second year no general salary increases were granted state employees.

An amnesty program was enacted to allow tax delinquents to pay back state income taxes without penalty. The 1910 law restricting "head of household" to males was altered, as was a law that made rape legally impossible within marriage. Bills were passed to loosen restrictions on state banks, make computer "hacking" a felony, tighten child pornography laws, allow recovery of unclaimed oil royalties, and "cap" the total state prison population, allowing early release upon declaration of an emergency by the governor. Strict drunk-driving penalties were enacted.

Reform. Gov. George Nigh appointed a commission on reform of the state's government. The commission made more than 250 recommendations for extensive changes in the structure and function of state government.

Petition. State Question 563 allowing county option on the sale of liquor by the drink was passed with 52% of the vote in the September run-off election. The state had ended prohibition in 1959 but restricted sale of liquor by the drink to private clubs. However, state Attorney General Mike Turpen ruled in December that the public bars and restaurants selling liquor (of which there were about 1,600) were

---

OKLAHOMA · Information Highlights

Area: 69,956 sq mi (181 186 km²).
Population (July 1, 1983 est.): 3,298,000.
Chief Cities (July 1, 1982 est.): Oklahoma City, the capital, 427,714; Tulsa, 375,300; Lawton (1980 census), 80,054.
Government (1984): *Chief Officers*—governor, George Nigh (D); lt. gov., Spencer Bernard (D). *Legislature*—Senate, 48 members; House of Representatives, 101 members.
State Finances (fiscal year 1983): *Revenues,* $4,805,000,000; *expenditures,* $4,772,000,000.
Personal Income (1983): $36,158,000,000; per capita, $10,963.
Labor Force (May 1984): *Civilian labor force,* 1,563,200; *unemployed,* 105,500 (6.8% of total force).
Education: *Enrollment* (fall 1982)—public elementary schools, 423,140; public secondary, 170,685; colleges and universities (fall 1983), 174,171. *Public school expenditures* (1982–83), $1,560,103,477 ($2,805 per pupil).

---

doing so illegally since no county had yet chosen to allow the sales of liquor by the drink.

Education. The State Regents for Higher Education raised standards for those seeking advanced education, now requiring them to complete a strengthened high school curriculum.

Court Cases. The U.S. Supreme Court found the plan of the National Collegiate Athletic Association (NCAA) for televised football games in violation of federal antitrust laws in *NCAA v. Board of Regents of the University of Oklahoma and University of Georgia Athletic Association.* Oklahoma's ban on wine advertisements on cable television was held to violate Federal Communications Commission regulations.

Pari-Mutuel Betting. Blue Ribbon Downs opened in Sallisaw to start pari-mutuel betting on horse racing. Voters have approved race tracks in five other counties.

The Economy. The Corporation Commission reported that gas and oil drilling in the lagging industry was up slightly over 1983. A small increase in employment was indicated, and there was improvement in the manufacturing sector.

JOHN W. WOOD, *University of Oklahoma*

ONTARIO

As Canada's most populous and wealthy province, Ontario led the country out of the economic recession in 1984 with an expected real growth rate of 4.7%. Ontario's economy was helped greatly by the buoyant automobile industry, largely centered in the province. Additional good news was a proposal by American Motors to build a new plant employing 4,000 at Brampton for its new Renault model. General Motors planned to spend C$250 million to upgrade its engine plant at St. Catharines, and Honda announced plans for a new plant at Alliston.

Budget. The improved economic climate was reflected in Treasurer Larry Grossman's May budget. Apart from a 4.9% increase in health insurance premiums, there was no tax increase. The deficit, held to $2 billion, was down from 1983, but the unemployment rate was expected to remain at 9.1%. At $450 million youth opportunities program was announced, part of a $600 million expenditure for job training and job creation with emphasis on new jobs in new industries. Innovation Centers were to be set up at some universities to support innovators trying to commercialize their ideas. Spending on day care and subsidized housing was to be increased. Total expenditures were expected to be $27 billion, of which 30.8% was for health and 19.9% for education. Municipalities were warned to curb tax increases or face controls.

Suspicions that this was a preelection budget were confounded in October when Premier William Davis announced his intention to retire from politics after 13 years as premier. He planned to resign as soon as the Progressive Conservative Party chose a new leader at a leadership convention in January 1985.

Education. Education became a lively issue during the year. Premier Davis reversed a long-standing position by indicating that the province would extend funding to grades 11 through 13 in the Separate (Roman Catholic) school system. This sparked opposition from public school officials, who feared a diversion of funds, and from leading figures in both the Anglican and United Churches. Even Catholics foresaw problems, since Education Minister Bette Stephenson made it clear that in return Catholic schools would be expected to take all applicants of any faith and would be unable to discriminate against non-Catholic teachers in hiring—requirements some felt would dilute the Catholic character of the schools.

Following several years of complaints of gross underfunding from the universities, a commission headed by Edmund Bovey was appointed to look into possible restructuring of the university system. The minister indicated her intention to implement the commission's recommendations.

Censorship. The Ontario Film Censor Board was once more in the headlines. Even though its activities were held unconstitutional under the new Canadian Constitution by the provincial court of appeal, it created a storm by banning some "Video Art," part of an International Art Exhibit in Toronto, which had not been "precleared." It also sought to extend its jurisdiction to sales and rentals of videocassettes. The issues remained unresolved pending possible legislation and probable litigation before the Supreme Court of Canada.

Bicentennial Celebration. The celebration of the bicentennial of the arrival of the Loyalist settlers in 1784, initially greeted with skepticism by some who saw it as a preelection move, seemed finally to have received general acceptance, especially after the September visit of Queen Elizabeth, who joined in the festivities in the St. Lawrence Valley and in Toronto. The queen's visit immediately followed that of Pope John Paul II, who came to the province twice on his Canadian tour—visiting Toronto and then Ottawa.

PETER J. KING, *Carleton University*

OREGON

In 1984, while most states began putting the effects of economic recession behind them, Oregon still awaited some sign of recovery in its devastated timber industry, traditionally the state's dominant economic activity.

Economic Conditions. Plywood-, lumber-, and paper-mill closures continued through 1984. High interest rates and shorter distances to national markets continued to work to the advantage of timber producers in the southern states. Local softwood markets, already decimated by recession, also suffered added competition from Canadian producers taking advantage of a favorable exchange rate. Boise Cascade Company, one of the region's largest producers, concentrated its activities in the drier ponderosa pine areas of eastern Oregon and Idaho. A company spokesman stated that the formerly lucrative fir and hemlock harvests of western Oregon and Washington probably would never return to their former prominence. Congress enacted a timber relief measure in the fall. The law provides for revision of contracts for federal timber, negotiated several years before at extremely high prices. According to most commentators, the effects of the new law would benefit the larger companies, but it came too late for many of the smaller independent operators.

ONTARIO · Information Highlights

Area: 412,582 sq mi (1 068 587 km²).

Population (April 1984 est.): 8,916,800.

Chief Cities (1981 census): Toronto, the provincial capital, 599,217; Ottawa, the federal capital, 295,163; North York, 559,521; Mississauga, 315,056; Hamilton, 306,434; London, 254,280.

Government (1984): *Chief Officers*—lt. gov., John Black Aird; premier, William G. Davis (Progressive Conservative); atty. gen., Roy McMurtry. *Legislature*—Legislative Assembly, 125 members.

Provincial Finances (1984–85 fiscal year budget): *Revenues,* $24,773,000,000; expenditures, $26,801,000,000.

Personal Income (average weekly earnings, May 1984): $400.44.

Labor Force (July 1984, seasonally adjusted): *Employed workers,* 15 years of age and over, 4,256,000; *unemployed,* 412,000 (8.8%).

Education (1984–85): *Enrollment*—elementary and secondary schools, 1,842,660 pupils; postsecondary (1984–85)—universities, 288,530; community colleges (full-time), 94,100.

(All monetary figures are in Canadian dollars.)

Sen. Mark Hatfield (front) discusses the funding of Nicaraguan rebels with Sen. Patrick Leahy (D-VT). In September the Senate Ethics Committee voted unanimously to drop charges of influence peddling against Oregon's senior senator. In November the Republican captured a fourth term by defeating Margie Hendriksen.

Tussock moth infestations, particularly in Lane County, threatened the Christmas tree market. The California Department of Agriculture imposed an embargo on trees grown in Lane County, denying them access to the California Christmas tree market.

The business climate appeared to have been improved by the repeal of the unitary tax, which imposed state taxes on the worldwide earnings of companies with units in Oregon. Gov. Victor Atiyeh was instrumental in attracting several high-tech firms to the state. N.E.C. Corporation of Japan said it planned to build a fiber optics plant in Hillsboro. Fujitsu Ltd. announced plans for two projects in Oregon: a semiconductor plant and one to build disk drives. Epson of Japan bought land for a computer printer factory near Portland, and National Semiconductor Corporation was building a factory in Hillsboro. Most political leaders agreed that high-tech industries represent the most probable solution to Oregon's economic woes. Before the repeal of the unitary tax, a survey by *Inc.* Magazine ranked Oregon's business climate 38th among the 50 states, and Alexander Grant Co. ranked Oregon 47th among the 48 contiguous states in its annual "manufacturing climate" index.

Elections. The most hotly contested issue before Oregon voters in 1984 was a sixth attempt since 1966 to limit property taxes. The initiative was beaten back by the narrowest margin to date: 16,000 votes or 1.6% of the voters. Despite being investigated by the Senate Ethics Committee for possible influence-peddling (the inquiry was later dropped), Sen. Mark Hatfield was returned to the U.S. Senate. Although several races were closer than anticipated, Oregon returned its entire congressional delegation to the House of Representatives. Democrat Barbara Roberts was elected secretary of state; Bill Rutherford, Republican appointee, was elected state treasurer; and Republican Dave Frohnmayer was reelected attorney general. Both houses of the state legislature remained in Democratic control, though both houses took on a more conservative flavor. Other initiatives passed severely restricted toxic waste disposal, initiated a state lottery, established a Citizens' Utility Board, and reinstituted the death penalty for certain crimes.

Education. Thirty-eight Oregon school districts began the 1984–1985 school year without voter-approved budgets. School officials called for a state sales tax to remove pressure from property tax, the only local source of school funds. Supplements appropriated by the state to the school districts amounted to 30% of district operating budgets.

L. CARL and JoANN BRANDHORST
Western Oregon State College

OREGON • Information Highlights

Area: 97,073 sq mi (251 419 km²).
Population (July 1, 1983 est.): 2,662,000.
Chief Cities (July 1, 1982 est.): Salem, the capital (1980 census), 89,233; Portland, 367,530; Eugene, 103,709.
Government (1984): *Chief Officers*—governor, Victor Atiyeh (R); secretary of state, Norma Paulus (R). *Legislative Assembly*—Senate, 30 members; House of Representatives, 60 members.
State Finances (fiscal year 1983): *Revenues,* $4,696,000,000; *expenditures,* $4,356,000,000.
Personal Income (1983): $28,585,000,000; per capita, $10,740.
Labor Force (May 1984): *Civilian labor force,* 1,314,500; *unemployed,* 122,800 (9.3% of total force).
Education: *Enrollment* (fall 1982)—public elementary schools, 308,964; public secondary, 139,220; colleges and universities (fall 1983), 141,172. *Public school expenditures* (1982–83), $1,417,392,505 ($3,504 per pupil).

OTTAWA

Ottawa, Canada's capital, was in the international spotlight more often than usual during 1984.

For many Ottawans the high point of the year was the visit by Pope John Paul II in September. His entrance into the city via a 5-mi (8-km) boat ride down the Rideau Canal was a novel departure in papal travel and offered an excellent viewing opportunity for the crowds. The visit culminated in an open-air Mass on LeBreton Flats celebrated by the pope before 300,000 people. Before the visit there had been considerable controversy over the site of the Mass, the public transport arrangement, and whether the day should be declared a public holiday (it was not).

Less than a week after the pope's departure, England's Queen Elizabeth and Duke of Edinburgh arrived to join in the bicentennial celebrations of the arrival in Ontario of the Loyalists in 1784. Scheduled for May, the visit had been postponed because of the federal election.

A new transit system inaugurated in 1984, based on the still-unfinished busways, produced a major shake-up of bus routes and a public outcry with protest meetings. By spring the problems appeared solved. The start of construction on the C$91 million National Gallery touched off a squabble between the federal government and the city. Failure to get a city building permit led Mayor Marion Dewar to threaten to deny the gallery municipal services after its completion if the $900,000 permit was not acquired.

In March, Ottawa hosted the world figure skating championships. Despite an embarrassing five-hour blackout that interrupted international TV coverage, they were both an artistic and financial success. The Ottawa 67s hockey team won the Memorial Cup in May.

PETER J. KING, *Carleton University*

PAKISTAN

Gen. Zia-ul-Haq, the leader of Pakistan's military regime, moved uncertainly in 1984 toward implementation of an electoral program outlined in August 1983. Despite partisan opposition, he frequently reaffirmed his intention to hold provincial elections and elections for a National Assembly on a nonpartisan basis by March 1985. Uncertainty concerning the prospect of retaining executive control prompted him to schedule a referendum for Dec. 19, 1984, in which 98% of those voting approved a five-year extension of his presidency and endorsed his policy of Islamization.

Political Developments. The opposition, which denounced the referendum as a fraud, had been weakened by the failure of its 1983

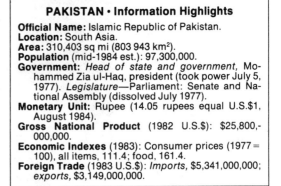

PAKISTAN • Information Highlights

Official Name: Islamic Republic of Pakistan.
Location: South Asia.
Area: 310,403 sq mi (803 943 km²).
Population (mid-1984 est.): 97,300,000.
Government: *Head of state and government,* Mohammed Zia ul-Haq, president (took power July 5, 1977). *Legislature*—Parliament: Senate and National Assembly (dissolved July 1977).
Monetary Unit: Rupee (14.05 rupees equal U.S.$1, August 1984).
Gross National Product (1982 U.S.$): $25,800,-000,000.
Economic Indexes (1983): Consumer prices (1977 = 100), all items, 111.4; food, 161.4.
Foreign Trade (1983 U.S.$): *Imports,* $5,341,000,000; *exports,* $3,149,000,000.

protest movement and the departure into exile of Pakistan People's Party leader Benazir Bhutto in January 1984. During the first half of 1984, Zia released numerous individuals arrested in the 1983 disturbances but forbade press coverage of political parties and disbanded university political organizations. The uncovering in January of an antigovernment plot in the military, though largely shrouded in secrecy, gave further indication of discontent with Zia's rule.

The process of Islamizing many of Pakistan's laws and institutions—a symbolic cornerstone of the military regime—was marked by promises to complete the introduction of interest-free banking in 1985, directives to replace English with Urdu in government offices, and further rulings restricting the role of women in national life. The Women's Action Forum protested the government's antifeminist policies, but figures indicated that the proportion of women in the labor force had been reduced from more than 9% to less than 3%. The minister for women's affairs resigned from the cabinet in protest over the inequality issue.

Economic Performance. Pakistan's economy continued to prosper despite notable setbacks in agriculture and foreign remittances. Growth in gross national product was approximately 5%. Over the previous five years, however, the economy had grown at about 6.2% per annum, or a net per capita rate of 3%. During the same period exports had risen by 165% and levels of foreign investment had nearly tripled. Pakistan's oil production increased in 1984.

Agriculture had its worst year since the military seized power in 1977. Wheat production fell by 1.5 million metric tons and cotton by 2 million bales. Remittances from Pakistani workers abroad fell, by about 4%, for the first time in a decade. The economic slowdown in the Persian Gulf region, where many Pakistanis were employed, thus threatened the country with both the loss of foreign exchange and the problem of finding jobs for large numbers of returning workers.

Consortium aid to Pakistan increased by 27% to $1.82 billion (U.S.). Although the assistance carried average interest rates of less than 3%, critical concerns were expressed over Pakistan's rising foreign debt.

Foreign Affairs. Despite continuing talks with India on normalization of relations, events in both countries clouded the prospects for such an agreement. India accused Pakistan of involvement in the Sikh disturbances in Indian Punjab. Pakistan expressed concern over Indian activities in disputed Kashmir. Both countries increased troop concentrations in border areas, particularly in Kashmir.

India continued to raise the specter of a Pakistani "Islamic bomb," charging early in 1984 that China had helped Pakistan test such a device. U.S. Sen. Alan Cranston (D-CA) picked up the theme in midyear and urged the United States to terminate military assistance to Pakistan. Zia's regime again denied any military intent in its nuclear program and warned India against attacking its nuclear facilities. The United States halted its nuclear cooperation agreement with China pending further clarification of Chinese involvement with Pakistan's nuclear program but chose not to cut off Pakistani aid. U.S. Vice-President George Bush visited Pakistan and India in May. The drug trade continued to be a major concern in U.S.-Pakistan relations, with more than 70% of illicit heroin in the United States estimated to be coming from Pakistan.

Several intrusions and bombings by Afghan aircraft led Pakistan to place antiaircraft installations along the border. Pakistan denied Soviet and Afghan charges of its involvement in hostilities within Afghanistan.

WILLIAM L. RICHTER
Kansas State University

PARAGUAY

Gen. Alfredo Stroessner completed 30 years in the presidency in August; no other chief executive in the Western Hemisphere continued to hold power so long. Much of the year's unrest was attributed to "the Argentine virus" and a persistent economic recession.

Political Activity. Antigovernment demonstrations occurred in downtown Asunción for the first time in 25 years. Some 1,500 members of the Authentic Radical Liberal party, opponents of the Stroessner regime, congregated at the Pantheon of National Heroes on September 29 to pay homage to Eusebio Ayala, the nation's Liberal president in 1932–36. When the crowd turned hostile toward the incumbent president, police moved in. They prevented the organizers of the protest from speaking and later blocked all roads into the capital.

The Liberal rally had been preceded on February 17 by an antigovernment protest of 2,000 militants from the Febrerista Revolutionary party. The dissidents shouted anti-Stroessner slogans and called for a democratic regime.

With the return to civilian rule in Argentina in December 1983, an "opening" of political tolerance became noticeable in Asunción. After 20 years in exile, Miguel Angel González Casabianca and Edgar Jiménez Mesa, leaders of the Colorado Popular Movement (MOPOCO), were allowed to return to Paraguay.

The closure of *ABC Color,* a daily newspaper whose objective analyses of the political situation had been widely read since the beginning of the year, demonstrated that the relaxation was only mild. The newspaper was shut down on March 22 and its director placed under house arrest. *ABC Color* was charged with fomenting subversion and provoking alarm.

After the September protest rally, Paraguay banned travel to and from Argentina for three days. Recently repatriated citizens were told to limit their activities to reporting for work and returning home at the end of the workday.

Economic Affairs. Because of bumper crops of soybeans and cotton, 1984 was expected to be a slightly better year, economically, than 1982 or 1983. Preparatory work began on the Yacyretá hydroelectric project on the Paraná River. The civil-works contract was valued at $1.43 billion (U.S.) and involved a 19-company consortium. The Paraguayan government and an American-owned company signed a petroleum exploration and exploitation contract.

The guaraní was being exchanged at 423 to the U.S. dollar in August after the official but unused rate of 126:1 was changed to 160:1 in May. An increase of 15% in the minimum wage was approved in June. Early in 1984, President Stroessner ordered his government to accept no more bankruptcy requests. Hundreds of firms had stopped paying their debts.

Foreign Affairs. An American human rights delegation arriving at the Asunción airport in April was denied entry into Paraguay because the delegates refused to have their documents copied. Four lawyers in the group were detained for eight hours without being able to contact their consulate and then were deported to Brazil.

LARRY L. PIPPIN, *University of the Pacific*

PARAGUAY • Information Highlights

Official Name: Republic of Paraguay.
Location: Central South America.
Area: 157,046 sq mi (406 750 km²).
Population (mid-1984 est.): 3,600,000.
Chief City (1982 census): Asunción, the capital, 455,517.
Government: *Head of state and government,* Gen. Alfredo Stroessner, president (took office Aug. 1954). *Legislature*—Congress: Senate and Chamber of Deputies.
Gross Domestic Product (1982 U.S.$): $5,800,000,000.
Foreign Trade (1983 U.S.$): *Imports,* $506,000,000; *exports,* $262,000,000.

PENNSYLVANIA

The elections so dominated the political agenda that 1984 seemed in other respects a quiet year in Pennsylvania. The controversies that caught public attention appeared to gain their relevance from their significance for the election.

Election. Although Democrats Walter Mondale and Geraldine Ferraro carried Philadelphia and Allegheny counties, the state's largest, Republicans Ronald Reagan and George Bush won 54% of the overall vote. Mondale and Ferraro carried only nine other counties, all in economically depressed western Pennsylvania.

In other races, incumbents triumphed with few exceptions. The three statewide winners were incumbent Republicans for state treasurer (R. Budd Dwyer) and attorney general (Leroy Zimmerman), and former Democratic Congressman Don Bailey for auditor. Dwyer won despite a scandal involving campaign contributions from state contractors. He was fortunate in that his opponent also was tainted by scandal. Zimmerman won with expenditures of well over $1 million, a state record for nongovernor races. Bailey used the Democrats' registration advantage of more than 900,000 to help overcome Susan Shanaman, the former head of the state Public Utilities Commission.

All but one of 23 incumbent congressmen were returned to Washington, as the Democrats retained their 13–10 advantage in the U.S. House of Representatives. Incumbent Frank Harrison lost the Democratic primary in the Wilkes-Barre area (eleventh district) to Paul Kanjorski, who held the seat for the Democrats in the general election. Incumbent Democrats Roger Edgar and Peter Kostmayer, both targeted by the National Republican Campaign Committee, held their seats from Philadelphia suburban districts in narrow victories. They overcame strong Republican registration advantages, well-financed opponents, and the popularity of President Reagan.

State legislative races showed similar results: incumbents of both parties won with few exceptions. Republicans maintained their slight majority in the Pennsylvania Senate, while Democrats retained their narrow margin in the House of Representatives. The absence of major new campaign themes made the 1984 election an affirmation of the status quo.

Economy. One explanation for the election results lies in the economy. The recovery was weaker in Pennsylvania than elsewhere, and traditional manufacturing segments of the Pennsylvania economy were still suffering. With this situation, the electorate did not reward Republicans with control of the state legislature or with more congressional seats. On the other hand, the electorate did not reject GOP incumbents in favor of Democrats.

PENNSYLVANIA • Information Highlights

Area: 45,308 sq mi (117 348 km²).
Population (July 1, 1983 est.): 11,895,000.
Chief Cities (July 1, 1982 est.): Harrisburg, the capital (1980 census), 53,264; Philadelphia, 1,665,382; Pittsburgh, 414,936; Erie, 118,493; Allentown, 104,324.
Government (1984): *Chief Officers*—governor, Richard L. Thornburgh (R); lt. gov., William W. Scranton III (R). *Legislature*—Senate, 50 members; House of Representatives, 203 members.
State Finances (fiscal year 1983): *Revenues,* $17,776,000,000; *expenditures,* $16,733,000,000.
Personal Income (1983): $136,176,000,000; per capita, $11,448.
Education: *Enrollment* (fall 1982)—public elementary schools, 1,157,356; public secondary, 626,613; colleges and universities (fall 1983), 545,112. *Public school expenditures* (1982–83), $5,465,364,449 ($3,329 per pupil).

By August, unemployment had dropped to 9.6%—an improvement over the double-digit figures of the recession, but still more than two percentage points higher than the national average. In western Pennsylvania, several counties had unemployment figures well into double digits. With steel production still lower than in 1983, President Reagan's decision not to place a quota on steel imports won him few friends in the steel towns and cities of western Pennsylvania. In those counties the president received fewer votes in 1984 than in 1980.

Legislation. Although election years rarely have major legislative initiatives, several controversial pieces were enacted. One such measure was a "right to know" bill strongly supported by organized labor and opposed by industrial manufacturers. The original bill would have required employers to provide workers with detailed information on the chemical content of all workplace materials. The compromise bill that passed into law was amended to limit the required information to a listing of the chemical components in all containers entering the workplace.

Nuclear Power. Cleanup work at the damaged Unit 2 reactor at Three Mile Island continued ahead of schedule. The only surprise came when an analysis of fragments of the damaged core suggested that the reactor came within a few hundred degrees of melting down during the March 1979 accident.

During the summer, the Nuclear Regulatory Commission moved toward approval of the restart of the undamaged Unit 1 reactor at Three Mile Island. But opposition from antinuclear groups and the state government successfully stalled efforts by the plant operator to generate electricity again. Opposition groups were aided by the release of new information on how hot the Unit 2 reactor had been during the accident and, by implication, how close the Unit 2 reactor had come to melting down.

ROBERT E. O'CONNOR
The Pennsylvania State University

PERU

President Fernando Belaúnde Terry's last full year in office was marked by the dismissal of an outspoken general fighting guerrillas in the southern Andes and by a continually deteriorating economic situation.

Guerrilla Warfare. Gen. Adrian Huaman Centeno, top military commander in three terrorist-ravaged southern departments, was fired on August 28, two days after blaming the spread of the Sendero Luminoso ("Shining Path") guerrillas on 160 years of government neglect and corruption. The officer, who commanded 7,000 troops in a region of 23,000 square miles (60 000 km²), complained that he never received funds promised to help peasants. "If exploitation of the people in rural areas is not stopped," he warned, "Peru will turn into another Nicaragua."

The Maoist-oriented Senderistas started attacking southern rural districts in May 1980 but spread into Lima and other areas in 1982–83 and into the Amazon oil fields in 1984. Since 1982 an estimated 3,000 civilians and 200 policemen had been killed. In December 1983 police captured number-two Senderista leader Emilio Díaz Martínez. Remaining at large a year later was Abimael Guzmán, the founder of the group, which calls itself the Communist Party of Peru. Some observers doubted that Guzmán was still in the country.

On June 3, government officials halted a well-known television program in the middle of a report on police corruption. Newscaster César Hildebrant also had reported on alleged military and police atrocities in Ayacucho department, including the discovery of at least 62 disfigured bodies in an unmarked grave. In August, Interior Minister Luis Antonio Percovich said that the war with the Sendero Luminoso was "brutalizing" the police: 5,218 policemen, about 8% of the force, were being prosecuted on charges that included robbery and murder.

Politics and the Economy. Alan García, 35-year-old secretary general of the American Revolutionary Popular Alliance (APRA), was expected to win the presidential election scheduled for April 1985. Belaúnde's Popular Action Party (AP) had won only 15% of the vote in November 1983 municipal elections. The AP nominated Vice President Javier Alva Orlandini as its presidential candidate. A coalition of leftist groups was expected to put up Alfonso Barrantes, the popular mayor of Lima.

Finance Minister Carlos Rodríguez Pastor resigned on March 19 after strong criticism of his economic policies. While Rodríguez sought to reduce inflation from 150% in 1983 to 50% in 1984, the rate was expected to reach at least 110% by December, and unemployment remained high at 14%. The nation's general malaise—alleviated only by a strong underground economy—led to a 24-hour general strike on

---

PERU · Information Highlights

Official Name: Republic of Peru.
Location: West Coast of South America.
Area: 496,000 sq mi (1 284 640 km²).
Population (mid-1984 est.): 19,200,000.
Chief Cities (1981 census): Lima, the capital, 3,968,972; Arequipa, 447,431; Callao, 441,374.
Government: *Head of state,* Fernando Belaúnde Terry, president (took office July 1980). *Head of government,* Luis Percovich Roca, prime minister (took office Oct. 1984). *Legislature*—Congress: Senate and Chamber of Deputies.
Monetary Unit: Sol (4,425 soles equal U.S.$1), Dec. 3, 1984.
Gross National Product (1982 U.S.$): $19,200,-000,000.
Economic Index (May 1984): *Consumer Prices* (1970 = 100), all items, 16,260; food, 18,706.
Foreign Trade (1983 U.S.$): *Imports,* $2,688,000,000; *exports,* $3,015,000,000.

March 22. Prime Minister Fernando Schwalb López resigned on March 30 after President Belaúnde announced plans to reactivate the economy through public spending, contrary to recommendations of the International Monetary Fund (IMF). Sandro Mariátegui was sworn in as the new prime minister and foreign minister on April 12. After resigning to run for the Senate in 1985, he was replaced in both posts by Interior Minister Percovich.

Peru's ability to meet payments on a $12 billion (U.S.) international debt was hampered by declining mineral prices. The Ministry of Energy and Mines forecast copper output at 385,700 tons in 1984, compared with 322,200 tons in 1983. Oil production increased, but falling prices were expected to reduce petroleum revenues to only $515 million. Good weather in 1984 led to increased production of wheat, potatoes, rice, and sugar.

International Relations. Although the IMF and other agencies criticized Peruvian public spending, the military paraded a new battleship, the *Montero*. It also revealed plans for a new naval base at Chimbote.

Direct flights between the United States and Peru were halted for four months because of a dispute over numbers of flights, seats, and intermediate stops.

NEALE J. PEARSON, *Texas Tech University*

PHILIPPINES

The Philippines experienced its worst storm on record in early September, as Typhoon Ike left thousands of people dead and more than a million homeless. But it was a continuing political storm, occasioned by the August 1983 murder of opposition leader Benigno Aquino, Jr., that gripped the nation. The authority of 67-year-old President Ferdinand Marcos was visibly eroded.

Aquino Inquiry. Fourteen months after the Aquino assassination, a special investigating panel concluded that the popular opposition figure, returning from a three-year self-imposed exile in the United States, could only have been shot by his army escorts. Rejecting the military's account of the slaying, originally endorsed by Marcos, four of the five tribunal members recommended the indictment for "premeditated murder" of 26 military men, including Armed Forces Chief of Staff Gen. Fabian Ver and two other senior officers—Gen. Luther Custodio and Gen. Prospero Olivas. In a minority report, the panel's chairwoman, Corazon Agrava, accused only General Custodio and six soldiers on duty at the airport.

General Custodio was placed under detention, but General Ver—a cousin and close confidant of Marcos—and Olivas—the chief military investigator in the case—were allowed to take leaves to prepare their defenses. President Marcos turned over the panel's report to the government ombudsman, who would determine the charges to be brought before a special court. Reacting to the charges, General Ver called the panel "a tool to destroy the protectors of the republic." He, along with President Marcos and the military, had contended that a single gunman had been hired by Communists to shoot Aquino.

Elections and Politics. The shadow of the Aquino assassination and mounting indications of military involvement (and perjury) hung over National Assembly elections on May 14. President Marcos' New Society Movement had held all but 14 seats in the 200-member body, but, in an apparent reaction against his handling of the Aquino affair, voters now gave the opposition 63 seats in the legislature; of those, 49 went to the United Nationalist Democratic Organization (UNIDO). Independent candidates won 8 seats.

Several other political actions reflected the turmoil in the Philippines and the Marcos regime's efforts to stabilize the situation. Businessmen and others increasingly took to the streets to demonstrate; in September the op-

position charged that 11 persons had been killed in a rally in Manila. The president, meanwhile, was so upset by criticisms made by Jaime Cardinal Sin that he openly attacked the popular prelate. In a January referendum, voters overwhelmingly favored restoration of the office of vice-president, which had been abolished by Marcos. And in mid-October, on the eve of the Aquino panel's report, General Ver announced a shake-up of the armed forces, with 40 officers resigning.

In mid-November, Mayor Cesar Climaco of Zamboanga City on the island of Mindanao, a vocal critic of President Marcos and a leader of UNIDO, was assassinated. Marcos ordered an investigation of the "heinous crime."

Marcos, who was not seen in public for weeks, finally appeared November 26 in a meeting with cabinet ministers and legislators to sign the budget bill for 1985. There were rumors of serious illness.

Insurgency. Muslim insurgent activity persisted in the south, but the chief rebel activity was that of the Communist New People's Army, which numbered about 12,500 armed regulars. In late June, President Marcos expressed shock at the strength of the rebels, and the government launched its largest offensive ever against the New People's Army in the northern highlands of Luzon island. A separate offensive was begun on Mindanao, where the insurgency was strongest. The Communists had called for a boycott of the May legislative elections. All in all, 91 persons died in election-related incidents involving the New People's Army.

Economy. The political unrest and persisting economic problems caused the flight of much capital from the Philippines in 1984. Prices, meanwhile, rose at an annual rate of about 60%, and unemployment reached some 35%. In October, President Marcos announced austerity measures as part of a tentative agreement with the International Monetary Fund for $630 million in new credits. Foreign exchange regulations would be eliminated, and the peso would be allowed to depreciate against the U.S. dollar; new taxes would be imposed; and key consumer prices would be raised. The cost of gasoline was increased from U.S. $1.55 per gallon to $1.74. The government still faced a $26 billion (U.S.) foreign debt.

Foreign Relations. Both President Marcos and the political opposition sought support from the United States, the Philippines' closest ally. Washington urged openness and justice in the Aquino case while supporting Marcos as the only alternative to communism. Despite its internal problems, the Marcos regime was active in the Association of Southeast Asian Nations (ASEAN) efforts to have Vietnam remove its troops from Cambodia.

RICHARD BUTWELL
California State University, Dominguez Hills

PHILIPPINES • Information Highlights

Official Name: Republic of the Philippines.
Location: Southeast Asia.
Area: 116,000 sq mi (300 440 km²).
Population (mid-1984 est.): 54,500,000.
Chief Cities (1980 census): Manila, the capital, 1,630,485; Quezon City, 1,165,865; Davao, 610,375; Cebu, 490,281.
Government: *Head of state,* Ferdinand E. Marcos, president (took office Dec. 30, 1965). *Head of government,* César Virata, premier (appointed April 8, 1981). *Legislature* (unicameral)—National Assembly.
Monetary Unit: Peso (18.3 pesos equal U.S.$1, floating rate, Jan. 11, 1985).
Gross National Product (1982 U.S.$): $39,000,000,000.
Economic Index (1983): *Consumer Prices,* (1972 = 100), all items, 190.5; food, 176.5. *Industrial Production* (June 1983, 1975 = 100), 205.
Foreign Trade (1983 U.S.$): *Imports,* $6,153,000,000; *exports,* $3,705,000,000.

PHOTOGRAPHY

In 1984 more computerized circuitry was squeezed into cameras, and tighter grain structures in film emulsions resulted in improved sharpness and a better quality of color photography. Major U.S. museums expanded space for photographs, and the death of Ansel Adams marked the passing of a giant (*see* page 414).

Cameras and Films. The ever-increasing electronification of 35mm single-lens reflex (SLR) cameras resulted in even more automation than in previous years. Ricoh's XR-P, for example, combined multiprogram capability—14 operating modes—with a two-stage data processing system, coupled with a microprocessor. The Olympus OM2S incorporated programmed automation. In compact non-SLRs, from Ansco to Yashica, manufacturers brought out automatic-everything cameras, and Chinon and Ricoh announced models with wide-angle and telephoto attachments and a close-up device. In the medium-format tribe (6×4.5 cm), the Pentax 645 full-system camera made its entry, offering SLR convenience plus full-system options, multimode (7) exposure with a built-in motor drive. In lenses, there was an increasing emphasis on sophisticated zooms, both wide-angle and telephoto, and at higher speeds, as well as one-touch (for focusing and zooming) capability. Of particular interest was Sigma's new group of lenses, headed by a 50—200mm f/3.5—4.5 apochromatic one-touch zoom. And Pentax reversed its hard line on not licensing its KA bayonet mount, so that independent lensmakers could supply KA-mounts as soon as royalty agreements could be settled.

In video cameras, Kodak introduced two models of an 8mm video camera recorder ("camcorder"), a cradle unit to play back and a compact camera recorder that is a self-contained unit with a camera portion and built-in recording component that will record and play back up to 90 minutes of videotaped recording on 8mm videocassettes. The Kodak 2200 camcorder sells for $1,599 and the 2400 for $1,899. With Kodak's introduction were announcements of 8mm videocameras from GE and RCA, and most major Japanese camera manufacturers were working on prototypes.

At the Photo Marketing Association's (PMA) annual meeting, Fuji showed its ISO 1600 color-print (Fujicolor HR 1600) and color-slide films, and Kodak responded with a new improved version of its highly successful 1000 color-print film (Kodacolor VR 1000). The most striking improvement came from 3M with its 400-speed color-print film. Agfa announced a new series of color transparency film in ISO 50, 100, 200, and 1000 speeds and its color-print Agfacolor "XRS" lineup in 100, 200, 400, and 1000. And Polaroid brought out several new SX-70-style films and its 600 color-print film in a rectangular format.

To improve exposure and final print quality and further automate and simplify photography, Kodak was phasing into DX (digital indexing) coding for all its 35mm films, i.e., four electronically readable codes were added to its film edges. Agfa has begun to do so, as would 3M. Though no DX-coded cameras were shown early in the year, most Japanese camera manufacturers indicated that many, if not most, were planning the DX shift on at least one model within the next year.

Shows, Publications, Collecting, Museum Expansion. "Color Photographs" were the subject of a "Recent Acquisitions" show at the Museum of Modern Art (MoMA) in New York City, as was "Color in the Summer" at the Brooklyn Museum. Grand masters were honored in retrospectives, along with accompanying publications. The MoMA featured the first comprehensive survey in more than 20 years of Irving Penn's works. The exhibit included 200 color and black-and-white pictures from the last four decades and a selection of early unpublished photographs. The humanistic work of 90-year-old André Kertész was scheduled to be shown at the Metropolitan Museum of Art in December but was postponed. "Bonjour Monsieur Lartigue," 125 pictures from the photographer's family albums in France before World War I, and "Eleanor and Barbara: Photography by Harry Callahan" of his wife and daughter were highlighted at the Nelson-Atkins Museum of Art in Kansas City and at the Detroit Institute of Arts, respectively.

Cindy Sherman's "Faces" was on view at the Akron Art Museum. She used herself as model and derived inspiration from the ways women have been portrayed in films and fashion. "Three Young Photographers: Photographs by Robert Adams, Jim Goldberg, and Joel Sternfeld" at MoMA explored the issues raised by the disintegration of the post World War II American dream. The latter exhibit exemplified the style "new documentary."

The market for fine photographic prints was recovering, and the outlook for investors was brighter than in years. According to a price index compiled by the monthly newsletter *The Photograph Collector,* prices for such fine prints rose 165% since 1975. The previous high of the index occurred in the spring of 1980 and was followed by a 30% slide in prices over the next two years. During that time many galleries closed. A two-day symposium, "Collecting Fine Art Photography for Pleasure and Profit," was held at the New School in New York City.

The Witkin gallery in New York City celebrated its 15th anniversary. New rooms at the MoMA's photography gallery tripled the space for exhibiting the medium, and the J. Paul Getty Museum in Malibu, CA, turned its attention to photographic collections. (*See* ART.)

BARBARA LOBRON
Free-lance Writer, Editor, and Photographer

At his studio near Carmel, CA, Ansel Adams posed in front of "Moonrise, Hernandez," one of his most famous photographs. The landscape masterpiece was taken in 1941 and sold at auction in 1979 for $15,000, then a record amount.

ANSEL ADAMS (1902–84)

Ansel Adams, probably the best-known U.S. photographer, died of heart disease near his Carmel, CA, home on April 21, 1984. A photographer of the Western landscape, Adams used his skills as a writer, teacher, and organizer to further the fortunes of his art form. He repeatedly photographed various Yosemite landmarks, including the rock face of Half Dome, and the West Coast artistic community. He also did portraiture. Moonrises fascinated him, and his most popular image, "Moonrise, Hernandez" (1941), was for a time the most expensive image sold at auction.

Adams also had great command of the controls of photographic printmaking. In the 1940s he invented the Zone System, a system of exposure and development control that allows the photographer to control the tones of black-and-white prints. In 1940 he helped establish a photography department at the Museum of Modern Art and in 1977 provided funding for a curatorial position there. In 1946 he started the first college photography department in what is now the San Francisco Art Institute. Fourteen years earlier he had joined Edward Weston, Imogen Cunningham, and other West Coast photographers in forming Group f/64, which championed sharp focus and unmanipulated images. In 1967 he founded the Friends of Photography in Carmel, now the leading organization for the appreciation and promotion of photography.

An ardent conservationist and environmentalist, Adams was affiliated with the Sierra Club for half a century. His writings include the classic *Basic Photo Series* on photographic techniques, *Eloquent Light,* and *Photographs of the Southwest. Ansel,* his autobiography, is due to be published in 1985.

BARBARA LOBRON

414

"Rose and Driftwood" (1932), above, typified Adams' work in Group f/64, which called for sharp detail focused through the smallest aperture of the lens (f/64). On a larger scale, the Sierra Nevada and Yosemite National Park in California provided the subject matter for many of Adams' best-known works—including "Moon and Half Dome, Yosemite Valley" (1960), right, and "Mount Williamson, Sierra Nevada, from Manzana" (1944), below. In the foreword to his 1979 book Yosemite and the Range of Light, Adams wrote: "Since June 1916 the Sierra has dominated my mind, art and spirit. . . . I think of the Sierra as sculptures in stone. . . . It is the detail of the Sierra that captures the eye and entices the camera."

Photos, Ansel Adams, Courtesy of Ansel Adams Publishing Rights Trust

PHYSICS

In 1984 the top quark was discovered, new accelerators were planned, and science education remained in the news.

Elementary-Particle Physics. In 1984 the long-sought top quark was found at the European Center for Nuclear Research (CERN) in Geneva, Switzerland. Quarks are considered the basic components of matter, with exotic properties such as fractional electrical charge. Quarks are thought to come in pairs, which together with their related leptons, are called generations. The first generation consists of the up and down quark, the electron, and the electron neutrino. The particles of the first generation form ordinary matter. The second generation includes the strange and charm quarks. The quarks of the third generation are called bottom and top. It was this last quark that was observed in 1984. A year earlier the key W and Z particles were observed at CERN. The electroweak theory combines the weak nuclear force and the electromagnetic force. The particles that transfer the force are the photon (the quantum of light) for electromagnetism and the intermediate vector bosons (W^+, W^-, and Z^0) for weak interaction. With the observation of the top quark, and with the W and Z particles discovered just as theory had predicted, physicists now want to test other predictions of this unified theory.

One prediction is that the proton is unstable. A number of experiments, including one in a salt mine underneath Cleveland, OH, and one under Mont Blanc in the Alps, are in progress. Using a huge detector (mainly 8,000 tons of water), a group of U.S. scientists has established that the proton lifetime is more than 6.5×10^{31} years. This value disagrees with the simplest of the Grand Unification Theories.

New Accelerators. To find the new particles of high-energy physics requires huge, expensive accelerators. The Super Proton Synchrotron (SPS) at CERN was converted into a proton-antiproton (p,p̄) colliding-beams machine to observe the W and Z particles. The United States had a similar proton synchrotron (Fermilab) but chose instead to double the energy and then build a pp̄ collider. This new system is called the Tevatron, since protons will be accelerated to a thousand billion eV (one TeV). It should be operational in 1986.

An electron-positron collider at CERN is now in the construction stage. This accelerator should produce many Z particles. Meanwhile construction of the proton-proton collider ("Isabelle") at Brookhaven National Laboratory was canceled. This billion-dollar project ran into major difficulties, primarily in producing high-field superconducting magnets. Although the magnet problem was resolved, elementary-particle physicists recommended canceling the entire project. The proposed alternative is a proton-proton collider with 10 to 20 TeV in each beam. The proposed new accelerator is called the Superconducting Super Collider. Price estimates start at several billion dollars. Since the accelerator would be so large—diameter of about 20 mi (32 km)—it could be built only in wide open spaces. It is often called the desertron.

Fractional Quantum Hall Effect. In the Hall effect when an electric field and a perpendicular magnetic field are applied to a conductor, an electric current is generated perpendicular to both fields. A novel new phenomenon has been observed at Bell Labs. In a special semiconductor thin-film structure, the electrons bound to the interface area (between crystals of GaAs and AlGaAs) are free only in the plane. They act as a two-dimensional electron gas. For a quantum two dimensional gas, the energy associated with the so-called cyclotron motion (induced by applied fields) is quantized. A few years ago the Hall conductance (induced current divided by the magnitude of the electric field) was found to be quantized in integral multiples of e^2/h, where e is the charge on the electron and h is Planck's constant.

A new and unexpected result was observed at Bell Labs when the Hall effect in the heterojunction was measured at low temperatures. Anomalous Hall effects also were observed at fractional multiples of e^2/h, such as $\frac{1}{3}$, $\frac{2}{3}$, $\frac{2}{5}$, $\frac{3}{5}$, and $\frac{4}{5}$. Initial theoretical investigations have explained some but not all of the observed phenomena. The excitations (quasiparticles) of these remarkable quantum liquids have fractional electric charge. The electrical resistance parallel to the applied electric field is nearly zero, far below normal metals. The low temperature and high magnetic field required may discourage applications.

Science Manpower and Education. The U.S. federal budget for fiscal year 1985 reflected support for basic scientific research, with significant increases in engineering and the physical sciences. Meanwhile the concern over science education and manpower continued at a high pitch.

The number of physics students in universities remained about the same as in recent years. An acute problem remained at the secondary school level, where science and mathematics enrollment and achievement seemed lower than ever. Enrollment in physics courses had plunged from more than 20% at the turn of the century to a few percent today. A recent survey showed that physics has the severest shortage of qualified teachers among the sciences.

Meanwhile, Congress passed and President Reagan signed into law a bill providing nearly $1 billion over a two-year period to improve the teaching of mathematics and science.

GARY MITCHELL
North Carolina State University

AP/Wide World

General Jaruzelski declared the Communist Party in full control of the nation, but the opposition remained active.

POLAND

The year 1984 was one of bitter conflict between the Communist regime and the opposition movement. It began with a letter from Solidarity leader Lech Walesa to government leader Gen. Wojciech Jaruzelski proposing reconciliation and partnership, but any prospects for greater harmony were soon upset by new government actions. The year 1984 was also one of much suffering for the Polish consumer.

Price Hikes. In the latter part of January 1984, the prices of several food items—including butter, cheese, chicken, and ham—were increased by more than 30%; bread prices were hiked 25%. During that one month, total food costs rose 10%. According to unofficial estimates, food prices in Poland had risen by about 300% since General Jaruzelski imposed martial law in December 1981.

The latest round of price hikes was part of Poland's most serious economic crisis since World War II. Most food staples—including meat, butter, sugar, flour, and rice—continued to be rationed in 1984. There was considerable public outcry against the regime's handling of the situation, with even the new government-sanctioned unions, supposedly more "loyal" to the regime than the outlawed Solidarity, sending letters of protest to party and government officials complaining that they had not been consulted on the harsh price policies. Church leaders, including Jozef Cardinal Glemp, Poland's Roman Catholic primate, also registered their objections to the new price hikes and to repression of dissent. Jailed Solidarity leader Wadyslaw Frasyniuk issued a statement de-

nouncing the increases as well as the lack of consultation that the government had promised in decisions on economic policy. The statement, smuggled out of prison and circulated clandestinely throughout Poland, also called for a boycott of the local elections scheduled for the summer.

Although the price increases did not lead to rioting—as they had in 1956, 1970, 1976, and 1980—factory workers at various locations did respond with shutdowns. On January 22 demonstrations and police clashes erupted in Gdansk following a meeting between Walesa and Cardinal Glemp and a Mass at St. Mary's Cathedral celebrated by the cardinal. Some 3,000 Solidarity supporters marched through the streets chanting "Down with food price hikes" and "No freedom without Solidarity."

Repression. In January the Polish police launched a purge of so-called "social undesirables" from public schools. Teachers and school administrators were instructed to help police by preparing lists of Western-style "punks," drug users, and "fascists." There was widespread concern that political dissidents were the real targets of the campaign.

At the beginning of February, the official Polish press published an open letter bitterly denouncing Lech Walesa as an alleged lawbreaker and a lazy and corrupt publicity seeker. Referring to his meetings with underground Solidarity leaders, the letter hinted at eventual prosecution of Walesa. Later that month, the government began legal proceedings against several priests, including the Rev. Henryk Jankowski, a friend of Lech Walesa, charging them with improper political activities. Cardinal Glemp resisted government pressure to muzzle, remove, or transfer pro-Solidarity priests but gave way in the case of the Rev. Mieczyslaw Nowak, whose pro-Solidarity sermons and activities especially angered the regime. Nowak was transferred from an industrial suburb of Warsaw to a parish in the countryside. Several of his parishioners were reported to have gone on a hunger strike to pressure Cardinal Glemp to reverse the transfer decision. In December, still another Warsaw area priest, Stanislaw Makowski, was forbidden to preach by the cardinal.

In March, stepping up its antireligious campaign, the government began actively enforcing its December 1983 decree that crucifixes be removed from public schools. This policy encountered substantial popular resistance, as well as strong opposition from the Catholic Church and Solidarity. Student protests and police confrontations broke out at various locations. In an agricultural school near the town of Garwolin, 400 students occupied the building to protest the removal of the crucifixes and were evicted by riot police. In Czestochowa, hundreds of students marched in protest to the holy shrine of the Black Madonna. Lech Walesa expressed his support of the student demonstrators. All of Poland's bishops declared their opposition to the government campaign, with one of them, Bishop Jan Mazur of Siedlce, going on a hunger strike in late March.

In early April, the government stepped up "the war of the crucifixes" by requiring students to sign statements recognizing church-state separation; those not signing would be barred from enrolling in school. Finally, on April 6, confronted by a wave of protests, the regime relented and announced that students could wear crucifixes to school and that crucifixes could be displayed in school libraries and dormitories—though still not in classrooms. Bishop Mazur ended his hunger strike. Late in the year, however, the government appeared to renew its anti-crucifix campaign.

Opposition. The spring months saw a rising tide of activism by the government opposition. In a statement issued April 11, four Solidarity leaders in hiding—Zbigniew Bujak, Bogdan Lis, Tadeusz Jedynak, and Eugeniusz Szumiejko—called on the Polish people to boycott the June local elections. May Day celebrations in Poland produced new confrontations between the regime and the opposition in several cities, including Warsaw. The most striking probably occurred in the city of Gdansk, where Lech Walesa himself infiltrated the official parade and, together with other Solidarity supporters, voiced opposition slogans directly to Communist officials on the reviewing stand. Riot police attacked the demonstrators, but Walesa returned home and was not arrested.

On June 8, an eight-member team of medical experts told a Warsaw court that Grzegorz Przemyk, a 19-year-old student arrested in 1983, had died as a result of a beating inflicted while he was in custody of the police. Przemyk's death continued to be a political cause célèbre against the regime. On June 10, Polish authorities announced the arrest of Bogdan Lis, the 31-year-old fugitive Solidarity leader, generally considered the second-in-command to Zbigniew Bujak (still at large) among the underground leaders.

The calls for a boycott of the June 17 local elections had a significant effect on voter turnout. According to official results, less than 75% of eligible voters went to the polls—the lowest percentage in the 40-year history of Poland's Communist regime. In 85 of the country's 23,214 election districts, the voting had to be repeated because fewer than half of the eligible voters took part in the poll. According to Solidarity sources, the turnout was only 60–65% of eligible voters.

In late June, a demonstration was held in the city of Poznan to mark the anniversary of the famed June 1956 riots there. Police clashed with about 1,000 of the demonstrators, using clubs and tear gas to break up the crowd.

Antigovernment rhetoric continued from the opposition through the summer. In mid-August, Lech Walesa warned that if the United States ever restores any economic aid to Poland, it would require careful monitoring by impartial sources to see that the program really benefited the Polish people. And in a statement commemorating the fourth anniversary of the Gdansk accords of August 1980, Walesa declared that, by abandoning the historic agreement with the trade unions, the government had "ignored the will of the nation." He warned that this policy bore a threat of conflict "the tragic outcome of which we are not able to imagine." Unlike some other Solidarity figures, however, Walesa cautioned followers against confrontational tactics.

POLAND • Information Highlights

Official Name: Polish People's Republic.
Location: Eastern Europe.
Area: 120,700 sq mi (312 612 km²).
Population (mid-1984 est.): 36,900,000.
Chief Cities (Dec. 1982): Warsaw, the capital, 1,628,900; Lodz, 845,700; Cracow, 730,900.
Government: *Head of state,* Henryk Jablonski, chairman of the Council of State (took office 1972). *Head of government,* Gen. Wojciech Jaruzelski, chairman of the Council of Ministers (Feb. 1981) and first secretary of the Polish United Workers' Party (Oct. 1981). *Legislature* (unicameral)—Sejm.
Monetary Unit: Zloty (109.00 zlotys equal U.S.$1, August 1984).
Gross National Product (1982 U.S.$): $186,800,-000,000.
Economic Indexes (1983): *Consumer Prices* (1980 = 100), all items, 294.5; food, 352.1. *Industrial Production* (1975 = 100), 116.
Foreign Trade (1983 U.S.$): *Imports,* $9,931,000,000; *exports,* $10,951,000,000.

Amnesty. In July, meanwhile, the regime had begun releasing political prisoners as part of a sweeping amnesty. Passed by a special session of the Sejm (parliament) called in commemoration of the 40th anniversary of Communist rule, the bill called for the release of 652 political prisoners and some 35,000 common criminals within 30 days. The first 80 dissidents were released on July 23, but the government declared that if any of them resumed their forbidden activities in the next 30 months they would be subjected to more substantial jail terms than those originally imposed. Many Solidarity activists released under the amnesty, such as Andrzej Gwiazda, expressed profound skepticism at the regime's motives. Indeed in December, Gwiazda was rearrested and sentenced to three months in jail for participating (with Walesa) in an unlawful demonstration in Gdansk. Several Solidarity leaders, including Walesa, responded with a short hunger strike.

One effect of the amnesty was to halt the trial, already underway, of four Solidarity advisers—Jacek Kuron, Adam Michnik, Henryk Wujec, and Zbigniew Romaszewski—charged with attempting to overthrow the regime by force. Among others, Bogdan Lis and Piotr Mierzejewski were released in December. A top Solidarity leader, Zbigniew Janas, came out of hiding. Walesa, however, declared the amnesty to be a "step in the right direction."

Popieluszko Incident. On October 21, Polish television informed the public of the abduction by unknown assailants of one of the regime's most celebrated opponents, the Rev. Jerzy Popieluszko. The 37-year-old Catholic priest was pastor of the St. Stanislaw Kostka church in Warsaw and was well known for his outspoken sermons. In August he reportedly was indicted for "abusing religious freedom" and stockpiling illegal pro-Solidarity literature and explosives in his apartment. Father Popieluszko denied all of the charges but continued to win a large following for his active support of Solidarity. His disappearance October 19 coincided with threats against the life of another prominent religious supporter of Solidarity, Father Jankowski.

The state media condemned Father Popieluszko's abduction, and government officials announced that the Polish police would work full force to solve the crime. General Jaruzelski called a special meeting of the Party's Central Committee and in a nationally televised speech sponsored a resolution condemning this "act of dangerous banditry which has shocked the people of our country."

On October 26, the government announced the arrest of three suspects in the kidnapping, Capt. Grzegorz Piotrowski, Lt. Waldemar Chmielewski, and Lt. Leszek Pekala of the Polish security force (SB). Four days later, acting on their testimony, police recovered Father

AP/Wide World

The abduction and murder of Father Jerzy Popieluszko, an outspoken supporter of Solidarity, became a cause célèbre.

Popieluszko's body from a reservoir in northern Poland; according to an official autopsy, he had been tortured. A fourth suspect, security police Col. Adam Pietruszka, was detained for "aiding and abetting" the murder. His superior, Gen. Zenon Platck, was suspended from office. The year ended with attention focused on the trial of Piotrowski, Chmielewski, Pekala, and Pietruszka, which had begun in Torin.

Because Popieluszko had been attacked in the Soviet newspaper *Izvestia* only weeks before his murder, there was suspicion among Poles of a possible KGB role in the case. Lech Walesa called the whole affair an attempt to provoke the opposition into a bloody and futile uprising against the regime. However, he urged restraint and expressed his disagreement with Solidarity leaders who urged a general protest strike. Popieluszko's funeral on November 3 drew an estimated 250,000 people to the streets of Warsaw. Walesa addressed the crowd, declaring "we shall never forget this death." In mid-November, he called for a reform of the whole Interior Ministry, while the government warned the opposition not to "exploit" the Popieluszko murder for "subversive purposes."

Foreign Affairs. The Communist regime in Warsaw continued to be closely tied to Moscow and the Soviet bloc. At the end of February, forces of the USSR, Poland, and East Germany held joint military maneuvers in western and northwestern areas of Poland. In early May, General Jaruzelski visited Moscow, where he assured Soviet leader Konstantin Chernenko of Poland's "close and unbreakable" union; Chernenko, in turn, assured his guest of Soviet backing against all "acts of subversion." The two leaders signed a 15-year economic cooperation pact, and Jaruzelski was presented with the Order of Lenin. In the second week of June, Poland participated in a Moscow summit of the Council of Mutual Economic Assistance (Comecon); it was the first full-scale meeting of the Communist-bloc alliance since 1971.

Poland's relations with the United States continued to be strained, though there was some improvement. In late July, President Ronald Reagan responded to the amnesty in Poland by announcing the lifting of two sanctions: LOT, the Polish airline, would be permitted to resume flights to the United States, and the ban on cultural exchange agreements was to be lifted; the Warsaw regime, however, attacked Washington for not lifting its other sanctions. These included a ban on Polish fishing in U.S. waters, a ban on government-to-government credits, and a suspension of Poland's "most-favored-nation" trade status. An official statement claimed that U.S. sanctions "stole $350 out of every Pole's pocket."

In November several hundred Polish tourists traveling on Polish vessels sought refuge in West Germany.

ALEXANDER J. GROTH
University of California, Davis

POLAR RESEARCH

Antarctic. During the 1983–1984 austral summer more than 300 researchers conducted 93 projects at four U.S. stations, aboard two U.S. Coast Guard icebreakers, and aboard the National Science Foundation's research ship *Hero.*

Aboard the research ship *Melville,* operated by the Scripps Institution of Oceanography, 41 marine scientists studied the physics, chemistry, and biology at the sea ice edge in the Weddell Sea. By analyzing temperature, salinity, and other factors, physical oceanographers found that two distinct features in this region may influence biological productivity—a hydrographic front near 59°S and an area of low salinity about 320 mi (200 km) north of the ice edge. Biologists found that marine organisms were distributed in distinct patterns. The highest levels of productivity were along the northern limit of the ice edge; productivity diminished toward the south as the ice cover increased and toward the north in the open ocean. Their findings acutely emphasize that high biological productivity in Antarctic waters is tied to the physical and chemical nature of the sea ice.

Investigations on Seymour Island, site of the first discovery of mammal fossils in Antarctica, revealed that fossils from this area predate their descendants from middle and lower latitudes by as much as 40 million years. Fourteen scientists from five institutions collected fossils of fish, birds, whales, other marine vertebrates, and invertebrates and searched for more mammal fossils. The data from the 1984 season and two previous ones provided scientists with new data on the geologic, climatic, and oceanic histories of the Southern Hemisphere. The island's fossil sequence is a nearly complete record of the breakup of the supercontinent Gondawana. Because of data obtained on Seymour Island, geologists now believe that the sudden appearance of plant and animal groups in the midlatitude geologic record may reflect major dispersals of animals from high latitudes to low and midlatitudes.

On Feb. 22, 1984, geologists and glaciologists visited Mt. Siple (73°15'S 126°6'W) for the first time. The mountain, a snow-covered volcano, was discovered in 1940 by U.S. aviators. The scientists collected soil and rock samples to study the region's geologic history.

In West Antarctica glaciologists studied the 1 million-sq mi (2.6 million-km²) West Antarctic ice sheet. This ice sheet, the world's only marine-based ice sheet, is subject to relatively rapid changes, and its response to climate change might provide scientists with critical information about climatic warming.

Arctic. During the summer (June to September), marine scientists investigated the shelves of the northern part of the Bering Sea and the Chukchi Sea. Their objective was to determine whether or not nutrients and other organic materials supplied by the Yukon River, North America's fifth-largest river, caused more marine animals to be present in shelf waters. They found instead that ocean currents and mixing processes cause high productivity. Near the northwest Alaskan coast, the continental shelf of the two seas is a broad plateau that is never deeper than 160 ft (50 m). Because the ocean waters continually move nutrients into the continental shelf area, the scientists suggested that this region resembles algae continuously cultured in a laboratory, where favorable growth conditions are maintained because nutrients are constantly added and cell yield is removed. During the summer these waters yield an estimated 2 to 4 grams of carbon per square meter per day (the world ocean average is 0.1 gram per day).

U.S. President Ronald Reagan signed the Arctic Research Policy Act in 1984. This act established a committee to coordinate the Arctic research by U.S. federal agencies, and it included the participation of the scientific community.

WINIFRED REUNING
National Science Foundation

The Problem of Growth

The United Nations' second International Conference on Population, held in Mexico City, Aug. 6–14, 1984, focused renewed attention on the complex issues related to the high rates of population growth. Some experts refer to this growth as a "population explosion"; others call it a "population crisis." No matter what the term, there is general agreement that the current rates of growth, particularly in the developing countries, pose a serious problem for the future.

The Problem. The world's population in the year 1 A.D. is estimated to have been 250 million people. Historically, growth rates were well below 0.1% (actually averaging as low as 0.002% for most of the known history of mankind), with birth and death rates being roughly equal. However, a dramatic shift occurred in the 18th and 19th centuries when death rates began to fall as a result of the many changes flowing out of the Industrial Revolution.

By the early 1800s, the world's population reached 1 billion people, having taken all of known human history to reach that point. However, it took only approximately 100 years to reach the second billion people, 30 years to reach the third, and 15 years to reach the 4 billion point. It is estimated that at present the world is adding an additional billion people every 11 to 12 years, a totally unprecedented situation. Current projections suggest a world population of about 6 billion people by the year 2000, with the world currently adding more than 70 million people every year or some 200,000 additional people every day.

The problems are particularly acute in the developing world where population growth rates range from 2–4%. The average rate of growth for the world is slightly less than 2%, which results in a doubling of the population in approximately 35 years. For those developing countries with population growth rates at the level of 3% or higher, the population will double in just 22 years or less. In North America and Europe, on the other hand, growth rates are well under 1%, with a few countries in Europe having reached zero or even negative growth.

Programs and Policies. During the past two decades, increasing numbers of developing countries have recognized the seriousness and the resultant problems of population growth on their overall economic and social development plans. As a result, they have declared population policies aimed at lowering population growth rates or have instituted family planning programs to improve the health and well-being of women and children.

The first official population policy was declared in India in 1952, with several other Asian countries following suit in the 1960s and 1970s. A major element of such population policies has been the implementation of national family planning programs. A number of countries in the Asian and Latin American regions have had major successes in implementing such programs and in beginning to lower the population growth rates. They have included, most notably, such countries as South Korea, Taiwan, Indonesia, Thailand, Mexico, Costa Rica, and Chile. Perhaps the most dramatic, and also the most controversial, is the program of the People's Republic of China in which major strides have been taken to slow the rate of growth in the first country to exceed a population of 1 billion (see also page 71).

In 1974 the first UN international conference was held in Bucharest, Rumania, at which population issues were debated by representatives from most of the world's countries. Some developing country representatives did not agree with the United States and other developed countries that population growth was a problem; they suggested, as did many of the socialist countries, that development was the best contraceptive. Despite the opposition, however, the meeting identified population growth as a world problem and urged that all couples should have the right to receive information and services about contraception.

At the 1984 UN meeting in Mexico City, the developing countries took the lead in preparing a strong statement on population and on the programs needed for impact on the problem. Delegates from 149 countries stated that population growth was an intrinsic part of the development process and that all people, including adolescents, have a right to family planning information and services. They stressed the adverse effects of early marriage and childbearing and the scourge of high rates of infant, child, and maternal mortality and morbidity in the developing world. They went on to stress the importance of increased funding support for population and family planning programs, the urgent need to improve the status of women, and the sovereign right of all countries to determine their own population programs and policies. Ironically, the stance of the U.S. government was different from 1974. In 1984, Reagan administration representatives took a more conservative position in regard to population growth as a developing problem, and to issues related to abortion.

ALLAN ROSENFIELD

PORTUGAL

In 1984, Socialist Prime Minister Mário Soares and his coalition government backed strict austerity measures because of difficult economic conditions and showed strong concern for international affairs.

Government and Politics. In January the Portuguese parliament liberalized abortion laws in cases involving rape, deformed fetuses, and danger to the mother's health. Supported by Socialists and Communists, the bill passed despite objections from both the Social Democrats, a partner in Soares' coalition, and the opposition Christian Democrats. The Roman Catholic Church mounted a vigorous campaign to defeat the measure, which was backed by two thirds of the population, according to a public-opinion poll. The strong position of the church in rural areas is offset by its declining influence among younger, urbanized Portuguese.

Equally controversial was parliament's approval by a 138 to 79 vote of an internal security statute. The law enables authorities to eavesdrop electronically, open mail, make arrests, and conduct warrantless searches and seizures when the government perceives a threat to internal security. Communist deputies excoriated the bill as reminiscent of the arbitrary violation of civil liberties practiced by the nation's secret police, which was disbanded a decade ago after the fall of the right-wing dictatorship. Soares justified the internal security legislation as a necessary tool in combating terrorism.

Since there were no elections in 1984, Soares was able to concentrate most of his energies on economic reforms, even as his popular support sagged. If recovery takes place thanks to his policies and the economic rebound of developed countries, the 59-year-old prime minister may seek the presidency in 1985 when incumbent António Ramalho Eanes, who is ineligible for reelection, steps down.

PORTUGAL • Information Highlights

Official Name: Portuguese Republic.
Location: Southwestern Europe.
Area: 36,400 sq mi (94 276 km²).
Population (mid-1984 est.): 10,100,000.
Chief Cities (1981 census): Lisbon, the capital, 812,400; Oporto, 329,100.
Government: *Head of state,* Antonio Ramalho Eanes, president (took office July 1976). *Head of government,* Mário Soares, prime minister (took office June 9, 1983). *Legislature* (unicameral)—Assembly of the Republic.
Monetary Unit: Escudo (160 escudos equal U.S.$1, Nov. 5, 1984).
Gross National Product (1982 U.S.$): $23,400,-000,000.
Economic Indexes (1983): *Consumer Prices* (1976 = 100), all items, 414.6; food, 423.5. *Industrial Production* (1975 = 100), 151.
Foreign Trade (1983 U.S.$): *Imports,* $8,245,000,000; *exports,* $4,608,000,000.

Economy. Sluggish economic growth and high unemployment aside, Portugal agreed to continue its stabilization program in order to receive additional assistance from the International Monetary Fund (IMF). In midyear the country received the second installment of a four-part $480 million IMF loan. In return, the Soares government pledged to impose a gradual devaluation of the peso by 1% a month and to lower the nation's 1984 balance-of-payments deficit to $1.25 billion (U.S.) from $1.6 billion. The IMF agreed to allow a budget deficit in 1984 of 8.5% of the gross national product, rather than the 7% level initially demanded by the international agency.

These actions conformed to a recommendation of the Organization for Economic Cooperation and Development that Portugal "maintain its restrictive fiscal and monetary stance in order to restore external equilibrium, reduce inflation and improve the position of public finance." Further, the organization urged "radical structural action" to spur price competition, expand the country's tax base, enhance labor market flexibility, and diminish dependence on agricultural imports.

In late July, Finance Minister Ernani Lopes announced receipt of a $401 million syndicated loan, involving 53 international banks. The economy was also buoyed by a 21% increase in tourism because of the strength of European currencies and the U.S. dollar against the escudo, combined with the opening of more hotels and vacation villas.

Foreign Affairs. In April, British Prime Minister Margaret Thatcher visited Portugal, the country with which Britain has its oldest treaty, dating from 1373. Thatcher sought to improve commercial relations between the two nations and to facilitate Portugal's joining the European Community (EC). She told Soares that Portugal's admission was long overdue and that negotiations should be concluded by year's end to assure the country's entry by Jan. 1, 1986, as scheduled. However, an internal dispute among the ten EC members concerning appropriate entry terms raised questions about achieving this goal.

Portugal demonstrated its continued interest in Africa in May when Soares signed a hydroelectric power accord with Mozambique, a former Portuguese territory, and South Africa. Portugal had also played a key role in the signing of a nonaggression treaty between the Pretoria regime and Maputo.

In late May, South African Prime Minister Pieter W. Botha visited Lisbon, where he expressed interest in a nonaggression pact with Angola, another former Portuguese colony. During the visit, Soares accepted an invitation to travel to South Africa.

See also AFRICA.

GEORGE W. GRAYSON
College of William and Mary

POSTAL SERVICE

By the time of his retirement as postmaster general (PMG) on Dec. 31, 1984, William F. Bolger had set a post-World War II record for fiscal solvency within the U.S. Postal Service (USPS). For the third successive year, the USPS accounts ended in the black.

The estimated surplus for fiscal year (FY) 1984, ending September 30, was $100 million. Final figures for FY 1983 and FY 1982 were $616 million and $802 million, respectively. Prior to FY 1979, the last year the books were in the black was 1945.

The FY 1984 surplus was unexpected, as most earlier estimates predicted a deficit. Given reasonably stable economic conditions, the immediate fiscal future of the agency would depend primarily on four factors: (1) the impact of the labor contract negotiations of late 1984, (2) income generated as a result of rate increases proposed in late 1983, (3) continued growth in mail volume, and (4) improved productivity.

Labor Relations. During 1984 the USPS underwent its most protracted labor negotiations. The postal labor contract of 1981 expired on July 20, 1984. When bargaining began on a new contract in late April, it quickly became clear that both sides were far apart. Under what became known as a "two-tier" wage package, the USPS proposed to hold the line on present worker wages but pay new workers 33% less, a figure later reduced to 23%. The USPS also requested several fringe-benefit reductions. Bolger's argument, based on a USPS study, was that postal pay and benefits exceeded comparable private compensation by 18 to 23%. "We plan to correct that," he said.

The four major postal unions with exclusive jurisdiction then unveiled their counterproposals, through which they hoped to boost pay and benefits by close to $8,000 during the next three years. Both sides declined to compromise, and the 1981 contract ran out in midsummer. The law then provides for 90 days of further negotiations between management and labor, followed by compulsory arbitration of remaining differences during an additional 45 days. Fact-finding under the auspices of the Federal Mediation and Conciliation Service is also authorized during the first half of the 90-day period.

On July 25 the USPS announced that, regardless of the labor negotiations, it would institute its two-tier pay arrangement for new employees on August 4. Amid heated objections from the unions, Congress responded and by an amendment of an appropriation bill later that month forbade the USPS to make major wage changes outside the bargaining process outlined in the Postal Reform Act of 1970.

When the existing contract ended, the two smaller unions—of rural carriers and mail handlers—invoked fact-finding, and in September a nonbinding report recommended a $2,000 wage increase over the next three years and withdrawal of the two-tiered wage proposal.

Meanwhile, the two largest postal unions—the National Association of Letter Carriers and the American Postal Workers Union—joined forces in negotiations and waived fact-finding. There were a few more inconclusive bargaining sessions. Then all contract differences between the four unions and the USPS went to arbitration on October 19. There was some delay in forming the arbitration teams, but by the middle of November three teams—one for the USPS and the two largest unions and the others for the USPS and the two smaller unions—were deliberating. They had the power to complete the contracts, and their decisions, which might not all be the same, would probably become binding some time in December 1984.

Rates. Personnel expenses form 83% of the USPS budget. Thus, with several billion dollars riding on the result of the labor contract process, the USPS took out insurance in the form of a rate increase request in late 1983. The postal governors sought an average rise in rates of 15%. In September 1984 the Postal Rate Commission (PRC) responded with approval of an increase of about 9%. This would mean a rise in first class postage of 2 cents, up from 20 to 22 cents. On December 12 the postal governors accepted most of the PRC rate increase proposals and named Feb. 17, 1985, as their effective date.

Volume. Volume figures continued to favor the USPS, with the total for FY 1984 figured at 131 billion pieces, up an extraordinary 12 billion over the total for FY 1983.

Technology. By the end of FY 1984 both mail volume and worker productivity were up close to 50% over 1970. Improved technology, related mainly to the sorting of letters and other flat pieces, was responsible for the latter. Much of the new machinery also assisted development of the new 9-digit code system, known as "ZIP + 4." Congress authorized this to begin in October 1983, and large bulk mailers were offered attractive discounts to use it.

By December 1984, U.S. postal productivity was by far the highest in the world, and U.S. first-class letter rates were tied with those of Belgium for the lowest. Paul Carlin succeeded Bolger as PMG on Jan. 1, 1985. A USPS staff member since 1969, Carlin headed the service's central region.

The main casualty of the year was E-COM, the service's first domestic form of electronic mail, initiated in 1982. Costs were high and volume too low. The postal governors put the system up for sale in the fall of 1984.

Canada. Under a government corporation formed in 1981, the Canadian postal deficit was halved, personnel cut by 3,000, and 1987 set as the target date for a balanced budget.

PAUL P. VAN RIPER, *Texas A&M University*

PRINCE EDWARD ISLAND

Economic development strategy and federal-provincial cooperation were twin themes in Prince Edward Island (P.E.I.) during 1984. The political landscape tilted with the September 4 federal election.

Economic and Financial. A new development strategy aimed at helping island businesses enter international markets was unveiled at the opening of the Legislature on March 6. The speech from the Throne outlined a plan to establish the P.E.I. Development Agency, a Crown corporation that would stimulate private investment and open new markets. "We've been out into the market place, to various countries outside Canada, and the business is there," Premier Jim Lee told reporters. "P.E.I. can share in that market but we have to identify it and then come back and produce the right products."

In a budget presentation on April 10, Finance Minister Lloyd MacPhail projected a 1984–85 fiscal year deficit of some C$9.8 million, down from the $18.2 million deficit projected for the previous year (which actually came in lower because of unexpected revenues). The budget, which introduced few new programs, called for spending of $440.3 million and revenues of $432 million.

A five-year, $120 million regional development agreement between P.E.I. and the federal government was signed June 13 in Charlottetown. The agreement was concluded under an umbrella accord providing for a joint approach to the province's economic development. Under a second agreement, Ottawa and P.E.I. would each contribute $500,000 toward a program to analyze prospects and programs for growth.

Education. The federal government is committed to spend a minimum of $2.9 million on French-language education in P.E.I. over three years, under a federal provincial agreement signed on May 10. In 1982–83 more than 500 students were enrolled in French first-language programs in P.E.I. schools and 15,600 in French second-language programs.

Politics. In the September 4 federal election, the Conservatives won three of the island's four seats, whereas previously the Tories had held two seats. Liberal Bennett Campbell, the island's representative in two successive Liberal cabinets, lost his Cardigan seat to Tory Pat Binns. Tom McMillan, who retained his Hillsborough seat, was later named tourism minister.

Federal Presence. The new, $20 million headquarters of the federal Veterans Affairs Department was officially opened on June 26 in Charlottetown. An estimated 1,400 permanent jobs have been created on the island as a result of the move of the Veterans Affairs operation from Ottawa.

JOHN BEST, *"Canada World News"*

PRINCE EDWARD
ISLAND • Information Highlights

Area: 2,184 sq mi (5 657 km²).
Population (April 1984 est.): 125,000.
Chief Cities (1981 census): Charlottetown, the capital, 15,282; Summerside, 7,828.
Government (1984): *Chief Officers*—lt. gov., Joseph Aubin Doiron; premier, James Lee (Progressive Conservative); atty. gen., Horace B. Carver, *Legislature*—Legislative Assembly, 32 members.
Provincial Finances (1984–85 fiscal year budget): *Revenues,* $434,970,000; *expenditures,* $464,222,000.
Personal Income (average weekly earnings, May 1984): $322.91.
Labor Force (July 1984, seasonally adjusted): *Employed workers,* 15 years of age and over, 50,000; *unemployed* 7,000 (11.9%).
Education (1984–85): *Enrollment*—elementary and secondary schools, 24,960 pupils; postsecondary (1983–84)—universities, 2,400; community colleges, 770.
(All monetary figures given in Canadian dollars.)

PRISONS

The U.S. prison population again reached record levels in 1984, as the effects of stricter sentencing laws became apparent throughout the country. Multibillion dollar prison building projects went into effect as officials tried to keep up with the increasing number of criminals being taken into custody for longer periods of time. Application of the death penalty reached its highest level in 20 years.

Overcrowding. The number of persons in a federal or state prison reached 438,830 at the end of 1983 and 454,136 by mid-1984, almost double the number of a decade earlier. Official figures do not include juveniles, persons incarcerated in jails and other short-term detention facilities, or the 1.5 million persons under supervised detention (probation or parole). About 10% of the prison inmates are kept in prisons built before 1875, and a majority are housed in facilities constructed before World War II.

The United States imprisons more people than any other country in the Western world. As of mid-1984, about one out of every 520 Americans was in a federal or state prison. In certain parts of the country, more than one out of every ten black males between the ages of 18 and 34 were in prison. Almost every prison in the country was filled beyond capacity, and the largest prison construction program in history was under way.

Politicians at most levels of government continued the trend of recent years to enact more stringent and severe prison terms. In October, Congress passed and President Reagan signed a crime package that included increased penalties for drug dealers, repeat offenders, and others. Provisions were also included that allow judges for the first time to detain certain allegedly dangerous defendants before trial. In June the Supreme Court ruled 6–3 that states

Virginia's Mecklenburg Correctional Center (right) was the scene of a two-day prisoner rebellion in August, when 32 inmates took nine hostages and seized a prison control center.

could constitutionally detain juvenile criminal suspects before bringing them to trial *(Schall v. Martin)*. Justice William H. Rehnquist, writing for the majority, argued that the freedom of a juvenile suspect had to "be qualified by the recognition that juveniles, unlike adults, are always in some form of custody. . . . Children, by definition, are not assumed to have the capacity to take care of themselves." In dissenting, Justice Thurgood Marshall noted that it was "difficult to take seriously" the majority's analogy between parental and state custody.

Voters in some states approved prison bond construction issues. In California, for example, they approved $550 million for construction of state and county prisons. In other states, such as New York, officials faced with voter rejection of bond issues found ways to underwrite massive new prison construction through diversion of funds from urban development agencies. In many cases official figures for prison construction are only the tip of the iceberg, since they do not take into account staffing and maintenance costs. The facilities must be staffed around the clock every day of the year, and, with conditions deteriorating and union activity increasing, the pay rates for prison personnel continue to rise. U.S. Sen. Alphonse D'Amato (R-NY) proposed tax incentives for private developers to build and lease buildings to state and local governments for use as prisons. He argued that prisons offer "a guaranteed stream of income" since there would never be any worry about vacancies; savings eventually could be passed on to the public.

Prison officials were being forced to learn new skills in crisis management as overcrowded conditions contributed to already high levels of tension and unrest. In August only a threat of direct assault by state police ended a two-day prisoner rebellion at Virginia's Mecklenburg Correctional Center. Several guards had been stabbed, and the 32 participants took nine hostages and seized a control center of the 300-bed prison. During the same month, the New York State Department of Correctional Services disciplined 182 inmates at the Attica prison for refusing to return to their cells after an inmate had been shot by a corrections officer.

Death Penalty. During 1984 the number of prisoners on death row passed 1,400. By mid-October the number of executions for the year reached 15 with the electrocution of Linwood Briley, convicted of shooting a country-western disc jockey during a robbery. In May, Briley had led an escape effort from the death row in Virginia where he had been held since 1979. All the escapees eventually were recaptured, although Briley and his brother, James, also on death row, avoided arrest for 19 days.

In September, Timothy Baldwin was executed in Louisiana for the 1978 murder of Mary James Peters, the godmother of his youngest son. Baldwin became the 24th person executed in the United States since the Supreme Court ruled in 1976 that the death penalty was constitutional. Baldwin to the end maintained his innocence, but appeals courts rejected arguments that his rights were violated when a prosecutor offered to let him plead guilty to second-degree murder, which does not carry a death penalty. Baldwin declined and elected to stand trial.

Also in September, Gov. James B. Hunt, Jr., of North Carolina, in the midst of a difficult political fight for the seat of Sen. Jesse Helms, indicated that he would not block the execution of Margie Velma Barfield. Mrs. Barfield was convicted in 1978 of poisoning her fiancé with arsenic. She was executed on November 2, the first woman put to death in the United States in 22 years.

According to the Justice Department, 252 death sentences had been handed down in 1983, and more than 100 inmates left death row: five were executed, five died of natural causes, three committed suicide, one was killed in an attempted escape, and 99 had their sentences either commuted or overturned. Some experts pointed out that additional security against suicide would have to be provided, since the resumption of executions made life on death row even more excruciating.

See also CRIME; LAW.

DONALD GOODMAN
John Jay College of Criminal Justice

PRIZES AND AWARDS

NOBEL PRIZES[1]

Chemistry: R. Bruce Merrifield, Rockefeller University, honored for his development of a rapid automated method for making proteins that "has created completely new possibilities in the field of peptide and protein chemistry . . . as well as in the field of nucleic acid chemistry. . . ."

Economics: Richard Stone, Cambridge University (retired), cited for being "mainly responsible for creating an accounting system for nations that has been indispensable in monitoring their financial position, in tracking trends in national development, and in comparing one nation's economic workings with another's."

Literature: Jaroslav Seifert, Czech poet. (*See* page 320.)

Peace Prize: Bishop Desmond Tutu, South African Council of Churches. (*See* BIOGRAPHY.)

Physics: Carlo Rubbia, Harvard University; Simon van der Meer, CERN, cited "for their decisive contributions to the large project, which led to the discovery of the field particles W and Z, communicators of weak interaction."

Physiology or Medicine: César Milstein, British Medical Research Council's Laboratory of Molecular Biology, Cambridge University; Georges J. F. Köhler and Niels K. Jerne (professor emeritus), Basel Institute of Immunology, honored for "giving science a revolutionary new technique for producing antibodies that is used today for countless purposes in laboratories throughout the world."

[1] about $190,000 each category

ART

American Academy and Institute of Arts and Letters Awards

Academy–Institute Awards ($5,000 ea.): art—Alice Adams, Donna Dennis, Nathan Oliveira, Tony Rosenthal, Herman Cherry; music—James Dashow, William Kraft, John Melby, Ellen Taaffe Zwilich

Arnold W. Brunner Memorial Prize in Architecture ($1,000): Peter Eisenman

Award of Merit for Sculpture: Raoul Hague

Charles Ives Fellowship ($10,000): Nicholas C. K. Thorne

Charles Ives Scholarships ($5,000 ea.): Richard Campanelli, Kenneth Fuchs, Laura Karpman, Bright Sheng, Larry Stukenholtz, Gregory Youtz

Distinguished Service to the Arts: Roger L. Stevens

Goddard Lieberson Fellowships ($10,000 ea.): Primous Fountain III, Peter Lieberson

Gold Medal in Architecture: Gordon Bunshaft

Marjorie Peabody Waite Award ($1,500): Herman Berlinski (composer)

Nathan and Lillian Berliawsky Award ($5,000): The American Composers Orchestra

Richard and Hinda Rosenthal Foundation Award ($5,000): James Brown (in art)

Walter Hinrichsen Award: Ross Bauer

American Institute of Architects Honor Awards: (*See* ARCHITECTURE.)

Capezio Dance Award: William, Harold, Lew Christensen

Dance Magazine Awards: Alexandra Danilova, Robert Irving, Donald Saddler, Tommy Tune

John F. Kennedy Center Honors for career achievement in the performing arts: Lena Horne, Danny Kaye, Gian Carlo Menotti, Arthur Miller, Isaac Stern

National Academy of Recording Arts and Sciences Grammy Awards for excellence in phonograph records

Album of the year: *Thriller*, Michael Jackson

Classical album: Mahler: Symphony No. 9 in D Major, Sir Georg Solti (conductor), James Mallinson (producer)

Country music song: *Stranger in My House*, Mike Reid (songwriter)

Jazz vocal performance—female: Ella Fitzgerald, *The Best Is Yet to Come*

Jazz vocal performance—male: Mel Tormé, *Top Drawer*

New artist: Culture Club

Record of the year: *Beat It*, Michael Jackson

Song of the year: *Every Breath You Take*, Sting (songwriter)

Naumburg Chamber Music Awards: Lydian String Quartet, Aspen Wind Quintet

Pritzker Architecture Prize ($100,000): Richard Meier

Pulitzer Prize for Music: Bernard Rands, *Canti del Sole*

Samuel H. Scripps–American Dance Festival Award ($25,000): Hanya Holm

JOURNALISM

George Polk Memorial Awards

Consumer reporting: Marcia Stepanek, Stephen Franklin, *The Detroit Free Press*

Economics reporting: Dennis Camire, Mark Rohner, Gannet News Service

Foreign-affairs reporting: Philip Taubman, *The New York Times*

Foreign reporting: Joseph Lelyveld, *The New York Times*

Local reporting: Jim McGee, *The Miami Herald*

Medical reporting: Benjamin Weiser, *The Washington Post*

National reporting: Robert R. Frump, Timothy Dwyer, *The Philadelphia Inquirer*

Regional reporting: Paul Lieberman, Celia Dugger, *The Atlanta Journal and Constitution*

Special interest reporting: *The Amicus Journal*, published by the National Resources Defense Council

Television documentary: WGBH, Boston, Public Broadcasting System

Television reporting—local: John Fosholt, Ward Lucas, KBTV News, Denver

Television reporting—network: Don McNeill, CBS News

Special award: Youssef M. Ibrahim, *The Wall Street Journal*

Career award: William L. Shirer

Maria Moors Cabot Prizes ($1,000 ea.): Kenneth Gordon, *The Trinidad Express*, Trinidad, W. I.; Alister and Cynthia Hughes, *The Grenada Newsletter*, Grenada, W. I.; Frank N. Manitzas, ABC News. Special citations to Harold Fitz-Herbert Hoyte, National Public Radio, John Hoagland (posthumously)

National Magazine Awards

Design: *House and Garden*

Essays and criticism: *The New Republic* for three essays by Charles Krauthammer

Fiction: *Seventeen* for "An Eighty Percent Chance," "The Education of Esther Eileen," and "Teenage Wasteland"

General excellence awards: *The American Lawyer*, *Outside*, *House and Garden*, *National Geographic*

Public service: *The New Yorker* for "Breaking the Spell"

Reporting: *Vanity Fair* for "When Memory Goes"

Single topic issue: *Esquire* for "Fifty Who Made the Difference"

Service to the individual: *New York* for "How Well Does Your Bank Treat You?"

Overseas Press Club Awards

Book on foreign affairs: David Shipler, *Russia: Broken Idols, Solemn Dreams*

Business news reporting from abroad: (magazines and books)—Michael Cieply, *Forbes Magazine*; (newspapers and wire services)—Paul A. Gigot, *The Wall Street Journal*

Cartoon on foreign affairs: Richard Locher, *Chicago Tribune*

Daily newspaper or wire service interpretation of foreign affairs: Karen Elliott House, *The Wall Street Journal*

Daily newspaper or wire service reporting from abroad: Don Bohning, *The Miami Herald*

Economic news reporting from abroad (magazines and books)—*Business Week*, "Can Mitterrand Remake France's Economy?" (newspapers and wire services)—Bob Gibson, *Los Angeles Times*

Magazine story on foreign affairs: *Newsweek*, "Nuclear War: Can We Reduce the Risk"

Magazine reporting from abroad: Christopher Dickey, *The New Republic*

Photographic reporting from abroad: (magazines and books)—Peter Jordan, *Time;* (newspapers and wire services)—Stan Grossfeld, *The Boston Globe*

Radio interpretation of foreign affairs: Robert Kotowski, KYW Newsradio

Radio spot news from abroad: Jim Laurie, ABC News Radio

Television interpretation or documentary on foreign affairs: Public Television, *Inside Story*, "Dateline: Moscow" and "Inside the USSR" (correspondent—Hodding Carter; producers—Philip Burton, Christopher Koch, Ned Schnurman, Joseph M. Russin)

Television spot news reporting from abroad: Richard Threlkeld, ABC News; Cable News Network

Robert Capa Gold Medal: Jim Nachtwey, *Time*

Madeline Dane Ross Award: Bob Adams, James B. Forbes, *St. Louis Post-Dispatch*

Pulitzer Prizes

Commentary: Vermont Royster, *The Wall Street Journal*

Criticism: Paul Goldberger, *The New York Times*

Editorial cartooning: Paul Conrad, *The Los Angeles Times*

Editorial writing: Albert Scardino, *The Georgia Gazette*

Feature photography: Anthony Suau, *The Denver Post*

Feature writing: Peter Mark Rinearson, *The Seattle Times*

General local reporting: *Newsday*

International reporting: Karen Elliott House, *The Wall Street Journal*

National reporting: John Noble Wilford, *The New York Times*

Public service: *The Los Angeles Times*

Special local reporting: *The Boston Globe*

Spot news photography: Stan Grossfeld, *The Boston Globe*

LITERATURE

Alfred and Ellen Knowles Harcourt Awards ($10,000 ea.): Lloyd Goodrich, *Thomas Eakins;* Edward Burns, *The Gertrude Stein–Carl Van Vechten Correspondence, 1913–1946*

American Academy and Institute of Arts and Letters Awards

Academy-Institute Awards ($5,000 ea.): Amy Clampitt, Don DeLillo, Sanford Friedman, Robert Hass, Lincoln Kirstein, Romulus Linney, Bobbie Ann Mason, Craig Nova

The American Academy in Rome Fellowship in Literature: David St. John

E. M. Forster Award ($5,000): Humphrey Carpenter

Gold Medal in History: George F. Kennan

Harold D. Vursell Memorial Award ($5,000): W. M. Spackman

Jean Stein Award ($5,000): Andrea Lee

Morton Dauwen Zabel Award ($2,500): Jamaica Kincaid

Richard and Hinda Rosenthal Foundation Award ($3,000): Danny Santiago

Sue Kaufman Prize for First Fiction ($1,000): Denis Johnson

Witter Bynner Prize for Poetry ($1,500): Henry Taylor

American Book Awards ($10,000 ea.)

Fiction: Ellen Gilchrist, *Victory Over Japan*

First fiction: Harriet Doerr, *Stones for Ibarra*

Nonfiction: Robert V. Remini, *Andrew Jackson and the Course of American Democracy, 1833–1845, Volume III*

Bancroft Prizes ($4,000 ea.): Louis R. Harlan, *Booker T. Washington: The Wizard of Tuskegee 1901–15;* Paul Starr, *The Social Transformation of American Medicine*

Bruce Catton Prize ($5,000): Duma Malone

Canada's Governor-General Literary Awards

English-language awards:

Drama—Anne Chislett, *Quiet in the Land*

Fiction—Leon Rooke, *Shakespeare's Dog*

Nonfiction—Jeffery Williams, *Byng of Vimy: General and Governor-General*

Poetry—David Donnell, *Settlements*

French–language awards:

Drama—René Gingras, *Syncope*

Fiction—Suzanne Jacob, *Laura Laur*

Nonfiction—Maurice Cusson, *Le contrôle social du crime*

Poetry—Suzanne Paradis, *Un goût de sel*

Edward MacDowell Medal: Mary McCarthy

National Book Critics Circle

Biography/autobiography: Joyce Johnson, *Minor Characters*

Criticism: John Updike, *Hugging the Shore: Essays in Criticism*

Fiction: William Kennedy, *Ironweed*

Nonfiction: Seymour M. Hersh, *The Price of Power: Kissinger in the Nixon White House*

Poetry: James Merrill, *The Changing Light at Sandover*

National Medal for Literature ($15,000): Mary McCarthy

Neustadt International Prize for Literature ($25,000): Paavo Haavikko

PEN Literary Awards

Ernest Hemingway Foundation Award for first fiction ($7,500): Joan Chase, *During the Reign of the Queen of Persia*

PEN Translation Prize ($1,000): William Weaver for *The Name of the Rose* by Umberto Eco

Renato Poggioli Translation Award ($3,000): Stephen Sartarelli for *Horcynus Orca* by Stefano D'Arrigo

PEN/Nelson Algren Fiction Award ($1,000 ea.): Chris Mazza, Martha Miyatake

PEN/Faulkner Award ($5,000): John Wideman, *Sent for You Yesterday*

Pulitzer Prizes

Biography: Dr. Louis R. Harlan, *Booker T. Washington: The Wizard of Tuskegee, 1901–1915*

Fiction: William Kennedy, *Ironweed*

General nonfiction: Paul Starr, *Social Transformation of American Medicine*

History: (no award given)

Poetry: Mary Oliver, *American Primitive*

Special citation: Theodor Seuss Geisel (Dr. Seuss)

(*See also Libraries.*)

MOTION PICTURES

Academy of Motion Picture Arts and Sciences ("Oscar") Awards

Actor—leading: Robert Duvall, *Tender Mercies*

Actor—supporting: Jack Nicholson, *Terms of Endearment*

Actress—leading: Shirley MacLaine, *Terms of Endearment*

Actress—supporting: Linda Hunt, *The Year of Living Dangerously*

Cinematography: Sven Nykvist, *Fanny and Alexander*

Costume design: Marik Vos, *Fanny and Alexander*

Director: James Brooks, *Terms of Endearment*

Film: *Terms of Endearment*

Foreign-language film: *Fanny and Alexander* (Sweden)

Music—original song score or adaptation: Michel Legrand, Alan and Marilyn Bergman, *Yentl*

Music—song: *Flashdance . . . What a Feeling* (*Flashdance*)

Screenplay—original: Horton Foote, *Tender Mercies*

Screenplay—adaptation: James Brooks, *Terms of Endearment*

Gordon E. Sawyer award: Dr. John G. Frayne

Jean Hersholt Humanitarian award: M. J. Frankovich

Honorary award: Hal Roach

Visual Effects Achievement: *Return of the Jedi*

American Film Institute's Life Achievement Award: Lillian Gish

Cannes Film Festival Awards

Golden Palm award: Wim Wenders, *Paris, Texas*

Best actor: Alfredo Lauda, Francisco Rabal, *The Holy Innocents* (shared)

Best actress: Helen Mirren, *Cal*

Best director: Bertrand Tavernier, *A Sunday in the Country*

Best screenplay: Theo Angelopoulos, Theo Vatinos, Tonino Guerra, *Voyage to Cythere*

Best artistic contribution: Peter Biziou, *Another Country*

PUBLIC SERVICE

American Institute for Public Service Jefferson Awards:
Donna Velnick, Sally K. Ride, William H. Webster, Campbell and Frances Cutler, Margaret Marshall, Betty Taylor, Maude Callen, Virginia Clemmer, J. Peter Grace

Harry S. Truman Public Service Award: Margaret Truman Daniel

Templeton Prize for progress in religion ($205,000): Rev. Michael Bourdeaux

UNESCO Peace Education Prize ($60,000): International Physicians for the Prevention of Nuclear War

U.S. Presidential Medal of Freedom: Howard H. Baker, Jr., James Cagney, Whittaker Chambers (posthumously), Leo Cherne, Terence Cardinal Cooke (posthumously), Denton Cooley, Tennessee Ernie Ford, Hector Garcia, Andrew Goodpaster, Henry M. Jackson (posthumously), Lincoln Kirstein, Louis L'Amour, Joseph M. A. H. Luns, Norman Vincent Peale, Jackie Robinson (posthumously), Carlos P. Romulos, Anwar el-Sadat (posthumously), Eunice Kennedy Shriver

SCIENCE

Albert Lasker Awards
   Basic research ($15,000, shared): César Milstein, Medical Research Council, Cambridge, England; Georges J. F. Köhler, Basel Institute of Immunology; Michael Potter, National Cancer Institute
   Clinic research ($15,000): Paul C. Lauterbur, State University of New York at Stony Brook
   Public service award (15,000): Henry J. Heimlich, Xavier University, Cincinnati, OH

Bristol-Myers Award for distinguished achievement in cancer research ($50,000): Robert A. Weinberg

General Motors Cancer Research Foundation Awards ($130,000 ea.): Michael Bishop and Harold E. Varmus (shared), Robert C. Gallo, Barnett Rosenberg

Hammer Prize for cancer research ($100,000): Michael J. Bishop, Harold E. Varmus, Raymond K. Erikson, Robert Weinberg

Louisa Gross Horwitz Prize for research in biology or biochemistry ($22,000 shared): Michael S. Brown, Joseph L. Goldstein, University of Texas Health Science Center, Dallas, TX

TELEVISION AND RADIO

Academy of Television Arts and Sciences ("Emmy") Awards
   Actor—comedy series: John Ritter, *Three's Company* (ABC)
   Actor—drama series: Tom Selleck, *Magnum, P.I.* (CBS)
   Actor—limited series: Laurence Olivier, *Laurence Olivier's King Lear* (SYN)
   Actress—comedy series: Jane Curtin, *Kate and Allie* (CBS)
   Actress—drama series: Tyne Daly, *Cagney and Lacey* (CBS)
   Actress—limited series: Jane Fonda, *The Dollmaker* (ABC)
   Children's program: *He Makes Me Feel Like Dancin'* (NBC)
   Classical program in the performing arts: "Plácido Domingo Celebrates Seville" *Great Performances* (PBS)
   Comedy series: *Cheers* (NBC)
   Drama series: *Hill Street Blues* (NBC)
   Informational series: *A Walk Through the 20th Century with Bill Moyers* (PBS)
   Informational special: *America Remembers John F. Kennedy* (SYN)
   Limited series: "Concealed Enemies" *American Playhouse* (PBS)
   Special drama: *Something About Amelia* (ABC)
   Supporting actor—comedy series: Pat Harrington, Jr., *One Day at a Time* (CBS)
   Supporting actor—drama series: Bruce Weitz, *Hill Street Blues* (NBC)
   Supporting actor—limited series or special: Art Carney, *Terrible Joe Moran* (CBS)
   Supporting actress—comedy series: Rhea Perlman, *Cheers* (NBC)
   Supporting actress—drama series: Alfre Woodard, *Hill Street Blues* (NBC)
   Supporting actress—limited series or special: Roxana Zal, *Something About Amelia* (ABC)
   Variety, music, or comedy program: *The 6th Annual Kennedy Center Honors: A Celebration of the Performing Arts* (CBS)

George Foster Peabody Awards
Radio: Thomas Looker, *New England Almanac: Portraits in Sound;* Don McGannon, Westinghouse Broadcasting Corp.; KMOX Radio, St. Louis, *Times Beach: Born 1925, Died 1983;* South Carolina Educational Radio Network, *Piano Jazz;* WCCO Radio, Minneapolis, MN, *Debbie Pielow: Waiting for a Heart;* WMAL Radio, Washington, *The Jeffersonian World of Dumas Malone;* WRAL Radio, Raleigh, NC, *Victims;* WSM Radio, Nashville, TN, *The Grand Ole Opry*

Television: ABC and Dick Clark Productions, *The Woman Who Willed a Miracle;* CBS Entertainment and Mendelson-Melendez Productions, *What Have We Learned, Charlie Brown;* CBS Entertainment and Smith-Hemion Productions, *Romeo and Juliet on Ice;* CBS News, *The Plane That Fell From the Sky;* CBS News, *60 Minutes* (segment on the life sentence of Lenell Geter); Chrysalis-Yellen Productions and NBC, *Prisoner Without a Name, Cell Without a Number;* KCTS, Seattle, WA, *Diagnosis: AIDS;* KRON-TV, San Francisco, *Climate of Death;* NBC and Edgar J. Scherick Associates, *He Makes Me Feel Like Dancin';* NBC and Motown Productions, *Motown 25: Yesterday, Today, Forever;* Sunbow Productions, NY, *The Great Space Coaster;* WBBM-TV, Chicago, *Studebaker: Less Than They Promised;* WBRZ-TV, Baton Rouge, LA, *Give Me That Bigtime Religion;* WCCO-TV, Minneapolis, *I-Team: Ambulances;* WGBH-TV, Boston, *Nova: The Miracle of Life;* WGBH-TV (plus two coproducers), for a 13-episode history of the Vietnam War; WNBC-TV, NY, *Asylum in the Streets;* WTBS-TV, Atlanta, *Portrait of America;* WTTW, Chicago, and the BBC, *The Making of a Continent;* WTTW, Chicago, *The Merry Widow*

Humanitas Prizes
   Long-form category ($25,000): John Pielmeier, *Choices of the Heart*
   One-hour category ($15,000): Peter Silverman, Steven Bochco, Jeffrey Lewis, David Milch for an episode of *Hill Street Blues*
   One-half-hour category ($10,000): Gary David Goldberg, Ruth Bennett, *Family Ties*

THEATER

Antoinette Perry ("Tony") Awards
   Actor—drama: Jeremy Irons, *The Real Thing*
   Actor—musical: George Hearn, *La Cage aux Folles*
   Actress—drama: Glenn Close, *The Real Thing*
   Actress—musical: Chita Rivera, *The Rink*
   Director—drama: Mike Nichols, *The Real Thing*
   Director—musical: Arthur Laurents, *La Cage aux Folles*
   Featured actor—drama: Joe Mantegna, *Glengarry Glen Ross*
   Featured actor—musical: Hinton Battle, *The Tap Dance Kid*
   Featured actress—drama: Christine Baranski, *The Real Thing*
   Featured actress—musical: Lila Kedrova, *Zorba*
   Musical: *La Cage aux Folles*
   Musical—book: Harvey Fierstein, *La Cage aux Folles*
   Musical—score: Jerry Herman, *La Cage aux Folles*
   Play: *The Real Thing*, Tom Stoppard
   Reproduction of a play or musical: *Death of a Salesman*
   Special awards: Joseph Papp; The Old Globe Theater, San Diego; Peter Brook and Alexander Cohen for "achievement in the lyric theater" for their production of *La Tragédie de Carmen;* Peter Feller; Al Hirschfeld.

New York Drama Critics Circle Awards
   Best new play: *The Real Thing* by Tom Stoppard
   Best American play: *Glengarry Glen Ross*
   Best musical: *Sunday in the Park with George* by Stephen Sondheim and James Lapine
   Special citation: Samuel Beckett

Pulitzer Prize for Drama: David Mamet, *Glengarry Glen Ross*

PUBLISHING

The U.S. print media shared in the nation's expanding economy in 1984. In an exciting news year, the U.S. presidential campaign and the Olympics provided opportunities for special reporting, increased ad sales, and special editions. Publishers recorded record profits. Despite an increase to $535 per metric ton of newsprint and a 20–25% hike for magazine paper, consumption by publishers continued to rise. Book sales were up, with familiar names on the best-seller lists. And new magazines appeared at a one-per-day pace, though many fell by the wayside.

Books. Book sales for 1984 were termed "mostly solid and stable" by *Publishers Weekly*'s John P. Dessauer, who viewed the year as "bright." The U.S. Commerce Department estimated that sales would approach $9.2 billion (U.S.), up 10% over 1983. An attendance record of 18,000 was set at the American Booksellers Association convention in Washington, DC, in May.

The Cambridge University Press celebrated its 400th anniversary in 1984. The Beacon Press reached 130. And children's author Theodor Seuss Geisel, known for his 44 Dr. Seuss books, reached 80; his books have sold in excess of 100 million copies. Louis L'Amour, known for his 89 Western books, was awarded the highest U.S. civilian honor, the Presidential Medal of Freedom; his newest book, *The Walking Drum,* has a 12th-century plot.

One problem that continued to disturb publishers was piracy. The Association of American Publishers told a Senate committee that "the problem is approaching crisis proportions." Twelve countries, mostly in the Far East and South America, were blamed. Firms estimated that losses could reach $100 million annually. All in all, however, it was a good year for book publishing, with several categories flourishing.

The market for computer-oriented books continued to expand. R. R. Bowker Co. tabulated some 3,000 new titles by mid-1984. *Publishers Weekly* carried a special supplement on software publishing and selling.

The romance market, meanwhile, became glutted. Silhouette Books was acquired by Simon and Schuster. Some 300 aspiring authors met for the Romance Writers of America convention to hear experts in this $300–$400 million market. Among individual authors, Leo Buscaglia remained popular. His *Living, Loving, and Learning* was followed by *Loving Each Other.*

Diet-fitness plans, cat cartoons, cookbooks, and religious volumes also continued to sell well. Movie-television stars revealed how to slim down, with advice from Stefanie Powers, Jaclyn Smith, Raquel Welch, Victoria Princi-

Larry Dale Gordon, Sygma

Theodor Seuss Geisel—better known as Dr. Seuss—turned 80 years old and won a special Pulitzer citation for his "contribution of nearly half a century to the education and enjoyment of America's children and their parents."

pal, and others. Jim Davis joined the fitness craze with *Garfield Tips the Scales.* Early in the year, *Garfield Eats His Heart Out* and *Garfield Sits Around the House* were best-sellers. Heathcliff, drawn by George Gately, joined the cat parade.

The Bible and other religious books were heavily promoted and sold well. Billy Graham's *Approaching Hoofbeats: The Four Horsemen of the Apocalypse* was a leader. Robert Schuller had two widely read volumes, *Tough Times Never Last, but Tough People Do* and *Tough-Minded Faith for Tenderhearted People.*

The 1983 report on U.S. schools by the National Commission on Excellence in Education, titled "A Nation at Risk," prompted a spate of new books detailing the plight of education in America. In the realm of politics, author and editor Ronald Steel pointed out the lack of any "serious campaign biography or a revelation of conscience" about the 1984 presidential candidates.

Few newcomers reached the best-seller lists. John Naisbitt's *Megatrends*, Carole Jackson's *Color Me Beautiful*, and Thomas J. Peters' and Robert Waterman, Jr.'s *In Search of Excellence* were on the 1982, 1983, and 1984 lists. Another longtimer was Erma Bombeck's *Motherhood: The Second Oldest Profession*.

Other popular books in early 1984 were James Michener's *Poland;* Stephen King's *Pet Sematary,* and Umberto Eco's *The Name of the Rose.* Paperback leaders were King's *Christine;* Danielle Steel's *Once Upon a Lifetime;* Michener's *Space,* and *The One Minute Manager* by Kenneth Blanchard and Spencer Johnson.

Later in the year, fiction leaders included Helen Hooven Santmyer's *. . . And Ladies of the Club;* Gore Vidal's *Lincoln;* Robert Ludlum's *The Aquitaine Progression;* Jeffrey Archer's *First Among Equals,* and Frederick Forsyth's *The Fourth Protocol.*

Nonfiction leaders were *The Kennedys: An American Dream* by Peter Collier and David Horowitz; Bob Woodward's *Wired;* David A. Yallop's *In God's Name;* Bob Greene's *Good Morning, Merry Sunshine,* and William L. Shirer's *The Nightmare Years: 1930–1940.*

Paperback leaders were Judith Rossner's *August;* Jackie Collins' *Hollywood Wives;* Steel's *Thurston House;* Lawrence Sanders' *The Seduction of Peter S.,* and Susan Schaeffer's *The Madness of a Seduced Woman.*

William Least Heat Moon's *Blue Highways* stayed on the list, as did others by Bombeck, Buscaglia, and Shirley MacLaine. *Fatal Vision* by Joe McGinniss, Robert Haas' *Eat to Win,* Norman Mailer's *Tough Guys Don't Dance,* and Margaret Truman's murder mysteries with a Washington background sold well. Eudora Welty's *One Writer's Beginnings* and Barbara Tuchman's *The March of Folly* also were popular. Bill Adler and Thomas Chastain wrote *Who Killed the Robins Family?* and offered $10,000 for a reader's solution; *The Revenge of the Robins Family* followed. And Andy Rooney was back with *Pieces of My Mind.*

Magazines. Healthy increases in advertising revenue and circulation, a glut in computer magazines, and the *Penthouse*–Miss America controversy highlighted a busy year in magazine publishing. According to the Magazine Publishers Association (MPA), there were 10,809 periodicals in 1984, up from 9,719 five years earlier. However, only 1,751 were consumer and farm magazines; others were for more specialized audiences.

The latest circulation and ad revenue statistics signaled the renewed health of magazine publishing. The per-issue circulation of consumer magazines in 1983 was 305,240,173, a record. Approximately 73% were sold by subscription. Single-copy prices averaged $1.97 in 1983, subscriptions $21.53. The industry realized a longtime goal when the share of overall revenues from circulation surpassed 50%. And the first half of 1984 showed advertising revenues up 17.3%, to more than $2 billion.

Computer magazines, with scores of new titles, appeared to be nearing the point of shakeout. The *Media Industry Newsletter* noted that while an estimated $1.46 billion would be spent on computer ads in 1984, this field had grown "too fast, too soon." According to *Advertising Age,* the "top ten magazines got 80% of the ad dollars, leaving most of the market to fight for leftovers." Business publications were doing well, with ad revenues up 20% the first half of 1984.

Special issues were noteworthy. In late 1983, *BYTE* had a record 728-page edition. *Esquire* had 618 pages in its Golden Anniversary Collection number. *Vogue,* in fall 1984, topped 800 pages. *Sports Illustrated* honored the Olympics in a 536-page edition that carried a record $24 million in advertising.

In the year's biggest publishing controversy, *Penthouse* sold out the five-million-copy run of its 15th anniversary edition, which featured nude photographs of Miss America Vanessa Williams. A reorder of 850,000 copies followed. At *Playboy,* President Christie Hefner reported the company's first profits in two years.

In other industry news, *Newsweek* moved into Australia and planned a Japanese-language edition. The *National Geographic Traveler,* a quarterly, made its debut. *Seventeen* marked its 40th birthday with record circulation and ad revenue. *U.S. News & World Report* was sold for some $160 million to Mortimer Zuckerman, also the owner of *The Atlantic.* At *Reader's Digest,* changes were underway following the death of the last of the cofounders, Lila Atcheson Wallace. And *The New Yorker* found itself in a controversy when it was revealed that one of its writers, Alastair Reid, apparently had made up items in some of his stories; editor William Shawn called it "a journalistic mistake," a violation of the weekly's principles.

Cable television remained an important competitive factor for magazines, though perhaps to their benefit. An MPA campaign claimed that magazine readership actually is higher in homes wired for cable. Such gains were noted for 86 of the 122 magazines studied by Simmons Market Research Bureau.

In mid-1984 the Audit Bureau of Circulation (ABC) reported that *Reader's Digest* was still the widest-circulating publication, with 18,012,397 copies per issue. *TV Guide* was second with 17,345,473; *National Geographic* had 10,202,854; *Modern Maturity,* 9,887,549; *Better Homes and Gardens* 8,003,399; *Family Circle,* 7,003,508; *Woman's Day,* 6,858,487; *McCall's,* 6,224,408; *Good Housekeeping,* 5,296,527; and *Ladies' Home Journal,* 5,123,096. Other leaders included *Time, Playboy, Redbook, Penthouse,* and *Newsweek.*

AP/Wide World

James F. Hoge resigned as publisher of the "Chicago Sun-Times" and was named publisher of New York's "Daily News."

In terms of advertising revenues, *Time* remained first with nearly $300 million in 1983 and more than $154 million in the first half of 1984. *TV Guide* remained second, with figures of $269 million and $142 million, respectively. As usual *Business Week* led in ad pages.

Newspapers. Growth was the key trend in U.S. newspaper publishing, with record expenditures of $917 million for new plants, additions, and modernization in 1984. Canadian newspapers allotted $57 million for similar expansion.

Circulation climbed slightly. *Editor & Publisher International Yearbook* listed 446 morning papers with a combined circulation of 33,842,142, and 1,284 evening editions, with 28,802,461. Twenty-nine were all-day papers. The 772 Sunday editions had 56,747,436 in circulation.

The American Newspaper Publishers Association reported that there were 7,547 weeklies with a combined circulation of 43 million. In Canada, the 26 morning and 92 afternoon papers had a combined circulation of 5,546,381, down slightly.

The circulation leaders in 1984, according to ABC, were the *Wall Street Journal*, with 2,100,000; *New York Daily News*, 1,374,858; *USA Today*, 1,200,000; *Los Angeles Times*, 1,057,536; *New York Times*, 970,051; *New York Post*, 963,069; *Washington Post*, 768,288; *Chicago Tribune*, 762,882; *Detroit News*, 657,015; *Detroit Free Press*, 631,087; *Chicago Sun-Times*, 628,285; and *San Francisco Chronicle*, 539,450. Sunday leaders were the *New York Daily News*, 1,813,671; *New York Times*, 1,593,107; *Los Angeles Times*, 1,321,244; *Chicago Tribune*, 1,145,387, and *Washington Post*, 1,042,821.

Group ownership expanded. The nation's 149 groups owned 1,173 dailies and 601 Sunday papers. Gannett, with 85 dailies, led the groups. The Black Press made some gains, with 185 newspapers in 34 states reporting a combined circulation of 3,600,000.

Time magazine's choices for the nation's ten best newspapers were, in alphabetical order, the *Boston Globe, Chicago Tribune, Des Moines Register, Los Angeles Times, Miami Herald, New York Times, Philadelphia Inquirer, St. Petersburg Times, Wall Street Journal,* and *Washington Post*. Other "worthy papers" included the *San Jose Mercury News, Sacramento Bee, Orlando Sentinel, Baltimore Sun, Long Island Newsday, Milwaukee Journal, Louisville Courier-Journal, Charlotte Observer, Dallas Morning News* and *Times Herald,* and *Detroit News* and *Free Press*.

Several important newspapers underwent change of ownership, while others made expansions. In late 1983, Rupert Murdock paid $90 million for the *Chicago Sun/Times,* and the Toronto Sun Publishing Co. acquired the *Houston Post* for $100 million. The *Memphis Press-Scimitar* closed, while the *St. Louis Globe-Democrat* fought for survival. Mergers of morning and afternoon editions occurred in several cities. Meanwhile, the *Atlanta Constitution* and *Journal* spent $50 million on construction, the *Boston Globe* opened a $42 million satellite plant, and the *Hartford Courant* and *Bakersfield Californian* each spent more than $25 million on additions. The *Washington Times,* despite losses of $150 million in its first two years, planned a West Coast edition. And in Window Rock, AZ, the *Navajo Times* became the first Indian daily newspaper. Publishers remained concerned about the expansion of shoppers and other free papers.

Major organizations also underwent change. The National News Council ceased operations because of insufficient financial support. In Canada, publishers considered establishing a similar watchdog operation. Meanwhile, The Newspaper Guild planned an all-out drive to increase its 32,000 membership. The Guild reported a minimum starting salary of $330 per week and a top minimum salary, usually reached after five years, of $520 weekly.

In other developments, the *Wall Street Journal* was caught in a scandal involving a reporter for its "Heard on the Street" column. But the paper covered the story itself, cooperated in the formal investigation, and fired the reporter.

WILLIAM H. TAFT
University of Missouri-Columbia

PUERTO RICO

Politics took center stage in Puerto Rico in 1984 as voters on November 6 turned out of office two-term Gov. Carlos Romero Barceló of the pro-statehood New Progressive Party and elected former Gov. Rafael Hernández Colón of the Popular Democratic Party.

Romero's defeat was a setback for the statehood cause. If reelected, Romero had planned to hold a plebiscite early in 1985 to pave the way for a request to Congress to admit Puerto Rico as the 51st state. But Hernández Colón, 48, who governed the island from January 1973 to January 1977 before losing two straight elections to Romero, has vowed to uphold the current commonwealth relationship between Puerto Rico and the United States.

In the elections, Hernández Colón received 822,040 votes (47.8%) to Romero's 767,710 (44.6%). San Juan Mayor Hernán Padilla, who ran for governor as candidate for the newly formed Puerto Rican Renewal Party, received 68,536 votes (4%). Fernando Martin of the Puerto Rican Independence Party got 61,101 votes (3.6%). Former Catholic University Chancellor Jaime Fuster of the Popular Democratic Party was elected resident commissioner to Washington, succeeding Baltasar Corrada del Rio of the New Progressive Party, who was elected mayor of San Juan.

The Popular Democratic Party widened its control of the legislature, where it has held a majority since 1980. It gained 16 of 27 Senate seats and 34 of 51 seats in the House of Representatives. The near-stalemate in government during the last four years escalated in 1984 into serious clashes between the executive and legislative branches with each accusing the other of abuse of power.

The notorious Cerro Maravilla case continued to haunt the Romero administration up until Election Day. Although the police slayings of two young supporters of Puerto Rican independence occurred on the Cerro Maravilla mountaintop on July 25, 1978, the case continued to draw great interest through televised Senate hearings. The hearings were reconvened just before the elections. Previous testimony had revealed that the police shot to death the two *independentistas*, who were allegedly on a terrorist mission, while they were on their knees after having surrendered, and that law enforcement officials had covered up the facts.

Many island residents were stunned by constant disclosures of corruption in government. The scandals ran the gamut from political kickbacks to personal gain by officials and reached into many government agencies and towns controlled by the New Progressive Party.

Economy. The economy made some progress, but unemployment remained a major problem. Although the Planning Board reported a 4.7% economic growth for fiscal

1983–84—as compared with a 2.2% decline the previous year—and a decreasing 3.7% inflation rate, official unemployment figures stayed at around 20% all year. Government figures revealed that three out of every five 16- to 24-year-olds looking for jobs could not find them.

The Commonwealth suffered a potential loss of hundreds of millions of dollars in liquor tax revenues as a result of a tax reform bill passed by Congress. Among other things, the bill ended Puerto Rico's liquor redistillation program, which would have brought to the island in fiscal 1984–85 some $221 million in revenues from rebates of federal excise taxes on liquor originating in mainland distilleries, shipped to the island for redistilling, then shipped back to the states for sale. Puerto Rico also was excluded from a general increase in liquor excise taxes but continued to receive a rebate of the current federal excise tax on Puerto Rican–produced rum sold in the states.

Papal Visit. An eight-hour stopover on October 12 by Pope John Paul II, the first visit ever of a pope to this predominantly Catholic island of 3.2 million people, buoyed spirits. About 650,000 of the faithful attended a twilight Mass celebrated by the pope, the largest crowd for any event in the island's history.

ROBERT FRIEDMAN, *"The San Juan Star"*

QUEBEC

Quebec political life in 1984 was dominated by one overriding question: how the independence issue should be presented in the next provincial general election, expected in the fall of 1985 or the spring of 1986. In a narrow sense it is a question for the government of the ruling Parti Québécois (PQ) to decide, but it cannot help but profoundly affect the province's future.

Political Showdown. At a policy convention on June 9, PQ delegates voted overwhelmingly to transform the next election, in effect, into a plebiscite on independence. They adopted a resolution stipulating that a vote for the PQ "is a vote for the sovereignty of Quebec."

Whether, in fact, that is the way the party plays it remained uncertain. Premier René Lévesque and some influential members of his cabinet were opposed to the party's tying its hands in this fashion. Opinion polls have shown that independence from Canada—on which the PQ lost a referendum in 1980—is not a popular cause. Therefore, in pushing for independence the party is asking for trouble as it faces a growing challenge from a resurgent Liberal Party.

The enormity of the PQ's task in trying to win a third term was underlined when the party lost four more by-elections to the Liberals—three in June and one in November, bringing to 22 straight the number of by-elections the government has lost since it first took office in 1976. A further blow to Premier Lévesque's leadership was the resignation of five proseparatist cabinet members on November 22.

Federal Election Consequences. The sovereignty issues was thrown into a new light by the election of a new Conservative federal government in the September 4 national election. The Tories not only won big across Canada, but they astounded everybody by winning 58 of Quebec's 75 seats in Parliament, with just 17 for the Liberals. In the preceding Parliament, the Tories held only one seat.

During the election campaign, members of the PQ worked diligently for the Tory candidates in Quebec and against the PQ's detested enemies, the federal Liberals. After the election, Premier Lévesque talked about the possibility of a new beginning in relations between the Quebec and federal governments. Addressing the Quebec National Assembly on October 16, the premier said his government was "completely disposed to maintain harmonious relations" with the new federal regime. It was also prepared to devote the "energy that is necessary" to working out a constitutional accord.

For its part, the federal government accepted the olive branch, pledging in the speech from the throne on November 5 to "work to create the conditions that will make possible the achievement of this essential accord." Thus the conditions appeared to be ripening for a renewed effort at associating Quebec with Canada's new Constitution, which it hitherto has rejected on the ground that the document infringes Quebec's provincial rights. If the effort to have Quebec approve the constitution should succeed, it would leave the independence movement in tatters, since a contradiction exists between a province pulling out of the federal union while at the same time supporting the new and dynamic constitution that governs that union.

For Lévesque, never a diehard separatist, this might be an attractive way out of a dilemma, transforming sovereignty into a more distant goal that need not preoccupy him as it has perforce preoccupied him since 1976. On the other hand, the independence struggle has given meaning to the PQ from the beginning, and without that goal to strive for, its members might quickly lose the drive and spirit that enabled the party to attain power.

AP/Wide World

Members of the Quebec police force surround the National Assembly after an armed man rushed into the legislature and killed three government workers and injured 12 others.

Assembly Mayhem. The National Assembly became a scene of carnage on May 8 when a man dressed in army combat fatigues burst in and opened fire with a submachine gun, killing three government workers and wounding more than a dozen others. Cpl. Dennis Lortie of the Canadian armed forces was later charged with three counts of first-degree murder.

Education. The Supreme Court of Canada in late July struck down provisions of Quebec's controversial Bill 101 restricting English-language education in the province. The provisions were held to be inconsistent with the federal Bill of Rights and therefore "inoperable."

JOHN BEST, *"Canada World News"*

QUEBEC • Information Highlights

Area: 594,860 sq mi (1 540 687 km²).
Population (April 1984 est.): 6,540,100.
Chief Cities (1981 census): Quebec, the capital, 166,474; Montreal, 980,354; Laval, 245,856; Longueuil, 124,320.
Government (1984): *Chief Officers*—lt. gov., Jean-Pierre Côte; premier, René Lévesque (Parti Québécois). *Legislature*—Legislative Assembly, 122 members.
Provincial Finances (1984–85 fiscal year budget): *Revenues,* $22,465,000,000; *expenditures,* $25,640,000,000.
Personal Income (average weekly earnings, May 1984): $394.62.
Labor Force (July 1984, seasonally adjusted): *Employed workers,* 15 years of age and over, 2,737,000; *Unemployed* 376,000 (12.1%).
Education (1984–85): *Enrollment*—elementary and secondary schools, 1,148,650 pupils; postsecondary (1984–85)—universities, 196,270; community colleges, (full-time), 141,600.
(All monetary figures are in Canadian dollars.)

RECORDINGS

The recording industry enjoyed a boom year in 1984. Exciting new technology, a broadening product-mix base, superstar releases with enormous domestic and international appeal, a return to record buying by older consumers, and the absence of major price increases contributed to what a National Association of Recording Merchandisers (NARM) representative dubbed "the biggest year in recorded product history." A NARM survey for the first six months of 1984 showed total recorded product sales up by 17% over the same period in 1983. This recovery was led by a sharp increase in cassette sales, balancing a small decline in long-playing (LP) and extended-play (EP) format sales. Singles showed a slight recovery. Surprisingly, 8-track cartridge sales went up due to demand in the direct-marketing sector. Although there were no 1983 statistics for comparison, 1.5 million compact discs (CDs) were sold in the first half of 1984, and sales figures accelerated rapidly toward the end of the year.

Classical. When digital CDs were introduced in 1983, most of the music available on them was classical. Although a great deal of popular music was released in the new format in 1984, it still had greatest impact in the classical field. CDs accounted for 25% of Deutsche Grammophon's sales in the United States. Joining the major labels in producing classical titles on CD were such smaller companies as Qualiton, Sine Qua Non, Vanguard, and the Moss Music Group of labels, which included Vox.

In June the PolyGram plant in Hanover, West Germany, pressed its ten millionth CD, a performance of Pachelbel's *Canon* by the Berlin Philharmonic conducted by Herbert von Karajan. Another milestone in the acceptance of the system was the release of the first all-digital recording of Richard Wagner's monumental four-opera cycle *Der Ring des Nibelun-*

RCA

Releases on compact disc included an all-digital recording of Wagner's four-opera "The Complete Ring."

gen. Recorded in East Germany by Eurodisc, it was sold in the United States by RCA on 18 CDs pressed in Japan. In September, CBS/Sony opened the first American CD pressing plant.

Among the labels attempting to improve the quality of their conventional LPs was Angel. That company had its premium classical line mastered and pressed in West Germany using Teldec's Direct Metal Mastering process.

In preparation for the 1985 tercentennial of the births of Johann Sebastian Bach, George Frideric Handel, and Domenico Scarlatti, a variety of artists recorded music by these composers. Guitarist Christopher Parkening taped a new album of Bach transcriptions for Angel, and the Cambridge Buskers made one for Deutsche Grammophon that included works by all three.

Popular. The top of the popular music charts was dominated by a very few blockbuster albums, which spun off numerous hit singles. Only ten albums hit the Number One spot in 1983 and 1984 combined. Chart-toppers in 1984 were Michael Jackson's *Thriller,* Prince's *Purple Rain* soundtrack, the *Footloose* soundtrack, Lionel Richie's *Can't Slow Down,* Huey Lewis and the News' *Sports,* and Bruce Springsteen's *Born in the U.S.A.* Statistics on these albums were record-shattering. Jackson's *Thriller* became the largest-selling album in the history of recording at 35 million copies worldwide. It produced seven Top Ten singles, an unprecedented feat.

The outstanding success of Prince's *Purple Rain* soundtrack challenged Jackson's supremacy on the charts. By the end of the year, it had held the Number One pop position for more than 25 weeks, beating *Saturday Night Fever's* record as the longest running Number One soundtrack in the past 20 years. It topped five *Billboard* charts, matching Jackson's accomplishment as the broadest Number One cross-

Prince's "Purple Rain" topped the pop album charts for some 25 weeks, longer than any soundtrack in 20 years.

© Warner Brothers Records

RECORDINGS | 1984

CLASSICAL

BEETHOVEN: Piano Concertos Nos. 1–5; Alfred Brendel, Chicago Symphony Orchestra, James Levine conductor (Philips).

BEETHOVEN: Violin Sonata No. 9, in A Major (*Kreutzer*), Violin Sonata No. 5, in F Major (*Spring*); Uto Ughi, Wolfgang Sawallisch (RCA).

BIZET: *Carmen;* Julia Migenes-Johnson, Placido Domingo, Faith Esham, Ruggero Raimondi, Orchestre National de France, Lorin Maazel conductor (Erato/RCA).

BOITO: *Mefistofele;* Nicholai Ghiaurov, Luciano Pavarotti, Mirella Freni, Montserrat Caballé, National Philharmonic Orchestra, Oliviero de Fabritiis conductor (London).

THE FALLA TRIO: Virtuoso Music for Three Guitars (Concord).

IVES: Songs; Roberta Alexander, Tan Crone (Etcetera).

MAHLER: Symphony No. 1, in D Major; Philadelphia Orchestra, Riccardo Muti conductor (Angel).

MENDELSSOHN: Violin Concerto, in E Minor, SAINT SAENS: Violin Concerto No. 3, in B Minor; Cho-Liang Lin, Philharmonia Orchestra, Michael Tilson Thomas conductor (CBS Masterworks).

NAZARETH: Brazilian Tangos and Waltzes; Arthur Moreira Lima (Pro Arte).

PUCCINI: *La Rondine;* Kiri Te Kanawa, Placido Domingo, London Symphony Orchestra, Lorin Maazel conductor (CBS Masterworks).

JAZZ

COUNT BASIE: *Kansas City Style* (RCA).

GENE BERTONCINI & MICHAEL MOORE: *Close Ties* (Omnisound).

ROSEMARY CLOONEY: *Sings the Music of Irving Berlin* (Concord Jazz).

MILES DAVIS: *Decoy* (Columbia).

JACK DeJOHNETTE'S SPECIAL EDITION: *Album Album* (ECM).

CHICO FREEMAN: *Tangents* (Elektra/Musician).

AL JARREAU: *High Crime* (Warner Bros.).

EARL KLUGH: *Nightsongs* (Capitol).

RAMSEY LEWIS & NANCY WILSON: *The Two of Us* (Columbia).

WYNTON MARSALIS: *Hot House Flowers* (Columbia).

BOBBY McFERRIN: *The Voice* (Elektra/Musician).

PAT METHENY GROUP: *First Circle* (ECM).

THE MODERN JAZZ QUARTET: *Echoes: Together Again* (Pablo).

THELONIUS MONK: *Blues Five Spot* (Milestone).

SONNY ROLLINS: *Sunny Days, Starry Nights* (Milestone).

ZOOT SIMS: *Quietly There* (Pablo).

MEL TORME & GEORGE SHEARING: *An Evening at Charlies* (Concord Jazz).

JOE WILLIAMS: *Everyday I Have the Blues* (Savoy Jazz).

MUSICALS, MOVIES

AGAINST ALL ODDS: soundtrack (Atlantic).

AMADEUS: soundtrack (Fantasy).

BREAKIN': soundtrack (Polydor).

EDDIE & THE CRUISERS: John Caferty & the Beaver Brown Band; soundtrack (Scotti Bros.).

FOOTLOOSE: soundtrack (Columbia).

GHOSTBUSTERS: soundtrack (Arista).

STOP MAKING SENSE: Talking Heads; soundtrack (Sire).

SUNDAY IN THE PARK WITH GEORGE: original cast (RCA).

POPULAR

BRYAN ADAMS: *Reckless* (A&M).

ALABAMA: *Roll On* (RCA).

JOHN ANDERSON: *Eye of the Hurricane* (Warner Bros.).

LAURIE ANDERSON: *Mister Heartbreak* (Warner Bros.).

BANANARAMA: *Bananarama* (London/PolyGram).

THE BANGLES: *All Over the Place* (Columbia).

THE BELLAMY BROTHERS: *Restless* (Curb/MCA).

PAT BENATAR: *Tropico* (Chrysalis).

BIG COUNTRY: *Steel Town* (Mercury/PolyGram).

DAVID BOWIE: *Tonight* (EMI/America).

LAURA BRANIGAN: *Self Control* (Atlantic).

PEABO BRYSON: *Straight from the Heart* (Elektra).

LINDSEY BUCKINGHAM: *Go Insane* (Elektra).

THE CARS: *Heartbeat City* (Elektra).

CHICAGO: *Chicago 17* (Full Moon/Warner Bros.).

EARL THOMAS CONLEY: *Treading Water* (RCA).

ELVIS COSTELLO & THE ATTRACTIONS: *Goodbye Cruel World* (Columbia).

CULTURE CLUB: *Waking Up with the House on Fire* (Epic/Virgin).

NEIL DIAMOND: *Primitive* (CBS).

THOMAS DOLBY: *The Flat Earth* (Capitol).

DURAN DURAN: *Arena* (Capitol).

SHEILA E.: *The Glamorous Life* (Warner Bros.).

EURYTHMICS: *Touch* (RCA).

THE EVERLY BROTHERS: *EB84* (Mercury).

THE FIXX: *Phantoms* (MCA).

FRANKIE GOES TO HOLLYWOOD: *Welcome to the Pleasure Dome* (Island).

GLENN FREY: *The Allnighter* (MCA).

THE GO-GO's: *Talk Show* (IRS/A&M).

MERLE HAGGARD: *It's All in the Game* (Epic).

DARYL HALL & JOHN OATES: *Big Bam Boom* (RCA).

SAM HARRIS: *Sam Harris* (Motown).

COREY HART: *First Offense* (EMI/America).

DAN HARTMAN: *I Can Dream About You* (MCA).

THE HONEYDRIPPERS: *Volume One* (Es Parnaza/Atlantic).

BILLY IDOL: *Rebel Yell* (Chrysalis).

JULIO IGLESIAS: *1100 Bel Air Place* (Columbia).

THE JACKSONS: *Victory* (Epic).

JEFFERSON STARSHIP: *Nuclear Furniture* (Grunt/RCA).

ELTON JOHN: *Breaking Hearts* (Geffen/Warner Bros.).

GEORGE JONES: *Ladies Choice* (Epic).

RICKIE LEE JONES: *The Magazine* (Warner Bros.).

THE JUDDS: *Why Not Me* (Curb/RCA).

CHAKA KHAN: *I Feel for You* (Warner Bros.).

KISS: *Animalize* (Mercury/PolyGram).

CYNDI LAUPER: *She's So Unusual* (Portrait/CBS).

JULIAN LENNON: *Valotte* (Atlantic).

MADONNA: *Like a Virgin* and *Madonna* (Sire/Warner Bros.).

BARBARA MANDRELL: *Clean Cuts* (MCA).

BOB MARLEY & THE WAILERS: *Legend* (Island).

ANNE MURRAY: *Heart Over Mind* (Capitol).

WILLIE NELSON: *City of New Orleans* (Columbia).

NENA: *99 Luftballoons* (Epic).

BILLY OCEAN: *Suddenly* (Jive/Arista).

JEFFREY OSBORNE: *Don't Stop* (A&M).

LUCIANO PAVAROTTI: *Mama* (London/PolyGram).

TEDDY PENDERGRASS: *Love Language* (Asylum/Elektra).

STEVE PERRY: *Street Talk* (Columbia).

POINTER SISTERS: *Break Out* (Planet/RCA).

THE PRETENDERS: *Learning to Crawl* (Sire/Warner Bros.).

QUIET RIOT: *Condition Critical* (Pasha/Epic).

RATT: *Out of the Cellar* (Atlantic).

LOU REED: *New Sensations* (RCA).

KENNY ROGERS: *What About Me* (RCA).

LINDA RONSTADT: *Lush Life* (Asylum/Elektra).

DIANA ROSS: *Swept Away* (RCA).

RUSH: *Grace Under Pressure* (Mercury/PolyGram).

SCANDAL/PATTY SMYTH: *The Warrior* (Columbia).

JOHN SCHNEIDER: *Too Good to Stop Now* (MCA).

THE SCORPIONS: *Love at First Sting* (Mercury/PolyGram).

SHALAMAR: *Heartbreak* (Solar).

FRANK SINATRA: *L.A. Is My Lady* (Qwest/Warner Bros.).

RICKY SKAGGS: *Country Boy* (Epic).

BRUCE SPRINGSTEEN: *Born in the U.S.A.* (Columbia).

BILLY SQUIER: *Signs of Life* (Capitol).

ROD STEWART: *Camouflage* (Warner Bros.).

BARBARA STREISAND: *Emotion* (Columbia).

DONNA SUMMER: *Cats Without Claws* (Geffen/Warner Bros.).

SURVIVOR: *Vital Signs* (Scotti Bros./Epic).

THE THOMPSON TWINS: *Into the Gap* (Arista).

THE TIME: *Ice Cream Castle* (Warner Bros.).

TOTO: *Isolation* (Columbia).

TINA TURNER: *Private Dancer* (Capitol).

TWISTED SISTER: *Stay Hungry* (Warner Bros.).

U2: *The Unforgettable Fire* (Island).

VAN HALEN: *1984* (Warner Bros.).

VANITY: *Wild Animal* (Motown).

STEVIE RAY VAUGHAN & DOUBLE TROUBLE: *Couldn't Stand the Weather* (Epic).

JOHN WAITE: *No Brakes* (EMI/America).

WHAM!: *Make It Big* (Columbia).

THE WHO: *Who's Last* (MCA).

HANK WILLIAMS, JR.: *Major Moves* (Curb/Warner Bros.).

PETER WOLF: *Lights Out* (EMI/America).

"WEIRD AL" YANKOVIC: *In 3-D* (Rock 'n' Roll/Epic).

Mobile Fidelity Sound Lab

Mobile Fidelity brought out a limited-edition, audiophile set of ten early Rolling Stones albums, priced at $250.

many of these stayed on the charts for extended 20-week periods and more, country legend Willie Nelson still dominated the field. Toward the end of the year, his *City of New Orleans* LP consistently held at Number One while six other Nelson solo and duet albums peppered the charts—including *Stardust,* with an incredible 340-plus weeks of chart activity.

CD technology spread from upscale buyers to the regular album consumer as prices of both hardware and software dropped. The WEA labels, CBS, PolyGram, and Denon agreed to keep software prices at $15 or below. NARM projected that the CD format would overtake LPs in five years. The number of mainstream pop titles began to gain on classical and jazz. RCA began subsidizing pop artists to record digitally for the new format. CD in-car-dash units and Walkman-type units were developed.

Although audiophile-quality vinyl pressings were overshadowed by interest in the CD format, Mobile Fidelity Sound Lab's Original Master Recordings limited-edition collection of the Rolling Stones stirred up wide interest. This magnificent package of high-quality half-speed masters of ten early Stones LPs became a valuable collector's item.

Cassettes continued to outsell LPs. A&M began releasing all its cassettes on audiophile BASF tape, and Columbia did the same for select artist product only. Jazz product on cassette lagged behind, although in 1984 cassettes leapt to 30–40% of jazz volume compared with 1983's 10–15%.

Video recording strongly influenced the audio recordings market, although home music video recordings did not sell as well as predicted. Based on the success of Vestron's *Making Michael Jackson's Thriller,* the largest-selling music video at 800,000 copies, industry experts forecast that 25% of video software sales would be music video by 1988. Volume in 1984 was closer to 5–6%.

Sony continued its successful marketing of music video, creating the Sony 45, EP, and LP categories. David Bowie's mini-movie, *Jazzin' for Blue Jean,* and Duran Duran's *Dancing on the Valentine* were two of its most important 1984 releases. Vestron made its bid with a Rolling Stones video collection, *Video Rewind.* Despite disappointing sales, interest in music video remained high. Three significant award programs for these recordings were established in 1984: The First Annual MTV Music Video Awards, the *Billboard* Music Video Awards, and the First International Music Video Festival of St. Tropez awards.

In other video hardware news, RCA abandoned the problem-ridden CS videodisc format and left the field to laserdiscs and the Beta and VHS tape systems.

Billboard, the recording industry bible, celebrated its 90th anniversary.

over success in chart history. Two hit singles from the LP, "When Doves Cry" and "Let's Go Crazy," topped three charts simultaneously, matching Jackson's historic first.

Besides *Purple Rain,* eight other soundtracks went platinum: *Footloose, Ghostbusters, Breakin', Hard to Hold, The Big Chill, Eddie and the Cruisers, Two of a Kind,* and *Yentl.*

Lionel Richie became the first artist in pop chart history to have a single from one album, *Can't Slow Down,* in the Top Forty every week for a full year. The LP itself spent a full year in the Top Ten (an accomplishment equaled only by *Thriller* and Fleetwood Mac's *Rumours*) and produced four Top Ten hits.

Singles by other black artists dominated the Top Ten, as well. Tina Turner's smash comeback put "What's Love Got to Do with It" in the Number One slot, a spot occupied by Stevie Wonder, Ray Parker, Jr., Billy Ocean, and Deniece Williams at various times throughout 1984.

Cyndi Lauper was the first female singer to reach the Top Three with her first three chart hits. Her album, *She's So Unusual,* was only the third album in history—the first by a female artist—to generate three Top Ten hits.

Julio Iglesias was the only solo pop artist to achieve two platinum LPs in one year. Attesting to the vigor of the heavy metal sound, the Scorpions were the only group to accomplish the same.

In the country arena, although a wide variety of artists had successful recordings and

PAULETTE WEISS

REFUGEES AND IMMIGRATION

As it did two years earlier in the 97th Congress, legislation making major changes in U.S. immigration law failed to pass the 98th Congress in 1984. The failed legislation, the Simpson-Mazzoli Bill, was agreed to by the Senate in May 1983 and won narrow approval in the House of Representatives (216–211) in June 1984. But, despite numerous compromises by members of both houses, it died in a joint House-Senate conference committee when Congress adjourned on October 12.

The bill, named for its principal sponsors, Sen. Alan Simpson (R-WY) and Rep. Romano Mazzoli (D-KY), would have established fines and prison sentences for employers who knowingly hire illegal aliens, offered legal resident status to at least 2 million illegals currently living in the United States, and permitted larger numbers of temporary foreign workers to enter the country. Similar to legislation that passed the Senate but not the House during the 97th Congress, the Simpson-Mazzoli Bill was the culmination of more than a decade of effort to control illegal immigration and to prevent the exploitation of alien workers. Supporters of the bill said they would reintroduce the proposal when the 99th Congress convenes in 1985.

The Senate version would have fined employers $1,000 for each illegal alien hired and $2,000 for a second offense. Repeated violations would have brought a six-month jail term. Aliens who entered the United States illegally before Jan. 1, 1980, would have been granted "amnesty," or legal resident status. In addition, the Senate agreed to relax restrictions on the immigration of workers under labor contracts and approved the creation of a foolproof national identification system.

The House bill set no criminal penalties for hiring illegals, providing civil fines instead. The House amnesty provision included illegal aliens who entered the country before Jan. 1, 1982. The House bill contained contract-worker provisions similar to the Senate version and in addition set up a more liberal program to permit agricultural workers without contracts to enter the country in search of farm jobs.

Virtually all the differences between the House and Senate were resolved in the conference committee. Criminal sanctions for employers were approved, with a two-year grace period during which citations or warnings would be issued to violators and an additional three-year grace period for farmers-employers. Amnesty was offered to illegals who entered the United States before Jan. 1, 1981. Welfare benefits would have been provided selectively to amnestied aliens, depending on their date of entry into the United States. The provision for a national identity card was killed, but a three-year study of the possible use of Social Security cards for identification purposes was authorized.

The conference committee nearly reached a stalemate over a House-approved ban on job discrimination against amnestied aliens. A last-minute compromise was reached under which persons "intending" to become U.S. citizens were declared to have the same rights as citizens. The bill finally foundered on a White House demand for a $1 billion (U.S.) cap on federal money to be devoted to resident alien welfare costs.

International Migration. Despite the failure of the Simpson-Mazzoli bill, pressure was expected to remain on Congress to deal with the problem of immigration, both legal and illegal. Immigration accounts for almost 50% of U.S. population growth, and the illegal alien population is estimated at between 4 and 8 million.

The developing countries of the Third World are the source of most of the immigration into the United States and other industrialized countries. The imbalance of wealth and resources between the rich and poor countries, and the rapid growth of population in the Third World are pushing international migration to new peaks. The United Nations projects a doubling of the population of less-developed countries between 1980 and 2025. Mexico is the largest single-country source of U.S. migration, with 59,298 legal immigrants in 1983 and many times that number of illegals. But 282,724 legal immigrants entered the United States from Asian countries in 1984, about half of all legal immigration.

Depressed economic and social conditions in the poor countries are exacerbated by violence and political strife. Refugee problems are on the rise around the globe. Afghanistan has generated the world's largest refugee population. At least 4 million Afghans have fled since the Soviet Union invaded in 1979. The United States has resettled more than 700,000 Southeast Asians in recent years, and the government announced in 1984 that it would accept up to 10,000 political prisoners from Vietnam and all of the estimated 15,000 children fathered there by American servicemen. Some 500,000 Salvadoreans, fleeing civil war in their country, now live in the United States, most of them illegally. The newest refugee flow detected by the office of the UN High Commissioner for Refugees is to Pakistan from Iran, which is ravaged by internal dissension and war with Iraq.

The High Commissioner's office spends more than $400 million per year caring for some of the 11 million refugees scattered around the world. The total refugee bill is much higher—estimated at $10 billion a year, of which more than $1 billion is spent by the United States. Under such conditions, experts predict that the problems of refugees and illegal immigrants will become worse rather than better.

Richard C. Schroeder, *"Vision" Magazine*

Chester Higgins, Jr., NYT Pictures

Archbishop Iakovos marked his 25th year as head of the Greek Orthodox Archdiocese of North and South America.

RELIGION

Survey

As American Methodism celebrated its 200th anniversary in 1984, it was important to remember that the denominations of Methodism emerged out of a movement that began within British Christianity in the 18th century. Methodism was a version of a similar enterprise called Pietism that occurred within the Lutheran and Reformed traditions of the continent. The first "methodists" were members of the Church of England who sought a disciplined and methodical development of personal religion. They met together in small groups of Bible study and prayer. These societies often engaged in disciplined self-examination and rigorous spiritual exercises. John Wesley, his brother Charles, and George Whitefield were leaders of this attempt at spiritual renewal.

After a very unsuccessful tenure as a Church of England missionary in Georgia, John Wesley returned to England full of self-reproach and spiritual dissatisfaction. He had been struggling to save his soul by self-discipline. It was not until May 24, 1738, when he attended the meeting of a Moravian society in Aldersgate that he felt his "heart strangely warmed." He had found inner liberation and it was out of this experience that a movement was launched that profoundly affected the his-

tory of British and American Christianity. Some historians have suggested that Methodism has been the most representative American religion. Methodism has tended to emphasize the intensity of personal religious experience and commitment. It led American spirituality away from its early Calvinistic stress on God's initiative in the experience of salvation to an emphasis on human decision. The Wesleyan message has been called perfectionism, with its accent on sanctification—the possibility of complete assurance of redemption which releases divine power in man to full effect. Holiness becomes a present reality.

After the War of Independence had been won, American Anglicanism had to restructure itself in keeping with the new political order. It obviously could no longer be the Church of England. As the Protestant Episcopal Church was being constituted out of this necessity, its Methodist constituency found itself less and less at home with the parent church. When the Bishop of London refused to ordain clergy to serve the Methodist societies in America, John Wesley ordained two men for the American ministry and under their leadership the Methodist Episcopal Church was organized in Baltimore on Dec. 24, 1784. During the 19th century several other denominations were founded, some of them the result of Wesleyan influence upon German Lutheran and Reformed peoples. In 1968 several of these denominations merged to form the United Methodist Church.

RICHARD E. WENTZ, *Arizona State University*

Far Eastern

During the Maoist years, the sayings of Chairman Mao attained an almost scriptural status in China. When the nation opened its doors to the United States and the West the spiritual isolation of China was challenged by the materialism of the capitalistic world. Recently there has been a campaign to halt this spiritual pollution. However, trade and production seemed to be affected by the campaign and the antagonism of youth was aroused. The campaign was terminated and China continues its agitation over what to do with the religious inclinations of the people. Meanwhile, it is estimated that Christianity continues to grow, sometimes in clandestine fashion. Although a policy of toleration toward publicly regulated Christianity was instituted in 1979, the government of China has found it difficult to curb the growth of the unauthorized house-church movement.

India. India continued to be a scene of interreligious and intercultural conflict in 1984. It is important to understand that the religions of humankind traditionally have provided the means of identity and worldview. When the integrity of social identity and worldview is threatened, conflict results. Sikhism is a blending of devotional Hinduism with Muslim theism. The founder of the Sikh tradition felt that the bitter animosity between Hindu and Muslim was the result of irrelevant externals. Thus was born a tradition that now has spawned a separatist movement seeking to avoid being engulfed by the Hindu tides. In June 1984, Indian Army troops, in an attempt to crush the terrorist campaign of Sikh extremists, fought their way into the holiest of Sikh shrines, the Golden Temple at Amritsar. More than 300 were killed, including the charismatic leader of the separatists, Sant Jarnail Singh Bhindranwale. The attack led ultimately to the assassination of Prime Minister Indira Gandhi in late October by Sikh bodyguards. Her murder was followed by a storm of public violence, in which Hindus sought bloody revenge against Sikhs. More than 1,000 persons were reported killed in the worst riots since 1947.

RICHARD E. WENTZ

Islam

The Organization of the Islamic Conference, consisting of 42 Muslim nations and the Palestine Liberation Organization (PLO), held its fourth summit conference in Casablanca, Morocco, in January 1984. Morocco's King Hassan II presided over the meeting, succeeding King Fahd of Saudi Arabia as chairman. The selection of President Kenan Evren of Turkey, President Abdou Diouf of Senegal, and PLO chairman Yasir Arafat as deputy chairmen gave the organization a leadership embracing a variety of political and religious views.

The solidarity that the meeting's planners hoped to demonstrate was hurt by Iran's boycott in protest over the attendance of its Gulf War rival, Iraq. The main order of business, the question of readmitting Egypt, further highlighted differences within the group. Debate over the status of Egypt, which had been suspended from the conference since 1979 because of its treaty with Israel, prolonged the conference for an additional day. In the end, a vote favoring Egypt's readmission passed, and Egyptian President Hosni Mubarak accepted the invitation to participate in future conference deliberations.

In a series of preliminary meetings, Muslim foreign ministers voiced their support for the Turkish Republic of Northern Cyprus. They condemned both superpowers: the United States for its security pact with Israel; the Soviet Union for its continuing occupation of Afghanistan.

A major concern of the Organization of the Islamic Conference that emerged later in the year centered on the relocation of foreign embassies in Israel from Tel Aviv to Jerusalem. Interest in this matter heightened when the U.S. Congress urged that the American Embassy be transferred to Jerusalem. The conference opposes such relocations on the grounds that they recognize Israeli sovereignty over Jerusalem and violate United Nations resolutions. The conference's Jerusalem Committee recommended that Muslim nations sever diplomatic relations with two Central American states, Costa Rica and El Salvador, both of which had recently opened embassies in the disputed city.

In many parts of the Muslim world, 1984 was a year of continuing political activism. Social and economic problems in Tunisia, for example, enabled critics of the regime to demand that it pay stricter attention to fundamental Islamic principles, including those of social justice, as means of solving these difficulties. Muslim organizations participated in riots in several Tunisian cities in January.

Rioting in northern Nigeria early in the year led to military intervention and the loss of as many as 1,000 lives. This violence coincided with the anniversary of the death of a fundamentalist leader.

Conversely, the 1983 decision to impose Islamic law in the Sudan, including the predominantly Christian and animist southern regions, aggravated an already tense situation there and necessitated the imposition of a state of emergency in April 1984.

Muslim minorities encountered serious difficulties in several countries. Muslim insurgents in the Philippines, who have long protested what they view as government neglect of and discrimination against their community, continued a long-standing guerrilla war. In Bombay, India, and the nearby city of Bhiwandi, communal tensions between Muslims and Hindus erupted in May into a series of riots, which were worsened by a sense of restlessness among a large mass of unemployed youths from both communities.

Islam also entered the American political scene during the 1984 primary campaign when Louis Farrakhan, leader of the Lost-Found Nation of Islam, denounced critics of the presidential candidacy of the Rev. Jesse Jackson. The Lost-Found Nation of Islam is a black organization that during the 1970s split from the older Nation of Islam, founded in the 1930s by Elijah Muhammad. In the 1970s, Elijah Muhammad's son, Warith Deen Muhammad, abandoned many of the racist views of the Nation of Islam and brought the movement, which came to be called the American Muslim Mission, more in line with true Islamic principles. Farrakhan and his followers, however, clung to the older black-supremacy views, which have no basis in Muslim beliefs.

KENNETH J. PERKINS
University of South Carolina

Rabbi Meir Kahane (center), controversial founder of the Jewish Defense League, was elected to the Israeli parliament as a member of the far-right Kach Party. Kahane called for the expulsion of all Arabs from Israel.

Judaism

Parliamentary elections in Israel and the presidential campaign in the United States precipitated issues of primary concern to world Jewry in 1984.

Jews everywhere viewed with alarm the manifestation of a radical trend in Israeli society, evidenced by the emergence of a militant Jewish underground and the election to the Knesset (parliament) of Rabbi Meir Kahane, a proponent of extreme religious-nationalistic policies. Prolonged political maneuvering after the inconclusive parliamentary elections in July added to the distress of the Conservative and Reform movements, as they focused on the question "Who Is A Jew?" in an attempt to accommodate demands by the religious parties to amend the existing definition along religious legal lines. Orthodox rabbis sharply criticized the Conservative and Reform position, which claimed that strict adherence to Jewish orthodoxy would splinter world Jewry.

In the United States, the Democratic campaign program included moving the U.S. Embassy from Tel Aviv to Jerusalem, an issue vital to Jews; the Reagan administration continued to oppose such a transfer. In an apostolic letter, Pope John Paul II called for an "internationally guaranteed status" for Jerusalem. Evangelical Christian leaders, on the other hand, testified before a U.S. congressional committee in favor of legislation requiring the move. Anti-Semitic statements made during the primary campaign by Democratic candidate the Rev. Jesse Jackson and some of his aides heightened Black-Jewish tensions.

In March the final report of the American Jewish Commission on the Holocaust caused agonizing controversy within the Jewish community. The commission, established in 1981 to study American Jewish responses to the Holocaust, determined that American Jewish organizations did not do everything in their power to save victims of the Holocaust.

In May, world Jewry welcomed two positive developments. One was an invitation from Morocco's King Hassan to an international panel of Jewish leaders, including an official delegation from Israel, for the biannual Congress of Moroccan Jews in Rabat. The congress was also attended by the crown prince and several Moroccan ministers of state. The other positive development was an overture by the Hungarian government for cultural exchanges with Israel. First was the participation of four prominent Hungarian historians at a Haifa University conference marking the 40th anniversary of Hungarian Jewry's Holocaust. This was followed by the opening at Tel Aviv University of a government-sponsored photographic exhibit called "The Jews of Hungary," attended by an official Hungarian delegation. In July dissidents in Hungary published an appeal in the local underground magazine for resumed diplomatic relations with Israel.

Italy's Jews, meanwhile, welcomed a concordat signed by the Vatican that transferred control of ancient Jewish catacombs to the Italian government. These catacombs contain artifacts said to be from the Second Temple in Jersualem destroyed by Roman legions nearly 2,000 years ago.

In the Soviet Union the tough line against teachers of Jewish culture adopted under the rule of late party leader Yuri Andropov was intensified in 1984 with the harassment and arrest of several teachers and the confiscation of Hebrew texts. At its June commencement exercises, Yeshiva University in New York City awarded Soviet dissident Anatoly Shcharansky an honorary Doctor of Humane Letters degree for his role as a symbol of struggle "for religious perseverance and human freedom." Scharansky is serving a 13-year sentence in a Soviet prison. The award was the first honorary degree in the history of the university to be granted in absentia. Jews the world over held prayer meetings in sympathy with his plight and that of 1975 Nobel Peace Prize winner Andre Sakharov, whose request to travel abroad for medical treatment was denied.

LIVIA E. BITTON-JACKSON
Herbert H. Lehman College, CUNY

Orthodox Eastern

While plans for the Great and Holy Synod of all Orthodox Churches remained at a standstill, various late 1983–1984 meetings between church leaders indicated an ongoing process of communication among Orthodox Churches in Socialist and Islamic-dominated regions. In the fall of 1983, Pimen, the patriarch of Moscow, visited the Rumanian Orthodox Church led by Patriarch Justin; Seraphim, the archbishop of Athens and head of the Church of Greece, traveled to Yugoslavia to confer with German, the patriarch of the Serbian Church; and Metropolitan Dorotheos, primate of the Orthodox Church of Czechoslovakia, was received in Constantinople by the Ecumenical Patriarch, Dimitrios I, demonstrating cordial relations between the Ecumenical Patriarchate and an autocephalous (self-governing) church established by the Church of Russia.

The Russian Orthodox Church continued to prepare for the millennium of Christianity in the Russian lands in 1988 with the restoration of the Danilov Monastery in Moscow. Dissenting Orthodox Christians, including the Rev. Gleb Yakunin, and recently arrested activists in remote parts of the country remained imprisoned. Russian and American church leaders exchanged several visits during 1984. A delegation of about 200 Christians from the National Council of Churches of Christ in the USA drew sharp criticism in the American media for their alleged failure to speak out clearly concerning government restrictions and persecutions of believers in the USSR during their spring visit. Western observers continued to debate the measure of freedom enjoyed by believers in the USSR. Many claim that the Russian Orthodox Church is no longer considered a major threat to the Soviet regime since the government controls its leadership.

The Orthodox Church in America (OCA) received the visit of Metropolitan Vasilly of Warsaw, head of the Orthodox Church of Poland, in May. Returning the visit of Metropolitan Theodosius, primate of the OCA, the aging hierarch told of the peculiar difficulties facing the Orthodox Poles, who number about 1 million, living in the Roman Catholic country now controlled by Soviet-backed Communists.

Pope John Paul II continued to foster friendly relations with the Orthodox. In December 1983 the pope met with the Greek Orthodox Metropolitan Chrysostomos of Myra in Bari, Italy. Earlier in November, on the feast of St. Andrew, the pope reaffirmed the statement of Vatican Council II in his letter to Dimitrios I of Constantinople that the Roman and Orthodox Churches "indeed have in common 'true sacraments and above all, in virtue of apostolic succession, the priesthood and the Eucharist.' " The pontiff added that "despite the vicissitudes of history and the obstacles which, in the past, have arisen between them, our churches remain united by very profound bonds."

Archbishop Iakovos celebrated his 25th anniversary as head of the Greek Orthodox Archdiocese of North and South America. The hierarch was hailed at the Greek Orthodox Clergy-Laity Congress in New York in July. His critics, including the suspended priest Eusebius Stephanou of the Logos Foundation, continued to criticize the archbishop and his supporters for neglecting the spiritual ministry of the Church and for violating traditional Orthodox canons of ecclesial conciliarity, including the direct participation of presbyters and lay people in the election and operation of the episcopate.

Father Alexander Schmemann, world famous theologian and ecumenist who served as dean of St. Vladimir's Seminary in Crestwood, NY, from 1962, died of cancer on Dec. 13, 1983. The Russian Orthodox priest, who was instrumental in the establishment of the autocephalous Orthodox Church in America in 1970, was succeeded as dean of St. Vladimir's by the Rev. John Meyendorff.

THOMAS HOPKO, *St. Vladimir's Seminary*

Protestantism

An intense public debate on relating religion, moral values, and politics drew the attention of Protestants during the 1984 U.S. election year. Some religious figures argued for Christians to make their values felt in government by electing politicians who shared their beliefs, especially on such issues as abortion. Others declared that public officials should not use the authority of their office to "impose" their private religious beliefs on fellow citizens who did not share them. (*See also* feature article, page 42.)

New Leaders. Much of the year's Protestant news focused on leadership changes. The Rev. Emilio Castro, 57, a Uruguayan Methodist clergyman who had headed evangelism work at the World Council of Churches in Geneva, Switzerland, was named the world ecumenical organization's top executive. He was expected to continue the social activist agenda initiated by his predecessor, the Rev. Philip Potter, 62, and to espouse a similar type of "liberation theology." But he also was expected to make new inroads in building bridges to both Catholic and evangelical Protestant constituencies that are not a part of the council.

The Rev. Arie Brouwer, 49, was nominated as general secretary of the National Council of Churches (NCC), the U.S. ecumenical agency with 31 Protestant and Orthodox member bodies. Former head of the Reformed Church in America, the nation's oldest organized demonination, Brouwer had headed the social-justice unit of the World Council of Churches. He came to the NCC's top job, succeeding Presbyterian laywoman Claire Randall, just in time to administer a planned structural overhaul of the council, which was suffering from financial problems and a dismal public image.

The NCC encountered sharp criticism for its Inclusive Language Lectionary, a set of Scripture readings for worship from which masculine terms for God had been expunged. The second cycle of readings was issued late in 1984. Unacceptable to some Scripture scholars, as well as grass roots church members, were alterations by the NCC's lectionary committee changing "God our Father" to "God our Father and Mother" and changing "Lord" to "Sovereign."

The Presbyterian Church (USA), formed by the reunion of major northern and southern branches of U.S. Presbyterianism, elected southerner James Andrews as its first chief executive, or "stated clerk." Andrews won an upset victory over respected veteran ecumenist William P. Thompson, a Kansas-born lawyer who had headed the (northern) United Presbyterian Church for 18 years.

Ultraconservatives continued to accrue power in the Southern Baptist Convention

(SBC). Atlanta pastor and television preacher the Rev. Charles Stanley was elected president. He was the candidate of the SBC's so-called "inerrancy" wing. The wing has battled moderates in the denomination, claiming that their view of Scripture as "infallible and inerrant Word of God" is the only valid belief about the authority of the Bible. The SBC passed a resolution opposing the ordination of women as clergy, stating that man was first in the Creation and woman first in the Edenic Fall; therefore women should not hold authority over women. The resolution was not binding on local congregations. Southern Baptists also went on record opposing the production or use of tobacco.

Episcopalians marked the tenth anniversary of the first "irregular" ordinations of women to the priesthood, and a coalition of activists called for the denomination to elect its first woman bishop.

United Methodists, who elected their first woman bishop in 1980, elected two more women to the office in 1984, including the first black woman bishop, the Rev. Leontyne Kelly. They also elected their first Hispanic bishop and the first Japanese-American bishop. United Methodists, celebrating their 200th anniversary as an organized denomination in America, voted to bar "self-avowed, practicing homosexuals" from the ordained ministry.

Merger Attempts. The Christian Church (Disciples of Christ) and the United Church of Christ, after six years of talks on possible union, backed away from proposing merger in the immediate future. The action came in response to grass roots opposition to union.

Major Lutheran denominations—the Lutheran Church in America, the American Lutheran Church, and the Association of Evangelical Lutheran Churches—continued talks aimed at merging to form a new body in 1988.

Other Political Developments. Congregations of several denominations joined the movement to violate the law by giving sanctuary to undocumented refugees from Central America, mostly Guatemala and El Salvador.

A coalition of Protestant groups filed suit opposing the naming of an ambassador to the Vatican, charging that the practice violated the 1st Amendment by giving preference to one religion over another.

A coalition of evangelical Protestants rallied to the defense of the Rev. Sun Myung Moon, the head of the Unification Church. Some Protestants believed his conviction and imprisonment on tax-evasion charges constituted "religious harassment" of an unpopular religious group. Another church-state battle concerned the closing down of an uncertified school in Nebraska and the jailing of its head.

JEAN CAFFEY LYLES
Associate Editor, Religious News Service

Uruguayan Methodist Parson Emilio Castro (right) was elected secretary general of the World Council of Churches.

AP/Wide World

Roman Catholicism

The role of religion in politics came to the fore in 1984 as the Roman Catholic Church, from the pope on down, became embroiled in government-related disputes in such diverse areas as Nicaragua, the Philippines, Poland, and the United States.

It was also the year of more trips for the most traveled of pontiffs as Pope John Paul II journeyed to Korea, the South Pacific, Canada, the Caribbean, and Switzerland, not to mention several jaunts around his adopted Italy.

Controversy took on such varied forms as nuns leaving the religious life to participate in political life; priests warned to leave government office or face suspension; imprimaturs (official approval) removed from books written by two U.S. theologians; and a major shuffle in the Roman Curia, the Vatican's administrative arm, that led to greater internationalization of the body.

During the year the Vatican renegotiated its concordat (treaty) with Italy, which reduced church privileges and resulted in Catholicism no longer being considered a state religion. The Vatican also agreed to pay a "goodwill" offering of $250 million to creditors of the scandal-ridden Banco Ambrosiano while claiming it had no legal responsibility in the matter.

In an impressive Easter ceremony, Pope John Paul ended the special Holy Year marking the 1,950th anniversary of Christ's redemptive act. He later consecrated the world to Mary, Christ's mother, defended marriage and family life in a number of declarations, and issued a series of warnings against the continuing spread of artificial birth control and abortion.

Early in the year, the United States established formal diplomatic relations with the Vatican. William Wilson became the first U.S. ambassador to the Vatican in 117 years, and the Apostolic Delegate, Archbishop Pio Laghi, became the Vatican Pro-Nuncio to the United States. (*See also* page 47.)

In Europe, tensions between the Polish Communist regime and the Polish bishops continued to deepen, despite the release of scores of members of the outlawed trade union, Solidarity, from prison. More recently, after protracted negotiations, Church and government leaders agreed to accept aid for Polish farmers offered by Western Catholic Church sources, principally in the United States. Pope John Paul disclosed that the Soviet Union had denied him the opportunity to travel to Lithuania to take part in the observance of the 500th anniversary of the death of St. Casimir, patron saint of Lithuania and Poland.

In September, the Vatican's doctrinal congregation issued a critique of some liberation theology, warning against the use of Marxist analysis in applying Gospel teachings to social change. At the same time, a well-known liber-

AP/Wide World

In March, Bernard F. Law, 52, became the eighth archbishop of Boston, the third-largest U.S. archdiocese.

ation theologian, Friar Leonardo Boff of Brazil, was brought to Rome to explain his teachings to the congregation's head, Joseph Cardinal Ratzinger. Several U.S. bishops warned against interpreting the Vatican critique as a condemnation of all liberation theology. They stressed that the document actually highlighted biblical foundations of such theological concepts.

Other U.S. News. The Catholic bishops' conference, led by Archbishop Rembert Weakland of Milwaukee, finalized the draft of a pastoral letter on the U.S. economy. The development of the pastoral included a broad consultation with a variety of economists and business experts. A lay commission, set up independently, undertook the development of a corollary document, but from a viewpoint more sympathetic to the American free enterprise system.

As the national elections approached, leading politicians and church leaders entered into the debate over abortion and other religious-related issues. In an effort to coalesce church pro-life factions, Chicago's Joseph Cardinal Bernardin sustained his earlier call for a consistent ethic of life based on the concept of a "seamless garment." Emerging as the top American church spokesman, he urged Catholics to support life at all levels and stages, condemning abortion and the arms race, as well as the denial of human rights.

During the year, Pope John Paul named Archbishop John O'Connor (*see* BIOGRAPHY) to head the New York archdiocese, and Archbishop Bernard Law to lead the Boston see. Lawrence Cardinal Shehan, former archbishop of Baltimore, died.

ROBERT L. JOHNSTON
Editor, "The Chicago Catholic"

443

RETAILING

Mergers and a push for better sales productivity dominated 1984 for American retailers. And as if that were not enough, they had to cope with the fact that their best business came at the year's beginning and end.

It was, however, a year of generally acceptable volume and profits. The uncertainty of the middle months, however, heightened the already pervading stress on increasing sales productivity in existing stores. Both Sears Roebuck and K mart Corporation, the nation's first- and second-largest chains, respectively, unveiled and expanded their "stores of the future." These featured additional higher-priced goods, a higher fashion element, easier access, and more national brands. In both old and new stores, the push was upscale to capitalize on rising income and taste levels.

Mergers and Acquisitions. The merger mill ran overtime with two takeover wars. The most notable was the effort by The Limited, Inc., a Columbus, Ohio, specialty store retailer, to acquire Carter Hawley Hale Stores, the Los Angeles operator of such stores as The Broadway, Neiman-Marcus, and Bergdorf Goodman. The confrontation turned bitter, with litigation and charges against Carter Hawley by the Securities and Exchange Commission (SEC), which lost its case in court. The West Coast company floated a new preferred stock issue that gave General Cinema Corporation a 37% interest for $300 million, which Carter Hawley spent for a huge block of its common stock to elude Limited's grasp. General Cinema, a leading film distributor and soft-drink bottler, had obtained an option to buy Carter Hawley's Waldenbooks' subsidiary. But when the takeover war ended, General Cinema reconsidered and Carter Hawley sold the book chain to K mart.

The second takeover squabble involved Woodward & Lothrop, Washington, DC, whose directors agreed to a merger with Taubman Holdings. But descendants of "Woodies" founding family filed suit against the proposal. Monroe G. Milstein, chairman of Burlington Coat Factory Company, and other investors then made a bid for Woodies. But Woodies' board refused the Milstein group's offer, turned back the family opponents in the courts, and again endorsed the Taubman bid.

In other takeovers, Petrie Stores Corporation acquired one of its largest competitors, Miller-Wohl Stores; Dillard Department Stores of Little Rock purchased the Stix Baer & Fuller stores in St. Louis from Associated Dry Goods Corporation and also acquired the Diamond, Phoenix, and John Brown Company, Oklahoma City, from Dayton Hudson Corporation, Minneapolis; and Brooks Fashion Stores agreed to be bought by Dylex, a Canadian retailer, and other investors.

Avon Products sold its Tiffany & Company to an investor group headed by Tiffany management. Alexander's Inc. said it was in merger talks with a group affiliated with the Bass Brothers' interests in Fort Worth and others, but the talks ended unsuccessfully. The Altman Foundation, which owns B. Altman & Company, invited bids for the seven-unit Altman's to increase the foundation's assets and to honor altered tax rules.

Expansion. Expansion was not far behind in making news. R. H. Macy advanced further into the Sunbelt, adding two stores in Houston to its Florida stores, and said it would open two stores in New Orleans. Bloomingdale's added a Miami store to its 1983 Dallas unit. The big fashion specialty stores, Saks Fifth Avenue and Lord & Taylor, also leaped into the Sunbelt. And a Southern company that had grown dramatically, Wal-Mart Stores, continued to launch 100 or more stores, becoming the second-largest discounter after K mart.

In the retail-food field, American Stores, Salt Lake City, bought the Jewel Companies, Chicago. The Great Atlantic & Pacific Tea Company rebounded from its earlier misfortunes by reporting consistent profits and even purchased Kohl's Supermarkets from Batus Retail. Safeway Stores, Oakland, which had been the nation's biggest supermarket chain, appeared to have surrendered that role to the Kroger-Dillon stores, which merged in 1983.

Pricing. "Off-price," the discounting of branded apparel, lost some of its steam due to rising costs, growing competition, and promotional rivalry by department stores. But the success of the Price Club in San Diego created a flurry of new "warehouse membership" stores.

ISADORE BARMASH, *"The New York Times"*

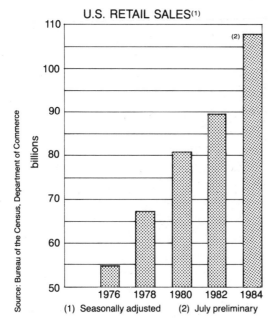

U.S. RETAIL SALES⁽¹⁾

Source: Bureau of the Census, Department of Commerce

billions

110
100
90
80
70
60
50

1976   1978   1980   1982   1984
(2)

(1) Seasonally adjusted   (2) July preliminary

444

The Sweepstakes Boom

Sweepstakes or giveaway promotions, supposedly spawned by economic recession, survived the most recent one by two years, delighting millions of Americans with the chance to get something for nothing. Few won. Many were disappointed. But in 1984 the corporations that sponsored them and paid out an estimated $195 million in prizes were pleased by the exposure from a relatively modest marketing expenditure.

Giveaways became more important in 1984 because many companies that had not used them before decided to participate. One attraction is that unlike cash refunds or cents-off coupons that are open-ended and therefore unpredictable, "sweeps" have a finite budget and a fairly accurate response can be estimated. The business giveaway boom also appeared to coincide with the rise in popularity of state lotteries. (*See also* PEOPLE, PLACES, and THINGS, page 75.)

Although prizes have grown more varied—from a lifetime windfall of $1 million to cameras, luggage, and tubes of toothpaste—Americans have long been subjected to giveaway offers in their mail and stores. Reader's Digest has given away more than $1 million annually for the last quarter-century, while the magazine subscription company, Publishers Clearing House, has paid more than $500,000 a year since 1967. But sweeps hit their best stride after 1975 when states decided that they were no longer just another form of gambling. While growing 10% or more in prize value in recent years, prize games had been used during the 1930s Depression to spur seriously lagging sales.

Biggest recent corporate sponsors resemble a Who's Who of American business. They include Warner-Lambert Company, General Foods Corporation, Nestlé Company, Campbell Soup Company, the Kellogg Company, General Mills, Inc., Ralston-Purina Company, and the McDonald's Corporation.

The trend in prizes has been toward goods and services rather than cash. "There's a lot of leverage for a company giving merchandise sweeps," observes Michael Ellman, executive vice-president of Don Jagoda Associates, a New York company active in marketing giveaways. "The goods are bought at wholesale at mass discounts but they have a retail value in customers' eyes." And recently, too, the economics of giveaways has been enhanced by a bartering arrangement between the sponsor and the manufacturer of the prize. Under the agreement, the advertising exposure is exchanged for the prize.

Robert R. McElroy, "Newsweek"

Don Jagoda (c) is president of Don Jagoda Associates, Syosset, NY. The company is one of several that specializes in the planning and conducting of sweepstakes.

But despite the states' more open policy, there are still some legal curbs against sweeps. In many states, consideration or purchases are not allowed. In others, only two of the three sweeps' elements—prize, chance, and consideration—are permitted. In general, the presence of all three is considered to constitute a lottery. And mostly for that reason, consideration is not used.

Much as many consumers cast the entry forms in the trash, the games' benefits to sponsors are multifaceted. Costs of the average $100,000 promotion are low in view of the exposure. Deadlines and limits on prizes make sweeps economical. Entrants' names can be used for other solicitations. For the bulk of consumers, it is all just another form of annoyance. But for others, it is a mingled source of fun, hope, even diversion.

ISADORE BARMASH

RHODE ISLAND

Nineteen eighty-four was a year of seemingly constant political turmoil in Rhode Island. A lively January legislative session was punctuated by final action on the felony conviction of Providence Mayor Vincent A. Cianci, Jr. The mayor, who was convicted on an assault charge, accepted a plea-bargaining agreement that brought him a suspended sentence and forced his resignation from office on April 25.

City Council President Joseph R. Paolino, Jr., became acting mayor and, with others, a candidate in a special election set for July. Cianci also filed to succeed himself but lost a court battle to stay on the ballot. When the delayed election was finally held on July 31, Paolino defeated Independent Frederick Lippitt by 117 votes.

The Legislature. The General Assembly adjourned May 9 after resolving a budget impasse between the House and the Senate. (The latter's aggressive Republican minority had been expanded in a June 1983 special election.) During the session a litter-control program was passed in lieu of a bottle-deposit bill, the drinking age was raised to 21, and legislation was enacted to purge the voter rolls. Also, provision was made to submit the "Greenhouse Compact," an economic development package with accompanying bond issue, to the voters in a special election on June 12. A state equal rights amendment was rejected.

The Greenhouse program, intended to strengthen existing industries and promote the development of new ones, had been hailed as innovative and imaginative when first announced in October 1983. Gradually doubts surfaced and opposition grew, and despite support from business, labor, and educational leaders, it was resoundingly defeated by the voters four to one, failing in every community in the state. Suspicion of politician control and concern about the high price tag were key factors in the defeat.

September Primary. While attention was still on the legislative session, Greenhouse referendum, and Providence mayoral problems, the stage was being set for a bruising Democratic primary struggle for nomination to succeed retiring Gov. J. Joseph Garrahy. Mayor Joseph W. Walsh of Warwick and State Treasurer Anthony J. Solomon were the contestants. Walsh had the support of the General Assembly leadership, and Solomon of Governor Garrahy and a sizable following from past elections.

In an increasingly bitter battle, Walsh, endorsed by the State Committee, questioned Solomon's qualifications, while the latter portrayed the mayor as allied with the party's bosses. Before the campaign ended with Walsh's defeat, each had spent more than $1 million in the most expensive primary in the state's history, and the Democrats were badly split.

General Election. The Republican Party approached the election campaign buoyed by its successes in the June 1983 Senate contests. Cranston's popular mayor, Edward D. DiPrete, was persuaded to run for governor, heading a ticket with an unprecedented number of female candidates: Senate Minority Leader Lila M. Sapinsley for lieutenant governor, incumbent Susan L. Farmer for secretary of state, and Arlene Violet, a former nun, for attorney general.

On November 6, Ronald Reagan carried the state by a paper-thin margin over Walter Mondale. DiPrete defeated Solomon handily, and Sapinsley lost narrowly to Sen. Richard A. Licht, while Violet defeated incumbent Dennis J. Roberts, II, by a similar narrow margin, and Democrat Roger N. Begin was elected state treasurer. U.S. Sen. Claiborne Pell was reelected, as were the state's two members of the U.S. House of Representatives. The GOP lost ten of its recently won state Senate seats but gained seven seats in the House. The loss of the governorship and of the attorney general's office were stunning blows to the Democrats.

The Economy. The debate over economic development in Rhode Island took place as the economy was rebounding strongly from the national recession. Almost every month brought reports of rising numbers of jobs and a declining unemployment rate. By September the latter had fallen to its lowest level since April 1970, at a seasonally adjusted rate of 4.9%. In October more Rhode Islanders held jobs (408,600) than ever before.

As economic activity accelerated, predictions of a substantial surplus of revenue over projected budget expenditures stirred dispute over what tax cuts might be made and when.

In the fall, Governor Garrahy led a delegation to Japan—in an effort to bring Japanese business concerns to Rhode Island.

ELMER E. CORNWELL, JR., *Brown University*

RHODE ISLAND • Information Highlights

Area: 1,212 sq mi (3 140 km²).
Population (July 1, 1983 est.): 955,000.
Chief Cities (1980 census): Providence, the capital (July 1, 1982 est.), 155,717; Warwick, 87,123.
Government (1984): *Chief Officers*—governor, J. Joseph Garrahy (D); lt. gov., Thomas R. DiLuglio (D). *General Assembly*—Senate, 50 members; House of Representatives, 100 members.
State Finances (fiscal year 1983): *Revenues,* $1,835,000,000; *expenditures,* $1,708,000,000.
Personal Income (1983): $11,151,000,000; per capita, $11,670.
Labor Force (May 1984): *Civilian labor force,* 481,500; *unemployed,* 30,500 (6.3% of total force).
Education: *Enrollment* (fall 1982)—public elementary schools, 89,467; public secondary, 49,895; colleges and universities (fall 1983), 70,811. *Public school expenditures* (1982–83), $454,061,845 ($3,570 per pupil).

Acting independent of Soviet policy line, Nicolae Ceauşescu (left) visited West Germany in October. On arrival in Bonn, the Rumanian leader was welcomed by West German President Richard von Weizsäcker.

Gaby Sommer, Gamma

RUMANIA

In 1984, Rumania faced a grim economic situation at home and walked a political tightrope in international affairs.

Domestic Affairs. Confronted with serious shortages of electric power and food, together with the need to increase Rumania's exports to pay its multibillion-dollar debt to the West, the government initiated a severe austerity program. A 50% cut in the use of electricity was ordered. Meat rations were cut by 15%, flour by 13%, and allocations of milk, cooking oil, and sugar were sharply reduced. In January, in an attempt to increase the supply of agricultural products, the government offered more favorable prices and tax incentives to those producing them on private household plots and state farms.

A reshuffling of top political officials took place in early 1984. The Minister of Agriculture and Food, Ion Teşu, was replaced by Gheorghe David; the Minister of Electric Power, Trandafir Cocîrlă, by Nicolae Busui; the Minister for the Chemical Industry, Gheorghe Caranfil, by Gheorghe Dinu; the Minister for Light Industry, Lina Ciobanu, by Ion Păţan; the Minister for Technical and Material Supply and Control of Fixed Assets Administration, Ion Păţan, by Richard Winter; the Minister for the Machine-Building Industry, Ioan Avram, by Petre Preoteasa; and the Chairman of the State Committee for Prices, Ion Tulpan, by Aneta Spornic. Manea Mănescu and Major General Constantin Olteanu, the Minister of National Defense, were elected to the Political Committee of the Rumanian Communist Party (RCP).

In March the Executive Committee of the RCP launched a campaign to stimulate the lagging Rumanian birthrate, setting a national population target of 25 million by 1990. It included a new minimum legal marriage age of 15 for women, a 5% surtax on single persons over 25, and monthly monitoring of all pregnancies to term, with investigations of all miscarriages and prison terms for illegal abortions.

In May, President Nicolae Ceauşescu inaugurated a 40-mi (65-km) canal that forms a shorter link between the Danube and the Black Sea. It was one of Rumania's biggest investment projects, costing almost $2 million (U.S.).

Foreign Relations. Rumania walked a careful line between independence of the Soviet bloc and cooperation with it. It was the only bloc country to send a team to the Summer Olympic Games in Los Angeles, garnering a handsome total of 53 medals. In October, Ceauşescu and his wife Elena visited West Germany, breaking the political quarantine imposed on West Germany by the Soviet Union and giving cautious approval to a rapprochement of the two Germanies. Ceauşescu was careful to ask both the United States and the USSR to halt nuclear missile deployment in Europe and to deny the utility of both the North Atlantic Treaty Organization (NATO) and the Warsaw Pact.

At the end of January, Soviet Foreign Minister Andrei Gromyko paid a three-day visit to Bucharest. Moscow agreed to supply Rumania with 1.5 million tons of oil on the same favorable terms received by other East European countries. In March, Rumania asked NATO and the Warsaw Pact to agree to hold military spending at current levels and to seek future reductions. In June, Ceauşescu met with Soviet President Konstantin Chernenko in Moscow, urging the resumption of Soviet-U.S. nuclear arms talks.

JOSEPH F. ZACEK
State University of New York at Albany

RUMANIA · Information Highlights

Official Name: Socialist Republic of Rumania.
Location: Southeastern Europe.
Area: 91,700 sq mi (237 499 km²).
Population (mid-1984 est.): 22,700,000.
Chief Cities (July 1, 1981): Bucharest, the capital. 2,165,997; Braşov, 320,168; Cluj-Napoca, 289,808.
Government: *Head of State,* Nicolae Ceauşescu, president (took office 1967) and secretary-general of the Communist Party (1965). *Head of government,* Constantin Dascalescu, premier (took office May 1982). *Legislature* (unicameral)—Grand National Assembly.
Monetary Unit: Leu (22.44 lei equal U.S.$1, Aug. 1984).
Gross National Product (1982 U.S.$): $104,800,-000,000.
Foreign Trade (1982 U.S.$): *Imports,* $9,836,000,000; *exports,* $11,714,000,000.

447

SAN FRANCISCO

The city of San Francisco, its 706,000 residents, and its 51-year-old mayor, Dianne Feinstein, were in the spotlight as they hosted the Democratic National Convention, July 16–19, 1984. And the city was ready. Nearly $9 million had been spent on street and building repairs, and the cable car system—under renovation for nearly two years—was rolling again. The convention, held at the George R. Moscone Center downtown, cost $5.6 million to put on but injected an estimated $60 million into a thriving economy. (The municipal budget had a surplus of $150 million.) With the success of the event, Mayor Feinstein, whom Democratic presidential nominee Walter Mondale had considered as a possible running mate, increased her already wide popularity at home.

On July 10, a record 57,756 fans crowded into Candlestick Park for baseball's 55th All-Star Game, won by the National League, 3–1. On April 24, the Bay Area was struck by an earthquake that registered 6.2 on the Richter Scale. And for 13 weeks in the fall, 26 city restaurants were closed by a strike.

SASKATCHEWAN

Two of Saskatchewan's Members of Parliament were appointed to cabinet positions in the new government of Prime Minister Brian Mulroney: Ray Hnatyshyn as government house leader and Bill McKnight as labor minister.

Agriculture. A serious drought across most of Saskatchewan's prime grain-producing area and an infestation of grasshoppers reduced the expected grain harvest in 1984. The projected yield of 16.07 million metric tons was down almost 4 million tons from 1983. However, the quality of the grain was generally high, with 60 to 70% of the red-spring wheat given top grade. To help livestock producers in drought-stricken areas, jointly funded federal-provincial grants became available.

Government. In March the provincial government's budget called for a deficit of C$267 million, 20% lower than in 1983. An attempt was made to reform the welfare system: the level of social assistance to single employables was cut, and a $9 million skill-development program was instituted.

SaskWater Corporation was created to consolidate the work of various departments and agencies now dealing with water issues. Other highlights included: a reduction of 304 civil service jobs, a Venture Capital Tax Credit (a 30% income tax credit on any investment in new manufacturing, processing, tourism, or research and development projects), savings bonds from SaskPower, and a participation bond in Saskoil (a lower fixed return and a share in the profits).

Legislative Assembly member Bill Sveinson, formerly a Conservative backbencher, left government ranks to sit as the single Liberal, against 55 Conservatives and 8 New Democrats. In the federal election on September 4, 9 Conservative candidates and 5 New Democratic candidates were elected from Saskatchewan.

Resources. Oil industry activity continued at a record-setting pace. Two heavy-oil upgrader projects were announced. Husky Oil, with Saskatchewan, Alberta, and federal government financing, has begun a $3.2 billion heavy-oil production and upgrading project at Lloydminster. Assisted by $600 million in federal government financing, the NewGrade Energy Inc. upgrader is to be integrated into the Consumers' Co-op Refinery in Regina.

Aiming at natural-gas self-sufficiency in Saskatchewan, the provincial government reduced royalties and encouraged development of reserves. As a result, the number of new gas wells has risen substantially. The potash industry apparently recovered from 1983's plunge in prices, and mines operated close to capacity.

The Key Lake uranium mine, a joint project of the Saskatchewan Mining and Development Corporation and other groups, opened in northern Saskatchewan in October 1983. It is said to be the world's purest uranium deposit (2% per metric ton of ore). On Jan. 5, 1984, at the Key Lake mine, overfilling of a holding reservoir with radium-contaminated water caused the largest radioactive spill in Saskatchewan history. The Saskatchewan Environment Department ordered the mine to pump the contaminated water off the muskeg before spring runoff, and decontaminate it.

Economy. Urban housing starts were down to 3,500 from a 14-year average of 7,000 (total Saskatchewan housing starts were 4,500). The late 1984 unemployment rate of 8% was one of the lowest in Canada.

SHARON MAIER, *Regina Public Library*

SASKATCHEWAN • Information Highlights

Area: 251,700 sq mi (651 942 km²).
Population (April 1984 est.): 1,003,300.
Chief Cities (1981 census): Regina, the capital, 162,613; Saskatoon, 154,210; Moose Jaw, 33,941.
Government (1984): *Chief Officers*—lt. gov., C. Irwin McIntosh; premier, Grant Devine (Progressive Conservative); atty. gen. Gary Lane. *Legislature*—Legislative Assembly, 64 members.
Provincial Finances (1985 fiscal year budget): *Revenues,* $3,010,000,000; *expenditures,* $3,270,000,000.
Personal Income (average weekly earnings, May 1984): $383.78.
Labor Force (July 1984, seasonally adjusted): *Employed workers, 15 years of age and over,* 435,000; *Unemployed* 38,000 (8.0%).
Education (1984–85): *Enrollment*—elementary and secondary schools, 212,140 pupils; postsecondary (1984–85)—universities, 28,400; community colleges (full-time), 2,370.
(All monetary figures are in Canadian dollars.)

Saudi Oil Minister Ahmed Zaki Yamani (right) chats with his Nigerian counterpart, Tam David-West, at an emergency meeting of OPEC oil ministers in Geneva in October. The purpose of the meeting was to curb production and prop up weakening prices.

AP/Wide World

SAUDI ARABIA

As the war between Iraq and Iran in the Persian Gulf intensified, Saudi Arabian production of oil increased and Saudi fear of full-fledged involvement in the war grew in 1984.

Oil and Finance. Saudi Arabia used its crucial role of "swing" producer among the Organization of the Petroleum Exporting Countries (OPEC) to keep prices and production levels stable in 1983–1984, despite a worldwide surplus of more than 1 million barrels of oil per day that placed great pressure on prices to move downward. In 1983, Saudi Arabia produced only 5 million barrels of oil per day, the lowest amount since 1971. Because of increasing attacks on oil tankers in the Gulf, the Saudis began to pump more oil in early 1984 and also doubled the local price of gasoline. Fearing a possible interruption in oil deliveries if Iran closed the Strait of Hormuz, Saudi Arabia placed more than 15 million barrels of oil on chartered tankers in the Indian Ocean as a floating reserve. The trans-Arabian pipeline to Yanbu on the west coast, outside any likely fighting zone, was opened. Oil Minister Ahmed Zaki Yamani on March 3 warned that a disruption of Gulf oil shipments would send world oil prices skyrocketing out of control. Other OPEC countries objected to increased Saudi production; they urged Saudi Arabia to lessen oil shipments so as to reduce the world oil glut. Saudi Arabia agreed to do so on October 31, cutting production by 674,000 barrels per day, as part of OPEC's planned total reduction of 1.5 million barrels per day.

The fiscal year 1984 budget deficit of $10 billion (U.S.) was expected to increase to $13 billion in fiscal 1984–85 as projected government income from oil decreased. Expenditures were projected at $75 billion and income at only $62 billion. Money to cover the deficit was to be taken from government-owned foreign investments.

Foreign Affairs and the Military. Since Saudi leaders felt that United States involvement in Lebanon and Soviet aid to Syria threatened to lead to a major conflict in the Middle East, they tried to help resolve the Lebanese crisis. Saudi Arabia sent observers to the Lebanese national reconciliation talks in late 1983 and again in March 1984. Saudi mediation helped lessen tensions between Syria and the United States but failed to resolve peacefully the fighting among Palestine Liberation Organization factions in northern Lebanon.

Traditional Saudi quiet diplomacy and mediation ended when attacks on Saudi-owned oil tankers by Iraq and Iran began in the spring of 1984. For three years Saudi Arabia had aided Iraq in its war effort with money and diplomacy, but Iraq attacked ships of all nationalities, including Saudi vessels, carrying Iranian oil.

In January joint Saudi-Kuwaiti air force maneuvers were held, and France agreed to sell the Saudis more than $4 billion worth of anti-aircraft weapons. King Fahd on March 26 again spoke publicly of the possible introduction of military conscription. In April and May three Saudi vessels were attacked in the Persian Gulf. U.S. President Ronald Reagan then assured the king on May 21 that the United States would support Saudi Arabia against Iran in the event of war. To demonstrate this support Reagan sold and immediately dispatched 400 small antiaircraft missiles and 200 missile launchers on May 29. American and allied European warships assembled in water near Saudi Arabia but outside the Gulf proper.

Despite a United Nations Security Council vote against Iran on June 1, Iranian airplanes came close to Saudi territory on June 5 and were attacked by Saudi F-15s. One Iranian jet

---

SAUDI ARABIA • Information Highlights

Official Name: Kingdom of Saudi Arabia.
Location: Arabian peninsula in southwest Asia.
Area: 900,000 sq mi (2 331 000 km²).
Population (mid-1984 est.): 10,800,000.
Capital: Riyadh.
Government: *Head of state and government,* Fahd ibn Abd al-Aziz, king and prime minister (acceded June 1982).
Monetary Unit: Riyal (3.56 riyals equal U.S.$1, Oct. 22, 1984).
Gross Domestic Product (fiscal year 1983 U.S.$): $120,000,000,000.
Economic Index (1982): *Consumer Prices* (1970 = 100), all items, 365.7; food, 290.6.
Foreign Trade (1983 U.S.$): *Imports,* $43,000,-000,000; *exports,* $40,000,000,000.

was shot down. Saudi Arabia then declared an air defense interception zone, where threatening aircraft would be destroyed as they came close to Saudi land.

In August, Libyans on their way to Mecca for the Muslim pilgrimage unsuccessfully tried to smuggle guns into Saudi Arabia. On September 1, Libyan leader Muammar el-Qaddafi told Libyans in Arabia to abandon their plans against the Saudi government.

Government. In contrast to the dramatic activity in the economy and foreign affairs, very little changed in Saudi politics. Power remained firmly in the hands of King Fahd. Ghazi al-Gosaibi, the minister of health, was dismissed on April 18, after serving for more than ten years in the cabinet in various capacities, because of his objections to the large commissions given to royal intermediaries who arranged government contracts with foreign corporations.

The Arabian American Oil Company (ARAMCO) had been completely owned by the Saudi government for more than three years, but top management continued to be mostly American. On November 8, Ali Na'imi became the first Saudi president of ARAMCO—an appointment that symbolized the transfer of Saudi Arabia's most valuable commodity, oil, from foreign to Saudi control.

WILLIAM OCHSENWALD
Virginia Polytechnic Institute

SINGAPORE

After years of talk, the ruling People's Action Party (PAP) acted to replace the leadership that had guided Singapore for 25 years. Meanwhile the party prepared for new elections.

Politics. At the biennial PAP conference in September, all older cabinet members relinquished their positions in the party's central committee, with the exception of Prime Minister Lee Kuan Yew. Emerging as foremost contenders to succeed Lee, who indicated that he may retire in 1988 at age 65, were three men in their forties: Trade and Industry Minister Tony Tan, Defense Minister Goh Chok Tong, and Minister without Portfolio and Secretary General of the National Trades Union Congress Ong Teong Cheong. However, an unknown element in the competition for leadership was added by 32-year-old Lee Hsien Loong, the prime minister's son, who resigned from the high command of the armed forces to campaign for a seat in Parliament.

Proposed legislation would provide greater executive powers for the ceremonial presidency, including a veto over future government actions that would result in reduction of the nation's accumulated financial reserves. The bill led to conjecture that the prime minister may seek the presidency when he retires, enabling him to oversee the transition to younger leadership.

Unlike past years, when elections were called on short notice, the PAP began early in the year to name new candidates for the elections, which were held on December 22. Almost one third of the PAP candidates for the 79 parliamentary seats were new. In contrast to recent prior elections, two women were included. Leading the retirees were first deputy prime minister and economic czar Goh Keng Swee, for health reasons, and Minister of Health Howe Yoon Chong. A new law ensured an opposition under carefully circumscribed conditions. In 20 years, opposition parties had won only a single seat in Parliament. Henceforth, if together they fail to win three seats in elections, up to three of their leading vote-getters will be given speaking privileges in the legislature.

In the elections the PAP, as expected, won a sweeping victory. However, the opposition did improve its position, winning two seats.

Social Issues. The prime minister's 1983 call for college educated women to have more children continued to attract attention. The government offered tax incentives and school preference for educated mothers with three children and rewards for less educated mothers who accepted sterilization. A government committee's recommendation that retirement be delayed from age 55 to age 60, and eventually to 65, proved unpopular. The proposal would deny until the new retirement ages access to savings of the Central Provident Fund (CPF), the public pension fund supported by employer and employee contributions.

The Economy. Spurred by economic recovery in the West, especially in the United States, Singapore's real growth in the first half of 1984 was almost 10%, up from 7.9% in 1983. Tensions between the Monetary Authority of Singapore and foreign bankers during the year culminated in the expulsion of the merchant bank Jardine Fleming for alleged improper practices and for giving faulty advice.

K. MULLINER, *Ohio University*

SINGAPORE · Information Highlights

Official Name: Republic of Singapore.
Location: Southeast Asia.
Area: 239 sq mi (618 km²).
Population (mid-1984 est.): 2,500,000.
Capital: Singapore City.
Government: *Head of state,* C. V. Devan Nair, president (took office October 1981). *Head of government,* Lee Kuan Yew, prime minister (took office 1959). *Legislature* (unicameral)—Parliament.
Monetary Unit: Singapore dollar (2.1675 S. dollars equal U.S.$1, Oct. 22, 1984).
Gross Domestic Product (1982 U.S.$): $14,200,-000,000.
Economic Index (1983): *Consumer Prices* (1978 = 100), all items, 128.4; food, 127.8.
Foreign Trade (1983 U.S.$): *Imports,* $28,158,-000,000; *exports,* $21,833,000,000.

SOCIAL WELFARE

A combination of natural and man-made disasters turned the worst fears of widespread famine in eastern and central Africa into a shocking reality toward the end of 1984.

African Famine. Starving children brought to relief centers in Ethiopia were dying there at the rate of 100 or more a day. In October graphic film on television news drew large-scale attention to the crisis for the first time, although it had been predicted for several years. Hurried relief efforts were mounted by various groups and nations. The United States at first had misgivings about aiding the Marxist government in Ethiopia, and the Reagan administration attempted to link increases in aid to Africa with passage of a bill to continue financial support for Nicaraguan rebels. Ultimately, U.S. exports of grain and other foods were doubled (by far the major share in the relief effort), partly in response to lobbying by the Catholic Relief Service. The Soviet government sent only military aid to its client state until late in the year.

It was still not clear at year end whether or not the aid was too little and too late. In Ethiopia alone 6 million people were in imminent danger of starving; the situation in Chad and Mozambique was nearly as bad. On a broader scale, 15 years of virtually continuous drought and mismanaged agricultural policies had placed 35 million people in 18 African nations in desperate jeopardy, with relief efforts severely hampered by ineffective or nonexistent distribution systems for getting food to those who needed it in what had become the worst crisis of its kind in decades. The dimensions of the calamity became clear enough by midsummer to prompt the World Bank to propose the creation of a special emergency fund for the most impoverished black African nations. The reason was that continuing concern among leaders of industrial nations about the debt problems of Latin America had distracted attention from the far more urgent and immediate needs in Africa. (*See also* AFRICA.)

Other Third World Issues. A furor erupted in August at the UN Conference on Population, when the U.S. government's delegation announced a more stringent policy of withholding assistance for population aid to organizations whose planning programs perform or promote abortions. The delegates from 149 countries at that meeting confronted the prospect of global population growth that threatened to outstrip resources by more than doubling in the next 50 years. They were told that 42% of the world's children under five years of age were malnourished, that 1 in 10 in the Third World countries would die before their first birthday, that 1 billion people lacked clean water to drink, and that one quarter of the world's families lived in inadequate dwellings.

W. V. Chandler's report for the World Watch Institute on world health, released in July, indicated that low-cost primary health-care procedures, along with better water and sanitation, could easily save the lives of 7 million children a year. Yet the World Bank and similar agencies had invested ten times more in energy production than in health, nutrition, and family planning in the Third World. Meanwhile, the U.S. Agency for International Development, which had done much of the basic work in health-care research, faced a 20% reduction in its budget for that activity.

By contrast, the return to market incentives in Chinese farming and the "Green Revolution" in India brought striking improvements in food supplies and generally better standards of living to those large nations. Other parts of Asia were not so fortunate. The United Nations High Commissioner for Refugees sought to provide incentives to encourage ship captains to pick up more Vietnamese "boat people." The numbers rescued had dropped sharply in 1983, raising fears that many had been left on the high seas to perish. During the commissioner's tours of Southeast Asia, he reported that at least 130,000 Cambodians and Vietnamese in Thailand camps were waiting for a chance to relocate where they could rebuild their lives. Political turmoil in the Philippines was matched during the year by a continued deterioration in the lot of most citizens due to rapid population growth, a decline in trade and worker productivity, and a sharp drop in real wages.

Social Programs. In spite of hard times in most places, the gradual spread of social-insurance programs continued in various parts of the world. Six developing countries in Asia and Africa introduced old-age and disability insurance, primarily benefiting government employees, while some improvements in the categories of people covered were made in West Germany and Portugal, and higher benefits were provided in a variety of places.

For the most part, however, the retreat in welfare spending continued in Western Europe as economic recovery slowed and budgets were strained again. Both poor and relatively prosperous countries made fresh cuts in their welfare systems. West Germany converted grants for university students to loans, reduced maternity-leave payments, imposed charges for previously free medical insurance, and cut unemployment benefits. General resentment mounted against Turkish "guest workers" in Germany receiving such aid. In France, a modest retreat from free medical and other benefits early in the year was only the beginning of intensified austerity; by October, the economic downturn had produced a sudden growth in the number of totally destitute persons and new emergency taxes to help them survive. Similar reductions were adopted in the cautiously socialist regime of Spain. In Britain, the Conservative Party's retreat was halted by spreading unemployment, among the worst in Europe, that placed a continued drain on the nation's resources. The situation forced a postponement of the national debate on the future of the welfare state that Prime Minister Margaret Thatcher had called for early in 1984.

United States. A three-year study financed by the U.S. Social Security Administration showed that a poor person was better off in most other countries than in the United States. Other countries generally had higher grants for the costs of raising children and for maternity benefits in particular. Additional studies showed that in spite of Reagan administration predictions, the number of Americans below the poverty line had increased. The average family's income rose slightly in 1983, but about 900,000 people fell into poverty during the year.

One study indicated that one fourth of Americans lived in poverty at one time or another in the 1970s, and that many continued to slip in and out of poverty. The persistently poor were found mostly among the aged and members of households in which the head of family was disabled. Two thirds of these "permanent poor" lived in the South, mostly in rural areas. Moreover, changes in the tax laws over the past few years imposed an additional burden on some low-income families. Between 1979 and 1982 the number of Americans below the poverty line ($9,862 for a family of four in 1982) rose from 26.1 million to 34.4 million. Of these, 849,000 paid federal income taxes in 1982, more than double the number in 1980. At the same time, stricter definitions and enforcement cut about 100,000 families headed by working women from benefits under Aid to Families with Dependent Children programs and pushed them into poverty-level incomes.

Such studies were grist for political mills in a presidential election year, but public opinion seemed to be more concerned with such problems as drug and alcohol abuse. More marijuana, cocaine, and heroin were produced in 1984 than ever before, and far more went to the United States than to any other country. Federal efforts to combat the problem at home and abroad seemed fruitless, and many states, such as California, turned to more vigorous enforcement of laws on their own, especially in combating the growing of marijuana on state and federal lands. The problem of drunk driving was labeled the "nation's number one safety and health" hazard by J. Burnett, chairman of the National Transportation Safety Board. One effort to grapple with it was a new federal law withholding highway construction assistance from states that failed to raise their minimum drinking age to 21 years within two years. Another was an anticrime law that tightened laws dealing with drug trafficking.

Constituent complaints regarding the seemingly arbitrary removal of disability benefits prompted a law providing a specific standard that must be met before any beneficiary can be removed from the rolls. The administration initially had resisted this solution following some fierce resistance and eloquent denunciations by several judges. The broader question of the future of Social Security became a much-debated topic in the election, but all sides stated the issue in terms too simplistic to shed much light on the strengths and weaknesses of the system. Most experts agreed that an overhaul of Medicare and Medicaid programs would be necessary very soon, and suggested the appointment of a commission similar to the one that aided in amending the Old Age and Survivors Insurance program. Meanwhile, Congress imposed a 15-month freeze on physicians' fees as a stopgap effort to keep health-care costs from further escalation.

Another major, often underlying, issue in the election was abortion; the Right-to-Life movement gained strength and adherents and on many connected issues may have mobilized a small majority of voters. Some extremists in the movement still used violence; several bombings of planned parenthood centers occurred in various parts of the nation. Undoubtedly, much of the drive for President Reagan's reelection by antiabortion groups came from the hope that the appointments to the Supreme Court anticipated during his second term would bring a reversal of the 1973 decision that legalized abortion on demand. Other issues concerning women were less controversial. A federal law gave spouses the right to pensions of vested workers who died before retirement, and other changes in pension regulation provided more equitable treatment. Congress also required states to develop systems for the automatic withholding of child-support payments from the wages of any person delinquent in such payments.

Perhaps the most shocking welfare issue of the year was the revelation of widespread sexual and physical abuse of women and children. Television dramatizations of the plight of battered wives swayed public opinion to support direct help at local and state levels. A series of sensational trials focused attention on child abuse as an apparently growing problem, whether it involved major physical mistreatment or sexual exploitation ranging from "kiddie porn" productions to constant sexual abuse by family members or friends. The failure to identify and confront such abuse in child-care centers added to the concerns of working mothers, and in one case forced the resignation of a city official in New York. Aside from possible indirect effects on law enforcement, there were no other appreciable results.

MORTON ROTHSTEIN
University of California-Davis

The U.S. Homeless

During the winter of 1983–84 a spate of journalistic pieces, photo essays, and other reports brought to the American public a new awareness of the plight of the homeless, whose numbers seemed to be increasing dramatically. There were certainly larger numbers of people with no place to live who were straining both public and private facilities, ironically at the very time when the lot of most Americans seemed to be improving in a recovering economy. Historically, there always had been a small proportion of the population without homes, who lived as migrants or derelicts in the skid rows of large cities and served as occasional casual laborers. Reliable statistics on the new homeless were unavailable, with estimates ranging from 250,000 to 2.5 million, but it was indisputable that their composition was varied and drawn from many different groups. There were strong differences of opinion, made sharper still by an impending election, about the causes, extent, and solutions for this mounting social problem.

Causes and Extent. The causes for a portion of the "underclass" being without shelter are pervasive; basically they are people who move outside the regular, ordinary patterns of life and of the system of social work, bureaucracy, and entitlements. They often resist any effort to conform to the requirements of the welfare system. They cannot, as people without addresses, receive food stamps or any but emergency welfare payments. Since they do not meet any definition or requirement of residency, they are not counted in unemployment figures and are impossible to count at all. But increasingly, they are made up of mental patients discharged from various institutions, of runaways or other young people separated from their families, and of workers unable to acquire needed skills. The disintegration of family life in a postindustrial society, the failure to deal with several categories of the mentally ill or deficient, and the failure to sustain the level of single-occupancy living units available —much less increase them—at affordable rates, even in flophouses, are all basic elements in the syndrome that produces these people. They come from all ethnic groups; many of them are women—the notorious "bag ladies" that now seem ubiquitous in most large cities.

Less clear is the reason for the rather sudden strain they have placed on relief facilities. The largest private organization addressing the problem, the Salvation Army, provides only 42,000 beds throughout the nation. New York City, which has the largest public shelter system, housed some 6,000 homeless nightly during the year, twice the number of 1981 and more than during the Great Depression of the 1930s, but hardly enough to deal with an estimated 20,000 homeless below the age of 21 years in that city alone. In Philadelphia, some 15,000 persons received emergency family housing in 1983, five times as many as in 1981, and there was evidence that whole families have joined the ranks of the single drifters. Detroit officials estimated that their case load had increased more than 50% over the previous winter. The District of Columbia shelters were full by September, long before winter came. Chicago had 100 city beds for about 20,000 homeless; as in most places, officials relied on church and community help to supplement their facilities.

Yet most of the homeless took refuge in abandoned buildings, over hot-air grates, under bridges, in phone booths and trash dumpsters, and on the traditional park benches, hazarding the elements every night, with tragic results. New York City's Board of Health reported that during the winter of 1983– 84 an average of one homeless person a day was found dead.

For many of the U.S. homeless, hot-air grates are one of the few places to go when temperatures fall.

J. L. Atlan, Sygma

E. Kashi, Gamma-Liaison

The growing number of homeless has increased substantially the burden of the nation's various assistance organizations, including local soup kitchens.

Assistance. Such obvious need stimulated a new wave of activism in several cities. In Washington, DC, the Community for Creative Non-Violence, led by the charismatic Mitch Snyder, uses intensely flamboyant tactics to attract attention to the problem. The organization advises private and religious groups in 35 major cities on how to deal with the homeless. Its leaders also testified before three Congressional hearings on the subject, obtained special intervention from President Reagan on behalf of special proposals they pushed, and have instituted a first amendment case due to come before the Supreme Court on access to housing as a basic right. The Community also had been instrumental in pressing for and obtaining more than 1,500 beds in Washington during the year, compared with the 174 available in 1979.

In New York City, the main champion of the homeless, Robert Hayes, who quit his job with a prestigious law firm to found the Coalition for the Homeless in 1982, sued both the city and state government for more and better housing for those without it. Both the mayor and governor admitted they had not and could not meet the need fully and sought to allocate more funds. Emergency shelter for more than 2,300 families (up from 900 in 1982–83) in the city's squalid welfare hotels was hardly sufficient to provide even temporary solutions. Massachusetts responded positively with special legislation that funded 13 shelters on a cost-sharing basis with the community groups involved, and it committed $200 million to build new housing units and renovate old ones to shelter the five or ten thousand estimated homeless in that state.

Other states have fought to shift the burden for this care somewhere else. The Phoenix (AZ) City Council adopted an anti–skid row ordinance in 1981 that discouraged blood banks, bars, soup kitchens, and flophouses. The city of Tucson is suing a church soup kitchen as a public nuisance. Pennsylvania tightened its welfare and work-fare rules, as did several other states; these actions, along with the paring of 200,000 from the rolls of Supplemental Security Income, added considerably to the number of homeless.

The Housing Problem. The basic problem, however, is the lack of low-cost housing throughout much of the United States. The revitalization of the central sections of cities destroyed many cheap, old hotels and boarding houses. Federally subsidized housing projects for the poor either became subsidies for the middle class if they were run well or deteriorated rapidly into hideous slums that gave all government housing a bad press. Fewer than half of the six million low-income units that Lyndon Johnson claimed were needed in the nation were built, and in the 1970s all federal housing programs were cut back while costs of private housing skyrocketed. In the same 1970s about one million single-occupancy dwellings were destroyed or converted to condominiums, according to one study. The number of Americans sharing living quarters with other families also increased dramatically, further evidence of the growing shortage of housing.

The Reagan administration has sought to deal with the housing shortage largely by makeshift programs for the homeless. The Pentagon, for example, offered 500 locations to cities or groups from their inventory of unoccupied military reserve centers, but there were no funds to make them habitable. The Federal Emergency Management Agency spent $140 million over two years in shelter aid, and by year-end it was reviewing the situation for possible means of subsidizing shelters directly. Meanwhile, the Federal Housing Act of 1983 was being denounced as a departure that virtually ended all federal government involvement in housing construction and began a still experimental system of housing "vouchers" for the poor that would rely on the private market to provide the needed additional shelters.

MORTON ROTHSTEIN

With tensions high in black townships near Johannesburg, security forces take time to play soccer with children.

SOUTH AFRICA

In September 1984 the basic structure of the white political system in South Africa was changed by the implementation of a new constitution. For President Pieter W. Botha this was "the threshold of a new dawn," but the country soon experienced the worst African unrest since the Soweto uprising in 1976.

Constitutional Changes. The new constitution replaced the Act of Union, which had brought South Africa into being in 1910. It established a tricameral Parliament, with chambers for Indians and Coloureds (a racially mixed group) in addition to that for whites. Africans, who constitute 73% of the population, were excluded because the government considered them to be citizens of the "black homelands" created from South African territory. The new Parliament gave the appearance of reflecting the views of three races, but real power remained firmly in white hands. In effect, both the office of the president and the powerful President's Council were controlled by the National Party, the majority party in the 178-member white House of Assembly.

While the new constitution had the general support of South Africa's 4.6 million whites, who voted in favor of the changes in November 1983, it had only minimal support from the country's 870,000 Indians and 2.1 million Coloureds. In August, 70% of the eligible Coloured voters boycotted elections for their 85-member House of Representatives and 80% of the Indians for their 45-member House of Delegates.

The United Democratic Front (UDF) led by Dr. Allan Boesak, a prominent Coloured religious leader, organized the national boycott, which was a clear rejection of the constitution and an indication of the strength of the new UDF coalition of antiapartheid groups.

Former Prime Minister Botha, whose office was abolished by the new constitution, became South Africa's first fully executive president on September 14. Until then the presidency had been largely ceremonial. The next day Botha announced a cabinet that for the first time in the country's history included a Coloured and an Asian. The Rev. H. J. Hendrickse, leader of the Labour Party, and Amichand Rajbansi, of the National People's Party, were appointed to the cabinet but were given ministries without portfolio. For many observers the appointments were mere tokens.

Black Urban Violence. From September onward, violence erupted in black townships surrounding Johannesburg. Hundreds of people were killed or injured. Rioting began in Sebokeng, Sharpeville, and Boipatong over such major grievances as rent increases, inferior schools, and the exclusion of blacks from complete participation in the political life of the country.

In October, 7,000 police and Defense Force troops conducted house-to-house searches that resulted in the arrest of more than 350 persons. The use of the Defense Force in domestic affairs for the first time since the Soweto uprising was highly criticized by opposition leaders and even by some government newspapers.

The Nkomati Accord. In March, South Africa altered the regional political configuration by entering into an accord with the Marxist government of Mozambique. The Mozambican regime was forced into the agreement by a third year of devastating drought, a major economic crisis, and attacks by the South African–backed Mozambique National Resistance (MNR) organization. The pact of "nonaggression and good neighborliness" was signed on March 16 on the banks of a river 300 miles (500 km) east of Johannesburg. It was a setback for the African National Congress (ANC), South Africa's exiled black liberation movement, since the signatories were committed to withhold support fom each other's internal enemies.

After March 16, Mozambique expelled 800 members of the ANC from its territory and cut back the organization's presence to a ten-member diplomatic mission. But by June there were no signs of the Mozambique National Resistance curtailing its activities; indeed, the MNR extended its operations into two more Mozambican provinces. In October, however, an agreement engineered by South Africa was reached by the Maputo government and the MNR. President Samora M. Machel was acknowledged as the leader of Mozambique; "armed activity and conflict within Mozambique" would be stopped; and the South African government would be called in to play an intermediary peacekeeping role. The cease-fire agreement was said to have come about because of Mozambique's threat to cancel the earlier nonaggression pact with South Africa if the activities of the MNR were not curtailed.

Prime Minister's Trip. In May and June, Prime Minister Botha made a 16-day official tour of Europe. He received formal but cool receptions from the political leaders in most of the eight countries he visited, and his trip was marred by antiapartheid demonstrations. The visit was nonetheless a significant diplomatic departure from South Africa's decades-long isolation. Many white South Africans saw it as a step closer to international acceptance and recognition of the impending constitutional changes.

The Economy. Gold accounted for half of South Africa's exports in 1984, and the steep decline in gold prices since 1981 continued to have a severe effect on the economy. Like Mozambique, South Africa was also experiencing one of the most serious droughts in its history. These factors, together with high interest rates, double-digit inflation, a negative balance of payments, and excessive government spending, had created the country's worst recession since the 1930s.

Nobel Prize. The 1984 Nobel Peace Prize was awarded to South African Bishop Desmond M. Tutu in recognition of his nonviolent campaign to end apartheid (*see* BIOGRAPHY).

Namibia. Although there were signs of a breakthrough, little progress was made on implementing UN Security Council Resolution 435 (1978), which called for the independence of Namibia, the former South West Africa. The United States had been participating in a five-power effort to get South Africa to implement the resolution by withdrawing from Namibia and accepting UN-supervised elections in the territory. But the Reagan administration and South Africa had added a further dimension to the problem by linking South Africa's agreement to the withdrawal of Cuban forces from Angola, and this continued to cause the major impasse throughout 1984.

South Africa's demand that the Cubans leave was unacceptable to the Marxist government of Angola, which was opposed by rebel groups and regarded the Cubans' presence as essential for its survival. The South West African People's Organization (SWAPO), which was conducting guerrilla operations in Namibia from Angola, demanded independence for Namibia free of South African–imposed conditions. Meanwhile, South African troops had attacked SWAPO bases in Angola.

In February 1984, South Africa and Angola signed a disengagement agreement for the withdrawal of Pretoria's support for the rebel National Union for the Total Independence of Angola (UNITA) in return for Angola's controlling SWAPO forces in the border area. By December, however, South Africa still had troops within Angolan territory.

In July, direct talks took place between SWAPO and South Africa for the first time. South Africa proposed that an interim government for Namibia be established under SWAPO leadership but with key ministerial appointments to be determined by South Africa. SWAPO found these terms to be unacceptable.

See also AFRICA.

PATRICK O'MEARA
African Studies Program, Indiana University

SOUTH AFRICA • Information Highlights

Official Name: Republic of South Africa.
Location: Southern tip of Africa.
Area: 476,218 sq mi (1 233 404 km²).
Population (mid-1984 est.): 31,700,000.
Chief Cities (1980 census): Pretoria, the administrative capital, 528,407; Cape Town, the legislative capital, 213,830; Johannesburg, 1,536,457; Durban, 505,963.
Government: *Head of state and government,* P. W. Botha, president (took office Sept. 1984). *Legislature*—Parliament (tricameral): House of Assembly, House of Representatives (Coloured), and House of Delegates (Indians).
Monetary Unit: Rand (1.8587 rands equal U.S. $1, Dec. 3, 1984).
Gross Domestic Product (1982 U.S.$): $71,668,-000,000.
Economic Index (October 1983): *Consumer Prices* (1970 = 100), all items, 423.2; food, 491.1.
Foreign Trade (1982 U.S.$): *Imports,* $16,700,-000,000; *exports,* $17,200,000,000.

At the age of 81, South Carolina's Strom Thurmond (R) won his sixth term in the U.S. Senate. It was expected that he would remain chairman of the Senate Judiciary Committee.

Office of the Senator

SOUTH CAROLINA

Pressured persistently by Gov. Richard Riley, the legislature added one cent to the sales tax to upgrade public school education. Quality education was mandated by law.

Government. President Ronald Reagan received 64% and Republican Sen. Strom Thurmond 67% of the vote in the general election, despite most blacks voting Democratic. All six congressmen were reelected, keeping representation evenly divided. In the state legislature, Republicans gained 7 seats, 4 in the senate and 3 in the house. However, the legislature remained overwhelmingly Democratic. For the first time, four blacks were elected to serve full terms in the senate; 16 blacks were elected to the house. In several of the metropolitan areas, Republicans made significant gains in county and school district elections.

After deliberations in the legislature and federal courts, the state senate was reapportioned into 46 single-member districts, with 10 having majority black population. Despite this adjustment, only 4 blacks were elected.

Constitutional amendments were approved restricting legislative spending and borrowing powers. Laws were enacted to increase pay for state employees and schoolteachers, impose an accommodations tax, simplify voting procedures, raise the age for consuming beer and wine to 20, permit blind jurors, authorize twin trailer trucks on major highways, make baby selling a felony, and impose heavier sentences for some crimes. The governor continued his effort to reduce the amount of nuclear waste brought into the state. Numerous cases against major drug offenders were prosecuted successfully, and large amounts of marijuana crops were destroyed.

Education. Providing more than $217 million in additional sales tax money, the state took a giant step to invigorate public school education. The comprehensive law providing for the use of the funds mandated additional credits for graduation, graduation examinations, periodic basic skills testing, extensive remedial pro-

grams, and strict attendance regulations. Teacher pay was geared to the southeastern average, and evaluation of teachers and principals was required. Overall, the laws directed that positive results must be achieved, and they empowered the state to enforce the regulations.

The scores on most basic skill and Scholastic Aptitude Tests (SATs) improved. In higher education, the state significantly increased funding; minority quotas in white universities lagged; and agreement was reached on the number of medical students to be enrolled.

Industry and Agriculture. Textile and apparel plants in the state continued to close, leaving several communities in dire conditions. New plants and expansions to existing ones outpaced 1983's growth. State agencies stressed the development of small businesses and the upgrading of vocational educational programs. A nuclear plant and a massive paper production industry began full operations without serious environmental disturbances.

Weather was a major factor in agriculture, with heavy rains in midsummer and drought in the late summer and fall. Hail damage was extensive in some areas. Because of drought, tobacco outpaced soybeans as the chief money

---

SOUTH CAROLINA • Information Highlights

Area: 31,113 sq mi (80 582 km²).
Population (July 1, 1983 est.): 3,264,000.
Chief Cities (1980 census): Columbia, the capital (July 1, 1982 est.), 101,457; Charleston, 69,510; Greenville, 58,242.
Government (1984): *Chief Officers*—governor, Richard W. Riley (D); lt. gov., Mike Daniel (D). *General Assembly*—Senate, 46 members; House of Representatives, 124 members.
State Finances (fiscal year 1983): *Revenues,* $4,598,000,000; *expenditures,* $4,229,000,000.
Personal Income (1983): $29,984,000,000; per capita, $9,187.
Labor Force (May 1984): *Civilian labor force,* 1,511,700; *unemployed,* 107,700 (7.1% of total force).
Education: *Enrollment* (fall 1982)—public elementary schools, 424,362; public secondary, 184,156; colleges and universities (fall 1983), 134,532. *Public school expenditures* (1982–83), $1,158,594,893 ($2,017 per pupil).

crop. There was a large peach crop, but prices lagged behind expectations. Numerous farmers experienced long-range financial difficulties.

General. In the spring, tornadoes devastated sections of four counties, killing 21 people and causing massive damage.

To remedy prison overcrowding, a new $45 million correctional institution was approved. Columbia continued to plan and improve the riverfront area of the city. The Columbia zoo was rated among the ten best in the nation.

ROBERT H. STOUDEMIRE
University of South Carolina

SOUTH DAKOTA

South Dakotans cast 63% of their ballots for the reelection of Ronald Reagan, while returning Republican Larry Pressler to the U.S. Senate (74%) and Democrat Tom Daschle to the U.S. House of Representatives (57%). They sent Republican majorities back to the state legislature: Senate—25R, 10D; House—55R, 13D, 2 Ind.

Exercising popular initiative, the voters declined to mandate a nuclear arms freeze but reserved the privilege of voter approval for.any project to dispose of low-level nuclear waste in their state, such as that under study at Edgemont by Chem-Nuclear Systems, Inc. With slight margins, they approved a law to fix the starting date for all public school terms after Labor Day, in order to prolong the availability of students for service in tourism and farming through summertime; and they rejected a proposed constitutional amendment to merge the office of School and Public Lands with that of State Treasurer.

Legislation. During its regular session, the legislature accomplished little of major importance except to approve the governor's proposed $897 million budget for fiscal year 1985. The budget was to use some $340 million in federal revenues and take the remainder from state sources to sustain the functions of government and improve education and other human services.

A special session reorganized water conservancy subdistricts created in 1959; after Jan. 1, 1985, new regional development units were to evolve by county option to stimulate water use with state encouragement and financial support. With this, the controversial Oahe subdistrict vanished after a quarter-century of tortuous effort to alleviate urban shortages and to supply water-parched farms in the arid northeastern counties.

The special session also passed legislation affecting the state college and university system. Professors had been accustomed to receiving only uniform percentage increases each year as negotiated by a recognized bargaining agency. In 1984 they were given an additional

fund, available to no more than 20% of the faculty at any institution, for special "merit pay." This was welcomed by productive faculty, but it was also perceived as a process that may lead to the destruction of the state-wide faculty union.

Three institutions of higher learning surrendered traditional charges and accepted new roles. A branch of the University of South Dakota (USD) at Madison that had served mainly to train teachers became a computer-training institution. The USD branch at Springfield was closed as a vocational school for the general public and changed to serve as a minimum security prison to alleviate occupancy at penal institutions in Yankton and Sioux Falls. Meanwhile, the old Presbyterian Huron College closed as a liberal arts school and reopened as a branch of the National College of Business at Rapid City, after Huron citizens accepted a bond issue to liquidate its debts.

Accordingly, the number of non-Indian public and private higher-education institutions in South Dakota diminished from 14 to 11. Total enrollment was barely affected.

The Economy. Melting snow cover and excessive rainfall caused flooding that destroyed as much as 40% of farm production in some counties. In the Yankton area, following a local feud over drainage, a farmer shot and killed two neighbors. Quiet anguish was more widespread; across the state, still more farmers left their land.

Various indicators reflected slow but steady recovery in the general economy. Unemployment fell to some 4.5% (but was more than 80% on Indian reservations). Although average personal income remained at the bottom of the national scale, most South Dakotans reported increases in salaries or other incomes. Profits from tourism were steady, and special industries experienced growth, including gold production and lumbering in the Black Hills.

HERBERT T. HOOVER
The University of South Dakota

SOUTH DAKOTA • Information Highlights

Area: 77,116 sq mi (199 730 km²).

Population (July 1, 1983 est.): 700,000.

Chief Cities (1980 census): Pierre, the capital, 11,973; Sioux Falls, 81,343; Rapid City, 46,492.

Government (1984): *Chief Officers*—governor, William J. Janklow (R); lt. gov., Lowell C. Hansen II (R). *Legislature*—Senate, 35 members; House of Representatives, 70 members.

State Finances (fiscal year 1983): *Revenues,* $961,000,000; *expenditures,* $859,000,000.

Personal Income (1983): $6,891,000,000; per capita, $9,847.

Labor Force (May 1984): *Civilian labor force,* 345,200; *unemployed,* 14,500 (4.2% of total force).

Education: *Enrollment* (fall 1982)—public elementary schools, 85,990; public secondary, 37,907; colleges and universities (fall 1983), 34,879. *Public school expenditures* (1982–83), $292,102,189 ($2,486 per pupil).

SPACE EXPLORATION

In 1984 a new manned space endurance record of 237 days was established by three Soviet cosmonauts aboard the Salyut 7 space station, eclipsing the old endurance record of 211 days set in 1982 by three other Soviet cosmonauts. *Discovery* joined *Columbia* and *Challenger* as part of the U.S. space shuttle fleet, and five successful shuttle missions were flown. Soviet cosmonaut Svetlana Savitskaya became the first woman to perform a space walk, and three months later Kathryn D. Sullivan became the first American woman to accomplish a similar feat. In interplanetary space exploration, the USSR launched two spacecraft to encounter Halley's comet when it returns in 1986, and the International Cometary Explorer continued on its trajectory toward an encounter with the comet Giacobini-Zinner in 1985.

Manned Space Flight. The Salyut 7 space station, which had been unoccupied since November 1983, was reactivated on February 9 by the Soyuz T-10 crew of mission commander Leonid Kizim, flight engineer Vladimir Solovyov, and research cosmonaut Oleg Atkov. On April 4 the Salyut 7 crew was visited by the Soyuz T-11 crew, which included Rakesh Sharma of India and Soviet cosmonauts Yuri Malyshev and Gennedy Strekalov, for seven days of combined activities. The crew returned to earth on April 11 in the Soyuz T-10 spacecraft and left behind their newer Soyuz T-11 vehicle for use by the remaining cosmonauts.

On April 23, April 26, April 29, May 4, and again on May 18, cosmonauts Kizim and Solovyov performed extravehicular activities (EVAs) to repair the Salyut 7's propellant system, which had been damaged by an explosive rupture in 1983, and to install additional solar arrays. On February 20, April 15, May 8, and May 28, supplies and fuel were delivered to the station by unmanned Progress spacecraft.

On July 17 the Soyuz T-12 crew, composed of mission commander Vladimir Dzhanibekov, flight engineer Svetlana Savitskaya, and research cosmonaut Igor Volk, was launched to join Kizim, Solovyov, and Atkov on board Salyut 7. On July 25, Dzhanibekov and Savitskaya conducted an EVA to demonstrate tools to be used in future repair and assembly operations. On July 29, Dzhanibekov, Savitskaya, and Volk flew a nominal reentry and returned to earth in their Soyuz T-12 spacecraft.

On August 8, Kizim and Solovyov performed their sixth EVA and completed the re-

Soyuz T-10 parachuted to earth October 2 carrying three cosmonauts who had spent a record 237 days in space: (l-r) Leonid Kizim, Vladimir Solovyov, and Oleg Atkov.

Photos, Tass/Sovfoto

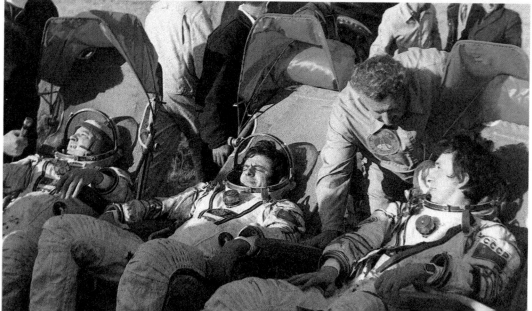

pairs on the Salyut 7 propulsion system. An unmanned Progress 23 transport was launched on August 14 to resupply Salyut 7 with fuel and bulk supplies.

On October 2, 1984, after occupying the Salyut 7 space station for a record 237 days, Kizim, Solovyov, and Atkov returned to earth in the Soyuz T-11 spacecraft. Following their flight, the cosmonauts were in good health but required an extended period of readaptation to earth's gravity. The new 237-day manned space endurance record broke the previous record of 211 days established on board the same Salyut 7 station in 1982 by Anatoly Berezovoy and Valentin Lebedev.

Five U.S. space shuttle missions were conducted in 1984 as *Discovery,* the third of four planned orbiters, joined *Columbia* and *Challenger* as part of the fleet. The first shuttle mission of 1984 and *Challenger*'s fourth flight, designated STS 10 (Space Transportation System Mission 10), began on February 3 with launch from the Kennedy Space Center (KSC) at Cape Canaveral, FL, and ended eight days later with the first shuttle landing on the runway at KSC. Vance D. Brand was the mission commander; the other crew members were pilot Robert L. Gibson and mission specialists Bruce McCandless II, Robert E. McNair, and Robert L. Stewart. The highlight of the mission came on Feburary 7, when McCandless and Stewart made untethered spacewalks using nitrogen-propelled backpacks. Two commercial communications satellites, Western Union's Westar 6 and Indonesia's Palapa B-2 were also successfully deployed from the shuttle, but neither achieved its desired geosynchronous orbit because of malfunctioning booster rockets.

The seven-day STS 11 mission, the fifth flight of *Challenger,* began on April 6 with launch from KSC and ended successfully with a landing at Edwards Air Force Base, CA. The mission was commanded by Robert L. Crippen, supported by pilot Francis R. Scobee and mission specialists Terry J. Hart, James D. van Hoften, and George D. Nelson. The highlight of the mission was the in-orbit repair of the malfunctioning Solar Maximum Mission satellite during extended EVAs by Nelson and van Hoften using the techniques demonstrated on *Challenger's* previous flight. In addition, the Long Duration Exposure Facility (LDEF), a large structure carrying a variety of experiments requiring direct exposure in space, was deployed. The LDEF will be retrieved by the shuttle in 1985 and returned to earth, where the results of the experiments will be analyzed.

After three disappointing postponements, *Discovery*'s maiden flight (STS 12) got underway with a successful lift-off from KSC on August 30. The six-member crew was made up of mission commander Henry W. Hartsfield, Jr.; pilot Michael L. Coats; mission specialists Steven A. Hawley, Richard M. Mullane, and Judith A. Resnik; and Charles D. Walker of the McDonnell Douglas Corporation, the first industrial payload specialist. Three communication satellites were successfully launched from *Discovery*'s cargo bay and boosted to geosynchronous orbit by payload assist modules— Satellite Business System's SBS-4, Hughes Aircraft Co.'s Syncom IV, and AT&T's Telestar 3-C. In addition, *Discovery* carried the Continuous Flow Electrophoresis Experiment, designed to separate biological materials for use in new pharmaceuticals, and a 102-ft (31-m) solar-power panel, which was unfurled from the payload bay and retracted several times. The STS 12 mission ended with a landing on September 5 at Edwards Air Force Base.

On the October flight of the shuttle "Challenger," Kathryn Sullivan became the first U.S. woman to walk in space.

Photos, NASA

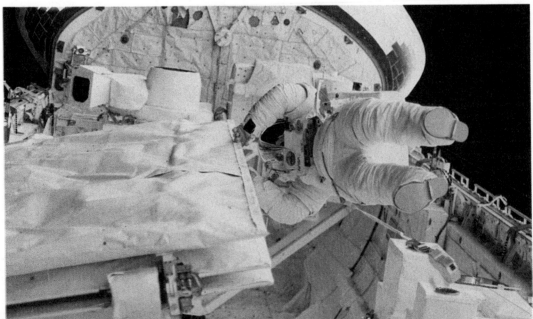

"Discovery" astronauts Dale Gardner and Joseph Allen retrieve—and advertise—a damaged communications satellite.

STS 13, *Challenger*'s sixth flight, was launched October 5 from KSC with a crew of seven, the most ever to fly on a space mission. The seven were: mission commander Robert L. Crippen; pilot Jon A. McBride; mission specialists David C. Leestma, Sally K. Ride, and Kathryn D. Sullivan; payload specialist Paul D. Scully-Power; and engineer Marc Garneau, the first Canadian to fly in space. A highlight of the mission was the deployment of the Earth Radiation Budget Satellite, which monitors thermal radiation from the earth and measures stratospheric aerosols and trace elements. The shuttle also carried an imaging radar that provided high-resolution imagery of surface geologic and oceanographic features and a camera that acquired high-resolution photographs for cartographic mapping. Kathryn Sullivan became the first U.S. woman to walk in space when she and Leestma exited the shuttle for three and a half hours on October 11 to demonstrate procedures for in-space satellite refueling. The mission ended successfully with a landing at KSC on October 13.

The second flight of *Discovery* and the last shuttle mission of 1984, STS 14, began on November 8 with a launch from KSC and ended eight days later, also at KSC. This time *Discovery* carried a crew of five—mission commander Frederick H. Hauck, pilot David M. Walker, and mission specialists Joseph P. Allen, Anna L. Fisher, and Dale A. Gardner. The highlight of the mission was the EVAs by Allen and Gardner to retrieve the Palapa B-2 and Westar VI communication satellites, which had been placed in improper orbits by malfunctioning booster rockets following deployment from *Challenger* in February. Both satellites were returned to earth and will be refurbished and sold for reuse. The crew also deployed two communications satellites during the mission—Anik D-2 for Telesat of Canada and Syncom IV-1 for Hughes Aircraft Co.—and successfully boosted them into geosynchronous orbit.

In his January 1984 State of the Union address, President Ronald Reagan announced plans to develop a permanently manned U.S. space station and invited other nations to participate in the program. Japan, Canada, and the European Space Agency continued studies on participating in the development and operation of the U.S. space station.

Science Satellites. The first direct evidence of the possible existence of other planetary systems was provided by the Infrared Astronomical Satellite (IRAS), launched in 1983, which detected small particles surrounding the stars Vega and Formalhaut out to distances of 7.5

billion mi (12 billion km). Analysis of some of the other celestial objects observed by IRAS indicated that more than 40 other nearby stars might also be surrounded by solid particles similar to those around Vega. This suggests that our galaxy, the Milky Way, may contain numerous stars surrounded by particles that could coalesce into larger bodies, eventually forming a planetary system around the star.

Three interactive AMPTE (Active Magnetospheric Particle Tracer Explorers) satellites were launched into space from Cape Canaveral by a single Delta rocket on August 16 to study the interaction of the solar wind with the earth's magnetosphere. Participants in the multinational project are West Germany, Great Britain, and the United States.

Planetary Probes. The U.S. Voyagers 1 and 2, Pioneer Venus Orbiter, and Pioneers 10 and 11 all continued operations in the extended mission mode during 1984. Voyager 2 continued toward its planned encounter with Uranus in 1986 and Neptune in 1989, while Voyager 1, on a highly divergent trajectory, continued outward toward the heliospheric boundary, the outermost limit of the Sun's sphere of influence. Pioneer 10, the only man-made object to have left the solar system, was more than 3 billion mi (4.8 billion km) from earth. The International Cometary Explorer, after having been diverted out of earth orbit, was on a trajectory that would intercept the comet Giacobini-Zinner in 1985.

Two Soviet spacecraft, Vega 1 and Vega 2, were launched in December to encounter Halley's comet in 1986, when it reappears after an absence of 76 years. As the two spacecraft fly by Venus in June 1985 on their way to intercept the comet, each will deploy a soft-landing probe into Venus' night side to obtain atmospheric and surface data.

The Soviet Venera 15 and 16 spacecraft in orbit around Venus continued to acquire high-resolution radar imagery of the surface through the obscuring cloud layer. The imagery, at a resolution of 1–2 km (.6–1.2 mi), provides a broad geological characterization of surface areas, including impact craters, major fractures, mountain ridges, and hills.

Application Satellites. U.S. weather satellites in geosynchronous and low-altitude polar orbit were restored to partial operational capability in 1984 with the launch of NOAA 9 and the reactivation of GOES 1. GOES 1, which had been inactive since 1983, was reactivated to replace the GOES 5 spacecraft, which failed in July 1984. GOES 1 and GOES 6 together make up a geosynchronous system that provides hourly weather observations over the Atlantic and Pacific. NOAA 9, launched December 12 to replace the older NOAA 7, and NOAA 8 together form an advanced low-earth-orbit meteorological system that provides global coverage four times daily.

The Soviet Union, meanwhile, launched an advanced Meteor 2 weather satellite on July 5 to join its constellation of low, polar-orbiting meteorological satellites.

Japan used an N-2 booster to launch its third geosynchronous weather satellite, GMS 3, on August 3 from the Tanegashima Space Center. GMS 3, the U.S. GOES 1 and GOES 6, the European Space Agency's Meteosat, and India's Insat constitute the world's geosynchronous weather satellite system.

The U.S. emphasis on civil remote sensing continued with the launch of Landsat 5 on March 1 to replace the malfunctioning Landsat 4. Landsat 5 provides imagery in seven spectral bands at a ground resolution of 98 ft (30 m) for a wide variety of scientific studies and applications in agriculture, forestry, urban studies, and geological mapping. Ownership and operation of the U.S. land remote-sensing system, including the spacecraft, was to be transferred in 1985 from the government to a commercial organization, the Earth Observing Satellite Corporation.

Two Soviet electronic imaging earth-resources spacecraft were launched in 1984 in addition to eight film-return satellites that returned their photographic canisters to earth after missions lasting between three weeks and three months.

Communication Satellites. In addition to the five geosynchronous communication satellites successfully launched by the space shuttle, 17 civilian communication satellites were placed in geosynchronous orbit by expendable launch vehicles in 1984. Of these 17, two were launched by the United States, six by France, seven by the USSR, and one each by Japan and the People's Republic of China. The Chinese used a CZ-3 booster to launch their first geosynchronous satellite on April 8 from their new space facility in Sichuan Province. An N-2 booster was used to launch Japan's third communications satellite, BS-2A, on January 23. The United States used an Atlas-Centaur to launch an Intelsat V-G for Intelsat and a Delta vehicle to launch a Galaxy-C for Hughes Aircraft Co. An Intelsat V-F8 and GTE Spacenet F-1 were launched aboard Ariane 1 rockets from the French launch complex at Kourou, French Guiana. On August 4 and again on November 9, French Ariane 3 growth vehicles were used to launch two satellites simultaneously; a Telecom 1A and a Eutelsat ECS-2 were put in orbit on the first mission, and an Inmarsat Marecs B2 and a GTE Spacenet 2 were lofted into space on the second.

The seven domestic communication satellites placed in geosynchronous orbit in 1984 by the USSR included two Radugas, two Gorizont, two Ekran television relay spacecraft, and a developmental version of the Luch communication satellite.

WILLIAM L. PIOTROWSKI

SPAIN

During its second year in office, Spain's Socialist government deepened economic reforms and fashioned an accord with workers amid controversy over the nation's security commitment.

Government and Politics. On June 3, approximately 100,000 demonstrators in Madrid protested both the presence of U.S. military bases in Spain and their country's two-year-long membership in the North Atlantic Treaty Organization (NATO). The NATO question sharply divided the Socialist Party (PSOE) of Prime Minister Felipe González. While his party did not endorse the rally, its youth and labor sectors swelled the ranks of protesters. Later, Foreign Minister Fernando Morán urged withdrawal from NATO's military committee.

Internal discord exposed the PSOE to attacks from opposition parties. Manuel Fraga, head of the conservative Popular Alliance, lamented the government's "incongruence" on NATO; the leader of the Social-Christian Democratic Popular Party characterized the position of the government as "shameful"; and the Communists bemoaned the Socialists' failure to keep a campaign promise and reduce Spain's participation in the military alliance.

In October, after two years of ambiguity on the issue, González stated that he favored remaining in NATO but that a national referendum on the question would be held within the next 16 months. He also called for a reduction of U.S. troops in Spain. The two issues were included in a ten-point defense plan that González said would be submitted to parliamentary debate before the referendum. The PSOE did not react favorably to the plan. The party debated the issue at its December congress. In a May visit to Madrid, West German Chancellor Helmut Kohl had called Spain's admission to the European Community (EC) "unthinkable" if it pulled out of the collective security pact.

Debate over NATO did not prevent the promulgation of a new electoral law. The statute reduces inequities in the size of voting districts, permits qualified foreigners to cast ballots in municipal elections, and imposes campaign spending limits on candidates and parties.

French President François Mitterrand lent fellow Socialist González a helping hand in the deadly conflict with the Basque separatist organization, ETA. Mitterrand pledged that his country would no longer treat ETA members in southwest France as refugees. The French government also extradited three ETA militants accused of murder—a move that sparked anti-French violence in the Spanish Basque region.

Economy. Spain's gross domestic product grew by more than 2.2% beyond the figure registered in 1983, thanks to the recovery in the industrial world, combined with prudent economic policies at home. These policies helped drive inflation below the 12.2% level of 1983.

Central to the government's effort to spur output was the closing of outmoded and inefficient steel-producing and shipbuilding plants. This action, projected to eliminate 17,000 jobs in the 1984–86 period, triggered strikes by Socialist- and Communist-dominated unions.

González' personal intervention gained the support of the Socialist union for an economic and social accord with government and business designed to target public spending in productive economic areas, create jobs, regulate employer taxes, and assure reasonable salary increases. Communist labor leaders ridiculed the agreement as an "insult" to the work force, nearly one fourth of whose members were unemployed at year's end.

In the first eight months of 1984, Spain imported $3.5 billion (U.S.) more in goods and services than it exported—a notable improvement over the $7 billion shortfall recorded in a comparable period the year before. From January to August, foreign investment shot up 60.1%, indicating renewed confidence.

Foreign Affairs. Negotiations for Spain's admission to the European Community (EC) went forward for much of 1984. At the EC summit in December, however, Greece threatened to veto Spain's and Portugal's memberships unless the EC agreed to a $5 billion aid plan for southern European farmers. The threat put a "new shadow of doubt" over an enlarged EC.

In late November, Spain and Great Britain agreed to restore free movement of people, goods, and vehicles across the Spanish-Gibraltar border. The two nations also agreed to resolve the issue of sovereignty.

In mid-May, King Juan Carlos and Queen Sofia paid a state visit to the Soviet Union. The trip, the first to the USSR by a Spanish head of state, completed the reestablishment of relations between the two countries, which had restored diplomatic ties in 1977 after a long hiatus.

GEORGE W. GRAYSON
College of William and Mary

SPAIN • Information Highlights

Official Name: Spanish State.
Location: Iberian Peninsula in southwestern Europe.
Area: 195,987 sq mi (507 606 km²).
Population (mid-1984 est.): 38,400,000.
Chief Cities (1982 est.): Madrid, the capital, 3,271,834; Barcelona, 1,720,998; Valencia, 770,277.
Government: *Head of state,* Juan Carlos I, king (took office Nov. 1975). *Head of government,* Felipe González Márquez, prime minister (took office Dec. 1982). *Legislature*—Cortés: Senate and Chamber of Deputies.
Monetary Unit: Peseta (165.7 pesetas equal U.S.$1, Nov. 5, 1984).
Gross Domestic Product (1982 est. U.S.$): $179,700,000,000.
Economic Indexes (1983): *Consumer Prices* (1970 = 100), all items, 608.9; food, 539.2. *Industrial Production* (March 1984, 1975 = 100), 125.
Foreign Trade (1983 U.S.$): *Imports,* $29,194,000,000; *exports,* $19,735,000,000.

At the Los Angeles Memorial Coliseum, 93,000 spectators witnessed lavish opening ceremonies for the Summer Games.

The Olympic Games

The highlight of the 1984 sports year was the quadrennial renewal of the Olympic Games. The Summer Games were held during July and August amid the freeways and sunny urban sprawl of Los Angeles, California. It was the second time the City of Angels had hosted the pageant, the first having come at the height of the Great Depression in 1932. The 1984 Winter Games were held during February in Yugoslavia, the first Socialist nation ever to stage the event. The host city, Sarajevo, located in the dark fir forest of Bosnia-Herzegovina, had been best known as the site of the 1914 assassination of Archduke Franz Ferdinand—the incident that set off World War I.

The Summer and Winter Games both featured excellent competition and produced some memorable moments. They also certified individual athletes—such as Carl Lewis, Mary Lou Retton, and Scott Hamilton—as heroes for the ages. Unfortunately, the Los Angeles Olympics had one major problem. In early May, as the Olympic torch relay was starting its winding, 9,000-mi (15,000-km) journey from New York to Los Angeles, the Soviet Union announced that it would not be taking part in these Games. Thirteen other Warsaw Pact nations joined the boycott, with only Rumania agreeing to compete. The Soviets accused the Reagan administration of interfering with the Olympics and fomenting anti-Soviet propaganda. They said their athletes would be unsafe in Los Angeles.

Many people close to the Olympic scene contended that the boycott had been ordained when the United States led a Western boycott of the 1980 Moscow Olympics. Under pressure from then President Jimmy Carter, 55 nations stayed away that year to protest the Soviet intervention in Afghanistan. Ironically, Afghanistan was one of the Soviet-bloc nations that boycotted the LA Games. The others included East Germany, Bulgaria, Czechoslovakia, Hungary, Poland, and Cuba, all among the world leaders in amateur sports.

In some sports, the boycott had little effect on the quality of competition. In others, such as women's track and field, women's swimming, weight lifting, boxing, gymnastics, team handball, canoeing, rowing, and wrestling, competition was radically weakened and did not live up to the level of the past.

The Soviet Union, East Germany, and the United States had been expected to be the major medal winners. As it turned out, the United States won by far the most gold medals —a record 83 to 20 for second-place Rumania —and total medals—174 to 59 for second-place West Germany.

Six days after the Olympics ended, the Soviet bloc staged Friendship '84. This Olympic-type competition in Moscow, Czechoslovakia, Poland, Hungary, Bulgaria, and Cuba was designed partly to allow athletes from the boycotting nations to match or surpass the performances in Los Angeles.

The results were mixed. The LA winners had better performances in 16 of the 24 events in men's track and field and 11 of the 15 in men's swimming. The Friendship performances were better in 12 of the 17 events in women's track and field and 7 of the 14 in women's swimming. As always, comparisons were not always valid because of different conditions.

Pessimists insisted the boycott had dealt the Olympic movement a fatal blow. They said the Soviets were sure to boycott the 1988 Olympics in Seoul because they had no diplomatic relations with South Korea. The International Olympic Committee (IOC), however, said that the 1988 Olympics would remain in Seoul and hoped it could persuade the Soviet Union to attend. The IOC also studied a proposal from Greece, the home of the ancient Olympics, to become a permanent home for the modern Olympics, though that course seemed unlikely. Finally, the committee considered punishment for nations that boycotted future Olympic Games.

The XXIII Summer Games

The Los Angeles Olympics, the first to be staged by private enterprise rather than by government, ran 16 days and cost less than $500 million, little by Olympic standards. Spending was kept down by financial support from corporations, the use of existing facilities, and help from 50,000 volunteers. The LA Organizing Committee ultimately reported a surplus of $150 million.

Despite the boycott, 140 nations, the most ever for an Olympics, took part. They sent more than 7,500 athletes and more than 8,000 journalists. Worldwide television audiences were estimated at more than 2 billion.

The United States, with 597 athletes, had the largest team. In the 26 official sports, it failed to win medals only in soccer, team hand-

U.S. Olympic Heroes: Carl Lewis, below left, matched the 1936 feat of Jesse Owens by winning gold medals in the 100-m and 200-m dashes, the long jump, and the 4 x 100-m relay. Joan Benoit won the first ever Olympic women's marathon, covering the 26 miles, 385 yards in 2 hours, 24 minutes, 52 seconds. Neither athlete was seriously challenged.

David Madison, Duomo   Paul J. Sutton, Duomo

ball, and rhythmic gymnastics. U.S. athletes won a total of 174 medals—83 gold, 61 silver, and 30 bronze. Next were West Germany, with 17-19-23—59; Rumania, with 20-16-17—53; Canada, with 10-18-16—44; and Great Britain, with 5-10-22—37. China, enjoying its first full-fledged Olympic competition, took 32 medals overall.

Track and Field. The drama in the Los Angeles Coliseum centered on the attempt of Carl Lewis to win the same four events that the late Jesse Owens had won in the 1936 Berlin Olympics. The 23-year-old Lewis, from Willingboro, NJ, achieved his goal without serious challenge. He won the 100-m dash by a record margin, earned a second gold in the long jump though taking only two of his six permitted attempts, breezed to victory in the 200-m dash, and anchored the United States to victory—and a world record—in the 400-m relay. (*See* BIOGRAPHY.)

The United States dominated track and field, winning 40 medals (16 gold, 15 silver, and 9 bronze) in 41 events. The Americans won 9 of the 24 events for men and 7 of the 17 for women.

The men's winners included Edwin Moses of Laguna Hills, CA, in the 400-m hurdles; Sebastian Coe of Great Britain in the 1,500 meters, and Daley Thompson of Great Britain in the decathlon. All had won Olympic gold medals before. The major winner among the women was Valerie Brisco-Hooks of Los Angeles, though her three gold medals came in events in which the boycotting nations were strong.

For the first time, the women's program included a 3,000-m run and a marathon. Both had

dramatic moments. Among the 3,000-m finalists were 26-year-old Mary Decker of Eugene, OR, and 18-year-old Zola Budd of Great Britain. In midrace the two runners made physical contact, and Decker, the world champion, fell to the infield. She did not move for five minutes as Maricica Puica of Rumania won the race. Budd left the stadium in tears, saying the incident was not her fault. Decker left in tears, saying it was. In the marathon, Joan Benoit of Freeport, ME, took an early lead and won the race easily. Several minutes later, Gabriela Andersen-Schiess of Switzerland staggered into the stadium. She was dehydrated and almost delirious as she staggered around the last lap and collapsed across the finish line. Two hours later, she was well.

Swimming. The United States won 9 of the 15 events for men and 11 of the 14 for women. It actually won a total of 21 gold medals because Nancy Hogshead of Jacksonville, FL, and Carrie Steinseifer of Saratoga, CA, finished in a dead heat in the women's 100-m freestyle.

Among the men, Michael Gross of West Germany won two gold medals and one silver in individual events. Alex Baumann of Sudbury, Ontario, Canada, won both individual medleys in world-record time, and Rick Carey of Mount Kisco, NY, took both backstroke finals.

Among the women, Tracy Caulkins of Nashville, TN, won both individual medleys; Mary T. Meagher of Louisville, KY, won both butterflies; and Tiffany Cohen of Mission Viejo, CA, won both distance freestyle finals. Including relays, Hogshead won three gold medals and one silver.

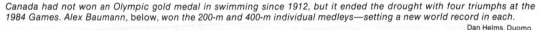

Canada had not won an Olympic gold medal in swimming since 1912, but it ended the drought with four triumphs at the 1984 Games. Alex Baumann, below, won the 200-m and 400-m individual medleys—setting a new world record in each.

Dan Helms, Duomo

Perfect 10s: Mary Lou Retton of the United States and Li Ning of China were shining lights in the gymnastics competition. Retton, 16, won a total of five medals, including a gold in the women's individual all-around. Li, 20, nicknamed the "Li Ning Tower of Power" by awestruck competitors, earned six medals overall, three of them gold.

Gymnastics. In the 14 traditional gymnastics events, the United States won 5 gold, 5 silver, and 6 bronze medals. The U.S. men and the Rumanian women won the team championships. Koji Gushiken of Japan and 16-year-old Mary Lou Retton of Fairmont, WV, took the all-around titles. Retton, with a perfect 10 in her final event, the vault, barely defeated Ecaterina Szabo of Rumania, 79.175 points to 79.125. The two women finished with five medals each; four of Szabo's were gold. Li Ning of China won six medals, including three gold in men's individual events.

New to the Olympic program in 1984 was the rhythmic gymnastics competition, won by Lori Fung of Canada.

Boxing. Of the 12 world amateur titles, U.S. boxers held six and Cubans held five in 1984. The two countries had been expected to share most of the honors in the Olympic competition. With the Cubans absent, however, the United States won 9 gold medals, 1 silver, and 1 bronze. Paul Gonzales of Los Angeles, the 106-pound champion, was chosen over Mark Breland of Brooklyn, NY, the 147-pound champion, as the outstanding boxer of the Games.

Basketball. The United States won every men's and women's game it played by a hefty margin and became the first nation to win both basketball gold medals in one Olympics. Michael Jordan of the University of North Caro-

lina led the men's team, and Cheryl Miller of Southern California starred on the women's squad. Much of the attention on the men's team, however, was paid to its tempestuous coach, Bobby Knight of Indiana University.

Other Sports. Greg Louganis of Mission Viejo easily won both men's diving titles. U.S. freestyle wrestlers won gold medals in 7 of their 10 classes. In yachting, every U.S. boat won a medal (3 gold and 4 silver). In synchronized swimming, a new Olympic sport, the United States won both gold medals. The United States also did well in men's archery, men's and women's cycling, equestrian show jumping, shooting, and men's volleyball.

Rumania excelled in men's canoeing, women's rowing, and weight lifting. China did well in weight lifting and women's diving, Japan in judo and women's volleyball, Italy in fencing and modern pentathlon, France in fencing and soccer, Yugoslavia in water polo and men's and women's team handball, and South Korea in judo and women's archery.

New Zealand was strong in men's kayaking, with Ian Ferguson winning three gold medals. Sweden starred in women's kayaking, West Germany in equestrian dressage, Pakistan in men's field hockey, and the Netherlands in women's field hockey.

Overall. The Los Angeles Olympics had many distinctions. It introduced two women's

Dan Helms, Duomo

Britain's Daley Thompson won his second straight Olympic decathlon. His 8,797 points set a new Olympic record.

sports (synchronized swimming and rhythmic gymnastics) to the Olympic program and added women's events in track and field, swimming, cycling, shooting, and canoeing. It introduced professionals to Olympic soccer and the demonstration sport of tennis.

The Games attracted 5,797,823 spectators, the highest total for any Olympics. The predominantly U.S. crowds cheered wildly for American athletes, but they also appreciated the wonderful moments that reflected the Olympic spirit of international sportsmanship. One came in the men's open judo final, in which Yashuhiro Yamashita of Japan pinned Mohamed Rashwan of Egypt. Though Yamashita had torn a calf muscle in an earlier match, Rashwan refused to attack the leg.

"That would be against my principles," he said. "I don't want to win that way."

It was an Olympics with almost everything —everything, that is, except the Soviet-bloc athletes.

XXIII SUMMER GAMES
Gold Medalists

Archery
Men: Darrell Pace, United States
Women: Hyang-Soon Seo, South Korea

Basketball
Men: United States
Women: United States

Boxing
Light Flyweight: Paul Gonzales, United States
Flyweight: Steve McCrory, United States
Bantamweight: Maurizio Stecca, Italy
Featherweight: Meldrick Taylor, United States
Lightweight: Pernell Whitaker, United States
Light Welterweight: Jerry Page, United States
Welterweight: Mark Breland, United States
Light Middleweight: Frank Tate, United States
Middleweight: Joon-Sup Shin, South Korea
Light Heavyweight: Anton Josipovic, Yugoslavia
Heavyweight: Henry Tillman, United States
Super Heavyweight: Tyrell Biggs, United States

Canoeing
Men's 500-m Kayak Singles: Ian Ferguson, New Zealand
Men's 1,000-m Kayak Singles: Alan Thompson, New Zealand
Men's 500-m Kayak Pairs: New Zealand
Men's 1,000-m Kayak Pairs: Canada
Men's 1,000-m Kayak Fours: New Zealand
Men's 500-m Canadian Singles: Larry Cain, Canada
Men's 1,000-m Canadian Singles: Ulrich Eicke, West Germany
Men's 500-m Canadian Pairs: Yugoslavia
Men's 1,000-m Canadian Pairs: Rumania
Women's 500-m Kayak Singles: Agneta Andersson, Sweden
Women's 500-m Kayak Pairs: Sweden
Women's 500-m Kayak Fours: Rumania

Cycling
Men's 1,000-m Time Trial: Fredy Schmidtke, West Germany
Men's 100-km Team Time Trial: Italy
Men's Individual Sprint: Mark Gorski, United States
Men's 4,000-m Individual Pursuit: Steve Hegg, United States
Men's 4,000-m Team Pursuit: Australia
Men's Individual Road Race: Alexi Grewal, United States
Men's Individual Points Race: Roger Ilegems, Belgium
Women's Individual Road Race: Connie Carpenter-Phinney, United States

Equestrian
Individual 3-Day Event: Mark Todd, New Zealand
Team 3-Day Event: United States
Individual Dressage: Reiner Klimke, West Germany
Team Dressage: West Germany
Individual Jumping: Joe Fargis, United States
Team Jumping: United States

Fencing
Men's Individual Foil: Mauro Numa, Italy
Men's Team Foil: Italy
Men's Individual Épée: Philippe Boisse, France
Men's Team Épée: West Germany
Men's Individual Sabre: Jean François Lamour, France

Men's Team Sabre: Italy
Women's Individual Foil: Luan Jujie, China
Women's Team Foil: West Germany

Field Hockey
Men: Pakistan
Women: Netherlands

Gymnastics
Men's All-Around: Koji Gushiken, Japan
Men's Floor Exercises: Li Ning, China
Men's Horizontal Bar: Shinji Morisue, Japan
Men's Vault: Lou Yun, China
Men's Parallel Bars: Bart Conner, United States
Men's Rings: K. Gushiken and Li Ning (tie)
Men's Pommel Horse: Li Ning and Peter Vidmar, United States (tie)
Men's Team: United States
Women's All-Around: Mary Lou Retton, United States
Women's Balance Beam: Simona Pauca, Rumania; Ecaterina Szabo, Rumania (tie)
Women's Floor Exercises: E. Szabo
Women's Vault: E. Szabo
Women's Uneven Parallel Bars: Ma Yanhong, China; Julianne Mc-Namara, United States (tie)
Women's Team: Rumania
Women's Rhythmic Gymnastics: Lori Fung, Canada

Handball
Men: Yugoslavia
Women: Yugoslavia

Judo
Extra Lightweight: Shinji Hosokawa, Japan
Half Lightweight: Yoshiyuki Matsuoka, Japan
Lightweight: Byeong-Keun Ahn, South Korea
Half Middleweight: Frank Wieneke, West Germany
Middleweight: Peter Seisenbacher, Austria
Half Heavyweight: Hyoung-Zoo Ha, South Korea
Heavyweight: Hitoshi Saito, Japan
Open: Yasuhiro Yamashita, Japan

Modern Pentathlon
Individual: Daniele Masala, Italy
Team: Italy

Rowing
Men's Single Sculls: Pertti Karppinen, Finland
Men's Double Sculls: United States
Men's Quadruple Sculls: West Germany
Men's Pairs With Coxswain: Italy
Men's Pairs Without Coxswain: Rumania
Men's Fours With Coxswain: Great Britain
Men's Fours Without Coxswain: New Zealand
Men's Eights: Canada
Women's Single Sculls: Valeria Racila, Rumania
Women's Double Sculls: Rumania
Women's Quadruple Sculls: Rumania
Women's Pairs Without Coxswain: Rumania
Women's Fours With Coxswain: Rumania
Women's Eights: United States

Shooting

Men's Rapid-Fire Pistol: Takeo Kamachi, Japan
Men's Free Pistol: Xu Haifeng, China
Men's Running Game Target: Li Yuwei, China
Men's Small Bore Rifle, Prone: Edward Etzel, United States
Men's Small Bore Rifle, Three Positions: Malcolm Cooper, Great Britain
Men's Air Rifle: Philippe Heberle, France
Men's Trapshooting: Luciano Giovannetti, Italy
Men's Skeetshooting: Matthew Dryke, United States
Women's Air Rifle: Pat Spurgin, United States
Women's Standard Rifle: Wu Xiaoxuan, China
Women's Sport Pistol: Linda Thom, Canada

Soccer

France

Swimming and Diving

Men's 100-m Backstroke: Rick Carey, United States
Men's 200-m Backstroke: R. Carey
Men's 100-m Breaststroke: Steve Lundquist, United States
Men's 200-m Breaststroke: Victor Davis, Canada
Men's 100-m Butterfly: Michael Gross, West Germany
Men's 200-m Butterfly: Jon Sieben, Australia
Men's 100-m Freestyle: Rowdy Gaines, United States
Men's 200-m Freestyle: M. Gross
Men's 400-m Freestyle: George DiCarlo, United States
Men's 1,500-m Freestyle: Michael O'Brien, United States
Men's 400-m Freestyle Relay: United States
Men's 800-m Freestyle Relay: United States
Men's 200-m Individual Medley: Alex Baumann, Canada
Men's 400-m Individual Medley: A. Baumann
Men's 400-m Medley Relay: United States
Men's Springboard Diving: Greg Louganis, United States
Men's Platform Diving: Greg Louganis
Women's 100-m Backstroke: Theresa Andrews, United States
Women's 200-m Backstroke: Jolanda De Rover, Netherlands
Women's 100-m Breaststroke: Petra Van Staveren, Netherlands
Women's 200-m Breaststroke: Anne Ottenbrite, Canada
Women's 100-m Butterfly: Mary T. Meagher, United States
Women's 200-m Butterfly: M. T. Meagher
Women's 100-m Freestyle: Carrie Steinseifer, United States; Nancy Hogshead, United States (tie)
Women's 200-m Freestyle: Mary Wayte, United States
Women's 400-m Freestyle: Tiffany Cohen, United States
Women's 800-m Freestyle: T. Cohen
Women's 400-m Freestyle Relay: United States
Women's 200-m Individual Medley: Tracy Caulkins, United States
Women's 400-m Individual Medley: T. Caulkins
Women's 400-m Medley Relay: United States
Women's Springboard Diving: Sylvie Bernier, Canada
Women's Platform Diving: Zhou Jihong, China

Synchronized Swimming

Solo: Tracie Ruiz, United States
Duet: United States

Track and Field

Men's 100-m: Carl Lewis, United States
Men's 200-m: C. Lewis
Men's 400-m: Alonzo Babers, United States
Men's 800-m: Joaquim Cruz, Brazil
Men's 1,500-m: Sebastian Coe, Great Britain
Men's 5,000-m: Said Aouita, Morocco
Men's 10,000-m: Alberto Cova, Italy
Men's Marathon: Carlos Lopes, Portugal
Men's 110-m Hurdles: Rober Kingdom, United States
Men's 400-m Hurdles: Edwin Moses, United States
Men's 3,000-m Steeplechase: Julius Korir, Kenya
Men's 400-m Relay: United States
Men's 1,600-m Relay: United States
Men's 20-km Walk: Ernesto Canto, Mexico
Men's 50-km Walk: Raul Gonzalez, Mexico
Men's Decathlon: Daley Thompson, Great Britain
Men's High Jump: Dietmar Moegenburg, West Germany
Men's Long Jump: C. Lewis
Men's Triple Jump: Al Joyner, United States
Men's Discus: Rolf Danneberg, W. Germany
Men's Shot Put: Alessandro Andrei, Italy
Men's Hammer Throw: Juha Tiainen, Finland
Men's Javelin: Arto Haerkoenen, Finland
Men's Pole Vault: Pierre Quinon, France
Women's 100-m: Evelyn Ashford, United States
Women's 200-m: Valerie Brisco-Hooks, United States
Women's 400-m: V. Brisco-Hooks
Women's 800-m: Doina Melinte, Rumania
Women's 1,500-m: Gabriella Dorio, Italy
Women's 3,000-m: Maricica Puica, Rumania
Women's Marathon: Joan Benoit, United States
Women's 100-m Hurdles: Benita Brown-Fitzgerald, United States
Women's 400-m Hurdles: Nawal El Moutawakel, Morocco
Women's 400-m Relay: United States
Women's 1,600-m Relay: United States
Women's Heptathlon: Glynis Nunn, Australia
Women's High Jump: Ulrike Meyfarth, West Germany
Women's Long Jump: Anisoara Stanciu, Rumania
Women's Discus: Ria Stalman, Netherlands
Women's Shot Put: Claudia Losch, West Germany
Women's Javelin: Tessa Sanderson, Great Britain

Volleyball

Men: United States
Women: China

Water Polo

Yugoslavia

Weight Lifting

Flyweight: Zeng Guoqiang, China
Bantamweight: Wu Shude, China
Featherweight: Chen Weiqiang, China
Lightweight: Yao Jingyuan, China
Middleweight: Karl-Heinz Radschinsky, West Germany
Light Heavyweight: Petre Becheru, Rumania
Middle Heavyweight: Nicu Vlad, Rumania
Heavyweight: Rolf Milser, West Germany
Second Heavyweight: Norberto Oberburger, Italy
Super Heavyweight: Dinko Lukim, Australia

Wrestling, Freestyle

Paperweight: Robert Weaver, United States
Flyweight: Saban Trstena, Yugoslavia
Bantamweight: Hideaki Tomiyama, Japan
Featherweight: Randy Lewis, United States
Lightweight: In-Tak You, South Korea
Welterweight: David Schultz, United States
Middleweight: Mark Schultz, United States
Light Heavyweight: Ed Banach, United States
Heavyweight: Lou Banach, United States
Super Heavyweight: Bruce Baumgartner, United States

Wrestling, Greco-Roman

Paperweight: Vicenzo Maenza, Italy
Flyweight: Atsuji Miyahara, Japan
Bantamweight: Pasquale Passarelli, West Germany
Featherweight: Weon-Kee Kim, South Korea
Lightweight: Vlado Lisjak, Yugoslavia
Welterweight: Jouko Salomaki, Finland
Middleweight: Ion Draica, Rumania
Light Heavyweight: Steven Fraser, United States
Heavyweight: Vasile Andrei, Rumania
Super Heavyweight: Jeff Blatnick, United States

Yachting

Windglider: Stephan Van Den Berg, Netherlands
Soling: United States
Flying Dutchman: United States
Star Class: United States
Finn Class: Russell Coutts, New Zealand
Tornado Class: New Zealand
470 Class: Spain

Final Medal Standings

Country	Gold	Silver	Bronze
United States	83	61	30
West Germany	17	19	23
Rumania	20	16	17
Canada	10	18	16
Great Britain	5	10	22
China	15	8	9
Italy	14	6	12
Japan	10	8	14
France	5	7	15
Australia	4	8	12
South Korea	6	6	7
Sweden	2	11	6
Yugoslavia	7	4	7
Netherlands	5	2	6
Finland	4	3	6
New Zealand	8	1	2
Brazil	1	5	2
Switzerland	0	4	4
Mexico	2	3	1
Denmark	0	3	3
Spain	1	2	2
Belgium	1	1	2
Austria	1	1	1
Portugal	1	0	2
Jamaica	0	1	2
Norway	0	1	2
Turkey	0	0	3
Venezuela	0	0	3
Morocco	2	0	0
Kenya	1	0	1
Greece	0	1	1
Nigeria	0	1	1
Puerto Rico	0	1	1
Algeria	0	0	2
Pakistan	1	0	0
Colombia	0	1	0
Egypt	0	1	0
Ireland	0	1	0
Ivory Coast	0	1	0
Peru	0	1	0
Syria	0	1	0
Thailand	0	1	0
Cameroon	0	0	1
Dominican Republic	0	0	1
Iceland	0	0	1
Taiwan	0	0	1
Zambia	0	0	1

With artistry, grace, and charm, the British team of Jayne Torvill, 26, and Christopher Dean, 25, won new fans for the sport of ice dancing. Their sensuous interpretation of Ravel's Bolero in the free-skating portion of the competition broke the mold of the traditional ballroom style. Their overall performance earned them record scores—and gold medals.

The XIV Winter Games

East Germany and the Soviet Union dominated competition at the XIV Winter Games held Feb. 7–19, 1984, in Sarajevo. The United States did well in Alpine skiing and figure skating, winning all of its eight medals (four gold and four silver) in those two sports. The only nations to win more gold medals than the United States were East Germany (9) and the Soviet Union (6). Finland and Sweden both equaled the U.S. total of four gold medals. The most total medals were captured by the Soviet Union (25), East Germany (24), Finland (13), and Norway (9). In all, 49 nations, a record, sent 1,437 athletes, also a record, to Sarajevo.

Alpine Skiing. A major surprise occurred when Bill Johnson of Van Nuys, CA, who had never won an important ski race until a World Cup downhill in Wengen, Switzerland, on January 15, finished first in the Olympic downhill. The 23-year-old Californian had brashly predicted that he would win at Sarajevo. When he did, he became the first American man to gain an Olympic gold medal in Alpine skiing. On the last day of the Games, Phil Mahre of Yakima, WA, won the men's slalom. His twin, Steve, finished second, and his wife gave birth to a boy. Earlier, Switzerland's Max Julen captured the gold in the giant slalom, and Jure Franko of Yugoslavia became a national hero by finishing second. It was Yugoslavia's first medal in Winter Olympic history.

In the women's giant slalom, Debbie Armstrong of Seattle took first; Christin Cooper of Sun Valley, ID, was second; and France's Perrine Pelen prevented an American sweep by finishing just ahead of Tamara McKinney of Olympic Valley, CA. Michela Figini, a 17-year-old Swiss, and Italy's Paoletta Magoni, a 19-year-old who had never finished better than sixth in four years of World Cup racing, were the victors in the downhill and slalom, respectively. Pelen added to her Olympic medal collection by taking the silver in the slalom.

Figure Skating. Scott Hamilton (*see* BIOGRAPHY) easily won the men's singles in figure skating, finishing first in compulsory figures, second in the short program, and second in free skating. Canada's Brian Orser took his country's only silver medal by finishing second in the event. For Americans a moment to remember occurred when, following the award ceremony, Hamilton skated a victory lap carrying a U.S. flag.

Rosalynn Sumners, the world champion from Edmonds, WA, was cofavorite with Katarina Witt of East Germany in the women's singles. Witt, 18, barely won the gold medal after Sumners omitted two difficult jumps toward the end of her free-skating program.

Kitty and Peter Carruthers of Wilmington, DE, provided another memorable moment when they finished a nearly flawless free-skating program and hugged for ten seconds at midice. However, the adopted brother and sister duo were second in the pairs competition to Elena Valova and Oleg Vasiliev, the Soviet world champions.

The artistic highlight at Sarajevo was the ice dancing of the British skaters Jayne Torvill and Christopher Dean. The judges gave them 19 perfect scores of 6 en route to their gold medal. The Americans were disappointed when Judy Blumberg and Michael Seibert of New York placed fourth in the event. Like Torvill-Dean, they skated with an interpretive and classical style rather than the conventional ballroom dancing style. The judges, not entirely comfortable with the revolutionary approach of Torvill-Dean, apparently did not want to encourage further innovations.

Speed Skating and Nordic Skiing. Gaetan Boucher, a 25-year-old speed skater from Quebec who captured the silver medal in the 1,000 meters at Lake Placid in 1980, "finally came first." At Sarajevo, he won the gold in both the 1,000-m and 1,500-m races and took a bronze in the 500 meters. East Germany's Karin Enke, another Olympic veteran speed skater, captured two gold and two silver medals.

Marja-Liisa Hamalainen of Finland won all three women's individual cross-country ski races and added a bronze in the relay. Gunde Svan of Sweden took two golds in the men's

The top medal-winner in the Winter Games was Finland's 28-year-old cross-country skier Marja-Liisa Hamalainen, who took three golds in individual competition and a bronze in the relay. In men's speed skating, Canada's Gaétan Boucher, 25-year-old Olympic veteran, raced to two golds and a bronze.

Photos Adam J. Stoltman, Duomo

Partice Habans, Sygma

Bill Johnson, a relative unknown, made good on his promise to win the men's downhill. The cocky 23-year-old became the first U.S. Alpine skier ever to wear an Olympic gold medal.

competition—the 15 kilometers and the relay. Nikolai Zimyatov, of the USSR, the holder of three gold medals from the 1980 Games, added to his collection by winning the 30 kilometers.

Other Sports. East Germany dominated bobsledding and did well in luge. The U.S. four-man bobsled, driven by Jeff Jost of Burke, NY, finished fifth, a heartening performance because the Americans had purchased the sled only three days before the race and could make only two practice runs in it.

The Soviet Union decisively won the gold medal in ice hockey. Czechoslovakia's and Sweden's teams were the silver- and bronze-medal winners, respectively. The United States, whose ice hockey team had upset the Soviet defenders and thrilled a nation in 1980, was seventh among the 12 teams.

Overall. The organizers staged the 1984 Winter Games almost flawlessly. The only major disappointment was the heavy snows that forced frequent rescheduling of the Alpine

skiing events. The ski postponements added to the problems of ABC, which had paid $91.5 million—more than half of the entire Winter Olympic budget—for U.S. television rights. The network also was hurt by the disappointing performance of the U.S. hockey team.

In addition, all ABC shows were taped, and the six-hour time difference between Sarajevo and the eastern United States meant that most potential viewers knew the results before the programs were shown. The television audiences were 25% below expectations, and ABC reimbursed many sponsors.

FRANK LITSKY, *"The New York Times"*

XIV WINTER GAMES
Gold Medalists

Alpine Skiing
Men's Downhill: Bill Johnson, United States
Men's Giant Slalom: Max Julen, Switzerland
Men's Slalom: Phil Mahre, United States
Women's Downhill: Michela Figini, Switzerland
Women's Giant Slalom: Debbie Armstrong, United States
Women's Slalom: Paoletta Magoni, Italy

Biathlon
10-kilometer Individual: Eirik Kvalfoss, Norway
20-kilometer Individual: Peter Angerer, East Germany
Relay: USSR

Bobsled
2-Man: East Germany
4-Man: East Germany

Figure Skating
Pairs: E. Valova-O. Vasiliev, USSR
Men's Singles: Scott Hamilton, United States
Women's Singles: Katarina Witt, East Germany

Ice Dancing: J. Torvill-C. Dean, Great Britain

Ice Hockey: USSR

Luge
Men's Singles: Paul Hildgartner, Italy
Men's Doubles: H. Stangassinger-F. Wembacher, West Germany
Women's Singles: Steffi Martin, East Germany

Nordic Skiing
Men's 15-kilometer: Gunde Svan, Sweden
Men's 30-kilometer: Nikolai Zimyatov, USSR
Men's 50-kilometer: Thomas Wassberg, Sweden
Men's 40-kilometer Relay: Sweden
Men's 70-meter Ski Jump: Jens Weissflog, East Germany
Men's 90-meter Ski Jump: Matti Nykanen, Finland
Men's Combined: Tom Sandberg, Norway
Women's 5-kilometer: Marja-Liisa Hamalainen, Finland
Women's 10-kilometer: M. L. Hamalainen
Women's 20-kilometer: M. L. Hamalainen
Women's 20-kilometer Relay: Norway

Speed Skating
Men's 500 meters: Sergei Fokichev, USSR
Men's 1,000 meters: Gaetan Boucher, Canada
Men's 1,500 meters: G. Boucher
Men's 5,000 meters: Tomas Gustafson, Sweden
Men's 10,000 meters: Igor Malkov, USSR
Women's 500 meters: Christa Rothenburger, East Germany
Women's 1,000 meters: Karin Enke, East Germany
Women's 1,500 meters: K. Enke
Women's 3,000 meters: Andrea Schone, East Germany

Final Medal Standings

	Gold	Silver	Bronze
East Germany	9	9	6
USSR	6	10	9
United States	4	4	0
Finland	4	3	6
Sweden	4	2	2
Norway	3	2	4
Switzerland	2	2	1
Canada	2	1	1
West Germany	2	1	1
Italy	2	0	0
Great Britain	1	0	0
Czechoslovakia	0	2	4
France	0	1	2
Japan	0	1	0
Yugoslavia	0	1	0
Liechtenstein	0	0	2
Austria	0	0	1

Auto Racing

Alain Prost of France won seven Formula One Grand Prix races in 1984, tying the record set in 1963 by Jim Clark, but he still fell one-half point short in his bid to become his country's first World Driving Champion. After 16 races on four continents, the 1984 Formula One champion was Austria's Niki Lauda, Prost's teammate on Team McLaren. It was Lauda's third title.

Mario Andretti, the only man ever to win both the World and U.S. titles, also had a sensational season. Andretti won six races, started from the pole position eight times, and earned $903,307. He won his fourth Championship Auto Racing Teams (CART) national title, but his first since 1969, when he also won the Indianapolis 500. In 1984, however, the checkered flag at Indy went to Rick Mears, who averaged a record of 163.621 mph (263.315 km/h).

The most famous race on the National Association of Stock Cars (NASCAR) circuit, the Daytona 500, was won by Cale Yarborough for the fourth time. Another all-time great, Richard Petty, reached a milestone by winning the 200th race of his career. The victory came in the Firecracker 400 at Daytona Speedway on July 4. And veteran driver Johnny Rutherford set a new world closed-course speed record of 215.189 mph (346.304 km/h). Taking over for Rick Mears, who had been injured in a race in Canada, Rutherford set the mark during qualifying for the Pocono 500, won by Danny Sullivan. Terry Labonte was the 1984 NASCAR champion.

BOB COLLINS
"The Indianapolis Star"

AUTO RACING

Major Race Winners

Indianapolis 500: Rick Mears
Michigan 500: Mario Andretti
Pocono 500: Danny Sullivan
Daytona 500: Cale Yarborough

1984 Champions

World Championship: Niki Lauda (Austria)
CART: Mario Andretti
NASCAR: Terry Labonte

Grand Prix for Formula One Cars, 1984

Austria: Niki Lauda
Belgium: Michele Alboreto (Italy)
Brazil: Alain Prost (France)
Canada: Nelson Piquet (Brazil)
Dallas: Keke Rosberg (Finland)
Detroit: Nelson Piquet
Europe: Alain Prost
France: Niki Lauda
Germany: Alain Prost
Great Britain: Niki Lauda
Italy: Niki Lauda
Monaco: Alain Prost
Netherlands: Alain Prost
Portugal: Alain Prost
San Marino: Alain Prost
South Africa: Niki Lauda

Baseball

The 1984 baseball season will be remembered as one of change. For the third straight season, all four major league divisions had new champions; players in their first full seasons won batting titles; rookie pitchers led both leagues in strikeouts; and the 15-year reign of Commissioner Bowie Kuhn ended when Peter V. Ueberroth took office on October 1.

Play-offs and World Series. After making several midseason trades to bolster their pitching staff, the Chicago Cubs roared to the top of the National League (NL) Eastern Division on August 1, then entered the play-offs as heavy favorites to win their first pennant since 1945. Entry into the World Series seemed certain after the Cubs took the first two games of the best-of-five Championship Series at Wrigley Field, their home park. But the San Diego Padres, a 1969 expansion team with no previous postseason experience, received heroic performances from high-priced free agent signees Steve Garvey and Goose Gossage to take all three games at Jack Murphy Stadium. Since the advent of divisional play in 1969, only the American League's Milwaukee Brewers had ever overcome a 2-0 deficit to win a play-off.

San Diego's World Series opponent, the Detroit Tigers, claimed the American League (AL) flag by sweeping the Kansas City Royals,

Second baseman Ryne Sandberg of the Cubs batted .314 with 19 homers and 84 RBIs to win NL MVP honors.

© Richard Pilling

Alan Trammel of the Tigers had nine hits in the World Series, including two home runs in Game 4. The Detroit shortstop was named MVP of the Fall Classic.

champions of the West, in three straight. The Tigers had captured the Eastern Division by winning 35 of their first 40 games, a major league record. They ended the season with a club record 104 victories, tops in the majors. Kansas City, on the other hand, squeaked to the Western Division title with 84 wins, the fewest of any AL champion since the advent of divisional play.

Most of the play-offs were held without the regular umpires, who went on strike for greater compensation for All-Star and postseason work. They returned to the field when Ueberroth agreed to arbitrate the dispute. After the season, the new commissioner awarded the umpires an increase of more than 100% for All-Star, play-off, and World Series duty.

In the 1984 World Series, Detroit took an early lead when Jack Morris fired an eight-hitter to top San Diego in the October 9 opener, 3–2. The Padres pulled even in Game 2 when little-used Kurt Bevacqua smacked a three-run homer to turn a 3–2 deficit into a 5–3 San Diego win. After the Series shifted to Detroit, however, San Diego could not find a way to win. In Game 3, Padre pitchers walked 11 batters, tying an embarrassing record, as the Tigers took a 5–2 win. The next day, two home runs by Alan Trammell knocked in all of Detroit's runs in a 4–2 victory. And in Game 5, Kirk Gibson also hit a pair of home runs, leading the Tigers to an 8–4 title clincher. Trammell, whose nine hits tied a record for a five-game Fall Classic, was named Most Valuable Player (MVP) of the Series.

Regular Season. Sensational pitching performances were a hallmark of the 1984 season from the first week through the last. Detroit's Jack Morris threw a 4–0 no-hitter against the Chicago White Sox on April 7. Two weeks later, Montreal's David Palmer pitched a 4–0 perfect game (shortened to five innings by rain) against the Cardinals in St. Louis. And on September 30, the final day of the regular season, California's Mike Witt pitched the majors' first nine-inning perfect game since 1981, whitewashing Texas, 1–0.

Rick Sutcliffe of the Cubs won the NL Cy Young Award, posting a 16–1 record and a 2.69 earned run average (ERA) after his June arrival from Cleveland. Sutcliffe thus became the first Cy Young recipient to win the citation after a midseason trade. The AL Cy Young winner, Detroit's left-handed relief ace Willie Hernández, had been traded from Philadelphia during spring training. By season's end he had posted a 9–3 record, with 32 saves and a 1.92 ERA in 80 appearances. Because his addition proved decisive in Detroit's march to the World Championship, Hernández was also named MVP in the American League. Only one relief pitcher, Rollie Fingers of the 1981 Milwaukee Brewers, had ever swept both honors.

Though Hernández reaped postseason honors, another relief pitcher found his way into the record book. Bruce Sutter of the St. Louis Cardinals saved 45 games, a National League record. Dan Quisenberry of the Kansas City Royals, who saved 45 in the American League in 1983, again led the Junior Circuit, this time with 44.

Only two starting pitchers, one in each league, won 20 games: Joaquin Andujar of the St. Louis Cardinals and Mike Boddicker of the Baltimore Orioles. Boddicker's 2.79 ERA also led the AL. Rookies Dwight Gooden of the New York Mets and Mark Langston of the Seattle Mariners led their respective leagues in strikeouts. Gooden, at 19, became the youngest man ever to pitch in the All-Star Game; he struck out the side in his All-Star debut, helping the Nationals post a 3–1 win in the July 10 game at San Francisco. On September 17, he fanned 16 batters for the second consecutive game, giving him a record 45 strikeouts over three straight games. Gooden finished the year with 276 whiffs, tops in the major leagues and the most ever by a rookie pitcher. His 17–9 record and 2.60 ERA (second in the league to 2.48 by Alejandro Peña of the Dodgers) earned Gooden NL Rookie of the Year honors.

At the plate, veteran outfielder Tony Armas of the Boston Red Sox led the majors with 43 home runs and 123 runs batted in (RBI). Dale

Murphy of Atlanta and Mike Schmidt of Philadelphia shared the NL home run lead with 36, while Schmidt and Montreal's Gary Carter tied for RBI leadership with 106 each. Though Murphy's .547 slugging percentage led both leagues, he was denied in his quest for an unprecedented third straight MVP award. Ryne Sandberg, second baseman of the Chicago Cubs, ended Murphy's string after hitting .314, with 200 hits, 19 homers, 84 RBI, and 32 stolen bases. The smooth fielder also hit .368 in the NL play-offs. Another former Phillie, Gary Matthews, fueled the Chicago charge with 19 game-winning hits and a .410 on-base percentage, both tops in the NL.

In the American League, Dave Winfield and Don Mattingly of the New York Yankees waged a fierce struggle for the batting title, with Mattingly winning on the last day of the season. His .343 was surpassed only by NL winner Tony Gwynn, who collected 213 hits en route to a .351 average for San Diego. Seattle's slugging first baseman Alvin Davis won AL rookie honors after hitting .284, with 27 homers and 116 runs batted in.

Montreal's Tim Raines led the majors with 75 stolen bases and became the first man to steal at least 70 bases for four straight seasons. Juan Samuel of Philadelphia stole 72, a rookie record that eclipsed Raines' 1981 mark. The St. Louis Cardinals became the first team since 1916 to top 200 stolen bases for three straight seasons. Rickey Henderson of the Oakland Athletics led the American League with 66 steals.

Among the older stars who excelled in 1984, Pete Rose became only the second player in major league history to get 4,000 hits, beginning to close in on Ty Cobb's record of 4,191 career hits. Rose started the 1984 season as a member of the Montreal Expos, but he was traded to the Cincinnati Reds in August and was named player-manager, baseball's first since 1979. A month later another longtime hitting star also found himself in exclusive company with the legendary Cobb. Rusty Staub of the New York Mets hit a pinch-hit home run to join Cobb as the only players to homer before age 20 and after age 40. And veteran slugger Reggie Jackson, now with the California Angels, reached a career milestone on September 17 when he connected for his 500th home run; only 12 players (all retired) have hit more.

Stamina was the quality that took center stage May 8–9, when the Chicago White Sox took two nights and 25 innings to defeat the Milwaukee Brewers, 7–6, in a game that was both the longest game by innings in AL history and the longest game by time (8 hours and 6 minutes).

Five players—catcher Rick Ferrell, pitcher Don Drysdale, and infielders Harmon Killebrew, Luis Aparicio, and Pee Wee Reese—were elected to the Baseball Hall of Fame.

The Minnesota Twins changed ownership during the year, as Carl Pohlad purchased the franchise from Calvin Griffith. The sale of the Cleveland Indians was pending, and the San Francisco Giants were placed on the market after the season.

DAN SCHLOSSBERG, *Baseball Writer*

BASEBALL

Professional—Major Leagues
Final Standings, 1984

AMERICAN LEAGUE

Eastern Division	W	L	Pct.	Western Division	W	L	Pct.
Detroit	104	58	.642	Kansas City	84	78	.519
Toronto	89	73	.549	California	81	81	.500
New York	87	75	.537	Minnesota	81	81	.500
Boston	86	76	.531	Oakland	77	85	.475
Baltimore	85	77	.525	Chicago	74	88	.457
Cleveland	75	87	.436	Seattle	74	88	.457
Milwaukee	67	94	.416	Texas	69	92	.429

NATIONAL LEAGUE

Eastern Division	W	L	Pct.	Western Division	W	L	Pct.
Chicago	96	65	.596	San Diego	92	70	.568
New York	90	72	.556	Atlanta	80	82	.494
St. Louis	84	78	.519	Houston	80	82	.494
Philadelphia	81	81	.500	Los Angeles	79	83	.488
Montreal	78	83	.484	Cincinnati	70	92	.432
Pittsburgh	75	87	.463	San Francisco	66	96	.407

Play-Offs—American League: Detroit defeated Kansas City, 3 games to 0; National League: San Diego defeated Chicago, 3 games to 2.

World Series—Detroit defeated San Diego, 4 games to 1. First Game (Jack Murphy Stadium, San Diego, Oct. 9, attendance 57,908): Detroit 3, San Diego 2; Second Game (Jack Murphy Stadium, Oct. 10, attendance 57,911): San Diego 5, Detroit 3; Third Game (Tiger Stadium, Detroit, Oct. 12, attendance 51,970): Detroit 5, San Diego 2; Fourth Game (Tiger Stadium, Oct. 13, attendance 52,130): Detroit 4, San Diego 2; Fifth Game (Tiger Stadium, Oct. 14, attendance 51,901): Detroit 8, San Diego 4.

All-Star Game (Candlestick Park, San Francisco, July 10, attendance 57,756): National League 3, American League 1.

Most Valuable Players—American League: Willie Hernández, Detroit; National League: Ryne Sandberg, Chicago.

Cy Young Memorial Awards (outstanding pitchers)—American League: Willie Hernández, Detroit; National League: Rick Sutcliffe, Chicago.

Managers of the Year—American League: Sparky Anderson, Detroit; National League: Jim Frey, Chicago.

Rookies of the Year—American League: Alvin Davis, Seattle; National League: Dwight Gooden, New York.

Leading Hitters—(Percentage) American League: Don Mattingly, New York, .343; National League: Tony Gwynn, San Diego, .351. (Runs Batted In) American League: Tony Armas, Boston, 123; National League: Mike Schmidt, Philadelphia, and Gary Carter, Montreal (tied), 106. (Home Runs) American League: Armas, 43; National League: Schmidt and Dale Murphy, Atlanta (tied), 36. (Hits) American League: Mattingly, 207; National League: Gwynn, 213. (Runs) American League: Dwight Evans, Boston, 121; National League: Sandberg, 114.

Leading Pitchers—(Earned Run Average) American League: Mike Boddicker, Baltimore, 2.79; National League: Alejandro Peña, Los Angeles, 2.48. (Victories) American League: Boddicker, 20; National League: Joaquin Andujar, St. Louis, 20. (Strikeouts) American League: Mark Langston, Seattle, 204; National League: Dwight Gooden, New York, 276. (Shutouts) American League: Geoff Zahn and Bob Ojeda, Boston (tied), 5; National League: Andujar, Peña, and Orel Hershiser, Los Angeles (tied), 4. (Saves) American League: Dan Quisenberry, Kansas City, 44; National League: Bruce Sutter, St. Louis, 45.

Stolen Bases—American League: Rickey Henderson, Oakland, 66; National League: Tim Raines, Montreal, 75.

Professional—Minor Leagues, Class AAA
American Association: Louisville
International League: Pawtucket
Pacific Coast League: Edmonton

Amateur
NCAA: Cal State-Fullerton
Little League World Series: Seoul, South Korea

Noren Trotman

The LA Lakers could not stop Larry Bird in the NBA championship series, as his Boston Celtics won their 15th league crown. Bird was the play-off and regular-season MVP.

Basketball

In professional basketball, the Boston Celtics, the most successful team in the history of the sport, once again ruled the roost in 1983–84. By beating the Los Angeles Lakers four games to three in the play-off finals, the Celts captured their record 15th National Basketball Association (NBA) championship.

The Georgetown University Hoyas, a team that had never won a national title, took the 46th National Collegiate Athletic Association (NCAA) crown with a convincing 84–75 triumph over the Houston Cougars in the final at Seattle. Michigan won the National Invitation Tournament (NIT), and Southern California took the women's NCAA championship.

The Professional Season

The Celtics began the season with new ownership and a new coach, former defensive star K. C. Jones. They also had acquired 6'4", 200-lb. (1.93-m, 91-kg) Dennis Johnson, who gave them needed size and strength at the guard position.

In the championship series, beginning in Game 4, Johnson guarded Earvin ("Magic") Johnson, the Lakers' backcourt wizard. Dennis Johnson did an extraordinary job guarding Magic, coming up with several key steals and forcing the clever ball handler into lapses and turnovers in Games 4 and 7, both Celtic victories.

Many observers believed the Lakers let the championship slip from their grasp. They were troubled by mental lapses in key situations, perhaps suffering from overconfidence. They had taken a 2–1 lead with a one-sided 137–104 victory in Game 3 at Los Angeles, but they were never quite the same. A team known for its finesse and fast break, the Lakers took a pounding from the Celtics, who had 31 more rebounds during the seven games. And both teams suffered from fatigue, brought on by the long series, coast-to-coast travel, and the sweltering heat of Boston Garden, which has no air conditioning.

Boston had posted the best regular-season record in the league (62–20) and was assured of the home-court advantage. The Lakers had finished with the second-best mark (54–28). The Celtics had won the Eastern Conference title by eliminating the tough Milwaukee Bucks, four games to one. The Bucks had recorded the league's fourth-best regular-season mark (50–32), with the defending champion Philadelphia '76ers posting the third best (52–30). The '76ers were upset in the first round of the play-offs, 3–2, by the New Jersey Nets. Los Angeles, meanwhile, had won the Western Conference title and a berth in the play-off finals by ousting the surprising Phoenix Suns four games to two.

The Lakers opened the championship series with a 115–109 victory at Boston Garden, but the Celtics came back to score a 124–121 overtime triumph in Game 2. Then at Los Angeles came the one-sided Laker victory that many seemed to think would seal the Celtics' fate. The loss prompted Larry Bird, Boston's 6'9" (2.06-m) star forward who would go on to be named most valuable player of the series as well as of the entire regular season, to say that his team "played like sissies." Bird averaged 27.4 points and 14 rebounds for the play-off finals.

PROFESSIONAL BASKETBALL

National Basketball Association
(Final Standings, 1983–84)

Eastern Conference

Atlantic Division	W	L	Pct.
*Boston	62	20	.756
*Philadelphia	52	30	.634
*New York	47	35	.573
*New Jersey	45	37	.549
*Washington	35	47	.427
Central Division			
*Milwaukee	50	32	.610
*Detroit	49	33	.598
*Atlanta	40	42	.488
Cleveland	28	54	.341
Chicago	27	55	.329
Indiana	26	56	.317

Western Conference

Midwest Division	W	L	Pct.
*Utah	45	37	.549
*Dallas	43	39	.524
*Denver	38	44	.463
*Kansas City	38	44	.463
San Antonio	37	45	.451
Houston	29	53	.354
Pacific Division			
*Los Angeles	54	28	.659
*Portland	48	34	.585
*Seattle	42	40	.512
*Phoenix	41	41	.500
Golden State	37	45	.451
San Diego	30	52	.366

*Made play-offs

Play-Offs
Eastern Conference

First Round	Boston	3 games	Washington	1
	Milwaukee	3 games	Atlanta	2
	New Jersey	3 games	Philadelphia	2
	New York	3 games	Detroit	2
Semifinals	Boston	4 games	New York	3
	Milwaukee	4 games	New Jersey	2
Finals	Boston	4 games	Milwaukee	1

Western Conference

First Round	Dallas	3 games	Seattle	2
	Los Angeles	3 games	Kansas City	0
	Phoenix	3 games	Portland	2
	Utah	3 games	Denver	2
Semifinals	Los Angeles	4 games	Dallas	1
	Phoenix	4 games	Utah	2
Finals	Los Angeles	4 games	Phoenix	2
Championship	Boston	4 games	Los Angeles	3
All-Star Game	East 154, West 145			

Individual Honors

Most Valuable Player: Larry Bird, Boston
Most Valuable Player (play-offs): Larry Bird, Boston
Most Valuable Player (all-star game): Isiah Thomas, Detroit
Rookie of the Year: Ralph Sampson, Houston
Coach of the Year: Ralph Layden, Utah
Leading Scorer: Adrian Dantley, Utah, 30.6 points per game
Leader in Assists: Earvin Johnson, Los Angeles, 13.1 per game
Leading Rebounder: Moses Malone, 13.4 per game

Bird's comment, as well as his play, rallied the Celtics, who won their second overtime game, 129–125, in Los Angeles and tied the series at two games apiece. Bird had 29 points and 21 rebounds, while Kareem Abdul-Jabbar led the Lakers with 32 points. Returning to a sold-out and sweltering Boston Garden for Game 5, the Celtics ran roughshod over the listless Lakers. Bird's 34 points and 17 rebounds led the Celts to a 121–103 rout and a 3–

2 edge in games. Two days later back in Los Angeles, however, Abdul-Jabbar (30 points) and Magic Johnson (21 points and 10 assists) revived the Laker assault, squaring the series at 3–3 with a 119–108 triumph. The stage was set for a seventh-game showdown in Boston on June 12.

The major question being asked was whether the 37-year-old Abdul-Jabbar, who during the regular season had broken Wilt Chamberlain's career scoring record of 31,419 points, could counter the hard-hitting rebounding of the Celtics. Twice in the series he had suffered painful migraine headaches, and he was near total exhaustion in Game 5 at the Boston Garden.

Abdul-Jabbar again rose to the occasion in the series finale, scoring a game-high 29 points. But the Celtics' attack was multipronged, as Bird had 20 points and 12 rebounds, Cedric Maxwell had 24 points and 8 rebounds, Robert Parish contributed 14 points and 16 rebounds, and Dennis Johnson scored 22 points. Bird, Maxwell, and Parish accounted for three more rebounds than the entire Laker team. Overall the Celtics outrebounded Los Angeles 52–33, which made the difference in light of Boston's weak 39.5% field-goal shooting accuracy.

The triumph marked the Celtics' fourth NBA title in 11 years. It was the seventh time they appeared in the seventh game of a championship series and the seventh time they won. It was the eighth time they faced the Lakers in the final round and the eighth time they won. In fact, the only play-off final the Celtics ever lost was to the St. Louis Hawks in 1958.

The College Season

The apparent favorite going into the 53-team NCAA tournament was the North Carolina Tar Heels, coached by Dean Smith and led by Player of the Year Michael Jordan and All-American Sam Perkins. The Tar Heels, from the tough Atlantic Coast Conference (ACC), had won the title in 1982 and had lost only two games in 1983–84. But in the Eastern Regional semifinals, the Indiana Hoosiers of the Big Ten, coached by Bobby Knight (also coach of the 1984 U.S. Olympic squad), upset North Carolina, 72–68. That left Georgetown, Houston, and Kentucky as the apparent favorites. A surprising Virginia team, also from the ACC, upset Indiana in the Eastern Regional final, 50–48, to round out the Final Four.

To reach the Final Four in Seattle, Georgetown had eliminated Southern Methodist (37–36), Nevada-Las Vegas (62–48), and Dayton (61–49). At Seattle, the Hoyas first came up against Kentucky, one of the tournament's finer teams with a great tradition of postseason success and an outstanding player in 7'1" (2.16-m) center Sam Bowie. With depth at every position, the powerful Hoyas won easily, 53–40.

Focus on Sports

In the NCAA finals, the Georgetown Hoyas seemed always to outnumber the Houston Cougars. With strength, discipline, and team depth, the Hoyas rolled to an 84-75 triumph.

The Houston Cougars, meanwhile, had advanced by beating Louisiana Tech (77–69), Memphis State (78–71), and Wake Forest (68–63). They reached the championship game for the second year in a row by defeating Virginia, 49–47, in overtime.

The Houston-Georgetown game, played before a crowd of 38,000 at the Seattle Kingdome, featured the matchup between college basketball's two most intimidating seven-foot centers: Pat Ewing, a Georgetown junior, and Akeem Abdul Olajuwon, a Nigerian in his junior year at Houston.

But fans who expected a dramatic one-on-one struggle between the two giants were largely disappointed. Olajuwon was charged with his fourth personal foul after only 23 seconds of the second half, and he played cautiously thereafter. He ended up with 15 points, 9 rebounds, and only 1 blocked shot. Ewing, meanwhile, finished with only 10 points, 9 rebounds, and 4 blocked shots. Most of the play was left to less-heralded players on both teams. With superior bench depth and overall strength, Georgetown proved too formidable for the Cougars, winning 84–75.

The Hoyas, who had won the Big East Conference title and had hovered at or near the top of the wire-service polls all season, were coached by John Thompson. His strict discipline and methodical style of play brought Georgetown to an overall season record of 34–3. That represented the most victories by a college team since Kentucky won 36 games in 1947–48. Thompson, a former pro center who had played in the shadow of Celtic Hall of Famer Bill Russell, became the first black coach to win an NCAA crown.

After the season, Olajuwon chose to go into the NBA college draft rather than remain at Houston for his senior year. He was, of course, the first selection in the draft. He was taken by the Houston Rockets, who already had Ralph Sampson, the 1983 Number 1 draft choice out of Virginia who went on to become NBA rookie of the year in 1984. Ewing, on the other hand, chose to play for the U.S. Olympic team and stay at Georgetown for his senior year.

In other postseason collegiate play, Michigan defeated Notre Dame, 83–63, in the NIT final at Madison Square Garden in New York City. Southern California beat Tennessee, 72–61, to win its second consecutive women's NCAA title. Janice Lawrence of Louisiana Tech won the Wade Trophy as the season's outstanding women's college basketball player.

GEORGE DE GREGORIO
"The New York Times"

BOXING

Boxing remained further factionalized during 1984 after the creation in 1983 of the International Boxing Federation (IBF), a splinter group that had won over Larry Holmes as its most visible adherent and in 1984 crowned champions or recognized others in all weight divisions. Holmes, who had been the World Boxing Council's (WBC's) heavyweight champion, relinquished that crown late in 1983 to help form and bolster the IBF. He had hoped it would be a venture by which he could promote his own title fights under the IBF umbrella. But in 1984, Holmes, who was sanctioned as the IBF champion, did not have a bout until early in November, when he scored a 12th-round TKO over James ("Bonecrusher") Smith, a relative unknown.

The WBC title Holmes had left vacant went up for grabs in March, when Tim Witherspoon (whom Holmes had defeated in 1983) scored a 12-round majority decision over Greg Page in Las Vegas. Witherspoon lasted as champion only until late August, when he dropped a majority decision to Pinklon Thomas in another Las Vegas 12-rounder. Gerrie Coetzee of South Africa, who won the World Boxing Association (WBA) title in 1983, lost it to Page on December 1 in Sun City, Bophuthatswana. Page scored an eighth-round knockout.

With the permanent retirement on May 11, 1984, of welterweight Sugar Ray Leonard, two men ascended to the top rung as boxing's biggest drawing cards—Marvelous Marvin Hagler and Thomas ("Hit Man") Hearns. Leonard, who had retired in 1982 because of a detached retina, made a comeback and scored a ninth-round knockout of Kevin Howard at Worcester, MA. But immediately after the bout, Leonard announced his permanent retirement, saying that he had nothing more to prove and did not want to risk further injury.

World Boxing Champions*

Junior Flyweight—Francisco Quiroz, Dominican Republic (1984), World Boxing Association (WBA); Chang Chong Koo, South Korea (1983), World Boxing Council (WBC); Dodie Penalosa, Philippines (1984), International Boxing Federation (IBF).
Flyweight—Santos Laciar, Argentina (1982), WBA; Sot Chitalada, Thailand (1984), WBC; Soon Chung Kwon, South Korea (1984), IBF.
Junior Bantamweight—Jiro Watanabe, Japan ((1982), WBC; Judo Chun, South Korea (1984), IBF; WBA title vacant.
Bantamweight—Richard Sandoval, United States (1984), WBA; Alberto Davila, United States (1983), WBC; Satoshi Shingaki, Japan (1984), IBF.
Junior Featherweight—Victor Callejas, Puerto Rico (1984), WBA; Juan (Kid) Meza, United States (1984), WBC; Seungin Soo, South. Korea (1984), IBF.
Featherweight—Eusebio Pedroza, Panama (1978), WBA; Wilfredo Gomez, Puerto Rico (1984), WBC; Mink Eun Oh, South Korea (1984), IBF.
Junior Lightweight—Rocky Lockridge, United States (1984), WBA; Julio Cesar Chavez, Mexico (1984), WBC; Hwan Kil Yuh, South Korea (1984), IBF.
Lightweight—Livingstone Bramble, Virgin Islands (1984), WBA; José Luis Ramirez, Mexico (1984), WBC; Harry Arroyo, United States (1984) IBF.
Junior Welterweight—Gene Hatcher, United States (1984), WBA; Billy Costello, United States (1984), WBC; Aaron Pryor, United States (1984), IBF.
Welterweight—Donald Curry, United States (1983), WBA and IBF; Milton McCrory, United States (1983), WBC.
Junior Middleweight—Mike McCallum, Jamaica (1984), WBA; Thomas Hearns, United States (1982), WBC; Carlos Santos, Puerto Rico (1984), IBF.
Middleweight—Marvin Hagler, United States (1980), WBA and IBF; WBC title vacant.
Light Heavyweight—Michael Spinks, United States (1981), WBA, WBC, and IBF.
Cruiserweight—Piet Crous, South Africa (1984), WBA; Carlos DeLeon, Puerto Rico (1983), WBC; Lee Roy Murphy, United States (1984), IBF.
Heavyweight—Greg Page, United States (1984), WBA; Pinklon Thomas, United States (1984), WBC; Larry Holmes, United States (1983), IBF.

* As of Dec. 1, 1984; year of achieving title in parentheses.

Hearns, the WBC junior middleweight titleholder, dispatched three opponents with ease and established himself as one of the most devastating punchers in the sport. In February he scored a unanimous decision over Luigi Minchillo in Detroit. Then in June, in a much-publicized bout, he put an end to the long career of Roberto Duran of Panama with a knockout at 1:07 of the second round at Las Vegas. And in September, Hearns scored a third-round knockout of Fred Hutchings in Saginaw, MI.

Hagler, meanwhile, stopped Juan Domingo Roldan in the 10th round of their March bout in

Focus on Sports

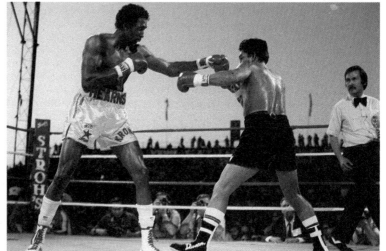

Thomas "Hit Man" Hearns (left) knocked out Roberto Duran in the second round of their WBC junior middleweight championship bout at Caesars Palace in Las Vegas. It was the first time in Duran's 17-year, 82-fight professional career that he was KOed.

Las Vegas. But then in October, Marvelous Marvin was stripped of his title after knocking out Mustafa Hamsho in the third round at New York's Madison Square Garden. Hagler, recognized by all sanctioning bodies as middleweight champion, lost the WBC version because he had violated council rules by participating in a fight scheduled for 15 rounds. All WBC title bouts must be scheduled for 12 rounds—an edict adopted as a safety measure. Hagler filed an appeal.

By far the biggest upset of the season was scored by Livingstone Bramble, a new face on the lightweight scene, who pounded out a 14th-round technical knockout of WBA champion Ray ("Boom Boom") Mancini on June 1 in Buffalo, NY. On the same card, Johnny Bumphus, the WBA junior welterweight champion, was dethroned by Gene Hatcher on a knockout in the 11th round. The WBC lightweight title changed hands on November 3, when José Luis Ramirez of Mexico, who was almost knocked out in the second round, came back to stop unbeaten Edwin Rosario of Puerto Rico in the fourth at San Juan; the loss was Rosario's first in 29 fights. Two other title bouts took place on November 3: Billy Costello won a 12-round unanimous decision from Saoul Mamby in Costello's hometown of Kingston, NY, to keep his WBC junior welterweight crown; on the same card, Juan (Kid) Meza knocked out Jaime Garza in the first round to take the WBC junior featherweight title.

GEORGE DE GREGORIO, *"The New York Times"*

Football

On Jan. 20, 1985, in front of more than 84,000 spectators in Stanford Stadium in Palo Alto, CA, the San Francisco 49ers gave an impressive all-around performance and defeated the Miami Dolphins, 38–16, in Super Bowl XIX. The 49er offense, with quarterback Joe Montana at the helm, tied the record for the most points scored in a Super Bowl. The versatile six-year professional passed for 331 yards—a Super Bowl record—and ran for another 59 yards. He threw three touchdown passes and scored a TD himself with a fine six-yard run. Fullback Roger Craig also played an excellent game. He scored three touchdowns, rushed for a total of 58 yards on 15 carries, and gained 82 yards on 8 receptions.

The San Francisco defense, meanwhile, allowed the high-powered Miami offense, led by quarterback Dan Marino, only one touchdown, three field goals, and no points at all in the second half. The victory was San Francisco's second Super Bowl triumph; they had beaten the Cincinnati Bengals, 26–21, in Super Bowl XVI. It also marked the second time that quarterback Joe Montana was named the most valuable player of a Super Bowl.

In the second year of its existence, the rival United States Football League (USFL) expanded from 12 to 18 teams for its spring-summer schedule. In the championship game on July 15, it came down to the Philadelphia Stars of the Eastern Division against the Arizona Wranglers of the Western Division. The Stars, who had been defeated in the 1983 title contest by the Michigan Panthers, this time emerged victorious, 23–3. The Philadelphia attack was led by the running of Kelvin Bryant—115 yards and a four-yard touchdown run—and the passing of Chuck Fusina, the game's most valuable player (MVP). By the end of the season, however, it became clear that expansion had been a mistake, as several teams were awash in red ink. The league was realigned to 14 teams for 1985, and, in a move spearheaded by New Jersey Generals' owner Donald Trump (*see* BIOGRAPHY), there was talk of moving to a fall-winter schedule for the 1986 season. The USFL also filed a $1.3 billion antitrust suit against the NFL.

In the Canadian Football League, the Winnipeg Blue Bombers won their first Grey Cup in 22 years by defeating the Hamilton Tiger-Cats, 47–17, in the championship game at Edmonton. Winnipeg quarterback Tom Clements was the game's MVP.

On the college level, the undefeated Brigham Young Cougars (12–0) were the top-ranked team, and Boston College quarterback Doug Flutie won the Heisman Trophy.

National Football League

The two teams in Super Bowl XIX were the class of the NFL throughout the 1984–85 season. It became clear early on that the San Francisco 49ers and Miami Dolphins were the ones to beat by anyone harboring ambitions of reaching Palo Alto. And by the end of the regular season, they had compiled the league's best records—15–1 for the 49ers (the most regular-season wins in NFL history) and 14–2 for the Dolphins.

The spark of the Miami offense was quarterback Marino, who made short shrift of the "sophomore jinx" with a sensational second-year performance. Marino set four major NFL single-season passing records: most yardage (5,084), most touchdown passes (48), most completions (362), and most 400-yard games (4). The first passer to throw for more than 5,000 yards, Marino made the Dolphins the league's number 1 team in passing and total offense. His two favorite targets were Mark Clayton (73 receptions for 1,389 yards and 18 touchdowns) and Mark Duper (71 receptions for 1,306 yards and 8 touchdowns).

In the first round of the play-offs, the Dolphins disposed of the Seattle Seahawks, 31–10, as Marino broke open the game with a pair of third-period scoring passes within two minutes

—including a 33-yarder to Clayton. Then in the American Conference title game, Miami whipped the Pittsburgh Steelers, 45–28, behind a typical Marino performance—421 yards and four TD passes. Duper had five receptions for 148 yards and two touchdowns.

The 49ers, meanwhile, had their own stellar passer in Montana. The former Notre Dame star was the highest-rated quarterback in the National Conference with 279 completions, 3,630 yards, and 28 touchtown tosses. In addition, San Franciso possessed a formidable ground attack. Wendell Tyler was the top 49er running back with 1,262 yards on 246 carries, and rookie Roger Craig contributed 649 yards.

To reach the Super Bowl, the 49ers first ousted the surprising New York Giants, 21–10, and then shut out the Chicago Bears, 13–0, for the conference crown. Ironically, Chicago had boasted the stingiest defense in the league, but the defensive crew of 49er Coach Bill Walsh beat the Bears at their own game by mounting a rush that bottled up even Chicago's great running back, Walter Payton.

In the American Conference, the Steelers reached the play-offs by leading the weak Central Division with a 9–7 record. Then they played defense like the powerful Steeler teams of the 1970s and upset the Denver Broncos, the Western Division champions, 24–17. Meanwhile, the Los Angeles Raiders, the defending Super Bowl champions, had been eliminated by the Seahawks, 13–7, in the wild-card game. Thus ended a tough season for the Raiders, who, after a 5–1 start, lost veteran quarterback Jim Plunkett to injury. A rusty Plunkett did play against Seattle, which mounted an effective rush against him. Because there were older players in other key positions, the Raiders appeared to face a major rebuilding task. Seattle, on the other hand, was quarterbacked by young Dave Krieg, who delighted hometown fans with an outstanding year. Krieg emerged as the fourth-rated passer in the conference, behind Marino, Tony Eason of the New England Patriots, and Dan Fouts of the San Diego Chargers.

In the National Conference, the Bears upset the Washington Redskins, 23–19, to gain the NFC final. Having led the league in six defensive categories, including a record 72 sacks, the Bears dumped Redskin quarterback Joe Theismann seven times in the game. Also of special note was the touchdown pass thrown by the Bears' star running back Walter Payton. Chicago, beset by injuries to its passers, had used six quarterbacks during the regular season—including Payton on a few plays. Washington's top rusher, meanwhile, the powerful John Riggins, at 35 the oldest running back in the league, was held to 50 yards on 21 carries by the Bears. Comeback honors of the year went to the Giants, who improved from 3-12-1 in 1983 to 9–7 in 1984 and upset the L.A. Rams in the National Conference wild-card game. The Giants contained the Rams' star rusher, Eric Dickerson, and came up with a goal-line stand in the fourth quarter to save the 16–13 victory.

AP/Wide World

Eric Dickerson of the L.A. Rams broke O.J. Simpson's single-season rushing record. By the end of the 16-game schedule, Dickerson had run for a total of 2,105 yards on 379 carries.

Miami's Dan Marino tossed a record 48 TD passes, became the first NFL quarterback to throw for more than 5,000 yards in one season, and led his team to Super Bowl XIX.

The 1984–85 NFL season was one in which several important records were set, in addition to those by Dan Marino. Perhaps the most important was the shattering of Jim Brown's career rushing mark by the Bears' Payton (*see* BIOGRAPHY). In his tenth season in the league, Payton ran for a total of 1,684 yards on 381 carries, giving him a career total of 13,309. That eclipsed the mark of 12,312 by the former Cleveland Brown great. Another rushing mark to fall was O.J. Simpson's single-season standard of 2,003, set in 1973 with the Buffalo Bills. The Rams' Dickerson ran for 2,105 yards on 379 carries in 1984–85. (Simpson's record, however, had been established in a 14-game

PROFESSIONAL FOOTBALL

United States Football League

Final Standings

EASTERN CONFERENCE

Atlantic Division	W	L	T	Pct.	Points For	Against
Philadelphia	16	2	0	.889	479	225
New Jersey	14	4	0	.778	430	312
Pittsburgh	3	15	0	.167	259	379
Washington	3	15	0	.167	270	492
Southern Division						
Birmingham	14	4	0	.778	539	316
Tampa Bay	14	4	0	.778	498	347
New Orleans	8	10	0	.444	348	395
Memphis	7	11	0	.389	320	455
Jacksonville	6	12	0	.333	327	455

PLAY-OFFS

Philadelphia 28, New Jersey 7
Birmingham 36, Tampa Bay 17
Philadelphia 20, Birmingham 10

WESTERN CONFERENCE

Central Division	W	L	T	Pct.	Points For	Against
Houston	13	5	0	.722	618	400
Michigan	10	8	0	.556	400	382
San Antonio	7	11	0	.389	309	325
Oklahoma	6	12	0	.333	251	459
Chicago	5	13	0	.278	340	466
Pacific Division						
Los Angeles	10	8	0	.556	338	373
Arizona	10	8	0	.556	502	284
Denver	9	9	0	.500	356	413
Oakland	7	11	0	.389	242	348

PLAY-OFFS

Arizona 17, Houston 16
Los Angeles 27, Michigan 21
Arizona 35, Los Angeles 23

CHAMPIONSHIP GAME: Philadelphia 23, Arizona 3

National Football League

Final Standings

NATIONAL CONFERENCE

Eastern Division	W	L	T	Pct.	Points For	Against
Washington	11	5	0	.688	426	310
N.Y. Giants	9	7	0	.563	299	301
Dallas	9	7	0	.563	308	308
St. Louis	9	7	0	.563	423	345
Philadelphia	6	9	1	.406	278	320
Central Division						
Chicago	10	6	0	.625	325	248
Green Bay	8	8	0	.500	380	309
Tampa Bay	6	10	0	.375	335	380
Detroit	4	11	1	.281	283	408
Minnesota	3	13	0	.188	276	484
Western Division						
San Francisco	15	1	0	.938	475	227
L.A. Rams	10	6	0	.625	346	316
New Orleans	7	9	0	.438	298	361
Atlanta	4	12	0	.250	281	382

PLAY-OFFS

N.Y. Giants 16, L.A. Rams 13
Chicago 23, Washington 19
San Francisco 21, N.Y. Giants 10
San Francisco 23, Chicago 0

AMERICAN CONFERENCE

Eastern Division	W	L	T	Pct.	Points For	Against
Miami	14	2	0	.875	513	298
New England	9	7	0	.563	362	352
N.Y. Jets	7	9	0	.438	332	364
Indianapolis	4	12	0	.250	239	414
Buffalo	2	14	0	.125	250	454
Central Division						
Pittsburgh	9	7	0	.563	387	310
Cincinnati	8	8	0	.500	339	339
Cleveland	5	11	0	.313	250	297
Houston	3	13	0	.188	240	437
Western Division						
Denver	13	3	0	.813	353	241
Seattle	12	4	0	.750	418	282
L.A. Raiders	11	5	0	.688	368	278
Kansas City	8	8	0	.500	314	324
San Diego	7	9	0	.438	394	413

PLAY-OFFS

Seattle 13, L.A. Raiders 7
Pittsburgh 24, Denver 17
Miami 31, Seattle 10
Miami 45, Pittsburgh 28

SUPER BOWL XIX: San Francisco 38, Miami 16

schedule, and Dickerson surpassed it in the 15th game of the season.) Also falling in 1984–85 were the career and single-season records for pass receptions. Charlie Joiner of the Chargers became the all-time leading receiver, ending the season with a career total of 657 (8 more than former Redskin Charley Taylor). And Art Monk of the Redskins hauled in a record 106 aerials during the year (5 more than Charley Hennigan in 1964).

Off the field, a discouraging development for football fans in Oakland came in early November, when the U.S. Supreme Court let stand a ruling that prevented the league from blocking the Raiders' 1982 move to Los Angeles. The court's action was seen by some as allowing owners to move their franchises at their own discretion—as Robert Irsay had done in the middle of the night, when he sent the Colts from Baltimore to Indianapolis earlier in the year. Philadelphia nearly lost the Eagles when owner Leonard Tose threatened a move to Arizona, but a last-minute financial package arranged by Mayor Wilson Goode kept the team in Philly.

The College Season

The player of the year made the play of the year in college football. The Boston College Eagles were playing the defending national champion Miami Hurricanes at the Orange Bowl in Miami. After a wildly exciting passing duel between the Eagles' Doug Flutie and the Hurricanes' Bernie Kosar, Miami scored a touchdown with 28 seconds left, to go ahead 45–41. The victory apparently was theirs. With a national television audience looking on, the diminutive (5'9¾") Flutie then moved the Eagles to Miami's 48 yard line. But only six seconds showed on the clock—only a desperation "Hail Mary" pass was left to try, and the Hurricanes would be waiting. Flutie took the snap and scrambled around the backfield while his receivers raced toward the goal line. Finally Flutie flung the ball—64 yards in the air—and it landed, miraculously, in the arms of his roommate, Gerard Phelan. Boston College had won, 47–45.

With his 472 yards that night, Flutie became the first collegian to pass for more than 10,000 yards in a four-year career. After piloting the Eagles to a 45–10 triumph over Holy Cross in the last game of the regular season, Flutie flew to New York to accept the Heisman Trophy—which he had won in a landslide vote. Keith Byars, Ohio State's fine tailback, was the runner-up; Robbie Bosco of Brigham Young (BYU), another standout passer, was third; and Miami's Kosar was fourth. Flutie became the first quarterback to win the award since Pat Sullivan of Auburn in 1971. After that, running backs had been selected for the honor 12 consecutive times.

By any measure, the surprise team of the year was Brigham Young, which was voted the national champion in both major wire-service polls, primarily because it finished as the only major undefeated team. The main objection voiced by some fans to rating BYU number 1 was its relatively weak schedule. The Cougars did not play any highly ranked teams and faced only four squads that had managed records of above .500.

AP/Wide World

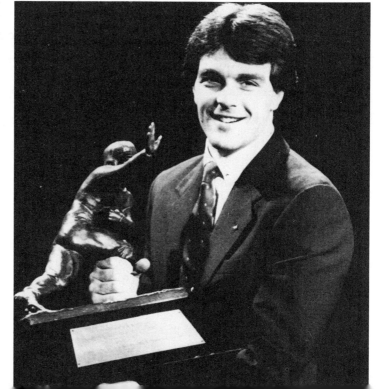

Quarterback Doug Flutie closed out his stellar career at Boston College with a record total of more than 10,000 yards passing, a Cotton Bowl victory over Houston, and the 1984 Heisman Trophy.

BYU had been expecting 1984 to be a rebuilding year. After an 11–1 record in 1983, the Cougars had lost several key players—most notably quarterback Steve Young, who signed a multimillion-dollar contract with the Los Angeles Express of the USFL. Thus, the 1984 Cougars were thought to be out of the race even for their own Western Athletic Conference title, let alone a national championship. But Coach LaVell Edwards' team, which had not lost since its 1983 opener against Baylor, kept rolling. By season's end it had extended the winning streak to 24 games. Bosco filled in so capably for Young that he ranked first in the nation in total offense.

As the Cougars were making a 24–17 comeback victory over Michigan in the Holiday Bowl—a triumph that convinced many doubting Thomases—Washington was helping BYU attain top honors by upsetting Oklahoma in the Orange Bowl. Oklahoma had been running second in the polls, but the Sooners gave up two touchdowns in a one-minute span in the final period, dashing their title hopes. By dint of their Orange Bowl victory, the Washington Huskies moved up to second place in the final polls.

For the first time in its history, Army went to a bowl game and downed Michigan State, 10–6, in the Cherry Bowl. The Cadets posted a 6–3–1 season record after Coach Jim Young installed a "wishbone" offense; the new attack rolled up 345.3 rushing yards per game, tops in the country. Navy (4–5–1), which had won the previous seven inter-service meetings, this time lost to Army, 28–11, before 73,180 fans in Philadelphia, the first Army-Navy sellout since 1971.

Coach Gerry Faust continued to have his problems at Notre Dame. A midseason slump dropped the Fighting Irish's record to 3–4, but they rebounded with four consecutive wins, including a 19–7 decision over Southern California in the traditional season finale. That win, along with a berth in the Aloha Bowl, settled the disquieted Notre Dame alumni somewhat. In Honolulu, however, the Irish came up against another late-surging team, Southern Methodist. The Mustangs, who had won their last five games and a share of the Southwest Conference title (with Houston), beat Notre Dame in the Aloha Bowl, 27–20.

In the "granddaddy of them all," the Rose Bowl again proved disastrous for the Big Ten representative: for the tenth time in 11 years and the 14th time in 16 years, the Big Ten team was defeated, as USC prevailed over Ohio State, 20–17.

The Sugar Bowl in New Orleans had an unexpected hero, as Nebraska quarterback Craig Sundberg, who had the flu the day before, threw three touchdown passes and ran for another as the Cornhuskers routed Louisiana State, 28–10. The hero of the Cotton Bowl was

COLLEGE FOOTBALL

Conference Champions	Atlantic Coast—Maryland Big Eight—Oklahoma Big Ten—Ohio State Pacific Coast—Nevada-Las Vegas Pacific Ten—USC Southeastern—Florida Southwest—Houston, SMU (tie) Western Athletic—Brigham Young
NCAA Champions	Division I-AA—Montana Division II-Troy State Division III-Augustana
NAIA Champions	Division I—Carson-Newman, Central Arkansas (tie) Division II—Troy State
Individual Honors	Heisman Trophy—Doug Flutie, Boston College Lombardi Trophy—Tony Degrate, Texas Outland Trophy—Bruce Smith, Virginia Tech

Major Bowl Games

Aloha Bowl (Honolulu, Dec. 29)—SMU 27, Notre Dame 20
Bluebonnet Bowl (Houston, TX, Jan. 1)—West Virginia 31, Texas Christian 14
California Bowl (Fresno, CA, Dec. 15)—Nevada-Las Vegas 30, Toledo 13
Cherry Bowl (Pontiac, MI, Dec. 22)—Army 10, Michigan State 6
Cotton Bowl (Dallas, TX, Jan. 1)—Boston College 45, Houston 28
Fiesta Bowl (Tempe, AZ, Jan. 1)—UCLA 39, Miami 37
Florida Citrus Bowl (Orlando, FL, Dec. 22)—Florida State 17, Georgia 17
Freedom Bowl (Anaheim, CA, Dec. 26)—Iowa 55, Texas 17
Gator Bowl (Jacksonville, FL, Dec. 30)—Oklahoma State 21, South Carolina 14
Hall of Fame (Birmingham, AL, Dec. 29)—Kentucky 20, Wisconsin 19
Holiday Bowl (San Diego, Dec. 21)—Brigham Young 24, Michigan 17
Independence Bowl (Shreveport, LA, Dec. 15)—Air Force 23, Virginia Tech 7
Liberty Bowl (Memphis, TN, Dec. 27)—Auburn 21, Arkansas 15
Orange Bowl (Miami, FL, Jan. 1)—Washington 28, Oklahoma 17
Peach Bowl (Atlanta, GA, Dec. 31)—Virginia 27, Purdue 24
Rose Bowl (Pasadena, CA, Jan. 1)—USC 20, Ohio State 17
Sugar Bowl (New Orleans, LA, Jan. 1)—Nebraska 28, Louisiana State 10
Sun Bowl (El Paso, TX, Dec. 22)—Maryland 28, Tennessee 27

Final College Rankings

	AP Writers	UPI Coaches
1	Brigham Young	Brigham Young
2	Washington	Washington
3	Florida	Nebraska
4	Nebraska	Boston College
5	Boston College	Oklahoma State
6	Oklahoma	Oklahoma
7	Oklahoma State	Florida
8	SMU	SMU
9	UCLA	Southern Cal
10	Southern Cal	UCLA

also somewhat unlikely. Boston College defeated Houston, 45–28, but the game's MVP was *not* Doug Flutie. It was Phelan, who had caught "The Pass" against Miami.

Disappointing seasons were turned in by Penn State, Pitt, and Alabama. The Nittany Lions, after starting the season with three victories, ended with a 6–5 mark, the worst since Coach Joe Paterno's first season in 1966. Pitt, highly rated in the preseason, faltered to a 3–7–1 record, their poorest in 13 years. And Alabama coach Ray Perkins, with the unenviable task of taking over for the late Paul ("Bear") Bryant, had a rough sophomore year at the Crimson Tide helm. Alabama struggled to its first losing season in 27 years, with a 5–6 mark.

LUD DUROSKA
"The New York Times"

Golf

Some exciting new faces—and some exciting old ones—surfaced on the professional golf tours in 1984.

On the Professional Golfers' Association (PGA) Tour, Tom Watson won three tournaments, was the leading money-winner for the fifth time with $476,260, and was named player of the year by the PGA for the sixth time. Watson was challenged for player-of-the-year honors by South Africa native Denis Watson, who had never won in three previous years on the tour but who took three tournaments in a late-season spurt in 1984. Mark O'Meara, the 1981 rookie of the year but also never a winner, triumphed at Milwaukee, had 14 other top-ten finishes, and ended up second in the money race with $465,873. Corey Pavin won one tournament and $260,536 and was named *Golf Digest*'s rookie of the year. Calvin Peete won the Vardon Trophy with a low scoring average of 70.56 strokes per round.

It was a glamorous year for the men's major championships. After 11 years of a successful but frustrating career, the popular Ben Crenshaw broke through to win the Masters. Crowd favorite Fuzzy Zoeller defeated Greg Norman in a play-off for the U.S. Open title at Winged Foot, and Seve Ballesteros, the dashing Spaniard, overcame Tom Watson to win the British Open at St. Andrews. And in the PGA Championship at Shoal Creek in Birmingham, AL, 45-year-old Lee Trevino, a Hall of Famer plagued by injury and personal problems the last two years, fired a 15-under-par 273 to win his sixth major tournament by four shots over Lanny Wadkins and veteran Gary Player.

Betsy King, who had failed to win in six full seasons on the Ladies Professional Golfers Association (LPGA) Tour, won three times and added four seconds and three thirds. She was the leading money-winner with $266,771 and was named the LPGA player of the year. Patty Sheehan won four tournaments, including the LPGA Championship, earned the Vare Trophy for having the lowest scoring average at 71.40, and was second on the money list with $255,185. Ayako Okamoto won three tournaments and was third in money winnings.

Hollis Stacy won her third U.S. Women's Open. Julie Inkster, the three-time U.S. Amateur champion now in her first full year on the LPGA Tour, won the other two majors, the Nabisco Dinah Shore and the du Maurier Classic, and was named the LPGA's rookie of the year. Kathy Whitworth, 45 and in the Hall of Fame, won three tournaments to boost her career total to 87 and surpass Sam Snead as the professional with the most official victories.

On the Senior Tour, Miller Barber won the U.S. Senior Open and three other tournaments; Don January was the leading money winner.

LARRY DENNIS, *"Golf Digest"*

GOLF

PGA 1984 Tournament Winners

Seiko-Tucson Match Play Championship: Tom Watson
Bob Hope Classic: John Mahaffey (340)
Phoenix Open: Tom Purtzer (268)
Isuzu-Andy Williams San Diego Open: Gary Koch (272)
Bing Crosby National Pro-Am: Hale Irwin (278)
Hawaiian Open: Jack Renner (271)
Los Angeles Open: David Edwards (279)
Honda Classic: Bruce Lietzke (280)
Doral-Eastern Open: Tom Kite (272)
Bay Hill Classic: Gary Koch (272)
USF&G Classic: Bob Eastwood (272)
Tournament Players Championship: Fred Couples (277)
Greater Greensboro Open: Andy Bean (280)
Masters: Ben Crenshaw (277)
Sea Pines Heritage Classic: Nick Faldo (270)
Houston Coca-Cola Open: Corey Pavin (274)
Mony Tournament of Champions: Tom Watson (274)
Byron Nelson Golf Classic: Craig Stadler (276)
Colonial National Invitation: Peter Jacobsen (270)
Memorial Tournament: Jack Nicklaus (280)
Kemper Open: Greg Norman (280)
Manufacturers Hanover Westchester Classic: Scott Simpson (269)
U.S. Open: Fuzzy Zoeller (276)
Georgia-Pacific Atlanta Golf Classic: Tom Kite (269)
Canadian Open: Greg Norman (278)
Western Open: Tom Watson (280)
Anheuser-Busch Golf Classic: Ronnie Black (267)
Miller High Life Quad Cities Open: Scott Hoch (266)
Sammy Davis Jr.-Greater Hartford Open: Peter Jacobsen (269)
Danny Thomas Memphis Classic: Bob Eastwood (280)
Buick Open: Denis Watson (271)
PGA Championship: Lee Trevino (273)
World Series of Golf: Denis Watson (271)
B.C. Open: Wayne Levi (275)
Bank of Boston Classic: George Archer (270)
Greater Milwaukee Open: Mark O'Meara (272)
Panasonic Las Vegas Invitational: Denis Watson (341)
LaJet Classic: Curtis Strange (273)
Texas Open: Calvin Peete (266)
Southern Open: Hubert Green (265)
Walt Disney World Golf Classic: Larry Nelson (266)
Pensacola Open: Bill Kratzert (270)

LPGA 1984 Tournament Winners

Mazda Classic of Deer Creek: Silvia Bertolaccini (280)
Elizabeth Arden Classic: Patty Sheehan (280)
Sarasota Classic: Alice Miller (280)
Uniden LPGA Invitational: Nancy Lopez (284)
Samaritan Turquoise Classic: Chris Johnson (276)
Tucson Conquistadores LPGA Open: Chris Johnson (272)
Women's Kemper Open: Betsy King (283)
Nabisco Dinah Shore: Juli Inkster (280)
J&B Scotch Pro-Am: Ayako Okamoto (275)
S&H Golf Classic: Vicki Bergon (275)
Freedom Orlando Classic: Betsy King (202)
Potamkin Cadillac Classic: Sharon Barrett (213)
United Virginia Bank Classic: Amy Alcott (210)
Chrysler-Plymouth Charity Classic: Barb Bunkowsky (209)
LPGA Corning Classic: JoAnne Carner (281)
LPGA Championship: Patty Sheehan (272)
McDonald's Kids' Classic: Patty Sheehan (281)
Mayflower Classic: Ayako Okamoto (281)
Boston Five Classic: Laurie Rinker (286)
Lady Keystone Open: Amy Alcott (208)
Jamie Farr Toledo Classic: Lauri Peterson (278)
U.S. Women's Open: Hollis Stacy (290)
Rochester International: Kathy Whitworth (281)
du Maurier Classic: Juli Inkster (279)
West Virginia Classic: Alice Miller (209)
Henredon Classic: Patty Sheehan (277)
Chevrolet World Championship of Women's Golf: Nancy Lopez (281)
Columbia Savings LPGA Classic: Betsy King (281)
Rail Charity Golf Classic: Cindy Hill (207)
Portland Ping Championship: Amy Alcott (212)
Safeco Classic: Kathy Whitworth (279)
San Jose Classic: Amy Alcott (211)
Hitachi Ladies British Open: Ayako Okamoto (289)
Smirnoff Ladies Irish Open: Kathy Whitworth (285)
Mazda Japan Classic: Nayoko Yoshikawa

Other Tournaments

British Open: Severiano Ballesteros (276)
U.S. Men's Amateur: Scott Verplank
U.S. Women's Amateur: Deb Richard
U.S. Men's Public Links: Bill Malley
U.S. Women's Public Links: Heather Farr
U.S. Men's Senior Open: Miller Barber (286)
Mid-Amateur: Mike Podolak
U.S. Senior Men's Amateur: Bob Rawlins
U.S. Senior Women's Amateur: Constance Guthrie
U.S. Junior Boys: Doug Martin
U.S. Junior Girls: Cathy Mockett
World Match Play: Severiano Ballesteros
NCAA Men: Houston
NCAA Women: Miami

Wild Again (2), a 31–1 long shot ridden by Pat Day, won the $3 million Breeders' Cup Classic at Hollywood Park. That race, the richest of all time, was one of seven in the new Breeders' Cup Series, worth a total of $10 million.

AP/Wide World

Horse Racing

John Henry, Slew o' Gold, Princess Rooney, Fit to Fight, and Swale were the thoroughbred stars of 1984, a year that introduced the Breeders' Cup series to the sport. Run on November 10 at Hollywood Park, the Breeders' Cup was made up of seven races with a total of $10 million in prize money. In the $3 million Breeders' Cup Classic, the richest horse race of all time, 31-1 long shot Wild Again, brilliantly ridden by Pat Day, was first across the wire. Gate Dancer finished second but was disqualified to third; Slew o' Gold was moved up from third to second.

John Henry, a nine-year-old gelding, won six of nine starts in 1984 and brought home $2,336,650 in purses, increasing his record career earnings to $6,597,947. His victories included the Budweiser-Arlington Million, a race he had won three years earlier.

Slew o' Gold won the Woodward, Marlboro Cup Handicap, and Jockey Club Gold Cup, an unprecedented sweep of Belmont's Fall Championship Series that netted him a $1 million bonus. The four-year-old son of Seattle Slew earned $2,627,944 in 1984, a single-season record, and retired with a total of $3,533,534.

The standout four-year-old filly Princess Rooney won the Breeders' Cup Distaff and the Spinster. Fit to Fight, a five-year-old owned by Rokeby Stable, captured the Metropolitan Handicap by a head, the Suburban Handicap by 3¾ lengths, and the Brooklyn Handicap by 12½ lengths to become only the fourth horse to win the Handicap Triple Crown.

Swale, trained by Woody Stephens, won the Kentucky Derby and Belmont Stakes. Just eight days after the Belmont, however, the three-year-old son of Seattle Slew suddenly collapsed and died. No official cause of death was ever determined.

Gate Dancer, trained by Jack Van Berg, set a track record in capturing the Preakness. Chief's Crown was the champion two-year-old colt, and Life's Magic ruled as the best three-year-old filly.

Harness Racing. Fancy Crown, a three-year-old filly, was selected the 1984 Harness Horse of the Year. During the year she equaled the world record for the mile trot with a clocking of 1:53.45.

On The Road Again's $1,751,695 set a single-season earnings record for harness racing. Baltic Speed set a single-season record for trotters with earnings of $1,062,611.

JIM BOLUS
"The Louisville Times"

HORSE RACING

Major U.S. Thoroughbred Races

Arkansas Derby: Althea, $600,250 (total purse)
Belmont: Swale, $516,700
Breeders' Cup Classic: Wild Again, $3,000,000
Breeders' Cup Distaff: Princess Rooney, $1,000,000
Breeders' Cup Juvenile: Chief's Crown, $1,000,000
Breeders' Cup Juvenile Fillies: Outstandingly, $1,000,000
Breeders' Cup Mile: Royal Heroine, $1,000,000
Breeders' Cup Sprint: Eillo, $1,000,000
Breeders' Cup Turf: Lashkari, $2,000,000
Brooklyn Handicap: Fit to Fight, $331,500
Budweiser-Arlington Million: John Henry, $1,000,000
Flamingo: Time for a Change, $365,000
Florida Derby: Swale, $300,000
Hollywood Gold Cup Handicap: Desert Wine, $500,000
Hollywood Invitational: John Henry, $300,000
Jockey Club Gold Cup: Slew o' Gold, $584,000
Kentucky Derby: Swale, $712 400
Marlboro Cup : Slew o' Gold, $400,000
Matriarch: Royal Heroine, $260,000
Meadowlands Cup Handicap: Wild Again, $500,000
Metropolitan Handicap: Fit to Fight, $348,500
Preakness: Gate Dancer, $338,600
Rothmans International: Majesty's Prince, $600,000
Santa Anita Handicap: Interco, $523,650
Spinster: Princess Rooney, $192,600
Suburban Handicap: Fit to Fight, $335,500
Travers: Carr de Naskra, $337,500
Turf Classic: John Henry, $625,250
Washington, D.C., International: Seattle Song, $250,000
Woodward: Slew o' Gold, $292,000
Yellow Ribbon Invitational: Sabin, $400,000

Major U.S. Harness Races

Cane Pace: On The Road Again, $600,000
Hambletonian: Historic Freight, $1,219,000
Kentucky Futurity: Fancy Crown, $168,010
Little Brown Jug: Colt Fortysix, $366,717
Meadowlands Pace: On The Road Again, $1,293,000
Peter Haughton Memorial Trot: Another Miracle, $1,000,000
Sweetheart Pace: Armbro Dazzler, $1,030,000
Wilson Pace: Nihilator, $2,161,000
World Trotting Derby: Baltic Speed, $601,950
Yonkers Trot: Baltic Speed, $431,780

Ice Hockey

The 1983–84 National Hockey League (NHL) season will be remembered as the one in which the brash Edmonton Oilers, led by Wayne Gretzky, finally took the air out of the New York Islanders. Trying to become only the second team in league history to win five consecutive Stanley Cup championships, the Islanders were deflated by the NHL's greatest offensive machine. The Oilers broke their own team scoring record (set in 1982–83) with 446 goals during the 80-game regular season, and their thirst for a first league crown was quenched with a smashing four-games-to-one victory over the Islanders in the Cup finals.

Regular Season. In the race for individual scoring honors, Gretzky easily outpointed his nearest rival, Oiler defenseman Paul Coffey, to win his fourth straight Ross Trophy. He had the most goals, 87, and the most assists, 118, for an astounding 205 points. He also set an NHL record by scoring at least one point in 51 straight games. From the Oilers' first game on Oct. 5, 1983, to Jan. 28, 1984, Gretzky had 153 points. Had he not played another game, he still would have won the scoring title by 27 points. The "Great One" won a record fifth straight Hart Trophy as the NHL's most valuable player (MVP).

Coffey's runner-up total of 126 points was the most by a defenseman since Hall of Famer Bobby Orr in the mid-1970s. Coffey scored 40 goals, joining Orr as the only defenseman ever to reach that total. The Oilers had two other players—Jari Kurri and Mark Messier—with more than 100 points, and yet another, Glenn Anderson, with 99. In all, 12 players in the league broke the 100-point plateau, and eight had 50 goals or more.

The Oilers were not the only offensive power, however. Islander winger Mike Bossy became the first player to score 50 or more goals in seven straight seasons. Los Angeles Kings' center Marcel Dionne became the fourth leading scorer (1,379 points) of all time, with 92 in 1983–84.

The Oilers sputtered only once in their drive for the Smythe Division title. They lost five straight games in February with Gretzky and Kurri out of the lineup, including a humiliating 11–0 loss to the weak Hartford Whalers. Except for that slide, they were awesome. They had the most points (119) and most wins (57) of any team in the league. The Isles and Boston Bruins each had 104 points to win the Patrick and Adams divisions, respectively.

Play-Offs. Gretzky continued his scoring dominance in the Oilers march to the Stanley Cup, with 35 points in 19 play-off games. The Conn Smythe Trophy (play-off MVP), however, went to Messier, who had 26 points and was also an important aggressive presence on the ice.

Rich Pilling

The Oilers and Wayne Gretzky (r) win the Stanley Cup.

The Oilers began their quest by beating the Winnipeg Jets three straight in the first round and the stubborn Calgary Flames in seven games in the Smythe Division final. Boston and Buffalo, however, could not avoid embarrassing early exits. The Bruins, who finished 29 points ahead of Montreal in the Adams Division, were bounced by the Canadiens in three straight games. Buffalo got the same treatment from the Quebec Nordiques. Then, in the "Battle of Quebec," the surprising Canadiens shot down the Nordiques in six games to win the division play-off title.

In the Patrick Division play-offs, the Isles went five tough games with the New York Rangers, winning the deciding game in overtime. Washington, meanwhile, was whipping the Philadelphia Flyers three in a row. The defending champion Islanders then got past Washington in five games for the division championship.

The Minnesota North Stars went seven games to beat the St. Louis Blues in the NHL's weakest division, the Norris. The Oilers then whipped Minnesota in four straight to take the Campbell Conference crown, and the Islanders overcame the hard-skating Canadiens for the Wales Conference championship. That set up a rematch of the 1982–83 Islander–Oiler Stanley Cup final.

In the opener, the Oilers stunned the Isles with an uncharacteristically strong defensive performance, winning 1–0. Goalie Grant Fuhr made 37 saves in the Oilers first-ever Stanley Cup shutout. Gretzky was held without a point for only the fourth time all season, but Kevin McClelland beat Islander goalie Billy Smith in the third period for the game's only goal. In their determined "Drive for Five" (fifth straight Stanley Cup), the Islanders regrouped in Game 2, whipping the Oilers 6–1. Star center Bryan Trottier scored two goals, including one in the first minute of play, and giant defenseman Clark Gillies scored a hat trick.

Game 2, however, proved to be the Islanders' last hurrah, as the Oilers easily won the next three games on home ice. Keyed by a dramatic end-to-end goal by Messier, Edmonton drove Smith from the nets in a 7–2 rout in Game 3. Game 4 was a similar story, also ending 7–2. Gretzky scored on a breakaway 30 seconds into the game—his first goal in seven play-off meetings with the Islanders—and slipped home the game's last goal on another breakaway. In what proved to be the series clincher, Game 5, Gretzky scored the first two goals in a 5–2 Oiler triumph.

For the Islanders, the loss to Edmonton marked the end of a remarkable string of 19 consecutive play-off series victories. As for the Oilers, they became the fastest expansion team to win the Cup. They joined the NHL in 1979 after seven years in the rival World Hockey League (WHL).

Canada Cup. In the six-nation Canada Cup tournament, Team Canada defeated Sweden, two games to none, in the best-of-three championship series. The winner had ousted the favored Soviet team, 3–2, in a semifinal match.

NCAA. Bowling Green defeated Minnesota-Duluth, 5–4, in four overtimes to capture the NCAA crown.

JIM MATHESON, *"The Edmonton Journal"*

Skiing

Two Swiss skiers dethroned two Americans for the overall World Cup championship in Alpine skiing in 1984, with Pirmin Zurbriggen and Erika Hess taking the men's and women's crowns from Phil Mahre of Yakima, WA, and Tamara McKinney of Squaw Valley, CA.

Zurbriggen won the men's overall title with 256 points, and Ingemar Stenmark finished second with 230 points. Mahre, who had won the crown three years in a row, finished in a disappointing tie for 15th place. The 22-year-old Hess captured the women's overall title by finishing fourth in the last race of the season, a slalom at Oslo, Norway, on March 24. That finish gave her enough points to surpass Hanni Wenzel of Liechtenstein, who missed a gate and was disqualified. Hess ended up with 247 points, Wenzel 238. McKinney placed third overall with 194 points.

In giant slalom competition, both Zurbriggen and Stenmark ended the World Cup tour with 115 points, but the Swede was awarded the title for actually having won more races—four to Zurbriggen's three. On the women's side, Hess beat out Wenzel for the title.

In the downhill, the Swiss made another clean sweep. Urs Raeber took the men's title, and the women's honors went to Maria Walliser.

ICE HOCKEY

National Hockey League
(Final Standings, 1983–84)

Wales Conference

Patrick Division	W	L	T	Pts.	Goals For	Against
*N.Y. Islanders	50	26	4	104	357	269
*Washington	48	27	5	101	308	226
*Philadelphia	44	26	10	98	350	290
*N.Y. Rangers	42	29	9	93	314	304
New Jersey	17	56	7	41	231	350
Pittsburgh	16	58	6	38	254	390
Adams Division						
*Boston	49	25	6	104	336	261
*Buffalo	48	25	7	103	315	257
*Quebec	42	28	10	94	360	278
*Montreal	35	40	5	75	286	295
Hartford	28	42	10	66	288	320

Campbell Conference

Norris Division	W	L	T	Pts.	For	Against
*Minnesota	39	31	10	88	345	344
*St. Louis	32	41	7	71	293	316
*Detroit	31	42	7	69	298	323
*Chicago	30	42	8	68	277	311
Toronto	26	45	9	61	303	387
Smythe Division						
*Edmonton	57	18	5	119	446	314
*Calgary	34	32	14	82	311	314
*Vancouver	32	39	9	73	306	328
*Winnipeg	31	38	11	73	340	374
Los Angeles	23	44	13	59	309	376

*Made play-offs

Stanley Cup Play-Offs
Wales Conference

Montreal	3 games	Boston	0
N.Y. Islanders	3 games	N.Y. Rangers	2
Quebec	3 games	Buffalo	0
Washington	3 games	Philadelphia	0
Montreal	4 games	Quebec	2
N.Y. Islanders	4 games	Washington	1
N.Y. Islanders	4 games	Montreal	2

Campbell Conference

Calgary	3 games	Vancouver	1
Edmonton	3 games	Winnipeg	0
Minnesota	3 games	Chicago	2
St. Louis	3 games	Detroit	1
Edmonton	4 games	Calgary	3
Minnesota	4 games	St. Louis	3
Edmonton	4 games	Minnesota	0

Championship

Edmonton	4 games	N.Y. Islanders	1

Individual Honors

Hart Trophy (most valuable player): Wayne Gretzky, Edmonton
Ross Trophy (leading scorer): Wayne Gretzky
Vezina Trophy (top goaltender): Tom Barrasso, Buffalo
Norris Trophy (best defenseman): Rod Langway, Washington
Selke Award (best defense forward): Doug Jarvis, Washington
Calder Trophy (rookie of the year): Tom Barrasso
Lady Byng Trophy (sportsmanship): Mike Bossy, N.Y. Islanders
Conn Smythe Trophy (most valuable in play-offs): Mark Messier, Edmonton
Coach of the Year: Bryan Murray, Washington

All-Star Game

Wales Conference 7, Campbell Conference 6

NCAA: Bowling Green

The men's World Cup slalom title went to Marc Girardelli of Luxembourg, with Stenmark second. Girardelli is actually an Austrian who defected from his country's ski federation. Among the women, McKinney salvaged her season by winning the slalom title with 110 points. Roswitha Steiner of Austria was second.

GEORGE DE GREGORIO

Soccer

The year 1984 was one of highs and lows for soccer in the United States.

Amateur. The high point came during the Summer Olympic Games, when 1,421,627 fans poured through turnstiles in Cambridge, MA, Annapolis, MD, Palo Alto, CA, and the Rose Bowl in Pasadena, CA, to see 16 nations compete for the gold medal. Soccer was the most-attended sport in the Olympics. Five times during the two-week tournament the U.S. attendance record of 77,691—set in 1977 at a North American Soccer League (NASL) play-off game between the New York Cosmos and Ft. Lauderdale Strikers—was broken.

The highlight of the Summer Games came on August 11 when France, displaying some of the world's top young players (professionals were allowed to participate in the Olympics for the first time), defeated Brazil, 2–0, for the gold medal in front of 101,799 Rose Bowl fans. Yugoslavia beat 1982 World Cup champion Italy, 2–1, for the bronze medal on August 10 in front of 100,374 Rose Bowl fans.

The U.S. Olympic Team, composed mainly of NASL players, defeated Costa Rica, 3–0, before 78,265 at Palo Alto in its first game, but then lost to Italy, 1–0, and tied Egypt, 1–1, to miss qualifying for the quarterfinals by one goal. Canada, with a team also composed of NASL players, reached the quarterfinals but lost to Brazil, 5–3, on penalty kicks.

In other United States Soccer Federation (USSF) activities, the U.S. National Team began the road to Mexico and the 1986 World Cup by defeating the Netherlands Antilles in a home-and-home first round CONCACAF (Confederation of North, Central American and Caribbean Federation) World Cup qualifying series. The two teams played to a scoreless tie on the island of Curaçao, and then the United States won 4–0 at Busch Stadium in St. Louis. The United States was scheduled to play Trinidad and Tobago and Costa Rica in second-round CONCACAF competition.

Also, the U.S. Junior National Team was defeated by Mexico, 1–0, in the semifinals of the CONCACAF tournament at Trinidad on September 12, and failed to qualify for the 1985 Junior World Cup in the USSR. It was the first time the United States failed to qualify for the Junior World Cup since 1979.

Professional. On the professional scene, the NASL conducted full indoor and outdoor seasons and crowned two different champions. Indoors, the San Diego Sockers won their third straight indoor championship with a three-game championship series sweep of the New York Cosmos. Outdoors, the Chicago Sting won the Soccer Bowl Championship Series with a two-game sweep of Toronto. It was the second Soccer Bowl triumph for the Sting, who won in 1981, and it was the second straight year Toronto lost in the finals. Award winners in the NASL included Steve Zungul of the Golden Bay Earthquakes, who won both the indoor and outdoor scoring championship and both Most Valuable Player (MVP) awards; Cosmos Coach Eddie Firmani, the indoor Metropolitan Insurance coach of the year; Sockers Coach Ron Newman, the outdoor Metropolitan Insurance coach of the year; and Tampa Bay forward Roy Wegerle, the rookie of the year.

Janis Rettaliata

The Baltimore Blast and St. Louis Steamers fought it out for the Major Indoor Soccer League (MISL) championship. The Blast won the best-of-seven series, 4 games to 1.

The MISL crowned a new champion, as the Baltimore Blast defeated the St. Louis Steamers, 4 games to 1, in a best-of-seven series. Award winners in the MISL included Stan Stamenkovic of Baltimore, the MVP, and Blast Coach Ken Cooper, the coach of the year.

After losing three teams—New York, Buffalo, and Phoenix—the MISL took in four NASL clubs—San Diego, Chicago, Minnesota, and New York—for 1984–85 as part of a historic accommodation between the two leagues. The four new clubs left the MISL with two seven-team divisions for the 1984–85 season. The NASL lost its president, Howard Samuels, who died of a heart attack in October. Executive Director of League Operations Ted Howard assumed command and spearheaded a movement for a new outdoor concept encompassing both regular-season and international cup games.

Elsewhere on the outdoor scene, a new league—the United Soccer League (USL)—was formed in 1984 as a replacement for the American Soccer League, which went dormant for one year. The Fort Lauderdale Sun won the first USL title, defeating Houston, two games to one, in the championship series.

JIM HENDERSON
North American Soccer League

SOCCER

NORTH AMERICAN SOCCER LEAGUE
(Final Standings, Outdoor Season 1984)
Eastern Division

	W	L	G.F.	G.A.	Pts.
*Chicago	13	11	50	49	120
*Toronto	14	10	46	33	117
New York	13	11	43	42	115
Tampa Bay	9	15	43	61	87

Western Division

	W	L	G.F.	G.A.	Pts.
*San Diego	14	10	51	42	118
*Vancouver	13	11	51	48	117
Minnesota	14	10	40	44	115
Tulsa	10	14	42	46	98
Golden Bay	8	16	61	62	95
*Made play-offs.					

NASL Outdoor Champion: Chicago Sting
NASL Indoor Champion: San Diego Sockers
MISL Champion: Baltimore Blast
USL Champion: Ft. Lauderdale Sun
European Cup Champion: Liverpool
European Nations Cup Champion: France
NCAA Championship: Clemson

Swimming

The Friendship '84 Games in late August, the Soviet Union's version of the Olympics, produced some outstanding swimming performances. Most notable was Sergei Zabolotnov's effort in the 200-m backstroke, in which he broke American Rick Carey's world record with a time of 1 minute, 58.41 seconds. Zabolotnov's mark was the first swimming record set at the Moscow event and erased Carey's

standard of 1:58.86, set in the U.S. Olympic Trials at Indianapolis. Carey won the gold medal at the Olympics with a time of 2:00.23.

Four other world marks fell at the Friendship Games. Sylvia Gerasch of East Germany swam the 100-m breaststroke in 1:08.29, and East German women's relay teams set standards in the 400-m freestyle (3:42.41) and 400-m medley relay (4:03.69). Ina Kleber's opening backstroke leg (1:00.59) in the medley relay also set a world record.

Kristin Otto, who swam the opening leg on the East German 400-m freestyle relay team, had lowered the 200-m freestyle mark to 1:57.75 in the spring; that bettered the four-year-old mark of Cynthia Woodhead of the United States by .48 second. In the same meet, Jens-Peter Berndt's 4:19.61 in the 400-m individual medley erased Ricardo Prado's 1982 standard by .17 second.

Tracy Caulkins of Nashville, TN, winner of three gold medals at the Olympics, also was outstanding at the NCAA championships in Indianapolis, where she won four individual titles representing the University of Florida. But Texas won the team title, defeating defending champion Stanford, 392–324. In the men's NCAA championships, held in Cleveland, Florida took the team title with 287½ points; Texas was second with 277.

GEORGE DE GREGORIO

Tennis

John McEnroe and Martina Navratilova propelled themselves so far in front of the other players on the 1984 tennis tour that their games seemed to belong to the stars while the rest of the circuit simply exhibited earthly excellence.

McEnroe won Wimbledon (defeating Jimmy Connors in the final, 6–1, 6–1, 6–2) and the U.S. Open (beating Ivan Lendl, 6–3, 6–4, 6–1) and would have won the French final over Lendl had he not become a victim of his own belligerence. McEnroe led two sets to love and had a service break in the third when the cumulative effect of his bickering with officials wore him down. Lendl won 3–6, 2–6, 6–4, 7–5, 7–5, for his first major championship.

Navratilova's straight-set victory (6–3, 6–1) over Chris Evert Lloyd in the finals of the French Open in June earned her a $1 million bonus for capturing the Grand Slam. Some purists contended that her Wimbledon, U.S., Australian, and French championships had not been accomplished during the same calendar year. The Czech-born U.S. citizen could not settle the controversy as she was upset in the Australian Open by another Czech, Helena Sukova, who deprived Martina of a record seventh straight grand slam title.

Martina's serve is a savage left-handed sweeper, her groundstrokes can alternate top-

The explosive Ivan Lendl of Czechoslovakia won his first Grand Slam tournament ever by defeating John McEnroe in the finals of the French Open, 3–6, 2–6, 6–4, 7–5, 7–5.

spin or underspin with power or off-pace, her volley is rapier sharp, and her court coverage is superior. She is a complete player with no weaknesses and an incredible array of strengths. As a result, Chris Evert Lloyd, the top women's player for six years, has been reduced to the unfamiliar role of runner-up. In 1984, Chris reached the finals of the French Open, Wimbledon, and U.S. Open, only to lose to Martina each time. No other woman in the top 10 was even close to Martina or Chris in WTA ranking points.

The child superstar phenomenon, which ironically started with Evert Lloyd herself 14 years earlier when she reached the semifinals of the U.S. Open at age 16, seemed to be unraveling in 1984. Tracy Austin and Andrea Jaeger, both of whom were ranked among the world's top four players two years earlier, dropped off the tour because of a series of injuries that their young bodies could not endure. Two former teen stars, Pam Shriver and Bettina Bunge, and 17-year-old Carling Bassett have managed to overcome crippling setbacks but not before the warning to all youngsters was clear: the physical and emotional strain of year-round professional tennis may threaten a young athlete's career.

Just as Navratilova and Evert Lloyd dominated women's tennis, McEnroe, Lendl, Connors, and Mats Wilander had a monopoly on the first four places in the men's rankings, with no one else in sight. Gone from the top 10 were perennial stars Guillermo Vilas, Vitas Gerulaitis, José Luis Clerc, and Gene Mayer. In their places were four Swedes—Wilander (4), Anders Jarryd (6), Henrik Sundstrom (7), and Joakim Nystrom (8), with yet another, Stefan Edberg, ranked 19.

Perhaps more than any other sport, problems with officiating and player behavior have preoccupied professional tennis in recent years. Slowly, the game's governing fathers are realizing that human eyes are not capable of precisely gauging the flight of a ball traveling at speeds of more than 100 mph (160 km/h). The difficult task of "calling lines" is slowly being

TENNIS

Davis Cup: Sweden
Federation Cup: Czechoslovakia
Wightman Cup: United States

Major Tournaments

U.S. Open—men's singles: John McEnroe; men's doubles: John Fitzgerald (Australia) and Tomas Smid (Czechoslovakia); women's singles: Martina Navratilova; women's doubles: Navratilova and Pam Shriver; mixed doubles: Manuela Maleeva (Bulgaria) and Tom Gullikson; men's 35 singles: Stan Smith; women's 35 singles: Laura DuPont; junior girls: Katerina Maleeva (Bulgaria); junior boys: Mark Kratzman (Australia).
U.S. Clay Courts—men's singles: Andres Gomez (Ecuador); men's doubles: Ken Flach and Robert Seguso; women's singles: Manuela Maleeva (Bulgaria); women's doubles: Beverly Mould and Pam Smith.
U.S. National Indoor—men's singles: Jimmy Connors; men's doubles: Fritz Buehning and Peter Fleming.
Volvo Grand Prix Masters—men's singles: John McEnroe; men's doubles: McEnroe and Peter Fleming.
Virginia Slims (New York): Martina Navratilova.
World Championship Tennis (Dallas): John McEnroe.
Wimbledon—men's singles: John McEnroe; men's doubles: McEnroe and Peter Fleming; women's singles: Martina Navratilova; women's doubles: Navratilova and Pam Shriver; mixed doubles: John Lloyd and Wendy Turnbull.
French Open—men's singles: Ivan Lendl (Czechoslovakia); men's doubles: Henri Leconte (France) and Yannick Noah (France); women's singles: Martina Navratilova; women's doubles: Navratilova and Pam Shriver; mixed doubles: Anne Smith and Dick Stockton.
Italian Open—men's singles: Andres Gomez (Ecuador); men's doubles: Ken Flach and Robert Seguso; women's singles: Manuela Maleeva (Bulgaria); women's doubles: Iva Budarova (Czechoslovakia) and Marcela Skuhersk (Czechoslovakia).
Canadian Open—men's singles: John McEnroe; men's doubles: McEnroe and Peter Fleming; women's singles: Chris Evert Lloyd; women's doubles: Kathy Jordan and Elizabeth Sayers.
Australian Open—men's singles: Mats Wilander (Sweden); men's doubles: Sherwood Stewart and Mark Edmondson (Australia); women's singles: Chris Evert Lloyd; women's doubles: Martina Navratilova and Pam Shriver.
N.B. All players are from the United States, unless otherwise noted.

Geoff Smith, a senior at Providence (RI) College and former fireman from Liverpool, England, won the 88th Boston Marathon in 2 hours, 10 minutes, 34 seconds, an exceptional time for the windy, drizzly conditions.

AP/Wide World

turned over to electronic devices. And it is being recognized that fining millionaires like McEnroe and Connors $1,000 per incident is merely a petty-cash punishment.

Among the tennis-playing public, mid-sized rackets have replaced oversized as the current rage, with conventional dimensions in wood nearly extinct. Engineering and style have improved in rackets, shoes, and clothing.

EUGENE L. SCOTT
Publisher, "Tennis Week" Magazine

Track and Field

Though he did not have a chance to compete in the Olympics because of the Soviet boycott, pole vaulter Sergei Bubka of the USSR was one of the outstanding track-and-field athletes of 1984. The 5'10", 176-pounder set a world record of 19'2¼" on May 25 at Bratislava, Czechoslovakia, breaking by three quarters of an inch the 1983 standard of Thierry Vigneron of France. A week later, on June 3, at St. Denis, France, Bubka scaled 19'3½". Then early in July, prior to the start of the Olympics and as if to offer a challenge to those competing at Los Angeles, Bubka cleared 19'4¼" in a meet in London. (Pierre Quinon of France took the Olympic gold with 18'10¼".) Later in the summer, at a meet in Rome, Vigneron reclaimed the world record with a vault of 19'4¾". But his supremacy was brief. Bubka came back minutes later with a vault of 19'5¾".

Bubka's record was one of 20, seven by women and 13 by men, established in 1984. The only one set at the Olympics was a time of 37.83 seconds in the 400-m relay by the United States. The only other American to set a world mark in 1984 was Evelyn Ashford, who lowered her 10.79-second clocking in the 100-m dash to 10.76 at Zurich, Switzerland, on August 22. Other new record holders included Fernando Mamede of Portugal in the men's 10,000 meters (27:13.81) and Olga Bondarenko of the Soviet Union in the women's 10,000 meters (31:13.78); China's Zhu Jianhua in the men's high jump (7'10"); West Germany's Jurgen Hingsen in the decathlon (8,798 points); Tatyana Kazankina of the Soviet Union in both the women's 2,000 meters (5:28.72) and 3,000 meters (8:22.62); Ingrid Kristiansen of Norway in the women's 5,000 meters (14:58.89); Uwe Hohn of East Germany in the men's javelin (343'10"); and Yuri Sedykh of the Soviet Union in the hammer (283'3").

Marathons. Although official world records are not kept, Steve Jones of Wales won the America's Marathon in Chicago with a best-ever time of 2:08.05; Rosa Mota of Portugal came in first among the women. In the New York Marathon, Orlando Pizzolato of Italy took the men's division; Norway's Grete Waitz won the women's race for the sixth time. And in the 88th Boston Marathon, the men's winner was Geoff Smith of Great Britain; the women's winner was Lorraine Moller of New Zealand.

GEORGE DE GREGORIO

SPORTS SUMMARIES[1]

ARCHERY—U.S. Champions: men: Darrell Pace, Hamilton, OH; women: Ruth Rowe, McLean, VA.

BIATHLON—U.S. Champions: men: Josh Thompson, Asford, WA; women: Julie Newman, Mercer Island, WA.

BILLIARDS—World Three-Cushion Champion: Nobuki Kobayashi, Japan.

BOBSLEDDING—U.S. Champions: two-man: Brent Rushlaw and Jim Tyler, Saranac Lake, NY; four-man: Jeff Jost, Burke, NY.

BOWLING—Professional Bowling Association: national champion: Bob Chamberlain, Pontiac, MI; Tournament of Champions: Mike Durbin, Chagrin Falls, OH; men's world cup: Jack Jurek, Tonawanda, NY; women's world cup: Eliana Rigato, Italy. **American Bowling Congress:** singles: (tie) Bob Antczak, Chicago, and Neal Young, Louisville, KY; doubles: Chris Cobus and John Megna, Milwaukee; all-events: Bob Goike, Detroit; masters: Earl Anthony, Dublin, CA; team: Minnesota Loons Number 1, St. Paul, MN. **Bowling Proprietors' Association of America:** men's open: Mark Roth, Spring Lake Heights, NJ; women's open: Karen Ellingsworth, Des Plaines, IL. **Women's International Bowling Congress:** open division, singles: Freida Gates, North Syracuse, NY; doubles: Bea Hoffman and Sue Reese, Novato, CA; all-events: Shinobu Saitoh, Japan; team: All Japan.

CANOEING—U.S. Champions (flatwater): kayak: men's 500 m: Greg Barton, Homer, MI; 1,000 m: Barton; 10,000 m: Barton; women's 500 m: Cathy Hearn, Garrett Park, MI. Canoe: men's 500 m: Jim Terrell, Milford, OH; 1,000 m: Rod McLain, Gloversville, NY.

CROSS COUNTRY—World Champions: men: Carlos Lopes, Portugal; women: Maricica Puica, Rumania. **U.S. Champions:** men: Pat Porter, Eugene, OR; women: Cathy Branta, Slinger, WI.

CURLING—World Champions: men: Eigil Ramsfjell, Norway; women: Connie Laliberte, Canada. **U.S. Champions:** men: Bruce Roberts, Hibbing, MN; women: Amy Hattan, Duluth, MN.

CYCLING—Tour de France: Laurent Fignon, France. **World Pro Champions:** sprint: Koichi Nakano, Japan; pursuit: Hans-Henrik Oersted, Denmark; road: Claude Criquelion, Belgium. **U.S. Amateur Road Racing Champions:** men: Therlow Rogers; women: Rebecca Daughton, Allentown, PA.

DOG SHOWS—Westminster: best: Ch. Seaward's Blackbeard, Newfoundland owned by Elinor Ayers, Manchester, VT.

FENCING—U.S. Champions: men's foil: Michael McCahey, Winnetka, IL; epée: Paul Soter, San Francisco; saber: Peter Westbrook, New York City; women's foil: Vincent Bradford, San Antonio; epée: Bradford. **NCAA:** men's team: Wayne State; women's team: Yale.

FIELD HOCKEY—NCAA (women): Old Dominion.

FIGURE SKATING—World Champions: men: Scott Hamilton, Bowling Green, OH; women: Katarina Witt, East Germany; pairs: Barbara Undserhill and Paul Martini, Canada; dance: Jayne Torvill and Christopher Dean, Great Britain. **U.S. Champions:** men: Hamilton; women: Rosalynn Sumners, Edmonds, WA; pairs: Caitlin and Peter Carruthers, Wilmington, DE; dance: Judy Blumberg, Tarvana, CA, and Michael Seibert, Washington, PA.

GYMNASTICS—U.S. Gymnastics Federation Champions: men's all-around: Mitch Gaylord, Van Nuys, CA; women's all-around: Mary Lou Retton, Fairmont, WV. **NCAA:** men's team: UCLA; women's team: Utah.

HANDBALL—U.S. Handball Association Champions (4-wall): men's singles: Naty Alvarado, Hesperia, CA; women's singles: Rosemary Bellini, New York City; collegiate team: Lake Forest.

HORSE SHOWS—World Cup: Mario Deslauriers, Canada, on Aramis; **U.S. Equestrian Team Champions:** show jumping: Conrad Homfeld, Petersburg, VA, on Abdullah; dressage: Hilda Gurnny, Moorpark, CA, on Keen; three-day event: Bruce Davidson, Chesterland, PA, on Doctor Peaches.

JUDO—U.S. Champions: men's 132-lb class: Fred Glock, New York City; 143: Doug Tono, Chicago; 156: Dan Augustine, Berkeley, CA; 172: Nicky Yonezuka, Watchung, NJ; 189: Tommy Martin, Stockton, CA; under 209: Leo White, U.S. Army; over 209: Eddie Arrarazcaeta, Hialeah, FL; open: Mike Mika, Little Rock, AK; women's 106-lb class: Darlene Anaya, Albuquerque, NM; 114: Mary Lewis; Albany, NY; 123: Ann Marie Burns, Spring Valley, CA; 134: Lynn Roethke, Indianapolis; 145: Christine Penick, San Jose, CA; 158: Belinda Binkley, Colorado Springs; over 158: Margaret Castro, New York City; open: Heidi Bauersachs, New York City.

LACROSSE—NCAA: men's Div. I: Johns Hopkins; Div. III: Hobart; women: Temple.

LUGE—U.S. Champions: men: Tim Nardiello, Lake Placid, NY; women: Bonnie Warner, Mount Baldy, CA.

MODERN PENTATHLON—World Champions: junior men: Igor Shvarts, USSR; women: S. Yakovleva, USSR. **U.S. Champions:** men: Mike Storm, Arlington, VA; women: Kim Dunlop, Tallahassee, FL.

PADDLEBALL—U.S. Champions (4-wall): men: Steve Wilson, Flint, MI; women: Carla Teare, Clarkston, MI.

POLO—World Cup: Boehm Porcelain. **Gold Cup:** White Birch, CT. **America Cup:** Old Pueblo, CA. **North America Cup:** Houston.

RACQUETBALL—U.S. Champions: men's amateur open: Dan Ferris, St. Cloud, MN; women's open: Marci Drexler, North Hollywood, CA; men's pro: Mike Yellen, Southfield, MI; women's pro: Heather McKay, Canada.

ROWING—International Rowing Federation Lightweight Champions: men's single sculls: Denmark; doubles: Italy; straight four: Spain; eight: Denmark; women's single sculls: West Germany; doubles: Denmark; straight four: West Germany; eight: United States. **U.S. Collegiate Champions:** pair without coxswain: Wisconsin; four with coxswain: Temple; four without coxswain: Princeton; eight: Navy.

RUGBY—Five-Nations Champion: Scotland. **U.S. Champions:** men's club: Dallas Harlequins; women's club: Florida St.; collegiate: Harvard.

SHOOTING—U.S. National Rifle and Pistol Champions: men's pistol: James Laguana, Ft. Benning, GA; small-bore rifle, 3-positions: Lones Wigger, Ft. Benning; small-bore rifle, prone: Ronald West, Zanesville, OH; high-power rifle: Patrick McCann, Staunton, IL; women's pistol: Cherrie Shaw, Rockford, IL; small-bore rifle, 3-positions: Deena Wigger, Ft. Benning; small-bore rifle, prone: Marsha Beasley, Arlington, VA; high-power rifle: Norma J. McCullough, Newhall, CA.

SOFTBALL—U.S. Amateur Softball Association Champions: men's major fast pitch: California Coors Kings, Merced, CA; class-A fast pitch: Hudson's Supply, Bakersfield, CA; major slow pitch: Lilly Air Systems, Chicago; class-A slow pitch: Bender Plumbing Supply, New Haven, CT; women's major fast pitch: California Diamonds, Los Angeles; class-A fast pitch: Arrow Butane Flames, Las Cruces, NM; major slow pitch: The Spooks, Anoka, MN; class-A slow pitch: Mr. A's Express, Sacramento, CA.

SPEED SKATING—World Champions: men's overall: Oleg Bojiev, USSR; 500 m: Hilbert van der Duim, Netherlands; 1,500 m: Bojiev; 5,000 m: Geir Karlstad, Norway; 10,000 m: Michael Hadgchieff, Austria; women's overall: Karin Enke, East Germany; 500 m: Enke; 1,500 m: Enke; 3,000 m: Enke; 5,000 m: Andrea Schone, East Germany.

SQUASH RAQUETS—World Champion: Janhangir Khan, Pakistan. **U.S. Champion:** Mark Talbott, Kudjoe Keys, FL.

TABLE TENNIS—U.S. Champions: men: Dan Seemiller, Pittsburgh, PA; women: In Sook Bhushan, Aurora, CO.

VOLLEYBALL—U.S. Champions: men: Nautilus Pacifica, Long Beach, CA; women: Carlsen Chrysler, Palo Alto, CA. **NCAA:** men: UCLA; women: Hawaii.

WEIGHTLIFTING—U.S. Weightlifting Federation Champions: men's 114-lb class: Brian Okada, Wailuku, HI; 123: Albert Hood, Los Angeles; 132: Phil Sanderson, Billings, MT; 148: Don Abrahamson, Cupertino, CA; 165: Chuck Jambliter, Jamestown, NY; 181: Mark Levell, Chicago; 198: Kevin Winter, San Jose, CA; 220: Ken Clark, Pacifica, CA; 242: Guy Carlton, Colorado Springs; over 242: Mario Martinez, Salinas, CA; women's 97-lb class: Dee Anna Hammock, Cumming, GA; 106: Mary Carr, Wichita, KS; 114: Rachel Silverman, San Francisco; 123: Colleen Colley, Chamblee, GA; 132: Jane Camp, College Park, GA; 149: Judy Glenney, Farmington, NM; 165: Jody Anderson, Geneva, IL; 182: Benita Carswell, Atlanta; over 182: Karyn Tarter, New Rochelle, NY.

WRESTLING—World Cup Champions (freestyle): 105.5-lb class: Bob Weaver, Lehigh, PA; 114.5: Joe Gonzalez, Bakersfield, CA; 125.5: Anatoly Belaglazou, USSR; 136.5: Steven Sarkisyan, USSR; 149.5: Mikhail Kharachura, USSR; 163: Vladimir Dzhuton, USSR; 180.5: Chris Campbell, United States; 198: Sanasar Oganasyan, USSR; 220: Magomad Magomadov, USSR; heavyweight: Bruce Baumgartner, Edinboro, PA.

YACHTING—U.S. Yacht Racing Union: champion of champions: Riaz Latifullah, Washington; Mallory Cup (men): Marc Eagan, Bay-Waveland Y.C., Mississippi; Adams Trophy (women): Betsy Gelenitis, Metedeconk Club, New Jersey.

[1] Sports not covered separately in pages 473–492.

SRI LANKA

Ethnic violence involving Sinhalese, the nation's majority, and Tamils, the largest minority, continued in 1984. It was marked by the growing strength of extremist Tamil groups seeking an independent homeland and by repressive and generally ineffective actions by the government.

Communal Violence. On January 10 an All-Party Peace Conference, convened on the initiative of the ruling United National Party (UNP), began what proved to be prolonged and intermittent discussions of ways to deal with ethnic problems and to achieve national reconciliation. On the day after the conference opened Tamil terrorists killed two policemen and injured several others in the northern town of Point Pedro. On March 28 at least seven persons were reported killed in another northern town when Air Force troops were ambushed by Tamil terrorists; and on the following day a Sinhalese government official and his driver were shot in Jaffna. In April, according to government reports, at least 50 "suspected terrorists" were killed (other estimates were much higher). In August the government reported that 95 people, including 26 security troops, were killed. And on November 30 and during the first week of December about 300 persons were reported to have been killed in a rebel attack on two prison camps, an attempted invasion of guerrillas from India, and retaliatory action by Sinhalese army troops following a guerrilla attack on an army convoy.

The government was criticized repeatedly both for its failure to arrest the growing terrorism and for its allegedly brutal methods of repression. When the All-Party Peace Conference reconvened in late August, the government made further concessions, including a proposal to create a second parliamentary chamber that would give better representation to minority groups.

Economic Developments. Largely because of higher prices for tea, its principal export, Sri Lanka had a favorable balance of trade in 1984. Thus it was able to increase its foreign exchange earnings and to cease importing rice, the staple food for its population.

The government suspended negotiations for a $50 million standby loan from the International Monetary Fund (IMF), allegedly because of the improvement in its foreign-exchange position but probably also because of its reluctance to accept some of the conditions insisted on by the IMF before the loan could be approved. President J. R. Jayewardene did order budget cuts of more than $100 million, in accordance with an IMF recommendation, but he resisted other IMF conditions, including devaluation of the rupee, reduced indexation of wages, and reduced subsidies on basic necessities. The World Bank granted Sri Lanka a "structural adjustment" loan of $210 million, and an aid consortium provided another loan of about $410 million.

Foreign Affairs. The troubled internal situation created new problems for Sri Lanka in its external relations. Many foreign governments expressed concern over the deteriorating situation, and some, including Israel, sent advisers to assist the government in dealing with the Tamil terrorists.

Relations with India were strained to an unprecedented degree because of the Sinhala-Tamil tensions in Sri Lanka. The government of India was understandably concerned over the possible spill-over effects of these tensions, for most Tamils live in the south Indian state of Tamil Nadu where they were openly sympathetic with those in Sri Lanka. As many as 40,000 from Sri Lanka took refuge in Tamil Nadu. The Sri Lankan government charged that India was giving assistance to the Tamil terrorists and that several thousand of them were being trained in guerrilla warfare in camps in Tamil Nadu. Both governments sought to prevent this delicate issue from creating major strains on their normally good relations. President Jayewardene discussed the whole matter with Prime Minister Indira Gandhi during a visit to New Delhi in late June and early July.

In June, prior to his visit to India, President Jayewardene made official visits to the United States and Britain. In November he returned to New Delhi for the funeral of Indira Gandhi.

NORMAN D. PALMER
University of Pennsylvania

STAMPS AND STAMP COLLECTING

After it published its 1984 stamp schedule, the U.S. Postal Service (USPS) added some for obvious political reasons and postponed others. The USPS contributed more than $200,000 to a Council of Philatelic Organizations to in-

Selected U.S. Commemorative Stamps, 1984

Subject	Denomination	Date
Alaska	20¢	Jan. 3
Olympics	4x20¢ block	Jan. 6
Fed. Dep. Insur. Corp.	20¢	Jan. 12
Harry Truman	20¢	Jan. 26
Love	20¢	Jan. 31
Carter Woodson	20¢	Feb. 1
Soil and Water Conservation	20¢	Feb. 6
Credit Union	20¢	Feb. 10
Lillian Gilbreth	40¢	Feb. 24
Orchids	4x20¢ block	March 5
Hawaii	20¢	March 12
Maryland	13¢ card	March 25
National Archives	20¢	April 16
Olympics	4x20¢ block	May 4
Louisiana World's Fair	20¢	May 11
Health Research	20¢	May 17
Douglas Fairbanks	20¢	May 23
Jim Thorpe	20¢	May 24
John McCormack	20¢	June 6
St. Lawrence Seaway	20¢	June 26
Wetlands Preservation	20¢	July 2
Roanoke Voyages	20¢	July 13
Herman Melville	20¢	Aug. 1
Horace Moses	20¢	Aug. 6
Smokey Bear	20¢	Aug. 13
Roberto Clemente	20¢	Aug. 17
Dr. Frank Laubach	30¢	Sept. 2
American Kennel Club	4x20¢	Sept. 7
Crime Prevention	20¢	Sept. 26
Family Unity	20¢	Oct. 1
Eleanor Roosevelt	20¢	Oct. 11
Nation of Readers	20¢	Oct. 16
Santa Claus Christmas	20¢	Oct. 30
Madonna Christmas	20¢	Oct. 30
Vietnam Veterans	20¢	Nov. 10

crease interest in and sales of its new stamps. The group hired a public relations firm for a $20,000 fee to place monthly publicity in daily and weekly newspapers asking the public to "Fall in Love with Stamp Collecting."

To stimulate interest among youngsters, Washington stepped up its Benjamin Franklin Stamp Clubs program in grammar schools. Though veterans felt that the figure was highly exaggerated, the USPS said that the programs were "conducted in 60,000 learning centers," or double the number reported only two years before. Also, it sponsored a stamp design contest and awarded top prizes to Molly LaRue, an Ohio Wesleyan University art student, and nine-year-old Danny LaBoccetta from Jamaica, NY. Their designs were used for stamps in October and intended for Christmas mail.

In addition to producing single stamps, the USPS continued the practice of producing blocks of four different designs for the same event. Among them were quartets showing orchids, pedigreed dogs, and two for the Olympics.

Another major event marked by stamps was the continuing travel schedule of Pope John Paul II. All the countries he visited produced commemorative stamps and postmarks. In October, Vatican City itself issued 12 new stamps for normal postal use, each of which recalled trips made by the pontiff in 1981 and 1982.

The major philatelic exhibitions of the year were staged in Zurich, Melbourne, Seoul, Montreal, and Sofia.

ERNEST A. KEHR, *Stamp News Bureau*

STOCKS AND BONDS

After two years of dramatic gains, the U.S. stock market flattened out in 1984 amid concern over slowing economic growth and a seemingly intractable federal budget deficit.

The Dow Jones average of 30 industrial stocks, the most widely recognized measure of market trends, never threatened to match its advances of 19.6% in 1982 and 20.3% in 1983. It closed December 31 at 1,211.57, down 47.07 points, or 3.7% for the year.

Trading volume at the New York Stock Exchange (NYSE) set a record for the third straight year, totaling 23.07 billion shares, against 21.59 billion in 1983. But it hardly qualified as a vintage year in the securities business. Brokers' profits were squeezed by such problems as high costs and pressure from large investing institutions for lower commission rates on securities transactions. The Big Board itself was faced with an increasing competitive challenge from the National Association of Securities Dealers, operator of the modernized "over-the-counter" market, and independent over-the-counter dealers offering to handle trades in stocks listed on the NYSE.

Brokers and their customers had their economic worries as well. In the first half of the year, with the gross national product (GNP) growing at an annual rate of better than 8%, after adjustment for inflation, there was widespread speculation that the economy might "overheat," causing a revival of inflation.

The Federal Reserve kept a tight rein on credit, and interest rates rose. That policy proved very effective, slowing the GNP growth rate to 1.9% by the third quarter of the year. As autumn arrived, some economists and investors began to worry that the policy had worked too well—that the desired slowing of business activity would give way to an undesired recession. Apparently mindful of this change in expectations, the Fed shifted gears, seeking to encourage renewed growth. On the eve of Thanksgiving, it took its most overt step in that direction by lowering the discount rate, the rate it charges on loans to private financial institutions, from 9% to 8.5%. In December the rate was lowered again to 8%.

All this helped foster a strong rally in the credit markets, where bond prices rise and fall in a direct inverse relationship with interest rates. Bond prices, depressed early in the year by fears of heavy demand for credit and resurgent inflation, rebounded vigorously as the economy slowed and inflation remained low, at an annual rate of about 4%. The stock market, which often takes its cues from the bond market, was slow to respond this time, however.

Though its overall showing was unspectacular, the stock market had its memorable moments during the year. One highlight was a short but exuberant buying spree in the first

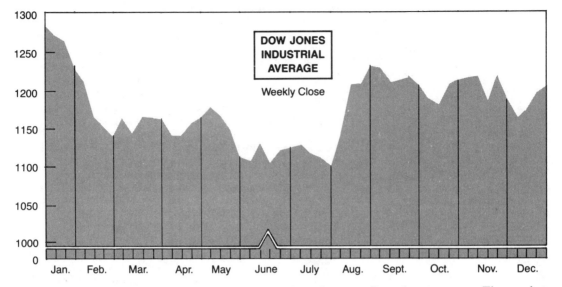

three days of August. With the evidence mounting that the dangers of a runaway boom had been averted, the Dow Jones Industrial Average soared almost 87 points in that brief span. Friday, August 3, brought a record volume of 236.57 million shares on the NYSE. And talk naturally arose of a reprise of the historic rally in stock prices that had begun two years before, in August 1982. But those hopes went unfulfilled.

The financial community's mergers-and-acquisitions specialists got the year off to a rousing start with such transactions as Texaco's takeover of Getty Oil, and the record $13.2 billion purchase of Gulf Oil by Standard Oil of California (since renamed Chevron). For much of the rest of the year, speculation simmered in the energy stocks as traders sought to cash in on "the next oil takeover."

Trends and Problems. In the year's financial wheeling and dealing, a particular controversy arose over a phenomenon known as greenmail. This occurred when the management of a corporation whose stock was being accumulated by an unfriendly outsider moved to forestall a takeover by buying the shares back from the "raider" at an above-market price (sometimes with an added payment for the hostile investor's expenses.) With each instance of greenmail, protests from other stockholders, lawsuits, and calls for action to prohibit this practice mounted.

Another source of serious concern in the financial world was the soundness of the banking system, strained by problem loans to developing countries and the energy industry. The most vivid manifestation of this issue came when federal authorities were forced to put together a financial rescue plan for Chicago's Continental Illinois bank.

It was not much of a year, either, for speculators in smaller, lesser-known stocks. These issues typically performed a good deal worse than the overall market averages. The market for new stock issues, regarded as a sensitive barometer of speculative enthusiasm, quieted down after its busiest year ever in 1983.

On balance, in fact, companies were not selling new stock; they were buying back existing shares, which they perceived as undervalued. Among the companies announcing major repurchase programs were Teledyne and Standard Oil (Indiana).

While many speculating sectors of the market languished, the long-neglected utility group was a surprise winner. Although many electric utilities continued to struggle with financial woes, stemming from new power projects, the Dow Jones average of 15 utilities climbed to its highest level since the 1960s.

The utilities benefited from low inflation rates, downward pressure of fuel costs, and, in the latter stages of the year, falling interest rates that made their generous dividend yields appealing to investors. They also had in their ranks a new group of companies that found favor in the market—the seven regional holding companies born with the breakup of American Telephone and Telegraph, which took effect on January 1. While the stock of the new, smaller AT&T went nowhere in the first year of trading, all seven of the "baby bells" rose in price.

International. As on Wall Street, it was a mixed year around the world. A world index of stock prices compiled by International SA, Geneva, and published by *The Wall Street Journal* showed a 0.1% decline from the start of the year through late November.

The often-volatile Hong Kong market turned in the best gain, rising 25.2%, followed by Britain, up 18.6%; France, up 17.2%; Japan, up 15.1%; West Germany, up 3.7%; and Switzerland, up 0.4%. The losers included Canada, down 4.6%, and Australia, down, 2.2%.

CHET CURRIER, *The Associated Press*

SUDAN

Opposition to the 15-year-old regime of President Jaafar al-Nemery grew steadily during 1984. Nemery's attempts to placate Sudan's various interest groups only served to alienate other groups and called into question his ability to continue to hold the country together.

Foreign Relations. In mid-March a Soviet-made bomber appeared out of the desert and dropped five bombs around the main Sudanese radio station at Omdurman, across the river from Khartoum. President Nemery immediately charged that Libya was responsible for the attack, but many Sudanese were skeptical. It was even speculated that Nemery may have ordered the bombing himself in order to convince his allies, Egypt and the United States, that he needed more military support. Despite these widespread doubts, the United States responded to the bombing by sending two Airborne Warning and Control System (AWACS) planes to Egypt. Cairo then invoked its 1976 joint defense pact with Sudan and sent troops to its southern neighbor.

Internal Security. Rebels in southern Sudan claimed that President Nemery had invoked the defense pact in order to free his own troops to put down the growing rebellion in the south. The Sudanese People's Liberation Movement (SPLM) carried out a series of kidnappings of expatriate workers and received international attention. The most daring and effective of these raids was an attack in February on a Chevron Oil installation in the south, killing four workers. The attack forced Chevron to suspend its Sudanese operations. Rebel attacks also put an end to construction of the pipeline designed to bring the oil from the fields to Port Sudan. Before the drilling stopped, Sudan was expecting to receive a projected $136 million per year in oil revenue.

There were also indications in 1984 that, for the first time, the southern rebels were cooperating with anti-Nemery forces in the north. Where the southern rebels generally have expressed the desire for an independent state in the south, rebel leaders have said that they would be satisfied with overthrowing the Nemery regime.

The southerners' hostility was further aggravated by the application of Islamic Law *(sharia)* to all citizens of Sudan, including those of the Christian south. Opposition to *sharia* also grew among Muslims in the north, most of whom felt that President Nemery had applied the law too strictly. Floggings and amputations became commonplace during the year, and even foreigners were not exempt from the rule that prescribes flogging as the punishment for possession of alcohol.

In reaction, Sudan's merchant and professional classes, once the bulwarks of Nemery's

---

SUDAN · Information Highlights

Official Name: Democratic Republic of Sudan.
Location: Northeast Africa.
Area: 966,988 sq mi (2 504 503 km²).
Population (mid-1984 est.): 21,100,000.
Government: *Head of state and government,* Gen. Jaafar Mohammed al-Nemery, president and prime minister. *Legislature* (unicameral)—National People's Assembly.
Monetary Unit: Pound (1.300 pounds equal U.S.$1, May 1984).
Foreign Trade (1983 U.S.$): *Imports,* $1,354,000,000; *exports,* $624,000,000.

---

support, deserted him. In May the president was forced to call a state of emergency, including curfews and bans on public meetings, partially in response to strikes by doctors and clerks.

Economy. Despite Sudan's mineral and agricultural potential, its economy and debt situations have been described as hopeless. The country's total debt of $7 billion (U.S.) is about equal to its Gross National Product. Sudan is the largest recipient of U.S. bilateral aid in sub-Saharan Africa, receiving $190 million in economic aid and $45 million in military assistance in 1984.

U.S. support for President Nemery may be waning, however, as U.S. officials have developed doubts about his ability to hold on to the country.

MICHAEL MAREN, *"Africa Report"*

SWEDEN

A strong growth in exports, a reduced budget deficit, and moderate rates of inflation and unemployment made 1984 a good year for the Swedish economy and business community.

Economy. Industrial production during the first half of 1984 was 8.1% higher than during the first six months of 1983. This was a new record level for the first half of the year, exceeding the previous peak, in 1974, by 2%. Order bookings for Swedish industry were up 9% in the first half of 1984.

Trade with the United States, which for a decade had shown a deficit, showed a surplus of 4 billion kronor ($500 million) in January-April 1984, the largest surplus on record for any of Sweden's trading partners. It made the United States Sweden's second-largest export market after West Germany. A major increase in car exports (the United States accounted for 56% of Sweden's car exports) and the high exchange rate of the dollar played an important part in this development.

Sweden's total foreign trade during the first seven months of 1984 resulted in a surplus of 16.2 billion kronor ($2 billion), an increase of 60% compared with 1983. At the same time that exports were booming, the rates of inflation

Svenskt Pressfoto/Pictorial Parade

Despite chilly relations, Sweden's King Carl XVI Gustaf (right) hosted Soviet Foreign Minister Gromyko in January.

and unemployment were decreasing. In July 1984 the former stood at 7.2% and the latter at 3.2%. As a consequence of the economic upswing, the Stockholm Stock Exchange during 1984 became the eighth largest in the world.

During 1984, Sweden consolidated its position as a high-tech manufacturer. On August 20, Infovox AB launched a new multilanguage text-to-speech system that automatically transforms computer texts into synthetic speech. The use of industrial robots also reached new heights, with Sweden boasting the highest number of industrial robots per employee in the world.

Domestic Policy. The big issue of debate in 1984 was still the wage-earners funds. Every wage earner and every company above a certain profit level must pay a share of their income to special union funds. The funds then put their money in the regular stockmarket. In about ten years, the wage-earners funds will be the largest single stockholder in Sweden. On October 4, more than 100,000 people demonstrated against what they called a socialistic experiment, and the nonsocialistic parties promised to liquidate the funds if they win the election in 1985.

Foreign Policy. The 35-nation Conference on Confidence- and Security-Building Measures and Disarmament in Europe was convened in Stockholm on Jan. 17, 1984. The conference was conceived as a follow-up to the Madrid Conference on Security and Cooperation in Europe, which came to a close in September 1983. The first round of talks in Stockholm focused on ways to reduce the threat of East-West armed conflict in Europe.

In a Parliament debate on foreign affairs on March 23, the Swedish government stressed the importance of remaining neutral.

Defense. On May 8 the Swedish Supreme Commanders released a report stating that there had been ten certain cases of alien underwater operations in the Swedish archipelago. Then on August 9 a Soviet military aircraft pursued a Swedish charter aircraft en route to Stockholm; the pursuit took place in Swedish airspace and lasted 4½ minutes. The Swedish government issued a strong protest, but Moscow denied the incident.

Because of the increasing number of such incidents in recent years, the Swedish Parliament on March 16 signed an agreement to raise the defense budget by 2.2 billion kronor.

SVERKER LITTORIN, *Free-Lance Writer*

SWEDEN • Information Highlights

Official Name: Kingdom of Sweden.
Location: Northern Europe.
Area: 173,732 sq mi (449 964 km²).
Population (mid-1984 est.): 8,300,000.
Chief Cities (Dec. 31, 1983): Stockholm, the capital, 649,686; Göteborg, 425,875; Malmö, 230,381; Uppsala, 149,300.
Government: *Head of state,* Carl XVI Gustaf, king (acceded Sept. 1973). *Head of government,* Olof Palme, prime minister (took office Oct. 7, 1982). *Legislature* (unicameral)—Riksdag.
Monetary Unit: Krona (8.7925 kronor equal U.S.$1, Oct. 18, 1984).
Gross Domestic Product (1983 U.S.$): $90,666,-000,000.
Economic Indexes (1983): *Consumer Prices* (1970 = 100), all items, 320.1; food, 359.0. *Industrial Production* (1975 = 100), 100.
Foreign Trade (1983 U.S.$): *Imports,* $26,100,-000,000; *exports,* $27,441,000,000.

SWITZERLAND

Many national referenda, plus the election of a woman to the Federal Council (cabinet), made 1984 an active year in Swiss politics.

Cabinet. On Dec. 7, 1983, the Federal Assembly rejected the Social Democratic Party's nomination of Liliane Uchtenhagen for one of the two seats allotted the Social Democrats on the Federal Council, electing instead a male member of the party. This rebuff led the Social Democrats to convene a national party congress on Feb. 12, 1984, at which the leadership unsuccessfully recommended that the party vote to withdraw from the four-party governing coalition, in existence since 1959. General negative public reaction to the Uchtenhagen affair was exacerbated by the action of male voters of the half-canton of Appenzell Ausser Rhoden when they voted on April 29 to continue denying women the right to vote in local affairs.

On October 2, however, 136 years of all-male membership on the Federal Council ended when the Federal Assembly elected Elisabeth Kopp, a Radical Democrat member of parliament and mayor of the Zurich suburb of Zumikon.

National Referenda. A national referendum on Feb. 26, 1984, rejected overwhelmingly the creation of a civilian national service corps that would provide an alternative to the existing requirement of military service for all 19-year-old males. On May 20, voters defeated an attempt to ban the sale of residential property to foreigners who had not obtained permanent resident status. They also vetoed a proposal requiring Swiss banks to open records to authorities investigating domestic and foreign tax-evasion cases. Finally, on September 23, 55% of the electorate rejected an attempt to halt current construction of nuclear power plants and require the phasing-out of existing plants by the year 2000.

International Affairs. On Jan. 1, 1984, Switzerland, along with the six other members of the European Free Trade Association (EFTA),

joined with the ten members of the European Community (EC) to form a gigantic free-trade area for industrial goods.

Swiss business circles greeted with relief the termination on January 27 of a seven-year international boycott of the products of Nestlé Corporation, one of Switzerland's largest business concerns. The boycott ended after Nestlé agreed to abide by World Health Organization guidelines regarding the promotion, marketing, and distribution of infant formula in underdeveloped countries.

On May 16, the Swiss Federal Tribunal for the first time ordered five international banks based in Switzerland to aid the U.S. Securities and Exchange Commission in its investigation of insider-trading violations. The banks were instructed to provide the names of traders who bought specified stock through their secret Swiss bank accounts prior to public announcement of a business merger. However, on September 26 the Swiss government refused to extradite to the United States Marc Rich and Pincus Green, who had been indicted by American authorities in 1983 on a $48 million tax evasion charge.

PAUL C. HELMREICH, *Wheaton College, MA*

SYRIA

The Baath Party leadership of Syria began 1984 in a much stronger position in regional politics than in 1983. Despite a power struggle over succession that began in November 1983, Syria reemerged in 1984 as a dominant force in the Middle East.

Role in Lebanon. Syrian policy reflected a fear of being outflanked by the Israelis in Lebanon and of being left out of a peace process that would leave the occupied Golan Heights under Israeli control. The Syrians enhanced their control over Lebanese politics, first by supporting rivals to the Amin Gemayel government and then by supporting that government. Syria also continued to exercise considerable influence over the Palestine Liberation Organiztion (PLO) through its support of a Damascus-based group competing with Yasir Arafat for control of the organization.

After the February withdrawal of U.S. Marines and the subsequent pullout of the rest of the multinational force from Lebanon, Syria became the undisputed outside power in that war-torn nation. With the Americans gone, the Lebanese government weak and ineffectual, and the Israelis entangled in a costly occupation of southern Lebanon, the Syrians sought to create a Lebanese government beholden to Damascus and not subject to Israeli influence. The Syrians supported Gemayel's rivals, drastically curtailing his ability to rule. On March 5, Gemayel bowed to Syria's longstanding demand to scrap the agreement of May 1983

SWITZERLAND · Information Highlights

Official Name: Swiss Confederation.
Location: Central Europe.
Area: 15,918 sq mi (41 228 km²).
Population (mid-1984 est.): 6,500,000.
Chief Cities (1981 est.): Bern, the capital, 147,300; Zurich, 371,600; Basel, 183,000.
Government: *Head of state,* Leon Schlumpf, president, (took office Jan. 1984). *Legislature*—Federal Assembly: Council of States and National Council.
Monetary Unit: Franc (2.5365 francs equal U.S.$1, Oct. 22, 1984).
Gross National Product (1982 U.S.$): $95,600,-000,000.
Economic Index (1983): *Consumer Prices* (1970 = 100), all items, 188.2; food, 196.1. *Industrial Production* (1983, 1975 = 100), 109.
Foreign Trade (1983 U.S.$): *Imports,* $29,117,-000,000; *exports,* $25,595,000,000.

Lebanon's Rashid Karami (left) met with Syrian President Hafez al-Assad in Damascus on April 23. Three days later, reportedly with Assad's consent, Karami was named premier in Lebanon's new national unity government. Syria's control of Lebanon's government strengthened Assad's role in Middle Eastern affairs.

AP/Wide World

under which Israel would withdraw its forces from Lebanon while continuing to police the south. Under Syrian pressure, Gemayel was now orienting his policy not toward the United States and the West but toward Damascus.

When the Lebanese reconciliation talks opened in mid-July in Lausanne, Switzerland, Syria clearly was playing the dominant role. Now Damascus was careful to avoid outright support for any of the Lebanese rivals and sought instead a delicate balance in which it would hold the central mediation role.

Regional and Big-Power Politics. President Hafez al-Assad aimed to parlay Syria's leading position in Lebanon into a key role in whatever international negotiations might take place on the future of the Middle East. In October he made his first official visit in four years to the USSR, where Soviet leader Konstantin Chernenko pledged "full support and all-around assistance." Assad's trip solidified Syria's position as the Soviets' chief client and arms recipient in the area.

Syria's relations with the United States were severely strained early in the year, with Syrian-supported groups targeting U.S. Marines in Lebanon and with intense retaliatory bombardment by U.S. forces. In July, however, long after the Marine withdrawal, U.S. Assistant Secretary of State Richard Murphy signaled a shift in U.S. thinking by describing Syria as playing a "helpful" role in restoring stability in Lebanon. A visit by Murphy to Damascus in September, preceding the opening of Israeli-Lebanese talks, led to speculation that a Syrian-U.S. deal had been struck with regard to those talks. It remained unclear at year's end just what role the United States envisaged for Syria in the region, but the apparent U.S. shift did underline the influence that Assad's regime had gained.

After Egypt and Jordan reestablished diplomatic relations in September, a move that enraged Assad, Syria feared a movement toward a new, moderate regional alliance that would include Saudi Arabia, Iraq, Jordan, and Egypt —and isolate Syria. Damascus' continued support for Iran against Iraq in the Gulf War added impetus to this movement.

Succession. In November 1983, President Assad, one of the longest-ruling leaders in the Middle East, was struck by an apparent heart attack. Assad had made a public appearance before the end of that year, but his illness touched off a struggle for power which on March 11, 1984, prompted Assad to reshuffle his cabinet and name three vice-presidents— Foreign Minister Abdel Halim Khadam; Rifaat al-Assad, head of the "defense companies," a division of troops guarding the capital; and Zuhair Mashariqah, a leader of the Baath Party. The struggle reached its peak in late March, when Rifaat, the president's younger brother, sent some of his heavily armed troops to seal off roads leading into Damascus and patrol the streets of the city. Inside Damascus, units of the Special Forces—elite commandos led by Rifaat's rival, Gen. Ali Haidar—went on alert, occupying rooftops and major intersections. The 3rd armored division, commanded by Shafiq Fayyad, deployed tanks west and north of the city in another apparent warning to Rifaat. Other rivals for power included Defense Minister Mustafa Talas and Chief of Staff Hikmat Shihabi.

To defuse the power struggle, President Assad in late May sent Rifaat, Haidar, and Fayyad on a visit to the Soviet Union. By midsummer Rifaat was reported to be "undergoing medical treatment" in Switzerland, while Haidar and Fayyad reappeared in Damascus. By the time Rifaat returned in late November, his guard units had been cut back and were taking their orders directly from the regular Army command. Despite uncertainty about his health, President Assad had emerged firmly in command.

Steven M. Riskin, *Middle East Specialist*

SYRIA • Information Highlights

Official Name: Syrian Arab Republic.
Location: Southwest Asia.
Area: 72,000 sq mi (186 480 km²).
Population (mid-1984 est.): 10,100,000.
Government: *Head of state,* Lt. Gen. Hafez al-Assad, president (took office officially March 1971). *Head of government,* Abdel Raouf al-Kassem, prime minister (took office Jan. 1980). *Legislature* (unicameral)—People's Council.
Monetary Unit: Pound (3.925 pounds equal U.S.$1, August 1984).
Gross Domestic Product (1981 U.S.$): $18,400,000,000.
Economic Index (1983): *Consumer Prices* (1970 = 100), all items, 409.0; food, 439.0.
Foreign Trade: (1983 U.S.$): *Imports,* $4,536,000,000; *exports,* $1,938,000,000.

Taiwan's President Chiang Ching-kuo (far left) hosted a U.S. congressional delegation in April. Taipei urged stronger ties with Washington as the Reagan administration moved closer to the People's Republic.

TAIWAN (Republic of China)

It was a year of political transition in Taiwan. The question of who would succeed President Chiang Ching-kuo continued to loom large, and the process of ''Taiwanization''—bringing more Taiwan-born citizens into positions of authority in the government—moved forward significantly. Meanwhile the Kuomintang (Nationalist Party) resisted steadfastly attempts by Peking to initiate negotiations on reunification of Taiwan with the mainland provinces.

Politics. Elections for positions in the Legislative Yuan in December 1983 resulted in a sweeping victory for Kuomintang candidates, who took 62 of 71 contested seats. During the election campaign the party made a point of the degree to which it had come to represent the Taiwan-born majority on the island, noting that only about 30% of its current members had been born on the mainland. Opposition politicians blamed their poor showing on election rules that favored the Kuomintang and on infighting among opposition candidates.

In March 1984, Chiang was elected by the National Assembly to a new six-year term as president. His vice-presidential running mate was Lee Teng-hui, a Taiwan-born agricultural economist and former governor of the province, who was seen as having little in common with conservative ''mainlander'' elements in the government. The previous vice-president,

Shieh Tung-min, was also born on Taiwan, but Lee's election constituted a more significant step forward in the process of Taiwanization. The difference was that the chief executive's failing health made Lee's eventual succession to the presidency a distinct possibility.

Another individual widely considered to be a potential successor to Chiang was Premier Sun Yun-suan. In February, however, Sun suffered a stroke and underwent brain surgery. To many people's surprise he was replaced on June 1 not by Kuomintang Secretary General Tsiang Yen-si but by Yu Kuo-hwa. Yu, who had begun his career as personal secretary to Chiang Kai-shek, was trained as an economist and since his arrival on Taiwan in 1955 had held a series of posts in banking and finance. Most recently he had served as governor of the Central Bank and chairman of the Council for Economic Planning and Development. Speculation had it that Tsiang was being held in reserve as Chiang's successor to the important position of Kuomintang chairman in 1986.

Reconstitution of the national government continued to be discussed in Taiwan political circles. The current government structure was based on a constitution adopted, and on an election conducted, prior to the departure of the Kuomintang from the mainland in 1949. Despite supplemental elections that had brought Taiwan-born politicians into the legislative branch of the government, natural attrition had reduced total membership in the National Assembly and the Legislative Yuan from more than 3,750 to fewer than 1,900. Reconstitution would permit the Kuomintang to abandon its claim to be the legitimate government of all China and to have as its principal goal the recapture of the mainland provinces.

The Economy. Statistics on the Taiwan economy released in January 1984 showed for 1983 a gross national product of $49.7 billion (U.S.), a growth rate of 7.1%, and a per capita income of $2,400. More than 350 American companies were doing business with Taiwan, and American investment there totaled some $6 billion. Total two-way trade between the United States and Taiwan exceeded $16 billion in 1984, some three times the volume of U.S. trade with the People's Republic of China

---

TAIWAN (Republic of China) · Information Highlights

Official Name: Republic of China.
Location: Island off the southeastern coast of mainland China.
Area: 13,892 sq mi (35 981 km²).
Population (mid-1984 est.): 19,200,000.
Chief Cities (Dec. 31, 1982): Taipei, the capital, 2,327,641; Kaohsiung, 1,248,175; Taichung, 621,566; Tainan, 609,934.
Government: *Head of state,* Chiang Ching-kuo, president (installed May 1978). *Head of government,* Yu Kuo-hua, premier (took office June 1984). *Legislature* (unicameral)—Legislative Yuan.
Monetary Unit: New Taiwan dollar (40.2 NT dollars equal U.S.$1, Dec. 1983).
Gross National Product (1983 est. U.S.$): $49,700,-000,000.

(PRC). Unofficial trade between Taiwan and the mainland provinces—most of it conducted indirectly through Hong Kong—was amounting to some $450 million a year, or about 1% of Taiwan's total two-way trade.

International Relations. President Reagan's visit to the PRC in April was largely ignored on Taiwan. Taipei continued to press for closer ties with Washington, but Reagan, who in his 1980 election campaign had commented favorably on such a move, avoided like references in 1984. Instead he emphasized the achievements of his administration in fostering relations with Peking. Nevertheless, in June it was announced that the United States would sell Taiwan a dozen C-130 military transports.

In September, at the annual meeting of the International Criminal Police Organization (Interpol), Taiwan delegates walked out after delegates from the People's Republic were seated as the representatives of China. Taipei had rejected Peking's proposal for comembership in Interpol, despite accepting a similar formula for Olympic competition.

In a report issued in September, Taiwan announced that it would try "every feasible means" to thwart the development of ties between South Korea and the PRC. The Seoul government was one of only 23 that maintained full diplomatic ties with Taipei.

On September 30, PRC Premier Zhao Ziyang called once again for reunification talks. He cited the new constitutional provision for "special administrative zones" within the PRC that, like Hong Kong for 50 years after 1997, could retain their own political and economic systems. He suggested that the terms of reunification for Taiwan would be even more generous than those just accepted by Britain for its Chinese colony. Taiwan rejected the idea of negotiations and denounced the agreement on Hong Kong as invalid for having been concluded with an illegitimate Chinese government.

See also CHINA, PEOPLE'S REPUBLIC OF.

JOHN BRYAN STARR, *Yale–China Association*

came to power after the resignation in January of Zanzibari President Aboud Jumbe, who had flaunted a lavish lifestyle in the poverty-stricken country, and who had done little to quell separatist tendencies in Zanzibar.

Zanzibar. Zanzibar constantly sought more self-rule during 1984, seeking in part to end the rigid political controls that the mainland-dominated ruling Chama Cha Mapinduzi Party had imposed on the island, and hoping to ease its economic crisis by a return to a freer economic system. Though fears of secession were probably overstated, Zanzibar's restlessness could spill over to the mainland. The Zanzibari nationality of Prime Minister Salim was a potential mitigating factor. The new administration also took steps to end political detention and to guarantee civil liberties on Zanzibar, hoping to undercut both secessionists and any attempt by the mainland to restore political centralization.

Economic Crisis. Tazania's economic decline continued during 1984, due largely to the bloated twin bureaucracies of the ruling party and governmental organizations that totally control, and suffocate, most economic activities. Food was scarce, imports were almost nonexistent for lack of foreign exchange, and consumer goods were rarely found. To ease the problem, Tanzania sought a massive loan from the International Monetary Fund, but the Fund's conditions, a cut in government spending and a drastic devaluation of the Tanzanian shilling, were rejected by Nyerere as interference in the nation's official socialist economy.

Nevertheless, Tanzania allowed a small return to private farming and took steps to revive the private tea plantations that were nationalized almost two decades before. The government also invested in new facilities for growing and refining pyrethrum, a potent natural insecticide. However, there was little initial return on these actions. Zanzibar's cloves, which earn 95% of its export income, lost buyers, thus adding to the island's problems.

ROBERT GARFIELD, *DePaul University*

TANZANIA

Major political transitions and a continuing economic malaise were the leading developments in Tanzania in 1984.

Presidential Succession. President Julius Nyerere, who has led Tanzania since its independence, announced his intention to retire at the end of his term in 1985. His heir apparent, Prime Minister Edward Sokoine, was killed in a car accident in April 1984, leading to a scramble for preferment. The winner was Foreign Minister Salim Ahmed Salim, who was named the new prime minister and thus Nyerere's probable successor. His only major rival was Ali Hassan Mwinyi, the new president of the semiautonomous province of Zanzibar. Mwinyi

TAXATION

Rising public expenditures and growing government deficits were a source of concern in most industrial nations. Accordingly, tax relief measures were modest and often were outweighed by provisions increasing tax revenues.

The United States

Congressional Action. As part of a deficit-reduction package, Congress approved the tax reform bill of 1984, which was signed by President Ronald Reagan on July 18. The law calls for revenue increases of $56,367,000,000 over the period 1984–87 and revenue reductions of $5,492,000,000, for a net increase of $50,875,000,000. Many of the provisions—labeled as a "tax freeze"—repealed or postponed reductions granted under earlier laws.

Provisions increasing taxes for individuals included repealing a provision under which net interest income up to $3,000 ($6,000 on joint returns) would be excluded from taxable income, beginning in 1985; postponing a scheduled cut in the maximum estate and gift tax rate; reducing the tax savings from income averaging; and providing that loans made at no interest or below market rates can be subject to income and gift taxes. For U.S. citizens working abroad, the law deferred scheduled increases in tax-exempt earned income; the permanent level of the exclusion of $95,000 was postponed to 1990.

The law also increased the diesel fuel excise tax from 9 cents to 15 cents a gallon, and the excise tax on liquor by $2 for a gallon of 100-proof liquor; extended the 3% telephone excise tax; imposed stricter tax rules on personal use of business property such as automobiles, computers, and airplanes; and required that tax shelters sold must be registered with the Internal Revenue Service (IRS).

Provisions of the new law affecting business included: phasing out graduated tax rates for large corporations; raising taxes on corporate preference income; increasing to 18 years from 15 years the write-off period for certain real estate; restricting sales of tax benefits by tax-exempt organizations; changes in accounting and record-keeping rules to close some tax shelters; and limitations on the issuance of tax-free industrial development bonds by state and local units.

In the foreign trade area, the law authorized the creation of Foreign Sales Corporations to promote trade by U.S. companies. Such corporations will replace the Domestic International Sales Corporations (DISCs) that some countries had criticized as providing illegal export subsidies. The law repealed a 30% withholding tax on foreigners' portfolio income.

Provisions of the new law tending to reduce taxes include shortening the holding period for long-term capital gains from 12 months to 6 months; extending the targeted jobs tax credit; and raising the earned income credit for lower-income taxpayers.

Supreme Court. The court handed down 12 tax decisions, evenly split between federal and state issues.

In *U.S. v. Arthur Young & Co.*, the court decided that the IRS has the right to see the working papers prepared by a certified public accountant to evaluate the adequacy of a company's tax reserves. The relationship of attorneys to their clients is not a "fitting analogue" to that of accountants, the court said. The attorney's duty, as a confidential adviser and advocate, is to present his client's case in the most favorable possible light. On the other hand, the court stated, an independent certified public accountant performs a public responsibility that "transcends any employment relationship with the client."

The court's decision, which came as a blow to the accounting profession, ended a nine-year battle by Amerada Hess, an oil company, and Arthur Young & Co., its accounting firm, to prevent the IRS from examining what they contended were sensitive documents concerning the accounting firm's view of potential taxes.

In another decision concerning IRS taxing powers, *Dickman v. Commissioner of Internal Revenue,* the court ruled that interest-free demand loans from one family member to another are subject to the federal gift tax. The case arose after a Florida couple made interest-free demand loans totaling more than $1 million to their son and a family-owned corporation. When a lower court ruled for the IRS in assessing gift taxes of $83,000 on the loans, the family appealed. Among other arguments, the taxpayers contended that the IRS should not be allowed to abandon its previous practice of not taxing such loans. In response to this claim, Chief Justice Warren Burger said that prior court decisions allow the IRS to "change earlier interpretations of the law, even if such a change is made retroactive in effect."

In another case, *Badaracco v. Commissioner of Internal Revenue; Deleet Merchandise Corporation v. U.S.,* the court also ruled in favor of the IRS. The court held that the filing of a nonfraudulent amended income-tax return after originally filing a fradulent return does not prevent the IRS from issuing a deficiency notice more than three years after the amended return was filed. The issue involved the interpretation of two sections of the Internal Revenue Code—Section 6501(a) and Section 6501(c). The taxpayers argued that their act of filing honest amended returns voided the effects of their fraudulent returns and that the IRS should be held to the three-year statute of limitations. The court agreed with the government's position that the fact of fraud was unchanged by the amended returns.

In state-tax decisions, the court ruled that four state-tax statutes were unconstitutional. Three of the laws—in Hawaii, New York, and West Virginia—were struck down because they violated the Commerce Clause of the Constitution by discriminating against interstate commerce.

In *Bacchus Imports, Ltd. v. Dias,* the case dealt with a Hawaii law that imposed a 20% tax on wholesale liquor sales. The law exempted fruit wine produced in Hawaii and okolehao (a locally produced brandy) from the tax. The purpose of the exemption was to aid Hawaiian industry, the court ruled, and the effect was clearly discriminatory.

In *Westinghouse Electric Corporation v. Tully,* the court invalidated a New York franchise tax law that allowed corporations a credit against the tax on accumulated income of their DISC subsidiaries. The credit applied only for gross receipts attributable to export shipments originating in New York. The credit thus discriminated against export shipping from other states, the court said.

The West Virginia case, *Armco Inc. v. Hardesty,* involved a state tax on wholesale gross receipts, from which local manufacturers were exempt. The fact that local manufacturers were subject to a higher manufacturing tax was not relevant, the court noted, because manufacturing and wholesaling are not "substantially equivalent events." The tax was held to discriminate against interstate commerce.

In another case involving a Hawaii law, *Aloha Airlines, Inc. v. Director of Taxation of Hawaii; Hawaiian Airlines, Inc. v. Director of Taxation of Hawaii,* the court invalidated the state's tax on the annual gross income of interisland airlines because it was contrary to a federal law. Federal law prohibits a state from levying most taxes on transactions involving air transportation but excludes property taxes from the prohibition. The fact that Hawaii's tax was "styled" as a property tax measured by gross receipts, rather than as a straightforward gross receipts tax, does not entitle the tax to escape preemption by federal law.

In *California Franchise Tax Board v. U.S. Postal Service,* the court ruled that the Postal Service must honor a state's order that it withhold wages of federal workers who are delinquent in their state income tax payments. Federal law provides that the Postal Service may "sue and be sued." The Postal Service had contended, however, that the California board's order was that of an administrative agency rather than a court and thus the service had not been "sued" within the meaning of the law. The Supreme Court rejected the service's contention, noting that to distinguish between administrative and judicial processes "would be to take an approach to sovereign immunity that this court rejected more than 40 years ago."

State and Local Taxes. State and local governments collected $320,545,000,000 in taxes during the 12 months ending June 30, 1984, an increase of $38,602,000,000 or 13.7% over the previous year. A year earlier, the corresponding increase had been only 5.7%.

Legislative action in 1984 raised state taxes by about $2.2 billion annually, on a net basis. Laws increasing taxes were approved in 11 states, for new annual revenues of $3.3 billion. Partly offsetting were reductions in nine states totaling $1.1 billion.

International

Canada. In February, Minister of Finance Marc Lalonde presented a budget calling for C$495 million in tax reductions for fiscal 1986. The budget cut personal income taxes mainly through tax assistance for pensions. Corporate income taxes were reduced by simplification of small business tax provisions and by tax credits for employee profit participation plans. Other changes reduced revenues from oil and from the sales tax.

Europe. Britain's Chancellor of the Exchequer Nigel Lawson presented a budget offering relief for some taxpayers, balanced against revenue increases elsewhere. Tax reductions include cutting the corporate income tax rate in stages from 52% to 35% by 1986–87; increasing personal-income allowances to reduce taxes for those with lower incomes and the elderly; and reducing the stamp tax on security and real property transfers from 2% to 1%. Higher revenues would come from raising excise taxes, phasing out the 50% tax exclusion given to foreign employees going to the United Kingdom to work for foreign companies; and reducing sharply the capital recovery deductions allowed for new plant and equipment investment.

The West German government considered measures to provide a two-stage tax relief totaling 20.2 billion Deutsche marks (about $7.5 billion) for the years 1986 through 1988. The provisions emphasized personal income tax relief by raising deductions and reducing the progressiveness of tax rates. Parliamentary debate on the measures was expected until mid-1985.

In November the French government approved its budget for 1985. Significant features included personal income tax cuts of 5% for all taxpayers, reductions of 10% in the business tax, and repeal of an additional 1% social security tax levy. On the other hand, the government called for a four-cent increase in the gasoline tax.

Japan. The 1984–85 budget for Japan included measures that lowered personal income taxes but raised the corporate income tax rate from 42% to 43.3% and increased taxes on commodities, liquor, and petroleum.

ELSIE M. WATTERS, *Tax Foundation, Inc.*

TELEVISION AND RADIO

A pair of headlines appearing within one month of each other in *The New York Times* pretty well summed up the prevailing trends in television during 1984. The first headline, "Making the Case for Serious Television Viewing," ran above an article that listed some of the outstanding programming that somehow continues to thrive, like cacti, in the so-called video wasteland. The Public Broadcasting Service (PBS), as usual, got the lion's share of praise, for such documentary series as *The Brain* and *Civilization and the Jews* and for such Masterpiece Theatre historical dramas as *The Jewel in the Crown.* But commercial TV held its own, with the American Broadcasting Companies' (ABC's) *A Streetcar Named Desire* starring Ann-Margret, and the Columbia Broadcasting System's (CBS') *A Christmas Carol* with George C. Scott. In fact, the *Times* article even detected some forward progress in the area of commercial TV "docudramas," citing ABC's *The Burning Bed,* CBS' *Silence of the Heart,* and the National Broadcasting Company's (NBC's) *Children in the Crossfire* as docudramas that treated explosive contemporary issues—battered wives, teenage suicide, and Northern Ireland, respectively—with surprising sensitivity and integrity.

The second *Times* headline read, "Where's That Promised New World of Cable?" The November article recounted the recent financial and artistic woes of cable television. A few weeks later, *Variety* began its report on the Windy City's tortuous negotiations for a cable operator with these words: "Will Chicago go down in the video history textbooks as the beach upon which the cable tide crested?" Neither article suggested that programming produced for cable is any worse on the average than broadcast programming—Broadway's *Master Harold and the Boys* on cable's Showtime channel may have been the most important TV drama of 1984–but rather that the cable pitchmen had promised so much more by this time.

Strangely enough, the Big Three of broadcast television—ABC, CBS, and NBC—could not take any comfort in the troubles of cable. The November ratings "sweeps" showed a loss of 4% of their combined audience "share" on top of similar losses the previous few years, meaning that Americans with television sets were increasingly tuning to cable, PBS, or independent stations—or else not tuning in at all. All of this pointed to a continuing uncertainty and shakedown in American television and a public that was getting plenty of viewing options but not, evidently, enough choice.

Network Ratings and Series. The three commercial networks finished their 1983–84 ratings race on April 15 with almost precisely the same numbers that had prevailed throughout the

AP/Wide World

Barry Bostwick and Patty Duke Astin starred in the eight-hour, three-part miniseries "George Washington" on CBS.

1980s. (Rating is the percentage of all U.S. households with TV sets.) CBS won again with a rating of 18.1, ABC sored 17.2, and NBC again brought up the rear with 14.9. The first half of the 1984–85 season, however, brought one of the most dramatic ratings shakeups in recent years. NBC climbed into a strong second place, mainly on the strength of *The Cosby Show.* The new comedy starring Bill Cosby was hailed for its warm, authentic portrait of a middle-class, two-career black family.

By late November, a *Variety* analyst wrote that *Cosby* was the "only true hit" among the fall series premieres and that "the two dominant programming genres remain the nighttime soap and the miniseries." The perennial favorite nighttime soaps, *Dallas* of CBS and *Dynasty* of ABC, seemed likely to finish among the ratings winners again, he predicted, with *Falcon Crest* and *Knots Landing* of CBS close behind.

Another *Variety* analyst identified the season's programming trend as "working women as series stars." But he added that the genre seemed overcrowded—*Jessie,* starring Lindsay Wagner, was canceled before the end of the year—and he predicted a ratings shakeout among such other women's series as *Cagney* and Lacey, Who's the Boss?, Paper Dolls, and Partners in Crime.

A more conservative trend, mirroring the national mood, showed in the popularity of Call to Glory, ABC's nostalgic portrait of a Kennedy-era test pilot and his family, as well as such action/adventure series as NBC's The A Team.

News. For the first time in several seasons, there were no major premieres of news programs, as the networks appeared to consolidate their news programming expansions of the early 1980s.

In an election year, television again came under fire for exercising—some said abusing—its political power. President Ronald Reagan's poor showing in his first televised debate with Democratic challenger Walter Mondale was considered his only major stumble on the road to reelection. After the president's landslide victory, Mondale conceded that he never did feel comfortable in front of TV cameras.

At the same time, the news departments crusaded for their constitutional rights. After criticism from the news media for its rigid control of coverage of the 1983 war in Grenada, the U.S. Defense Department agreed to create a specially trained team of representatives from each of the major news organizations that would be allowed freer access to war zones and detailed military information.

People. Established stars headlined some of the more successful new series of the 1984–85 season. Bill Cosby on NBC was most prominent, but veteran Broadway performer Angela Lansbury also pleased the critics as an Agatha Christie-type sleuth on CBS' Murder, She Wrote. ABC tried to bolster its faltering fall lineup with a December replacement, Off the Rack, a fashion industry comedy starring Edward Asner and Eileen Brennan. And the film actor Jack Warden was cast in a CBS replacement, Crazy Like a Fox. CBS moved two of its female personalities into higher-profile positions: the stylish Diane Sawyer moved from CBS Morning News to become the fifth correspondent on the popular 60 Minutes; and she was replaced by Phyllis George, who brought her girl-next-door charm from The NFL Today. Meanwhile, the departure of the ever-controversial Howard Cosell was blamed for the ratings tailspin of ABC's Monday Night Football. Finally, critics noted sadly the retirement of NBC's Edwin Newman, one of television's most literate and respected commentators.

Cable and Pay TV. With the words, "Take that, MTV," Ted Turner, colorful kingpin of Cable News Network, turned on the switch to his new Cable Music Channel, the first rival to the fast-growing pioneer of continuous rock music videos, MTV. Only a month later, however, having failed to attract the target number of subscribers, the Cable Music Channel was sold to MTV Networks Inc.

AP/Wide World

Jane Fonda won an Emmy Award for her portrayal of Gertie Nevels, a rural Kentucky mother, in ABC's "The Dollmaker."

But Turner's was one of the few major new programming ventures on cable TV, which seemed to enter a period of retrenchment in 1984. Home Box Office, the leading pay channel for new movies and entertainment specials, which had signed on between 2 million and 5 million subscribers each year since 1980, slowed in 1984 to just 1.5 million new subscribers. Qube, Warner-Amex's two-way cable channel, joined a growing casualty list of cable's enlightened specialty channels.

The program woes seemed to reflect the problems of the cable operators who distributed them. Warner Amex, the leading U.S. cable systems operator, faced losses of nearly $100 million in 1984 and had to cut service in Pittsburgh, Milwaukee, and Dallas. In December, Boston Cablevision asked that city to bail it out of financial trouble.

Sports programming continued to thrive on cable, however. The 24-hour sports channel, ESPN, and the sports-heavy USA Network both had healthy subscriber gains in 1984, and SportsChannel grew in a quantum leap with the $57 million investment that accompanied a new partnership with CBS.

TV and the Law, Public Issues. The trial of Gen. William Westmoreland vs. CBS News, in full swing as 1984 ended, was watched as a watershed case for the future of television news and the interpretation of the 1st Amendment. Westmoreland named correspondent Mike Wallace and producer George Crile as principal defendants in his $120 million libel suit, which charged that their 1982 60 Minutes report,

TELEVISION | 1984
Some Sample Programs

Anatomy of an Illness—A dramatization of the true-life story of editor Norman Cousin's struggle against a crippling painful disease. With Eli Wallach, Edward Asner. ABC, May 15.

Aurora—A 1984 TV-movie about a woman's search for funds from her former lovers in order to restore the sight of her illegitimate son. With Sophia Loren, Daniel Travanti, Eduardo Ponti. NBC, Oct. 22.

Barchester Chronicles—A dramatization in seven parts of the Anthony Trollope works *Barchester Towers* and *The Warden.* With Donald Pleasence, David Gwillim. PBS, Oct. 28.

Ben Kingsley as Edmund Kean—One man show in which the English actor Edmund Kean was portrayed. With Ben Kingsley. PBS, May 21.

The Brain—An eight-part series on the strides in uncovering the mysteries of the human brain. PBS, Oct. 10.

The Burning Bed—A 1984 fact-based TV-movie about a Michigan woman who killed her abusive former husband. With Farrah Fawcett, Paul Le Mat. NBC, Oct. 8.

Camille—Dramatization of the Alexandre Dumas (fils) novel. With Colin Firth, Greta Scacchi. CBS, Dec. 11.

Celebrity—A three-part dramatization of Thomas Thompson's novel depicting three friends' lives over a period of 25 years. With Joseph Bottoms, Michael Beck, Ben Masters. NBC, Feb. 12.

La Cenerentola—Rossini's opera of the Cinderella story was performed at Milan's La Scala. With Frederica von Stade. PBS, Feb. 6.

A Choreographer's Notebook—The New York City Ballet performed dances choreographed by Peter Martins. PBS, Feb. 13.

Crossing the Distance—A Smithsonian World telecast depicting how science, technology, and art were used to conquer distance. PBS, Feb. 15.

D-Day and Eisenhower—*CBS Reports* rebroadcast on the 40th anniversary of D-Day an edited version of the reminiscences of Dwight Eisenhower on the occasion of the 20th anniversary of the Normandy landing of World War II; other film footage was included. CBS, June 5.

D-Day Plus 40 Years—Commemorative ceremonies for the Allied landings in Normandy. NBC, June 6.

Diana—Musical special. With Diana Ross. CBS, April 12.

The Dollmaker—A 1984 TV-movie about an Appalachian woman who left Kentucky with her family to live in Detroit. With Jane Fonda. ABC, May 13.

Don Quixote—An American Ballet Theater production of the Cervantes novel, staged by and starring Mikhail Baryshnikov. PBS, March 5.

Fatal Vision—Two-part 1984 movie about a murder case involving the Green Beret physician Jeffrey MacDonald. With Gary Cole, Barry Newman, Karl Malden, Eva Marie Saint. NBC, Nov. 18.

George Washington—A three-part miniseries, based on the James T. Flexner biography, that dramatized the life of George Washington from his youth to the end of the American Revolutionary War. With Barry Bostwick, Patty Duke Astin, Jaclyn Smith. CBS, April 8.

The Gin Game—Hume Cronyn and Jessica Tandy enacted their stage roles in the TV adaptation of the play about two old-age home residents. PBS, March 6.

Heartsounds—A 1984 TV-movie about a New York doctor who suffered a heart attack. With James Garner, Mary Tyler Moore. ABC, Sept. 30.

The Irish R.M.—A six-part *Masterpiece Theatre* presentation about a British officer who resigned his commission to go to Ireland as a resident magistrate. With Peter Bowles, Bryan Murray. PBS, Jan. 29.

Jesse Owens Story—A two-part docudrama on the life of the U.S. Olympian. With Dorian Harewood. Independent, July 9.

The Jewel in the Crown—Dramatization in 14 parts of the four Paul Scott novels called *The Raj Quartet* about the last years of British rule in India. With Dame Peggy Ashcroft, Tim Pigott-Smith, Art Malik, Charles Dance, Saeed Jaffrey, Geraldine James, Judy Parfitt, Susan Wooldridge. PBS, Dec. 16.

Kim—A TV-movie based on Rudyard Kipling's story. With Peter O'Toole, Ravi Sheth. CBS, May 16.

King Lear—Television adaptation of Shakespeare's tragic masterpiece. With Sir Laurence Olivier, Anna Calder-Marshall, Diana Rigg, Dorothy Tutin, John Hurt, Leo McKern. Independent, Jan. 26.

Lace—Two part 1984 TV-movie, adapted from the Shirley Conran novel. With Bess Armstrong, Brook Adams, Arielle Dombasle, Angela Lansbury, Phoebe Cates. ABC, Feb. 26.

The Last Days of Pompeii—Three-part TV spectacular adapted from the Edward Bulwer-Lytton novel. With Sir Laurence Olivier, Lesley-Anne Down, Ernest Borgnine. ABC, May 6.

Lena Horne: The Lady and Her Music—A one-woman show first presented on Broadway in 1981. With Lena Horne. PBS, Dec. 7.

The Lost Honor of Kathryn Beck—A 1984 TV-movie about a woman who becomes a material witness, harassed by police and the media. With Marlo Thomas, Kris Kristofferson. CBS, Jan. 24.

Love Those Trains—A *National Geographic* special about trains and the enthusiasts that love them. PBS, Feb. 8.

The Magic Flute—A *Great Performances* telecast of the Mozart opera, taped at the 1982 Salzburg Festival. PBS, Jan. 9.

The Master of Ballantrae—A television adaptation of the Robert Louis Stevenson classic. With Richard Thomas, Michael York, Sir John Gielgud. CBS, Jan. 31.

Master of the Game—A three-part adaptation of the Sidney Sheldon best-seller about the rise of a multinational corporate dynasty headed by Kate Blackwell (Dyan Cannon). CBS, Feb. 19.

The Mikado—The Gilbert and Sullivan classic opera. With William Conrad. PBS, June 6.

Mistral's Daughter—A dramatization of the Judith Krantz novel, about the life and loves of an artist. With Stacy Keach, Stefanie Powers, Lee Remick. CBS, Sept. 24.

Nancy Astor—*Masterpiece Theatre*'s eight-part biography of the first woman elected to Britain's House of Commons. With Lisa Harrow. PBS, April 15.

Pavarotti Live at Madison Square Garden—Luciano Pavarotti joins with flutist Andrea Griminelli, conductor Emerson Buckley, and the New Jersey Symphony Orchestra in a classical recital. PBS, August 16.

Pope John Paul II—A 1984 TV-movie on the life of Karol Wojtyla. With Albert Finney. CBS, April 22.

Pudd'nhead Wilson—Television adaptation of Mark Twain's novel. With Ken Howard, Lisa Hilboldt, Steven Weber. PBS, Jan. 24.

Shakespeare Plays—The 1984 presentations included *The Comedy of Errors,* with Roger Daltrey, Michael Kitchen; *Pericles, Prince of Tyre,* with Mike Gwilym, Amanda Redman; and *Much Ado About Nothing,* with Cherie Lunghi, Robert Lindsay. PBS, Feb. 20, June 11, Nov. 30.

A Streetcar Named Desire—Tennessee Williams' play about a neurotic fading belle was adapted for television. With Ann-Margret, Treat Williams, Beverly D'Angelo. ABC, March 4.

To the Lighthouse—A dramatization of Virginia Woolf's novel. With Rosemary Harris. PBS, Oct. 12.

True West—Sam Shepard's play of the struggle between two brothers. With John Malkovich, Gary Sinise, PBS, Jan. 31.

U.S.–Soviet Relations—Reflections on the First 50 Years —Hosted by Harrison Salisbury; with Richard Nixon, Averill Harriman, George Kennan, Walter Stoessel, Thomas Watson. PBS, April 17.

V: The Final Battle—This three-part miniseries was a sequel to the 1983 TV-movie and depicted a battle between evil humanoids and human freedom fighters in Los Angeles. With Faye Grant, Marc Singer. NBC, May 6.

A Voyage Round My Father—About a father, blinded in middle age, who continues his law practice. With Sir Laurence Olivier, Alan Bates. Independent, April 19.

Walk Through the 20th Century—Nineteen-part series exploring ''the vivacity of the past.'' With Bill Moyers. PBS, Jan. 11 (debut).

War and Peace—The Rise of Syria. ABC, June 14.

A Woman of Substance—A six-hour miniseries about a young servant girl who rises to rule a business empire. With Deborah Kerr, Jenny Seagrove. Independent, Nov. 26.

You Can't Take It With You—Telecast of the Moss Hart-George Kaufman play. With Jason Robards, Colleen Dewhurst. PBS, Nov. 21.

"The Uncounted Enemy: A Vietnam Deception," had unfairly accused him of deliberately falsifying enemy troop counts during his command of U.S. forces in Southeast Asia. "Outtakes," or unused portions of taped interviews, were weighed as evidence to determine whether the newsmen had edited the material in a deliberately misleading fashion.

Interestingly, PBS won a 1984 Emmy Award for investigating Westmoreland's investigator; its *Frontline* segment, "Uncounted Enemy, Unproven Conspiracy," cast doubts on CBS' journalistic methods. And PBS' own chronicle of the war, *Vietnam: A Television History,* won six of that network's 19 awards, as PBS dominated the news Emmys.

The cable TV industry was also challenged, by such groups as Morality in Media, for "pornographic" programming. The Playboy Channel, which according to *Variety* was one of the "more tame" but widespread sources of spicy viewing, was attacked by many groups, but a Utah referendum to ban such channels from state cable systems was defeated 2–1.

Another grass-roots organization, the National Coalition on TV Violence, reported that prime-time violence had increased 75% since 1980, with *V, The A Team,* and *Blue Thunder* the chief 1984 offenders.

Regulation. New legal rulings set significant precedents for television in 1984. The U.S. Supreme Court ruled, 5–4, that taping programs with home video recorders (VCRs) does not violate copyright law, reversing a 1981 appeals court ruling which grew out of a suit by the Disney and Universal film studios against Sony Corporation. As part of its movement toward broadcast regulation under the Reagan administration, the Federal Communications Commission rejected a proposal to require a specific amount of children's programming on commercial TV stations.

Radio. A front-page banner headline in a September issue of *Variety* read: "Radio Breaking Racial Barriers." The article went on to document a dramatic movement of black musical acts—such as Michael Jackson, Prince, and Tina Turner—into the mainstream of white-dominated Top-40 radio stations. Two major black, or "urban contemporary," radio stations—WXKS-FM in Boston and WKTU-FM in New York—switched to the broader-based "contemporary hit" format in 1984.

The year also saw a sudden rise of "outrageous" radio talk show hosts, who followed the lead of WNBC's Don Imus in stretching the bounds of good taste to the point of ethnic slurs and other attention-getting devices.

Variety reported that, a year after federal budget cuts had threatened its existence, a streamlined National Public Radio was "very much alive and bouncing back" with a wider audience than ever before, although the network had a $7 million deficit to repay within three years.

DAN HULBERT, *"The Dallas Times Herald"*

AP/Wide World

Broadway luminary Angela Lansbury (right) *plays an Agatha Christie-type detective in CBS' new hit series "Murder, She Wrote." Film stars Van Johnson and June Allyson appeared with her for the first time since the trio was together at MGM in the early 1950s.*

and funds for supplies and equipment. To fund the costly legislation, one cent was added to the general sales tax, a measure designed to bring in nearly $300 million in the first year. Opponents of the tax were able to write in a provision that would remove the sales tax on food by 1988. By late fall, the state had built up more than $3 million in surplus funds. Gov. Lamar Alexander, who had urged a "Better Schools" program two years earlier, was given much of the credit for the legislation.

Tax reform was widely discussed during the year as legislators realized that the sales tax—now 5.5% with options for local governments to add 2.25%—was one of the highest in the nation. Hearings were held across the state and indicated strong sentiment in favor of an income tax, providing the sales tax could be lowered.

Higher Education. In a significant decision that came after 16 years of court battles, U.S. District Judge Thomas Wiseman ordered an end to a dual system in higher education by declaring that the "heart of the problem is traditionally black Tennessee State University" (in Nashville). That institution, whose freshman enrollment this fall consisted of more than 90% blacks as contrasted with the state's overall black population of only 16%, was ordered to have within five years a faculty of at least 50% whites and an enrollment by 1993 of 50% whites. Predominantly white institutions nearby, such as Middle Tennessee State and Austin Peay State, were ordered to develop plans designed to enhance the mission of TSU as "the regional urban university" of Middle Tennessee. Seventy-five black college sophomores are to be prepared annually for postgraduate study and are to be treated preferentially. U.S. Justice Department attorneys objected to some of the settlement and appealed the ruling.

Banking, Crops, Other News. Tennessee continued to lead the nation in bank failures, as

AP/Wide World

Albert Gore, Jr., 36-year-old Harvard-educated Vietnam veteran, easily won election to the U.S. Senate. The victorious Democrat had served four terms in the U.S. House.

TENNESSEE

Politics, education, tax reform, and banking were items of major concern in Tennessee. As had been predicted, President Ronald Reagan swept Tennessee—normally a Democratic state—by a large majority, winning eight of the nine congressional districts. Democrat Albert Gore, Jr., seeking the U.S. Senate seat vacated by Majority Leader Howard Baker, turned back state Sen. Victor Ashe by a substantial vote. The only congressional contest was that in the sixth district, which was won handily by Democrat Bart Gordon of Murfreesboro. Slightly more than 65% of the registered voters appeared at the polls, a figure down from the 73.3% of 1980.

Legislature. Earlier, the state legislature in a historic session enacted several significant pieces of legislation, the most important of which was the comprehensive Educational Reform Act. The heart of the measure provided for substantial salary increases for instructors who attained a classification of "master teacher," merit pay based on periodic evaluations as teachers climbed a "career ladder,"

TENNESSEE • Information Highlights

Area: 42,144 sq mi (109 152 km²).
Population (July 1, 1983 est.): 4,685,000.
Chief Cities (July 1, 1982 est.): Nashville-Davidson, the capital, 455,252; Memphis, 645,760; Knoxville, 175,298; Chattanooga, 168,016; Clarksville (1980 census), 54,777.
Government (1984): *Chief Officers*—governor, Lamar Alexander (R); lt. gov., John S. Wilder (D). *General Assembly*—Senate, 33 members; House of Representatives, 99 members.
State Finances (fiscal year 1983): *Revenues,* $4,783,000,000; *expenditures,* $4,578,000,000.
Personal Income (1983): $44,743,000,000; per capita, $9,549.
Labor Force (May 1984): *Civilian labor force,* 2,205,800; *unemployed,* 182,100 (8.3% of total force).
Education: *Enrollment* (fall 1982)—public elementary schools, 590,839; public secondary, 237,425; colleges and universities (fall 1983), 207,777. *Public school expenditures* (1982–83), $1,577,914,998 ($2,027 per pupil).

shock waves from the demise in 1983 of the massive Butcher banking empire subsided. At midyear, the FDIC planned an examination of at least 242 cases of possible wrongdoing associated with the Butcher-related banks. When the Coalmont Savings Bank of Grundy County closed in late summer, it became Tennessee's ninth failure of the year and the 21st since the Butcher empire folded.

Sufficient rains and sunshine during the crop year enabled farmers to produce record crops of corn, wheat, and tobacco. Early frosts curtailed crops that normally mature late, such as soybeans and cotton.

Reporting for prison terms were former Gov. Ray Blanton and Blanton aides Clyde Edd Hood and Jim Allen, all convicted for conspiracy to sell liquor licenses. They joined Eddie Sisk, a Blanton aide already serving a term for corruption in office, and state Rep. Tommy Burnett, house leader convicted for failure to file timely income tax returns. Even while in prison, Burnett was chosen in the November elections for another legislative term.

ROBERT E. CORLEW
Middle Tennessee State University

TERRORISM

Explosives-filled trucks driven by suicide drivers, members of a fanatical Muslim sect, destroyed the French and U.S. embassies in Beirut and the U.S. embassy in Kuwait. The same group threatened to kill the president of the United States. Car bombs exploded in Paris, London, Port-au-Prince (Haiti), Bogotá (Colombia), and Pretoria (South Africa). The prime minister of Great Britain narrowly escaped an assassination attempt by the Irish Republican Army. Assassins killed the prime minister of India. An Italian court indicted Bulgarian officials for their alleged complicity in the attempted assassination of the pope. Terrorism continued to gain media attention in 1984.

Terrorist groups are diverse. Ideological extremism, ethnic separatism, and religious fanaticism are the major forces behind today's terrorists. They share six common tactics—bombings, which alone account for half of all terrorist attacks; assassinations; armed assaults; kidnappings; hijackings; and the seizure of buildings with hostages.

Terrorism is most likely defined by the nature of the act, not by the identity of the perpetrator or the nature of the cause. Terrorism is violence, or the threat of violence, calculated to create an atmosphere of fear and alarm. All terrorist acts are crimes like murder, kidnapping, or arson. Many, such as the taking of hostages, would also be violations of the rules of war, if a state of war existed. The violence is often directed against civilian targets and is carried out in a way that will achieve maximum publicity, intending to produce psychological effects beyond the immediate damage caused. Still, lack of agreement on this simple definition impedes international cooperation.

Terrorists are able to attract publicity to themselves and their causes. Thus far, however, they have been unable to translate these consequences of terrorism into concrete political gain. Since the colonial era, no terrorist group has been able to achieve its own declared long-range goals. In spite of apparent failure, the terrorists persist, although defections have increased. Terrorists explore ways to continue their struggle in prison. They have indicated a willingness to negotiate cease-fires.

Ill-prepared and uncertain how to confront the terrorist threat in the early 1970s, governments since have become more rigorous and more effective. U.S. Secretary of State George Shultz in October 1984 advocated the use of military force, not only in retaliation to an attack but also in preventive strikes. In fact most governments have adopted hard-line, no-concession, no-negotiation policies in dealing with hostage situations. Physical security around the likely targets of terrorist attack has increased. Embassies are becoming virtual fortresses. Diplomats and top executives often travel in armored limousines with armed bodyguards. The collection and analysis of intelligence have improved as well as knowledge of the terrorists' mindset.

Thousands of terrorists are in jail worldwide, with some groups destroyed and others hard-pressed by authorities. But the total volume of terrorist activity in the world has increased. More alarmingly, terrorism has become bloodier and more indiscriminate. The numbers of large-scale bombings and fatalities have increased. A December bombing of a packed train traveling between Bologna and Florence, Italy, that killed 25 persons constituted an example of the killing of innocent bystanders, people who happen to be in the wrong place at the wrong time, a group that makes up the fastest-growing category of victims.

There are several reasons for the increased volume. Terrorists have become more proficient and brutalized. Killing becomes easier. Terrorists, in order to overcome the apathy of a public numbed by growing terrorism, must escalate in order to hold their audience. Religious fanaticism, a growing factor in the terrorist struggles of the 1980s, provides the sanction of God in the mind of the terrorist. Growing state sponsorship provides terrorists with additional resources and reduces constraints.

But terrorism is not simply the mode of fanatic groups. A growing number of governments themselves use terrorist tactics, employ terrorist groups, or exploit terrorist incidents as a mode of surrogate warfare.

BRIAN JENKINS, *The Rand Corporation*

TEXAS

Politics and the economy remained the dominant issues in Texas in 1984. The weather also made headlines; much of West Texas suffered under continuing drought conditions, while flooding racked other parts of the state. A freeze in the Rio Grande valley also caused distress among citrus farmers and growers.

Politics. As has been predicted, Ronald Reagan carried Texas with relative ease. Responding to the low national rate of inflation and to Reagan's posture on defense spending, Texans gave the incumbent president a substantial mandate. The Republican candidate ran very well in the state's large urban areas, particularly Houston and Dallas. In a bitterly contested senatorial race to fill the seat vacated by John Tower, Republican Phil Gramm defeated his Democratic opponent, Lloyd Doggett. An attorney and former state legislator, Doggett emphasized local issues while trying to disassociate himself from Walter Mondale and the national Democratic platform. Surprisingly, the state's Hispanics and blacks did not play the pivotal role in the election that some political analysts had forecast for them. Gov. Mark White and San Antonio Mayor Henry Cisneros maintained their status as significant figures in the Democratic Party.

Economy. While other Sunbelt states, particularly Florida and Arizona, appeared to be participating in the nation's financial recovery, the economy in Texas remained somewhat stagnant. Dperessed oil prices, resulting from an international petroleum surplus, tended to discourage local drilling and exploration. Oil field equipment sales and employment in the industry generally tended to lag as well. For the first time in recent years, real-estate values declined, as homes proved difficult to sell. Houston and Dallas experienced a glut in rentals of office space, a development that further discouraged investment building.

On the positive side, however, persistent efforts to attract high-tech industries to Texas appeared to be succeeding. Continued expansion in the Austin-San Antonio corridor was noticeably facilitated by this development. A number of colleges and universities in the state banded together in research consortiums to encourage high-tech development.

Education. As pledged by Gov. Mark White, public school teachers in Texas received a moderate across-the-board increment in 1984. This was accomplished in a special session of the state legislature, called to deal with problems of education as a whole. Ross Perot, a graduate of the U.S. Naval Academy and a multimillionaire investor, chaired a committee of private citizens that submitted a report for the legislature's consideration. Controversial from its inception, the report called for an appointive, rather than elective, state board of education and for teacher testing to determine qualifications. With regard to students, academic standards required for graduation were also made more rigorous. A passing grade in all subjects now is required in order to remain eligible for extracurricular activities, including athletics. After intense and often acrimonious debate, the basic provisions of the Perot plan were approved. Supporters of the reforms believe that the plan's standards will serve as benchmarks for educational betterment in other states.

"Proposition Two"—a proposal creating a dedicated fund for construction at state universities other than the University of Texas and Texas A&M—was endorsed in a statewide vote. The University of Texas and Texas A&M already share in income from the oil-rich "Permanent University Fund," so this development was widely considered to be an equitable solution. On the private school level, Trinity University in San Antonio and Rice University in Houston remained among the nation's leaders in the recruitment of merit scholars.

Sports. For the second year in a row, the University of Houston basketball team made it to the finals of the NCAA tournament. Defeated by Georgetown, as it had been by North Carolina State the previous year, the Cougars faced a period of rebuilding. Akeem Olajuwon, their All-American center from Nigeria, signed with the Houston Rockets of the NBA. In college football, the University of Texas Longhorns enjoyed a 7-4-1 season but lost to Iowa, 55–17, in the first Freedom Bowl; the Houston Cougars, 7–5 during the season, were defeated by Boston College, 45–28, in the Cotton Bowl.

Again the legislature would probably consider the question of legalized thoroughbred horse racing in 1985. An argument heard against the objections of religious groups was the need to increase the state's revenue base.

STANLEY E. SIEGEL, *University of Houston*

TEXAS • Information Highlights

Area: 266,807 sq mi (691 030 km²).
Population (July 1, 1983 est.): 15,724,000
Chief Cities (July 1, 1982 est.): Austin, the capital, 368,135; Houston, 1,725,617; Dallas, 943,848; San Antonio, 819,021; El Paso, 445,071; Fort Worth, 401,402; Corpus Christi, 246,081.
Government (1984): *Chief Officers*—governor, Mark White (D); lt. gov., William P. Hobby (D). *Legislature*—Senate, 31 members; House of Representatives, 150 members.
State Finances (fiscal year 1983): *Revenues,* $17,-400,000,000; *expenditures,* $15,796,000,000.
Personal Income (1983): $183,730,000,000; per capita, $11,685.
Labor Force (May 1984): *Civilian labor force,* 7,924,500; *unemployed,* 442,100 (5.6% of total force).
Education: *Enrollment* (fall 1982)—public elementary schools, 2,149,813; public secondary, 835,-846; colleges and universities (fall 1983), 795,741. *Public school expenditures* (1982–83), $7,442,-158,754 ($2,731 per pupil).

Marking 38 years on the Thai throne in 1984, King Bhumibol (left) *remained a dominant figure on the national scene. He and Queen Sirikit hosted a state dinner for West German President Karl Carstens and Mrs. Carstens during their late February-March visit.*

Camera Press/Photo Trends

THAILAND

Three leaders dominated the Thai political scene in 1984—King Bhumibol Adulyadej, Prime Minister Prem Tinsulanonda, and Gen. Arthit Kamlang-ek, the army commander and supreme commander of the armed forces. The king continued to support the prime minister, who completed four years in office in 1984.

Neither the 57-year-old king nor his 64-year-old prime minister were in very good health, leading to continued speculation about who would succeed them. The prime minister visited the United States in September to undergo an examination for heart disease.

Political Events. General Arthit often denied wanting to succeed Prem, but he frequently expressed his views on domestic and foreign policy issues and gave every sign of being ambitious. The military has been powerful for many years in Thai politics but has allowed a gradual return of representative government.

General Arthit supported constitutional amendments that would go far toward restoring military rule in Thailand. Prem appeared to oppose them. One amendment would allow active-duty military officers to hold cabinet posts. Another would restore the legislative powers of the appointed Senate, which includes many former military officers. The amendments were first defeated in a parliamentary vote in March 1983. However, they were introduced again in 1984 with strong support from the military, and Parliament voted to defer debate until 1985.

Clearly linked with the constitutional amendments was the issue of whether General Arthit's term as supreme commander would be extended. Prem, who held the post of defense minister as well as prime minister, deferred action on this subject, but he and Arthit jointly signed a promotion list that advanced many of Arthit's followers. For example, Gen. Pichit Kullavanich became commander of the important First Army Region.

Economy. Burdened with a fairly large foreign debt and unable to control the prices it received for exports, the Thai government was forced to impose strict limits on government spending and imports in order to avoid a serious balance-of-payments problem. The results of this austerity program were expected to be reasonably good in 1984—modest growth, manageable inflation, and a much smaller gap in the balance of payments than in 1983, partly because of continued low prices for oil imports.

Perhaps the most serious cloud on the economic horizon was rising unemployment. The country needed to create more jobs in industry because it was running out of surplus agricultural land. To do this, one of the urgent needs was to make Thai exports more competitive in world markets. Some progress in this regard was recorded in 1984.

Foreign Relations. Foreign Minister Siddhi Savetsila continued to implement the policy of aiding Cambodian resistance groups and isolating Vietnam from Western economic aid. This policy was again endorsed by the UN General Assembly.

In March, Thai military sources reported that Vietnamese troops had advanced into Thailand in pursuit of Khmer Rouge rebels from neighboring Cambodia. Thailand lodged a complaint with the United Nations against Vietnamese aggression. In the United States as part of a six-nation tour in April, Prem met with President Reagan, who agreed to sell 40 M-48 tanks to Thailand to help it protect its borders.

PETER A. POOLE
Author, "The Vietnamese in Thailand"

THAILAND • Information Highlights

Official Name: Kingdom of Thailand (conventional); Prathet Thai (Thai).
Location: Southeast Asia.
Area: 198,772 sq mi (514 820 km²).
Population (mid-1984 est.): 51,700,000.
Chief City (1983 est.): Bangkok, the capital, 5,535,048.
Government: *Head of State,* Bhumibol Adulyadej, king (acceded June 1946). *Head of government,* Gen. Prem Tinsulanonda, prime minister (took office March 1980).
Monetary Unit: Baht (23.000 baht equal U.S.$1, June 1984).
Gross National Product (1982 U.S.$): $38,400,-000,000.
Economic Index (1983): *Consumer Prices* (1970 = 100), all items, 298.2; food, 307.8.
Foreign Trade (1983 U.S.$): *Imports,* $10,232,-000,000; *exports,* $6,368,000,000.

THEATER

A generation ago, Broadway was the fountainhead of American theater. That has changed. Musicals still originate on Broadway, although less frequently since they began costing upward of $1 million apiece to produce. Broadway's plays, however, almost always originate elsewhere—regional theaters, off Broadway, or London. The pattern held in 1984.

Outstanding Productions. Broadway launched one distinguished new musical, Stephen Sondheim's *Sunday in the Park with George*. Its two plays of distinction—Tom Stoppard's *The Real Thing* and David Mamet's *Glengarry Glen Ross*—first were staged in London.

Sondheim's *Sunday in the Park with George* is one of the most exhilarating theatrical works of the decade, adding to Sondheim's reputation as the American musical theater's great innovator of the post-World War II era. Nominally, the musical is about how the French pointillist, Georges Seurat, painted his famous "Sunday Afternoon on the Island of La Grande Jatte." But the play is really about the creative process, not just the business of getting a canvas filled, although it is a stunning *coup de theatre* when director James Lapine starts with a blank canvas and ends the first act by filling it with figures familiar from reproductions of that painting.

As Seurat's painting comes into being, and as his inner world is wafted into life by Sondheim's music, so do his imperatives. Actor Mandy Patinkin's grave, somber Seurat intones his artistic priorities: "Design. Tension. Balance. Composition. Light. Harmony." Those familiar with Sondheim's gracefully probing and suavely iconoclastic music will note that he and Seurat value many of the same attributes.

Clearly, Seurat's biography is also Sondheim's veiled autobiography. The self-consciousness in Seurat is attuned to the postmodernist sensibility, epitomized by Sondheim. Like Seurat, Sondheim often has been accused of creating clever, but bloodless, work. But the fierce stare in Patinkin's Seurat argues against this and so does the conviction that percolates through the gracefully turned score that more than once echoes Ravel and other French composers. The fact that Seurat, like Sondheim, remains a passionately dispassionate observer is made to seem a heroic virtue. Sondheim's music, like Seurat's painting, is marked by rigorous order, precision, organization. By intention, there is no dance, but everyone glides.

The Real Thing represents a breakthrough for Stoppard, too. Like Sondheim, he is often accused of glib facility and emotional avoidance. In *The Real Thing* he retains the wit and verbal trapeze acts that coruscate through such earlier works as *Travesties* and *Jumpers,* but he no longer uses dazzle as something to hide behind. His play is about a playwright who moves from writing brittle, Noel Coward–like farces to growth through pain. At first, it is pain he causes others, as he breaks with his wife to pursue an adulterous affair with the wife of his leading man. Soon, it is pain he feels himself as he tries to build a second marriage and finds his own emotional reserves inadequate to the task of meeting his partner's needs, which ultimately leads to her infidelity.

Under Mike Nichols' direction, the cast brings to the writing a degree of fine tuning remarkable for its nuance and economy. As the

Bert Andrews

David Mamet's scalding comic drama "Glengarry Glen Ross" presents a painful view of the dog-eat-dog world of real estate salesmen, passing off worthless Florida land to unsuspecting and naive customers. Through the efforts of several gifted performers, the struggle for dominance and survival is vividly portrayed. Veteran actor Vincent Gardenia (seated on desk) joined the cast several months after the play opened.

BROADWAY OPENINGS | 1984

MUSICALS

The Human Comedy, book and lyrics adapted by William Dumaresq from William Saroyan's novel, music by Galt MacDermot; directed by Wilford Leach; with Rex Smith, Stephen Geoffreys; April 5–15.

Oliver, book, music, and lyrics by Lionel Bart, based on the Charles Dickens novel *Oliver Twist;* directed by Peter Coe; with Ron Moody, Braden Danner, Patti LuPone; April 29–May 13.

Quilters, by Molly Newman and Barbara Damashek, music and lyrics by Miss Damashek; directed by Miss Damashek; with Rosemary McNamara; Sept. 25–Oct. 14.

The Rink, book by Terrence McNally, music by John Kander, lyrics by Fred Ebb; directed by A. J. Antoon; with Liza Minnelli, Chita Rivera; Feb. 9–Aug. 4.

Sunday in the Park with George–book by James Lapine, music and lyrics by Stephen Sondheim; directed by Mr. Lapine; with Mandy Patinkin, Bernadette Peters; May 2–.

The Three Musketeers, original book by William Anthony McGuire, new version by Mark Bramble, music by Rudolf Friml, lyrics by P. G. Wodehouse and Clifford Grey, based on the novel by Alexandre Dumas; with Brent Spiner, Ron Taylor, Chuck Wagner; Nov. 11–18.

The Wiz, book by William F. Brown, music and lyrics by Charlie Smalls; directed by Geoffrey Holder; with Stephanie Mills; May 24–June 3.

PLAYS

Accidental Death of an Anarchist, by Dario Fo, adapted by Richard Nelson; directed by Douglas C. Wager; with Jonathan Pryce; Nov. 15–Dec. 1.

Alone Together, by Lawrence Roman; directed by Arnold Mittelman; with Kevin McCarthy, Janis Paige; Oct. 21–.

Awake and Sing!, by Clifford Odets; directed by Theodore Mann; with Nancy Marchand, Thomas G. Waites, Harry Hamlin; March 8–April 29.

The Babe, by Bob and Ann Acosta; directed by Noam Pitlik; with Max Gail; May 17–22.

Beethoven's Tenth, by Peter Ustinov; directed by Robert Chetwyn; with Peter Ustinov, George Rose; April 22–May 13.

Cyrano de Bergerac, by Edmond Rostand, translated and adapted by Anthony Burgess; directed by Terry Hands; with Derek Jacobi, Sinead Cusack; Oct. 16–.*

Death of a Salesman, by Arthur Miller; directed by Michael Rudman; with Dustin Hoffman, Kate Reid, John Malkovich, Stephen Lang; March 29–July 1; Sept. 14–Nov. 18.

Design for Living, by Noel Coward; directed by George C. Scott; with Jill Clayburgh, Frank Langella, Raul Julia; June 20–.

End of the World, by Arthur Kopit; directed by Harold Prince; with John Shea, Barnard Hughes, Linda Hunt; May 6–June 2.

Glengarry Glen Ross, by David Mamet; directed by Gregory Mosher; with Robert Prosky, J. T. Walsh, James Tolkan, Mike Nussbaum, Joe Mantegna, Lane Smith, Jack Wallace; March 25–.

The Golden Age, by A. R. Gurney, Jr.; directed by John Tillinger; with Irene Worth, Stockard Channing, Jeff Daniels; April 12–May 6.

Hurlyburly, by David Rabe; directed by Mike Nichols; with William Hurt, Harvey Keitel, Ron Silver, Judith Ivey, Cynthia Nixon, Jerry Stiller, Sigourney Weaver; Aug. 7–.

Ian McKellen Acting Shakespeare, presented by Arthur Cantor, Bonnie Nelson Schwartz, and Rebecca Kuehn; with Ian McKellen; Jan. 19–Feb. 19.

Kipling, by Brian Clark, based on the works of Rudyard Kipling; directed by Patrick Garland; with Alec McCowen; Oct. 10–21.

Ma Rainey's Black Bottom, by August Wilson; directed by Lloyd Richards; with John Carpenter, Charles S. Dutton, Theresa Merritt, Leonard Jackson, Robert Judd, Lou Criscuolo, Joe Seneca, Aleta Mitchell, Scott Davenport-Richards, Christopher Loomis; Oct. 11–.

A Moon for the Misbegotten, by Eugene O'Neill; directed by David Leveaux; with Kate Nelligan, John Bellucci, Jerome Kilty, Ian Bannen; May 1–June 9.

Much Ado About Nothing, by William Shakespeare; directed by Terry Hands; with Derek Jacobi, Sinead Cusack; Oct. 14–.*

Open Admissions, by Shirley Lauro; directed by Elinor Renfield; with Calvin Levels, Marilyn Rockafellow; Jan. 29–Feb. 12.

Play Memory, by Joanna M. Glass; directed by Harold Prince; with Donald Moffat, Jo Henderson, Valerie Mahaffey; April 26–29.

The Real Thing, by Tom Stoppard; directed by Mike Nichols; with Jeremy Irons, Glenn Close, Christine Baranski, Kenneth Welsh; Jan. 5–.

A Woman of Independent Means, by Elizabeth Forsythe Hailey, based on her novel; directed by Norman Cohen; with Barbara Rush; May 3–13.

OTHER ENTERTAINMENT

Doug Henning and His World of Magic; with Doug Henning; Dec. 11–.

Haarlem Nocturne, conceived by Andre De Shields; written and directed by Mr. De Shields and Murray Horwitz; with Andre De Shields; Nov. 18–.

Shirley MacLaine on Broadway, original music and lyrics by Marvin Hamlisch and Christopher Adler; staged and choreographed by Alan Johnson; with Shirley MacLaine; April 19–May 27.

Whoopi Goldberg, production supervised by Mike Nichols; with Whoopi Goldberg; Oct. 24–.

* Royal Shakespeare Company (in repertory)

---

emotional pilgrim, Jeremy Irons always makes sure that the playwright's clever witticisms are transparent, never hiding his bewilderment and, later, the vulnerability he writhes under as he scrambles to cover the nakedness of his exposed heart. As the woman in his life, Glenn Close has the more difficult assignment. Her selfishness could render her unsympathetic; that it does not is a tribute to Close's ability to project earthy warmth. Aside from being the most brilliant play about love and marriage in years, *The Real Thing* also projects an optimism about its entwined subjects that is far from commonplace on the contemporary stage.

Glengarry Glen Ross blazes with a verbal inventiveness and energy of a different sort. Mamet has for years been praised for his ear, for his ability to compose soaring arias of ver-

nacular. What has been less noticeable, until now, is the increasing degree of precision and economy in his writing. Here, he becomes an American Pinter, whose characters speak in jagged fragments that seem to resonate with several layers of meaning simultaneously.

The subject of *Glengarry Glen Ross* is the driving viciousness of a competitive office of real estate hustlers in Chicago. They recall the inept lowlifes in Mamet's earlier *American Buffalo*. The grubby office that the salesmen each want so fiercely to dominate, to conquer with sales of worthless Florida land to suckers, grinds their souls to powder, yet they are addicted to the fast-talking voraciousness that is its music. Mamet is acute enough and honest enough, though, to like and be excited by his characters. He sees them as the ultimate vic-

Ken Howard

Martha Swope

Martha Swope

BROADWAY AWARD WINNERS

Among 1984's award-winning shows were the musicals "Sunday in the Park with George" (right), featuring the music of Stephen Sondheim, and "The Rink" (top), which meshed the talents of Liza Minnelli and Chita Rivera and brought Miss Rivera a Tony as best supporting actress in a musical. Glenn Close (above, left) and Jeremy Irons, stars of Tom Stoppard's "The Real Thing," received Tonys as best dramatic actress and actor. One of the most powerful dramas of the season, this revised British import captured five Tonys in all, including awards for best director, best supporting actress, and best play.

tims. The ensemble under director Gregory Mosher is incisively orchestrated, from Joe Mantegna's self-prodder to Robert Prosky's aging go-getter.

Broadway Musicals. As usual, not all meritorious work succeeded, even in the musical arena, which was meagerly populated. Galt MacDermot's *The Human Comedy* set William Saroyan's novel to perky, lyrical music that seemed an outpouring of sweet vitality in the midst of life's negation by World War II. It could not make a successful jump to Broadway from Joseph Papp's Public Theater. *The Rink* proved that star power could carry sour, tepid material only so far. Chita Rivera and Liza Minnelli threw themselves into their roles of an estranged mother and daughter who reconcile on the eve of the demolition of their family-owned roller-skating rink, but it was not enough.

Broadway also had little patience with *Quilters*, a musical about pioneer women that first was staged in Denver and moved to New York with its charm intact. *Haarlem Nocturne* was designed to showcase the songwriting ability and ambisexual dancing of Andre De Shields, but the powerhouse singing of Ellia English and Debra Byrd were the most electrifying elements, especially in traditional blues. Two revivals came and went quickly. Lionel Bart's *Oliver!* flopped despite the presence of Fagin from the original London cast, Ron Moody. A good-naturedly rambunctious updating of Rudolf Friml's *The Three Musketeers* vanished quickly, too.

Finally, the year of Sondheim was augmented further by a successful off-Broadway revival of his *Pacific Overtures* and New York City Opera performances of his *Sweeney Todd*.

English actress Billie Whitelaw, a foremost interpreter of Samuel Beckett plays, performed in three in 1984.

AP/Wide World

Broadway Plays. Among the so-called straight plays, August Wilson's *Ma Rainey's Black Bottom* comes close to being a musical. Set in 1927 at a Chicago recording session of the great blues singer, the play is filled with harsh and sometimes funny riffs of black speech. The Yale Repertory Company production was chiefly ignited by Charles S. Dutton's performance as an angry, frustrated sideman. David Rabe's *Hurlyburly*, originally given an all-star production off-Broadway under Mike Nichols' direction, was powered by corrosive energy, too. But Rabe's study of divorced men more or less connected to the movie business and each other seems to turn against its characters and go sour after a darkly funny first act.

Joanna Glass's *Play Memory*, about a girl growing up in Saskatchewan with a bitter, self-pitying drunken father, was well staged, with Donald Moffat compelling in the downbeat central role. Shirley Lauro's *Open Admissions*, expanded from a one-act play originally staged off-Broadway, took on a worthy subject—the deterioration of educational standards under the so-called open admissions system. Calvin Levels, as a young black man angrily clamoring for a better education than he knew he was getting, was a standout. *End of the World*, Arthur Kopit's attempt to wrap an antinuclear war message in a private eye parody, was unsuccessful. And while the writing of A. R. Gurney, Jr., about WASPs has often been successful, his attempt to refashion Henry James' *The Aspern Papers* into a romance called *The Golden Age* was not. Nor did Peter Ustinov's tour de force, *Beethoven's Tenth*, find an audience, despite frequent eruptions of humane good humor as Ustinov's Ludwig visited an English musical family. After years of being denied a visa by the U.S. State Department, Italian political satirist Dario Fo brought his *Accidental Death of an Anarchist* to Broadway. Dealing with an actual incident in which a police suspect dropped to his death from a police station window, it was most notable for Jonathan Pryce's inspired burlesque in the role of a holy fool sent to haunt the police. *Alone Together*, with Janis Paige and Kevin McCarthy, was a comedy about parents who find that their children have not left the nest for college. It seldom rose above TV sitcom.

Solo performances and revivals figured, as well. *Ian McKellen Acting Shakespeare* adroitly displayed the mercurial talents of that English actor. *Whoopi Goldberg* showcased that mime-comedienne frequently outreaching her often dated material. Alec McCowen labored bravely, but vainly, to bring *Kipling* to dramatic life. And Barbara Rush was unable to generate much sympathy for her portrayal of a wealthy Texan in *A Woman of Independent Means*. *The Babe* (Babe Ruth) struck out, but Shirley MacLaine gamely took on Broadway with her one-woman show.

Dustin Hoffman brought star power to an uneven revival of Arthur Miller's *Death of a Salesman,* with John Malkovich and Kate Reid. The Circle in the Square offered a lively reprise of Clifford Odets' *Awake and Sing!* and followed it with a far less convincing but much more successful staging of Noel Coward's *Design for Living.* Kate Nelligan was a luminous Josie in the American Repertory Theatre revival of Eugene O'Neill's *A Moon for the Misbegotten,* which originated in Cambridge, MA. From England came the Royal Shakespeare Company (RSC) with a pair of bright productions, each starring Derek Jacobi and Sinead Cusack. *Cyrano de Bergerac* was the crowd-pleaser, but Anthony Burgess' fussy translation dampened its billowing romanticism. Shakespeare's *Much Ado About Nothing,* staged with all its levels of reality delicately intact and echoed in Ralph Koltai's gossamer designs, was near perfect.

Los Angeles Arts Festival. Before opening in New York, the Royal Shakespeare Company joined a number of international colleagues for a Los Angeles arts festival designed to be a theatrical equivalent of the Olympic athletic events there during the summer of 1984. The offerings that won the most acclaim, in addition to the RSC, were Shakespeare in French and Euripides in Japanese, as Ariane Mnouchkine's Théâtre du Soleil staged *Richard II* and Tashida Suzuki directed *The Trojan Women* as a nightmarish aftermath of World War II.

Off Broadway. Even off-Broadway stages, once so trailblazing, frequently housed revivals or material first staged elsewhere. At age 78, Samuel Beckett not only has an off-Broadway theater named after him, but found it presenting a steady flow of his plays. A triple-bill of short Beckett plays performed by Billie Whitelaw—*Rockaby, Footfalls,* and *Enough*—was followed by a revival of *Endgame* directed by and starring Alvin Epstein. Arthur Miller's *After the Fall* was revived with Frank Langella in the role many deem Milleresque and Dianne Wiest playing the Marilyn Monroe figure sans blond wig. The Circle Repertory Company revived a 1965 Lanford Wilson play, *Balm in Gilead,* along with Chicago's Steppenwolf Theatre Company under John Malkovich's direction.

The offerings at Joseph Papp's New York Shakespeare Festival ranged from Janusz Glowicki's allegory of oppression in Poland, *Cinders,* with Christopher Walken, to Puccini's *La Bohème,* with Linda Ronstadt. Russian playwright Victor Rozov's *The Nest of the Wood Grouse,* focused on a diplomat and his family in Moscow. The cast included Eli Wallach, Anne Jackson, Mary Beth Hurt, and Phoebe Cates, and the director was Joseph Papp. Ted Tally's *Terra Nova,* about Robert F. Scott's doomed Antarctic expedition, and Beth Henley's *The Miss Firecracker Contest,* about

David S. Talbott

The Louisville Festival of New American Plays presented "Danny and the Deep Blue Sea." It later went to New York.

Mississippi eccentrics, got first New York stagings at the American Place Theater and Manhattan Theater Club, respectively. Each had been staged years ago outside New York. *Woza, Albert!,* an antiapartheid satire, came from South Africa, and from the fertile Festival of New American Plays at the Actors Theater in Louisville, KY, came John Patrick Shanley's *Danny and the Deep Blue Sea,* about a couple groping for love in a Bronx bar.

Little of the experimentation of previous years surfaced in the new theatrical offerings off-Broadway. *A . . . My Name Is Alice,* by Joan Micklin Silver and Julianne Boyd, was a cheerful post-feminist feminist musical, full of verve and self-sufficiency in standard cabaret format. Plays about loneliness, in naturalistic style, also were plentiful. Craig Lucas' *Blue Window,* intercutting seven lonely Manhattanites' conversations before and after a party, was typical, and perhaps the most lighthanded. Dennis McIntyre's *Split Second* dramatized the spiritual crisis experienced by a policeman who may have been too quick on the trigger. A couple of plays even took on broad visions of the America of yesteryear: Peter Parnell's *Romance Language* and Michael Weller's *The Ballad of Soapy Smith.* The latter could not quite float its American Falstaff—a Klondike con man. Parnell's play, staged with remarkable resourcefulness at the Playwrights Horizons, second to none in encouraging young writers, tried unconvincingly to present Walt Whitman, Henry David Thoreau, Louisa May Alcott, Emily Dickinson, Charlotte Cushman, and George Custer as sexual outlaws. Laurence Carr's *Kennedy at Colonus* honorably grappled with the last eight years of Robert F. Kennedy's life.

JAY CARR
Critic-at-large, "The Boston Globe"

THIRD WORLD

Although mounting protectionism and declining oil prices raised questions about the ability of certain large debtor states to meet huge obligations to international banks and lending institutions, the robust economic recovery in industrialized nations brightened the prospects for the Third World.

Economic Recovery. In late September, finance ministers and central bankers from 148 nations swarmed into Washington for the annual meetings of the World Bank and International Monetary Fund (IMF). In recent years, gloom pervaded these sessions because of weak economic growth, unimpressive international trade, and strident threats that some less developed countries (LDCs) owing billions of dollars might forge a debtors' cartel to exact softer repayment terms or—worse still—simply refuse to pay. Default by a Mexico, Brazil, or Nigeria might tumble the international financial structure and plunge the world into a severe depression.

Smiles replaced frowns at the 1984 gathering when Jacques de Larosiere, the IMF's managing director, reported that the industrial world was enjoying its strongest economic gains in eight years. He predicted that the U.S. gross national product (GNP) would shoot up 7.3% in 1984, while the 19 most industrialized countries would register an overall 5% upswing. These advances would stimulate demand for goods and services—with the volume of world trade expected to expand 8.5%.

The economic resurgence gave a material as well as a psychological boost to large LDCs that, until recently, appeared hopelessly mired in debt and poverty. The United States rebound whetted the American appetite for imports while the dollar's strength vis-à-vis other currencies slashed the price of foreign products entering the U.S. market. For instance, shipment of Brazilian goods to the United States had soared 44% in the two years to nearly $7 billion (U.S.) for 1984, while Mexico's climbed 15% to $18 billion.

Debt Rescheduling. Once a ragged stepsister of the international economic community because of its $96 billion debt, Mexico became a dazzling Cinderella thanks to the imposition of painful austerity measures. The IMF-monitored plan cut the growth of government spending, curbed increases in public employment, and diminished subsidies on gasoline, electricity, and other vital items. In September, foreign creditors rewarded Mexico for its assiduous belt-tightening by allowing repayment of its $48.5 billion public sector debt at an average rate of 1.11 percentage points above the London interbank rate, by 1998—eight years beyond the initial deadline. Mexico will save approximately $400 million annually by this arrangement.

Recognizing the possibility of rescheduling their own debts on more favorable terms, Argentina ($45 billion debt), Brazil ($98 billion), Nigeria ($20 billion), and the Philippines ($25 billion) are among important developing countries that agreed to IMF-approved stabilization programs in 1984. Meanwhile, nationalistic sensibilities led Venezuela ($37 billion) to adopt an independent retrenchment·scheme.

The Reagan administration modified its hard-line opposition to profligate Third World borrowing when it agreed that countries could borrow up to 450% of their IMF limit or "quota," a ceiling that the U.S. government had once wanted lowered to 325%.

Growth and flexibility silenced proponents of a debtors' cartel. Yet, while its tick was softer than before, the debt bomb was not defused. To begin with, a surge of 11 to 13% by midyear in the U.S. prime interest rate, to which many loan repayments are pegged, raised debt service costs by $5 billion for Latin American nations alone. A reversal of the late-year decline in U.S. interest rates could more than offset the benefits conferred by debt renegotiations. Growing protectionism by developed countries through higher tariffs, sturdier quotas, and special accords posed an even greater threat to export-driven recovery among developing nations.

That oil prices fell during the last quarter of 1984 proved a blessing for energy importers—Argentina, Brazil, India, and Pakistan, for instance—which form a vast majority of LDCs. However, the decline imperiled the economic recuperation of such important petroleum-dependent countries as Algeria, Indonesia, Iran, Mexico, Nigeria, and Venezuela. A representative country is Mexico where a $1.00 per barrel drop in oil charges deprives the economy of $600 million in foreign exchange. Still, cheaper energy spurs growth in the United States, Europe, and Japan, which—in turn—swells demand for Third World exports.

Population Policy. Population increases offset more than half of the 3.7% rise in GNP accomplished in the Third World in 1984. Concern over the social and economic consequences of unwanted high fertility rates dominated the agenda of the second UN International Conference on Population that convened in Mexico City in August. Delegates from 149 nations learned that global population growth had dropped from 2% to 1.7% in the previous decade. Yet, 90% of the future expansion would occur in the Third World. (*See also* POPULATION.)

Indira Gandhi. Third World leaders mourned the October 31 assassination of Indira Gandhi, the prime minister of India and a longtime leader of the Third World's nonaligned nations movement.

GEORGE W. GRAYSON
College of William and Mary

D. Henschel, Picture Group

Alon Reininger, Contact Press Images

The October 31 assassination of Prime Minister Indira Gandhi and the December industrial accident at the Union Carbide plant in Bhopal focused attention on India (above); with a population of 746.4 million, the nation has a per capita GNP of a mere $260. Mexico City's crowded subway (left) is indicative of the city's rapidly growing population, which is expected to reach 18.1 million in 1985. In Cairo, Egypt, another Third World city, work continued on a needed but trouble-ridden subway (below left). Meanwhile, the Overseas Education Fund assists Third World women; in a rural area of Sri Lanka (below), representatives of the fund teach women to make coffee from palymra palm.

OEF International

Christine Osborne, Middle East Pictures & Publicity

TRANSPORTATION

The continued strong performance of the U.S. economy in 1984 benefited most modes of transportation, though quite unevenly. By mid-year, cumulative rail ton-miles were running some 16% above the prior year, truck traffic was up about 12%, and air cargo had increased some 18%. As the year proceeded, however, slower economic growth in comparison with the exceptionally rapid economic improvement of late 1983 was expected to reduce these rates of increase. Rail traffic was favorably affected in the third quarter by the building of coal stocks in expectation of a possibly prolonged coal strike. Passenger-traffic growth was slower and was most vigorous in the private automobile segment, which represents about 83% of all intercity-passenger movement. Intercity-bus traffic experienced an actual decline as competitive fare cutting by some of the more aggressive airlines diverted long-haul traffic. In some markets, airline rates stood at less than half the level of bus fares.

The gradual decline of freight ton-miles and of total estimated freight costs in relation to Gross National Product (GNP) continued through 1983, but the sharp increase in industrial production in the early part of 1984 sent total ton-miles up more rapidly than GNP, a relation often found during a strong industrial recovery. Passenger miles, on the other hand, lagged behind the growth in GNP. The declining trend of total transport volume and costs in relation to GNP appeared likely to continue indefinitely, albeit with occasional departures from the trend, as in early 1984. The long-term decline reflects the continuing transition of the economy from heavy freight-producing industries to high-tech and service industries.

Price pressure on the carriers was relieved to some degree by the continued revival of traffic. Freight rates by rail, barge, and air had been lower in 1983 than in 1981, and only modest recovery was in evidence in 1984. Truck carriers had succeeded in pushing less-than-truckload rates up slightly, but truckload rates remained depressed in the face of continuing new entry and overcapacity. Improved efficiency in car movement enabled the railroads to handle exceptionally heavy traffic in September, with little evidence of car shortage. The passenger air carriers, however, continued to face reduced yields and sharp fare competition in some markets. While carrier earnings were expected to improve in most sectors of the industry, highly disparate results were to be expected among individual carriers.

Legislation and Regulation. Two major legislative enactments in 1984 promised to change the outlook for international shipping to and from the United States and for motor carrier costs. After seven years of effort by legislators, the Shipping Act of 1984 replaced the Shipping Act of 1916. Of major importance to shipowners was a resolution of the long-standing dispute over antitrust immunity. The new law specifies seven types of action that may be undertaken by shipping companies jointly within conference organizations; among these are the ability to fix rate and service conditions, to regulate the types and amount of cargo carried, and the right to allot ports and regulate sailings. Agreements must be filed with the Federal Maritime Commission (FMC) and approved within specified time limits. In the event it finds any such agreement substantially anticompetitive, the FMC may seek injunctive relief in the courts, where it assumes the burden of proof.

The act continues the requirement that carriers must file and maintain tariffs containing all their rates, charges, and services except on certain bulk and low-value products. Time/volume rates may now be published in tariffs. For the first time, shippers and carriers may also enter into normal contract relations with an ocean common carrier operating in the foreign trade. And shippers may collectively bargain with carriers, a provision designed to afford protection to small shippers who, by creating associations, may generate bargaining power similar to that enjoyed by any large shipper under the contract provisions of the act.

Unlike the trend toward deregulation of domestic transport in recent years, the Shipping Act of 1984 provides more comprehensive regulation for ocean carriers in the foreign trade. It also retains the prohibition against deferrals and other tariff rebates.

Another new piece of legislation allayed much of the concern generated by 1983 federal highway tax increases. Without reducing the prospective tax income intended for the benefit of the Highway Trust Fund, the new law converts most of the tax falling on heavy trucks to a variable charge rather than a fixed charge per vehicle regardless of the usage obtained from the vehicle. The former method was expected to put many truckers out of business. Instead, the new legislation provides a use tax of $100 for vehicles weighing more than 55,000 lbs (25 000 kg), plus $22 for each additional 1,000 lbs (454 kg) up to 75,000 lbs (34 000 kg). The maximum fixed tax becomes $550 for the largest class of vehicle. To avoid current loss from this major reduction in the use tax, Congress approved a six-cent differential diesel fuel tax. A great deal of highway repair and improvement work was already underway as a result of the increased funding generated by the Surface Transportation Assistance Act of 1982.

Safety. The year was one of unusual concern for safety in several modes of transportation. In particular, sharpened attention was placed on the dangers of alcohol and drug abuse, not only by the drivers of private passenger cars but by professional drivers as well. Railroads, too, came under scrutiny, as an in-

Amtrak's northbound "Montrealer" derailed and crashed into a ravine near Williston, VT, on July 7. It was one of four Amtrak crashes during that month, killing a total of ten persons.

creased number of train accidents were attributed to such abuse. With Secretary of Transportation Elizabeth H. Dole deeply concerned about safety, serious consideration was given to a federal regulation that might supplement the railroads' own Rule G, which has governed the use of alcohol by train service employees for most of the industry's history. Railroad unions were reluctant to see such a development and put their emphasis on rehabilitation rather than discipline.

Federal pressure on state legislatures to increase the minimum drinking age showed great success. Several states also mandated the use of seat belts, but controversy continued over the effectiveness of passive restraints, including air bags, in the face of conflicting interpretation of available statistics and tests. In air safety, concern continued over the adequacy of staffing, training, and equipment for the air traffic control system in the face of increasing numbers of aircraft operations.

Railroads. Earnings from piggyback (TOFC-COFC) service remained marginal, though volume continued to grow more rapidly than traffic as a whole. Competition with trucks in a deregulated environment resulted in depressed rates, while increased investment in terminal facilities has been required. A number of car types designed to reduce weight and cut air resistance were under test. But a major problem for the railroads in this large segment of their business was the noncompetitive structure of wages, benefits, and work rules. The rail unions had yet to recognize the impact of nonunion truck competition spawned by deregulation. Thus, despite excellent on-time performance and minimal damage to freight, the road-railer Empire State Express between New York and Buffalo was discontinued. The operating unions did make some concessions, but not in sufficient measure to make the service truck competitive.

The major mergers of recent years appeared to be working well, affording new through-services to shippers and generating some of the hope-for economies. The Santa Fe-Southern Pacific case was as yet undetermined by the Interstate Commerce Commission (ICC); the Southern Pacific Transportation Co. stock remained in a trust although the parent companies merged. After extended proceedings, the ICC recommended to the bankruptcy court that the remaining core of the Milwaukee Road be awarded to the SOO Line (controlled by Canadian Pacific). And the disposition of Conrail was being actively sought by the Department of Transportation. Fourteen bids were received, but it appeared that Congressional action would be required before a final decision could be reached.

The ICC's exemption of box-car traffic was challenged because of its prospective impact on short-line railroads and box-car owners. Certain of the commission's proposed rules were therefore deferred. The ICC's exemption of export coal traffic from all regulation was overruled by a circuit court and remanded for further proceedings. Discontent on the part of "captive" shippers with the lack of restraint on rate increases grew to the degree that political activity was organized to seek redress in Congress. Other shippers concerned about the closing of through routes and the discontinuance of reciprocal switching were joining in this activity. The position taken by shippers in general was that the ICC had failed to preserve the balance between competitive freedom in railroads and the protection of captive shippers facing railroad monopoly.

The Staggers Act of 1980, intended to preserve that balance, and the national economic recovery have no doubt helped improve rail profitability. There are those who believe, however, that the railroads have abused the freedom accorded them and that a four-member commission generally oriented toward deregulation has aided in producing this result. After a long hiatus, three new appointees to the commission were confirmed, restoring the body to its statutory composition.

Motor Carriers. Continued price pressures were felt in the industry as more than 10,000 new entrants, many of them small firms or owner operators, struggled for a share of a slowly growing volume of available freight traffic. More failures occurred among older carriers, which were unable to adjust to the changed competitive situation. Other carriers found it possible to survive by developing employee stock ownership plans (ESOPs) as compensation for the acceptance of lower rates of pay. A good example was Transcon, a major long-haul carrier restored to health by an ESOP and a 12% cut in employee compensation.

Despite petitions by major groups of shippers concerned with continued rate bureau activity in promulgating rates on small shipments and the rapid escalation of rates on such traffic, the ICC refused to cancel the antitrust immunity (already reduced) of motor carrier rate bureaus with respect to such traffic. The commission also continued to resist efforts to persuade it to examine and restrain rate-cutting activities that were regarded by both motor carriers and shippers as destructive competitive practices.

The commission had earlier removed the special conditions attached to railroad use of their motor carrier subsidiaries for over-the-road transportation. In general, railroads had been restricted in their use of trucks to service that was ancillary or supplemental to rail carriage of goods. The ICC later removed these conditions with respect to the acquisition of new authority or of existing motor carriers. These actions were challenged in the courts.

Meanwhile, however, Norfolk Southern sought authority to acquire North American Van Lines, which, though usually thought of as a household-goods mover, is in fact well entrenched in other categories of motor carriage. Curiously, Burlington Northern, which had previously disposed of its air freight forwarding subsidiary, was in the process of dispensing with its two motor carrier subsidiaries.

The Surface Transportation Assistance Act of 1982 also required the designation of a system of highways over which vehicles 102 inches (2.55 m) wide (as opposed to the previous 96 inches—2.44 m) could be operated and on which 48-ft (14.6-m) semitrailers or doubles composed of two 28-ft (8.5-m) units could be employed. Reasonable access was to be afforded to customer's premises and carrier terminals. The final system designated by the Department of Transportation in 1984 was regarded by the trucking industry as deficient in many respects. State opposition to the designation of highways off the interstate system was a major reason for this situation, which has caused many motor carriers to defer purchase of the larger vehicles.

Air Transportation. Passenger traffic showed modest increases, less than had been hoped for. Air cargo responded much more briskly to economic recovery. Many carriers enjoyed increased earnings, though a number of large carriers remained on the endangered list. The TWA spin-off was accomplished, and its future earning capacity was uncertain. Pan American, Eastern, and Western airlines remained in perilous positions. Continental's reduced operations brought the company into the black, but Braniff's restored services failed to generate hoped-for volume. The major success story was the continued rapid growth and profitability of People Express, which entered many

One consequence of airline deregulation in 1978 has been a gradual bunching of arrivals and departures. In September 1984, representatives of 100 airlines agreed on more than 1,300 schedule changes to help alleviate runway congestion.

Nik Kleinberg, Picture Group

new markets—including the transcontinental—in direct low-priced competition with longtime incumbents on those routes. Many of the major trunk carriers continued to seek additional concessions from employees to assist them in meeting the price competition that was precipitated on many routes.

The years since deregulation in 1978 have been marked by a great deal of revision of the route patterns of many of the airlines. The hub system of organizing routes and connecting service, pioneered by Delta at Atlanta many years ago, has become a prime element in the competitive strategy of many other lines. A result has been the bunching of arrivals and departures in prime time at a number of major airports. Delays produced by such scheduling caused the percentage of on-time performance to fall to the low 70s and generated significant additional fuel costs as well as passenger complaint. Missed connections, too, were not uncommon. After much deliberation, the Civil Aeronautics Board in 1984 conferred antitrust immunity for carrier discussion of schedule adjustments. In a series of meetings led by Federal Aviation Administration personnel, some 1,300 schedules were altered in an effort to resolve the problem.

Landing slots as well as gate and counter space were prime elements in Midway Airlines' proposed takeover of Air Florida. The latter airline had indulged in overexpansion and, despite successive curtailments of operations, was ultimately obliged to seek refuge under Section 11 of the Bankruptcy Act. Despite heavy opposition, particularly by Eastern, Midway was able to resume some Air Florida operations in late September.

Dec. 31, 1984, marked the demise of the Civil Aeronautics Board (CAB) under the terms of the 1978 Airline Deregulation Act. A number of CAB functions passed to other agencies under the terms of that act: contracting for mail transportation to the Postal Service; control of operating authority, rates, and practices to the Department of Transportation; and antitrust issues to the Department of Justice. Such consumer protection issues as the rules relating to overbooking, smoking on aircraft, and baggage liability would presumably pass to the Federal Trade Commission, which expressed little interest in such jurisdiction. Further Congressional action may be necessary.

Inland Water and Ocean Transportation. The barge industry, particularly on the Mississippi River and its tributaries, suffered significant overcapacity and depressed rates. Rail competition through the service of contract rates has provided more opportunity for the rail carriers to divert some traditional barge cargo. The low level of activity in the steel industry, though improving, continued to affect barge and Great Lakes carriers adversely. The Tennessee-Tombigbee Waterway, long under con-

struction in the face of continuing challenge by environmentalists and railroads, was opened across the divide between the Tennessee River and Gulf of Mexico drainage. An early opening was anticipated for the route, which would greatly shorten the distance for water traffic moving west to the Mississippi, then east from New Orleans via the Gulf Intracoastal Canal.

The 1983 purchase of Texas Gas Resources by CSX Rail System brought up the issue of railroad control of a barge line—in this case American Commercial Lines, Inc., the largest barge operation in the United States. No railroad had been allowed to control a significant barge operation since the Panama Canal Act of 1913 required ICC approval of such control. In 1984 the stock of American Commercial was trusted pending ICC action. On July 24 the commission voted to approve the merger and on September 7 issued its formal report. Barge interests immediately sought a stay and filed an appeal with the U.S. Court of Appeals for the 6th Circuit.

The total tonnage of the world's merchant fleets declined in 1983 for the first time since 1945. In view of continued over-tonnaging in the petroleum and other bulk trades, a further decline seemed likely in 1984. Laid-up tonnage continued at a high level, and the demand for tankers was stagnant. Despite air attacks on tankers moving in the Persian Gulf, exports from that area continued; however, some Gulf countries did restrain oil production in an effort to hold price levels.

In the liner trades, the high level of the U.S. dollar generated large increases in imports while restraining exports. One consequence was a change in directional balance-of-traffic on the Atlantic, as westbound cargo offerings exceeded those available eastward to liner vessels. Similarly, the usual eastward imbalance of cargo on the Pacific routes increased. Controversies with Venezuela and the Philippines over issues of cargo preference for vessels of particular flags were resolved during the year as the United States sought to preserve a larger share for cross traders.

Transit. Available federal funds were far short of those called for by light- and heavy-rail transit projects being proposed by municipalities across the country. Meanwhile, questions were being raised in the face of sharp cost escalation of some still partially completed systems, the limited coverage within the metropolitan areas that even the largest of such systems would provide, and the failure of ridership to develop up to the levels forecast by planners. Rehabilitation and improvement continued on various commuter lines operated by public transit authorities and on the deteriorated transit systems of New York and Philadelphia.

ERNEST W. WILLIAMS, JR.
Columbia University

With the U.S. dollar very strong, overseas travel as well as goods were excellent bargains.

OH, WHAT A LOVELY TOWN! LET'S BUY IT!

ROMA FIRENZE

U.S. $

Gene Basset, "The Atlanta Journal"

TRAVEL

The prospect of trading their U.S. dollars for more French francs, British pounds, and Italian lire than they had ever been worth before proved irresistible for millions of Americans in 1984. With the strength of the dollar providing even greater overseas travel bargains as the year wore on, U.S. travelers applied for passports and boarded airplanes in record numbers.

Europe was again the number one destination. It was estimated that by year's end, 5.5 million Americans would have traveled to Europe, an all-time high and a 40% increase since 1982. And as people discovered when they tried to make airline reservations, Europe was no longer a seasonal destination. Charter flights were filled right to year's end.

The strong dollar took travelers in other directions as well, being credited for healthy jumps in U.S. travel to such diverse places as New Zealand and Japan, Hong Kong and Mexico. By the end of the year, it was estimated that 11.2 million Americans had traveled overseas, another 4 million to Mexico, and 11.85 million to Canada. Increases of 20% and more in U.S. tourist arrivals were not uncommon. U.S. passport offices had to struggle to keep up with applications during the busy April-to-July rush. Of an estimated 4.5 million passport applications during the year, 600,000 of them came in May alone.

At the same time, events conspired to put a damper on travel within the United States. The dollar exchange rate discouraged many overseas travelers from visiting the country. Overseas arrivals just barely held their own with the previous year. The Summer Olympic Games in Los Angeles did not turn out to be a significant factor in attracting foreign visitors. And the World's Fair in New Orleans also failed to attract the anticipated number of visitors, both foreign and domestic.

As for Americans themselves, for many it was a choice of a European trip in 1984 instead of traveling at home or to such nearby vacation spots as the Caribbean. The feeling seemed to be that currency exchange rates were just too good to last. And many people with extra cash in hand for the first time in several years seemed to be spending it on cars or refrigerators rather than travel. While travel revenue in the United States did go up, the total number of trips taken by Americans was down. Travelers were taking longer and more expensive trips—but fewer of them.

Cruising. More travelers than ever before took to the seas, attracted by a host of special fares and offbeat ports of call. For even though passenger numbers were at an all-time high, there were also more ships to fill. To woo passengers, cruise lines offered free air fare to embarkation points, price discounts, and certificates good for price cuts on future cruises.

Major new cruise ships attracting American passengers in 1984 included Sitmar's *Fairsky,* Holland America's *Noordam,* the Mediterranean-based *Sea Goddess I,* and, by year's end, Princess Cruises' *Royal Princess.* More ships were expected over the next two years, as a commitment to shipbuilding made in the cruising boom years of the late 1970s comes to fruition. For the most part, these are the jumbo jets of the cruising industry, much bigger than cruise liners used to be—1,200 passengers has become standard, and one line is even studying the feasibility of a 5,000-passenger ship.

With the popular cruising waters of the Caribbean, the Mexican Riviera, and Alaska becoming more crowded, ships went everywhere in an effort to attract passengers. Cruise ships sent people down the Danube and the Yangtze rivers, navigated the "Northwest Passage" from Newfoundland to Alaska, and dropped anchor off remote Southeast Asian shores and such offbeat spots as Napolean's mid-Atlantic island exile of St. Helena. Never before had passengers been given such a wide choice of unusual destinations.

Cruise lines also reached out to a new type of passenger—no longer necessarily affluent and elderly. One study showed that 41% of first-time cruise passengers were 35 years old or under, nearly half were under 45, and 48% earned less than $25,000 annually. An increasing number of short cruises, even one-day sails, allowed travelers to sample the cruising life without a big investment of time or money.

An important center of the short-cruise business was San Diego, where Crown Cruise Line introduced one-day cruises to and from Ensenada, Mexico, aboard the *Viking Princess* for less than $100. San Diego became an increasingly significant base for longer cruises to Mexico as well, and late in the year it was made the home port for one of Princess Cruises' ships.

A number of West Coast cities were in the midst of beefing up their cruise passenger facilities—San Diego, Los Angeles, and Seattle all had major pier development under way.

Continuing Trends. Despite heavily booked flights on some routes, airlines continued to suffer financial problems because of high operating costs and the need to replace aging aircraft with new-generation jets. For the traveler, the scramble to fill airline seats meant that attractive fares were available on the most competitive routes. From New York/Newark (NJ) to Europe, where People Express had launched low-cost, no-frills service the year before, bargain fares continued to be offered.

And in 1984, People Express also entered the domestic fray with $240 round-trip transcontinental flights (Oakland, CA, to Newark), prompting immediate competitive response from other airlines.

Low fares between the West Coast and Hawaii also were available throughout the year, as were economical air-accommodation packages. Thus, the tourist business in Hawaii was brisk.

Airlines also made intense efforts to attract business travelers. Almost all of them offered special sections for business travelers with more spacious seating, special meals, and various other attentions. Many airlines gave full-fare passengers credit toward free flights as they accumulated mileage.

The business traveler was not the only one being offered personalized attention in 1984. A continuing travel trend was the availability of more individualized tours and services. Small hotels in a number of cities were elegantly refurbished to appeal to travelers who did not want to be one in a thousand. Bed-and-breakfast inns continued to proliferate, and associations were organized to simplify making reservations.

More and more destinations offered "special interest" touring programs—such as wine-tasting, wildlife-viewing, and hot-air ballooning —designed to appeal to small groups of travelers bound by common hobbies or interests. There were even "literary" tours tracing the plots of *Brideshead Revisited* and *Far Pavilions*. And participation was another growing trend, with groups of Americans taking to bicycles, rafts, camelback, and their own two feet to explore some of the farthest corners of the earth.

PHYLLIS ELVING, *Free-lance Travel Writer*

The Louisiana World Exposition, held in New Orleans, May 12–Nov. 11, 1984, failed to attract the hoped-for crowds.

Mitchel L. Osborne

The deteriorating situation in the Persian Gulf was the topic at an emergency meeting of the foreign ministers of the Arab League in Tunis in May.

TUNISIA

The year 1984 began tragically when rioting with loss of life swept through Tunisia in January. Thousands of Tunisians took to the streets to protest the government's decision to raise bread and other food prices more than 80% by rescinding grain subsidies. Heavily armed soldiers clashed with the rioters for nearly a week, and at least 89 people were killed in the disturbances. The rioting ceased after President Habib Bourguiba made a nationwide broadcast in which he announced restoration of the subsidies.

Politics. The food riots represented a setback for the 83-year-old Bourguiba. Hoping to bequeath a stable and more liberal society as his legacy, Bourguiba, just before the riots, had designated Prime Minister Mohamed Mzali as his official successor and had legalized two opposition parties, making Tunisia a multiparty state for the first time.

But fallout from the riots continued to dominate the political scene throughout the year. Dozens of rioters received long sentences in a series of trials lasting through August. There also was a crackdown on the press and on Islamic fundamentalist groups. Bourguiba sacked Interior Minister Driss Guiga, saying that Guiga had let the riots get out of control. But many Tunisians felt that Mzali had been the main proponent of the food-price increases, and Bourguiba did little to dispel criticism of his designated successor. Consequently, the popularity of a Mzali-led government, should Bourguiba resign or die in the near future, remained in serious doubt.

Economy. Economically, 1984 was a difficult year. Despite the food riots, austerity measures, including an 11% increase in the price of bread, were instituted in July. Unemployment rose above 25%, partly because the recession in France, where many Tunisians traditionally found work, forced thousands to return home.

In regard to export problems, domestic demand for petroleum products expanded, threatening Tunisia's status as a net oil exporter. While the production of phosphate fertilizers continued to grow, worldwide markets remained stagnant. Tunisia, the world's second-largest exporter of olive oil, is increasing its efforts to produce other agricultural goods for export in order to limit the revenue losses that will result when Spain and Portugal—also large producers of olive oil—enter the European Community.

The 1984 budget deficit was estimated at $578 million, but Tunisia's image as a fundamentally stable nation enabled the government to obtain easily a credit of more than $100 million from European banks. Further aid may come from the U.S. Agency for International Development, which was considering a resumption of its assistance program for Tunisia.

Foreign Relations. Tunisia, seeking to maintain good relations with its neighbors, reacted cautiously to the Libyan-Moroccan "treaty of union." Bourguiba's government, while it stopped short of criticizing the new pact, was careful to reaffirm the validity of the treaty of "fraternity and concord" that Tunisia signed in 1983 with Algeria and Mauritania.

To demonstrate its dedication to the cause of Maghreb unity, Tunisia hosted Ali Triki, Libya's foreign minister, only a week after the Libyan-Moroccan treaty was announced. A joint Tunisian-Libyan development bank was established, initially capitalized at $100 million. Cooperative projects also were proposed.

MICHAEL MAREN, *"Africa Report"*

TUNISIA · Information Highlights

Official Name: Republic of Tunisia.
Location: North Africa.
Area: 63,400 sq mi (164 206 km²).
Population (mid-1984 est.): 7,000,000.
Chief City (1975 census): Tunis, the capital, 550,404.
Government: *Head of state,* Habib Bourguiba, president-for-life (took office 1957). *Chief minister,* Mohamed Mzali, prime minister (took office April 1980). *Legislature* (unicameral)—National Assembly.
Monetary Unit: Dinar (.761 dinar equals U.S.$1, June 1984).
Gross National Product (1982 U.S.$): $8,700,-000,000.
Economic Indexes (1983): *Consumer Prices* (1977 = 100), all items, 168.5; food, 175.9.
Foreign Trade (1983 U.S.$): *Imports,* $3,108,000,000; *exports,* $1,852,000.000.

TURKEY

For Turkey, 1984 was a year primarily devoted to political and economic settling under the new government elected in November 1983. At that time, power was returned to the parliament following three years of military government.

Political Affairs. The highlight of 1984 was local elections held in March. They were won by the Motherland Party, which received 41% of the vote and won more than 50% of the mayoralties, including those of the largest cities and 54 of the 67 province capitals. The results were important because they confirmed the popularity of Prime Minister Turgut Ozal, whose victory in the parliamentary voting of 1983 had been under a cloud because of allegations that only parties backed by the armed forces had been allowed to compete. In the local elections two new parties, the Social Democracy and True Path parties, finished second and third with 23% and 13%, respectively. The other parties finished far behind.

The government again gave major attention to economic development in 1984. A legislative landmark was adoption of the 5th five-year development plan, which set ambitious growth targets and emphasized moving toward more integration with the world economy and continuing to increase Turkish exports.

Trials of accused terrorists continued. They had been started when the armed forces took power in 1980 in response partly to the high level of urban guerrilla violence. Martial law was lifted in 13 provinces in July and generally eased elsewhere. Controversy persisted about allegations of mistreatment of prisoners, however, although the government opened the prisons to inspection by the Council of Europe. During the year, some Turkish prisoners engaged in hunger strikes to protest prison conditions.

Foreign Relations. President Kenan Evren led the Turkish delegation to the Islamic Summit Conference in Casablanca in January and was elected chairman of its economic and social cooperation committee. He also paid a state visit to Saudi Arabia. Prime Minister Ozal visited Libya, Iran, and the USSR. Foreign visitors to Turkey included President Li Xiannian of the People's Republic of China. Among countries with which economic protocols or agreements were concluded were Iran, Iraq, Poland, Rumania, and Bulgaria. An agreement was initialed for financing of the Ataturk High Dam, which is expected to increase electricity production by about one third, and several large credits were obtained from the World Bank for industrial development. Military and economic aid to Turkey from the United States remained at a high level in 1984.

On other issues the record was mixed. A visit to Ankara in March by West German Foreign Minister Hans-Dietrich Genscher produced an optimistic report on Turkish progress toward restoration of full democracy. Turkey received a generally warm response from the Council of Europe, which had suspended Turkish participation in 1980.

Little progress was made on the Cyprus issue. Turkey and Pakistan remained the only two states to recognize the Turkish Republic of Northern Cyprus, which had declared its independence in 1983. Turkey made a conciliatory gesture in January by withdrawing 1,500 of its estimated 25,000 troops on the island. Efforts by United Nations Secretary General Javier Pérez de Cuellar to work out settlements of specific territorial and economic issues were not successful. In March tensions with Greece were heightened when a short clash took place between Greek and Turkish naval vessels in the Aegean Sea. The incident caused little damage but symbolized continuing tensions in that area.

Two more incidents of Armenian terrorism took place in 1984. In April a Turkish businessman was killed and two Turkish diplomats wounded in Tehran, and in June the Turkish labor counselor was killed in Vienna. Some encouragement came from the January conviction in Los Angeles of an Armenian for the 1982 murder of the Turkish consul there, and an Armenian accused of the 1983 killing of the Turkish ambassador to Yugoslavia was convicted in Belgrade. An international symposium on terrorism was held in Ankara in the spring, but on the whole little progress was made in controlling terrorism.

The Economy. Some progress was made in reducing inflation, and exports again increased moderately, particularly to Middle East and East European countries. The economy was aided by a year of general labor peace and by continued income from Turkish workers and contractors in Europe and several Arab states.

Other Matters. It was reported that, despite generous severance pay offers from the government of West Germany, only about 10% of the

TURKEY · Information Highlights

Official Name: Republic of Turkey.
Location: Southeastern Europe and southwestern Asia.
Area: 296,000 sq mi (766 640 km²).
Population (mid-1984 est.): 50,200,000.
Chief Cities: (1980 census): Ankara, the capital, 1,877,755; Istanbul, 2,772,708; Izmir, 757,854.
Government: *Head of state,* Gen. Kenan Evren, president (took office Nov. 10, 1982). *Head of government,* Turgut Ozal, prime minister (took office Dec. 13, 1983). *Legislature*—Grand National Assembly.
Monetary Unit: Lira (414 liras equal U.S.$1, Oct. 29, 1984).
Gross Domestic Product (1982 U.S.$): $53,800,000,000.
Economic Index (1983): *Consumer Prices* (1970 = 100), all items, 3,624.8; food, 3,853.4.
Foreign Trade (1983 U.S.$): *Imports,* $9,348,000,000; *exports,* $5,694,000,000.

estimated 550,000 Turkish workers there want to return home. Permission to explore on Mt. Ararat for the remains of Noah's Ark was made more liberal, and several expeditions took place, though again with inconclusive results. Turkish athletes won three bronze medals in boxing and wrestling at the Olympic Games, and the Turkish entrant in the Miss Europe contest won that title for the second year in a row.

WALTER F. WEIKER
Rutgers—The State University of New Jersey

UGANDA

Some economic improvement, darkened by growing political violence and bloodshed, marked the year in Uganda.

Economy. A slight economic upturn continued in Uganda in 1984, as the government drastically restricted imports, created a two-tier exchange system for the Ugandan shilling, and provided enough security in the capital, Kampala, to allow the revival of shops and places of entertainment. The return of some Asian-Ugandans who had been stripped of their possessions and expelled by former dictator Idi Amin also aided the newly revived economy.

Internal Security. Random violence and mass murder became frequent in Uganda in 1984. Some of the incidents were perpetrated by rebels opposed to President Milton Obote's regime, some by simple bandits, and many by the Ugandan army. The poorly disciplined army was divided by tribal rivalries and a lack of effective command due to the death of its commander, Maj. Gen. Oyite Ojok, in a helicopter crash in December 1983.

Rebels of the "National Resistance Army" kidnapped 11 foreign Red Cross workers in January (releasing 9 of them unharmed a week later) and successfully raided a government barracks and arsenal in Masindi in February, capturing many advanced weapons. The army, which was retrained by Tanzanian and North Korean advisers, then moved with great and often random violence against any place or population that might be linked to rebel activity or infested with "bandits." By year-end, it was estimated that the army's activities had resulted in almost 100,000 civilian deaths and the displacement of more than 750,000 people, who either fled the country or were herded into refugee camps. Besides the human losses, nearly 90,000 houses and farms had been destroyed or looted by Ugandan soldiers, causing hunger in many parts of the nation.

Ethnic Violence. Besides the lack of discipline, much of the violence in Uganda was due to ethnic rivalries within the army and within the government of President Obote's ruling Uganda People's Congress (UPC). A power struggle between the two tribes most heavily represented in the army, the Acholi and the Langi, resulted in the massacre of many officers of the latter group, and the refusal of President Obote, a Langi himself, to name a new army commander, who would almost certainly be an Acholi.

Ethnic rivalry also resulted in the systematic murder of thousands of Karamojong and Pokot, who inhabit northern Uganda and neighboring parts of Kenya. These two tribes in turn have retaliated against the army and other ethnic groups, leading to widespread death, starvation, and displacement of whole communities. The army has also carried out a special campaign in central Uganda against the Ganda ethnic group, who traditionally have been anti-Obote and who largely support Obote's main legal opposition, the Democratic Party. Thousands of dead and the internment of more than 120,000 Ganda in camps were the results of this policy. This campaign also witnessed the assassination of several Democratic Party members of Parliament, whose vacant seats were all won by Obote's UPC. By year-end, it seemed that Uganda was almost back to the times of Idi Amin.

ROBERT GARFIELD, *DePaul University*

UGANDA · Information Highlights

Official Name: Republic of Uganda.
Location: Interior of East Africa.
Area: 91,075 sq mi (235 885 km²).
Population (mid-1984 est.): 14,300,000.
Chief City (1980 census): Kampala, the capital, 458,423.
Government: *Head of state,* Milton Obote, president (elected Dec. 1980). *Head of government,* Erifasi Otema Allimadi, prime minister (appointed Dec. 1980). *Legislature* (unicameral)—National Assembly, 126 members.
Monetary Unit: Uganda shilling (293.5 shillings equal U.S.$1, May 1984).
Gross Domestic Product (1982 U.S.$): $4,800,-000,000.
Foreign Trade (1982–83, U.S.$): *Imports,* $345,-000,000; *exports,* $325,000,000.

At May Day celebrations in Moscow, a giant propaganda poster says that the actions of Washington threaten the entire world. Soviet-U.S. relations remained extremely frigid.

USSR

In the Soviet Union the year 1984 was marked by the selection of a new leader and, rather than any major shifts in policies or political structures, a high degree of stability and continuity. Essentially the same ruling elite that had been formed during the leadership of President Leonid Brezhnev (1964 to 1982) remained in power. Relations with the United States continued to be tense, with serious negotiations on arms control suspended. The USSR and most of its allies refused to participate in the Los Angeles Olympics and held their own "Friendship Games" in Moscow, a graphic symbol of the deep division between East and West. While the United States was involved in election campaigns, the Soviet Union was primarily concerned with its structural economic problems, the maintenance of its military defense, the continuing war in Afghanistan, and an ambitious educational reform. At the very end of the year, steps were taken to renew talks with the United States on a range of arms-control issues. Plans were made for arms talks between Soviet Foreign Minister Andrei Gromyko and U.S. Secretary of State George Shultz in January 1985.

Domestic Affairs

Leadership. Only a little more than a month into 1984, the Soviet leadership changed hands once again. After a long and mysterious illness, which turned out to be chronic kidney disease, Yuri Vladimirovich Andropov, 69, general secretary of the Communist Party since November 1982, died on February 9 (*see* OBITUARIES). Four days later, the Central Committee elected 72-year-old Politburo member Konstantin Ustinovich Chernenko as head of the party (*see* BIOGRAPHY). The elevation of this faithful follower of Brezhnev was widely interpreted in the West as signaling the reemergence of the older generation of party officials and a moderate challenge to the more aggressively reformist elements in the party elite, which had held sway during Andropov's brief tenure. Chernenko made it clear to the Central Committee, which was still largely composed of people elected at the last Brezhnev party congress early in 1981, that he would continue his mentor's policy of slow turnover of party personnel. While cadres might relax and enjoy their secure positions, Chernenko's hold on the Politburo was considerably weaker than either Brezhnev's or Andropov's had been, and the policies of the collective leadership continued through 1984 to reflect the general recognition that reform of the economy and the educational system was imperative.

Chernenko repeatedly praised the late President Andropov's policies, and the younger leaders promoted by Andropov—Mikhail Gorbachev (53), Grigory Romanov (61), Vitaly Vorotnikov (58), and Heidar Aliev (61)—continued to play leading roles in policy formation and execution. Gorbachev, often referred to in the West as the second-in-command and likely successor to Chernenko, became particularly visible in 1984. He substituted for the ill Chernenko at the opening of the Friendship Games in August, and he made a highly publicized visit to Great Britain in December.

The available evidence suggested that Chernenko was quite weak—both physically and politically—early in the year but that he managed to consolidate his position. In April he was elected president of the Supreme Soviet of the USSR, the highest state post in the country. The transition of power thus was completed, with Chernenko, like Brezhnev and Andropov before him, heading both the party and state apparatuses.

But Chernenko's administration was still widely regarded as something of a holding operation between two periods of more dynamic leadership. A Soviet anecdote told of a subway conductor announcing: "Next stop Chernenko. Transfer from Brezhnev to Andropov." The real Andropov period, it was suggested, lay not in the past but in the hands of his protégés. Of the 11 full members of the Politburo at year's end, six were in their seventies: Chernenko (73), Gromyko (75), Premier Nikolai Tikhonov (79), Dinmukhammed Kunayev (72), Mikhail Solomentsev (71), and Viktor Grishin (70). But of this older group only Chernenko was simultaneously a member of both the Politburo, the highest decision-making body in the party, and the Secretariat, the executive office that carries out Politburo policy. Both Gorbachev and Romanov of the younger generation were in both bodies. Clearly the leading figures in the younger group seemed well-placed.

The role of Gromyko increased noticeably during the course of the year, and most observers viewed him as the key figure in the making of Soviet foreign policy. But in contrast to Gromyko's ascendancy, his counterpart in the military, Marshal Dmitri Ustinov, suffered an eclipse, due to serious illness. On December 20, the 76-year-old defense minister and Polit-

Mikhail Gorbachev, at 53 the youngest member of the Politburo, appeared to be the eventual successor to Chernenko.

Tass from Sovfoto

buro member died in Moscow. Two days later, his successor as head of the military was named—Deputy Defense Minister Sergei Sokolov. The 73-year-old career officer was not a member of the Politburo, however, and did not hold nearly the high-level policy influence of his venerated predecessor. The future of party-military relations, a field in which Ustinov had been the pivotal figure, became uncertain.

Also dying during the year were Deputy Premier Leonid Konstandov and Col. Gen. Semyon F. Romanov, chief of staff of air defense forces.

The Military. Under Ustinov, the Soviet military was highly influential during the smooth transition from Brezhnev to Andropov in 1982. In contrast, the military was much less prominent in the emergence of Chernenko. In their public statements early in the year, military spokesmen were quite cool about Chernenko, though as the year progressed relations between the party chief and the military seemed to improve. In time, Chernenko was referred to in the press as the commander in chief of Soviet armed forces, the same title held previously by Brezhnev and Andropov.

The operational military commander of the Soviet armed forces was the chief of the general staff, Marshal Nikolai Ogarkov, the man who had masterfully defended Soviet actions in the Korean Air Lines incident at a public press conference late in 1983. Ogarkov, who seemed quite secure in his position, gave an interview in May in which he called for greater peacetime preparation throughout Soviet society and greater emphasis on conventional, nonnuclear forces. The suggested introduction of military priorities at every level of society may have been seen by party officials as a threat to their prerogatives and power. Increased military spending would also threaten the "broad social program" intended to benefit the Soviet public. Whatever the reasons, Ogarkov was suddenly dismissed as chief of staff on September 6. He was replaced by Marshal Sergei Akhromeyev, a deputy hitherto known as a principal spokesman on arms-control issues. With the removal of Ogarkov and the death of Ustinov, there had been a major shakeup at the General Staff, and the policy implications of the changes were still unclear at year's end. The military budget for 1985, however, showed a 12% increase over the previous year.

Economy. There were no major changes in Soviet economic policy during 1984, with the mild reforms of the Andropov period being continued. A few experimental initiatives in the decentralization of economic decision making begun in the Georgian Republic were widely discussed, and the general campaign against corruption started by Andropov was continued. Though there was much enthusiasm for increases recorded in national income (3.1%), industrial output (4%), agricultural output

(5%), and labor productivity (3% in industry, 6% in agriculture) in 1983, these gains were the result more of increased discipline imposed by the government than of significant structural changes. Nevertheless, the Andropov record did represent a reversal of the steady decline seen during the last years of the Brezhnev era and offered hope that the Chernenko leadership would carry on the reforming tendency.

Certain chronic economic problems did continue into 1984, however. The rise in wages and salaries was not matched by consumer production, and the imbalance between spending power and available commodities remained acute. Soviet consumers had plenty of cash but not enough goods to buy. Consumer items were still shoddy, and the excess demand could only be satisfied in the illegal and semilegal "second economy." Outside the state-controlled sector, goods and services were available at "market prices." A second major problem was the overdevelopment of extractive and primary industries. The USSR relied mainly on its own natural resources, and an enormous amount of capital was used to extract raw materials and fuel. Costs rose as the quality of the raw materials declined. The Soviet Union remained, however, the largest producer of oil in the world, even while it found it more difficult to subsidize its exports to its allied customers in Eastern Europe.

The perennial food problem continued to point up the failures of the collectivized agricultural sector. At the end of June, the Soviets went on a buying spree of U.S. grain, making purchases at twice the rate of the previous year. While its own domestic needs remained great, the Soviet Union was also required to supply grain to many of its allies, most immediately to the famine-ridden people of Ethiopia. The Soviet grain harvest, however, was once again, for the fourth year in a row, below expectation. The plan called for 240 million metric tons, but the U.S. Department of Agriculture estimated that the actual 1984 crop would reach only about 180 million tons.

From the first day of his administration, Chernenko emphasized the need for a "serious restructuring" of the Soviet economy. The program instituted by Andropov in July 1983 by which five ministries would be allowed to experiment with more local planning was reaffirmed, and efforts were made to increase the rights and responsibilities of Soviet enterprises. By the end of the year, Chernenko felt compelled to emphasize the achievements of the economy. He told the Politburo that "the Soviet economy has started developing more dynamically. The past two years saw positive changes." A particular source of pride was the completion of the 2,000-mi (3 200-km) Baikal-Amur railroad in Siberia (though it was not yet ready for full operation). The optimistic tone of Chernenko's speech was tempered by admis-

Butler, Gamma-Liaison

Oleg Khlan (r) and Igor Rykov, Soviet soldiers who had deserted in Afghanistan and escaped to Britain, accused the Soviets of atrocities. In November, however, they returned to the USSR. Also returning was Svetlana Alliluyeva, the daughter of Stalin, who had defected to the West in 1967.

Tass from Sovfoto

USSR · Information Highlights

Official Name: Union of Soviet Socialist Republics.
Location: Eastern Europe and northern Asia.
Area: 8,649,498 sq mi (22 402 200 km²).
Population (mid-1984 est.): 274,000,000.
Chief Cities (Jan. 1, 1982 est.): Moscow, the capital, 8,301,000; Leningrad, 4,719,000; Kiev, 2,297,000.
Government: *Head of state,* Konstantin U. Chernenko, chairman of the Presidium of the Supreme Soviet, president (elected April 11, 1984). *Head of government,* Nikolai A. Tikhonov, premier (took office Oct. 1980). Secretary-general of the Communist Party, Konstantin U. Chernenko (elected Feb. 13, 1984). *Legislature*—Supreme Soviet: Soviet of the Union Soviet of Nationalities.
Monetary Unit: Ruble (0.831 ruble equals U.S.$1, August 1984—noncommercial rate).
Gross National Product (1982 U.S.$): $1,715,-000,000,000.
Economic Index (1983): Industrial Production (1975 = 100), 138.
Foreign Trade (1983): *Imports,* $80,410,000,000; *exports,* $91,336,000,000.

sions that oil and coal production had fallen below target, that one third of Soviet trucks were not working properly, and that consumer goods were still of poor quality.

School Reform. Just after New Year's Day 1984, an extensive draft of a school reform law was published in the Soviet press. The purpose of the reform was to improve the scientific, technological, and vocational training of the school-age population. Education was to begin at age six (instead of seven) and to continue through eleven grades (instead of ten). All children were to complete nine grades and then determine which course to follow for the final two years. At this point more and more students would be guided toward vocational-technical schools.

For the next three months, meetings were held throughout the country to discuss the legislation. More than 7 million people were involved in the meetings, and letters were sent to state and party bodies with suggestions. According to the official press, "Soviet citizens have unanimously approved the aims and basic principles of the reform." But, in fact, there had been considerable opposition, particularly to the proposal of beginning school one year earlier. On April 12 the reform was presented to the Supreme Soviet, the nominal parliament of the USSR. Since it had been accepted the day before by the Central Committee, its passage was a foregone conclusion. Despite suggestions during the public debate that competition should determine the admission of pupils to the tenth grade, it was decided that students be allowed to choose freely whether to enter vocational-technical school or a specialized educational program.

A huge expenditure—11 billion rubles (U.S. $13 billion)—was allocated to implement the reform. New schools were to be built to accommodate the expected 7 million new pupils during the next Five-Year Plan, and teachers' salaries were to be raised by 30–35%. The educational reform was conceived as the necessary first step in the renovation of the Soviet economy. The development of skilled and competent workers and administrators would, in the future, raise productivity and efficiency. Training in computers was to be stressed, and the non-Russian peoples were to improve their fluency in the Russian language.

Dissent. After nearly two decades of exporting their dissidents to the West, the Soviet government had largely eliminated organized opposition to its rule. Because of the restrictions on emigration, many Jews who had hoped to leave for Israel or the United States continued to agitate for visas. But Jewish emigration had always been linked to improvements in East-West relations, and in the Reagan years the "new Cold War" resulted in a reduction of the number of exit visas to only a few thousand. Prominent "refuseniks" like Anatoly Shcharansky languished in prison camps, while a few demonstrated openly before Western news cameras to publicize their plight.

Tass from Sovfoto

Soviet officials welcomed a Spanish head of state for the first time, as King Juan Carlos made an official state visit in May. In his talks with Kremlin leaders, the king emphasized the theme of human rights.

The most famous dissident in the USSR, Andrei Sakharov, began a hunger strike on May 2 to protest the government's refusal to allow his wife, Yelena Bonner, to travel abroad for medical treatment. Sakharov was in forced exile in the city of Gorky, and news of his condition reached Moscow only sporadically. At the end of May, Soviet authorities declared that the Nobel laureate was eating regularly, but in August a videotape was released showing a much-aged Sakharov. As much as the Soviets tried to contain the Sakharov case, they failed to prevent it from becoming a major concern of the international community. During his visit to Moscow in June, President François Mitterrand of France embarrassed his hosts by raising the issue in private talks and then in a toast. But the Soviets were unwilling to compromise, and it was soon announced that Yelena Bonner had been sentenced to five years of internal exile for "slandering the Soviet state."

The Soviet theater lost one of its most distinguished innovators when Yuri Lyubimov, the controversial director of Moscow's avant-garde Taganka Theater, was stripped of his citizenship. The action was taken when Lyubimov refused to return home from an extended stay in London. On the other hand, on November 2 the Kremlin announced the return of one of its most illustrious defectors, Svetlana Alliluyeva, the 58-year-old daughter of Joseph Stalin. After 17 years abroad, Alliluyeva had become disenchanted with life in the West and homesick for her country and children. She returned to Moscow with her daughter, Olga, whose father is an American architect, and both were granted Soviet citizenship. It was speculated that the approaching 40th anniversary of the victory over Nazi Germany might be a time of official recognition of Stalin's role in the war effort and therefore part of a general effort to rehabilitate the dictator. Earlier in the year, Stalin's closest associate, Vyacheslav Molotov, who had been expelled from the party in 1962, was quietly reinstated.

Foreign Affairs

The year 1984 was a particularly frustrating one for the Kremlin leadership in the area of international diplomacy.

U.S. Relations. In December 1983, after the United States had begun deployment of its Cruise and Pershing II missiles in West Europe, the Soviet Union, as it had warned, walked out of the arms talks (both INF and START) in Geneva. All Soviet efforts to wean the Europeans from their support of U.S. policy had failed, and Moscow's repeated calls for new initiatives were rebuffed by Washington. In his first major speech of 1984, Gromyko told the Stockholm Conference that American missiles were undermining security in Europe.

Jasmin, Gamma-Liaison

The Soviets hosted Friendship '84, a sports festival for the nations that had followed its boycott of the Olympics.

Yet, he suggested, "the dangerous slide toward the abyss can be stopped." At first the Kremlin simply insisted on removal of the new American missiles before the Soviet delegation would return to the talks. In May it announced that additional Soviet missiles were being placed in East Germany and European Russia to balance the U.S. deployments and that more submarines were being added to the Soviet fleet. A month later the news agency Tass reported that the USSR was prepared to talk about banning weapons in space. The Kremlin was anxious about President Reagan's "strategic defensive initiative," the so-called "Star Wars" plan to develop an antinuclear space defense system. Washington relayed its willingness to discuss space weapons but requested that other arms-control issues also be placed on the agenda. Caught offguard, the Soviets refused to expand the talks.

In the tense atmosphere of late spring, the Soviet Union decided not to send its athletes to the Los Angeles Olympic Games. Though this had probably been a foregone conclusion ever since the United States had boycotted the Moscow Games of 1980, the decision simply underscored the continued decline of U.S.-Soviet relations during the Reagan presidency. That deterioration was hastened in August when, in a radio voice check, President Reagan was accidently overheard making a joke about bombing the Soviet Union.

More than a month passed before any improvement could be discerned in the tone of communiqués. Election-year politics may have played a role in the softening of rhetoric from the American side, and late in September both Reagan and Democratic presidential nominee Walter Mondale held talks with Gromyko. Nothing substantive came out of the meetings. Only after Reagan's landslide victory in November were serious overtures made by Moscow. It was soon agreed that Gromyko and U.S. Secretary of State Shultz would meet early in 1985 to discuss the possibility of further arms talks. The year ended with a slight improvement in the tone of interchanges between the superpowers, but no agreements of any significance were reached.

Afghanistan and Eastern Europe. Other areas of major concern to the Soviet Union in 1984 were the persistence of the resistance to the Soviet-imposed government in Afghanistan and the unpopularity of the military regime in Poland. While Soviet forces managed to hold on to major centers of population and prevent major losses to the Afghan rebels, they were unable to knock out the Western-backed insurrection. No significant victories were reported on either side. The Soviet Union expressed willingness to discuss the Afghan question internationally but primarily in order to end the supplying of the rebels from outside and to secure the leftist government in Kabul.

In Poland, Gen. Wojciech Jaruzelski maintained firm control over the political scene and attempted to win popular support for his government by moderating military rule. But the kidnap and murder of a popular dissident priest, Father Jerzy Popieluszko, by members of the Polish police set off a new round of protests and demonstrations. The Soviet Union stood aloof from Polish matters, at least publicly, and simply reiterated its support of the Jaruzelski government.

More ominous for the Soviet government was the growing rapprochement between East and West Germany. When East German party leader Erich Honecker decided to pay a state visit to West Germany, the Kremlin pressured him to call it off. The hoary arguments about West German designs on East Germany were resurrected in a campaign to discourage closer relations between the two Germanys.

All in all, the Soviet Union's hold over its allies in Europe appeared strained in 1984. Rumania remained virtually independent of Soviet control, particularly in foreign policy. Hungary continued to enjoy relative prosperity resulting from its reformed economic system. Only Bulgaria and Czechoslovakia did not officially or by example question Soviet hegemony and the standard model of socialist development.

Central America, Africa, and the Middle East. Despite its many public expressions in favor of peaceful coexistence and willingness to negotiate on a range of issues, the Kremlin also issued some strong rhetoric supporting the national liberation movements in Central America and Africa. The USSR continued to send military and economic aid to Nicaragua, which was under attack by U.S.-backed counterrevolutionaries. Immediately after the American elections, a mysterious shipment of Soviet arms to Nicaragua produced a tough response from the White House, which feared that MiG fighter planes were being added to the Sandinista arsenal. Nicaragua assured the United States that it had received no MiGs, only helicopters. The crisis quickly subsided, but it was clear that Nicaragua would be on its own in any military confrontation with the United States. Short of military intervention, however, the USSR would continue to aid the Sandinista revolution.

In Africa the Soviet Union's principal allies, the Marxist governments of Ethiopia and Angola, were both in difficult straits. Ethiopia was racked by civil war and a devastating famine caused by three successive years of drought, incompetence of local officials, and the inadequate delivery of Western and Soviet food aid. Western critics castigated the USSR and Ethiopia for being more concerned about weapons supplies than food for the starving. In Angola, 2,000 Soviet advisers worked alongside a similar number of East Germans and 30,000 Cubans to stabilize the economy and defend the government from South African–backed guerrillas.

In the Middle East, the Soviet Union restored diplomatic ties with Egypt in July. However, no other new initiatives were taken by the USSR in the ongoing conflicts in the region. Moscow continued to back Syria and the Palestine Liberation Organization (PLO). And in the dispute between Yasir Arafat's more moderate Palestinian faction and his radical opponents, the Soviets supported Arafat.

China. In late December there was some evidence of a shift in Sino-Soviet relations, as First Deputy Prime Minister Ivan Arkhipov made a nine-day visit to Peking. It was described as the most important visit to China by any Soviet official in 15 years. The trip was highlighted by a series of agreements on Chinese plant modernization and scientific and technological cooperation. The trade level between the two countries was raised to $1.8 billion (U.S.) for 1985. There was no suggestion, however, of any major reconciliation.

RONALD GRIGOR SUNY
University of Michigan

On September 27, the U.S. delegation to the UN General Assembly, headed by Secretary of State George Shultz (second row, left), *listened intently to a 75-minute address by Soviet Foreign Minister Andrei Gromyko.*

UNITED NATIONS

A surprising resurgence of U.S. diplomatic power manifested itself at the United Nations over the course of a year that otherwise saw few political developments of import in either the Security Council or General Assembly. Secretary-General Javier Pérez de Cuéllar was able to demonstrate his skills as a mediator in three major disputes—in Cyprus, in the Middle East, and in the war between Iraq and Iran. Attention was also focused on the crisis in Africa, as the General Assembly and the UN specialized agencies sought to spur the flow of aid to the more than 20 countries on that continent experiencing drought, famine, and economic difficulties.

The scope of U.S. success was recognized by allies and enemies alike, and it was generally attributed to the unorthodox confrontational tactics of American representative Jeane Kirkpatrick. The U.S. withdrawal from UNESCO (*see* special report, page 536) helped the Americans achieve budgetary restraint by other UN agencies, and a policy of linking American bilateral aid programs to the UN voting patterns of recipient nations helped produce —for the first time in years—pro-American majorities on political issues ranging from southern Africa to Central America. "The U.S. situation at the UN is very substantially improved, no question about that," Kirkpatrick said at a year-end press briefing. This result, she added, helped the "restoration of the UN as an effective instrument for promoting international cooperation."

There was also evidence at the UN late in the year that the long period of intense confrontation between the United States and the Soviet Union—a major factor in the UN's political paralysis—was thawing. In an appearance before the Assembly on September 24, U.S. President Ronald Reagan made a conciliatory appeal to Moscow for cooperation on regional issues as well as nuclear-arms negotiations. And although Soviet Foreign Minister Andrei Gromyko responded with a harsh speech on September 27, he did meet at the UN with U.S. Secretary of State George Shultz in preparation for talks with President Reagan later that week at the White House, the first high-level U.S.-Soviet contact since Reagan took office. The two powers also cooperated in staving off a challenge to the existing Antarctic Treaty and keeping a lid on the UN budget, although a coolness continued to pervade other debates.

General Assembly. Ambassador Paul Lusaka of Zambia was elected president of the General Assembly's 39th annual regular session, which opened September 18. Brunei Darussalam was admitted as the UN's 159th member.

Apart from the statement by Reagan, the most dramatic speech by a visiting national leader was that by Salvadoran President José Napoleón Duarte on October 8, in which he offered to travel unarmed to a neutral site in his country to meet rebel leaders for the first time. The meeting was held a week later.

Over the three-month span of the session, delegates spent most of their time discussing and drafting a declaration on the African crisis, which was adopted by acclamation on December 3. UN agencies had warned of the famine danger and started providing aid as far back as 1983, more than a year before public awareness of the situation became widespread. The declaration, devoid of ideological polemics, called for a broad range of immediate relief measures and spoke of the need to promote long-term

UNESCO

The United States terminated its membership in the United Nations Educational, Scientific and Cultural Organization (UNESCO) on Dec. 31, 1984. The move left that most controversial of UN agencies in a political and economic crisis and served notice to other international institutions that anti-American policies could jeopardize U.S. support.

"The circumstances that impelled us last year [1983] to announce our plan to withdraw have not changed sufficiently this year to warrant a change in our decision," said Assistant Secretary of State Gregory Newell on December 19, as he announced the action. "Extraneous politicization continues, as does, regrettably, an endemic hostility toward the institutions of a free society. . . . UNESCO's mismanagement also continues. . . . "

For the 160-member agency, the U.S. pullout meant the loss of a quarter of its funding, which was to have been $187 million for 1985. UNESCO officials said no plans had been made by year's end but expressed hope that cutbacks and voluntary contributions would compensate for the loss. "I don't think this will have any adverse effect on UNESCO's financial situation," said Amadou-Mahtar M'Bow of Senegal, the director-general. But Britain served notice in November that it would leave the agency at the end of 1985 unless further reforms were made. The departure of Britain, which provides 8% of the UNESCO budget, could imperil the institution's survival.

Under the UNESCO constitution (written in 1946 by American poet Archibald MacLeish), a nation must give 12 months' notice before withdrawing. The agency was chartered "to contribute to peace and security by promoting collaboration among the nations through education, science and culture," and promoting "the free flow of ideas by word and image."

It operates 182 programs in these fields, with a budget focus (40%) on education programs, such as the eradication of illiteracy and the training of educators in the Third World. In science, the "Man and Biosphere" program coordinates some 1,000 environmental projects, and the Oceanographic Commission provides global data vital to scientists—and to the U.S. Navy. Newell said the United States hoped to retain links to some of these programs.

Other activities include support of hundreds of publications and conferences in various fields, the protection and rescue of monuments, and a reevaluation of the role of media.

This last program, which called for a "New World Information and Communication Order," was cited in most criticisms of UNESCO because it was used to promote government limits on journalistic freedom and to redress the perceived Western orientation of news flows. The U.S. list of "politicized" programs also included "Soviet-inspired" educational curricula that boost the rights of states over individuals, promote world disarmament, and criticize capitalism.

In response to Western criticisms, M'Bow cut back support for some of these programs and conferences, but so grudgingly that he generated even more distrust. Much of the dissatisfaction focused on M'Bow personally, but he vowed to stay on the job until the end of his term in 1987.

Politics aside, UNESCO had been viewed for years by Western and UN officials as the most inefficient of the UN agencies, spending four of every five budget dollars at its Paris headquarters rather than in field projects. (By contrast, the UN Children's Fund spends 88% of its money in the field.) UNESCO admittedly suffers from program duplication, uncontrolled budget growth, and an inability to pinpoint and shut down useless programs. In these areas, internal efforts and outside pressures produced some reform in 1984.

Critics of U.S. policy charged that UNESCO's vulnerability made it a target for conservative ideologists whose hidden motive was to reduce U.S. involvement in all multinational organizations. They complained that Washington did not specify until too late the changes required for the United States to remain in the agency. When the American demands were put forward in October, many were not backed by other Western nations.

The European Community appealed to Washington to postpone the withdrawal decision for a year, as did the U.S. National Commission for UNESCO, a citizens' liaison group set up by Congress. Fears were expressed that the withdrawal would be damaging to the U.S. scientific community and corporate interests.

The exit from UNESCO was not the first American walkout. In 1974, Congress suspended the U.S. contribution to UNESCO because it excluded Israel from participation in regional activities. Funding was restored two years later, and anti-Israel bias had been minimal since.

The United States said it would rejoin UNESCO when it "returns to its original purposes and principles." To promote reform, Washington set up an observer mission in Paris to monitor the agency's progress.

MICHAEL J. BERLIN

recovery. On December 18, the final day of its session, the Assembly also allocated $73.5 million to build a new conference center in Addis Ababa, the Ethiopian capital. The action was taken despite private opposition from the secretary-general and an American warning that the UN would send the wrong signal to potential donors ''by spending so lavishly on a status symbol for a country where millions are threatened with starvation.''

The United States was successful in helping to block credentials challenges to the delegations of Grenada (without a vote) and Israel (by a vote of 80 to 41, with 22 abstentions). A number of resolutions critical of Israel were adopted, including one that called for the convening of a UN-sponsored peace conference on the Middle East with the participation of Israel, the Arab states, the Palestine Liberation Organization, and the major powers. The United States and Israel, however, reaffirmed their opposition to such a conference.

One of the most telling symbols of renewed American influence was the deletion from a number of resolutions of paragraphs condemning the United States and Israel for cooperating with South Africa.

U.S. efforts also helped in Assembly elections that shifted the political balance on the Security Council in the West's favor for 1985. Two Soviet allies—Mongolia and Ethiopia— were blocked from Council seats in elections won by Thailand and Madagascar. Denmark, Australia, and Trinidad and Tobago were also chosen to serve two-year Council terms, providing the West with an edge it had not enjoyed for a decade.

In the debate on Central America, the Assembly adopted a resolution reflecting the U.S. position by recognizing the need for more negotiations on a peace agreement among the five nations of the region. Because of lack of support, Nicaragua was obliged to withdraw its own resolution, implicitly critical of U.S. policy.

The United States also supported resolutions calling for the withdrawal of Soviet troops from Afghanistan (adopted by 119 to 20, with 14 abstentions) and Vietnamese troops from Cambodia (adopted by 110 to 22, with 18 abstentions).

The Americans stood alone, however, as all 147 other nations present approved the annual UN publication of a list of products that have been banned as harmful by a number of countries. The United States and other Western nations also opposed without success a resolution endorsing UNESCO and the ''New World Information Order.''

In other actions, the Assembly called for negotiations between Britain and Argentina over the Falkland Islands, and adopted 64 resolutions on a wide range of disarmament issues. In the area of human rights, it also

AP/Wide World

Jeane Kirkpatrick met with reporters following a December meeting with the president. Earlier the U.S. ambassador to the UN had said that she would resign in 1985.

adopted by consensus an international convention against torture and resolutions critical of human rights violations by El Salvador, Chile, and Guatemala.

The session was suspended until early 1985 without action being taken on 12 agenda items, including Cyprus, the war between Iran and Iraq, and the launching of a dialogue on economic issues between rich and poor nations.

Security Council. The Council experienced a relatively quiet year. It met four times to hear complaints against South Africa for its invasion of Angola, its promulgation of a new constitution, and its repression of black demonstrators protesting their lack of representation under that constitution. The vote was unanimous on two resolutions, but the United States abstained on the other two.

There were also four debates on Nicaragua, three of them brief sessions in which complaints were aired but no action was proposed. Early in April, however, a long debate on the mining of Nicaraguan ports ended with a U.S. veto of a resolution put forward by Nicaragua that was critical of the ''acts of aggression'' committed against it.

There were two debates on Lebanon and two vetoes—one by Washington, the other by Moscow. On February 29 the Soviet Union vetoed a French proposal calling for an immediate cease-fire in the factional fighting in Beirut and the deployment of a new UN peace force to replace a force of U.S., French, British, and Italian troops. On September 6, the United

States vetoed a Lebanese resolution calling on Israel to ease restrictions on the population of southern Lebanon, an area it occupied in 1982.

In the Cyprus dispute, the Council adopted a resolution in May encouraging mediation by the secretary-general. The 15 members urged both sides in the Iran-Iraq war not to use chemical weapons, and the council called on Iran to halt its attacks against civilian shipping in the Persian Gulf. The members also heard statements on disputes between Sudan and Libya and between Laos and Thailand. And it renewed the mandates of UN peacekeeping forces in Cyprus, Lebanon, and the Golan Heights.

Secretariat. Javier Pérez de Cuéllar scored a major triumph with the first breakthrough in a decade in the dispute between the Greek and Turkish communities on Cyprus. He launched negotiations in September between the leaders of the two groups, and after three rounds produced enough concessions from each side to announce on December 12 the scheduling of a summit meeting in New York City early in 1985. UN officials said Greek Cypriot President Spyros Kyprianou and Turkish Cypriot leader Rauf Denktash each compromised on the key issues of how much territory each community should occupy and the veto powers to guarantee the rights of the ethnic Turkish minority under a federated government.

In November the secretary-general's aides were able to launch negotiations between Israel and Lebanon on security arrangements for the withdrawal of Israeli troops from southern Lebanon. Eleven rounds of talks were held at the headquarters of the UN peace force in Lebanon before a year-end recess, but little progress was reported.

Although the Iran-Iraq war continued without letup, Pérez de Cuéllar remained the only one able to produce even minimal progress toward an agreement. In March he sent a team of four experts to investigate Iranian charges that Iraq had used outlawed chemical weapons in the fighting, and they came back with hard evidence to that effect. In June the secretary-general won a commitment from both sides not to attack civilian population centers. He also appealed to the combatants on the treatment of prisoners of war, and at year's end he dispatched a mission to investigate the matter on both sides.

Pérez de Cuéllar also remained involved in negotiating a withdrawal of Soviet troops from Afghanistan, without visible signs of progress. And in June he made a visit to Israel and the Arab nations.

In a precedent-breaking speech to the General Assembly in December, Pérez de Cuéllar accused the United States and Soviet Union of "arrogance" for allowing their ideological confrontation to "jeopardize the future of humanity" through the nuclear-arms race.

Amid controversy over whether Secretariat members are overpaid, some 2,000 members of the UN staff staged a brief protest in December against a decision to roll back a portion of the 9.6% pay hike they had been granted.

Specialized Agencies. In Montreal on March 7, the Governing Council of the International Civil Aviation Organization voted—20 to 2, with 19 abstentions—to condemn the Soviet Union for shooting down a South Korean airliner the previous September, killing all 269 people aboard. The vote endorsed a report concluding that Soviet authorities did not try hard enough to identify the plane before deciding to down it.

The Trusteeship Council heard a plea in May from former residents of Bikini atoll in Micronesia that the United States should clean up the radiation from nuclear tests held there in the 1950s, so that they can return home.

The International Labor Organization issued a report in June that Poland had breached two treaties on trade union rights. In November, Poland announced its withdrawal from the agency.

In August a World Population Conference in Mexico City adopted 88 proposals to update the "world plan of action," despite deep disagreements on the funding of abortions and the need for birth-control programs. (See also POPULATION.)

Legal Activities. For the first time in a number of years, the International Court of Justice played an active political role, taking action in two major cases.

In April, after the mining of Nicaraguan ports by U.S.-backed rebels, the Managua government appealed to the court for a ruling that would halt the use of military force and the U.S. intervention in its internal affairs. Three days before Nicaragua presented its case in The Hague, Washington informed the UN that it was placing a two-year moratorium on its acceptance of World Court jurisdiction over Central American cases. In November, however, the court ruled that it does have jurisdiction to decide the case. The decision itself was still pending at year's end. In the interim, the court called on the United States to refrain from any military action against Nicaragua.

The tribunal handed down a decision in October on a maritime border dispute between the United States and Canada, giving about two thirds of the 30,000-sq mi (78 000-km²) ocean area, which has fertile fisheries and potential offshore oil, to the United States. But the Canadian third includes the choicest fishing sites.

On another legal matter, the deadline for countries to sign the UN Convention on the Law of the Sea passed on December 9 with 159 signatures received. The United States, which opposed the treaty, was not among them.

MICHAEL J. BERLIN
"The Washington Post"

ORGANIZATION OF THE UNITED NATIONS

THE SECRETARIAT

Secretary-General: Javier Pérez de Cuéllar (until Dec. 31, 1986)

THE GENERAL ASSEMBLY (1984)

President: Paul John Firmino-Lusaka, Zambia
The 159 member nations were as follows:

Afghanistan
Albania
Algeria
Angola
Antigua and
Barbuda
Argentina
Australia
Austria
Bahamas
Bahrain
Bangladesh
Barbados
Belgium
Belize
Belorussian SSR
Benin
Bhutan
Bolivia
Botswana
Brazil
Brunei Darussalam
Bulgaria
Burkina Faso
Burma
Burundi
Cambodia
Cameroon
Canada

Cape Verde
Central African
Republic
Chad
Chile
China, People's
Republic of
Colombia
Comoros
Congo
Costa Rica
Cuba
Cyprus
Czechoslovakia
Denmark
Djibouti
Dominica
Dominican
Republic
Ecuador
Egypt
El Salvador
Equatorial Guinea
Ethiopia
Fiji
Finland
France
Gabon
Gambia

German Demo-
cratic Republic
Germany, Federal
Republic of
Ghana
Greece
Grenada
Guatemala
Guinea
Guinea-Bissau
Guyana
Haiti
Honduras
Hungary
Iceland
India
Indonesia
Iran
Iraq
Ireland
Israel
Italy
Ivory Coast
Jamaica
Japan
Jordan
Kenya
Kuwait

Laos
Lebanon
Lesotho
Liberia
Libya
Luxembourg
Madagascar
Malawi
Malaysia
Maldives
Mali
Malta
Mauritania
Mauritius
Mexico
Mongolia
Morocco
Mozambique
Nepal
Netherlands
New Zealand
Nicaragua
Niger
Nigeria
Norway
Oman
Pakistan
Panama

Papua New
Guinea
Paraguay
Peru
Philippines
Poland
Portugal
Qatar
Rumania
Rwanda
Saint Christopher
and Nevis
Saint Lucia
Saint Vincent and
The Grenadines
São Tomé and
Principe
Saudi Arabia
Senegal
Seychelles
Sierra Leone
Singapore
Solomon Islands
Somalia
South Africa
Spain
Sri Lanka
Sudan

Surinam
Swaziland
Sweden
Syria
Tanzania
Thailand
Togo
Trinidad and Tobago
Tunisia
Turkey
Uganda
Ukrainian SSR
USSR
United Arab Emirates
United Kingdom
United States
Uruguay
Vanuatu
Venezuela
Vietnam
Western Samoa
Yemen
Yemen, Democratic
Yugoslavia
Zaire
Zambia
Zimbabwe

COMMITTEES

General. Composed of 29 members as follows: The General Assembly president; the 21 General Assembly vice presidents (heads of delegations or their deputies of Bahrain, Bangladesh, Bolivia, Bulgaria, Chad, China, Cuba, Cyprus, Djibouti, France, Ghana, Guatemala, Iceland, Italy, Malaysia, Morocco, Togo, USSR, United Kingdom, United States, Yemen); and the chairmen of the following main committees, which are composed of all 159 member countries.

First (Political and Security): Celso Antonio de Souza E. Silva (Brazil)
Special Political: Alpha Ibrahima Diallo (Guinea)
Second (Economic and Financial): Bryce Harland (New Zealand)
Third (Social, Humanitarian and Cultural): Ali Abdi Madar (Somalia)
Fourth (Decolonization): Renagi Renagi Lohia (Papua New Guinea)
Fifth (Administrative and Budgetary): Ernest Besley Maycock (Barbados)
Sith (Legal): Gunter Goerner (German Democratic Republic)

THE SECURITY COUNCIL

Membership ends on December 31 of the year noted; asterisks indicate permanent membership.

Australia (1986)
Burkina Faso (1985)
China*
Denmark (1986)
Egypt (1985)

France*
India (1985)
Madagascar (1986)
Peru (1985)
Thailand (1986)

Trinidad and Tobago (1986)
Ukrainian SSR (1985)
USSR*
United Kingdom*
United States*

THE TRUSTEESHIP COUNCIL

President: Laurent Rapin (France)

China[2] France[2] USSR[2] United Kingdom[2] United States[1]

[1] Administers Trust Territory. [2] Permanent member of Security Council not administering Trust Territory.

THE INTERNATIONAL COURT OF JUSTICE

Membership ends on February 5 of the year noted

President: Taslim O. Elias (Nigeria, 1994)
Vice-President: José Sette Camara (Brazil, 1988)

Roberto Ago (Italy, 1988)
Mohammed Bedjaoui
(Algeria, 1988)
Guy Ladreit De Lacharrière
(France, 1991)
Jens Evensen (Norway, 1994)
Robert Y. Jennings
(United Kingdom, 1991)
Manfred Lachs (Poland,
1994)

Kéba Mbaye (Senegal,
1991)
Platon D. Morozov (USSR,
1988)
Ni Zhengyu (China, 1994)
Shigeru Oda (Japan, 1994)
José María Ruda (Argentina,
1991)
Stephen Schwebel (United
States, 1988)
Nagendra Singh (India,
1991)

THE ECONOMIC AND SOCIAL COUNCIL

President: S. Correa da Costa (Brazil)
Membership ends on December 31 of the year noted.

Algeria (1985)
Argentina (1986)
Bangladesh (1987)
Botswana (1985)
Brazil (1987)
Bulgaria (1985)
Canada (1986)
China (1986)
Colombia (1987)
Congo (1985)
Djibouti (1985)
Ecuador (1985)
Finland (1986)
France (1987)
German Democratic
Republic (1986)
Germany, Federal
Republic of (1987)
Guinea (1987)

Haiti (1987)
Iceland (1987)
India (1987)
Indonesia (1986)
Japan (1987)
Lebanon (1985)
Luxembourg (1985)
Malaysia (1985)
Mexico (1987)
Morocco (1987)
Netherlands (1985)
New Zealand (1985)
Nigeria (1987)
Papua New Guinea
(1986)
Poland (1986)
Rumania (1987)
Rwanda (1986)
Saudi Arabia (1985)

Senegal (1987)
Sierra Leone (1985)
Somalia (1986)
Spain (1987)
Sri Lanka (1986)
Surinam (1985)
Sweden (1986)
Thailand (1985)
Turkey (1987)
Uganda (1986)
USSR (1986)
United Kingdom
(1986)
United States
(1985)
Venezuela (1987)
Yugoslavia (1986)
Zaire (1986)
Zimbabwe (1987)

INTERGOVERNMENTAL AGENCIES

Food and Agricultural Organization (FAO); General Agreement on Tariffs and Trade (GATT); International Atomic Energy Agency (IAEA); International Bank for Reconstruction and Development (World Bank); International Civil Aviation Organization (ICAO); International Fund for Agricultural Development (IFAD); International Labor Organization (ILO); International Maritime Organization (IMO); International Monetary Fund (IMF); International Telecommunication Union (ITU); United Nations Educational, Scientific and Cultural Organization (UNESCO); Universal Postal Union (UPU); World Health Organization (WHO); World Intellectual Property Organization (WIPO); World Meteorological Organization (WMO).

The White House

The American electorate gave a popular president a new four-year lease on 1600 Pennsylvania Avenue.

UNITED STATES

"There is renewed energy and optimism throughout the land," President Ronald Reagan reported to the Congress in his State of the Union address on January 25. "America is back—standing tall, looking to the 80s with courage, confidence, and hope."

Although it was only to be expected that the president would offer a rosy assessment of the national condition in a year in which he would seek reelection (*see* pages 26–41), there was considerable evidence to support the chief executive's appraisal. The economy seemed relatively stable and strong, certainly by comparison with the period under the Carter administration, which was marked by skyrocketing inflation and interest rates, or with the dark days of the recession earlier in Reagan's own administration. And with the withdrawal of the Marine contingent from Lebanon, U.S. troops were no longer endangered by active combat elsewhere in the world.

Domestic Affairs

Americans could relax and enjoy the competition of the summer Olympics in Los Angeles, where the achievements of U.S. athletes engendered a surge of national pride. In September, *Time* magazine in a cover story on

"America's Upbeat Mood" reported in words that Reagan himself might have chosen: "Americans are feeling more sanguine and comfortable about their country than they felt in two decades." Still, some critics contended, there were flaws in the picture and limits to the economic gains the Reagan administration had wrought. In a 415-page assessment of "The Reagan Record," issued on August 15, the Urban Institute, a private, nonprofit research group, reported: "Even under optimistic assumptions, standards of living for most people will rise less than they did in the 1970s and far less than they did in the 1960s." The institute's report concluded that the "foremost" legacy of the administration was the federal deficits projected for years ahead, which the report warned could undermine confidence in government and threaten future economic growth.

Deficit and Taxes. While President Reagan's advisers challenged the conclusions of the report, and other similar criticism, no one could deny that the deficits cast a long shadow over the administration's plans and policies. As the president's fiscal experts grappled with the problem, their estimates of its scope fluctuated during the year. On February 1, when the president presented his proposed budget to Congress, it projected a deficit for fiscal 1985, beginning Oct. 1, 1984, of $180.4 billion. On April 10 that estimate was lowered slightly to $179 billion, and on August 15, in anticipation of vigorous economic growth, the figure was reduced even more to $172 billion. But in November, shortly after the president's reelection, David Stockman, director of the Office of Management and Budget, sharply altered the estimate upward. In meetings with other administration officials, Stockman was reported to have put the new deficit figure at $210 billion. The administration blamed the big jump on Congress spending more than it had been expected to and on the economy slowing down faster than had been anticipated.

Whatever the reasons, the changed arithmetic put the administration in a difficult position, particularly because during the campaign the president had promised not to raise taxes and also not to cut Social Security benefits or to squeeze so-called safety net programs for the poor. As the administration struggled to curb the tide of red ink, it was reported to be considering cuts in farm price supports, veterans' medical benefits, and retirement benefits for federal employees.

Meanwhile there was also speculation that the tax reforms to be recommended by a special Treasury Department study group might be modified to raise additional revenue—despite the president's previous pledge not to boost taxes. On November 26 the Treasury Department presented to the president its plan for a new, more simplified tax system. Basically the plan is a variant of the "flat rate" tax and would lower the taxes paid by individuals and increase corporate taxes. It was understood that the president would "review the Treasury's recommendations carefully, along with congressional and public reaction" and then submit his plan for tax reform, probably in his 1985 State of the Union address.

The Administration. Along with its fiscal headaches the administration was plagued by allegations of misconduct against high level officials. The first of these cases resulted from the resignation of Attorney General William French Smith, announced on January 22, and the president's decision to replace him with White House counsellor Edwin Meese III. When his nomination was submitted to the Senate Judiciary Committee in March, Meese, a longtime Reagan adviser and a staunch conservative, came under attack from liberal Democratic senators who complained he was too close to the president to be independent as attorney general and criticized his civil-rights views. But another line of attack, focusing on Meese's personal finances, developed.

Democratic Sen. Howard Metzenbaum of Ohio raised questions about Meese's relationships with several persons. Some were connected with the Great American Federal Bank of California, had helped Meese get financial help, and had themselves received federal appointments. Meese denied any wrongdoing. Then it was disclosed that Meese had failed to report, as required by disclosure laws for federal employees, that his wife had received a $15,000 interest-free loan from a friend, Edwin Thomas, who worked for Meese at the White House and later was appointed regional administrator of the General Services Administration in San Francisco.

Meese said he had "inadvertently" failed to report the loan. He accused his critics of making "false and misleading statements" about his conduct and asked for the appointment of a special prosecutor to clear his name. On April 2 a federal court panel, acting on the request of Attorney General Smith, appointed Washington trial lawyer Jacob Stein to investigate allegations about Meese's financial affairs, along with the circumstances surrounding his promotion to colonel in the Army Reserve, which the Army's inspector general subsequently had found to be improper. President Reagan expressed his continued full confidence in Meese. Meanwhile, though, the confirmation hearings were suspended pending outcome of the probe, Meese's nomination was set aside, and Smith agreed to stay on at the Justice Department.

Michael Evans, The White House

President Reagan confers with Chief of Staff James A. Baker. A former Texas lawyer, Baker not only ran the White House but also oversaw the president's reelection campaign.

Vice-President George Bush (center) *joined the new baseball commissioner, Peter Ueberroth (right),* Hall of Famer George Kell, *and more than 50,000 fans to watch the Detroit Tigers take the World Series. Earlier, the 46-year-old Ueberroth had served as president of the Los Angeles Olympic Organizing Committee.*

On September 20, Stein reported that he had found "no basis" for bringing criminal charges against Meese. His report made no judgment on whether Meese's conduct had been improper or unethical. President Reagan called the report a "vindication" of Meese and announced that if reelected he would resubmit his name to the Senate for the top post at Justice.

No sooner was Meese cleared of wrongdoing than trouble developed for another high administration figure. This was Labor Secretary Raymond J. Donovan who was named October 1, along with seven other persons, in a 137-count indictment charging him with grand larceny, falsifying documents, and filing false documents in a multimillion dollar scheme to defraud the New York City Transit Authority. The charges stemmed from Donovan's business dealings before he joined the Reagan administration in 1981, when he was head of a construction firm in New Jersey.

The first sitting cabinet officer in modern history to be indicted, Donovan pleaded innocent to the charges, took a leave of absence from his post, and denounced the indictment,

New Senate Majority Leader Robert Dole (right) *joins House Minority Leader Robert Michel as a GOP spokesman.*

which came five weeks before the presidential election, as politically motivated. The Bronx County district attorney, Mario Merola, who brought the indictment against Donovan is a Democrat. Donovan's activities had been investigated in 1982 by a U.S. special prosecutor who found no evidence to support criminal charges. However, the special prosecutor's probe was focused solely on the question of whether federal law had been violated. The Bronx County indictments were based on alleged violations of New York State law and according to the District Attorney Merola drew on evidence not available to the special prosecutor. Trial was expected to occur in 1985.

Following the president's reelection, another cabinet member, Education Secretary T. H. Bell, announced November 8 that he would resign at the end of the year to return to a teaching post at the University of Utah. Bell was credited with helping maintain the life of the Education Department, which President Reagan initially had intended to dismantle. On November 20, Jeane J. Kirkpatrick, whose post as U.S. representative to the United Nations has cabinet rank, disclosed that she planned to return to private life at the end of the United Nations General Assembly session in December. And as the month drew to a close, Lee M. Thomas was named to succeed William D. Ruckelshaus as administrator of the Environmental Protection Agency (EPA). Ruckelshaus, who had taken over the EPA in May 1983, had resigned for "a whole lot of personal things." When named, Thomas was overseer of the EPA's toxic-waste program.

Congress. As might be expected in an election year, the second session of the 98th Congress was marked by considerable partisan maneuvering and bickering. President Reagan's influence, which had been dominant in the early days of his administration, was noticeably diminished as the Democratic majority in the House of Representatives, reinforced by the 1982 congressional elections, sought to deny the Republican incumbent any advantage at the polls. A number of politically sensitive issues were sidetracked, and substantive legislative accomplishments were few.

In the national security and foreign policy area, Congress balked at the president's original request for $313 billion in defense spending, which would have represented a real increase of 13%. What was agreed to instead was a $293 billion appropriation, which amounted to a 5% real increase in spending. A presidential request for 40 additional MX missiles also encountered stiff opposition. A compromise agreement provided for appropriation of $2.5 billion for no more than 21 missiles. But actual production would require further congressional action in March. And Congress prohibited any tests of the antisatellite (ASAT) missile against a target in space until March 1985—and limited the number of such tests in fiscal 1985 to three.

The president's freedom of action in Central America also was restricted. Congress prohibited further aid to rebels against the leftist Sandinista government in Nicaragua until March, when approval of both Houses of Congress would be required for a presidential stipulation that the Sandinista government was undermining its neighbors. But a House measure to bar the sending of U.S. combat forces to Nicaragua or El Salvador was turned down by the Senate. And Congress did approve a substantial package of military and economic aid to the administration-backed government of José Napoleón Duarte in El Salvador.

Senate conservatives, led by Republican Sen. Jesse Helms of North Carolina, prevented approval of a treaty designed to outlaw genocide for which Reagan had sought ratification. The treaty's foes contended that it would undermine U.S. sovereignty.

Economic policy turned into one of the most bitter battlegrounds between the Republican White House and the Democratic House. The struggle over spending continued until the last hours of the session, becoming so heated that on October 4 the president sent 500,000 nonessential government employees home from work. He contended there was no money to pay them because Congress had approved only 4 of 13 individual spending bills.

On October 11, the day before it adjourned, Congress ended the impasse by approving a $470 billion spending bill to fund most government agencies through the end of the 1985 fiscal year. Earlier, after months of wrangling, Congress approved a budget resolution that set total outlays for fiscal 1985 at $932 billion. Also approved was a deficit reduction package designed to cut the deficit by $149 billion over three years. Included in the package was a tax component for raising $50.8 billion in additional revenues, mainly by closing loopholes, increasing taxpayer compliance, and raising cigarette and telephone excise taxes. In its final action of the session the Congress approved raising the limit on the national debt to $1.824 trillion. This was the third increase in the debt ceiling approved during the year.

Congress refused to give its approval to a Reagan-backed constitutional amendment to require a balanced budget. But the House, in an apparent attempt to exploit the deficit as a campaign issue against Reagan, approved a measure requiring the president to submit a balanced budget to Congress.

One of the most important accomplishments of the session was approval of a package of anticrime bills. These measures require federal judges to follow new sentencing guidelines, restrict use of the insanity defense, allow for pretrial detention of dangerous defendants, and establish a new interagency program for enforcing drug laws. Omitted, however, were proposals by the president to establish federal capital punishment and to modify the rules excluding illegally obtained evidence from being used against defendants in criminal trials.

Also, approved was an administration-backed proposal to curb drunken driving by

Sloan, Gamma-Liaison

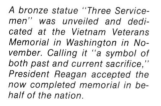

A bronze statue "Three Servicemen" was unveiled and dedicated at the Vietnam Veterans Memorial in Washington in November. Calling it "a symbol of both past and current sacrifice," President Reagan accepted the now completed memorial in behalf of the nation.

young people by withholding federal highway funds from states unless they raise their minimum drinking age to 21, a requirement on the states to strengthen procedures for collecting delinquent child support payments by withholding such payments from wages, a measure giving spouses the right to the pensions of vested workers who die before retirement age, a law establishing a specific standard that must be met before a beneficiary can be denied Social Security disability benefits, and a "Baby Doe" bill requiring states to establish procedures to ensure that severely handicapped babies receive adequate medical attention.

The Congress refused to act on presidential initiatives to provide tax and minimum wage incentives to economically rehabilitate inner city areas and to give tuition tax credits to parents with children in private and parochial schools. Also rejected was a Reagan-backed amendment to the Constitution to allow prayer in public schools—although a measure was approved requiring public schools receiving federal funds to allow use of school facilities by student religious or political groups if similar groups are permitted access to the school. On the civil-rights front, the Senate refused to act on legislation passed by the House to overturn a Supreme Court decision limiting federal action against educational institutions that discriminate on the basis of sex.

Another major proposal that Congress failed to enact was a broad reform of the immigration laws.

On ethical problems involving its own members, the House reprimanded Rep. George

Although an unknown number of aliens continued to cross the U.S.-Mexico border illegally, Congress was unsuccessful in its attempt to pass a new immigration law.

J.P. Laffont, Sygma

UNITED STATES • Information Highlights
Official Name: United States of America.
Location: Central North America.
Area: 3,618,770 sq mi (9 372 614 km²).
Population (mid-1984 est.): 236,300,000.
Chief Cities (July 1, 1982, est.): Washington, DC, the capital, 633,425; New York, 7,086,096; Los Angeles, 3,022,247; Chicago, 2,997,155; Houston, 1,725,617; Philadelphia, 1,665,382; Detroit, 1,138,717
Government: *Head of state and government,* Ronald Reagan, president (took office Jan. 20, 1981). *Legislature*—Congress: Senate and House of Representatives.
Monetary Unit: Dollar.

Hansen, an Idaho Republican who was convicted of filing false financial statements in violation of the 1978 Ethics in Government Act. Hansen later narrowly lost his bid for reelection. The Senate Ethics Committee called off an inquiry into allegations that Republican Sen. Mark O. Hatfield of Oregon had improperly helped a Greek businessman who had paid Hatfield's wife $55,000 for real-estate help. The committee decided there was insufficient evidence to make a case against Hatfield, who easily won reelection. The House Ethics Committee voted to investigate charges that Congresswoman Geraldine Ferraro of New York, the Democratic vice-presidential nominee, had failed to adequately disclose her husband's financial holdings. In December the House Ethics Committee found that Representative Ferraro had violated the act—but unintentionally. Accordingly, no sanctions against her were recommended.

With the retirement of Howard Baker (R-TN) from the Senate in January 1985, a major battle developed over who would succeed him as majority leader. In a tight five-way race on November 28, Sen. Robert Dole of Kansas emerged the winner. The Republican senators also chose Sen. Alan K. Simpson of Wyoming to succeed Alaska's Sen. Ted Steven as majority whip, and Robert Packwood of Oregon became Senator Dole's successor as chairman of the Senate Finance Committee. Since Sen. Charles Percy of Illinois was defeated in his reelection bid, the chairmanship of the Foreign Relations Committee became vacant. Senator Helms, the second-ranking Republican member of the committee, decided to remain head of the Agriculture Committee, paving the way for Sen. Richard G. Lugar of Indiana to take over as leader of the Foreign Relations Committee.

On the Democratic side, Rep. Thomas P. O'Neill of Massachusetts was chosen to remain speaker of the House, probably his final term, and Florida's Sen. Lawton M. Chiles, Jr., unsuccessfully challenged Sen. Robert C. Byrd of West Virginia for the post of Senate minority leader.

ROBERT SHOGAN, *"Los Angeles Times"*

Former Presidents and Their Families

During 1984, a year in which Ronald Reagan and Walter Mondale campaigned for the presidency, former White House occupants and their families were also prominent in the news.

Centennials. The 100th anniversary of the birth of Harry S. Truman, the nation's 33d president, was celebrated during May 1984. Although Truman's prestige was at a low level during his final days as chief executive, a recent polling of historians gave him a rating of "near great." Clark Clifford, Truman's former counsel and chairman of the centennial committee, pointed out that "every year he has risen in the esteem of the American people."

On the birthday itself, May 8, the president's only child, Margaret Truman Daniel, addressed a special joint meeting of Congress. Later in May, the Truman family home in Independence, MO, became part of the National Park Service.

Another centennial, the 100th anniversary of the birth of Eleanor Roosevelt, also was marked in 1984. In October, Val-Kill, the former first lady's home near Hyde Park, NY, was dedicated as a national historic site.

Nixon Comeback. Aug. 9, 1984, marked the tenth anniversary of Richard M. Nixon's resignation from the presidency. Although Nixon left the White House a disgraced individual, by 1984 he had become a sort of elder statesman. He now was a commentator and adviser, especially on foreign affairs; an author—his latest book, *No More Vietnams,* was scheduled for spring 1985 publication; a lecturer—in May, he addressed the American Society of Newspaper Editors; and a world traveler. The former chief executive was also involved in fund-raising for the Nixon library, which is to be built near the former summer White House in California.

In spite of his resurgence, the former president continued to refuse to apologize directly for the Watergate scandal that led to his resignation. In a 90-minute interview with Frank Gannon in April, he said, however, "There's no way that you could apologize that is more eloquent, more decisive, more finite, which would exceed resigning the presidency of the United States."

Presidential scholar Thomas E. Cronin called Nixon's comeback "astonishing." According to Cronin, "historians do not rate Mr. Nixon well because of the unforgivable strains on the presidency and the fact that he weakened the institution through his excesses of power. But aside from Watergate, his achievements with respect to détente and other foreign policies would have to be rated high."

Ford, Carter, Literary News. Both former Presidents Gerald Ford and Jimmy Carter addressed their parties' political conventions in 1984. President Ford maintained his busy speechmaking schedule and campaigned actively for Republican candidates. Although President Carter was an enthusiastic supporter of Walter Mondale for the presidency, he pretty much stayed away from the campaign trail. The 39th president devoted part of his time to his hobby, woodworking. Four chairs made by Carter sold for $41,000, which was to be used for the Carter library. In early September the former chief executive joined members of a nonprofit Christian organization that builds low-cost housing for the poor in rehabilitating a building in New York City.

Rosalynn Carter, meanwhile, enjoyed success as an author. *First Lady from Plains,* her memoirs, was a best-seller. New mystery novels by Miss Truman and Elliott Roosevelt, the son of Franklin Roosevelt, appeared in 1984.

First Ladies Conference. "Modern First Ladies: Private Lives and Public Duties"—"a substantive and serious inquiry into the evolving role" of the American first lady—was held at the Gerald R. Ford Museum in Grand Rapids, MI, April 18–20. It was attended by two former first ladies, Betty Ford and Rosalynn Carter; three presidential daughters, Susan Ford Vance, Lynda Bird Johnson Robb, and Luci Johnson Turpin; and Eleanor Seagraves, the granddaughter of President Roosevelt and a White House resident from 1933 until 1937.

First-family leadership, the first family and the media, and White House family life were areas that received special attention during the conference. The participants agreed that there was a real empathy among White House occupants and that the role of first families merits ongoing consideration. Mrs. Ford, its organizer, noted that the participants "have started not only what I hope will be a new but continuing project."

Benefits. In March the Senate Governmental Affairs Committee approved a bill that would limit Secret Service protection for former presidents and put new limits on funds for office staff and presidential libraries. Such expenditures for former Presidents Nixon, Ford, and Carter totaled $29 million in fiscal 1984. According to Sen. William Roth (R-DE), a sponsor of the bill, Americans "want former presidents to be treated with dignity and grace, but dignity and opulence should not be confused." Congress adjourned, however, without taking final action on the measure.

JAMES E. CHURCHILL, JR.

The Economy

It surged powerfully, even beyond the expectations of the White House, putting people to work, lifting incomes, boosting corporate profits, and even, some said, reelecting the president of the United States. The American economy was on a roll.

It defied warnings. It ignored forecasters, almost all of whom said the economy could not continue expanding at such a swift pace. By midyear, said the economists, the credit needs of public and private sectors would have them fighting for the same limited pool of funds. Interest rates would rise, perhaps prices too. The economy would overheat and the good times would end in a puff.

Prosperity and Fear. Even as the good times rolled they were accompanied by incessant worries, about the high valuation of the dollar, the preponderance of imports over exports, the big federal budget deficit, the fragility of the banking system, and the inability of America to compete worldwide in areas it once had dominated.

No matter, it was a year of enormous successes. Gross national product soared, personal income rose, employment reached record highs, inflation was held in check, interest rates fell, and consumer and business confidence were at levels that seemed unlikely or even impossible just two years before.

Weakness in the trade balance, however, was to an extent never even approached before. For the first time ever, imports exceeded exports by more than $100 billion, a consequence in part of a highly valued dollar that made U.S. goods expensive and, relatively speaking, lowered the price of goods imported.

Meanwhile, the 1985 fiscal year budget deficit—the shortfall between government revenues and expenditures—was projected at $200 billion, all of which would have to be financed from the same credit pool needed for business expansion and consumer purchases. Would

there be enough to go around? Already, critics said lenders had become too liberal in their terms, and as if to confirm it, 800 of the nation's 14,700 banks were classified as problems by the Federal Deposit Insurance Corp.

Continental Illinois Corp., one of the ten largest U.S. bank holding companies, was among them, requiring a federal government rescue mission to put up $4.5 billion to bail it out of trouble in the summer. Nothing of such magnitude had been tried before, but regulators maintained that if Continental failed, so would smaller institutions. Before the year was out, 79 banks would be closed, surpassing the 1937 total of 75 but remaining far below the 4,000 failures in 1933.

The banking system's problems were not limited to the domestic economy. Enticed by high rates obtainable on foreign loans, and assured by the feeling that entire nations seldom default, billions of dollars in loans were made to Third World nations. The debt of less-developed countries (LDCs) to Western banks, governments, and international agencies such as the International Monetary Fund stood at $810 billion as the year began, according to the World Bank, up from $766 billion in the previous year. Large borrowings tapered off in 1984, as commercial banks and the IMF demanded that potential borrowers first set their houses in order.

Bankers were encouraged as many of the LDC nations, including Mexico (owing some $96 billion), Brazil ($98 billion), and Argentina ($45 billion), strengthened their economies by restraining inflation and spurring exports. The modest worldwide recovery and the strong U.S. economy gave a major assist, creating markets for LDC goods that ranged from food to airplanes.

For the most part, U.S. farmers failed to participate in the good times. Crop prices remained low, interest rates on loans taken to expand during the good times in the 1970s became burdens, commodities markets were glut-

THE U.S. ECONOMY

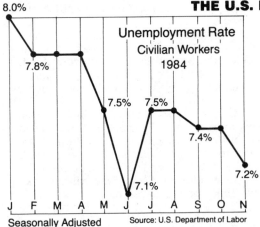

Unemployment Rate
Civilian Workers
1984

8.0%
7.8%
7.5%   7.5%
7.4%
7.1%
7.2%

J F M A M J J A S O N

Seasonally Adjusted   Source: U.S. Department of Labor

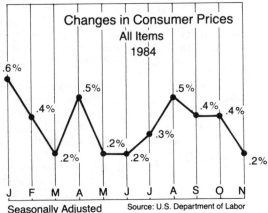

Changes in Consumer Prices
All Items
1984

.6%
.4%
.5%
.2%
.2%   .2%
.3%
.5%
.4%   .4%
.2%

J F M A M J J A S O N

Seasonally Adjusted   Source: U.S. Department of Labor

Productivity

Such economic indicators as consumer prices, Dow Jones average, and housing starts are regularly in the headlines and familiar terms for most Americans. In 1984, however, another economic barometer, productivity, received special attention. In fact, productivity was the concern of a national advisory commission. In its June report to President Ronald Reagan, the National Productivity Advisory Commission recommended additional reform of the nation's tax structure as a way to further encourage productivity and private savings and investment.

U.S. Outlook. During the U.S. economic recovery that began in late 1982, real gross national product (GNP) grew strongly through mid-1984. Productivity, as measured by real business product per labor hour, accounted for about one third of the rebound. In the latter half of 1984, productivity and real GNP were growing less rapidly. But by late 1984, many economists believed that the productivity slowdown that took place between 1973 and 1982 was over, and that productivity was returning to its long-run trend rate of between 2% and 3% per year. This view was based on the apparent reversal during the past several years of most of the factors that were responsible for the slowdown. A stronger productivity trend would continue to help hold down increases in labor costs per unit of output and in the general price level.

As indicated in the table below, business sector productivity rose at an average annual rate of 3% from 1948 to 1973. From 1973 to the last business cycle peak in 1981, the rate of increase was only 0.8%. This small increase was associated with accelerating cost and price inflation. Since the cycle trough in the last quarter of 1982, productivity rose at a 3.4% annual rate through mid-1984. The durable goods manufacturing sector has been particularly strong. Increases in rates of utilization of plant capacity have been a major cause of the productivity rebound. The slowing of the expansion in the last half of 1984 suggests that productivity gains also are decelerating. From here on the underlying trend factors will supersede cyclical forces in determining productivity growth.

Productivity advance averaging about 2.5% a year is a reasonable expectation for the rest of the 1980s. After declining as a proportion of GNP, research and development outlays have been rising for several years. New technology is being diffused more rapidly through a strong upsurge in new plant and equipment expenditures in 1983–84. Outlays for education and

U.S. Domestic Business Economy
Productivity, Labor Costs, and Prices
(Average annual percentage rates of change)

	Real gross Product	Product per hour	Average hourly compensation	Unit labor costs	Implicit price deflator
1948–66	3.7	3.2	5.0	1.8	1.8
1966–73	3.6	2.3	6.9	4.5	4.2
1973–81	2.3	0.8	9.2	8.3	8.1
1981–82	−2.8	−0.1	7.7	7.9	5.4
1982–83	4.4	2.7	4.3	1.6	3.0
1983–84 [a]	9.6	3.1	4.0	1.0	3.3

[a] Second quarter 1983 to second quarter 1984

Source: Bureau of Labor Statistics, U.S. Department of Labor.

training continue to rise, and the quality of education, as measured by Scholastic Aptitude Test scores, has been improving since 1981 after a long decline. Costs of regulatory compliance are leveling off after rising throughout the 1970s.

Stronger growth is promoting economies of scale, as well as raising rates of utilization of plant capacity. Labor-management relations have improved during recent years, with the spread of employee involvement systems that increase efficiency and reduce restrictive work rules and practices.

The productivity recovery and brighter future prospects have helped subdue cost and price inflation in the United States. In conjunction with a deceleration of average wage-rate increases to little more than 4% for 1983–84, the strong productivity performance has cut the rise in labor costs per unit of output to less than 1%. With price inflation of near 3.5%, there has been a smart recovery in corporate profits which continues to give fuel to the recovery.

International View. Most other industrialized countries, which also experienced a productivity slowdown after 1973, have not enjoyed as sharp a rebound in real GNP and productivity since 1982 as the United States. As a result, most have had a higher inflation rate, which contributed to the strength of the dollar. The rising dollar has helped to hold down U.S. inflation but has contributed to a widening trade deficit. Particularly hard hit are such U.S. industries as steel and footware whose productivity gains have lagged behind those of its major trading partners in recent years. But high-technology industries such as electrical machinery, computers, and pharmaceuticals, are doing well in the various world markets.

See also BUSINESS AND CORPORATE AFFAIRS; INDUSTRIAL REVIEW.

JOHN W. KENDRICK

ted, and many nations offered more intense competition in world grain markets.

In contrast, the automobile industry looked healthy again, but some observers wondered if it were so. They wondered if Detroit's success could have been achieved without Japan's agreement to restrain its exports to the United States. And they mused over what might happen should restraints be removed, as Japan repeatedly asserted they should be. For the time being the figures were impressive.

In addition, the success of autos disguised another deep concern about the future of America's industrial heartland, that geographic arc that dips from the Northeast beneath the Great Lakes and then northwest again, and which contains many heavy metal maufacturers with old plants, dated technology, and products unsuited to an affluent marketplace turning more to services than manufactures. Steel capacity, for example, fell to about 135 million tons at year-end, compared with 160 million tons in 1977. Imports, which American steelmakers claimed were subsidized, accounted for 25% of the domestic market.

While civilian unemployment dropped to a national rate of 7.2% by the end of the year, pockets of unemployment in the Midwest sometimes doubled that figure. And in geographic areas where high technology was king, the rate sometimes was only half the national average. At Christmastime, retailers in the Boston area, ringed by computer manufacturers, pleaded in vain for sales help. More than 5 million computers priced under $1,000 were sold throughout the nation during 1984, but manufacturers still were disappointed.

Indicators. But, in keeping with the style of economic 1984, for every disappointment there seemed to be a corresponding satisfaction, revealed by the statistics:

• Unemployment dropped from 8.2% in December 1983 to 7.2% in November 1984.

• Employment rose to 105.9 million, which was "more people employed than at any time in the history of the nation," said President Ronald Reagan late in the year.

• Consumer prices rose just a bit above 4% for the year, marking the third straight year of single-digit percentages after years of destructive inflation.

• Real gross national product (GNP), the total production of goods and services denominated in 1972 dollars to offset the impact of inflation, rose more than $100 billion, from $1.53 trillion in 1983 to $1.64 trillion in 1984. In current, or 1984, dollars, the GNP reached about $3.69 trillion.

• Disposable personal income, the amount left after taxes, rose to nearly $2.7 trillion from $2.5 trillion a year earlier.

• The prime lending rate held firm against expectations of a rise. It did reach 13% in midsummer, two points higher than in January, but it fell back to under 11% by December. And fixed-rate home mortgage rates declined to less than 13.5% in the final month of the year.

The stock market, however, seemed to reflect more anxiety than enthusiasm, with prices alternating between flurries and declines. The Dow Jones Industrial Average reached its high of 1286.64 points in the first week of January, fell to a low of 1086.57 on July 24, and closed the year at 1211.57.

The broadest measure of the economy, gross national product, raced ahead in the first quarter at a 10.1% annual rate, which almost everyone agreed could not be sustained. But the second quarter proved strong as well, registering a 7.1% rate of growth. Then came the shock. The July-September quarter showed a gain of only 1.6%, and the fear quotient rose. Economists forecast a recession to arrive early in 1985, and some even said the country was in a "growth recession," meaning a rate of growth so small that unemployment might rise and business might postpone expansion plans.

Outlook. Their fears were premature. While the economy had indeed run out of energy, it showed renewed signs of life even before the year was out. In a "flash" estimate in December, government economists said quarterly growth would approach 2.8%. The November jobless rate fell unexpectedly, and just as surprisingly, retail sales rose a strong 1.8%. Housing received good news in the form of lower mortgage rates, with conventional fixed-rate loans falling to an average of 13.42% from 14.05% a month earlier. And, a consensus seemed to be building that any recession was still many months away and that in the meantime a 3% growth rate seemed likely early in 1985. Other imponderables developed quickly, however, and with them came new worries and uncertainties. There would be tax changes, and at last the budget deficit—which had declined to $175 billion in fiscal 1984 but which seemed headed toward $200 billion in 1985—was to be faced.

The Department of the Treasury let it be known that it favored a sweeping tax overhaul that would simplify tax returns, lower the taxes of the poor, greatly expand the tax base by eliminating loopholes, and remove many of the tax deductions that business had become accustomed to. The pervasiveness of the plan surprised many people, but none more than those in business. The president was noncommittal.

A few days later the president unveiled to his cabinet a plan for reducing spending that would do away with many popular social and business programs. He also proposed that federal civilian workers be asked to take a one-year 5% wage cut, and he conceded that cuts might be needed in defense if budget deficits were to be reduced.

JOHN CUNNIFF, *The Associated Press*

UNITED STATES / SPECIAL REPORT

The Budget Deficit

Election year 1984 may well be remembered as the year of the deficit debate. As the campaign season drew to a close, no topic had generated more comments by the candidates than the record difference between revenues and spending by the federal government. Democratic presidential candidate Walter Mondale risked alienating voters by presenting a deficit reduction package that called for tax increases, while incumbent President Ronald Reagan defended his tax-slashing record of the previous four years and promised that the deficit would come down on its own. Growing prosperity accompanying the economic recovery, he said, would automatically result in increased tax revenues.

Reagan came to office denouncing his Democratic predecessors' propensity to "tax and tax, spend and spend" and promised to balance the federal budget in 1984. His economic plan called for massive tax and spending cuts. By the end of his first year in office, Reagan had largely succeeded in translating the first part of his plan into law. The Economic Recovery Tax Act of 1981 (ERTA) called for a 25% cut in personal income taxes over three years and included provisions that significantly reduced corporate taxes as well. But he was less successful on the spending side. Although Congress passed many of his proposals to cut spending for social programs, these were not equal to the drop in revenues provided for by ERTA. At the same time, an increase in military spending called for by the president pushed the budget further into the red.

The 1981–82 recession, the worst the country had experienced since the Great Depression of the 1930s, doomed Reagan's budget-balancing goal. The depressed economy generated fewer dollars than expected in tax revenues, while federal spending for such welfare programs as unemployment insurance soared as the recession put thousands of people out of work. Tax increases introduced in 1982 and 1984 were not large enough to correct the growing imbalance. By the end of fiscal 1984—Sept. 30, 1984—the federal budget deficit had ballooned from $59.6 billion in 1980 to an estimated $174.3 billion.

Deficits of this magnitude are without precedent in the United States. In the past, the federal budget has tended to register deficits in times of war, which necessitate sudden and massive spending increases. The imbalance was usually corrected, however, at war's end. This trend changed during the 1960s, when the administration of President Lyndon Johnson coupled spending for the U.S. involvement in

Marlette, "Charlotte Observer"

Although the Reagan economic plan has had success in certain areas, a $175 billion deficit is a big trouble spot.

the Vietnam War with increased outlays for its Great Society social programs. Since 1969 the federal budget has never been in balance.

But it was not until recent years—as the red ink passed the $100 billion mark—that the budget deficit became the focus of widespread public concern. While adherents to "supply-side" theory continue to believe that increased prosperity brought on by tax cuts will eliminate the deficit over time, most other observers dispute this outcome and say the federal budget deficit has serious effects on the economy.

Effects. In order to finance the deficit, say critics, the federal government must compete with consumers and private businesses for a limited pool of credit. By "crowding out" private borrowers, it is said, the government saps the credit markets for money that might otherwise be used for productive investment or for consumer purchases, and may thus retard the recovery now in progress or even disrupt it altogether and plunge the country into another recession.

This "crowding-out" phenomenon is also said to place upward pressure on interest rates. In vying for large sums of money to finance the deficit, the federal government increases the price of credit, the interest rate charged by lending institutions to their borrowers. Interest rates remained stubbornly high throughout the recession and eased only slightly in early 1984. A dip in the prime lending rate from 13% to 12.75% in late September—which the administration hailed as evidence of the validity of its economic policy—was attributed instead to a slowdown in the economy by many outside observers.

In addition to dampening economic growth, sustained high interest rates also make the dollar an attractive investment vehi-

THE BUDGET DEFICIT

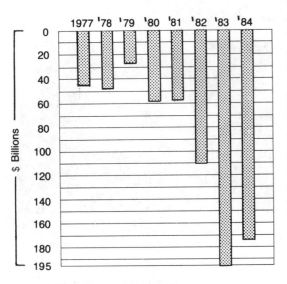

1977 '78 '79 '80 '81 '82 '83 '84

cle worldwide. As foreign investors have flocked to dollar-denominated securities, the value of the U.S. currency has risen steadily. As their own currency values have plummeted against the dollar, many European nations have complained that the United States is using their reserves to finance its own deficit. Another facet of the strong dollar, however, works to the investor nations' favor. As the value of their currencies falls in relation to the dollar, their exports to the United States become increasingly attractive to American consumers. At the same time, cheap imports put many U.S. businesses at a competitive disadvantage both at home and abroad.

Some observers of exchange-rate movements fear that foreign investors, convinced that the dollar is overvalued, may lose confidence and abruptly pull out of their U.S. investments. According to this scenario, the dollar's value will collapse and the vast pool of foreign reserves that has helped satisfy the federal government's borrowing needs will suddenly dry up. The resulting scarcity of credit would push interest rates even higher, precipitating another serious recession.

The federal budget deficit has also been blamed for aggravating the international debt crisis of recent years. By driving up interest rates at home, it is said, the deficit has made it all the more difficult for such Third World nations as Mexico, Brazil, and Nigeria to pay back the huge sums they borrowed during the 1970s to speed internal development. Many of these loans were made by U.S. banks, and interest payments are determined according to current rates in the United States. As a result, the amounts due by many of these countries have skyrocketed. Although Mexico's near-

default was averted in 1982 by a rescheduling of its loans, the fear remains that other debtor nations could face similar crises if U.S. interest rates do not subside in the near future.

The Candidates' Plans. The two presidential candidates addressed these fears in different ways. President Reagan continued to defend his policies and predicted that the budget deficit, after peaking at $184.8 billion in fiscal 1987, would fall to $161.7 billion in 1989. He promised not to increase personal income taxes in 1985 and blamed Congress for failing to pass the deeper cuts in federal spending he had requested during his first term. Reagan did, however, repeat his call for two controversial measures aimed at preventing future budget deficits. One is the "line-item veto," which would allow the president to veto single items of appropriations bills. Under current law such bills must be signed into law or vetoed in their entirety. Congress is considered unlikely to pass such legislation, as it would erode its own power in favor of the executive branch.

Reagan also voiced support for a balanced-budget amendment to the U.S. Constitution, which would flatly prohibit the federal government from spending more than it receives in taxes. Congressional approval of such an amendment does not appear to be forthcoming. But its supporters have come close to forcing Congress to call a constitutional convention for the purpose of writing such an amendment. By mid-October 1984, 32 state legislatures—only two short of the necessary three fourths—had approved resolutions in favor of the convention.

Both these solutions to the budget deficit were strongly opposed by Democrats, who called instead for an economic policy that would result in a balanced budget. Mondale based his call for tax increases on the budget projections of the bipartisan Congressional Budget Office, which foresaw a far more pessimistic budget outcome than the Reagan administration. By 1989, it predicted, the deficit would total $263 billion, over $100 billion more than the administration estimated for the same year. Mondale's solution would be a rise in income taxes, a cut in projected defense spending, and a cap on most nondefense spending.

But not all critics of the Reagan administration's budget policy embraced Mondale's alternative. The Bipartisan Budget Appeal, a trade association made up of some of the nation's largest corporations and headed by former Commerce Secretary Peter Peterson, called for immediate action to reduce the budget deficit but rejected the tax increases called for by Mondale as excessive. The coalition drew up its own plan to reduce spending and planned to lobby Congress for its support in 1985.

MARY H. COOPER

Foreign Affairs

The United States tried to steer a steady foreign-policy course during the election year of 1984. The Reagan administration sought to avoid the dramatic shifts in personnel and policy that had characterized its first three years. It also attempted to achieve successes in key world trouble spots to show the electorate. Its record was mixed.

Personnel, Management, and Oversight. The major policymakers remained George Shultz (secretary of state), Caspar Weinberger (secretary of defense), Robert McFarlane (national security adviser), William Casey (director of the Central Intelligence Agency, CIA), Donald Regan (secretary of the treasury), Jeane Kirkpatrick (ambassador to the UN) and William Brock (special trade representative). Unlike their behavior in previous years, the principals managed to avoid noisy public disagreements. The major exception to this picture of amity was Secretary of State Shultz's October 25 call for the United States to cease being "the Hamlet of nations" and retaliate swiftly against terrorism, even if that meant jeopardizing the lives of innocent bystanders. Most observers believed the secretary was criticizing the approach favored by Weinberger's Pentagon. In addition, there were year-end reports of general disagreement between Shultz and Weinberger.

Significant personnel shifts did occur, however, just below the top. In May, Donald Rumsfeld dropped his efforts as a special mediator of the Arab-Israeli dispute and returned to his position as head of the G. D. Searle Co. The administration did not name a replacement for him, relying instead on Assistant Secretary of State for Near Eastern and South Asian Affairs Richard Murphy. He did not resume conversations with Israel, Egypt, Jordan, and Syria until August. Similarly, Richard Stone, the special envoy to Central America, also left the administration on March 1 after a confrontation with Assistant Secretary of State for Inter-American Affairs Langhorne Motley. The administration replaced Stone with Harry Shlaudeman, a career diplomat who served in 1983 as the staff director of the Kissinger Commission on Central America. The highest-ranking career foreign service officer, Lawrence Eagleburger, also retired as under secretary of state for political affairs. Eagleburger, a symbol of continuity with previous administrations, joined his patron as a member of Henry Kissinger Associates, an international consulting firm. Michael Armacost, another career man, took over as under secretary.

More significant upheavals in congressional oversight of foreign policy took place. The new head of the House Foreign Affairs Committee, Dante Fascell (D-FL), was a much more aggressive critic of the administration than his predecessor, the late Clement Zablocki (D-WI). More changes were in the offing as a result of the November elections. Sen. Charles Percy (R-IL) became the third chairman of the influential Foreign Relations Committee to be defeated by the voters since 1974. He was to be succeeded by Sen. Richard Lugar (R-IN). In the House, Rep. Clarence Long (D-MD), chairman of the subcommittee charged with supervising foreign aid, also was rejected at the polls. Long, a loud dissenter from the administration's Central American policy, stood to be replaced by David Obey (D-WI), another outspoken critic of U.S. activities.

Relations With the Soviet Union. Washington and Moscow continued to be locked in a bitter and dangerous cold war. President Reagan appeared both to moderate his tone and assail the Soviets, who remained highly suspicious of the United States. On January 16 the president offered an olive branch with the hope that 1984 would be a "year of opportunities for peace." A week later Soviet President Yuri Andropov shot back that his country required "practical deeds" from America before relations between the two giants could improve. Already ill when he spoke, Andropov died on February 9. Vice-President George Bush represented the United States at the funeral and spoke briefly with Andropov's successor, Konstantin Chernenko, 72, a protégé of Leonid Brezhnev.

Relations stalled as Chernenko consolidated his power in the spring. Moscow watched in annoyance as President Reagan made a triumphal tour of the People's Republic of China in late April. Like Jimmy Carter before him, the president tried to enlist Peking in the struggle against Moscow. In May, Chernenko struck back with the surprise announcement on the 7th that Soviet athletes would not participate in the Summer Olympics scheduled for Los Angeles. Most of the Soviets' allies in Eastern Europe and Asia as well as Cuba and Ethiopia joined the boycott.

Little progress took place over arms control. Despite Washington's predictions, the Soviets did not return to the negotiations on strategic or intermediate-range missiles. In the winter and early spring, Democratic presidential candidates berated the administration for not enticing Moscow back to the table, a theme that the eventual nominee, Walter Mondale, hammered at during the fall campaign. Mondale assailed Reagan for being the first president since Herbert Hoover not to have met with his Soviet counterpart and the first since 1945 not to actively pursue arms control.

Partly to blunt these charges, the administration looked for signs of Soviet accommodation. In late June, Moscow proposed a September meeting in Vienna to discuss a treaty banning development of antisatellite and antiballistic missile weapons. These systems, designated a Strategic Defense Initiative by the administration and derided as a "Star Wars" fantasy by its critics, alarmed Moscow. Washington accepted Moscow's invitation to Vienna with the proviso that other weapons might be included in the conversations too. Resentful that the United States wanted to renew the conversations without first removing its Pershing II and cruise missiles from Europe (Moscow's condition for returning to the table), the Soviets canceled the Vienna initiative.

Relations deteriorated further in August. As President Reagan prepared for his weekly paid political radio broadcast on the 11th, he joked into what he thought was a dead microphone that he had "signed legislation outlawing Russia forever. We begin bombing in five minutes." Democrats charged him with irresponsibility, while the Russians considered the remark "unprecedentedly hostile."

Moscow, however, anticipated Reagan's victory in November. Accordingly, they looked for progress in the fall before polling day. Foreign Minister Andrei Gromyko, who had missed the 1983 session of the UN General Assembly because of the uproar over the Soviets' downing of a Korean airliner, came to the 1984 meeting in New York. He heard President Reagan make a conciliatory speech and met with both Shultz and Reagan during the week of September 23. White House officials were pleased to receive the Soviet foreign minister as a sign that relations had not collapsed totally. Once more, the Soviets asserted that they required "positive deeds" by the United States on several arms-control treaties or a declaration eschewing the first use of nuclear weapons before relations could improve. Additional Shultz-Gromyko talks were later scheduled for early 1985, however.

The Middle East. The administration tried to keep the Middle East from becoming an explosive issue during the campaign. Despite President Reagan's pledge in his January 25 State of the Union message that the contingent of 1,500 U.S. Marines were in Lebanon to stay, he removed them within a month. In early Febru-

ary, Lebanon's government collapsed and chaos reigned in Beirut. Restless Democratic members of the House of Representatives prepared a resolution demanding the Marines' withdrawal. On the 7th the president ordered them to ships offshore, but he allowed the battleship *New Jersey* to shell Muslim and Druze positions in the hills east of Beirut. House Speaker Thomas P. O'Neill (D-MA) complained that the shelling was "absolutely not" authorized by congressional resolutions.

The United States kept a low profile in the Middle East over the next several months. In mid-February two of its moderate Arab allies, Egypt and Jordan, had criticized American vacillation and unwillingness to push Israel toward peace. But America preferred to wait for a new government in Jerusalem before resuming an active mediation role. Washington hoped that Israel's Labor Party would return to power with a strong majority in the July 23 elections. That was not to be. The elections produced a deadlock in Israeli politics, not resolved until mid-September when Labor Party leader Shimon Peres patched together a national unity coalition of the nationalist Likud bloc and the more moderate Laborites. Deeply divided over the future of Israeli settlements on the West Bank, the new government did not appear to be in a position to make dramatic departures in the search for peace.

With the American presidential campaign in full swing by September, the Reagan administration had no desire to reopen the wounds of the Middle East. The calm was shattered, however, on the morning of September 20 when a suicide truck bomb once more devastated the U.S. embassy. Two Americans and several Lebanese were killed in this, the third attack on an American installation in 17 months. Lebanon once more became an issue in the presidential election campaign. Democratic vice-presidential candidate Geraldine Ferraro blasted the "negligence and incompetence" of the Reagan administration for the loss of life. The president avoided personal responsibility

AP/Wide World

In early February, President Reagan spoke in favor of the findings of the National Bipartisan Commission on Central America. Left to right: Sen. Charles Percy, commission chairman Henry Kissinger, Sen. Claiborne Pell, National Security Adviser William McFarlane, and Vice-President George Bush listen to the president's remarks.

for the lapses in physical security. He also suggested that congressional efforts to rein in the CIA had contributed to intelligence failures to predict the attack.

Representatives of Israel and Lebanon met in November to try to arrange a withdrawal of Israeli troops from the south of Lebanon. The United States played a subsidiary role in these talks. Having been burned in 1983 when an American-sponsored treaty between the two was rejected in Lebanon, the United States pledged only to support an agreement nailed down by the parties themselves.

Central America. The administration also tried to prevent events in Central America from clouding the electoral horizon. The National Bipartisan Commission on Central America, headed by Henry Kissinger, reported its findings on January 11. It acknowledged the local roots of discontent in Central America but also proclaimed that the region was ripe for Soviet and Cuban mischief. Noting a vital U.S. interest in the area, the commission recommended quick military aid to El Salvador and a five-year program of $8 billion in economic aid to the entire region.

The administration hoped that the commission's findings and the elections scheduled for El Salvador in March and May would quiet discontent. On March 25, Christian Democrat José Napoleon Duarte received the most votes, but Roberto D'Aubuisson, the leader of the extreme right, polled enough to force a runoff on May 6. A balky U.S. Congress refused to authorize additional military aid to El Salvador until after the runoff, won by Duarte. As soon as Duarte's victory seemed assured, President Reagan addressed the nation with a plea for additional military aid to the region.

Duarte proved an effective advocate for his cause. His visits to Washington in May, Western Europe in July, and the United Nations in October generated much sympathy among previously skeptical liberals. The meeting between government and leftist representatives on October 15 also encouraged hopes for a peaceful end to El Salvador's agony.

No such optimism prevailed on the subject of relations between the United States and Nicaragua, which slumped throughout the year. In late March, Nicaragua accused CIA-backed counterrevolutionaries (the *contras*) of planting mines in its harbors. The United States first denied the accusations but reversed itself in early April. Sen. Barry Goldwater, chairman of the Select Committee on Intelligence, erupted at William Casey, director of the CIA, and the Senate voted 84–12 for a resolution condemning the mining. The House followed suit.

Undeterred, the administration continued to pressure Nicaragua. In April the United States announced that it was not bound by any decision of the World Court taken in response to Nicaragua's complaints against U.S. harass-

ment. Washington denounced Managua's plans for elections on November 4, proclaiming that the voting would be a Soviet-style sham. When the vote took place as scheduled without the participation of the major opposition parties, Washington complained bitterly that the election of Sandinista leader Daniel Ortega to the presidency made a mockery of democracy.

China and East Asia. President Reagan's trip to China from April 26 to May 1 provided a grand opportunity for him to appear as a statesman. He dropped references to Taiwan while in China, but he did try to warn his hosts that communism is evil and religion vital for civilization. The Chinese television network prevented the broadcast throughout the country of such inflammatory statements, but China's leaders were pleased to have America's president extend a hand in the common struggle against the USSR. The two powers signed accords on scientific and cultural exchanges, economic relations, and nuclear energy.

South Africa. Just prior to receiving the 1984 Nobel Peace Prize, Bishop Desmond Tutu, general secretary of the South African Council of Churches and a leading opponent of South Africa's policy of apartheid, accused the Reagan administration of not doing enough to improve the racial situation in his homeland. At a White House meeting with the president, the bishop argued that the administration should impose economic sanctions against South Africa. The president, meanwhile, defended his policy of "constructive engagement" toward Pretoria. At the same time, antiapartheid demonstrations were occurring at the South African embassy in Washington and at consulates across the United States.

Throughout the year, the Reagan administration linked independence for South-West Africa (Namibia) with the withdrawal of Soviet-backed Cuban troops from Angola. In addition, the Reagan administration supported Mozambique as it reached a security pact with South Africa.

International Economics and Relations With the Allies. America's large budget deficit of $175 billion in fiscal year 1984 and foreign trade gap of more than $130 billion caused considerable difficulties for the United States in its relations with other industrial nations, most of which had not fully emerged from the recession of 1982–83. At the annual summit meeting of the seven largest non-Communist industrial nations, held in London from June 7 to 9, the six other powers pleaded with the United States to lower its interest rates. They pressed President Reagan for a guarantee of lower federal budget deficits as a way of reducing the debt burden of Third World nations. They pointed out that some $250 billion of Third World debts would come due in 1985.

ROBERT D. SCHULZINGER
University of Colorado, Boulder

URUGUAY

Amid much turmoil, attention in Uruguay centered throughout the year on elections that would bring a return to democratic government after 11 years of military rule. On November 25, 48-year-old centrist Julio María Sanguinetti was elected president.

Politics and Unrest. The year began with a crackdown on dissent by the government of Gen. Gregorio Alvarez. On January 18, however, a general strike was called in demand for wage increases, amnesty for political prisoners, and early elections. The government closed down three news magazines that carried reports of the strike and outlawed the Inter-Union Plenum, which had organized it. In February a number of political groups demanded the release of Gen. Liber Seregni, a leftist presidential candidate in 1971 and one of Latin America's best-known political prisoners. Also in February, the government announced that it was holding "only" 830 political prisoners.

In spite of setbacks to the democratization process in the early months, the National Episcopal Conference was acting as intermediary between the military government and the opposition. And by March there began to be results. On March 19 the government released General Seregni, although it barred him from voting or running for office for two years.

On April 1 a "day of peaceful national protest" was called by the political opposition—the National Party, Colorado Party, Civic Union Party, and the Broad Front. Two weeks later the government closed down two more opposition publications, and protesters took to the streets demanding press freedom and political amnesty. Police broke up the march.

Following 11 years of military rule in Uruguay, President-elect Julio María Sanguinetti, a former congressman, hoped to form "a government of national understanding."

AP/Wide World

URUGUAY · Information Highlights

Official Name: Oriental Republic of Uruguay.
Location: Southeastern coast of South America.
Area: 68,036 sq mi (176 215 km²).
Population (mid-1984 est.): 3,000,000.
Government: *Head of state,* Gregorio Alvarez, president (took office Sept. 1981). *Legislature*—Council of state.
Monetary Unit: Peso (72.38 pesos equal U.S.$1, Jan. 5, 1985).
Gross Domestic Product (1982 U.S.$): $30,000,000,000.
Economic Index (1983): Consumer Prices (1970 = 100), all items, 34,916.8; food, 34,870.7.
Foreign Trade (1982 U.S.$): *Imports,* $647,000,000; *exports,* $1,015,000,000.

A new element in the situation was the return on June 16 of Uruguay's most famous political exile, Wilson Ferreira Aldunate of the National Party. Returning by ferry on the River Plate, he was arrested by the Uruguayan navy and put in jail. The National Party broke off all negotiations with the government until his release, and other opposition groups also voiced disapproval. Then on June 27, the 11th anniversary of the military regime, another nationwide strike was called.

In early August the government reached agreement with the opposition (except the National Front) on a return to civilian rule. The regime agreed to repeal laws that permitted it to dismiss public officials without reason and to ban citizens from political activity, and also agreed to legalize the parties making up the Broad Front. Elections would be held November 25, and civilian government would begin March 1, 1985.

Still in jail, Ferreira could not run for the presidency, and the National Party named Alberto Zumarán, a journalist active in human rights, as its candidate. The Broad Front put up Juan José Crottigini. And the Colorado Party chose Sanguinetti, who had played a key role in the negotiations with the regime.

In a heavy voter turnout—about 1.9 million, of whom 400,000 cast ballots for the first time—Sanguinetti was elected with some 39% of the vote. In a speech the next day, he called for the support of the other parties "so that this government can consolidate Uruguayan democracy and forever bury the past." Ferreira, however, was expected to be released before the March 1 presidential inauguration and to challenge the legitimacy of the new government.

Economy. The economic crisis from which the country had been suffering for several years continued. Among the biggest problems that Sanguinetti would inherit are an unemployment rate of more than 15%, an annual inflation rate of about 50%, and a foreign debt in excess of $5 billion (U.S.).

ROBERT J. ALEXANDER
Rutgers University

In mid-May the city of Provo, Utah, fought unusually heavy spring flooding by laying down sandbag drainage channels.

AP/Wide World

UTAH

A Republican landslide in the 1984 election, a mine disaster along with an early "monstrous" snowstorm, and the selection of Sharlene Wells of Salt Lake City as Miss America were some of the highlights in Utah in 1984.

Politics. Republicans enjoyed a complete sweep of national and major state elective offices in the 1984 elections. With approximately a 77% turnout of the electorate, one of the highest participation rates in the United States, Utah supported the Reagan-Bush ticket by a 74% to 25% margin, far exceeding the differential in the national popular vote. In statewide elections, Republican House Speaker Norman H. Bangerter easily turned back a challenge from former Democratic Congressman Wayne Owens to become Utah's 13th governor and—under a new constitutional amendment—brought along State Auditor Val Oveson (R) lieutenant governor. Bangerter would be Utah's first Republican governor in 20 years.

All of Utah's three congressional district seats went to Republicans. There was "no contest" in the first and third districts, where James V. Hansen and Howard C. Nielsen, both incumbents, defeated challengers by majorities of more than 70%. In the second congressional district (Salt Lake County), the contest between Lt. Gov. David S. Monson (R) and Frances Farley (D) gave Monson a slim 143-vote margin after the outcome was delayed until all absentee ballots were received and certified a week after the election. Monson received 676 votes of the 1,023 absentee ballots certified and counted, increasing his margin over Farley to 472 (49.46% to 49.14%).

In the Utah Senate, the Republicans retained their 23–6 domination. Republicans added three seats to their predominant majority in the Utah House of Representatives (now 61–

14). Salt Lake County, the largest in the state, elected an exclusively GOP County Commission.

Utahans also approved five constitutional amendments, including one strengthening the individual right to bear arms and another revising the way judges are elected and permitting the legislature to create an intermediate appellate court to alleviate the Supreme Court's heavy caseload. Other amendments approved included the establishment of a trust fund to increase revenue for educational purposes; the creation of a 45-day annual legislative session; and a uniform registration fee for motor vehicles, boats, and airplanes in lieu of a property tax. A referendum on the regulation of cable television programming was rejected by a nearly three-to-two ratio. The constitutionality of the referendum was considered questionable, and a similar attempt by proponents had failed to pass the legislature.

Natural Disasters. A coal mine disaster brought grief and shock to the small commu-

---

UTAH • Information Highlights

Area: 84,899 sq mi (219 889 km²).
Population (July 1, 1983 est.): 1,619,000.
Chief Cities (1980 census): Salt Lake City, the capital (July 1, 1982 est.), 163,859; Provo, 74,108; Ogden, 64,407.
Government (1984): *Chief Officers*—governor, Scott M. Matheson (D); lt. gov., David S. Monson (R). *Legislature*—Senate, 29 members; House of Representatives, 75 members.
State Finances (fiscal year 1983): *Revenues,* $2,442,000,000; *expenditures,* $2,304,000,000.
Personal Income (1983): $14,555,000,000; per capita, $8,993.
Labor Force (May 1984): *Civilian labor force,* 696,400; *unemployed,* 45,300 (6.5% of total force).
Education: *Enrollment* (fall 1982)—public elementary schools, 275,145; public secondary, 95,038; colleges and universities (fall 1983), 103,324. *Public school expenditures* (1982–83), $702,033,143 ($2,013 per pupil).

nity of Castle Dale, in central Utah, just before Christmas. A fire in the Wilberg Mine, operated by the Emery Mining Co. and owned by the Utah Power & Light Co., trapped and killed 27 miners.

Salt Lake City experienced the worst snowstorm in its history on October 18. The storm, rising off the Great Salt Lake, had dropped 18.6 inches (47 cm) of heavy snow by noon at the Salt Lake International Airport. The storm triggered a 50-car accident north of the city, closed all schools, and temporarily cut electric service.

LORENZO K. KIMBALL, *University of Utah*

VENEZUELA

President Jaime Lusinchi's Democratic Action Party (AD) assured itself of political control for four years with a resounding victory in May municipal elections. Under an economic recovery program announced in February the bolivar regained most of the ground it had lost in 1983.

Political Developments. AD won an estimated 60% of the municipal vote, or 10% more than it had won in the December 1983 national legislative elections. In the Federal District (Caracas), AD took 46.3% of the vote while COPEI, the main opposition party, fell to 20.6% and the leftist Movement for Socialism (MAS) received only 7.3%. Opposition groups had tried to make the vote a referendum on economic policies introduced by Lusinchi after he took office on February 2. Despite compulsory voting laws, 40% of the electorate abstained.

Among the key appointees in a new cabinet was Manuel Azpurúa Arreaza, minister of finance, who was linked to big industrial groups on which the regime depended for the creation of new jobs. In other moves aimed at reviving the economy, Lusinchi named Benito Raúl Losada as president of the Central Bank in place of Leopoldo Díaz Bruzual, and Brigido Natera as president of the Petroven state oil company replacing Humberto Calderón Berti. The new minister of foreign affairs was Isidro Morales Paúl, an expert on international law and the maritime dispute between Venezuela and Colombia.

VENEZUELA • Information Highlights

Official Name: Republic of Venezuela.
Location: Northern coast of South America.
Area: 352,143 sq mi (912 050 km²).
Population (mid-1984 est.): 18,600,000.
Government: *Head of state and government,* Jaime Lusinchi, president (took office Feb. 2, 1984). *Legislature*—Congress: Senate and Chamber of Deputies.
Gross National Product (1982 U.S.$): $71,000,-000,000.
Foreign Trade (1981 U.S.$): *Imports,* $6,667,000,000; *exports,* $15,002,000,000.

The Economy. On February 24, Lusinchi revised the February 1983 tiered exchange rate for the bolivar in an effort to create 200,000 to 250,000 new jobs in the private sector. The preferential rate of 4.3 bolivars to the dollar was to be extended to business firms that employed more than ten persons and increased the size of their work force by 10% or more. Austerity measures included a cut in subsidies that had kept the price of gasoline at 40 cents per gallon in U.S. equivalents; a proposed sale or reorganization of state-owned companies such as the national airline and several banks; and a freeze on government employment—estimated at 20% of the work force of 6 million. New restrictions on price increases, money supply, and imports contributed to a slowdown of inflation, which was not expected to exceed 20% in 1984, compared with 25% in 1983 and 8.3% in 1982.

Lusinchi's measures closely paralleled suggestions of the International Monetary Fund in 1983 when Venezuela first attempted to refinance an estimated $34 billion international debt. Formal negotiations on rescheduling the public sector's share of this debt—about $27.5 billion—began on July 23. A combination of dollar sales by the Central Bank and rescheduling of the debt appeared to have reversed the bolivar's slide on the free market, where it had gone from 8 to the dollar in February 1983 to 17 in August 1983. By October 1984 it had recovered to a floating rate of 9.8 to 1.

The announcement in October that Great Britain, Norway, and Nigeria were cutting the price of their low-sulfur oil by $1 to $2 a barrel jolted Venezuela. The cuts were sure to have an impact on Venezuelan exports of high-sulfur oil to the United States for home-heating use and electricity production.

On August 3, Venezuela and Mexico renewed for one year the 1980 San José Energy Cooperation Agreement. The two oil exporters would continue to supply 20% of the requirements of Central American and Caribbean nations at a special interest rate of 8% on unpaid balances—or 6% if the balance was used for economic development projects.

Foreign Relations. Venezuela agreed with Colombia on February 17 to cooperate in eliminating drug trafficking between the two countries. And in response to a proposal of Colombian President Belisario Betancur, Caracas expressed hope on July 11 that agreement would be reached on their sea and undersea boundary.

Venezuela alienated the Sandinista government of Nicaragua by accepting Edén Pastora as a political refugee after an unsuccessful assassination attempt on the guerrilla leader's life in Costa Rica. Efforts were made to ease the Essequibo border dispute with Guyana through United Nations mediation efforts.

NEALE J. PEARSON, *Texas Tech University*

VERMONT

The year 1984 was one of dramatic political change in Vermont. In January, four-term Republican Gov. Richard Snelling indicated that he would not seek reelection. The Republican House speaker and Senate president pro tempore subsequently announced plans to retire.

Politics and Legislation. In the state's nonbinding presidential primary in March, Sen. Gary Hart won an overwhelming Democratic endorsement while President Ronald Reagan was unopposed on the Republican side. The president carried Vermont easily in November. At the same time, history was made by the election of Vermont's first woman governor, Democrat Madeleine Kunin, in a razor-thin victory over Republican Attorney General John Easton. While Republicans won all other statewide offices, the Democrats for the first time ever won a majority in the state Senate and narrowed the Republican advantage in the state House of Representatives to four seats.

The January-to-April legislative session focused on erasing a $44 million deficit, the largest in the state's history, without cutting deeply into social programs. Presented with a number of tax reform proposals, the legislature rejected the governor's plan to decouple the state income tax from the federal income tax. Currently the state tax is calculated as a percentage of the federal tax. The legislature chose instead to increase corporate and rooms and meals taxes and to impose a new tax on banks.

Environmentalists achieved a victory when the state legislature closed a decade-old loophole in a law that had exempted projects on lots of ten or more acres (four or more hectares) from development permits.

Legal Developments. A state Supreme Court decision curbed the jurisdiction of Vermont's unique system of lay assistant judges and called into question a large class of suits in which they had participated. The legislature attempted to affirm the voting power of the assistant judges in matters of fact, in order to eliminate the likelihood of mass appeals. The Supreme Court ruled this action a violation of the separation of powers, but itself affirmed the role of the assistant judges.

In a break with tradition, Frederic Allen, a Burlington attorney, was chosen as Vermont's chief justice to replace Franklin Billings, who became a federal district judge. Allen was the first nonjudge chosen to head the Supreme Court since the early 19th century.

Late in 1983 it was learned that Chittenden County (including the city of Burlington and the University of Vermont) had been placed on the U.S. State Department's list of areas declared off-limits to Soviet diplomats in reprisal for Soviet travel restrictions. A protest by Burlington's Socialist Mayor Bernard Sanders was overruled by the Board of Aldermen.

Train Disaster. On the morning of July 7, after a severe rainstorm, the Amtrak Montrealer was derailed near Burlington. With five dead and 150 injured, it was the nation's worst train accident since 1979 and Amtrak's worst accident in 13 years.

ROBERT V. DANIELS AND SAMUEL B. HAND
University of Vermont

Governor-elect Madeleine M. Kunin

Madeleine M. Kunin (D) joins Martha Layne Collins of Kentucky as one of two women governors. Born in Zurich, Switzerland, Sept. 28, 1933, the future politician was educated at the universities of Massachusetts and Vermont and Columbia's School of Journalism. Before entering politics, she was a journalist and college professor. The governor-elect has served as a state representative (1973–79), Democratic whip (1975, 1977), and lieutenant governor (1979–83). She is married and has four children.

VERMONT • Information Highlights

Area: 9,614 sq mi (24 900 km²).
Population (July 1, 1983 est.): 525,000.
Chief Cities (1980 census): Montpelier, the capital, 8,241; Burlington, 37,712; Rutland, 18,436.
Government (1984): *Chief Officers*—governor, Richard A. Snelling (R); lt. gov., Peter Smith (R). *General Assembly*—Senate, 30 members; House of Representatives, 150 members.
State Finances (fiscal year 1983): *Revenues,* $900,000,000; *expenditures,* $890,000,000.
Personal Income (1983): $5,242,000,000; per capita, $9,979.
Labor Force (May 1984): *Civilian labor force,* 265,600; *unemployed,* 17,200 (6.5% of total force).
Education: *Enrollment* (fall 1982)—public elementary schools, 64,181; public secondary, 27,273; colleges and universities (fall 1983), 31,306. *Public school expenditures* (1982–83), $266,700,052 ($3,051 per pupil).

VIETNAM

The Vietnamese economy continued to recover slowly in 1984 from years of war and peacetime mismanagement, but Vietnam remained one of the poorest countries in Asia.

As the year drew to a close, Vietnamese forces staged a massive attack against rebel Cambodian bastions along the Thai-Cambodian border. The attack left a large number of civilians dead and caused others to flee to Thailand.

Internal Developments. The government claimed that despite some bad weather, the agricultural sector produced almost enough food to feed Vietnam's rapidly growing population. However, the government sold some of the high-quality rice produced in Vietnam to pay foreign debts and imported lower-grade rice to feed its people. Industrial production also grew, but basic consumer goods such as textiles were scarce because some had to be sold abroad. According to foreign press reports, inflation was running at more than 70%, and many government officials felt compelled to moonlight just to make ends meet.

In July 1984, Communist Party Secretary-General Le Duan urged his party colleagues to accept pragmatic solutions to the key problems facing Vietnam. First of all, he defended the liberal economic policies that had been instituted about five years earlier—and that had recently come under attack by party theorists. These policies included a system of production contracts giving farmers an economic incentive to raise production; a system of piece work and production bonuses for factory workers; and the granting of considerable autonomy to the managers of export industries.

During the first half of 1984, the government conducted a campaign to crack down on all forms of private enterprise, which according to foreign press reports accounted for as much as 40% or 50% of wholesale and retail trade in some areas. The method used was to try to tax the private firms out of existence. But according to the Vietnamese press many of the private firms survived by bribing tax collectors.

In his July 1984 speech, Le Duan quoted Karl Marx to justify the system of production incentives. He told his Communist colleagues that only one thing would make workers produce: "their own interest." He quoted Marx as saying that "once ideology is separated from benefit, it is certain to disgrace itself." People who work harder, Le Duan concluded, "should receive higher pay and enjoy a better standard of living."

Foreign Relations. Broadening trade relations with the outside world was also of the utmost importance, according to Le Duan. Most of the non-Communist nations had sharply limited their economic ties with Vietnam since Hanoi's forces occupied Cambodia in 1979. Le Duan urged his colleagues to try to end this isolation while continuing to emphasize close economic ties with the Soviet bloc and Laos and Cambodia. He said that Vietnam badly needed Western markets and know-how in order to rebuild its ailing economy.

As a first step in this direction, Le Duan led a mission to India in September. He was accompanied by Foreign Minister Nguyen Co Thach and senior trade officials. India had developed a large modern sector in its economy, and it was a good place to send Vietnamese students to learn modern production techniques. India was also one of Vietnam's closest friends in the non-Communist world—and one of the few that had recognized the Hanoi-backed government in Cambodia.

Besides visiting India, Thach traveled to many Asian and European nations seeking to broaden Vietnam's foreign ties. Most countries in the United Nations had so far refused to recognize the pro-Vietnam government in Cambodia, but they wished to see an end to the guerrilla warfare that had claimed so many lives.

Before visiting Tokyo in October, Thach issued a statement that seemed to invite Japan and other nations to play a mediating and peacekeeping role in the Cambodian struggle. A few days later, however, a Vietnamese official at the United Nations explained that Thach's remark had been "distorted" by the press; what he had meant, the official said, was that Vietnam would accept international supervision or monitoring of a Cambodian peace settlement only after an agreement had been reached between the parties directly involved.

Meanwhile, representatives of the United States and Vietnam continued to discuss certain issues, although the two countries did not have diplomatic relations. According to press reports, there had been discussion of the question of allowing Amerasian children of American soldiers who served in Vietnam to go to the United States.

See also CAMBODIA.

PETER A. POOLE
Author, "Eight Presidents and Indochina"

VIETNAM · Information Highlights

Official Name: Socialist Republic of Vietnam.
Location: Southeast Asia.
Area: 127,300 sq mi (329 707 km²).
Population (mid-1984 est.): 58,300,000.
Chief Cities (1979 census): Hanoi, the capital, 2,570,905; Ho Chi Minh City, 3,419,067; Haiphong, 1,279,067.
Government (1984): Communist Party secretary, Le Duan; State Council chairman, Truong Chinh; Council of Ministers, chairman, Pham Van Dong.
Monetary Unit: Dong (9.79 dongs equal U.S.$1, March 1984).
Gross National Product (1982 U.S.$): $10,700,-000,000.
Foreign Trade (1982 U.S.$): *Imports,* $1,438,000,000; *exports,* $595,000,000.

VIRGINIA

In a year in which President Ronald Reagan swept the state in his reelection bid, a year in which Sen. John Warner became the first Virginia candidate to garner 1 million votes, and a year in which Warner's opponent, Democrat Edythe Harrison, was the first woman major party candidate ever to run in a statewide race, the name Virginians probably will remember most is that of Linwood Briley.

In October, Briley, who was implicated in 11 killings in the Richmond area, became the first person to die unwillingly in the state's electric chair in more than 20 years. But that was not before he had led five other killers in an exquisitely planned escape from death row. It happened the night of May 31—when the inmates, dressed as guards, disguised a television set as a smoking bomb and arranged for prison officials to provide them a van to drive away from Virginia's top maximum security prison. It was the biggest breakout from death row in U.S. history. Briley himself remained free for 19 days before being caught by a force of FBI agents and police officers in a South Philadelphia garage.

Elections. The November election results in the state mirrored those of the nation. Reagan won 63% of the vote, but Republicans did not manage any gains in the congressional delegation. Though Republican Warner, with 70%, won even more comfortably than the president, the two Democratic congressmen who had GOP opponents held their seats. The only new face in the delegation belongs to D. French Slaughter, a Republican and former state legislator, who won the seventh district race to replace the retiring J. Kenneth Robinson.

Legislature. The 1984 session of the General Assembly appropriated $10 million to support efforts to clean up the Chesapeake Bay. That's the same amount Congress approved as a start for the cleanup—an unprecedented, long-term effort involving Virginia, Maryland, Pennsylvania, and the District of Columbia.

The state lawmakers made the most news, however, by not taking action. It put aside for more study one of the most controversial issues of recent years—the proposed construction of a slurry pipeline to move liquefied coal from the mines in far southwestern Virginia across the state to the port of Hampton Roads.

Sports. Like the rest of the nation, Virginia cheered the winners in the Olympic Games, especially those from Virginia. Joe Fargis and Conrad Homfeld, two men from the Petersburg area who were little known before the games, became instant celebrities by winning gold and silver medals in the equestrian events. Pernell "Sweet Pea" Whitaker brought home to Norfolk a gold medal in the 132-pound class in boxing.

Long-suffering University of Virginia football fans also had reason to rejoice. The team made the national rankings for the first time in 32 years, and ended the university's dubious distinction of being the only major college never to go to a bowl game; it won the Peach Bowl, 27-24. The football success duplicated that of the basketball team, which fought its way to the NCAA's Final Four after almost not getting picked for the tournament.

ED NEWLAND
"Richmond Times-Dispatch"

VIRGIN ISLANDS

More than 70% of the 30,430 registered voters in the U.S. Virgin Islands (VI) turned out for the 1984 general election November 6 to select the territory's delegate to Congress, 15 members for the local legislature, and members of two territorial boards. The Democratic incumbent delegate to Congress Ron de Lugo, a nonvoting member of the U.S. House of Representatives, scored an overwhelming victory over independent challenger Janet Watlington. De Lugo garnered approximately 75% of the total vote cast. The successful reelection bid translated to a sixth term for De Lugo, who was the first to serve as VI delegate when the post was established in 1972. He sat out just one term (1979–81), when he ran unsuccessfully for VI governor. His goal in the next Congress, he said, is to sponsor enactment of the territory's basic "economic tools," such as the $35 million a year rum matching fund.

Twelve of 15 incumbent senators sought reelection to a two-year term in the VI legislature; only five were successful. Poll watchers predicted that the voters were seeking radical change in the local Senate makeup, but nearly all expressed surprise when official election tallies revealed ten new faces replacing many senior senators. Among the defeated candidates were Senate President Hugo Dennis and Vice-

---

VIRGINIA • Information Highlights

Area: 40,767 sq mi (105 586 km²).

Population (July 1, 1983 est.): 5,550,000.

Chief Cities (July 1, 1982 est.): Richmond, the capital, 218,237; Virginia Beach, 282,588; Norfolk, 266,874; Newport News, 151,240; Hampton, 124,966; Chesapeake, 119,749.

Government (1984): *Chief Officers*—governor, Charles S. Robb (D); lt. gov., Richard J. Davis (D). *General Assembly*—Senate, 40 members; House of Delegates, 100 members.

State Finances (fiscal year 1983): *Revenues,* $7,540,000,000; *expenditures,* $6,747,000,000.

Personal Income (1983): $67,240,000,000; per capita, $12,116.

Labor Force (May 1984): *Civilian labor force,* 2,808,300; *unemployed,* 120,100 (4.3% of total force).

Education: *Enrollment* (fall 1982)—public elementary schools, 682,630; public secondary, 293,097; colleges and universities (fall 1983), 288,588. *Public school expenditures* (1982–83), $2,381,954,532 ($2,620 per pupil).

President Bent Lawaetz. Of the senate turnover, Dennis said, "The 15th legislature has been extremely productive, but much of what we did was misunderstood."

Controversial measures approved by the 15th legislature include revision and stiffening of penalties for sexual offenders as outlined in the VI code; approval of a multimillion dollar turnkey development agreement between the territorial government and the West German firm Rogge General Contractors, including contracts for construction of a new cruise port on St. Croix, schools on St. Thomas and St. Croix, a marina on St. John, and an airport terminal on St. Thomas; extension of tax exemption benefits on a number of tourist-oriented products; and a number of rezoning proposals to allow the development of resort hotels, primarily on St. Thomas.

The 15th legislature also resurrected the question of status between the islands and the United States. Panel discussions on the issue were sponsored by a special Senate Select Committee throughout 1984, and a referendum containing various status options—including independence, statehood, or retention of current territorial status—is to come up for vote in 1986.

While tourism was up, industry was suffering. Hess Oil Virgin Islands Corp. threatened to close its St. Croix refinery—which employs some 800 workers—because of dwindling profits, and the Martin Marietta Aluminum plant also on St. Croix said it would close.

MARGARET ENOS, *The Associated Press*

WASHINGTON

The Green River murders, so-called because most of the bodies have been found near the Green River in southern King County, remained unsolved in 1984. Authorities say the killer has claimed 28 victims, all female, and 15 other missing women are believed to have been murdered. Most of the women were prostitutes or closely associated with prostitution.

On October 4, Wai-Chiu "Tony" Ng was arrested in Calgary, Alberta, and held for aggravated murder in Washington's worst mass homicide, when 13 people were killed in a gambling club in Seattle's International District in February 1983. Two other gunmen had been convicted for their roles in the homicide.

WPPSS Default. In November 1984 the Washington Supreme Court reaffirmed its June 1983 decision that sent the Washington Public Power Supply System (WPPSS) into default of $2.25 billion worth of bonds to build two nuclear power plants. The Supreme Court had ruled that 23 public utility districts and municipal utilities in Washington had exceeded their authority when they decided to sponsor WPPSS nuclear projects 4 and 5. King County

Superior Court Judge H. Joseph Coleman then ruled that the Supreme Court decision had so gutted the original agreement between WPPSS and the 88 sponsoring utilities in Washington, Idaho, and Oregon that the agreements were no longer enforceable. The WPPSS's announcement that it could not meet bond payments triggered the largest default in municipal bond history. Chemical Bank of New York and a group of investors then initiated suits seeking recovery of the indebtedness.

Despite the default on Nuclear Projects 4 and 5, the WPPSS celebrated the completion of Nuclear Project 2 in September. The 1,100-megawatt plant started generating electricity in mid-1984, almost 12 years after the groundbreaking ceremony.

The WPPSS's financial problems caused Nuclear Projects 1 and 3 to be mothballed until new energy forecasts could be made and financing arranged. Work had been scheduled to restart on Nuclear Project 3 in July 1985 and on Project 1 in July 1986. In September the Bonneville Power Administration recommended that the restart of Project 3 be delayed an additional 27 months and Project 1 be delayed an additional 15 months. When work was halted, Project 1 was 63% complete and Project 3 was 75% complete.

Elections. In the general election, the incumbents in every elective state office were returned with the exception of Gov. John Spellman (R), who was replaced by Pierce County Executive Booth Gardner (D). In the congressional races, each incumbent was returned except in the first district, where Joel Pritchard (R) had retired. His seat was won by former Seattle City Councilman John Miller (R).

Ballot Initiatives. Since a controversial 1974 ruling by federal Judge George Boldt that only Indians may fish commercially for steelhead and that Indians, under treaty rights, have the right to catch half the salmon in certain state

---

WASHINGTON • Information Highlights

Area: 68,139 sq mi (176 479 km²).
Population (July 1, 1983 est.): 4,300,000.
Chief Cities (July 1, 1982 est.): Olympia, the capital (1980 census), 27,447; Seattle, 490,077; Spokane, 171,903; Tacoma, 161,351.
Government (1984): *Chief Officers*—governor, John Spellman (R); lt. gov., John A. Cherberg (D). *Legislature*—Senate, 49 members; House of Representatives, 98 members.
State Finances (fiscal year 1983): *Revenues,* $8,353,000,000; *expenditures,* $7,908,000,000.
Personal Income (1983): $52,368,000,000; per capita, $12,177.
Labor Force (May 1984): *Civilian labor force,* 2,068,700; *unemployed,* 200,400 (9.7% of total force).
Education: *Enrollment* (fall 1982)—public elementary schools, 507,515; public secondary, 231,700; colleges and universities (fall 1983), 229,639. *Public school expenditures* (1982–83), $2,206,230,814 ($3,211 per pupil).

waters, the commercial fishing industry in Washington has sought, through various means, to negate the Boldt decision. In November voters approved an initiative to ask Congress to make steelhead a game fish off-limits to commercial fishermen and to declare that no one shall be denied equal access to fishery resources because of race, sex, or any treaty. Despite the favorable vote for the initiative, prevailing legal opinion is that the initiative will face serious legal challenge.

In an initiative that was watched closely by national observers, voters turned back by a narrow margin an attempt to repeal state-funded abortions for poor women.

WARREN W. ETCHESON
University of Washington

WASHINGTON, DC

The District of Columbia resisted the national trend and voted for Walter F. Mondale for president. Mondale had not been DC's original Democratic choice; the predominantly black electorate supported Jesse L. Jackson in the May presidential primary.

District Elections. Incumbent John Ray (D) and Carol Schwartz (R), a former school-board member, won at-large city council seats. The ward-based council positions were won by incumbents John A. Wilson (D), Charlene Drew Jarvis (D), H. R. Crawford (D), and Wilhelmina J. Rolark. Walter E. Fauntroy (D), unopposed, won an eighth term as the nonvoting delegate to Congress. Also elected were 323 members of 37 advisory neighborhood commissions throughout the city.

Shelter for the Homeless. The nation's first initiative guaranteeing homeless people the right to adequate overnight shelter was overwhelmingly approved, over the opposition of City Hall, which had argued that it would cost more than $60 million to provide overnight housing to as many as 15,000 persons.

Rhodes Tavern. The 184-year-old Rhodes Tavern, the city's first town hall and oldest commercial building, was torn down when appeals judges refused to issue an injunction order to stop demolition despite voters' approval of an initiative supporting preservation.

Home Rule. New federal corrective legislation provides that laws passed by the city go into effect unless both houses of Congress and the president disapprove any criminal bills within a 60-day review period, and any other legislation within a 30-day period.

Statehood. A bill to grant statehood was introduced in the U.S. Senate. The Senate bill matched one being debated by the House of Representatives.

Amendment. Iowa, Louisiana, and Delaware expanded the list to 16 states that have ratified the Voting Rights Amendment that would permit DC residents to elect full voting representation in Congress. The constitutional amendment requires the ratification of 22 more states by Aug. 22, 1985.

New Attractions. The Three Fightingmen statue, depicting black, white, and Hispanic servicemen in combat gear, was installed near the Vietnam Veterans Memorial wall, on which are inscribed the names of more than 58,000 men and women who died in the Vietnam War. (*See* page 543.)

The National Theatre reopened after a $6 million renovation at National Place, a new hotel-office-retail complex on Pennsylvania Avenue. Nearby, the 315-foot (96 m) Old Post Office bell tower and observation deck opened for visitors.

A memorial on granite blocks arranged in a semicircle, bearing the names of the 56 signers of the Declaration of Independence, was dedicated in Constitution Gardens.

Metro. The Red Line subway route was extended 6.8 mi (11 km) from the Northwest section into Maryland, adding five new stations and the longest escalator in the United States.

MORRIS J. LEVITT, *Howard University*

S. Dudley Ripley, retiring Smithsonian director, inspects construction of the institution's new museum.

WEST VIRGINIA

West Virginia's beleaguered bituminous coal industry continued to make the state's unemployment the nation's worst in 1984. By November, some 16% of the work force still was idle, a 1% improvement over 1983, but West Virginia was still one of only four states to have unemployment in double digits.

During a heated political campaign, marked by record expenditures by many candidates, leaders of both parties pledged to find ways of creating more jobs and of joining the national economic upswing.

Elections. Voters put the state in President Reagan's column and returned Republican Arch A. Moore, Jr., West Virginia's first two-term governor (1969–77), to the gubernatorial chair in a close win over former House of Delegates Speaker Clyde M. See, Jr. But they followed traditional Democratic lines in most other races. Retiring Gov. John D. (Jay) Rockefeller IV, 47, narrowly won the Senate seat being vacated by Jennings Randolph, a member of the Senate since 1959 and a former U.S. Congressman. Rockefeller reputedly spent almost $9 million in defeating Morgantown businessman John Raese, 34, who requested an impoundment of ballots shortly after midnight on Election Day. Nothing came of the challenge.

All four incumbent Democratic congressmen—Alan B. Mollohan, Harley O. Staggers, Jr., Bob Wise, and Nick J. Rahall II—were reelected. All five Board of Public Works positions went to Democrats, also—Charlie Brown, attorney general; former Congressman Ken Hechler, secretary of state; incumbent Glen Gainer, auditor; incumbent Gus Douglass, commissioner of agriculture; and A. James Manchin, moving from secretary of state to treasurer. The GOP recorded slight gains in the legislature, gaining 13 seats in the House of Delegates, where they now trail Democrats, 74–26, and two in the Senate, where the Democratic margin is 29–5.

Legislature. The legislative session early in the year was marked by expected struggles to overcome slumping revenues and to meet strident demands from public workers and teachers whose salary levels were among the nation's poorest—in many instances below the poverty level. A modest pay raise was implemented, and interim committees worked through the summer and fall to find revenues for continuing increases. But much of the session's work simply resulted in five amendments to the state constitution, which were submitted to the electorate in November.

Four amendments—empowering the legislature to institute a state lottery, authorizing a support program for veterans' housing, approving "voluntary contemplation, meditation, or prayer in school classrooms," and exempting

AP/Wide World

Jay Rockefeller (D-WV) was elected to the U.S. Senate. His wife, Sharon, was delighted by the win but disappointed that her father, Sen. Charles Percy (R-IL), lost.

intangible property from taxation—were approved. A multipurpose amendment, which, among other things, would have tacked on a sixth cent to the state sales tax and would have authorized a 100% excess levy in every county, primarily aimed at school construction and upgrading, was defeated.

Immediately after his victory, Governor-elect Moore said that his proposals to the legislature would include elimination of the con-

---

WEST VIRGINIA • Information Highlights

Area: 24,231 sq mi (62 759 km²).

Population (July 1, 1983 est.): 1,965,000.

Chief Cities (1980 census): Charleston, the capital, 63,968; Huntington, 63,684; Wheeling, 43,070.

Government (1984): *Chief Officers*—governor, John D. Rockefeller IV (D); secy. of state, A. James Manchin (D). *Legislature*—Senate, 34 members; House of Delegates, 100 members.

State Finances (fiscal year 1983): *Revenues,* $3,202,000,000; *expenditures,* $3,046,000,000.

Personal Income (1983): $17,997,000,000; per capita, $9,159.

Labor Force (May 1984): *Civilian labor force,* 760,600; *unemployed,* 104,500 (13.7% of total force).

Education: *Enrollment* (fall 1982)—public elementary schools, 266,950; public secondary, 108,165; colleges and universities (fall 1983), 83,202; *Public school expenditures* (1982–83), $957,532,433 ($2,764 per pupil).

troversial business and occupation tax, and the state's inheritance tax. He also indicated he would try to approach two political hot potatoes—the state liquor monopoly and collective bargaining for state employees.

DONOVAN H. BOND, *Professor Emeritus*
West Virginia University

WISCONSIN

Legislative action and controversies regarding Indian rights and school integration highlighted the year in Wisconsin.

Legislature. A ten-week session early in the year ended the legislature's biennial schedule, with incremental, rather than unconditional, progress on several issues.

The most notable achievement of the session was passage of a marital property law that makes fundamental changes in the system of property ownership that had been in effect since the state's territorial days. The new law establishes a shared-ownership or community-property concept for property acquired during marriage. It replaces the historic principle that property generally belongs to the breadwinner of the family.

With an eye to the November elections, legislators took advantage of an improving economy to eliminate a 10% income-tax surcharge that was imposed in 1983. The state in that year faced a revenue gap but in 1984 found that it might have a surplus of up to $500 million by mid-1985.

But the Democratic-controlled legislature put its own stamp on other measures. A bill endorsed by Democratic Gov. Anthony S. Earl to impose 24 credits as a minimum graduation standard for local schools was reduced to 13.5 credits. A measure to control acid rain ended up as a version establishing limits on sulfur-dioxide emissions of electric generating plants but setting no limits at all on paper mills. A measure designed to protect groundwater shifted to the taxpayer the cost of a program helping to pay for replacement of contaminated private wells.

Elections. With no statewide office up for election, there was little excitement beyond the presidential campaign for Wisconsin voters. There were also a few surprises in the results. President Reagan carried the state by a 55%–45% margin. All five Democratic congressmen and the four Republicans were reelected easily. Republicans gained seven seats in the Assembly, giving them 47 seats in the 99-member body. Democrats, however, gained one seat in the state Senate, and the 1985 Senate will have 19 Democrats and 14 Republicans.

Indian Controversy. The normal tranquility of Wisconsin's north woods was jarred by a controversy over hunting and fishing rights granted Chippewa Indians. The ruling, issued by a federal court in 1983, upheld the rights of about 12,000 Chippewas to hunt, fish, and gather wild rice on territory the tribes had ceded to the United States in the mid-1800s. As Indians started a 71-day rifle deer season, non-Indians voiced opposition. A group called Equal Rights for Everyone gained thousands of members; white hunters picketed the opening day of the deer season; bumper stickers proclaimed "Shoot an Indian, save 25 deer"; and people were warned not to walk in the woods. State and Indian leaders were attempting to cool tempers.

School Desegregation. In an action that capped two years of controversy, the Milwaukee School Board filed suit against the state of Wisconsin and 24 suburban school districts, charging that longtime policies had confined black students to city schools. The suit charged that the policies had created a racially dual structure of public education, and it asked the federal court to declare the schools unconstitutionally segregated. It asked the court to reorganize and consolidate school districts, create magnet schools, assign students to reduce segregation, desegregate faculty and staff, and order other programs to overcome the effects of past discrimination. The suit was being watched because it has been filed by the School Board, rather than a private group, and because it alleges violations of both the Wisconsin and U.S. constitutions.

Economy. Since the worst of the recession of the early 1980s, the state has recovered more than 60,000 jobs in nonfarm wage and salary employment but still remained below the prerecession total. For 1984 as a whole, employment growth was expected to be 3.4%; manufacturing job growth was expected to be up 5.3% over 1983. Personal income, adjusted for inflation, was projected to be $23.6 billion, a gain of 6.4% over 1983.

PAUL SALSINI
"The Milwaukee Journal"

WISCONSIN • Information Highlights

Area: 56,153 sq mi (145 436 km²).
Population (July 1, 1983 est.): 4,751,000.
Chief Cities (July 1, 1982 est.): Madison, the capital, 172,640; Milwaukee, 631,509; Green Bay (1980 census), 87,899.
Government (1984): *Chief Officers*—governor, Anthony S. Earl (D); lt. gov., James T. Flynn (D). *Legislature*—Senate, 33 members; Assembly, 99 members.
State Finances (fiscal year 1983): *Revenues,* $8,545,000,000; *expenditures,* $7,633,000,000.
Personal Income (1983): $53,935,000,000; per capita, $11,352.
Labor Force (May 1984): *Civilian labor force,* 2,428,600; *unemployed,* 167,600 (6.9% of total force).
Education: *Enrollment* (fall 1982)—public elementary schools, 503,871; public secondary, 280,959; colleges and universities (fall 1983), 277,751. *Public school expenditures* (1982–83), $2,308,552,461 ($3,237 per pupil).

WOMEN

Women's issues gained increased public attention during 1984. In the United States this was partly a result of the role being played by women in politics (*see* feature article, page 36), but concern over women's economic position and status in society also was in evidence. The economic and social position of women drew attention in other countries as well. In Japan new legislation promoting equal opportunity in employment for women was widely debated. In Canada women voters were considered a key factor in the September election that brought the Progressive Conservative Party, led by Brian Mulroney, to power.

Economic Issues. A U.S. Census Bureau study released early in the year showed that women continued to lag behind men in earning power. Women have joined the work force in increasing numbers (some 63% of women above the age of 16 held jobs in 1984, compared with about 31% in 1954) and have made inroads in such traditionally male professions as law, medicine, and engineering. But the study showed that a woman with a four-year college education could expect to earn just 83% of what a similarly qualified man would earn as a starting salary, and that she could expect her lifetime earnings to be considerably less.

One explanation for the disparity, according to women's rights groups, was that such traditional "pink-collar" occupations as secretarial work had been undervalued by men who set salaries. In 1984, lawsuits demanding comparable pay for "comparable worth" were brought to court in several states, including Michigan, New York, and Washington.

Meanwhile, although greater numbers of women held management positions, top-level jobs continued to elude them. Women won two lawsuits charging discrimination in high-level employment. Christine Craft, a news anchor, won $325,000 in a retrial of her 1983 suit against a Kansas City TV station that she said had demoted her because of her appearance. And the U.S. Supreme Court ruled in favor of Elizabeth Hishon, a lawyer who contended that an Atlanta law firm had practiced discrimination by not inviting her to become a partner after seven years of employment.

Congress in 1984 passed legislation designed to help the two groups of women most often afflicted with poverty—older women and single mothers. The Retirement Equity Act of 1984 prohibits pension plans from counting a one-year maternity leave as a break in service, increases the access of widows to survivor's benefits, and allows state courts to apportion pension benefits in divorce cases. A second new law was adopted to set up a system for enforcing child support payments.

Pension benefits, however, continued to be lower for women than for men. Payments from private pensions, based on actuarial tables showing women living longer than men, averaged about $3,000 per year for women and about $4,700 per year for men. At the same time, other actuarial tables resulted in higher rates for women for health and other insurance. After the defeat in Congress early in the year of a bill requiring equal insurance, the National Organization for Women (NOW) took its case to court and filed suit against Mutual of Omaha, the country's largest health insurer, charging that the company illegally overcharged women.

Social Issues. Coupled with the increase in working women has been a tendency for women to postpone childbearing and to have fewer children. In 1984 this trend continued to be strongest among white and highly educated groups. It was seen as a boon to some sectors of the economy and a bane to others. Couples with few or no children have more income available for luxury items, but they are less likely to support schools and other child-related services.

Outside the workplace, there were both gains and setbacks in the area of women's rights. The year saw the end of a 12-year court battle between the U.S. Jaycees, a civic organization for young men, and the Minnesota chapter of the group, which wanted to admit women. The U.S. Supreme Court ruled in July that laws barring discrimination in public accommodations applied to the organization.

Another Supreme Court decision was seen by many women as a setback. In a case involving Grove City College in Pennsylvania, the court gave a narrow interpretation to federal civil rights laws. It ruled that laws banning federal funds for institutions that discriminate apply only to the specific programs that are funded, not to the entire school. In an effort to restore the broader meaning, a new civil rights bill was passed by the House of Representatives, but a similar Senate bill was blocked in committee. In early October, as the end of the congressional session drew near, there was an unsuccessful attempt to attach it as a rider to a last-minute spending bill.

The problems of battered women also received attention during the year. In another key court decision, the New Jersey Supreme Court ruled that expert testimony on the behavior of battered women could be admitted to help such women establish claims of self-defense in murder cases. Expert testimony, the court said, could help bring out the fact that battered women are often unable to leave their abusers for psychological or financial reasons. The ruling came on an appeal by a New Jersey woman who was convicted of reckless manslaughter for killing her husband in 1980 after numerous beatings. Similar testimony has been allowed by high courts in Washington, Maine, and Georgia but barred in Ohio and Wyoming.

ELAINE PASCOE, *Free-lance Writer*

WYOMING

Marginal improvement in the state's economy and the politics of a general election year dominated the news in Wyoming during 1984.

The Economy. Agricultural economic news of significance included a report by the U.S. Department of Agriculture indicating that farmland, including buildings, had an average worth in Wyoming of $165 per acre, the lowest amount of any of the states in the country. In late April, typically unpredictable weather dealt ranchers a severe blow when blizzards with subzero temperatures swept northern portions of the state. Much young livestock perished, and stockmen in some counties lost up to 80% of their sheep and cattle.

Less dramatic but more significant was the recession that continued to weaken the state's mineral industry. Accounting for 70% of Wyoming's tax base, the industry includes five key products: coal, natural gas, oil, trona (soda ash), and uranium. Where found on federal lands, the minerals also provide the state with federal royalty payments. In 1984 the market price for each resource fell appreciably. The production of coal, gas, oil, and trona increased, but only slightly. The price drop was good news for the national economy, but the state continued in a budgetary squeeze, lacking substantial production increases. Royalty payments, $165 million in 1984, were down 16% from the previous year, and the state's total mineral valuation dropped about a percentage point as well. Cost and marketing problems and legal and political opposition by the railroad industry triggered cancellation of several large-scale coal slurry pipelines. Indicating some recovery, oil drilling activity in the state increased by about 10% in 1984.

The adjusted unemployment rate, about 5% by late summer, was down three percentage points from 1983. This differential appeared to be more the result of an out-migration of workers than any solid expansion in the economy.

WYOMING • Information Highlights

Area: 97,809 sq mi (253 326 km²).
Population (July 1, 1983 est.): 514,000.
Chief Cities (1980 census): Cheyenne, the capital, 47,283; Casper, 51,016; Laramie, 24,410.
Government (1984): Chief Officers—governor, Ed Herschler (D); secy. of state, Thyra Thomson (R). Legislature—Senate, 30 members; House of Representatives, 64 members.
State Finances (fiscal year 1983): Revenues, $1,597,000,000; expenditures, $1,263,000,000.
Personal Income (1983): $6,126,000,000; per capita, $11,911.
Labor Force (May 1984): Civilian labor force, 259,900; unemployed, 16,300 (6.3% of total force).
Education: Enrollment (fall 1982)—public elementary schools, 74,396; public secondary, 27,269; colleges and universities (fall 1983), 23,844. Public school expenditures (1982–83), $382,181,627 ($4,045 per pupil).

Budget and Politics. In February the legislature met in its off-year budget session and made supplementary appropriations to Gov. Ed Herschler's "no-growth" budget, adopted in 1983. A total expenditure of $1.954 billion was authorized. Included in that amount was $643.3 million from the general fund for state operations and $24.9 million for capital construction.

In the November elections Wyoming voters cast 196,153 ballots (official count), clearly a state record. The figure represented a 82% voter turnout, one of the nation's highest. President Reagan carried every county and 68% of the total vote, six percentage points better than he had done in 1980. U.S. Sen. Alan Simpson (R) was returned for a second term with 78% of the vote. He defeated Victor Ryan (D), a political unknown and retired professor from Laramie. Simpson subsequently was chosen Senate majority whip.

Incumbent Rep. Dick Cheney (R) carried 74% of the vote in his victory over Laramie lawyer Hugh McFadden, Jr. (D). The elections strengthened a Republican majority in the state House of Representatives by eight seats. The split in the newly elected legislature is 46 Republicans and 18 Democrats. The party division in the Senate remains unchanged with 19 Republicans and 11 Democrats.

Other Events. Great Britain's Queen Elizabeth II spent several days during her October U.S. visit as a guest of the Wallop family on their ranch near Sheridan. Owned by U.S. Sen. Malcolm Wallop, the property dates from the 1880s when it was settled by his grandfather, a son of the Earl of Portsmouth.

H. R. DIETERICH
University of Wyoming

YUGOSLAVIA

Disagreements among the leaders of the ruling League of Communists of Yugoslavia (LCY), the name of Yugoslavia's Communist Party, dominated the political life of the country in 1984 and intensified Yugoslavia's socioeconomic crisis. The nation was particularly proud, however, to serve as host of the 1984 Winter Olympic Games (*see* page 470).

Domestic Affairs. On May 15 both chambers of the Assembly of the Socialist Federal Republic of Yugoslavia (SFRY) confirmed the election of Yugoslavia's collective presidency, which consists of a nine-member leadership that serves five years. On the same day the government was reshuffled. The ethnic Muslim Raif Dizdarević became foreign minister, while Dobroslav Ćulafić, a Montenegrin with a reputation as a hard-liner, was given the post of minister of the interior.

The 13th plenum of the LCY's central committee took place in Belgrade on June 12–13. It

Renate Flottau, Photo Trends

A new memorial to the late Marshal Tito was unveiled in the city of Skopje. Ideological and policy differences now divide the party, but the cult of Tito endures.

was devoted to ideological questions. Deep conflicts were revealed among the committee's 163 members, who could not even agree on a statement summarizing the conclusions of the meeting. The committee, however, took an unprecedented step in submitting to 2.2 million LCY members in their 70,000 organizations a long questionnaire dealing with the party's role in Yugoslavia. The answers were to be used in the preparation of the next party congress. A preliminary report on the results of the questionnaire proved to be startling. The London *Economist* of October 27 reported that party members at the grass roots level expressed resentment over the perquisites and privileges enjoyed by members in the higher echelons of the party and denounced corruption in party ranks.

Although the party seemed so badly split that a showdown between the leading antagonists might prove to be unavoidable, the party did act decisively in its handling of political dissenters. On April 20 a group of 28 people attending a seminar in Belgrade, including Milovan Djilas, the world-famous critic of Titoism, was held for questioning, then released. It was reported later that one of the group, Ra-

domir Radović, the only worker among the 28, had subsequently taken his life. A petition addressed to the authorities by his friends asked for a full disclosure of the events surrounding his death. Early in the summer a participant in the seminar, Vojislav Šešelj, a former sociology instructor at the University of Sarajevo, was arrested and sentenced to eight years in prison for "committing the criminal act of posing as a counterrevolutionary threat to the social system" in Yugoslavia. Six Serbians, all of them intellectuals who had attended the seminar, also were arrested and accused of activities aimed at overthrowing Communist rule. But in spite of these arrests there were signs that the leaders of the LCY disagreed on how to cope with intellectual dissenters, just as they disagreed on how to deal with nonconformist writers and artists.

There was no major change in the situation plaguing the autonomous province of Kosovo, where more than three quarters of the population are ethnic Albanians. The authorities responded to the anti-Yugoslav activity of the militant Albanians with arrests and stiff court penalties. Continuing antagonism between the Serbian minority and the Albanian majority in the province led to further Serbian emigration from Kosovo. Military leaders indicated their displeasure with the inability of the party's civilian leaders to solve the Kosovo problem and hinted that the Army's patience had its limits.

Church-state relations were complicated by a religious revival in Yugoslavia. The activities of all the major churches had an ethnic and political coloration that was not acceptable to the regime. On September 8–9 the Catholic Church of Croatia celebrated 13 centuries of Christianity in Croatia. A huge crowd attended the Mass held in Marija Bistrica, a small village near Zagreb. A papal envoy attended the ceremony. The Serbian Orthodox Church continued to express its alarm over the situation in Kosovo, where churches and monasteries were being destroyed or desecrated. An Islamic revival with fundamentalist undertones worried the authorities, although the Muslims in Yugoslavia were far from being united in their aspirations.

Economy. The first half of 1984 witnessed a modest economic recovery as industrial production increased and exports rose. The nation's grain harvest was satisfactory, though smaller than in 1983. However, despite two price freezes during the year, the rate of inflation spiraled upward, threatening to exceed 100% by the end of the year. Unemployment was also high, with at least 13% of the labor force out of work.

The Long-Term Stabilization Program, adopted in principle in July 1983, was to have introduced elements of private enterprise into Yugoslavia's socialist economy. While Prime

YUGOSLAVIA · Information Highlights

Official Name: Socialist Federal Republic of Yugo-slavia.
Location: Southwestern Europe.
Area: 99,000 sq mi (256 409 km²).
Population (mid-1984 est.): 23,000,000.
Chief Cities (1981 census): Belgrade, the capital, 1,470,073; Osijek, 867,646; Zagreb, 768,700; Niš, 643,470.
Government: *Head of state,* Veselin Djuranović, president (took office May 15, 1984). *Head of government,* Milka Planinc, prime minister (took office May 1982). *Legislature*—Federal Assembly: Federal Chamber and Chamber of Republics and Provinces.
Monetary Unit: New Dinar (165.7 dinars equal U.S.$1, August 1984).
Gross National Product (1982 U.S.$): $53,900,-000,000.
Economic Indexes (1983): *Consumer Prices* (1970 = 100), all items, 1,470.6; food, 1,704.7; *Industrial Production* (1975 = 100), 146.
Foreign Trade (1983 U.S.$): *Imports,* $11,104,-000,000; *exports,* $9,038,000,000.

Minister Milka Planinc argued forcefully in favor of the plan, influential segments within the party claimed that private enterprise might undermine Yugoslavia's brand of socialism. An acrimonious meeting of the party's central committee, held in mid-October, led to a delay in the introduction of the first phase of the stabilization program.

Aware that Yugoslavia's huge foreign debt could not be repaid without the help of the International Monetary Fund (IMF) and other Western banks, the prime minister warned of an economic collapse and threatened to resign, though her term of office had two more years to run. The threat became moot when the IMF in early September and the U.S. Export-Import Bank a few days later agreed to refinance the country's debt.

Foreign Relations. In February, Vidoje Žarković, a member of the collective presidency, visited the Soviet Union and talked with top Soviet leaders. The LCY's weekly *Komunist* wrote on March 23 that the Žarković meeting with the Soviet leader Konstantin Chernenko confirmed that Soviet-Yugoslav relations were "stable and inviolable."

Yugoslavia cultivated cordial relations with the United States. The U.S. ambassador in Belgrade declared on August 31 that his government's policy toward Yugoslavia "will continue to be based on full support for independence, unity, and territorial integrity of that nation and respect for its nonaligned policies."

Relations between Yugoslavia and the People's Republic of China were close in 1984, with the Chinese president and foreign minister both making official visits. On the other hand, relations with Albania and Bulgaria continued to be tense, despite meetings of officials at various levels.

MILORAD M. DRACHKOVITCH
The Hoover Institution, Stanford University

YUKON

The reelection of Yukon Member of Parliament Erik Nielsen resulted in his appointment as deputy prime minister in the new national Progressive Conservative Government. Yukoners returned Nielsen to Parliament for his sixth term, representing 26 years of service.

On October 16, Government Leader Christopher Pearson announced his intention to retire from political life in early 1985. He spent six years in office.

Indian Land Claims. Yukon's 6,000 to 8,000 Indians, at a general assembly in July, voted overwhelmingly in favor of renegotiating the land claims agreement-in-principle. This will provide for monetary and land settlements along with certain political guarantees and involvement in the territory's resource management.

Economy. Sluggish world markets for lead and zinc continued to plague a start-up of the territory's largest mine, at Faro. However, a reduced work force continued to work on an overburden stripping program in the hope of making ore extraction and milling more viable economically.

The stripping program at the Cyprus Anvil Mine, a subsidiary of Dome Petroleum, represents a C$50 million investment supported equally by company and government funding. Dome Petroleum continued to seek a buyer for the Cyprus Anvil Mine and surrounding properties. The ongoing shutdown of the mine resulted in continuing closure of the White Pass railway.

Government. A major government-wide reorganization announced in July by Yukon Government Leader Christopher Pearson resulted in the consolidation of 15 departments and three crown corporations into nine central ministries. The initiative also caused a reduction in the executive council from six to four ministers, with Education and Tourism Minister Bea Firth and Justice Minister Clarke Ashley returning as private caucus members. Negotiations continued between the territorial and federal governments for the transfer of land blocks to territorial control.

ANDREW HUME, *Whitehorse, Yukon*

YUKON · Information Highlights

Area: 207,037 sq mi (536 223 km²).
Population (April 1984 est.): 21,700.
Chief City (1981 census): Whitehorse, the capital, 14,814.
Government (1984): *Chief Officers*—commissioner, Douglas Bell; government leader, Christopher Pearson. *Legislature*—16-member Legislative Assembly.
Public Finance (1984–85 fiscal year budget est.): *Revenues,* C$152,320,000; *expenditures,* C$148,-214,000.
Education (1984–85): *Enrollment*—elementary and secondary schools, 4,390 pupils.

Zaire's President Mobutu Sese Seko (left), *reelected to a seven-year term in July, visited French President François Mitterrand in September to discuss the situation in Chad.*

AGIP Pictorial Parade

ZAIRE

Amid economic problems and a few signs of opposition, President Mobutu Sese Seko won reelection for a third seven-year term with 99.16% of the vote. (A vote for or against Mobutu, the sole candidate, was mandatory for citizens of voting age.)

Economy and Mining. The 1984 budget deficit was revised upward because of the fall in copper prices and an increase in the U.S. dollar exchange rate. Despite this, the International Monetary Fund gave Zaïre a favorable report on its economic reforms and reduction of government spending, allowing Kinshasa to draw further credit as agreed.

Copper, diamond, and oil production were increased, as well as exports of crude oil and agricultural products. Private investment expanded with the privatization of some state enterprises. Inflation moderated only slightly.

Domestic Affairs. Early in the year, Mobutu reshuffled his cabinet with the departure of two ministers (finance and budget). Later, new ministers were appointed to education and justice. Additionally, Nyiwa Mobutu, the eldest son of the head of state, was appointed secretary at the ministry of foreign affairs.

In July, Mobutu was reelected president of the ruling Popular Movement of the Revolution (MPR) and hence leader of Zaire under the constitution, written by Mobutu. Under the Zairian constitution, the MPR is the only legal party. Exiled opposition groups exist in Belgium, the former colonial ruler of Zaire, and in Paris. The government blamed several bomb explosions in Kinshasa on the foreign-based

Lumumba National Congolese Movement and the Zairian Socialist Party.

Foreign Affairs. Kinshasa also accused Libya of some of the bombings. Zairian sources said that Libya never forgave Kinshasa for renewing diplomatic ties with Israel in 1982. They also stated that nearly 2,000 Zairian troops in Chad, sent there to support the regime of President Hissène Habré, were viewed by Libyan leader Muammar el-Qaddafi as an act of aggression against Libya, which opposed Hissène.

One explosion at Kinshasa airport was attributed to the Soviet airline Aeroflot. Zaire terminated a 1984 air agreement with Moscow and required all Aeroflot personnel to leave.

France signed four aid agreements with Zaire for road construction and crop development. In September, Mobutu met with French President François Mitterrand in Paris to discuss the presence of the Zairian troops in Chad.

THOMAS H. HENRIKSEN, *Hoover Institution*

ZAIRE • Information Highlights

Official Name: Republic of Zaire.
Location: Central equatorial Africa.
Area: 905,000 sq mi (2 243 950 km²).
Population (mid-1984 est.): 32,200,000.
Chief City (1980 est.): Kinshasa, the capital, 3,000,000.
Government: *Head of state,* Mobutu Sese Seko, president (took office 1965). *Legislature* (unicameral)—National Legislative Council.
Monetary Unit: Zaire (35.41 zaires equal U.S.$1, May 1984).
Foreign Trade (1982 U.S.$): *Imports,* $480,000,000; *exports,* $569,000,000.

ZIMBABWE

In 1984, Zimbabwe entered its fifth year of independence. The ruling Zimbabwe African National Union (ZANU) consolidated its power at the party's first congress since 1964 and articulated plans for a more socialist-oriented state. In the Matabeleland region, conflict persisted between government forces and former guerrillas of the Zimbabwe African People's Union (ZAPU). The year brought no improvement to the economy, which continued to be plagued by problems including a third successive year of severe drought.

Political Developments. Important changes in government preceded ZANU's huge outdoor party congress. Early in January, Prime Minister Robert Mugabe reduced the size of his cabinet and demoted the controversial minister of home affairs, Herbert Ushewokunze, to minister of transportation. Ushewokunze, who had been criticized for his use of emergency powers, antiwhite statements, and advocacy of a socialist state, was replaced by Simbi Mubako, the minister of justice. Eddison Zvogbo added Mubako's portfolio to his existing one, legal and parliamentary affairs.

The ZANU congress took place from August 8 to 12 in the capital city, Harare. Those attending the meetings included President Samora Machel of Mozambique, President Kenneth Kaunda of Zambia, President Quett Masire of Botswana, Oliver Tambo of the African National Congress of South Africa, and representatives from North Korea and Hungary. The congress adopted a new party constitution and reelected Prime Minister Mugabe as its president and Simon Muzenda as its vice-president.

The more than 6,000 party delegates discussed a new draft constitution for Zimbabwe that aimed at the eventual establishment of a one-party state. While reaffirming the party's commitment to "scientific socialism," the congress decided that a one-party state would not be created in the near future—an indication that Mugabe was unwilling to meet the demands of those who favored such a fundamental change at once. Since independence, ZANU had commanded a parliamentary majority large enough to ensure the achievement of any of its goals; immediate implementation of a one-party state was important primarily to the more radical members of the party.

The Lancaster House constitution, drafted in London in 1979 at the end of the liberation war, specified that entrenched clauses of the constitution could not be amended without a unanimous vote of the House of Assembly. In 1984 the Assembly included a bloc of 20 white seats, which were protected by an entrenched clause until 1987. Another 20 seats were held by Joshua Nkomo's ZAPU and 3 by Bishop Abel Muzorewa's United African National

---

ZIMBABWE • Information Highlights

Official Name: Republic of Zimbabwe.
Location: Southern Africa.
Area: 151,000 sq mi (391 090 km²).
Population (mid-1984 est.): 8,300,000.
Chief Cities (provisional census, Aug. 1982): Harare (formerly Salisbury), the capital, 656,000; Bulawayo, 413,800.
Government: *Head of state,* Canaan Banana, president (took office April 1980). *Head of government,* Robert Mugabe, prime minister (took office March 1980). *Legislature*—Parliament: Senate and House of Assembly.
Monetary Unit: Zimbabwe dollar (1.316 Z. dollars equal U.S.$1, July 1984).
Gross Domestic Product (1982, U.S.$): $7,100,-000,000.
Economic Indexes (1983): *Consumer Prices* (1970 = 100), all items, 318.4; food, 314.6. *Industrial Production* (March 1983, 1975 = 100), 104.
Foreign Trade (1982, U.S.$): *Imports,* $1,430,-000,000; *exports,* $1,273,000,000.

Council. Prime Minister Mugabe's ZANU held 57 seats of the 100 total.

On August 12, the prime minister announced the composition of a newly created 15-member Politburo and of an enlarged, 90-member Central Committee, the two most important decision-making bodies within the party. Their membership reflected Mugabe's efforts to achieve a political balance between competing ideological factions and among the clans within the majority Shona ethnic group.

The membership of the Politburo reflected the dominance of one powerful Shona clan, the prime minister's Zezuru, which received 7 of the 15 seats. Strong representation also was given to the Karanga, a fighting clan of great importance in maintaining any form of Shona equilibrium; both Simon Muzenda, the deputy prime minister, and Emmerson Munangagwa, who represented this important clan, were named to the Politburo.

One of the main surprises was that powerful cabinet minister Eddison Zvogbo was not placed on the Politburo, although he was elected to the Central Committee. Edgar Z. Tekere, who in 1980 was acquitted of charges of murdering a white farmer, was elected to the Central Committee. Callistus Ndlovu, a former member of ZAPU who had defected to ZANU and was currently minister of mines, was also chosen for the Central Committee.

Perhaps the most significant result of the congress was the clear affirmation of Mugabe's firm control of the party and of the country.

After the congress it was announced that government leaders would be asked to fill out forms declaring their assets. The congress had adopted a leadership code requiring politicians to relinquish their businesses and holdings or lose their positions. The code was a response to the corruption of some government officials and an indication of ZAPU's increasing commitment to a socialist model. Some Zimbabweans were skeptical about the extent to which the code would be implemented.

In November the prime minister ousted the two remaining ZAPU members of his cabinet: Cephas Msipa, minister of water resources, and John Nkomo (unrelated to Joshua Nkomo), minister of state in the deputy prime minister's office. The immediate reason for the dismissals was that ZAPU had been blamed for the assassination of Sen. Ndou Ndhlovu of ZANU, but possibly this may have been an excuse to remove the ministers for not having defected to ZANU.

Matabeleland Unrest. In April attention was focused on Matabeleland, home of the Ndebele, a non-Shona group, and of Joshua Nkomo, the leader of the opposition. The country's seven Roman Catholic bishops accused the Zimbabwean army and specifically its North-Korean–trained Fifth Brigade of waging a campaign of terror in the region. In a report based on investigations by the church's Justice and Peace Commission, the bishops charged the army with committing "atrocities" against farmers and provided evidence of more than 24 civilian deaths as well as numerous instances of beating, rape, or torture.

Troops had been sent into Matabeleland because of the activities of nearly 2,000 antigovernment rebels (called "dissidents"), many of whom had fought in the war of liberation as ZAPU guerrillas loyal to Nkomo. The Zimbabwean government had frequently accused South Africa of furnishing weapons and supplies to the rebels, and Prime Minister Mugabe was angry at Nkomo's unwillingness to condemn publicly their violence. By August relative stability had returned to Matabeleland, partly because Mugabe had pulled back troops from the region. In late November, however, tensions were revived by the assassination in Matabeleland of Jini Ntuta, a senior member of ZAPU, allegedly by antigovernment dissidents.

The Economy. Zimbabwe's economic crisis worsened in 1984. The gross domestic product and exports fell, inflation and government debt service rose, and the availability of foreign exchange declined. One factor exacerbating these problems was an almost total lack of major new foreign investment since 1980. Another was the continuing drought, which forced Zimbabwe to become an importer of food. The drought also led to an influx of an estimated 100,000 refugees from hard-hit Mozambique.

In February, Finance Minister Bernard Chidzero presented the 1983–84 supplemental budget to Parliament. Chidzero announced that Zimbabwe would need $271 million in extra appropriations and that the anticipated budget deficit for the year would be $640 million, 60% larger than had been anticipated. Spending on drought relief was increased by 23% and for agriculture by 67%. Later in February the International Monetary Fund suspended its programs in Zimbabwe in part because of the country's extraordinary budget deficit.

At the end of March, Chidzero introduced tough measures to deal with the critical foreign-exchange shortage. Among these was a temporary embargo on profit and dividend remittances by multinationals to their headquarters overseas. The government excluded from this provision any foreign investment after 1979, such as that of the Heinz Food Group, the only substantial new foreign investor in Zimbabwe since independence.

In his 1984–85 budget speech to Parliament in July, Chidzero said that the Zimbabwean economy had been through yet another year of difficulties and contraction, with almost all productive sectors registering negative growth. He outlined the drastic effects of the drought and the recession on all sectors of the economy.

The extent to which Zimbabwe would be able to implement the socialist goals expressed at the ZANU party congress would depend largely on a strengthening of its fragile economy. In 1984 the gross domestic product fell below its 1983 low of -3%, and inflation was running at an annual rate of 30%. The government was not able to provide resources for new resettlement programs, especially for ex-guerrillas for whom there were no longer government stipends. Indeed, the government was unable to continue to finance agricultural projects for existing resettlement schemes. An end to the drought would certainly alleviate some of Zimbabwe's economic problems, but the country would continue to have long-range economic difficulties unless it could find new outlets for its declining manufacturing sector.

White Emigration. The white population in 1984 was estimated to be between 100,000 and 125,000 out of a total population of 8.3 million. White emigration remained close to 20,000 a year, and many who left moved to South Africa or Britain. While a number of those emigrating were workers with essential skills, no severe dislocations occurred. Those who remained included more than 4,000 commercial farmers, who were essential for the economic survival of the country. While this number was down from 5,000 at independence, the government had done much to encourage them to stay and there had been no expropriation of commercial farming land. White farmers survived the drought, and the price of maize, tobacco, and cotton reached record levels.

Whites had been encouraged to remain in Zimbabwe by the delay in establishing one-party rule. They had also been reassured by Mugabe's removal of the controversial Herbert Ushewokunze from the home ministry and by the government's decision not to enforce a requirement that all schools in the country should have a 60% African majority.

PATRICK O'MEARA, *Indiana University*

The St. Louis Zoo was awarded a special citation for its successful campaign to breed the rare Speke's gazelle, left. Meanwhile at the Bronx (NY) Zoo, a Przewalski's wild horse stallion, one of the rarest species, sired two foals. Virgil, below, and his brother Victor were introduced to the public in June.

ZOOS AND ZOOLOGY

While zoos and aquariums in the United States continue to enjoy great popularity, the national organization that represents them—the American Association of Zoological Parks and Aquariums (AAZPA)—has not enjoyed high recognition. In September 1984, newly installed AAZPA President Elvie Turner, Jr., said that he intended to generate greater public recognition for the organization. Turner, also the director of the Fort Worth (TX) Zoo, pointed out that much of the AAZPA's work in conservation and education goes unnoticed, even though the group has led the way in organizing captive breeding of rare wildlife species.

Meanwhile, breeding and relocation efforts, behavioral research, field expeditions, and work on new zoological exhibits continued throughout 1984.

Breeding. Two zoos and two aquariums received AAZPA awards for achievements in breeding: the San Antonio Zoo was cited for breeding the Madagascar angulated tortoise; the St. Louis Zoo was awarded for the Speke's gazelle; the Seattle Aquarium was honored for the giant Pacific octopus; and Sea World in San Diego was singled out for the king and emperor penguins.

Another breeding success took place at the Jacksonville (FL) Zoo on February 27, when the first Aldabra tortoise ever hatched in the Northern Hemisphere emerged from its egg. The giant species rivals the huge tortoises of the Galápagos Islands in size. Living on the Indian Ocean's Seychelles archipelago, the Aldabra tortoise can grow to more than 4 ft. (1.2 m) long and weigh more than 500 lbs (227 kg).

Two foals sired by a Przewalski's wild horse stallion from the Soviet Union were born at the Bronx (NY) Zoo. Przewalski's wild horse is one of the rarest species in the world. Native to central Asia, it is believed to be ex-

Photos, AP/Wide World

tinct in the wild. The Przewalski's species, closely related to the ancestor of domestic horses, is the only truly wild horse in nature; other so-called wild horses are really domestic horses living in a feral state. The Soviet stallion was brought to the Bronx Zoo in 1982 and was transferred to the San Diego Zoo in the fall of 1984 for breeding with females. In exchange, a stallion from the Bronx and a mare from San Diego were sent to the Soviet Union.

A zoological first took place at the Louisville (KY) Zoo in May, when a quarter horse mare gave birth to a male Grant's zebra. Although other embryo transfers and cross-species deliveries had been made, this was said to be the first successful embryo transfer between two equine species. Zoologists believed that the procedure could be used to save endangered equine breeds.

Relocation. As the biblical story of Sampson and the lion testifies, lions once roamed the Middle East. In August 1984, Asiatic lions returned to the Middle East when four cubs bred at the San Diego Zoo's Wild Animal Park were shipped to a preserve in Israel's Negev Desert. The lions, two males and two females, were among 12 Asiatic lions born at the park. The destination of the cubs was the Hai Bar Reserve, located on 8,000 acres (3 200 ha) of desert 25 mi (40 km) north of the Red Sea resort of Eilat. Framed by barren, craggy mountains, the reserve was established in 1969 to preserve species that lived in Palestine during biblical times.

In September the National Zoo in Washington, DC, returned 14 captive-bred golden lion tamarins to their native forest habitat in Brazil. These small, rare monkeys had been trained for survival in a special primate acclimation facility. Threatened by deforestation, the golden lion tamarin numbers less than 100 in the wild.

Research. The San Diego Zoo launched a major research study of the special behavior and reproductive potential of another rare species of monkey, the lion-tailed macaque. Under a federal grant, the zoo will probe infant social development, adult sexual behavior, and aggression among the 33 macaques in its colony. Less than 1,000 lion-tailed macaques remain in the wild in their native India.

The New England Aquarium began research into a marine creature called the gribble, which causes $1 billion (U.S.) in damage yearly by burrowing into waterfront structures and the hulls of ships. Crustaceans only one millimeter long, gribbles have confounded efforts to thwart burrowing. The aim of the project is to find ways to protect such structures from gribble damage.

A tiny tree frog called the coqui is familiar in Puerto Rico because of its call, which sounds like its name. Carvings and ceramics depicting the coqui are sold throughout the island. Researchers from Cornell University and the State University of New York at Albany have been studying the coqui for half a decade. In 1984 they reported that the male coqui is an amphibian version of the "house husband." The female leaves its eggs long before the tadpoles develop and hatch. The male remains with them, guarding against enemies and keeping them moist, perhaps by urination.

Expeditions. The Mystic (CT) Aquarium and the New York Aquarium sent a major expedition to Canada's Hudson Bay in July to capture white whales, also known as belugas. The expedition, based in Churchill, Manitoba, captured five of the whales—two for Mystic and three for the New York institution—with the help of native Eskimos and Indians. Inshore whales, the belugas were caught in the mouth of the Churchill River, where about 1,500 of them normally feed. Roughly 10 ft (3 m) long and 1,000 lbs (450 kg) each, the whales were driven into shallow water by small, outboard-powered boats. Members of the capture teams jumped from the craft into the water and wrestled the whales onto canvas stretchers, which were then lifted into the boats. The whales were held for a few days in holding pools, then shipped to the aquariums by air.

Exhibits. Elephants were on the minds of exhibit designers at several zoos during the year. At the Fort Worth Zoo, construction began on a major exhibit for Asian elephants. Covering 3 acres (1.2 ha), the exhibit will house two males and between four and six females. Funded by the city, the $1.2 million exhibit will include a high-ceilinged concrete building and an outdoor enclosure surrounded by stockade fencing. Zoo officials said they hope to breed Asian elephants, which are rare in the wild, at the facility.

The Woodland Park Zoo in Seattle announced that deteriorating conditions in its elephant exhibit, which houses four of the animals, have created health and safety problems. The zoo hoped to raise more than $2 million to build a new exhibit that would simulate the native habitat of the elephants in Thailand.

In the fall, renovation of the elephant house at New York's Bronx Zoo was begun. The redesigned building, to be called "Elephant Palace," will consist of a central domed main building flanked by two wings. One wing will house Asian elephants, the other rare African black rhinoceroses. A visitors center will be created under the dome, and an amphitheater holding 1,000 people will feature public demonstrations of elephant training and behavior.

Atlanta Scandal. A major scandal erupted at the Atlanta (GA) Zoo during the spring. The city of Atlanta and federal investigators launched an investigation of the zoo because of appalling conditions there. Animals were found to be living in filth, sick, and, in some cases, missing. Zoo officials allowed two bears to be loaned to a tourist attraction where the bears were destroyed because they were said to be "unruly." An elephant, which the zoo said had been retired to a farm, actually had died while in the hands of a circus. A tiger, lion, and two Kodiak bears perished, and four rare cheetahs seemed to be missing.

The troubles at the zoo appeared to stem from lack of funds. In 1983, a $21 million renovation of the 95-year-old zoo was scrapped because the money was not available. According to investigators, dissention among the staff added to the problems. Authorities at other zoos that had loaned animals to Atlanta asked for them back. To the credit of the nation's zoos, however, the Atlanta facility had been suspended from membership by AAZPA before the scandal broke.

EDWARD R. RICCIUTI
Free-lance Environment and Wildlife Writer

Statistical and Tabular Data

Table of Contents

NATIONS OF THE WORLD

A Profile and Synopsis of Major 1984 Developments

Nation, Region	Population in millions	Capital	Area Sq mi (km²)	Head of State/Government
Angola, S.W. Africa	7.8	Luanda	481,000 (1 245 790)	José Eduardo dos Santos, president

Some 25,000 Cuban troops continued to aid the Marxist government of Angola in fighting rebels of the National Union for the Total Independence of Angola (UNITA) and other groups. In January, South African forces completed a month-long offensive in southern Angola against bases used by guerrillas of the South West Africa People's Organization (SWAPO) for raids into Namibia (South West Africa). In February, Angola and South Africa signed a disengagement agreement calling for Angola to freeze SWAPO strikes across the border in return for South Africa's evacuation of Angolan territory and withdrawal of support for UNITA. At the year's end this agreement was not fully implemented.

Nation, Region	Population in millions	Capital	Area Sq mi (km²)	Head of State/Government
Antigua and Barbuda, Caribbean	0.1	St. John's	171 (443.6)	Sir Wilfred E. Jacobs, governor-general Vere C. Bird, prime minister

Prime Minister Vere Bird was reelected to another five-year term in April. His Antigua Labour Party won 16 of the 17 seats contested in Parliament, a gain of three. Gross Domestic Product, GDP (1982 est. U.S.$): $125.6 million. Foreign Trade (1981 est.): Imports, $139.3 million; exports, $33.6 million.

Nation, Region	Population in millions	Capital	Area Sq mi (km²)	Head of State/Government
Bahamas, Caribbean	0.2	Nassau	5,380 (13 934)	Sir Gerald C. Cash, governor-general Lynden O. Pindling, prime minister

In April the Bahamian government signed a pact with the United States for the lease of three U.S. military facilities in the Bahamas. The agreement was reached after more than ten years of negotiations. Opening the July summit meeting of the Caribbean Community and Common Market (Caricom), Prime Minister Pindling charged that "external agencies" had attempted "to extend extraterritorial jurisdiction and destabilize the Bahamas." GNP (1981): $1.4 billion. Foreign Trade (1982): Imports, $740 million; exports, $222 million.

Nation, Region	Population in millions	Capital	Area Sq mi (km²)	Head of State/Government
Bahrain, W. Asia	0.4	Manama	261 (676)	Isa bin Sulman Al Khalifa, emir

Work continued on the $540 million causeway the Saudis are building to link the island of Bahrain to the Saudi mainland. It is scheduled to be completed in 1985. Gross National Product, GNP (1982): $11 billion. Foreign Trade (1982): Imports, $3.6 billion; exports, $3.7 billion.

Nation, Region	Population in millions	Capital	Area Sq mi (km²)	Head of State/Government
Barbados, Caribbean	0.3	Bridgetown	166 (430)	Sir Hugh Springer, governor-general John M. G. Adams, prime minister

On a nine-day tour of Latin America and the Caribbean, U.S. Secretary of State George Shultz visited Barbados, where he stated that the Reagan administration would consider a request from the Organization of Eastern Caribbean States for aid in developing a security force. GDP (1982): $997.5 million. Foreign Trade (1983): Imports, $616 million; exports, $303 million.

Nation, Region	Population in millions	Capital	Area Sq mi (km²)	Head of State/Government
Benin, W. Africa	3.9	Porto Novo	43,483 (112 622)	Mathieu Kérékou, president

In February the ruling National Revolutionary Assembly (parliament) voted to extend the presidential and legislative tenures from three to five years and to reduce the assembly's membership from 336 to 196. On August 1, Mathieu Kérékou was sworn in as president after his reelection by the assembly. GNP (1982): $1.1 billion. Foreign Trade (1982): Imports, $590.3 million; exports, $304.3 million.

Nation, Region	Population in millions	Capital	Area Sq mi (km²)	Head of State/Government
Bhutan, S. Asia	1.4	Thimphu	18,000 (46 620)	Jigme Singye Wangchuk, *king*

GDP (fiscal year 1981–82): $131 million. Foreign Trade (fiscal year 1981–82): Imports, $50.8 million; exports, $20.2 million.

Botswana, S. Africa	1.0	Gaborone	231,804 (600 372)	Quett Masire, *president*

In the first general elections since 1980, President Quett Masire and his ruling Botswana Democratic Party were returned to power. GNP (1981–82 fiscal): $721.6 million. Foreign Trade (1982): Imports, $580.0 million; exports, $456.2 million.

Burkina Faso, W. Africa	6.7	Ouagadougou	106,000 (274 540)	Thomas Sankara, *head of state*

A planned coup to overthrow the military government headed by Thomas Sankara was foiled on May 27. Seven soldiers were executed for treason, and five received long prison terms at hard labor. Formerly known as Upper Volta, the nation was renamed Burkina Faso, meaning "land of incorruptible men," on August 4. In a national day speech celebrating the event, Sankara called for economic progress, especially in regard to food production. On August 31, he appointed a new cabinet, including a number of his close associates, to end factionalism in government. GNP (1982 U.S.$): $1.1 billion. Foreign Trade (1982): Imports, $346 million; exports, $56 million.

Burundi, E. Africa	4.7	Bujumbura	10,747 (27 834)	Jean-Baptiste Bagaza, *president*

GDP (1982 U.S.$): $1.2 billion. Foreign Trade (1983): Imports, $194 million; exports, $76 million.

Cameroon, Cen. Africa	9.4	Yaoundé	183,567 (475 439)	Paul Biya, *president*

Incumbent President Paul Biya was elected to his first full term in January. Although he was the only candidate, a heavy voter turnout indicated that he had strong public support. In February exiled former President Ahmadou Ahidjo was convicted of treason on charges of having plotted to overthrow Biya in 1983. From April 6 to 9, elements of the presidential palace guard staged a bloody but unsuccessful revolt, which according to some reports was an effort to restore Ahidjo to power. GDP (1981): $7.0 billion. Foreign Trade (1983): Imports, $1.2 billion; exports, $942 million.

Cape Verde, W. Africa	0.3	Praia	1,560 (4 040)	Aristides Pereira, *president* Pedro Pires, *prime minister*

GDP (1981): $100 million. Foreign Trade (1981): Imports, $95 million; exports, $79 million.

Central African Republic, Cen. Africa	2.6	Bangui	242,000 (626 780)	André-Dieudonne Kolingba, *president of the Military Committee for National Recovery*

Gen. André-Dieudonne Kolingba reshuffled the Military Committee for National Recovery. The post of secretary of state for defense and war veterans was abolished. GDP (1982): $658 million. Foreign Trade (1981): Imports, $95 million; exports, $79 million.

Comoros, E. Africa	0.5	Moroni	838 (2 171)	Ahmed Abdallah Abderemane, *president*

GNP (1981): $90 million. Foreign Trade (1981): Imports, $33 million; exports, $17 million.

Congo, Cen. Africa	1.7	Brazzaville	135,000 (349 650)	Denis Sassou-Nguesso, *president* Ange Edouard Poungui, *prime minister*

On July 30 the Central Committee of the Congolese Labor Party (PCT), the only legal party, unanimously reelected Col. Denis Sassou-Nguesso president. A constitutional change made the president head of government, reducing the premier to coordinating functions. PCT ideology director Jean-Pierre Thystère-Tchicaya was implicated in antigovernment activities and removed from the Politburo. Statistics released in 1984 reported a 13% increase in GDP for 1983. GDP (1983): $2.03 billion. Foreign Trade (1982): Imports, $807 million; exports, $977 million.

Djibouti, E. Africa	0.3	Djibouti	9,000 (23 310)	Hassan Gouled Aptidon, *president* Barkat Gourad Hamadou, *premier*

In Djibouti in March, Ethiopia's Lt. Col. Mengistu Haile Mariam and President Hassan Gouled Aptidon discussed the issue of refugees. GDP (1980): $160 million. Foreign Trade (1981): Imports, $152 million; exports, $66 million.

Dominica, Caribbean	0.1	Roseau	291 (752.7)	Clarence A. Seignoret, *president* Mary Eugenia Charles, *prime minister*

GNP (1983): $56.4 million. Foreign Trade (1982): Imports, $48.5 million; exports, $28.5 million.

Dominican Republic, Caribbean	6.3	Santo Domingo	18,712 (48 464)	Salvador Jorge Blanco, *president*

In April, three days of riots over government-ordered price increases caused more than 50 deaths and hundreds of injuries. The price hikes, in foodstuffs, imported goods, and medicines, were part of austerity measures required by the International Monetary Fund (IMF) as a condition of continuing a three-year loan. The government closed two radio stations and a television station and ordered police to occupy the headquarters of five labor unions in response to the riots. In June and September the Dominican Republic met with ten other Latin American nations to discuss their foreign debt crisis. GNP (1981): $7.6 billlion. Foreign Trade (1983): Imports, $1.282 billion; exports, $811 million.

Equatorial Guinea, Cen. Africa	0.3	Malabo	10,830 (28 051)	Teodoro Obiang Nguema Mbasogo, *president* Cristino Seriche Bioko, *premier*

In Paris in June, M. Manuel-Ruben N'Dongo presented the program of his new opposition movement in exile, the Social Democratic Convergence (CSD). M. N'Dongo urged "all the opposition groups in Equatorial Guinea to create the necessary means for the rapid liberation of the country." GNP (1980): $100 million.

Fiji, Oceania	0.7	Suva	7,095 (18 376)	Sir Penaia Ganilau, *governor-general* Sir Kamisese Mara, *premier*

In June, Fiji joined 13 other South Pacific nations on the island of Tuvalu for a meeting of the South Pacific Forum. The participants accepted a proposal by Australian Prime Minister Robert Hawke to work on a treaty establishing a nuclear-free zone in their region. The plan would forbid the possession or testing of nuclear weapons by forum members and ban the dumping of nuclear waste in the Pacific Ocean. GDP (1982): $1.85 billion. Foreign Trade (1983): Imports, $484 million; exports, $240 million.

Nation, Region	Population in millions	Capital	Area Sq mi (km²)	Head of State/Government
Gabon, Cen. Africa	1.0	Libreville	102,712 (266 024)	El Hadj Omar Bongo, *president* Léon Mébiame, *premier*

Good relations with France were restored in April during a visit to Libreville by French Premier Pierre Mauroy. Relations had declined since 1982 because of publicity in France alleging misconduct by Gabonese officials and a scandal involving the president and his wife. France, which had a 70% interest in Gabon's lucrative oil production, agreed to build a 300-megawatt nuclear reactor for Gabon. Gabon and Mauritius agreed in principle to establish diplomatic relations; representatives of the two nations signed agreements concerning cultural, scientific, and technical cooperation. GDP (1982): $3.5 billion. Foreign Trade (1982): Imports, $724 million; exports, $2.16 billion.

Nation, Region	Population in millions	Capital	Area Sq mi (km²)	Head of State/Government
Gambia, W. Africa	0.7	Banjul	4,361 (11 295)	Sir Dawda Kairaba Jawara, *president*

On February 1, President Sir Dawda Jawara declared that the Senegambian confederation had become a political reality and its political and administrative institutions were working well. Liberia and Gambia agreed to revive their 1974 treaty of friendship and cooperation. GNP (1981): $240 million. Foreign Trade (1983): Imports, $115 million; exports, $48 million.

Nation, Region	Population in millions	Capital	Area Sq mi (km²)	Head of State/Government
Ghana, W. Africa	12.2	Accra	92,100 (238 538)	Jerry Rawlings, chairman, Provisional National Defense Council

Ghana's economy improved in 1984, reversing a decade of decline due chiefly to mismanagement. A 5% growth was expected, with inflation reduced from 140% to 35%. The improvement was attributed to more reliable rains, to the government's success in encouraging productivity and self-help, and especially to an economic austerity program endorsed by the International Monetary Fund. Ghana was granted more than $800 million in Western aid for its 1983–86 recovery program, which featured incentives for farmers, the business community, and foreign investors. Political tensions eased in 1984. The government lifted a curfew in force since the 1981 coup and reopened Ghana's borders. Plans were being formulated for a representative national assembly. In the interim, the membership of the ruling Provisional National Defense Council was increased to seven. The 1984 census revealed a population of 12,205,574. GNP (1982 est.): $10.5 billion. Foreign Trade (1982): Imports, $705 million; exports, $873 million.

Nation, Region	Population in millions	Capital	Area Sq mi (km²)	Head of State/Government
Guinea-Bissau, W. Africa	0.8	Bissau	14,000 (36 260)	João Bernardo Vieira, *president*

Guinea-Bissau returned to constitutional government on May 16. After the election of eight regional councils in March, the councils chose representatives for a 150-member National Assembly. The assembly in turn approved a new constitution and elected a 15-member Council of State to replace the ruling Council of the Revolution. The assembly unanimously named João Bernardo Vieira as chairman of the new council—and thus head of state—for a five-year term. Vieira had been in power since a coup in 1980. GDP (1982 fiscal year): $177 million. Foreign Trade (1982): Imports, $50 million; exports, $12 million.

Nation, Region	Population in millions	Capital	Area Sq mi (km²)	Head of State/Government
Guyana, Northeast South America	0.8	Georgetown	83,000 (214 970)	Forbes Burnham, *president* Hugh Desmond Hoyte, *prime minister*

In January the government announced that the Guyana dollar would be devalued by almost 20%. Later that month a $40.7 million loan to Guyana for irrigation and drainage systems was approved by the Inter-American Development Bank. In June, President Burnham signed $250 million worth of trade agreements with Bulgaria, China, and North Korea. In August, Prime Minister Ptolemy Reid retired due to ill health and was replaced by Vice-President for Production Hugh Desmond Hoyte. GNP (1982): $430 million. Foreign Trade (1982): Imports, $280 million; exports, $241 million.

Nation, Region	Population in millions	Capital	Area Sq mi (km²)	Head of State/Government
Haiti, Caribbean	5.5	Port-au-Prince	10,714 (27 749)	Jean-Claude Duvalier, *president*

In March, President Duvalier guaranteed freedom of the press and respect for human rights in Haiti. But on May 10 the government forbade all political activity and pamphleteering except by the president's party. On May 14, U.S. Secretary of State George Shultz reported that Haiti's progress in improving human rights was sufficient to justify continued U.S. aid. Food riots May 21–30 began in the town of Gonaives and spread to Milot and Cap Haitien, where mobs raided CARE food warehouses. CARE food reportedly had been sold instead of distributed to the needy. In response to the riots, President Duvalier ordered the distribution of the food, replaced five of his cabinet ministers, and ousted virtually the entire local government of Gonaives. GNP (1982): $1.5 billion. Foreign Trade: Imports (1981), $461 million; exports (1983), $166 million.

Nation, Region	Population in millions	Capital	Area Sq mi (km²)	Head of State/Government
Ivory Coast, W. Africa	9.2	Yamoussoukro	124,903 (323 500)	Félix Houphouët-Boigny, *president*

An "anti-gang brigade," a special unit to combat crime in the Ivory Coast, became operational on July 31. GDP (1982 est.): $7.7 billion. Foreign Trade (1982): Imports, $2.09 billion; exports, $2.34 billion.

Nation, Region	Population in millions	Capital	Area Sq mi (km²)	Head of State/Government
Jamaica, Caribbean	2.4	Kingston	4,244 (10 991)	Florizel Glasspole, *governor-general* Edward Seaga, *prime minister*

In 1984, Jamaica worked to meet conditions set by the International Monetary Fund (IMF) for receiving a $143.5 million loan. The government agreed to raise taxes, cut the budget deficit, and devalue the Jamaican dollar. The loan, which went into effect June 21, was expected to help Jamaica repay its $3 billion foreign debt. GNP (1982): $3 billion. Foreign Trade (1983): Imports, $1.5 billion; exports, $738 million.

Nation, Region	Population in millions	Capital	Area Sq mi (km²)	Head of State/Government
Kiribati, Oceania	0.06	Tarawa	.266 (690)	Reginald Wallace, *governor-general* Ieremia Tabai, *president*

In June, Kiribati joined 13 other South Pacific nations in an agreement to work toward establishing a nuclear-free zone in their region. See also FIJI.

Nation, Region	Population in millions	Capital	Area Sq mi (km²)	Head of State/Government
Kuwait, W. Asia	1.6	Kuwait	6,880 (17 818)	Jabir al-Ahmad Al Sabah, *emir* Saad al-Abdallah Al Sabah, *prime minister*

In March six men were sentenced to hang for their participation in the terrorist attacks in December 1983 on the U.S. and French embassies and on several Kuwaiti installations. Kuwaiti oil exports suffered as a result of bombings of Gulf shipping in the nearby Iran-Iraq war zone. Per capita income (1983), $25,850. Foreign Trade: Imports (1981), $6.9 billion; exports (1983), $11.8 billion.

Nation, Region	Population in millions	Capital	Area Sq mi (km²)	Head of State/Government
Lesotho, S. Africa	1.5	Maseru	11,761 (30 460)	Moshoeshoe II, *king* Leabua Jonathan, *prime minister*

In an August reshuffling of the cabinet, Vincent Montsi Makhele became foreign minister. GNP (1980): $569.0 million. Foreign Trade (1982): Imports, $420 million; exports, $139 million, including $102 million in remittances of Basotho workers in South Africa.

Nation, Region	Population in millions	Capital	Area Sq mi (km²)	Head of State/Government
Liberia, W. Africa	2.2	Monrovia	43,000 (111 370)	Samuel K. Doe, *head of state*

In July voters approved a revised draft constitution. Head of State Gen. Samuel K. Doe then lifted a four-year ban on political activity in preparation for 1985 presidential and legislative elections that would complete Liberia's return to civilian rule. In August, however, Doe announced the arrest "for security reasons" of University of Liberia Professor Amos Sawyer, a chief architect of the constitution and a candidate for the presidency. The arrest touched off student protests dispersed by troops with dozens of casualties. GDP (1982): $800 million. Foreign Trade (1982): Imports, $422 million; exports, $464 million.

Liechtenstein, Cen. Europe	0.03	Vaduz	62 (160)	Franz Josef II, *prince* Hans Brunhart, *prime minister*

In a referendum held on July 1, women won the right to vote, after having been denied the right in two earlier referenda. Prince Hans Adam, son of Prince Franz Josef II and de facto ruler of Liechtenstein since July 1983, was given executive authority in August. However, his father remained the principality's titular head.

Luxembourg, W. Europe	0.4	Luxembourg	998 (2 586)	Jean, *grand duke* Jacques Santer, *prime minister*

Parliamentary elections in June resulted in the replacement of the Christian Socialist Pierre Werner by the Social Democrat Jacques Santer as prime minister of a coalition government. Grand Duke Jean paid an official visit to the United States in November. GNP (1982): $3.4 billion. Foreign Trade (1983, Belgium-Luxembourg Economic Union): Imports, $54 billion; exports, $51 billion.

Madagascar, E. Africa	9.8	Antananarivo	230,000 (595 700)	Didier Ratsiraka, *head of government* Desire Rakotoarijaona, *premier*

Creditors agreed to reschedule $210 million of Madagascar's $1.56 billion foreign debt. The government's 1984–85 economic adjustment program aimed at liberalizing domestic pricing and marketing in order to raise exports and thereby improve debt-servicing capacity. GDP (1980): $3.2 billion. Foreign Trade (1981): Imports, $540 million; exports, $316 million.

Malawi, E. Africa	6.9	Lilongwe	45,747 (118 484)	Hastings Kamuzu Banda, *president*

The national executive committee of the ruling Malawi Congress Party (MCP) was reorganized by President Banda. Minister without Portfolio Robson Chirwa and Minister at Large Sydney Somanje were reappointed. GDP (1982): $1.34 billion. Foreign Trade (1983): Imports, $312 million; exports, $230 million.

Maldives, S. Asia	0.2	Malé	115 (298)	Maumoon Abdul Gayoom, *president*

GDP (1982): $74 million. Foreign Trade (1982): Imports, $46 million; exports, $17.3 million.

Mali, W. Africa	7.6	Bamako	464,871 (1 204 015)	Moussa Traoré, *president*

Mali rejoined the Monetary Union of West Africa and adopted the Communauté Financière Africaine (CFA) franc, worth twice the old Mali franc. The move was expected to curtail smuggling and black-market activities. GDP (1982): $1 billion. Foreign Trade (1982): Imports, $332 million; exports, $146 million.

Malta, S. Europe	0.4	Valletta	121 (313)	Agatha Barbara, *president* Carmelo Mifsud Bonnici, *prime minister*

As part of its attempt to check the influence of the Catholic Church, the government closed eight Catholic schools in the fall, claiming they were in contravention of the law by charging fees. Archbishop Mercieca closed all 72 Catholic schools in protest. There followed a strike and lockout in the state schools and a general sympathy strike by the general work force on October 10. On December 22, Dom Mintoff resigned the premiership and was succeeded by Carmelo Mifsud Bonnici. Mintoff, who earlier in the month had reaffirmed Malta's ties with the Soviets during a visit to the USSR, announced that he would retain his House seat. GDP (1982): $1.14 billion. Foreign Trade (1983): Imports, $733 million; exports, $363 million.

Mauritania, W. Africa	1.8	Nouakchott	419,212 (1 085 760)	Maouya Ould Sidi Ahmed Taya, *president*

On December 12, in a bloodless coup, Col. Maouya Ould Sidi Ahmed Taya overthrew Mohammed Khouna Ould Haidalla as president of the ruling Military Committee for National Salvation. Taya had served as prime minister from April 1981 to March 1984, when Haidalla assumed that post as well as the presidency. GNP (1982 est.): $720 million. Foreign Trade (1983): Imports, $226 million; exports, $291 million.

Mauritius, E. Africa	1.0	Port Louis	720 (1 865)	Sir Seewoosagur Ramgoolam, *governor-general* Aneerood Jugnauth, *prime minister*

Opposition leader M. Paul Berenger was suspended from parliament on June 16. The government dropped plans to enforce a law that would have required newspapers on the island to pay a security deposit in case they are sued for libel. The government closed down Libya's embassy in Port Louis for "interfering in the internal affairs" of Mauritius. Prime Minister Aneerood Jugnauth reshuffled his government early in the year. GDP (1983 est.): $960 million. Foreign Trade (1983): Imports, $433 million; exports, $369 million.

Monaco, S. Europe	0.03	Monaco-Ville	0.6 (1.5)	Rainier III, *prince* Jean Herly, *minister of state*

A son, Andrea Albert Grace, was born to Princess Caroline and her husband Stefano Casiraghi on June 8.

Mongolia, E. Asia	1.9	Ulan Bator	604,100 (1 564 619)	Jambyn Batmonh, *prime minister and head of the Mongolian Communist Party*

In March, Mongolia refused to ask Soviet troops to leave the country, despite demands by China for the withdrawal as a condition for improving Chinese-Soviet relations. In August the president of the state presidium and secretary-general of the Mongolian Communist Party, Yumjaagiyn Tsedenbal, stepped down due to ill health. He was replaced as party leader by Prime Minister Jambyn Batmonh. Foreign Trade (1981): Imports, $655 million; exports, $436 million.

Nauru, Oceania	0.008	Nauru	8 (20.7)	Hammer DeRoburt, *president*

Nauru was among 14 South Pacific nations participating in a forum in June to discuss establishing a nuclear-free zone in the region. See also FIJI. GNP (1981): $155 million. Foreign Trade (1981): Imports, $11 million; exports, $75 million.

Nepal, S. Asia	16.6	Katmandu	56,136 (145 391)	Birendra Bir Bikram, *king* Lokendra B. Chand, *prime minister*

GDP (fiscal year 1982–1983): $2.3 billion.

Nation, Region	Population in millions	Capital	Area Sq mi (km²)	Head of State/Government
Niger, W. Africa	6.3	Niamey	489,000 (1 266 510)	Seyni Kountché, *president* Hamid Algabid, *prime minister*

An "interim program for economic consolidation" was adopted for 1984–85 after the 1979–83 development plan failed to meet its goals because of a sharp decrease in the price of uranium, Niger's chief export. The new program called for reductions in public spending and turning over certain state monopolies to private business. GDP (1982 U.S.$): $2 billion. Foreign Trade (1982): Imports, $442 million; exports, $333 million.

Oman, W. Asia	1.0	Muscat	ca. 82,000 (212 380)	Qabus bin Said, *sultan and prime minister*

GNP (1981 U.S.$): $6.3 billion. Foreign Trade (1983): Imports, $2.5 billion; exports, $4 billion.

Papua New Guinea, Oceania	3.4	Port Moresby	183,540 (475 369)	Kingsford Dibela, *governor-general* Michael Somare, *prime minister*

In May, Pope John Paul II visited Papua New Guinea, where he said Mass for a group of nearly 200,000 Stone Age tribesmen in Mount Hagen. Port Moresby was the site of a meeting of 18 Asian and Pacific Commonwealth leaders in August. GNP per capita (1982): $820. Foreign Trade (1983): Imports, $974 million; exports, $734 million.

Qatar, W. Asia	0.3	Doha	4,247 (11 000)	Khalifa bin Hamad Al Thani, *emir and prime minister*

GDP (1982 U.S.$): $7.9 billion. Foreign Trade (1983): Imports, $1.5 billion; exports, $3.4 billion.

Rwanda, E. Africa	5.8	Kigali	10,169 (26 338)	Juvenal Habyarimana, *president*

On January 9, following presidential and legislative elections in late December 1983, President Habyarimana announced a cabinet shuffle, including three new ministers. At the same time, he stressed the need for economic austerity and achieving self-sufficiency in food production. GDP (1981 U.S.$): $1.4 billion. Foreign Trade (1983): Imports, $279 million; exports, $80 million.

Saint Christopher and Nevis, Caribbean	0.04	Basseterre	101 (261)	Clement A. Arrindell, *governor-general* Kennedy A. Simmonds, *prime minister*

In March, St. Christopher and Nevis was admitted to the Organization of American States (OAS). In June, in the first elections since the nation gained independence in 1983, Prime Minister Simmonds' coalition government was returned to power. GNP (1982): $41.6 million. Foreign Trade (1983): Imports, $47.3 million; exports, $30.6 million.

Saint Lucia, Caribbean	0.1	Castries	239 (619)	Sir Allen Lewis, *governor-general* John Compton, *prime minister*

GDP (1982 proj.): $121.5 million. Foreign Trade (1982): Imports, $117 million; exports, $41.6 million.

Saint Vincent and the Grenadines, Caribbean	0.1	Kingstown	150 (389)	Sir Sydney Gunn-Munro, *governor-general* James F. Mitchell, *prime minister*

The New Democratic Party, led by James Mitchell, defeated Prime Minister Milton Robert Cato's St. Vincent Labour Party in July elections. The New Democrats won 9 of 13 seats in the legislature. GNP (1981): $69.2 million. Foreign Trade (1981 est.): Imports, $65.4 million; exports, $52 million.

San Marino, S. Europe	0.022	San Marino	24 (62)	Co-regents appointed semiannually

São Tomé and Principe, W. Africa	0.1	São Tomé	372 (963)	Manuel Pinto da Costa, *president*

In March, President António Romalho Eanes of Portugal visited São Tomé and Principe, a former Portuguese colony, in an effort to strengthen the bonds between the two countries. GDP (1981 est. U.S.$): $30 million. Foreign Trade (1981 est.): Imports, $20 million; exports, $8.8 million.

Senegal, W. Africa	6.5	Dakar	76,000 (196 840)	Abdou Diouf, *president*

Rival factions of the National Workers Federation of Senegal (CNTS) clashed in Dakar in July, with one worker killed and several injured. The CNTS has been associated with the dominant Socialist Party, but disaffection with the Socialists arose among certain CNTS elements who were beginning to lean toward other political groups. GDP (1982 est.): $2.5 billion. Foreign Trade (1982): Imports, $974 million; exports, $477 million. See also GAMBIA.

Seychelles, E. Africa	0.1	Victoria	171 (444)	France Albert René, *president*

On June 15, President René was reelected with more than 92% of the vote. Opposition leaders called for a boycott of the election, but observers considered that the turnout was good. GDP (1982 est.): $128 million. Foreign Trade (1982): Imports, $97.9 million; exports, $15.3 million.

Sierra Leone, W. Africa	3.9	Freetown	27,925 (72 325)	Siaka Stevens, *president*

Student rioting early in 1984 at Fourah Bay College in Freetown focused attention on opposition to President-for-life Siaka Stevens. Anti-Stevens groups living abroad joined in an effort to achieve unity in order to bring "democracy and development" to Sierra Leone. GDP (1981 est.): $1.2 billion. Foreign Trade (1982): Imports, $298 million; exports, $111 million.

Solomon Islands, Oceania	0.3	Honiara	11,500 (29 785)	Sir Baddeley Devesi, *governor-general* Solomon Mamaloni, *prime minister*

In May, Pope John Paul II visited the Solomon Islands, where he stopped at the World War II battleground of Guadalcanal. Governor-General Devesi used the occasion to criticize French nuclear testing in the South Pacific. GNP per capita (1982): $660. Foreign Trade (1981): Imports, $76 million; exports, $66 million.

Somalia, E. Africa	5.7	Mogadishu	265,175 (686 803)	Mohamed Siad Barre, *president*

It was announced in January that Cuban troops occupying the Ogaden region in dispute between Somalia and Ethiopia were to be withdrawn by June. State visits to Somalia included those by Egyptian President Mubarak in January and Kenyan President Moi in July. GDP (1982 est.): $1.9 billion. Foreign Trade (1982): Imports, $221 million; exports, $185 million.

Nation, Region	Population in millions	Capital	Area Sq mi (km²)	Head of State/Government
Surinam, S. America	0.4	Paramaribo	63,037 (163 265)	Desire Bouterse, *head of National Military Council* Willem Udenhout, *prime minister*

In January, military leader Col. Desire Bouterse dismissed the civilian government of Prime Minister Errol Alibux and canceled tax and price increases instituted by the government. The increases had caused labor unrest, including strikes by bauxite workers. (Some 80% of Surinam's foreign earnings are derived from the sale of bauxite.) An interim government formed in February was instructed to restore economic order. GDP (1980): $1.044 billion. Foreign Trade (1982): Imports, $511 million; exports, $429 million.

Swaziland, S. Africa	0.6	Mbabane	6,704 (17 363)	Ntombi Thwala, *queen regent* Prince Bhekimpi Dlamini, *prime minister*

On March 31, Swaziland and South Africa revealed that the two countries secretly had signed a peace accord in 1982 by which each pledged to prevent the use of its territory as a base for guerrilla activity against the other. GDP (1982): $500 million. Foreign Trade (1982): Imports, $501 million; exports, $306.1 million.

Togo, W. Africa	2.9	Lomé	22,000 (56 980)	Gnassingbé Eyadéma, *president*

Ceremonies were held in Togo to mark 100 years of German-Togo relations. GNP (1982 est.): $950 million. Foreign Trade (1982): Imports, $290 million; exports, $202 million.

Tonga, Oceania	0.1	Nuku'alofa	385 (997)	Taufa'ahau Tupou IV, *king* Prince Fatafehi Tu'ipelehake, *premier*

In June, Tonga joined 13 other members of the South Pacific Forum in an agreement to work toward establishing a nuclear-free zone in their region. See also FIJI. GNP (1980): $50 million. Foreign Trade (1982): Imports, $47 million; exports, $5 million.

Trinidad and Tobago, Caribbean	1.2	Port-of-Spain	1,980 (5 128)	Ellis Clark, *president* George Chambers, *prime minister*

In June, Trinidad and Tobago agreed to reschedule a $70 million loan made to Jamaica in 1976. At the July summit meeting of the Caribbean Community and Common Market (Caricom), Prime Minister Chambers questioned the benefits of Trinidad's continued membership in Caricom. Trinidad had been criticized by fellow members for its trade barriers and for its opposition to the 1983 U.S.-led invasion of Grenada. GNP (1982): $7.3 billion. Foreign Trade (1983): Imports, $2.558 billion; exports, $2.387 billion.

Tuvalu, Oceania	0.008	Funafuti	10 (26)	Sir Fiatau Penitala Tea, *governor-general* Tomasi Puapua, prime minister

In June, Tuvalu was the site of a forum of 14 South Pacific nations, at which they agreed to work toward establishing a nuclear-free zone in their region. See also FIJI. GNP (1980 est.): $4 million. Foreign Trade (1981): Imports, $2.8 million; exports, $26,789.

United Arab Emirates, W. Asia	1.5	Abu Dhabi	32,000 (82 880)	Zayid bin Sultan Al Nuhayyan, *president* Rashid ibn Said Al Maktum, *prime minister*

GDP (1982 est.): $30,000 per capita. Foreign Trade (1982): Imports, $9.4 billion; exports, $16.8 billion.

Upper Volta (See Burkina Faso.)

Vanuatu, Oceania	0.1	Port-Vila	5,700 (14 763)	George Ati Sokomanu, *president* Walter Lini, *prime minister*

Vanuatu joined 13 other South Pacific nations in June to discuss establishing a nuclear-free zone in their region. See also FIJI. Foreign Trade (1983): Imports, $64 million; exports, $31 million.

Vatican City, S. Europe	0.001	Vatican City	0.17 (0.438)	John Paul II, *pope*

A new concordat between the Vatican and Italy, replacing the one of 1929, was signed by the Vatican and the Italian government on February 18. See also ITALY, page 287.

Western Samoa, Oceania	0.2	Apia	1,133 (2 934)	Malietoa Tanumafili II, *head of state* Tofilau Eti, *prime minister*

In June, Western Samoa participated in a meeting of the South Pacific Forum. See also FIJI. Foreign Trade (1982): Imports, $50 million; exports, $13 million.

Yemen, North, S. Asia	5.9	San'a	75,000 (194 250)	Ali Abdallah Salih, *president* Abdel Aziz Abd al-Ghani, *prime minister*

The government announced in June that oil in "promising quantities" had been discovered not far from the border with Saudi Arabia. GNP Per Capita (1982): $500. Foreign Trade (1981 U.S.$): Imports, $1.7 billion; exports, $47 million.

Yemen, South, S. Asia	2.1	Aden	111,139 (287 849)	Ali Nassir Muhammad al-Hasani, *chairman,* Council of Ministers

The so-called hard-liners, who wish for even closer ties with the Soviet Union, gained a substantial foothold in May in the party and government when four of them joined the Politburo and three won ministerial appointments. GNP Per Capita (1982 U.S.$) $470.

Zambia, E. Africa	6.6	Lusaka	290,584 (752 614)	Kenneth David Kaunda, *president* Nalumino Mundia, *prime minister*

Zambia reached agreement on rescheduling much of its foreign debt with its three principal creditors: Britain, Belgium, and the United States. On September 18, Paul John Fermino Lusaka, Zambia's representative to the United Nations, became president of the 39th General Assembly. GDP (1981): $2.9 billion. Foreign Trade (1982): Imports, $831 million; exports, $1.06 billion.

POPULATION
Vital Statistics of Selected Countries

	Estimated population mid-1984 (millions)	Birthrate per 1,000 population [1]	Death rate per 1,000 population [1]	Infant mortality [2]	Life expectancy at birth	Urban population (%)
World	4,762.0	28	11	84	61	40
Afghanistan	14.4	48	23	182	40	16
Albania	2.9	28	7	47	70	33
Algeria	21.4	44	11	116	57	52
Angola	7.8	47	22	153	42	21
Argentina	29.1	24	9	38.5	70	82
Australia	15.5	16	8	10.3	75	86
Austria	7.6	12	12	12.8	73	55
Bangladesh	99.6	49	18	148	47	11
Belgium	9.9	12	11	11.7	72	95
Bolivia	6.0	42	16	130	50	45
Brazil	134.4	31	8	76	63	68
Burma	38.9	38	14	99	54	29
Cambodia	6.1	38	19	201	43	15
Cameroon	9.4	44	18	108	47	35
Canada	25.1	15	7	9.6	74	76
Cen. Afr. Republic	2.6	46	20	147	43	35
Chile	11.9	24	6	23.6	68	81
China	1,034.5	21	8	35	65	21
Colombia	28.2	28	7	56	63	64
Cuba	9.9	16	6	17.3	74	69
Cyprus	0.7	22	8	17.2	74	53
Czechoslovakia	15.5	15	12	16.1	70	67
Denmark	5.1	10	11	8.4	74	83
Ecuador	9.1	41	9	81	61	44
Egypt	47.0	38	11	80	56	44
El Salvador	4.8	34	8	44	64	39
Ethiopia	32.0	47	23	146	40	14
Finland	4.9	14	9	6.5	74	60
France	54.8	15	10	9.3	74	73
Germany, East	16.7	14	14	12.3	72	76
Germany, West	61.4	10	12	10.9	73	94
Ghana	14.3	48	16	102	50	36
Greece	10.0	14	9	14.3	73	65
Guatemala	8.0	42	7	65.9	59	39
Haiti	5.5	36	14	113	52	26
Hungary	10.7	12	14	19.7	70	54
India	746.4	34	14	125	50	23
Indonesia	161.6	34	13	92	49	22
Iran	43.8	44	12	106	55	49
Iraq	15.0	47	13	77	56	68
Ireland	3.6	20	9	10.6	73	56
Israel	4.2	24	7	13.9	74	87
Italy	57.0	11	10	13.1	73	69
Japan	119.9	13	6	6.6	76	76
Jordan	3.5	46	9	68	61	60
Kenya	19.4	53	13	86	55	13
Korea, North	19.6	32	8	34	64	33
Korea, South	42.0	23	7	34	67	57
Laos	3.7	42	18	128	45	13
Lebanon	2.6	30	8	41	66	78
Liberia	2.2	45	15	153	54	33
Libya	3.7	46	13	99	57	52
Malaysia	15.3	31	7	31	64	30
Mexico	77.7	32	6	55	66	67
Morocco	23.6	41	12	106	57	42
Netherlands	14.4	12	8	8.3	76	88
New Zealand	3.2	16	8	11.8	72	83
Niger	6.3	51	22	144	43	13
Nigeria	88.1	49	17	134	49	28
Norway	4.1	12	10	7.5	76	70
Pakistan	97.3	43	15	124	51	28
Panama	2.1	26	5	25	70	49
Paraguay	3.6	35	8	46	65	39
Peru	19.2	37	12	101	58	65
Philippines	54.5	32	7	54	61	37
Poland	36.9	19	9	20.4	71	59
Portugal	10.1	16	10	26	71	30
Rumania	22.7	15	10	28.6	71	50
Saudi Arabia	10.8	42	12	112	55	70
South Africa	31.7	35	10	95	61	53
Spain	38.4	13	7	9.4	73	91
Sweden	8.3	11	11	6.8	76	83
Syria	10.1	46	8	61	66	48
Taiwan	19.2	23	5	9.1	72	66
Tanzania	21.2	46	14	102	52	13
Thailand	51.7	26	6	54	61	17
Tunisia	7.0	33	7	98	59	52
Turkey	50.2	31	10	121	62	45
Uganda	14.3	46	15	96	54	7
USSR	274.0	20	10	32	69	64
United Kingdom	56.5	13	12	11	73	76
United States	236.3	16	9	10.9	74	74
Uruguay	3.0	18	9	33.7	70	84
Venezuela	18.6	33	5	41	67	76
Vietnam	58.3	34	10	99	66	19
Yugoslavia	23.0	16	9	29.9	70	39
Zaire	32.2	46	17	111	47	34
Zambia	6.6	48	16	105	50	43
Zimbabwe	8.3	47	13	73	53	23

[1] More Developed Countries—1981–82 data
 Less Developed Countries—early 1980s data

[2] Deaths under age one per 1,000 live births

Source: 1984 World Population Data Sheet, Population Reference Bureau, Inc., Washington, DC

	Barley[1]	Corn[1]	Eggs (million pieces)	Milk	Rice[2]	Soybeans	Sugar[3]	Wheat
Afghanistan	365	800	—	—	480	—	10	3 000
Albania	15	350	—	—	—	—	20	400
Algeria	560	1	—	—	1	—	11	810
Angola	—	250	—	—	20	—	45	11
Argentina	170	10 000	3 200	5 250	475	6 200	1 621	12 000
Australia	4 800	183	3 492	6 110	635	85	3 420	21 903
Austria	1 486	1 500	1 732	3 670			385	1 415
Bangladesh	10				21 937		161	1 198
Belgium[4]	939	36	3 260	4 100	—		782	1 062
Bolivia	56	489			61	75	225	40
Brazil	155	22 500	8 500	10 500	9 000	15 400	9 400	2 100
Bulgaria	1 100	3 100	2 500		60	83	171	3 600
Burma	—	200	—		14 800	19	60	118
Canada	10 200	7 000	5 900	8 105	—	722	132	26 588
Chile	60	650		950	115	1 (1982)	227	850
China	8 360	67 672			168 870	9 765	3 803	81 390
Colombia	35	900			1 780	100	1 288	77
Costa Rica	—	104			277		241	
Cuba		95			518		8 200	
Czechoslovakia	3 250	650	5 500	6 700	—	5	790	5 823
Denmark	5 933		1 370	5 300			380	1 577
Dominican Republic		65			394		1 160	
Ecuador	33	300			270	6	220	23
Egypt	120	3 600	2 400		2 442	162	767	1 996
El Salvador		502			52		240	
Ethiopia	1 000	1 150			—		182	600
Finland	1 700	—	1 510	3 155			155	550
France	11 460	10 128	14 543	27 900	40	24	3 870	24 835
Germany, E.	3 730	12	5 950	8 100	—		920	3 550
Germany, W.	10 265	950	13 100	26 600			2 725	8 998
Ghana	—	524			60		10	
Greece	866	1 728	2 530	677	84		298	2 026
Guatemala		1 105			44	2	515	53
Guyana	—	5			213		265	
Haiti	—	195			133	—	46	
Honduras	—	495			68		215	
Hungary	950	6 500	4 500	2 835	41	51	450	6 000
India	2 000	7 000		16 300	88 509	600	7 025	42 502
Indonesia		4 000			35 237	625	1 758	
Iran	1 200	50			1 261	70	500	5 300
Iraq	250	90			200		35	965
Ireland	1 534	—	650	5 890			214	330
Israel	7	28	1 870		—		10 (1981)	335
Italy	1 450	6 600	10 900	11 100	1 020	61	1 353	8 514
Japan	380	3	34 280	7 175	12 957	217	830	695
Kenya	50	1 275			36	—	350	205
Korea, N.		2 300			5 000	330		400
Korea, S.	804	130			7 608	226	5	112
Lebanon	8	2			—		100	15
Madagascar	—	115			2 100		100	
Malaysia		22			1 813		82	
Mexico	360	9 500	9 900	6 500	435	600	3 242	3 200
Morocco	1 198	224			6		395	1 971
Mozambique	—	200			65		100	3
Nepal	25	750			2 700	—	17	626
Netherlands	194	1	11 200	12 550			808	1 043
New Zealand	550	175		7 200			—	294
Nicaragua	—	200			123		229	
Nigeria		1 800			1 280	50	65	35
Norway	558	—	—	1 967				85
Pakistan	160	1 050			5 215	4	1 219	12 414
Panama	—	80			207		180	
Paraguay	—	600			52	550	95	107
Peru	120	650		610	632	10	620	75
Philippines		3 743			7 851	7	2 367	
Poland	4 143	76	7 700	16 400	—		2 000	5 131
Portugal	65	500	1 280	730	100	—	11	327
Rumania	3 100	11 000	7 200	3 630	71	300	598	5 350
Saudi Arabia	12	5			3	—		710
South Africa	140	9 000	3 080	2 480	—	28	1 462	1 734
Spain	10 300	2 400	11 750	6 300	223	2	1 348	4 330
Sri Lanka					2 310		30	
Sudan					4		285	170
Sweden	2 765		—	3 798			284	1 722
Switzerland	262	144	780	3 751			124	410
Syria	270	80			—		90	1 600
Taiwan	—	215			3 345	8	610	2
Tanzania	—	950			160		115	70
Thailand	—	4 500			19 000	165	1 920	
Tunisia	350				—		12	618
Turkey	5 600	1 500			338	45	1 770	13 300
USSR	40 500	12 100	77 000	97 500	2 500	500	8 700	78 000
United Kingdom	10 800	—	13 300	16 200			1 155	10 880
United States	13 188	190 454	68 392	61 610	4 522	44 519	4 836	65 857
Uruguay	115	120			389	14	91	380
Venezuela		397	2 888	1 665	449	5 (1980)	423	1
Vietnam		500			14 000	—	200	
Yugoslavia	700	11 200	4 600	4 730	42	210	778	5 524
Zaire	—	525			250	—	52	5
Zambia	—	800			10	7	140	12
Zimbabwe	14	1 700			—	86	452	124

Source: U.S. Department of Agriculture.   [1] October 1984 estimate   [2] Rough rice   [3] Centrifugal sugar   [4] Includes Luxembourg

INDUSTRIAL PRODUCTION: SELECTED COUNTRIES (1983)
(in thousand metric tons)

	Cotton yarn	Cement	Gas, manufactured (terajoules)	Newsprint	Rubber, synthetic	Steel, crude	Wool yarn
Algeria	—	3 744[1]	—	—	—	—	—
Argentina	82.8	5 868	—	94.8[1]	48	2 892	—
Australia	16.8	5 088	435 948	375.6	32.76	5 304	17.76
Austria	16.8	4 908	8 964	176.4	—	4 848	8.28
Bangladesh	46.8	300	—	26.4	—	—	—
Belgium	44.4	5 724	9 864	114	108	10 200	86.76
Brazil	—	20 880	—	105.6	220.92	14 664	—
Bulgaria	85.2	5 640	—	—	—	2 820	34.8
Burma	19.2[1]	324	—	—	—	—	—
Canada	—	8 184	37 788[1]	8 493.6	180.84	12 828	—
Chile	—	1 128[1]	—	156	—	600	—
China	3 360.0[1]	95 196	—	—	132.96	40 140	92.52[1]
Colombia	—	4 572[1]	—	—	—	216[1]	—
Cuba	26.4	3 228	2 556[2]	—	—	—	—
Cyprus	—	948	—	—	—	—	—
Czechoslovakia	140.4	10 500	139 776	67.2	67.2	15 024	—
Denmark	—	1 656	4 296	—	—	492	—
Egypt	237.6[1]	4 260[1]	—	—	—	—	12[3]
Ethiopia	7.2[2]	—	360[2]	—	—	—	—
Finland	6.0	1 944	300	1 285.2	9	2 412	—
France	199.2	24 504	204	217.2	511.56	17 616	107.88
Germany, E.	134.4[2]	11 784	105 192	105.6[2]	155.04	7 224	36.84
Germany, W.	181.2	29 568	199 644	660	432.36	36 108	46.80
Greece	117.6	14 124	144	—	—	—	—
Haiti	—	216	—	—	—	—	—
Hong Kong	140.4	1 728	5 928	—	—	—	—
Hungary	56.4	4 248	7 656	—	—	3 612	10.8
India	948.0[1]	25 356	—	159.6	31.2	10 116	—
Indonesia	—	6 144	—	—	—	—	—
Ireland	—	1 488	3 396[2]	—	—	—	—
Israel	16.8	2 172[1]	—	2.4	—	—	6.24
Italy	159.6[1]	39 768	54 636	193.2	216.12[1]	21 684	—
Jamaica	—	240[1]	—	—	—	—	—
Japan	438.0	80 892	204 888	2 562	1 002.48	96 984	110.04
Jordan	—	1 272	—	—	—	—	—
Kenya	2.4[1]	1 320[1]	—	—	—	—	—
Korea, S.	271.2	21 276	—	207.6	91.2	5 064	21.12
Malaysia	10.8	3 984	—	—	—	—	—
Mexico	—	17 028	—	74.4[1]	108	7 152	7.8[1]
Morocco	—	3 852	—	—	—	—	—
Netherlands	9.6	3 240	18 228	176.4	195.96	4 488	6.48
New Zealand	—	756	396	—	—	228	19.32
Nigeria	—	1 800[2]	—	—	—	—	—
Norway	2.4[1]	1 620	84	704.4	—	828	3.24
Pakistan	448.8	3 936	—	—	—	—	—
Panama	—	—	12[2]	—	—	—	—
Philippines	—	4 560	264	—	—	—	—
Poland	172.8	16 164	—	82.8	120	16 236	74.04
Portugal	98.4[1]	5 988	2 568	—	—	384	3.6[1]
Rumania	189.6[2]	13 932[1]	—	91.2[1]	144.96	13 056[1]	—
Singapore	—	—	25 632	—	—	—	—
South Africa	48.0[1]	7 908	—	225.6[2]	27.48	7 068	2.28[1]
Spain	—	31 284	29 760[1]	108.0[2]	50.64	12 864	—
Sri Lanka	7.2	480	—	—	—	—	—
Sweden	4.8	2 232	—	1 363.2	—	4 212	2.28
Switzerland	—	4 176[1]	—	—	—	—	—
Syria	42.0[1]	2 676[1]	—	—	—	—	2.88[1]
Tanzania	—	264[1]	—	—	—	—	—
Thailand	—	7 272	—	—	—	—	—
Tunisia	—	2 520	480[1]	—	—	108[1]	—
Turkey	51.6	13 596	—	147.6	21.96	1 728	5.28
USSR	1 645.2[2]	127 992	612 240[2]	1 508.4[1]	—	152 496	—
United Kingdom	97.2	13 392	59 400[1]	79.2	259.68	15 972	121.20
United States	988.8[1]	63 000	277 344[1]	4 688.4	1 978.32	75 420	62.52[1]
Venezuela	—	—	—	—	—	2 316	—
Yugoslavia	120.0	8 724	3 024[2]	27.6	—	2 004	49.56
Zambia	—	324[1]	—	—	—	—	—
Zimbabwe	—	612	—	—	—	—	—

Source: *Monthly Bulletin of Statistics*, United Nations, August 1984.   [1] 1982   [2] 1981   [3] 1980

WORLD MINERAL AND METAL PRODUCTION

ALUMINUM, primary smelter (thousand metric tons)

	1982	1983
United States	3,274	3,353
USSR[e]	1,875	2,000
Canada	1,065	1,091
West Germany	723	730[e]
Norway	637	715
Australia	381	475
Brazil	299	400[e]
China[e]	370	380
France	390	361
Spain	367	358
Venezuela	244	343
Yugoslavia	246	284
Japan	351	256
New Zealand	167	236
Other countries[a]	2,913	2,872
Total	13,302	13,854

ANTIMONY, mine[b] (metric tons)

	1982	1983
Bolivia	13,978	10,500[e]
China[e]	10,000	10,000
USSR[e]	9,000	9,100
South Africa	9,135	6,302
Mexico	1,564	1,540[e]
Yugoslavia	1,400	1,360
Australia	1,203	1,180[e]
Thailand	666	1,180[e]
Turkey	1,079	1,100
Morocco	905	1,000[e]
Other countries[a]	4,845	5,092
Total	53,775	48,354

ASBESTOS[c] (thousand metric tons)

	1982	1983
USSR[e]	2,180	2,250
Canada	834	829
South Africa	212	220[e]
Zimbabwe	194	190[e]
Brazil	140	135
Italy	116	120[e]
China[e]	110	110
Other countries	294	303
Total	4,080	4,157

BARITE[c] (thousand metric tons)

	1982	1983
China[e]	900	1,000
United States	1,674	684
USSR[e]	520	520
Mexico	364	350
India	326	300
Morocco	538	275
West Germany	362	250
Other countries[a]	2,806	2,380
Total	7,490	5,759

BAUXITE[d] (thousand metric tons)

	1982	1983
Australia	23,625	24,000[e]
Guinea	11,827	11,080
Jamaica	8,361	7,300[e]
Brazil	6,289	7,000[e]
USSR[e]	6,180	6,180
Yugoslavia	3,668	3,500
Hungary	2,627	2,917
Greece	2,853	2,900[e]
India	1,854	1,923
Guyana	1,430	1,791
Surinam	3,059	1,750[e]
France	1,662	1,716
China	1,500	1,500
Other countries[a]	4,438	3,539
Total	79,373	77,096

CEMENT[c] (thousand metric tons)

	1982	1983
USSR	123,681	128,000
China	94,072	108,250
Japan	80,686	80,650
United States	58,369	64,725
Italy	39,727	39,217
Brazil	25,644	38,225
West Germany	31,168	31,000
Spain	29,000	30,633
India	22,498	25,000[e]
France	26,141	24,504
South Korea	17,887	21,282
Mexico	19,298	16,850
Poland	16,035	16,163
Other countries[a]	295,217	301,156
Total	879,423	925,655

COAL, anthracite and bituminous[c] (million metric tons)

	1982	1983
China	651	715
United States	711	665
USSR	555	554
Poland	189	191
South Africa	140	146
India	128	136
Australia	119	121
United Kingdom	125	118
West Germany	89	82
North Korea[e]	45	45
Canada	35	37
Other countries[a]	163	164
Total	2,950	2,974

COAL, lignite[cf] (million metric tons)

	1982	1983
East Germany	276	280[e]
USSR	163	162
West Germany	127	124
Czechoslovakia	99	100
Yugoslavia	54	58
United States	49	47
Poland	38	43
Australia	38	35
Other countries[a]	182	192
Total	1,026	1,041

COPPER, mine[b] (thousand metric tons)

	1982	1983
Chile	1,241	1,190[e]
United States	1,148	1,038
USSR[e]	970	1,000
Canada	612	625
Zambia	568	543[e]
Zaire	519	535[e]
Poland	376	380[e]
Peru	369	336
Philippines	292	309
Australia	245	256
Mexico	239	250[e]
South Africa	189	211
China[e]	200	200
Papua New Guinea	170	183
Other countries[a]	934	971
Total	8,072	8,027

COPPER, refined, primary and secondary (thousand metric tons)

	1982	1983
United States	1,694	1,584
USSR[e]	1,180	1,200
Japan	1,075	1,092
Chile	852	813
Zambia	585	575
Canada	328	544
Belgium	458	455
West Germany	394	420
Poland	348	357
China[e]	280	280
Zaire	175	227
Australia	178	200
Peru	228	191
Spain	172	159
South Africa	143	152
Other countries[a]	1,134	1,196
Total	9,224	9,445

DIAMOND (thousand carats)

	1982	1983
Zaire	9,000	11,438
Botswana	7,769	10,731
USSR[e]	10,600	10,700
South Africa	9,154	10,311
Australia	557	6,200
China[e]	2,000	2,000
Other countries[a]	5,287	4,739
Total	44,367	56,119

FLUORSPAR[g] (thousand metric tons)

	1982	1983
Mongolia	670	690
Mexico	631	605[e]
USSR[e]	540	540
China[e]	480	480
South Africa	331	274
Thailand	241	257
France	244	240[e]
United Kingdom	98	200[e]
Spain	194	187
Other countries[a]	849	831
Total	4,278	4,304

GAS, natural[h] (billion cubic feet)

	1982	1983
USSR	17,682	18,929
United States	18,520	16,657
Netherlands	2,548	2,500[e]
Canada	2,683	2,465
Algeria	1,048	1,650
United Kingdom	1,263	1,304
Mexico	1,279	1,274
Rumania[e]	1,200	1,200
Indonesia	926	1,032
Other countries[a]	8,234	8,531
Total	55,383	55,542

GOLD, mine[b] (thousand troy ounces)

	1982	1983
South Africa	21,355	21,847
USSR[e]	8,550	8,600
Canada	2,081	2,274
United States	1,466	1,957
China[e]	1,800	1,900
Brazil[e]	1,500	1,600
Australia	867	1,035[e]
Philippines	834	802[e]
Papua New Guinea	564	582
Other countries[a]	4,040	3,936
Total	43,057	44,533

GRAPHITE (thousand metric tons)

	1982	1983
China[e]	185	185
USSR[e]	105	110
Czechoslovakia[e]	45	45
Mexico	36	36[e]
India	52	35
South Korea	27	31
North Korea[e]	25	25
Other countries[a]	112	118
Total	587	585

GYPSUM[c] (thousand metric tons)

	1982	1983
United States	9,560	11,688
Canada	5,443	7,484
Japan	6,363	6,622
France	6,039	5,990[e]
USSR[e]	5,400	5,400
Iran[e]	5,000	5,400
Spain	5,049	5,000
China[e]	3,500	3,600
United Kingdom	2,740	3,100
Mexico	1,866	2,360
West Germany	1,721	1,815[e]
Australia	1,730	1,796
Italy	1,335	1,270[e]
Other countries[a]	15,894	16,333
Total	71,640	77,858

IRON ORE[c] (thousand metric tons)

	1982	1983
USSR	244,411	245,000
Brazil	95,000	89,000
Australia	87,694	71,500
China[e]	69,000	71,000
India	40,902	38,800[e]
United States	36,002	38,600
Canada	35,425	33,495
South Africa	24,554	16,605
France	19,411	15,967
Liberia	18,268	14,937
Sweden	16,138	13,212
Venezuela	11,200	9,715
Other countries[a]	83,302	81,302
Total	781,307	739,133

IRON, steel ingots (thousand metric tons)

	1982	1983
USSR	147,165	153,000
Japan	99,548	97,164
United States	72,903	76,761
China	37,160	39,950
West Germany	35,880	35,730
Italy	23,981	21,674
France	18,416	17,612
Czechoslovakia	14,992	15,024
United Kingdom	13,704	14,993
Brazil	12,990	14,659
Poland	14,795	13,600
Rumania	13,055	13,100[e]
Canada	11,762	12,828
Spain	13,160	12,731
South Korea	11,753	11,915
Belgium	9,900	10,155
India	10,715	10,305
South Africa	8,271	7,004
East Germany	7,169	7,000[e]
Other countries[a]	69,385	72,019
Total	646,704	657,224

LEAD, mine (thousand metric tons)

	1982	1983
Australia	455	477
United States	513	449
USSR[e]	430	435
Canada	341	252
Peru	176	206
China[e]	160	160
Mexico	146	150[e]
Yugoslavia	115	120[e]
Morocco	104	102
Other countries[a]	968	973
Total	3,408	3,324

LEAD, refined, primary and secondary[i] (thousand metric tons)

	1982	1983
United States	1,088	1,018
USSR[e]	730	745
Japan	302	355
West Germany	348	352
United Kingdom	310	315
Canada	239	242
Australia	247	224
France	209	206
China[e]	175	175
Mexico	163	165[e]
Italy	134	130[e]
Spain	132	130
Other countries[a]	1,150	1,172
Total	5,227	5,229

	1982	1983
MAGNESIUM, primary (thousand metric tons)		
United States	93	105
USSR	81	83
Norway	35	35 [e]
France	10	9 [e]
Canada [e]	5	8
Italy	7	8
China [e]	7	7
Other countries [a]	9	9
Total	247	264
MANGANESE ore (thousand metric tons)		
USSR	9,821	10,400 [e]
South Africa	5,217	2,886
Brazil	2,340	2,100 [e]
Gabon	1,511	1,857
China [e]	1,600	1,600
Australia	1,132	1,353
India	1,448	1,320
Other countries [a]	1,070	917
Total	24,139	22,433
MERCURY [b] (76-pound flasks)		
USSR [e]	64,000	64,000
Spain	48,808	48,000 [e]
United States	25,760	25,070
China	20,000	20,000
Algeria	11,000	10,000
Other countries [a]	28,128	21,423
Total	197,696	188,493
MOLYBDENUM, mine [b] (metric tons)		
United States	38,274	15,400
Chile	20,048	15,000 [e]
USSR	11,000	11,000
Canada	13,961	10,478
Peru	2,893	2,630 [e]
China [e]	2,000	2,000
Other countries [a]	5,874	6,025
Total	94,050	62,533
NATURAL GAS LIQUIDS (million barrels)		
United States	566	571
Algeria	105	180
USSR [e]	145	145
Saudi Arabia	157	125 [e]
Canada	117	114
Mexico [e]	95	95
Other countries [a]	195	239
Total	1,380	1,469
NICKEL, mine [b] (thousand metric tons)		
USSR [e]	165	170
Canada	89	122 [e]
Australia	89	90 [e]
New Caledonia	60	63 [e]
Indonesia	55	47
Cuba	36	37
South Africa	22	21
Dominican Republic	6	20
Other countries [a]	126	119
Total	648	689
NITROGEN, content of ammonia (thousand metric tons)		
China [e]	12,711	15,000
USSR [e]	14,000	14,500
United States	11,764	10,202
India	3,287	3,200 [e]
Rumania	2,587	2,600 [e]
Canada	2,062	2,374
Mexico	2,031	2,160
France	1,900	1,900 [e]
Netherlands	1,655	1,744
West Germany	1,570	1,703
Other coutries [a]	21,126	21,457
Total	74,693	76,840
PETROLEUM, crude (million barrels)		
USSR	4,503	4,528
United States	3,157	3,159
Saudi Arabia	2,366	1,834
Mexico	1,002	973
Iran	873	892
United Kingdom	741	798 [e]
China	745	774 [e]
Venezuela	692	656
Canada	464	495
Indonesia	488	490

	1982	1983
PETROLEUM, crude (cont'd.)		
Nigeria	472	452
United Arab Emirates	456	409
Libya [a]	418	402
Iraq [e]	310	400
Other countries [a]	2,861	3,130
Total	19,548	19,392
PHOSPHATE ROCK [c] (thousand metric tons)		
United States	37,414	42,573
USSR	26,700	27,000 [e]
Morocco	17,754	20,106
China	11,720	12,500
Tunisia	4,196	5,924
Jordan	4,390	4,749
Brazil	2,732	3,208
Israel	2,148	2,969
South Africa	3,173	2,742
Togo	2,128	2,081
Other countries [a]	9,847	10,774
Total	122,202	134,626
POTASH, K₂0 equivalent basis (thousand metric tons)		
USSR	8,079	9,300
Canada	5,309	6,203
East Germany	3,434	3,430 [e]
West Germany	2,057	2,100
France	1,701	1,900 [e]
United States	1,784	1,429
Other countries [a]	2,300	2,316
Total	24,664	26,678
SALT [c] (thousand metric tons)		
United States	34,392	31,387
USSR [e]	15,800	16,200
China	16,384	15,872
West Germany	10,978	10,500 [e]
India	7,312	10,004 [e]
Canada	7,940	8,590
United Kingdom	7,637	7,600 [e]
France	6,694	7,120 [e]
Australia	6,100	6,000 [e]
Mexico	5,480	5,500 [e]
Rumania	5,000	5,000
Italy	4,605	4,700 [e]
Poland [e]	4,300	4,300
Brazil	3,724	3,850 [e]
Other countries [a]	28,791	28,975
Total	165,137	165,598
SILVER, mine [b] (thousand troy ounces)		
Mexico	59,175	61,435
Peru	53,639	55,871
USSR	46,900	47,200
United States	40,248	43,415
Canada	42,246	35,560
Australia	29,156	32,150 [e]
Poland	21,058	24,900 [e]
Chile	12,288	11,600 [e]
Japan	9,843	9,877
South Africa	6,943	5,559
Bolivia	5,472	5,090
Sweden	5,626	5,500
Other countries [a]	51,172	52,461
Total	383,766	390,618
SULFUR, all forms [j] (thousand metric tons)		
USSR [e]	9,640	9,590
United States	9,787	9,290
Canada	6,281	6,625
Poland	5,285	5,240
Japan	2,595	2,645
China [e]	2,300	2,600
France	2,061	2,063
Mexico	1,916	1,633
West Germany	1,821	1,540
Spain	1,167	1,131
Other countries [a]	7,923	8,115
Total	50,776	50,472
TIN, mine [b] (thousand metric tons)		
Malaysia	52,330	42,000
USSR [e]	37,000	37,000
Indonesia	33,806	27,000 [e]
Bolivia	26,773	24,400 [e]
Thailand	26,109	19,943
China [e]	15,000	15,000

	1982	1983
TIN, mine [b] (cont'd.)		
Other countries [a]	46,158	46,277
Total	237,176	211,620
TITANIUM MINERALS [c] [k] (thousand metric tons) ILMENITE		
Australia	1,169	893 [e]
Norway	552	544
USSR [e]	430	435
United States	207	NA
Finland	168	160
India	153	150 [e]
Other countries [a]	324	427
Total	3,003	2,609
RUTILE		
Australia	221	170 [e]
Sierra Leone	48	72
South Africa	47	56
Other countries [a]	24	28
Total	340	326
TITANIFEROUS SLAG		
Canada [e]	670	610
South Africa [e]	380	380
Total	1,050	990
TUNGSTEN, mine [b] (metric tons)		
China [e]	12,500	12,500
USSR [e]	9,000	9,100
Bolivia	2,534	2,400 [e]
South Korea	2,420	2,293
Australia	2,618	2,060
Portugal	1,358	1,360 [e]
Brazil [e]	1,100	1,200
Austria	1,714	1,117
United States	1,521	980
Burma	844	930
Peru	688	720
Other countries [a]	9,768	9,222
Total	46,065	43,882
URANIUM OXIDE (U₃0₈) [b] [l] (metric tons)		
United States	12,156	9,344
Canada	9,525	8,845
South Africa	6,858	7,128
Niger	5,023	5,024
Namibia	4,453	4,379
France	3,397	3,857
Australia	5,251	3,795
Other countries [a]	2,024	2,083
Total	48,687	44,455
ZINC, mine [b] (thousand metric tons)		
Canada	1,189	1,070
USSR [e]	800	805
Australia	665	695
Peru	507	553
United States	303	275
Mexico	242	257
Japan	251	256
Sweden	185	203
Ireland	167	186 [e]
Spain	173	175 [e]
China	160	160
Poland	145	146 [e]
Other countries [a]	1,451	1,465
Total	6,238	6,246
ZINC, smelter, primary and secondary (thousand metric tons)		
USSR [e]	920	930
Japan	662	701
Canada	512	617
West Germany	335	356
United States	302	305
Australia	296	303
Belgium	228	263
France	244	250 [e]
Spain	187	190 [e]
Netherlands	186	188
Mexico	127	179
Poland	165	170
China [e]	160	160
Finland	144	155
Other countries [a]	1,397	1,408
Total	5,865	6,175

[a] Estimated in part. [b] Content of concentrates. [c] Gross weight. [d] Includes calculated bauxite equivalent of estimated output of aluminum ores other than bauxite (nepheline concentrate and alunite ore). [e] Estimate. [f] Includes coal classified in some countries as brown coal. [g] Marketable gross weight. [h] Marketed production (includes gas sold or used by producers, excludes gas reinjected to reservoirs for pressure maintenance and that flared or vented to the atmosphere, which is not used as fuel or industrial raw material, and which thus has no economic value). [i] Excludes bullion produced for refining elsewhere. [j] Includes (1) Frasch process sulfur, (2) elemental sulfur mined by conventional methods, (3) by-product recovered elemental sulfur, and (4) elemental sulfur equivalent obtained from pyrite and other materials. [k] Excludes output (if any) by China. [l] Excludes output (if any) by Albania, Bulgaria, China, Czechoslovakia, East Germany, Hungary, North Korea, Mongolia, Poland, Rumania, and Vietnam.

Compiled by Charles L. Kimball, U.S. Bureau of Mines

THE UNITED STATES GOVERNMENT

EXECUTIVE BRANCH
(selected listing, as of Jan. 15, 1985)

President: Ronald Reagan

Vice-President: George Bush

Executive Office of the President
The White House

Counsellor to the President: Edwin Meese III[1]
Chief of Staff and Assistant to the President: Donald T. Regan[2]
Deputy Chief of Staff and Assistant to the President: Michael K. Deaver[3]
Assistant to the President and Press Secretary: James S. Brady
Assistant to the President and Deputy to the Chief of Staff: Richard G. Darman
Counsel to the President: Fred F. Fielding
Assistant to the President for Cabinet Affairs: Craig L. Fuller
Assistant to the President for National Security Affairs: Robert McFarlane
Assistant to the President for Legislative Affairs: M. B. Oglesby
Assistant to the President and Deputy Press Secretary: Larry M. Speakes

Assistant to the President for Policy Development: John A. Svahn
Assistant to the President for Intergovernmental Affairs: Lee Verstandig
Assistant to the President for Public Liaison: Faith Ryan Whittlesey
Office of Management and Budget, Director: David A. Stockman
Council of Economic Advisers, Chairman: (vacant)
Office of United States Trade Representative, U.S. Trade Representative: William E. Brock
Council on Environmental Quality, Chairman: A. Alan Hill
Office of Science and Technology Policy, Director: George A. Keyworth II
Office of Administration, Director: John F. W. Rogers II

The Cabinet

Department of Agriculture
Secretary: John R. Block
Deputy Secretary: Richard E. Lyng

Department of Commerce
Secretary: Malcolm Baldrige
Deputy Secretary: Clarence Brown
National Oceanic and Atmospheric Administrator: Anthony J. Calio
National Bureau of Standards, Director: Ernest Ambler
Bureau of the Census, Director: John Keane

Department of Defense
Secretary: Casper W. Weinberger
Deputy Secretary: Frank C. Carlucci
Joint Chiefs of Staff
    Chairman: Gen. John W. Vessey, Jr., USA
    Chief of Staff, Army: Gen. John A. Wickham, Jr., USA
    Chief of Staff, Air Force: Gen. Charles A. Gabriel, USAF
    Chief of Naval Operations: Adm. James D. Watkins, USN
    Commandant, Marine Corps: Gen. P. X. Kelley, USMC
Secretary of the Air Force: Verne Orr
Secretary of the Army: John O. Marsh, Jr.
Secretary of the Navy: John F. Lehman, Jr.

Department of Education
Secretary: William J. Bennett[4]

Department of Energy
Secretary: John S. Herrington[4]
Deputy Secretary: W. Kenneth Davis

Department of Health and Human Services
Secretary: Margaret Heckler
Undersecretary: Charles Baker
Surgeon General: C. Everett Koop
Alcohol, Drug Abuse, and Mental Health Administrator: Donald I. MacDonald
Centers for Disease Control, Director: James O. Mason
National Institutes of Health, Director: James B. Wyngaarden
Social Security Administration, Commissioner: Martha A. McSteen

Department of Housing and Urban Development
Secretary: Samuel R. Pierce, Jr.
Undersecretary: John Knapp (acting)

Department of the Interior
Secretary: Donald P. Hodel[4]
Undersecretary: Anne Dore McLaughlin
Fish and Wildlife Service, Director: Robert A. Jantzen
National Park Service, Director: Russell E. Dickenson
Bureau of Mines, Director: Robert C. Horton

Department of Justice
Attorney General: William French Smith[1]
Deputy Attorney General: Carol E. Dinkins
Solicitor General: Rex E. Lee
Federal Bureau of Investigation, Director: William H. Webster
Drug Enforcement Administrator: Francis M. Mullen, Jr.
Immigration and Naturalization Service, Commissioner: Alan C. Nelson
Bureau of Prisons, Director: Norman A. Carlson

Department of Labor
Secretary: Raymond J. Donovan[5]
Undersecretary: Ford B. Ford (also acting secretary)
Women's Bureau, Director: Lenora Cole-Alexander
Commissioner of Labor Statistics: Janet L. Norwood

Department of State
Secretary: George P. Shultz
Chief of Protocol: Selwa Roosevelt
Undersecretary for Political Affairs: Michael Armacost
Undersecretary for Security Assistance, Science and Technology: William Schneider, Jr.
Undersecretary for Management: Ronald I. Spiers
Assistant Secretary for Human Rights and Humanitarian Affairs: Elliott Abrams
Assistant Secretary for African Affairs: Chester A. Crocker
Assistant Secretary for East Asian and Pacific Affairs: Paul D. Wolfowitz
Assistant Secretary for European and Canadian Affairs: Richard R. Burt
Assistant Secretary for Inter-American Affairs: Langhorne A. Motley
Assistant Secretary for Near Eastern and South Asian Affairs: Richard W. Murphy
Assistant Secretary for Administration: Robert E. Lamb
United Nations Representative: Jeane J. Kirkpatrick

Department of Transportation
Secretary: Elizabeth Dole
Deputy Secretary: James Burnley IV
U.S. Coast Guard, Commandant: Adm. James S. Gracey, USCG
Federal Aviation Administrator: Donald D. Engen
Federal Highway Administrator: R. A. Barnhart
Federal Railroad Administrator: John H. Riley

Department of the Treasury
Secretary: James A. Baker III[4]
Deputy Secretary: R. T. McNamar
Undersecretary for Monetary Affairs: Beryl W. Sprinkel
Comptroller of the Currency: C. T. Conover
Internal Revenue Service, Commissioner: Roscoe L. Egger, Jr.

Independent Agencies

ACTION, Director: Thomas W. Pauken
Appalachian Regional Commission, Federal Cochairman: Winifred A. Pizzano
Central Intelligence Agency, Director: William J. Casey
Commission on Civil Rights, Chairman: Clarence M. Pendleton, Jr.
Commission of Fine Arts, Chairman: J. Carter Brown
Consumer Product Safety Commission, Chairman: Nancy H. Steorts
Environmental Protection Agency, Administrator: Lee M. Thomas[4]
Equal Employment Opportunity Commissioner: Clarence Thomas
Export-Import Bank, President and Chairman: William H. Draper III
Federal Communications Commission, Chairman: Mark S. Fowler
Federal Deposit Insurance Corporation, Chairman: William M. Isaac
Federal Election Commission, Chairman: Lee Ann Elliott
Federal Emergency Management Agency, Director: Louis O. Giuffrida
Federal Farm Credit Board, Chairman: Dwight L. Tripp, Jr.
Federal Home Loan Bank Board, Chairman: Edwin J. Gray
Federal Labor Relations Authority, Chairman: Henry Bowen Frazier III (acting)
Federal Maritime Commission, Chairman: Alan Green, Jr.
Federal Mediation and Conciliation Service, Director: Kay McMurray
Federal Reserve System, Chairman: Paul A. Volcker
Federal Trade Commission, Chairman: James C. Miller III
General Services Administrator: Ray Kline (acting)

Interstate Commerce Commission, Chairman: Reese H. Taylor, Jr.
National Aeronautics and Space Administration, Administrator: James M. Beggs
National Foundation on the Arts and Humanities
 National Endowment for the Arts, Chairman: Francis S. M. Hodsoll
 National Endowment for the Humanities, Chairman: William J. Bennett[6]
National Labor Relations Board, Chairman: Donald L. Dotson
National Science Foundation, Director: Erich Bloch
National Transportation Safety Board, Chairman: James E. Burnett
Nuclear Regulatory Commission, Chairman: Nunzio J. Palladino
Peace Corps, Director: Loren Miller Ruppe
Postal Rate Commission, Chairman: Janet D. Steiger
Securities and Exchange Commission, Chairman: John S. R. Shad
Selective Service System, Director: Maj. Gen. Thomas K. Turnage
Small Business Administrator: James C. Sanders
Tennessee Valley Authority, Chairman: Charles H. Dean, Jr.
U.S. Arms Control and Disarmament Agency, Director: Kenneth L. Adelman
U.S. Information Agency, Director: Charles Z. Wick
U.S. International Development Cooperation Agency, Director: M. Peter McPherson (acting)
U.S. International Trade Commission, Chairman: Alfred E. Eckes
U.S. Postal Service, Postmaster General: Paul Carlin
Veterans Administrator: Harry N. Walters

THE SUPREME COURT

Warren E. Burger, chief justice
William J. Brennan, Jr.
Byron R. White

Thurgood Marshall
Harry A. Blackmun
Lewis F. Powell, Jr.

William H. Rehnquist
John Paul Stevens
Sandra Day O'Connor

THE 99TH CONGRESS

Senate Committee Chairmen

Agriculture, Nutrition, and Forestry: Jesse Helms (NC)
Appropriations: Mark O. Hatfield (OR)
Armed Services: Barry Goldwater (AZ)
Banking, Housing, and Urban Affairs: Jake Garn (UT)
Budget: Peter V. Domenici (NM)
Commerce, Science, and Transportation: John C. Danforth (MO)
Energy and Natural Resources: James A. McClure (ID)
Environment and Public Works: Robert T. Stafford (VT)
Finance: Bob Packwood (OR)
Foreign Relations: Richard Lugar (IN)
Governmental Affairs: William V. Roth, Jr. (DE)
Judiciary: Strom Thurmond (SC)
Labor and Human Resources: Orrin G. Hatch (UT)
Rules and Administration: Charles McC. Mathias, Jr. (MD)
Small Business: Lowell P. Weicker, Jr. (CT)
Veterans' Affairs: Frank Murkowski (AK)

Select Senate Committee Chairmen

Ethics: (vacant)
Indian Affairs: Mark Andrews (ND)
Intelligence: David Durenberger (MN)

House Committee Chairmen

Agriculture: E. de la Garza (TX)
Appropriations: Jamie L. Whitten (MS)
Armed Services: Les Aspin (WI)
Banking, Finance and Urban Affairs: Fernand J. St. Germain (RI)
Budget: William H. Gray III (PA)
District of Columbia: Ronald V. Dellums (CA)
Education and Labor: Augustus F. Hawkins (CA)
Energy and Commerce: John D. Dingell (MI)
Foreign Affairs: Dante B. Fascell (FL)
Government Operations: Jack Brooks (TX)
House Administration: Frank Annunzio (IL)
Interior and Insular Affairs: Morris K. Udall (AZ)
Judiciary: Peter W. Rodino, Jr. (NJ)
Merchant Marine and Fisheries: Walter B. Jones (NC)
Post Office and Civil Service: William D. Ford (MI)
Public Works and Transportation: James J. Howard (NJ)
Rules: Claude Pepper (FL)
Science and Technology: Don Fuqua (FL)
Small Business: Parren J. Mitchell (MD)
Standards of Official Conduct: Louis Stokes (OH)
Veterans' Affairs: G. V. Montgomery (MS)
Ways and Means: Dan Rostenkowski (IL)

Select House Committee Chairmen

Aging: Edward R. Roybal (CA)
Intelligence: Lee H. Hamilton (IN)
Narcotics Abuse and Control: Charles B. Rangel (NY)

1) Edwin Meese is to be nominated attorney general; 2) named (Senate confirmation not required); 3) resignation announced; 4) named (Senate confirmation required); 5) on leave of absence; 6) named secretary of education (no new appointee to Humanities).

SENATE MEMBERSHIP

(As of January 1985: 53 Republicans, 47 Democrats) Letters after senators' names refer to party affiliation—D for Democrat, R for Republican. Single asterisk (*) denotes term expiring in January 1987; double asterisk (**), term expiring in January 1989; triple asterisk (***), term expiring in January 1991.

Alabama
*** H. Heflin, D
* J. Denton, R

Alaska
*** T. Stevens, R
* F. H. Murkowski, R

Arizona
* B. Goldwater, R
** D. DeConcini, D

Arkansas
* D. Bumpers, D
*** D. Pryor, D

California
* A. Cranston, D
** P. Wilson, R

Colorado
* G. Hart, D
*** W. Armstrong, R

Connecticut
** L. P. Weicker, Jr., R
* C. J. Dodd, D

Delaware
** W. V. Roth, Jr., R
*** J. R. Biden, Jr., D

Florida
** L. M. Chiles, Jr., D
* P. Hawkins, R

Georgia
*** S. Nunn, D
* M. Mattingly, R

Hawaii
* D. K. Inouye, D
** S. M. Matsunaga, D

Idaho
*** J. A. McClure, R
* S. D. Symms, R

Illinois
* A. J. Dixon, D
*** P. Simon, D

Indiana
** R. G. Lugar, R
* D. Quayle, R

Iowa
* C. E. Grassley, R
*** T. Harkin, D

Kansas
* R. J. Dole, R
*** N. Kassebaum, R

Kentucky
* W. H. Ford, D
*** M. McConnell, R

Louisiana
* R. B. Long, D
*** J. B. Johnston, D

Maine
*** W. Cohen, R
** G. Mitchell, D

Maryland
* C. M. Mathias, Jr., R
** P. S. Sarbanes, D

Massachusetts
** E. M. Kennedy, D
*** J. F. Kerry, D

Michigan
** D. W. Riegle, Jr., D
* C. Levin, D

Minnesota
** D. Durenberger, R
*** R. Boschwitz, R

Mississippi
** J. C. Stennis, D
*** T. Cochran, R

Missouri
* T. F. Eagleton, D
* J. C. Danforth, R

Montana
** J. Melcher, D
*** M. Baucus, D

Nebraska
** E. Zorinsky, D
*** J. Exon, D

Nevada
* P. Laxalt, R
** C. Hecht, R

New Hampshire
*** G. Humphrey, R
* W. Rudman, R

New Jersey
*** B. Bradley, D
** F. R. Lautenberg, D

New Mexico
*** P. V. Domenici, R
** J. Bingaman, D

New York
** D. P. Moynihan, D
* A. D'Amato, R

North Carolina
*** J. Helms, R
* J. P. East, R

North Dakota
** Q. N. Burdick, D
* M. Andrews, R

Ohio
* J. H. Glenn, Jr., D
** H. M. Metzenbaum, D

Oklahoma
*** D. Boren, D
* D. Nickles, R

Oregon
*** M. O. Hatfield, R
* B. Packwood, R

Pennsylvania
** J. Heinz, R
* A. Specter, R

Rhode Island
*** C. Pell, D
** J. H. Chafee, R

South Carolina
*** S. Thurmond, R
* E. F. Hollings, D

South Dakota
*** L. Pressler, R
* J. Abdnor, R

Tennessee
** J. Sasser, D
*** A. Gore, Jr., D

Texas
** L. M. Bentsen, D
*** P. Gramm, R

Utah
* E. J. Garn, R
** O. Hatch, R

Vermont
** R. T. Stafford, R
* P. J. Leahy, D

Virginia
*** J. Warner, R
* P. S. Trible, Jr., R

Washington
** D. J. Evans, R
* S. Gorton, R

West Virginia
* R. C. Byrd, D
*** J. D. Rockefeller IV, D

Wisconsin
* W. Proxmire, D
* R. W. Kasten, Jr., R

Wyoming
** M. Wallop, R
*** A. Simpson, R

HOUSE MEMBERSHIP

(As of January, 1985, 252 Democrats, 182 Republicans, 1 undecided) "At-L." in place of Congressional district number means "representative at large." * Indicates elected Nov. 6, 1984; all others were reelected in 1984.

Alabama
1. *H. L. Callahan, R
2. W. L. Dickinson, R
3. W. Nichols, D
4. T. Bevill, D
5. R. Flippo, D
6. B. Erdreich, D
7. R. Shelby, D

Alaska
At-L. D. Young, R

Arizona
1. J. McCain, III, R
2. M. K. Udall, D
3. B. Stump, R
4. E. Rudd, R
5. *J. Kolbe, R

Arkansas
1. W. V. Alexander, Jr., D
2. *T. Robinson, D
3. J. P. Hammerschmidt, R
4. B. Anthony, Jr., D

California
1. D. H. Bosco, D
2. E. A. Chappie, R
3. R. Matsui, D
4. V. Fazio, D
5. S. Burton, D
6. B. Boxer, D
7. G. Miller, D
8. R. V. Dellums, D
9. F. H. Stark, Jr., D
10. D. Edwards, D
11. T. Lantos, D
12. E. Zschau, R
13. N. Y. Mineta, D
14. N. Shumway, R
15. T. Coelho, D
16. L. E. Panetta, D
17. C. Pashayan, Jr., R
18. R. Lehman, D
19. R. J. Lagomarsino, R
20. W. M. Thomas, R
21. B. Fiedler, R
22. C. J. Moorhead, R
23. A. C. Beilenson, D
24. H. A. Waxman, D
25. E. R. Roybal, D
26. H. L. Berman, D
27. M. Levine, D
28. J. Dixon, D
29. A. F. Hawkins, D
30. M. G. Martinez, D
31. M. Dymally, D
32. G. M. Anderson, D
33. D. Dreier, R
34. E. Torres, D
35. J. Lewis, R
36. G. E. Brown, Jr., D
37. A. McCandless, R
38. *R. K. Dornan, R
39. W. Dannemeyer, R
40. R. E. Badham, R
41. W. D. Lowery, R
42. D. Lungren, R
43. R. Packard, R
44. J. Bates, D
45. D. L. Hunter, R

Colorado
1. P. Schroeder, D
2. T. E. Wirth, D
3. *M. L. Strang, R
4. H. Brown, R
5. K. Kramer, R
6. D. Schaefer, R

Connecticut
1. B. Kennelly, D
2. S. Gejdenson, D
3. B. Morrison, D
4. S. B. McKinney, R
5. *J. G. Rowland, R
6. N. L. Johnson, R

Delaware
At-L. T. R. Carper, D

Florida
1. E. Hutto, D
2. D. Fuqua, D
3. C. E. Bennett, D
4. W. V. Chappell, Jr., D
5. B. McCollum, Jr., R
6. K. H. MacKay, D
7. S. M. Gibbons, D
8. C. W. Young, R
9. M. Bilirakis, R
10. A. Ireland, R
11. B. Nelson, D
12. T. Lewis, R
13. C. Mack, R
14. D. A. Mica, D
15. E. C. Shaw, Jr., R
16. L. Smith, D
17. W. Lehman, D
18. C. Pepper, D
19. D. B. Fascell, D

Georgia
1. R. L. Thomas, D
2. C. Hatcher, D
3. R. Ray, D
4. *P. L. Swindall, R
5. W. Fowler, Jr., D
6. N. Gingrich, R
7. G. Darden, D
8. J. R. Rowland, Jr., D
9. E. L. Jenkins, D
10. D. D. Barnard, Jr., D

Hawaii
1. C. Heftel, D
2. D. K. Akaka, D

Idaho
1. L. Craig, R
2. *R. Stallings, D

Illinois
1. C. A. Hayes, D
2. G. Savage, D
3. M. A. Russo, D
4. G. M. O'Brien, R
5. W. O. Lipinski, D
6. H. J. Hyde, R
7. C. Collins, D
8. D. Rostenkowski, D
9. S. R. Yates, D
10. J. Porter, R
11. F. Annunzio, D
12. P. M. Crane, R
13. *H. W. Fawell, R
14. *J. E. Grotberg, R
15. E. R. Madigan, R
16. L. Martin, R
17. L. Evans, D

18. R. H. Michel, R
19. *T. L. Bruce, D
20. R. J. Durbin, D
21. M. Price, D
22. *Kenneth J. Gray, D

Indiana
1. *P. J. Visclosky, D
2. P. R. Sharp, D
3. J. Hiler, R
4. D. Coats, R
5. E. H. Hillis, R
6. D. Burton, R
7. J. T. Myers, R
8. undecided
9. L. H. Hamilton, D
10. A. Jacobs, Jr., D

Iowa
1. J. A. S. Leach, R
2. T. Tauke, R
3. C. Evans, R
4. N. Smith, D
5. *J. R. Lightfoot, R
6. B. W. Bedell, D

Kansas
1. P. Roberts, R
2. J. Slattery, D
3. *J. Meyers, R
4. D. Glickman, D
5. B. Whittaker, R

Kentucky
1. C. Hubbard, Jr., D
2. W. H. Natcher, D
3. R. L. Mazzoli, D
4. G. Snyder, R
5. H. Rogers, R
6. L. Hopkins, R
7. *C. C. Perkins, D

Louisiana
1. R. L. Livingston, Jr., R
2. L. Boggs, D
3. W. J. Tauzin, D
4. B. Roemer, D
5. J. Huckaby, D
6. W. H. Moore, R
7. J. B. Breaux, D
8. G. W. Long, D

Maine
1. J. R. McKernan, Jr., R
2. O. Snowe, R

Maryland
1. R. Dyson, D
2. *H. D. Bentley, R
3. B. A. Mikulski, D
4. M. S. Holt, R
5. S. Hoyer, D
6. B. Byron, D
7. P. J. Mitchell, D
8. M. Barnes, D

Massachusetts
1. S. O. Conte, R
2. E. P. Boland, D
3. J. D. Early, D
4. B. Frank, D
5. *C. G. Atkins, D
6. N. Mavroules, D
7. E. J. Markey, D
8. T. P. O'Neill, Jr., D
9. J. J. Moakley, D
10. G. E. Studds, D
11. B. Donnelly, D

Michigan
1. J. Conyers, Jr., D
2. C. D. Pursell, R
3. H. Wolpe, D
4. M. Siljander, R
5. *P. B. Henry, R
6. B. Carr, D
7. D. E. Kildee, D
8. B. Traxler, D
9. G. A. Vander Jagt, R
10. *B. Schuette, R
11. R. Davis, R
12. D. E. Bonior, D
13. G. Crockett, Jr., D
14. D. Hertel, D
15. W. D. Ford, D
16. J. D. Dingell, D
17. S. Levin, D
18. W. S. Broomfield, R

Minnesota
1. T. J. Penny, D
2. V. Weber, R
3. B. Frenzel, R

4. B. F. Vento, D
5. M. Sabo, D
6. G. Sikorski, D
7. A. Stangeland, R
8. J. L. Oberstar, D

Mississippi
1. J. L. Whitten, D
2. W. Franklin, R
3. G. V. Montgomery, D
4. W. Dowdy, D
5. T. Lott, R

Missouri
1. W. L. Clay, D
2. R. A. Young, D
3. R. A. Gephardt, D
4. I. Skelton, D
5. A. Wheat, D
6. E. T. Coleman, R
7. G. Taylor, R
8. W. Emerson, R
9. H. L. Volkmer, D

Montana
1. P. Williams, D
2. R. Marlenee, R

Nebraska
1. D. Bereuter, R
2. H. Daub, R
3. V. Smith, R

Nevada
1. H. Reid, D
2. B. Vucanovich, R

New Hampshire
1. *R. C. Smith, R
2. J. Gregg, R

New Jersey
1. J. J. Florio, D
2. W. J. Hughes, D
3. J. J. Howard, D
4. C. Smith, R
5. M. Roukema, R
6. B. J. Dwyer, D
7. M. J. Rinaldo, R
8. R. A. Roe, D
9. R. G. Torricelli, D
10. P. W. Rodino, Jr., D
11. *D. A. Gallo, R
12. J. Courter, R
13. *H. J. Saxton, R
14. F. Guarini, D

New Mexico
1. M. Lujan, Jr., R
2. J. Skeen, R
3. B. Richardson, D

New York
1. W. Carney, R
2. T. J. Downey, D
3. R. J. Mrazek, D
4. N. F. Lent, R
5. R. McGrath, R
6. J. P. Addabbo, D
7. G. L. Ackerman, D
8. J. H. Scheuer, D
9. *T. J. Manton, D
10. C. E. Schumer, D
11. E. Towns, D
12. M. R. Owens, D
13. S. J. Solarz, D
14. G. V. Molinari, R
15. B. Green, R
16. C. B. Rangel, D
17. T. Weiss, D
18. R. Garcia, D
19. M. Biaggi, D
20. *J. J. DioGuardi, R
21. H. Fish, Jr., R
22. B. A. Gilman, R
23. S. S. Stratton, D
24. G. B. H. Solomon, R
25. S. L. Boehlert, R
26. D. Martin, R
27. G. C. Wortley, R
28. M. F. McHugh, D
29. F. Horton, R
30. *F. J. Eckert, R
31. J. F. Kemp, R
32. J. J. LaFalce, D
33. H. J. Nowak, D
34. S. N. Lundine, D

North Carolina
1. W. B. Jones, D
2. T. Valentine, D

3. C. O. Whitley, Sr., D
4. *W. W. Cobey, R
5. S. L. Neal, D
6. H. Coble, R
7. C. Rose, D
8. W. G. Hefner, D
9. *J. A. McMillan, R
10. J. T. Broyhill, R
11. *W. M. Hendon, R

North Dakota
At-L. B. Dorgan, D

Ohio
1. T. A. Luken, D
2. W. D. Gradison, Jr., R
3. T. Hall, D
4. M. Oxley, R
5. D. L. Latta, R
6. B. McEwen, R
7. M. DeWine, R
8. T. N. Kindness, R
9. M. Kaptur, D
10. C. E. Miller, R
11. D. E. Eckart, D
12. J. R. Kasich, R
13. D. J. Pease, D
14. J. F. Seiberling, D
15. C. P. Wylie, R
16. R. Regula, R
17. *J. A. Traficant, D
18. D. Applegate, D
19. E. F. Feighan, D
20. M. R. Oakar, D
21. L. Stokes, D

Oklahoma
1. J. R. Jones, D
2. M. Synar, D
3. W. W. Watkins, D
4. D. McCurdy, D
5. M. Edwards, R
6. G. English, D

Oregon
1. L. AuCoin, D
2. R. F. Smith, R
3. R. Wyden, D
4. J. Weaver, D
5. D. Smith, R

Pennsylvania
1. T. Foglietta, D
2. W. Gray, III, D
3. R. A. Borski, Jr., D
4. J. P. Kolter, D
5. R. T. Schulze, R
6. G. Yatron, D
7. R. W. Edgar, D
8. P. H. Kostmayer, D
9. B. Shuster, R
10. J. M. McDade, R
11. *P. E. Kanjorski, D
12. J. P. Murtha, D
13. L. Coughlin, R
14. W. Coyne, D
15. D. Ritter, R
16. R. S. Walker, R
17. G. W. Gekas, R
18. D. Walgren, D
19. W. F. Goodling, R
20. J. M. Gaydos, D
21. T. J. Ridge, R
22. A. J. Murphy, D
23. W. Clinger, Jr., R

Rhode Island
1. F. J. St Germain, D
2. C. Schneider, R

South Carolina
1. T. Hartnett, R
2. F. D. Spence, R
3. B. C. Derrick, Jr., D
4. C. Campbell, Jr., R
5. J. Spratt, Jr., D
6. R. M. Tallon, Jr., D

South Dakota
At-L. T. Daschle, D

Tennessee
1. J. H. Quillen, R
2. J. J. Duncan, R
3. M. Lloyd, D
4. J. Cooper, D
5. W. H. Boner, D
6. *B. Gordon, D
7. D. Sundquist, R
8. E. Jones, D
9. H. E. Ford, D

Texas
1. S. B. Hall, Jr., D
2. C. Wilson, D
3. S. Bartlett, R
4. R. Hall, D
5. J. Bryant, D
6. *J. Barton, R
7. B. Archer, R
8. J. Fields, R
9. J. Brooks, D
10. J. J. Pickle, D
11. J. M. Leath, D
12. J. C. Wright, Jr., D
13. *B. Boulter, R
14. *M. Sweeney, R
15. E. de la Garza, D
16. R. Coleman, D
17. C. Stenholm, D
18. G. T. Leland, D
19. *L. Combest, R
20. H. B. Gonzalez, D
21. T. Loeffler, R
22. *T. DeLay, R
23. *A. G. Bustamante, D
24. M. Frost, D
25. M. Andrews, D
26. *R. Armey, R
27. S. P. Ortiz, D

Utah
1. J. Hansen, R
2. *D. S. Monson, R
3. H. C. Nielson, R

Vermont
At-L. J. M. Jeffords, R

Virginia
1. H. H. Bateman, R
2. G. W. Whitehurst, R
3. T. Bliley, Jr., R
4. N. Sisisky, D
5. D. Daniel, D
6. J. R. Olin, D
7. *D. F. Slaughter, Jr., R
8. S. Parris, R
9. F. C. Boucher, D
10. F. Wolf, R

Washington
1. *J. Miller, R
2. A. Swift, D
3. D. L. Bonker, D
4. S. Morrison, R
5. T. S. Foley, D
6. N. D. Dicks, D
7. M. Lowry, D
8. R. Chandler, R

West Virginia
1. A. B. Mollohan, D
2. H. O. Staggers, Jr., D
3. R. E. Wise, Jr., D
4. N. J. Rahall, II, D

Wisconsin
1. L. Aspin, D
2. R. W. Kastenmeier, D
3. S. Gunderson, R
4. G. D. Kleczka, D
5. J. Moody, D
6. T. E. Petri, R
7. D. R. Obey, D
8. T. Roth, R
9. F. J. Sensenbrenner, Jr., R

Wyoming
At-L. R. Cheney, R

AMERICAN SAMOA
Delegate, Fofó Sunia, D

DISTRICT OF COLUMBIA
Delegate, W. E. Fauntroy, D

GUAM
Delegate, *Ben Garrido Blaz, R

PUERTO RICO
Resident Commissioner
*J. B. Fuster, D

VIRGIN ISLANDS
Delegate, Ron de Lugo, D

UNITED STATES: Major Legislation Enacted During Second Session of the 98th Congress

SUBJECT	PURPOSE
Water Research	Authorizes a continuing program of water-resources research. Enacted over presidential veto. Public Law 98-242.
Fish and Wildlife	Established a National Fish and Wildlife Foundation. Signed March 26. Public Law 98-244.
Black Americans	Recognizes the contributions of blacks to American independence. Signed March 27. Public Law 98-245.
Omnibus Budget Reconciliation	Saves the federal government some $8 billion in payment to federal employees and retirees. Signed April 18. Public Law 98-270.
Children	Strengthens federal laws involving the production and distribution of pornographic material involving children. Signed May 21. Public Law 98-292.
Bankruptcy Courts	Restructures the nation's bankruptcy courts, giving overall authority for bankruptcy matters to federal district courts. Signed July 10. Public Law 98-353.
Transportation Safety	Amends the Surface Transportation Assistance Act of 1982 to withhold a portion of federal highway funds from states that do not enact a minimum alcoholic drinking age of 21 and to require states to use at least 8% of their highway safety apportionments for developing child-restraint systems in motor vehicles. Signed July 17. Public Law 98-363.
Landsat Satellites	Paves the way for the U. S. government to sell its private sector satellites that take photos of the earth. Signed July 17. Public Law 98-365.
Christopher Columbus	A 30-member Christopher Columbus Quincentenary Jubilee Commission will plan celebrations to mark the 500th anniversary of Columbus' discovery of the New World. Signed August 7. Public Law 98-375.
Math and Science Education; Equal Access	Authorizes $1 billion over two years to improve math and science education; also requires public schools receiving federal funds to allow access to school facilities by any voluntary student religious or political group if the facilities are opened for other extracurricular activities. Signed August 11. Public Law 98-377.
Child Support	Strengthens the procedure for collecting delinquent child-support payments. Signed August 16. Public Law 98-378.
Pensions	Gives spouses the right to the pensions of vested workers who die before retirement age, allows workers to participate in pension plans at an earlier age. Signed August 23. Public Law 98-397.
Dams	Authorizes a $650 million fund to repair and modify federally owned dams. Signed August 28. Public Law 98-404.
Drugs	Makes many more inexpensive "generic" versions of brand-name drugs available to consumers. Signed September 24. Public Law 98-417.
Airlines	Effective Jan. 1, 1985, the Civil Aeronautics Board will cease to exist, and passenger rights on airplanes will be enforced by the Department of Transportation. Signed October 4. Public Law 98-443.
Child Abuse	Ensures that severely handicapped infants will receive proper medical treatment. Also provides shelters for victims of domestic violence. Signed October 9. Public Law 98-457.
Public Health	Approves new health warnings for cigarette packages and advertisements. Signed October 12. Public Law 98-474.
Public Debt	Raises the public debt limit from $1.573 trillion (the limit enacted in June 1984) to $1.824 trillion. Signed October 13. Public Law 98-475.
Children's Safety	Gives the Consumer Product Safety Commission more power to order federal safety and recall warnings on toys, cribs, playpens, and other items used by children. Signed October 17. Public Law 98-491.
Organ Transplants	Seeks to ease problems associated with organ transplant surgery. Signed October 19. Public Law 98-507.
Peace	Authorizes the establishment of a U. S. Institute for Peace. Signed October 19. Public Law 98-525.
Terrorism	Authorizes $355.3 million to improve security at U. S. embassies; establishes a new program of rewards for persons providing conclusive information about terrorist acts against the United States. Signed October 19. Public Law 98-533.
Veterans	Requires the Veterans Administration to establish guidelines for compensating Vietnam veterans suffering from the effects of the herbicide Agent Orange. Signed October 24. Public Law 98-542.
Cable Television	Clarifies the rights of cities to grant franchises for local cable-television operators, while limiting city authority over rates and programs. Signed October 30. Public Law 98-549.
Trade	Extends for 8½ years the generalized system of preferences, which lift duties on some imports from some developing nations; gives the president authority to enforce voluntary restraints on steel imports. Signed October 30. Public Law 98-573.
Crime	See page 194.

Environment
  Toxic Waste
  Wilderness Areas
	
	See page 215.
	See page 216.

Taxation	See page 503.

Contributors

ADRIAN, CHARLES R., Professor of Political Science, University of California, Riverside; Coauthor, *Governing Urban America:* CALIFORNIA; LOS ANGELES

ALEXANDER, ROBERT J., Professor of Economics and Political Science, Rutgers University: BOLIVIA; ECUADOR; URUGUAY

AMBRE, AGO, Economist, Bureau of Economic Analysis, U.S. Department of Commerce: INDUSTRIAL PRODUCTION

BARMASH, ISADORE, Business-Financial Writer, *The New York Times;* Author, *Always Live Better Than Your Clients, More Than They Bargained For,* and *The Chief Executives:* RETAILING; RETAILING—*Sweepstakes*

BATRA, PREM P., Professor of Biochemistry, Wright State University: BIOCHEMISTRY

BECK, KAY, School of Urban Life, Georgia State University: GEORGIA

BERGEN, DAN, Professor, Graduate Library School, University of Rhode Island, Kingston, RI: LIBRARIES

BERLIN, MICHAEL J., United Nations Correspondent, *New York Post* and *The Washington Post:* UNITED NATIONS; UNITED NATIONS—*UNESCO*

BEST, JOHN, Chief, *Canada World News,* Ottawa: NEW BRUNSWICK; PRINCE EDWARD ISLAND; QUEBEC

BITTON-JACKSON, LIVIA E., Professor of Judaic and Hebraic Studies, Herbert H. Lehman College of City University of New York; Author, *Elli: Coming of Age in the Holocaust* and *Madonna or Courtesan? The Jewish Woman in Christian Literature:* ISRAEL; ISRAEL—*Jerusalem;* RELIGION—*Judaism*

BÖDVARSSON, HAUKUR, Free-lance Journalist, Reykjavik, Iceland: ICELAND

BOLUS, JIM, Sports Department, *The Louisville Times;* Author, *Run for the Roses:* SPORTS—*Horse Racing*

BOND, DONOVAN H., Professor Emeritus of Journalism, West Virginia University: WEST VIRGINIA

BOULAY, HARVEY, Senior Administrator, Rogerson House: Author, *The Twilight Cities:* MASSACHUSETTS

BRAMMER, DANA B., Associate Director, Bureau of Governmental Research, University of Mississippi: MISSISSIPPI

BRANDHORST, L. CARL, Associate Professor of Geography, Western Oregon State College, Monmouth, OR: OREGON

BURANELLI, VINCENT, Biographer and Historian, Coauthor, *Spy/Counterspy: An Encyclopedia of Espionage:* ESPIONAGE

BURKS, ARDATH W., Professor Emeritus of Asian Studies, Rutgers University: Author, *Japan: A Postindustrial Power:* JAPAN

BUSH, GRAHAM W. A., Associate Professor of Political Studies, University of Auckland, New Zealand; Author, *Local Government & Politics in New Zealand;* Editor, *New Zealand—A Nation Divided?:* NEW ZEALAND

BUTWELL, RICHARD, President and Professor of Political Science, California State University, Dominguez Hills, CA; Author, *Southeast Asia: A Political Introduction, Southeast Asia Today and Tomorrow, U Nu of Burma,* and *Foreign Policy and the Developing State:* ASIA; BURMA; LAOS; PHILIPPINES

CARR, JAY, Critic-at-Large, *The Boston Globe:* THEATER

CHALMERS, JOHN W., Concordia College, Edmonton, Alberta; Editor, *Alberta Diamond Jubilee Anthology:* ALBERTA

CLARKE, JAMES W., Professor of Political Science, University of Arizona: ARIZONA

CLIFT, ELEANOR, White House Correspondent, Washington Bureau, *Newsweek:* THE 1984 U.S. ELECTIONS—*Women in Politics;* BIOGRAPHY—*George Bush, Geraldine Ferraro, Gary Hart, Walter Mondale, Ronald Reagan*

CLIFTON, TONY, London Bureau Chief, *Newsweek;* Author, *God Cried:* GREAT BRITAIN

COHEN, SIDNEY, Clinical Professor of Psychiatry, Neuropsychiatric Institute, UCLA School of Medicine; Author, *The Substance Abuse Problems* and *The Alcohol Problems:* DRUG AND ALCOHOL ABUSE

COLE, GORDON H., George Meany Center for Labor Studies: LABOR

COLE, JOHN N., Contributing Editor, *Maine Times;* Author, *From the Ground Up, Cityside/Countryside,* and *In Maine:* MAINE

COLLINS, BOB, Sports Editor, *The Indianapolis Star:* SPORTS—*Auto Racing*

COMMANDAY, ROBERT, Music Critic, *San Francisco Chronicle:* MUSIC—*Classical*

CONRADT, DAVID P., Professor of Political Science, University of Florida; Author, *Germany at the Polls, The German Polity,* and *The West German Party System:* GERMANY

COOPER, MARY H., Staff Writer, *Editorial Research Reports:* UNITED STATES—*The Budget Deficit*

CORLEW, ROBERT E., Dean, School of Liberal Arts, Middle Tennessee State University: TENNESSEE

CORNWELL, ELMER E., JR., Professor of Political Science, Brown University: RHODE ISLAND

CUNNIFF, JOHN, Business News Analyst, The Associated Press; Author, *How to Stretch Your Dollar:* UNITED STATES—*The Economy*

CUNNINGHAM, PEGGY, Staff Reporter, *Baltimore News American:* MARYLAND

CURRIER, CHET, Financial Writer, The Associated Press; Author, *The Encyclopedia of Investments* and *Careers in the '80s:* STOCKS AND BONDS

CURTIS, L. PERRY, JR., Professor of History, Brown University: IRELAND

DANIELS, ROBERT V., Professor of History, University of Vermont: VERMONT

DARBY, JOSEPH W., III, Reporter, *The Times-Picayune/States-Item:* LOUISIANA

DAVIES-JONES, ROBERT, National Severe Storms Laboratory, National Oceanic and Atmospheric Administration (NOAA): TORNADOES

De GREGORIO, GEORGE, Sports Department, *The New York Times;* Author, *Joe DiMaggio, An Informal Biography:* SPORTS—*Basketball, Boxing, Skiing, Swimming, Track and Field*

DELZELL, CHARLES F., Professor of History, Vanderbilt University; Author, *Italy in the Twentieth Century:* ITALY

DENNIS, LARRY, Senior Editor, *Golf Digest;* Coauthor, *How to Become a Complete Golfer:* SPORTS—*Golf*

DIETERICH, H. R., Professor, History/American Studies, University of Wyoming, Laramie: WYOMING

DRACHKOVITCH, MILORAD, Professor, The Hoover Institution on War, Revolution, and Peace, Stanford University; Author, *U.S. Aid to Yugoslavia and Poland:* YUGOSLAVIA

DRIGGS, DON W., Professor of Political Science, University of Nevada; Coauthor, *The Nevada Constitution: Its Origin and Growth:* NEVADA

DUFF, ERNEST A., Professor of Political Science, Randolph-Macon Women's College; Author, *Agrarian Reform in Colombia* and *Violence and Repression in Latin America:* COLOMBIA

DUROSKA, LUD, *The New York Times;* Author/editor, *Football Rules in Pictures, Great Pro Quarterbacks,* and *Great Pro Running Backs:* SPORTS—*Football*

DURRENCE, J. LARRY, Department of History and Political Science, Florida Southern College; Mayor of Lakeland, FL: FLORIDA

ELKINS, ANN M., Fashion Director, *Good Housekeeping Magazine:* BIOGRAPHY—*Ralph Lauren;* FASHION

ELVING, PHYLLIS, Free-lance Travel Writer; Editor, *Pacific Travel News* magazine: TRAVEL

ENOS-KEARNS, MARGARET, Writer, The Associated Press, St. Thomas: U.S. VIRGIN ISLANDS

ENSTAD, ROBERT H., Writer, *Chicago Tribune:* CHICAGO; ILLINOIS

ETCHESON, WARREN W., Graduate School of Business Administration, University of Washington: WASHINGTON

EWEGEN, BOB, Editorial Writer, *The Denver Post:* COLORADO

FAGEN, M. D., AT&T Bell Laboratories (retired); Editor, *A History of Engineering and Science in the Bell System,* Vols. I and II: COMMUNICATION TECHNOLOGY

FRANCIS, DAVID R., Economic Columnist, *The Christian Science Monitor:* INTERNATIONAL TRADE AND FINANCE; INTERNATIONAL TRADE AND FINANCE—*Tariffs*

FRIEDMAN, ROBERT, Reporter, *The San Juan Star:* PUERTO RICO

FRIIS, ERIK J., Editor and Publisher, *The Scandinavian-American Bulletin;* Coeditor, *Nordic Democracy* and *Scandinavian Studies:* DENMARK; FINLAND

GAILEY, HARRY A., Professor of History and Coordinator of African Studies, San Jose State University, California: CHAD; GUINEA; NIGERIA

GARFIELD, ROBERT, Associate Professor of History, Director of Common Studies, DePaul University, Chicago, IL; Editor, *Readings in World Civilizations:* KENYA; TANZANIA; UGANDA

GEIS, GILBERT, Professor, Program in Social Ecology, University of California, Irvine; Author, *Man, Crime and Society:* CRIME

GJESTER, THØR, Editor, *Økonomisk Revy,* Oslo: NORWAY

GOODMAN, DONALD, Associate Professor of Sociology, John Jay College of Criminal Justice, City University of New York: PRISONS

GORDON, MAYNARD M., Editor, *Motor News Analysis:* AUTOMOBILES; AUTOMOBILES—*Leasing*

GRAHAM, FRED, Law Correspondent, CBS News: CHURCH AND STATE

GRAYSON, GEORGE W., John Marshall Professor of Government and Citizenship, College of William and Mary; Author, *The Politics of Mexican Oil* and *The United States and Mexico: Patterns of Influence:* BRAZIL; PORTUGAL; SPAIN; THIRD WORLD

GREEN, MAUREEN, British Author and Journalist: GREAT BRITAIN—*The Arts;* LITERATURE—*English;* LONDON

GROTH, ALEXANDER J., Professor of Political Science, University of California, Davis; Coauthor, *People's Poland: Government and Politics:* POLAND

GRUBERG, MARTIN, Professor of Political Science, Coordinator, Criminal Justice, University of Wisconsin, Oshkosh: LAW

HADWIGER, DON F., Professor, Iowa State University; Author, *Politics of Agricultural Research;* Coauthor, *Policy Process in American Agriculture:* AGRICULTURE

HAKKARINEN, IDA, Research Meteorologist, Severe Storms Research Program Support Group (Goddard Space Flight Center), General Software Corporation: METEOROLOGY—*The Weather Year*

HAND, SAMUEL B., Professor of History, University of Vermont: VERMONT

HANLEY, KAREN STANG, Assistant Editor, *Booklist;* Book Reviewer, "About Books": LITERATURE—*Children's*

HARVEY, ROSS M., Assistant Director of Information, Government of the Northwest Territories, Yellowknife, N.W.T.: NORTHWEST TERRITORIES

HATHORN, RAMON, Professor of French Studies, University of Guelph, Ontario: LITERATURE—*Canadian Literature in French*

HAYES, KIRBY M., Professor of Food Science and Nutrition, University of Massachusetts, Amherst, MA: FOOD

HELMREICH, ERNST C., Professor of History, Emeritus, Bowdoin College, Bowdoin, ME; Author, *The German Churches Under Hitler: Background, Struggle, and Epilogue:* AUSTRIA

HELMREICH, PAUL C., Professor of History, Wheaton College, Norton, MA: SWITZERLAND

HENBERG, MARVIN, Department of Philosophy, University of Idaho: IDAHO

HENDERSON, GREGORY, Professor, Research Associate, Fairbank Center for East Asian Studies, Harvard University; Author, *Korea: The Politics of the Vortex* and *Divided Nations in a Divided World:* KOREA

HENDERSON, JIM, Director of Public Relations, North American Soccer League; Former Publisher, *Annual Soccer Guide:* SPORTS—*Soccer*

HENRIKSEN, THOMAS H., Associate Director and Senior Research Fellow, The Hoover Institution on War, Revolution, and Peace, Stanford, CA; Author, *Mozambique: A History;* Coauthor, *The Struggle for Zimbabwe: Battle in the Bush:* MOZAMBIQUE; ZAIRE

HOOVER, HERBERT T., Professor of History, University of South Dakota; Author, *The Chetemacha People* and *The Sioux:* SOUTH DAKOTA

HOPKO, THE REV. THOMAS, Assistant Professor, St. Vladimir's Orthodox Theological Seminary, Crestwood, NY: RELIGION—*Orthodox Eastern*

HOYT, CHARLES K., Associate Editor, *Architectural Record;* Author, *More Places for People:* ARCHITECTURE

HULBERT, DAN, *The Dallas Times-Herald:* TELEVISION AND RADIO

HUME, ANDREW, Free-lance Writer; Author, *The Yukon:* YUKON

HUTH, JOHN F., JR., Free-lance Writer; Former Reporter, *The Plain Dealer,* Cleveland, OH: OHIO

JAFFE, HERMAN J., Department of Anthropology and Archaeology, Brooklyn College, City University of New York: ANTHROPOLOGY

JENKINS, BRIAN MICHAEL, Director of Research on Guerrilla Warfare and International Terrorism, The Rand Corporation, Santa Monica, CA: TERRORISM

JENNINGS, PETER, Anchor and Senior Editor, ABC's "World News Tonight": THE YEAR IN REVIEW

JEWELL, MALCOLM E., Professor of Political Science, University of Kentucky; Coauthor, *Kentucky Politics:* KENTUCKY

JOHNSTON, ROBERT L., Editor/Associate Publisher, *The Chicago Catholic:* BIOGRAPHY—*John J. O'Connor;* RELIGION—*Roman Catholicism*

JONES, H. G., Curator, North Carolina Collection, University of North Carolina Library; Author, *North Carolina Illustrated, 1524-1984:* NORTH CAROLINA

JOSEPH, LOU, Senior Writer, Hill and Knowlton: MEDICINE AND HEALTH—*Dentistry*

KARNES, THOMAS L., Professor of History, Arizona State University; Author, *Latin American Policy of the United States* and *Failure of Union: Central America 1824-1960:* CENTRAL AMERICA

KASH, DON E., George Lynn Cross Research Professor of Political Science, University of Oklahoma; Coauthor, *Our Energy Future* and *Energy Under the Oceans;* Author, *U.S. Energy Policy: Crisis and Complacency:* ENERGY

KEHR, ERNEST A., Director, Stamp News Bureau; Author, *The Romance of Stamp Collecting:* STAMPS AND STAMP COLLECTING

KENDRICK, JOHN W., Professor of Economics, The George Washington University, Washington, DC; Author, *Understanding Productivity: An Introduction to the Dynamics of Productivity Changes* and *Improving Company Productivity;* Coauthor, *Productivity in the United States: Trends and Cycles:* UNITED STATES—PRODUCTIVITY

KIMBALL, LORENZO K., Professor of Political Science, University of Utah: UTAH

KIMBELL, CHARLES L., Senior Foreign Mineral Specialist, U.S. Bureau of Mines: STATISTICAL AND TABULAR DATA—*Mineral and Metal Production*

KING, PETER J., Associate Professor of History; Carleton University, Ottawa: ONTARIO; OTTAWA

KINNEAR, MICHAEL, Professor of History, University of Manitoba: MANITOBA

KISSELGOFF, ANNA, Chief Dance Critic, *The New York Times:* BIOGRAPHY—*Peter Martins;* DANCE

KRAUSE, AXEL, Economic Correspondent, *International Herald Tribune,* Paris: FRANCE

LAI, CHUEN-YAN DAVID, Associate Professor of Geography, University of Victoria, B.C.: HONG KONG

LAURENT, PIERRE-HENRI, Professor of History and Director of International Relations Program, Tufts University, Medford, MA: BELGIUM

LAWRENCE, ROBERT M., Professor of Political Science, Colorado State University; Coeditor, *Arms Control and Disarmament: Practice and Promise* and *Nuclear Proliferation: Phase II:* ARMS CONTROL; MILITARY AFFAIRS; MILITARY AFFAIRS—*Chemical Weapons*

LEE, STEWART M., Chairman, Department of Economics and Business Administration, Geneva College, Beaver Falls, PA; Coauthor, *Economics for Consumers:* BUSINESS AND CORPORATE AFFAIRS; CONSUMER AFFAIRS

LEMERT, JAMES B., Professor of Journalism, Director, Division of Communication Research, School of Journalism, University of Oregon; Author, *Does Mass Communication Change Public Opinion After All?:* OBITUARIES—*George H. Gallup*

LEVINE, LOUIS, Department of Biology, City College of New York; Author, *Biology for a Modern Society* and *Biology of the Gene:* GENETICS; MICROBIOLOGY

LEVITT, MORRIS J., Professor, Department of Political Science, Howard University; Coauthor, *Of, By and For the People: State and Local Government and Politics:* WASHINGTON, DC

LEWIS, JEROME R., Director for Public Administration, College of Urban Affairs and Public Policy, University of Delaware: DELAWARE

LIDDLE, R. WILLIAM, Professor of Political Science, The Ohio State University; Author, *Political Participation in Modern Indonesia:* INDONESIA

LISTOKIN, DAVID, Professor, Center for Urban Policy Research, Rutgers University; Author, *Fair Share Housing Allocation;* Coauthor, *Revitalizing the Older Suburb;* Coeditor, *Cities Under Stress: The Fiscal Crisis of Urban America:* HOUSING

LITSKY, FRANK, Sportswriter, *The New York Times;* Author, *New York Times Official Sports Record Book (1965–1969), Superstars,* and *The Winter Olympics:* BIOGRAPHY—*Scott Hamilton;* SPORTS—*The Olympic Games*

LITTORIN, SVERKER, Free-lance Writer, Swedish-American Chamber of Commerce, New York, NY: SWEDEN

LOBRON, BARBARA L., Writer, Editor, Photographer; Former Copy Editor, *Camera Arts:* PHOTOGRAPHY

LYLES, JEAN CAFFEY, Associate Editor, Religious News Service; Editor-at-Large, *The Christian Century;* Author, *A Practical Vision of Christian Unity:* RELIGION—*Protestantism*

MABRY, DONALD J., Professor of History, Mississippi State University; Author, *The Mexican University and the State* and *Mexico's Acción Nacional;* Coauthor, *Neighbors—Mexico and the United States:* MEXICO

MAIER, SHARON, Library Assistant, Regina Public Library: SASKATCHEWAN

MARCOPOULOS, GEORGE J., Associate Professor of History, Tufts University, Medford, MA: CYPRUS; GREECE

MAREN, MICHAEL, Free-lance Writer, Former Assistant Editor, *Africa Report,* The African-American Institute: ALGERIA; MOROCCO; SUDAN; TUNISIA

MASOTTI, LOUIS H., Professor of Political Science, Urban Affairs and Policy Research, Northwestern University, Evanston, IL; Author, *The New Urban Politics* and *The City in Comparative Perspective:* CITIES AND URBAN AFFAIRS

MATHESON, JIM, Sportswriter, *Edmonton Journal:* SPORTS—*Ice Hockey*

McCORQUODALE, SUSAN, Associate Professor of Political Science, Memorial University of Newfoundland: NEWFOUNDLAND

McFADDEN, ROBERT D., Reporter, *The New York Times;* Coauthor, *No Hiding Place:* NEW YORK CITY

McGILL, DAVID A., Professor of Marine Science, U.S. Coast Guard Academy, New London, CT: OCEANOGRAPHY

MEYER, EDWARD H., President and Chairman of the Board, Grey Advertising Inc.: ADVERTISING

MICHAELIS, PATRICIA A., Curator of Manuscripts, Kansas State Historical Society: KANSAS

MIRE, JOSEPH, George Meany Center for Labor Studies: LABOR

MITCHELL, GARY, Professor of Physics, North Carolina State University, Raleigh: PHYSICS

MORRIS, MILTON D., Director of Research, Joint Center for Political Studies: THE 1984 U.S. ELECTIONS—*Blacks and the Vote*

MORTON, DESMOND, Professor of History, University of Toronto; Author, *A Short History of Canada, Working People: An Illustrated History of the Canadian Labour Movement,* and *Canada and War;* BIOGRAPHY—*Brian Mulroney, Jeanne Sauvé, John Turner;* CANADA

MULLINER, K., Assistant to the Director of Libraries, Ohio University; Coeditor, *Southeast Asia: An Emerging Center of World Influence?* and *Malaysian Studies II:* MALAYSIA; SINGAPORE

MURPHY, ROBERT F., *The Hartford Courant:* CONNECTICUT

NADLER, PAUL S., Professor of Finance, Rutgers University; Author, *Commercial Banking in the Economy* and *Paul Nadler Writes About Banking:* BANKING

NAFTALIN, ARTHUR, Professor of Public Affairs, Hubert H. Humphrey Institute of Public Affairs, University of Minnesota: MINNESOTA

NEUMANN, JIM, *The Forum,* Fargo, ND: NORTH DAKOTA

NEWLAND, ED, *Richmond Times-Dispatch:* VIRGINIA

NOLAN, WILLIAM C., Professor of Political Science, Southern Arkansas University: ARKANSAS

OCHSENWALD, WILLIAM, Department of History, Virginia Polytechnic Institute, Blacksburg, VA; Author, *The Hijaz Railroad* and *Religion, Society and the State in Arabia;* Coeditor, *Nationalism in a Non-National State: The Dissolution of the Ottoman Empire:* SAUDI ARABIA

O'CONNOR, ROBERT E., Associate Professor of Political Science, The Pennsylvania State University; Coauthor, *Politics and Structure:* PENNSYLVANIA

OLSON, ROBERT, Associate Professor, Middle Eastern History and Politics, University of Kentucky; Coeditor, *Iran: Essays on a Revolution in the Making;* Editor, *The Fundamental Principles and Precepts of Islamic Government* and *Iranian Society: An Anthology of Writings by Jalal Al-e Ahmad:* IRAN; IRAQ; IRAN-IRAQ WAR

O'MEARA, PATRICK, Director, African Studies Program, Indiana University, Bloomington, IN; Coeditor, *Africa, International Politics in Southern Africa,* and *Southern Africa, The Continuing Crisis:* AFRICA; BIOGRAPHY—*Desmond Tutu;* SOUTH AFRICA; ZIMBABWE

PALMER, NORMAN D., Professor Emeritus of Political Science and South Asian Studies, University of Pennsylvania; Author, *Elections and Political Development: The South Asian Experience* and *The United States and India: The Dimensions of Influence:* BIOGRAPHY—*Rajiv Gandhi;* INDIA; OBITUARIES—*Indira Gandhi;* SRI LANKA

PARKER, FRANKLIN, Benedum Professor of Education, West Virginia University; Author, *Battle of the Books, British Schools and Ours,* and *U.S. Higher Education: A Guide to Education Sources;* Coauthor, *Crucial Issues in Education:* EDUCATION

PASCOE, ELAINE, Free-lance Writer and Editor: BIOGRAPHY—*Robert Ludlum, Shirley MacLaine, Stephen Sondheim;* CHILDREN; FAMILY—*Grandparents;* OBITUARIES—*Ethel Merman;* WOMEN

PAWEL, MIRIAM, Bureau Chief, *Newsday,* Albany, NY: NEW YORK STATE

PEARSON, NEALE J., Professor of Political Science, Texas Tech University, Lubbock, TX: CHILE; PERU; VENEZUELA

PERKINS, KENNETH J., Assistant Professor of History, University of South Carolina: LIBYA; RELIGION—*Islam*

PIOTROWSKI, WILLIAM L., National Aeronautics and Space Administration: SPACE EXPLORATION (article written independent of NASA)

PIPPIN, LARRY L., Professor of Political Science, Elbert Covell College, University of the Pacific; Author, *The Rémon Era:* ARGENTINA; BIOGRAPHY—*Raúl Alfonsín;* PARAGUAY

PLATT, HERMANN K., Professor of History, Saint Peter's College, Jersey City: NEW JERSEY

POOLE, PETER A., Author, *ASEAN in the Pacific Community, Eight Presidents and Indochina,* and *The Vietnamese in Thailand:* CAMBODIA; THAILAND; VIETNAM

POULLADA, LEON B., Professor of Political Science, Center for Afghanistan Studies, University of Nebraska; Author, *Reform and Rebellion in Afghanistan:* AFGHANISTAN

QUIRK, WILLIAM H., Construction Consultant; Former North American Editor, *Construction Industry International* magazine: ENGINEERING, CIVIL

RAGUSA, ISA, Research Art Historian, Department of Art and Archaeology, Princeton University: ART

REUNING, WINIFRED, Writer, Polar Programs, National Science Foundation: POLAR RESEARCH

RICCIUTI, EDWARD R., Free-lance Writer; Author, *Audubon Society Book of Wild Animals* and *The Beachwalker's Guide:* ENVIRONMENT; ZOOS AND ZOOLOGY

RICHTER, WILLIAM L., Director, South Asia Center, Kansas State University: BANGLADESH; PAKISTAN

RIGGAN, WILLIAM, Associate Editor, *World Literature Today,* University of Oklahoma; Author, *Picaros, Madmen, Naifs, and Clowns* and *Comparative Literature and Literary Theory:* LITERATURE—*World*

RIORDAN, MARY MARGUERITE, Chair/Professor of English, City College of San Francisco; Author, *Lillian Hellman, A Bibliography: 1926–1978:* OBITUARIES—*Lillian Hellman*

RISKIN, STEVEN M., Middle East Specialist, Washington, DC: JORDAN; LEBANON; SYRIA

ROBINSON, LEIF J., Editor, *Sky and Telescope* magazine: ASTRONOMY

ROEDER, RICHARD B., Professor of History, Montana State University: MONTANA

ROSENFIELD, ALLAN, Director, Center for Population and Family Health, Faculty of Medicine, Columbia University; Contributor, *Studies in Family Planning* and *Population and Development: Challenges and Prospects:* POPULATION—*The Problem of Growth*

ROSS, RUSSELL M., Professor of Political Science, University of Iowa; Author, *Government and Administration of Iowa:* IOWA

ROTHSTEIN, MORTON, Professor of History, University of California, Davis, Davis, CA: SOCIAL WELFARE; SOCIAL WELFARE—*The Homeless*

ROWEN, HERBERT H., Professor, Rutgers University, New Brunswick, NJ; Author, *John de Witt: Grand Pensionary of Holland, 1625–1672;* Editor, *The Low Countries in Early Modern Times: A Documentary History:* THE NETHERLANDS

ROWLETT, RALPH M., Professor of Anthropology, University of Missouri, Columbia; Editor, *Personal Ornament in the Ancient World:* ARCHAEOLOGY

RUFF, NORMAN J., Assistant Professor, University of Victoria; Coauthor, *Reins of Power: Governing British Columbia:* BRITISH COLUMBIA

SALSINI, PAUL, *The Milwaukee Journal:* WISCONSIN

SAVAGE, DAVID, Course Supervisor, Continuing Studies Department, Simon Fraser University: CANADA—*The Arts;* LITERATURE—*Canadian Literature in English*

SCHLOSSBERG, DAN, Author, *The Baseball Book of Why, The Baseball Catalog, Baseballaffs, Barons of the Bullpen,* and *Hammerin' Hank: The Henry Aaron Story:* SPORTS—*Baseball*

SCHROEDER, RICHARD C., Washington Bureau Chief, *Visión;* Syndicated Writer, U.S. Newspapers: CARIBBEAN; GRENADA; LATIN AMERICA; REFUGEES AND IMMIGRATION

SCHULZINGER, ROBERT D., Professor of History, University of Colorado, Boulder; Author, *American Diplomacy in the Twentieth Century* and *The Wise Men of Foreign Affairs: The History of the Council on Foreign Relations:* UNITED STATES —*Foreign Affairs*

SCHWAB, PETER, Professor, Political Science, State University of New York at Purchase; Author, *Decision Making in Ethiopia, Haile Selassie I,* and *Ethiopia: Politics, Economics and Society:* ETHIOPIA

SCOTT, EUGENE L., Publisher and Founder, *Tennis Week;* Author, *Bjorn Börg: My Life & Game, Tennis: Game of Motion, Ivan Lendl's Power Tennis,* and *The Tennis Experience:* SPORTS—*Tennis*

SETH, R. P., Professor of Economics, Mount Saint Vincent University, Halifax: CANADA—*The Economy;* NOVA SCOTIA

SEYBOLD, PAUL G., Professor, Department of Chemistry, Wright State University, Dayton, OH: CHEMISTRY

SHEPRO, CARL E., Professor of Political Science, University of Alaska, Fairbanks, AL: ALASKA

SHOGAN, ROBERT, National Political Correspondent, Washington Bureau, *Los Angeles Times;* Author, *A Question of Judgment* and *Promises to Keep:* THE 1984 U.S. ELECTIONS; UNITED STATES—*Domestic Affairs*

SIEGEL, STANLEY E., Professor of History, University of Houston; Author, *A Political History of the Texas Republic, 1836–1845* and *Houston: Portrait of the Supercity on Buffalo Bayou:* TEXAS

SILVER, LARRY B., Acting Director, National Institute of Mental Health: MEDICINE AND HEALTH—*Mental Health*

SIMMONS, MARC, Author, *Albuquerque: A Narrative History* and *New Mexico: A Bicentennial History:* NEW MEXICO

SIMON, RITA J., Dean, School of Justice, College of Public & International Affairs, The American University; Author, *The Jury: Its Role in American Society;* Editor, *The Jury System: A Critical Assessment:* LAW—*The Jury System*

SNODSMITH, R. L., Ornamental Horticulturist; Author, *Tips from the Garden Hotline:* GARDENING AND HORTICULTURE

SPERA, DOMINIC, Professor of Music, Indiana University; Author, *The Prestige Series—16 Original Compositions for Jazz Band:* MUSIC—*Jazz;* OBITUARIES—*Count Basie*

STARR, JOHN BRYAN, Lecturer, Department of Political Science, Yale University; Executive Director, Yale-China Association; Author, *Continuing the Revolution: The Political Thought of Mao;* Editor, *The Future of U.S.-China Relations:* CHINA; TAIWAN

STERN, JEROME, Associate Professor of English, Florida State University: LITERATURE—*American*

STEWART, WILLIAM H., Associate Professor of Political Science, The University of Alabama; Author, *The Alabama Constitutional Commission* and *Alabama and the Energy Crisis:* ALABAMA

STOKES, W. LEE, Professor, Department of Geology and Geophysics, University of Utah; Author, *Essentials of Earth History* and *Introduction to Geology:* GEOLOGY

STOUDEMIRE, ROBERT H., Distinguished Professor of Government Emeritus, University of South Carolina: SOUTH CAROLINA

SUNDERLIN, LISA A., Editorial Assistant, *The Numismatist:* COINS AND COIN COLLECTING

SUNY, RONALD GRIGOR, Alex Manoogian Professor of Modern Armenian History, University of Michigan, Ann Arbor; Author, *The Baku Commune, 1917–1918: Class and Nationality in the Russian Revolution* and *Armenia in the Twentieth Century:* BIOGRAPHY—*Konstantin Chernenko, Andrei Gromyko;* OBITUARIES—*Yuri Andropov;* USSR

SYLVESTER, LORNA LUTES, Associate Editor, *Indiana Magazine of History,* Indiana University, Bloomington; Editor, *No Cheap Padding: Seventy-Five Years of the "Indiana Magazine of History":* INDIANA

TABORSKY, EDWARD, Professor of Government, University of Texas, Austin; Author, *Communism in Czechoslovakia, 1948–1960* and *Communist Penetration of the Third World:* CZECHOSLOVAKIA

TAFT, WILLIAM H., Professor Emeritus of Journalism, University of Missouri, Columbia; Author, *American Journalism History, American Magazines for the 1980s:* PUBLISHING

TATTERSALL, IAN, Curator, Department of Anthropology, American Museum of Natural History: ANTHROPOLOGY—*The "Ancestors" Exhibition*

TAYLOR, WILLIAM L., Professor of History, Plymouth State College, Plymouth, NH: NEW HAMPSHIRE

TESAR, JENNY, Medicine and Science Writer: COMPUTERS; MEDICINE AND HEALTH; MEDICINE AND HEALTH—*Trauma and Trauma Centers*

THEISEN, CHARLES W., Assistant News Editor, *The Detroit News:* MICHIGAN

THOMPSON, OWEN, Professor, Department of Meteorology, University of Maryland: METEOROLOGY

TOWNE, RUTH W., Professor of History, Northeast Missouri State University: MISSOURI

TURNER, ARTHUR CAMPBELL, Professor of Political Science, University of California, Riverside; Author, *Tension Areas in World Affairs;* Coauthor, *Control of Foreign Relations:* EGYPT; MIDDLE EAST

TURNER, CHARLES H., Staff Writer, *The Honolulu Advertiser:* HAWAII

VAN RIPER, PAUL P., Professor and Head (retired), Department of Political Science, Texas A&M University: POSTAL SERVICE

VOLSKY, GEORGE, Center for Advanced International Studies, University of Miami: CUBA

WATTERS, ELSIE M., Vice President-Research, Tax Foundation, Inc.: TAXATION

WEEKS, JEANNE G., Member, American Society of Interior Designers; Coauthor, *Fabrics for Interiors:* INTERIOR DESIGN

WEICKER, LOWELL P., JR., United States Senator, Chairman, Small Business Committee: THE SMALL BUSINESS—*The Backbone of the U.S. Economy*

WEIKER, WALTER F., Professor, Rutgers University, Newark, NJ: TURKEY

WEISS, PAULETTE, Free-lance Writer and Consultant to the Music Industry: BIOGRAPHY—*Michael Jackson;* MUSIC—*Popular;* RECORDINGS

WENTZ, RICHARD W., Professor of Religious Studies, Arizona State University; Author, *The Contemplation of Otherness: The Critical Vision of Religion* and *Saga of the American Soul:* RELIGION—*Survey, Far Eastern*

WILLIAMS, DENNIS A., General Editor, *Newsweek:* ETHNIC GROUPS

WILLIAMS, EDDIE N., President, Joint Center for Political Studies: THE 1984 U.S. ELECTIONS—*Blacks and the Vote*

WILLIAMS, ERNEST W., JR., Professor of Transportation, Graduate School of Business, Columbia University; Coauthor, *Transportation and Logistics* and *Shipping Conferences in the Container Age:* TRANSPORTATION

WILLIS, F. ROY, Professor of History, University of California, Davis; Author, *France, Germany and the New Europe, 1945–1968, Italy Chooses Europe,* and *The French Paradox:* EUROPE

WINCHESTER, N. BRIAN, Associate Director, African Studies Program, Indiana University; Contributor, *Political Handbook of the World* and *World Encyclopedia of Political Systems and Parties:* AFRICA

WOLF, WILLIAM, Film Critic, Gannett News Service; Author, *The Marx Brothers, The Landmark Films,* and *The Cinema and Our Century:* MOTION PICTURES

WOOD, JOHN, Professor of Political Science, University of Oklahoma: OKLAHOMA

YOUNGER, R. M., Author, *Australia and the Australians, Australia's Great River,* and *Australia! Australia! March to Nationhood:* AUSTRALIA; BRUNEI

ZABEL, ORVILLE H., Midland Lutheran College, Fremont, NE; Professor Emeritus, Creighton University, Omaha, NE: NEBRASKA

ZACEK, JOSEPH FREDERICK, Professor of History, SUNY at Albany; Author, *Palacký: The Historian as Scholar and Nationalist:* ALBANIA; BULGARIA; HUNGARY; RUMANIA

ZAGORIA, DONALD S., Professor, Hunter College and CUNY Graduate Center; Author, *The Sino-Soviet Conflict* and *Vietnam Triangle:* CHINA—A TIME OF CHANGE

Index

Main article headings appear in this index as bold-faced capitals; subjects within articles appear as lower-case entries. Both the general references and the subentries should be consulted for maximum usefulness of this index. Illustrations are indexed herein. Cross references are to the entries in this index.